Life Insurance

THE IRWIN SERIES IN RISK AND INSURANCE

EDITORS

EDISON L. BOWERS
The Ohio State University

DAVIS W. GREGG
The American College of Life Underwriters

ATHEARN *General Insurance Agency Management*

BLACK, KEIR, & SURREY *Cases in Life Insurance*

BRAINARD *Automobile Insurance*

DICKERSON *Health Insurance* Revised Edition

DONALDSON *Casualty Claim Practice*

EILERS & CROWE *Group Insurance Handbook*

FOLLMANN *Medical Care and Health Insurance: A Study in Social Progress*

FRAINE *Valuation of Securities Holdings of Life Insurance Companies*

GOSHAY *Information Technology in the Insurance Industry*

GREGG *Life and Health Insurance Handbook* Second Edition

GREIDER & BEADLES *Law and the Life Insurance Contract*

HABER & COHEN *Social Security: Programs, Problems, and Policies*

HABER & MURRAY *Unemployment Insurance in the American Economy*

LONG & GREGG *Property and Liability Insurance Handbook*

MAGEE *Life Insurance* Third Edition

MAGEE *Property Insurance* Third Edition

MAGEE & BICKELHAUPT *General Insurance* Seventh Edition

McGILL *Legal Aspects of Life Insurance*

McGILL *Life Insurance* Revised Edition

MEHR & CAMMACK *Principles of Insurance* Fourth Edition

MEHR & HEDGES *Risk Management in the Business Enterprise*

MELONE & ALLEN *Pension Planning: Pensions, Profit Sharing, and Other Deferred Compensation Plans*

MYERS *Social Insurance and Allied Government Programs*

REDEKER & REID *Life Insurance Settlement Options* Revised Edition

SNIDER *Readings in Property and Casualty Insurance*

STALNAKER *Life Insurance Agency Financial Management* Revised Edition

LIFE
INSURANCE

by

DAN M. McGILL, Ph.D., C.L.U.

Frederick H. Ecker, Professor
of Life Insurance
and
Chairman, Department of Insurance,
Wharton School of Finance and Commerce
University of Pennsylvania

Revised Edition · 1967
RICHARD D. IRWIN, INC.
Homewood, Illinois

To My Parents-in-Law
CLIO AND VELMA KEM
With Respect and Affection

Preface

THIS is a basic text on life insurance. It presupposes no prior knowledge of the subject, and it treats of all the topics that constitute the foundation for the study of the more specialized phases of the subject. Emphasis is placed on principles, and throughout the book the underlying reasons for the various contract provisions, actuarial computations, underwriting practices, and legal doctrines are stressed. All technical terms are carefully defined and consistently employed. Visual demonstrations of concepts are liberally interspersed throughout the more technical sections of the book.

The volume reflects more than a decade of experimentation by the author as to the best manner in which to present ideas and concepts to students of insurance. Perhaps the most distinctive feature of the book is the integration of the subject matter of each section with that of all other sections. Attention is at all times focused on principles or concepts that are common to many aspects of the life insurance mechanism. To illustrate the inherent unity of the subject, a set of expense assumptions was developed, and in successive chapters the impact of these expenses was demontrated with respect to gross premiums, reserves, surrender values, and dividends. For purposes of comparability, uniform actuarial assumptions were used throughout the book. A body of internally consistent legal principles was evolved, and conflicting legal doctrines were specifically identified and, where possible, reconciled. The result is a highly integrated and coherent book.

While the analysis of each topic proceeds from the most elementary conceptual base, it is carried to a greater depth than is customary with basic texts. This comprehensiveness of treatment stemmed from the author's desire to leave no question of real substance unanswered in the mind of the inquiring student. The need for an approach of this sort seemed particularly pressing with respect to the actuarial and legal aspects of the subject. Some of the most fundamental concepts of great practical import have been available only in actuarial and legal publications not readily accessible, nor always intelligible, to the typical student of life insurance. The mathematical foundation of the life insurance mechanism is thoroughly explored, but at no point does the explanation progress beyond simple arithmetic and uncomplicated verbalization.

The legal facets of life insurance are subjected to a rather rigorous examination, the emphasis being placed not on legal abstractions but on the legal realities of business transactions affecting the welfare of tens of millions of persons. The treatment of the legal environment is so broad in scope that it need not be supplemented, for beginning classes, by specialized treatises on the subject.

Another topic which is developed more extensively than has been the custom with basic texts is programming. The amount of space devoted to programming itself is deceptively small, but the groundwork for the analysis is laid in the chapters on the beneficiary, supplementary agreements, and settlement options. Again, this material need not be supplemented in beginning classes by specialized manuals or treatises on programming.

The institutional material has been greatly expanded in this edition and is believed to embrace most of the areas that are of interest to teachers and students. Time and space limitations prevented the inclusion of some topics covered in other texts or suggested by colleagues at other institutions.

This text is designed for use in college classes of life insurance, institutional educational programs, such as those of the American College of Life Underwriters and the Life Office Management Association, and company training programs. It is best suited for a course with approximately sixty hours of instruction but can be adapted to shorter or longer courses. Several chapters, and portions of other chapters, can be omitted without impairing the essential unity of the book. For example, some teachers may elect not to assign the chapter on modified reserve systems or certain portions of the chapter on gross premiums. In some schools, the subject of programming is studied in an advanced course, so that the material on that subject could be omitted in a basic course. On the other hand, the book, properly supplemented by collateral readings, could serve as the foundation for a year's course in life insurance, or ninety hours of instruction.

I am indebted to many individuals for generously and graciously given assistance in the preparation of both the original and present editions of the book. The acknowledgments in the preface to the first edition are reaffirmed, and I again express my heartfelt thanks to those who helped to bring that project to fruition. I would mention specifically the very great contribution of William A. Spare, F.S.A.,

Controller and Associate Actuary of the Provident Mutual Life Insurance Company; Berkeley Cox, formerly General Counsel of the Aetna Life Insurance Company; Willis H. Satterthwaite, Vice President and General Counsel of the Penn Mutual Life Insurance Company; and Dr. Charles Kelly Knight, Professor Emeritus of Insurance at the University of Pennsylvania.

In connection with the present edition, my greatest debt is to J. Alan Lauer, F.S.A., Assistant Actuary of the Provident Mutual, who performed all the actuarial calculations incident to the change to the 1958 C.S.O. Mortality Table and the 1955 American Annuity Table, as well as providing general advice on company practices. I am only slightly less indebted to J. Edwin Dowling, Associate General Counsel of the Metropolitan Life Insurance Company, for his extremely meticulous and constructive review of the legal materials in the book. William H. Greenwood, Jr., Vice President—Underwriting of Provident Mutual read all the material on underwriting and offered many helpful suggestions. The chapter on reinsurance was reviewed by George W. Young, F.S.A., Senior Vice President of the Connecticut General Life Insurance Company, and his associates, and John G. Phillips, Vice President—Reinsurance of the Business Men's Assurance Company of America, but they should not be identified with any particular views expressed therein.

My deep thanks go to Edwin B. Lancaster, F.S.A., Vice President—Personal Insurance of the Metropolitan Life Insurance Company and J. Henry Smith, F.S.A., Vice President and Actuary of the Equitable Life Assurance Society of the United States, for their expert updating of the materials on industrial and group life insurance, respectively. Robert Jackson, F.S.A., Vice President and Actuary of the Phoenix Mutual Life Insurance Company, provided helpful insights on the subject of surplus and dividends.

William B. Harman, Jr., Associate General Counsel of the American Life Convention furnished invaluable assistance in connection with the chapters on taxation of life insurance companies. Generous and knowledgeable guidance in this area was also provided by Alfred N. Guertin, F.S.A., former Actuary of the American Life Convention, and Henry F. Rood, F.S.A., President of Lincoln National Life Insurance Company and several of his colleagues.

This revision could not have been completed at this time and never in this form without the wonderful cooperation and efforts of a number of persons who undertook the preparation of material in areas not embraced within the first edition. These persons whose specific contributions are identified by name in both the table of contents and the body of the text are listed herewith in the order in which their chapters appear: Dr. Joseph M. Belth, Associate Professor of Insurance, Indiana University; Dr. Stuart Schwarzschild, Professor of Insurance, and Dr. Eli A. Zubay, Professor of Actuarial Science and Mathematics, both of Georgia State College; Dr. J. Robert Ferrari, Assistant Professor of Insurance, Wharton School, University of Pennsylvania; Robert G. Espie, F.S.A., Vice President and Comptroller, Aetna Life Affiliated Companies; and Stuart McCarthy, Vice President and Associate General Solicitor, Equitable Life Assurance Society of the United States. Needless to say, I am profoundly grateful to these individuals for their willingness to participate in this venture and for the high quality of their product.

My thanks also go out to my colleagues at the University of Pennsylvania and other institutions who from time to time have made suggestions for improving and enhancing the usefulness of this book. I ask their indulgence if they do not find all their suggestions reflected in this edition.

Finally, I record my continuing dependence on the administrative talents of my able secretary, Milly A. Brill, who assumed a myriad of responsibilities in this undertaking that would normally fall to the lot of the author.

While I gratefully recognize my indebtedness to the foregoing persons and others too numerous to mention by name, I assume sole and exclusive responsibility for any errors and shortcomings that this edition may contain.

Dan M. McGill

Philadelphia, Pennsylvania
December, 1966

Table of Contents

LIST OF FIGURES   xvii

LIST OF TABLES   xix

Part One—Introduction

CHAPTER   PAGE

I. ECONOMIC BASES OF LIFE INSURANCE   3
    Family Purposes   4
    Business Purposes   19

II. BASIC PRINCIPLES   25
    Illustration of the Insurance Principle   26
    Application to Life Insurance   26
    Assessment Insurance   27
    Yearly Renewable Term Insurance   29
    The Level Premium Plan   32

Part Two—Types of Contracts: Nature and Uses

III. TERM INSURANCE   43
    Nature of Term Insurance   43
    Renewability   44
    Convertibility   46
    Long-Term Contracts   49
    Nonlevel Term Insurance   51
    Critique of Term Insurance   52

IV. WHOLE LIFE INSURANCE   58
    Principal Types of Whole Life Insurance   58
    Joint Life Insurance   66
    "Special" Whole Life Policies   68
    Functions of Whole Life Insurance   70

V. ENDOWMENT INSURANCE   71
    Nature of Endowment Insurance   71
    Alternative Concept of Endowment Insurance   73
    Investment Feature of an Endowment   75
    Uses of the Endowment Insurance Contract   76

VI. ANNUITIES   81
    Nature of Annuities   81
    Single-Life Annuities   85
    Joint Annuities   96
    Variable Annuities   98
    Actuarial Considerations   102
    Uses of the Annuity   105

xi

CHAPTER | PAGE

VII. SPECIAL LIFE AND ANNUITY CONTRACTS ... 107
   Combination Contracts ... 108
   Contracts with Income Settlements ... 119
   Contracts with Unusual Premium Features ... 123
   Miscellaneous Contracts ... 125

Part Three—The Arithmetic of Life Insurance

VIII. BASIS OF RISK MEASUREMENT ... 133
   Theory of Probability ... 133
   Construction of a Mortality Table ... 137
   Characteristics of Tables in General Use ... 146
   Portrayal of Death Rates ... 162

IX. INTEREST ... 166
   Definition of Terms ... 166
   Compound Interest Functions ... 168
   Current Interest Assumptions ... 180

X. NET PREMIUMS ... 182
   Net Single Premium ... 183
   Net Level Premium ... 207

XI. THE RESERVE ... 218
   Types of Reserves ... 218
   Methods of Determining the Reserve ... 221
   Statutory Regulation of Reserves ... 241
   Safety Margins in the Legal Reserve ... 242
   Deficiency Reserves ... 243
   Voluntary Reserves ... 245

XII. GROSS PREMIUMS ... 246
   General Considerations ... 247
   Loading of Participating Premiums ... 252
   Gross Nonparticipating Premiums ... 260
   Derivation of Participating Gross Premiums through
      Technique of Tentative Gross Premiums ... 274

XIII. MODIFIED RESERVE SYSTEMS ... 276
   The Problem ... 276
   Full Preliminary Term Valuation ... 278
   Modified Preliminary Term Valuation ... 283
   Select and Ultimate Valuation ... 290

XIV. SURRENDER VALUES ... 291
   Guiding Principles ... 291
   Nonforfeiture Legislation ... 296
   Relationship between Surrender Values and Other Values ... 311

XV. SURRENDER OPTIONS ... 315
   Cash ... 316
   Reduced Paid-Up Insurance ... 318
   Extended Term Insurance ... 320
   Automatic Premium Loan ... 325

CHAPTER   PAGE

XVI. SURPLUS AND DIVIDENDS   330
    Concept of Gains and Losses   330
    Sources of Surplus   332
    Apportionment of Surplus   335

XVII. SURPLUS AND DIVIDENDS (CONTINUED)   353
    Illustrative Dividend Computation   353
    General Equity of the Dividend Scale   356
    The Experience Premium Method   357
    Other Considerations   360
    Special Forms of Surplus Distribution   363
    Dividend Options   366

Part Four—Selection, Classification, and Treatment of Risks

XVIII. SELECTION AND CLASSIFICATION OF RISKS   375
    Purpose of Selection   375
    Guiding Principles   377
    Factors Affecting the Risk   380

XIX. SELECTION AND CLASSIFICATION OF RISKS (CONTINUED)   398
    Sources of Information   398
    Classification of Risks   404
    Nonmedical Insurance   409
    Insurability Option   415
    Insurance at Extremes of Age   416

XX. INSURANCE OF SUBSTANDARD RISKS   419
    Incidence of Extra Risk   420
    Treatment of Substandard Risks   421
    Removal of Substandard Rating   428
    Value of Substandard Insurance   429

XXI. REINSURANCE   431
    Purpose of Reinsurance   431
    Proportional Reinsurance   435
    Nonproportional Reinsurance   447

Part Five—Legal Aspects of Life Insurance

XXII. FUNDAMENTAL LEGAL CONCEPTS   453
    Forms of Law   454
    Relationship of the Judiciary to Legislative Law   462
    American Judicial System   465
    General Nature of a Life Insurance Contract   471

XXIII. FORMATION OF A LIFE INSURANCE CONTRACT   477
    Legal Capacity of the Parties   477
    Mutual Assent   482

XXIV. FORMATION OF A LIFE INSURANCE CONTRACT
    (CONTINUED)   499
    Consideration   499
    Legality of Purpose   502
    Form   518

CHAPTER	PAGE

XXV. AVOIDANCE OF THE CONTRACT BY THE INSURER   520
- Breach of Warranty   521
- Misrepresentations   523
- Concealment   536

XXVI. WAIVER, ESTOPPEL, AND ELECTION BY THE INSURER   542
- Law of Agency   543
- Meaning of Waiver, Estoppel, and Election   548
- Waiver Situations   551

XXVII. THE INCONTESTABLE CLAUSE   559
- Nature and Purpose of the Clause   559
- Types of Incontestable Clauses   565
- Matters Specifically Excluded from Operation of the Incontestable Clause   568
- Relationship to Other Policy Provisions   570

XXVIII. THE BENEFICIARY   576
- Types of Beneficiaries   576
- Succession in Interest   588
- Ownership Rights   591

XXIX. THE BENEFICIARY (CONTINUED)   594
- Simultaneous Death and Short-Term Survivorship   594
- Effecting Change of Beneficiary   598
- The Minor as Beneficiary   600
- The Trustee as Beneficiary   602
- Remarriage Clause   604

XXX. ASSIGNMENT OF LIFE INSURANCE CONTRACTS   606
- Right of Assignment   606
- Effect of Assignment on Rights of Beneficiary   608
- Effect of Assignment on Ownership Rights   612
- Notice to the Company of Assignment   619
- Other Matters Relating to Assignment   621

XXXI. PROTECTION AGAINST CREDITORS   624
- Non-statutory Protection   624
- Statutory Protection   627
- Scope of Exemption Statutes   635

Part Six—Settlement Options and Programming

XXXII. GENERAL CONCEPTS AND RULES   639
- Settlement Agreements   639
- Contract Rates versus Current Rates   642
- Right of Withdrawal   644
- Right of Commutation   646
- Minimum Amount Requirements   646

XXXIII. STRUCTURE AND FUNCTIONAL CHARACTERISTICS OF SETTLEMENT OPTIONS   647
- Retention of Proceeds at Interest   647
- Systematic Liquidation without Reference to Life Contingencies   650
- Systematic Liquidation with Reference to Life Contingencies   659

CHAPTER   PAGE

XXXIV. USE OF SETTLEMENT OPTIONS   665
    Adaptation of Settlement Options to Basic Family Needs   665
    Illustration of Programming Principles   672

Part Seven—Special Forms of Life Insurance

XXXV. GROUP LIFE INSURANCE   679
    General Characteristics   679
    General Principles   680
    State Regulation of Group Life Insurance   683
    Basic Features   686

XXXVI. GROUP LIFE INSURANCE (CONTINUED)   700
    Types of Plans   700
    Other Aspects of Group Life Insurance   707

XXXVII. INDUSTRIAL LIFE INSURANCE   711
    General Characteristics   711
    Origin and Recent Developments   713
    Plans of Insurance   716
    Policy Provisions   717
    Administration   723
    Compensation of Agents and Managers   727
    Cost   729

XXXVIII. TOTAL DISABILITY AND ACCIDENTAL DEATH BENEFITS   732
    Total Disability Benefits   732
    Accidental Death Benefits   752

Part Eight—Institutional Aspects of Life Insurance

XXXIX. REGULATION   759
    Regulatory Structure   760
    Agencies of State Regulation   766
    Subject Matter of Regulation   769

XL. TYPES OF LIFE INSURANCE CARRIERS *by Joseph M. Belth*   780
    Commercial Life Insurance Companies   781
    Other Types of Life Insurance Carriers   796

XLI. ORGANIZATION AND STRUCTURE OF LIFE INSURANCE
COMPANIES *by Stuart Schwarzschild and Eli A. Zubay*   812
    Basic Concepts of Organization   812
    Home Office Organization   815
    Field Organization   823
    Types of Agency Organization   836

XLII. LIFE INSURANCE COMPANY INVESTMENTS *by J. Robert
Ferrari*   840
    The Company Investment Process   840
    Life Insurance Companies in the Capital Markets   852

XLIII. FINANCIAL STATEMENTS *by Robert G. Espie, F.S.A.*   860
    The NAIC Blank   860
    Concepts of Insurance Company Accounting   860
    Structure of Financial Statements   862
    Interpretation of Operating Results   885
    Use of the Annual Statement   888

CHAPTER   PAGE

XLIV. TAXATION OF LIFE INSURANCE COMPANIES   893
  Federal Income Taxation   893
  Conceptual Approach to Taxation of Life Insurance Companies 896
  Evolution of the Present Tax Structure   903

XLV. TAXATION OF LIFE INSURANCE COMPANIES (CON-
  TINUED)   910
  The Life Insurance Company Income Tax Act of 1959   910
  Taxation by State and Local Governments   928

XLVI. TAX TREATMENT OF LIFE INSURANCE *by Stuart A. Mc-*
  Carthy   931
  Income Tax Laws   933
  Estate Tax Laws   937
  Gift Tax Laws   941
  State Laws   942
  Employer-Employee Plans   942

APPENDIXES
A. APPLICATION FOR LIFE INSURANCE POLICY   951
B. SPECIMEN WHOLE LIFE INSURANCE CONTRACT   953
C. SPECIMEN INSPECTION REPORT FORM   962
D. SPECIMEN FORM RELATING TO SETTLEMENT ELECTION AND
 DESIGNATION BY DIRECT BENEFICIARY   964
E. A.B.A. ASSIGNMENT FORM   966
F. NAIC MODEL GROUP LIFE INSURANCE BILL   967
G. SPECIMEN GROUP LIFE CERTIFICATE   975
H. DEATH RATES AND EXPECTATION OF LIFE UNDER VARIOUS MOR-
 TALITY AND ANNUITY TABLES   978
I. NET SINGLE PREMIUMS PER $1,000, 1958 C.S.O. MORTALITY
 TABLE, $2\frac{1}{2}\%$ INTEREST CURTATE FUNCTIONS   984
J. NET SINGLE PREMIUMS, ANNUITY DUE, 1958 C.S.O. MORTAL-
 ITY, $2\frac{1}{2}\%$ INTEREST, CURTATE FUNCTIONS   990
K. TYPICAL SCHEDULE OF COMMISSIONS FOR CAREER AGENCY
 AGREEMENT   992

Index

INDEX   1001

List of Figures

FIGURE PAGE

1. HYPOTHETICAL ILLUSTRATION OF ECONOMIC VALUE OF A HUMAN LIFE 9

2. TYPICAL PATTERN OF EARNINGS 10

3. COMPARISON OF YEARLY RENEWABLE TERM PREMIUM WITH LEVEL PREMIUM FOR TERM TO 65 33

4. COMPARISON OF YEARLY RENEWABLE TERM PREMIUM WITH LEVEL PREMIUM FOR ORDINARY LIFE POLICY 35

5. PROPORTION OF PROTECTION AND INVESTMENT ELEMENTS IN ORDINARY LIFE CONTRACT 38

6. BASIC STRUCTURE OF A RETIREMENT ANNUITY CONTRACT ISSUED AT MALE AGE THIRTY-FIVE AND MATURING AT AGE SIXTY-FIVE 95

7. RELATIVE PROPORTIONS OF WHOLE LIFE AND TERM INSURANCE IN A $10,000 TWENTY-YEAR FAMILY INCOME POLICY 109

8. RELATIVE PROPORTIONS OF WHOLE LIFE AND TERM INSURANCE IN A $10,000 FAMILY MAINTENANCE POLICY 113

9. BASIC STRUCTURE OF A $10,000 RETIREMENT INCOME CONTRACT ISSUED AT MALE AGE THIRTY-FIVE AND MATURING AT AGE SIXTY-FIVE 117

10. SOURCE OF THE RESERVE: PROSPECTIVE METHOD 233

11. TERMINAL RESERVES FOR $1,000 OF WHOLE LIFE INSURANCE 235

12. RELATIONSHIP BETWEEN RESERVES AND SLOPE OF THE MORTALITY CURVE 236

13. COMPARISON OF MODIFIED NET PREMIUM UNDER FULL PRELIMINARY TERM METHOD OF VALUATION WITH FULL NET LEVEL PREMIUM, ORDINARY LIFE, AGE THIRTY-FIVE 281

14. IMPACT OF CASH SURRENDER ON THE STRUCTURE OF A WHOLE LIFE CONTRACT 317

15. IMPACT OF REDUCED PAID-UP INSURANCE OPTION ON THE STRUCTURE OF THE WHOLE LIFE CONTRACT 320

16. IMPACT OF EXTENDED TERM INSURANCE OPTION ON THE STRUCTURE OF THE WHOLE LIFE CONTRACT 325

xvii

FIGURE   PAGE

17. IMPACT OF AUTOMATIC PREMIUM LOANS ON THE STRUCTURE
    OF THE WHOLE LIFE INSURANCE CONTRACT   328

18. RELATIVE FREQUENCY OF MORTALITY EXPECTATIONS OF A
    GROUP OF PERSONS AT ANY PARTICULAR AGE   376

19. ADAPTATION OF SETTLEMENT OPTIONS TO FAMILY INCOME
    NEEDS   673

20. STRUCTURE OF GROUP PAID-UP AND REDUCING TERM INSUR-
    ANCE, BASIS OF $1,000   704

List of Tables

TABLE   PAGE

1. INFLUENCE OF THE RESERVE ON THE COST OF INSURANCE   37

2. SURRENDER VALUES UNDER ORDINARY LIFE POLICY   61

3. NONPARTICIPATING ANNUAL PREMIUM RATES PER $1,000 OF ENDOWMENT INSURANCE   73

4. MONTHLY INCOME PER $1,000 OF ACCUMULATIONS UNDER VARIOUS ANNUITY FORMS   90

5. COMMISSIONERS 1958 STANDARD ORDINARY MORTALITY TABLE   140

6. SELECT MORTALITY TABLE RATES PER 1,000   144

7. DEATH RATES AND EXPECTATION OF LIFE UNDER FOUR RECENT MORTALITY TABLES   163

8. AMOUNT OF 1 AT VARIOUS RATES OF COMPOUND INTEREST   169

9. PRESENT VALUE OF 1 AT VARIOUS RATES OF COMPOUND INTEREST   172

10. AMOUNT OF 1 PER ANNUM AT VARIOUS RATES OF COMPOUND INTEREST   175

11. PRESENT VALUE OF 1 PER ANNUM AT VARIOUS RATES OF COMPOUND INTEREST   179

12. 1958 C.S.O. MORTALITY TABLE   188

13. 1955 AMERICAN ANNUITY TABLE   199

14. PROGRESSION OF RESERVE FUNDS UNDER RETROSPECTIVE METHOD OF VALUATION, LEVEL PREMIUM BASIS   224

15. COST OF INSURANCE FOR $1,000 ORDINARY LIFE POLICY ISSUED AT AGE 35; 1958 C.S.O. TABLE AND 2½ PER CENT INTEREST; NET LEVEL PREMIUM RESERVES   227

16. COMPARISON OF TERMINAL RESERVES UNDER THE AMERICAN EXPERIENCE TABLE, THE 1941 C.S.O. TABLE, AND THE 1958 C.S.O. TABLE AT 3 PER CENT INTEREST, ORDINARY LIFE POLICY OF $1,000   238

17. TERMINAL RESERVES, ORDINARY LIFE POLICY OF $1,000; 1958 C.S.O. TABLE AND INTEREST AT 2½ PER CENT AND 3 PER CENT   240

18. HYPOTHETICAL EXPENSE AND LOADING FACTORS FOR ORDINARY LIFE POLICY ISSUED AT AGE 35 IN FACE AMOUNT OF $10,000   256

xix

TABLE   PAGE

19. NUMBER LIVING AND PERSISTING   267

20. ASSET SHARE CALCULATION, $1,000 TEN-PAYMENT LIFE POLICY ISSUED AT AGE 35   269

21. ACCUMULATION OF ANNUAL PREMIUM OF $1   272

22. COMPARISON OF ADDITIONAL FIRST-YEAR EXPENSE ALLOWANCES UNDER FULL PRELIMINARY TERM AND COMMISSIONERS RESERVE METHODS OF VALUATION   286

23. TERMINAL RESERVES UNDER VARIOUS METHODS OF VALUATION: 25-YEAR ENDOWMENT ISSUED AT AGE 35   289

24. ASSET SHARE CALCULATION; $1,000 ORDINARY LIFE POLICY ISSUED AT AGE 35   312

25. MINIMUM PAID-UP SURRENDER BENEFITS AT VARIOUS DURATIONS UNDER ORDINARY LIFE, 20-PAYMENT LIFE, AND 20-YEAR ENDOWMENT POLICIES   321

26. COMPARISON BETWEEN ASSUMED AND ACTUAL EXPERIENCE DURING TENTH POLICY YEAR OF 10,000 ORDINARY LIFE POLICIES FOR $1,000, ISSUED AT AGE 35   333

27. ILLUSTRATIVE MORTALITY SAVINGS PER $1,000 AT VARIOUS DURATIONS AND AGES AT ISSUE   342

28. ANNUAL DIVIDENDS PER $1,000 FROM EXCESS INTEREST EARNINGS OF 1.05 PER CENT   347

29. DIVIDENDS PER $1,000 FOR FIRST TWENTY YEARS UNDER ORDINARY LIFE POLICY ISSUED AT AGE 35   355

30. AMOUNT OF PAID-UP INSURANCE PURCHASABLE WITH $1 OF DIVIDENDS AT VARIOUS ATTAINED AGES   368

31. BUILD TABLE—MALE AND FEMALE AGES 15 AND OVER   383

32. ILLUSTRATIVE GROSS ANNUAL PREMIUM RATES AT QUINQUENNIAL AGES FOR ORDINARY LIFE CONTRACT UNDER SUBSTANDARD TABLES A, B, C, AND D   424

33. AMOUNT OF PRINCIPAL NEEDED TO PROVIDE STIPULATED PERIODIC INTEREST INCOME   648

34. GUARANTEED INSTALLMENTS PER $1,000 OF PROCEEDS   653

35. AMOUNT OF PRINCIPAL NEEDED TO PROVIDE GUARANTEED INCOME FOR VARYING DURATIONS   654

36. LENGTH OF PERIOD FOR WHICH MONTHLY INCOME IS PROVIDED BY VARYING PRINCIPAL SUMS   657

37. DISTRIBUTION OF PRINCIPAL SUM AS BETWEEN INSTALLMENT TIME OPTION AND DEFERRED LIFE ANNUITY UNDER LIFE INCOME OPTION WITH VARYING PERIODS OF GUARANTEED INSTALLMENTS   661

TABLE   PAGE

38. AMOUNT OF PRINCIPAL NEEDED TO PROVIDE LIFE INCOME OF
    $10 PER MONTH—AT VARIOUS AGES   662

39. MONTHLY LIFE INCOME PER $1,000 OF PROCEEDS AT VARIOUS
    AGES   663

40. CALCULATIONS OF AVERAGE ANNUAL PREMIUM PER $1,000 OF
    GROUP TERM INSURANCE   701

41. ACTUARIAL FUNCTIONS AND NET ANNUAL LEVEL PREMIUMS
    FOR WAIVER-OF-PREMIUM AND DISABILITY INCOME BENE-
    FITS AT SELECTED AGES OF ISSUE   747

42. ACCIDENTAL DEATH RATE PER 1,000 AT QUINQUENNIAL AGES
    UNDER THE 1959 ACCIDENTAL DEATH BENEFITS TABLE   755

43. NET ANNUAL PREMIUMS PER $1,000 OF ACCIDENTAL DEATH
    BENEFITS AT SELECTED AGES AND VARIOUS PERIODS OF PRO-
    TECTION   755

44. NET RATE OF INTEREST EARNED ON INVESTED FUNDS   850

45. PERCENTAGE DISTRIBUTION OF ASSETS OF U.S. LIFE INSURANCE
    COMPANIES   854

Part One

INTRODUCTION

CHAPTER I

Economic
Bases of
Life
Insurance

A HUMAN life is possessed of many values, most of them irreplaceable and not susceptible of measurement. These values are founded on religious, moral, and social relationships. From a religious standpoint, for example, the human life is regarded as immortal and endowed with a value beyond the comprehension of mortal man. In man's relationship with other human beings, a set of emotional and sentimental attachments is created which cannot be measured in monetary terms or supplanted by material things. A human life may be capable of artistic achievements which contribute in a unique way to the culture of a society. Such values, however, are not the subject matter of life insurance. Life insurance is concerned with the *economic* value of a human life, which is derived from its earning capacity and the financial dependence of other lives on that earning capacity. Life insurance is not oblivious to the other values associated with a human life; in fact, the life insurance transaction has strong moral and social overtones. Yet, the foundation of life insurance is the economic value of the human life. Since such economic value may arise out of either a family or a business relationship, it seems advisable to discuss the functions of life insurance under the headings of (1) family purposes and (2) business purposes.

3

FAMILY PURPOSES

Economic Value of the Human Life

Source of the Value. In terms of its physical composition, the human body is worth only a few dollars. In terms of earning capacity, however, it may be worth hundreds of thousands of dollars. Yet, earning power alone does not create an economic value that can logically serve as the basis of life insurance. A human life has an economic value only if some other person or organization can expect to derive a pecuniary advantage through its existence. If an individual is without dependents and no other person or organization stands to profit through his living, either now or in the future, then his life, for all practical purposes, has no monetary value that needs to be perpetuated. Such an individual is rare. Most income producers either have dependents or can expect to acquire them in the normal course of events. In either case, a basis exists for insurance.

In the majority of cases, the family of an income producer is completely dependent upon his personal earnings for subsistence and the amenities of life. In other words, the "potential" estate is far more substantial than the existing estate—the savings which the family head has been able to accumulate. The family's economic security lies in the earning capacity of the family head, which is represented by his "character and health, his training and experience, his personality and power of industry, his judgment and power of initiative, and his driving force to put across in tangible form the economic images of his mind."[1] Over a period of time, these economic forces are gradually converted into income, a portion of which is devoted to self-maintenance, a portion to support of dependents, and, if the income is large enough, a portion is saved to meet future needs and contingencies. If the individual lives and keeps his health, his total income potential will eventually be realized, all to the benefit of his family and others who derive financial gain from his efforts. If he should die or become permanently and totally disabled, the unrealized portion of his total earnings potential would be lost and, in the absence of other measures, the family would soon find itself destitute or reduced to straitened circumstances. This need not happen, however, since there is a device by means of which an individual can project his in-

---

[1] S. S. Huebner, *Life Insurance* (4th ed.; New York: Appleton-Century-Crofts, Inc., 1950), p. 14.

come for an indefinite period beyond his death. That device, of course, is life insurance. By means of life insurance, an individual can assure himself that his family will receive the monetary value of those income-producing qualities that lie within his physical being, whether he lives or dies. By capitalizing his life value, he can leave his family in the same economic position that they would have enjoyed had he lived.

Most men voluntarily assume responsibility for the support and maintenance of their wives and dependent children during their lifetime. In fact, they consider it one of the rewarding experiences of life. In any case, the law attaches a legal obligation to the support of a wife and children. Thus, if there is a divorce or a legal separation, the court will normally decree support payments for dependent children and alimony for the wife, if she be the aggrieved party. In some cases, such payments, including alimony, are to continue beyond the husband's death, if the children are still dependent or if the wife has not remarried.[2] Nevertheless, it takes a high order of responsibility for a man voluntarily to provide for continuation of income to his dependents after his death. It virtually always involves a reduction in the individual's own standard of living. Yet, few would deny that any person with a dependent wife, children, or parents has a moral obligation to provide them with the protection afforded by life insurance, as far as his means permit.

Dr. S. S. Huebner has the following to say concerning the obligation to insure:

From the family standpoint, life insurance is a necessary business proposition which may be expected of every person with dependents as a matter of course, just like any other necessary business transaction which ordinary decency requires him to meet. The care of his family is man's first and most important business. The family should be established and run on a sound business basis. It should be protected against needless bankruptcy. The death or disability of the head of this business should not involve its impairment or dissolution any more than the death of the head of a bank, railroad or store. Every corporation and firm represents capitalized earning capacity and good will. Why then, when men and women are about to organize the business called a family should there not be a capitalization in the form of a life insurance policy of the only real value and good will behind that business? Why is it not fully as reasonable to have a life insurance policy accompany a marriage certificate as it is to have a marine insurance

---

[2] In such event, the husband is required to provide life insurance or to set funds aside in trust.

certificate invariably attached to a foreign bill of exchange? The voyage in the first instance is, on the average, much longer, subject to much greater risk, and in case of wreck, the loss is of infinitely greater consequence.

The growth of life insurance implies an increasing development of the sense of responsibility. The idea of providing only for the present must give way to recognition of the fact that a person's responsibility to his family is not limited to the years of survival. Emphasis should be laid on the "crime of not insuring," and the finger of scorn should be pointed at any man who, although he has provided well while he was alive, has not seen fit to discount the uncertain future for the benefit of a dependent household. . . . Life insurance is a sure means of changing uncertainty into certainty and is the opposite of gambling. He who does not insure gambles with the greatest of all chances and, if he loses, makes those dearest to him pay the forfeit.[3]

Measurement of Monetary Value. It seems agreed that an individual should protect his earning capacity for the benefit of his dependents by carrying life insurance in an appropriate amount. The question logically arises at this point as to how much is an "appropriate" amount.

Some have suggested that a person should capitalize his economic value at an amount large enough to yield, at a reasonable rate of interest, an income equal to the family's share of his earnings. In an attempt to obtain the same general result, others have recommended that a person capitalize his value at a figure large enough to yield an annual income equal to a specified percentage, such as 50 per cent, of his personal earnings at the time of his death. Both of these approaches are based on the assumption that the income from personal efforts is a perpetuity. They would preserve the capitalized value of a portion of his earnings into perpetuity. Such an assumption is patently invalid. Personal earnings are subject to termination at any time by death or disability of the producer and, in any case, will not continue beyond the date of retirement. Therefore, in capitalizing the earnings of an individual, account must be taken of their terminable nature.

The technically accurate method of computing the monetary value of a man is too complex for general use.[4] It would involve an estimate of the individual's personal earnings for each year from his present age to the date of retirement, taking into account the normal trend of earnings. From each year's income would be deducted the cost of self-maintenance, life insurance premiums, and personal income taxes.

---

[3] Huebner, *op. cit.*, p. 23.

[4] See Louis J. Dublin, and Alfred J. Lotka, *The Money Value of a Man* (rev. ed.; New York: Ronald Press Co., 1946), for a comprehensive discussion of the subject.

The residual income for each year would then be discounted at an assumed rate of interest and against the possibility of its not being earned. In the latter calculation, the three contingencies of death, disability, and unemployment would have to be considered. The sum of the discounted values for each year of potential income would be the present value of future earnings or the monetary value of the life in question. Using this method, Dublin and Lotka found that a man aged thirty with a potential net income of $3,500 per year has a monetary value of $53,200.[5] A person aged forty with a potential net income of $7,000 per year has a present worth of $99,000.

In determining the economic value of a human life for purposes of insuring this value against loss by reason of death, one should not discount the projected flow of income to the family for the probability of death of the life involved. The objective is to determine the present value of the income flow to the family if the family head survives to the end of his income-producing period, since ideally the insurance should be sufficient to permit the family to enjoy the same standard of living that it would have enjoyed had the breadwinner not died.

A reasonably accurate estimate of a man's economic value for purposes of life insurance can be derived by a method which is simple to understand and which can be used by anyone with access to a compound discount table. There are five steps in this procedure:

1. Estimate the individual's *average* annual earnings from personal efforts over the remaining years of his productive lifetime.
2. Deduct federal and state income taxes, life insurance premiums, and the cost of self-maintenance.
3. Determine the number of years between the individual's present age and the contemplated age of retirement.
4. Select a reasonable rate of interest at which future earnings will be discounted.
5. Multiply (1) minus (2) by the present value of $1 per annum for the period determined in (3), discounted at the rate of interest selected in (4).

With respect to the first step, an effort should be made to anticipate the pattern of future earnings. In the majority of cases, particularly among semiskilled and clerical workers, earnings will reach their maximum at a fairly early age, perhaps around forty, and will remain at that level until retirement. The earnings of professional people continue to increase until about fifty-five, after which they level off or

---

[5] *Ibid.*, p. 195.

decline somewhat. The earnings of still other groups may continue to rise until shortly before retirement. It is usually possible to estimate rather accurately the average annual income that can be expected.

The second step is a little more difficult, but income taxes and the cost of self-maintenance can be approximated within a reasonably close margin of error. The purpose of step 2, of course, is to arrive at the family's share of personal earnings. If the individual can estimate directly what portion of his earnings goes to the support of his family, the determination of the income tax liability, life insurance premiums, and the cost of self-maintenance can be dispensed with. In the typical case, it is probably not too inaccurate to assume that one half of the man's gross personal earnings is devoted to the support of his family. In the low income brackets, the percentage would undoubtedly be a little higher but in no event more than two thirds; while in the higher income brackets, the percentage might be slightly lower.

The purpose of step 3 is to determine how long the family can expect to receive the income projected in step 2, ignoring, for reasons indicated above, the probability that the individual may die before reaching normal retirement age.

The rate of interest selected in step 4 should be in line with the rate generally payable on proceeds left with the insurance company, since it is usually assumed that the proceeds will be left with the insurance company, to be liquidated under one or more of the customary settlement options. The lower the rate assumed, the greater will be the present value of the future income. A rate of 3 per cent is generally selected.

The present value of $1 per annum, the only new element involved in step 5, is obtained from that type of compound discount table that shows the present value of a series of future income payments for various periods of time and at various rates of interest. Specifically, it is the type that shows the present value of 1 per annum for various durations and at different assumed rates of interest. The present value of 1 per annum for forty years at 3 per cent interest, for example, is 23.11. If the 1 may be taken to represent $1, the present value of a series of annual payments of $1 for forty years, discounted at 3 per cent, is $23.11. If a $2\frac{1}{2}$ per cent interest rate were to be assumed, the present value would be $25.10. Such a computation recognizes that a dollar due some years hence is not worth a dollar now in the pocket. A dollar due forty years from now is worth only thirty-one cents today, if a discount rate of 3 per cent is assumed. This is equivalent to saying that thirty-one cents (actually $0.306557) invested at 3 per cent compound interest will amount to $1 at the end of forty years.

The entire process of computing the monetary value of a human life can be illustrated with the example of a married man aged thirty-five, with gross annual earnings of $8,000, whose income is expected to remain at that level until retirement. It can probably be assumed that $4,000 per year will be devoted to the family. If the person is to retire at sixty-five, the income can be expected to flow in for the next thirty years. At 3 per cent interest, $1 per year for thirty years is worth $19.60 today. Therefore, an income flow of $4,000 per year for thirty years is worth $4,000 × $19.60, or $78,400. A person aged thirty-five who can be expected to devote an average of $5,000 per year to his family over the next thirty years is worth $98,000 to his family today, if the income is discounted at 3 per cent. If possible, that income should be capitalized in the form of a life insurance policy on the producer of the income.

Diminishing Nature of the Economic Value. It must be apparent that from any given point, the economic value of a producer will have a tendency to diminish with the passage of time. His earnings level may continue to increase for a certain period or indefinitely; but with each passing year, the remaining period of productivity becomes shorter. Each year of income that is realized, the less that remains to be earned. Since the economic value of a man is nothing more than the unrealized earning capacity represented by his native ability and acquired skills, his value must diminish as potential income is converted into actual income. This principle is illustrated diagrammatically in Figure 1.

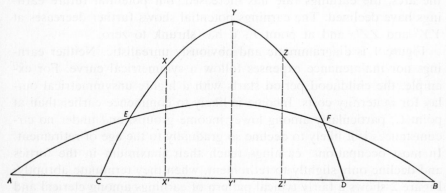

FIG. 1. Hypothetical illustration of economic value of a human life.

The chord *AB* represents the lifetime of an individual born at point *A* and dying at point *B*. The arc *AB* represents his cost of maintenance and, during his productive years, his income tax liability. The arc *CD* represents earning capacity. During the period *A* to *C,* there are no earnings, but there are costs of maintenance represented by the triangle *AEC.* Earnings commence at *C* and may represent part-time work or sums earned for running errands. The area of arc *CD* that extends above arc *AB* represents earnings in excess of taxes and the cost of self-maintenance. Point *D* marks the age of retirement; and the area *DFB* symbolizes the second major period in the individual's life, during which the cost of self-maintenance exceeds his income.

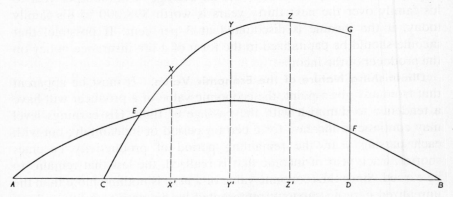

FIG. 2. Typical pattern of earnings.

The monetary value of the individual is at its peak at point *E,* since net earnings are just commencing. At the point where *XX'* intersects the arcs, the earnings rate has increased, but potential future earnings have declined. The earnings potential shows further decreases at *YY'* and *ZZ';* and at point *F,* it has shrunk to zero.

Figure 1 is diagrammatic and obviously unrealistic. Neither earnings nor maintenance expenses follow a symmetrical curve. For example, the childhood period starts with a highly unsymmetrical outlay for maternity costs. Income is likely to commence earlier than at point *C,* particularly among lower income groups, and under no circumstances is it likely to decline so gradually to the age of retirement. In most occupations, earnings reach their maximum in the forties and decline only slightly to retirement, when they terminate abruptly. Figure 2 shows a fairly typical pattern of earnings among clerical and professional groups.

Bases for Insurance. The foregoing diagrams illustrate in rough fashion the economic foundation of three broad categories of life insurance. The first is represented by the area *AEC*. The needs of the individual are met during this period by the parents or other persons responsible for the welfare of the child. If the child should die before becoming a producer, the investment in his maintenance and education is sacrificed. That this can be a sizable sum was demonstrated by Dublin and Lotka in their book, *The Money Value of a Man*, previously cited. They estimate that on the basis of the 1939 price level and the standard of living of a family in the $5,000–$10,000 income bracket (also on the 1939 basis), it takes $16,337 to rear a child to age eighteen.[6] This sum is broken down as follows:[7] food, $3,628; clothing, $1,697; shelter, $5,774; medical care, $1,596; transportation and recreation, $2,787; education, $283; and miscellaneous, $572. At today's prices these figures would more than double. While most parents regard such expenditures as one of the duties and privileges of parenthood and justifiably shrink from labeling them as an investment, to be recovered, if practicable, in the event of the child's death, they do create a substantial insurable value which can logically serve as one of the bases for juvenile insurance—a rapidly growing segment of the life insurance business.

Another type of insurance need is portrayed by the area in arc *CD* lying above arc *AB*. The surplus earnings represented by this area are the source of support for the individual's dependents and a broad measure of the economic loss to the family if the producer should die. A portion of such earnings will have to go into insurance premiums, and another portion should be set aside for the old-age needs of the producer and his wife; but the share that is destined for the care and maintenance of the family should be capitalized and preserved for the family through the medium of life insurance. This is family insurance in the purest sense.

Finally, the retirement needs of the individual, represented by the area *DFB*, should be met, at least in part, through life insurance and annuities. The income vacuum may be partially filled by Federal OASDI benefits, but the most realistic source of the additional income needed is life insurance and annuities, provided through either an industrial pension plan or a personal insurance program.

---

[6] *Ibid.*, p. 57.

[7] *Ibid.*, p. 55.

Analysis of Needs

The foregoing approach to the problem of determining how much life insurance a person should carry has been termed the "human life value" approach. It is based on the proposition that a person should carry life insurance in an amount equal to the capitalized value of his net earnings. Another approach to the problem is to analyze the various needs that would be experienced by the family in the event that the income producer should die. The presumption is that the needs would have to be met through life insurance, although other resources, particularly Federal OASDI benefits, are taken into account in the ultimate determination of the amount of insurance needed. This technique is identified as the "needs approach" and, purely from a sales standpoint, is regarded as more realistic than the "human life value" approach.

It would be difficult, if not impossible, to prepare a list of all needs that might possibly arise after the death of the income producer. Family circumstances differ, and a list of needs that would be appropriate for one family might be quite unsuited for another. Moreover, within any particular family, the needs picture changes from time to time. The most that can be attempted in this section is to outline the general categories of needs that are likely to be found in any family situation. These categories are discussed in the order in which they arise, which in most cases is also the order of importance.[8]

Cleanup Fund. The first need in point of time is a fund to meet the expenses that grow out of the death of the insured and to liquidate all current outstanding obligations. There are many types of obligations to be met, and ready cash should be available for that purpose. Such a fund is usually referred to as a "cleanup fund," although an effort is currently being made to substitute the term "probate fund" or "estate clearance fund."

The principal items of expense to be considered include (1) hospital, doctors', and nurses' bills incident to last illness; (2) burial expense, including funeral costs, cemetery lot, and marker; (3) personal obligations, including unpaid notes, household bills, installment payments, personal loans, and unsatisfied judgments, if any; (4) unpaid pledges, whether or not they are legally binding obligations; (5) cost

---

[8] For a highly logical and comprehensive description of needs, see Harold L. Sullivan, *Needs and the Life Underwriter* (Philadelphia: American College of Life Underwriters, 1957).

of estate administration, including executor's or administrator's fee, appraisers' fees, legal fees, and court costs; and (6) estate, inheritance, income, and property taxes. Mortgages might well be included in the foregoing list; but in view of their size and the special problems frequently encountered in their connection, they are usually treated as a separate need.

It is difficult to estimate precisely the size of the fund that will be needed, since the obligations of an individual vary from year to year. Moreover, last-illness expenses can be estimated only within a broad range, since the individual may die suddenly or may linger for months or years. The needs will vary with the size of the estate. In the typical estate, for example, estate and inheritance taxes will be insignificant items, if present at all; while in a sizable estate, they may constitute the largest item of expense, running into tens or hundreds of thousands of dollars. Executors' or administrators' fees and legal expenses are based on the size of the estate, the former normally being a fixed percentage of the probate estate. In the typical estate, however, a cleanup fund of $2,000 to $5,000 should suffice.

Readjustment Income. Few individuals are able to leave an estate, including life insurance, substantial enough to provide their dependents with an income as large as they enjoyed while the family head was alive. This means that an adjustment will generally have to be made in the standard of living. In order to cushion the economic and emotional shock, it is considered highly desirable that the adjustment be postponed for a period following the producer's death. The income during this period should be approximately equivalent to the family's share of the producer's earnings at the time of his death. The length of the period should depend largely on the magnitude of the change that will have to be made in living standards. If the adjustment is slight, a year should suffice. If the adjustment is to be drastic, two years or more should be allowed. If the widow must prepare herself for a position, an even longer period may be needed.

Income during Dependency Period. After expiration of the readjustment period, income should be provided in a reduced amount until the children, if any, are able to support themselves. This is sometimes called the "critical period" income. Two concepts are involved: How much income should be provided, and for how long?

Obviously, as much income as is consistent with other needs should be provided. As a minimum, enough should be provided that the family can remain intact and the widow can devote full time to the care and guidance of the children during their formative years. The children may have to engage in part-time employment, but it should not be so extensive as to impair their health or interfere with their education. This period is considered so important that life insurance companies have created special policies to meet the needs of the period.

The most important determinants of the duration of the income are the present ages of the children and the type of education with which they are to be provided. In any case, income should be provided until the youngest child is eighteen. If there are several children, the income can be reduced somewhat as each reaches the age of self-sufficiency. If the children are to receive a college education, income will have to be provided for a longer period. In that event, the income during the period the children are in college may be provided by special educational insurance policies. For planning purposes, the immediate death of the income producer is assumed. The projected income is then presumed to be needed for a period equal to the difference between the present age of the youngest child and the age at which the child is expected to become self-supporting.

Life Income for Widow. The needs that exist during the readjustment and dependency periods are primarily family needs. It is presumed that the family unit will be preserved, under the guidance of the widow, and that the resources of the various members of the family will be pooled to meet the needs of the group. After the children have become self-supporting, however, the widow will still have needs as an individual and will require an income from some source. She may be able to obtain employment; but at that age, her earning power has declined substantially. Upon marriage, the wife usually gives up her job or the opportunity to train herself to become self-supporting. As the years pass, she loses whatever occupational skills she may have possessed and would likely have to return to the labor market as an unskilled, middle-aged woman. Under such circumstances, her employment opportunities are extremely limited. Most husbands feel a moral obligation to provide their widows with incomes that will continue throughout the remaining years of their lives. The income may be modest, but it can be the difference between complete dependency and reasonable self-sufficiency.

Special Needs. There are certain needs that are not found in every family situation and, even when found, are not likely to enjoy as high a priority as those previously discussed. Three of the most prominent of these are mortgage redemption, educational, and emergency needs.

1. *Mortgage redemption needs.* Home ownership is very prevalent among American families today; but most of the homes are burdened with a mortgage, frequently financed by a life insurance company. These mortgages are amortized over a period of years, but it is highly probable that an unliquidated balance will still be outstanding upon the death of a person with dependent children. In some cases, of course, the widow may want to sell the house and move into a smaller one or possibly into an apartment, and it would not be essential to provide funds for the liquidation of the mortgage. In fact, it may be easier to dispose of a home if it has a mortgage on it than if it is clear of debt. In many—if not most—cases, however, it is contemplated that the survivors will continue to occupy the family residence, and funds to pay off the mortgage will be needed. If the family can occupy the home rent-free, it will greatly reduce the amount of income that would otherwise be required.

2. *Educational needs.* The income provided for a widow during the period when the children are dependent should normally be adequate for secondary school expenses, as well as for general maintenance. If a college education for one or more of the children is envisioned, however, additional income will be needed. Under present conditions, college expenses tend to range from about $2,000 to $3,500 per year. The cost might be less if the family happens to live in the vicinity of a college or university and the college student resides at home or it might be considerably higher than the indicated upper range if the institution has a high tuition schedule. In any event, there is no question that a college or professional education is beyond the means of many children who lose their fathers in childhood. Life insurance companies have prepared attractive educational policies that will meet this need in a very convenient manner; but in many cases, the limited funds available for life insurance premiums must be devoted to higher priority needs.

3. *Emergency needs.* From time to time in the life of a family, there arise unforeseen needs for money. The need may arise out of an illness, surgical operation, major dental work, repairs to the home, or many other sources. It is obviously unrealistic for the family head to leave just enough income for the family to subsist if everything goes

well and no unusual expenditures are incurred. A liquid fund should be set up from which additional income can be provided if and as needed. Some estate planners assign an emergency fund a priority one step below that of the readjustment income.

Retirement Needs. This, of course, is not a type of need that falls within the categories previously described. On the contrary, it is a type that arises only if the others do not. Yet, it is a contingency that the estate planner must anticipate, and one that must be considered in arriving at the amount of insurance which a family head should carry. To be more precise, it is a contingency which should be considered in determining the *type* of insurance which the family head should purchase, since if the family needs are met with the right kind of insurance (assuming adequate funds for premiums), the cash values under such insurance will usually be sufficient to take care of the old-age needs of the insured himself, as well as those of his wife, if still living. This will be demonstrated below.

Monetary Evaluation of the Foregoing Needs. It is interesting to compare the monetary value of these needs with the economic value of the human life, computed earlier. For purposes of comparison, assume —as in the earlier illustration—that the family head is age thirty-five, has gross annual earnings of $8,000, and devotes $4,000 per year to his family. Assume further that he has a wife aged thirty, and two children, ages two and five, and that an income of $350 per month is to be provided during the first two years, $300 per month during the next fourteen years, and $200 per month thereafter for the life of the widow.

In computing the present value of the foregoing series of income payments, it is advisable to treat them as a life income of $200 per month payable from the widow's age thirty, with an additional income of $100 per month for sixteen years, and still another $50 per month for two years. Superimposed on each other, these series of income payments produce $350 per month for the first two years, $300 per month for the next fourteen years, and $200 per month for the life of the widow. On the basis of the 1955 American Annuity Table, with male ages set back one year and female ages set back six years,[9] and 3 per cent interest, a life income of $200 per month for a female aged thirty, with payments guaranteed for twenty years, has a present value of $62,700. Provision must be made for guaranteed payments during

---

[9] See p. 103 for an explanation of the nature and purpose of an age setback.

the dependency of the children, since in the event of the early death of the widow, the income to the children would be reduced to $100 per month ($150 per month during the first two years). Guaranteed installments are available only in multiples of five years, up to twenty years; and at age thirty, a twenty-year guarantee can be obtained at a sacrifice of only 1 cent per $1,000 of principal sum, as compared to a fifteen-year guarantee which would have been closer to the sixteen-year dependency period. The present value, on a 3 per cent interest basis, of $100 per month for sixteen years is $15,314, and the present value of $50 per month for two years is $1,167. Rounding the figures to the closest hundred dollars, one obtains a sum of $79,-181 as the present value of the income needs, compared to $78,400 as the capitalized value of the family's share of earnings. The similarity ends, however, when the lump-sum needs—cleanup fund and mortgage redemption fund—educational needs, and emergency needs are added to the total. Even if no provision is made for the college education of the children, a cleanup fund of $2,000, a mortgage redemption fund of $8,000, and an emergency fund of $3,000 would increase the total to $92,000. If $8,000 were provided each of the children for a college education, the total requirements would reach $108,000.

It is not likely that these needs will have to be met entirely through personal life insurance. If the individual in question is covered under the Federal OASDI program with benefits approaching the maximum, which, in view of his earnings, is very probable, virtually all the income needed until the youngest child is eighteen will be provided by the federal government.[10] This would reduce the personal insurance requirements by approximately $45,000. If the husband were "fully" insured at the time of his death—a reasonable assumption—the widow, at age sixty-two, would become entitled to a life income of $112 per month, which would reduce the personal insurance requirements by another $21,000. The individual may have been covered by group life insurance, with benefits of possibly $15,000 or more. Therefore, it is not beyond the realm of possibility that all the needs, including those requiring lump-sum payments, may be met in full.

It was stated earlier that the retirement needs of the husband do not impose additional *quantitative* requirements. This is clear when it is realized that $80,000 of insurance (the equivalent of the income

---

[10] This assumes that the widow will not remarry during the period and that both children survive the period.

needs) purchased on the ordinary life plan, the lowest premium type of permanent insurance, before age thirty-five, will have accumulated at least $42,000 in cash values by age sixty-five. This would provide him with a life income, with payments guaranteed for ten years, of more than $260 per month. If his wife were alive and in need of old-age protection, the accumulated sum could be converted into a joint-and-last-survivor annuity,[11] which would provide an income of $200 per month as long as either the husband or the wife should survive. Such an income, supplemented by Federal OASDI benefits and possibly retirement benefits from an employer pension plan, should meet their old-age needs with ample margins. If an effort were made to keep down premium outlays through a liberal use of term insurance, the cash values available to the insured at age sixty-five would be reduced accordingly.

Amount of Insurance to Be Carried

Ideally, the life of each productive member of society should be insured for an amount equal to his full economic value, as measured by his contributions to those who are dependent upon him. Then, upon the death of the income producer, the insured sum should be liquidated in a manner consistent with the purposes to be served, the various needs being met in the order of importance. If the insured should live to retirement, the sums which he has accumulated through his premium payments should, with the exception of amounts required for cleanup and other necessary purposes, be used to satisfy his own old-age needs and those of his wife, if living.

As a practical matter, attainment of this ideal is difficult, even when recognition is given to death benefits available under the Federal OASDI program and employer welfare plans. The basic obstacle is that when both the economic value and the needs are at their maximum—at the younger ages—the funds available for premium payments are at their minimum. In the lower income groups, the bulk of the family income goes into the necessities of life, very little being saved. As the family income rises, aggregate expenditures for consumer goods increase, but they constitute a smaller percentage of total income. Thus, more money is available for insurance premiums and other forms of savings. By that time, however, the need for insurance may have declined somewhat.

---

[11] See pp. 96–97 for a description of the joint-and-last-survivor annuity.

Various formulas have been developed in an attempt to establish the proper relationship between family income and the amount of insurance to be carried. A rule of thumb that has gained wide acceptance is that 10 per cent of gross family income should be devoted to life insurance premiums. This ratio is probably unrealistic at incomes below $5,000 per year; but as the income goes above that figure, the ratio becomes attainable. Another rule states that the typical wage earner should carry insurance equal to three years' gross income, while persons in the higher income brackets should capitalize seven years' earnings.

It is interesting to note that in 1965, only 3.94 per cent of the disposable personal income of American families went into premiums for life insurance and annuities.[12] This is approximately the same rate that has prevailed during the last decade.

The average American family in 1965 owned enough life insurance of all types to replace twenty-three months of its disposable income after federal income taxes.

BUSINESS PURPOSES

Life insurance serves a wide variety of purposes in the business world, but most of the services can be grouped under the headings of (1) key-man indemnification, (2) credit enhancement, (3) business continuation, and (4) employer welfare plans.

Key-Man Indemnification

Perhaps the most direct application of the principles of family insurance to the business world is that represented by key-man insurance. The purpose of this insurance is to indemnify a business concern for the loss of earnings occasioned by the death of a key officer or employee. In many business concerns, there is one man whose capital, technical knowledge, experience, or business connections make him the most valuable asset of the organization and a necessity to its successful operation. This is more likely to be true of a small organization, but innumerable examples of key men can be found in large organizations. A manufacturing or mining enterprise may be dependent upon one or a few men whose engineering talents are vital to the concern. With the splitting of the atom, a new classification of key

---

[12] Disposable personal income is gross income minus federal income taxes.

men came into existence—nuclear physicists. However, a man with unusual administrative ability or perhaps the ability to develop and motivate a superior sales organization may also be a key man. A highly successful fund raiser is entitled to be regarded as a key man by an educational institution or other organization partly dependent upon public subscriptions.[13]

Naturally, it is difficult to estimate the economic loss that would be suffered by the organization in the event of the key man's death. In most cases, the loss is measured in terms of earnings; but occasionally, it is based on the additional compensation that would have to be paid to a replacement. In some cases, it is assumed that the reduction in earnings will be of temporary duration, such as five years; while in other cases, a permanent impairment of earning power is envisioned. The basis for indemnity can usually be established rather accurately when the key-man protection is required in connection with some specific research project or other undertaking of temporary duration.

The insurance is taken out on the life of the key man by the business and is made payable to the business as beneficiary. In most cases, some form of permanent insurance, usually ordinary life, is taken out; and the accumulating cash values are reflected as an asset on the books of the business. If key-man protection is needed for only a temporary period, term insurance is normally used. Premiums paid for key-man insurance are not deductible as a business expense; but in the event of death, the proceeds are received free of federal income tax.

Credit Enhancement

Life insurance can serve to enhance the credit of a business concern in two general ways: improvement in the general credit rating of the concern and availability as collateral.

The first credit function of life insurance is closely allied to, if not identical with, key-man insurance. Anything that stabilizes the financial position of a business concern improves its credit rating. Insuring the lives of key personnel not only assures banks and other prospective lenders that the business will have a financial cushion in the event that a key person should die but improves the liquidity of the firm through the accumulation of cash values which are available at

---

[13] A few years ago, a southern college insured the life of its president for $1 million as he was about to embark on a fund-raising campaign.

all times. As a result, the firm will not only be able to command more credit but will be able to obtain it on better terms.

A more specific use of life insurance for credit purposes is found in its pledging for collateral. It is important to note, however, that the collateral may serve two different purposes. It may protect the lender only against loss arising out of the death of a key man or the borrower, or it may provide protection against both the unwillingness and the inability of the borrower to repay the loan. In connection with the first situation, a business firm may have borrowed as much as is justified on the basis of conventional operating ratios but would like to borrow additional sums to take advantage of an unusual business opportunity. If the bank has confidence in the business and feels that the only contingency to fear is the death of the business head or other key person, it can safely extend the additional credit upon the assignment to the bank of a life insurance policy in an appropriate amount on the life of the proper official. The policy need not have cash values, term insurance frequently being used. The basic security behind the loan is the earning capacity of the business and the integrity of the officials. The policy provides protection only against the death of the person whose business genius would assure repayment of the loan. Such loans, secured only by the assignment of a term insurance policy on the life of the borrower, are very common in connection with personal or nonbusiness transactions. The classic example is the aspiring doctor who borrows money from a benefactor to finance his college and medical school expenses, the funds to be repaid after the young doctor has established his practice on a firm foundation and the benefactor to be protected in the interim by a term insurance policy on the life of the budding physician. This is a character loan, pure and simple; the only hazard to repayment is premature death.

A loan based on cash values is in a different category. The basic security lies in the policy values, and the amount of the loan is always something less than the cash value under the policy assigned to the lender. If the borrower dies before the loan is repaid, the lender recovers his funds from the death proceeds, the difference being paid to the insured's estate or designated beneficiary. If the borrower lives but the loan is not paid at maturity, the lender can recover his funds through surrender of the policy for cash or through exercise of the policy loan privilege. If the loan is repaid at maturity, the policy is reassigned to the borrower. Life insurance policies are widely used for this purpose, in both business and personal connections. The insured frequently borrows from the insurance company, through the policy loan privilege, rather than through assignment to a bank or other lender.

Business Continuation

One of the important forms of business organization in this country is the general partnership. There are several advantages to this form of organization, but it is subject to the general rule of law that any change in the membership of the partnership causes its dissolution. In accordance with this rule, the death of a general partner dissolves the partnership; and the surviving partners become liquidating trustees, charged with the responsibility of paying over to the estate of the deceased his fair share of the liquidated value of the business. Liquidation of a business, however, almost invariably results in severe shrinkages among the assets. Accounts receivable yield only a fraction of their book value, inventory is disposed of at sacrifice prices, furniture and fixtures are sold as secondhand merchandise, and good will is lost completely. Moreover, liquidation deprives the surviving partners of their means of livelihood. In the absence of a prior agreement among the partners, any attempt to avoid liquidation would be beset with legal and practical complications. Even if the surviving partners could raise the cash to purchase the interest of the deceased —an unrealistic assumption in most cases—they would have to prove, as liquidating trustees, that the price paid for the interest was fair. In some states, their fiduciary status would prevent their purchasing the deceased's interest at any price, since it would be virtually tantamount to trustees purchasing trust property. Seldom is it practicable for the widow or other heir to become a member of the reorganized partnership or to purchase the interests of the surviving partners.

In order to avert this impasse, it is becoming increasingly common for the members of a partnership to enter into an agreement which binds the surviving partners to purchase the partnership interest of the first partner to die at a price set forth in the agreement and obligates the estate of the deceased partner to sell his interest to the surviving partners. The various interests are valued at the time the agreement is drawn up and revised from time to time thereafter. Each partner is insured for the amount of his interest, the insurance being owned by either the partnership or the other partners. Upon the first death among the partners, the life insurance proceeds are used by the partnership or the partners, as the case may be, to purchase the interest of the deceased. Thus, the business continues in operation for the benefit of the surviving partners, and the heirs of the deceased receive in cash the going-concern value of his business interest. All parties benefit by the arrangement. After the first death, the surviving partners can enter into a new buy-and-sell agreement, or they can continue under the original agreement with the necessary valuation and insurance adjustments. Life insurance is uniquely suited to the financing of such agreements, since the very event which creates the need for cash provides the cash.

The same sort of agreement is desirable for the stockholders in a close corporation. While the death of a stockholder does not legally dissolve the corporation, the same practical difficulties may be encountered in any attempt to continue the business in operation. These difficulties stem from the fact that the stockholders of a close corporation are also its officers, earnings are distributed primarily in the form of salaries, and no ready market exists for the stock. So similar in basic characteristics are close corporations and partnerships that the former have been described as "incorporated partnerships."

Upon the death of a principal stockholder in a close corporation, the surviving stockholders are faced with three choices (apart from liquidation), all of which may prove undesirable: (1) to accept the widow or other adult heir of the deceased into the active management of the corporation; (2) to pay dividends, approximately equivalent to the salary of the deceased stockholder, to the widow or other heir without any participation in management on her part; or (3) to admit into active management of the company outside interests to whom the stock of the deceased may have been sold. The widow, on her part, faces the possibility of having to dispose of the deceased's stock at a sacrifice price, either to the surviving stockholders or to outsiders, neither of whom would normally be inclined to offer a fair price; or the threat of receiving no dividends if she should decide to retain the stock. These difficulties can be avoided by a binding buy-and-sell agreement financed by life insurance. The surviving stockholders get the stock, and the widow receives cash for a speculative business interest.

Similar agreements are worked out between a sole proprietor and one or more key employees, with at least a portion of the purchase price being provided by life insurance and the remainder being financed by interest-bearing notes, to be paid off from earnings of the business after the proprietor's death.

Employer Welfare Plans

Employer welfare plans provide three broad types of benefits that can be financed through the insurance mechanism: disability benefits, including income replacement and indemnification of medical, surgical, and hospital costs; death benefits; and old-age benefits. The plans which provide such benefits are usually referred to, respectively, as group health insurance; group life insurance; and pensions, including group annuity plans. While *accidental* death benefits may be and usually are provided under a group health plan, life insurance contracts, per se, are used only in connection with group life insurance and certain forms of pensions. Suffice it to say here that death benefits under a group life insurance contract may be provided in the form of yearly renewable term insurance, permanent types of contracts, or a combination of the two. The employer always bears a portion of the cost and may pay all. The benefits payable on behalf of any particular employee are determined by a formula which precludes selection against the company. In other words, the employees are not permitted to choose the amount of coverage, since those in poor health could be expected to apply for the largest amount of insurance.

Life insurance benefits, as such, are provided only under the individual contract type of pension plan (sometimes called a "pension trust") or the so-called "group permanent contract." The latter is the same type of contract used under a group life plan when the death benefits are provided by permanent forms of insurance. Death benefits under other types of pension plans are usually limited to a refund, with or without interest, of the sums contributed by the employee.

CHAPTER II

Basic Principles

INSURANCE has been defined in many different ways. Willett, for example, has defined it as "that social device for making accumulations to meet uncertain losses of capital which is carried out through the transfer of the risks of many individuals to one person or to a group of persons."[1] Kulp states that "insurance is a formal social device for the substitution of certainty for uncertainty through the pooling of hazards."[2] In the same vein, Riegel and Miller say that from a functional standpoint, "insurance is a social device whereby the uncertain risks of individuals may be combined in a group and thus made more certain, small periodic contributions by the individuals providing a fund out of which those who suffer loss may be reimbursed."[3] Finally, Pfeffer, in his search for a generic definition, concludes that "Insurance is a device for the reduction of the uncertainty of one party, called the insured, through the transfer of particular risks to another party, called the insurer, who offers a restoration, at least in part, of economic losses suffered by the insured."[4]

Underlying all these definitions is the concept of risk pooling—of group sharing of losses. That is, persons exposed to loss from a particular source combine their risks and agree to share losses on some equitable basis. The risks may be combined under an arrangement whereby the participants mutually insure each other, a plan which is

[1] Allan H. Willett, *The Economic Theory of Risk and Insurance* (Philadelphia: University of Pennsylvania Press, 1951), p. 72.

[2] C. A. Kulp, *Casualty Insurance* (3d ed.; New York: Ronald Press Co., 1956), p. 9.

[3] Robert Riegel and Jerome S. Miller, *Insurance Principles and Practices* (New York: Prentice-Hall, Inc., 1947), p. 19.

[4] Irving Pfeffer, *Insurance and Economic Theory* (Homewood, Ill.: Richard D. Irwin, Inc., 1956), p. 53.

25

appropriately designated "mutual insurance"; or they may be transferred to an organization which, for a consideration, called the "premium," is willing to assume the risks and pay the resulting losses. In life insurance, such an organization would be a stock life insurance company. While several elements must be present in any sound insurance plan, the essence of the arrangement is the pooling of risks and losses.

Illustration of the Insurance Principle

The basic principle involved in the insurance technique can best be illustrated in terms of a simple form of insurance such as fire insurance. Suppose that in a certain community, there are 1,000 houses, each worth $20,000, and each exposed to approximately the same probability of destruction by fire. The probability that any one of these houses will be destroyed by fire in any particular year is extremely remote, possibly no more than one out of 1,000. Yet if that contingency should occur, the loss to the owner would be staggering—$20,000. If it could be assumed, however, that only one of the 1,000 houses would be destroyed by fire in a particular year, a contribution of only $20 by each home owner would provide a fund large enough to reimburse in full the unfortunate person whose home was lost. If each home owner were willing to assume a certain loss of $20, he could rid himself of the risk of a $20,000 loss. Over the years, only a relatively small percentage of the homes would be destroyed; and through their willingness to contribute a series of small annual sums to a mutual indemnity fund, the property owners would eliminate the possibility of a catastrophic loss to any of their group.

Application to Life Insurance

The principle of loss sharing can be applied in identical fashion to the hazard of death.

The simplest illustration would involve insurance for one year, with all members of the group the same age and possessing roughly similar prospects for longevity. The members of such a group might mutually agree that a specified sum, such as $1,000, would be paid to the estate or designated beneficiaries of such members as might die during the year, the cost of such payments being borne equally by the members of the group. In its simplest form, this arrangement might envision an assessment upon each member in the appropriate amount as each death occurs. In a group of 1,000 persons, each death would produce an assessment of $1 per member. Among a group of 10,000 persons aged 35, 25 persons could be expected to die within a year, according to the Commissioners 1958 Standard Ordinary Mortality Table (1958 C.S.O. Table); if expenses of operation are ignored, cumulative assessments of $2.50 per person would provide the funds for payment of $1,000 to the estate of each of the 25 deceased persons. Larger death payments would produce proportionately larger assessments.

Assessment Insurance

At one time, plans based on the assessment technique were widely used in the United States, though confined to fraternal societies and so-called "business assessment associations."[5] In practice, however, assessments were levied to cover future claims rather than to pay claims which had already been incurred. For example, the Ancient Order of United Workmen, organized in 1868 and the first society to provide death benefits—$2,000—levied an assessment of $1 against each member after the payment of each death claim, in order that funds would be available for the prompt settlement of the next claim. Later plans adopted the practice of levying assessments at regular intervals—usually, once a year—rather than after each death.

The early societies generally levied the same assessment on all members, irrespective of age. This "flat assessment" plan was based upon the theory that there would be a continual flow of new members at the younger ages, with little variation from year to year in the average age of those in the group. Hence, the total death rate would not increase, and the annual assessments would remain relatively constant over the years.

Unfortunately, this assumption was invalid. It is not true that the total death rate will not increase so long as the average age of the group does not rise. Suppose, for example, that a fraternal society was organized with 2,000 members, all thirty years of age, and that after several years, its membership was composed of 1,000 persons aged twenty and 1,000 aged forty—an admittedly unrealistic assumption. The average age would still be thirty, as it was at the organization of the society. However, since the death rate increases more rapidly from ages thirty to forty than it decreases from ages thirty to twenty, the

---

[5] Business assessment associations were local societies which were organized for the sole purpose of offering insurance at rates much lower than those charged by regular or old-line life insurance companies. They were neither fraternal in character nor organized on the lodge system.

number of deaths in the group will be greater under the later distribution of ages than under the original. The 1958 C.S.O. Table shows a death rate of 2.13 per 1,000 at age thirty, 1.79 per 1,000 at age twenty, and 3.53 per 1,000 at age forty. With 2,000 members aged thirty, the society could expect 4.26 deaths in one year; whereas with 1,000 members aged twenty and 1,000 aged forty, it could expect 5.32 deaths. The disparity would have been even larger if a higher average age had been assumed.

Moreover, the average age was virtually certain to increase. Newly organized societies consisted predominantly of young and middle-aged members. Applicants at the older ages were not solicited, since their admission to the group would have increased the assessments and placed the younger members at a greater financial disadvantage. As the society grew older, there was a tendency for the average age to climb because of the difficulty of offsetting the increase in the age of the current membership by the flow of new entrants. This difficulty can be explained by a simple example. If a society should commence operations with five members at ages twenty, twenty-one, twenty-two, twenty-three, and twenty-four, the average age of the group would be twenty-two. Assume that during the first year of operation the youngest member, aged twenty, dies and is replaced by a new member. If the new member is also twenty years of age, the average age of the group will be 22.8, since each of the surviving members is now one year older. If any one, except the oldest, of the original five members dies and is replaced by a member twenty years of age or more, the average age will be increased. The practical effect of this phenomenon is such that deceased and withdrawing members of a fraternal society had to be replaced by more than an equivalent number of younger members if the average age of the group was not to increase.

As assessments increased in magnitude and frequency, young and healthy members tended to withdraw from the society, frequently to join a younger society where protection could be obtained at a lower cost, while the old and infirm members remained. This would have the obvious effect of increasing the average age even more rapidly, thus further accelerating the withdrawal of the young and healthy members. Under such circumstances, it would soon become impossible to attract new members. The increase in the proportion of aged and infirm members was accompanied by a corresponding increase in death rates. The inevitable result was an abnormally high rate of assessment and, not infrequently, a collapse of the organization. The attendant loss to those aged members who had all their lives contributed to the benefits of others was disheartening and often tragic.

Once the weakness of the flat assessment plan became apparent, many societies began to grade the assessment according to the age at entry, a typical scale ranging from $0.60 at age twenty to $2.50 at age sixty. However, the rate for any given member remained fixed and did not increase as the member grew older and constituted a heavier mortality risk. While not as crude as the flat assessment plan, the graded assessment arrangement proved unsatisfactory and, like the former, worked a hardship upon the younger members.

A third plan called for assessments that would increase as the member grew older. If based on valid mortality data, such increasing premiums were theoretically sound; but from a practical standpoint, the arrangement was defective, in that it required low premiums in the younger productive years and high premiums in the older years of lessening productive capacity. More serious, it prompted healthy members to withdraw from the plan as premiums increased, lowering the health level of the residual group and producing an abnormal increase in mortality rates. This process is called *adverse selection* and, while present in many aspects of life insurance and in many different forms, is particularly identified with an insurance plan which provides for premiums that increase with age.

Finally, some plans provided for a reduction in benefits with advancing age, the assessment rate remaining level. This technique is defensible and is found today in many plans of group life insurance.

As a result of the weaknesses explained above, the assessment plan of insurance no longer occupies an important place in the field of life insurance. Most plans established on that basis either have become insolvent or have been reorganized in accordance with more commonly accepted principles of life insurance management.

Yearly Renewable Term Insurance

Similar in many respects to assessment insurance is yearly renewable term insurance, a plan widely used in connection with group insurance[6] and reinsurance[7] but having only a limited appeal for individuals. An understanding of its nature and limitations is essential to an appreciation of the more complex forms of insurance.

---

[6] See Chapter XXXVI.
[7] See Chapter XXII.

Yearly renewable term insurance is the simplest form of insurance offered by regular life insurance companies. It provides insurance for a period of one year only, but permits the policyholder to renew the policy for successive periods of one year each without the necessity of furnishing evidence of insurability. In other words, the policyholder can renew the policy without submitting to a medical examination or providing other evidence of good health. For reasons which will be apparent later, the right to renew is limited to a specified period or to specified ages. If the insured should die while the policy is in force, the face amount would be paid to his estate or designated beneficiaries. If the insured does not die during the period of protection, no benefits are payable at the expiration of the policy or upon his subsequent death. The premiums he paid to the insurance company would have been used by the latter to pay the claims of those who died during the period of protection. It should not be inferred, however, that the surviving policyholder did not receive any return on his contributions to the company. The protection he enjoyed while his insurance was in force had a definite monetary value which was reflected in the premium charged by the insurance company. It will be demonstrated later that the cost of insurance protection for those who do not die is a most important element in the financial operations of a life insurance company.

The premium for yearly renewable term insurance is determined by the death rate for the attained age of the individual involved.[8] This is attributable to the fact that each premium purchases only one year of insurance protection. Moreover, each group of policyholders of a given age is considered to be a separate class for premium purposes; and each group must pay its own death claims, the burden being borne pro rata by the members of the group. Since the death rate increases with age, the premium for yearly renewable term insurance increases each year.

To illustrate, the death rate at age twenty-five, according to the 1958 C.S.O. Table, is 1.93 per 1,000. If an insurance company should insure a group of 100,000 persons aged twenty-five for $1,-000 for one year, it could expect 193 death claims, aggregating $193,000. Inasmuch as premiums are paid in advance to life insurance companies, the cost of the anticipated death claims would be distributed pro rata over the 100,000 policyholders, and a premium

---

[8] This ignores expenses of operation and interest in prepaid premiums, but the omissions do no violence to the principle involved.

of $1.93 would be exacted from each policyholder. It should be noted (1) that the premium is precisely the same as the death rate; and (2) that those policyholders who, according to the mortality projection, will die during the year contribute on the same basis as those who will survive. The implication of the latter is that each policyholder pays a share of his own death claim, a principle that underlies all life insurance contracts, the proportion, however, varying with the type of contract, age of issue, and duration of the protection. The implications of the former are made clear in the following paragraphs.

If the 99,807 survivors of the original group of 100,000 policyholders should be insured for another year, they would be exposed to the death rate for persons aged twenty-six, or 1.96 per 1,000, which would theoretically produce 196 deaths and claims totaling $196,-000. That sum divided equally among the 99,807 participants would yield a share, or premium, of $1.96 per person. If the 99,611 survivors should desire insurance for another year, provision would have to be made for $198,000 in death claims, necessitating a premium of $1.99. For the first several years, the premium would continue to increase slowly, being only $2.13 at age thirty, $2.51 at age thirty-five, and $3.53 at age forty. Thereafter, however, the premium would rise sharply, reaching $5.35 at age forty-five, $8.32 at fifty, $13.00 at fifty-five, $20.34 at sixty, and $31.75 at sixty-five. If the insurance should be continued beyond age sixty-five, the cost would soon become prohibitive, soaring to $49.79 per $1,000 at age seventy, $73.37 at seventy-five, $109.98 at eighty, and $161.14 at eighty-five. The premium at ninety would be $228.14 per $1,000; and at ninety-five, $351.24. Finally if a person aged ninety-nine should want $1,000 of insurance on the yearly renewable term basis, he would have to pay a premium of $1,000, since the 1958 C.S.O. Table assumes that the limit of life is one hundred and that a person aged ninety-nine would die within the year.

If the surviving members of the aforementioned group should continue to renew their insurance year after year, the steadily increasing premiums would cause many to question the advisability of continuing the insurance. After a point, there would be a tendency for the healthy individuals to give up their protection, while those in poor health would continue to renew their policies, regardless of cost. This is the adverse selection to which reference has previously been made. The withdrawal of the healthy members would accelerate the increase in the death rate among the continuing members and, unless ample margins were provided in the premium rates of the insurance company, could produce death claims in excess of premium income. In such event, the loss would be borne by the company, since the rates at which the policy can be renewed are guaranteed for the entire period of renewability. It is for this reason that companies which offer yearly renewable term insurance on an individual basis invariably place a limit on the period during which the insurance can be renewed.

Even though the insurance companies were not to place restrictions on the period during which the insurance can be renewed, yearly renewable term insurance would not be feasible for long-term protection. Dissatisfaction with increasing premiums causes many policyholders to discontinue their insurance, often at a time when, because of physical condition or other circumstances, they cannot obtain other insurance. Such action is likely to be accompanied by resentment that after years of premium payments at increasing financial sacrifice, the insurance protection is lost, with no tangible benefits for the sacrifice involved. More important, however, is the fact that few, if any, individuals are able and willing to continue their insurance into the advanced ages where death is most likely to occur. Yet, the great majority of individuals need insurance which can be continued until death, at whatever age it might occur. This need led to the development of *level premium* insurance.

The Level Premium Plan

Nature. Level premium insurance is just what the name implies—a plan of insurance under which premiums do not increase from year to year but, instead, remain constant throughout the premium-paying period. It does not imply that the insured must pay premiums as long as he has insurance protection, only that all premiums required will be of equal size.[9]

It must be apparent that if premiums which have a natural tendency to increase with each passing year are leveled out, the premiums paid in the early years of the contract will be more than sufficient to meet current death claims, while those paid in the later years will be less than adequate to meet current claims. This is a simple concept, but it has manifold ramifications and far-reaching significance.

The chief significance of the level premium technique lies in the

---

[9] As a matter of fact, arrangements are sometimes found under which the premium for the first few years of the contract is lower than that required for the remainder of the premium-paying period. See "modified life" policies, pp. 123–24.

fact that the redundant premiums in the early years of the contract create a fund which is held "in trust"[10] by the insurance company for the benefit and to the credit of the policyholders. This fund is called a *reserve*, which is not merely a restriction on surplus, as in the ordinary accounting sense, but is a fund which must be accumulated and maintained by the insurance company in order to meet definite future obligations. Since the manner in which the fund is to be accumulated and invested is strictly regulated by law, it is usually referred to in official literature as the *legal reserve*. Technically, the reserve is a

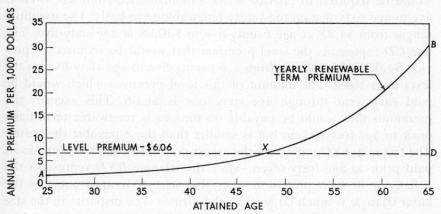

FIG. 3. Comparison of yearly renewable term premium with level premium for term to sixty-five; age of issue, twenty-five.

composite liability account of the insurance company, not susceptible of allocation to individual policies; but for present purposes, it may be viewed as an aggregate of individual accounts established to the credit of the various policyholders.[11]

From the standpoint of an individual policy, the excess portions of the premiums paid in the early years of the contract are accumulated at compound interest and used to supplement the inadequate premiums of the later years. This process can be explained most simply in connection with a contract which provides protection for only a temporary period, as opposed to one which provides insurance for the whole of life. Figure 3, therefore, shows the working of the level

---

[10] This is not a trust fund in the legal sense, which would require the insurance company to establish separate investment accounts for each policyholder and render periodic accountings.

[11] In practice, each policy is credited with a cash value or surrender value which is not the same as the reserve but has its basis in the redundant premiums of the early years.

premium mechanism in connection with a term policy issued at age twenty-five, to run to age sixty-five. The premiums are based on the 1958 C.S.O. Table and an interest assumption of $2\frac{1}{2}$ per cent. In other words, it is assumed, with respect to the level premium calculations, that the reserves are invested at $2\frac{1}{2}$ per cent; and with respect to the yearly renewable term premiums, that each premium earns $2\frac{1}{2}$ per cent for one year before being disbursed in the form of death benefits. No allowance is made for expenses.

The curve AB represents the premiums at successive ages that would be required to provide $1,000 of insurance from age twenty-five to age sixty-five on the yearly renewable term basis. The premium ranges from $1.88 at age twenty-five to $30.98 at age sixty-five. The line CD represents the level premium that would be required to provide $1,000 of insurance from age twenty-five to age sixty-five on the level term basis. The amount of this level premium which would be paid each year through age sixty-four is $6.06. This exceeds the premiums that would be payable on the yearly renewable term basis prior to age forty-seven, but is smaller than those payable thereafter. The triangle AXC represents the excess portions of the level premiums paid prior to age forty-seven, while the triangle BXD represents the deficiency in such premiums after that age. It is apparent that the latter triangle is much larger than the former. The disparity in the size of the two areas is attributable to the fact that the sums represented by the triangle AXC, which constitute the reserve under the contract, are invested at compound interest and the interest earnings are used along with the principal sum to supplement the inadequate premiums of the later years. The reserve is completely exhausted at age sixty-five, having been used to pay the policy's share of death claims submitted under other policies, which is another way of saying that the reserve, including the investment earnings derived therefrom, is gradually used up after age forty-six in the process of supplementing the then deficient level premium. The reserve under this particular contract—term to sixty-five, issued at age twenty-five—reaches its maximum size at age fifty-three, when it stands at $110.32, diminishing thereafter at an accelerating rate until exhausted at the expiration of the policy.

The functioning of the level premium plan is even more striking—though more difficult to grasp—when applied to a policy providing insurance for the whole of life. A comparison of the level premium required under an ordinary life policy with that required on the yearly renewable term basis is presented in Figure 4. As in the case of Figure

3, the age of issue is twenty-five, and the premiums are based on the 1958 C.S.O. Table and $2\frac{1}{2}$ per cent interest, with no allowance for expenses.

In this case, an annual level premium of $12.55, per $1,000, paid as long as the insured lives, would be the mathematical equivalent of a series of premiums on the yearly renewable term basis, ranging from $1.88 per $1,000 at age twenty-five to $975.59 at age ninety-nine.

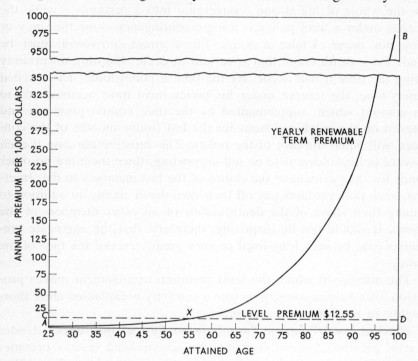

FIG. 4 Comparison of yearly renewable term premium with level premium for ordinary life policy; age of issue, twenty-five.

The 1958 C.S.O. Table assumes that everyone who survives to age ninety-nine will die during the year, producing a net premium on the yearly renewable term basis equal to the face of the policy, less the interest that will be earned on the premium during the year. Line *CD* bisects the curve *AB* between the ages of fifty-four and fifty-five.

The disparity between the areas bounded by *AXC* and *BXD* is very much greater in this case than in Figure 3. Even more amazing, however, is the fact that the excess premiums, area *AXC,* in the early years of an ordinary life contract (or, for that matter, any type of insurance contract except term) will not only offset the deficiency in the premiums of the later years, when the term premium is in the hundreds of dollars, but with the aid of compound interest, will accumulate a reserve equal to the face of the policy by the time the insured reaches the terminal age in the mortality table. This is in contrast to the level premium term contract, under which the reserve is completely used up at the expiration of the contract. The difference is due to the fact that the hazard under a contract providing protection for the whole of life is one "converging into a certainty," while the hazard under a term policy is a mere contingency—one that may or may not occur. Under a whole life contract, provision must be made for a death claim that is certain to occur, the only uncertainty being the time it will occur. By the time a policyholder has reached ninety-nine, the reserve under his policy must have accumulated to an amount which, supplemented by the final annual premium and interest on the combined sums for the last twelve months of the contract, will equal the face of the policy. This must be the case if each class of policyholders is to be self-supporting, since there are no other funds for the payment of the claims of the last members to die. In effect, such policyholders pay off their own death claims, in addition to paying their share of the death claims of all other members of the group. It should not be surprising, therefore, that the aggregate premiums paid by such long-lived persons greatly exceed the face of the policy.

The manner in which the level premium arrangement makes provision for a hazard converging into a certainty is explained more thoroughly in the following section.

Effect of Level Premium Technique on Cost of Insurance. Under a level premium type of contract, the accumulated reserve becomes a part of the face amount payable upon the death of a policyholder. From the standpoint of the insurance company, the effective amount of insurance is the difference between the face of the policy and the reserve. Technically speaking, this is the *amount at risk*. As the reserve increases, the amount at risk decreases. The significance of this relationship to the subject under discussion is that as the death rate increases, the effective amount of insurance decreases, producing a *cost of insurance*[12] within practicable limits. This process is illustrated in Table 1.

---

[12] The cost of insurance is an actuarial term referring to the sum obtained by multiplying the death rate at the attained age of the insured by the net amount at risk. Its derivation and significance are described in Chapter XI.

TABLE 1

INFLUENCE OF THE RESERVE ON COST OF INSURANCE,
ORDINARY LIFE CONTRACT FOR $1,000 ISSUED AT AGE 25;
1958 C.S.O. TABLE AND 2½ PER CENT INTEREST

Year	Attained Age, Beginning of Year	Reserve, End of Year (Even Dollars)	Net Amount at Risk	Death Rate per 1,000	Cost of Insurance
1...........25		$ 11	$989	1.93	$ 1.91
5...........29		57	943	2.08	1.96
10...........34		122	878	2.40	2.11
20...........44		269	731	4.92	3.60
30...........54		431	569	11.90	6.77
40...........64		592	408	29.04	11.85

As was stated earlier, the net level premium for an ordinary life contract issued at age twenty-five, calculated on the basis of the 1958 C.S.O. Table and 2½ per cent interest, is $12.55. Since the death rate at age twenty-five is 1.93 per 1,000, about $11 of the first premium is excess and goes into the policy reserve. If the policyholder should die during the first year, the company would use the $11 in settling the claim and would have to draw only $989 from the premiums contributed by the other policyholders in the age and policy classification of the deceased. This would mean that each member's prorata share of death claims in the first year would be only $1.91 (1.93 × 0.989), instead of $1.93, the yearly renewable term premium for $1,000 of insurance at age twenty-five (with no allowance for interest). By the end of the fifth year, the reserve, or accumulation of excess payments, will have increased to $57 per $1,000, which sum would be available for settlement of a death claim under the policy. The net amount at risk would have decreased to $943, which would necessitate a contribution from the other policyholders (and the deceased) of only $1.96, instead of the yearly renewable term premium of $2.08. The reserve will have grown to $269 per $1,000 by the end of the twentieth year, which would reduce the cost per $1,000 from $4.92 to $3.60. By the time the insured has reached sixty-five, the reserve under his policy will have accumulated to $592, and the actual amount of protection will have shrunk to $408. A death claim in the fortieth year of the contract would be settled by payment of the $592 in the reserve and $408 from the current year's premium payments (of all the policyholders). The prorata share of each policyholder for all death claims during the year would be only $11.85, as compared to $29.04 if no reserve had been available. The influence of the reserve on the cost of insurance is even more striking at the advanced ages.

The true nature of level premium insurance should now be apparent. Under the level premium plan, a $1,000 policy does not provide $1,000 of insurance. The company is never on the risk for the face amount of the policy—even in the first year. The amount of actual insurance is always the face, less the policyholder's own accumulated excess payments. Since the excess payments may be withdrawn by the policyholder at any time through the cash surrender or loan privilege,[13] they may be regarded as a savings or investment account. Thus, a level premium policy does not provide pure insurance but a combi-

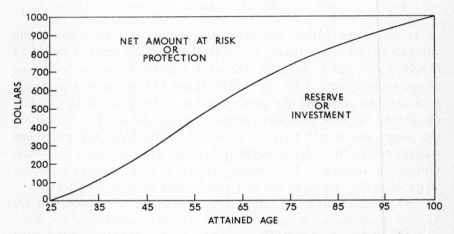

FIG. 5. Proportion of protection and investment elements in ordinary life contract, issued as of age twenty-five; 1958 C.S.O. Table and 2½ per cent interest.

nation of decreasing insurance and increasing investment, the two amounts being computed in such a manner that in any year their sum is equal to the face of the policy. This is illustrated in Figure 5 for an ordinary life policy of $1,000 issued at age twenty-five, the calculations being based on the 1958 C.S.O. Table and 2½ per cent interest.

The area below the curve represents the reserve under the contract or, as mentioned above, the policyholder's equity in the contract. The area above the curve represents for the company the net amount at risk and for the policyholder the amount of protection. As the reserve increases, the amount of protection decreases. At any given age, however, the two combined will equal the face of the policy. By age eighty-five, the reserve has increased to $834.35; and by ninety-five, it

---

[13] Cash surrender and other surrender options are discussed in Chapter XV.

has reached $916.98. By that time, the protection element of the contract has become relatively minor; and by age one hundred—the end of the contract—it has completely disappeared. At age one hundred, the policyholder will receive $1,000, composed entirely of the investment element.

This combination of protection and investment is characteristic of all level premium plans, with the exception of most term contracts; and, fundamentally, one contract differs from another only in the proportion in which the two elements are combined. This basic truth should be kept in mind as the study of contract forms is undertaken.

Further Significance of Level Premium Plan. The impact of the level premium plan is felt throughout nearly all operations of a life insurance company. It accounts for the fact that the composite assets of the life insurance companies exceed $160 billion and are increasing at the rate of about $7 to $8 billion per year. The investment of these funds has presented the life insurance institution with one of its most challenging problems but, at the same time, has enabled the institution to contribute in a most material way to the dynamic expansion of the American economy. The level premium plan underlies the system of cash values and other surrender options which has made the life insurance contract one of the most flexible and valuable contracts in existence. It has caused the life insurance contract to be regarded as one of the most acceptable forms of collateral for credit purposes. Despite these positive contributions—and the complications introduced into company operations—the transcendent significance of the plan lies in the fact that it is the only arrangement under which it is possible to provide insurance protection to the uppermost limits of the human life span without the possibility that the cost will become prohibitive.

Part Two

TYPES OF CONTRACTS:
NATURE AND USES

CHAPTER III

Term Insurance

THERE are four basic types of life insurance contracts: term, whole life, endowment, and annuity. The function of the first three is to create a principal sum or estate, either through the death of the insured or through the accumulation of funds set aside for investment purposes. The function of the annuity, on the other hand, is to liquidate a principal sum, regardless of how created, in a scientific manner. This dissimilarity in the basic function of life insurance and annuities has caused some to question the propriety of classifying annuities as a type of life insurance contract, but there appear to be enough similarities to justify the practice. The term insurance contracts are discussed in this chapter.

Nature of Term Insurance

Term insurance provides life insurance protection for a limited period only, the face of the policy being payable if death should occur during the specified period, and nothing being paid in the event of survival. The period may be as short as one year, or it may run to age sixty-five. The customary terms are five, ten, fifteen, and twenty years. Such policies may insure for the agreed term only, or they may give the insured the option of renewing the protection for successive terms without evidence of insurability. Applications for term insurance are carefully underwritten; and various restrictions may be imposed as to the amount of insurance, the age before which it must be obtained, the age beyond which it cannot be renewed, and the like.

Term insurance may be regarded as temporary insurance and, in principle, is more nearly comparable to property and casualty insurance contracts than any of the other life insurance contracts in use. For example, if a building is insured against direct loss or damage by fire under a five-year term policy, the owner will be indemnified for any loss or damage that is sustained from that source during the term. If the term expires without a loss having occurred, the obligation of the fire insurance company ceases, and the policy is without further effect. If the policy is not renewed and a fire thereafter ensues, the company is absolved of all liability, since it was not on the risk. Similarly, if a person insures his life under a five-year term contract, no obligation is incurred by the insurance company unless the death of the insured occurs within the term. All premiums paid for the term protection are considered to be fully earned by the company by the end of the term, whether or not a loss has occurred, and the policy has no further value.

The premium for term insurance is relatively low, despite the fact that it contains a relatively high expense "loading" and an allowance for adverse selection. The reason for this is that term contracts do not cover the period of old age, when death is most likely to occur, and when the cost of insurance is high. In other words, a term policy insures against a contingency only and not a certainty, as do other kinds of policies.

Renewability

Many term insurance contracts contain an option to renew for a limited number of additional periods of term insurance, usually of the same length. The simplest policy of this type, of course, is the yearly renewable term policy, which is a one-year term contract, renewable for successive period of one year each. However, even the longer term contracts, such as the ten-year term, may be renewable. The following is a typical renewal provision:

Renewal Privilege. The insured may renew this policy for further periods of ten years each without medical examination, provided there has been no lapse in the payment of premiums, by written notice to the company at its home office before the expiration of any period of the insurance hereunder and by the payment in each year, on the dates above specified, of the premium for the age attained by the insured at the beginning of any such renewal period in accordance with the table of rates contained herein.

The key to the renewable feature is the right to renew the contract without a medical examination or other evidence of insurability. Where the term policy contains no renewal privilege, or where it can be renewed only upon evidence of insurability satisafactory to the company, the insured may find himself at the expiration of the term still in need of protection but—because of poor health, hazardous occupation, or other reason—unable to secure a renewal of the contract or to obtain any other form of life insurance protection. The renewal feature prevents this sort of situation. Its chief function is to protect the insurability of the policyholder.

The premium increases with each renewal, being based on the attained age of the insured at the time of any such renewal. Within the period, however, the premium is level. Over a long period of time, punctuated by several renewals, the premium will consist of a series of level premiums, each higher than the previous one. By the time the insured is in his fifties, he will be paying a premium that is higher than that which he would be paying for an ordinary life contract acquired in his early thirties. Moreover, the rate will continue to increase with each renewal. The scale of rates at which the insurance can be renewed is published in the original contract and cannot be changed by the company as long as the contract remains in force.

Evidence of renewal is usually provided in the form of a certificate to be attached to the original contract, although some companies issue a new contract with each renewal.

The companies view renewable term insurance with mixed feelings. There is no question that, properly used, it fills a real need. However, it presents certain problems to the company which writes it. Whether the policy is on the yearly renewable term plan or a longer term basis, there is likely to be strong selection against the company at time of renewal; and this selection will become increasingly great as the age of the policyholder—and hence, the renewal premium—increases. Resistance to increasing premiums will cause many of those who remain in good health to fail to renew each time a premium increase takes effect, while those in poor health will tend to take advantage of the right of renewal, with the result that as time goes on, the mortality experience among the surviving policyholders will become increasingly unfavorable. While adverse mortality experience from this source can be provided for through dividend adjustments, if the policy is on a participating basis, it requires substantial margins in the premium rates. As a result, each dollar of protection on the term basis tends to cost the policyholder more than under any other type of contract. As a further safeguard against adverse selection, the companies do not permit renewals to carry the coverage beyond age sixty or, at the latest, sixty-five. Limitations on yearly renewable term are usually more stringent, the coverage frequently being restricted to ten or fifteen years or, occasionally, fifteen years or age sixty-five, whichever is earlier. The fact is that renewable term insurance is satisfactory for individual coverage, as to both the policyholder and the company, only when the coverage does not extend into the higher ages.[1]

Convertibility

In addition to the renewable privilege, a term policy may contain a provision that permits the policyowner to exchange the term contract for a contract on a permanent plan, likewise without evidence of insurability.[2] In other words, a term insurance policy may be both renewable and convertible. The convertible feature serves the needs of those who want permanent insurance but are temporarily unable to afford the higher premiums required for whole life and endowment insurance. It is also useful when the policyholder desires to postpone the final decision as to the type of permanent insurance he will purchase until a later date when, for some reason, it may be possible to make a wiser choice. Thus, convertible term insurance provides a means of obtaining, in the same policy, temporary insurance and an option on permanent insurance. The insurability of the insured is protected by the convertible feature in an even more valuable manner than under the renewable feature, since it guarantees access to permanent insurance—not just continuation of temporary protection. The two features together afford complete protection against loss of insurability.

The conversion may be effective as of the date of the exchange or as of the original date of the term policy. If the term policy is converted as of the current date, the premium rate for the new contract is

---

[1] A classic experiment with renewable term insurance is that represented by the Provident Savings Life Assurance Society of New York, which was organized in 1875 to write insurance solely on that basis. Some of the most distinguished names in the life insurance business were associated with it or gave it their blessing. Sheppard Homans, whose name will always be known to insurance historians as the compiler of American Experience Table of Mortality, was one of the active proponents. Elizur Wright, the putative father of legal reserve life insurance, gave his support and approval, and in a letter to Mr. Homans, foresaw "a new era in life insurance" if the plan received the appreciation it deserved. The Provident Savings Society, the name by which the company came to be known, operated for approximately twenty years, with about $200 million of renewable insurance issued by 1895. By 1900, mortality was running so far ahead of the anticipated rate that the company found itself in serious difficulties. Operations were discontinued in 1911 with the reinsurance of outstanding policies.

[2] The expressions "permanent plan" or "permanent insurance" refer to whole life and endowment insurance, as distinguished from the temporary protection afforded by term insurance.

that for the insured's attained age, and the form of the policy is the one currently being issued. A conversion value, based on the reserve under the term policy, may be allowed toward payment of the premium on the new policy. This would usually be of small amount, since most term policies accumulate only a small reserve, which, incidentally, can be obtained by the insured only in the form of a conversion credit. Such conversion is usually referred to as the "attained age" method.

A policy can normally be converted retroactively only within the first five years after issue. When the conversion is effective as of the original date, the premium rate for the permanent contract is that which would have been paid had the contract been taken out originally, and the policy form is that which would have been issued originally. It is these two features which motivate the insured in most instances to convert retroactively. The advantage of the lower premium is obvious; but in many cases, the contract being issued at the original date contains actuarial assumptions or other features more favorable than those being incorporated in current policies. Offsetting these advantages, however, is the fact that a financial adjustment—involving a payment by the insured to the company—is required, which may be quite substantial if the term policy has been in force for several years. This adjustment may be computed on a variety of bases, but a great number of companies specify that the payment will be the larger of (1) the difference in the reserves (in some companies, the cash surrender values) under the policies being exchanged, or (2) the difference in the premiums paid on the term policy and those that would have been paid on the permanent plan, with interest on the difference at a stipulated rate (normally, 5 or 6 per cent). Under (2), an allowance is frequently made for any larger dividends that would have been payable under the permanent form. Some companies require a payment equal to the difference in reserves, plus a charge of 5 or 6 per cent.

It can be seen that the purpose of this adjustment, regardless of how computed, is to place the insurance company in the same financial position it would have enjoyed had the permanent contract been issued in the first instance. Therefore, it would not seem to bestow any financial advantage on the insured to convert retroactively, apart from the possibility of obtaining the benefit of more favorable actuarial assumptions. The insured will admittedly pay a smaller premium but—by making up the deficiency in the term premium—will, in effect, pay it over a longer period of time. Actuarially, the two sets of premiums are equivalent. Some persons are under the mistaken impression that by making the financial adjustment required for conversion as of the original date, they are, in effect, investing money retroactively and being credited with retroactive interest. The fact of the matter is that the insured pays the company the interest which it would have earned (more under adjustment [2]) had the larger premium been paid from the beginning.

Many factors should be considered by the insured in making a choice between the two bases of conversion, one of the most important being the state of the insured's health. He would be ill-advised to convert retroactively—and pay a substantial sum of money to the insurance company—if his health were impaired. Such sum would immediately become a part of the reserve under the contract and would not increase the amount of death benefits in the event of the insured's early demise—or ever, for that matter. The payment simply reduces the effective amount of insurance. In most cases, if the insured has surplus funds to invest in insurance, he should consider the purchase of additional insurance or perhaps the prepayment of premiums on existing policies, including the newly converted one. Subject to certain limitation, most companies permit the insured to prepay premiums, either in the form of so-called "premium deposits" or through the discounting of future premiums. The two procedures are very similar, the principal difference being that under the discount method, credit is taken in advance for the interest to be earned on the funds deposited. Under both arrangements, the funds deposited with the company are credited with interest at a stipulated rate and, in some instances, are credited with the interest earned by the company in excess of the stipulated rate. Some companies permit withdrawal of premium deposits at any time, in which case a lower rate of interest may be credited, while others limit the withdrawals to anniversary or premium due dates. A few companies permit withdrawals only in case of surrender or death. Some companies credit no interest or otherwise penalize the insured if the funds are withdrawn. In the event of the insured's death, the balance of any such deposits is returned to the insured's estate or designated beneficiaries in addition to the face of the policy.

In opposition to the above, it should be said that retroactive conversion, since it produces a larger reserve and, hence, larger interest earnings, will lead to a lower net cost of insurance if the insured survives a sufficiently long period. As with so many other aspects of the insured's insurance program, the decision should rest on the relative importance to the insured of the investment and protection features of the contract.

As was previously noted, a retroactive conversion must take place within five years after issue. If the term of the policy is no longer than ten years, a conversion as of a current date can usually be accomplished throughout the full term. If the term is longer than ten years, the policy may stipulate that the conversion privilege must be exercised, if at all, before the expiration of a period shorter than the term of the policy. For example, a fifteen-year term policy must usually be converted, if at all, within twelve years from date of issue, while a twenty-year term policy must be converted within fifteen years.

The purpose of such a time limit is to minimize adverse selection. There is always a substantial degree of adverse selection in the conversion process. Those policyholders in poor health as the time for conversion approaches are more likely to convert and pay the higher premiums than those who believe themselves to be in good health. If the decision with respect to conversion must be made some years before the expiration of the term policy, a higher percentage of healthy policyholders, uncertain of their health some years hence, will elect to convert. Even so, experience has shown that the death rate among those who convert is higher than normal. This accounts for the fact that premium rates for convertible term insurance are somewhat higher than those for term policies not containing the conversion privilege.

If the policy is renewable, the only limitation that may be found is that it be converted before age sixty or sixty-five. In other cases, the contract will state that it must be converted a certain period before the expiration of the last term for which it can be renewed.

In all cases, conversion may be permitted beyond the time limit, but within the policy term, upon evidence of insurability.

Some companies issue term policies which are automatically converted at the expiration of the term to a specified plan of permanent insurance. It is doubtful that this procedure is effective in reducing adverse selection, since the healthy individuals may fail to continue the permanent insurance.

Long-Term Contracts

While most term contracts provide protection for a relatively short period, subject to renewal for successive periods of the same duration, there are three types of term contracts which are designed to provide long-period protection in the first instance.

Life Expectancy Contract. As its name implies, this contract provides protection for the life expectancy of the insured, the premium being level throughout the period. The life expectancy refers to the number of years, *on the average,* that an individual may expect to live after having attained any given age, so that the exact term of this contract depends upon the age of the insured at date of application. At age fifteen, the term would be fifty-five years, according to the 1958 C.S.O. Table; while at age fifty, it would be twenty-four years. The rationale of the policy is that it provides protection during the productive years of the individual, when the need for insurance is greatest. Its appeal is derived from the fact that it furnishes maximum protection during the productive period of the individual's life at a very low annual outlay. It is strictly a protection as opposed to an investment contract.

Since the premiums are leveled over a long period, however, the contract provides surrender values. As in other term contracts, the cash value of the policy at the end of the term is zero. The policy may be issued with such disability provisions as the company writes, together with accidental death benefits.[3]

Provision is made for automatic conversion of the contract, at the end of the term, into a whole life form for a reduced amount of insurance with no increase in premium; or, at the option of the insured, the original amount of insurance can be continued with an increase in premium. If at the expiry of the term policy, premiums are being waived under a total disability provision, premiums on the whole life policy will also be waived during the continuance of the disability. The policy also contains a conventional conversion provision, which permits the insured to convert to a number of permanent forms at any time prior to the expiration of the term.

Term Expectancy Contract. The term expectancy contract is virtually identical with the life expectancy form, except that the former contains no conversion privileges. Not only does it not convert automatically into a whole life policy at the expiry of the term, but it cannot be converted on any earlier date. These privileges were omitted in order to permit the issuance of the contract at the lowest possible premium

---

[3] Accidental death benefits are available under many forms of term insurance. Disability benefits are usually limited to long-period term contracts, although waiver of premium is sometimes available in the short-term contracts.

rate. The conversion privilege of the life expectancy contract carries an additional premium. The period covered by the term expectancy policy is the life expectancy of the applicant.

This policy provides protection during the insured's life expectancy at the lowest possible annual outlay. If the need for protection is clearly temporary and only limited funds are available for premium payments, the term expectancy policy may well be more suitable than the life expectancy contract. The disadvantage of the contract is that it may lead to misunderstanding and disappointment. There is real danger that the insured—and particularly his dependents—will assume, as the years go by, that coverage is provided for the whole of life. If the insured outlives his expectancy and dies without insurance protection, it is of little avail to argue with the dependents that the insured was conversant with the contract and was satisfied to have the protection of the policy during his lifetime. The term expectancy policy is ordinarily recommended as an adjunct, where temporary protection on a long-term basis is needed, to an adequate amount of permanent insurance. Even here, the possibility of dissatisfaction exists; but to the life insurance adviser, it is a calculated risk which must be assumed.

Term to Sixty-Five Contract.   This contract provides protection on a level premium basis from age of issue to age sixty-five. It is not to be confused with yearly renewable or other forms of term insurance which can be renewed until the insured reaches age sixty-five. The period covered by this contract is normally somewhat shorter than the life expectancy, but its termination date coincides with the age generally regarded as the normal retirement age and, hence, probably comes closest to limiting its protection to the years when the insured's income is derived from personal efforts. Since the term is usually shorter than that of the other two long-period term contracts, the premium will be slightly smaller. It is customary to provide for cash and other surrender values. A conversion privilege may be offered; but if so, it must usually be exercised some time before the expiration of the policy. A typical form requires conversion prior to age sixty.

Nonlevel Term Insurance

The preceding discussion has presumed that the amount of insurance is level or uniform throughout the term of the policy. This is not necessarily the case, since the amount of insurance may increase or decrease throughout the term. As a matter of fact, a substantial—if not predominant—portion of term insurance is on a basis that provides for systematic decreases in the amount of insurance from year to year. This type of term insurance, appropriately called *decreasing term insurance,* may be written in the form of a separate contract, a rider to a new or existing contract, or as an integral part of a combination contract. The first two forms are illustrated by family income policies or riders, while the integration of decreasing term insurance with some other basic type of coverage is exemplified by the retirement income policy. These special forms of coverage are discussed in a later chapter.

Increasing term insurance in the form of a "return-of-premium" provision has been around for a long time but in recent years the concept has enjoyed a much wider application in connection with various arrangements, specifically split-dollar, minimum deposit, and bank loan plans, which contemplate the borrowing or encumbering of the cash value of an underlying policy. In order to provide a uniform death benefit to the insured's personal beneficiaries, contracts developed for these uses frequently make provision for the automatic purchase of an additional amount of term insurance each year in the exact or approximate amount by which the cash value increases, the latter being fully encumbered at all times. Increasing term insurance may be provided on a year-to-year basis through the operation of the so-called "fifth dividend option" which is described at a later point.

Critique of Term Insurance

Term insurance has long been a controversial type of insurance. Many people, not familiar with or perhaps not sympathetic to the principle of level premium insurance, advocate the use of term insurance in all situations, to the virtual exclusion of permanent insurance. There are certain insurance "consultants" who, when they find permanent plans in an insurance program, will advise their surrender for cash and replacement with term insurance. On the other hand, the insurance companies, mindful of the limitations of term insurance and fearful of possible adverse public reaction, tend to discourage its indiscriminate use. This has given rise to a widespread impression that insurance companies are opposed to term insurance, preferring the higher premium forms which add more to income and assets. It might be helpful, therefore, to point out the areas which can legitimately be served by term insurance and to analyze briefly some of the fallacious arguments that have been advanced in favor of term insurance.

Areas of Usefulness. Term insurance is suitable where either (1) the need for protection is purely temporary or (2) the need is permanent but the insured temporarily cannot afford the premiums for permanent insurance. In the first case, term insurance is the complete answer, but it should be renewable in the event that the temporary need should extend over a longer period than that which was originally anticipated. Theoretically, the policy need not be convertible; but since relatively few people carry an adequate amount of permanent insurance and the loss of insurability is a constant threat, it would be advisable to obtain a policy with the conversion privilege. The second broad use of term insurance requires that the policy be convertible. The conversion privilege is the bridge that spans the gap between the need for permanent insurance and the financial ability to meet the need. In this case, since the insured's financial situation might persist longer than anticipated, the policy should be renewable as well as convertible. Thus, it can be seen that the renewable and convertible features serve quite different functions and, ideally, should be incorporated in all term policies.

Examples of temporary needs which can and should be met through term insurance are encountered daily. One of the most obvious is the need to hedge a loan. A term policy in the amount of the loan payable to the lender not only protects the lender against possible loss of principal but, in the event of the insured's death, would relieve his estate of the burden of repaying the loan. A mortgage redemption policy serves the same purpose. An individual who has invested heavily in a speculative business venture should protect his estate and family by obtaining term insurance in the amount of the investment. If a business firm is spending a considerable sum in an experimental project, the success of which depends on the talents and abilities of one individual or a few individuals, term insurance on the appropriate person or persons will protect the investment. A family man with young children is likely to need more insurance while the children are dependent than he will need when they have grown up and become self-sufficient. The additional insurance during the child-raising period can be—and usually is—provided through term insurance. In many of these cases, the term insurance is of a decreasing variety and is frequently superimposed on a plan of permanent insurance. The family income policy, which is described later, is an example of the use of term insurance in combination with permanent insurance.

The second function of term insurance is important to young people who are so situated that they can expect substantial improvement in their financial situation as the years go by. Prime examples are professional men who have made a considerable investment in education and training but whose practice must be built up gradually. Young business executives also constitute good prospects for term insurance.

Fallacious Arguments in Favor of Term Insurance. The arguments which are here characterized as fallacious arguments in favor of term insurance could just as aptly be described as unfounded criticism of level premium insurance, since the arguments turn out to be just that. Upon analysis, most of the criticisms can be merged into the two sweeping allegations that (1) level premium insurance overcharges the policyholder and (2) the investment and protection elements should be separated.

The basis for the first allegation is the indisputable fact that if a policyholder dies in the early years of his contract, his premium outlay under the level premium plan is considerably larger than it would have been under a term plan. It follows, then, according to the term advocates, that the policyholder paid a larger premium than was necessary. They question whether it is wise for the insured to pay in advance for something he may never need or live to enjoy. They argue that it is better "to pay as you go and get what you pay for."

There is no question that the insured would be far better off with term insurance if he could be sure that he would die within a relatively short time; on the other hand, he would be far worse off if he guessed wrong and lives to a ripe old age. Moreover, the chances of living to an age where the total term premiums will have exceeded the total premiums paid under the level premium plan are better than the chances of not surviving to that age. Insurance is a group proposition, and no one knows whether it is to be his lot to die young or to live to an excessively old age. The level premium plan is a scheme which protects the insured against the consequences of living too long and having to pay prohibitive premiums for insurance protection. In effect, it shifts a portion of the premium burden of those who live beyond their life expectancy to those who die young and receive an exceedingly large return on their premium outlay. Since, at the outset, no one can know which group he will be in, payment of the level premium by all is an eminently fair and satisfactory arrangement.

The "overcharge" argument sometimes takes the form of an assertion that the reserve under permanent forms of insurance is forfeited to the company in the event of the insured's death. To correct this "inequity," it is argued, the normal death benefit should be increased by the amount of the reserve.

This argument, it should be apparent, strikes at the very heart of the level premium plan. As has been stated, the essence of this plan is a gradual reduction in the net amount at risk as the reserve increases. If the reserve is to be paid in addition to the face of the policy, this reduction in the amount at risk does not occur, and premiums which were calculated on the assumption that the risk is to be a decreasing one will clearly be inadequate. Some companies offer a contract which promises to return the reserve in addition to the face of the policy, but the premium is increased accordingly.

The second broad argument—that the investment and protection elements of the contract should be separated—is based upon the proposition that an individual can invest his surplus funds more wisely and with a greater return than can the life insurance company. Those who believe this recommend that the individual buy term insurance and then place in a separate investment program the difference between the term premium and the premium that he would have paid for level premium insurance. Some recommend that this difference in premiums be placed in government bonds, others recommend investment trusts or mutual funds, while others recommend an individual investment program in common stocks.

This argument needs to be analyzed in terms of the objectives of any investment program. The principal objectives are generally regarded to be safety of principal, yield, and liquidity.

With respect to the first, the life insurance industry has compiled a solvency record over the years that is unmatched by any other type of business organization. It has survived wars, depressions, and inflations with composite losses to policyholders that can only be termed as inconsequential.[4] This record has been achieved through concentration on government bonds—federal, state, and local—high-grade corporate bonds, and real estate mortgages, and emphasis on diversification. Investments are diversified as to type of industry, geographical distribution, maturity, and size. Many of the larger companies have from

---

[4] Dr. David McCahan's study of the solvency record of life insurance, covering the period 1910–32, revealed that the average annual loss to policyholders during the twenty-three-year period did not exceed 29 cents for each $1,000 of net reserve. S. S. Huebner and David McCahan, *Life Insurance as Investment* (New York: D. Appleton-Century, Inc., 1933), pp. 122–23. The period encompassed by the study covered three depressions and World War I.

100,000 to 200,000 different units of investment. The reserve or investment of the individual policyholder is commingled with the reserves of all other policyholders and invested as a unit. In effect, therefore, each policyholder owns a prorata share of each investment unit in the company's portfolio. The insured may have as little as one cent invested in some units. Such diversification—which is the keystone of safety—is obviously beyond the reach of the individual investor. Only by investing exclusively in federal and state government bonds, with the consequent sacrifice of yield, could the individual investor hope to match the safety of principal that his funds would enjoy with a reputable life insurance company.

Life insurance companies unquestionably obtain the highest possible yield commensurate with the standard of safety which they have set for themselves. As a group, the life insurance companies domiciled in the United States earned 4.61 per cent of their mean ledger assets during the calendar year 1965. This figure represents the net investment income, after deducting all expenses allocable to investment operations but before deduction of federal income taxes. This figure which does not reflect capital gains and losses, was the highest since 1932 but was still below the rate of 5.07 per cent earned in the 1920's. In today's booming economy, many individuals may be able to secure a higher yield than that provided by a life insurance company by investing in common stocks or other equity investments, especially if unrealized capital appreciation is taken into account, and some exceptional investors will be able to do it under virtually any circumstances. It is highly questionable, however, that the *typical* life insurance policyholder can, over a long period, earn a consistently higher yield than a life insurance company, regardless of the type of investment program which he pursues. Moreover, it should be noted that the annual accretions in cash values are not subject to federal income taxes as they accrue,[5] while the earnings from a separate investment program would be taxed as ordinary income.

With respect to the third objective of an investment program, it can be said that the liquidity of a life insurance contract is unsurpassed. The policyholder's investment can be withdrawn at any time, with no loss of principal. This can be accomplished through surrender for cash or through policy loans. The insured never faces the possibility of

---

[5] Except in the case of death, most of the earnings on the reserve of a life insurance contract are eventually taxed to the insured but usually at a time when he is in a much lower tax bracket.

liquidating his assets in an unfavorable market, nor can his policy loans be called because of inadequate collateral. The liquidity of certain types of investment approaches that of life insurance cash values, but no investment whose value depends upon the market can aspire to the liquidity of the demand obligation represented by the life insurance contract.

More important, perhaps, than any of the preceding factors is the question of whether the savings under a separate investment program would be accomplished in the first instance. Life insurance is a form of "forced" saving. Not only does life insurance, with its periodic premiums, provide a simple and systematic mechanism for saving; but when the savings feature is combined with the protection feature, there is far more incentive for the insured to save than there would otherwise be. An individual who is voluntarily purchasing a bond a month or setting aside so much per month in some other type of savings account may skip a month or two if some other disposition of his money appeals to him more. If, however, failure to set aside his predetermined contribution to a savings account would result in loss of insurance protection which he prizes very highly and which might be irreplaceable, the insured will be far more likely to make the savings effort. He saves because it is the only way of preserving his protection.

The foregoing is not to disparage other forms of investment. All have their place in the financial program of an individual. Level premium life insurance, however, should be the foundation of any such financial program.

CHAPTER IV

Whole
Life
Insurance

IN CONTRAST with term insurance, which pays benefits only if the insured dies during a specified period of years, whole life insurance provides for the payment of the face amount upon the death of the insured, regardless of when it may occur. It is this characteristic—protection for the whole of life—that gives the insurance its name. The expression has no reference to the manner in which the premiums are paid, only to the duration of the protection. If the premiums are to be paid throughout the lifetime of the insured, the insurance is known as *ordinary life;* if premiums are to be paid only during a specified period, the insurance is designated *limited-payment life.* Hence, it may be said that there are two principal types of whole life contracts: ordinary life and limited-payment life.

PRINCIPAL TYPES OF WHOLE LIFE INSURANCE

Ordinary Life Insurance

Ordinary life insurance is that type of whole life insurance the premiums for which are based on the assumption that premiums will be paid until the death of the insured. It seems desirable to define ordinary life in that manner, since in an increasing number of cases, the insurance is purchased with no intention on the part of the insured of paying premiums as long as he lives. In many cases, the insurance is purchased as part of a program that contemplates the use of dividends to pay up the insurance by the end of a period shorter than the life expectancy of the insured; in other cases, the plan may be to surrender the insurance for an annuity or for a reduced amount of insurance. The point is that ordinary life should not be envisioned as a type of insurance on which the insured is irrevocably committed to pay premiums as long as he lives, even into extreme old age. Rather, it should be viewed as a type of policy which provides permanent protection for the lowest premium outlay, with the greatest degree of flexibility to meet changing needs and circumstances. It is the most basic policy offered by any life insurance company, and it enjoys the widest sale. It should be the foundation of any insurance program and, in an adequate amount, could well serve as the entire program. Its distinctive features are discussed below.

Permanent Protection. The protection afforded by the ordinary life contract is permanent in the sense that the term never expires and hence never has to be renewed or converted. If the insured continues to pay premiums, or pays up the policy, he has protection as long as he lives, regardless of the condition of his health; and eventually, the face of the policy will be paid. This is a valuable right, since virtually everyone has need of some insurance as long as he lives, if for nothing more than to pay his last-illness and funeral expenses. In most cases, the need is much greater than that.

In one sense, ordinary life may be regarded as an endowment. It will be learned later that an endowment insurance contract pays the face of the policy if the insured should die during the endowment period or if he should survive to the end of the period. If age one hundred is considered to be the end of the endowment period—as well as the end of the mortality table—then an ordinary life policy becomes a contract which pays the face as a death claim if the insured should die before age one hundred or as a matured endowment if he should survive to one hundred. During the years when the American Experience Table of Mortality (which has a terminal age of ninety-six) was being used for new insurance, many companies labeled their ordinary life contract as an "endowment at 96." For that matter, many companies today offer an "endowment at 85" in lieu of an ordinary life contract. Many prospects will buy an "endowment at 85" when they will not buy an ordinary life policy! Of course, the ordinary life policy could just as aptly be described as a "term to 100," if it were to be assumed that all individuals who survive to age ninety-nine die before their one hundredth birthday.

Lowest Premium Outlay. Inasmuch as the premium rate for an ordinary life contract is calculated on the assumption that premiums will be payable throughout the whole of life, the lowest rate is produced. As will be noted later, the net single premium for a whole life policy is computed without reference to the manner in which the periodic premiums will be paid and, at any particular age, is the same for ordinary life and any form of limited-payment life. Naturally, the longer the period over which the single-sum payment is spread, the lower will be each periodic payment. Thus, the *net* annual level premium per $1,000 of ordinary life insurance, issued as of age twenty and calculated on the basis of the 1958 C.S.O. Table and $2\frac{1}{2}$ per cent interest, is only $10.75, while the comparable premium for a twenty-payment life policy is $19.48. The *gross* annual premium[1] per $1,000 charged by a certain nonparticipating company for the same two contracts at age twenty is $11.67 and $20.03, respectively.[2] The gross annual premium for these two contracts at age thirty-five is $18.81 and $28.48, respectively. The comparable rates for endowment insurance are much higher. For example, the net annual level premium for a twenty-year endowment insurance contract, issued at age twenty, is $39.28 per $1,000, while the gross premium for the contract at ages twenty and thirty-five is $43.01 and $44.81, respectively.

Limited-payment and endowment insurance contracts provide benefits that justify the higher premium rates, of course; but if the objective of the insured is to secure the maximum amount of permanent insurance protection per dollar of premium outlay, then his purposes will be best served by the ordinary life contract. Its moderate cost brings the policy within reach of all except those in the older age brackets.

Investment Element. As level premium permanent insurance, ordinary life accumulates a reserve which gradually reaches a substantial level and eventually equals the face of the policy. As is to be expected, however, the reserve at all durations is lower than that of the other forms of permanent insurance. In other words, the protection element tends to be relatively high. Nevertheless, it is the opinion of many that the ordinary life contract offers the optimum combination of protection and investment. The contract emphasizes protection; but it accumulates an investment element that can be used to accomplish a variety of purposes, some of which are mentioned below.

---

[1] The gross premium is the premium actually paid by the policyholder. It is the net premium increased by an allowance for expenses and contingencies.

[2] A nonparticipating life insurance company is a stock company that pays no dividends to policyholders. A participating or mutual company will usually charge a somewhat higher gross premium but will make a dividend refund to the policyholder at the end of the year.

The cash values which will accumulate under an ordinary life contract at three different ages of issue and at varying durations are shown in Table 2. Also shown are the other surrender values, paid-up insurance and extended term insurance, whose significance will be explained below. Cash values are not available during the first year or

TABLE 2

SURRENDER VALUES UNDER ORDINARY LIFE POLICY FOR $1,000,
ISSUED AS OF AGES 20, 30, AND 40,
1958 C.S.O. TABLE AND 2½ PER CENT INTEREST
(1958 C.E.T. for Extended Term*)

YEARS	AGE 20 (GROSS PREMIUM: $11.67)				AGE 30 (GROSS PREMIUM: $15.78)				AGE 40 (GROSS PREMIUM: $22.75)			
	Cash	Paid Up	Extended Term		Cash	Paid Up	Extended Term		Cash	Paid Up	Extended Term	
			Yrs.	Days			Yrs.	Days			Yrs.	Days
1..	—	—	—	—	—	—	—	—	—	—	—	—
2..	—	—	—	—	$ 3	$ 10	1	12	$ 12	$ 29	2	77
3..	$ 5	$ 19	1	356	16	47	5	111	31	71	4	336
4..	14	52	5	257	29	83	8	205	49	110	6	292
5..	24	86	9	342	43	120	11	46	68	149	8	116
6..	33	116	13	129	56	153	12	304	87	186	9	176
7..	43	147	16	72	71	189	14	142	107	223	10	169
8..	53	177	18	98	85	220	15	156	127	259	11	80
9..	64	208	20	4	100	253	16	117	146	291	11	269
10..	74	235	21	37	115	283	16	363	167	325	12	89
11..	85	263	22	21	130	312	17	177	187	356	12	209
12..	97	292	22	326	146	342	17	337	207	385	12	295
13..	108	317	23	132	162	371	18	83	228	415	13	4
14..	120	344	23	288	178	398	18	154	248	442	13	34
15..	132	369	24	22	194	423	18	192	269	470	13	58
16..	145	395	24	111	211	450	18	226	290	496	13	62
17..	158	419	24	158	227	473	18	211	311	522	13	50
18..	171	443	24	169	244	496	18	196	332	546	13	23
19..	184	464	24	152	262	521	18	182	353	570	12	352
20..	198	487	24	138	279	542	18	129	374	592	12	308
Age 60..	508	804	17	338	458	725	15	319	374	592	12	308
Age 65..	588	853	15	305	547	794	14	107	478	694	12	14

* The 1958 C.E.T., an abbreviation for the Commissioners 1958 Extended Insurance Table, is a special table approved for the computation of extended term insurance. It contains extra margins of conservatism in recognition of the adverse selection associated with term insurance and the fact that no allowance is made for expenses incurred in connection with extended term insurance.

two of the insurance because of the cost to the company of putting the business on the books. The interdependence of expenses and cash values will be described in Chapter XIV.

Flexibility. Ordinary life, in common with other forms of whole life insurance, provides a high degree of flexibility. This flexibility is derived from several different contract provisions, but one of the most significant is that set of provisions referred to as "nonforfeiture" or "surrender" options. Designed originally to preserve the policyholder's equity in the policy reserve, the surrender provisions are being increasingly used to adapt the coverage of the policy to changing circumstances and needs. Most policies stipulate that the surrender value may be taken in one of three forms: cash, reduced amount of paid-up whole life insurance, and paid-up term insurance.

The policy may be surrendered at any time for its cash value; but in that event, the protection terminates, and the company has no further obligation under the policy. While this privilege provides a ready source of cash to meet a financial emergency or to take advantage of a business opportunity, it should be exercised with restraint, since it destroys the further usefulness of the policy. A policy that has been surrendered for cash cannot be reinstated, except by special permission of the company.

The second option permits the insured to take a reduced amount of paid-up whole life insurance, payable upon the same conditions as the original policy. The amount of the paid-up insurance is that amount which can be purchased at the insured's attained age by the net cash value (cash value, less any policy indebtedness, plus any dividend accumulations) applied as a net single premium. It is to be noted that the paid-up insurance is purchased at *net* rates, which constitutes a sizable saving. Reference to Table 2 will reveal that the cash value at the end of twenty years on an ordinary life contract issued at age thirty is $279, which is sufficient, as a net single premium, to purchase $542 of paid-up whole life insurance. The protection continues in the reduced amount until the insured's death, unless the reduced policy is surrendered for cash; and no further premiums are called for under this plan.

The third option provides paid-up term insurance in an amount equal to the original face of the policy, increased by any dividend additions or deposits, and decreased by any policy indebtedness. The length of the term is that which can be purchased at the insured's attained age with the net cash value applied as a net single premium. The aforementioned cash value of $279 would purchase, at age fifty, term insurance for 18 years and 129 days. If the insured fails to elect an option within a specified period after default of premiums, this option automatically goes into effect.

If the financial status of the insured makes it impracticable to continue premium payments, or if the need for insurance protection undergoes a change, the insured may wish to avail himself of the surrender options. After the dependents have become self-supporting, he may elect to discontinue premium payments and continue his protection on a reduced scale for the remainder of his life. If, on the other hand, the need for insurance continues, he may elect to eliminate premium payments but continue the full amount of protection for a definite period of time. The elimination of fixed payments may be particularly attractive as the insured approaches retirement and anticipates a curtailment in his income.

Another use of surrender values which is growing in popularity is to apply them to the purchase of an annuity or retirement income. Recent contracts of many companies specifically give the insured the right to take the cash value in the form of a life income, purchased at net rates. Other companies will grant the privilege upon request. More and more insureds are purchasing ordinary life to protect their family during the child-raising period, with the specific objective of using the cash values for their own retirement. The cash value of an ordinary life policy purchased at age twenty-five will amount to about 60 per cent of the face at age sixty-five. The comparable percentage for an ordinary life policy purchased at age thirty-five is 52 per cent, and even a policy issued as late as age forty will accumulate a cash value at age sixty-five only slightly less than one half of the face. Therefore, if an individual should procure $50,000 of ordinary life insurance at age thirty-five, for example, he would have approximately $26,000 in cash values at sixty-five, which at net rates would provide a life income of about $180 per month. Supplemented by Federal OASDI benefits, private retirement plan benefits, and income from other savings, this would provide the insured with a substantial retirement income.

Some might feel that the interruption of premium payments on an ordinary life policy would in some way amount to failure to complete the program. There are, of course, situations where this might be the case. However, if the ordinary life plan is deliberately selected with the idea of discontinuing premiums at an advanced age, there can be no suggestion of failure in completing the undertaking. Neither should an insured be reluctant to convert ordinary life insurance to reduced paid-up insurance if a change of circumstance makes the reduced amount adequate for his needs, particularly if retirement status makes life insurance premiums an unjustified burden. Life insurance is designed to provide protection where the need exists. It can be a burden and may represent very real sacrifice on the part of the insured. If, however, the need for protection ceases, the burden may be lightened. This is an advantage of the ordinary life contract that should be recognized at the outset and utilized as the occasion arises.

Another broad source of flexibility is found in the latitude provided the insured in the disposition of dividends. The insured has various options, which will be analyzed in due course;[3] but the two which are of particular interest in the present connection are those that permit the insured to use the dividends to pay up the policy or to mature it as an endowment. Either option makes it possible for the insured to discontinue premium payments within the foreseeable future, which may be a prime consideration. On the basis of the dividend record of one large company, an ordinary life policy purchased at any age in the twenties can be paid up within twenty-seven years or can be made to mature as an endowment within thirty-eight years, through the application of dividends to that purpose. The period becomes shorter as the age of issue goes up.

A final source of flexibility that should be mentioned is the right to convert to other forms of insurance. It is customary to include a provision in all whole life policies giving the insured the right to exchange the policy for another type of contract, sometimes subject to certain conditions. Whether such privilege is specifically granted or not, an exchange can usually be negotiated. Virtually all companies will permit any form of permanent insurance to be converted to another form, without evidence of insurability, as long as the new contract calls for a larger premium. Most companies, however, will not permit a higher premium contract to be exchanged for a lower premium contract without evidence of insurability. Such an exchange not only reduces future premiums but requires the company to return a portion of the reserve to the insured, thereby increasing the actual amount at risk. The company always suspects an impairment of health under such circumstances.[4] If the insured is converting to a higher premium form, the net amount at risk will be reduced more rapidly, and the company does not have to fear adverse selection. The ordinary life contract has a unique advantage in this regard, in that it is the lowest premium form of permanent insurance and hence can be converted to any other form of permanent insurance without evidence of insurability. The insured, therefore, whose savings objective may envision substantial amounts of endowment and limited-payment insurance, but whose current financial circumstances limit the funds available for insur-

---

[3] Chapter XVII.

[4] Some companies are willing to issue a policy on a lower premium plan without evidence of insurability if the amount of insurance is increased to such an extent that the company is relieved of the obligation to refund a portion of the reserve and suffers no reduction in premium income.

ance, might well inaugurate his insurance program with ordinary life, with the idea of converting it later to higher premium forms. If feasible, ordinary life is preferable to term insurance under such circumstances, since if the more ambitious program is never realized, the insured still has permanent protection and a modest investment. Moreover, if conversion is ultimately effected, the financial adjustment involved—whether it be the lump-sum payment of the difference in reserves or merely a shift to the higher premium basis—will not be so drastic.

Limited-Payment Life Insurance

Limited-payment life insurance is that type of whole life insurance the premiums for which are limited by contract to a specified number of years. The limitation may be expressed in terms of the *number* of annual premiums or of the *age* beyond which premiums will not be required. Policies whose premiums are limited by number usually stipulate ten, fifteen, twenty, twenty-five, or thirty payments, although some companies are willing to issue policies calling for any desired number of premiums. The greater the number of premiums payable, naturally, the more closely the contract approaches the ordinary life form. For those who prefer to limit their premium payments to a period measured by a terminal age, companies make available policies which are paid up at a specified age—typically, sixty, sixty-five, or seventy. The objective is to permit the policy to be paid for during the working lifetime of the insured. Many companies issue contracts the premiums for which are payable to an advanced age, such as eighty-five; but for all practical purposes, such contracts can be regarded as the equivalent of ordinary life contracts.

Since, at the date of issue, the value of a limited-payment whole life contract is precisely the same as that of a contract to be purchased on the ordinary life basis, and since it is presumed that there will be fewer premium payments under the limited-payment policy, it follows that each premium must be larger than the comparable premium under an ordinary life contract. Moreover, the fewer the premiums specified or the shorter the premium-paying period, the higher will be each premium. However, the higher premiums are offset by greater cash and other surrender values. Thus, the limited-payment policy will provide a larger fund for use in an emergency and will accumulate a larger fund for retirement purposes than will an ordinary life contract issued at the same age. On the other hand, if death takes place within the first several years after issue of the contract, the total premiums paid under the limited-payment policy will exceed those payable under an ordinary life policy. The comparatively long-lived policyholder, however, will pay considerably less in premiums under the limited-payment plan than on the ordinary life basis. There is no presumptive financial advantage as between one form and the other. The choice depends upon circumstances and personal preference. The limited-payment policy offers the assurance that premium payments will be confined to the productive years of the insured, while the ordinary life contract provides maximum permanent protection for any given annual outlay. The limited-payment policy contains the same surrender options, dividend options, settlement options, and other features that make for a high degree of flexibility.

An extreme form of limited-payment contract is the single-premium life insurance policy. Under this plan, the number of premiums is limited to one. The effective amount of insurance protection is, of course, substantially less than the face of the policy and the investment element correspondingly great. Such contracts, therefore, are purchased largely for investment purposes. As investments, they offer a high degree of security, a satisfactory interest yield, and ready convertibility into cash on a basis guaranteed by the company for the entire duration of the contract. Since the single premium represents a substantial amount of money and is computed on the basis that there will be no return of any part of it in the event of the early death of the insured, it has only limited appeal for protection purposes.

The limited-payment principle is applicable to any type of contract and is frequently used in connection with endowment contracts.

JOINT LIFE INSURANCE

The typical life insurance contract is written on the life of one person and is technically known as "single-life insurance." A contract can be written on more than one life, however, in which event it is known as a joint-life contract. Strictly speaking, a joint-life contract is one written on the lives of two or more persons and payable upon the death of the *first* person to die. If the face is payable upon the death of the *last* of two or more lives insured under a single contract, it would be called a *last survivor* policy. Such a policy would be useful only under the most exceptional circumstances and hence is rarely issued. Joint-life policies, on the other hand, are fairly common.

The joint-life policy may cover as many as four lives (even more, theoretically); but because of expense and other practical obstacles, most companies limit the number to three. The contract is usually written on the whole life plan, either ordinary life or limited-payment; but it can be obtained on the endowment plan. In the latter case, the face is payable upon the first death or at the end of the endowment period. It is virtually never written on the term plan, since separate term policies on each life for the same amount would cost little more than a joint policy and would offer the advantage of continued protection to the survivor or survivors.

The premium for a joint-life policy is somewhat greater than the combined premiums on separate policies providing an equivalent amount of insurance. In other words, the premium for a $20,000 joint-life policy covering two lives is larger than the sum of the premiums on two separate contracts providing $10,000 each. This is so, since with separate policies, only $10,000 is payable upon the death of the first of the two insureds to die; while under the joint-life policy, $20,000 would be payable. Moreover, since two lives are covered, the "cost of insurance" is relatively high, and cash values are relatively low.

The provisions of the joint-life contract follow closely those of the single-life contract. The clause allowing change to other forms of policy differs in that it provides a privilege of change to policies on separate lives. This privilege of change provides for (1) conversion to single-life policies on the same plan as that of the joint policies; (2) division of the amount of insurance equally among the insured lives, the total amount so written not to exceed the face amount of the joint policy; and (3) dating of the new policies as of the original date of issue of the joint policy.

The joint-life contract has been largely confined to two types of situations: business associates, and husbands and wives. In the financing of a partnership buy-and-sell agreement, for example, partners sometimes take out a joint policy covering the lives of all partners and written for an amount equal to the largest interest involved. Upon the death of the first partner, the surviving partners will be provided the funds with which to purchase the partnership interest of the deceased. The same practice may be followed by stockholders in a close corporation. It is doubtful, however, that the joint-life policy is suitable in the majority of such cases. Since the insurance terminates upon the first death among the partners or close corporation stockholders, the remaining members of the firm will not only be without insurance but—of greater consequence—may be uninsurable. Furthermore, a change in the membership of the organization may make it difficult or impossible to adjust the insurance coverage. Differences in the ownership interests of the members may also create a problem. Finally, there is always the possibility of confusion or misunderstanding if one of the firm members is declined for insurance. For these reasons, it is usually better for a separate policy to be placed on each partner or stockholder, in the amount of his ownership interest, with the premiums being shared on some equitable basis.

A joint-life policy may be suitable for a husband and wife where the death of either will create a need for funds, as would be true if death taxes were involved. Even here, dissatisfaction sometimes arises when the survivor is brought face to face with the fact that he no longer has any coverage under the contract.

"SPECIAL" WHOLE LIFE POLICIES

One of the most controversial developments of recent years has been the widespread introduction and vigorous promotion of "special" policies. Usually on the ordinary life plan, these policies carry a premium rate lower than those of the regular forms. Such policies have long been offered by many companies; but in recent years, numerous other companies have adopted the practice to meet the growing "price" competition.

A company may justify a special low rate on a particular policy—which, in all other respects, is identical with the regular policy form—by (1) limiting the face to a specified *minimum amount* or (2) limiting its issue to *preferred risks*—that is, to groups which because of more rigorous underwriting requirements, should experience a lower rate of mortality than that among insured lives generally. In some cases, both practices are a factor.

The purpose of the minimum amount is to reduce the expense rate per $1,000 of insurance. Many items of expense reflected in the gross premium of a policy are not affected by the face amount of the policy. Examples of such expenses are the medical examiner's fee, inspection fee, accounting costs, and general overhead. If the average size of the policy can be increased, therefore, the expense rate per $1,000 will be lower. Then, because the gross premium is lower, expenses which vary directly with the size of the premium—notably, commissions and premium taxes—will also be less per $1,000 of insurance. In fact, in many companies, the commission *rate* on special policies is lower than that on other whole life policies. A class of policies in which the minimum face amount is $5,000 can be expected to develop an *average* face amount double that of the regular classes in which the minimum is $1,000. Some companies do not offer their "special" policy in an amount less than $25,000. The savings in the expense rate alone can be quite substantial.

The savings garnered by superior selection depend upon the nature of the standards imposed, the test of which is actual mortality experience. The potential area of savings is fairly large, since selection standards have a significant impact on mortality rates. Furthermore, "preferred risk" policies are almost always issued on a minimum-amount basis, and thus reap the expense savings described above. At most ages, and in most companies, the difference in premiums between a "special" whole life policy and the regular ordinary life policy ranges from $2 to $3 per $1,000. On a large policy, the savings can be especially attractive.

The case for "special" policies is based largely on the grounds of equity. If a policyholder takes out a policy of such size that its expense rate is lower than average, or if he is a better risk than average, he should be given the benefit of the savings in the form of a lower premium. The principal argument against the bargain policies is the arbitrary nature of the underlying classification. For example, the reasons which justify a lower expense loading per $1,000 for a policy of $5,000 than for one of $2,000 argue just as forcefully for an even lower rate for a $10,000 policy, a $20,000 policy, and so on. In fact, the logical conclusion is that premium rates per $1,000 should decrease as the size of the policy increases. However desirable such a practice might be from the standpoint of equity, it would tremendously complicate the operation of the business and might, in fact, be impracticable. Limiting the expense discount to policies of $5,000 or over, or to any other arbitrary amount, is only partial recognition of the relatively lower expenses on large policies.

By the same token, if the principle of granting a lower rate to superior risks is sound, it should be extended to all other kinds of policies and not be limited to the whole life variety.[5] The soundness of the

---

[5] As a matter of fact, this is now being done on an increasingly broader basis through a system of graded premiums. See pp. 250–51 for a discussion of this development.

principle has been questioned in some quarters, however, on the grounds that it is contrary to the basic insurance principle of averaging. It is argued that to get average results, coverage of large groups is essential—which, from a practical standpoint, requires inclusion in the same group of persons with widely varying prospects of longevity. Some insureds must bear more than their theoretically accurate share of mortality costs, while others will contribute less than their true share.

While not a part of the argument for or against "special" policies, it should be observed that the placing of the larger policies or the superior risks in a separate class, with a lower premium rate, inevitably results in a higher cost of insurance for the smaller policies and those insureds who cannot qualify as preferred risks.

FUNCTIONS OF WHOLE LIFE INSURANCE

At this point, the purposes served by whole life insurance should be clear. In summary, however, it may be stated that the whole life policy (1) provides protection against long-range or permanent needs and (2) accumulates a savings fund that can be used for general purposes or to meet specific objectives. The first function is particularly applicable to the life income need of the widow, last-illness and funeral expenses, expenses of estate administration, death taxes, philanthropic bequests, and the needs of dependent relatives other than the widow. The general savings feature of the policy is useful in times of financial emergency or as a source of funds to take advantage of an unusual business or investment opportunity. The policy may be used for the specific purpose of accumulating funds for the college education of the children, to set a son up in business, to provide a dowry for a daughter, or to supplement the retirement income of the insured.

CHAPTER V

Endowment Insurance

TERM and whole life insurance provide for payment of the face amount of the policy only in the event of death. Endowment insurance, on the other hand, provides not only for payment of the face of the policy in the event of the insured's death during a specified period of years, but also for payment of the full face amount at the end of such period if the insured still be living. The endowment insurance policy, therefore, introduces a concept not heretofore encountered. That concept is the "pure endowment."

NATURE OF ENDOWMENT INSURANCE

A "pure endowment" is a contract which promises to pay the face of the policy only if the insured be living at the end of a specified period, nothing being paid in case of prior death. It is rarely—if ever—sold, since few individuals are willing to take the chance of dying during the endowment period and forfeiting the entire consideration paid for the contract. In contrast, a term insurance contract promises to pay the face of the policy only if the insured should die during a specified period, nothing being paid in the event of his survival to the end of such period. The two promises are, therefore, exactly opposite in their nature. They may be combined in one contract, however, in which case the resulting policy will pay the face whether the insured lives or dies. Such a contract is designated "endowment insurance" in order to distinguish it from a "pure endowment." From the standpoint of structure, therefore, it may be said that an endowment insurance policy is a combination of pure or level term insurance and a pure endowment.[1]

---

[1] The same description may be applied to a whole life policy, which is simply a combination of term insurance for a period extending to age one hundred and a pure endowment for the same term.

71

Endowment insurance policies may be classified in various ways; but with respect to the manner in which the *maturity date* is expressed, they may be subdivided into (1) those that mature at a specified age, such as fifty-five, sixty, or sixty-five; and (2) those that mature at the end of a specified number of years, such as ten, fifteen, or twenty. Those in the first category tend to be long-term endowments and are usually taken out to combine insurance protection during the working years of life with provision for old age. Those in the second category may be regarded as short-term endowments and are more likely to be acquired for investment purposes or to meet some special need, such as repayment of a mortgage or some other type of loan. Of course, for a prospect aged forty-five, a twenty-year endowment and an endowment at sixty-five are exactly equivalent, and it would be a matter of indifference as to which he selected. The same is true of other durations. Some companies offer twenty-five- and thirty-year endowments, whose endowment period at many ages would closely approximate that of the policies which mature at specified ages.

As was noted earlier, many companies issue an "endowment at 85" in lieu of, or perhaps in addition to, an ordinary life policy. In the latter case, the ordinary life is frequently a "special" policy, and an "endowment at 85" is used to avoid offering two ordinary life policies at different premium rates. A "life paid up at 85" is sometimes used for the same purpose. Finally, it should be noted that a few companies offer "double endowments" and "semi-endowments," under which, in the first case, the amount payable in the event of survival is twice that paid in the event of death, and, in the second case, the sum payable upon survival is only half that paid in the event of death.

Endowment insurance policies are usually issued with premiums payable throughout the endowment period. In the case of short-term endowments, the premiums are very large, since the face of the policy must be accumulated over a relatively short period. The premiums on long-term endowments are much more moderate and, at some ages, are only slightly higher than those for ordinary life. The relative magnitude of annual premium rates for endowment insurance policies of varying durations and at different ages of issue can be observed in Table 3. The rates are those of nonparticipating policies issued by a well-known stock company.

Long-term endowments are frequently issued on the limited-payment plan, a twenty-payment endowment at sixty-five being quite common. Under that plan, premium payments, if made annually, would cease at the end of nineteen years (the first premium being paid

TABLE 3
NONPARTICIPATING ANNUAL PREMIUM RATES
PER $1,000 OF ENDOWMENT INSURANCE
Policy Fee of $10.00 to Be Added

AGE	ENDOWMENTS OF SPECIFIED DURATIONS					ENDOW-MENT AT 60	ENDOW-MENT AT 65	ORDI-NARY LIFE RATE
	10 Years	15 Years	20 Years	25 Years	30 Years			
20.........	$ 93.57	$58.59	$42.01	$31.88	$25.30	$17.28	$14.37	$10.67
25.........	93.62	58.64	42.45	32.33	25.70	20.94	17.27	12.44
30.........	93.83	59.02	43.05	32.89	26.22	26.22	21.20	14.78
35.........	94.42	60.06	43.81	33.62	26.80	33.62	26.80	17.81
40.........	95.35	61.16	44.87	34.55	28.96	44.87	34.55	21.75
45.........	96.60	62.12	46.31	37.40	32.46	62.12	46.31	26.94
50.........	97.38	63.38	48.34	40.77	36.98	97.38	63.38	33.14
55.........	99.32	66.05	52.21	45.60	—	—	99.32	40.95
60.........	103.56	71.20	58.43	—	—	—	—	51.78

at time of issue), but the policy would not mature until age sixty-five or upon the insured's earlier death. Endowments are also issued on joint lives, the policy being payable at the first death, if it occurs prior to the maturity date.

ALTERNATIVE CONCEPT OF ENDOWMENT INSURANCE

Some people wonder how a life insurance company can afford to offer a contract which pays the face amount whether the insured lives or dies. To them, it looks like a situation in which the insured cannot fail to win. If he dies, his family receives a sum which is normally much in excess of the premiums he paid; if he lives, he receives the sum himself. In either case, the insurance company "loses." Others, however, view the endowment insurance contract as one under which the insured cannot fail to lose. They argue that to derive a benefit under the pure endowment portion of the contract, the insured must outlive the endowment period. If he does not, the consideration paid for the pure endowment is forfeited. To derive a benefit under the term portion of the contract, the insured must die before the end of the endowment period; otherwise, the premiums paid for the term insurance are forfeited. It is obviously impossible to receive payment under both portions of the contract. Therefore, it is inevitable that the insured will lose one set of premiums.

The same line of reasoning has led such people to argue that the reserve under an endowment of insurance contract is forfeited if the policyholder dies before the policy matures as an endowment. To take an extreme example, the reserve under a twenty-year endowment insurance policy at the end of the nineteenth year is nearly equal to the face of the policy. If the insured were to surrender the policy for its cash value at the end of the nineteenth year and obtain a one-year term policy for the same face amount, his estate would be in receipt of both the cash value of the endowment and the face amount of the term insurance in the event of the insured's death during the twentieth year. Consequently, it is contended that the company should pay upon the death of the policyholder not only the face of the policy but, in addition, the accumulated reserve.

To counter such criticism, another concept of the endowment insurance contract has been developed. Under this concept, the contract is not viewed as a combination of level term insurance and a pure endowment but rather as *decreasing term insurance* and *increasing investment*. The investment portion of the contract is not regarded as a pure endowment, all of which is forfeited in the event of the insured's death before the end of the term, but as a savings account credited to the policyholder and available at any time to the insured through surrender of the policy or exercise of the loan privilege. This investment feature is supplemented by term insurance, which is not, however, level term insurance for the face of the policy throughout the term, but insurance for a constantly decreasing amount which, when added to the investment accumulation at the date of death, will make the amount payable under the contract equal to its face. The insurance portion of the contract is almost equal to the face in the first year but decreases throughout the term of the endowment. Finally, when the investment portion of the contract equals the face of the policy—at maturity—the decreasing term insurance will have declined to zero. At any particular time, the accumulated savings fund on the one side and the decreasing term insurance on the other will always equal the face of the policy. In other words, there is no forfeiture in the event of death. Upon death, the insured's estate or heirs receive the savings accumulation standing to his credit and, in addition, decreasing term insurance proceeds equal to the difference between the investment accumulation and the face of the policy.

The foregoing concept, which will be recognized as the one underlying all forms of permanent insurance, has been termed the *economic* concept of endowments, as distinguished from the *mathematical*.[2] Both are mathematically sound, and one is the actuarial equivalent of the other.

---

[2] The premium for an endowment insurance contract is calculated as if it were composed of level term insurance and a pure endowment.

INVESTMENT FEATURE OF AN ENDOWMENT

The endowment insurance contract definitely emphasizes the investment element, particularly the short-term endowments. In most cases, the endowment contract is taken out with the objective of accumulating a specific sum, and the protection element is merely a corollary to the main objective. The protection or decreasing term feature assures the accomplishment of the objective, whether the insured lives or dies. With this emphasis on investment, it is only natural that the insured be curious about the rate of return that he can expect to enjoy on his savings account.

A number of methods have been advanced for computing the yield on an endowment insurance contract. The first—and crudest—is to regard the entire premium as the contribution to the savings account and then to ascertain the rate of compound interest at which these payments must be accumulated in order to equal the face of the policy at the maturity date. This method ignores the fact that a portion of the premium goes for insurance protection and thus is *spent,* not invested. Therefore, this method produces an unrealistically low yield on the insured's "investment."

The second method goes to the other extreme. It treats the investment element of the premium as the difference between the full premium for the endowment insurance policy in question and the premium for a level term insurance policy for the same amount, issued at the same age, and covering the same number of years. The fallacy in this method is that the insurance protection under an endowment contract is not level but is a decreasing function. The effective amount of protection averages about half the face of the policy, so that the cost of protection is greatly overstated. The resulting yield, therefore, is higher than the true yield.

The third—and proper—method of calculating the yield on an endowment contract is to deduct from each annual premium the cost of one-year term insurance for the net amount at risk (technically, the "cost of insurance") and to ascertain, by trial and error, the rate of compound interest at which the remainders must be accumulated in order to equal the face of the policy at the maturity date. This method gives proper recognition to the decreasing nature of the protection but involves laborious calculations.

For all practical purposes, the simplest lay method of determining the yield upon the investment element of an endowment contract—or of any life insurance contract, for that matter—is to find the net rate of interest actually earned by the company on its invested funds. A company that operates on an equitable basis and makes the proper charges against individual contracts for operating expenses and claims will, in theory, earn exactly the same rate on the investment feature of every contract it issues. In practice, however, the yield, as calculated in accordance with the third method described above, may vary as among policies issued by the same company because of variations in the loading formula. Moreover, the yield on some or all of the contracts may exceed the rate of interest earned by the company on its invested funds. This apparent anomaly is explained by the fact that not all liabilities of the company against which invested funds are held are interest-bearing. The legal reserve *is* interest-bearing, since the company must earn a return equal to the rate assumed in the actuarial computations. Surplus, however, is *not* interest-bearing; and its investment earnings may, in effect, be allocated to certain or all of the contracts written by the company through the dividend formula. Since, in most companies, surplus approaches 10 per cent of the legal reserve, this source of investment earnings could, if fully and equitably allocated, produce an investment yield on all contracts 10 per cent greater than the published rate of return on invested funds.

USES OF THE ENDOWMENT INSURANCE CONTRACT

Misuse of the Contract

The endowment insurance contract is one of the most useful forms issued by life insurance companies but one that has lent itself to widespread misuse. It is essentially a savings plan—with insurance to protect the program against premature death of the insured—and is not suitable where the primary need is for protection. The premiums are the largest of any life insurance plan, but they provide the smallest amount of protection per dollar of premium outlay. Yet, many people see in the endowment contract a refutation of the old adage that with life insurance, one must "die to win." It is particularly appealing to young people who, without dependents, have not developed a sense of family responsibility and are interested only in a proposition that promises a financial return to them. It seems to offer the possibility of "having your cake and eating it, too."

There would be no particular disadvantage in an insurance program based on endowments if the insured remained without dependents. In the usual course of events, however, he will acquire dependents and will experience the need for a substantial amount of insurance protection which, at his stage in life, should be met with the lowest premium forms of insurance. Instead, he finds that the limited funds which he can allocate to insurance premiums are committed to heavy-premium forms of insurance which provide relatively little protection. Moreover, if the contracts are short-term endowments, as is usually the case, they will mature at the peak of the insured's earning capacity at a time when his need for protection is still very great and his insurability is in question. Unless he were able to supplement the endowment contracts with other insurance, upon maturity he would find himself without protection and possibly without the insurability to replace the protection. Even if new insurance could be obtained, the premiums would be much higher than they would have been had the insurance been purchased at an earlier age. In such cases, the best solution frequently is to use the proceeds of the matured endowments to prepay premiums on the new insurance, on either the discounted or the premium deposit basis.

The only basis on which any contract should be criticized is that it fails to provide the optimum combination of investment and protection in the situation for which it has been prescribed or is being used. Endowment insurance is highly unsuited for many purposes but is ideally adaptable to other needs. It may be of interest to review briefly the early uses of the endowment principle before proceeding to two important modern uses.

Early Uses of Endowment

The earliest use of the endowment idea was to provide a sum of money for children at a given age or upon the happening of some event. There is a reference to such use in a treatise on usury published in 1572,[3] in which the author questioned whether or not the purchaser of such a contract is a usurer. The particular contract to which the writer made reference was one which provided that in consideration of

---

[3] Thomas Wilson, *A Discourse Upon USUARIE, by waie of Dialogues and Oracions, for the better Varietie, and more delight of all those that shall read this treatise* (London, 1572, 1584; also New York: Harcourt, Brace & Co., Inc., 1925; and London: G. Bell & Sons, 1925).

£100 paid on behalf of a child aged one, the corporation would pay £500 to the child at age fifteen, if living. It is interesting that the author of the treatise felt the contract to be usurious.

For boys, these contracts provided the funds for an education or for getting a start in some business, trade, or profession; for girls, they provided the dowries necessary for the contracting of satisfactory marriages. In neither situation was there the slightest intimation of providing for the old-age needs of the insured. One type of contract which gained some prominence was "apprenticeship insurance," which was designed to provide the necessary funds for an apprentice to set himself up in business at the end of the apprenticeship term.

In the early part of the eighteenth century, when insurance projects of almost every description were introduced in London, and especially during that period noted for the orgy of gambling and speculation that culminated in the South Sea Bubble, numerous schemes involving the endowment principle were concocted for children. Some of the arrangements were underwritten by life insurance companies, but many were not. In most instances, death of the insured child relieved the company of all liability under the contract. The agreements, therefore, were in the form of pure endowments.

The writing of endowment insurance on adult lives is of comparatively recent origin. The earliest record of such policies is that relating to policies issued in 1839 by a company known as the "British Empire." The idea proved popular, and other companies jumped on the band wagon. From the outset, these policies combined death benefits with the pure endowment.

Educational Funds

One of the most important modern uses of the endowment is to accumulate funds for the higher education of children. The contract may be written on the life of the child or on the life of a parent, usually the father. If the insurance is written on the life of the child, it is highly desirable that the policy be endorsed with a provision, called the *payor clause,* that all future premiums are to be waived if the premium payor, who is named in the endorsement, should die or become disabled. Such a clause is used with all forms of juvenile insurance. Both the child and the premium payor must satisfy the underwriting requirements of the company.

The contract is written for the number of years that will elapse between the child's present age and the age at which he is expected to enter college. If the child is one year old and is expected to be ready for college at eighteen, for example, the term of the contract will be seventeen years. If the child is three years old, a fifteen-year endowment is written, and so on, except that in most companies, the minimum term is ten years.[4]

The settlement plan is set up in a manner designed to meet the needs of the typical college student. It is usually stipulated that the proceeds are to be paid out in equal monthly installments over a four-year period, with no payments to be made, however, during the three vacation months. If desired, a larger payment can be prescribed for October 1 and February 1, in order to meet tuition and other fees payable around those dates. A larger payment can also be specified for June 1 of the senior year, in order to take care of any unusual expenses that might develop at that time or to provide a graduation gift. If nine monthly payments are specified, they usually run from October 1 through June 1; if ten payments are stipulated, the first falls on September 1 and the last on June 1. Payment throughout the twelve months can be specified, if desired, as well as distribution over a period longer than four years.

The settlement agreement usually provides that the monthly income will commence upon receipt by the insurance company of satisfactory evidence that the beneficiary is enrolled in an accredited university or college. To preclude dispute about the status of any particular university or college, some insurance companies require that a list of educational institutions satisfactory to the insured be filed with the company. Other companies are willing to accept the language "recognized college or university." If the policy matures before the child is ready for college, the proceeds are held at interest, with the interest being paid monthly or quarterly to the beneficiary. In order to take care of the possibility that the child may not wish to go to college, the settlement plan normally provides for payment of the proceeds to the beneficiary in a lump sum at age twenty-five if, by that time, he has not enrolled in a recognized college or university.

It may be pointed out that funds for educational purposes may be

---

[4] If the child is within less than ten years of college age, a ten-year endowment can be taken out with a face of such amount that the cash value will provide the necessary funds within the time desired. Life insurance companies have computed tables showing the amount of insurance necessary at the end of any given number of years to provide an income of a designated amount over any particular period. Reference to the table of surrender values under a ten-year endowment will reveal how much insurance is needed to accumulate a cash value equal to the desired sum.

accumulated under other than endowment contracts. If the only concern is that the premature death of the breadwinner will prevent the accumulation of the necessary funds, term insurance will serve the need for protection. If a means of accumulating the funds is also desired, any form of whole life insurance in the appropriate amount will serve both purposes. This, of course, presupposes the surrendering of the insurance for its cash value at the time the child enters college. If the additional protection afforded by the whole life insurance is not needed and it is desired to avoid the higher "cost of insurance" involved under that form, then the endowment form should by all means be utilized.

Old-Age Income

Another important use of endowment insurance is to provide funds for the old-age support of the insured and his wife. It is possible to determine what principal sum will be needed at retirement to supplement the income of the insured from Federal OASDI, a private retirement plan, and other sources. Theoretically, it is immaterial how the principal sum is accumulated; but it should be liquidated in a scientific manner, which means through an annuity or the life income option of a life insurance contract. If the sum is also accumulated by life insurance means (including annuities), the basis on which the principal sum can be converted to income is set forth by contract. In effect, an annuity is purchased at net rates guaranteed from the inception of the contract.

The principal sum can be accumulated through whole life insurance, endowment insurance, or an annuity. The choice will depend upon the "mixture" of protection and investment desired. If a mixture heavy with protection and light with investment is desired, the appropriate form of whole life insurance should be used. If all investment and no protection are wanted, a deferred annuity is suitable. If a mixture of light protection and heavy investment is desired, an endowment maturing at the anticipated retirement age is ideal. The choice does not depend upon the attributes of any one contract, but upon the nature and objectives of the insured's complete insurance and financial program.

CHAPTER VI

Annuities

THE TERM "annuity" is derived from the Latin word *annus,* meaning year, and hence connotes an annual payment. A broader definition of an *annuity,* however, is a periodic payment to commence at a stated or contingent date and to continue throughout a fixed period or for the duration of a designated life or lives. The person whose life governs the duration of the payments is called the *annuitant.* The annuitant may or may not be the person who receives the periodic payments, although he usually is. The income under the annuity contract may be paid annually, semiannually, quarterly, or monthly, depending upon the conditions of the agreement. Normally, the income is paid monthly.

If the payments are to be made for a definite period of time, without regard to life contingencies,[1] the agreement is known as an annuity *certain.* If the payments are to be made for the duration of a designated life, the agreement is called a *life* annuity or, more accurately, a *single-life* annuity. It is also referred to as a *whole life* annuity to distinguish it from a *temporary life* annuity, under which payments are to be made during a specified period of time, but only as long as a designated person is alive. In other words, a temporary life annuity terminates with the death of the designated individual or at the expiration of the specified period of time, whichever occurs earlier. The word "life" in the title of an annuity indicates that the payments are based on life contingencies or continue only as long as a designated person is alive. This chapter is concerned primarily with whole life annuities.

NATURE OF ANNUITIES

The Annuity Principle

As has been said earlier, the primary function of life insurance is to *create* an estate or principal sum, while the primary function of an an-

---

[1] This means that the obligation of the insurer is not measured by the duration of a human life.

nuity is to *liquidate* a principal sum, regardless of how created. Despite this basic dissimilarity in function, life insurance and annuities are based on the same fundamental principles. In the first place, both protect against loss of income. Life insurance furnishes protection against loss of income arising out of premature death; an annuity provides protection against loss of income arising out of excessive longevity. It might be said that life insurance provides a financial hedge against dying too soon, while an annuity provides a hedge against living too long. From an economic standpoint, both contingencies are undesirable. A second common feature is the utilization of the pooling technique. Insurance is a pooling arrangement whereby all make contributions so that the dependents of those who die prematurely may be indemnified for loss of income, whereas the annuity is a pooling arrangement whereby those who die prematurely make a contribution on behalf of those who live beyond their life expectancy and would otherwise outlive their income. A third common feature is the fact that the contributions in each case are based on probabilities of death and survival, as reflected in a mortality table. For reasons which will be apparent later, the same mortality table is not used for both sets of calculations. Finally, under both arrangements, contributions are discounted for the compound interest that will be earned on them by the insurance company.

The annuity concept is founded on the unpredictability of human life. A person may have accumulated a principal sum for his old-age support, which, on the assumption that it is to be liquidated over his remaining years, should be adequate for the purpose. Such a procedure, however, involves an estimate of the future lifetime of the individual. He might assume that he is of average health and vitality for his age and could expect just to live out his life expectancy. He could not be sure that he would not survive his expectancy, however, and to be on the safe side, would have to plan to spread his principal over a much longer period than he is likely to live. Even then, there would be some danger of surviving the period and finding himself without income. On the other hand, he might die after only a few years, leaving to his estate funds which could and should have been used to provide him with more of the comforts of life. If the individual, however, would be willing to pool his savings with those of other people in the same predicament, the administering agency, through reliance on the laws of probability and large numbers, could provide each of the participants with an income of a specified amount as long as he lives—

regardless of his longevity. No one could outlive his income. Such an arrangement, however, implies a willingness on the part of each participant to have all or a portion of his unliquidated principal at the time of his death used to supplement the exhausted principal of those who live beyond their life expectancy.

Each payment under an annuity is composed partly of principal and partly of the income on the unliquidated principal. For each year that goes by, a larger proportion of the payment is composed of principal. If a person just exactly lived out his life expectancy, as computed at the time he entered on the annuity, his principal would be completely exhausted with the last payment prior to his death. If he lived beyond his life expectancy, each payment would be derived from funds forfeited by those who failed to survive their expectancy. It is an equitable arrangement since, at the outset, no one can know into what category he will fall. There is no other arrangement under which a principal sum can with certainty be completely liquidated in equal installments over the duration of a human life.

Classification of Annuities

Annuities may be classified in many different ways, depending upon the point of emphasis.[2] For most purposes, they can be classified as to (1) number of lives covered, (2) time when payments commence, (3) method of premium payment, and (4) nature of the insurer's obligation.

Number of Lives Covered. This is a simple dichotomy and refers only to whether the annuity covers a single life or more than one life. The conventional form is a single-life annuity. If the contract covers two or more lives, it may be a *joint* annuity or a *joint-and-survivor* annuity. A joint annuity provides that the income will cease upon the first death among the lives involved; it is seldom issued. A joint-and-survivor annuity, on the other hand, provides that the income will cease only upon the last death among the lives insured. In other words, payments under a joint-and-survivor annuity continue as long as either of two or more persons lives. This is a very useful contract, and it enjoys a wide market. Contracts involving more than two lives are rarely sold.

Time when Payments Commence. Under this heading, annuities may be classified as *immediate* or *deferred*. An immediate annuity is

---

[2] For an exhaustive classification of annuities, see Clyde J. Crobaugh, *Handbook of Insurance* (New York: Prentice-Hall, Inc., 1949), Vol. I, p. 25.

one under which the first payment is due one payment interval from the date of purchase. If the contract provides for monthly payments, the first payment is due one month from the date of purchase; if annual payments are called for, the first payment is due one year from the date of purchase. However, the annuity is "entered on" immediately. The first payment begins to accrue immediately after purchase. This type of annuity is always purchased with a single premium. The annuitant exchanges a principal sum for the promise of an income for life or for a term of years, as the case might be.

The immediate annuity has been supplanted in importance by the deferred annuity, under which a period longer than one payment interval must elapse after purchase before the first payment is due. As a matter of fact, there is normally a spread of several years between the date of purchase and the time when payments commence. This contract is usually, but not always, purchased with periodic premiums payable over a period of years, up to the date of income commencement. It is a type suitable for a person of ordinary means desirous of accumulating a sum for his old-age maintenance.

Method of Premium Payment. Annuities may be purchased with either single premiums or periodic premiums. Originally, an annuity was envisioned as a type of contract one would buy with a lump sum, accumulated perhaps from a successful business venture or possibly inherited, in exchange for an immediate income of a stipulated amount. Immediate annuities are still purchased with a lump sum, but most annuities today are purchased on an installment basis. High death and income taxes have made it difficult for persons to accumulate in one sum the consideration for a single-premium annuity. The deferred annuity provides an attractive and convenient method of accumulating the necessary funds for an adequate old-age income.

Nature of the Insurer's Obligation. The dichotomy here is pure versus refund annuities. The pure annuity, frequently referred to as a "straight life annuity," provides periodic—usually monthly—income payments that continue as long as the annuitant lives but terminate upon his death. The annuity is considered fully liquidated upon the death of the annuitant, no matter how soon that may occur after purchase, and no refund is payable to the deceased's estate. Moreover, no guarantee is given that any particular number of monthly payments will be paid. This nonrefund feature may be applied to either an immediate or a deferred annuity. In other words, it is possible to obtain a contract under which no part of the purchase price would be refunded if the annuitant should die before the income commences. On the other hand, the contract could call for a refund of all premiums paid, with or without interest, in the event of the insured's death before commencement of the annuity income, with no refund feature after the annuitant enters on the annuity. Under a deferred annuity, therefore, it is necessary to distinguish between the accumulation and liquidation periods in describing the contract as pure or refund.

A refund annuity is any type that promises to return in one manner or another a portion or all of the purchase price of the annuity. These contracts take several forms, the most important of which are discussed in the next section. As might be expected, refund annuities are far more popular than pure annuities.

SINGLE-LIFE ANNUITIES

Immediate Annuities

The discussion in this section is not limited to immediate annuities in the technical sense but includes the liquidation phase of deferred annuities. In other words, it is a description of the various arrangements under which a principal sum can be liquidated on the basis of life contingencies. The principles involved are equally applicable to the life income options of life insurance contracts.

Pure Annuities. As stated above, a pure annuity is one that provides periodic payments of a stipulated amount as long as the annuitant lives, with the payments ceasing upon the death of the annuitant and the consideration paid for the annuity being regarded as fully earned by the insurance company. The payments may be made monthly, quarterly, semiannually, or annually. The more frequent the periodic payments, the more costly is the annuity in terms of annual income. That is, twelve monthly payments of $100 each, the first due one month hence, are more costly than one annual payment of $1,200 due one year hence. This is due to the greater expense of drawing twelve checks, loss of interest by the company, and the greater probability that the annuitant will live to receive the payments. If the annuitant should die six months and one day after purchasing the annuity, he would receive six monthly payments of $100 each in one case and nothing in the other. The principle would hold true regardless of the year in which the annuitant dies. Occasionally, annuities are made "apportionable"—i.e., they provide for a prorata fractional payment covering the period from the date of the last regular payment to the date of death. This feature necessitates an increase in the purchase price, since premiums for the usual type of annuity are calculated on the assumption that there will be no such prorata payment.

The pure annuity provides the maximum income per dollar of outlay and for that reason is perhaps most suitable for persons with only a limited amount of capital. According to typical actuarial assumptions, $1,000 of capital will provide income to a man aged sixty-five of $6.68 per month on a straight life income basis, whereas if payments had been guaranteed for twenty years, whether the annuitant lives or dies, the monthly income would have been only $5.15.[3] On an investment of $20,000, the difference in monthly income would be $30.60, which for an aged person might be the difference between dependency and self-sufficiency. At age seventy, the difference in monthly income from $20,000 would be $52.60; and at seventy-five, the difference would be $88.20—too large to ignore. At the younger ages, however, because of the high probability of survival, the difference in income between an annuity without a refund feature and one with a refund feature is too small to take a chance on an early death. At age thirty-five, an annuity with a five-year guarantee can be obtained for the same cost as a pure annuity, and a twenty-year guarantee can be obtained at the sacrifice of only 4 cents of monthly income per $1,000 of outlay. Even at age fifty-five, a ten-year guarantee can be obtained at a reduction in monthly income of only 10 cents. It might be stated as a generalization that a pure annuity should not be purchased below age sixty (age sixty-five for female), unless the limited amount of capital makes it imperative. Below that age, the annuitant's chances of surviving the typical periods of guaranteed payments are so good that he gains little in monthly income by giving up the refund feature.

Refund Annuities. Most people have strong objections to placing a substantial sum of money into a contract that promises little or no return if they should suffer an early death. Therefore, insurance companies have found it necessary to add a refund feature to annuities to make them salable. The refund feature may take two general forms: a promise to provide a certain number of annuity payments whether the

---

[3] The income figures in this chapter reflect the amounts of monthly life income payable per $1,000 of capital accumulated with an insurance company through periodic premiums. Due to expense allowances, the same income could not be obtained from a lump-sum payment of $1,000 to an insurance company at the ages mentioned.

annuitant lives or dies, or a promise to refund all or a portion of the purchase price in the event of the annuitant's early death.

The first type of contract goes under various names, including "life annuity certain," "life annuity certain and continuous," "life annuity with installments certain," and "life annuity with minimum guaranteed return." The essence of the agreement is that a stipulated number of monthly payments will be made whether the annuitant lives or dies, with payments to continue for the whole of the annuitant's life if he should live beyond the guaranteed period. Contracts may be written with payments guaranteed for five, ten, fifteen, or twenty years, although any one company is not likely to offer such a wide range of choices. A few companies will guarantee payments for twenty-five years.

It may be recognized that this type of refund annuity is composed of two elements: an annuity certain and a pure deferred life annuity. The annuity certain covers the period of guaranteed payments and, true to its characteristics, provides the payments whether the annuitant is alive or not. The deferred life annuity is effective as of the end of the period of guaranteed payments and provides benefits only if the annuitant survives the term of the annuity certain. The benefits are deferred and are contingent upon the annuitant's being alive to receive them. Therefore, the second portion of the company's promise can properly be described as a *pure deferred* life annuity. If the annuitant does not survive the period of guaranteed payments, no payments are made under the deferred life annuity, and no refund is forthcoming. If the annuitant does survive the term of the annuity certain the deferred life annuity provides benefits for the remainder of the annuitant's life.

An annuity certain is always more expensive per dollar of income than a life annuity, since it is not based on life contingencies. The payments are a certainty, the only cost-reducing factor being the compound interest earned on the unliquidated portion of the purchase price. Therefore, the longer the term of the annuity certain—or, to put it more specifically, the longer the period of guaranteed payments—the more costly will be this type of refund annuity, or the lower will be the yield on the purchase price. Since it is not based on life contingencies, the cost of an annuity certain does not depend upon the age of the annuitant; it varies directly with the length of the term. At any particular age, however, the longer the period of guaranteed payments, the less expensive will be the deferred life annuity, since the higher the age at which the deferred life annuity commences, the smaller the probability that the annuitant will survive to that age. This means that the larger the number of guaranteed payments, the smaller the portion of the purchase price going into the deferred life annuity.

There are two important types of contracts which promise to return all or a portion of the purchase price. The first of these is called the "installment refund annuity." This contract promises that in the event the annuitant dies before receiving monthly payments equal to the purchase price of the annuity, the payments shall be continued to a contingent beneficiary or beneficiaries until the full cost has been recovered. According to the rates of the same company quoted earlier, $30,000 would provide a monthly life income of $173.40 on the installment refund basis to a male annuitant aged sixty-five at the time of purchase. If the annuitant should die after receiving one hundred payments, or $17,340, the payments would be continued to a contingent beneficiary until an additional $12,660 was paid out, making an aggregate of $30,000. If he should die after fifteen years, there would be no further payments, since the entire purchase price would already have been recovered. It is understood, of course, that payments to the annuitant continue as long as he lives, even though the purchase price may long since have been recovered in full.

The contract may promise, upon the death of the annuitant, to pay to the annuitant's estate or a contingent beneficiary in a lump sum the difference, if any, between the purchase price of the annuity and the sum of the monthly payments, in which case the contract is called a "cash refund annuity." The only difference between the "cash refund" and "installment refund" annuities is that under the former, the unrecovered portion of the purchase price is refunded in a lump sum at the time of the annuitant's death; whereas in the latter case, the monthly installments are continued until the purchase price has been completely recovered. The former is naturally somewhat more expensive, because the insurance company loses the interest it would have earned while liquidating on the installment basis the remaining portion of the purchase price.

It is frequently asked how a life insurance company can afford to promise to return in full the annuitant's investment in an annuity contract, whether he lives or dies, and yet continue the monthly payments to annuitants who have already recovered their investment. It would seem that every dollar paid to an annuitant in excess of his investment would have to be offset by the forfeiture of a dollar by an annuitant who died before recovering the purchase price. The answer lies in compound interest. It will be noted that the company does not promise to pay out benefits equal to the purchase price *plus interest*. Interest earnings on the unliquidated portion of the premiums of all annuitants receiving benefits under this type of refund annuity provide the funds for payments in excess of the investment of any particular annuitant.

As a compromise between the straight life annuity and the 100 per cent refund annuity, there is a contract which guarantees a minimum return of one half of the purchase price. Logically enough, it is called a "50 per cent refund annuity." Under its terms, if the annuitant dies before receiving benefits equal to half of the cost of the annuity, monthly installments are continued until payments to both annuitant and beneficiary equal half of the cost of the annuity. It is customary to provide that, if the beneficiary so elects, he can receive the present value of the remaining payments in a lump sum. Since the guarantee under this contract is smaller than that under the 100 per cent refund annuity, the cost is lower; or, conversely, the income per dollar of outlay is larger.

Another variation of the refund annuity is found among contributory pension plans. Called a "modified" cash refund annuity, this form promises that should the employee die before receiving retirement benefits equal to the accumulated value of *his* contributions, with or without interest, the difference between his benefits and his contributions will be refunded in a lump sum to his estate or a designated beneficiary. In other words, the refund feature is based on the employee's contributions and not on the total cost of the annuity.

Finally, a form of annuity sometimes written provides that, regardless of the number of payments received prior to the annuitant's death, 50 per cent of the cost of the contract will be returned in the form of a death benefit. This contract is not, in the strict sense, a refund annuity. Instead, one half of the premium is used by the company to provide a straight life annuity, and the other half is held on deposit. Earnings from the half of the premium held on deposit are used to supplement the annuity benefits provided by the other half of the premium. Upon the annuitant's death, the premium deposit is returned to the annuitant's estate or a designated beneficiary in the form of a death benefit.

The amount of monthly income that would be provided under the various important forms of annuities per $1,000 of premium accumulations with a life insurance company is shown in Table 4. The principal sum of $1,000 does not refer to a single premium of that amount, paid at the various ages, but to a sum accumulated through periodic

TABLE 4

MONTHLY INCOME PER $1,000 OF ACCUMULATIONS
UNDER VARIOUS ANNUITY FORMS

MALE AGES*	LIFE ANNUITY					INSTALL-MENT REFUND ANNUITY	FULL CASH REFUND ANNUITY
	No Period Certain	5-Year Certain	10-Year Certain	15-Year Certain	20-Year Certain		
25...........	$3.20	$3.20	$3.20	$3.20	$3.19	$3.18	$3.17
30...........	3.35	3.35	3.35	3.34	3.33	3.31	3.30
35...........	3.54	3.54	3.53	3.52	3.50	3.48	3.47
40...........	3.78	3.77	3.76	3.74	3.71	3.68	3.67
45...........	4.08	4.08	4.05	4.02	3.96	3.94	3.51
50...........	4.48	4.47	4.43	4.35	4.24	4.25	4.21
55...........	5.00	4.98	4.90	4.76	4.56	4.65	4.59
60...........	5.72	5.67	5.50	5.23	4.88	5.15	5.05
65...........	6.68	6.56	6.22	5.71	5.15	5.78	5.64
70...........	7.98	7.72	7.03	6.17	5.35	6.57	6.37
75...........	9.76	9.18	7.87	6.52	5.35	7.60	7.29

* Benefits for women are those for a man five years younger. Thus, a woman aged sixty-five would receive the same income as a man aged sixty.
Rate basis: 1955 American Annuity Table and 3 per cent interest; male ages set back one year and female ages set back six years; no loading for expenses.

premiums, which contained an allowance for expenses, or through the maturity by death of an insurance contract purchased with gross premiums. In other words, these benefits, which may be augmented by dividends, are based on net premiums and could not be purchased with a lump-sum payment on quite so favorable a cost basis, but they illustrate the variations in yield among the various annuity forms.

Table 4 reveals the inconsequential cost of a refund feature at the younger ages and the high cost of such a feature at the advanced ages. It is interesting to note that at the higher ages, both the installment refund and the cash refund forms are less expensive—or, conversely, yield more—than a life annuity with a twenty-year guarantee. At the advanced ages, they cost less than even a fifteen-year guarantee. It should be remembered, however, that the benefits under each of the forms are the actuarial equivalent of those under all the other forms, and the annuitant must choose the form which is most appropriate to his financial and family circumstances.

Deferred Annuities

It is helpful, in considering deferred annuities, to distinguish between (1) the accumulation period and (2) the liquidation period. The preceding discussion of immediate annuities related entirely to the liquidation phase of annuities. It was assumed that the funds needed to provide the various income payments were on hand, and no consideration was given to the manner in which the funds were accumulated.

With deferred annuities, however, there is always a period during which there are accumulated with the insurance company the funds necessary to provide the benefits promised at a specified date in the future. The sum may be accumulated through a lump-sum premium to which compound interest is added during the intervening years, or it may be accumulated through a series of periodic level premiums. In either case, a question arises as to the obligation of the company in the event that the purchaser dies prior to the date when the income is scheduled to commence.

The agreement might provide that there is to be no refund of premiums if the annuitant should die before receiving any payments. If so, the annuity could be described as a "pure" annuity with respect to the period of accumulation. Such a contract has little popular appeal; but under private pension plans, employer contributions are almost invariably applied to the purchase of pure deferred annuities. If the employee should terminate his employment before retirement, the employer recovers his contributions, plus interest; but if the employee should die, employer contributions on his behalf would remain with the insurance company to provide benefits to employees who remain with the employer to retirement. Such an annuity can be purchased at a much lower premium than one which promises to return contributions to the date of death, with the result that the employer can either finance his pension plan at the lowest possible outlay or, if he is so minded, can provide larger retirement benefits than he could otherwise afford.

Deferred annuities sold to individuals almost without exception promise to return all premiums, with or without interest, in the event of the annuitant's death before "entering on" the annuity. The usual contract provides for a return of gross premiums without interest or the cash value, whichever is larger, under such circumstances. Such a contract, therefore, is a refund annuity with respect to the period of accumulation.

Everything said about immediate annuities in the earlier discussion applies with equal force to the liquidation phase of deferred annuities. Once the necessary funds have been accumulated and the annuitant is ready to enter on his annuity, he normally has the option of taking the income on any of the plans described. Thus, he might choose a straight life annuity, a life annuity with guaranteed installments, an installment refund annuity, or a cash refund annuity. As a matter of fact, he may be given the privilege of taking cash in lieu of a life income. It is not inconsistent for the annuitant to choose a pure or straight life annuity for the liquidation phase of an annuity that was of the refund type during the accumulation phase. Conceivably, he might purchase an annuity that provides for no refund during the period of accumulation and elect to liquidate it on a refund basis. Most annuitants, however, prefer the refund basis during both the accumulation and the liquidation phases.

The most popular annuity form offered today is a deferred annuity that generally goes under the name of a *retirement annuity*. Virtually all companies offer such a contract, and its sales exceed by a wide margin those of all other forms combined.

Perhaps the most distinctive characteristic of the retirement annuity is its flexibility. A wide range of options permits the annuitant to adjust the contract during the deferred period to changes of circumstances not anticipated when the contract was purchased. Such flexibility can be provided since, prior to maturity, the contract is nothing more than a method of accumulating a principal sum through the use of the investment facilities of an insurance company.

The premiums for the contract may be quoted in units of $100 annual premium or in terms of the annual premium needed to provide a monthly life income of $10 at a designated age. In the first case, the premium will be an even amount, and the income will vary with the age of issue and the age at which the income will commence; whereas in the second case, the income will be a fixed, even amount, and the premium will vary. It is customary to base premium computations on the assumption that the annuitant will receive a life income with payments guaranteed for ten years. If, at the time of maturity, the annuitant elects another option, the income is adjusted accordingly.

The structure of the contract can best be understood by reference to a numerical example. In accordance with the rate basis of several leading companies, $1,608 would have to be on hand at age sixty-five for each $10 unit of monthly life income to be paid to a male annuitant, with payments guaranteed for ten years.[4] This is the sum that must be accumulated for each $10 unit of income by every male annuitant who wants his income to begin at age sixty-five, regardless of the age at which he purchased the annuity. Obviously, the younger the age at which the annuitant begins to contribute toward his accumulation objective, the smaller each annual contribution or deposit can be. To accumulate $16,080, the amount needed to provide $100 per month at age sixty-five, with payments guaranteed for 120 months, a man aged twenty-five would have to contribute only $236 per year to age sixty-five, while a man aged forty-five would have to deposit $655.40 per year.[5] A person aged fifty-five would have to deposit $1,547.70 per year for ten years.

The level premiums or deposits, as they are usually called, are accumulated at a rate of compound interest specified in the contract— 3 per cent in this case. In the event of the annuitant's death before age sixty-five, or whatever the maturity date, the company will return the accumulated gross premiums, without interest, or the cash value, whichever is larger. The cash value is equal to the gross premiums improved at a guaranteed rate of interest after deduction of a charge for expenses. After about ten years, the cash value exceeds the accumulated value of premiums paid, without interest, and thus becomes the effective death benefit. It is of interest to note that, while this is an annuity contract, there is an insurance element during the period, and to the extent, that the death benefit exceeds the cash value.

The annuitant may withdraw the cash value at any time, whereupon the contract would terminate and the company would have no further obligation. Under some contracts, he may borrow against the cash value, which would not bring about a termination of the contract. The contract normally stipulates that if there is a default on premium payments and the cash value is not withdrawn within thirty-one days, a paid-up deferred annuity in a reduced amount will be provided.

---

[4] Rate basis: 1955 American Annuity Table and 3 per cent interest; male ages set forward one year and female ages set back four years; no loading for expenses.

[5] These deposits, or level premiums, include a charge for insurance company expenses and vary among the companies whose policies have the same maturity value. The deposits illustrated are for a contract on which dividends are paid prior to maturity.

Such paid-up annuity can itself be surrendered for cash at any time.

At the maturity date, the annuitant may elect to have the accumulated sum—$16,080 in the example—applied under any of the annuity forms offered by the company, even though the premium deposits were predicated on the assumption that the income would be provided under a life annuity with 120 guaranteed installments. The actual monthly income might be more or less than the amount originally anticipated, depending upon the option elected. Moreover, the annuitant is usually given the privilege of taking cash in lieu of an annuity. This is known as the *cash option,* and it exposes the company to serious adverse selection. Persons in poor health tend to withdraw their accumulations in cash, while those in excellent health usually choose an annuity. To offset this selection, some companies provide a somewhat smaller income per $1,000 of accumulations under a retirement annuity than under annuities that do not offer the cash option.

Under most contracts, the annuitant may choose to have the income commence at an earlier or a later date than the one originally specified in the contract, with an appropriate adjustment in the amount of income. The privilege of having the income commence at an earlier age than that specified in the contract is, it should be recognized, an option to convert the cash value to an *immediate* annuity, as contrasted with the option, mentioned above, to convert the cash value into a paid-up *deferred* annuity. There is usually no age limit below which the income cannot commence, although the option is subject to the general requirement that the periodic income payments equal or exceed a stipulated minimum. On the other hand, there is usually a limit, sometimes as high as age eighty, beyond which commencement of the income cannot be postponed. The option to postpone the commencement of income payments may be particularly attractive if the annuitant at the original maturity date is still in good health and plans to work for a few more years. The life income payable at any particular age, whether the maturity date is moved ahead or set back, is the same amount that would have been provided had the substituted maturity date been the one originally selected.

A final feature offered by some companies is the privilege of converting the retirement annuity contract into a life insurance contract. This can be a useful feature for the individual who purchased the retirement annuity contract when young and without dependents, and who, after acquiring family obligations, decides that his premium payments should be devoted to family protection. When the conversion option is present, it permits the annuitant to exchange his contract for any whole life or endowment policy offered by the company on the same terms and conditions and at the same premium rates prevailing as of the original date of purchase of the annuity contract, subject to the usual financial adjustment. However—and this is important—the annuitant must furnish evidence of insurability at the time of conversion. Therefore, the only advantage to the conversion privilege is the opportunity it might afford the annuitant to obtain a life insurance contract on more favorable terms than those on which it could be obtained by outright purchase.

The basic structure of the retirement annuity contract is illustrated in Figure 6. Before maturity, the contract is nothing more than a

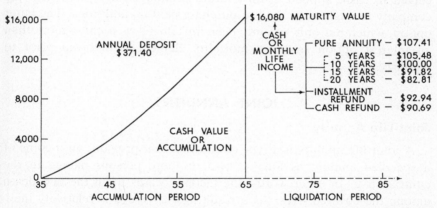

FIG. 6. Basic structure of a retirement annuity contract issued at male age thirty-five and maturing at age sixty-five; death benefits prior to maturity equal to gross premiums during first eight years and cash value thereafter.

savings plan, under which can be accumulated the principal sum needed to provide a life income of any specified magnitude. In the example, $16,080 is needed to provide a monthly life income at age sixty-five of $100 with payments guaranteed for 120 months. The maturity value of the contract is always determined by the age at which the income is to commence and is not affected by the age at which the accumulation is begun. The maturity value of a contract which promises to provide $100 per month for life at male age sixty is $18,180, whereas the same income from age seventy would require an accumulation of only $14,220. With any particular accumulation objective, however, the annual deposit depends upon the age at which the accumulation begins. In the present example, the annual deposit is $371.40. Over the thirty-year period, the annuitant will pay in a total of $11,142. Interest on the premiums, less expenses, will amount to $4,938, bringing the total accumulation to $16,080. The annuitant is assured of recovering his premiums if he should die before the contract matures; and after several years, his estate would receive considerably more than the purchase price. The refund feature after maturity depends upon the option elected by the annuitant. The income available from the $16,080 ranges from $82.81 to $107.41.

Retirement annuities written by mutual companies are virtually always participating during the accumulation period and may be participating on some basis during the liquidation phase. The contract provides that dividends during the accumulation period may be received in cash, applied against future premiums, deposited with the company at interest, or used to purchase paid-up additions. The latter option, which has only recently been introduced, is nothing more than an interest option since no mortality element is involved prior to maturity.

JOINT ANNUITIES

Joint-Life Annuity

A joint-life annuity is a type of contract that provides an income of a specified amount as long as two or more persons named in the contract live. In other words, the income ceases upon the first death among the covered lives. As a result, the coverage is relatively inexpensive.

This contract has a very limited market. It might be appropriate for two persons, elderly sisters, for example, who have an income from a stable source large enough to support one but not both of the sisters. If a joint-life annuity can be purchased, without disturbing the other income, in an amount adequate to support one sister, the combined income while both sisters are alive will be adequate for their needs; and upon the death of one of the sisters, the original income from investments will meet the needs of the survivor. Such a contract is always sold as a single-premium immediate annuity.

Joint-and-Last-Survivor Annuity

This is a far more appealing contract than the joint-life annuity, in that the income continues as long as either of two or more persons lives. It is ideal for a husband and wife or for other family relationships.

For most combinations of ages, the joint-and-last-survivor annuity is the most expensive of all annuity forms. To provide an income of $100 per month on the joint-and-survivor basis to a man and woman both aged sixty-five, an accumulation of $20,120 is needed. This is to be compared to the $14,970 required to provide a life income of $100 per month with no refund feature to a man aged sixty-five. If the man is sixty-five and the woman sixty, a more common situation, a sum of $21,740 would be needed to provide $100 per month on the joint-and-survivor basis.

The joint-and-survivor annuity may be purchased as a single-premium immediate annuity, in which event the cost will be somewhat higher than the accumulation figures quoted above; or it may be one of the optional forms made available under an annual premium deferred annuity, such as the retirement annuity previously described. The form may also be made available for the settlement of life insurance and endowment proceeds. The typical form does not contain a refund feature, although a number of companies offer a contract under which 120 monthly installments are guaranteed, and a few offer 240 guaranteed installments. When so written, if the last survivor dies before the minimum number of payments have been made, the remaining installments will be continued to a contingent beneficiary. As under single-life annuities, the contingent beneficiary may be permitted to take the present value of the remaining installments. When both husband and wife are sixty-five, a life income of $100 per month with 120 guaranteed installments requires an accumulation of $20,240—only $120 more than such an annuity without a refund feature.

In its conventional form, the joint-and-survivor annuity continues the same income to the survivor as is payable while both annuitants are alive. A common modification provides that the income to the survivor will be reduced to two thirds of the original amount, on the theory that the survivor does not require as much income as do the two annuitants—and to reduce the cost. This contract or option, as the case may be, is called a *joint-and-two-thirds annuity*. Such a contract written in an original amount of $100 on the lives of a husband and wife, both aged sixty-five, requires an accumulation of slightly more than $17,500. The benefits can be duplicated by placing a single-life immediate annuity in the appropriate amount on each annuitant, and a conventional joint-and-survivor annuity on both lives. Thus, an immediate annuity on each life for $100 per month and a joint-and-survivor annuity in the amount of $100 per month would provide $300 per month as long as both annuitants live and $200 per month to the survivor.

A form is available under which the income to the survivor is reduced to one half the original amount, such modification being known as the *joint-and-one-half annuity*. This form does not have the appeal of the joint-and-two-thirds annuity.

The joint-and-last-survivor form is widely used in private pension plans. It is common to provide that where the joint-and-two-thirds annuity has been elected by the employee, the income is to be reduced only when the employee dies first. If the wife or other dependent should die first, the employee continues to receive the full income.

VARIABLE ANNUITIES

The conventional concept of an annuity is that of a contract which promises to provide payments of a fixed amount over a specified period or throughout the lifetime of one or more persons. The persistent rise in prices over the last quarter century, however, has focused attention on the need for protecting the purchasing power of annuity benefits and has given rise to a type of contract which attempts to achieve that objective by providing benefits that tend to vary inversely with changes in the purchasing power of the dollar. Such a contract has appropriately been named a *variable annuity*.

If a contract is to provide benefits with a stable purchasing power, it must provide more dollars when prices rise and fewer dollars when prices decline. Such a result could theoretically be brought about by adjusting the benefits to changes in an appropriate price index, such as the Consumer Price Index published by the Bureau of Labor Statistics. This is not practicable from the standpoint of the insurance companies, however, since there is no mechanism by which the value of the assets backing the annuity promises can be adjusted automatically, or otherwise, to changes in the dollar value of the promises. As a practical solution, contracts have been developed which provide benefits adjusted to changes in the market value of the assets—typically, common stocks—in which the annuity reserves are invested. The theory is that over a long period of time, the market value of a representative group of common stocks will tend to conform rather faithfully to changes in the consumer price level. Moreover, inasmuch as the insurance company's liabilities to its annuitants are expressed in terms of the market value of the assets offsetting the liabilities, funds for the payment of annuity benefits will at all times be available in the proper proportions.

At present, variable annuities are issued almost exclusively on a deferred basis. During the accumulation period, premium payments—or deposits, as they are frequently called—are applied to the purchase of accumulation units. The accumulation unit is assigned an arbitrary value, such as $10, at the inception of the plan; and the initial premiums purchase accumulation units at that price. Thereafter, the units are revalued each month to reflect changes in the market value of the common stock making up the company's variable annuity portfolio. On any valuation date, the value of each accumulation unit is determined by dividing the market value of the common stock underlying the accumulation units by the aggregate number of units. Dividends are usually allocated periodically to the participants and applied to the purchase of additional accumulation units, although they may simply be reinvested without allocation and permitted to increase the value of each existing accumulation unit. Capital appreciation or depreciation is always reflected in the value of the accumulation units, rather than in the number of units. (In other words, both realized and unrealized gains and losses are reflected for individual participants through an increase or decrease in the value of their accumulation units.) A portion of each premium payment is deducted for expenses, and the remainder is invested in accumulation units at their current market value.

At the beginning of the liquidation period, the accumulation units are exchanged for annuity units. The number of annuity units that will be acquired by the annuitant depends upon the company's assumptions as to mortality, dividend rates, and expenses, and upon the market value of the assets underlying the annuity units. In essence, the number of annuity units is determined by dividing the dollar value of the accumulation units by the present value of a life annuity at the participant's attained age in an amount equal to the current value of one annuity unit, adjusted for monthly payments. Whereas the number of accumulation units of a particular person increases with each premium payment and each allocation of dividends; the number of annuity units remains constant throughout the liquidation period. The units are revalued each year, however, the value at each valuation date reflecting the current market price of the common stock and the mortality, investment, and expense experience for the preceding year.[6] The dollar income payable to the annuitant each month is determined by multiplying the number of annuity units by the current value of each unit. During the annuity—or liquidation—period, the higher the market price of the stock and the greater the dividends, the greater will be the dollar income of the annuitant. During the accumulation stage, however, it is to the advantage of the annuitant for stock prices to be relatively low, since he will thus be able to acquire a larger number of accumulation units for each premium payment.

Some of the more recent variable annuity contracts differ from the foregoing type by (1) using only one unit rather than two, (2) discounting for mortality before as well as after retirement, and (3) limiting variations in the unit value to investment experience only.

A participant in a variable annuity plan should not normally be permitted to surrender his accumulation units for cash or take other action that might involve temptations to "play" the stock market. Where the variable annuity is used as part of a pension plan, surrender values are not generally made available. Where the variable annuity is sold as an individual contract, surrender privileges are made available, but on a much more restricted basis than in connection with ordinary annuities. Under all plans, the current value of the accumulation units is payable, usually as a continuing income, upon the death of the participant during the accumulation period.

The pioneer and still outstanding adaptation of the variable annuity concept is the College Retirement Equities Fund (CREF), a nonprofit corporation established in 1952 by a special act of the New York State Legislature to issue variable annuities to participants in college and university retirement plans underwritten by the Teachers Insurance and Annuity Association. The economic research which preceded the establishment of CREF and the essential features of the plan that was finally evolved have been described in various publications and should be consulted by the interested student.[7]

---

[6] More precisely, the value of an annuity unit at the end of each fiscal year is obtained by dividing the current market value of the funds supporting the annuity units by the present value of the total number of annuity units expected to be paid over the future lifetimes of all participants then receiving annuity payments, in accordance with the assumptions as to mortality, investment earnings, and expense rates for the future.

[7] The following studies were published by the Teachers Insurance and Annuity Association: *A New Approach to Retirement Income,* by William C. Greenough; *An*

Since the establishment of CREF a number of companies have been organized to sell variable annuities, on either an individual or group basis, to members of the general public. In most jurisdictions the insurance law had to be modified or given liberal administrative interpretation in order to permit the sale of variable annuities, not only because of the unusual features of the contract but also, and more importantly, because of the nature of the investment program that would be involved. The great majority of the states now permit the writing of variable annuities on a group basis, i.e., in connection with a pension plan, and a substantial but smaller number authorize their issue on an individual basis.

In a landmark decision,[8] the United States Supreme Court held that an individual variable annuity contract is a security within the meaning of the Securities Act of 1933 and that any organization which offers such a contract is an investment company and subject to the Investment Company Act of 1940. Hence, any company which offers individual variable annuity contracts is subject to dual supervision by the Securities and Exchange Commission and the various state insurance departments. Group variable annuity contracts are currently exempt from supervision by the Securities and Exchange Commission provided certain restrictions are observed.

Supporters of the variable annuity feel that some kind of protection against inflation is needed by annuitants and believe that a common stock investment program administered by a life insurance company is the best approach to this need that has yet been developed. Opponents of the plan argue that the traditional and only legitimate function of a life insurance company is to issue fixed-dollar benefits. They fear an adverse reaction against the entire life insurance institution if the dollar benefits provided by variable annuity contracts fall short of those the annuitants were led to expect. They warn that in their enthusiasm, the agency forces might make unduly optimistic estimates as to the future performance of the common stock portfolio, thus paving the way for possible disillusionment and resentment at a later date. In a different vein, critics of the variable annuity approach

---

Experiment with the Variable Annuity, by George E. Johnson; and *A Retirement System Granting Unit Annuities and Investing in Equities,* by Robert M. Duncan. See also *Transactions of the Society of Actuaries,* Vol. IV (1952), pp. 317–44; and "Pension-Meeting Price Level Changes," by William C. Greenough, in *Pensions: Problems and Trends,* Dan M. McGill, ed. (Homewood, Ill.: Richard D. Irwin, Inc., 1955), pp. 138–60.

[8] *Securities and Exchange Commission* v. *Valic,* 359 U.S. 65 (1959).

question whether continuing inflation is inevitable and, even if it should be, whether common stock investments would provide an effective hedge against rising prices.

ACTUARIAL CONSIDERATIONS

The cost to the insurance company of providing annuity benefits is based on the probability of survival rather than the probability of death. In itself, this fact would seem to have no greater significance than that the insurance company actuaries, in computing premiums for annuities, would have to refer to the actuarial functions reflecting probabilities of survival rather than probabilities of death. As a matter of fact, however, the writing of annuities poses a unique set of actuarial problems for an insurance company.

In the first place, the companies have found that the mortality among persons who purchase annuities tends to be lower, age for age, than that of persons who purchase life insurance. There may be several reasons for this, including the peace of mind that comes with an assured income for life; but certainly, one of the most important is the selection practiced against the company. Individuals who know themselves to have serious health impairments rarely, if ever, purchase annuities. In fact, many persons contemplating the purchase of immediate annuities subject themselves to a thorough medical examination to make sure that they have no serious impairments before committing their capital to annuities. On the other hand, persons who know or suspect that they have an impairment usually seek to obtain life insurance. Whatever its origin, the mortality difference between life insurance policyholders and annuitants is so substantial that special annuity mortality tables must be used for the calculation of annuity premiums.[9]

Secondly, the secular trend toward lower mortality which has been such a favorable development with respect to life insurance has been very unfavorable with respect to annuities. Many annuity contracts run for sixty to seventy-five years, counting the accumulation period; and rates which were adequate at the time the contract was issued may, with continued improvement in longevity, prove inadequate over

---

[9] Selection against the company is present in the use of settlement options under life insurance contracts. Some companies are so concerned about adverse selection under settlement options that a smaller monthly income is provided under the life income option when the beneficiary elects the option than when the insured elects it for the beneficiary.

the years. All mortality tables, of course, contain a margin for safety —which, in the case of life insurance mortality tables, means higher death rates than those which are likely to be experienced and, in the case of annuity mortality tables, means lower rates of mortality than those anticipated. While a long-run decline in mortality rates increases the safety margin in life insurance mortality tables, it shrinks the margin in annuity mortality tables, sometimes to the point of extinction. Therefore, an annuity mortality table which accurately reflected the mortality among annuitants at the time it was compiled gradually becomes obsolete and eventually overstates the mortality that can be expected.

Finally, a high percentage of annuitants, are women, who, as a group, enjoy greater longevity than men. This has intensified the first two factors mentioned above and forced the companies to introduce a rate differential between male and female annuitants long before a rate differential based on sex was applied to the sale of life insurance policies.

The companies have attempted to cope with these problems, or complications, in various ways. In the first place, they compute annuity considerations on the basis of mortality tables that reflect the lower mortality of annuitants. A number of annuity tables have been constructed and used, the 1937 Standard Annuity Table being in common use until the 1950's. The Annuity Table for 1949, or some modification thereof, is the most widely used table today for the writing of individual annuities, but the 1955 American Annuity Table, on which all annuity calculations in this volume are based, is gaining favor.

The specific problem associated with the continuing decline in mortality rates among annuitants was dealt with for many years through the introduction of age "setbacks," a practice still in common use though not always for this particular purpose. In other words, a person may be assumed to be one, two, or three years younger than his actual age. Thus, a person who is actually sixty-five presumably with the life expectancy of an individual that age, may be presumed for the purpose of premium calculations to have the life expectancy of a person aged sixty-four, sixty-three, or even sixty-two, thereby increasing the premium for a given amount of income. Female ages are usually set back four or five years, in addition to the male setback, in recognition of the sex differential in mortality. Thus, if male ages are set back one year, female ages will be set back six years. If the reduction in mortality is reflected equally at all ages, the setback technique can be utilized indefinitely without serious distortion of the equities among annuitants at different ages. However, the reduction has not proceeded at a uniform rate at the various ages, which has definitely limited the efficacy of the setback technique.

The most recent approach to the "problem" of declining mortality is the rise of an annuity table which, by means of projection factors, attempts to forecast and make suitable adjustment for future reductions in mortality rates. For example, the aforementioned Annuity Table for 1949 contains a set of projection factors which with some administrative complications can be used to adjust the mortality assumptions for all ages from year to year or, in lieu thereof, can be used to project the basic rates of mortality to some future date. The American Annuity Table, through a set of adjustment factors, also makes allowance for future reduction in mortality.

Until recent years, companies attempted to hedge future improvement in annuitant mortality through the use of an unrealistically low interest assumption in the premium formula. The rates were substantially lower than those used in the calculation of life insurance premiums. The effectiveness of this technique can be judged by the fact that an interest margin of $\frac{1}{4}$ per cent is capable of absorbing a general reduction in mortality of 6 or 7 per cent. Competition among insurance companies and between insurance companies and competing investment media has caused the companies to adopt interest assumptions much closer to the level of their actual investment earnings. Considerations for individual deferred annuities are generally being computed today on the basis of interest assumptions running from $2\frac{1}{2}$ to $3\frac{1}{2}$ per cent, while immediate annuities may be priced on the basis of assumptions running to 4 per cent or more.

A final approach to the actuarial complexities of annuities is to compute the premiums, or considerations, on a participating basis, which permits conservative assumptions with respect to all factors entering into the computations. Annual premium annuities issued by mutual companies are almost invariably participating during the accumulation period and may be participating on some basis during the liquidation period. Stock companies may also issue annuities that are participating during the accumulation period. Single premium immediate annuities, whether written by mutual or stock companies, are usually not participating for reasons explained in the chapter on dividends.

USES OF THE ANNUITY

Because it is the single-premium life annuity that most frequently comes to mind when annuities are mentioned, and since this form requires the deposit of a substantial sum of money, most people have the impression that annuities are of interest only to the wealthy. This is not at all the case. The field of usefulness of the annuity is nearly as wide as that of the life insurance contract, and forms have been devised to fit every conceivable need or circumstance.

The market for annuities is composed of two broad classes of individuals: those who have already accumulated an estate, either through inheritance or by their own personal efforts, and those who are merely seeking to accumulate an estate. The first class may be subdivided into the wealthy and those with only moderate resources.

Wealthy persons purchase annuities as a hedge against adverse financial developments. Large estates can be wrecked through business reverses, unwise investments, and reckless spending. The records of insurance companies abound with cases of individuals who at one time were wealthy but whose fortunes melted away, leaving as a sole source of income payments from annuities purchased in their more affluent days. There are, in fact, numerous individuals dependent upon relatives for whom they had purchased annuities during a more solvent period. Wealthy people, then, purchase annuities in a search for security. To them, yield is a secondary consideration.

Yield, on the other hand, is a primary consideration for those persons, mostly middle-aged and elderly, who have accumulated a modest estate and are hopeful that it will be the source of financial security during the remaining years of their lives. The life annuity, perhaps in the joint-and-survivor form, is the answer to the problem of this group, since it maximizes income by including in each monthly payment a portion of the principal and at the same time promises a continuation of the income as long as the annuitant or annuitants live. Some persons in these circumstances are reluctant to invest their capital in annuity, since they wish to leave an estate to their children or other close relatives. Many parents, however, feel that, having reared and educated their children, their greatest responsibility is providing for their own old-age maintenance, thus relieving the children of that burden. The annuity is an ideal instrument for accomplishing this objective.

There are situations where the entire capital accumulation may not be needed to provide for the old-age support of the parents. In such cases, a portion of the estate can be used to purchase an annuity of suitable form and size, making it possible for the remainder of the estate to be distributed to the children during the parents' lifetime, when it may be of the greatest use to the children. Most young people would probably prefer to receive a smaller share of their parents' estate when their need for capital is the greatest than to wait for a larger share when the need may be less urgent. Moreover, many parents, if they could safely do so, would prefer to distribute a portion of the estate to the children during their lifetime in order to witness the enjoyment that it would bring. Annuities can be used in like manner to provide living bequests to charitable, educational, and religious organizations.

The annuity is an attractive savings medium for the person who has not yet accumulated an estate but is desirous of achieving financial independence in old age. Professional people find annuities especially attractive for that purpose. The same is true of professional athletes, entertainers, and others who enjoy a very large income but for a limited period of time. Retirement annuities are appropriate for this purpose and can be purchased through periodic premiums or through single-premium deposits as the annuitant comes into possession of large sums.

CHAPTER VII

Special

Life and

Annuity

Contracts

IN ADDITION to the regular life insurance and annuity contracts described in the preceding chapters, life insurance companies offer a wide range of policies that can only be characterized as special or combination policies. They are not to be confused with the "special" whole life contract described in Chapter IV.

These special forms present few principles different from those already discussed. They differ only in that they combine two or more basic forms, such as term and whole life, distribute the proceeds in a special manner, or provide for an unusual pattern of premium payments. They are designed to fit particular situations and hence do not offer the same flexibility as do the regular contracts. In many cases, the coverage could be duplicated by writing separate contracts, frequently at less expense to the company and with more satisfaction to the policyholder. Nevertheless, the industry has felt an institutional obligation to make life insurance available on terms and conditions convenient to the public. The adjustment of coverages, disbursing methods, and premium payments to fit public needs and preferences is regarded as a part of the character and quality of life insurance service. Several of the special contracts have met a real need and enjoy wide popularity. As a group, however, these contracts account for a fairly small percentage of life insurance sales in the United States.

For purposes of discussion, these special contracts can be classified into four groups: (1) those that combine the various types of coverages, (2) those that distribute proceeds in a particular manner, (3) those that possess unusual premium features, and (4) those that defy classification and must be termed "miscellaneous."

COMBINATION CONTRACTS

Family Income Policy

This is one of the most popular of all special contracts and is designed for young men with family responsibilities who are unable to afford a sufficient amount of insurance under one of the regular forms of protection. Its purpose is to provide funds for the period during which the children are dependent.

In its simplest form, the family income policy stipulates that in the event of the insured's death within a specified period—usually ten, fifteen, or twenty years, running from date of issue—monthly payments equal to 1 per cent of the face of the policy ($10 for each $1,000 of insurance) will be paid to the designated beneficiary from the date of the insured's death to the end of the specified period, with the face of the policy being payable upon termination of the income payments. If the insured should die beyond the specified period, only the face of the policy is payable. The length of the period is determined by the age of the youngest child and, ideally, should be long enough to protect the family until the youngest child is self-supporting. Some companies offer a contract under which the period extends to age sixty-five, rather than for a specified number of years.

To illustrate, if a young man should purchase a $10,000 twenty-year family income policy and die two years from the date of issue, $100 per month would be payable for the next eighteen years and $10,000 at the end of eighteen years. If he should die fifteen years from the date of issue, $100 per month would be paid for five years and $10,000 at the end of five years. If he should die twenty years and one day after the effective date of the contract, only the face would be paid, but it would be payable immediately.

Structurally, the family income contract is a combination of whole life insurance and decreasing term insurance. The whole life contract provides for payment of the face whenever the insured dies, whether it be during the specified term or at any time thereafter. Term insurance is superimposed on the whole life insurance in an amount sufficient, when supplemented by interest on the proceeds from the whole life policy, to provide the monthly payments during the specified period.

The maximum number of income payments that would be called for under a contract with a twenty-year period is 240. If the policy is for $10,000 and the entire $100 per month had to be provided by term insurance, the effective amount of term insurance at the date of issue would be $18,975 (present value at 2½ percent of 240 monthly payments of $100 each). However, the proceeds of the whole life policy, which technically become payable upon the death of the insured, are held at interest by the insurance company, and the interest income is applied against the contractual monthly payments. At 2½ per cent interest, each $1,000 of insurance proceeds provides $2.06 per month, which means that $20.60 of the necessary $100 per month comes from interest on the $10,000 of whole life proceeds.[1]

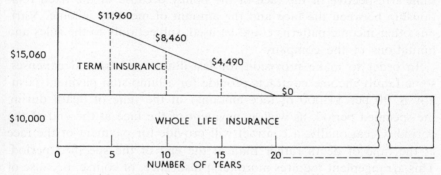

FIG. 7. Relative proportions of whole life and term insurance in a $10,000 twenty-year family income policy; 2½ per cent interest.

Therefore, only slightly more than $15,000 ($15,060, to be exact) of term insurance would be needed to provide the maximum of 240 payments. Each month that the insured lives reduces the amount of term insurance protection by an average of $62.75 until at the end of twenty years, the protection is zero. If the insured should die thereafter, only the $10,000 of whole life insurance is payable. The average amount of protection provided by the decreasing term insurance is $8,460, as illustrated in Figure 7.

The proceeds of the whole life policy may be taken in a lump sum or in accordance with any of the settlement options offered by the company. In programming a client's insurance estate, provision is usually made for distribution of the whole life proceeds under one of the

---

[1] If the insurance is participating, the actual monthly payments will be increased by the excess interest credited to the proceeds. These increments to the contractual payments do not operate to reduce the amount of term insurance.

income options. If a life income is elected for the widow, as is frequently done, the income from the combined contract will decrease somewhat at the end of the twenty-year period (or whatever period was originally selected) but will continue at the reduced level for the remainder of the beneficiary's life. If the widow's age at the expiration of the term insurance period should be forty-five, for example, the $10,000 of whole life proceeds would provide a life income of $37.60 per month, with payments guaranteed for ten years. Under another option, the income payable during the specified period could be continued beyond the period at the same level until the whole life proceeds are exhausted, which, under a $2\frac{1}{2}$ per cent interest assumption, would be nine years and three months. The period would be the same irrespective of the face of the policy because of the fixed relationship between the face and the amount of monthly income. Various other income patterns could be used, subject only to the rules and limitations of the company.

In order to make provision for last-illness and funeral expenses, some family income contracts provide for a lump-sum payment (usually $200 per $1,000 of face amount) at the time of death during the specified period, as well as payment of the face at the end of the period. Occasionally, a contract will provide for payment of the face at the time of death rather than at the end of the specified period. This arrangement requires more term insurance, of course, because of the loss of interest on the whole life proceeds. Finally, some companies will provide a monthly income in excess of the conventional $10 per $1,000 of insurance, with an appropriate adjustment in premium. In such a case, more term insurance is added to the whole life insurance to provide the additional income.

The benefits described above may be provided within a single contract, called the family income *policy,* or by means of a family income *rider* attached to any form of permanent insurance, including endowments. The rider provides the decreasing term insurance and specifies that in the event of the insured's death during the term period, the proceeds of the policy to which it is attached are to be held by the company under the interest option, the interest being used to provide a portion of the income payments. The rider can be attached to any form of permanent insurance with premiums payable throughout the term of the rider, which may be written for any period desired. In most companies, it can be added to either a new or an old policy. If it is to be added to an existing policy, the insured must furnish evidence of insurability. Because of its flexibility, the rider arrangement has all but supplanted the special policy form.

The premium for a family income policy or rider is level throughout the period of term protection but, at the expiration of the period, drops down to that payable for the permanent insurance. During the later years of the specified period, the level premium for the decreasing term insurance exceeds the cost of insurance allocable to the term portion of the contract. Consequently, some companies provide for payment of the term insurance costs by means of level premiums payable throughout only a portion of the period, such as during the first fifteen years of a twenty-year term.

The insurance may be written with such disability benefits as the company is prepared to write under the permanent contracts of insurance. The amount of any disability income benefits, however, depends only on the face of the underlying policy and is not increased on account of the term insurance. Likewise, if the contract is written with accidental death benefits and the insured is killed during the term insurance period, the double death benefit ordinarily applies only to the basic amount of insurance and not to the income.

The family income contract provides income protection when most needed and at minimum cost. The income period is measured from the date of the policy and not from date of the insured's death, which makes possible the use of decreasing term insurance. On the debit side, however, the contract lends itself to the same possibility of misunderstanding as do all other contracts utilizing term insurance. The insured may misunderstand the limitations as to income protection. Reference to specified periods for income protection not infrequently creates the impression that income will be paid from the date of the death of the insured for the full number of months or years mentioned in the policy rather than for the number of years remaining in the period. Confusion is increased by the fact that the family maintenance policy, presently to be noticed, does in fact provide for income payments for a definite and certain period commencing with the death of the insured. There are also instances where the insured has fully understood the nature of the coverage but the beneficiary is disappointed when the income period proves to be shorter than expected. The life underwriter should seek to avoid misunderstanding by clearly setting forth to the insured—and to the beneficiary—the exact nature of the protection.

The term feature of the contract is also subject to the limitations of temporary insurance. The protection may expire at a time when the need is still great. Additional children may have been born after the contract was purchased, extending the need for family protection beyond the period originally anticipated. To meet these objections, some companies provide that the term feature of the contract may be converted, without evidence of insurability, into any of the regular forms of whole life or endowment insurance. The amount of permanent insurance which can be obtained under this privilege is limited to the commuted value of the term insurance at the date of conversion or, under the rules of some companies, to a specified percentage, such as 75 or 80 per cent, of the commuted value at the date of conversion. The exchange must usually occur some years prior to the expiration of the term period.

Family Maintenance Policy

The family maintenance policy is very similar to the family income policy, with the important exception that *the period during which income payments are to be made commences to run with the death of the insured,* rather than with the date of issue of the policy. Income may be provided for a period of ten, fifteen, or twenty years from the death of the insured. However, the income will be payable only if the insured dies within a specified period *running from the date of issue of the policy.* This period is the same length as that of the income period. Irrespective of the point within the specified period at which the insured dies—even though it be the last day of the period—the income will be payable for the number of years set forth in the contract. The face amount of the policy, unless otherwise provided, is payable at the expiration of the income period.

Like the family income policy, the family maintenance policy is a combination of permanent insurance and term insurance. However, since the amount and duration of income payments remain the same, regardless of the date of the insured's death (within the specified period, of course), the term insurance is said to be level, rather than decreasing. Hence, the structure of the policy may be more accurately described as a combination of permanent insurance and level term insurance. Interest on the proceeds of the underlying policy serves to reduce the amount of term insurance, as with the family income policy. The benefits may be provided by a special package policy or by attachment of a term rider on permanent insurance. The structure of the policy is portrayed in Figure 8.

Since the family maintenance policy provides level term protection, it is substantially more expensive than a comparable family income policy. One large company quotes a nonparticipating premium rate of $7.40 per $1,000 at age twenty-five for its twenty-year family maintenance rider and a comparable rate of $4.50 per $1,000 for its twenty-year family income rider. At age thirty, the comparable rates are $9.19 and $4.98, respectively, and the spread becomes greater as the age of issue increases. Above thirty-five, the rate for the family maintenance policy is more than double that for the family income policy.

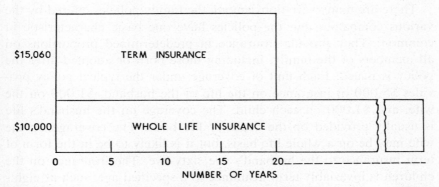

FIG. 8. Relative proportions of whole life and term insurance in a $10,000 family maintenance policy; 2½ per cent interest.

This is understandable, since the amount of term protection under the family maintenance policy is just double the average amount under the family income policy.

In order to permit a reduction in the premium burden, some companies allow the insured to shorten the income period as the children grow older, thus reducing the effective amount of insurance. Most contracts restrict such adjustments to five-year intervals. To the extent that the privilege is exercised, the coverage of the family maintenance policy tends to approach that of the family income policy.

The family maintenance policy is somewhat more flexible than the family income policy. If family circumstances change—for example, if additional children are born after the contract is taken out—the level protection of the family maintenance contract is more likely to meet the needs of the family than is the decreasing protection of the family income policy. Moreover, misunderstandings as to the benefits available are not so likely to arise. Nevertheless, the family income policy is far the more popular of the two contracts and is favored by most companies. Few companies offer both contracts.

Family Life Insurance Policy

Not to be confused with either of the two foregoing policies is the policy which goes under the name of the "family life insurance policy" or, sometimes, the "family plan." Introduced in its present form in 1956, this contract has achieved remarkable popularity and is now being offered by a large number of companies. It produces as much as a third of the premium volume of many companies.

There are many variations among the family policies offered by the various companies, but the policies have one basic characteristic in common: They provide insurance in predetermined proportions on all members of the family, including those born or adopted after the policy is issued. Each unit of coverage under the typical policy provides $5,000 of insurance on the life of the husband, $1,000 on the wife, and $1,000 on each child. The coverage on the husband's life is usually provided on the ordinary life basis. The coverage on the wife may be on a whole life basis, but it is likely to be in the form of term insurance to the husband's age sixty-five. The insurance on the children is invariably term insurance to a specified age, such as eighteen, twenty-one, or twenty-five.

Under most policies, the premium rate for the entire package of protection depends entirely upon the age of the insured. The premium is computed on the assumption that the wife is the same age as the husband, and that the number and ages of the children conform to a particular pattern. If the wife is not the same age as the husband, the predetermined premium will be used to purchase whatever amount of insurance can be obtained at her actual age. If the wife is younger than the husband, the amount of insurance on her life will be somewhat more than $1,000; while if she is older than her husband, she will have less than $1,000 of coverage. A limitation on the age differential is usually imposed in order that the surrender values under the policy will comply with the legal requirements. Under the rules of most companies, the wife must not be more than twelve years younger or seven years older than the husband. Under some policies, the amount of insurance on the wife bears a fixed relationship to that on the husband, the aggregate premium varying with the age of the wife as well as that of the husband. The insurance on the wife is usually one fifth of that on the husband, but some policies provide one fourth.

When the premium reflects the age of the wife, it is not necessary or customary to impose any limitations on the age differential between the husband and wife.

The premium for the family policy reflects neither the number nor the ages of the children covered by the policy. As stated above, the premium does reflect an *assumption* as to the number and age distribution of the children, but deviations from the assumption are ignored for both premium and dividend purposes. This is practicable, since the premium for the children's insurance constitutes such a small portion of the total premium. The relative insignificance of the cost of the children's coverage stems from the extremely low death rates at the ages involved and the use of term insurance. The studies of one company showed that the administrative expense of establishing and maintaining records on the individual children would exceed the cost of providing protection during the entire period of coverage. Hence, it is not customary to maintain individual records for the children, and children born or legally adopted after the policy is issued are automatically covered, without notice to the company, upon the attainment of a specified age, usually fourteen days.

It is common to include a waiver of premium benefit which provides that if the husband dies or becomes totally disabled, further premiums on the entire policy are waived. An accidental death benefit, which may be optional or automatic, is usually included on the husband and is frequently applied to the wife. If the wife predeceases her husband, it is the usual practice to reduce the premium; but some companies continue the original premium, using the portion of the premium that had been charged for the wife's insurance to provide an appropriate increase in insurance on the life of the husband.

The usual surrender and loan values are generally available, although under most policies, paid-up insurance is provided only on the husband's life. Some policies make provision for a few months of extended term insurance on the lives of the dependents to bridge short gaps between surrender and reinstatement. Automatic premium loans are available under some policies.

The usual dividend options are available; but here again, it is the practice to specify that any paid-up insurance purchased by dividends will be on the life of the husband only.

It is customary to permit conversion on the attained age basis of the term insurance on the lives of the dependents upon expiry of such insurance. The children are generally permitted to acquire

$5,000 of permanent insurance for each $1,000 of term insurance.

The husband is generally designated as owner of the policy. However, the policy itself usually specifies the disposition of the insurance on the various lives. The typical arrangement is for the insurance on the husband's life to be payable to the wife, if living, otherwise to his estate; the insurance on the wife's life to be payable to the husband, if living, otherwise to her estate; and that on a child's life to be payable to the father, if living, otherwise to the mother, if living, otherwise to the child's estate.

All persons to be insured under the family policy initially must be insurable, although less rigorous selection standards may be applied to the dependents than to the husband. If either the husband or the wife is uninsurable, the family policy cannot be issued, but the company may make available a "parent's" policy covering only one parent and all insurable children. If a child is uninsurable, the family policy can still be issued, with such child being excluded from coverage. Children born or legally adopted after the policy is issued are automatically covered upon attaining the minimum age for inclusion, irrespective of their health. The amount of insurance during the first six months of life may be smaller than that provided thereafter.

Retirement Income Contract

This contract goes under several names, including *income endowment, retirement endowment, endowment annuity,* and *insurance with annuity.* It is an extremely popular contract and is offered under some name by virtually all companies. It has all but supplanted the long-term endowment as a means of providing old-age income for the policyholder. It is widely used in connection with *pension trusts,* a form of industrial pension plan for small employers, and is frequently used in other types of pension plans.

The retirement income contract is practically identical with the retirement annuity contract previously discussed, except for the death benefit available before maturity. The objectives of the two contracts are the same—to provide old-age income to the policyholder and possibly his wife—and the accumulation required for each $10 unit of monthly income is the same, ranging from about $1,200 to $2,000, depending upon age at maturity and sex of the insured. However, the retirement income contract provides a larger death benefit in the early years of the contract. Whereas the retirement annuity promises only the return of premiums or the cash value, whichever is larger, the retirement income contract promises $1,000 for each $10 unit of monthly life income or the cash value, whichever is larger. As a matter of fact, some contracts provide up to $2,000 of insurance for each $10 unit of monthly income.

The additional death benefits are provided by means of decreasing term insurance. The insurance element is represented by the excess of the face amount of the contract over the cash value. The amount of insurance decreases as the cash value increases and ultimately declines to zero as the cash value equals the face of the policy. Thereafter, the death benefit is the same as that of the retirement annuity—namely, the cash value.

The structure of the contract is illustrated in Figure 9. The maturity

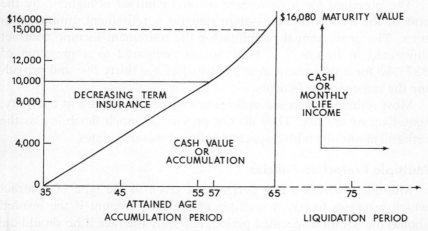

FIG. 9. Basic structure of a $10,000 retirement income contract issued at male age thirty-five and maturing at age sixty-five; gross annual premium, $450.50

value of a $10,000 retirement income contract maturing at age sixty-five, according to the actuarial assumptions being used, is $16,080, the same as that of a retirement annuity providing a life income of $100 per month, with payments guaranteed for ten years. The maturity value may be taken in cash or in accordance with the customary options available under a retirement annuity, including the joint-and-survivor annuity. If the insured should die during the early years of the contract, his estate or designated beneficiary would receive $10,000, instead of a refund of premiums paid. The $10,000 could be taken in a lump sum or under any of the customary settlement options. The death benefit would be composed of the cash value plus a sufficient amount of term insurance to equal the face of the policy. For a policy issued at age thirty-five, however, the cash value would reach the face at age fifty-seven; and thereafter, the contract is precisely the same as a retirement annuity. The insurance element would have completely evaporated.

On the other hand, if the face of the policy is $1,500 for each $10 unit of monthly income, the term insurance protection continues almost to maturity. This can be seen in Figure 9. The area between the broken horizontal line and the solid diagonal line represents the insurance protection in that case. Policies which provide more than $1,500 of insurance for each $10 unit of income usually have a larger maturity value than $1,608, but a few companies write a contract whose face is larger than the maturity value.

The premium for a retirement income contract is higher—by the cost of the term insurance—than that for a retirement annuity contract. The gross annual premium for the retirement income contract illustrated in Figure 9 is $450.50, as compared to a premium of $371.40 for a retirement annuity issued at age thirty-five and providing the same income benefits.

Most retirement income policies are written to mature at age sixty, sixty-five, or seventy. They do not provide as much flexibility as the retirement annuity with respect to optional maturity dates.

Multiple Protection Policies

Multiple protection is a designation given to the type of contract which promises to pay a multiple of the face amount if the insured should die within a specified period, and only the face if he should die after the expiration of the period. The period may run for a stipulated number of years, typically ten, fifteen, or twenty, or to a specified age, usually sixty or sixty-five. The death benefits during the specified period are usually double or triple the face of the policy. Thus, a particular policy may be referred to as "double protection to 65" or "triple protection to 60."

This coverage illustrates one of the simplest applications of term insurance. If double protection is involved, it represents a combination of term insurance and an equal amount of permanent insurance; if triple protection is promised, the term insurance is double the amount of permanent insurance. The coverage may be provided by a special package policy or by attachment of a term rider to a whole life or endowment policy. The similarity between a twenty-year double protection policy and a twenty-year family maintenance policy should be apparent. The former expresses the coverage in terms of a principal sum, while the latter expresses it in terms of monthly income. Like the family maintenance policy, the term insurance portion of the coverage is convertible into permanent insurance, subject to the usual limitations.

Premiums for the policy may be level throughout the premium-paying period of the permanent insurance or may be higher by the cost of the term insurance during the period of multiple protection. Surrender values of the permanent insurance are not affected by the term supplement, but the term supplement itself may develop surrender values which would disappear upon expiration of the term insurance. Neither disability income nor accidental death benefits are applicable to the term coverage.

An interesting application of the multiple protection concept is the combination of a "life paid-up at 65" policy with an equal amount of term to sixty-five. The resulting policy provides double protection to sixty-five and paid-up insurance for the full face amount thereafter.

CONTRACTS WITH INCOME SETTLEMENTS

There are two types of contracts that make no provision for a lump-sum settlement: the *survivorship annuity* and the *life income* policy. The benefits under these contracts are payable only in the form of income.

Survivorship Annuity

The survivorship annuity, sometimes referred to as a "reversionary annuity," is not really an annuity but a life insurance contract. More accurately, it is a life insurance policy coupled with an annuity agreement. The contract promises to pay a life income of a specified amount to a designated beneficiary if the beneficiary should survive the insured—hence the name. If the beneficiary should predecease the insured, however, the contract terminates, and no benefits are payable. Benefits are payable only as long as the beneficiary is living, there being no guaranteed payments. The contract is one of life insurance, in that one person—sometimes called the "nominator"—is insured to provide the funds for the payment of a life income to another person. The amount at risk at any particular time is the principal sum needed to provide a life income of the specified amount to the beneficiary at her attained age. Since the present value of an immediate life annuity declines with each increase in age, the effective amount of insurance under a survivorship annuity is at the maximum at the time of issue and decreases as the years go by. Inasmuch as the age of the beneficiary determines the amount at risk, the contract does not permit a change of beneficiary.

The insured, or nominator, must furnish evidence of insurability, since his death fixes the date on which the income payments begin. On the other hand, no medical examination is required of the beneficiary, inasmuch as her death relieves the company of any further obligation under the contract. Evidence of insurability is never required of annuitants. Premiums are paid as long as the insured lives or until the death of the beneficiary. The contract has no cash or loan values; but after a prescribed number of premiums have been paid, the reserve can be used to provide a paid-up survivorship annuity. Accidental death benefits may be provided, which means that the amount of the annuity payments will be doubled if the insured's death is caused by accident. The contract may also provide disability benefits; but since the policy is written for the benefit of the annuitant, the disability benefit is usually confined to waiver of premiums.

The survivorship annuity offers a unique advantage, in that it provides the beneficiary a life income of a fixed amount, regardless of the age of the beneficiary at the time of the insured's death. No other contract can duplicate that feature. The proceeds of a life insurance contract can be taken in the form of a life income for the beneficiary, but the amount of each income payment is determined by the age of the beneficiary at the time of the insured's death and cannot be known in advance. With a survivorship annuity, however, the insured can select the income which he wants payable to the beneficiary and rest secure in the knowledge that the beneficiary, if living, will receive such income, regardless of when death occurs.

A second attractive feature of the survivorship annuity is its low cost when the insured is young and the beneficiary is elderly—the typical situation. It is usually purchased by a young person to assure the means of support to an elderly person, such as a parent. According to the rates quoted by one large company, an insured aged thirty can purchase for an annual premium of $101.70 a survivorship annuity that will provide a life income of $100 a month for a female beneficiary aged sixty at the time of issue. The premium is low, of course, because of the high probability that the beneficiary will predecease the insured. The closer the ages of the insured and the beneficiary, the higher the premium. It might be said that the premium for the survivorship annuity is relatively low because it provides an income only if the beneficiary is alive to need it, whereas under all other contracts of insurance, the need is presumed and the proceeds provided whether the original beneficiary is dead or alive.

There are certain disadvantageous features to the survivorship annuity. In the first place, it is extremely inflexible. It provides income only to the person originally designated in the contract. No other person can be substituted for the original beneficiary, either before or after the insured's death. It is rather unsuitable for the protection of a wife, since in the event of her death and the subsequent remarriage of the husband, the protection of the original contract could not be extended to the second wife, and a new contract would be conditioned on the husband's insurability. The same difficulties would be encountered in the event of divorce. A second disadvantage is that the contract makes no provision for others who may be dependent upon the insured. Specifically, it provides no protection to the insured's children except while the wife-beneficiary is alive. If the wife should die shortly after the husband's death, the contract would provide no income to the dependent children. The same would be true if the wife should predecease the husband; but in that case, the husband could procure additional insurance, if insurable. Finally, there is no old-age protection. The contract does not provide cash values, and no income will be paid until the insured dies, even though he might live to an advanced age.

A modified form of the survivorship annuity is available under which the income to the beneficiary does not commence until the expiration of a specified period following the insured's death. If the beneficiary does not survive the specified period, no payments are made under the contract, and the company retains all premiums paid. This form is very appropriately called a *deferred survivorship annuity*. Its appeal lies in its low cost. If an insured aged thirty wishes to provide, by means of a conventional survivorship annuity, a life income of $100 a month to a wife also aged thirty, the annual premium would be $322.40. If, however, the insured were willing to defer the income for twenty years after his death, the contract could be procured for an annual premium of $62.80. Such deferral of income places a contract written for the benefit of a young beneficiary in the same general price range as that of a conventional survivorship annuity purchased for an older beneficiary. In order to provide for the beneficiary's needs during the years immediately following the insured's death, most companies offering the deferred survivorship annuity insist, as an underwriting requirement, that the insured carry sufficient insurance with the company involved to provide an income during the deferred period at least equal to that payable under the deferred survivorship annuity. Then, the company may point out, as a cost argument, that income is being provided during the period when there are likely to be dependent children but that a life income, always costly, is being provided only if the beneficiary is alive at the end of the period to need it.

Life Income Policy

The life income policy differs from the survivorship annuity only in that payments are guaranteed for a specified period following the insured's death, whether the beneficiary is alive to receive them or not. In all other respects, the two contracts are identical. If the beneficiary survives the specified period, which may run as long as twenty years, she will receive income for life. If she does not survive the insured, the guaranteed payments will go to contingent beneficiaries. Thus, this arrangement protects dependents other than the primary beneficiary, removing the principal objection to the unmodified form of the survivorship annuity.

The insurance value of the policy is composed of two elements: (1) the principal sum required to provide the specified number of payments certain and (2) the sum required to provide for the continuation of the payments if the beneficiary be alive at the end of the period. The value of the first element will depend upon the number of payments—usually 120, 180, or 240—and will be the same irrespective of the age of the beneficiary at the time the contract is issued. For example, if the contract promises to provide $100 a month for a minimum of twenty years, the company must have $18,975 on hand at the insured's death to meet this portion of its obligation.[2] This sum, generally referred to as the *commuted value* of the guaranteed installments, can be provided by any form of whole life insurance. The second element of the coverage depends upon the age of the beneficiary and is, in fact, a deferred survivorship annuity, commencing, in this case, twenty years after the insured's death. Thus, it may be said that the life income policy is a combination of (1) a whole life policy

---

[2] This assumes an interest basis of 2½ per cent.

in the amount of the commuted or present value of the guaranteed payments and (2) a deferred survivorship annuity for the amount of income stipulated in the contract.

If the beneficiary should predecease the insured, the deferred survivorship annuity portion of the contract will terminate; but the whole life portion will remain in effect for the protection of the contingent beneficiaries, usually the insured's children. The premium will, of course, be reduced at the beneficiary's death by the cost of the annuity. The whole life portion of the contract has surrender values which, however, cannot be obtained without terminating the entire contract. The beneficiary designation with respect to the guaranteed installments may be changed at will. If the beneficiary has predeceased the insured, most contracts will permit the contingent beneficiaries to take the commuted value of the guaranteed payments in a lump sum.

A few companies offer the life income policy on the endowment plan. Such a contract provides for an annuity income upon the insured's death or upon his survival to a specified age, such as sixty or sixty-five. Payments are made throughout the guaranteed period and as long thereafter as either the insured or the beneficiary is alive. This contract is expensive, but it affords complete protection to husband, wife, and children, especially if provision is made for the permanent and total disability of the insured.

It should be clear that there is no difference, in substance, between a life income policy and an arrangement whereby the insured takes out a deferred survivorship annuity and a separate insurance policy capable of providing the same income during the deferred period as the annuity will provide thereafter.

CONTRACTS WITH UNUSUAL PREMIUM FEATURES
Modified Life Policies

"Modified life" is an appellation given to those policies the premiums for which are lower during the first few years of the contract than they are thereafter. Such contracts can be subdivided into two categories: (1) those that represent an adaptation of the term insurance principle and (2) those that represent only a *redistribution* of premiums.

One type of policy in the first category provides level term insurance for the first few years, usually five, and whole life thereafter. The premium during the preliminary period is at the term rate, jumping up at the end of the period to the whole life rate at the insured's attained age. There are no surrender values during the first five years; but thereafter, the contract is a whole life policy in every respect. Under another general type of contract embodying the term principle, the protection is wholly on the term basis only during the first year, the amount of term insurance decreasing each year during the remaining portion of the preliminary period and the amount of whole life insurance increasing each year until, at the end of the period, all of the protection is on the whole life basis. The premium during the preliminary period increases with each increment of whole life insurance but, as a result, will be slightly lower after the preliminary period than under the previous contract described. There may be surrender values, though necessarily small, during the latter portion of the preliminary period.

Policies in the second category utilize whole life insurance from the outset, with no element of term insurance involved. One type of policy provides that the premium during the first three or five years will be exactly one half the premium payable thereafter. Another provides for a premium during the first five years approximately 70 per cent of that payable thereafter. Under either one of these plans, the premium after the preliminary period will be larger than the level premium at the original age of issue but smaller than the level premium for the insured's attained age at the end of the period. It is generally agreed that any such redistribution of premiums is practicable when the reduced premium during the preliminary period lies between (1) the regular level premium at age of issue and (2) the premium for term insurance with automatic continuance on a permanent plan. The greater the excess of the "reduced" premium over the term rate, the smaller will be the level premium at the end of the preliminary period. In every case, the present value of the redistributed premiums is exactly the same as that of the level premiums payable from the date of issue. There are cash and other surrender values during the preliminary period; but naturally, they are smaller than those that would be available if the full level premium had been paid.

Modified life policies are designed to overcome the sales resistance of life insurance prospects. They are intended for persons who feel that they cannot afford to purchase permanent insurance at regular rates but who hope to improve their financial status within a few years. They are particularly attractive to young men just out of school and embarking upon a business career. Principally, however, they cater to the human tendency to discount the future heavily. Many people prefer to pay a smaller premium immediately and a considerably larger one some time in the future than to pay the normal premium from the beginning.

In a different vein, modified life policies may be used by companies selling participating insurance to help meet the price competition from nonparticipating policies which are typically offered at lower gross premiums.

Return Premium Policy

The return premium policy provides not only for payment of the face upon maturity but also for the return of all or a portion of the premiums paid. This refund feature is usually added to a policy to offset some objectionable feature which militates against its sale. For example, it might be added to a survivorship annuity to eliminate the forfeiture of premiums involved when the beneficiary predeceases the insured. These policies may provide for the return of the exact premium. If the annual premium were $53.85, for instance, the policy might promise to return $50, thus simplifying premium calculations, since an extra premium is charged for the refund feature. In effect, the face of the policy is increased each year by the amount of the premium or the portion thereof which the company promises to refund. The premium for the contract is level, however.

Under some contracts, the premium refund feature operates only if the insured dies before a specified age, such as, sixty-five. In such policies, the premium refund feature is underwritten through *increasing* term insurance.

MISCELLANEOUS CONTRACTS

Income and Principal Policy

The distinctive characteristic of the income and principal policy is the provision upon the death of the insured for payment of a life income of a specified amount to the primary beneficiary, with the face of the policy being payable to a secondary beneficiary upon the death of the first. If the primary beneficiary predeceases the insured, the face of the policy is paid directly to the secondary beneficiary upon the death of the insured.

This policy is designed for the person who wants his insurance to provide for the lifetime needs of one person—e.g., his widow—but wants the proceeds ultimately distributed intact to certain other persons—normally, the children. The conventional method of accomplishing such an objective would be to leave the insurance proceeds with the company under the interest option, with the interest to go to the widow as long as she lives and the proceeds to be distributed to the children as secondary beneficiaries upon the death of the widow. The only weakness to this plan is that few individuals can leave insurance in such quantity that the interest from it will be adequate for the needs of the primary beneficiary. The income and principal policy purports to solve this dilemma by guaranteeing a rate of interest on the proceeds greatly in excess of that normally payable under the interest option, thus reducing the amount of insurance necessary to provide any given income. Most of these contracts guarantee a return of 6 per cent, which, quite naturally, looks very attractive to the prospect.

As in all contracts which appear to offer a "bargain," however, the insured pays for the extra feature. This contract is really a combination of a whole life policy and a survivorship annuity. The whole life policy provides the proceeds that will ultimately be paid to the secondary beneficiary or beneficiaries, while the survivorship annuity provides the *difference* between the rate of return that the company can reasonably expect to earn on proceeds held at interest and the rate promised under the contract. For example, if the company can reasonably expect to earn only 3 per cent interest but promises 6 per cent, the additional income of $30 per year for each $1,000 of proceeds must be provided by a survivorship annuity at an appropriate extra premium. The extra premium would depend upon the age of the primary beneficiary, as well as that of the insured, as is true of the premium for all survivorship annuities. If the primary beneficiary predeceases the insured, the survivorship annuity terminates, and the premium is reduced to the rate payable for the whole life contract. Then, upon the insured's death, the proceeds of the whole life policy are payable immediately to the secondary beneficiaries, either in a lump sum or under one or more of the available settlement options.

Some contracts promise the income not for the lifetime of the primary beneficiary, but for a definite term of years. In that case, the extra income, which must be paid in any event, is provided by additional insurance on the whole life plan. Extra income of $30 per year for twenty years, for example, would be equivalent on a 3 per cent interest basis to $460 of insurance. Thus, under a $20,000 contract, the additional insurance involved would be $9,200, and the premium would be adjusted accordingly.

There is certainly no theoretical objection to the income and principal policy. There is a practical objection, however, that the insured may be misled into believing that he is getting a "6 per cent investment" for his beneficiary, when, in reality, he is paying an extra premium for the additional income promised.

Guaranteed Dividend Policy

This is a nonparticipating contract which promises the payment of an annual "dividend" of a specified amount. It usually contains a sheet of coupons for such dividends, resembling the coupons attached to bonds. In life insurance, the term "dividend" refers to a policy's share in the divisible surplus earnings of the company, and the size of such dividends obviously cannot be accurately predicted at the date of issue of the policy. Guaranteed dividends, therefore, are not true dividends in the insurance sense but an additional benefit for which an extra premium must be charged. The reserve for such a policy includes the present value of future guaranteed dividends, which, after all, are as much a part of the contractual liability as the face amount itself.

Face Amount plus Cash Value Policies

This contract was introduced to meet the objection of uninformed persons that the reserve under a level premium contract should be paid in addition to the face amount. This contract does just that—but at a price. It is a combination of two whole life contracts, one of which provides for payment of the face amount, the other providing for payment of the cash value. The effective amount of insurance increases each year under the latter, but the premium for the composite contract is level. Once again, the insured gets precisely what he pays for.

Juvenile Insurance

Juvenile insurance does not involve special policies of the type discussed in this chapter but, rather, represents only a modification of the regular forms of insurance to meet the needs of young children. Technically, juvenile insurance refers to insurance written on the lives of children from the age of one day to fourteen or fifteen years, issued on the application of a parent or some other person responsible for the support of the child. The principal appeal of juvenile insurance is the opportunity it affords to start a child on a thrift program at an early age. It lends itself admirably to the accumulation of funds for the higher education of the child. This type of insurance is now an important branch of the life insurance industry.

In the beginning, life insurance companies viewed juvenile insurance with a certain amount of skepticism because of the limited insurable value of a young child (unless his earnings potential is considered). It was feared that indiscriminate insuring of children would lead to speculation in the lives of young children and perhaps even to homicide or murder. As a result, the companies established rather strict limits on the amount of insurance which they would write on the lives of young children, and several states enacted statutes for the same purpose. The companies have gradually relaxed their restrictions, however, and, unless prohibited by statute, will now write substantial amounts on juvenile lives. Some companies have no fixed limit on the amount of insurance which they will write on children over a specified age, such as thirty-two days.

Those states that restrict the writing of juvenile insurance usually specify the amount of insurance that can be in force on the life of a child at each age during the early years. In most cases, the statutory limitations apply only up to age five, but they may extend to age ten or fifteen. The New York Insurance Law, for instance, provides for graded amounts ranging from $400 at ages below six months up to $1,500 at ages between thirteen and one-half and fourteen and one-half. Notwithstanding these limits, a person with an insurable interest in the minor, or one upon whom the minor is dependent for support, may procure up to $5,000 of insurance on a child at any age below fourteen and one-half, provided that the total amount of insurance on the life of the minor does not exceed 25 per cent of the insurance in force upon the life of the person effecting the insurance if the minor is under four and one-half years of age, and 50 per cent of the insurance on the life of the applicant if the minor is above four and one-half years of age. Interestingly, the New York law imposes no limit on the amount of insurance that may be issued on the life of a minor to a person who has an insurable interest and pays premiums but *upon whom the minor is not dependent for support*. This latter feature was introduced into the law in 1959 in order to permit grandfathers to build life insurance estates for their grandchildren.[3] Companies writing

---

[3] J. Edwin Dowling and Richard E. Erway, *The Life Insurance Law of New York* (New York: The Association of Life Insurance Counsel, 1963), p. 378.

juvenile insurance in states with statutory limitations usually issue policies with benefits which are graded in accordance with state law. The benefits may go as low as $75 during the first year and as high as $1,000 at age five. Other companies prefer to issue in such states policies that promise, in the event of death before a specified age, such as fifteen or eighteen, only to return all premiums paid with interest. Such a contract does not provide *insurance* prior to the specified age and hence can be issued in any face amount without contravening state statutes. Policies with graded insurance benefits cannot be issued with large "ultimate" face amounts unless the fraction of the face that is payable at the lowest age is very small, since otherwise the effective amount of insurance during the early years might exceed the legal limit.

In those jurisdictions that do not impose restrictions on juvenile insurance, it is now possible to obtain coverage for the face amount of the policy from age one. If the policy is issued at age zero, it is customary to restrict the first-year death benefit to $250 per $1,000 of face amount. Most companies will insure a child one day old, but many require the child to be at least one month old. No medical examination is required for nominal amounts, but sizable policies may necessitate evidence of insurability. Policies are usually issued to age fourteen or fifteen, with the ownership in the applicant until the child reaches age twenty-one. Most companies will issue regular policies to applicants above the juvenile age limit but below the age of twenty-one, on their own application, even though, in many states, this involves the risk of disaffirmation of the contract by the applicant. Some states, including New York, have by statute conferred legal capacity on minors above a certain age, usually fourteen, to enter into a life insurance transaction.

Juvenile insurance is usually written on the following forms: (1) twenty-payment endowment at age sixty-five, (2) twenty-payment endowment at age eighty-five, (3) twenty-year endowment, (4) life paid-up at sixty-five, and (5) educational endowment at age eighteen. Ordinary life policies are generally available, but long-term endowments and limited-payment policies can be obtained at such a small premium differential that they tend to be more popular.[4]

An interesting policy introduced in recent years is the "jumping

---

[4] For example, according to the rates of one company, the premium for an ordinary life policy issued at age zero is $11.14 per $1,000, while the premium for a life paid-up at age sixty-five policy at the same age is only $11.49.

juvenile" or "estate builder." Usually issued on the limited-payment plan, this contract probably deserves to be classified as a "special" policy. It is obtainable from age zero to fifteen; and at age twenty-one, the face amount jumps to five times the original face, with no increase in premium. In other words, a $1,000 policy issued at age one is automatically converted into a $5,000 whole life policy at age twenty-one, with no increase in premium. This is just the reverse of the multiple protection contract, which in one form provides extra protection during the first twenty years with the premium level throughout the premium-paying period. Under the "jumping juvenile" policy, a substantial portion of the premium in the early years of the contract is used to meet the cost of the additional protection in the later years. According to the rates of one prominent company, the premium for a $1,000 "jumping juvenile" policy issued at age one on the life paid-up at sixty-five plan is $43.77, as compared to a premium of $11.49 on a conventional juvenile life paid-up at sixty-five policy issued at the same age. However, the premium for the former remains at $43.77 after the face has increased to $5,000, while the extra $4,000 of protection under the life paid-up at sixty-five contract would cost $17.79 per $1,000 at age twenty-one. In the one case, the total cost after age twenty-one is $43.77; in the other case, $82.65.

Provision can be made in all forms of juvenile insurance for continuance of the insurance in the event of the death or total disability of the person who applies for the insurance and assumes responsibility for payment of the premiums. Generally called the "payor clause," this provision stipulates that premiums will be waived until the insured (the child) reaches a specified age—usually, eighteen, twenty-one, or twenty-five,—should the premium payor, designated in the clause, die or become disabled. In the case of an educational endowment, premiums would be waived to maturity of the contract. Attachment of this rider to a contract is conditioned upon the insurability of the premium payor.

Part Three

THE ARITHMETIC OF
LIFE INSURANCE

CHAPTER VIII

Basis
of Risk
Measurement

AS WAS pointed out in an earlier chapter, insurance is a mechanism through which certainty is substituted for uncertainty. This is accomplished by having those persons who are exposed to loss from a particular hazard contribute to a common fund, from which those who suffer a loss from that cause can be indemnified. Thus, the certain loss of the contribution or premium replaces the uncertainty that a larger loss will be sustained. If a plan of insurance is to be scientific, however, there must be an acceptable method of measuring the risk of loss, in order to determine the sum which should be contributed to the fund by each participant. Such measurement is dependent upon a fundamental principle of mathematics known as the *theory of probability*.

THEORY OF PROBABILITY

Statement of the Theory

The theory of probability is composed of several *laws* of probability, the most important of which, from an insurance standpoint, is the law of *simple probability*. This law states that the chance that a particular event will happen can be expressed by a fraction, the numerator of which indicates the number of times that the event may happen and the denominator of which indicates the number of times the event can happen. A corollary of this law states that the sum of the separate probabilities may be expressed by unity, or one. It follows, then, that the probability that a particular event will happen is

1 minus the probability that it will not happen. These principles can be made clear by an illustration.

The classic example of simple probability is the tossing of a coin. If the coin is not defective, the chance that it will fall "heads" when tossed is one out of two. There are only two possibilities, and only one will satisfy the condition; therefore, the probability is $\frac{1}{2}$. The probability that the coin will fall *either* heads *or* tails is 1, or a certainty.

To take a slightly more complicated example, there are fifty-two cards in a deck of playing cards. The chance that the ace of spades will be drawn from the deck at random, therefore, is $\frac{1}{52}$. There are fifty-two possibilities, but only one will satisfy the condition. The probability of drawing an ace of any kind is $\frac{4}{52}$, since there are four suits and one ace in each suit. The probability that a card drawn at random will *not* be an ace is $\frac{48}{52}$, or 1 minus the probability that it will be an ace.

The probability that both of two mutually independent events will happen is equal to the product of the simple probabilities that the events, taken separately, will happen. This is compound probability, which can be illustrated by the tossing of two coins. The probability that both coins will fall heads up is $\frac{1}{2} \times \frac{1}{2}$, or $\frac{1}{4}$, since it is known that the chance is $\frac{1}{2}$ that each separate coin will fall heads up. That this is the correct result may easily be demonstrated. If it is assumed that the two coins are a nickel and a dime, the different ways in which they may fall are:

Nickel	*Dime*
Heads up	Heads up
Heads up	Tails up
Tails up	Heads up
Tails up	Tails up

These are the only combinations that can be made with the two coins, and the first combination is the only one of the four that satisfies the stipulated condition—namely, both coins heads up. Hence, since the joint events are equally likely to happen, there is one chance in four that this combination will appear, or the probability of its occurrence is $\frac{1}{4}$. The probability that three or more coins tossed simultaneously would all fall heads up could be determined in like manner.

Application to Life Insurance

If a life insurance plan is to operate successfully, it is necessary to forecast mortality among insured lives within a relatively narrow margin of error. In theory, this could be accomplished deductively or inductively. The validity of a priori or deductive reasoning depends upon the completeness with which all the causes at work in the determination of a given phenomenon are known, and the limitations of the human mind are such that deductive reasoning does not provide that degree of certainty that must underlie an insurance undertaking. Inductive reasoning, which is based on the assumption that what has happened in the past will happen again in the future if the same conditions are present, does not require an analysis of causes of phenomena in order to predict future events. Inductive reasoning is based on the assumption that all events are governed by a natural law. In the example of coin tossing, the law of pure chance is illustrated. It is an even chance that either side of the coin will be up. Then, if in a great number of trials, it is found that the coin falls heads up one half of the time, the conclusion may be drawn that approximately the same results will be obtained if the same number of trials are taken again.

It is also assumed that there is a *law of mortality* which governs the rate at which human beings die; that certain causes are in operation which determine that out of a large group of persons at birth, a definite number of lives will fail each year until all have died. However, it is not necessary to analyze this law of mortality completely and to know all the operating causes to predict the probable rate of mortality among a large group of persons. By studying the rate of mortality among any group and noting all the circumstances that, according to the best knowledge available, might affect that rate, it is possible to predict fairly accurately the death rate that may be experienced by any other group surrounded by approximately the same set of circumstances. Thus, without complete knowledge of the law of mortality, a working basis is found for predicting future rates of mortality.

The validity of mortality forecasts formulated by inductive reasoning depends upon two factors: (1) accuracy of the mortality statistics underlying the estimates and (2) the number of exposure units or the volume of mortality experience. With respect to the first factor, it might be pointed out that mortality statistics have been drawn from two broad sources: the general population and insured lives. General population death rates are derived from census enumerations and the returns of deaths from registration offices, and are known to contain elements of error. There are errors in both sets of records. Errors creep into census statistics from a number of sources. The census enumerators frequently record the information in the wrong classification; mistakes are made in the process of tabulation; and the individuals being interviewed occasionally provide incorrect information, deliberately or unintentionally. Inaccurate statements may stem from the vanity of the person reporting or from information being furnished by one member of the family about all the others. In the latter instance, the answers not infrequently are guesses or approximations. Sometimes, willful misstatements are made in an effort to conform to a social pattern. There is a tendency for the very young and the very old to overstate their ages, while those in between may understate their ages, particularly those approaching old age. There is a disproportionate number of persons at all ages ending in zero or five. Finally, a large number of ages are reported as unknown.

On the other side of the picture, there are serious defects in the reporting of deaths in the United States. Only in recent decades have all states been reporting deaths to the National Office of Vital Statistics. Moreover, in no section of the country are all deaths recorded. Therefore, death rates based on population and death registration returns do little more than approximate the law of mortality.[1]

The mortality statistics of insured lives tend to be highly accurate. Both the date of birth and the date of death are matters of record, so the death rate for the various ages can easily be derived. Virtually all mortality tables used by life insurance companies today are based on the experience of insured lives.

Not only must the recorded mortality statistics be accurate, but they must be available in sufficient quantity to reflect the true underlying probabilities. The significance of the body of experience is based on a statistical principle known in actuarial circles as *Bernoulli's Theorem* and in lay circles as the *law of average*. A formal statement of the theorem is that as the number of trials increases, the proportion

---

[1] The rates of mortality among the general population in this country are recorded in the United States Life Tables which are prepared by the National Office of Vital Statistics. The most recent series of tables are based on the 1960 census of population and the registered deaths of the three-year period, 1959–61. The tables contain separate tabulations for male and female lives, each being further subdivided to show the rate of mortality among white persons and colored persons, among native-born and foreign-born, and among those residing in cities and those residing in rural areas.

The first population tables of historical importance were the English Life Tables, the first series of which were compiled by Dr. William Farr, Compiler of Abstracts in the General Register Office. They were based on the census enumeration for England and Wales of 1841, and registered deaths for the same year.

of successes tends to approach the underlying probability. Thus, the probability that a coin tossed into the air will fall heads up is known to be $\frac{1}{2}$. Yet, there is no assurance that in ten tosses, for example, the coin will fall heads up five times and tails up five times. Neither will the theoretical ratio be achieved with certainty in one hundred throws. As the number of tosses increases, however, the variation from the theoretical ratio will become smaller and smaller; and eventually, after an infinite number of trials, the proportion of heads up will be exactly $\frac{1}{2}$. In most real situations, the true underlying probability will not be known; but as the number of cases under observation increases, the actual experience will tend to approach the "probable" experience. It is not necessary that the true or objective probability ever be known with exactitude. In practice, it is essential only that the number of cases under observation be sufficiently large to produce a result that is reasonably close to actual conditions. In applying the theory, it can be expected that variations from the assumed probability will occur from time to time. In the long run, however, if the number of cases is sufficiently large, the variations will have the effect of canceling one another, and the actual results will tend to approach the assumed results.

With reference to the prediction of future mortality rates, the law of average has a double application. The rates which purport to reflect the true law of mortality, to which reference has previously been made, must rest on a body of mortality experience broad enough and large enough to insure the operation of the law of average. Such rates, however, will serve as a measure of future mortality among a particular group only if the group is large enough to develop an average death rate or is large enough to permit the law of average to operate. In practice, the major insurance companies pool their experience in an effort to determine the true rate of mortality, age by age, for the various groups which they insure. The problem of obtaining an average experience for a particular group of policyholders is one of securing an adequate number of lives of the type and quality represented in the mortality projections. This is a problem for both the agency and the underwriting departments of the insurance company.

CONSTRUCTION OF A MORTALITY TABLE

The theory of probability is applied in life insurance through the use of a mortality table. A mortality table is a record of mortality observed in the past, usually adjusted to provide a margin of safety, and arranged in a manner to show the probabilities of death and survival at each separate age. Since it is the instrument used by an insurance company to price its product and to establish the necessary financial safeguards, it is important to understand the construction of a mortality table. In the following discussion, it will be assumed that insured lives form the basis of the table, which is actually the case.

Derivation of Rates of Mortality

The first and most basic step in the construction of a mortality table is to determine the rate of death for each separate age to be included in the mortality table. The ages usually run from age one to the assumed maximum limit of life, which may be 96, 100, or 115, for example. The form of the table would suggest that a group of policyholders, numbering possibly 100,000 or 1,000,000, was brought under observation at age one and kept under observation until the last of the group had died, with the rate of death at each separate age being recorded. This is not at all the manner in which the rates of mortality are derived. It would obviously be impossible to obtain the records of such a large group of persons, all of whom were born on the same day, and record the deaths from year to year until all the members of the group have died. Moreover, even if such data were available, they would not accurately reflect the mortality that could be expected among succeeding generations. It is practicable, however, for one company or a group of companies to assemble data on the number of insured lives exposed to the risk of death at each separate age during a selected period, such as one year, five years, or ten years, and the number of policyholders in each age category who died during the period. If this is done, the raw materials for the fashioning of a mortality table will be available.

Suppose, for illustration, that the following data have been collected for a period of one year:

Age	Number under Observation	Number Dying during the Year
1.............	10,000	60
2.............	30,000	120
3.............	80,000	240
4.............	60,000	180
Etc............	Etc.	Etc.

From these figures, death rates may be computed for the respective ages in the following manner:

Age	Rate of Death Expressed as a Fraction	Rate of Death Expressed as a Decimal
1...........	$\dfrac{60}{10,000}$	0.006
2...........	$\dfrac{120}{30,000}$	0.004
3...........	$\dfrac{240}{80,000}$	0.003
4...........	$\dfrac{180}{60,000}$	0.003

The death rate for the other ages to be included in the table can be derived in like manner.

In the foregoing illustration, a large number of lives was assumed to be under observation at each age. In practice, such a large "exposure" is not likely to be obtained during any one year. If the investigation is limited to a single year, the results, even in a very large company, will be subject to considerable distortion because of the small number of lives involved. It is customary, therefore, to study the experience of several years in deriving death rates to be incorporated into a mortality table. If the experience of more than one year is used, the "number under observation" would have to be adjusted to reflect the number of years of exposure; and the deaths are recorded, not for any one year, but for the entire period under observation. In technical language, the deaths during the entire period would be compared, not with the number of persons insured, but with the number of "years' exposure to risk" of death. Thus, if rates are being derived for a five-year period, the deaths that occur at each age during the five years would be compared with the total "exposure" at that age, which would have been contributed by five different sets of insured persons. Each person who survived the period would have contributed five years' exposure, one year at each attained age. Most mortality tables in use today are based on the combined experience of the principal companies over a period of years.

The rate of mortality at any given age is *the proportion of persons of that age who die during a period of one year.*[2] This proportion may be—and usually is—expressed in terms of the number of deaths "per thousand," but it may be expressed in terms of other numbers such as "per hundred" or "per hundred thousand." Thus, mortality rates from specified diseases are usually expressed "per hundred thousand" living, since such rates are much smaller than the total rate from all causes. In actuarial calculations, the rate of mortality is usually quoted on a unit basis—e.g., "3 per thousand" becomes .003.

Elements of a Mortality Table

Once the rates of mortality have been derived, a mortality table can be constructed by applying the schedule of death rates to the survivors of an arbitrary number of persons assumed to be alive at the youngest age for which data are available. The process is illustrated in the excerpt from the Commissioners 1958 Standard Ordinary Mortality Table (1958 C.S.O. Table) shown in Table 5.

TABLE 5

COMMISSIONERS 1958 STANDARD ORDINARY MORTALITY TABLE

Age	Number Living	Number Dying	Rate of Mortality	Age	Rate of Living	Number Dying	Rate of Mortality
0.......	10,000,000	70,800	.00708	50.......	8,762,306	72,902	.00832
1.......	9,929,200	17,475	.00176	51.......	8,689,404	79,160	.00911
2.......	9,911,725	15,066	.00152	52.......	8,610,244	85,758	.00996
3.......	9,896,659	14,449	.00146	53.......	8,524,486	92,832	.01089
4.......	9,882,210	13,835	.00140	54.......	8,431,654	100,337	.01190
..	....	......	......	..	....	......	......
..	....	......	......	..	....	......	......
45.......	9,048,999	48,412	.00535	95.......	97,165	34,128	.35124
46.......	9,000,587	52,473	.00583	96.......	63,037	25,250	.40056
47.......	8,948,114	56,910	.00636	97.......	37,787	18,456	.48842
48.......	8,891,204	61,794	.00695	98.......	19,331	12,916	.66815
49.......	8,829,410	67,104	.00760	99.......	6,415	6,415	1.00000

The arbitrary number to which the earliest death rate is applied is called the *radix* of the table. In connection with the 1958 C.S.O. Table, the radix is 10,000,000; under the 1941 C.S.O. Table it was 1,000,-000 and under the American Experience Table of Mortality, it was

---

[2] This is a definition of a "central death rate," which refers to the rate of dying among a group of persons who are a specified age at the *beginning of the year.* The *probability of death,* on the other hand, refers to the rate of dying among a group of persons who are just entering on a specified age at the beginning of the year. On the average, the first group would be six months older than the latter group. Probabilities of death are used in the construction of a mortality table, but the distinction will not be observed in this chapter. Probabilities of death are derived from central death rates.

100,000.[3] The previously determined death rate of 7.08 per 1,000 at age zero is applied to the radix of 10,000,000 persons, producing 70,800 deaths the first year. This leaves 9,929,200 survivors, who will be exposed to a death rate of 1.76 per 1,000 during the second year, resulting in 17,475 deaths. The 9,911,725 persons alive at the beginning of age two are exposed to a death rate of 1.52 per 1,000, and so on. This process of attrition is continued until, at age ninety-nine, only 6,415 of the original group remain, and they are assumed to die during the year.

Since the radix of the table is arbitrary, the numbers in the columns headed "Number Living" and "Number Dying" are not significant within themselves. The column headed "Rate of Mortality" is the heart of the table and the source from which the figures in the other two columns are derived.

Sometimes, a mortality table has an additional column showing the "expectation of life" or "life expectancy" at each age. The figure in this column opposite any age is the *average* number of years lived after attaining that age by all who reach such age. Under most mortality tables the life expectancy is at its longest at age one,[4] but at any given age, the sum of the life expectancy plus the number of years already lived will be larger than the life expectancy at age one. Thus, in accordance with the latest United States Life Tables, reflecting death rates in 1960, life expectancy at age one is 70.75 years; while at age fifty, it is only 25.29 years. However, 25.29 years added to the fifty already lived produces an expected *total* lifetime of 75.29 years. The term "expectation of life" is rather misleading, since it has no significance with respect to any particular individual. The probable future lifetime of any individual depends upon his state of health and may be much longer or much shorter than the average.

Contrary to the general impression, premium rates are not calculated on the assumption that everyone will live for the period of his life expectancy. For reasons too complex to explain here, rates computed

---

[3] The original radix of the 1941 C.S.O. Table was 1,000,000 lives at age one; but a new radix at age zero was later substituted, producing a rate of mortality at age zero. The American Experience Table was similarly modified after it was published.

[4] It might be thought that life expectancy at birth would be the longest under all mortality assumptions; but the assumed death rate during the first year of life may be so much higher than that of the next several years that the child aged one can expect a longer life, *on the average*, than one who has just been born. Under some of the older mortality tables, the life expectancy continued to increase for several years after birth, one table showing a greater expectancy at ten than at birth. Under the 1958 C.S.O. Table life expectancy is greatest at age zero.

on such an assumption would be inadequate for life insurance contracts and redundant for annuity contracts.

Adjustments to Mortality Data

Rarely, if ever, does a mortality table adopted for premium calculations by a life insurance company reflect the precise rates of mortality derived from the underlying mortality investigation. In the evolution of actuarial science, several mathematical formulas have been evolved, seeking to explain the true law of mortality. Some have gained general acceptance in the actuarial field. The death rates produced by such formulas, when plotted, form a smooth and continuous curve, suggesting that mankind's resistance to disease and degeneration declines in continuous and minute gradations. Yet, observed data, when plotted, usually produce an irregular curve, punctuated with inexplicable deviations. Hence, the actuaries introduce a series of corrections or adjustments to the actual, observed data in order to make them conform more closely to the mathematically derived curve which seems to fit the particular data involved. This process is called *graduation,* of which there are several methods, most of them complex and requiring a high degree of technical competence.

Graduation is particularly necessary in those areas where the data are scanty and unreliable. This is likely to be true at the extreme ranges of age—at the very young and the very old ages. In most tables, the death rates at both extremities are derived by formula. In some cases, a portion of one table is inserted into another.

The method of graduation used in a particular situation depends upon the nature of the data, the purpose of the computation, and the judgment of the actuary. Different methods will produce different numerical values from the same set of data. In fact, values vary as between different actuaries using the same method of graduation. One method may be used for one section of a mortality table and a different one for another section. Whatever method is used, the objective is to introduce smoothness and regularity into the observed values, without distorting their basic characteristics.

Another type of adjustment that may be introduced into a mortality table is one designed to provide a margin of safety. In a life insurance mortality table, this means showing higher death rates than those that are actually anticipated; while in an annuity table, it means lower rates of mortality than those actually expected. In some of the older tables, such margins were implicitly provided through the use of data for a period known to have had rates of mortality higher than those currently being experienced or expected to be experienced in the future. In recent mortality tables, based upon relatively current experience, the margins were explicitly provided through arbitrary adjustments of the underlying data. For example, the data for the 1941 C.S.O. Table were deliberately adjusted to provide a margin of 5 per cent of the reciprocal of the expectation of life, as reflected by the observed rates of mortality. In the construction of the 1941 Standard Industrial Mortality Table, the observed rates were adjusted in such a manner that at ages thirty-five through sixty-five, the actual rates were only 80 per cent of the final tabular rates, variable margins being provided at all other ages. On the other hand, the rates entering into the *Ga*-1951 Table, an annuity table presently to be described, were reduced by 10 per cent at all ages for males and 12½ per cent for females. The insertion of such margins is regarded as sound business practice and not inimical to the interests of the policyholders. The security behind insurance contracts is enhanced by conservative actuarial assumptions; and with participating insurance, at least, any savings can be passed on to the policyholders in the form of dividends.

Select, Ultimate, and Aggregate Mortality Tables

Studies have conclusively proved that the rate of mortality among a group of recently insured lives is lower, age for age, than that among policyholders who have been insured for some years. This is attributed to the influence of medical selection, which should—as a minimum—screen out those applicants for insurance who are suffering from a disease or physical condition likely to prove fatal in the near future. As might be expected, the disparity in death rates is at its maximum during the first year of insurance, diminishing gradually thereafter, but never disappearing altogether. There is a measurable disparity for at least fifteen years; but for practical purposes, it is generally assumed that the effect of selection "wears off" after approximately five years.

To illustrate, the death rate among a group of policyholders twenty-five years of age who have just become insured will be substantially lower than that of a group of policyholders now twenty-five who were insured more than five years previously. The difference in the death rate among the two groups at age twenty-six will be somewhat smaller, the disparity decreasing each year until, at age thirty, the two rates should be virtually the same.

A table which undertakes to show the reduced mortality in the early years of insurance is called a *select* mortality table. Technically, a select mortality table is one which shows the rate of mortality not only by age but also by "duration of insurance" or time since selection. In theory, a select table would be an entire series of mortality tables, one for each age of issue. Since the effect of selection wears off in about five years, however, the rates, for all practical purposes, need not be differentiated by duration for more than that period of time. It is found, therefore, that a select mortality table is usually constructed in the form shown in Table 6.

TABLE 6

SELECT MORTALITY TABLE—RATES PER 1,000*

| AGE AT ISSUE | YEAR OF INSURANCE | | | | | | AT-TAINED AGE |
	1	2	3	4	5	6 and Over	
35............	.92	1.10	1.33	1.61	1.95	2.36	40
36............	.97	1.19	1.46	1.79	2.19	2.64	41
37............	1.04	1.30	1.62	2.00	2.44	2.95	42
38............	1.13	1.44	1.80	2.22	2.72	3.28	43
39............	1.24	1.59	1.99	2.47	3.01	3.63	44
40............	1.36	1.74	2.20	2.72	3.32	4.02	45

* Mortality Table X_{18} with select modification by James C. H. Anderson.

Some conception of the mortality reduction brought about through selection can be gained by comparing the death rate in the column headed "6 and over" opposite age thirty-five with the rate shown in Column 1 opposite age forty. Column 1 shows the death rate at the various ages during the first year of insurance, when the effect of selection is greatest, while Column 6 reflects the rate after the effect of selection has worn off. The disparity in death rates for the same attained age at various durations can be observed by comparing Column 2 opposite age thirty-five with Column 1 opposite age thirty-six, Column 3 opposite age thirty-five with Column 1 opposite age thirty-seven, and so on to Column 6.

If, in the construction of a mortality table, there is excluded the experience which is thought to reflect the effects of selection, the table is said to be an *ultimate* mortality table. That is, it reflects the rates of mortality that can ultimately be expected after the beneficent influence of selection has worn off. Column 6 of Table 6 constitutes an ultimate mortality table.

Ultimate mortality tables, or the ultimate rates in a select table, are usually used in the calculation of net premiums, reserves, surrender values, and dividends. While a select table more accurately represents the experience of insured lives, its use for computing the foregoing values would introduce administrative complications, while exerting only an inconsequential effect on over-all equity.

A mortality table may be constructed from the experience of all insured lives, irrespective of duration of insurance, in which case the table is referred to as an aggregate mortality table. An aggregate table includes the experience of recently selected lives, but does not segregate it by duration in the fashion of the select table.

Select tables are widely used in developing gross premiums for both participating and nonparticipating insurance and for testing, through asset share calculations, the appropriateness of existing or proposed schedules of dividends and surrender values. They are also used in projecting profits on new blocks of nonparticipating business. Another important use is in the tabulation of mortality experience for purposes of analysis and comparison. Comparisons among companies, or of the experience of different periods in the same company, would be vitiated unless account were taken of the relative proportions of new business and the lower rates of mortality experienced on recent issues. The significant basic tables prepared by the Mortality Committee of the Society of Actuaries, from data supplied on a continuous basis since 1934 by a group of the principal companies, are constructed in select form.

There are no theoretical or practical objections to the use of an aggregate table apart from the fact that an ultimate table provides the companies with a source of extra mortality savings during the early years of the contract that helps to offset the heavy expenses incurred in placing the business on the books.

Additional Decremental Factors

In the mortality tables used in the calculation of life insurance premiums, death is the only factor assumed to decrease the number of persons living at each age. However, for certain specialized computations, tables which are based on additional decremental factors may be needed. In projecting the cost of a pension plan, for example, it is necessary to know, in addition to the number of employees who will die, the number who will leave the service of the employer before reaching retirement. If disability benefits are to be provided, it will also be necessary to predict the number of employees who will become disabled and the period of time during which they will remain disabled. In public pension plans which provide widows' benefits, it is necessary to estimate the probabilities of remarriage. This is true of the Federal Old-Age, Survivors and Disability Insurance program. In calculating the present value of renewal commissions for purposes of commutation, recognition must be given not only to the number of anticipated deaths but also to the number of policies which will be terminated through nonpayment of premiums.

Tables with more than one decremental factor are constructed in the same manner as an ordinary mortality table. A table which projects the number of policy terminations, in addition to the death rate, may serve as an example. A radix is selected, and the number of deaths *before* withdrawal during the first year is set down. Then, the number of lapses and surrenders during the year is computed. The two totals are added, and their sum is deducted from the number living at the beginning of the year under observation. The remainder represents the number of survivors at the beginning of the second year. The process is continued until all the policies are assumed to have terminated through death or surrender. The completed table shows *rates* of death and withdrawal, as well as the number of deaths and withdrawals.

CHARACTERISTICS OF TABLES IN GENERAL USE

It is well recognized that mortality varies among different types of lives and that a life insurance company must utilize that body of mortality experience that seems most appropriate for the category or categories of risks being written. This means that a company writing a variety of risks will utilize several different mortality tables for new business at the same time. Moreover, there will always be a considerable amount of business on the books written on the basis of older mortality tables currently regarded as obsolete—or, at least, obsolescent. Therefore, it is desirable to have a familiarity with several different mortality and annuity tables.

American Experience Table of Mortality

One of the best known of all mortality tables is the American Experience Table of Mortality. Published in 1868, it is based upon the experience of the Mutual Life Insurance Company of New York for the period 1843–58, the data encompassing all the accumulated experience of the company from the inception of operations. It was constructed and graduated by Sheppard Homans, actuary of Mutual Life, and was the first mortality table to be based on the experience of insured lives in America. In its original form the table showed death rates from age ten through age ninety-six, no one in the observed group having lived beyond the latter age. Many years later, the table was extended down to age zero. Until two decades ago, it was almost universally used for the calculation of life insurance premiums and reserves, and is the basis upon which much of the ordinary insurance now in force was issued. It is no longer an accurate measure of mortality rates, particularly at the lower ages, and for ordinary business issued since 1947, has been supplanted by the tables developed under the aegis of the National Association of Insurance Commissioners.

The American Men Mortality Table

The American Men Mortality Table was prepared by the Actuarial Society of America in co-operation with the American Institute of Actuaries and the National Convention (now Association) of Insurance Commissioners. It was constructed from mortality data furnished by fifty-nine American and Canadian companies for the period 1900–1915 and was published in 1918. In order to avoid giving undue weight to the experience of the larger companies, the amount of data taken from any one company was limited to $50 million of "exposure" per year. Only the experience of male insured lives was studied. In the final construction of the table, the experience during the first five years of coverage was excluded, an ultimate mortality table thus being derived.

The American Men Table shows much lower death rates at the younger ages than those under the American Experience Table. At age twenty, for example, the death rate under the American Men Table is only half that of the American Experience Table. The disparity between the two sets of rates declines with increasing ages until age sixty, after which the rates under the American Experience Table are slightly lower. At the advanced ages, the rates of the American Men Table are again lower, because of the assumption under the American Men Table that the limit of life is age 104.

For a considerable period after its publication, the American Men Table found little acceptance. Since the period studied was free from wars and epidemics and the data had not been adjusted to provide a specific margin of safety, many companies questioned whether the table could safely be used for the calculation of premiums and reserves. The influenza epidemic of 1918 strengthened such doubts. As mortality rates continued to decline, however, several companies—mostly those writing insurance on a nonparticipating basis—adopted the table for *premium* calculations on ordinary insurance. Moreover, it came to be widely used for the calculation of group life insurance premiums. However, it enjoyed only limited use for valuation purposes, partly because it was never authorized in all states for the calculation of reserves and partly because minimum surrender values would have been increased to an undesirable extent.[5]

The Commissioners 1941 Standard Ordinary Table

The Commissioners 1941 Standard Ordinary Table, generally referred to as the 1941 C.S.O. Table, was prepared by the Committee to Study the Need for a New Mortality Table and Related Topics, and was published in 1941.[6] It is based on the experience of the principal companies for the period 1930–40, the observed rates being increased slightly, as was explained earlier, to provide a margin of safety for life insurance operations. The table runs from ages one to one hundred, with one million persons assumed to be alive at age one. The death rates are lower than those of the American Experience Table at all ages, but are lower than those of the American Men Table only through age thirty-six and above age sixty.

The 1941 C.S.O. Table was developed to meet the widespread criticism of the continued use of the American Experience Table. The impression was general that the insurance companies were making an unconscionable profit through the use of an obsolete table. As will be clear after a study of dividend policy, such was not the case. Since the mortality table is an instrument subject to adjustment, an obsolete table with a *known* error can serve the purpose for which it was constructed almost as well as a table which is absolutely accurate. Just as a magnetic compass rarely points true north, but must have its findings corrected by a navigator, so must a mortality table with redundant rates be adjusted to produce proper charges. Nevertheless, the life insurance industry finally came to realize that on the ground of appearances alone, it was necessary to develop a mortality table that

---

[5] This latter point is discussed in the chapter on surrender values.

[6] As a matter of strict accuracy, the 1941 C.S.O. Table, in final form, was prepared by a successor group, called the Committee to Study Nonforfeiture Benefits and Related Topics.

would accurately reflect recent mortality experience of insured lives. Consequently, a committee was appointed in 1936 by the National Association of Insurance Commissioners to study the need for a new mortality table and related topics.

The committee was composed of five actuaries nominated by five state insurance departments, one actuary nominated by the Actuarial Society of America, and one actuary nominated by the American Institute of Actuaries. The chairman of the committee was Alfred N. Guertin, then actuary of the New Jersey Insurance Department; and the legislation which enacted into law the recommendations of the committee, and a successor committee, came to be known as the *Guertin legislation.* The committee not only constructed a new mortality table but also developed a new basis for the calculation of minimum surrender values and a new reserve valuation method. Following the report of the Guertin Committee, virtually all states enacted legislation prescribing the use of the 1941 C.S.O. Table in the calculation of minimum reserve and surrender values for all ordinary insurance issued after January 1, 1948. Thereupon, many companies voluntarily adopted the 1941 C.S.O. Table for the calculation of premiums on all new issues of ordinary insurance, the switch being effective in most cases on January 1, 1948. Other companies continued to use or switched to tables which reflected even more accurately the status of current mortality.

The 1941 Standard Industrial Table

Industrial life insurance is one of the three broad categories of life insurance, the other two being ordinary and group, and is characterized by small amounts of insurance (less than $1,000 face amount) and weekly or monthly collection of premiums at the home or business of the policyholders by representatives of the insurance company. It is sold to the lower income groups, with no medical examination, many of the policyholders being employed in hazardous or unhealthful occupations and living in the less desirable neighborhoods. Moreover, a large percentage of the policyholders are Negroes, particularly in the South. As a result, the death rate among industrial policyholders is considerably higher than that among ordinary insureds; and special mortality tables must be used in the calculation of premiums, reserves, and surrender values.

The first special table was constructed on the basis of the industrial experience of the Metropolitan Life Insurance Company during the years 1896 to 1905. This table, the Standard Industrial Mortality Table, was in general use until 1948. A new table, reflecting the industrial experience of the Metropolitan Life Insurance Company for the period 1930–39, was prepared by Malvin E. Davis of the Metropolitan and published in 1941. This table, which came to be known as the 1941 Standard Industrial Mortality Table, was legalized by New York and later adopted by the Guertin Committee. For about twenty years after its publication, the 1941 Standard Industrial Mortality Table was specified as the mortality basis for the calculation of minimum reserve and surrender values for industrial life insurance policies then being issued and it can still be used on an optional basis for policies currently being issued. Effective Jan. 1, 1968, however, minimum reserve and surrender values for all new policies will have to be computed on the basis of the Commissioners 1961 Standard Industrial Mortality Table, a table discussed below.

The 1941 Substandard Industrial Mortality Table was constructed for the use of companies that write predominantly Negro lives. As might be expected, this table shows considerably higher rates of mortality than the 1941 Standard Industrial Mortality Table, since Negro lives are subject to relatively high rates of mortality of all ages. No table is prescribed by law for the calculation of minimum reserve and surrender values for substandard insurance of any kind, but the regulatory authorities usually have to approve the basis actually used.

The 1937 Standard Annuity Table

As was stated earlier, mortality experience among annuitants is quite different from that among insured lives, making it necessary to use specially constructed mortality tables for the calculation of annuity premiums. Furthermore, it is necessary to distinguish between male and female lives, a practice only recently adopted for life insurance purposes. Not only are death rates among female annuitants much lower than those among male annuitants, but a substantial proportion of all annuities issued are on female lives. The difference between the mortality of male and female annuitants can be represented approximately by taking for females the mortality rate of the male table for an age four or five years younger. In this way, the necessity of constructing separate male and female tables can be avoided.

A variety of annuity mortality tables has been used over the years, a new table being adapted for future transactions as experience revealed the death rates under the table in current year to be unrealistically high. One of the most widely used and best known of these tables is the 1937 Standard Annuity Table.[7] This table, with female ages set back five years, was used to predict mortality experience not only for individual annuities and life income options but also for group annuities and uninsured pension plans. At ages below sixty, this table is based on the experience of clerical employees covered under *group life insurance* contracts during the period 1932–36, while the death rates at ages sixty and above reflect the mortality among individual annuitants for the same period. The original table assumed 1,000,000 persons alive at age ten and followed through until the last person died at age 109. The unusually high limiting age of 110 reflects the superior longevity of annuitants. The table was later extended down to age zero by mathematical formula. No margin of safety was provided other than that implicit in the use of individual annuitant experience, which is assumed to be subject to a high degree of adverse selection, and group life clerical experience, which reflects a sizable proportion of female lives. Apart from this margin, no specific provision was made for future improvement in mortality, which, with respect to annuities, is an unfavorable development from the standpoint of the insurer. This deficiency in the 1937 Standard Annuity Table, also associated with all earlier annuity tables, led to the development of annuity tables with explicit allowance for future mortality improvement. These latter tables, in one form or the other, have generally replaced the 1937 Standard Annuity Table for the writing of new annuities and for the valuation of pension plan liabilities. The pioneer table of the most recent type is the Annuity Table for 1949.

The Annuity Table for 1949

The Annuity Table for 1949 was developed by Wilmer A. Jenkins, of the Teachers Insurance and Annuity Association, and Edward A. Lew, of the Metropolitan Life Insurance Company.[8] Their objective was to construct a table that would not only accurately reflect current mortality among annuitants, but would also make allowance, on a realistic and equitable basis, for future improvement in mortality. The table was constructed from the annuitant mortality experience (active lives under group annuity contracts at the younger ages and individual

---

[7] Other important annuity tables that have been used (and the years in which they were published) include the McClintock Table (1896), the American Annuitants Table (1920), and the Combined Annuity Table (1928).

[8] See W. A. Jenkins, and E. A. Lew, "A New Mortality Basis for Annuities," *Transactions of the Society of Actuaries,* Vol. 1 (1949), pp. 369–466, for an account of the study of annuitant experience and the derivation of a new annuity table.

annuitants at the older ages[9] of the principal life companies for a number of years centering around 1943. The experience was adjusted to bring it up to the level of the 1949 current mortality.

To provide a margin for future improvement in mortality, two sets of projection factors were prepared. One set, known as "projection scale A," assumes that annuitant mortality will continue to decline indefinitely into the future at the same annual rates of decrease that have prevailed in recent decades. The other set, "projection scale B," assumes that the future will produce smaller rates of decrease in mortality at the younger ages, where past reductions have already engendered very low mortality rates, and somewhat higher rates of decrease than those of the past at ages over sixty, which ages should derive the greatest benefit from current medical research into cardio-vascular renal diseases and malignancies. Projection scale A might be regarded as retrospective in its outlook, while projection scale B is prospective in nature.

The practical effect of using projection factors with an annuity table is that the death rate at all ages becomes smaller with each passing calendar year, the table always remaining up to date—if the projection factors are accurate. The death rates at the various ages are not static but depend upon the calendar year of experience. Thus, for a group of annuitants, the expected mortality rates at a given attained age will vary by year of birth.

The Annuity Table for 1949, or any other table so constructed, can be used with or without the projection factors or with the projection factors being used to adjust the basic mortality rates to some current or future date. For example, the 1949 rates could be brought up to the 1967 level of mortality, with the resulting rates being used to form a static annuity table. Various modifications of the basic table are in common use.

The Group Annuity Table for 1951

In recognition of the need for an annuity table that would reflect the special characteristics of employee annuitants, a rapidly growing number, Ray M. Peterson, of the Equitable Life Assurance Society, undertook an investigation of group annuitant mortality, out of which grew a table designated the Group Annuity Table for 1951.[10]

---

[9] The volume of experience under individual immediate nonrefund annuities at the younger ages was too meager to be reliable.

[10] See Ray M. Peterson, "Group Annuity Mortality," *Transactions of the Society of Actuaries,* Vol. IV (1952), pp. 246–307.

This table was basically derived from the mortality experience of group annuitants—the first published table to be so derived. At ages below fifty-six, the rates are those of the Annuity Table for 1949 adjusted for one year's decrease according to the Jenkins and Lew projection scale B. At ages over sixty-five, the rates are based on the intercompany group annuity retired lives experience for the years 1946–50, with an allowance for three years' decrease in mortality according to projection scale B.[11] Mortality rates for the gap between ages fifty-six and sixty-five were derived by extrapolation.

The use of projection factors was designed to adjust the mortality rates to the 1951 level. At that point, the basic table was considered to be representative of the *average* actual experience of all occupational groups for the year 1951. On the theory that certain groups of employees, which cannot be identified on an a priori basis, will experience lighter mortality than the average, it was deemed necessary to introduce an arbitrary margin of safety. This was accomplished by reducing the observed mortality rates for males at all ages by 10 per cent and those for females by $12\frac{1}{2}$ per cent. This type of adjustment provides a margin that increases with age, which was thought desirable in view of the relative unreliability of the data at the advanced ages.

Peterson then prepared a set of projection factors through which the table can be kept up to date. He designated his set of factors as "projection scale C," in deference to scales A and B prepared by Jenkins and Lew. Projection scale C is $1\frac{1}{2}$ times projection scale B, subject to a maximum annual reduction of $1\frac{1}{4}$ per cent. Peterson reasoned that since death rates for group annuitants are currently higher than those of individual annuitants, future progress in medical care, sanitation, and nutrition should exert a slightly stronger influence on group annuitant mortality. In other words, there is more room for improvement. The same reasoning would seem to dictate a higher scale of factors for males than for females, but the desire to avoid undue complexity motivated Peterson to use the same scale for both sexes.

The Group Annuity Table for 1951 with some form of projection scale C is almost universally used for group annuity and pension purposes. Some companies and consulting actuaries are using the table with the full projection applied. Others are using the table with some

---

[11] The data centered around 1948, producing a three-year spread between that date and 1951, the effective date of the new table.

modification of projection scale C, the modification usually being designed to lessen the administrative complications. A modification of the table that has gained wide acceptance is to project the basic mortality rates to a current date and then, to allow for some further decline in mortality, to set all ages back one year.

The 1955 American Annuity Table

Concern with the problem of developing adequate and equitable rates for annual premium deferred annuities and life income options under ordinary insurance policies, where the period between policy issue and settlement may run to fifty years or more—averaging twenty-five years—led to the construction of still another annuity table, namely the 1955 American Annuity Table.[12]

This table was developed by William C. McCarter of the Northwestern Mutual Life Insurance Company from mortality data submitted by the principal life insurance companies on a continuing basis to the Society of Actuaries. Specifically, the data reflected the experience under individual immediate annuities between the 1948 and 1953 anniversaries. The exposure included over 22,000 deaths at ages eighty and above, a group whose mortality appeared to be overstated in the Annuity Table for 1949. This possible overstatement of mortality at the older ages was thought to be significant in view of the fact that the average age at which males and females were entering on life income settlements and immediate annuities was sixty-five and sixty, respectively, and showing a tendency to increase over time.

The table reflects the combined experience of male and female lives, females being treated as males five years younger in age. The use of a five-year age setback for females overstates the mortality at the younger ages and understates it at the older ages, the overstatement of annuity values increasing with age.

In order to take into account future decreases in mortality, McCarter introduced a procedure for adjusting the annuity payments to the year of settlement. Through the use of a set of adjustment factors, the annuity income per unit of premium or accumulation could be related to the level of mortality assumed to prevail at the time the income commences. However, the annuity payments, once their amount was fixed by the date of commencement, would be level

---

[12] See William C. McCarter, "A New Annuity Mortality Table and a Graded Rate System for the Life Income Settlement Options," *Transactions of the Society of Actuaries,* Vol. VIII (1956), pp. 127–165 and discussion on pp. 483–503 for a description of this table.

throughout the lifetime of the annuitant. The annual adjustment factors were based on the assumption that mortality at ages forty and above would decrease at the annual rate of about 0.9 per cent, approximately equivalent to the decrease envisioned in the Jenkins and Lew projection scale A except at the higher ages. Stated differently, the decreases was expected to be the rough equivalent of a $\frac{1}{10}$-year age setback per calendar year. The use of a constant age setback assumes fairly level rates of mortality decrease at all ages above forty and especially at the upper ages, as contrasted with projection scale A which assumes that the future rate of mortality reduction tapers off to zero by age ninety.

The 1955 American Annuity Table is being used by a number of important insurance companies. It is used, without the scale of adjustment factors, as the mortality basis for all annuity values in this volume. In lieu of the annual adjustment factors, male ages are set back one year and female ages six years. With these age setbacks, the assumed mortality rates should be reasonably close to those prevailing today.

Commissioners 1958 Standard Ordinary Mortality Table

The latest table to be developed for general ues in connection with ordinary insurance is the 1958 C.S.O. Table. This table was developed jointly by the Society of Actuaries and the National Association of Insurance Commissioners, in an effort to eliminate the need for deficiency reserves which within recent years had become a matter of serious concern to many stock life insurance companies.[13]

The 1958 C.S.O. Table grew out of an earlier mortality table, called Table X_{17}, which had been prepared by a special committee of the Society of Actuaries and recommended to the National Association of Insurance Commissioners for its approval. Table X_{17} was, in turn, based on an experience table, tentatively designated X_{18}.

Table X_{18} was constructed from the data contributed each year to the Society of Actuaries Committee on Mortality under Lives Individually Insured. It comprised the mortality experience for the period 1950–54 of lives individually insured on a standard basis by fifteen large companies. All experience during the first five policy years was excluded, as were war deaths, regardless of the duration of the policies. Only the experience of standard medically examined lives was included in the tabulations for the sixth through the fifteenth

---

[13] See pp. 243–45 for a discussion of deficiency reserves.

policy years; but for the sixteenth and subsequent policy years, the experience of all standard lives, whether or not medically examined, was reflected. Data for male and female lives were merged.

In order to provide a margin of safety, the experience of thirty-three smaller companies during the period 1950–54 was analyzed, and the X_{18} rates were increased by a percentage sufficient to provide for the mortality experienced at any age by any of the thirty-three companies (ignoring chance fluctuations). This method of determining the size of the safety margins to be incorporated in a mortality table represented in new principle in the construction of mortality tables. The margins finally adopted were 15 per cent at ages fifty-two to ninety-two,with higher percentage margins at other ages. The resulting set of mortality rates was identified as Table X_{17}.[14]

Upon consideration of Table X_{17} as a possible standard for minimum reserves and surrender values, many companies voiced the fear that the margins in the rates would not be adequate at all ages for universal usage throughout the country.[15] Particular concern was expressed over the margins at the younger ages, which in some cases were as low as 0.25 deaths per 1,000 lives. The low level of these margins was the result of a deliberate policy, suggested by a committee of the National Association of Insurance Commissioners, of avoiding rates in excess of those reflected in the United States White Males 1949–51 Table.

In order to remove any possible doubts about the adequacy of the margins in a table to be used for valuation purposes, additional margins were introduced into Table X_{17} at all ages from zero to sixty-two. After such adjustment, the *absolute* margins at the younger ages were approximately the same as those contained in the 1941 C.S.O. Table, while the *percentage* margins were greater at all ages than the corresponding margins in the 1941 C.S.O. Table (since the basic rates of Table X_{17} were lower). The absolute margin at age zero, after the adjustment, was 0.75 deaths per 1,000 and increased steadily with increase in age. The percentage margins ranged from 236 per cent at the younger ages to 15 per cent at the older ages.

---

[14] For a complete and authoritative account of the construction of Tables X_{17} and X_{18}, see Charles M. Sternhell, "The New Standard Ordinary Mortality Table," *Transactions of the Society of Actuaries,* Vol. IX (1957), pp. 1–23.

[15] Other companies opposed adoption of the table on the grounds that it would permit large companies to lower their gross premiums without the penalty of establishing deficiency reserves and hence would enable them to gain a competitive advantage over smaller, less affluent companies.

The mortality rates contained in the adjusted table were compared with the ultimate mortality experience for the period 1950–54 of the forty-eight companies whose experience was considered in the construction of Table X_{17} This comparison revealed that the total mortality of the individual companies, as a percentage of the mortality provided for under the adjusted table, ranged from a low of about 50 per cent to a high of 93 per cent. In other words, the company with the highest mortality ratio would have had a margin of 7 per cent for the period 1950–54, had it been operating on the basis of the adjusted table.

In response to criticism that the data used in the construction of Table X_{17} represented too brief a period, the industry actuarial committee appointed by the National Association of Insurance Commissioners to recommend changes in Table X_{17} studied, for the period 1954–57, the mortality experience of the fifteen companies which contributed data for the construction of the table. This study indicated that the average mortality for the fifteen companies was about 5 per cent lower than the corresponding experience for the 1950–54 period. As a further test, the committee analyzed the impact of the 1957–58 influenza epidemic on United States population mortality rates. This analysis indicated that the average mortality level between 1957 and 1958 policy anniversaries, the period experiencing the maximum impact of the influenza epidemic, would probably not exceed the average mortality level for the period 1950–54.

On the basis of the above findings, the National Association of Insurance Commissioners, at its meeting in December, 1958, approved X_{17}, as adjusted, as a minimum standard for reserves and surrender values and designated it as the Commissioners 1958 Standard Ordinary Mortality Table. The NAIC recommended that the states approve the new table as a permissive standard until January 1, 1966, after which it would become a mandatory standard. This recommendation was implemented by all jurisdictions and the use of the table for the purposes indicated is mandatory for all policies of ordinary insurance issued on or after Jan. 1, 1966.

Net premiums calculated on the basis of the 1958 C.S.O. Table are lower at all ages than the comparable premium rates under the 1941 C.S.O. Table. For example, the net level premium at $2\frac{1}{2}$ per cent interest for an ordinary life policy issued at age thirty-five is $17.67 per $1,000 under the 1958 C.S.O. Table, as compared to $20.50 under the 1941 C.S.O. Table.

Reserves under the 1958 C.S.O. Table are slightly lower than those computed on the basis of the 1941 C.S.O. Table. Aggregate reserves under the new table are expected to be about 2 or 3 per cent lower than under the old table.

In recognition of the extra mortality associated with extended term insurance and the use of net rates for the calculation of the benefit, the NAIC approved a special table, called the Commissioners 1958 Extended Term Insurance Table, for determining the period of extended term insurance. The Commissioners Extended Term Insurance Table was constructed by adding a loading of 0.75 deaths per 1,000, or 30 per cent of the mortality rates under the 1958 C.S.O. Table, whichever is greater, to the 1958 C.S.O. Table mortality rates. The Industry Actuarial Advisory Committee had recommended that the special table reflect a loading of 30 per cent of the 1958 C.S.O. Table rates *and* 0.75 deaths per 1,000, the latter to take care of the expense of maintaining the benefit in force; but the NAIC rejected the special expense loading of 0.75 deaths per 1,000. Except for the *minimum* loading of 0.75 deaths per 1,000, this is the same sort of adjustment permitted in the calculation of premiums for extended term insurance under the 1941 C.S.O. Table. Mortality rates under the Commissioners 1958 Extended Term Insurance Table are lower at all ages than 130 per cent of the 1941 C.S.O. Table mortality rates, but are at approximately the same level as 1941 C.S.O. Table mortality rates. If the companies use the Commissioners 1958 Extended Term Insurance Table for the calculation of premiums for extended term insurance, it will mean that periods of extended term insurance will be no longer than those currently available, since, in general, companies have not availed themselves of the privilege of calculating extended term insurance premiums on the basis of 130 per cent of the 1941 C.S.O. Table mortality rates.

The Industry Actuarial Advisory Committee suggested that it would be appropriate to permit the companies to use the special table to determine the amount of reduced paid-up insurance, in view of the small average size of reduced paid-up policies, with a consequent high expense rate. The commissioners, however, did not include this departure from previous practice in their final recommendations.

Mortality data for male and female lives were combined in unknown proportions in the construction of the 1958 C.S.O. Table, which makes it impossible to determine precisely how large a reduction should be made in the rates in calculating premiums for female lives. The NAIC recommended, however, that in the determination of minimum reserve and surrender values, the companies be permitted to use an age for female lives not more than three years younger than the actual age. This modification was approved not only for policies issued on the basis of the 1958 C.S.O. Table, but also for those issued on the basis of the 1941 C.S.O. Table.

Table X_{18}—which, as was indicated earlier, served as the basis of the 1958 C.S.O. Table—was officially designated by the NAIC as the 1958 C.S.O. Basic Table and is identified in that manner in Table 7.

Commissioners 1960 Standard Group Mortality Table

The second in a trilogy of mortality tables developed in recent years under the aegis of the National Association of Insurance Commissioners NAIC is the Commissioners 1960 Standard Group Mortality Table. While mortality tables have been constructed from time to time, for special purposes, from tabulated group mortality experience, this was the first group mortality table to be prepared for general use and for official approval. Its construction was a joint effort of an Industry Advisory Committee and a Technicians Committee of the NAIC.

The table is based upon the group mortality experience compiled on a continuing basis by the Society of Actuaries from data submitted by the ten companies writing the bulk of group life insurance. The data covered the period 1950 through 1958, including an exposure of 59,000,000 life years and claims totaling 400,000. In order to make the data as homogeneous as possible and to minimize the effect of varying underwriting standards, the investigators confined their analysis to the experience relating to employer-employee groups covering twenty-five or more employees and qualifying for standard rates. The excluded data comprised only a small percentage of the total.

Explicit margins were introduced into the observed data in order to permit the writing of groups in all except the most hazardous industries at standard rates, and for other reasons. In its final form, the 1960 C.S.G. Table shows mortality rates about 20 per cent lower on the average than those in the 1941 C.S.O. Table and about 10 per cent above the rates in the 1958 C.S.O. Table. The observed group mortality, weighted by exposure to risk, is approximately 10 per cent higher than the *ultimate* mortality under ordinary insurance policies, the higher level of group mortality being primarily attributable to the coverage of both standard and substandard risks without distinction (except as to hazardous industries) and to the unfavorable experience on group conversions which for accounting purposes is reflected in the group experience.

The 1960 C.S.G. Table was approved by the NAIC in November, 1960 and recommended to the various states as a basis for minimum first-year premiums and legal reserves for group term life insurance. Within a year all five states having minimum premium requirements had designated the 1960 C.S.G. Table, with prescribed allowances for expenses. as the official basis for the minimum premiums. The rates derived from this table, loaded in the prescribed manner, are designated as the 1961 Standard Group Life Insurance Premium Rates.[16]

Commissioners 1961 Standard Industrial Mortality Table

The most recent mortality table to be promulgated by the National Association of Insurance Commissioners is the Commissioners 1961 Standard Industrial Mortality (1961 C.S.I.) Table. This table rounds out the trilogy of mortality tables developed in recent years under the auspices of the NAIC and relating to the three broad subdivisions of the life insurance business: ordinary, group, and industrial.

The 1961 C.S.I. Table was developed from the mortality experience during the calendar years 1954–58 under industrial life insurance policies issued on white male and female lives by eighteen companies. This is in contrast to the 1941 Standard Industrial Table which was based entirely on the experience under one plan of insurance of the Metropolitan Life Insurance Company. The experience during the first calendar year was excluded, the data otherwise being aggregate in nature. Because of variations in company practice relating to the grading of benefits of juvenile ages, the experience is based on *number of policies* for ages one through nine and on *amounts of insurance* for ages ten above. At ages below ten, 17,004,693 policy years of exposure were involved, with 18,689 policies terminating as death claims. The exposure at ages ten and above was $86,356,443,374 of insurance years, with death claims amounting to $674,043,039. This exposure was about twice that of juvenile lives and five times the adult exposure underlying the 1941 Standard

---

[16] For an authoritative description of the construction and characteristics of the 1960 C.S.G. Table, see Morton D. Miller, "The Commissioners 1960 Standard Group Mortality Table and 1961 Standard Group Life Insurance Premium Rates," *Transactions of the Society of Actuaries,* Vol. XIII (1961), pp. 586–606.

Industrial Table. Female lives accounted for about half of the exposure. The data for ages seventy-five and above were so thin and variable that rates from the 1949–51 U.S. Life Table for Total Whites were used for ages seventy-five to one hundred, the terminal age.[17]

Substantial margins were introduced into the basic data to allow for differences in company underwriting standards and the racial composition of the policyholder group. The level of the margins was determined in part by an examination of the experience for the same period of eleven smaller companies, as well as some combined white and nonwhite data. The final margins ranged from 195.5 per cent of the observed experience at age twelve down to 25 per cent at ages sixty-three and over. The rates actually reflected in the 1961 C.S.I. Table were high enough to cover 99 per cent of the observed rates of the original eighteen companies on their white business. They cover about 82 per cent of the rates submitted by the eleven additional companies and roughly 70 per cent of the reported mortality on white and nonwhite lives combined. The table covers approximately 87 per cent of all mortality rates reviewed by the constructing committee, a slightly lower percentage than that associated with the 1958 C.S.O. Table.

The 1961 C.S.I. Table reflects a considerable improvement in the mortality of industrial policyholders. As compared with the 1941 Standard Industrial Table, the rates show a percentage reduction ranging from 68.1 per cent at age one down to 20.7 at age ninety-two. At the adult ages through sixty-five the reduction grades down from about 50 per cent to 35 per cent.

The 1961 C.S.I. Table must be used as the basis for minimum reserve and surrender values for all industrial policies issued on or after Jan. 1, 1968, and it may be used for that purpose, at the option of the insurer, for policies issued prior to that date.

In recognition of the higher mortality associated with extended term insurance and the absence of any specific loading for expenses, the states have approved the Commissioners 1961 Industrial Extended Term Insurance Table for use in computing premiums and reserves for extended term insurance under industrial policies. Like its counterpart in ordinary insurance, this table was constructed by in-

---

[17] For a description of the construction of the 1961 C.S.I. Table, see William C. Brown, "A Proposed New Industrial Valuation Table," *Transactions of the Society of Actuaries,* Vol. XIII (1961), pp. 457–70, with exhibits running to p. 494.

creasing the mortality rates in the underlying table by 30 per cent, or 0.75 deaths per 1,000, whichever is greater.

PORTRAYAL OF DEATH RATES

The death rates and expectation of life under the 1941 C.S.O. Table, the 1958 C.S.O. Table, the 1958 C.S.O. Basic Table, and the United States Life Tables for the years 1959–61 are shown in Table 7, pages 163–165. Such data for the other mortality and annuity tables discussed in this chapter are given in Appendix H, which should be consulted.

The death rate at age zero for the general population reflects still-births, whereas the rate at that age under the other tables reflects the number of deaths among persons born alive.

TABLE 7

DEATH RATES AND EXPECTATION
OF LIFE UNDER FOUR RECENT MORTALITY TABLES

AGE	1958 C.S.O. TABLE, 1950–54		1958 C.S.O. BASIC TABLE, 1950–54		1941 C.S.O. TABLE, 1930–40		UNITED STATES TOTAL POPULATION, 1959–61	
	Deaths per 1,000	Expectation of Life (Years)	Deaths per 1,000	Expectation of Life (Years)	Deaths per 1,000	Expectation of Life (Years)	Deaths per 1,000	Expectation of Life (Years)
0	7.08	68.30	6.33	71.79	22.58	62.33	25.93	69.89
1	1.76	67.78	1.00	71.25	5.77	62.76	1.70	70.75
2	1.52	66.90	0.75	70.32	4.14	62.12	1.04	69.87
3	1.46	66.00	0.68	69.37	3.38	61.37	.80	68.94
4	1.40	65.10	0.61	68.42	2.99	60.58	.67	67.99
5	1.35	64.19	0.55	67.46	2.76	59.76	.59	67.04
6	1.30	63.27	0.49	66.50	2.61	58.92	.52	66.08
7	1.26	62.35	0.44	65.53	2.47	58.08	.47	65.11
8	1.23	61.43	0.40	64.56	2.31	57.22	.43	64.14
9	1.21	60.51	0.37	63.58	2.12	56.35	.39	63.17
10	1.21	59.58	0.36	62.61	1.97	55.47	.37	62.19
11	1.23	58.65	0.37	61.63	1.91	54.58	.37	61.22
12	1.26	57.72	0.39	60.65	1.92	53.68	.40	60.24
13	1.32	56.80	0.44	59.68	1.98	52.78	.48	59.26
14	1.39	55.87	0.50	58.70	2.07	51.89	.59	58.29
15	1.46	54.95	0.56	57.73	2.15	50.99	.71	57.33
16	1.54	54.03	0.63	56.76	2.19	50.10	.82	56.37
17	1.62	53.11	0.70	55.80	2.25	49.21	.93	55.41
18	1.69	52.19	0.76	54.84	2.30	48.32	1.02	54.46
19	1.74	51.28	0.80	53.88	2.37	47.43	1.08	53.52
20	1.79	50.37	0.84	52.92	2.43	46.54	1.15	52.58
21	1.83	49.46	0.87	51.96	2.51	45.66	1.22	51.64
22	1.86	48.55	0.89	51.01	2.59	44.77	1.27	50.70
23	1.89	47.64	0.91	50.05	2.68	43.88	1.28	49.76
24	1.91	46.73	0.92	49.10	2.77	43.00	1.27	48.83
25	1.93	45.82	0.93	48.14	2.88	42.12	1.26	47.89
26	1.96	44.90	0.95	47.19	2.99	41.24	1.25	46.95
27	1.99	43.99	0.97	46.23	3.11	40.36	1.26	46.00
28	2.03	43.08	1.00	45.28	3.25	39.49	1.30	45.06
29	2.08	42.16	1.04	44.32	3.40	38.61	1.36	44.12
30	2.13	41.25	1.08	43.37	3.56	37.74	1.43	43.18
31	2.19	40.34	1.13	42.41	3.73	36.88	1.51	42.24
32	2.25	39.43	1.18	41.46	3.92	36.01	1.60	41.30
33	2.32	38.51	1.24	40.51	4.21	35.15	1.70	40.37
34	2.40	37.60	1.31	39.56	4.35	34.29	1.81	39.44
35	2.51	36.69	1.41	38.61	4.59	33.44	1.94	38.51
36	2.64	35.78	1.53	37.66	4.86	32.59	2.09	37.58
37	2.80	34.88	1.68	36.72	5.15	31.75	2.28	36.66
38	3.01	33.97	1.88	35.78	5.46	30.91	2.49	35.74
39	3.25	33.07	2.10	34.85	5.81	30.08	2.73	34.83
40	3.53	32.18	2.36	33.92	6.18	29.25	3.00	33.92

TABLE 7 (_Continued_)

Age	1958 C.S.O. Table, 1950–54		1958 C.S.O. Basic Table, 1950–54		1941 C.S.O. Table, 1930–40		United States Total Population, 1959–61	
	Deaths per 1,000	Expectation of Life (Years)	Deaths per 1,000	Expectation of Life (Years)	Deaths per 1,000	Expectation of Life (Years)	Deaths per 1,000	Expectation of Life (Years)
41.........	3.84	31.29	2.65	33.00	6.59	28.43	3.30	33.02
42.........	4.17	30.41	2.95	32.09	7.03	27.62	3.62	32.13
43.........	4.53	29.54	3.28	31.18	7.51	26.81	3.97	31.25
44.........	4.92	28.67	3.64	30.28	8.04	26.01	4.35	30.37
45.........	5.35	27.81	4.03	29.39	8.61	25.21	4.76	29.50
46.........	5.83	26.95	4.46	28.51	9.23	24.41	5.21	28.64
47.........	6.36	26.11	4.94	27.63	9.91	23.65	5.73	27.79
48.........	6.95	25.27	5.47	26.77	10.64	22.88	6.33	26.94
49.........	7.60	24.45	6.06	25.91	11.45	22.12	7.00	26.11
50.........	8.32	23.63	6.71	25.07	12.32	21.37	7.74	25.29
51.........	9.11	22.82	7.42	24.23	13.27	20.64	8.52	24.49
52.........	9.96	22.03	8.19	23.41	14.30	19.91	9.29	23.69
53.........	10.89	21.25	9.03	22.60	15.43	19.19	10.05	22.91
54.........	11.90	20.47	9.94	21.80	16.65	18.48	10.82	22.14
55.........	13.00	19.71	10.93	21.01	17.98	17.78	11.61	21.37
56.........	14.21	18.97	12.02	20.24	19.43	17.10	12.49	20.62
57.........	15.54	18.23	13.22	19.48	21.00	16.43	13.52	19.87
58.........	17.00	17.51	14.54	18.74	22.71	15.77	14.73	19.14
59.........	18.59	16.81	15.98	18.00	24.57	15.13	16.11	18.42
60.........	20.34	16.12	17.56	17.29	26.59	14.50	17.61	17.71
61.........	22.24	15.44	19.26	16.59	28.78	13.88	19.17	17.02
62.........	24.31	14.78	21.10	15.91	31.18	13.27	20.82	16.34
63.........	26.57	14.14	23.09	15.24	33.76	12.69	22.52	15.68
64.........	29.04	13.51	25.25	14.59	36.58	12.11	24.31	15.03
65.........	31.75	12.90	27.61	13.95	39.64	11.55	26.22	14.39
66.........	34.74	12.31	30.21	13.33	42.96	11.01	28.28	13.76
67.........	38.04	11.73	33.08	12.73	46.56	10.48	30.53	13.15
68.........	41.68	11.17	36.24	12.15	50.46	9.97	33.01	12.55
69.........	45.61	10.64	39.66	11.59	54.70	9.47	35.73	11.96
70.........	49.79	10.12	43.30	11.05	59.30	8.99	38.66	11.38
71.........	54.15	9.63	47.09	10.52	64.27	8.52	41.82	10.82
72.........	58.65	9.15	51.00	10.02	69.66	8.08	45.30	10.27
73.........	63.26	8.69	55.01	9.53	75.50	7.64	49.15	9.74
74.........	68.12	8.24	59.23	9.06	81.81	7.23	53.42	9.21
75.........	73.37	7.81	63.80	8.60	88.64	6.82	57.99	8.71
76.........	79.18	7.39	68.85	8.15	96.02	6.44	62.96	8.21
77.........	85.70	6.98	74.52	7.71	103.99	6.07	68.67	7.73
78.........	93.06	6.59	80.92	7.29	112.59	5.72	75.35	7.26
79.........	101.19	6.21	87.99	6.89	121.86	5.38	83.02	6.81
80.........	109.98	5.85	95.64	6.51	131.85	5.06	92.08	6.39
81.........	119.35	5.51	103.78	6.14	142.60	4.75	102.19	5.98
82.........	129.17	5.19	112.32	5.80	154.16	4.46	112.44	5.61
83.........	139.38	4.89	121.20	5.47	166.57	4.18	121.95	5.25
84.........	150.01	4.60	130.45	5.15	179.88	3.91	130.67	4.91

TABLE 7 (*Continued*)

Age	1958 C.S.O. Table, 1950–54		1958 C.S.O. Basic Table, 1950–54		1941 C.S.O. Table, 1930–40		United States Total Population, 1959–61	
	Deaths per 1,000	Expectation of Life (Years)	Deaths per 1,000	Expectation of Life (Years)	Deaths per 1,000	Expectation of Life (Years)	Deaths per 1,000	Expectation of Life (Years)
85.........	161.14	4.32	140.12	4.85	194.13	3.66	143.80	4.58
86.........	172.82	4.06	150.27	4.56	209.37	3.42	158.16	4.26
87.........	185.13	3.80	160.98	4.28	225.63	3.19	173.55	3.97
88.........	198.25	3.55	172.39	4.00	243.00	2.98	190.32	3.70
89.........	212.46	3.31	184.75	3.73	261.44	2.77	208.35	3.45
90.........	228.14	3.06	198.38	3.46	280.99	2.58	227.09	3.22
91.........	245.77	2.82	213.71	3.19	301.73	2.39	245.98	3.02
92.........	265.93	2.58	231.24	2.93	323.64	2.21	264.77	2.85
93.........	289.30	2.33	251.47	2.65	346.66	2.03	282.84	2.69
94.........	316.66	2.07	274.90	2.38	371.00	1.84	299.52	2.55
95.........	351.24	1.80	303.03	2.09	396.21	1.63	314.16	2.43
96.........	400.56	1.51	343.36	1.78	447.19	1.37	329.15	2.32
97.........	488.42	1.18	409.79	1.45	548.26	1.08	344.50	2.21
98.........	668.15	0.83	522.66	1.12	724.67	0.78	360.18	2.10
99.........	1,000.00	0.50	708.55	0.79	1,000.00	0.50	376.16	2.01
100.........	...	...	1,000.00	0.50	...	...	392.42	1.91
101.........	...	...	...	...	...	...	408.91	1.83
102.........	...	...	...	...	...	...	425.62	1.75
103.........	...	...	...	...	...	...	442.50	1.67
104.........	...	...	...	...	...	...	459.51	1.60
105.........	...	...	...	...	...	...	476.62	1.53
106.........	...	...	...	...	...	...	493.78	1.46
107.........	...	...	...	...	...	...	510.95	1.40
108.........	...	...	...	...	...	...	528.10	1.35
109.........	...	...	...	...	...	...	545.19	1.29
110.........	...	...	...	...	...	...	...	...

CHAPTER IX

Interest

THE PREMIUMS charged by life insurance companies reflect not only life contingencies, but also the functioning of compound interest. The level premium basis of operation leads to the accumulation of large sums of money which are held by the companies many years before being disbursed in satisfaction of their obligations. These funds are invested in income-producing assets and the earnings credited on a compound interest basis to the accounts of the various policyholders. These earnings are reflected not only in the premiums paid by the policyholders but also in the reserves, surrender values, and dividends under the various contracts.

Interest plays such a vital role in the actuarial computations and actual operations of a life insurance company that it seems essential to consider some of the more important concepts associated with the interest function before proceeding to the derivation of premiums and other values.

DEFINITION OF TERMS

The term "interest" is derived from the Latin word *interesse,* meaning "to be between" or "to be different." It represents the difference between the principal sum lent by a creditor and the amount which must be repaid by the borrower at the end of a specified term. Simply stated, it is the price or money consideration paid for the use of money.

From the standpoint of an investor, interest may be regarded as the income from invested capital. In this connection, the value of the original capital invested is called the *principal*. The sum to which the principal has accumulated by the end of a specified term is called the *amount*. The difference between the *amount* and the *principal* is, of course, *interest*.

Interest income is usually expressed as a *rate per cent* of the principal *per annum.* Rate per cent means rate per hundred. Thus, if an invested principal of $100 earns $3 during a twelve-month period, the rate of return is 3 per cent. The rate of interest may be expressed in various forms, such as $\frac{2.5}{100}$, $2\frac{1}{2}$ per cent, and 2.5 per cent; but in financial computations, it is customary to express it as a decimal fraction, such as .025. Then, to obtain the interest earnings on any given principal sum for a specified period, it is necessary only to multiply the appropriate decimal fraction by the principal sum. For example, the interest earnings on $1 invested for one year at $2\frac{1}{2}$ per cent is $1 × .025 = $0.025, or $2\frac{1}{2}$ cents. The interest on $100 invested for one year at $2\frac{1}{2}$ per cent is $100 × .025, or $2.50; and the amount or sum to which $100 will grow in one year is $100 × 1.025 = $102.50.

To determine the amount to which any given principal sum will accumulate in one year when invested at a specified rate of interest, the following algebraic equation may be used: $S = P\,(1 + i)$. In this equation, S represents the *amount,* or sum at the end of the year; P represents the *principal;* and i is the rate of interest. If the principal is assumed to be $1, the equation can be simplified to $S = 1 + i$. Once the amount to which $1 will accumulate in one year has been determined, the amount to which any principal sum will accumulate can be determined by simple multiplication.

If interest is credited against only the original principal invested, the resulting increment is described as *simple interest.* Simple interest would characterize the situation in which the principal sum is invested for only one interest period—normally, one year—or that in which the principal sum is invested over a number of interest periods, with the interest earnings being paid in full at the end of each interest period. If, however, interest earnings are not distributed but are added to the original principal, and the augmented sum, or amount, is then reinvested at the same or a different rate of interest, the resulting increment is *compound interest.* Simply and familiarly stated, compound interest is "interest on interest." Interest may be compounded annually, semiannually, monthly, or at other agreed-upon intervals; but the prevailing practice is to compound annually.

Life insurance calculations are based on compound interest. Premium and reserve computations are based on the assumption that funds contributed by policyholders are kept continuously invested until paid out in settlement of claims, with interest earnings being added to the original principal and reinvested. To understand the relationship of this process to the calculation of premiums and other values, it will be helpful to examine four basic compound interest series.

COMPOUND INTEREST FUNCTIONS

Accumulations

The first series is concerned with the determination of the sum, or amount, to which a principal sum of $1, or unity, invested for a number of years or other units of time, will increase at a specified rate of interest per unit of time. This is perhaps the simplest application of compound interest and involves nothing more than an accumulation of interest earnings. To illustrate, if $1 is invested at $2\frac{1}{2}$ per cent for one year, the combined amount of principal and interest at the end of the year, according to the algebraic equation previously set forth, will be $1 $\times$ 1.025, or $1.025. If the $1.025 is then invested as a new principal for another year at $2\frac{1}{2}$ per cent, the combined amount of principal and interest at the end of the second year will be $1.025 $\times$ 1.025, or $1.0506. This is equivalent to multiplying $1 by $(1.025)^2$. If the sum of $1.0506 is again invested for another year at $2\frac{1}{2}$ per cent, the principal and interest at the end of the third year will be $1.0506 $\times$ 1.025, or $1.076891, which is the equivalent of $(1.025)^3$. This process can be continued for any number of years, and the accumulated principal and interest will always equal the sum obtained by multiplying $1 by 1.025 raised to the power equivalent to the number of years involved. The amount of any principal sum invested for any number of years or other units of time at any rate of interest can be ascertained by the same process. If S represents the amount, or sum, at the end of the period, i the rate of interest, P the principal invested, and n the number of years, the general formula becomes $S = P (1 + i)^n$. If the principal is assumed to be $1, or 1, as is true in most compound interest tables, the formula can be stated as $S = (1 + i)^n$.

Table 8 shows the amount of 1 at the end of each unit of time for fifty units at various rates of compound interest. If it is desired to find the amount of $500, for example, at the end of twenty-three years, with interest at $2\frac{1}{2}$ per cent compounded annually, multiply the figure opposite 23 in the column headed $2\frac{1}{2}$ per cent, 1.764611, by 500, which yields $882.31.

TABLE 8

AMOUNT OF 1 AT VARIOUS RATES OF COMPOUND INTEREST

$$(1 + i)^n$$

Units of Time	2 Per Cent	2½ Per Cent	3 Per Cent	3½ Per Cent	4 Per Cent
1	1.020000	1.025000	1.030000	1.035000	1.040000
2	1.040400	1.050625	1.060900	1.071225	1.081600
3	1.061208	1.076891	1.092727	1.108718	1.124864
4	1.082432	1.103813	1.125509	1.147523	1.169859
5	1.104081	1.131408	1.159274	1.187686	1.216653
6	1.126162	1.159693	1.194052	1.229255	1.265319
7	1.148686	1.188686	1.229874	1.272279	1.315932
8	1.171659	1.218403	1.266770	1.316809	1.368569
9	1.195093	1.248863	1.304773	1.362897	1.423312
10	1.218994	1.280085	1.343916	1.410599	1.480244
11	1.243374	1.312087	1.384234	1.459970	1.539454
12	1.268242	1.344889	1.425761	1.511069	1.601032
13	1.293607	1.378511	1.468534	1.563956	1.665074
14	1.319479	1.412974	1.512590	1.618695	1.731676
15	1.345868	1.448298	1.557967	1.675349	1.800944
16	1.372786	1.484506	1.604706	1.733986	1.872981
17	1.400241	1.521618	1.652848	1.794676	1.947900
18	1.428246	1.559659	1.702433	1.857489	2.025817
19	1.456811	1.598650	1.753506	1.922501	2.106849
20	1.485947	1.638616	1.806111	1.989789	2.191123
21	1.515666	1.679582	1.860295	2.059431	2.278768
22	1.545980	1.721571	1.916103	2.131512	2.369919
23	1.576899	1.764611	1.973587	2.206114	2.464716
24	1.608437	1.808726	2.032794	2.283328	2.563304
25	1.640606	1.853944	2.093778	2.363245	2.665836
26	1.673418	1.900293	2.156591	2.445959	2.772470
27	1.706886	1.947800	2.221289	2.531567	2.883369
28	1.741024	1.996495	2.287928	2.620172	2.998703
29	1.775845	2.046407	2.356566	2.711878	3.118651
30	1.811362	2.097568	2.427262	2.806794	3.243398
31	1.847589	2.150007	2.500080	2.905031	3.373133
32	1.884541	2.203757	2.575083	3.006708	3.508059
33	1.922231	2.258851	2.652335	3.111942	3.648381
34	1.960676	2.315322	2.731905	3.220860	3.794316
35	1.999890	2.373205	2.813862	3.333590	3.946089
36	2.039887	2.432535	2.898278	3.450266	4.103933
37	2.080685	2.493349	2.985227	3.571025	4.268090
38	2.122299	2.555682	3.074783	3.696011	4.438813
39	2.164745	2.619574	3.167027	3.825372	4.616366
40	2.208040	2.685064	3.262038	3.959260	4.801021
41	2.252200	2.752190	3.359899	4.097834	4.993061
42	2.297244	2.820995	3.460696	4.241258	5.192784
43	2.343189	2.891520	3.564517	4.389702	5.400495
44	2.390053	2.963808	3.671452	4.543342	5.616515
45	2.437854	3.037903	3.781596	4.702359	5.841176
46	2.486611	3.113851	3.895044	4.866941	6.074823
47	2.536344	3.191697	4.011895	5.037284	6.317816
48	2.587070	3.271490	4.132252	5.213589	6.570528
49	2.638812	3.353277	4.256219	5.396065	6.833349
50	2.691588	3.437109	4.383906	5.584927	7.106683

Present Values

The second series is concerned with the determination of the present value of a sum due at a designated time in the future. This process is called *discounting,* and it is particularly vital to life insurance company operations, since the companies deal heavily in "futures." They promise benefits that will be paid in the future—in the distant future, in some cases—and they expect to finance these benefit payments through premium income and interest earnings to be received in the future. It is essential to the solvency of the companies to establish an equivalence between future benefit payments and future income. Such equivalence can be established only through the discounting process, through reducing all values to a common basis—*present values.*

Justification for Discounting.   Implicit in the discount process is the recognition that a dollar due one year from now is worth less than a dollar due now or in hand. Furthermore, a dollar due five years from now is worth less than a dollar due one year hence. These differences in value stem predominantly from the productivity of capital.[1] Money in hand can be invested to produce more money or capital. The difference in value between money in hand and money due in the future is measured by the rate of return that can be obtained from invested capital. The higher the rate of return obtainable on invested capital, the greater the difference between the value of present and future money, and vice versa. Moreover, the longer the period before the future money will be received, the greater the loss of interest earnings and, hence, the greater the disparity between the value of the present and future capital.

It should be apparent from the foregoing that the present value of an amount due at a specified date in the future is that principal sum which, if invested now at an assumed rate of interest, would accumulate to the required amount by the due date. For example, it is known that $1 invested at $2\frac{1}{2}$ per cent compound interest will accumulate in ten years to $1.28. That is equivalent to saying that $1 is the present value at $2\frac{1}{2}$ per cent compound interest of $1.28 due in ten years. This suggests that the present value of a sum due in the future can be obtained by reversing the process by which is determined the amount to

---

[1] Differences between present and future values also reflect the degree of risk associated with the future payment. Other things being equal, the greater the uncertainty that the future sum will be received, the higher will be the rate used to discount the payment. In this discussion, it is assumed that payment of the sum due in the future is certain.

which a given sum will accumulate in a specified number of years.

Derivation of Present Values. It was explained earlier that the amount to which a given sum will accumulate in a specified number of years is found by multiplying the principal by 1 plus the rate of interest raised to the power equal to the number of time units in the period. If, instead, the amount at the end of the period is given, the principal may be found by dividing the amount by 1 plus the rate of interest raised to the proper power. For example, $1 invested for one year at $2\frac{1}{2}$ per cent interest will accumulate to $1.025 by the end of the year. If the process is to be reversed, the principal is found by dividing $1.025 by 1.025. If the amount due two years hence is $1.0506, the present value of the amount at $2\frac{1}{2}$ per cent compounded annually, is $1.0506 \div (1.025)^2 = 1.0506 \div 1.0506 = \$1$. Similarly, if $1 is due one year hence, it is worth only $1 \div 1.025$, or $0.9756, today, assuming a discount rate of $2\frac{1}{2}$ per cent. If $1 is to be paid two years hence, its value at the moment is only $1 \div (1.025)^2 = 1 \div 1.0506 = \$0.9518$. Conversely, $0.9518 invested at $2\frac{1}{2}$ per cent compound interest will, at the end of two years, amount to $1. By use of the general formula, $P = \dfrac{S}{(1+i)^n}$, the present value of 1 at $2\frac{1}{2}$ per cent compound interest can be derived for any number of years or time units and arranged in tabular form for convenient use. As a matter of fact, the formula can be ignored and one step saved by dividing 1, or unity, by the amount of 1 accumulated at $2\frac{1}{2}$ per cent compound interest for n number of years, which values are available in specially compiled tables, such as Table 8 of this volume. It may be said, therefore, that tables of present values are constructed from tables of amounts of 1 accumulated at various rates of compound interest. Table 9 was derived in that manner. Since this table will be utilized for premium calculations which may involve a long span of years, present values for one hundred years or time units are shown.

It is customary to represent the present value of 1 due n years hence by the symbol v^n. Thus, at $2\frac{1}{2}$ per cent compound interest:

$$
\begin{aligned}
v &= 1 \div 1.025 & \text{or } 1 \div 1.02500 &= 0.975610 \\
v^2 &= 1 \div (1.025)^2 & \text{or } 1 \div 1.050625 &= 0.951814 \\
v^3 &= 1 \div (1.025)^3 & \text{or } 1 \div 1.076891 &= 0.928599 \\
\text{and } v^{100} &= 1 \div (1.025)^{100} & \text{or } 1 \div 11.813716 &= 0.084647
\end{aligned}
$$

Once a set of values for v^n has been derived, it is no longer necessary to divide the sum to be discounted by the amount of 1 plus the rate of

TABLE 9
Present Value of 1 at Various Rates of Compound Interest

$$v^n = \frac{1}{(1+i)^n}$$

Units of Time	2 Per Cent	2½ Per Cent	3 Per Cent	3½ Per Cent	4 Per Cent
1	0.980392	0.975610	0.970874	0.966184	0.961538
2	0.961169	0.951814	0.942596	0.933511	0.924556
3	0.942322	0.928599	0.915142	0.901943	0.888996
4	0.923845	0.905951	0.888487	0.871442	0.854804
5	0.905731	0.883854	0.862609	0.841973	0.821927
6	0.887971	0.862297	0.837484	0.813501	0.790315
7	0.870560	0.841265	0.813092	0.785991	0.759918
8	0.853490	0.820747	0.789409	0.759412	0.730690
9	0.836755	0.800728	0.766417	0.733731	0.702587
10	0.820348	0.781198	0.744094	0.708919	0.675564
11	0.804263	0.762145	0.722421	0.684946	0.649581
12	0.788493	0.743556	0.701380	0.661783	0.624597
13	0.773033	0.725420	0.680951	0.639404	0.600574
14	0.757875	0.707727	0.661118	0.617782	0.577475
15	0.743015	0.690466	0.641862	0.596891	0.555265
16	0.728446	0.673625	0.623167	0.576706	0.533908
17	0.714163	0.657195	0.605016	0.557204	0.513373
18	0.700159	0.641166	0.587395	0.538361	0.493628
19	0.686431	0.625528	0.570286	0.520156	0.474642
20	0.672971	0.610271	0.553676	0.502566	0.456387
21	0.659776	0.595386	0.537549	0.485571	0.438834
22	0.646839	0.580865	0.521893	0.469151	0.421955
23	0.634156	0.566697	0.506692	0.453286	0.405726
24	0.621721	0.552875	0.491934	0.437957	0.390121
25	0.609531	0.539391	0.477606	0.423147	0.375117
26	0.597579	0.526235	0.463695	0.408838	0.360689
27	0.585862	0.513400	0.450189	0.395012	0.346817
28	0.574375	0.500878	0.437077	0.381654	0.333477
29	0.563112	0.488661	0.424346	0.368748	0.320651
30	0.552071	0.476743	0.411987	0.356278	0.308319
31	0.541246	0.465115	0.399987	0.344230	0.296460
32	0.530633	0.453771	0.388337	0.332590	0.285058
33	0.520229	0.442703	0.377026	0.321343	0.274094
34	0.510028	0.431905	0.366045	0.310476	0.263552
35	0.500028	0.421371	0.355383	0.299977	0.253415
36	0.490223	0.411094	0.345032	0.289833	0.243669
37	0.480611	0.401067	0.334983	0.280032	0.234297
38	0.471187	0.391285	0.325226	0.270562	0.225285
39	0.461948	0.381741	0.315754	0.261413	0.216621
40	0.452890	0.372431	0.306557	0.252572	0.208289
41	0.444010	0.363347	0.297628	0.244031	0.200278
42	0.435304	0.354485	0.288959	0.235779	0.192575
43	0.246769	0.345839	0.280543	0.227806	0.185168
44	0.418401	0.337404	0.272372	0.220102	0.178046
45	0.410197	0.329174	0.264439	0.212659	0.171198
46	0.402154	0.321146	0.256737	0.205468	0.164614
47	0.394268	0.313313	0.249259	0.198520	0.158283
48	0.386538	0.305671	0.241999	0.191806	0.152195

TABLE 9
(*Continued*)

Units of Time	2 Per Cent	2½ Per Cent	3 Per Cent	3½ Per Cent	4 Per Cent
49.............	0.378958	0.298216	0.234950	0.185320	0.146341
50.............	0.371528	0.290942	0.228107	0.179053	0.140713
51.............	0.364243	0.283846	0.221463	0.172998	0.135301
52.............	0.357101	0.276923	0.215013	0.167148	0.130097
53.............	0.350099	0.270169	0.208750	0.161496	0.125093
54.............	0.343234	0.263579	0.202670	0.156035	0.120282
55.............	0.336504	0.257151	0.196767	0.150758	0.115656
56.............	0.329906	0.250879	0.191036	0.145660	0.111207
57.............	0.323437	0.244760	0.185472	0.140734	0.106930
58.............	0.317095	0.238790	0.180070	0.135975	0.102817
59.............	0.310878	0.232966	0.174825	0.131377	0.098863
60.............	0.304782	0.227284	0.169733	0.126934	0.095060
61.............	0.298806	0.221740	0.164789	0.122641	0.091404
62.............	0.292947	0.216332	0.159990	0.118495	0.087889
63.............	0.287203	0.211055	0.155330	0.114487	0.084508
64.............	0.281572	0.205908	0.150806	0.110616	0.081258
65.............	0.276051	0.200886	0.146413	0.106875	0.078133
66.............	0.270638	0.195986	0.142149	0.103261	0.075128
67.............	0.265331	0.191206	0.138009	0.099769	0.072238
68.............	0.260129	0.186542	0.133989	0.096395	0.069460
69.............	0.255028	0.181992	0.130086	0.093136	0.066788
70.............	0.250028	0.177554	0.126297	0.089986	0.064219
71.............	0.245125	0.173223	0.122619	0.086943	0.061749
72.............	0.240319	0.168998	0.119047	0.084003	0.059374
73.............	0.235607	0.164876	0.115580	0.081162	0.057091
74.............	0.230987	0.160855	0.112214	0.078418	0.054895
75.............	0.226458	0.156931	0.108945	0.075766	0.052784
76.............	0.222017	0.153104	0.105772	0.073204	0.050754
77.............	0.217664	0.149370	0.102691	0.070728	0.048801
78.............	0.213396	0.145726	0.099700	0.068336	0.046924
79.............	0.209212	0.142172	0.096796	0.066026	0.045120
80.............	0.205110	0.138705	0.093977	0.063793	0.043384
81.............	0.201088	0.135322	0.091240	0.061636	0.041716
82.............	0.197145	0.132021	0.088582	0.059551	0.040111
83.............	0.193279	0.128800	0.086002	0.057537	0.038569
84.............	0.189490	0.125659	0.083497	0.055592	0.037085
85.............	0.185774	0.122595	0.081065	0.053712	0.035659
86.............	0.182132	0.119605	0.078704	0.051896	0.034287
87.............	0.178560	0.116687	0.076412	0.050141	0.032969
88.............	0.175059	0.113841	0.074186	0.048445	0.031701
89.............	0.171627	0.111065	0.072026	0.046807	0.030481
90.............	0.168261	0.108356	0.069928	0.045224	0.029309
91.............	0.164962	0.105713	0.067891	0.043695	0.028182
92.............	0.161728	0.103135	0.065914	0.042217	0.027098
93.............	0.158556	0.100619	0.063994	0.040789	0.026056
94.............	0.155448	0.098165	0.062130	0.039410	0.025053
95.............	0.152400	0.095771	0.060320	0.038077	0.024090
96.............	0.149411	0.093435	0.058563	0.036790	0.023163
97.............	0.146482	0.091156	0.056858	0.035546	0.022272
98.............	0.143609	0.088933	0.055202	0.034344	0.021416
99.............	0.140794	0.086764	0.053594	0.033182	0.020592
100.............	0.138033	0.084647	0.052033	0.032060	0.019800

interest raised to the power equal to the number of time units involved. The present value of any sum due at the end of any number of years can be ascertained by *multiplying* the sum by the appropriate value of v^n. Thus, the present value of $1,000 due fifteen years hence is, at $2\frac{1}{2}$ per cent compound interest, $1,000 × 0.690466, or $690.47. This type of calculation will be utilized repeatedly in premium computations.

Contrast with Bank Discount Method. It should be observed that the method of deriving present values described above differs from the method of discounting used by banks and other commercial organizations. In banking and commercial transactions, it is customary to multiply the sum to be discounted by the discount rate and then to deduct the product from the original sum. For example, if a bank were to lend $1,000 for one year at $2\frac{1}{2}$ per cent interest, it would multiply $1,000 by $2\frac{1}{2}$ per cent and deduct the $25 thus obtained from the $1,000, turning over $975 to the borrower. Likewise, a department store entitled to a 2 per cent discount for payment of its invoices within ten days would remit only $980 in settlement of an invoice for $1,000. The *true* present value of a sum to be discounted, however, is that amount which, increased by the rate of interest for the period under consideration, will just equal the sum to be discounted. Reverting to the example of the bank, $975 invested at $2\frac{1}{2}$ per cent interest will amount to only $999.38, not $1,000. However, $975.61, the true value of $1,000 discounted for one year at $2\frac{1}{2}$ per cent interest, will, if invested at $2\frac{1}{2}$ per cent interest, accumulate to $1,000 at the end of one year.

For small amounts and short terms, the differences produced by the two methods of discounting are inconsequential. For financial transactions involving large sums and long periods of time, the differences represent substantial sums. The "true" discount method is used in most life insurance calculations.

The Amount of Annual Payments

The third compound interest series is concerned with the determination of the amount to which a number of equal annual payments will accumulate at various rates of interest. This series is useful to life insurance companies in calculating premiums for deferred refund annuities, estimating dividend accumulations, and for other purposes. The values are derived for annual payments of $1, on the assumption that such payments are made *at the beginning* of each year.

TABLE 10

AMOUNT OF 1 PER ANNUM AT VARIOUS RATES OF COMPOUND INTEREST

$$\ddot{S}_{\overline{n}|} = (1 + i) + (1 + i)^2 + \ldots + (1 + i)^n$$

Units of Time	2 Per Cent	2½ Per Cent	3 Per Cent	3½ Per Cent	4 Per Cent
1........	1.020000	1.025000	1.030000	1.035000	1.040000
2........	2.060400	2.075625	2.090900	2.106225	2.121600
3........	3.121608	3.152516	3.183627	3.214943	3.246464
4........	4.204040	4.256329	4.309136	4.362466	4.416323
5........	5.308121	5.387737	5.468410	5.550152	5.632975
6........	6.434283	6.547430	6.662462	6.779408	6.898294
7........	7.582969	7.736116	7.872336	8.051687	8.214226
8........	8.754628	8.954519	9.159106	9.368496	9.582795
9........	9.949721	10.203382	10.463879	10.731393	11.006107
10........	11.168715	11.483466	11.807796	12.141992	12.486351
11........	12.412090	12.795553	13.192030	13.601962	14.025805
12........	13.680332	14.140442	14.617790	15.113030	15.626838
13........	14.973938	15.518953	16.086324	16.676986	17.291911
14........	16.293417	16.931927	17.598914	18.295681	19.023588
15........	17.639285	18.380225	19.156881	19.971030	20.824531
16........	19.012071	19.864730	20.761588	21.705016	22.697512
17........	20.412312	21.386349	22.414435	23.499691	24.645413
18........	21.840559	22.946007	24.116868	25.357180	26.671229
19........	23.297370	24.544658	25.870374	27.279682	28.778079
20........	24.783317	26.183274	27.676486	29.269471	30.969202
21........	26.298984	27.862856	29.536780	31.328902	33.247970
22........	27.844963	29.584427	31.452884	33.460414	35.617889
23........	29.421862	31.349038	33.426470	35.666528	38.082604
24........	31.030300	33.157764	35.459264	37.949857	40.645908
25........	32.670906	35.011708	37.553042	40.313102	43.311745
26........	34.344324	36.912001	39.709634	42.759060	46.084214
27........	36.051210	38.859801	41.930923	45.290627	48.967583
28........	37.792235	40.856296	44.218850	47.910799	51.966286
29........	39.568079	42.902703	46.575416	50.622677	55.084938
30........	41.379441	45.000271	49.002678	53.429471	58.328335
31........	43.227030	47.150278	51.502759	56.334502	61.701469
32........	45.111570	49.354034	54.077841	59.341210	65.209527
33........	47.033802	51.612885	56.730177	62.453152	68.857909
34........	48.994478	53.928207	59.462082	65.674013	72.652225
35........	50.994367	56.301413	62.275944	69.007603	76.598314
36........	53.034255	58.733948	65.174223	72.457869	80.702246
37........	55.114940	61.227297	68.159449	76.028895	84.970336
38........	57.237238	63.782979	71.234233	79.724906	89.409150
39........	59.401983	66.402554	74.401260	83.550278	94.025516
40........	61.610023	69.087617	77.663298	87.509537	98.826536
41........	63.862223	71.839808	81.023196	91.607371	103.819598
42........	66.159468	74.660803	84.483892	95.848629	109.012382
43........	68.502657	77.552323	88.048409	100.238331	114.412877
44........	70.892710	80.516131	91.719861	104.781673	120.029392
45........	73.330564	83.554034	95.501457	109.484031	125.870568
46........	75.817176	86.667885	99.396501	114.350973	131.945390
47........	78.353519	89.859582	103.408396	119.388257	138.263206
48........	80.940590	93.131072	107.540648	124.601846	144.833734
49........	83.579401	96.484349	111.796867	129.997910	151.667084
50........	86.270989	99.921458	116.180773	135.582837	158.773767

Derivation of Values. On the basis of 2½ per cent interest, the first payment will amount to $1.025 at the end of the first year. At the beginning of the second year, another payment of $1 will be made, bringing to $2.025 the sum which will be invested during the second year. The amount at the end of the second year will be $2.025 × 1.025, or $2.075625. At the beginning of the third year, another payment of $1 will be made, raising the amount at interest to $3.075625; and at the end of the third year, the accumulated sum would be $3.075625 × 1.025, or $3.15251563. This process can be continued for an indefinite number of years, the results being arranged to produce a table such as Table 10.

Table 10 can be constructed from Table 8 by the simple process of addition. To illustrate, the first five figures in the 2½ per cent column of Table 8 are reproduced below:

	Amount of 1 at End of
One year	1.025000
Two years	1.050625
Three years	1.076891
Four years	1.103813
Five years	1.131408

The first figure above is the same as the first figure in the 2½ per cent column of Table 10. Thereafter, of course, the figures vary, since they portray different compound interest functions. However, to obtain the second figure in Table 10, the first two figures above are added. If, then, the third figure above, 1.076891, is added to 2.075625, the result is 3,152516, the third figure in Table 10. To this, 1.103813 is added, yielding 4.256329, the fourth figure in Table 10, and so on.

Modification for Payments at End of Year. It should be noted that Table 10 can be used to find the amount to which a series of annual payments made *at the end* of each year will accumulate. Clearly, if a person is to receive $1 at the end of a particular year, he will earn no interest on that $1 during the year of receipt. If he then invests the $1 at 2½ per cent interest, it will amount to $1.025 at the end of the *second* year. At that time, however, another dollar will be received, and $2.025 can be placed at interest during the third year. By the end of the third year, $3.075625 will have accumulated, including the payment due at the end of the year. This compares with $3.152516 that would have been on hand at that time had each of the three payments been made at the beginning of the year. The difference, $0.076891, is the compound interest on $1 for three years. By the end of the fourth year, $4.152516 will have accumulated, including the fourth payment. This is $0.103813 less than the amount that would have accumulated had the four payments been made at the beginning of each year, the difference in this case being compound interest at $2\frac{1}{2}$ per cent interest on $1 for four years. With each passing year, the difference will become larger, the disparity being attributable in each case to compound interest on $1 for the number of years involved. This being true, the amount to which a series of annual payments of $1 made at the end of each year will accumulate by the end of any number of years will always equal the amount of $1 per annum, payable at the beginning of each year, for a period one year shorter, plus $1. Thus, the amount of $1 per annum at the end of each year for ten years is $10.203382, the amount of $1 per annum *at the beginning* of each year for *nine* years, plus $1, or a total of $11.203382. This is $0.280085 less than the amount of $1 per annum at the beginning of the year for ten years, which, by reference to Table 8, is seen to be the accumulated interest on $1 at $2\frac{1}{2}$ per cent for ten years.

An example may help to clarify the procedure used in adapting Table 10 to a series of payments due at the end of each year. Suppose it is desired to find the amount to which $50 per year, payable for thirty years at the end of each year, will accumulate by the end of such period at $2\frac{1}{2}$ per cent interest. Since the first payment is not due until one year hence, interest will be earned for only twenty-nine years. From Table 10, the amount of $1 per annum in advance at $2\frac{1}{2}$ per cent interest for twenty-nine years can be obtained, which amount is $42.902703. There are to be thirty payments, however, the last of which is to be made at the end of the period. This last payment of $1, added to $42.902703, yields $43.902703, the amount of $1 per annum payable at the end of each year over a thirty-year period at $2\frac{1}{2}$ per cent. Since $1 payable in such manner will amount to $43.902703, then $50 payable in the same manner will amount to $50 × 43.902703, or $2,195.14.

Present Value of Annual Payments

The fourth, and final, compound interest series is concerned with the determination of the present value of a number of equal annual payments at various rates of interest. This series is used by life insurance companies to ascertain amounts payable under the "installment time" and "installment amount" methods of liquidating insurance proceeds[2] and, in combination with life contingencies, is also

---

[2] Settlement options are discussed in Chapters XXXII, XXXIII, and XXXIV.

utilized to calculate the present value of a life annuity due.[3] The latter is used to determine benefits under life income options, to convert net single premiums into net level premiums, and for other purposes. An understanding of this series is, therefore, particularly important to a comprehension of insurance company actuarial computations. The values in this series are derived for annual payments of $1 due *at the end* of each year, although tables reflecting these values can be adapted to payments due *at the beginning* of each year.

Derivation of Values. This series is derived from the values presented in Table 9 in the same manner that Table 10 was derived from the values in Table 8. It was observed in Table 9 that at 2½ per cent interest, the present value of $1 payable one year hence is $0.975610. The present value of the second payment of $1 due two years hence is $0.951814, while the third payment is worth $0.928599 at the present time. The present value of all three payments is, of course, the sum of the present values of each taken separately, or $2.856024. By the process of cumulative addition, the present value of a series of annual payments of $1 for any number of years can be found. Table 11 shows such values at various rates of interest for a period of fifty years. It will be noted that the value for two years in Table 11 is the sum of the first two figures in Table 9, the value for three years the sum of the first three figures in Table 9, and so on.

A contract calling for a series of annual (or more frequent) payments for a definite period of years is referred to as a "temporary annuity" or, sometimes, an "annuity certain." The present value of a temporary annuity of any amount for any period of time can be found from Table 11 by multiplying the amount of the annuity by the present value of an annuity of 1 for the appropriate number of years. Thus, the present value at 2½ per cent of a temporary annuity of $2,500 for thirty years is 20.930293 × $2,500 = $52,325.73.

Application of the Values. Tables have been constructed showing for a wide range of years and interest rates the temporary annuity whose present value is 1, so that the precise amount of income which can be purchased with a given sum can be readily determined. Such tables are constructed by dividing into 1 the present value of a temporary annuity of $1 for various durations and interest rates. For example, to determine the amount of a temporary annuity for twenty years at 2½ per cent interest that can be purchased with $1, the present value of 1 per annum for twenty years, $15.589162, is divided into 1, yielding $0.064147. In other words, at 2½ per cent compound inter-

---

[3] See p. 208.

TABLE 11

PRESENT VALUE OF 1 PER ANNUM AT VARIOUS RATES
OF COMPOUND INTEREST

$$a_{\overline{n}|} = v + v^2 + \ldots + v^n$$

Units of Time	2 Per Cent	2½ Per Cent	3 Per Cent	3½ Per Cent	4 Per Cent
1.........	.980392	.975610	.970874	.966184	.961538
2.........	1.941561	1.927424	1.913470	1.899694	1.886095
3.........	2.883883	2.856024	2.828611	2.801637	2.775091
4.........	3.807729	3.761974	3.717098	3.673079	3.629895
5.........	4.713460	4.645828	4.579707	4.515052	4.451822
6.........	5.601431	5.508125	5.417191	5.328553	5.242137
7.........	6.471991	6.349391	6.230283	6.114544	6.002055
8.........	7.325481	7.170137	7.019692	6.873956	6.732745
9.........	8.162237	7.970866	7.786109	7.607687	7.435332
10.........	8.982585	8.752064	8.530203	8.316605	8.110896
11.........	9.786848	9.514209	9.252624	9.001551	8.760477
12.........	10.575341	10.257765	9.954004	9.663334	9.385074
13.........	11.348374	10.983185	10.634955	10.302738	9.985648
14.........	12.106249	11.690912	11.296073	10.920520	10.563123
15.........	12.849264	12.381378	11.937935	11.517411	11.118387
16.........	13.577709	13.055003	12.561102	12.094117	11.652296
17.........	14.291872	13.712198	13.166118	12.651321	12.165669
18.........	14.992031	14.353364	13.753513	13.189682	12.659297
19.........	15.678462	14.978891	14.323799	13.709837	13.133939
20.........	16.351433	15.589162	14.877475	14.212403	13.590326
21.........	17.011209	16.184549	15.415024	14.697974	14.029160
22.........	17.658048	16.765413	15.936917	15.167125	14.451115
23.........	18.292204	17.332110	16.443608	15.620410	14.856842
24.........	18.913926	17.884986	16.935542	16.058368	15.246963
25.........	19.523456	18.424376	17.413148	16.481515	15.622080
26.........	20.121036	18.950611	17.876842	16.890352	15.982769
27.........	20.706898	19.464011	18.327031	17.285365	16.329586
28.........	21.281272	19.964889	18.764108	17.667019	16.663063
29.........	21.844385	20.453550	19.188455	18.035767	16.983715
30.........	22.396456	20.930293	19.600441	18.392045	17.292033
31.........	22.937702	21.395407	20.000428	18.736276	17.588494
32.........	23.468335	21.849178	20.388766	19.068865	17.873551
33.........	23.988564	22.291881	20.765792	19.390208	18.147646
34.........	24.498592	22.723786	21.131837	19.700684	18.411198
35.........	24.998619	23.145157	21.487220	20.000661	18.664613
36.........	25.488842	23.556251	21.832252	20.290494	18.908282
37.........	25.969453	23.957318	22.167235	20.570525	19.142579
38.........	26.440641	24.348603	22.492462	20.841087	19.367864
39.........	26.902589	24.730344	22.808215	21.102500	19.584485
40.........	27.355479	25.102775	23.114772	21.355072	19.792774
41.........	27.799489	25.466122	23.412400	21.599104	19.993052
42.........	28.234794	25.820607	23.701359	21.834883	20.185627
43.........	28.661562	26.166446	23.981902	22.062689	20.370795
44.........	29.079963	26.503849	24.254274	22.282791	20.548841
45.........	29.490160	26.833024	24.518713	22.495450	20.720040
46.........	29.892314	27.154170	24.775449	22.700918	20.884654
47.........	30.286582	27.467483	25.024708	22.899438	21.042936
48.........	30.673120	27.773154	25.266707	23.091244	21.195131
49.........	31.052078	28.071369	25.501657	23.276564	21.341472
50.........	31.423606	28.362312	25.729764	23.455618	21.482185

est, $1 will provide 6.4 cents per year for twenty years. Therefore, $1,000 would provide $1,000 × 0.064147, or $64.15.

While such tables are convenient, the same results can be obtained from Table 11, with little more effort. The values in that table may be viewed as the sums needed to purchase an annuity of $1 for the various terms involved. Thus, at 2½ per cent, $15.59 will provide $1 per year, the first payment due one year hence, for twenty years; and $20.93 will provide the same amount per year for thirty years. If $15.59 will provide $1 per year for twenty years, then $1,000—to use the above example—will provide an annual payment as much larger than $1 as $1,000 is greater than $15.59. Stated as a proportion, $1,000 : 15.589163 = x : 1$. Dividing $1,000 by 15.589163, it is found that $1,000 will provide an annual payment of $64.15, the figure previously obtained. Thus, the rule may be stated as follows: To determine the amount of annual payments due at the end of each year that will be provided by a given principal sum, divide the sum by the present value of 1 per annum at the stipulated rate of interest for the period over which the installments are to be paid.

Amounts payable under life insurance settlement options are payable *at the beginning* of the year.[4] Likewise, annual premiums are due at the beginning of the year. Therefore, life insurance companies must modify the values shown in Table 11 to reflect the present value of a series of periodical payments due at the beginning of the year. The adjustment involved is very simple. Consider, for example, a series of annual payments of $1, due at the beginning of each year, for twenty-five years. The first payment is due immediately and, obviously, is worth $1. There remain twenty-four additional payments, the first of which is due one year hence. The present value of the entire series is obtained by adding $1 to the present value of $1 per annum for twenty-four years, the result at 2½ per cent being 17.884986 + 1, or $18.88.

CURRENT INTEREST ASSUMPTIONS

Throughout this chapter—and, in fact, throughout the entire book —all illustrations have been in terms of a 2½ per cent interest assumption. This rate is perhaps representative of the rate used by most companies today in computing premiums and reserves on new life insur-

---

[4] As a matter of fact, life insurance settlement options usually provide for *monthly* payments, which necessitates a further modification, as will be explained in Chapter XXXII.

ance contracts, although many companies use a 3 per cent assumption and some use other rates. Most companies use a somewhat lower interest assumption in connection with their annuity contracts than with their insurance contracts, in order to provide an additional margin of safety against continued improvement in mortality. Interest assumptions in general are much lower than those of fifty years ago, a reflection of the decline in the return on invested funds. Many life insurance contracts still in force are based on interest assumptions of $3\frac{1}{2}$ per cent, 4 per cent, and even $4\frac{1}{2}$ per cent. In most cases, as is pointed out later, the reserves under such contracts have been recalculated on an interest basis in line with current assumptions.

A life insurance company must exercise sound judgment in selecting the interest rate or rates that are to be used in its computations, since rates are established for the lifetime of the contract. Companies tend to select a conservative rate, perhaps one percentage point less than they expect to earn on their investments over a long period. This is feasible for mutual companies and stock companies which issue participating policies, since interest earnings in excess of the assumed rate can be distributed to the policyholders through the dividend formula. Nonparticipating companies must select an interest rate more in line with expected earnings, since there is no provision in their contracts for adjusting premium rates which turn out to be ultraconservative.

CHAPTER X

Net

Premiums

THE PRICE charged by a life insurance company for an insurance or annuity contract is called the *premium*. This is a rather unfortunate term, stemming from the bottomry and respondentia loans[1] of the Middle Ages in connection with which the lender—for an additional payment, or "premium," over the interest charge—would agree to waive repayment of the loan if the vessel or cargo, as the case might be, should be lost at sea. The expression has survived the practice and is still used to designate the monetary consideration for the insurance company's promise.

The premium for a life insurance contract is usually expressed as a *rate* per $1,000 of face amount, while the premium for an annuity contract is normally expressed as a rate per specified amount of income, such as $100 per year or $10 per month. The premium may be paid in one sum, in which event it is referred to as a *single premium;* or it may be paid at periodic intervals, such as annually, semiannually, quarterly, or monthly. It was formerly the universal custom to compute periodic premiums on the assumption that they would be paid annually, with any smaller premiums, based on semiannual, quarterly, or monthly payments, being considered installments of the annual premium and, if unpaid at the date of death, deductible from the proceeds of the insurance. As will be explained later, however, companies now compute semiannual, quarterly, and monthly premiums on a basis which does not treat such payments as installments of an annual premium and which does not require deduction from proceeds of any "fractional premiums" which would have been payable after the date of death. As a matter of fact, many companies refund that portion of any quarterly, semiannual, or annual premium

---

[1] Bottomry loans were those made on the security of a ship or vessel, while respondentia loans were those made on the security of the cargo.

applicable to the period beyond the month in which the insured dies.

Premiums are computed on the basis of three fundamental assumptions: (1) a rate of mortality, (2) a rate of interest, and (3) a rate of expense, in which is included any provision for contingencies not absorbed in the margin available under the mortality and interest rates assumed. Only the first two factors, the rate of mortality and the rate of interest, enter into the calculation of the *net premium*. The net premium is designed to provide all benefits under the contract, whether payable by reason of death, survival, or surrender. If the actual experience conforms precisely to the projected experience, the net premiums received by a company will, in the aggregate, be just exactly adequate to pay all claims.

The amount added to the net premium to cover expenses of operation and to provide for contingencies is called *loading*.[2] The net premium increased by the loading is the *gross premium,* which is the premium payable by the policyholder. In the case of participating policies, the loading is usually much greater than is likely to be needed; and under the typical system of distributing surplus, the excess over the actual requirement, together with any mortality savings and excess interest earnings, will be returned to the policyholder as a *dividend*.[3]

The derivation of net premiums will be discussed in this chapter, the additional steps involved in the development of the gross premium being described in Chapter XII.

NET SINGLE PREMIUM

Whether the ultimate premium is to be paid in a single sum, annually, semiannually, quarterly, monthly, or weekly, the first step in the derivation of such premium is to determine the net *single* premium for the policy in question. Then, by a process to be explained later, the single premium is converted into an annual or a more frequent premium. Finally, the periodic premium is loaded for expenses and contingencies to produce the gross premium charged the policyholder. This section, therefore, will describe the calculation of the net single premium for the basic insurance and annuity contracts.

Assumptions Underlying Rate Computations

Rate computations of life insurance companies are based on three

---

[2] In a stock life insurance company, the loading will normally contain an allowance for profit, as well.

[3] The subject of dividends is discussed in Chapter XVI.

fundamental assumptions: (1) premiums are paid at the beginning of each policy year, (2) claims are paid at the end of the policy year in which they arise, and (3) the death rate is uniform throughout the policy year. None of these assumptions conform precisely to the facts.

The first assumption *tends* to be true. If a policy is purchased with a single premium, this sum is paid at the inception of the risk, and the portion attributable to any particular year may be regarded as having been paid at the beginning of such policy year. If annual premiums are to be paid, the first premium must be paid on or before the effective date of the contract; and, except for the operation of the grace period provision, each subsequent premium must be paid on or before the anniversary date of the policy. Premiums paid more frequently than annually may be treated as "true" or separate premiums, paid in advance of the period to which they pertain, or as installments of a premium due at the beginning of the policy year; but in any case, an adjustment must be made for the fact that the full annual premium was not received in advance of the applicable policy year.

At one time, the second assumption was fairly realistic. In the early days of American life insurance, it required about three months to render satisfactory proof of death; and the companies were permitted by contract to defer payment of claims for three additional months after the claim had been established to the satisfaction of the company. If death occurred, on the average, in the middle of the policy year, it worked out that the average claim was paid at the end of the policy year in which it arose. Today, however, with improved communication facilities and better service from insurance company field representatives, proof of death is established more promptly, and claims are paid immediately upon proof of death and entitlement. Since deaths do occur, on the average, near the middle of the policy year and the necessary claim documents are ordinarily submitted within a few days after the insured's death, the typical claim is paid not at the end of the policy year but almost six months earlier. The practical significance of this is that the company loses approximately six months' interest on the sum insured. At $2\frac{1}{2}$ per cent interest, this amounts to $12.36 per $1,000 of proceeds. The company may choose to absorb the deficiency in the margins available in the rate structure; or it may elect to treat it as an additional benefit to the policyholder, to be financed by an increase in the net premium or an upward adjustment in the loading. If the company decides to meet the loss of interest through an adjustment of the net premium, it will simply add the amount of the deficiency ($12.36 in the above example) to the face of the policy for purposes of premium computation, and the resulting net single premium will reflect the additional benefit. If the adjustment is made through the loading formula, the interest deficiency will be treated as a separate item of expense, to be amortized over the premium-paying period of the policy. The practice of adjusting premium rates to reflect immediate payment of claims is becoming more general, but the computations in this chapter will be based on the simpler assumption that claims are paid at the end of the policy year in which death occurs.

Like the second assumption, the third assumption set forth above is not consistent with actualities. The fact is that the death rate decreases constantly up to about age ten, after which it begins to increase, slowly at first, but at a constantly accelerating rate to the end of life. From a financial standpoint, the chief significance of this assumption—and the divergence of the facts from the assumption—attaches to policies whose premiums are paid at intervals more frequent than one year. In the case of annual premiums, funds are received in advance by the company and are on hand at any time during the year to pay the claims that arise. In the case of monthly premiums, however, if only one twelfth of the annual premium is collected in advance, but one sixth of the total mortality for the year, for example, should occur during the first month, the company would suffer a loss from the policies involved. This situation is likely to occur only at ages zero through ten, when the mortality rate is constantly decreasing. After age ten or eleven, however, the mortality rate is increasing; and the discrepancy between assumption and fact becomes increasingly favorable to the company and presents no problem, since the company will collect one twelfth of the premiums but will experience less than one twelfth of the year's claims during the first month.

With respect to annuities payable more often than annually, the reverse is true; and at the extreme ages, the losses arising out of the falsity of the assumption could be substantial.

Other factors contribute to the divergence between the third assumption and reality. For instance, the death rate fluctuates by calendar season, as does the sale of new policies. For certain blocks of policies, these influences may strengthen the assumption; but for others, the opposite is true.

Concept of the Net Single Premium

The underlying objective of life insurance rate making is to collect from each insured the precise monetary value of the benefits promised under his contract. If the contract is to be purchased with a single-sum payment—the assumption at this point—that sum must be the exact equivalent of the benefits contained in the contract. The net single premium is nothing more or less than the present value of future benefits. The essence of rate making, then, is the valuation of the promises embodied in the contract. Three steps are involved in this process.

The first step obviously is to ascertain the benefits promised under the contract. In a life insurance contract, these benefits take two basic forms: (1) a promise on the part of the company to pay the face of the policy in the event that the insured dies during a specified period and (2) a promise on the part of the company to pay the face of the policy if the insured should survive to the end of a specified period. Some contracts contain both promises, while others contain only the first. Moreover, contracts differ as to the period during which the company's promise or promises apply. Therefore, it is essential to identify precisely the type of contract whose premium is to be calculated.

The second step is to select the mortality table for the measurement of the life contingencies involved. Whether the company's promise is to pay upon death, survival, or both, the rate of mortality is the basic determinant of the value of the promise. In practice, a company must adopt a mortality table which is appropriate for the class of persons to be insured and, depending upon the nature of its operations, may use several tables concurrently. Unless otherwise stated, the Commissioners 1958 Standard Ordinary Mortality Table will be used for the premium computations in this volume.

Since the consideration for the contract is to be paid in the present and the promise of the company is to be fulfilled in the future, a third step must be introduced, linking the two actions to a common time basis. This linkage is accomplished through the discounting process, which was described earlier. The mortality table will indicate the relative probabilities of the company's promise or promises being fulfilled year by year, while the discount factor will reduce the monetary value of those separate yearly probabilities to a present value basis. The net single premium will equal the sum of the present values of all the probable benefits involved. The magnitude of the net single premium is greatly influenced by the rate at which the life contingencies are discounted; the lower the rate, the higher the premium, and vice versa. All calculations in this section will be based on 2½ per cent interest.

Two Techniques of Calculation

Life insurance premiums can be calculated according to two fundamental techniques, the first of which—for want of a more imaginative term—can be called the "individual approach" and the second the "aggregate approach." The first approach assumes that the calculation is being made for one individual and that his chances of dying or living year by year can be measured by the probability fractions in the mortality table. Implicit in this approach, however, is the assumption that a sufficiently large number of individuals, including all ages and all kinds of policies, are being insured to yield average results— i.e., that the *law of large numbers* is given an opportunity to operate. The "aggregate approach," on the other hand, assumes that each premium calculation is being made for a group of persons of identical age equal in size to the tabular number alive at the age of issue and that all members of the group contribute pro rata to a mutual fund, out of which all claims will be paid according to the tabular experience.

These two approaches can be illustrated in connection with the calculation of the net single premium for a one-year term policy in the amount of $1,000 issued at age thirty-five. It will be remembered that this type of contract pays the face of the policy if the insured should die during the year of coverage and nothing if he should survive.

Under the individual approach, the first step is to determine the probability that a person thirty-five years of age will die before attaining age thirty-six. Reference to the 1958 C.S.O. Table, reproduced in Table 12, reveals that 9,373,807 persons are assumed to be alive at age thirty-five, out of 10,000,000 persons alive at age zero and that 23,528 persons will die during the year, according to the assumption. Therefore, the probability that a person aged thirty-five will die during the year is $\dfrac{23,528}{9,373,807}$. This fraction multiplied by $1,000 yields the amount of money that an insurance company would have to have on hand *at the end* of the year for this policyholder and

TABLE 12
1958 C.S.O. MORTALITY TABLE

Age	Number Living	Number Dying	Rate of Mortality per Thousand	Age	Number Living	Number Dying	Rate of Mortality per Thousand
0...	10,000,000	70,800	7.08	50....	8,762,306	72,902	8.32
1...	9,929,200	17,475	1.76	51....	8,689,404	79,160	9.11
2...	9,911,725	15,066	1.52	52....	8,610,244	85,758	9.96
3...	9,896,659	14,449	1.46	53....	8,524,486	92,832	10.89
4...	9,882,210	13,835	1.40	54....	8,431,654	100,337	11.90
5...	9,868,375	13,322	1.35	55....	8,331,317	108,307	13.00
6...	9,855,053	12,812	1.30	56....	8,223,010	116,849	14.21
7...	9,842,241	12,401	1.26	57....	8,106,161	125,970	15.54
8...	9,829,840	12,091	1.23	58....	7,980,191	135,663	17.00
9...	9,817,749	11,879	1.21	59....	7,844,528	145,830	18.59
10...	9,805,870	11,865	1.21	60....	7,698,698	156,592	20.34
11...	7,794,005	12,047	1.23	61....	7,542,106	167,736	22.24
12...	9,781,958	12,325	1.26	62....	7,374,370	179,271	24.31
13...	9,769,633	12,896	1.32	63....	7,195,099	191,174	26.57
14...	9,756,737	13,562	1.39	64....	7,003,925	203,394	29.04
15...	9,743,175	14,225	1.46	65....	6,800,531	215,917	31.75
16...	9,728,950	14,983	1.54	66....	6,584,614	228,749	34.74
17...	9,713,967	15,737	1.62	67....	6,355,865	241,777	38.04
18...	9,698,230	16,390	1.69	68....	6,114,088	254,835	41.68
19...	9,681,840	16,846	1.74	69....	5,859,253	267,241	45.61
20...	9,664,994	17,300	1.79	70....	5,592,012	278,426	49.79
21...	9,647,694	17,655	1.83	71....	5,313,586	287,731	54.15
22...	9,630,039	17,912	1.86	72....	5,025,855	294,766	58.65
23...	9,612,127	18,167	1.89	73....	4,731,089	299,289	63.26
24...	9,593,960	18,324	1.91	74....	4,431,800	301,894	68.12
25...	9,575,636	18,481	1.93	75....	4,129,906	303,011	73.37
26...	9,557,155	18,732	1.96	76....	3,826,895	303,014	79.18
27...	9,538,423	18,981	1.99	77....	3,523,881	301,997	85.70
28...	9,519,442	19,324	2.03	78....	3,221,884	299,829	93.06
29...	9,500,118	19,760	2.08	79....	2,922,055	295,683	101.19
30...	9,480,358	20,193	2.13	80....	2,626,372	288,848	109.98
31...	9,460,165	20,718	2.19	81....	2,337,524	278,983	119.35
32...	9,439,447	21,239	2.25	82....	2,058,541	265,902	129.17
33...	9,418,208	21,850	2.32	83....	1,792,639	249,858	139.38
34...	9,396,358	22,551	2.40	84....	1,542,781	231,433	150.01
35...	9,373,807	23,528	2.51	85....	1,311,348	211,311	161.14
36...	9,350,279	24,685	2.64	86....	1,100,037	190,108	172.82
37...	9,325,594	26,112	2.80	87....	909,929	168,455	185.13
38...	9,299,482	27,991	3.01	88....	741,474	146,997	198.25
39...	9,271,491	30,132	3.25	89....	594,477	126,303	212.46
40...	9,241,359	32,622	3.53	90....	468,174	106,809	228.14
41...	9,208,737	35,362	3.84	91....	361,365	88,813	245.77
42...	9,173,375	38,253	4.17	92....	272,552	72,480	265.93
43...	9,135,122	41,382	4.53	93....	200,072	57,881	289.30
44...	9,093,740	44,741	4.92	94....	142,191	45,026	316.66
45...	9,048,999	48,412	5.35	95....	97,165	34,128	351.24
46...	9,000,587	52,473	5.83	96....	63,037	25,250	400.56
47...	8,948,114	56,910	6.36	97....	37,787	18,456	488.42
48...	8,891,204	61,794	6.95	98....	19,331	12,916	668.15
49...	8,829,410	67,104	7.60	99....	6,415	6,415	1,000.00

all others in his age and policy classification to pay the claims that will occur during the year among the group. Since this amount of money need be on hand only at the end of the policy year, the sum to be paid in advance by the policyholder can be reduced by the amount of interest that will be earned on such sum during the year. The actual premium, then, is calculated as follows:

$$\frac{23,528}{9,373,807} \times \$1,000 \times .975610 = \$2.45$$

Under the aggregate approach, it will be assumed that 9,373,807 persons aged thirty-five apply for a one-year term policy in the amount of $1,000 and that 23,528 persons in the group die during the ensuing year. This means that the company must have $23,528,000 on hand at the end of the year in order to pay claims. However, this entire amount need not have been collected from the policyholders, since the company is able to earn interest on the premiums paid in at the beginning of the year. For every dollar collected at the beginning of the year, the company will have $1.025 at the end of the year when the claims mature. Therefore, the amount of money that must be collected from the group is obtained by dividing $23,528,000 by $1.025, or by multiplying 23,528,000 by .975610, either of which procedures yields $22,954,146. Since it is not known at the beginning of the year which of the 9,373,807 persons will die, each must pay the same amount into the fund. To obtain the amount which must be collected from each participant, it is necessary only to divide the total contribution by the number contributing, namely:

$$\$22,954,146 \div 9,373,807 = \$2.45$$

In actual premium computations, the above premium would have been derived by the following equation:

$$\frac{23,528 \times \$1,000 \times .975610}{9,373,807} = \$2.45$$

Inasmuch as each of the foregoing techniques has certain expository advantages, all premium calculations in this chapter will be illustrated by both techniques.

Term Insurance

If the premium calculations for the yearly renewable term policy for $1,000 which served to illustrate the two computational techniques were carried forward for another year, it would be found that the premium is derived as follows:

$$\frac{24,685}{9,350,279} \times \$1,000 \times .975610 = \$2.58$$

or, according to the aggregate approach, as follows:

$$\frac{24,685 \times \$1,000 \times .975610}{9,350,279} = \$2.58$$

The insurance is considered to have commenced anew at age thirty-six, and the probability involved is that a person *now* thirty-six will die during the current year. Since the claim or claims, as the case may be, will be paid at the end of the current year, the premium is discounted at $2\frac{1}{2}$ per cent for only one year. Subsequent premiums would be calculated in the same manner, the probability fraction always being the number dying during the year over the number living at the beginning of that year, and the premium always being discounted for one year.

While yearly renewable term insurance serves as the simplest example of premium computations, it is rarely sold to individuals and is greatly exceeded in importance by term policies which provide protection on a level premium basis for a period of years. It is desirable, therefore, to illustrate the calculation of a net single premium for a term policy of the latter type. A five-year term policy for $1,000, issued at age thirty-five, can serve as an example. The individual approach will be explained first.

A new factor is introduced into the rate-making process with the five-year term policy, or any policy which provides protection beyond the current year. The problem in this specific instance is to determine the single sum payable now which is the equivalent of the company's promise to pay the face of the policy if the insured should die at any time within the next five years. Two facts should be kept firmly in mind: (1) the premium is paid only once, in a single sum at the inception of the risk; and (2) the death claim, if any, will be paid at the end of the year in which death occurs, and not at the end of the five-year period. Manifestly, the premium cannot be correctly determined by multiplying the total probability that the insured will die during the five-year period by the face value of the policy and discounting this amount in one operation, since the sum paid in by the insured might earn interest for as brief a period as one year and as long a period as five years. It is necessary to compute the cost of each year's mortality separately.

The cost of the first year's mortality is determined in precisely the same manner as the premium for the yearly renewable term policy at age thirty-five, the equation being:

$$\frac{23,528}{9,373,807} \times \$1,000 \times .975610 = \$2.45$$

The probability insured against during the second year is *not* $\frac{24,685}{9,350,279}$, which reflects the probability that a person now thirty-six will die within the next twelve months, but $\frac{24,685}{9,373,807}$, which reflects the probability that a person now *thirty-five* will die at age thirty-six, or during his thirty-seventh year. It should be noted that the latter is a smaller probability, reflecting the chance that the person will die during age thirty-five and will, therefore, not be exposed to the hazard of death during age thirty-six. If the person now thirty-five dies between ages thirty-six and thirty-seven, the money which he pays in now will earn two years' interest. Hence, the cost of mortality during the second year can be discounted for two years. The equation for the second year's mortality cost becomes:

$$\frac{24,685}{9,373,807} \times \$1,000 \times .951814 = \$2.51$$

The probability insured against during the third year of insurance is that a person now thirty-five will die during age thirty-seven, the fraction being $\frac{26,112}{9,373,807}$. That portion of the single premium allocable to the third year's cost of mortality will be held by the company for three years and hence can be discounted for three years. Therefore, the equation for the third year's mortality cost is:

$$\frac{26,112}{9,373,807} \times \$1,000 \times .928599 = \$2.59.$$

The probabilities of death during the fourth and fifth years are $\frac{27,991}{9,373,807}$ and $\frac{30,132}{9,373,807}$, respectively, the corresponding discount factors being .905951 and .883854. The cost of mortality for the entire five years can be summarized as follows:

Age 35: $\dfrac{23,528}{9,373,807}$ × $1,000 × .975610 = $ 2.45   Cost of 1st year's mortality

Age 36: $\dfrac{24,685}{9,373,807}$ × $1,000 × .951814 = $ 2.51   Cost of 2d year's mortality

Age 37: $\dfrac{26,112}{9,373,807}$ × $1,000 × .928599 = $ 2.59   Cost of 3d year's mortality

Age 38: $\dfrac{27,991}{9,373,807}$ × $1,000 × .905951 = $ 2.70   Cost of 4th year's mortality

Age 39: $\dfrac{30,132}{9,373,807}$ × $1,000 × .883854 = $ 2.84   Cost of 5th year's mortality

Net single premium = $13.09

This computation shows that $13.09 deposited with the company by each policyholder and placed at 2½ per cent interest will provide enough money to pay all death claims arising under this particular classification of policies during the five-year period. It will be observed that under this method, the net single premium is the sum of a series of values representing the cost of mortality for each separate year of insurance and obtained by *multiplying the probability insured against by the amount of the policy multiplied by the value of $1 discounted for the period the money is held*. In determining the probability insured against, the denominator remains the same throughout the period covered by the policy. The face of the policy is always assumed to be $1,000, except in the case of annuity contracts; and the net single premium which is derived is the premium *rate* per $1,000 of insurance.

Under the aggregate approach, it is assumed—as with the yearly renewable term policy—that 9,373,807 persons aged thirty-five are insured for $1,000 under a five-year term policy. It is further assumed that 23,528 persons die during the first year and that $23,528,000 in claims will be paid out at the end of the year. Since the money deposited at the inception of the contract for first-year claims will earn interest at 2½ per cent for one year, only $23,528,000 × .975610, or $22,954,146, need be paid in. It is assumed that 24,685 persons will die during the second year, requiring a sum of $24,685,000 at the end of the year for payment of claims. The sum deposited at the inception of the contract for these claims will earn interest for two years and can be reduced to $24,685,000 × .951814, or $23,495,529. Deaths during the third, fourth, and fifth years are assumed to follow the tabular pattern; and the sums deposited in advance to meet the resulting claims are discounted for three, four, and five years, respectively. The computations appear as follows:

Age 35: 23,528 × $1,000 × .975610 = $ 22,954,146 Present value of 1st-year claims
Age 36: 24,685 × $1,000 × .951814 = $ 23,495,529 Present value of 2nd-year claims
Age 37: 26,112 × $1,000 × .928599 = $ 24,247,577 Present value of 3rd-year claims
Age 38: 27,991 × $1,000 × .905951 = $ 25,358,474 Present value of 4th-year claims
Age 39: 30,132 × $1,000 × .883854 = $ 26,632,289 Present value of 5th-year claims

   Total discounted value of death
     claims   = $122,688,015

$$\$122,688,015 \div 9,373,807 = \$13.09$$

The present value of all death claims to be paid during the five-year period is, according to the assumptions, $122,688,015. Since there are 9,373,807 participants, the amount which each must contribute is obtained by dividing $122,688,015 by 9,373,807, giving $13.09, the same amount as was derived under the individual method.

To summarize, under the aggregate method, deaths are assumed to occur in exact accordance with the mortality table. The number of claims for each year of insurance is multiplied by the face amount of insurance discounted for the period the money is held. Then, the sum of the discounted yearly claims is divided by the number of entrants to give the net single premium or amount contributed by each entrant.

Whole Life Insurance

The distinctive feature of whole life insurance is that protection is provided for the whole of life. The face of the policy is payable upon the insured's death, regardless of his age at the date of death. Eventual payment of the face is a certainty, the only uncertainty being the year in which the policy will become a claim. Yet, the techniques for the computation of the net single premium are the same as those for a term policy. In fact, for purposes of premium calculation, whole life insurance is treated as term insurance expiring at the last age in the mortality table.

Under the individual approach, the net single premium for a whole life insurance policy issued at age thirty-five must reflect the probability that the insured will die during his thirty-sixth year, his thirty-seventh year, and every year up to and including his one-hundredth. Sixty-five separate probabilities are involved. To shorten the calculations, and to conserve space, only the equations for the first five and last five years are shown:

$$\text{Age 35: } \frac{23,529}{9,373,807} \times \$1,000 \times .975610 = \$2.45 \quad \text{Cost of 1st year's mortality}$$

Age 36: $\dfrac{24,685}{9,373,807} \times \$1,000 \times .951814 = \$\quad 2.51$ Cost of 2nd year's mortality

Age 37: $\dfrac{26,112}{9,373,807} \times \$1,000 \times .928599 = \$\quad 2.59$ Cost of 3rd year's mortality

Age 38: $\dfrac{27,991}{9,373,807} \times \$1,000 \times .905951 = \$\quad 2.70$ Cost of 4th year's mortality

Age 39: $\dfrac{30,132}{9,373,807} \times \$1,000 \times .883854 = \$\quad 2.84$ Cost of 5th year's mortality

. . . .

Age 95: $\dfrac{34,128}{9,373,807} \times \$1,000 \times .221740 = \$\quad 0.81$ Cost of 61st year's mortality

Age 96: $\dfrac{25,250}{9,373,807} \times \$1,000 \times .216332 = \$\quad 0.58$ Cost of 62nd year's mortality

Age 97: $\dfrac{18,456}{9,373,807} \times \$1,000 \times .211055 = \$\quad 0.42$ Cost of 63rd year's mortality

Age 98: $\dfrac{12,916}{9,373,807} \times \$1,000 \times .205908 = \$\quad 0.28$ Cost of 64th year's mortality

Age 99: $\dfrac{6,415}{9,373,807} \times \$1,000 \times .200886 = \underline{\$\quad 0.14}$ Cost of 65th year's mortality

Net single premium = $\$420.13$

The sum $420.13 represents the present value of the separate probabilities that the insured will die in each of the years from age thirty-five to ninety-nine, inclusive. Despite the fact that the 1958 C.S.O. Table assumes that all persons alive at age ninety-nine will die during the ensuing year, the cost of mortality during the insured's one-hundredth year in the above tabulation is the lowest of all the years. Two factors account for this curious result. In the first place, the probability that a person now aged thirty-five will survive to age ninety-nine, to die during the following year, is remote, only 6,415 persons out of 9,373,807 achieving that distinction. In the second place, if the individual now thirty-five should survive the next sixty-four years and die during his one-hundredth year, the sum deposited at the inception of the contract to hedge this possibility would earn interest for sixty-five years. The net result is that only $0.14 per policyholder need be set aside at age thirty-five to take care of death claims that occur at age ninety-nine.

One other interesting—and significant—fact should be noted. Inasmuch as it is a certainty that a whole life policy will sooner or later become a claim, the net single premium at any age of issue would be $1,000 per $1,000 of insurance were it not for the discount factor— the earnings on the advance deposit. The entire process of calculating the probabilities that death will occur at each of the possible ages is for the sole purpose of determining the amount of interest that will be earned on the advance premium before such premium and accumulated interest will have to be paid out in settlement of the death claim.

The aggregate approach illustrates more forcefully, perhaps, the impact of the discount factor on the net single premium for a whole life policy. Observe, in the following illustration, how clearly is revealed the sum of money that will earn one year's interest, two years' interest, and so on. Once again, only the equations for the first five and last five years are shown:

Age 35: 23,528 × $1,000 × .975610 = $ 22,954,146 Present value of 1st-year claims
Age 36: 24,685 × $1,000 × .951814 = $ 23,495,529 Present value of 2nd-year claims
Age 37: 26,112 × $1,000 × .928599 = $ 24,247,577 Present value of 3rd-year claims
Age 38: 27,991 × $1,000 × .905951 = $ 25,358,474 Present value of 4th-year claims
Age 39: 30,132 × $1,000 × .883854 = $ 26,632,289 Present value of 5th-year claims

. . . .

Age 95: 34,128 × $1,000 × .221740 = $ 7,567,543 Present value of 61st-year claims
Age 96: 25,250 × $1,000 × .216332 = $ 5,462,383 Present value of 62nd-year claims
Age 97: 18,456 × $1,000 × .211055 = $ 3,895,231 Present value of 63rd-year claims
Age 98: 12,916 × $1,000 × .205908 = $ 2,659,508 Present value of 64th-year claims
Age 99: 6,415 × $1,000 × .200886 = $ 1,288,684 Present value of 65th-year claims

Total discounted value of death
claims = $3,938,192,413

$3,938,192,413 ÷ 9,373,807 = $420.13 Net single premium

Sums set aside for the payment of the claims of those persons who will die during the fifth year, for example, will earn only 13 cents on the dollar, while the money destined for payment of claims of the sixty-fifth year will earn $4.98 on the dollar. The greatest number of deaths, according to the tabular assumptions, will occur at age seventy-six, when 303,014 claims will be filed; and each dollar set aside at the outset for payment of these claims will amount to $2.82 at that time. Truly, compound interest is a potent cost-reducing factor.

Endowment Insurance

An endowment insurance contract promises to pay the face of the policy if the insured should die during the term of the contract, or a like sum if he should survive to the end of the term. In the earlier analysis of the endowment insurance contract, it was pointed out that such a contract is a combination of a pure endowment, which pays only if the insured survives the specified period of years, and term insurance, which pays only if the insured does not survive the prescribed period of time. As might be expected, the net single premium for the endowment insurance contract is the sum of the respective net single premiums for the pure endowment and term insurance contracts. In order to use a different set of probabilities, the net single premium for a $1,000 ten-year endowment contract issued at age forty-five will be derived.

The first step is to calculate the premium for a ten-year term contract issued at age forty-five. There are no new principles involved in this step. The net single premium is the sum of the separate discounted probabilities that a person now forty-five will die during the next ten years or before the attainment of age fifty-five. A listing of the equations for each of the ten years is presented in the following illustration:

Age 45: $\dfrac{48,412}{9,048,999} \times \$1,000 \times .975610 = \$\ 5.22$ Cost of 1st year's mortality

Age 46: $\dfrac{52,473}{9,048,999} \times \$1,000 \times .951814 = \$\ 5.52$ Cost of 2nd year's mortality

Age 47: $\dfrac{56,910}{9,048,999} \times \$1,000 \times .928599 = \$\ 5.84$ Cost of 3rd year's mortality

Age 48: $\dfrac{61,794}{9,048,999} \times \$1,000 \times .905951 = \$\ 6.19$ Cost of 4th year's mortality

Age 49: $\dfrac{67,104}{9,048,999} \times \$1,000 \times .883854 = \$\ 6.55$ Cost of 5th year's mortality

Age 50: $\dfrac{72,902}{9,048,999} \times \$1,000 \times .862297 = \$\ 6.95$ Cost of 6th year's mortality

Age 51: $\dfrac{79,160}{9,048,999} \times \$1,000 \times .841265 = \$\ 7.36$ Cost of 7th year's mortality

Age 52: $\dfrac{85,758}{9,048,999} \times \$1,000 \times .820747 = \$\ 7.78$ Cost of 8th year's mortality

Age 53: $\dfrac{92,832}{9,048,999} \times \$1,000 \times .800728 = \$\ 8.21$ Cost of 9th year's mortality

Age 54: $\dfrac{100,337}{9,048,999} \times \$1,000 \times .781198 = \$\ 8.66$ Cost of 10th year's mortality

$$\text{Net single premium} = \$68.28$$

The calculation of the net single premium for the pure endowment does present a new principle. Here, there is only one contingency insured against—the probability that the insured will survive the ten-year period. If the insured dies within this period, the company has no obligation under the pure endowment. Therefore, the probability that the face amount of the pure endowment will have to be paid is measured by a fraction, the numerator of which is the number of persons living at age fifty-five, or 8,331,317, and the denominator of which is the number of persons living at age forty-five, or 9,048,999. Since the premium is paid at the beginning of the period and the claim is paid at the end of the period, the sum will be discounted for ten years. Hence, the equation for the derivation of the net single premium for a ten-year pure endowment issued at age forty-five is simply:

$$\frac{8,331,317}{9,048,999} \times \$1,000 \times .781198 = \$719.24$$

Once the net single premium has been derived for each of the two elements of the endowment insurance contract, the net single premium for the combined contract is obtained by adding the two sums together. Thus:

Net single premium, 10-year term policy, at age 45............$ 68.28
Net single premium, 10-year pure endowment, at age 45........$719.24
Net single premium, 10-year endowment insurance contract......$787.52

It is interesting to note that the pure endowment portion of the premium for the combined contract reflects two cost-reducing factors: compound interest and the "benefit of survivorship." If nothing were involved except compound interest, the $719.24 deposited with the company at the beginning of the period would amount to only $719.24 × 1.280085, or $920.69, at the end of the ten-year period. Yet, the policy promises $1,000 if the insured is alive on that date. From what source does the difference $1,000 − $920.69, or $79.31 come? The difference is attributable to the benefit of survivorship, which is the prorata share of each survivor in a fund created by the premiums, plus accumulated interest, of those persons, who failed to survive the period. According to the 1958 C.S.O. Table, 717,682 persons out of 9,048,999 alive at age forty-five die within the next ten years. Each of those persons deposits $719.24 with the company at the inception of the contract, which sum is not returnable in the event of death. By the end of the period, each deposit has accumulated to $920.69, creating an aggregate fund of $920.69 × 717,682, or $660,762,641, forfeited by those who died and available to the survivors. Divided by the number of survivors, 8,331,317, the fund yields $79.31 per survivor. This sum added to the accumulation of $920.69 provides the $1,000 promised under the contract.

The benefit of survivorship may be computed separately by dividing the number of living at age forty-five who contributed premiums by the survivors at age fifty-five who shared them. Thus, $\frac{9,048,999}{8,331,317} =$ 1.08614, and $920.69 × 1.08614 = \$1,000$, as before. Interest and survivorship may be combined: $1.08614 × 1.28008 = 1.39035$, and $1.39035 × \$719.24 = \$1,000$.

It may be observed that while interest is assumed to be credited at the annual rate of 2.5 per cent, in this case the benefit of survivorship boosts the total gain to 39.0 per cent—that is, from $719.24 to $1,000, over the ten-year period.

This concept underlies all contracts which provide benefits based upon survival to the end of a specified period. The longer the period and the higher the rate of mortality, the greater the benefit of survivorship. For purposes of comparison, it might be pointed out that the benefit of survivorship under a twenty-year endowment issued at age forty-five is $248.48 per survivor.

The benefit of survivorship can be demonstrated only by reference to a group of insured persons. For a demonstration of how the entire premium for an endowment insurance contract can be derived by the group or aggregate approach, the following exhibit is presented:

```
Age 45:  48,412 × $1,000 × .975610 = $   47,231,231 Present value of 1st-year claims
Age 46:  52,473 × $1,000 × .951814 = $   49,944,536 Present value of 2d-year claims
Age 47:  56,910 × $1,000 × .928599 = $   52,846,569 Present value of 3rd-year claims
Age 48:  61,794 × $1,000 × .905951 = $   55,982,336 Present value of 4th-year claims
Age 49:  67,104 × $1.000 × .883854 = $   59,310,139 Present value of 5th-year claims
Age 50:  72,902 × $1,000 × .862297 = $   62,863,176 Present value of 6th-year claims
Age 51:  79,160 × $1,000 × .841265 = $   66,594,537 Present value of 7th-year claims
Age 52:  85,758 × $1,000 × .820747 = $   70,385,621 Present value of 8th-year claims
Age 53:  92,832 × $1,000 × .800728 = $   74,333,182 Present value of 9th-year claims
Age 54: 100,337 × $1,000 × .781198 = $   78,383,064 Present value of 10th-year claims
```

Present value of death claims = $ 617,874,391

Age 55: 8,331,317 × $1,000 × .781198 = $6,508,408,178   Present value of benefits to survivors

Present value of death and survivor benefits = $7,126,282,569

$7,126,282,569 ÷ 9,048,999 = $ 787.52   Net single premium

Whole Life Annuity

A whole life annuity is a contract which provides periodic payments of a specified amount throughout the remaining lifetime of a designated individual, called the "annuitant." The payments may be made annually, semiannually, quarterly, or monthly, depending upon the provisions of the contract. Payments may begin one payment interval from the date of purchase, in which event the contract is called an *immediate* whole life annuity; or they may commence at a date more distant than one payment interval from the date of purchase, in which event the contract is properly called a *deferred* whole life annuity. Attention will first be directed to the calculation of premiums for an immediate whole life annuity.

Immediate Whole Life Annuity. From the standpoint of premium computations, a life annuity is nothing but a series of pure endowments. A pure endowment provides a benefit only if the insured survives to the end of a specified period; payments under a life annuity are made only if the annuitant is alive on the date the payment is due.

TABLE 13

1955 AMERICAN ANNUITY TABLE*

AGE x		NUMBER LIVING l_x	NUMBER DYING d_x	RATE OF MORTALITY PER 1,000 $1,000q_x$	PRESENT VALUE OF $1 PER ANNUM a_x AT 3% INTEREST
Male	Female				
5	10	10,000,000	3,700	.370	28.658
6	11	9,996,300	3,799	.380	28.529
7	12	9,992,501	3,897	.390	28.396
8	13	9,988,604	3,995	.400	28.259
9	14	9,984,609	4,094	.410	28.118
10	15	9,980,515	4,192	.420	27.974
11	16	9,976,323	4,290	.430	27.825
12	17	9,972,033	4,398	.441	27.672
13	18	9,967,635	4,505	.452	27.515
14	19	9,963,130	4,613	.463	27.353
15	20	9,958,517	4,730	.475	27.187
16	21	9,953,787	4,857	.488	27.016
17	22	9,948,930	4,994	.502	26.840
18	23	9,943,936	5,141	.517	26.659
19	24	9,938,795	5,307	.534	26.473
20	25	9,933,488	5,493	.553	26.282
21	26	9,927,995	5,699	.574	26.085
22	27	9,922,296	5,924	.597	25.883
23	28	9,916,372	6,168	.622	25.675
24	29	9,910,204	6,432	.649	25.462
25	30	9,903,772	6,725	.679	25.243
26	31	9,897,047	7,047	.712	25.018
27	32	9,890,000	7,408	.749	24.787
28	33	9,882,592	7,817	.791	24.550
29	34	9,874,775	8,285	.839	24.306
30	35	9,866,490	8,811	.893	24.056
31	36	9,857,679	9,394	.953	23.800
32	37	9,848,285	10,045	1.020	23.538
33	38	9,838,240	10,773	1.095	23.269
34	39	9,827,467	11,587	1.179	22.993
35	40	9,815,880	12,496	1.273	22.711
36	41	9,803,384	13,509	1.378	22.422
37	42	9,789,875	14,636	1.495	22.126
38	43	9,775,239	15,875	1.624	21.824
39	44	9,759,364	17,245	1.767	21.515
40	45	9,742,119	18,754	1.925	21.200
41	46	9,723,365	20,409	2.099	20.878
42	47	9,702,956	22,220	2.290	20.550
43	48	9,680,736	24,192	2.499	20.215
44	49	9,656,544	26,333	2.727	19.874
45	50	9,630,211	28,650	2.975	19.526
46	51	9,601,561	31,147	3.244	19.171
47	52	9,570,414	33,831	3.535	18.811
48	53	9,536,583	36,706	3.849	18.444
49	54	9,499,877	39,776	4.187	18.071
50	55	9,460,101	43,043	4.550	17.691
51	56	9,417,058	46,549	4.943	17.305
52	57	9,370,509	50,395	5.378	16.913
53	58	9,320,114	54,690	5.868	16.514
54	59	9,265,424	59,558	6.428	16.110

*As published in the *Transactions of the Society of Actuaries*, Vol. VIII (1956), pp. 144–5, this table showed number living and number dying to four decimal places up to male age ninety-one and up to eight decimal places at the extreme old ages. To simplify the presentation in this table and the premium calculations, the decimal has been moved four places to the right and the figures at the higher ages have been rounded.

TABLE 13 (*Continued*)

Age x Male	Age x Female	Number Living l_x	Number Dying d_x	Rate of Mortality per 1,000 $1,000q_x$	Present Value of $1 per Annum a_x at 3% Interest
55	60	9,205,866	65,113	7.073	15.701
56	61	9,140,753	71,462	7.818	15.287
57	62	9,069,291	78,703	8.678	14.870
58	63	8,990,588	86,903	9.666	14.450
59	64	8,903,685	96,000	10.782	14.029
60	65	8,807,685	105,930	12.027	13.607
61	66	8,701,755	116,612	13.401	13.186
62	67	8,585,143	127,927	14.901	12.766
63	68	8,457,216	139,764	16.526	12.348
64	69	8,317,452	152,093	18.286	11.932
65	70	8,165,359	164,875	20.192	11.519
66	71	8,000,484	178,059	22.256	11.109
67	72	7,822,425	191,579	24.491	10.703
68	73	7,630,846	205,354	26.911	10.300
69	74	7,425,492	219,282	29.531	9.903
70	75	7,206,210	233,243	32.367	9.510
71	76	6,972,967	247,094	35.436	9.123
72	77	6,725,873	260,668	38.756	8.742
73	78	6,465,205	273,776	42.346	8.368
74	79	6,191,429	286,205	46.226	8.000
75	80	5,905,224	297,724	50.417	7.639
76	81	5,607,500	308,082	54.941	7.286
77	82	5,299,418	317,016	59.821	6.941
78	83	4,982,402	324,260	65.081	6.604
79	84	4,658,142	329,550	70.747	6.275
80	85	4,328,592	332,639	76.847	5.956
81	86	3,995,953	333,306	83.411	5.645
82	87	3,662,647	331,363	90.471	5.344
83	88	3,331,284	326,669	98.061	5.051
84	89	3,004,615	319,141	106.217	4.769
85	90	2,685,474	308,768	114.977	4.495
86	91	2,376,706	295,615	124.380	4.232
87	92	2,081,091	279,836	134.466	3.978
88	93	1,801,255	261,676	145.274	3.734
89	94	1,539,579	241,469	156.841	3.499
90	95	1,298,110	219,643	169.202	3.275
91	96	1,078,467	196,701	182.389	3.060
92	97	881,766	173,206	196.431	2.855
93	98	708,560	149,756	211.355	2.659
94	99	558,802	126,952	227.186	2.473
95	100	431,850	105,349	243.947	2.296
96	101	326,502	85,432	261.659	2.128
97	102	241,070	67,582	280.342	1.969
98	103	173,488	52,049	300.015	1.818
99	104	121,439	38,945	320.696	1.676
100	105	82,494	28,246	342.402	1.541
101	106	54,248	19,804	365.150	1.413
102	107	34,439	13,395	388.956	1.293
103	108	21,044	8,709	413.836	1.179
104	109	12,335	5,425	439.806	1.071
105	110	6,910	3,226	466.881	.970
106	111	3,684	1,824	495.076	.874
107	112	1,860	975	524.406	.782
108	113	885	498	554.886	.695
109	114	394	231	587.551	.607
110	115	162	101	624.586	.516
111	116	61	41	670.361	.416
112	117	20	15	733.619	.301
113	118	5	4	831.839	.163
114	119	1	1	1000.000	

If the contract under consideration were a ten-year *temporary* life annuity, providing an annual income of $1,000, it could properly be regarded as a series of pure endowments, the first maturing one year hence, the second two years, and so on, the last maturing ten years hence. The whole life annuity differs from the temporary life annuity only in that the payments continue as long as the annuitant lives. If the terminal age for an annuitant is assumed to be 114, a whole life annuity purchased at age sixty-five would be the equivalent of a series of pure endowments, the first maturing at age sixty-six and the last at age 114.

In view of the superior longevity of annuitants, annuity premiums cannot safely be calculated on the basis of the same mortality table used in the derivation of life insurance premiums. A table must be used which reflects the peculiar experience of annuitants. Unless otherwise stated, annuity calculations in this chapter will be based upon the 1955 American Annuity Table, reproduced in Table 13, with interest at 3 per cent. Although the great majority of annuity contracts provide monthly income, the premiums derived herein will be the *rates* per $100 of annual income. No distinction will be made between male and female annuitants, all calculations being based on male ages.

The first annuity contract to be considered is an immediate whole life annuity purchased at age sixty-five to provide $100 per year, with the first payment to begin at age sixty-six and no payments to be made beyond the date of the annuitant's death. It will be recognized that this contract, in addition to its other characteristics, is a pure annuity.

The probability that the first payment of $100 will be made is $\frac{8,000,484}{8,165,359}$, the numerator indicating the number of persons alive at age sixty-six and the denominator the number alive at age sixty-five. Since one year will elapse before the payment is made, if at all, the sum set aside at the time of purchase can be discounted at 3 per cent. The present value of the first payment, therefore, is determined as follows:

$$\frac{8,000,484}{8,165,359} \times \$100 \times .970874 = \$95.13$$

The probability that the second payment will be made is the probability that a person now aged sixty-five will be alive at age sixty-seven.

This contingent payment can be discounted for two years. The present value of the second payment can be derived as shown in the following equation:

$$\frac{7,822,425}{8,165,359} \times \$100 \times .942596 = \$90.30$$

Observe that the denominator does not change. The determination of the net single premium for the entire series of contingent payments involves forty-four separate equations, of which the first five and last five are shown below:

Age 66: $\dfrac{8,000,484}{8,165,359} \times \$100 \times .970874 = \$\quad 95.13$ Present value of 1st annuity payment

Age 67: $\dfrac{7,822,425}{8,165,359} \times \$100 \times .942596 = \$\quad 90.30$ Present value of 2d annuity payment

Age 68: $\dfrac{7,630,846}{8,165,359} \times \$100 \times .915142 = \$\quad 85.52$ Present value of 3d annuity payment

Age 69: $\dfrac{7,425,492}{8,165,359} \times \$100 \times .888487 = \$\quad 80.80$ Present value of 4th annuity payment

Age 70: $\dfrac{7,206,210}{8,165,359} \times \$100 \times .862609 = \$\quad 76.13$ Present value of 5th annuity payment

. . . .

Age 110: $\dfrac{162}{8,165,359} \times \$100 \times .264439 = \$\quad 0.00$ Present value of 40th annuity payment

Age 111: $\dfrac{61}{8,165,359} \times \$100 \times .256737 = \$\quad 0.00$ Present value of 41st annuity payment

Age 112: $\dfrac{20}{8,165,359} \times \$100 \times .249259 = \$\quad 0.00$ Present value of 42d annuity payment

Age 113: $\dfrac{5}{8,165,359} \times \$100 \times .241999 = \$\quad 0.00$ Present value of 43d annuity payment

Age 114: $\dfrac{1}{8,165,359} \times \$100 \times .234950 = \$\quad \underline{0.00}$ Present value of 44th annuity payment

Present value of all payments or
net single premium = $1,151.88

Thus, in consideration of $1,151.88 paid in a single sum at the inception of the contract, an insurance company could afford to promise a person now aged sixty-five an income of $100 per year as long as he lives, the first payment being made at age sixty-six. This obviously presupposes that the company is entering into a sufficient number of such contracts to experience average results.

The net single premium for such an annuity can also be computed on an aggregate basis. The first five and the last five equations of the process are given herewith:

Age 66: 8,000,484 × $100 × .970874 = $ 776,746,190.30 Present value of 1st-year payments

Age 67: 7,822,425 × $100 × .942596 = $ 737,338,651.53 Present value of 2d-year payments

Age 68: 7,630,846 × $100 × .915142 = $ 698,330,767.01 Present value of 3d-year payments

Age 69: 7,425,492 × $100 × .888487 = $ 659,745,311.06 Present value of 4th-year payments

Age 70: 7,206,210 × $100 × .862609 = $ 621,614,160.19 Present value of 5th-year payments

. . . .

Age 110:   162 × $100 × .264439 = $ 4,283.91 Present value of 40th-year payments

Age 111:   61 × $100 × .256737 = $ 1,566.10 Present value of 41st-year payments

Age 112:   20 × $100 × .249259 = $ 498.52 Present value of 42d-year payments

Age 113:   5 × $100 × .241999 = $ 121.00 Present value of 43d-year payments

Age 114:   1 × $100 × .234950 = $ 23.50 Present value of 44th-year payments

Present value of all payments = $9,405,513,724.92
$9,405,513,724.92 ÷ 8,165,359 = $ 1,151.88 Net single premium

Once the net single premium for an immediate pure annuity has been derived, it is a simple matter to compute the premium for an annuity which promises to continue the payments for a specified number of years, whether the annuitant survives or not. The only modification that needs to be introduced is to substitute 1, or certainty, for the probabilities of survival used in the original equations. There is no contingency involved; the payments will be made whether the annuitant lives or dies. The only cost-reducing influence in the picture is the discount factor.

To take a simple example, consider an annuity purchased at age sixty-five to provide an income of $100 per year, with the payments guaranteed for five years. It will be recognized that this is a combination of a temporary annuity and a deferred whole life annuity. The cost of the first five payments—i.e., the temporary annuity element of the contract—would be determined as follows:

Age 66: 1' × $100 × .970874 = $ 97.09 Present value of 1st annuity payment
Age 67: 1 × $100 × .942596 = $ 94.26 Present value of 2d annuity payment
Age 68: 1 × $100 × .915142 = $ 91.51 Present value of 3d annuity payment
Age 69: 1 × $100 × .888487 = $ 88.85 Present value of 4th annuity payment
Age 70: 1 × $100 × .862609 = $ 86.26 Present value of 5th annuity payment
Present value of annuity
   certain   = $457.97

All payments following the fifth would stem from the deferred whole life annuity and hence would be dependent on the probability of survival. Their present value would be determined in the manner previously described. For example:

Age 71: $\dfrac{6,972,967}{8,165,359} \times \$100 = .837484 = \$71.52$ Present value of 6th annuity payment

Age 72: $\dfrac{6,725,873}{8,165,359} \times \$100 \times .813092 = \$66.98$ Present value of 7th annuity payment

and so on to age 114.

Under the aggregate method, 8,165,359 would be used as the number of payments during each of the first five years in place of the actual number of persons alive at the appropriate ages. The normal procedure would then be used, beginning with the sixth payment.

The net single premium for a *temporary* life annuity is calculated according to the same principles underlying the previous calculations. The only change is that the computations end with the age at which the last payment is to be made. For a ten-year life annuity issued at age seventy, for instance, the first probability would be the chance of survival to age seventy-one, or

$$\frac{6,972,967}{7,206,210},$$

and the last probability would be the chance that the annuitant would survive to age eighty, or

$$\frac{4,328,592}{7,206,210}.$$

Deferred Whole Life Annuity. It was found above that $1,151.88 must be on hand at age sixty-five to provide a life income of $100 per year, with no minimum number of payments guaranteed. This amount may be turned over to the insurance company in a single sum at the purchaser's age sixty-five, or the present value of that amount may be deposited with the company in a single sum some years prior to the time the income is to commence. More likely yet, it might be accumulated through a series of periodic deposits with the insurance company before the income is to begin. If the consideration for the life income is deposited with the company in advance of the annuity starting date,[4] either in a single sum or through periodic payments, a modification of the premium is required. The adjustment can be most clearly explained in terms of a nonrefund annuity purchased with a single premium some years prior to the annuity starting date. Specifically,

---

[4] The annuity starting date is the date the annuitant "enters on" the annuity and not the date on which the first payment is due, unless the two dates happen to coincide.

assume that a person aged thirty purchases an annuity contract which will pay him an annual income of $100 for life beginning at age sixty-five, with nothing being paid or refunded in the event of his death before age sixty-five. Note that in this example, the income is to begin one year earlier than in the example illustrating the derivation of the premium for an immediate annuity.

There are two ways to calculate the premium for this deferred annuity. The first, sometimes called the "pure endowment approach," consists of calculating the net single premium for an *immediate* life annuity providing $100 per year, with the first payment at sixty-five, and then discounting it to its value at age thirty in one operation. The second treats each annuity payment as a separate deferred annuity, to be discounted to age thirty.

It has been determined that a sum of $1,151.88 would have to be on hand at age sixty-five to provide a life income of $100 per year beginning at age sixty-six. If $100 were added to this sum, the payments could begin at age sixty-five, the additional amount taking care of the first payment which would be made on the effective date of the contract, with no interest being earned and no life contingency involved. Therefore, the present value at age sixty-five of an annuity which will provide $100 immediately and $100 per year thereafter as long as the annuitant lives is $1,251.88.

Something less than this amount, however, need be deposited with the company at the purchaser's age thirty. In the first place, the sum deposited at age thirty will earn interest for thirty-five years. In the second place, there is a substantial probability that the purchaser will not survive to age sixty-five to begin realizing on his income. The sums forfeited by those who fail to survive to that age reduce, through the benefit of survivorship, the amount which each annuitant must pay at the outset. Therefore, the sum that must be deposited with the company at age thirty is determined as follows:

$$\frac{8,165,359}{9,866,490} \times \$1,251.88 \times .355383 = \$368.19, \text{ or the net single premium}$$

Under the second method mentioned above, each payment would have to be discounted to age thirty and multiplied by the probability of surviving from age thirty to the particular age at which the payment is due. For example, the first payment of $100 would be discounted for thirty-five years and multiplied by the probability of the annuitant's surviving to age sixty-five. The second payment would be discounted for thirty-six years and multiplied by the probability of survival to sixty-six, and so on to age 114. The first five and last five equations of the process are set forth below:

Age 65: $\dfrac{8,165,359}{9,866,490} \times \$100 \times .355383 = \$\ 29.41$ Present value of 1st annuity payment

Age 66: $\dfrac{8,000,484}{9,866,490} \times \$100 \times .345032 = \$\ 27.98$ Present value of 2d annuity payment

Age 67: $\dfrac{7,822,425}{9,866,490} \times \$100 \times .334983 = \$\ 26.56$ Present value of 3d annuity payment

Age 68: $\dfrac{7,630,846}{9,866,490} \times \$100 \times .325226 = \$\ 25.15$ Present value of 4th annuity payment

Age 69: $\dfrac{7,425,492}{9,866,490} \times \$100 \times .315754 = \$\ 23.76$ Present value of 5th annuity payment

. . . .

Age 110: $\dfrac{162}{9,866,490} \times \$100 \times .093977 = \$\ \ 0.00$ Present value of 41st annuity payment

Age 111: $\dfrac{61}{9,866,490} \times \$100 \times .091240 = \$\ \ 0.00$ Present value of 42d annuity payment

Age 112: $\dfrac{20}{9,866,490} \times \$100 \times .088582 = \$\ \ 0.00$ Present value of 43d annuity payment

Age 113: $\dfrac{5}{9,866,490} \times \$100 \times .086002 = \$\ \ 0.00$ Present value of 44th annuity payment

Age 114: $\dfrac{1}{9,866,490} \times \$100 \times .083497 = \$\ \ 0.00$ Present value of 45th annuity payment

Present value of all payments or
net single premium = $368.19

The latter method of computing the net single premium can be illustrated by the aggregate approach. As usual, only the first five and last five equations are given:

Age 65: $8,165,359 \times \$100 \times .355383 = \$\ \ 290,182,977.75$ Present value of 1st-year payments

Age 66: $8,000,484 \times \$100 \times .345032 = \$\ \ 276,042,299.55$ Present value of 2d-year payments

Age 67: $7,822,425 \times \$100 \times .334983 = \$\ \ 262,037,939.38$ Present value of 3d-year payments

Age 68: $7,630,846 \times \$100 \times .325226 = \$\ \ 248,174,952.12$ Present value of 4th-year payments

Age 69: $7,425,492 \times \$100 \times .315754 = \$\ \ 234,462,880.10$ Present value of 5th-year payments

. . . .

Age 110: $162 \times \$100 \times .093977 = \$\ \ 1,522.43$ Present value of 41st-year payments

Age 111: $61 \times \$100 \times .091240 = \$\ \ 556.56$ Present value of 42d-year payments

Age 112: $20 \times \$100 \times .088582 = \$\ \ 177.16$ Present value of 43d-year payments

Age 113: $5 \times \$100 \times .086002 = \$\ \ 43.00$ Present value of 44th-year payments

Age 114: $1 \times \$100 \times .083497 = \$\ \ 8.35$ Present value of 45th-year payments

Present value of all payments = $3,632,742,953.10
$3,632,742,953.10 ÷ 9,866,490 = \$\ \ \ \ 368.19$ Net single premium

NET LEVEL PREMIUM

Relatively few life insurance contracts are purchased with single premiums. There are two very cogent reasons why this should be so. In the first place, few persons can accumulate a sufficiently large fund of savings to buy an adequate amount of life insurance on a single-premium basis. To attempt to do so would run counter to the prevailing practice in the field of consumer finance, where installment purchases have become the pattern. Entirely apart from the trends of the times, it seems peculiarly appropriate that life insurance should be financed on an installment basis. Since the fundamental purpose of life insurance is to provide protection against the loss of income from personal efforts—which, by definition, is received in periodic installments—it is only logical that the cost of the protective mechanism should be borne on a current basis out of the income that is being protected.

A second reason why most persons prefer installment financing of life insurance is the lower cost in the event of the early death of the insured. One monthly premium will purchase as much life insurance protection as a single premium—but not for as long a period, obviously. If the insured should die within a few years after the single-sum purchase of a life insurance policy, the cost would be many times greater than it would have been had annual, or more frequent, payments been made. Under an ordinary life policy issued at age thirty-five, a policyholder would have to remit twenty-four annual payments before his total outlay would equal the amount of the single premium. Ignoring interest, the annual premium method is cheaper for a policyholder aged thirty-five if he should die within twenty-three years after taking out the policy. With interest this period would be increased to almost forty years. On the other hand, if such policyholder should live beyond the period, he would pay more on the annual premium basis than under the single-premium arrangement; and with each passing year, the disparity would become greater.

Concept of the Level Annual Premium

If a policyholder is to be given the choice of paying for his insurance by a single premium or by a level annual premium, the latter must be determined in such a manner that the financial position of the company would be unaffected by the method chosen by the policyholder. This means that the net annual premium must be the mathematical equivalent of the net single premium. To be the mathematical equivalent of the net single premium, the net level premium must reflect (1) the possibility that the insured may die prematurely, with the attendant loss to the company of future premiums; and (2) the smaller sum which will be invested at compound interest, with the resultant loss of interest earnings to the company. Expressed in positive terms, the net level premium must reflect (1) the probability that the insured will survive to pay premiums and (2) the period during which the premiums will be invested at compound interest.

In considering this problem, actuaries noted the basic similarities between a life annuity and an annual premium. Both are paid annually during the lifetime of a designated person, or for a limited number of years during the person's lifetime; both cease upon the death of the designated person (except for certain types of refund annuities) and both are discounted to reflect interest earnings of the company. The only significant difference between the two is the date on which the first payment is due. Under an immediate life annuity, the first benefit payment is due one year from the date of purchase; under a life insurance contract, on the other hand, the first annual premium payment is due on the effective date of the contract. Therefore, a series of annual premiums is the equivalent of a life annuity of the ordinary variety plus one payment made immediately. In order to distinguish an annual premium from an ordinary life annuity, the former has been designated a *life annuity due*. To be more precise, if the level annual premium is to be paid throughout the lifetime of the insured—as is characteristic of the ordinary life contract—the premium is referred to as a *whole life annuity due*. If the premium is to be paid only during a specified period of time—as is true of term policies, limited-payment whole life policies, and endowments—the premium is known as a *temporary life annuity due*.

It should be understood that a life annuity due is only a concept, not a contract, and is used only in certain insurance calculations, prime examples of which are the conversion of a net single premium into a net level premium and the payment of insurance proceeds under a life income option, where the first payment is due upon maturity of the contract.

In attempting to arrive at the net level annual premium which is the equivalent of the net single premium for a particular policy, the present value of a life annuity due of $1 for the premium-paying period is determined. This technique is identical to the one employed in the computation of values under the various compound interest series. It consists of calculating any value under consideration on the basis of unity, or 1, and then—through the use of simple proportion —obtaining the corresponding value of a larger integer. Once the present value of a life annuity due of $1 is known, it is a simple matter to determine the precise annuity whose present value would be equivalent to the net single premium. This is accomplished by dividing the net single premium by the present value of the appropriate life annuity due of $1.

The rule for the derivation of net level annual premiums may be stated as follows: *Divide the net single premium for the policy in question by the present value of a life annuity due of $1 for the premium-paying period*. The process will be illustrated in the following pages in connection with the net single premiums heretofore derived in this chapter.

Term Insurance

It was found earlier that the net single premium for a five-year term policy issued at age thirty-five is $13.09. What level annual premium paid at the inception of the contract and on the next four anniversary dates, if the insured then be living, is the equivalent of $13.09? Following the rule stated above, the present value of a temporary life annuity of $1 for a term of four years plus $1 due immediately must be determined as of age thirty-five. The 1958 C.S.O. Table is used for this calculation, rather than the 1955 American Annuity Table, inasmuch as the persons involved are insurance policyholders, not annuitants. In other words, the same mortality and interest assumptions must be used to determine the present value of the annual premiums as are used to determine the present value of benefits. Since the present value of an annuity due calculated according to the 1958 C.S.O. Table is smaller than one based on the 1955 American Annuity Table, the 1958 C.S.O. basis results in higher premiums than would the 1955 American Annuity Table. The present value is computed in the following manner:

Age 35: $1 due immediately $= \$1.000000$ Present value of 1st payment

Age 36: $\dfrac{9,350,279}{9,373,807} \times \$1 \times .975610 = \$0.973161$ Present value of 2d payment

Age 37: $\dfrac{9,325,594}{9,373,807} \times \$1 \times .951814 = \$0.946919$ Present value of 3d payment

Age 38: $\dfrac{9,299,482}{9,373,807} \times \$1 \times .928599 = \$0.921236$ Present value of 4th payment

Age 39: $\dfrac{9,271,491}{9,373,807} \times \$1 \times .905951 = \underline{\$0.896062}$ Present value of 5th payment

Present value of all payments $= \$4.737378$

The alternative process—i.e., the aggregate approach—would appear as follows:

```
Age 35: 9,373,807 × $1 × 1.000000 = $ 9,373,807  Present value of 1st payment
Age 36: 9,350,279 × $1 ×  .975610 = $ 9,122,226  Present value of 2d payment
Age 37: 9,325,594 × $1 ×  .951814 = $ 8,876,231  Present value of 3d payment
Age 38: 9,299,482 × $1 ×  .928599 = $ 8,635,490  Present value of 4th payment
Age 39: 9,271,491 × $1 ×  .905951 = $ 8,399,517  Present value of 5th payment
              Present value of all payments = $44,407,271
                    $44,407,271 ÷ 9,373,807 = $ 4.737378  Present value of a five-year
                                                          life annuity due of $1 at age
                                                          thirty-five
```

The foregoing computations reveal that the present value of a five-year term annuity due of $1 at age thirty-five is $4.74. This means that an annual premium of $1 for this period will purchase any policy the present value, or net single premium, of which is equal to $4.74. The net single premium for the policy in question, however, is $13.09. Hence, to determine the size of the temporary life annuity payable at age thirty-five and annually during the next four years which would be equivalent to $13.09, simply divide $13.09 by $4.74. Thus, $13.09 ÷ $4.74 = $2.76, or the net level annual premium for a five-year term policy issued at age thirty-five.

If $2.76 is multiplied by five, it will be found that the product exceeds the net single premium of $13.09. This is only a reflection of the principle, explained earlier, that the net level annual premium must make an allowance for loss of interest and the chance that the insured will die before making all the installment payments contemplated. If the net single premium is paid, the company has $13.09 on which to earn interest from the beginning; whereas under the net level premium arrangement, only $2.76 is available at the outset, and not until the fifth premium is paid does the company hold as large a fund as under the net single-premium procedure. Likewise, if the insured should die during the first policy year, the company would collect only $2.76 under the annual premium method of financing, and not until the fifth premium is paid does the company receive from the policyholder as much as it would have received in the beginning under the single-premium arrangement. The longer the period involved, the greater the disparity between the net single premium and the sum potentially payable by the insured under the annual premium arrangement.

Ordinary Life Insurance

Ordinary life insurance is that type of whole life insurance the premiums for which are based on the assumption that premiums will be paid throughout the lifetime of the insured. To obtain the net level annual premium for an ordinary life policy, the net single premium for a whole life policy is divided by the present value of a *whole* life annuity due of $1. Since the whole of life is the longest premium-paying period contemplated under any policy, the present value per $1 of future premiums is greater than under any other type of policy, producing the lowest level annual premium of any policy of permanent insurance. This stands to reason, inasmuch as the net single premium for a whole life policy at any particular age is the same, irrespective of the pattern which the periodic premiums take. The longer the period over which the premiums are spread, the smaller each periodic premium will be.

The present value of a life annuity due of $1 for the whole of life at age thirty-five must take into account the probability that the insured will be alive at age thirty-six and each age thereafter to the end of the mortality table to pay the second and subsequent premiums. The first five and last five computations are shown below:

Age 35: $1 due immediately $= \$\ 1.000000$ Present value of 1st payment

Age 36: $\dfrac{9,350,279}{9,373,807} \times \$1 \times .975610 = \$\ 0.973161$ Present value of 2d payment

Age 37: $\dfrac{9,325,594}{9,373,807} \times \$1 \times .951814 = \$\ 0.946919$ Present value of 3d payment

Age 38: $\dfrac{9,299,482}{9,373,807} \times \$1 \times .928599 = \$\ 0.921236$ Present value of 4th payment

Age 39: $\dfrac{9,271,491}{9,373,807} \times \$1 \times .905951 = \$\ 0.896062$ Present value of 5th payment

. . . .

Age 95: $\dfrac{97,165}{9,373,807} \times \$1 \times .227284 = \$\ 0.002356$ Present value of 61st payment

Age 96: $\dfrac{63,037}{9,373,807} \times \$1 \times .221740 = \$\ 0.001487$ Present value of 62d payment

Age 97: $\dfrac{37,787}{9,373,807} \times \$1 \times .216332 = \$\ 0.000872$ Present value of 63d payment

Age 98: $\dfrac{19,331}{9,373,807} \times \$1 \times .211055 = \$\ 0.000435$ Present value of 64th payment

Age 99: $\dfrac{6,415}{9,373,807} \times \$1 \times .205908 = \underline{\$\ 0.000141}$ Present value of 65th payment

Present value of all payments = $23.77

There is a chance that a person who acquires an ordinary life policy at age thirty-five will live to pay sixty-five annual premiums; and that chance, along with all the other probabilities, must be evaluated. The present value of the sixty-fifth payment is very slight, only $0.000141, but it must be taken into account. The present value of all the separate probabilities that the annual premium of $1 will be paid is $23.77.

Dividing this sum into the net single premium of $420.13 for a whole life policy issued at age thirty-five produces a net level annual premium of $17.67. Thus, $420.13 ÷ $23.77 = $17.67, the net level annual premium.

Under the aggregate approach, the present value of the whole life annuity of $1 is found as follows:

Age 35: 9,373,807 × $1 × 1.000000 = $	9,373,807	Present value of 1st payment
Age 36: 9,350,279 × $1 × .975610 = $	9,122,226	Present value of 2d payment
Age 37: 9,325,594 × $1 × .951814 = $	8,876,231	Present value of 3d payment
Age 38: 9,299,482 × $1 × .928599 = $	8,635,490	Present value of 4th payment
Age 39: 9,271,491 × $1 × .905951 = $	8,399,517	Present value of 5th payment

. . . .

Age 95:	97,165 × $1 × .227284 = $	22,084.05	Present value of 61st payment
Age 96:	63,037 × $1 × .221740 = $	13,977.82	Present value of 62d payment
Age 97:	37,787 × $1 × .216332 = $	8,174.54	Present value of 63d payment
Age 98:	19,331 × $1 × .211055 = $	4,079.90	Present value of 64th payment
Age 99:	6,415 × $1 × .205908 = $	1,320.90	Present value of 65th payment

Present value of all payments = $222,860,199.19

$222,860,199.19 ÷ 9,373,807 = $23.77   Present value of whole life annuity due of $1 at age thirty-five

Limited-Payment Life Insurance

The net single premium for a whole life policy can be spread over any desired number of years by means of the appropriate life annuity due. For example, if a policyholder, aged thirty-five, wants to pay for his policy in twenty annual installments, there is computed the present value of $1 paid immediately and on each anniversary thereafter for nineteen years, contingent on the insured's survival, the last payment being made at the insured's age fifty-four. The present value of such an annuity is $15.43. This is a smaller sum than the corresponding whole life annuity due and, divided into the same net single premium, $420.13, produces a larger level annual premium than that payable under the ordinary life policy. The level annual premium for a twenty-payment life policy issued at age thirty-five is $420.13 ÷ $15.43 = $27.23.

For a ten-payment life policy, the computations would have ended at age forty-four, in compliance with the formula previously given, yielding a present value for the temporary life annuity of $8.86. Dividing this sum into $420.13 gives a ten-payment life premium of $47.42. Finally, if the policy is to be paid up at sixty-five, the present value of a series of payments of $1 per year, extending from age thirty-five to sixty-four and contingent on the insured's survival, would be calculated.

Endowment Insurance

The net level premium for an endowment insurance policy is derived in exactly the same manner as that of any other policy. All endowment policies, of course, are limited-payment policies, in the sense that the premium is not payable for the whole of life. In the great majority of cases, premiums are payable throughout the term of an endowment insurance contract. Some long-term endowments can be purchased with a premium-paying period of shorter duration than that of the policy. The procedure for converting the net single premium into the net level annual premium is the same: Divide the net single premium by the present value of a temporary life annuity due of $1 for the premium-paying period.

It was found earlier that the net single premium for a ten-year endowment issued at age forty-five is $787.52. The present value of a ten-year temporary life annuity due of $1 at age forty-five is $8.71. The net level annual premium, therefore, is $787.52 ÷ $8.71, or $90.42.

Deferred Annuity

Deferred annuities are usually financed by means of annual— rather than single—premiums. Such premiums may be paid throughout the period of deferment or may be limited to a specified period of years. The contract may provide for return of the annuitant's premiums, with or without interest, in the event of his death before the annuity income commences; or it may provide that the company shall retain all premiums paid, there being no refund to the premium payer's estate. The annual premium in the former case does not involve life contingencies, being merely the sum of money which must be set aside annually to accumulate at an assumed rate of compound interest to a predetermined amount at a specified date, that amount being the net single premium for an immediate annuity beginning at the specified date. For example, it has been determined that $1,-151.88 must be on hand at age sixty-five to provide a life income of $100 per year, the first payment due at age sixty-six. How much would a person aged thirty have to set aside each year, including a payment on his thirtieth birthday, to accumulate a sum of $1,151.88 by his sixty-fifth birthday, assuming that such annual payments earn compound interest at the rate of 3 per cent? Under such a program, thirty-five payments would be made, the first at age thirty and the last at age sixty-four. The period of accumulation would be thirty-five years. Reference to Table 10 on page 170 discloses that at 3 per cent interest, $1 per annum, payable at the beginning of the year, will accumulate to $62.275944 at the end of thirty-five years. Therefore, by dividing $1,151.88 by $62.275944, it can be determined that $18.50 must be set aside during each of thirty-five years to accumulate the required single premium, if premiums are to be returned in caes the annuitant dies before age sixty-five.

If no refund of premiums is contemplated, the net level annual premium for a deferred annuity is computed in the same manner as for life insurance contracts, except that the value of the annuity due, like the net single premium, is calculated on the basis of the 1955 American Annuity Table. The calculation of the net level premium for a nonrefund deferred annuity purchased at thirty, with income to begin at sixty-five, would utilize a temporary life annuity due, the value of which equals the present value of $1 due immediately and thirty-four subsequent annual payments of $1 contingent on survival, the final payment being due at age sixty-four. The net level premium is equal to $368.19 ÷ $21.3745, or $17.23.

Premiums Paid at Intervals of Less than One Year

All of the preceding calculations in this section have been based on the assumption that annual premiums are to be paid. However, many companies permit premiums to be paid semiannually, quarterly, or monthly; and such modes of premium payment are becoming increasingly popular. It seems desirable to note the basis on which such premiums are derived.

Theoretically, premiums paid at intervals of less than one year should be calculated in precisely the same manner as annual premiums, except that the underlying probability and interest functions should be based on time units commensurate with the premium-paying intervals involved. To derive true monthly premiums, for example, the mortality table should show the rate of mortality month by month rather than annually, and claim payments should be discounted by the month instead of by the year. This scientifically accurate procedure is ruled out, however, since none of the mortality tables in existence is graded for periods of less than one year. This means that an attempt must be made to approximate the theoretically correct results through some modification of the annual premium.

It should come as no surprise that the gross annual premium is modified in such a manner as to produce a larger payment to the company than would be true if the premium were being paid annually. The usual procedure is to make a percentage addition to the annual premium, more or less arbitrary in amount, and then divide the result into the requisite number of parts. The more frequent the interval at which the premiums are to be paid, the greater the percentage addition to the annual premium. The percentages vary among the companies; but an increase of 2, 4, and 6 per cent for a semiannual, quarterly, and monthly premium, respectively, might be regarded as typical. These percentages are applied to the gross premium, or the premium actually paid by the policyholder. A collection fee, expressed as a fixed amount per premium payment but usually integrated into the over-all premium, may also be charged.

To illustrate, if the gross annual premium for an ordinary life policy issued at age thirty-five were $27.69 per $1,000, the monthly premium, exclusive of the collection fee, would be obtained by adding $1.66 ($27.69 × .06) to the gross premium of $2.45 per $1,000. The quarterly premium would be derived by adding $1.11 ($27.69 × .04) to the gross premium and dividing the result, $28.80, by four, giving a quarterly premium of $7.20. Finally, $0.55 ($27.69 × .02) would be added to the gross premium and the result divided by two to arrive at the semiannual premium, which would be $14.12 per $1,000. If a collection fee is charged, the foregoing premiums might be increased, for example, by about fifty cents.[5]

The companies justify the higher rate on premiums paid more frequently than annually on several grounds. The primary justification lies in the greater administrative expense involved. In the extreme case, twelve collections must be processed and accounted for in contrast to the one that would be required under the annual premium arrangement. The collection fee is intended to cover this additional expense. There is also loss of interest due to the assumption in the computation of annual premiums that the premium is paid at the beginning of the year and earns interest for the whole year. Under the monthly premium basis, $11/24$ of one year's interest is lost; and even on

---

[5] Some companies vary the collection fee *per premium payment* by the number of payments to be made each year. For example, one company levies an additional charge per payment of 36, 56, and 52 cents for semiannual, quarterly, and monthly payments, respectively. These variations are introduced in recognition of the fact that the annual gross premium includes an allowance for one premium collection which must be taken into account in arriving at the total annual charge to be made for premium collections.

a semiannual premium basis, six months' interest on one half of the annual premium is lost, this being the equivalent of one year's loss of interest on one fourth of the annual premium. It is argued by some companies that policies paid for by semiannual, quarterly, or monthly premiums are subject to a higher lapse ratio and hence should carry a somewhat higher premium rate to compensate the company for the loss sustained thereby. Finally, if a company does not deduct unpaid "installments" of the annual premium from the proceeds payable at the time of death, the cost of this additional benefit may be included in the percentage addition to the gross premium.

In connection with the last-mentioned point, it was formerly the universal custom for companies to view semiannual, quarterly, and monthly premiums as installments of the annual premium, which was due and payable at the beginning of the policy year. It followed that if the contract should mature by reason of death before the total installments for the year were paid, the unpaid installments should be deducted from the proceeds. This adjustment was frequently not understood by the beneficiary, who felt that the company was improperly charging for insurance after the death of the insured. The desire to avoid public misunderstanding and dissatisfaction has led most companies to waive this deduction where the policy calls for it and to delete the provision from new policies being issued. If the premium for the policies in question was calculated on the assumption that the annual premium would be paid in at the beginning of the policy year, waiver of the right to collect any unpaid portions of the annual premium constitutes an additional benefit to the beneficiary, for which a charge must be made. The company can make an allowance for this additional benefit through the percentage addition to the gross premium described above or through a direct adjustment to the net premium identical in principle to the adjustment for payment of death claims before the end of the policy year in which they occur.

Premium Rates for Women

Lower mortality among female lives has long been recognized in the form of higher rates for annuities and life income settlements under life insurance policies. Until recently, however, females were granted no rate reduction for life insurance primarily on the grounds that the average amount of insurance per female life was so much lower than on male lives that the administrative costs more than offset the mortality advantage. Now that grading of premium rates by size of policy has become prevalent, the justification for ignoring the mortality differential has largely disappeared. (It is asserted by some that within each size classification or "band" established for the grading of premiums, the average amount of insurance per female life may be enough lower than for male lives to warrant overlooking some or all of the mortality differential.) Thus, most companies now give female policyholders a rate reduction in one form or the other.

The lower premiums may reflect the use of a separate set of mortality rates for female lives, such as those contained in the 1955–60 Basic Tables constructed by the Society of Actuaries or those in the reports on intercompany mortality experience published annually by the Society.[6] In that event, the policy reserves, surrender values, and dividend scales are usually the same as those applicable to policies on male lives issued at somewhat higher premium rates.[7]

The rate reduction may be produced by using mortality data undifferentiated by sex but setting female ages back an appropriate number of years, as is commonly done in connection with annuity mortality tables. With this approach, the premiums, policy reserves, surrender values, and dividends are geared directly to the setback age. Recognizing that this practice might violate the nonforfeiture laws of some states, the National Association of Insurance Commissioners, when promulgating the 1958 C.S.O. Table, recommended that the companies in computing policy reserves and surrender values be permitted to use an age for female lives not more than three years younger than the actual age. A number of states have acted on this recommendation, and the use of a three-year age setback for female lives has become increasingly common.

---

[6] These reports have separated the data for male and female lives since 1957.

[7] The amount of the premium reduction for female lives can be determined by inserting female mortality rates in an asset share computation which uses the same policy reserves, surrender values, and dividend scales as those applicable to male lives and which in all other respects is identical to the model for male lives. The use of the same dividend scale assumes that the margins in the female mortality rates are the same as those in the comparable male rates.

CHAPTER XI

The
Reserve

THE CALCULATION of a net single premium involves an equation, one side of which represents the present value of the benefits promised under the contract and the other the sum of money that must be on hand to provide the benefits. At the inception of the contract, the two sides of the equation are in balance. Moreover, the net single premium can be converted into a series of net level premiums without impairing the balance of the equation. However, once the contract has run for one or more premium-paying periods, the situation is changed. The present value of future benefits and the present value of future net premiums are no longer equal. As the years go by, the present value of future benefits increases, since the date of death draws steadily nearer; while the present value of future premiums declines, since there are fewer to be received. The side of the equation representing benefits increases each year until it eventually equals the face of the policy, whereas the side representing premium payments declines until it ultimately reaches zero.[1] If the equation is to remain in balance, a third element must be introduced; that element is the reserve. Thus, *the reserve may be defined as the difference between the present value of future benefits and the present value of future net premiums*. It is the balancing factor in the basic insurance equation.

TYPES OF RESERVES

The foregoing definition of the reserve reflects the so-called *prospective* view or concept of the reserve, the nomenclature stemming

---

[1] It will be recognized that the first part of this statement is not applicable to term insurance.

from the emphasis on or preoccupation with the future. Under the prospective method of valuation, no consideration is given to past experience apart from the basic mortality and interest assumptions entering into the formula. On the other hand, the reserve may be derived entirely by reference to past experience, such a reserve being known appropriately as the *retrospective* reserve. In such event, the reserve represents the net premiums collected by the company for a particular class of policies, plus interest at an assumed rate, less the death claims paid out. Both concepts are mathematically sound and, with the same set of actuarial assumptions, will produce identical reserves at the end of any given period. If the actual experience is more favorable than that assumed in the reserve computations, the savings will go into surplus, to be disposed of in accordance with the judgment of the company, the greater portion normally being distributed to policyholders as dividends.

In theory, the reserve can be calculated on the basis of either the gross premium or the net premium. Under gross premium valuation, the loading element is taken into consideration; while under net premium valuation, only mortality and interest are taken into account. Viewed prospectively, the gross premium reserve is equal to the excess of the present value of future claims and future expenses over the present value of future gross premiums; viewed retrospectively, it is the excess of gross premiums collected in the past over death claims and expenses incurred, improved at an assumed rate of interest. Gross premium valuation was the accepted practice among American life insurance companies until the year 1858, when the state of Massachusetts enacted legislation requiring the use of the net premium basis. Other states followed Massachusetts' lead; and today, net premium valuation is prescribed in every state. This is a stricter standard of solvency, the implications of which will be discussed later.

Finally, policies may be valued on either the full net level premium basis or in accordance with a method which permits all or a portion of the normal first-year reserve to be used in meeting the excess of first-year expenses over first-year loading. There are a number of methods designed to accomplish the latter objective, distinguished by the general designation of *modified reserve plans*. They will be described in a later chapter.

With respect to the time of valuation, reserves may be classified as terminal, initial, and mean. As its name implies, the *terminal* reserve is the reserve at the end of any given policy year. The *initial* reserve for any particular policy year is the reserve at the beginning of the policy year and is equal to the terminal reserve for the preceding year increased by the net level annual premium for the current year. The *mean* reserve is the arithmetic average of the initial reserve and terminal reserve for any year of valuation. For example, the initial reserve, computed on the basis of the 1958 C.S.O. Table and $2\frac{1}{2}$ per cent interest, for the fifth policy year of a $1,000 ordinary life contract issued as of age twenty-five is $57.97. This sum is obtained by adding the net level annual premium of $12.55 to the terminal reserve for the fourth policy year—namely, $45.42. The initial reserve of $57.97 will earn interest of $1.44 during the fifth year, producing a fund of $59.41 at the end of the year, from which the cost of insurance, $1.96, is deducted to yield the fifth-year terminal reserve of $57.45. The mean reserve for the fifth policy year then becomes

$$\frac{57.97 + 57.45}{2}, \text{ or } \$57.71.$$

In this illustration, the initial reserve is larger than the terminal reserve since the cost of insurance is greater than the interest on the initial reserve. This relationship does not always obtain, however, and under many circumstances, including policies issued at the younger ages and those with high interest assumptions, the terminal reserve is larger than the initial reserve. This relationship would obviously prevail at all ages of issue and at all durations in connection with policies purchased with a single premium.

The initial reserve is used principally in connection with the determination of dividends under participating policies. It will be shown later that one of the major sources of surplus from which dividends can be paid is a rate of investment earnings in excess of that assumed in the calculation of premiums. In allocating excess interest earnings to individual policies, the initial reserve is generally selected as the base to which the excess interest factor is applied, on the theory that it represents the amount of money invested throughout the year on behalf of a particular policy and hence is the measure of that policy's contribution to the pool of excess interest earnings.

The terminal reserve is also used in connection with dividend distributions. The companies allocate mortality savings on the basis of the net amount at risk, and the terminal reserve must be computed to determine the net amount at risk. On policies issued prior to 1948, the terminal reserve also serves as a basis for surrender values, the benefits being equal to the terminal reserve less a surrender charge (during the early years only). For policies issued since that time, surrender values are calculated in accordance with the terminal reserve *concept* but with a so-called "adjusted premium" rather than with the net annual level premium.[2]

The chief significance of the mean reserve is found in connection with annual statements. One of the most important items that must be reported is the aggregate amount of reserves. Inasmuch as policies are written throughout the year, on any given reporting date, some policies will just be commencing a policy year, some will just be completing a policy year, and some—the overwhelming majority—will be somewhere between one policy anniversary and the next. To calculate the exact reserve on all outstanding policies would be a tremendous— and unnecessary—task. Therefore, it is assumed, for purposes of the annual statement, that as of the date of valuation, all policies are exactly at the mid-point between two policy anniversaries. This involves the assumption that policies are written at a uniform rate throughout the year, which is not precisely the case, but is accurate enough for all practical purposes. Since the annual statements of life insurance companies are invariably prepared as of December 31, all policies are valued as if they were written on June 30, the mean reserve thus being used.

Except where otherwise indicated, the remainder of this chapter is devoted to *terminal* reserves computed on the *full net level premium basis*.

METHODS OF DETERMINING THE RESERVE

As was stated earlier, reserves may be ascertained prospectively or retrospectively. Since the retrospective method is the more easily grasped, it will be discussed first.

Retrospective Method

The retrospective method of valuation can be explained in terms of either one policy or all policies in a given classification. The group approach will be described first.

The retrospective reserve arises out of the level premium plan of operation. Under that arrangement, premiums in the early years of insurance are more than adequate to take care of the death claims that

---

[2] See pp. 302–8 for an explanation of the adjusted premium.

are submitted, creating a fund that can be drawn upon in the later years of coverage, when death rates rise sharply and claims exceed current premium income. In that sense, the reserve may be regarded as an accumulation of unearned premiums. In fact, the retrospective reserve is sometimes described as the *unearned premium reserve*. The overcharge is held to the credit of the surviving policyholders, showing up on the company's financial statement as a liability item. As a matter of fact, reserves in the aggregate constitute the major liability item in the balance sheet, typically accounting for about 90 per cent of all liabilities. It follows, therefore, that most of the assets of an insurance company are held in offset to policy reserves and, in effect, are earmarked for the benefit and protection of the policyholders. The exact manner in which overcharges lead to the creation of reserves is demonstrated in Table 14.

Table 14 shows the progression of reserve funds on a group of ordinary life contracts issued at age thirty-five and written in the amount of $1,000. According to the 1958 C.S.O. Table, 9,373,807 persons would be alive at age thirty-five out of an original group of 10,000,000 individuals alive at age zero. Therefore, it is assumed in the illustration that the group of persons taking out an ordinary life contract at age thirty-five is composed of the survivors of the original group of 10,000,000. The net level premium for an ordinary life contract issued at age thirty-five, computed on the basis of the 1958 C.S.O. Table and 2½ per cent interest, is $17.67 per $1,000 of face amount. Thus, the group will contribute a total of $165,645,801 (9,373,807 × $17.67) in premiums at the beginning of the first policy year. Since it is assumed that no death claims will be paid until the end of the year, the entire sum of $165,645,801 will earn interest throughout the year at the rate of 2½ per cent, producing earnings of $4,141,145. Thus, a sum of $169,786,946 will have accumulated by the end of the year, from which tabular death claims in the amount of $23,528,000 will be deducted. This will leave a fund of $146,-258,946, which, divided equally among the 9,350,279 survivors, will yield an individual reserve of $15.64.

The sum of $146,258,946 is carried over to the beginning of the second policy year and is augmented by the second annual premium of $165,230,035 (9,350,279 × $17.67), producing a sum of $311,-488,981, which will likewise be invested at 2½ per cent interest throughout the year. Interest earnings of $7,787,225 will bring the accumulated sum up to $319,276,206. According to the 1958

C.S.O. Table, 24,685 persons will die during the year; and the payment of their claims at the end of the year will reduce the fund to $294,591,206, or $31.59 per surviving policyholder. The terminal reserve for the second policy year will be carried forward to the beginning of the third policy year; and the process of adding annual premiums, crediting interest on the combined sum, and subtracting death claims is repeated. The process is continued until the last of the policyholders is assumed to have died.

It will be noted that in the early years, net premium income greatly exceeds the tabular death claims. During that period, therefore, both premium and investment income contribute to the building-up of the reserve fund. For each year that goes by, however, premium income declines (because of the reduction in the number of policyholders); while for a long period, the dollar value of death claims increases. By the twenty-fifth policy year, death claims catch up with premium income and exceed it thereafter to the end of the mortality table. For a few years thereafter, interest on the accumulated fund (including current premiums) is more than adequate to absorb the deficiency in net premium income, the aggregate fund thus continuing to grow. Beginning in the thirty-first policy year, however, death claims exceed both premium income and interest earnings, and the total fund commences to decline. In other words, after the thirty-first policy year, a portion of the principal must be used to pay death claims. Death claims reach a maximum in the forty-second policy year[3] totaling $303,014,000, but, even after tapering off, continue to exceed current premiums and investment earnings. The reserve fund continues to shrink until, with the payment of the death claims of the last 6,415 survivors in the sixty-fifth policy year, it is completely exhausted.

A sharp distinction must be drawn between the aggregate reserve and the prorata portion of that reserve allocable to an individual policyholder. Reference to Column 12 of Table 14 reveals that the individual reserve increases each year, eventually equaling the face of the policy (before payment of the last set of death claims). It continues to increase after the aggregate reserve begins its decline, due to the fact that the number of survivors decreases at a faster rate than the aggregate fund. The individual reserve must accumulate to the face of the policy since, if each group of policyholders is to be self-supporting,

---

[3] The *number* of deaths begins to decline after the forty-second policy year because of the shrinking number of survivors; but the death *rate*, of course, continues to increase.

TABLE 14

PROGRESSION OF RESERVE FUNDS UNDER RETROSPECTIVE METHOD OF VALUATION;
LEVEL PREMIUM BASIS; 1958 C.S.O. TABLE AND 2½ PER CENT INTEREST;
ORDINARY LIFE OF $1,000 ISSUED AT AGE 35;
NET LEVEL PREMIUM, $17.6711342

(1) Policy Year	(2) Attained Age at Beginning of Policy Year	(3) Tabular Number Living at Beginning of Policy Year (Equals Number Insured)	(4) Aggregate Reserve at End of Previous Year [see Col. 10]	(5) Annual Premiums Paid at Beginning of Policy Year [= (3) × $17.6711342]	(6) Total Sum on Hand at Beginning of Policy Year [= (4) + (5)]
1........	35	9,373,807		$165,645,801	$ 165,645,801
2........	36	9,350,279	$ 146,258,946	165,230,035	311,488,981
3........	37	9,325,594	294,591,206	164,793,823	459,385,029
4........	38	9,299,482	444,757,655	164,332,394	609,090,049
5........	39	9,271,491	596,326,300	163,837,762	760,164,062
6........	40	9,241,359	749,036,164	163,305,295	912,341,459
7........	41	9,208,737	902,527,995	162,728,827	1,065,256,822
8........	42	9,173,375	1,056,526,243	162,103,941	1,218,630,184
9........	43	9,135,122	1,210,842,939	161,427,967	1,372,270,906
10........	44	9,093,740	1,365,195,679	160,696,700	1,525,892,379
..	..	....	....	....	....
21........	55	8,331,317	2,937,104,694	147,223,821	3,084,328,515
22........	56	8,223,010	3,053,129,728	145,309,913	3,198,439,641
23........	57	8,106,161	3,161,551,632	143,245,059	3,304,796,691
24........	58	7,980,191	3,261,446,608	141,019,026	3,402,465,634
25........	59	7,844,528	3,351,864,275	138,621,707	3,490,485,982
26........	60	7,698,698	3,431,918,132	136,044,726	3,567,962,858
27........	61	7,542,106	3,500,569,929	133,277,567	3,633,847,496
28........	62	7,374,370	3,556,957,683	130,313,482	3,687,271.165
29........	63	7,195,099	3,600,181,944	127,145,560	3,727,327,504
30........	64	7,003,925	3,629,336,692	123,767,299	3,753,103,991
31........	65	6,800,531	3,643,537,591	120,173,096	3,763,710,687
32........	66	6,584,614	3,641,886,454	116,357,598	3,758,244,052
33........	67	6,355,865	3,623,451,153	112,315,343	3,735,766,496
34........	68	6,114,088	3,587,383,658	108,042,870	3,695,426,528
35........	69	5,859,253	3,532,977,191	103,539,646	3,636,516,837
36........	70	5,592,012	3,460,188,758	98,817,195	3,559,005,953
37........	71	5,313,586	3,369,555,102	93,897,091	3,463,452,193
38........	72	5,025,855	3,262,307,498	88,812,558	3,351,120,056
39........	73	4,731,089	3,140,132,057	83,603,709	3,223,735,766
40........	74	4,431,800	3,005,040,160	78,314,933	3,083,355,093
41........	75	4,129,906	2,858,544,970	72,980,123	2,931,525,093
42........	76	3,826,895	2,701,802,220	67,625,575	2,769,427,795
43........	77	3,523,881	2,535,649,490	62,270,974	2,597,920,464
44........	78	3,221,884	2,360,871,476	56,934,345	2,417,805,821
45........	79	2,922,055	2,178,421,967	51,636,026	2,230,057,993
..	..	....	....	....	....
60........	94	142,191	127,248,382	2,512,676	129,761,058
61........	95	97,165	87,979,084	1,717,016	89,696,100
62........	96	63,037	57,810,502	1,113,935	58,924,437
63........	97	37,787	35,147,548	667,739	35,815,287
64........	98	19,331	18,254,669	341,601	18,596,270
65........	99	6,415	6,145,177	113,360	6,258,537

TABLE 14 (*Continued*)

PROGRESSION OF RESERVE FUNDS UNDER RETROSPECTIVE METHOD OF VALUATION;
LEVEL PREMIUM BASIS; 1958 C.S.O. TABLE AND 2½ PER CENT INTEREST;
ORDINARY LIFE OF $1,000 ISSUED AT AGE 35;
NET LEVEL PREMIUM, $17.6711342

(7) 2½ Per Cent Interest for One Year on Sum in Column (6) [= .025 × (6)]	(8) Sum at End of Policy Year, before De- duction of Death Claims [= (6) + (7)]	(9) Death Claims by 1958 C.S.O. Mortality Table, Due at End of Policy Year	(10) Aggregate Re- serve at End of Policy Year after Deduction of Death Claims [= (8) − (9)]	(11) Tabular Number Living at End of Policy Year	(12) Individual Reserve at End of Policy Year, per $1,000 Insurance [= (10) ÷ (11)]
$ 4,141,145	$ 169,786,946	$ 23,528,000	$ 146,258,946	9,350,279	$ 15.64
7,787,225	319,276,206	24,685,000	294,591,206	9,325,594	31.59
11,484,626	470,869,655	26,112,000	444,757,655	9,299,482	47.83
15,227,251	624,317,300	27,991,000	596,326,300	9,271,491	64.32
19,004,102	779,168,164	30,132,000	749,036,164	9,241,359	81.05
22,808,536	935,149,995	32,622,000	902,527,995	9,208,737	98.01
26,631,421	1,091,888,243	35,362,000	1,056,526,243	9,173,375	115.17
30,465,755	1,249,095,939	38,253,000	1,210,842,939	9,135,122	132.55
34,306,773	1,406,577,679	41,382,000	1,365,195,679	9,093,740	150.12
38,147,309	1,564,039,688	44,741,000	1,519,298,688	9,048,999	167.90
. . . .	. . . .	. . . .	. . . .	. . . .	. . . . .
77,108,213	3,161,436,728	108,307,000	3,053,129,728	8,223,010	371.29
79,960,991	3,278,400,632	116,849,000	3,161,551,632	8,106,161	390.02
82,619,917	3,387,416,608	125,970,000	3,261,446,608	7,980,191	408.69
85,061,641	3,487,527,275	135,663,000	3,351,864,275	7,844,528	427.29
87,262,150	3,577,748,132	145,830,000	3,431,918,132	7,698,698	445.78
89,199,071	3,657,161,929	156,592,000	3,500,569,929	7,542,106	464.14
90,846,187	3,724,693,683	167,736,000	3,556,957,683	7,374,370	482.34
92,181,779	3,779,452,944	179,271,000	3,600,181,944	7,195,099	500.37
93,183,188	3,820,510,692	191,174,000	3,629,336,692	7,003,925	518.19
93,827,600	3,846,931,591	203,394,000	3,643,537,591	6,800,531	535.77
94,092,767	3,857,803,454	215,917,000	3,641,886,454	6,584,614	553.09
93,956,101	3,852,200,153	228,749,000	3,623,451,153	6,355,865	570.10
93,394,162	3,829,160,658	241,777,000	3,587,383,658	6,114,088	586.74
92,385,663	3,787,812,191	254,835,000	3,532,977,191	5,859,253	602.97
90,912,921	3,727,429.758	267,241,000	3,460,188,758	5,592,012	618.77
88,975,149	3,647,981,102	278,426,000	3,369,555,102	5,313,586	634.14
86,586,305	3,550,038,498	287,731,000	3,262,307,498	5,025,855	649.10
83,778,001	3,434,898,057	294,766,000	3,140,132,057	4,731,089	663.72
80,553,394	3,304,329,160	299,289,000	3,005,040,160	4,431,800	678.06
77,083,877	3,160,438,970	301,894,000	2,858,544,970	4,129,906	692.16
73,288,127	3,004,813,220	303,011,000	2,701,802,220	3,826,895	706.00
69,235,695	2,838,663,490	303,014,000	2,535,649,490	3,523,881	719.56
64,948,012	2,662,868,476	301,997,000	2,360,871,476	3,221,884	732.76
60,445,146	2,478,250,967	299,829,000	2,178,421,967	2,922,055	745.51
55,751,450	2,285,809,443	295,683,000	1,990,126,443	2,626,372	757.75
. . . .	. . . .	. . . .	. . . .	. . . .	. . . . .
3,244,026	133,005,084	45,026,000	87,979,084	97,165	905.46
2,242,402	91,938,502	34,128,000	57,810,502	63,037	917.09
1,473,111	60,397,548	25,250,000	35,147,548	37,787	930.15
895,382	36,710,669	18,456,000	18,254,669	19,331	944.32
464,907	19,061,177	12,916,000	6,145,177	6,415	957.94
156,463	6,415,000	6,415,000	0	0	0

there is no other source of funds from which the final death claims can be paid.

In theory, of course, the aggregate reserve cannot be allocated to individual policyholders. Insurance is a group proposition, and the reserve is a group concept. To be sure, the fund is held to guarantee performance under individual contracts, but it is computed on a group basis. If an occasion should ever arise whereby the total reserve fund would have to be apportioned among the various policyholders, as in the event of liquidation, such apportionment should, strictly speaking, take into account the relative state of health of the various policyholders and their respective chances of survival. A policyholder in poor health would be entitled to a relatively greater share of the aggregate reserve than one who is in good health, since the value of his contract, as measured by the relative chances of death, would be greater. Apportionment on the basis of the relative _value_ of the policies would clearly be impossible; so for all practical purposes, the reserve under a particular policy is considered to be its prorata share of the aggregate reserve.

The retrospective method of reserve valuation may also be illustrated with reference to an individual policy. Such an illustration, however, presupposes a familiarity with the "cost-of-insurance" concept which was touched upon briefly in Chapter II. It was pointed out there that under level premium insurance, the company is never on the risk for the full amount of the policy face. This is attributable to the fact that a reserve is created under the contract with the payment of the first premium and, if the policy remains in force, is available for the settlement of any death claim that may arise. In the event of a policyholder's death, the company returns the reserve under the contract and adds enough to it from sums contributed by all policyholders in the deceased's age and policy classification, including a contribution from the deceased himself, to make up the amount due under the contract. The sum which each policyholder must contribute as his prorata share of death claims in any particular year is called the "cost of insurance." It is the amount he must pay for protection. It is determined by multiplying the net amount at risk (face of the policy less the reserve) by the tabular probability of death at the insured's attained age. Thus, if at the end of twenty years the reserve under an ordinary life policy issued at age thirty is $309.76, the cost of insurance for the twentieth year is $\dfrac{\$690.24 \times 7.60}{1,000}$, or $5.25. The net amount at risk is $690.24; and the probability of death at age forty-nine, according to the 1958 C.S.O. Table, is 7.60 per 1,000. Therefore, that policy's share of death claims during the twentieth year of insurance is $5.25 per $1,000 of face amount.

The cost of insurance for a $1,000 ordinary life policy issued at

TABLE 15

COST OF INSURANCE FOR $1,000 ORDINARY LIFE POLICY
ISSUED AT AGE 35; 1958 C.S.O. AND $2\frac{1}{2}\%$ INTEREST;
NET LEVEL PREMIUM RESERVES

(1) Policy Year $[t]$	(2) Attained Age at Beginning of Policy Year $[= 35 + (t-1)]$	(3) 1958 C.S.O. Mortality Rate $[= q_{35} + (t-1)]$	(4) Amount at Risk During Year $[= 1,000\,(1 - {}_tV_{35})]$	(5) Cost of Insurance $[= (3) \times (4)]$
1	35	.00251	$984.36	$ 2.47
2	36	.00264	968.41	2.56
3	37	.00280	952.17	2.67
4	38	.00301	935.68	2.82
5	39	.00325	918.95	2.99
6	40	.00353	901.99	3.18
7	41	.00384	884.83	3.40
8	42	.00417	867.45	3.62
9	43	.00453	849.88	3.85
10	44	.00492	832.10	4.09
11	45	.00535	814.15	4.36
12	46	.00583	796.03	4.64
13	47	.00636	777.76	4.95
14	48	.00695	759.37	5.28
15	49	.00760	740.88	5.63
16	50	.00832	722.29	6.01
17	51	.00911	703.65	6.41
18	52	.00996	684.95	6.82
19	53	.01089	666.21	7.26
20	54	.01190	647.46	7.70
21	55	.01300	628.71	8.17
22	56	.01421	609.98	8.67
23	57	.01554	591.31	9.19
24	58	.01700	572.71	9.74
25	59	.01859	554.22	10.30
26	60	.02034	535.86	10.90
27	61	.02224	517.66	11.51
28	62	.02431	499.63	12.15
29	63	.02657	481.81	12.80
30	64	.02904	464.23	13.48
31	65	.03175	446.91	14.19
32	66	.03474	429.90	14.93
33	67	.03804	413.26	15.72
34	68	.04168	397.03	16.55
35	69	.04561	381.23	17.39

TABLE 15 (*Continued*)

COST OF INSURANCE FOR $1,000 ORDINARY LIFE POLICY
ISSUED AT AGE 35; 1958 C.S.O. AND 2½% INTEREST;
NET LEVEL PREMIUM RESERVES

(1) Policy Year [t]	(2) Attained Age at Beginning of Policy Year [$= 35 +$ $(t-1)$]	(3) 1958 C.S.O. Mortality Rate [$= q_{35} + (t-1)$]	(4) Amount at Risk During Year [$= 1,000\ (1 - {}_tV_{35})$]	(5) Cost of Insurance [$= (3) \times (4)$]
36.............	70	.04979	$365.86	$18.21
37.............	71	.05415	350.90	19.00
38.............	72	.05865	336.28	19.72
39.............	73	.06326	321.94	20.37
40.............	74	.06812	307.84	20.97
41.............	75	.07337	294.00	21.57
42.............	76	.07918	280.44	22.21
43.............	77	.08570	267.24	22.90
44.............	78	.09306	254.49	23.68
45.............	79	.10119	242.25	24.51
46.............	80	.10998	230.55	25.36
47.............	81	.11935	219.39	26.18
48.............	82	.12917	208.72	26.96
49.............	83	.13938	198.49	27.67
50.............	84	.15001	188.64	28.30
51.............	85	.16114	179.10	28.86
52.............	86	.17282	169.81	29.35
53.............	87	.18513	160.69	29.75
54.............	88	.19825	151.66	30.07
55.............	89	.21246	142.65	30.31
56.............	90	.22814	133.58	30.47
57.............	91	.24577	124.37	30.57
58.............	92	.26593	114.93	30.56
59.............	93	.28930	105.09	30.40
60.............	94	.31666	94.54	29.94
61.............	95	.35124	82.92	29.12
62.............	96	.40056	69.85	27.98
63.............	97	.48842	55.70	27.20
64.............	98	.66815	42.08	28.12
65.............	99	1.00000	0.00	0.00

age thirty-five is shown in Table 15 for each policy year to the end of the mortality table. As might be expected, the figure increases each year through the fifty-seventh year, or age ninety-one, at which point it amounts to $30.57. It declines thereafter, with the exception of the sixty-fourth policy year, since the net amount at risk is *decreasing* at a more rapid rate than the death rate is *increasing*. It is not until the thirty-sixth policy year, or age seventy, that the cost of insurance exceeds the net level premium of $17.67 for an ordinary life policy of $1,000 issued at age thirty-five. This means that through the thirty-fifth policy year, each annual premium makes a net addition to the policy reserve.[4]

In applying the cost-of-insurance concept to the determination of a retrospective reserve, it is necessary to know the terminal reserve for the policy year in question—the very value which is being sought. This poses no problem if the computation is being performed algebraically, but it creates a mathematical impasse if the reserve is being computed arithmetically. In order to avoid the introduction of algebraic symbols, this arithmetic contradiction will be ignored in the following illustrations.

The net level premium for an ordinary life policy of $1,000 issued as of age thirty-five is $17.67. Invested at $2\frac{1}{2}$ per cent interest, this sum will amount to $18.11 at the end of the first year. The policy's share of death claims during the first year is $2.47 $\left(\dfrac{\$984.36}{1,000} \times 2.51\right)$, which, deducted from the accumulated sum of $18.11, leaves $15.64 as the terminal reserve for the first year. This sum will be supplemented at the beginning of the second policy year by the second net level premium of $17.67, producing a sum of $33.31 that will be invested at an assumed rate of $2\frac{1}{2}$ per cent interest throughout the year and will earn $0.83. Thus, a fund of $34.14 will have accumulated by the end of the second year, from which will be deducted $2.56, as the cost of insurance $\left(\dfrac{\$968.41}{1,000} \times 2.64\right)$, producing a second-year terminal reserve of $31.59. This process is continued until, by the end of the tenth policy year, the reserve is $167.90. The accumulation during the eleventh year then takes the following form:

Terminal reserve for tenth year	$167.90
Add: Net level annual premium	17.67
Initial reserve for eleventh year	$185.57
Interest earnings at $2\frac{1}{2}$ per cent	4.64
Fund at end of eleventh year	$190.21
Deduct: Cost of insurance	4.36
Terminal reserve for eleventh year	$185.85

---

[4] It might be argued just as validly that through the thirty-fifth policy year, interest on the accumulated fund makes a net addition to the policy reserve, depending upon whether the cost of insurance is assumed to have been charged to net premiums or interest.

Thus, it may be said that the retrospective terminal reserve for any particular policy year is obtained by adding the net level annual premium for the year in question to the terminal reserve of the preceding year, increasing the combined sum by one year's interest at the assumed rate, and deducting the cost of insurance for the current year. If the policy is paid up or was purchased with a single premium, there will be no annual premiums to consider, and the cost of insurance must be met entirely from interest earnings on the reserve. Thus, the terminal reserve for the eleventh year under a ten-payment life policy issued as of age thirty-five in the amount of $1,000 would be obtained as follows:

Terminal reserve for tenth year	$517.49
Interest earnings at 2½ per cent	12.94
Fund at end of eleventh year	$530.43
Deduct:Cost of insurance	2.53
Terminal reserve for eleventh year	$527.90

If an ordinary life policy issued at age thirty-five should become a death claim during the eleventh policy year, it would contribute a total of $190.21 toward the payment of its own claim, leaving only $809.79 to be contributed by other policyholders. If the policy is still in force at the end of the year, it contributes $4.36 toward the payment of death claims under other policies in its classification, leaving $185.85 as the terminal reserve. It will be noted that the policy makes a contribution toward the cost of insurance whether it becomes a claim or not, a fact which has been alluded to on several previous occasions but not statistically demonstrated. It is interesting to note the difference in the eleventh-year cost of insurance between the ordinary life and ten-payment life policies, which is attributable solely to the difference in the reserves or, conversely, the amount at risk.

Prospective Method

While the retrospective method of computation provides a clear demonstration of the origin and purpose of the reserve, it is seldom used in actual reserve calculations. State valuation laws invariably express reserve requirements in terms of the prospective method. This does not mean that a company must use the prospective approach, since any method that will produce reserves equal to or in excess of those that would be derived by the statutory formula is acceptable. Nevertheless, the companies tend to prefer the prospective method because of its simplicity.

The prospective reserve, V, under a policy issued at age x, at the end of any given number of years, t, is equal to the net single premium for the policy in question at the age of valuation, A_{x+t}, minus the net level premium at age of issue, P_x, multiplied by the present value of a life annuity due of \$1 for the balance of the premium-paying period calculated as of the age of valuation, represented by $\ddot{a}_{x+t}$.[5] This can be illustrated in connection with an ordinary life contract for \$1,000 issued at age thirty-five. If it is desired to determine the full net level reserve under such contract ten years after issue, the verbal statement of the method can be formularized as follows:

$$_{10}V_{35} = A_{35+10} - (P_{35} \times \ddot{a}_{35+10})$$

or

$$_{10}V_{35} = A_{45} - (P_{35} \times \ddot{a}_{45})$$

Substituting known values in the formula, the computation of the reserve becomes a mere arithmetic exercise. Thus:

$$_{10}V_{35} = \$517.49 - (\$17.67 \times 19.783) = \$167.90$$

Stated verbally, the tenth-year reserve for an ordinary life policy of \$1,000 issued as of age thirty-five is equal to the net single premium for a whole life policy issued as of age forty-five, or \$517.49, minus the product of the net level premium for an ordinary life policy issued at age thirty-five, or \$17.67, and the present value of a whole life

---

[5] The general formula for the calculation of prospective reserves is:

$$_{t}^{k}V_{x:\overline{n}|} = A_{x+t:\overline{n-t}|} - _{k}P_{x:\overline{n}|}\ddot{a}_{x+t:\overline{k-t}|}$$

when

V = full net level premium reserve
x = age of issue
k = number of years in premium-paying period
t = number of years elapsed since date of issue
n = number of years in policy period
A = net single premium
P = net level premium
$\ddot{a}$ = present value of a life annuity due of \$1

The notation n is used only in connection with term and endowment insurance contracts and temporary life annuities. A whole life policy is known to run to the end of the mortality table, so it is not necessary to show n values for it. If it is the ordinary life form, the k values can likewise be omitted from the formula, since it is known that the premium-paying period is coterminous with the policy period. Thus, the prospective reserve formula for an ordinary life policy can be expressed as follows:

$$_{t}V_x = A_{x+t} - P_x\ddot{a}_{x+t}$$

annuity due of $1 calculated as of age forty-five, or $19.78. The present value of a *whole* life annuity due of $1 was used, since premiums are to be paid throughout the insured's life.

This formula symbolizes the earlier definition of a reserve that described it as the difference between the present value of future benefits and the present value of future premiums. The A_{x+t} represents the present value of future benefits, and the product of the values within the parentheses represents the present value of future premiums. For any particular policy, except term insurance, the present value of future benefits increases each year, since the insured is one year older and the policy one year closer to maturity. This is the same as stating that the net single premium for a policy increases with the attained age of the insured. On the other hand, the present value of future premiums declines, since each year, fewer premiums remain to be paid. Under any particular policy, the net level premium paid by the policyholder remains the same throughout the premium-paying period, but the present value of each dollar to be received by the company decreases with each passing year. At age thirty-five, for example, the present value of a whole life annuity due of $1, computed on the basis of the 1958 C.S.O. Table and 2½ per cent interest, is $23.77. By age forty-five, however, it has declined to $19.78; and by fifty-five, sixty-five, and seventy-five, it has fallen to $15.39, $11.04, and $7.32, respectively. The manner in which the present value of future benefits and the present value of future premiums diverge to create the necessity for a reserve is illustrated in Figure 10.

Line *AB* represents the present value of future benefits or the net single premium for a whole life policy at each of the attained ages from thirty-five to one hundred. Line *AC* represents the present value of future premiums, the values for which are derived by multiplying the net level premium for an ordinary life policy issued at age thirty-five—namely, $17.67—by the present value of a whole life annuity due of $1 at each of the attained ages from thirty-five to one hundred. At any point on the horizontal axis, the difference between lines *AB* and *AC* represents the reserve.

At age thirty-five, the net single premium for an ordinary life policy is $420.13, and the present value of future net level premiums at the inception of the contract is likewise $420.13. Therefore, there is no reserve at that point. The net single premium for an ordinary life policy issued at age thirty-six is $429.20, while the present value of future net level premiums for a policy issued at age *thirty-five* is only

$413.56. Therefore, a terminal reserve of $15.64 comes into existence at the end of the first policy year. By the end of the tenth policy year, the present value of future net level premiums will have declined to $344 ($17.37 × $19.78), while the net single premium for an ordinary life policy at the beginning of the next year—i.e., at the insured's age forty-five—will have risen to $517.49. The difference of

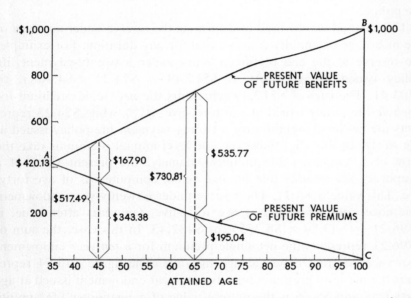

FIG. 10. Source of the reserve: prospective method. Annual premium ordinary life policy of $1,000 issued as of age thirty-five; 1958 C.S.O. Table and 2½ per cent interest.

$167.90 must be on hand in the form of a reserve. At age sixty-five, the net single premium for an ordinary life policy is $730.81, while the present value of future premiums at the age thirty-five rate is only $195.04. The reserve at the end of the thirtieth policy year, therefore, is $535.77. The two sets of values continue to diverge until at age one hundred, the present value of future premiums is zero, there being no more premiums to be paid; whereas the net single premium for an ordinary life policy at age one hundred, if one could be purchased at such an advanced age, would be $1,000, since the policy would immediately become a claim. Thus, the reserve at age one hundred would be equal to the face of the policy, a principle noted on earlier occasions.

The values for line AB would remain the same for the attained ages shown for any whole life policy, irrespective of the age of issue; but the values for line AC depend upon a specific age of issue, since the net level premium remains constant. Hence, the slope of the curves will differ with different ages of issue and with different types of policies; nevertheless, for any permanent form of insurance, the disparity between the two sets of values will ultimately equal the face of the policy.

This method can be used to determine the reserve under any type of life insurance or annuity contract and for any duration. For example, the reserve at the end of fifteen years under a twenty-payment life policy issued at age thirty is $517.49 — ($24.23 \times 4.708), or $403.41. The sum of $517.49 represents the net single premium for a *whole* life policy issued at age forty-five, A_{x+t}, while $24.23 represents the net level premium for a twenty-payment life policy issued at age thirty. In this case, however, the level annual premiums take the form of a *temporary* life annuity—namely, the present value of a temporary life annuity due for five years, computed as of age forty-five. This value is $4.71. The reserve under a twenty-year endowment insurance contract issued at age forty-five, ten years after issue, is $796.21— ($43.54 \times 8.355), or $432.43. In this case, the sum of $796.21 represents the net single premium for a *ten-year* endowment insurance contract issued at age fifty-five. The figure $43.54 represents the net level premium for a twenty-year endowment issued at age forty-five, and $8.36 is the present value of a *temporary* life annuity due of $1 for ten years computed as of age fifty-five. The reserve at the end of ten years under a fifteen-year term policy issued at age twenty-five is $13.09 — ($2.27 \times 4.737), or $2.34. Finally, the twentieth-year reserves under an annual premium nonrefund deferred annuity purchased at age thirty-five to provide $100 per month at age sixty-five is $9,551.77 — ($255.40 \times 8.439), or $7,396.45. These values represent, respectively, the net single premium at age fifty-five for a nonrefund deferred annuity of $100 per month commencing at age sixty-five, the net annual level premium for such annuity at age thirty-five, and the present value of a temporary life annuity due of $1 for ten years at age fifty-five.

Under limited-payment policies, whether of the whole life or endowment variety, the present value of the temporary life annuity due becomes zero after all premiums have been paid, and the reserve becomes the net single premium for the policy in question at the insured's attained age. Thus, the reserve under a twenty-payment life policy issued at age thirty-five, at the end of thirty years, is the net single premium for a whole life policy issued at sixty-five. This means that at any particular attained age, the reserves under all paid-up whole life policies are identical, irrespective of age of issue. The same is true of all paid-up endowment policies with the same maturity date. This principle is illustrated in Figure 11, which portrays the reserves under different forms of whole life policies issued as of age thirty-five.

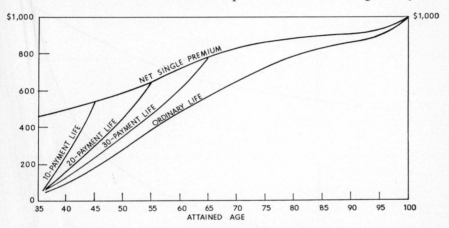

FIG. 11. Terminal reserves for $1,000 of whole life insurance; 1958 C.S.O. Table and 2½ per cent interest.

Significance of Actuarial Assumptions

In measuring its liabilities under outstanding contracts, whether accomplished retrospectively or prospectively, an insurance company must assume certain rates of mortality among its policyholders and a certain rate of earnings on the assets underlying the reserves. The assumptions as to mortality are reflected in the choice of the mortality table to be used in the valuation, while the appraisal of investment potential is reflected in the rate of interest selected for the computations. The reserve values heretofore cited were based on the 1958 C.S.O. Table and 2½ per cent interest. However, other assumptions have been and are being used in reserve computations. It is important, therefore, to note the impact on reserves of the choice of basic actuarial assumptions.

Mortality. There is a widespread belief that the higher the rates of mortality assumed in a reserve computation, the greater will be the reserve. Thus, there was a popular impression that the continued use of the American Experience Table of Mortality for premium and reserve computations resulted in the creation of excessive reserves. The fact of the matter is that the *level* of mortality, per se, is not a determinant of the size of the reserves. A mortality table that shows a much higher death rate at every age than another table could produce a much lower reserve than that computed on the basis of the latter.

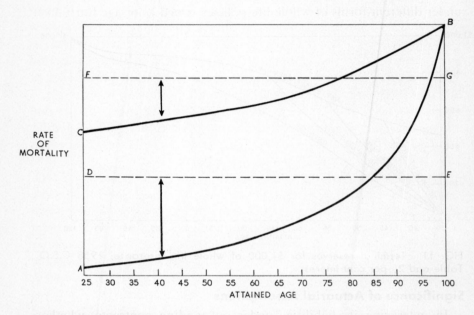

FIG. 12. Relationship between reserves and slope of the mortality curve.

The factor that governs the size of the reserve is the *steepness* of the mortality curve or the rapidity of increase in the rate of mortality from age to age. The steeper the slope of the mortality curve, the greater will be the reserve. This is true even though the steeper curve shows a lower rate of mortality at all ages up to the terminal age. This principle is illustrated in a crude fashion in Figure 12.

Curves *AB* and *CB* represent the death rates from ages twenty-five to one hundred under two *hypothetical* mortality tables, one reflecting unrealistically high rates of mortality and the other showing more normal rates. Lines *DE* and *FG* represent level premiums and are placed at such a distance above points *A* and *C*, respectively, as to create a triangle beneath the dotted line in each case approximately equivalent in area to the triangle above the dotted line. This obviously ignores the influence of compound interest and grossly exaggerates the redundancy of the level premiums in the early years of the insured's life, but it graphically illustrates the effect of leveling out mortality curves of differing slopes and does no violence to the principle involved. It is apparent that the table represented by curve *AB* would produce the higher reserves.

In practice, it is not always possible to predict by visual inspection the relative magnitude of reserves under different mortality tables at various ages and durations.[6] A particular mortality table may show higher death rates at some ages and lower death rates at other ages, as compared with another table. In such event, the reserves under the specified table may be higher at some ages and durations than those of another table, and lower at other ages and durations. For example, a select mortality table, which shows a rapidly increasing death rate during the early years of coverage as the effect of selection wears off, produces larger reserves for short durations than does a table which does not exhibit such a sharp increase in death rates.

It should now be clear that the reserves under the 1941 C.S.O. Table are greater at most ages of issue and most durations than those under the American Experience Table, since the former shows much lower death rates at the younger ages and only slightly lower rates at the older ages than those of the latter. In other words, the death rates under the 1941 C.S.O. Table increase at a more rapid rate from the younger to the older ages. The effect on reserves is shown in Table 16.

At the younger ages, and at the shorter durations, the reserves under the 1941 C.S.O. Table are substantially greater than those under the American Experience Table. At the older ages and longer durations, the disparity becomes smaller; and at some ages and durations, the American Experience Table reserves are larger than the reserves under the 1941 C.S.O. Table. This is due to the fact that the two mortality curves converge around age sixty, with the death rates under the American Experience Table rising more rapidly thereafter and the probability of death reaching 1, or certainty, four years earlier than under the 1941 C.S.O. Table. Thus, the slope of the American Experience Table mortality curve is slightly steeper after

---

[6] As a matter of fact, the determination of the effect on reserves that would be brought about by a change in mortality assumptions poses a mathematical problem of extreme complexity. For a discussion of the problem and the mathematical techniques, see C. Wallace Jordan, Jr., *Life Contingencies* (Chicago: Society of Actuaries, 1952), pp. 114–20; and E. F. Spurgeon, *Life Contingencies* (London: Cambridge University Press, 1947), pp. 112–16 and 188–90.

TABLE 16

COMPARISON OF TERMINAL RESERVES UNDER THE
AMERICAN EXPERIENCE TABLE, THE 1941 C.S.O. TABLE, AND THE 1958 C.S.O.
TABLE AT 3 PER CENT INTEREST, ORDINARY LIFE POLICY OF $1,000

End of	American Experience Table			1941 C.S.O.			1958 C.S.O.		
	Age 15	Age 35	Age 55	Age 15	Age 35	Age 55	Age 15	Age 35	Age 55
First year...	$ 5.85	$ 12.88	$ 28.87	$ 7.78	$ 15.19	$ 28.42	$ 6.95	$ 14.30	$ 27.62
Fifth year...	31.24	68.16	145.61	41.00	78.56	141.72	36.24	74.72	138.14
Tenth year..	67.79	146.01	290.50	87.37	163.19	279.88	77.35	156.29	273.33
Twentieth year......	160.02	327.58	551.19	196.98	344.95	527.71	179.14	334.23	512.38

age sixty than that of the 1941 C.S.O. Table, creating larger reserves for policies issued after that age or issued in the fifties, but with durations reflecting the steeper slope of the American Experience Table. It may be observed in Table 16 that after ten years, an ordinary life policy issued at age fifty-five has developed a larger reserve under the American Experience Table than under the 1941 C.S.O. Table.

The foregoing pertains to reserves under individual policies. It is of some interest to note that the total reserves of a typical life insurance company would be about 2 or 3 per cent higher under the 1941 C.S.O. Table than under the American Experience Table.

The reserves under the 1958 C.S.O. Table reflect roughly the same pattern as those under the 1941 C.S.O. Table, and, hence, the relationship to reserves under the American Experience Table is similar. While the death rates under the 1958 C.S.O. Table are lower at all ages than those under the American Experience Table, the slope of the mortality curve after age sixty is steeper under the American Experience Table than under the 1958 C.S.O. Table since the terminal age under the American Experience Table is four years lower. This produces larger reserves under the American Experience Table at the older ages of issues and longer durations.

The relationship of the reserves at the various ages of issue and durations under the 1941 and 1958 C.S.O. Tables does not lend itself to easy generalization since after about age thirty-five the death rates under the 1958 table is a constantly increasing percentage of the rates under the 1941 table. The effect of this is to produce a set of reserves that at all but the oldest ages will be larger under the 1941 C.S.O. Table, with the percentage difference in reserves being greatest at the youngest ages. With a typical and comparable distribution of policies, ages of issue, and durations, the reserves under the 1958 C.S.O. Table, computed on either a 2½ or 3 per cent assumption, should be around 97 per cent of those under the 1941 C.S.O. Table. Thus, on an aggregate basis, the reserves under the 1958 C.S.O. Table should be about the same as those under the American Experience Table.

Interest. Unlike a change in mortality assumptions, which may produce either an increase or a decrease in reserves, depending upon age of issue and duration, a change in the interest assumption will affect the magnitude of reserves in the same direction—but not necessarily to the same extent—at all ages of issue and durations.[7] Specifically, a decrease in the assumed rate of interest operates to increase reserves, while an increase in the rate decreases reserves.

The impact on reserves of a change in interest assumption is not easily explained in terms of the conventional retrospective and prospective approaches. For example, it might be concluded, retrospectively, that a reduction in the assumed rate of interest would result in the accumulation of a smaller reserve at the end of any given period short of the maturity of the contract or the end of the mortality table. Such a conclusion, however, ignores the fact that the lower interest assumption implies a larger net premium, and the problem becomes one of measuring the effect of accumulating a series of larger net premiums at a lower rate of interest. Inasmuch as the augmentation of net premiums more than compensates for the loss of interest earnings involved in the lower interest rate, a larger reserve results. On the other hand, an increase in the assumed rate of interest would require a smaller net premium, offsetting for a period of time the influence of the higher rate of interest earnings and producing a reserve that is smaller at all durations up to the end of the mortality table or earlier maturity of the contract than that computed on the basis of a lower interest assumption.

Prospectively, the analysis is complicated by the fact that the present value of future benefits and the present value of future premiums are affected in the same direction by a change in the interest assumption. However, inasmuch as the present value of future benefits is always influenced to a greater degree than is the present value of future premiums, a decrease in the assumed rate of interest always

---

[7] This is not true of term and other types of insurance policies whose reserves do not increase continuously to date of expiry or maturity.

produces a larger reserve, and an increase in interest a smaller reserve.

The simplest explanation revolves around the fact that the reserve must accumulate to the face of the policy by the end of the mortality table if a whole life contract, or by the maturity date if an endowment policy. Therefore, the lower the rate of interest at which the reserve is to be accumulated, the larger at any given time must be the fund to which the lower rate is to be applied. To take a very elementary example, if $1,000 must be accumulated by the end of any particular year and only 2½ per cent interest can be earned on invested funds, a sum of $976 must be on hand at the beginning of the year. If a yield of 3 per cent can be realized, only $971 need be on hand at the beginning of the year.

The impact of a change in interest assumption on the reserves of an individual contract can be observed in Table 17, which shows the terminal reserves at various durations on an ordinary life contract of $1,000 issued at various ages, on both a 2½ per cent and a 3 per cent interest basis. In each case, mortality in accordance with the 1958 C.S.O. Table is assumed. It will be noted that the percentage difference in reserves is greatest at the younger ages and the shorter durations. For example, for an ordinary life policy issued at age fifteen, the first-year terminal reserve computed on the basis of 2½ per cent

TABLE 17

TERMINAL RESERVES, ORDINARY LIFE POLICY OF $1,000;
1958 C.S.O. TABLE AND INTEREST AT 2½ PERCENT AND 3 PERCENT

End of	2½%			3%		
	Age 15	Age 35	Age 55	Age 15	Age 35	Age 55
First year.........	$ 8.07	$ 15.64	$ 28.96	$ 6.95	$ 14.30	$ 27.62
Fifth year........	41.80	81.05	144.01	36.24	74.72	138.14
Tenth year........	88.24	167.90	283.00	77.35	156.29	273.33
Twentieth year.....	199.36	352.54	524.54	179.14	334.23	512.38
Thirtieth year......	333.79	535.77	708.65	307.43	516.21	698.27
Fortieth year.......	481.62	692.16	853.98	453.49	675.36	847.40
Forty-fifth year....	556.27	757.75	1000.00	528.99	743.20	1000.00

interest is 16 per cent greater than that computed on the basis of 3 per cent interest. By the end of the twentieth year, the difference has declined to less than 11 per cent; and by the forty-fifth year, to 5 per cent. By age 100, the disparity between reserves will have disappeared altogether, as is true of all other ages of issue. This is illustrated in Table 17 by the reserves for age fifty-five.

With the decline in the general level of interest rates during the decades of the 1930's and 1940's, virtually all companies found it necessary to lower the rate of interest assumed in premium and reserve computations for new life insurance and annuity contracts. Many of the older contracts were issued on a $3\frac{1}{2}$ per cent or even higher interest basis, and new contracts were being written quite generally on a 3 per cent basis in the early years of the 1940's. During the next few years, widespread lowering of interest assumptions took place, with most companies adopting assumptions of $2\frac{1}{4}$ or $2\frac{1}{2}$ per cent for insurance contracts and even lower rates for annuity contracts. Interest rates turned upwards in the 1950's and have now approached the level of the late 1920's. Many companies have again adopted a 3 per cent assumption, usually at the time they were promulgating new rates on the basis of the 1958 C.S.O. Table, although the $2\frac{1}{2}$ per cent basis appears still to be the predominating pattern.

During the decline in interest rates during the 1930's and 1940's, many companies reduced the interest assumption in the computation of reserves under old contracts. This, of course, meant that the reserves under such contracts were increased. This was accomplished by a transfer of funds from the surplus account to the reserve account, at one time or over a period of years, or through diversion to the reserve account of a portion of current mortality, interest, and loading savings which would otherwise be distributed as dividends. Once the necessary funds were transferred to the reserve account, the policies thereafter were treated as if they had been written on the lower interest basis in the first instance, except that surrender and loan values were usually not increased. The companies were then in a position to meet their reserve requirements with lower earnings on their invested funds. In some states, notably New York, a reserve strengthening program of this sort can be undertaken only with the consent of the insurance commissioner and having been carried out can be reversed only with official consent. This requirement is in the interest of preserving equity among the various classes of policyholders.

STATUTORY REGULATION OF RESERVES

The basis on which the policy liabilities of a life insurance company are to be computed is subject to regulation by the various states. This has caused such liabilities to be termed *legal reserves*. As a matter of fact, the states only prescribe the basis on which *minimum* reserves are to be calculated, the companies being permitted to use any other basis which will yield reserves equal to or larger than those produced by the statutory method. The specifications are couched in terms of the mortality table to be used, the maximum rate of interest to be assumed, and the formula to be applied. The specifications differ as between life insurance and annuities and—in the life insurance category—as among ordinary, group, and industrial insurance. Special rules apply to proceeds left with the insurance company under supplementary agreements.

Prior to 1948, the universal legal basis for computing minimum net level premium reserves for ordinary insurance was the American Experience Table and 3½ per cent interest, applied under the prospective method of valuation. In most states, some modification of the net level premium reserve was recognized and approved. Under the Standard Valuation Law, which became effective in all states in 1948 and with a few exceptions was applicable to all policies issued between December 31, 1947 and December 31, 1965, the minimum reserve basis for all ordinary policies was the 1941 C.S.O. Table and 3½ per cent interest, likewise applied under the prospective formula.[8] However, a modified reserve standard, the details of which are described in a later chapter, was prescribed in lieu of the net level premium reserve basis. As of January 1, 1966, the use of the 1958 C.S.O. Table for all new ordinary insurance became mandatory, the other features of the Standard Valuation Law remaining unchanged. Other tables are prescribed for the valuation of group insurance, industrial insurance, and annuities.

Annual valuation of policy liabilities is required in every state.

SAFETY MARGINS IN THE LEGAL RESERVE

In practice, the insurance companies compute their legal reserves on a more conservative basis than that required by law. Most companies use the same mortality and interest assumptions for the computation of reserves that they use in the calculation of premiums. Even though state valuation laws permit the use of a 3½ per cent interest assumption, the majority of companies are using a 2½ per cent reserve basis for policies currently being issued; and many have converted all outstanding policies to that basis, regardless of the assumptions used at the time of issue. Obviously, this provides a margin of safety beyond that contemplated in the valuation laws.

---

[8] In New York, the maximum rate of interest that could be assumed was 3 per cent. That limitation still applies under the standards that became effective January 1, 1966.

Another margin of safety is provided through the use of net premium valuation. This, however, is a matter of law. Under this method of valuation, it is assumed that only the net premium (whether calculated in accordance with the actuarial assumptions prescribed by law or in accordance with assumptions actually being used by the company) is available year by year, including the first year, for the payment of death claims, and that the rates of mortality experienced and the rate of interest earned have been and will continue to be in exact accordance with the assumptions underlying the net premiums. Loading, whether in connection with past or future premiums, is not taken into account.

This has not always been the case. In the early years of insurance in this country, gross premium valuation was the rule. Furthermore, it was customary to ignore future expenses and to assume that the entire gross premium would be available for the payment of claims. The present practice, the outgrowth of legislation designed to eradicate the evils of the earlier system, assumes that the whole of the loading will be required for expenses. The truth lies somewhere between these two assumptions. The entire loading is normally not needed for expenses, and the excess portion might well be taken into account in evaluating a company's financial position. Certainly, that portion of loading in excess of future expense requirements constitutes a source of financial stability.

DEFICIENCY RESERVES

If the gross premium charged by an insurance company for a particular class of policies should be less than the valuation net premium,[9] the company must establish and maintain for such policies a supplemental reserve, which has been given the general appellation of *deficiency reserve*. Such a requirement has long been a feature of state insurance laws, currently being found in the statutes of thirty-four states; but only in recent years, when continued improvement in mortality and investment earnings and increasing emphasis on price competition brought nonparticipating gross premiums to levels approaching or even below valuation net premiums, has the requirement assumed practical significance. As was pointed out earlier, the require-

---

[9] The *valuation* net premium is the net premium used in the calculation of the company's policy reserves, whether the latter be computed on the net level premium basis or in accordance with one of the modified systems.

ment became so burdensome on companies, especially those writing nonparticipating insurance, that it resulted in the construction and legalization of a new mortality table.

Deficiency reserve laws are founded on the premise that the use, in the prospective reserve formula, of a net level premium larger than the gross premium which will actually be received overstates the present value of future premiums and, consequently, understates the amount of reserves required. The extent of the deficiency is assumed to be represented by the present value of the excess of the valuation net premium over the gross annual premium. This presumes that the entire gross premium is available for the payment of policy claims— which, of course, is contrary to the facts. Thus, the formula for the calculation of deficiency reserves understates, by the present value of future expenses, the sum of money needed to supplement the conventional policy reserves.

The deficiency reserve at any particular age is computed by multiplying the excess of the valuation net premium over the gross annual premium by the present value of a life annuity due of $1 for the remainder of the premium-paying period. If a company calculates its reserves on the basis of the 1958 C.S.O. Table and $2\frac{1}{2}$ per cent interest, the valuation net premium for an ordinary life policy issued at age thirty-five is $17.67 per $1,000, and the present value of a whole life annuity due of $1 at that age is $23.77. For each dollar by which the gross premium falls short of the valuation net premium at that age, a deficiency reserve of $23.77 must be set up. If the gross premium is $15.42, for example, the required deficiency reserve will be $23.77 $\times$ $2.25 ($17.67 — $15.42), or $53.48.

In contrast to ordinary policy reserves which increase with duration, deficiency reserves for a given class of policies decrease as the years go by. This is a natural consequence of the fact that the present value of a life annuity due of $1 declines with each premium payment, or with each increase in attained age. From a retrospective point of view, it is assumed that the deficiency reserve is drawn upon with each premium payment to offset the deficiency in the gross premium. Hence, it must decline with duration. Under either the prospective or the retrospective point of view, it is apparent that the deficiency reserve will disappear altogether at the end of the premium-paying period.

Inasmuch as deficiency reserves are computed on the basis of actual valuation net premiums rather than the *smaller* net premium that would be used in the computation of minimum reserves, a company may be penalized for adopting conservative assumptions. This has led to the suggestion that deficiency reserve laws be amended to authorize the use of the valuation net premium for *minimum* reserves in the calculation of deficiency reserves.

VOLUNTARY RESERVES

In addition to the legal reserve, which is held to meet specific policy obligations, life insurance companies set aside various *voluntary* reserves, some of which may serve a special purpose and some of which may simply be another name for surplus. Special purpose reserves may be set up to cover future declines in the market value of nonamortizable securities, to smooth out mortality fluctuations, to meet expenses under supplementary agreements, and the like. A general purpose reserve is likely to be called a "contingency reserve." In some companies, the contingency reserve constitutes the balancing item between assets and liabilities, no surplus being shown. Since all of such special reserves are voluntary in nature, they can be used to meet any of the obligations of an insurance company.

In some states, the amount of voluntary reserves, including surplus, which can be accumulated by a mutual life insurance company is limited by law. The purpose of such a limitation is to insure that the major portion of surplus earnings will be currently distributed to policyholders in the form of dividends. The accumulation is usually limited to 10 per cent of the legal reserve, as computed by the company. Therefore, the more conservative the basis on which a company computes its policy liabilities, the larger the surplus or special reserves it can accumulate. Many mutual companies have accumulated a surplus, in whatever manner it may be designated, close to the statutory maximum, and a feeling has developed in recent years that the maximum may be too low. Particular concern has been shown over the large amounts of term insurance being written, primarily in the form of group insurance, which magnifies the need for a contingency fund but makes a relatively small contribution to the statutory base limiting the size of the contingency reserve. Surplus limitation laws are generally directed at participating life insurance.[10]

---

[10] For discussion of surplus limitation laws see Joseph M. Belth, *Participating Life Insurance Sold by Stock Companies* (Homewood, Ill.: Richard D. Irwin, Inc., 1965), pp. 68, 69, and 155–56.

CHAPTER XII

Gross
Premiums

THE DISCUSSION of rate making up to this point has been confined to the derivation of the *net* premium, that sum of money which, with interest, is designed to meet the payment of benefits under the contract. To operate successfully, however, an insurance company must collect from the policyholder a premium which, supplemented by interest, will enable it to meet all the costs under the contract, including benefit payments and the policy's share of the company's operating expenses. Furthermore, if the company is a stock company, the policy should yield a return to stockholders. The premium which is intended to accomplish this multiple objective is designated as the *gross premium*. It is the premium quoted in the rate book and actually paid by the policyholders.

The gross premium may be regarded as either the net premium augmented by an amount called *loading* or a sum derived independently of the valuation net premium and based on all the factors that enter into a gross premium—namely, mortality, interest, expenses, contingency allowances, and, in the case of a stock company, an allowance for profit. The gross premiums of mutual companies are typically arrived at by the former method, while the nonparticipating premiums of stock companies are usually derived by the latter method.

Regardless of the procedure followed in arriving at the loading or its equivalent, a company is guided by three major considerations:

1. The total loading from all policies should, subject to the qualifications stated below, cover the total operating expenses of the company, provide such margins of safety as the management deems desirable, furnish a margin for a minimum dividend scale for participating policies, and—in the case of a stock company—make a contribution to profits. The foregoing is true only as a broad generalization. In some companies, margins in the

246

mortality and interest assumptions are used to meet a portion of the expenses, while margins for safety and dividends are frequently built into the net premium assumptions.

2. The expenses of the company, including the margins necessarily embodied in the loading, should be apportioned over the various plans and ages of issue on as equitable a basis as possible. In other words, each class of policies should pay its own costs, as nearly as those costs can be determined.

3. The resulting gross premium should enable the company to maintain or improve its competitive position in the business. This objective often conflicts with (1) and (2), so that the final gross premium may well represent a compromise.

The manner in which a company, whether it be a mutual or a stock company, attempts to fulfill these objectives is described in the following sections.

GENERAL CONSIDERATIONS

Nature of Insurance Company Expenses

A great variety of expenses is involved in the operation of a life insurance company.[1] They may be divided into two broad categories: investment expenses and insurance expenses. The former include all the costs incurred in making, servicing, and safeguarding the investments of the company and are treated as deductions from gross investment income. They are indirectly taken into account in determining the rate of interest to be used in net premium calculations but are not considered in connection with the loading of a net premium. Insurance expenses include all items of costs not related to the investment function. Only insurance expenses will be considered in the present connection.

Insurance expenses may be classified in various ways, depending upon the purpose to be served. One broad functional classification places all such expenses under one of the following three subdivisions: *production, distribution,* and *maintenance.*

Under production are listed those items of cost incurred before the agent has a policy to deliver. These would include fees for medical examinations and inspection reports, home office underwriting expenses, printing costs for applications and policies, and the cost of

---

[1] Analysis of the expenses of one large life insurance company turned up 222 separate functions to which costs could be assigned. See C. F. B. Richardson, "Cost Analysis," *The Record* (American Institute of Actuaries), Vol. XXXV, Part 1, No. 71 (June, 1946).

preparing the policy and establishing the records at the home office. Among the costs of distribution would be included outlays for advertising, first-year commissions, agency allowances and expenses (excluding a minor portion of such expenses which are incurred for clearly maintenance function), and agency supervision. Maintenance costs embrace renewal commissions, premium taxes, the expense of collecting renewal premiums, reinstatement costs, costs of executing policy loans, expenses incidental to issuance of settlement agreements, and costs of settling claims. Many items do not fit neatly under any of the subdivisions and must be prorated among the three. Such items include executive salaries, certain clerical salaries, rent, and home office maintenance.

A functional classification that is widely used for operating purposes shows the following categories of expenses: (1) acquisition, (2) agency, (3) selection, (4) issue, and (5) maintenance. Nevertheless, the most meaningful classification for purposes of deriving gross premiums stratifies insurance expenses into:

1. Those that vary with the rate of *premium*
2. Those that vary with the amount of *insurance*
3. Those that vary with the number of *policies*

The primary items which vary with the premium rate are commissions to agents, state premium taxes, acquisition expenses other than commissions, and agency expenses. The first two items are expressed directly as a percentage of the gross premium involved, while the last two items may be expressed as a percentage of either the premiums collected or the commissions paid. A portion of agency expenses and acquisition expenses other than commissions may be charged on a per policy basis. Agency renewal expenses may be assessed entirely on a per policy basis, as they are in the illustration given later in this chapter.

Very few, if any, expenses vary in direct proportion to the amount of the policy, but a number of expenses reflect to some degree the amount of insurance. Selection costs are the most sensitive to the size of the policy. For example, many companies will issue policies up to a certain size without a medical examination—so-called "nonmedical" insurance. If a medical examination is prescribed, the medical examiner's fee for small- and moderate-size policies will usually run from $7.50 to $10. Where a large amount of insurance is involved, however, the company may require an electrocardiogram, X rays, and other expensive diagnostic procedures, in which event the examiner's fee may run to $75 or $100. In some cases, two or more independent examinations may be required. The investigation of the applicant also tends to be more thorough as the size of the policy increases, a larger inspection fee thus being incurred. Other expenses which reflect the size of the policy to some degree are those associated with the issue, maintenance, and settlement of the policy.

Examples of expenses which can be assessed primarily on a per policy basis include the cost of issuing policies, establishing the necessary accounting records, sending of premium notices, accounting for premium remittances, settling of claims, and general overhead. Also, as indicated above, certain agency and acquisition expenses may be assessed on a per policy basis.

Nature of the Loading Formula

The foregoing suggests that the loading to a net premium should consist partly of a percentage of the premium, partly of a constant amount for each $1,000 of insurance, and partly of a constant amount for each policy. If the loading formula were to incorporate all three of these elements, the premium rate per $1,000 would vary with the face of the policy. Since the volume of expenses assessable on a per policy basis would remain constant, the greater the number of $1,000 units of insurance represented in the policy, the smaller the amount of expenses that would have to be borne by each unit.

British life insurance companies have long graded their premiums by size of policy through the use of a policy-writing fee,[2] but until the middle 1950's American companies considered this to be an unnecessary and impracticable refinement. Moreover, there was a question as to whether the practice would be in violation of the so-called "antidiscrimination" statutes found in many states, including New York.[3] The first step toward general adoption of premium grading by size of plan

---

[2] The policy fee is added to the normal loading and is the same for all policies, irrespective of size or plan. This produces an effective gross premium that varies with each $1,000 of insurance.

[3] Section 209 of the New York Insurance Law reads as follows: "No life insurance company doing business in this state shall make or permit any unfair discrimination between individuals of the same class and equal expectation of life, in the amount or payment or return of premiums or rates charged by it for policies of life insurance or annuity contracts or in the dividends or other benefits payable thereon, or in any of the terms and conditions thereof. . . ."

The issue under such statutes was whether the size of the policy could serve as the basis for a separate classification or whether "class" referred solely and exclusively to the expectation of life.

was taken when some companies years ago began issuing "special" policies, usually on the ordinary life plan, subject to a minimum amount of insurance per policy and possibly special underwriting requirements.[4] With increasing price competition, greater mechanization of insurance company operations, changing concepts of equity, and a series of favorable insurance department rulings (supported by a resolution of the National Association of Insurance Commissioners which, in effect, stated that there is no inherent discrimination in the principle of gradation of premiums by size of policy) the grading of premiums by size of policy, irrespective of policy plan or age of issue, has become a widespread practice.

The initial approach by American companies to the grading of premiums was generally through the establishment of rather broad amount classifications called "bands." Customarily, about four classifications or bands were established with the rate per $1,000 being uniform within each band. For example, a rate schedule might specify separate and progressively decreasing rates for the following size groups: $2,000–$4,999; $5,000–$9,999; $10,000–$24,999; and $25,000 and over. The spread between the highest and lowest rates might be about $3 per $1,000 with the greatest reduction occurring between the lowest two bands. This method is still used by some companies, but the more common approach today seems to be the policy fee technique.

The policy fee approach may be applied in its pure form, utilizing a constant charge per policy and producing a composite rate that varies with each $1,000 of insurance without limit, or it may be modified in various ways. One of the most common modifications is to levy a smaller fee on policies below a certain size, such as $4,000 or $5,000, in the interest of minimizing the expense charge on small policyholders. Above the specified size, the per policy charge is constant, ranging in amount among the various companies from about $10 to $25. Another modification is to use classifications or bands up to some level, such as $15,000 or $20,000, and a flat fee for policies over that amount.[5]

---

[4] The discrimination issue was avoided by limiting the ordinary life plan to "specials" and using similar but sufficiently different plans, such as life paid-up at 85 or endowment at age 85, when the amounts involved were less than the minimum required for a "special."

[5] For a scholarly and comprehensive analysis of graded premiums, see Elgin G. Fassel, "Premium Rates Varying by Policy Size," *Transactions of the Society of Actuaries,* Vol. VIII (1956), pp. 390–419, as well as the discussion beginning on p. 420.

Even when premiums are graded by size it is necessary, or at least desirable, to convert expenses that vary with the number of policies into an amount per $1,000 by relating them to a policy of *average* size. If per policy expenses are being assessed on a band basis, an average size policy must be assumed within each band. On the other hand, the policy fee approach would suggest that no assumption would have to be made as to the average size of policy, since the policy fee is designed to cover those expenses that are roughly constant per policy. However, in order to avoid a burdensome charge on small policies most companies assess a policy fee that is smaller than the constant expense per policy. The excess per policy cost must be allocated on the basis of an assumed average size policy. In the interest of simplicity, the expense allocations described in this chapter are based on the assumption that premiums are *not* being graded by size, through either a policy fee or the band technique.

The assumption used with respect to the average size policy is an important factor in the allocation of expenses. For example, if the cost studies of a company indicate that the share of each policy in the annual overhead of a company is $4.00 and the average-size policy issued in recent years is $10,000,[6] the overhead expenses of the company would be met by levying a charge of $0.40 per $1,000 in the loading formula. In order to inject greater refinement into their cost calculations, most companies compute the average size of policy for each of the principal plans, and some companies introduce a further differential by age at issue. It is well to note in this connection that the competitive position of a company can be materially affected, for better or for worse, by the average-size policy it issues.

Once the expenses which vary with the number of policies have been converted to a per $1,000 basis, the hypothetical loading formula can be reduced to two factors: a percentage of the premium and a constant per $1,000 of insurance. The manner in which the appropriate percentage and constant are arrived at for participating premiums is explained in the following section.

For an extremely critical view of the philosophy and practice of graded premiums, see Halsey D. Josephson, *Discrimination* (New York: Wesley Press, New York, 1960).

[6] In any cost study undertaken in connection with a proposed revision of rates, the company will be primarily concerned with the average size of policies expected to be issued under the new set of rates. Therefore, the average size of policies issued in recent years will usually be given more weight than the average size of all policies in force. In any such cost study, paid-up policies are excluded from consideration because (1) they usually represent old issues, (2) they include reduced paid-up insurance, and (3) no premium collection expense is involved.

LOADING OF PARTICIPATING PREMIUMS

Basic Principle Involved

The basic theoretical principle underlying the derivation of the loading formula is the same as that on which is based the computation of the net single and net level premiums. In connection with the latter, the present value of the benefits promised under the contract is computed, and the resulting sum is designated the net single premium. Then, this sum is converted into equivalent annual installments by dividing it by the present value of a life annuity due of $1 for the period over which the payments are to be made.

In similar fashion, the present value of the expenses to be incurred under a particular policy is computed as an essential step in the development of a loading formula. Then, this sum is likewise spread over the premium-paying period by dividing into it the present value of an appropriate life annuity due. After additions to provide the margins for contingencies and dividends, the resulting values can be expressed in the form of a percentage of the premium plus a constant, or in some other equivalent form, as will be explained later. It may be helpful to view the combination of the net single premium and the present value of future expenses as that sum of money which, with interest, will enable the company to meet all the monetary obligations under the policy in question.

A difference of great practical significance in the derivation of the two sets of present values is found in the fact that the benefits under the policy, being contractual, are known with certainty, whereas the expenses attributable to the policy can be determined, if at all, only after a painstaking analysis of operating costs and the probable future trend of such costs. The allocation of joint costs to the various policies and ages of issue presents the actuary with one of his most difficult tasks and is accomplished with only substantial—not absolute—equity.

Computation of Present Values

Ideally, more or less elaborate cost studies precede the adoption of a loading formula or formulas; and all items of expense are reduced to a unit basis for allocation among the various policy plans and ages at issue. As indicated earlier, these unit expense rates will be expressed either as a percentage of the premium or as an amount per $1,000 of face value. The first type of rate is easily obtained, since the expenses to which the rate is applied are already expressed, directly or indirectly, as a percentage of the premium. The real problem lies in the development of rates for all other types of expenses. These rates may be derived from the expense data of the company in question, as revealed by their own cost studies; or they may be based on the experience of other companies and modified as necessary.

Since the objective is to calculate the present value of these expenses, they must be further classified as to the time of their occurrence. Specifically, it must be known whether the expenses are incurred at the inception of the contract, at periodic intervals thereafter, or only upon the occurrence of some particular event in the future. In view of the differences among the various expenses as to the time at which and the circumstances under which they occur, it is necessary to arrange the various elements into a form lending itself to mathematical treatment. A formula is set up, and values are assigned to the integral elements. A typical formula might contain values for the following elements:

1. Expenses expressed as a percentage of the premium
   a) Those incurred only at time of issue
   b) Those incurred only during a limited number of renewal years
   c) Those incurred every year, including the first
2. Expenses expressed as an amount per $1,000 of insurance
   a) Those incurred only at time of issue
   b) Those incurred each year
   c) Those incurred only in year of death

First-year commissions, agency expense allowances, and other acquisition costs would be included under 1 (a). First-year commissions to the soliciting agent vary widely among companies and, to a lesser extent, among policy plans of the same company; but they have the common characteristic of being many times higher than the renewal commission. A typical first-year commission on an ordinary life policy issued at age thirty-five, which will serve as an example for the development of a loading formula, might be 55 per cent of the gross premium.[7] The other expenses, including the commission to the general agent, if any, might amount to another 55 per cent of the gross premium. Thus, the combined expenses that are incurred only at the time of issue can be assumed to equal at least 110 per cent of the first

---

[7] Typical first-year commissions for small companies range from 60 to 80 per cent of the gross premium.

premium. While these costs are actually paid by the company during the first policy year, it is assumed, for purposes of loading, that they are fully recovered from the policyholder only after all premiums due under the contract have been received. In other words, they must be amortized over the entire premium-paying period. The level percentage of the premium that will have to be liquidated each year can be obtained by dividing 110 per cent by the present value of a whole life annuity due of $1 as of age thirty-five, which has previously been determined to equal $23.77. Thus, $110 \div 23.77 = .0471$, or 4.71 per cent. It can be seen, therefore, that this category of expenses alone will add more than 5 per cent to the net level premium.

The items of expense included in 1 (*b*) are renewal commissions to the soliciting agent and agency expense allowances. Under recent compensation agreements, many patterns of renewal commissions can be found, some providing for a minimum commission or service fee throughout the lifetime of the policyholder; but for the sake of simple illustration, it will be assumed here that a renewal commission of 5 per cent will be paid for nine years. A policy charge of $2 will be added for agency allowances during the period. Since these commissions and agency allowances will be paid only if the corresponding premiums are paid, they should be discounted against the probability of death of the policyholder, lapse or surrender of the policy, termination of the agent without vested rights, and for interest. In practice, however, it is not customary in this particular calculation to discount these expenses for termination of the policy or the agent. Discounting only for mortality and interest, and employing the 1958 C.S.O. Table and $2\frac{1}{2}$ per cent interest, the present value of the renewal commissions is found to be 40.4 per cent of the gross premium. This sum must also be spread over the premium-paying period of the policy. The percentage addition to the annual premium that will be necessary to amortize these commissions is obtained by dividing 40.4 per cent by 23.77, which yields 1.7 per cent. By the same process, the annual premium needed to amortize the agency allowances is found to be 0.06 per cent per $1,000 of insurance.

The only item in 1 (*c*) of any significance is state premium taxes. These taxes vary among the various states but average about 2 per cent. Since the tax must be paid on each premium, it is not necessary to reduce it to a present value. It can be assumed to add 2 per cent to the loading formula.[8]

---

[8] Some companies now ignore premium taxes on annuity consideration in computing the basic gross premium for individual annuity contracts. Then the rates for

The principal expenses not expressed as a percentage of premium and incurred only at the time of issue are those connected with the selection procedure and the preparation of the policy for issue. It would perhaps be accurate enough for present purposes to assume that selection costs amount to $25 per policy plus $0.75 per $1,000 of insurance, and the expense of issuing a policy amounts to $12.50 plus $0.10 per $1,000. The expression of costs on both a per policy and a per $1,000 basis represents an attempt to recognize any differences in costs that can be attributed to the amount of insurance involved. In the case of selection costs, for instance, the $0.75 per $1,000 is considered to be a rough measure of the extra medical and inspection charges incurred on large policies. If an average-size policy of $10,-000 is assumed, the rates per $1,000 for these two types of expense become $3.25 and $1.35, respectively. These amounts are disbursed immediately and need not be discounted, but they must be spread over the premium-paying period of the policy. Using the annuity factor as before, it is found that $0.25 ($4.60 ÷ $23.77) must be added to each annual premium to cover these expenses.

The only expenses which would fall under 2 (*b*) are those that may be described as maintenance expenses. They include maintenance of policy records; year-end and other valuations of reserves; premium collections; dividend allocations; and miscellaneous correspondence with policyholders, beneficiaries, and assignees. Such expenses will vary with the average size of the policies involved; but in the present illustration, the rate will be assumed to be $0.58 per $1,000. Since this expenditure will be incurred each year, it need not be discounted but can be added directly to the loading.

Finally, certain costs are incurred in settling a death claim, and 2 (*c*) recognizes these costs. It is estimated that settlement costs amount to $22 per policy and $0.30 per $1,000, the latter rate representing the extra expense connected with larger policies. For the average policy of $10,000, settlement charges would amount to $2.20 + $0.30, or $2.50 per $1,000. The present value of this sum would be obtained in exactly the same manner as that of the face of the policy (in actual formulas used by actuaries, settlement costs are added to the face of the policy) and would come out to be $0.95. The level annual addition to loading to provide for this expense would be $0.95 ÷ $23.77 = $0.04 per $1,000 of insurance.

---

annuities in states that tax annuity considerations are increased by the amount of the tax.

The foregoing assumptions and calculations are summarized in Table 18. It will be noted that the expenses which can be expressed as a percentage of the gross premium total 8.4 per cent. Those which are expressed as an amount per $1,000 aggregate $0.93. If no other factors were to be considered, the loading formula might well call for 8.4 per cent of the gross premium and $0.93 per $1,000 of insurance. Other factors must be considered, however.

TABLE 18

HYPOTHETICAL EXPENSE AND LOADING FACTORS
FOR ORDINARY LIFE POLICY ISSUED AT AGE 35
IN FACE AMOUNT OF $10,000

Type of Expense or Loading Factor	When Incurred	Expense Rate				Addition to Annual Premium	
		Per Cent of Gross Premium	Per Policy	Per $1,000	Rate per $1,000	Per Cent of Gross Premium	Amount per $1,000
First-year commission....	At issue	55%				2.3%	
Agency expense allowance..	At issue	44	$20.00		$1.00	1.9	$0.04
Other acquisition expenses...	At issue	11	2.50		.25	0.5	0.01
Renewal commissions......	Second to tenth policy years	5				1.7	
Agency expense allowance..	Second to tenth policy years		2.00		.20		0.06
State premium	Annually	2				2.0	
Selection.........	At issue		25.00	$0.75	3.25		0.14
Issue............	At issue		12.50	0.10	1.35		0.06
Maintenance.....	Annually		4.75	0.10	0.58		0.58
Settlement costs..	At maturity		22.00	0.30	2.50		0.04
Total Expenses						8.4%	0.93
Allowance for contingencies....						3.0	0.50
Allowance for dividends..						2.4	1.16
Grand Total.						13.8%	$2.59

Adding of Margins

In the first place, an allowance will be made for contingencies. Most life insurance policies are long-term contracts, the premiums for which cannot be changed after issue; and many unforeseen developments may occur before the company discharges its obligations thereunder. Developments unfavorable to the company might take the form of epidemics, unexpectedly heavy investment losses, long-run decline in interest rates, adverse tax legislation, and unanticipated increases in operating expenses. A specific increment to the loading enables the company to accumulate a fund to meet such contingencies if and when they arise. Since any overcharges can be returned through the dividend formula, the allowance for contingencies is usually a generous one. An addition to loading of 3 per cent of the gross premium would not be out of line.

Secondly, it is customary for mutual companies to make an arbitrary addition to loading for the specific purpose of creating a surplus from which dividends can be paid. While some margins for dividends will be provided in the mortality and interest assumptions underlying the net premium, provision for minimum dividends will usually be made in the loading formula. The extent to which the loading formula will be used to create dividends will depend upon broad managerial viewpoints. It is primarily a question of whether the company wants to be a high-premium, large-dividend company or a low-premium, small-dividend company. If the management leans in the former direction, the addition to the loading formula will be large; if it favors the latter approach, the increment will be at minimum level.[9] A moderate increase might be 5 or 10 per cent of the gross premium, a portion of which could be in the form of a constant per $1,000.

The adjustment of the loading formula to provide allowances for contingencies and dividends produces a final loading of 13.8 per cent of the gross premium plus $2.59 per $1,000. Some companies, however, prefer to express the loading formula in terms of the *net* premium. If it is assumed that the foregoing expense rates and allowances were stated in terms of a gross premium of $23.50, the loading formula which has just been derived can be restated as 16 per cent of the net premium and $3.00 per $1,000.

Testing the Formula

Before the foregoing formula, or any other loading formula, would be officially adopted, it would be tested at various pivotal ages, such as

---

[9] It should be noted in this connection that the conventional method of calculating net costs (gross premiums for a specific period—e.g., twenty years—adjusted for dividends during the period, minus the cash value at the end of the period equals net cost) favors the high-premium company, since interest on the redundant portion of the premium is ignored (as well as interest earnings on the reserve). Other things being equal, the larger the participating gross premium, the lower the net cost at the end of any given period. There are, of course, offsetting disadvantages, including larger commissions and—unless reduced by dividend credits—larger premium taxes.

fifteen, twenty-five, thirty-five, forty-five, and fifty-five, to see whether under realistic assumptions as to mortality, interest earnings, expenses, and terminations, the resulting gross premium would develop sufficiently high asset accumulations to provide the surrender values promised under the contract, to meet the reserve requirements imposed by law or voluntarily adopted by the company, and to support a reasonable dividend scale. The gross premiums would also be compared with the corresponding premiums being charged by other companies operating in the same territory to see whether they are low enough to meet competition.

The adequacy tests are based on so-called "asset share calculations," the purpose of which is to determine, for any block of policies written on the same plan and at the same age of issue, the expected actual amount of money per $1,000 of insurance held by the company at the end of each policy year (for a maximum period of twenty or thirty years) after payment of death claims, expenses, dividends, and surrender values and allowance for actual interest earnings. The accumulated fund at the end of any policy year is divided by the number of surviving and persisting policyholders to obtain the share of assets allocable to any particular policyholder (on the assumption that each policyholder is insured for $1,000). The process is analogous to a retrospective reserve calculation based on anticipated actual rather than tabular experience and with allowance for terminations.[10]

If the surrender values promised at each duration were precisely equal to the asset share at each duration, surrender would cause neither profit nor loss; and as a result, termination rates would not have to be consiedred in premium and asset share calculations. Under most policies, however, the surrender value excees the asset share for a number of years. Since the surrender of a contract at those durations during which the surrender value exceeds the asset share creates an additional loss for the company, it is necessary to estimate the number of policyholders who will surrender at each duration and to increase the final premium by an amount sufficiently large in the aggregate to absorb the losses caused thereby. In effect, all policyholders—those persisting and those terminating—must make a contribution toward the sums withdrawn by terminating or surrendering policyholders. This is identical in principle to the leveling of single premiums, under which procedure surviving policyholders pay a portion of the premiums that would have been paid by the deceased policyholders had the latter

---

[10] See pp. 265–75 for an illustration of an asset share calculation.

survived. After the first few policy years, the asset share may exceed the surrender value, in which event the company would realize a gain or profit from a surrender; but the losses from surrenders at the early durations almost invariably exceed the gains from surrenders at the later durations. The normal effect, therefore, of employing termination rates in asset share calculations is to increase the premium.

Although the company may experience a gain on surrenders after the first few policy years, it does not fully recover its acquisition expenses (or more exactly, the portion of first-year expenses in excess of first-year loading) until the asset share equals or exceeds the reserve.[11] Up to that point, there exists a deficiency in reserves which must be made good out of surplus or dealt with through a modification of reserve requirements.[12] The date by which the full policy reserve is to be accumulated or, conversely, the acquisition expenses are to be fully recovered, is a matter for top management decision; but the decision will be greatly influenced by the competitive situation. The shorter the period over which the expenses are to be recouped, the larger must be the gross premium, and the higher will be the net cost during those years, and vice versa. It is not unusual for a well-established company to take twenty or twenty-five years to amortize the acquisition expenses of a particular class of policies. Newly established companies, or those with a relatively limited surplus, usually amortize their acquisition expenses within a much shorter period, such as five to ten years.

If the asset share exceeds the full reserve, the policy has made a contribution to company surplus. All policies are expected to make some contribution to surplus; but the extent of the contribution is governed by considerations of equity, safety, and competition. In some states—specifically, New York—the contribution which participating policies can make to surplus in the aggregate is regulated by law.

If the asset shares produced by the tentative or provisional premium are deficient in the light of company objectives, the loading must be increased in some fashion. If the accumulation appears to be excessive

---

[11] It should not be assumed from this statement that the asset share must exceed the surrender value before the full reserve can be accumulated. While such a condition would obviously accelerate the recovery of acquisition expenses, it is not an essential factor in the process of accumulating the reserve. In many cases, the surrender value after the first year or two is equal to the asset share.

[12] See Chapter XIII.

—if the asset share exceeds the surrender value by too great a margin or equals the reserve in too brief a period—the loading must be reduced. In the process of adjusting the loading to balance the various factors involved, the original percentage and constant factors will have to be modified and may lose all identity to the expense rates on which they were initially based. The only logic behind the percentage and constant factors that frequently evolve from the balancing process is that they represent the only combination which at all ages of issue will produce the desired fit among the factors involved.

It is frequently found that the type of loading formula which will produce the best balance, all plans and ages of issue considered, is one which provides for a specified percentage of the net premium for the plan in question and a specified percentage of the net premium for an ordinary life policy issued at the same age. This plan is usually referred to as the "modified percentage" plan. An example of such a plan would be a loading formula calling for $12\frac{1}{2}$ per cent of the net premium of the policy in question plus $12\frac{1}{2}$ per cent of the ordinary life net premium. Such a formula recognizes that the dollar amount of loading on the higher premium forms should be larger than under an ordinary life contract (because of expenses which vary with the premium) but not proportionately more (because of expenses which are constant per policy and because commissions are generally lower on the higher premium plans). The arbitrary nature of the percentage additions must be corrected through the expense factor of the *dividend* formula. The modified percentage formula may also incorporate a constant amount per $1,000. An example of such a formula would be 13 per cent of the net premium for the plan under consideration, plus 5 per cent of the ordinary life net premium at the same age, plus a constant of $3.50 per $1,000.

The general procedure for arriving at the gross premium which has just been described is not followed by all mutual companies. Some mutual companies calculate their gross premiums in a manner similar to that by which the nonparticipating premiums of stock companies are generally calculated, which process is explained in the following section.

GROSS NONPARTICIPATING PREMIUMS

Except as to interest to be earned, the gross nonparticipating premium fixes irrevocably the amount of money available to the company for claims, expenses, possible adverse contingencies, and profit to stockholders. The calculation of the gross nonparticipating premium, therefore, demands judgment of the highest order and the application of the most skillful actuarial techniques. The premium which is finally developed must be low enough to meet the competition of mutual companies and other stock companies, and high enough to insure the discharge of the company's mortality and expense obligations and to afford a margin for contingencies and profit.

The chief difference between the derivation of gross participating premiums and gross nonparticipating premiums is that the point of departure for the former is a net premium based on the same mortality and interest assumptions as those underlying the net level premium reserve, while the starting point for the latter is a net premium based on realistic assumptions as to mortality and interest earnings. Both procedures entail the development of reliable expense rates, the addition of these expense rates to the net premium to produce a provisional gross premium, and the testing of the provisional gross premium by an asset share calculation.

Two Basic Approaches

There are two basic approaches to the derivation of a gross nonparticipating premium, within the procedural framework sketched above, the divergence stemming from the treatment of the profit element. The first computes the premium on the basis of the most probable assumptions as to mortality, interest, expenses, and terminations; and a specific addition, either a constant or percentage, is made for profit. Several advantages are claimed for this approach, the principal one being that equal profits may be projected for each plan of insurance and each age of issue.

The second approach uses factors more conservative than the most probable, although less conservative than those which would be used for participating premiums, but makes no specific allowance for profit. The latter is expected to emerge from the more favorable experience than that assumed. Contrary to the situation under the first approach, the profit under this method varies widely among the various plans and issue ages. This is regarded as an advantage by some, on the ground that the profit is a function of the risk assumed. For example, the profit that would be realized from using a $2\frac{3}{4}$ per cent interest assumption when a return of 3 per cent is expected should be proportional to the sum of money exposed to the risk that the return will be less than 3 per cent or even less than $2\frac{3}{4}$ per cent. On this basis, the potential profit from a spread between the assumed and actual interest return would be larger under an endowment policy than under a term policy. The reverse would be true with respect to mortality assumptions. This second method is sometimes used as an adjunct to the first to indicate how large a profit margin is needed to provide the company with a minimum return in the event that a reasonable deviation from the most probable assumptions should occur.

The demonstration of the premium computation which is presented in the following pages is based on the first approach.

Selection of Most Probable Assumptions

Mortality. If a reasonable allowance for profit has been made by a specific addition to the loading of a nonparticipating policy, then—in theory—the other elements of the premium should be selected on such a basis as to produce a premium which, in the aggregate, would provide just exactly enough funds to enable the company to meet its obligations, leaving a residuum precisely equal to the predetermined profit. In practice, of course, this utopian result is impossible of attainment. Yet, the factors must be chosen with great care, since the premium is fixed for the lifetime of the contracts and adjustments cannot be made to reflect deviations of actual from expected results.

The mortality factor is particularly troublesome, in view of the fact that during the last half century, striking reductions in the death rate have taken place at virtually all ages and further—but less spectacular —reductions are expected in the decades to come. It might be argued that the premium should reflect anticipated improvement in future mortality, in order that the nonparticipating policyholder might share in the savings that would flow from such a development. While a few companies are beginning to adjust *annuity* rates in anticipation of future longevity gains, there has been no disposition on the part of the companies to adjust *insurance* premiums on that basis. Nevertheless, stock companies do attempt to utilize the latest available experience on *past* mortality.

In recent years, the best source of information on the trends, incidence, and level of current mortality among ordinary policyholders has been the *Reports* of the Committee on Mortality under Ordinary Insurances and Annuities, published annually by the Society of Actuaries. These data are compiled by the committee from mortality statistics supplied by eighteen of the largest life insurance companies. The experience is published on a select basis for the first fifteen policy years, and on an ultimate basis for all policies with a duration of fifteen years and more. The death rates are shown for only quinquennial age groups with respect to adult lives, but at all ages on juvenile lives. Occasionally, however, the committee publishes a graduated mortality table based on this body of experience; and such tables are widely used in the calculation of premiums for nonparticipating policies and the calculation of dividends under participating policies.[13] The latest table published by the committee reflects the death rates on a select and ultimate basis for the period 1955–60.

Many companies, mainly the large ones, construct mortality tables from their own experience and use them, sometimes with modifications, to calculate their premiums.

Interest. The rate of interest used in the calculation of nonparticipating premiums on a most probable basis must be selected with great care. It involves a guess as to the rates at which future investments will be made over the next twenty-five or fifty years. This guess must be made with full knowledge of the fact that the long-range effect of the interest rate is greater than that of the mortality rate, inasmuch as the funds being invested are increasing while the amount at risk is decreasing. Moreover, the profits of a stock company are very sensitive to the margin between actual interest earnings and assumed rates. The leverage is enormous from the standpoint of the stockholder.

A range of possible rates will be considered, the upper limit of which will usually be the rate being earned on current investments and the lower limit the valuation rate of interest for policies currently being issued. The latter rate, of course, is subject to the same considerations as those governing the rate used in premium calculations. Some companies use the same rate for premium and reserve calculations, but most adopt a higher rate for premium computations. A fairly common combination is a $3\frac{1}{2}$ per cent assumption for premium computations and a 3 per cent assumption for reserve valuations.

The use of a lower rate for reserve calculations has significant implications. Since one of the criteria the final gross premium will be expected to satisfy is its ability to accumulate a fund equal to the policy reserve for all policies remaining in force at the end of a specified number of years—e.g., ten—it is apparent that the effective rate of interest after the full terminal reserve has been accumulated is the valuation rate. In other words, the company could meet its obliga-

---

[13] See Chapter XVI.

tions under the contracts, after the full reserve has been accumulated, by earning interest just equal to the rate assumed in the reserve calculation. The situation is comparable to that of any company, stock or mutual, which has revalued its reserve requirements on a lower interest basis than that used in the computation of its premiums. This practice was touched upon in the preceding chapter.

Operating Expenses. Stock companies compute their expense rates in the same manner as mutual companies. The insurance expenses are classified broadly as first-year and renewal expenses, and expressed as constants per $1,000 of insurance, per $1 of premium (same as a specified percentage of the premium), and per policy. The average size of new policies is computed by plan and age of issue, and applied to the constant expense per policy to permit the expression of expense rates in terms of a percentage of the premium plus a number of dollars per $1,000 of insurance.[14] Since the expense factors are based upon the average collection frequency of the business, the final premium must be adjusted to reflect the particular frequency with which it will be paid.

Termination Rates. The selection of the most probable future termination rates is usually found to be more difficult than is the selection of the three factors previously discussed. This factor is of somewhat less importance, however, than are the other three—except, perhaps, for small companies with extremely high lapse rates during the early policy years; and variations from expected results have a less significant effect on financial results than would a comparable variation in other assumptions. The difficulty is caused by the extreme fluctuations over the years, largely as a result of economic conditions.

As in the case of rates of mortality, interest, and expense, it is customary to use termination rates based on the company's individual experience, although reference is usually made to the rates developed in broader studies.[15] Termination rates are influenced by the quality of the agency force, plan of insurance, amount of premium, frequency of premium payment, age at issue, and other factors as well. It would be

---

[14] This statement is based upon the previously stated assumption that expenses which are constant per policy are not being allocated by means of a policy fee or a "band" approach. See p. 251.

[15] Two sets of rates which are widely used are those developed by M. A. Linton in his pioneer study, *The Record of the American Institute of Actuaries,* Vol. XIII (1924), pp. 283–316, and those developed a quarter century later by C. F. B. Richardson and John M. Hartwell in *Transactions of the Society of Actuaries,* Vol. III (1951), pp. 338–72.

possible to derive different termination rates for each appropriate combination of these enumerated factors; but in practice, the termination rates are usually differentiated only by plan of insurance. Under all plans, the termination rate is high the first two years and decreases with duration, leveling out eventually.

It should be recalled that termination rates are used in premium calculations only because of the disparity between surrender values and the funds available for distribution to withdrawing policyholders.

Illustrative Premium Calculation

The process by which a set of gross nonparticipating premiums is derived can be explained most effectively by means of a numerical example. Therefore, an illustration of the calculation and testing of the gross premium for a ten-payment life policy issued at age thirty-five has been prepared. This particular policy was selected for the illustration only in order to minimize the arithmetic work involved.

This illustration is concerned primarily with the testing of a tentative or provisional premium by means of an asset share calculation; and the principles involved are equally applicable to the testing of a provisional participating premium, except for the fact that the tentative premium in the present case is based on a more realistic set of actuarial assumptions and that no consideration need be given to a proposed dividend scale.

Under this method of deriving premiums, the tentative premium can be based on any set of actuarial assumptions, or none at all. If the calculations are a phase of a general rate revision, the tentative premium for any particular policy and age of issue is usually the premium currently being charged. It may be the premium charged by a competing company. In the present example a representative net premium was selected and then loaded by an amount sufficient to take care of anticipated actual expenses and to provide a reasonable profit. The loading was based on an average-size policy of $10,000 with expense rates (including an allowance for profit) of 56 per cent of the gross premium and $6.51 per $1,000 for the first year and 12 per cent of the gross premium and $1.85 per $1,000 during each of the next nine years. The resulting trial gross premium was $48.50.

In asset share calculations, it is customary to subtract the annual expense charges from the trial gross premium to arrive at the "effective premium" for each year, although the same result would be obtained by using the trial gross premium and treating expenses as deductions along with death claims and surrender values. In the present example, the calculation of set of effective premiums has been simplified by the use of renewal expense assumptions which do not vary with duration. The format, however, is the same as that used in more complex computations. The effective premiums are derived as follows:

Policy Year	Trial Gross Premium	Expenses and Profit		Total Expenses and Profit	Effective Premium
		Per $1 of Premium	Per $1,000 of Insurance		
1	$48.50	$0.56	$6.51	$33.67	$14.83
2–10.............	48.50	0.12	1.85	7.67	40.83

Once a set of effective premiums has been derived, it is necessary to determine how many of the premiums will be received by the company each year. This involves consideration of death and withdrawal rates. The mortality assumptions used in this phase of the process may or may not be the same as those used in the computation of the tentative gross premium. It is essential that the mortality rates used in the testing of a trial gross premium be the most realistic available. In this example, the death rates shown in the 1955–60 select table were used.[16] The death rates per 1,000 at ages thirty-five through forty-four are shown below for both this table and the 1958 C.S.O. Table, those for the latter table being included only for purposes of comparison.

Age	1955–60 Select Table	1958 C.S.O. Table
35...............	0.78	2.51
36...............	0.99	2.64
37...............	1.24	2.80
38...............	1.43	3.01
39...............	1.62	3.25
40...............	1.83	3.53
41...............	2.12	3.84
42...............	2.42	4.17
43...............	2.77	4.53
44...............	3.18	4.92

Withdrawals were assumed to take place in accordance with the following pattern, the rates representing the number of withdrawals per 1,000 of policyholders:

---

[16] This table reflects the benefit of selection for a period of fifteen years.

First year..............150	Sixth year..............36
Second year............ 60	Seventh year............32
Third year............. 50	Eighth year..............29
Fourth year............ 44	Ninth year..............27
Fifth year.............. 40	Tenth year..............25

By applying a set of death and withdrawal rates to an arbitrary number of persons assumed to be alive at the beginning of any given period, a table can be prepared showing the number of persons living and persisting at the beginning and end of each policy year thereafter. Then, by means of such a table, the number of premiums that will be received at the beginning of each policy year can be predicted, as well as the number of persons who, by virtue of having survived and persisted, will theoretically be entitled to a prorata share of the fund standing to the credit of the group at the end of each policy year. Such a tabulation, based on a radix of 100,000 persons and the death and withdrawal rates given above, is presented in Table 19.

TABLE 19
NUMBER LIVING AND PERSISTING

Policy Year	Number Living and Persisting, First of Year	Rate of Death	Number Dying during Year*	Rate of Termination	Number Terminating, End of Year*	Number Living and Persisting, End of Year
1..............	100,000	.00078	78	.150	15,000	84,922
2..............	84,922	.00099	84	.060	5,095	79,743
3..............	79,743	.00124	99	.050	3,987	75,657
4..............	75,657	.00143	108	.044	3,329	72,220
5..............	72,220	.00162	117	.040	2,889	69,214
6..............	69,214	.00183	127	.036	2,492	66,595
7..............	66,595	.00212	141	.032	2,131	64,323
8..............	64,323	.00242	156	.029	1,865	62,302
9..............	62,302	.00277	173	.027	1,682	60,447
10..............	60,447	.00318	192	.025	1,511	58,744

* Theoretically, the death rates for each year should be applied to the number of persons alive and persisting at the beginning of the year, *less* one half of the number of persons assumed to withdraw during the year; while the withdrawal rate, in turn, should be applied to the number of persons alive and persisting at the beginning of the year, less one half the number of persons assumed to die during the year. In practice, such refinements are not usually introduced into the computations, in view of the wide margins of error that are likely to exist in the withdrawal rates in the first place.

One more set of values is needed before the asset share calculation can be undertaken, that being the sum per $1,000 of insurance made available in each policy year to a terminating policyholder. For the purposes of this example, it was assumed that the minimum values required under the Standard Nonforfeiture Law on a 3 per cent interest basis are available. These values for the first ten policy years under a ten-payment life policy issued at age thirty-five are as follows:

First year............$ 3.24		Sixth year...........$241.62
Second year......... 48.21		Seventh year........ 293.55
Third year.......... 94.51		Eighth year......... 347.02
Fourth year........ 142.15		Ninth year......... 402.11
Fifth year.......... 191.18		Tenth year......... 458.90

It will be learned in a later chapter[17] that under the Standard Nonforfeiture Law, the minimum surrender value at the end of the premium-paying period must equal the net level premium reserve at that time. Thus, the tenth-year surrender value above, $458.90, is also the tenth-year net level premium reserve for a ten-payment life policy issued at age thirty-five.

With a set of assumptions as to the number and volume of premiums that will be received each year, the number of death claims of $1,000 each that will be incurred each year (based on the same death rates as those used to determine the number of premiums to be received), the number and amount of surrender payments that will be disbursed each year, and the rate of interest which will be earned on accumulated funds (3½ per cent), the raw materials are available for the construction of the main body of the asset share calculation. The various assumptions are combined in the manner shown in Table 20 to arrive at the asset share per $1,000 at each duration.

According to Table 20, 100,000 policyholders will pay in a total of $1,483,000 in effective premiums at the beginning of the first year. This sum is assumed to earn interest throughout the year at 3½ per cent, amounting to $1,534,905 at the end of the year. Seventy-eight policyholders are assumed to die during the first year; the payment of these claims at the end of the year would reduce the fund by $78,000. Since the deaths will occur throughout the year, however, and the claims will be paid, on the average, six months before the end of the year, the drain on the fund must be increased by $1,365 ($78,000 × .0175) to compensate for the loss of a half year's interest on the claims payable. Death claims, therefore, are shown at $79,365. It is assumed that 15,000 policyholders will surrender their policies at the end of the first year, receiving $3.24 individually and $48,600 in the aggregate.

At the end of the year, a fund of $1,406,940 is assumed to be on hand, which, divided on a prorata basis among the 84,922 surviving and persisting policyholders, would give each $16.57. The latter sum is the asset share per $1,000 at the end of the first year. The terminal reserve at each duration is shown for purposes of comparison; and it may be observed that at the end of the first year, the reserve exceeds

---

[17] Chapter XIV.

TABLE 20

Asset Share Calculation,
$1,000 Ten-Payment Life Policy Issued at Age 35;
Gross Premium per $1,000 = $48.50

Policy Year	(1) Number Living and Persisting	(2) Effective Premiums per $1,000	(3) Total Effective Premiums [(1) × (2)]	(4) Initial Fund [(10)n − 1 + (3)]	(5) Initial Fund plus 3½ Per Cent Interest [(4) × 1.035]	(6) Death Claims*	(7) Cash Value	(8) Number Withdrawing	(9) Amount Paid on Surrender [(7) × (8)]	(10) Fund Balance [(5) − (6) − (9)]	(11) Asset Share [(10) ÷ (1)n + 1]	(12) Net Level Premium Terminal Reserve
1	100,000	14.83	$1,483,000	$ 1,483,000	$ 1,534,905	$ 79,365	$ 3.24	15,000	$ 48,600	$ 1,406,940	$ 16.57	$ 40.18
2	84,922	40.83	3,467,365	4,874,305	5,044,906	85,470	48.21	5,095	245,630	4,713,806	59.11	81.55
3	79,743	40.83	3,255,907	7,969,713	8,248,653	100,733	94.51	3,987	376,811	7,771,109	102.72	124.13
4	75,657	40.83	3,089,075	10,860,184	11,240,290	109,890	142.15	3,329	473,217	10,657,183	147.57	167.93
5	72,220	40.83	2,948,743	13,605,926	14,082,133	119,048	191.18	2,889	552,319	13,410,766	193.76	213.00
6	69,214	40.83	2,826,008	16,236,774	16,805,061	129,223	241.62	2,492	602,117	16,073,721	241.37	259.36
7	66,595	40.83	2,719,074	18,792,795	19,450,543	143,468	293.55	2,131	625,555	18,681,520	290.43	307.07
8	64,323	40.83	2,626,309	21,307,829	22,053,603	158,730	347.02	1,865	647,192	21,247,681	341.04	356.18
9	62,302	40.83	2,543,791	23,791,472	24,624,174	176,023	402.11	1,682	676,349	23,771,797	393.27	406.77
10	60,447	40.83	2,468,051	26,239,848	27,158,243	195,360	458.90	1,511	693,398	26,269,485	447.19	458.90

* These death claims have been adjusted to reflect a loss of six months' interest. The adjustment consists of increasing the claims by 1.75 per cent, which is equivalent to 3½ per cent annual interest for six months.

the asset share by $23.61. However, the asset share exceeds the surrender value by $13.33.

At the beginning of the second year, 84,922 surviving and persisting policyholders pay in a total of $3,467,365 in effective premiums, which, when added to the fund at the end of the first year, produces a total fund at the beginning of the second year of $4,874,305. Improved at $3\frac{1}{2}$ per cent interest, this fund amounts to $5,044,906 at the end of the second year, before deduction of death and surrender claims. Death claims, adjusted for loss of interest, and surrender payments reduce the fund to a net balance of $4,713,806. Divided prorata among the 79,743 surviving and persisting policyholders, this fund yields an asset share of $59.11, which falls short of the second-year terminal reserve by $22.44 per $1,000, but surpasses the surrender value by $10.90.

This process is continued through the next eight years; and by the end of the tenth policy year, the fund is seen to have grown to $26,269,485, which is sufficient to provide $447.19 to each of the 58,744 surviving and persisting policyholders. This is $11.71 less than the full net level premium reserve and the surrender value at that point, the latter two values being identical at the end of the tenth year, as explained above.

By comparing the asset share at each duration with the comparable surrender value and reserve, the company can evaluate the adequacy and equity of the trial gross premium. Unless and until the asset share equals or exceeds the surrender value, each termination is a direct drain on the surplus of the company. Under such circumstances, the company gives back to each withdrawing policyholder more money than that policyholder contributed to the surplus of the company. This situation may prevail for several years under many plans and ages at issue; but under a high-premium type of policy, such as the ten-payment life, the asset share would normally exceed the surrender value by some amount even at the end of the first year.

A more fundamental test used by the companies is the period of time required for the asset share to equal or exceed the full net level premium reserve. Until that occurs, the company has not recovered its acquisition expenses and is still showing a *book* loss for the block of business represented in the asset share calculation. Once the asset share exceeds the reserve, the acquisition expenses have been recovered in full, and the policies are making an annual contribution to the surplus of the company. Based on many considerations, including the interests of stockholders a company, in testing a trial gross premium, decides how long it can afford—and is willing—to wait before recovering its outlay on behalf of a group of policies. If it decides that it should take ten years in recouping its acquisition expenses, it will want to use a gross premium which will accumulate an asset share exactly equal to the reserve at the end of the tenth policy year. For convenience, such period is called the *validation period.*

It would be a sheer accident if the trial gross premium should produce an asset share precisely equal to the full net level premium reserve at the end of the validation period. There will always be a disparity, in one direction or the other; and the trial gross premium will have to be adjusted upward or downward. This adjustment is accomplished by dividing the difference between the asset share and the reserve at the end of the validation period by the so-called "accumulation of an annual premium of $1," and adding or subtracting the result, depending upon whether the asset share is smaller or greater than the reserve, to the trial gross premium. The technique is similar in principle to the life annuity due concept, despite the fact that in one case, an accumulation is involved, while in the other, a present value is derived. The technique will be illustrated in connection with the example of the ten-payment life policy.

It will be assumed that a validation period of ten years has been decided upon by the company. In this case, the trial gross premium is too small, as indicated by the fact that the asset share falls short of the reserve at the end of the validation period by $11.71. To determine the size of the correction that will be required, it is necessary to ascertain the effect which a change of $1 in the trial gross premium would have on the accumulation at the end of ten years and then, by simple proportion, find the exact change in the premium which would increase the accumulation by the desired amount.

It is helpful at this stage to visualize the change in the trial gross premium as an *increase* of $1, regardless of the direction of the adjustment actually needed. Then, it will be apparent that this additional annual payment of $1 will not have to bear any share of the death and surrender claims, since these were met through the original premium payments. However, the additional $1 will have to bear its proportionate share of those expenses that vary directly with the size of the premium. Since these expenses were earlier assumed to amount to 56 per cent of the first-year premium and 12 per cent of the renewal premium, the effective additional premium will be $0.44 the first year and $0.88 for each of the other nine years. The number of surviving and persisting policyholders at each duration remains the same, and so does the assumed rate of interest earnings. Therefore, the additional premium of $1 will bring in an additional sum of $44,000 the first year, which, at $3\frac{1}{2}$ per cent interest, will accumulate to $45,540 by the end of the first year. Because of lower renewal expenses, the additional effective premiums for the second year will aggregate $74,731.36, which, when supplemented by the fund at the end of the first year and interest at $3\frac{1}{2}$ per cent on the composite fund, will amount to $124,480.86, at the end of the second year. By the end of the tenth year, the additional premium of $1 paid each year by the surviving and persisting policyholders will have accumu-

TABLE 21

ACCUMULATION OF ANNUAL PREMIUM OF $1

(1)	(2)	(3)	(4)	(5)	(6)
Policy Year	Number Living and Persisting	Effective Premium	Total Effective Premiums [(2) × (3)]	Fund at Beginning of Year [Current (4) + (6) for Preceding Year]	Fund at End of Year [(5) × 1.035]
1........	100,000	$0.44	$44,000.00	$ 44,000.00	$ 45,540.00
2........	84,922	0.88	74,731.36	120,271.36	124,480.86
3........	79,743	0.88	70,173.84	194,654.70	201,467.61
4........	75,657	0.88	66,578.16	268,045.77	277,427.37
5........	72,220	0.88	63,553.60	340,980.97	352,915.30
6........	69,214	0.88	60,908.32	413,823.62	428,307.45
7........	66,595	0.88	58,603.60	486,911.05	503,952.94
8........	64,323	0.88	56,604.24	560,557.18	580,176.68
9........	62,302	0.88	54,825.76	635,002.44	657,227.53
10........	60,447	0.88	53,193.36	710,420.89	735,285.62

Asset share, end of ten years: $735,285.62 ÷ 58,744 = $12.52
Correct gross premium: $48.50 + ($11.71 ÷ $12.52) = $49.44

lated to $735,285.62. Divided prorata among the 58,744 policyholders surviving and persisting at that point, this sum would provide an additional $12.52 to each person. In other words, an increase in the trial gross premium of $1.00 would increase the asset share at the end of ten years by $12.52. This reflects not only the influence of compound interest but also the benefit of survivorship and persistency.

This is a greater correction than that needed in the case under consideration, where the asset share is only $11.71 short of the predetermined objective. However, in order to determine the exact amount by which the illustrative trial gross premium need be increased in order to accumulate the desired asset share, it is necessary only to divide $11.71 by $12.52, which yields $0.94. Thus, the correct gross premium is $49.44 ($48.50 + $0.94). This premium will accumulate an asset share at the end of ten years just exactly equal to the net level premium reserve, if the actual results conform precisely to the projected results.

The supporting calculations for the foregoing adjustment are presented in Table 21.

Development of a Schedule of Competitive Premiums

In the construction of a complete set of gross premium rates, a company will calculate the gross premium in the manner described above at either the quinquennial or the decennial ages of issue for all of its plans and then, by formula or by interpolation, will derive the rates for all other ages of issue. If a company can find a complete set of net premiums which, when loaded in a particular manner, will approximately reproduce the predetermined gross premiums at the specimen ages, it may derive a complete set of gross premiums by plan and age by means of that particular combination of net premiums and loading. The source and actuarial bases of the net premiums are immaterial; they may be based on published rates of mortality or may be based entirely on the company's own experience. They may be based on the same mortality and interest assumptions that were used in testing the trial gross premium or an assumption quite unrelated to those underlying the asset share calculation. The only thing that matters is that, when loaded in a specified manner, they will reproduce gross premium rates which are founded on realistic assumptions related to the company's own operations. Most companies do not attempt to find this happy combination of net premiums and loading and, instead, derive gross premiums for the intermediate ages entirely by interpolation.

Before the rates are derived for each age of issue, however, the gross premiums at the representative ages are compared with the corresponding rates of other companies operating in the same territory to determine whether they are competitive. This is an essential step in the rate-making process, since the asset share calculation is concerned only with the *adequacy* of the proposed gross premium. If a company's premium rates are clearly out of line, it will experience difficulty in holding its agency force and in all likelihood will lose ground in the struggle for new business. If the survey of other companies' rates reveals the skeletal set of premiums to be competitive, the company can proceed with the derivation of the complete set of rates. If its rates appear to be too high, however, the company will have to consider one or more of the adjustments outlined below.

If the "most probable" mortality, interest, expense, and termination rates have been used in the calculation of the gross premiums, there is little possibility that the competitive situation can be improved by changing any of those assumptions. Even with the same basic assumptions, however, the premiums can be reduced by extending the period over which acquisition expenses are to be amortized. This means that the drain on surplus will be increased, but it may be the most practicable solution among the various alternatives. If a specific allowance for profit has been made in the calculations, the shaving of this margin may pave the way for a small reduction in premiums. If the reductions made possible by extending the validation period and narrowing the profit margin are not substantial enough, adjustments of a more fundamental nature may have to be undertaken. Such adjustments could take the form of more stringent underwriting requirements, less conservative (and thus higher yielding) investments, greater operating economies, or the elimination of the less persistent policies.

The final step in the derivation of a set of premium rates is to review the over-all results for consistency as among the various plans and ages at issue. In all cases, identical premiums should be charged for identical benefits. There should be no "bargain rates" in the scale of premiums, since, entirely apart from considerations of equity, such rates are likely to attract an undue volume of business at those points, creating a serious disbalance among the various plans and ages of issue.

DERIVATION OF PARTICIPATING GROSS PREMIUMS THROUGH TECHNIQUE OF TENTATIVE GROSS PREMIUMS

The technique which underlies the calculation of the nonparticipating gross premiums of the larger stock companies is used by some mutual companies, with the modifications necessitated by the payment of policyholder dividends, to calculate participating gross premiums.

In using this technique, a mutual company computes a set of specimen gross premiums, at quinquennial or decennial ages, on the basis of the most probable" assumptions as to mortality, interest, and expenses, and tests such premiums for adequacy by means of the familiar asset share calculation. At this stage, no allowance is made for dividend distributions, the margins in the basic assumptions being so narrow that no funds are presumably available for distribution to policyholders. The trial gross premiums, adjusted to reflect the redundancy or deficiency in the asset share, as the case might be, are compared with the gross premiums (after dividends, in the case of participating gross premiums) of competing companies in order to ascertain whether they will stand up in competition. Once the premiums have been pitched to the optimum level from a competitive standpoint, the company is in a position to consider its dividend policy.

A dividend scale of any desired level and pattern can be developed, without the necessity of relating the resulting dividends to any particular sources of surplus. The margins needed to support the proposed dividend scale are added directly to the gross premiums. Several sets of premium rates, based on various assumed margins, are usually constructed and compared before the final set of representative gross premiums, with the built-in dividend scale, are selected. Gross premiums for all ages of issue are usually computed by loading the valuation net premiums—or, occasionally, some other set of net premiums—in accordance with a formula which, by experimentation, was found to develop gross premium rates approximately equivalent to the desired gross premiums when applied to valuation—or other selected—net premiums. As pointed out earlier, such a formula usually takes the form of a percentage of the gross of net premium plus a constant amount per $1,000 of insurance. The constant may vary slightly by age of issue.

Some companies vary the procedure by calculating the trial gross premiums on a nonparticipating basis and then adding the margins for the predetermined dividend scale before running the various asset share tests. Under such a procedure, dividend distributions operate as a decremental factor, along with death claims and surrender payments, in the asset share calculation. The general results should be the same under either procedure.

CHAPTER XIII

Modified Reserve Systems

THE PROBLEM

IT WAS explained in an earlier chapter that the net level premium reserve is based on the assumption that the loading in the gross premium for a particular policy will be just exactly adequate to take care of the expenses that will be incurred in connection with such policy, leaving only the net premium to absorb the cost of insurance and to accumulate the necessary policy reserve. By the same token, it assumes that the entire net premium will be available each year—including the first—to meet those obligations. Yet, it was noted in the preceding chapter that the costs of acquisition are such that the first-year expenses greatly exceed the loading in the first-year gross premium. Indeed, under many policies, first-year expenses will exceed the entire gross premium. The following situation relative to an ordinary life contract of $1,000 issued at age thirty-five may be regarded as a conservative example of the problem. In other words, first-year expenses in many companies would be much larger than those shown here.[1]

---

[1] The net premium and reserve shown in this illustration are based on the 1958 C.S.O. Table and interest at 3 per cent. Loading is equal to 16 per cent of the net premium plus a constant of $3.00 per $1,000.

Net premium.............................		$17.67
Loading....................................		5.83
Gross premium............................		$23.50
Initial expense...........................		17.53
Balance at beginning of year.............		$ 5.97
Interest at actual rate (3.95 per cent).........		.24
Sum at end of year......................		$ 6.21
Deduct:		
Actual cost of insurance (42 per cent of tabular cost)..........................	$ 1.04	
Other first-year expenses..................	15.27	
First-year terminal reserve...............	15.64	$31.95
Deficit, end of first year[2]....................		$25.74

Thus, it can be seen that the company's out-of-pocket costs during the first year, ignoring the reserve liability, exceeds by a wide margin the gross premium collected from the policyholder.

Offsetting this unfavorable financial picture at the end of the first policy year is the fact that the loading on renewal premiums, $5.83, will be far more than adequate to take care of renewal expenses, or expenses incurred after the first year. This suggests that the redundant portion of future loadings could be utilized to meet the excess of first-year expenses over first-year loading, provided a way could be found to cope with the deficit at the end of the first year.

If a company enjoys a strong surplus position, which is characteristic of the older, well-established companies, the deficit can be met out of surplus, with the latter being reimbursed or replenished from the redundant loading in future premiums. As the years go by, aggregate repayments from renewal loadings on business previously written will tend to offset the deficiencies being created by newly issued policies, thus lessening the *net* strain on surplus from new business. Eventually, repayments might more than offset the withdrawals.

In a small, recently organized company, the deficits arising out of new business cannot be met wholly by drawing on surplus. Typically, such a company has a relatively small surplus, and its new issues constitute a significantly large proportion of total business in force. If a company in that position should attempt to absorb its entire first-year deficit out of surplus, the latter would be quickly depleted, and the company might be forced to limit the amount of new business it

---

[2] Apart from the probable understatement of first-year expenses in the first instance, this statement of the deficit is not strictly accurate, inasmuch as the "other first-year expenses" will be incurred throughout the year and hence will reduce the sum at interest. Moreover, the reserve which would have to be reflected in the financial statement prepared as of the end of the calendar year in which the policy is written would be the *mean reserve,* which in this case would be $16.66. But, if the mean reserve were used, only a half year's cost of insurance would be reflected.

could accept. In any case, it would probably have to reinsure a heavier proportion of its business than underwriting requirements would dictate. Theoretically, the problem could be solved by charging a higher premium in the first year than in subsequent years, the difference being equal to the deficiency in the first-year loading; but the practical difficulties of this approach are so formidable as to preclude its use. From a sales standpoint, the companies would prefer to charge a *lower* premium for the first year, rather than a higher one.[3] This leaves no other solution than a modification of the reserve requirement of such nature that the company is relieved of the obligation of setting up a reserve—or, at least, the full net level premium reserve—at the end of the first policy year. Under most policies, this would not obviate the need for drawing on surplus, but would greatly reduce the drain. The amount "borrowed" from the net level premium reserve could be repaid from renewal loadings in the same manner and at the same time as the "loan" from surplus is repaid. Obviously, repayments to the reserve account should take priority over replenishment of surplus. Such a plan is practicable as long as the margin in renewal loadings is large enough to repay the loan from the reserve and the amount drawn from surplus. The qualification as to surplus is necessary, since otherwise, the surplus account would gradually be exhausted and the company would eventually be unable to accept new business. The principle of reserve modification has long been accepted by regulatory authorities and authorized for use in the computation of legal reserves. The most recent evidence of this acceptance is the incorporation of the concept in the Commissioners Reserve Valuation Method, which has been approved for use in all states.

Reserve valuation methods which contemplate something less than the full net level premium reserve at the end of the first policy year are broadly referred to as "modified reserve" plans or systems. There are several variations of such systems, the major subdivisions being *full preliminary term, modified preliminary term,* and *select and ultimate.*

FULL PRELIMINARY TERM VALUATION

The concept underlying the full preliminary term method of valuation is that the full first-year reserve can be properly be used to help meet the excess of first-year expenses over first-year loading, regardless

---

[3] As was noted in the study of contracts, some companies offer a contract the premium for which is lower during the first three or five years than that payable thereafter.

of the type of contract involved or the age at issue. This means that there will be no reserve at the end of the first year. The concept also implies that the repayment of the amount borrowed from the reserve can be spread over the entire premium-paying period. However, inasmuch as the reserve under the full preliminary term method of valuation at the end of the premium-paying period must be equal to the full net level premium reserve, a larger proportion of each renewal premium must be allocated to the accumulation of the reserve than under the full net premium method of valuation. Moreover, since the net amount at risk is somewhat greater throughout the premium-paying period than under the net level premium reserve method, the cost of insurance is slightly higher. The implication of the foregoing is that the net premium after the first year must be larger under the full preliminary term method of valuation than under the conventional method.

The technique by which the first-year reserve is released for application against expenses is to treat the first year of insurance as term insurance, irrespective of the contract form actually involved, and to assume that the original contract of permanent insurance goes into effect at the beginning of the second policy year. In other words, for the purpose of reserve calculation, all contracts are regarded as a combination of term insurance for the first year and permanent insurance—whole life or endowment insurance, as the case may be—issued at an age one year older and for a period one year shorter than that of the contract actually written. Thus, a twenty-year endowment issued at age thirty becomes, for purposes of reserve computation, a combination of a one-year term policy issued at age thirty and a nineteen-year endowment issued at age thirty-one. A thirty-payment life policy issued at age twenty-five is transformed into a one-year term policy written at age twenty-five and a twenty-nine-payment life policy issued at age twenty-six. The origin of the expression "preliminary term" should now be apparent.

If the first year is regarded as term insurance, no reserve need be set up at the end of the year, and the sum which would otherwise have to be set aside for that purpose can be diverted to the meeting of expenses. By the same token, if the permanent contract is viewed as one written at an age one year older and for a period one year shorter than the original contract, the hypothetical net premium must be larger than the actual one. The difference will be equivalent to the annual sum necessary to amortize the first-year reserve—the amount of the loan—over the remaining premium-paying period. For example, it was noted earlier in this discussion that the first-year reserve under an ordinary life contract issued at age thirty-five is $15.64 per $1,000. If the preliminary term method of valuation were to be used, the entire $15.64 would be released to help meet acquisition costs, but would have to be repaid in equal annual installments over the remaining premium-paying period of the policy. The amount which must be repaid each year can be obtained by dividing $15.64 by the present value of a whole life annuity due of $1 computed as of age thirty-six, or $23.40. The result, $0.67, added to the net level premium of $17.67 for an ordinary life policy issued at thirty-five, yields $18.34, the net level premium for an ordinary life policy issued at age thirty-six. Since the gross premium remains the same, that for an ordinary life policy issued at thirty-five, the effective amount of loading in renewal premiums is reduced by $0.67. If the gross premium is $23.50, the figure cited earlier, the effective loading in each renewal premium becomes $5.16 instead of $5.83. In effect, the company commutes or anticipates $0.67 out of every renewal premium. Stated differently, it borrows the first-year reserve, promising to repay the loan out of renewal loadings at the rate of $0.67 per year. By the end of the premium-paying period (in this case, the end of the mortality table), the loan will have been completely repaid, and the reserve will equal the full level premium reserve; but on any earlier date, the preliminary term reserve will be smaller than the latter by the present value of future contributions from renewal loadings. The impact of such reserve deficiency on the cost of insurance is reflected in the higher net premium for age thirty-six, or whatever age might be involved.

The effective amount of loading for an ordinary life contract issued at age thirty-five under the full preliminary term method of valuation, for both the first and subsequent policy years, is set forth in the following exhibit:

First Year:
1. Gross premium.................................$23.50
2. Net level premium.............................. 17.67
3. Loading..$ 5.83
4. Net premium for one-year term insurance.......... 2.45
5. Additional loading [(2) − (4)]..................... 15.22
6. Total loading available [(3) + (5)] = [(1) − (4)].... 21.05
Second and subsequent years:
7. Net premium required........................... 18.34
8. Effective renewal loading [(1) − (7)].............. 5.16
9. Additional net premium [(7) − (2)]................ 0.67

It can be seen that the effective amount of loading *at the beginning* of the first year is $21.05, as compared to the nominal loading of

$5.83.[4] Thereafter, however, the effective loading is only $5.16, since $0.67 of the original renewal loading must be diverted to reserve accumulation.

The foregoing relationships are graphically presented in Figure 13. In the case of full net level premium reserve valuation, the loading is $5.83 per $1,000 each year, including the first. In contrast, the loading under the full preliminary term method of valuation is $21.05

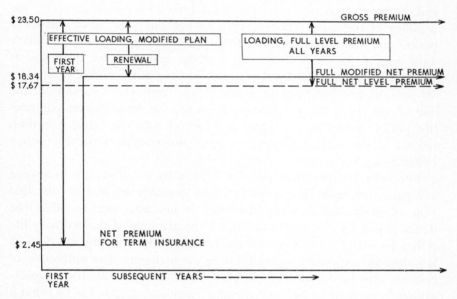

FIG. 13. Comparison of modified net premium under full preliminary term method of valuation with full net level premium, ordinary life, age thirty-five; 1958 C.S.O. Table and 2½ per cent interest. (Adapted, with permission, from Henry T. Owen, *Fundamentals of Life Insurance* [Englewood Cliffs, N.J.: Prentice-Hall, Inc., 1951], Fig. 1, p. 89.)

the first year and only $5.16 thereafter. The increase in the loading for the first year under the modified plan is just exactly offset actuarially by the reduction in loading for the subsequent years. In other words, the present value of the two loading patterns is the same at the inception of the contract. With respect to the net premiums under the two plans, one is a combination of $2.45 for the first policy year and $18.34 for subsequent years, while the other envisions a level pre-

---

[4] It should be noted that the amount of $21.05, which represents the loading available *at the beginning* of the year, differs from the sum of $21.47, obtained by adding $5.83 to $15.64, which, with certain refinements, might be viewed as representing the loading *at the end* of the policy year. The two sums can be reconciled.

mium of $17.67 throughout the life of the policy. In this case, like-wise, the present values are identical.

Full preliminary term reserves can be computed on either the pro-spective or the retrospective basis; but if the latter method is used, the first-year premium for term insurance must be taken into considera-tion. No new principles are involved in the calculation of such re-serves. The preliminary term reserve for any particular policy at the end of any given period is simply the full net level premium reserve for a policy of the same type issued at an age one year older and for a period one year shorter. Thus, at the end of ten years, the preliminary term reserve for an ordinary life contract issued at age thirty-five is $154.67, or the full net level premium reserve at the end of nine years for an ordinary life contract issued at age thirty-six. Likewise, at the end of ten years, the preliminary term reserve for a twenty-payment life policy issued at age forty is $289.53—the net level premium reserve at the end of *nine* years for a *nineteen-payment* life policy issued at age forty-one.

For most low-premium policies written by a typical life insurance company, the additional loading made available by treating the first year of insurance as term insurance is not adequate to offset the deficiency in the first-year loading. In the example of the ordinary life policy issued at age thirty-five, the total effective loading was $11.75 less than the expenses incurred during the first year. The difference, of course, must be drawn from surplus. Thus, it is possible for a rapidly growing company to have a "capacity" problem, despite the fact that it is using a modified reserve plan.

On the other hand, it must be recognized that the reserves released under the higher premium forms of insurance by the full preliminary term method of valuation may provide more funds than are required by a well-managed company to supplement the loading in the first-year premium. Consider, for instance, the situation with respect to a twenty-year endowment insurance contract issued at age thirty-five:

First year:
1. Gross premium...................................$48.85
2. Net level premium................................ 40.44
3. Loading..$ 8.41
4. Net premium for one-year term insurance........... 2.45
5. Additional loading [(2) — (4)]..................... 37.99
6. Total loading available [(3) + (5)]................. 46.40

Second and subsequent years:
7. Net premium required............................. 43.07
8. Effective renewal loading [(1) — (7)]............... 5.78
9. Additional net premium [(7) — (2)].................. 2.63

Under such a contract, $46.40 per $1,000 would be made available to meet acquisition expenses, but only $5.78 would be available for renewal expenses. In the case of a ten-year endowment contract, likewise issued at age thirty-five, the comparable figures—assuming loading of $14.38 per $1,000—would be $100.46 and $3.42, respectively. Clearly, some limitation on the extent to which the first-year reserve can be used to pay first-year expenses is necessary.

In attempting to arrive at a reasonable limitation on the use of the first-year reserve for such purpose, supervisory authorities have been guided by two considerations: (1) the amount of reserve released should not be so large as to encourage extravagance on the part of the companies in the acquiring of new business, and (2) the amount to be repaid in subsequent years should not exceed the margin in renewal loadings. Violation of the first consideration would lead to a needlessly high cost of insurance to policyholders; whereas violation of the second could lead to a permanent impairment of surplus by the policies involved, depending upon the margins available in the mortality and interest assumptions. In extreme cases—namely, very short term endowments—the renewal net premium under the full preliminary term system might exceed the full gross premium payable by the policyholder, all renewal expenses having to be paid out of surplus or out of earnings that could otherwise be distributed in the form of dividends. The limitations which have been arrived at are discussed in the next section.

MODIFIED PRELIMINARY TERM VALUATION

Modified preliminary term valuation, as its name implies, refers to any system of preliminary term valuation which imposes a limitation or restriction on the amount of first-year reserve that can be used for the payment of first-year expenses. Over the years, various states developed their own modifications of the full preliminary term basis of valuation, or adopted the modifications of other states, and required that the limitations embodied therein be observed with respect to policies written within their jurisdictions. One of the most widely adopted modifications was that developed by the State of Illinois, which appropriately became known as the *Illinois Standard*. The Illinois law limited the borrowing from the reserve to an amount equal to the first-year reserve under a twenty-payment life policy, except for policies with fewer than twenty annual premiums, in which case the amount was somewhat smaller. The full first-year reserve could be used for expenses under any policy having a "premium"[5] not greater than that for a twenty-payment life policy for the same age of issue, but a portion of the normal first-year reserve had to be held under any policy the premium for which was greater than the premium for a twenty-payment life policy of the same issue age.[6] Moreover, the full net level premium reserve had to be accumulated by the end of twenty years or, if shorter, the end of the premium paying period.

In Ohio, the law embodied the _principle_ of the Illinois Standard but required a modification of the full preliminary term method only for limited payment life and endowment policies providing for fewer than twenty payments. Thus, the Ohio Standard permitted full preliminary term reserves for all endowment insurance policies with premiums payable for twenty years or more, whereas the Illinois Standard allowed such reserves only when the premium was not greater than the comparable premium for a twenty-payment life policy.

The approach adopted in New Jersey rested on a different principle. Under the New Jersey Standard, the reserve required at the end of the first year under _any_ policy was the full net level premium reserve for the policy in question _less_ the excess of the full reserve on an _ordinary life_ policy over the reserve for a one-year term policy—which, of course, is zero. Therefore, at the end of the first policy year, no reserve was required for an ordinary life policy; while under other plans, the permissible _reduction_ from the full reserve (or, conversely, the additional expense allowance) was the same, irrespective of the type of plan or the number of premiums payable. Then the amount "borrowed" from the full reserve had to be repaid in prorata annual installments over the next nineteen years. Thus, by the end of the twentieth policy year, the full net level premium reserve was required under all policies.

Other modifications prevailed in various states and Canada. Needless to say, the multiplicity of valuation standards imposed a substantial administrative burden on companies operating in various jurisdictions. Consequently, one of the major objectives of the Guertin Com-

---

[5] The Illinois statute referred to the "premium charged," which would imply the gross premium. In the administration of the law, however, the net premium was used as a basis of comparison.

[6] See pp. 275–80 of the first edition of McGill, _Life Insurance,_ for a detailed description of the Illinois Standard and the method used to determine the amount of the first-year reserve (and subsequent reserves) for any policy having a premium in excess of that for a twenty-payment life policy issued at the same age.

mittee[7] was to develop a reserve valuation method which would deal with the first-year expense problem in such a manner as to be acceptable to all states, thus bringing about a higher degree of uniformity in this area than had ever prevailed before.

The Committee's efforts were crowned with success. The method that it recommended was embodied in the Standard Valuation Law which has been adopted by all states and—with minor exceptions—is applicable to all ordinary insurance issued since December 31, 1947.

The description of the Commissioners Reserve Valuation Method, as the uniform system is known, in the Standard Valuation Law is highly technical, partly because of the need for precision of language and partly to avoid use of the expression "preliminary term" which lends itself to the mistaken impression that under such a reserve system, the first year's insurance is term insurance. Stripped of its technical verbiage, however, the present law prescribes a method that is virtually identical with the Illinois Standard method. The principal difference lies in the treatment of policies with a premium-paying period of longer than twenty years. Under the Illinois Standard, those policies subject to a limitation on the use of the first-year reserve must accumulate the full net level premium reserves by the end of twenty years or the premium-paying period, *whichever is the shorter;* under the Commissioners Reserve Valuation Method the full net level premium reserve need not be accumulated until the end of the premium-paying period, even though such period should exceed twenty years. This modification, which permits slightly lower reserves throughout the premium-paying period and hence a proportionately larger first-year expense allowance, does not reflect a difference in principle or philosophy but was merely intended to eliminate the inconsistency encountered under the Illinois Standard in connection with certain plans under which the net premium at the lower ages at issue was greater than the net premium for a twenty-payment life policy but was less at the higher ages.

The procedure for determining the additional first-year expense allowances (over and above the normal loading) for various policies and ages of issue under the Commissioners Method is too complex to be described here. Suffice it to say that the entire first-year reserve may be used for all policies whose "modified"[8] net premium does not

---

[7] See p. 149.

[8] The "modified premium" is the net level annual premium for the actual age of issue increased by the amount necessary to amortize over the full premium-paying

exceed the modified net premium for a twenty-payment life policy issued at the same age. In other words, those policies may be valued on the basis of the full preliminary term method of valuation. For policies with higher premiums, the additional allowance for first-year expenses is limited to an amount approximately equal to the first-year net level premium reserve for a twenty-payment life policy issued at corresponding ages. The maximum additional expense allowance is precisely the same as the first-year reserve for a twenty-payment life policy when the policy calls for twenty annual premiums; it is somewhat smaller when fewer than twenty annual premiums are payable and slightly larger when more than twenty premiums are contemplated. These differences reflect the fact that the amount "borrowed" from the reserve is "repaid" by a level annual premium payable for the whole of the premium-paying period, including the first year.

TABLE 22

COMPARISON OF ADDITIONAL FIRST-YEAR EXPENSE ALLOWANCES UNDER FULL PRELIMINARY TERM AND COMMISSIONERS RESERVE METHODS OF VALUATION; AGE 35; 1958 C.S.O. AND 2½ PER CENT INTEREST

Type of Contract	Net Level Premium	Additional Expense Allowance	
		Full Preliminary Term Basis	Commissioners Method
Ordinary life.................	$17.67	$15.22	$15.22
25-payment life..............	23.42	20.97	20.97
20-payment life..............	27.24	24.79	24.79
15-payment life..............	33.86	31.41	24.36
10-payment life..............	47.44	44.99	23.51
25-year endowment...........	31.36	28.91	25.03
20-year endowment...........	40.44	37.99	24.79
15-year endowment...........	56.21	53.76	24.36
10-year endowment...........	88.53	86.08	23.51

A comparison of the additional first-year expense allowances made available under the full preliminary term and the Commissioners Reserve Valuation bases for various policies issued at age thirty-five is presented in Table 22. The allowances under the full preliminary term basis for policies with net premiums in excess of the twenty-payment life net premium are largely hypothetical since few states have ever permitted the unrestricted use of that method. Nevertheless, a comparison of the potential allowances under the two systems illustrates the restrictive effect of the Commissioners Method.

period the sum "borrowed" from the first-year reserve. The modified premium for an ordinary life policy issued at age thirty-five is the net level annual premium for the same policy issued at age thirty-six. See pp. 279–81 for an explanation of the manner in which the modified premium is derived for various policies.

The computation of minimum reserves under the Commissioners Reserve Valuation Method is relatively simple. Such reserves are computed in exactly the same manner as net level premium reserves except that a modified annual level premium, called the "modified premium," is substituted in the prospective reserve formula for the net level premium applicable to the policy in question. The "modified premium" is designed to spread the net single premium and the amount borrowed from the first-year reserve over the premium-paying period of the policy. It is derived by first taking the net single premium at actual age of issue; adding to it the net level annual premium for the same type of policy issued at an age one year older and for a period one year shorter, but not more than the net level premium for a nineteen-payment life policy issued at an age one year older than the actual age of issue; then subtracting the net natural premium (the premium for one-year term insurance) for the year of issue; and finally dividing the result by the present value of a life annuity due for the *full* premium-paying period.

For an ordinary life policy issued at age thirty-five on the basis of the 1958 C.S.O. Table and 2½ per cent interest, the modified premium would be:

$$\text{M.P.} = \frac{420.127 + 18.340 - 2.449}{23.775} = \$18.34$$

The same premium would have been obtained by dividing 23.775 into 420.13 (which yields $17.67, the net level premium at age thirty-five) and adding to the results the sum derived by dividing 23.40, the present value of a whole life annuity due at age thirty-six, into 15.64, the amount borrowed from the reserve the first year.

The CRVM reserve at the end of the first policy year would be:

1st CRVM Reserve = $429.20 − ($18.34 × 23.40) = $0, when enough decimal places are used.

This indicates that the full amount of the first-year reserve is available for expenses, in addition to the normal loading, a characteristic of full preliminary term valuation. The valuation basis is further identifiable by the fact that the modified premium, $18.34, is the same as the net level premium at age thirty-six.

At the end of ten years, the CRVM reserve would be:

10th CRVM Reserve = $517.49 − ($18.34 × 19.78) = $154.67, when the calculations are taken to enough decimal places.

The modified premium for a twenty-payment life policy issued at age thirty-five, on the basis of the 1958 C.S.O. Table and $2\frac{1}{2}$ per cent interest, would be:

$$\text{M.P.} = \frac{\$420.127 + 28.954 - 2.449}{15.42546} = 28.954 \text{ or } \$28.95$$

The CRVM reserves for the first and tenth policy years, respectively, would be computed as follows:

1st CRVM Reserve = $429.20 − ($28.95 × 14.823) = $0
10th CRVM Reserve = $517.49 − ($28.95 × 8.712) = $265.25

Again this is full preliminary term valuation, as evidenced by the related facts that the first-year reserve is zero and the modified premium, $28.95, is identical to the net level premium for a nineteen-payment life policy issued at age thirty-six.

When the net renewal premium on the full preliminary term basis for a policy such as a short-term endowment is greater than the net level premium for a nineteen-payment life policy issued at an age one year older, however, the Commissioners method modifies the full preliminary term results. Thus, the modified premium for a twenty-year endowment issued at age thirty-five would be computed in the following manner:

$$\text{M.P.} = \frac{\$623.769 + \$28.954 - \$2.449}{\$15.42546} = \$42.156 \text{ or } \$42.16$$

When this modified premium is inserted into the prospective reserve formula, a positive value is produced in the valuation of the first-year liabilities:

1st CRVM Reserve = $638.46 − ($42.16 × $14.823) = $13.57

This means, of course, that $13.57 of the net level premium reserve is not available for the meeting of first-year expenses.

The tenth-year reserve would be:

10th CRVM Reserve = $787.52 − ($42.16 × $8.712) = $420.28

As regards all policies issued at age thirty-five, on the basis of the 1958 C.S.O. Table and $2\frac{1}{2}$ per cent interest, $26.50 ($28.95 − $2.45) is the maximum amount that can be added to the net single premium for purposes of calculating the modified premium.[9] Other values

---

[9] It should be noted, however, that this is not the amount considered to have been borrowed from the first-year reserve. The extra amount made available for first-year expenses as a "loan" from the reserve is $26.50 less $1.71, the portion of $26.50 that must be repaid during the first year. In other words, a portion of the modified premium for the first year must be applied toward the amortization of the loan.

would, of course, apply to other ages of issues, but the maximum for any age of issue, irrespective of the type of policy involved, would be the net level premium for a nineteen-payment life policy issued at an age one year older than the policy being valued, minus the net premium for one-year term insurance at the actual age of issue. By limiting the size of the modified premium that can be used in the reserve computation, the Standard Valuation Law in effect prescribes the *minimum* level of reserves—the primary objective of any valuation law.

The amount of reserve that will be required under each of the methods of valuation described to this point is shown in Table 23 for a twenty-five-year endowment issued at age thirty-five.

TABLE 23

TERMINAL RESERVES UNDER VARIOUS METHODS OF VALUATION;
25-YEAR ENDOWMENT ISSUED AT AGE 35;
1958 C.S.O. TABLE AND 2½ PER CENT INTEREST

Years in Force	Net Level Premium	Full Preliminary Term	Illinois Standard	Commissioners Method
1	$ 29.71	$ 0.00	$ 4.24	$ 3.99
2	60.11	31.33	35.70	35.20
5	155.47	129.61	134.39	133.08
10	328.63	308.07	313.66	310.83
20	741.80	733.89	741.80	734.96
25	1,000.00	1,000.00	1,000.00	1,000.00

As might be expected, the largest reserves are required under the full net level premium method, while the smallest are required under the full preliminary term method. It is of particular interest to note the relationship of the reserves under the Commissioners Method to those required under the other methods. It has been estimated that for an established company with normal distribution of insurance by age, duration, and plan, the aggregate reserves under the Commissioners Reserve Valuation Method would be about 95 per cent of those computed on the net level premium basis. In a young company, or in any company in which new business is relatively large, the difference between aggregate reserves on the two bases may be much larger.

Although not an inherent feature of the Commissioners Reserve Valuation Method, the Standard Valuation Law prescribes, as the minimum basis, the use of the 1958 C.S.O. Table and 3½ per cent interest for the valuation of ordinary reserves.

SELECT AND ULTIMATE VALUATION

One other type of modified reserve method should be mentioned, inasmuch as it embodies a principle completely different from that underlying the modifications previously described. Devised by Miles M. Dawson, consulting actuary to the Armstrong Committee,[10] this method is called the "select and ultimate" method. It was incorporated into the New York Insurance Law in the general revision that followed the Armstrong investigation.

The select and ultimate method of valuation is based on the observed phenomenon, discussed and illustrated earlier, that the mortality experience among recently selected lives is more favorable than that among comparable lives not recently selected. This has led the companies to exclude the experience on recently selected lives in the construction of mortality tables to be used for premium computations. Since the premiums collected by an insurance company are based on *ultimate* experience, while the actual death rates reflect the effects of selection, a surplus is created, against which excess first-year expenses can be charged. The select and ultimate method permits a reduction in reserves during the first five years of a contract equivalent to the present value of the anticipated mortality savings. By the end of five years, the full net level premium reserve must be accumulated and maintained thereafter. The distinctiveness of this method lies in the fact that the deficiency in reserves during the first five years is made good, not out of renewal expense loadings, but out of mortality savings.

While perfectly sound from an actuarial standpoint, this method never gained acceptance, primarily because the mortality savings during the first five years are not adequate to absorb excess first-year expenses.

---

[10] The Armstrong Committee was a committee of the New York State legislature which conducted the historic investigation of the life insurance business in New York in 1905. Senator Armstrong was chairman of the committee, and Charles Evans Hughes was the examining counsel.

CHAPTER XIV

Surrender Values

ONE OF the corollaries of the level premium system of life insurance is the accumulation of large sums of money by the insurance company. Such accumulation arises out of the fact that in the early years of a contract, the policyholder pays in more money to the company than is needed to pay his share of the claim payments and operating expenses of the company. The excess is held by the company until such time as it is applied in settlement of a death or an endowment claim under the policy. The question naturally arises as to the disposition of the money accumulated on behalf of a particular policy if before maturity of the policy, it should terminate because of default in premium payments.

GUIDING PRINCIPLES

Three Concepts of Equity

The treatment of the withdrawing policyholder might be resolved according to any one of three possible views of the transaction. One possible view is that such policyholder has no claim against the company and is entitled to no refund of any amount. This view would be predicated on the assumption that the sole function of a life insurance contract is to provide certain designated benefits in the event of the death of the policyholder or, in the case of an endowment, his survival to the end of the endowment period. Failure of the policyholder to continue his participation in the venture until the happening of the designated contingency or contingencies would cause him to forfeit all his payments and all interest in the contract. The principle would be the same as that underlying the pure endowment. Naturally, the absence of termination benefits should be reflected in the cost of insurance. In the case of nonparticipating policies, the premiums should be discounted for anticipated withdrawals; while under participating policies, the adjustment could take the form of either lower premiums or higher dividends. The reductions in cost would be substantial.

This is an admittedly extreme view but one which was generally accepted—and applied—in the early days of life insurance in this country, unmitigated even by an advance adjustment in premiums. Such a view would not be seriously entertained today because of the generally adverse reaction to forfeitures of any kind. Moreover, premiums based upon forecasts of future withdrawal rates would be of questionable reliability because of the diverse influences to which withdrawal rates are subject and the wide fluctuations which occur.

At the other extreme is the view that the terminating policyholder should be entitled to the return of all premiums paid, plus interest at the contractual rate, less his prorata share of death claims and over-all operating expenses of the company. This view has broader implications than might be apparent from the mere statement of the proposition. Implicit in this view is the concept that the termination benefit should not be affected by the incidence of expenses. Such values would be based on the assumption that all expenses are incurred at a level rate throughout the premium-paying period of the policy and that the loading is sufficient to absorb the expenses that arise each year. This would mean that the withdrawing policyholder would receive as a surrender value an amount exactly equal to the full reserve under the contract, irrespective of the policy year in which the surrender occurs. Unliquidated acquisition expenses under policies surrendered during the early durations would be borne by persisting policyholders.

Adherents to the foregoing view argue that the healthy growth of a company benefits all policyholders alike and, consequently, the cost of securing the volume of new business essential to the continued growth of the company should be a charge on all policies rather than a specific assessment against new policies. Strictly applied, this concept would have *all* acquisition expenses borne by the entire body of policyholders, in which event the surrender value would equal the full reserve, even at the end of the first policy year. A modified form of the concept would have the existing policyholders bear only a portion of the acquisition costs of new policies, in which event the surrender value would lie somewhere between the asset share and the full reserve until acquisition costs have been fully amortized, after which it would equal the full reserve.

The third and prevailing view is that the withdrawing policyholder should receive a benefit, either in cash or in some form of paid-up insurance, as nearly as possible equivalent to his contribution to the funds of the company, less the cost of the protection which he received, and less any expenses incurred by the company in establishing and maintaining his policyholder status.[1] Such benefit would be subject to the controlling consideration that it should not be so liberal as to impair the equities or undermine the security of the remaining policyholders. This view holds that, ideally, the withdrawal of a policyholder should neither benefit nor harm the continuing policyholders; but if any conflicts of interests should develop in the process of balancing the two sets of equities involved, they should be resolved in favor of the persisting policyholders. This assignment of priority to the interests of continuing policyholders is asserted to be consistent with the general principle of contract law that the party to a contract who is willing to continue under the original terms of the contract shall not be made to suffer loss through the inability or unwillingness of the other party to adhere to the terms of the contract. It might be argued, on the other hand, that the modern insurance contract includes surrender value as part of the benefits under the policy; and if the insured chooses to withdraw and demand the surrender value, he is acting within the terms of his contract just as fully as the insured who keeps his policy in effect until it matures. Nevertheless, there does seem to be some justification for favoring the policyholders who wish to *continue* under the original terms of the contract.

Under this concept, the maximum benefit to which a withdrawing policyholder would be entitled is his prorata share of the assets accumulated by the company on behalf of the block of policies to which his policy belongs—in other words, the asset share. The actual benefit should be somewhat less, for the reasons outlined below.

Deductions from Asset Share

There are five possible reasons why a company might make available as a termination benefit an amount less than the asset share imputable to a surrendered policy: (1) adverse mortality selection, (2) adverse financial selection, (3) contribution to a contingency reserve, (4) contribution to profits, and (5) cost of surrender.

---

[1] Some persons would argue that the amount which a withdrawing policyholder receives should also reflect deductions for the expense of the surrender transaction and a contribution to the permanent surplus of the company.

Adverse Mortality Selection. Over the years, there has been considerable speculation among actuaries and in actuarial literature as to the effect of voluntary withdrawals on the mortality among the remaining members of the insured group. Many actuaries reason that since persons in extremely poor health are not likely to surrender their policies and—if necessary—will borrow to maintain their protection, those who do surrender are, *on the average,* in better health and can be expected to live longer than those who do not surrender. If that be true, the present value of future benefits for the remaining policyholders is greater than their prorata share of the assets accumulated for the payment of death claims; and by the same token, the present value of future benefits for the surrendering policyholders in the instant before withdrawal is less than their prorata share of the fund. If, several years after issue of a group of policies, all surviving and persisting policyholders should be divided into two categories—those in better health than the average for the group and those in poorer health than the average—and all those in the better health category should withdraw, taking with them their prorata share of the accumulated assets, the residual fund would not be sufficient to pay the death claims of the remaining policyholders. The same influence would be at work—though not on as broad a scale—in ordinary surrenders if it be true that surrendering policyholders are healthier, on the average, than those who continue their protection.

Other actuaries maintain that a large proportion of voluntary terminations are the result of either (1) cessation of the need for the policy or (2) a change in the financial circumstances of the insured, and are carried out without much regard for the state of the insured's health. Such actuaries see little adverse mortality selection in withdrawals and would not compel the surrendering policyholder to contribute, through a reduction in the termination benefit, toward the anticipated higher mortality among the persisting insureds.

There is little question, however, that an informed person in need of the equities in his insurance policies and aware that his health is impaired would be inclined to negotiate policy loans rather than surrender his policies. This was confirmed by an investigation in 1930 of the rate of mortality among a group of 50,000 policies of a large mutual company subject to policy loans. It was found that the mortality among the policies encumbered by loans was 30 per cent higher than that of all policies combined, the selection against the company being most marked at ages under 55. It was also found that the termination rates among the encumbered policies were much higher than the average for all policies, which offset to some extent the higher mortality among such policies.

In view of the foregoing and the general lack of conclusive data on the subject, some companies withhold from surrendering policyholders a small portion of the asset shares, in order to offset any adverse selection that might be involved.

Adverse Financial Selection. It has been observed that terminations, particularly cash surrenders, tend to increase sharply during periods of economic crises and depressions. These terminations not only reduce the inflow of cash to the company but, if cash is demanded, also increase the outflow of cash. Such a development can adversely affect the financial operations of the company in that (1) it has fewer funds to invest at the attractive rates of interest generally prevailing at such time; and (2) under the most extreme circumstances, the company may have to liquidate some assets at depressed prices. Apart from surrenders at a time of economic crisis, the right of the policyholder to demand the cash value of his policy at any time forces the company to maintain a more liquid investment portfolio than would otherwise be necessary, thus reducing the over-all yield on the portfolio.[2]

It can be argued with a great deal of logic that those policyholders who avail themselves of the cash surrender privilege, or any of the other surrender options, should be charged with the loss of investment earnings, including any capital losses, attributable to that privilege. Most companies recognize the force of this argument in fixing the amount of the termination value.

Contribution to Contingency Reserve. Sound life insurance procedure demands that each group of policies pay its own way in the long run, including provision for such adverse contingencies as wars, epidemics, asset losses, and so on. Obviously, newly issued policies must depend upon accumulations already on hand for these protective margins during the early years, and it is reasonable that something less than the actual accumulations under such policies be made available as a surrender value in the early years by reason of the risk which these policies imposed on existing funds. It is also reasonable that in

---

[2] As will be pointed out later, all policies issued in recent years give the company the *legal right* to postpone payment of the cash surrender value for a period of six months; but because of competition and other factors, this right would be invoked only under the most trying financial circumstances.

later years, some deduction should be made from the actual accumulations to avoid any weakening in the security of the remaining policies in the group. Finally, it is generally agreed that all policies should make some contribution to the permanent surplus of the company, in order to provide the same sort of safety cushion and reservoir for the payment of acquisition expenses that was provided them by the surplus contributed by earlier policies. This all means that the surrendering policyholder should receive something less than his policy's share of the total accumulation.

Contribution to Profits. Little need be said on this point, except that in a stock company, a deduction may be made from the asset share of the surrendering policyholder in recognition of the risk borne by capital funds. In any such deduction, allowance would be made for any profits already distributed to stockholders.

Cost of Surrender. All companies incur a certain amount of expense in processing the surrender of a policy. Some companies estimate the aggregate expenses that will be incurred in such transactions and spread the cost over all policies by adding it to the loading, in the same manner as the cost of settlement was treated in Table 18 (p. 256). Other companies charge the cost of the transaction to the particular policies involved by deducting it from the surrender value that would otherwise be available. Under the latter practice, the cost of surrender is, in effect, a deduction from the asset share.

NONFORFEITURE LEGISLATION

Early laws requiring the payment of benefits to policyholders who voluntarily terminate their contracts were given the name "nonforfeiture laws," in that their purpose was to prevent the forfeiture of equities built up in level premium policies. The term has persisted; and laws with similar purpose today are called nonforfeiture laws, the refunds required by such laws are called nonforfeiture values, and the form in which such values may be taken are referred to as nonforfeiture options. Except in reference to legislation, the term "surrender," used as an adjective, is synonymous with the expression "nonforfeiture" and, because of its simplicity, is preferred in this text. Thus, nonforfeiture values are referred to as "surrender values" and nonforfeiture options as "surrender options."

Reference might be made to another terminological distinction that will be observed in this text. The terms "lapse" and "surrender," as nouns or verbs, are used interchangeably by many persons; but, strictly speaking, "lapse" refers to the termination of an insurance policy through nonpayment of premiums prior to the time when surrender values are available, while "surrender" refers to the termination of a policy through nonpayment of premiums after termination or surrender values are available. Terminations during the first year or two are usually "lapses," while those thereafter are "surrenders." The terms have no reference to whether the termination occurs through inaction on the part of the policyholder or through some positive act on his part prior to the expiration of the grace period, as is sometimes mistakenly assumed. The terms will be used in their proper sense in this volume.

Legislation Prior to the Standard Nonforfeiture Law

Early insurance policies issued in this country made no provision for refunds in the event of termination prior to maturity. As the years passed, some companies began to recognize with varying degrees of liberality the interest of the withdrawing policyholder in the funds accumulated through his redundant premiums, but the forfeiture of all equities was still prevalent when Elizur Wright became Commissioner of Insurance in Massachusetts in the 1850's. Shocked by the injustice of such a practice, Wright, whose crusading spirit produced many reforms in the insurance business, was successful in securing legislation which required the payment of surrender values. Enacted in 1861, the Massachusetts law required that a terminating policyholder be credited with a sum equal to the terminal reserve computed on the basis of the Combined Experience or Actuaries Table and 4 per cent interest, less a "surrender charge" of 20 per cent, with such sum being applied as a net single premium to purchase term insurance in the face amount of the original policy. Other states followed Massachusetts' example; and eventually, by statute or administrative ruling, surrender values in some amount and in some form were made compulsory in virtually every state.

The basic assumptions underlying these statutes at the time of their enactment were (1) that the reserve under the policy, calculated on the basis of the valuation standard and realistic mortality and interest factors, represented the equitable interest of the policyholder in the funds of the company; (2) that the company was entitled, on discontinuance of a policy, to a substantial "surrender charge" as an offset to impaired mortality and *as a fund with which to cover the cost of issuing a new policy to a new policyholder;* and (3) that the expenses of operation were largely chargeable to all policyholders generally, without specific attempt at allocation in accordance with the incidence of such expenses.[3]

No changes in the rationale of the laws occurred over the next seventy-five years, although certain modifications were introduced. The most important modification was the approval of preliminary term valuation, which carried with it substantial reductions in the level of legal reserves—and indirectly, surrender values—and a recognition of the incidence of expenses. However, failure to provide for the use of tables of mortality based on current experience nullified to a substantial degree one of the original assumptions underlying the early legislation.

At the time of the Guertin legislation, surrender values were still based on the reserve under the policy, less a surrender charge. The laws of most states limited the surrender charge to $2\frac{1}{2}$ per cent of the face or $25 per $1,000 of insurance, but the charge could be levied irrespective of the duration of the policy. No values were required under any policy until three annual premiums had been paid, or at any duration for a term insurance policy of twenty years or less. Some statutes stipulated that the various surrender benefits had to be the mathematical equivalent of each other on the basis of a specified mortality table and rate of interest, usually those underlying the reserve valuation.

In practice, the companies were providing more liberal surrender values than the law required. In the first place, many companies levied a smaller surrender charge in the first year than the maximum permitted by law. For example, the maximum charge under some policies was only $10 per $1,000 of insurance. In the second place, the surrender charge was almost invariably graded downward with duration, the full reserve usually being payable after a maximum of twenty years. In many companies, the period during which a surrender charge was levied was much shorter. In the third place, some companies provided a surrender value for durations of less than three years in the case of short-term endowment policies and whole life policies with short premium-paying periods, under which substantial asset shares are accumulated in the early years.

---

[3] *Reports and Statements on Non-Forfeiture Benefits and Related Matters* (New York: National Association of Insurance Commissioners, 1941), p. 148.

Defects in the Old Nonforfeiture Legislation

Several criticisms were leveled at the old statutory basis for surrender values, but they can be summarized under the two headings of (1) linkage of surrender values and reserves, and (2) inequitable nature of the results.

Linkage of Surrender Values and Reserves. The most fundamental criticism that can be directed at the old nonforfeiture legislation is that it linked surrender and reserve values to the same actuarial base. While both of these values arise out of the leveling of premiums, they have no other connection and serve quite different purposes.

The surrender values represent the company's best estimate as to the amount of funds that will have accumulated from the contributions of a group of insureds at the end of each policy year throughout the lifetime of the contract. Once determined and incorporated in the contract, these values become binding obligations on the company. There is every reason, therefore, why surrender values should be projected on a conservative basis, with the interests of continuing policyholders being accorded preferential status. The projection should assume that *prior to any particular policy year,* death claims will have been larger than might reasonably have been anticipated, interest earnings lower than those which should have been earned, and expenses higher than those which might have been expected. In other words, the benefits should be as low as consistent with the dictates of equity and pressure from competing companies.

The reserve, on the other hand, represents the difference between future benefits and future premiums. It is also a projected value but is always concerned with developments *beyond any particular policy year*. The reserve at any particular point in time should always be in excess of that amount which, under reasonable assumptions as to mortality and interest earnings, would enable the company to meet its future obligations. Clearly, a fund cannot be conservative as to both surrender values and reserve liabilities.

The fallacy of coupling the two sets of values can be further illustrated by the example of a group of policies issued, through an actuarial error, at a grossly inadequate premium rate. At the end of any particular policy year, the accumulations under such policies, after payment of claims and expenses, should be relatively small or nonexistent. Yet, the sum that should be on hand to assure payment of all future claims should be larger than that which would have been necessary under the correct premium, in order to compensate for the smaller premiums to be received in the future. Thus, the same feature of the policy—namely, inadequate premiums—which calls for small surrender values demands large reserves.

The lesson to be drawn from the foregoing is that under the former relationship between reserves and surrender values, a company could not strengthen its financial position by adopting a more stringent reserve basis without at the same time undermining its solvency to some extent by increasing surrender values to unjustified levels.

Inequitable Nature of the Results. An equally serious criticism of the former statutory basis of surrender values is that it produced inequitable results. Several features of the system contributed to this broad criticism.

The first goes back to the linkage of reserves and surrender values. If it be conceded that reserves are not the proper measure of a policyholder's prorata interest in the accumulated assets of a company, then any system which relates surrender values to such a criterion is inequitable from the outset. The basic inequity inherent in such a procedure is the preferential treatment of withdrawing policyholders vis-à-vis continuing policyholders. However, inequities as among the surrendering policies were introduced through the continued use of the antiquated American Experience Table of Mortality for the computation of reserves, since reserves under this table are distorted somewhat as among the various plans, ages, and durations.

The second inequitable feature of the system was found in the fact that the maximum permissible surrender charge was the same, irrespective of the plan, age of issue, or duration. Since the primary purpose of the surrender charge was to reduce the reserve by the amount of the acquisition expenses incurred under the policy—or, under the original concept, which would be incurred in replacing the policy with one of like kind—the charge should have varied with the plan and age of issue. Since acquisition expenses are gradually amortized, the charge should also have been graded by duration, perhaps being removed altogether after a prescribed number of years.

A third inequitable feature was the failure to distinguish between types of reserve valuation methods. The surrender charge was the same whether the reserve liabilities were calculated on the basis of full level premium reserves or full preliminary term reserves. Inasmuch as the reserves under the latter system of computation already reflect the incidence of expenses, something less than the full surrender charge would have been appropriate. The failure to distinguish between reserve valuation methods meant that minimum reserve values under policies issued by companies using the preliminary term reserve system were lower than those in policies issued by net level premium reserve companies, even though the amounts accumulated and available for surrender values in the early policy years were not affected by the reserve systems employed.

A fourth inequity was produced by the provision that no surrender values need be granted until three annual premiums had been paid. Under certain high-premium policies, values are produced in the first year and should rightfully be made available to a withdrawing policyholder. Many policies produce values by the end of the second year.

A similar criticism can be leveled against the failure of the statutes to require surrender values under term policies of twenty years or less. If there is an accumulation under a policy, it should be made available in some form, regardless of the type of policy involved. It may be that the accumulations under some policies are too small to be made available in cash; but unless they are negligible, they should be provided in the form of paid-up insurance.

Standard Nonforfeiture Law

One of the matters with which the Guertin Committee concerned itself was the development of a new method for deriving surrender values which would eradicate the inequities and other deficiencies associated with the old method. The recommendations of the committee were embodied in model legislation which has been adopted or made effective[4] in substantially the original form in every jurisdiction. Referred to as the Standard Nonforfeiture Law, the new legislation became effective, with a few exceptions, on January 1, 1948; and policies issued since that date have had to provide the minimum surrender values prescribed by that law. The surrender values in policies issued prior to January 1, 1948, continue to reflect the method prescribed by the previous legislation.

Rationale of the New Law. The basis for minimum surrender values under the Standard Nonforfeiture Law is a radical departure from that prescribed under the old legislation. It evolved out of two fundamental conclusions of the Guertin Committee: (1) that surren-

---

[4] In some states, the legislation is permissive and not compulsory.

der values should be derived independently of the policy reserves and (2) that such values should reflect with reasonable fidelity the asset shares accumulated under the policies. The technique by which these two objectives were to be accomplished is called the "adjusted premium" method.

The adjusted premium method rejects the concept that the cost of acquiring a new policyholder should be a charge on all policyholders and, instead, embraces the philosophy that each group of policies issued on the same plan and at the same age should pay its own way, including the costs of acquisition. In effectuating this principle, the adjusted premium method adopts the basic assumptions and technique underlying the preliminary term method of reserve valuation. In other words, it recognizes that expenses are not incurred evenly throughout the policy period but, rather, are concentrated heavily in the first year. It recognizes, further, that first-year loading is not sufficient to absorb the special first-year expenses; but it assumes that the total loading over the premium-paying period is sufficient to absorb all expenses incurred under the policy at any time, including the first year. Thus, it assumes that acquisition expenses in excess of first-year loading can be amortized over the premium-paying period out of renewal loadings. Whereas the excess first-year expenses under the preliminary term method of valuation are charged against or "borrowed" from the first-year reserve, which sum or "loan" is repaid out of renewal loadings, such expenses under the adjusted premium method are charged against the sum which would otherwise be available to the policyholder in the event of surrender, and the "loan" against the surrender value is gradually amortized out of renewal loadings in the same manner as under the preliminary term method. The "loan" against the surrender value is not fully amortized until the end of the premium-paying period. Thus, it can be seen that the concepts underlying the preliminary term system of valuation and the adjusted premium method are identical, except that under the former, the excess first-year expenses are charged against the reserve, while under the latter, they are charged against the surrender value.

The manner in which the surrender values are made to reflect unamortized acquisition expenses gives the adjusted premium method its name. That portion of first-year expenses in excess of normal, recurring expenses is treated as an additional obligation or "amount at risk" under the policy, to be amortized over the premium-paying period in precisely the same manner that the present value of policy benefits is amortized. The annual sum that must be added to the net level premium to amortize this additional obligation is obtained by dividing the excess first-year expenses by the present value of an appropriate life annuity due. The result added to the net level premium produces the "adjusted premium." That is, the net level annual premium is "adjusted" to reflect the annual cost of liquidating the special acquisition expenses. Then, the surrender value at any duration is determined by finding the difference between the present value of the benefits under the policy and the present value of future "adjusted premiums."

The similarity between the foregoing and the definition of the prospective reserve should be apparent. The only difference is in the use of "adjusted premiums" in one case and net level premiums in the other case. Since, with the same mortality and interest assumptions, the present value of future benefits would be identical under either calculation and the present value of future adjusted premiums would be larger than the present value of future net level premiums, it follows that the surrender value would be smaller than the reserve. With identical mortality and interest assumptions, the difference between the reserve and the surrender value at any particular point in time represents the unamortized portion of excess first-year expenses. This lessens with each premium payment, finally disappearing when the last payment is made.

It is important to note, however, that the mortality and interest assumptions employed by a company in the calculation of surrender values need not be the same as those used by the company in the calculation of its premiums and reserves. The new law, as amended after the promulgation of the 1958 C.S.O. Table,[4a] specifies that *minimum* surrender values for ordinary insurance must be computed on the basis of the 1958 C.S.O. Table and $3\frac{1}{2}$ per cent; but the actual values promised under the company's contracts can be computed on any basis, including the method in effect before 1948, which produces values at least equal to the minimum values. Moreover, the reserves may be calculated on the basis of any actuarial assumptions selected by the company, provided the values equal or exceed those required by law and subject to the restriction against the use of an interest assumption more than $\frac{1}{2}$ per cent lower than the rate used in the calculation of surrender values.[5] This dissociation of reserve and surrender values was not possible under the old legislation.

[4a] As originally enacted, the Standard Nonforfeiture Law prescribed the use of the 1941 C.S.O. Table in computing *minimum* values. Use of the 1958 C.S.O. Table became mandatory on January 1, 1966.

[5] See pp. 310–11 for an explanation of the nature and purpose of this restriction.

The law further safeguards the interests of terminating policyholders by limiting the amount of first-year expenses that can be taken into account in computing the surrender values. The maximum special first-year expense allowance that can be used to determine the adjusted premium is the sum of (1) 40 per cent of the adjusted premium for the plan under consideration; (2) 25 per cent of the adjusted premium for the plan under consideration or an ordinary life policy issued at the same age, whichever is less; and (3) a flat $20 per $1,000 of insurance. In any case in which the adjusted premium exceeds $40, the appropriate percentage is applied to $40 rather than to the actual adjusted premium. This means that the maximum first-year expense allowance that can be taken into account under any policy is $46 per $1,000 of insurance [$20 + (40% × $40) + (25% × $40)]. If the adjusted premium for a particular policy should be less than $40 per $1,000, then the maximum special expense allowance would clearly be less than $46 per $1,000. The exact amount would have to be determined by an algebraic formula, since the expense limitation is expressed in terms of the adjusted premium itself.[6]

The percentage factors in the foregoing expense limitation formula were designed to take into account those expenses which are dependent upon the amount of the premium and the plan of insurance. The constant factor of $20 per $1,000 was intended to reflect those expenses which are dependent upon the number of policies or the amount of insurance. They were set at a level which would provide ample expense margins for any well-managed company. Furthermore, they contain margins for general contingencies, adverse mortality selection, adverse financial selection, and profit or contribution to permanent surplus. Therefore, the values obtained by substituting the adjusted premium for the net level premium in the prospective reserve formula represent the full surrender values, with no specific deductions being made to hedge the factors mentioned above.

Illustration of the Adjusted Premium Method. The first step in deriving surrender values under the Standard Nonforfeiture Law is to determine the special first-year expense allowance. This may be the maximum amount permitted by statute or a lesser sum based on the

---

[6] For a clear demonstration of how the expense limitation and the adjusted premium are derived algebraically, see Frederic P. Chapman, *The Standard Nonforfeiture and Valuation Legislation* (Philadelphia: American College of Life Underwriters, 1956), p. 8.

company's expense situation, competitive pressures, or other considerations.

The second step in the process is to calculate the adjusted premium.
This entity may be regarded as either that level annual premium
required to amortize a principal sum equal to the present value of the
benefits under the policy and the special first-year expense allowance
or that sum obtained by adding to the net level premium the annual
increment needed to amortize the special acquisition expenses over the
premium-paying period. The first concept may be illustrated with an
ordinary life policy issued at age thirty-five. The maximum special
first-year expense allowance for such a policy, calculated in accordance with the formula prescribed, is $32.37 per $1,000. That sum is
added to $420.30, the net single premium for an ordinary life policy
issued at age thirty-five, to obtain the amount that must be on hand at
the inception of the contract to meet the obligations under the contract
—namely, $452.50. To obtain the equivalent annual sum, $452.50
is divided by $23.78, the present value of a whole life annuity due
of $1 as of age thirty-five. The result, $19.03, is the adjusted
premimum.

The second concept is equally simple. To obtain the sum that must
be set aside out of each gross annual premium—including the first—
to amortize the special costs of acquisition, it is necessary only to divide $32.37 by $23.78, which yields $1.36. This amount added to
the net level premium for an ordinary life policy issued at thirty-five,
$17.67, gives $19.03, the same sum obtained above, as the adjusted
premium.

The third step is to substitute the adjusted premium for the net level
premium in the formula employed in the computation of prospective
reserves. It will be recalled that the tenth-year terminal reserve for an
ordinary life policy issued at age thirty-five was obtained as follows:
$517.49 − ($17.67 × $19.78) = $167.90. The first sum in the
equation, $517.49, represents the net single premium for a whole life
policy issued at age forty-five; the second sum, $17.67, the net level
premium for an ordinary life policy issued at age thirty-five; and the
last sum, $19.78, the present value of a whole life annuity due of $1
calculated as of age forty-five, with all values being computed on
the basis of the 1958 C.S.O. Table and $2\frac{1}{2}$ per cent interest. If the
surrender value under this policy at the end of ten years is sought, the
adjusted premium, $19.03, is substituted for the net level premium,
$17.67, in the foregoing equation; and the result, $517.49 −

($19.03 × $19.78) = $140.96, is the surrender value. The difference between the reserve at the end of ten years and the surrender value for the same period, $167.90 — $140.96, or $26.94, represents the "surrender charge," or unamortized portion of the special first-year expenses. The surrender value under the same policy at the end of twenty years would be: $624.55 — ($19.03 × $15.39) = $331.58. Since the twentieth-year terminal reserve for an ordinary life policy issued at thirty-five is $352.54, it is clear that the unamortized portion of the acquisition expenses has been reduced to $20.96. The disparity will not disappear in this case or under any other ordinary life policy until the end of the mortality table.

The detailed steps in the calculation of the tenth-year surrender value for an ordinary life policy issued at age thirty-five, with all values computed on the basis of the 1958 C.S.O. Table and 2½ per cent interest, can be summarized as follows:

1. Find net single premium for ordinary life policy at age 35.........$420.13
2. Find allowance for special first-year expenses.................... 32.37
3. Add (1) and (2).. 452.50
4. Find present value at age 35 of whole life annuity due of $1....... 23.78
5. Divide (3) by (4) to find adjusted premium...................... 19.03
6. Find net single premium for ordinary life policy at age 45......... 517.49
7. Find present value at age 45 of whole life annuity due of $1....... 19.78
8. Multiply (5) by (7) to find present value at age 45 of future
   adjusted premiums... 376.53
9. Subtract (8) from (6) to find tenth-year surrender value.......... 140.96

The surrender value under the adjusted premium method may also be found retrospectively by accumulating the annual adjusted premiums, less the excess first-year expenses, at the assumed rate of interest, and deducting death claims at the tabular rate. The process is identical with the calculation of retrospective reserves except for the use of the adjusted premium and the deduction of excess first-year expenses. It is a particularly useful concept in considering some of the modifications of the adjusted premium method.

Modifications of the Adjusted Premium Method. The foregoing is an illustration of the computation of *minimum* surrender values under a 2½ per cent interest assumption. Many companies, however, provide surrender values in excess of those required by law. This may be accomplished within the framework of the Standard Nonforfeiture Law either by assuming lower first-year expenses than the maximum permitted by the law or by assuming the maximum expenses and amortizing them over a shorter period than the number of years for which premiums are payable or at an uneven rate over the entire period of premium payments.

If first-year expenses are assumed to be lower than the maximum and the liquidation period is the same, it stands to reason that the annual increment to the net premium needed to amortize such expenses will produce a smaller adjusted premium (net premium plus the increment) than that used to compute minimum values. The substitution of a smaller adjusted premium in the prospective reserve formula will yield a lower present value of future adjusted premiums and hence a higher surrender value. Retrospectively, a lower expense assumption means a larger accumulation, even with a lower adjusted premium, and thus more funds for distribution to terminating policyholders.[7]

If, on the other hand, maximum first-year expenses are assumed but larger than minimum surrender values are desired, it is necessary only to use an adjusted premium that is larger in the early years than thereafter. For example, if it is desired that surrender values equal the net level premium reserve at the end of twenty years, the net premium can be increased by an amount sufficient to liquidate the special first-year expenses within twenty years and such adjusted premium used for the first twenty years, with the net level premium being used thereafter. Retrospectively, it is apparent that, by definition, this higher adjusted premium will amortize the acquisition expenses during the first twenty years and enable the company thereafter to grant surrender values equal to the reserve. It is also clear that once surrender values have accumulated to a level equal to the reserve, they can be maintained at that level thereafter by the same premium that supports the reserve—namely, the net level premium. The result of substituting such unlevel premiums in the prospective reserve formula cannot be reasoned through so simply; but at the end of the first policy year, and at every duration thereafter, the present value of the combination of premiums mentioned above is smaller than the present value of a level adjusted premium sufficient to amortize the special acquisition expenses over the entire premium-paying period. At the time of issue, the present value of the two patterns of adjusted premiums is the same, but the equivalence is destroyed with the payment of the first premiums of unequal amount.

---

[7] Since the asset share under most policies is negative for the first year or two, a smaller expense assumption means a *lower negative* fund during the first year or two, rather than a *larger positive* accumulation.

The same principle would apply if the company wants larger surrender values at every duration than those required by law but does not want them to equal the reserve until the end of the premium-paying period. This can be achieved by employing an adjusted premium during the early years of the contract larger than that needed to accumulate minimum values and a smaller one than the conventional adjusted premium for the remaining years of the premium-paying period. A number of such modifications are in use today.

All methods of deriving surrender values which rely upon the technique of an adjusted premium are classified as "standard nonforfeiture value methods." Only the method which employs a modified premium just exactly adequate to amortize the *maximum* special first-year expense allowance over the premium-paying period is properly called the "adjusted premium method." Hence, minimum values are derived by the "adjusted premium method." The larger values discussed above are derived by other forms of the "standard nonforfeiture value method."

Similarly, the term "adjusted premium" is usually used to represent only the premium defined in the Standard Nonforfeiture Law, which produces minimum values. Any other modified premium used to compute surrender values is usually referred to as a "nonforfeiture factor."[8] A "nonforfeiture factor" is employed to produce larger values than those required by law. In some of the more complex methods of computing surrender values, several nonforfeiture factors may be used in the same policy.

The Standard Nonforfeiture Law requires that each policy contain a statement of the method used to determine the surrender values and benefits provided under the policy. In New York and certain other states, the law was modified to require such statement only for the durations not shown in the contract, provided a description of the method used in the calculation of the earlier values has been filed with the Commissioner of Insurance.[9] This provision is of practical significance, in that it permits use of a formula during the first twenty

---

[8] The "nonforfeiture factor" is sometimes referred to as a "modified premium"; but in the minds of most actuaries, at least, the expression "modified premium" is usually associated with the net premium employed in the derivation of modified reserves, such as those computed under the Commissioners Reserve Valuation Method. On the other hand, the term "nonforfeiture factor" is sometimes used in lieu of "adjusted premium" in policies which provide *minimum* values in order to avoid any possible confusion in the minds of policyholders.

[9] It is customary to include in the policy only the surrender values and benefits for the first twenty years. Thus, in New York, it is not necessary to describe in the policy the method used to calculate the values for the first twenty years.

years (or premium-payment period, if shorter) which might be difficult to describe contractually.

The law does not require that surrender values be calculated in accordance with the principles of the standard nonforfeiture method. The only requirement is that the values be at least as large as those that would be produced by the adjusted premium method. Some companies still use a formula based on the reserve less a specified deduction and so describe it in their policies.

Surrender Dividends. It is likely that in any well-managed company, be it stock or mutual, the asset share allocable to any particular policy will, after a few years, exceed the surrender value provided thereunder and eventually will exceed the reserve. The reasons why the surrender value should be somewhat smaller than the asset share have been previously discussed; and one of the reasons, it will be recalled, is the general consensus that each policy should make a contribution to the surplus or contingency reserves of the company. From a purely accounting standpoint, the only way in which this can be accomplished is for the asset share eventually to exceed the reserve. If, after this has occurred, the policy should go off the books and, with it, the need for the protection of the surplus which it has helped to accumulate, considerations of equity would seem to demand that the withdrawing policyholder be permitted to take with him a reasonable proportion of the surplus created through his premiums. Equity does not demand that the withdrawing policyholder be entitled to his full contribution to surplus, since it is generally agreed that all policies should make a permanent contribution of some amount to surplus, in order to support the writing of an increasing percentage of new business. Such a final settlement with a withdrawing policyholder is called a *surrender dividend*.

The subject of surrender dividends was thoroughly explored by the Guertin Committee, which pointed out that the concept has been successfully applied to policies terminating not only by surrender, but by death as well. On the theory that a material disparity between surrender values and asset shares is most likely to arise out of the use of a lower interest assumption in the calculation of reserves than in the derivation of surrender values, the Guertin Committee proposed, in its final report, that the payment of an equitable surrender dividend be made compulsory under participating policies and optional under nonparticipating policies whenever the rate of interest employed in the calculation of reserves is $\frac{1}{2}$ per cent or more below the rate used in the calculation of surrender values. Such dividends were to be "based on the excess of the reserve held by the Company on the policy over the corresponding cash surrender value." The thought behind this recommendation was that under participating policies, the sums necessary to accumulate the higher reserves required by the lower interest assumption, which would not benefit the withdrawing policyholder, are likely to be withheld from dividends which would otherwise have been payable to the policyholder over the years. This would be particularly true under participating policies whose reserve basis was strengthened some years after issue. In the case of nonparticipating policies, the additional sums would have to come from higher premiums, which would not be reflected in the surrender values. It was the conclusion of the Guertin Committee, however, that competitive forces would cause nonparticipating premium rates to "find their level close to that supporting a minimum or near-minimum scale of nonforfeiture benefits" and thus make unnecessary a mandatory provision for surrender dividends.

The specific recommendation of the Guertin Committee was opposed by industry representatives on several grounds, including the possibility that the provision might be interpreted in such a manner as to require a surrender dividend equal to the full difference between the reserve and the surrender value. Under such an interpretation, the total surrender value under participating policies subject to the provision would always have equaled the reserve, which would have been a worse situation than that prevailing under the old system. The concept behind the recommendation was adopted, however, and made a part of the Standard Valuation Law in order to preserve the distinction between reserves and surrender values created in the Standard Nonforfeiture Law.

The Standard Valuation Law specifies that if the rate of interest used in the calculation of reserves under participating policies is more than $\frac{1}{2}$ per cent lower than the rate underlying the surrender values, a plan must be adopted for providing such "equitable increases" in surrender values as the Commissioner of Insurance shall approve. The law contains no implications as to the level of such surrender dividends or as to the method by which they shall be computed. The provision applies whether the rate used in the calculation of reserves was adopted at the time of issue or at some later date in connection with a general reserve-strengthening program. If, in the latter case, it can be demonstrated to the Commissioner of Insurance that the funds for the higher reserves were taken from the general surplus of the company, with no reduction in the dividends of the policies involved, the Commissioner would probably authorize the company to forego an increase of any sort in surrender values.

It should be noted that, except in New York, an interest differential of ½ per cent can exist, without the necessity of increasing surrender values. This permits a company some flexibility in estimating its future liabilities. In New York, however, if there is *any* differential in the interest rates underlying the reserve and surrender value calculations for participating policies, the company must make provision for a surrender dividend or prove to the satisfaction of the Insurance Commissioner that no increase in surrender values is justified.[10]

RELATIONSHIP BETWEEN SURRENDER VALUES AND OTHER VALUES

The relationship between surrender values, asset shares, and reserves, both level premium and modified, can be observed in Table 24. The basic elements of this table reflect an asset share calculation for a participating ordinary life policy issued at age thirty-five; but for purposes of comparison, certain other values are shown.

The death rates used in determining the number of living and persisting policyholders, and the volume of death claims, are based on varying percentages of the rates of mortality shown in the 1958 C.S.O. Table. The rates for the first five policy years are 42, 52, 60, 66, and 70 per cent, respectively, of the corresponding rates in the 1958 C.S.O. Table. At age forty, the mortality rate is assumed to be 72.5 per cent of that reflected in the 1958 C.S.O. Table; and it is assumed to increase one-half percentage point for each year of attained age thereafter, reaching 79.5 per cent at the twentieth policy year. Except for the first five years, these are the same mortality rates used in the calculation of dividends for this policy, the details of which are given in Table 29 on page 355. The rates for the first five years are lower than those employed in the dividend formula, in order to reflect the influence of selection. As will be learned in the following chapter, the rates used in the calculation of dividends usually do not reflect the savings from selection, the funds withheld by this stratagem being applied to the amortization of excess first-year expenses.

Withdrawals were assumed to take place at Linton A rates, except in the first year. Combined with the assumed rates of mortality and

---

[10] See Sec. 205, Subsec. 3(d) of New York Insurance Law.

TABLE 24

ASSET SHARE CALCULATION;
$1,000 ORDINARY LIFE POLICY ISSUED AT AGE 35;
GROSS PREMIUM PER $1,000 = $23.50

(1)	(2)	(3)	(4)	(5)	(6)	(7)	(8)
Policy Year	Number Living and Persisting	Effective Premiums per $1,000	Total Effective Premiums [(2) × (3)]	Initial Fund [(13)n − 1 + (4)]	Initial Fund plus 3.95 Per Cent Interest [(5) × 1.0395]	Death Claims*	Cash Value per $1,000
1........	100,000	−$ 9.29	−$ 929,000	−$ 929,000	−$ 965,696	$107,074	$ 0.00
2........	84,895	21.04	1,786,191	604,621	628,504	118,603	13.83
3........	79,685	21.04	1,676,572	1,980,191	2,058,409	136,515	32.29
4........	75,567	21.04	1,589,930	3,229,389	3,356,950	153,348	51.00
5........	72,092	21.04	1,516,816	4,374,772	4,547,575	167,616	69.95
6........	69,044	21.04	1,452,686	5,432,656	5,647,246	180,244	89.13
7........	66,382	21.04	1,396,677	6,424,613	6,678,385	189,541	108.51
8........	64,072	21.04	1,348,075	7,368,133	7,659,174	199,932	128.11
9........	62,018	21.04	1,304,859	8,269,144	8,595,775	211,863	147.90
10........	60,136	21.04	1,265,261	9,126,228	9,486,714	225,058	167.90
11........	58,412	22.41	1,309,013	10,026,054	10,422,083	238,858	185.85
12........	56,776	22.41	1,272,350	10,884,845	11,314,796	254,748	203.97
13........	55,220	22.41	1,237,480	11,704,113	12,166,425	271,981	222.24
14........	53,738	22.41	1,204,269	12,486,327	12,979,537	291,532	240.63
15........	52,324	22.41	1,172,581	13,231,260	13,753,895	312,140	259.12
16........	50,971	22.41	1,142,260	13,940,428	14,491,075	335,256	277.71
17........	49,623	22.41	1,112,051	14,599,034	15,175,696	359,788	296.35
18........	48,278	22.41	1,081,910	15,205,366	15,805,978	384,990	315.05
19........	46,935	22.41	1,051,813	15,758,100	16,380,545	411,613	333.79
20........	45,593	22.41	1,021,739	16,256,704	16,898,884	439,828	352.54

* These death claims have been adjusted to reflect a loss of six months' interest. The adjustment consisted of increasing the claims by 1.975 per cent, which is equivalent to 3.95 per cent for six months.

applied to a radix of 100,000 insureds, these withdrawal rates produced, at the various durations, the number of living and persisting policyholders shown in Column 2.

A gross premium of $23.50 was assumed, this being the net premium, computed on the basis of the 1958 C.S.O. Table and 2½ per cent, loaded 16 per cent of itself plus $3.00. Expenses were assumed to occur at the rate and according to the incidence shown in Table 18 on page 256. This yielded an effective premium of −$9.29 the first year, $21.04 for the second through the tenth policy years, and $22.41 for each year thereafter. Reference to Table 18 reveals that the only expenses involved after the tenth year are the premium tax, maintenance expenses, and the cost of settlement. The first two types of expenses are incurred annually; and the cost of settlement, while incurred only once per policy, is spread over the entire premium-

TABLE 24 (*Continued*)

(9)	(10)	(11)	(12)	(13)	(14)	(15)	(16)	(17)
Num-ber With-draw-ing	Amount Paid on Surrender [(8) × (9)]	Dividend per $1,000	Total Dividends Paid [(2) × (11)]	Fund Balance [(6) − (7) − (10) − (12)]	Asset Share [(13) ÷ (2)$_{n+1}$]	1958 C.S.O. 2½ Per Cent Net Level Terminal Reserve per $1,000	1958 C.S.O. 2½ Per Cent Mini-mum Cash Value per $1,000	1958 C.S.O. 2½ Per Cent CRVM Terminal Reserve per $1,000
15,000	$ 0	$1.28	$108,800†	−$ 1,181,570	−$ 13.92	$ 15.64	$ 0	$ 0
5,094	70,450	1.60	135.832	303,619	3.81	31.59	0.24	16.20
3,984	128,643	1.93	153,792	1,639,459	21.70	47.83	17.00	32.70
3,325	169,575	2.33	176,071	2,857,956	39.64	64.32	34.03	49.45
2,884	201,736	2.75	198,253	3,979,970	57.64	81.05	51.31	66.45
2,486	221,577	3.15	217,489	5,027,936	75.74	98.01	68.81	83.67
2,124	230,475	3.59	238,311	6,020,058	93.96	115.17	86.53	101.11
1,858	238,028	4.01	256,929	6,964,285	112.29	132.55	104.47	118.76
1,674	247,585	4.44	275.360	7,860,967	130.72	150.12	122.61	136.62
1,503	252,354	4.86	292,261	8,717,041	149.23	167.90	140.96	154.67
1,402	260,562	5.31	310,168	9,612,495	169.31	185.85	159.50	172.91
1,306	266,385	5.76	327,030	10,466,633	189.54	203.97	178.20	191.32
1,215	270,022	6.20	342,364	11,282,058	209.95	222.24	197.06	209.88
1,128	271,431	6.66	357,895	12,058,679	230.46	240.63	216.04	228.56
1,046	271,040	7.12	372,547	12,798,168	251.09	259.12	235.14	247.35
1,019	282,986	7.57	385,850	13,486,983	271.79	277.71	254.32	266.23
992	293,979	8.03	398,473	14,123,456	292.54	296.35	273.57	285.17
966	304,338	8.50	410,363	14,706,287	313.33	315.05	292.88	304.17
939	313,429	8.96	420,538	15,234,965	334.15	333.79	312.22	323.20
912	321,516	9.43	429,942	15,707,558	354.97	352.54	331.58	342.25

† Dividends paid to the 85,000 persons who either entered the second policy year or died during the first policy year.

paying period. Thus, all three operate to reduce the effective premium.

The assumption was made that the effective premiums are accumulated at the rate of 3.95 per cent, which is considerably higher than the rate of interest currently being used in premium and reserve calculations, but is a realistic measure of the interest being earned on interest-bearing liabilities.[11]

Cash values assumed to be made available to withdrawing policyholders are substantially higher than the minimum cash values computed on a 2½ per cent interest basis, as can be seen from a comparison of Columns 8 and 16 of Table 24. After the first ten years, the cash values are assumed to be identical with the net level premium reserves, calculated on a 2½ per cent interest basis.

[11] See pp. 343–46 for a brief description of the bases on which interest earnings may be expressed.

Dividends were assumed to be paid in accordance with the scale derived in Table 29 on page 355, with the full amount of the dividend for any particular year going to all persons who enter upon that year, even though they failed to survive or persist to the end of the year. First-year dividends, however, were assumed to be paid only to those policyholders who either survived and persisted or died during the year. In other words, first-year dividends were not paid to those who withdrew during the year.

The asset share which was developed from the foregoing assumptions is shown in Column 14 of Table 24. It will be observed that the asset share is negative the first year, which is normal for a policy of this type and premium, and is less than the cash value until the nineteenth year. This means that through the eighteenth policy year, the withdrawing policyholder would receive back more than his net contribution to the funds of the company. The difference must come out of surplus, to be repaid out of the gross premiums or dividends of the persisting policyholders.

The asset share is likewise less than the net level premium reserve until the nineteenth year. As has been pointed out earlier, this indicates that the company does not recover its acquisition expenses for this group of policies as a whole until the nineteenth year. This is perhaps normal for mutual companies, but stock companies usually amortize their first-year expenses over a shorter period. The excess of the asset share over the net level premium reserve—which, by the end of the twentieth year, amounts to $2.43 per $1,000—measures the contribution of each $1,000 policy to the surplus of the company. If, in the years beyond those included in Table 24, the disparity should become too great, the asset share would be reduced through an increase in the dividend scale.

CHAPTER XV

Surrender Options

THE SURRENDER values provided under the Standard Nonforfeiture Law, as well as those available under earlier legislation, can be taken by the policyholder in one of three forms: (1) cash, (2) paid-up whole life or endowment insurance, and (3) paid-up term insurance. These are properly referred to as *surrender benefits;* but since the policyholder has the option or privilege of choosing the form under which the surrender value is to be paid, the benefits are usually referred to as *surrender options.*

Under the old legislation, surrender benefits were not required until three annual premiums or their equivalent had been paid. The Standard Nonforfeiture Law requires that a surrender benefit be granted whenever a value appears under the formula. This may be as early as the end of the first year under some policies and later than three years under other policies. Under most plans, and at most ages of issue, a surrender value will appear in the second policy year. Formerly, no cash or other surrender benefits were required in the case of term insurance policies of twenty years or less. Under the new law, a level term policy for more than fifteen years[1]—or one which expires after age sixty-five, regardless of its duration—must provide surrender benefits.

The old laws generally specified that both paid-up term and paid-up reduced insurance had to be made available as a surrender benefit, one of which, upon default of premium, had to go into effect automatically unless the policyholder specifically elected another. The new law does not dictate the form of the paid-up benefit. Only one type need be made available; but if more than one is offered, one must be automatic.

---

[1] Twenty years in some states.

315

In general, the companies are continuing to offer both of the paid-up benefits required under the old laws. However, a company could grant some other type of benefit, such as term insurance for less than the face amount, if it so desired. The only requirement with which the companies must comply is that the present value of the paid-up benefit, based on the mortality and interest assumptions specified in the law, must be at least equal to the surrender value developed under the adjusted premium formula.

The paid-up benefits available under the new law are more favorable than those granted under the old legislation by reason of the lower mortality reflected in the C.S.O. Tables. Moderate increases in the amount of reduced paid-up insurance were registered at most ages and under most plans of insurance. The period of time for which paid-up term insurance is provided is longer at all ages under the new law, the extension being very pronounced at the younger ages, where the death rates under the C.S.O. Tables are very much lower than the corresponding rates under the American Experience Table.

The recent change to the 1958 C.S.O. Table has produced greater paid-up benefits per $1 of cash values because of lower mortality. The cash values may be larger or smaller than those developed under the 1941 C.S.O. Table, the relationships at various ages of issue and durations under various types of contracts being determined by the same factors governing the level of reserves. The widespread use of the Commissioners 1958 Extended Term Insurance Table in calculating premiums for extended term insurance has offset to some extent the advantages that would otherwise have been derived from the lower mortality rates in the 1958 C.S.O. Table.

The nature and significance of the various standard forms of surrender benefits will be discussed in the following sections.

Cash

The simplest form in which the surrender value may be taken is cash. There is an exact equivalence between the surrender value of a policy and the cash that can be obtained upon its surrender, leading many persons to refer to the surrender value generically as the *cash* surrender value. As under the old legislation, the new law requires that the surrender value of a policy be made available in the form of cash, but it does not compel a company to grant cash values until the end of three years in the case of ordinary insurance and five years in the case of industrial insurance. This limitation on cash values was provided in order to relieve the companies of the expense of drawing checks for the relatively small values that might have developed during the first and second policy years. It does not, however, relieve the company of the obligation of making available in some form of paid-up benefit any surrender value that might accumulate during the first two years. Most companies waive this statutory provision and provide a cash value as soon as any value develops under the policy.

The new law permits a company to postpone payment of the cash surrender value for a period of six months after demand therefor and surrender of the policy. This *delay clause* was given statutory sanction in order to protect the companies against any losses that might otherwise arise from excessive demands for cash during an extreme financial emergency such as occurred in 1933. The voluntary inclusion of such a clause in all new policies had become fairly general following

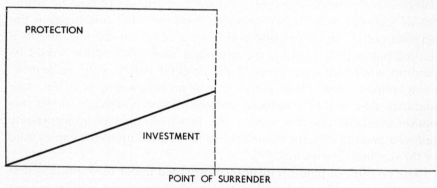

POINT OF SURRENDER

FIG. 14. Impact of cash surrender on the structure of a whole life contract.

the series of state-imposed moratoria on the payment of cash values and the granting of policy loans during the depression of the 1930's. Provision was usually made for a delay of either three or six months. The new law has made the inclusion of a delay clause mandatory and has provided a uniform delay period of six months. It is contemplated that the clause would be invoked only under the most unusual circumstances.

As might be expected, provision is made for deduction of any policy indebtedness from the cash value that would otherwise be available.

In connection with the discussion of each surrender benefit, the impact of its election on the structure of the underlying insurance contract will be illustrated diagrammatically. In each case, the underlying contract will be assumed to be a whole life policy; but the principle involved is applicable, with some modification, to any type of contract.

The change wrought in a whole life contract by the exercise of the cash surrender option is illustrated in Figure 14. The figure indicates that up to the point of surrender, the contract is a combination of protection and investment. By surrendering the policy for cash, however, the policyholder takes the investment element of the contract and, in so doing, terminates the protection element, as well. Subject only to any reinstatement privilege that might exist, the company has no further obligations under the contract.

Reduced Paid-Up Insurance

This form of surrender benefit is referred to as "reduced paid-up insurance," in recognition of the fact that under this option, the withdrawing policyholder receives a reduced amount of paid-up whole life or endowment insurance, payable upon the same conditions as the original policy. If the original policy were either an ordinary life or a limited-payment life policy, the insurance under this option would be paid-up whole life insurance. If the original policy were an endowment contract, this option would provide an endowment with the same maturity date but in a reduced amount. Some companies make this option available under a term policy in which case an appropriately reduced amount of term insurance would be paid up to the expiry date of the original term policy.

The amount of paid-up insurance provided under this option is that sum which can be purchased at the insured's attained age by the net surrender value (cash value, less any policy indebtedness, plus the cash value of any dividend additions or deposits) applied as a net single premium computed on the mortality and interest bases specified in the policy for the calculation of the surrender value. The reduction in amount is substantial in the earlier policy years; and even at the longer durations, the amount of paid-up insurance obtainable seems small in relation to the premiums paid. This option is more attractive in the case of limited-payment life and endowment policies, since the amount of paid-up insurance, except at the higher ages of issue, bears approximately the same relationship to the face of the original policy as the number of premiums paid bears to the total number payable.[2] This appeals to policyholders as reasonable. The amount of paid-up

---

[2] At one time, it was customary to grant paid-up insurance under limited-payment life and endowment policies which was exactly proportionate to the number of premiums paid. For example, under a twenty-payment life policy, the paid-up

insurance available at various durations under an ordinary life, an twenty-payment life, and a twenty-year endowment policy, issued at age thirty-five, is shown in Table 25.

Paid-up insurance is provided under this option at net premium rates, despite the fact that maintenance and surrender or settlement expenses will be incurred on the policies.[3] The law made no specific allowance for expenses, on the theory that the margins in the mortality and interest assumptions underlying the net rates will be sufficient to absorb any expenses that will be involved. In the case of participating insurance, however, any margins available for this purpose are reduced by the payment of dividends on the paid-up insurance.

It is interesting to note that there is a surrender privilege under reduced paid-up whole life and endowment policies. The law states that such policies can be surrendered for cash within thirty days after any policy anniversary, provided the original policy was in force long enough to grant a cash value. In other words, the cash surrender privilege of the paid-up policy cannot be used to subvert the provision in the law that cash values need not be granted until the end of three years.

This option is viewed with mixed emotions by the companies. On the favorable side, it does not involve a cash withdrawal and hence poses no threat of a forced liquidation of assets during a financial emergency. Moreover, it does not invite adverse mortality selection, as does the paid-up term insurance option. As a matter of fact, available evidence indicates that the mortality under reduced paid-up insurance is slightly lower than that under corresponding policies not in default, except for the first few years after default.

On the unfavorable side, paid-up values are usually small and hence disproportionately expensive to maintain. Unless surrendered for cash, the policy remains in force until it becomes a claim, which may be many years after default of the original policy. In the meantime, the policyholder and his beneficiary may have lost interest in the policy by reason of the small sum involved, with the result that no claim is filed with the company. The company is then faced with the problem of tracing a policyholder to pay a claim which is too small to justify the expense involved. On the other hand, if the policyholder dies within a short time after default, considerable ill will may be

---

insurance available at the end of ten years would be exactly half the face of the policy. Such an option was called "proportionate paid-up insurance."

[3] It should be noted that certain other types of expenses—e.g., commissions, premium taxes, underwriting expenses, and service fees—are not incurred.

created among the family and friends of the insured because of the smallness of the death benefit, as compared to what would have been paid under the paid-up term insurance option. This reduction in coverage is particularly susceptible to misunderstanding when the surrender is regarded by the policyholder as a temporary measure and ultimate reinstatement is contemplated. It is quite understandable, therefore, that reduced paid-up insurance is seldom designated in the policy as the *automatic* paid-up benefit.

The impact of the reduced paid-up insurance option on the structure of the whole life policy is illustrated in Figure 15. It is clearly

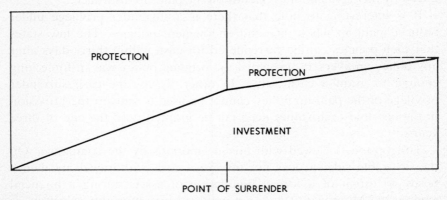

FIG. 15. Impact of reduced paid-up insurance option on the structure of the whole life contract.

apparent that the impact is on the protection element of the contract. In the example, the cash value before surrender had accumulated to a sum half the face of the policy, which at age sixty, for instance, would purchase a paid-up whole life policy in an amount approximately 75 per cent of the original face. The entire shrinkage comes out of the protection element, however, since the investment element continues to increase until, at the end of the mortality table, it equals the reduced face. The same phenomenon occurs with a surrender at any duration. As was pointed out above, this investment element of a reduced paid-up policy can be converted into cash by surrendering the policy pursuant to its terms.

Extended Term Insurance

The extended term insurance option provides paid-up term insurance in an amount equal to the original face of the policy, increased by any dividend additions or deposits and decreased by any policy indebtedness. The length of the term is such that can be purchased at the insured's attained age by the application of the net surrender value as a net single premium. This gives effect to the statutory requirement that the present value at the time of surrender of any paid-up surrender benefit must be at least the equivalent of the surrender value. The period for which term insurance would be provided for various durations under an ordinary life, a twenty-payment life, and a twenty-year endowment policy, issued at age thirty-five, is shown in Table 25.

In the case of endowment policies, paid-up term insurance is not provided beyond the maturity date of the policy. Yet, the surrender

TABLE 25

Minimum Paid-Up Surrender Benefits at Various Durations under
Ordinary Life, 20-Payment Life, and 20-Year Endowment Policies
Issued at Age 35 on Basis of the 1958 C.S.O. Table and
2½ Per Cent

Du-ration	Ordinary Life			20-Payment Life			20-Year Endowment				
	Cash Values	Extended Term*		Reduced Paid-Up	Cash Values	Extended Term*		Reduced Paid-Up	Cash Values	Extended Term*		Pure Endowment*	Reduced Paid-Up
		Years	Days			Years	Days			Years	Days		
3....	$ 17.00	4	38	$ 37.97	$ 45.93	9	190	$102.57	$ 84.12	14	313	—	$125.76
5....	51.31	9	47	109.84	103.95	15	125	222.53	172.42	15	—	$119.14	246.02
10....	140.96	14	91	272.40	259.55	21	291	501.56	412.23	10	—	462.39	523.45
15....	235.14	15	183	412.25	431.88	24	352	757.17	684.38	5	—	755.79	772.52
20....	331.58	15	72	530.91	624.55	Fully	Paid	Up	1,000.00	A	t	Maturi	ty
25....	427.84	14	60	630.46	—	—	—	—	—	—	—	—	—
30....	520.74	12	310	712.57	—	—	—	—	—	—	—	—	—

* Based on 1958 C.E.T. Table.

value under all endowment policies will eventually exceed the sum needed to purchase term insurance to the end of the endowment period and, under many policies, will do so within a few years after issue. This problem is met by applying the excess to the purchase of a paid-up *pure* endowment with a maturity date the same as that of the original policy.

For example, it can be observed in Table 25 that the minimum cash value at the end of ten years under a twenty-year endowment policy issued at age thirty-five is $412.23 per $1,000.[4] However, the net single premium at age forty-five for a ten-year term policy for $1,000

[4] In this illustration cash values and amounts of reduced paid-up insurance are based on the 1958 C.S.O. Table and 2½ per cent interest; periods of extended term insurance and amounts of pure endowment are based on the 1958 C.E.T. Table and 2½ per cent interest.

is only $87.86, leaving a balance of $324.37. Since the net single premium at age forty-five for a pure endowment of $1,000 maturing at age fifty-five—the maturity date of the original policy—is $701.52, the excess cash value, $329.37, will purchase a pure endowment maturing on that date in the amount of $462.39. It will be recognized that extended term insurance of $1,000 for ten years and a *pure* endowment of $462.39 are the same as a ten-year endowment insurance policy for $462.39 plus a ten-year term policy of $537.61. Thus, at most durations, the extended term option under an endowment policy is a combination of a reduced paid-up endowment *insurance* policy and a reduced paid-up term insurance policy. Theoretically, the surrender value could be applied equally well to the purchase of a $1,000 *pure* endowment, or a smaller amount, if the cash value were insufficient, any balance being applied to the purchase of term insurance in a reduced amount for the remainder of the endowment period.

Like reduced paid-up insurance, the insurance under this option is purchased at net rates, despite the fact that certain expenses will be incurred and, unless advantage is taken of the provision mentioned below, mortality margins will be thinner, if not nonexistent, because of adverse mortality selection. In recognition, however, of the substantial degree of adverse mortality selection thought to be associated with this option, the law permits the net single premium to be calculated on the basis of the Commissioners 1958 Extended Term Insurance Table, which, it will be recalled, was constructed by adding a loading of 0.75 deaths per 1,000, or 30 per cent of the mortality rates under the 1958 C.S.O. Table, whichever is greater, to the 1958 C.S.O. Table mortality rates. Most companies have exercised this prerogative, which materially shortens the period of extended term insurance and enables a company to get off the risk sooner than otherwise.[5]

The law provides that if there is any indebtedness against the policy at the time of its surrender, both the amount of term insurance and the surrender value used as a net single premium shall be reduced by the amount of the loan. By the same token, if there are any dividend additions standing to the credit of the policy, the *amount* of the additions will be added to the face amount of the extended insurance,

---

[5] During the period when the 1941 C.S.O. Table was prescribed for the calculation of minimum surrender values, companies were authorized to compute extended term premiums on the basis of 130 per cent of the 1941 C.S.O. Table mortality rates. For competitive reasons, however, most companies did not avail themselves of the privilege.

and the *cash value* of the additions will be added to the sum applied as a net single premium.[6]

This may be illustrated by a $1,000 policy which at the time of surrender has a surrender value of $500, dividend additions of $100 which have a cash value of $75, and a policy loan of $250. Under such circumstances, the face of the extended policy would be $850 ($1,000 + 100 − 250), and the net single premium would be $325 ($500 + 75 − 250).

It is readily apparent that the policy loan should be deducted from the surrender value to determine the net single premium, since it is only the *net* value that is available for the purchase of extended insurance, but many persons do not understand why it is also necessary to deduct it from the face of the policy. The requirement is founded on underwriting considerations. If the policy indebtedness were not deducted from the face of the extended policy, the companies would be exposed to a most virulent form of antiselection.

Consider the case of a person suffering from an incurable malady who has a $20,000 life insurance policy with a $10,000 cash value. If, to meet the cost of medical treatment or for any other reason, he should borrow the maximum amount against the cash value, say $9,500, and then die shortly thereafter, the company would be obligated to pay only $10,500, since the policy loan is an encumbrance against both the cash value and the death proceeds. The total return would thus equal the face of the policy, or $20,000. If, on the other hand, he could borrow $9,000, for example, surrender the policy, and apply the remaining equity, $1,000, to the purchase at net rates of $20,000 of extended term insurance, his death within the next few years would result in a total payment—the face plus the loan—of $29,000. Under present practice, as required by law, the ill policyholder could extend only $11,000, thus limiting the total obligation of the company to $20,000, as was the original intent.

The theory on which the deduction of policy loans is based is that the cancellation of an unliquidated policy loan constitutes a prepayment of a portion of the face amount. To ignore policy indebtedness in determining the face amount of extended insurance would be to make available, without medical or other evidence of insurability, additional term insurance equivalent to the policy indebtedness. This would violate all the tenets of sound underwriting.

The effect of deducting the policy loan from both the surrender

---

[6] Dividend *deposits* will also be added to the sum applied as a net single premium and *may* be added to the face amount of the extended insurance.

value and the amount of extended insurance is to produce a shorter period of term insurance than would be available if no loan existed. This is a natural consequence of the fact that the deduction is a much greater proportion of the cash value than it is of the face amount of the policy. Theoretically, the amount of term insurance should be, not the face amount less the loan, as required by law, but the face amount less the portion thereof having a cash value equal to the loan; in other words, a proportionate part of the *policy* would be *surrendered* to pay the loan, and only the remainder would be continued as term insurance. If this method were used, the *period* of term insurance would not be affected by policy indebtedness. The rule laid down by law in effect *increases* the total insurance and thus reduces the term, since the net cash value remains the same. Thus, if a policy of $1,000 has a cash value of $500 and policy indebtedness of $250, the cash value of *one half* of the policy is required to repay the loan, so that the proper amount of extended insurance would be $500, instead of $750, as presently provided. In other words, the *amount* of the term insurance is reduced by one fourth, whereas the *cash value* available to purchase it is reduced by one half. The *period* of insurance, therefore, must be less than it would be if no indebtedness existed.

From the standpoint of the companies, paid-up term insurance is a more attractive surrender benefit than paid-up whole life or endowment insurance. Among the favorable features of extended term insurance from the viewpoint of the companies are (1) the relatively large amount of insurance involved, with the correspondingly low expense *rate;* (2) the definite date of expiry, which limits the maintenance expenses and minimizes the problem of tracing policyholders; (3) the uninterrupted continuation of the original amount of coverage, as modified by dividend additions and policy loans, for those persons who contemplate eventual reinstatement; and (4) its adaptability to liberal reinstatement requirements, which stems from the fact that the amount at risk is normally decreased by reinstatement, in contrast to the increase in the amount at risk which occurs on the reinstatement of reduced paid-up insurance.

The only real disadvantage of extended term insurance from the standpoint of the companies is the adverse mortality selection encountered, and this can be hedged through the use of the higher mortality assumptions authorized by law or minimized through making the extended term option the *automatic* paid-up benefit. All things considered, the extended term option is so attractive that most companies designate it as the option to go into effect automatically, if the insured does not elect another available option within sixty days after the due date of the premium in default.

The change wrought in the structure of a whole life insurance policy by its surrender for extended term insurance is plotted in Figure 16. This diagram reveals that, in direct contrast to the situation under reduced paid-up insurance, the protection element grows progressively larger, and the investment element progressively smaller, until the policy finally expires. The investment element is at a peak at the time of surrender but is gradually used up in the payment of term insurance premiums, being completely exhausted at the point of expiry. Because of the complementary nature of the protection and investment elements in any insurance contract, this means that the protection ele-

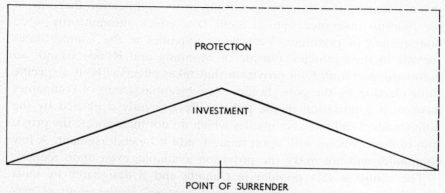

FIG. 16. Impact of extended term insurance option on the structure of the whole life insurance contract.

ment becomes constantly larger, eventually equaling the face of the extended insurance. This explains why the amount at risk is *reduced* through the reinstatement of a policy which has been running under the extended term option.

The investment element of a paid-up term insurance policy can be obtained by surrendering the insurance for cash, subject to the same conditions governing the surrender of reduced paid-up insurance. Extended term insurance is normally nonparticipating with respect to dividends.

AUTOMATIC PREMIUM LOAN

A policy provision found in some—but not all—policies that bears a close resemblance to the paid-up term insurance option but is technically not a surrender option (since the policy is not surrendered) is the automatic premium loan feature. It grew out of the conventional premium loan clause which states that, at the request of the policyholder, any premium may be paid by means of a loan against the surrender value, provided that a surrender value is then available and sufficiently large to cover the loan. Such a loan usually bears interest at the rate applicable to all policy loans. The automatic premium loan clause provides that any defaulted premium will be automatically paid and charged against the cash value without request from the policyholder unless he elects to surrender the policy for cash or one of the paid-up insurance options. In two states—Rhode Island and Montana —all policies of ordinary insurance must contain provision for automatic premium loans; but the policyholder is permitted to set aside this election by the state by specifying in the application that one of the paid-up insurance options shall take effect automatically upon nonpayment of premium. Very few companies in the United States include in their policies, outside of Montana and Rhode Island, an automatic premium loan provision that takes effect without a specific prior election by the policyholder. A substantial group of companies have such a provision in the policy, effective only if elected by the policyholder; and most companies which do not incorporate the provision in their policies will, upon request, add it by endorsement. A few companies will not make the provision available, even upon request.

The clause is very popular in Canada and is designated by most Canadian companies as the automatic "option" in the event of premium default.

The effect of the premium loan clause is to extend the original plan of insurance for the original face amount decreased by the amount of premiums loaned with interest. Such extension will continue as long as the cash value at each premium due date is sufficient to permit the advance of another premium. It should be noted that each premium loan increases the cash value, lengthening the period during which the process can be continued. At the same time, however, the indebtedness against the cash value is growing, not only by the granting of additional premium loans but also by the accrual of interest. Eventually, a premium due date will be reached when the unencumbered cash value is no longer large enough to permit the loan of an additional full premium. Some companies provide in their policies that at this point, the premium loan clause will cease to operate, and the then net cash value will be used to provide automatic extended insurance for whatever period the net cash value will purchase. Other companies stipulate that coverage for the fractional period will be provided on the premium loan principle by advancing the necessary proportionate premium to carry the policy to the exact point where the then cash value (obtained by interpolation) equals the total loan with interest.

The principal advantage to the policyholder of an automatic premium loan provision is that, in the event of inadvertent nonpayment of premium or temporary inability to pay the premium, the policy is kept in full force. Several collateral advantages flow from this basic fact. In the first place, premium payments can be resumed at any time (as long as the equity in the policy remains sufficient to pay premiums as they become due) without furnishing evidence of insurability. This is in contrast to the reinstatement of policies surrendered for paid-up insurance, in which case evidence of insurability is almost invariably required. Secondly, special benefits—such as waiver of premium, disability income, and double indemnity—remain in full force, contrary to the situation under the paid-up insurance options. Finally, if the policy is participating, the policyholder continues to receive dividends, which would usually not be true of paid-up term insurance and might not be true under reduced paid-up insurance.

On the other hand, unless the provision is used—as intended—only as a temporary convenience, it may prove to be disadvantageous to the policyholder. If premium payments are not resumed, not only will the *period* during which the policy will be kept in force usually be less than under extended insurance; but the *amount* payable in the event of death will be less, and the disparity will become greater with each passing year. The former situation arises from the fact that the insurance is kept in force through the payment of gross premiums, as compared to the net rates at which extended term insurance is purchased, while the smaller death benefit is simply attributable to the fact that each unpaid premium becomes a charge against the policy which will be deducted, with interest, from the proceeds payable at death.

During the earlier policy years, the period of coverage available under the premium loan arrangement may be as great or greater than that under extended term insurance. This is due to the fact that the surrender of the policy is postponed and the cash value at the date when the coverage finally terminates is a relatively greater proportion of the reserve than where extended insurance takes effect by surrender of the policy immediately upon default in payment of the premium. In other words, a greater proportion of first-year expenses will have been amortized, producing a larger surrender value. In the later policy years, however, extended term insurance will usually give a longer period of coverage than an automatic premium loan provision.

Another disadvantage, from the policyholder's standpoint, is that where an automatic premium loan provision is included in the policy, he may be inclined to use it too readily; and abuse of the privilege can lead to eventual termination of the plan. To overcome this objection, some companies use a form of automatic premium loan provision which will not take care of two consecutive premiums on an automatic basis. The policyholder must apply for a loan for the second of two consecutively unpaid premiums. Subsequent to such positive action of

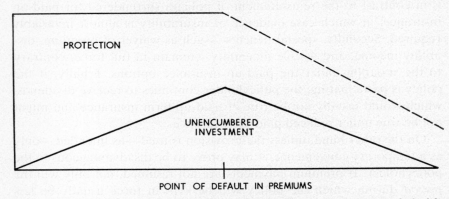

FIG. 17. Impact of automatic premium loans on the structure of the whole life insurance contract.

the policyholder, the automatic feature is again operative for the next default in premium payment. This modification takes care of premium defaults due to oversight or a temporary shortage of funds—the primary, if not the only, purpose of the provision—but does not permit the provision to be used as a substitute for systematic payment of premiums.

From the company's point of view, the automatic premium loan provision offers both advantages and disadvantages. When premium payment is resumed promptly, the system is simpler and much less expensive than to terminate the policy, set up some form of paid-up insurance, and then reverse the operations by reinstating the original policy. If premium payments are not resumed, however, the automatic premium loan arrangement will prove to be the most cumbersome and expensive method of continuing the coverage.

In the event of the insured's death during the period covered, the company is better off financially under the automatic premium loan arrangement than under extended term insurance, since it receives additional premiums by way of deduction from the policy proceeds; but offsetting this advantage to some extent are the additional outlays for commissions, premium taxes, and dividends (if participating).

The impact of the automatic premium loan feature on the structure of a whole life policy is portrayed in Figure 17. Upon default of the first premium, the effective amount of protection is reduced by the amount of the *gross* premium. Each year thereafter that the feature is permitted to operate, the amount of protection is reduced by the gross premium due that year, plus interest on that premium and all unpaid premiums of previous years. Hence, the protection element will decline at a constantly increasing rate. The surrender value will be exhausted, however, before the protection element is reduced to zero.

The effective or unencumbered investment element also turns downward, but not immediately; and it never declines at the same rate as the protection element. Therefore, the solid and broken lines are not parallel. The nominal investment element—the reserve—increases with the payment of each gross premium, irrespective of the source of the funds, by the amount of the net premium, plus interest at the contractual rate and benefit of survivorship, less the cost of insurance. Furthermore, it is increased each year by the amount of interest earned on the terminal reserve of the preceding year. If a substantial reserve has been accumulated, the normal annual increase in the tabular reserve may exceed the gross premium, with the result that the effective—as well as the nominal—investment element may continue to increase for a time after the automatic premium loan feature goes into operation. Within a few years, however, the accumulated premiums in default, plus interest, will exceed the annual increment to the tabular reserve, and the effective investment element will turn downward. Contrary to the behavior of the protection element, the decline in the investment element will continue until it reaches zero. At that point, the policy terminates, and both the protection and the investment elements cease to exist.

CHAPTER XVI

Surplus
and
Dividends

CONCEPT OF GAINS AND LOSSES

IT HAS been stressed in earlier chapters that the long-term obligation assumed by a life insurance company, coupled with the fixed terms of its contracts, forces the company to calculate its premium charges on a conservative basis. The nature of mutual life insurance is such that the adequacy of the gross premium can be given the highest priority; and consequently, it is found that mutual companies incorporate ample margins of safety into each of the basic assumptions entering into their gross premiums. The premiums of stock life companies must likewise meet the test of adequacy; but careful consideration must also be given to the competitiveness of the premiums, since no adjustments in the charges are made after the policy is issued. The margins in stock company premiums will be narrower, therefore, but still present. Thus, it is to be expected that both mutual and stock companies will normally show a gain from each year's operations.

The immediate result of a gain is to increase the surplus of the company; that is, the assets of the company will show a greater increase than the liabilities. The disposition of the gain, however, will depend upon whether it was realized by a stock or a mutual company. The gain in the case of a stock company will have been realized from either a specific margin for profit in the gross premium or favorable deviations of actual experience from assumed experience, or both. Irrespective of the source, the gain is analogous to the net earnings of an ordinary commercial organization and is available for distribution to the stockholders as compensation for the use of their capital. However, only a portion of the gain will normally be distributed to stock-holders in cash, the remainder being left in surplus to finance the acquisition of new business and to provide a financial buffer against adverse contingencies.

The addition to surplus in the case of a mutual company will likewise come predominantly from favorable deviations of actual experience from assumed experience, but they cannot be regarded as earnings in the usual sense. They represent overcharges made for the sake of safety, and it is understood by all concerned that adjustments in the company's charges will be made on the basis of actual experience. The basis for calling the deviations of actual from assumed experience "earnings" in the case of stock companies and merely "overcharges" in the case of mutual companies is that, in the one case, the gains go to third parties (stockholders) while, in the other case, they go back to the persons from whom they originated. Aggregate gains in a participating company are essentially a yardstick for measuring the proper proportion of the gross premiums to be returned to the policy-holders and are in no sense a measure of the profitability of the business.

The refund to mutual policyholders is called a "dividend." This is an unfortunate term, since only with respect to the excess of actual over assumed investment earnings can such a refund be regarded as a return on invested capital—the usual connotation of the word. It is nothing more than a refund of a deliberate overcharge and should not be confused with ordinary dividends payable to corporate stock-holders.

It is possible, of course, that a company will, during the course of a year, experience a loss with respect to one or more of the basic assumptions entering into the gross premium. During the influenza epidemic of 1917–18, for example, the death claims of many—if not all—companies exceeded the anticipated death rates; with the general decline in interest rates during the 1930's and 1940's, many companies found themselves earning a lower rate of interest than that assumed under some of their older policies, leading to the transfer of large sums from surplus to strengthen the reserves under such policies. Nevertheless, under normal circumstances, the over-all operations of a company should produce a net addition to surplus.

No further consideration will be given to the gains or losses of stock life insurance companies. While the sources of surplus are the same as those of mutual companies, the disposition of the gains is subject to quite different considerations from those governing the treatment of surplus in a mutual company—which is the primary concern of this chapter. The remainder of this chapter will be devoted to a discussion of the principal sources of surplus of a mutual company, the principles followed in apportioning surplus among policyholders, and the form in which the distributions may be taken.

SOURCES OF SURPLUS

Favorable Deviations from Premium Assumptions

Favorable deviations from the assumptions entering into the gross premium constitute the primary source of additions to surplus. This means fewer deaths than those assumed, a higher rate of interest than that used in the premium calculations, and lower expenses than the loading in the premiums. These sources of surplus are usually designated as *mortality savings, excess interest* (sometimes called interest *savings*), and *loading savings*. The use of the word "savings" in this sense is somewhat misleading, in that it connotes a residue from more efficient and economical operations than were anticipated in fixing the premiums, whereas the "savings" actually reflect margins known to be in the premiums and relied upon to produce additions to surplus. This is not to minimize the importance of the managerial factor in the production of a surplus. With any given set of assumptions and volume of insurance, the more capable the management in the areas of underwriting, investments, and administration, the greater the additions to surplus.

The basic equation for measuring gains or losses from deviations in the premium assumptions hearkens back to the retrospective reserve formula. For a group, that formula, it will be recalled, employs the following equation:

> Reserve at beginning of year (terminal reserve of preceding year) + Net premium + Interest on both at assumed rate − Tabular cost of insurance = Aggregate reserve at end of year

Substituting the gross premium minus loading for the net premium, the equation can be rewritten as follows:

> Reserve at beginning of year + Gross premium − Loading + interest on difference at assumed rate − Tabular cost of insurance = Reserve at end of year

The foregoing equation can be restated in a form that will reflect gains and losses. Thus:

Gross premiums + Assumed interest earnings − Loading − Tabular cost of insurance − Increase in reserves = Gain or loss (in this case, zero)

By substituting actual results for assumed experience in the above equation, either a positive or a negative value—indicating a gain or loss, respectively—will be reflected. Thus, the general equation for the derivation of gains or losses becomes:

Gross premiums + Actual net interest earnings − Actual expenses − Actual cost of insurance − Increase in reserves = Gain or loss for the period

These fundamental relationships can be illustrated by a hypothetical comparison of the actual experience under a group of policies during a particular year with the tabular or assumed experience. A reasonably realistic demonstration can be given on the basis of the tenth policy year of a group of 10,000 ordinary life policies for $1,000 issued at age thirty-five. Such a demonstration is presented in Table 26.

TABLE 26

Comparison between Assumed and Actual Experience
during Tenth Policy Year of 10,000 Ordinary Life Policies
for $1,000, Issued at Age 35*

Item	Nature of Adjustment	Assumed Experience	Actual Experience	Difference
Gross premiums.............		$235,000	$235,000	None
Interest income............	+	42,000†	66,000‡	+$24,000
Expenses..................	−	58,000	44,000	− 14,000
Death claims..............	−	49,000	37,000	− 12,000
Increase in reserves.........	−	170,000	172,000	+ 2,000
Gain or loss...............		None	+$ 48,000	

* All computations rounded to nearest $1,000.
† Interest at 2½ per cent on aggregate initial reserve of $1,677,900 ($167.79 × 10,000) which includes net premiums for tenth year. Expenses are assumed to be disbursed at beginning of year and hence earn no interest.
‡ Interest at 3.95 per cent on aggregate initial reserve of $1,677,900. Interest on difference between assumed and actual expenses is ignored in this calculation.

The assumed experience is based on the 1958 C.S.O. Table and 2½ per cent interest, with a loading of $5.83 per $1,000 of insurance. The actual experience is based on mortality at 74.5 per cent of the tabular rate, interest earnings of 3.95 per cent, and expenses at 76 per cent of the loading. The assumption is made that there are no voluntary terminations during the year, although the termination factor must be taken into account in testing an actual dividend formula. Dividend distributions are likewise ignored.

It can be observed from Table 26 that if the assumptions underlying the gross premium had been exactly realized during the tenth policy year, there would have been no addition to or deduction from surplus for the year's operations. On the basis of the hypothetical actual experience, however, the operations of the tenth policy year produced a net addition to surplus of $48,000.

As a result of the fact that the company earned 3.95 per cent on its investments, rather than the assumed rate of $2\frac{1}{2}$ per cent, interest earnings were $24,000 higher than "expected." Since interest is an additive factor, this deviation exerted a direct, positive effect on the surplus. Expenses were $14,000 less than the loading provided in the gross premium, which indirectly increased surplus by the same amount. Twelve fewer deaths occurred than the number "predicted" by the 1958 C.S.O. Table, and it would appear from the table that the mortality savings aggregated $12,000. The net savings, however, were smaller than that sum. As has been learned previously, a portion of each death claim is made up of the reserve under the policy—in this case, $167.90 per $1,000; and the net strain on a company from a death claim is the difference between the face amount and the reserve, or the net amount at risk. The real saving, therefore, was 12 × $832.10, or $9,985.20.

This sum can be reconciled with the gross savings of $12,000 when considered in conjunction with the increase in reserves. The projected increase of $170,000 was based on the assumption that forty-nine persons would die during the tenth year and reserves of 49 × $167.90, or $8,227.10, would be released. The reserves for the twelve who did not die were not released, however, but had to be carried forward to help meet the death claims when they do occur. Thus, the actual reserves are $2,000 higher than anticipated, which, subtracted from the $12,000 gross mortality savings, produces the net savings of $10,000.

Other Sources of Surplus

Any transaction that increases assets more than liabilities or decreases liabilities to a greater extent than assets is a source of surplus. In the latter category are voluntary terminations at early durations. Surrender values are usually less than reserves during the early years of a policy and, under the Standard Nonforfeiture Law, may be less until the end of the premium-paying period. A termination of a policy at any time before the surrender value equals the reserve increases surplus, since a liability item (reserves) is decreased more than an asset item (cash); or if one of the paid-up surrender benefits is elected by the withdrawing policyholder, the reserve released by the surrender of the original policy is greater than the reserve or present value of the paid-up benefit. It is recognized, of course, that this is not a net addition to surplus, since it merely replaces funds which were withdrawn earlier in order to finance the acquisition of the surrendered policy. Nevertheless, in the year of termination, the surplus account is increased by the difference, if any, between the reserve and the surrender value. Gains from surrenders do not usually enter directly into the dividend formula, but the over-all level of dividends is influenced by the relative liberality of surrender values.

Surplus may also be created through the sale of an asset for more than its book value or through the writing-up of the book value of an asset. Such gains may be taken into account in selecting the excess interest factor of the dividend formula, which would have the effect of distributing them; or, more commonly, they may be earmarked in a special surplus account to be used in offsetting future capital losses.[1] During the 1940's, when substantial capital gains were realized from the refunding operations of corporations seeking the advantages of lower interest rates, many companies applied such gains to the strengthening of their reserves, in recognition of the fact that the investments which produced the capital gains were being replaced with lower yielding assets.

Supplementary features of the insurance contract, such as disability income and accidental death provisions, may be an additional source of surplus; but they may also be a source of loss, as witness the disability income losses of the 1930's. These features are frequently taken into account as an additional factor in the dividend formula.

APPORTIONMENT OF SURPLUS

Divisible Surplus

There is no fixed relationship between the net gains to surplus in a particular calendar year and the dividends distributed to policyhold-

---

[1] Since 1951, gains—both realized and unrealized—on bonds and stocks must, by law, be held in the so-called Mandatory Security Valuation Reserve to offset possible losses in future years and hence are not available for current distribution. Gains on mortgages, real estate, and other earning assets may still be disposed of in accordance with the discretion of the company.

ers on the next policy anniversaries. The gains are credited to the appropriate surplus account as they accrue; and at the end of the calendar year, the directors of the company, on the basis of information then available and in the light of all the factors involved, decide what portion of the *total* surplus should be distributed in dividends the following year and what portion should be withheld as a contingency reserve. The amount earmarked for distribution is designated *divisible surplus,* and the payment of the sum indicated becomes a definite obligation of the company. Once set aside by action of the directors, the divisible surplus is converted into a liability and is no longer regarded as a part of the surplus of the company.

The sum withheld to meet contingencies—the difference between gross and divisible surplus—may be carried under various surplus accounts, identifying the special purposes for which it is held. Despite the fact that the annual statement blank provides a line for "Unassigned Surplus," many companies prefer to label their residual account "Unassigned Funds."

The decision with respect to the amount of funds to be set aside for dividends requires a balancing of the need for a general contingency fund against the advantages of pursuing a liberal dividend policy. The minimum objective of most companies is to continue the current dividend scale, which—for reasons that will be apparent later—usually implies a larger absolute distribution of surplus than that of the preceding year. Current additions to surplus will normally be sufficient to support the existing dividend scale; but if they should be deficient in a particular year or two because of temporary fluctuations with respect to the basic assumptions, the company may draw on funds accumulated in previous years to avoid a reduction in the scale. By the same token, if, during a temporary period, additions to surplus are more than adequate to support the existing dividend scale, the excess will usually be added to existing surplus, in order to avoid the expense and other complications of changing the scale. If, however, there should develop a significant disparity between the funds needed to maintain the existing scale and those currently available for distribution, and the disparity is expected to continue over a relatively long period, consideration must be given to a change in the scale. Such a disparity normally develops gradually out of a basic trend in mortality or interest rates, and the nature and magnitude of the modification of the dividend scale will reflect the directors' judgment as to the duration and future course of the trend or trends.

It is well to remember, in this connection, that the aggregate dividends distributed to any block of policies over their entire duration will be somewhat less than the sum of their individual contributions to surplus. This is necessarily so if the company is to accumulate and maintain a contingency reserve equal to a certain percentage of its liabilities, which is an objective of all well-managed companies. As the reserves increase, whether from the sale of new policies or the natural progression under old policies, the absolute size of the contingency reserve must also increase. Apart from interest earnings on the contingency reserve or "free surplus,"[2] the only source of funds for the necessary increments are the current earnings from policies. Therefore, in the long run, something less than the net additions to surplus from all blocks of policies must be returned to policyholders in the form of dividends, and equity demands that each block of policies bear its fair share of the burden involved in this practice. This is just another way of saying that the asset share of a policy should eventually exceed the reserve and that each policy is expected to make a permanent contribution to the surplus of the company.

In some companies, the importance attached to the contingency reserve is such that the portion of the total surplus to be set aside for contingencies is first determined, and the remainder is treated as the divisible surplus. There are undoubtedly times in the experience of all companies when this procedure is followed. In no well-managed company would the share of the total surplus to be distributed ever be determined without careful consideration of the impact on the safety cushion of the company.

Guiding Principles in the Distribution of Divisible Surplus

The apportionment of the divisible surplus among the various policyholders is a complex matter and one which should measure up to a set of guiding principles or criteria which, over the years, have been found valid. Stated in the approximate order of importance, these criteria stipulate that the system of distribution should be (1) equitable, (2) flexible, (3) reasonably simple in operation, and (4) capable of being understood by policyholders and the agency force.

Equity. There is general agreement that a system of surplus distribution should, above all other things, be equitable. There is also agreement that equity would be achieved if each policy could share

---

[2] In many companies, interest on these funds is taken into account in determining the excess interest factor. See pp. 343–45.

in the surplus in the exact proportion in which it contributed to the surplus. However, this objective cannot be attained in reality.

Mortality experience, for example, varies widely with duration, occupation, residence, amount of insurance, and plan of insurance. It is obviously impracticable to distinguish between all these factors in computing the individual contributions to surplus from favorable mortality. The rate of expense is likewise affected by many factors, including the size of the policy and the variation in the premium tax rates among the different states. Recognition of all these factors would unduly complicate the dividend formula. It would seem that the interest contribution of a particular policy could be easily traced, but strict equity would require consideration of the different times and interest rates at which the premiums were invested.

Furthermore, as was pointed out above, the divisible surplus will not, except by accident, equal the total "profits" or aggregate contributions to surplus, but is affected by considerations which are quite unrelated to the sources of surplus and which cannot be related to individual policies or even to classes of policies. Hence, a method of distribution which calls for the computation of individual contributions to surplus would require modification in order to reproduce in the aggregate the actual sum available for distribution. Such modification is likely to disturb the relationship between the assumed contributions from different sources.

Thus, under practical conditions, it is not possible to refund the excess payments of individual policyholders with exactitude, nor is it necessary to do so. In such matters, as in other respects, policies cannot be considered individually but must be dealt with on the basis of groups or classes; and the system of computing refunds or dividends should be one which aims at approximate equity between classes and among individual policies within classes. As a minimum standard of equity, the system of surplus distribution should take into account, as far as practicable, the principal sources of surplus and should not be simplified to the extent of causing injustice to any group of policyholders. This is likely to be the maximum standard, as well.

Flexibility. To say that the system of distribution must be adaptable to changing conditions is merely an enlargement of the statement that the method must be equitable. Flexibility is secured by (1) separate recognition in the dividend formula of as many as possible of the sources of surplus, (2) use of a type of formula which permits proper adjustments to be made in any of the factors involved, and (3) avoidance of arbitrary expedients in adjusting dividend scales as between one year and the other.

Unless supplementary features are present in the policies under consideration, it is not deemed practicable or necessary that the dividend formula accord separate recognition to more than the three primary elements of the premium. The manner in which this is done will be fully demonstrated in a later section. The formulas should be such that it can be modified so as to give effect, for example, to changes in the mortality experience as between different ages or plans, or to changes in the expense rate as between plans, ages at issue, or durations. Otherwise, there might be a tendency to continue a basis of distribution after it ceases to reflect the incidence of surplus earnings or to make changes which disturb the true equities involved. Temporary expedients such as constant percentage changes in the total dividend or elimination of the normal increase with duration, while possibly justifiable under certain circumstances, tend to destroy the simplicity and rationale of the dividend formula and its relationship to the actual factors experienced.

Simplicity. It is desirable, for practical reasons, that the method of distribution be reasonably simple in operation. A complicated formula is troublesome, expensive, and difficult to explain to policyholders and others, while the increase in accuracy may be more apparent than real. This does not mean that the divisible surplus should be apportioned on the basis of either the premium, the amount of insurance, or the reserve, as was the custom in earlier days. It simply means that complicated refinements—which, because of the fundamental limitations on the degree of equity attainable, can have only minor significance—should not be introduced into the procedure.

Comprehensibility by Policyholders and Agency Force. This is a minor consideration, but policyholders occasionally do make inquiry as to the basis of their dividends, particularly if the dividend scale on their policy has been reduced. Such an inquiry may be addressed to the home office or to a field representative. In the interest of good public relations, the formula should lend itself to a reasonably simple explanation. Certainly, it is important that the field force have a general understanding of the sources of surplus and how they are combined to produce a final dividend scale.

The Three-Factor Contribution Plan

Most companies in the United States and Canada employ a system of surplus distribution called the *contribution plan*. This designation is given to any procedure of dividend distribution which is based upon an analysis of the sources of surplus and which attempts to return to each class of policyholders a share of the divisible surplus approximately proportionate to the contribution of the class to the distributable surplus. It should be noted that his plan does not envision the return of *all* contributions to surplus. It merely requires that the *divisible surplus* be allotted to the participating policyholders in the approximate proportion in which they contributed to the total surplus. Such a procedure develops dividends which vary with the plan of insurance, age at issue, and duration of policy.

In the interest of simplicity, and for the other reasons outlined above, consideration is usually limited to the three major sources of surplus: mortality savings, excess interest, and loading savings. A distribution plan which recognizes only these sources of surplus is called the *three-factor contribution plan*.[3]

Theoretically, at least, there should be as many factors in the dividend formula as there are elements in the total gross premium. This means that if special benefits, such as those related to total disability and accidental death, should be provided in the contract for an additional premium, additional factors should be incorporated into the dividend formula to reflect the experience under the special clauses. Such factors may be positive or negative. During the 1930's, many companies inserted negative dividend factors in their distribution formula for policies which provided disability income benefits, in recognition of the net losses being suffered under total disability clauses. In recent years, this factor has become positive for most companies. The premium charged for accidental death benefits has, in the main, produced a profit, which is often reflected in a positive dividend factor added to the formula for those classes of policies providing accidental death benefits.

The manner in which the three-factor contribution plan operates to

---

[3] There are three other methods of apportioning surplus that are based on the contribution concept: experience premium method, asset share method, and the fund method. In common usage, the term "contribution" method is reserved for the method described herein as the "three-factor contribution" plan.

produce dividends, when no special benefits are involved, is described in the following sections.

Mortality Factor. The mortality factor of the dividend formula normally takes the form of a scale of percentages of the tabular cost of insurance, decreasing with attained age, and reflecting the company's actual mortality experience age by age as compared with the rates shown in the mortality table used in the calculation of premiums. The percentages may range from a high of 50 per cent at the lower ages to a low of 5 per cent at the higher ages, depending on the mortality table used. They will normally be the same for all plans except term insurance. Since the mortality under term policies is considerably higher age by age than under permanent insurance policies, a lower scale of mortality savings must be used for term insurance. Some companies still follow the older method of expressing the factor as a *constant amount* per $1,000 at risk, which, in view of the constantly decreasing amount at risk under any plan of permanent insurance, constitutes a *decreasing percentage* of the tabular cost of insurance as the attained age increases. A few companies express the factor as a varying amount per $1,000 at risk, the amount increasing with attained age. Regardless of the form in which the factor is expressed, the effect is to provide a mortality saving which, as a percentage of the tabular cost of insurance, grows smaller with attained age, in recognition of the shrinking margins in the mortality table. Applied to the entire volume of business, the mortality factors will approximately reproduce the aggregate amount of mortality savings available for distribution.

The percentage is usually expressed in terms of the *ultimate* mortality experience, thus excluding from consideration under this factor the mortality savings attributable to the effect of selection. The savings so excluded are assumed to be applied toward the payment of excess first-year expenses and hence are distributed indirectly in accordance with the method used to assess expenses. Normal mortality savings—i.e., those based on ultimate experience at the attained ages involved—are reflected in the dividends of the early policy years.

The various percentages are applied to the tabular cost of insurance rather than to the tabular rates of mortality, in recognition of the fact that the former reflects the net amount at risk, the true cost of a death claim. From the standpoint of an entire class of policies, the savings from fewer deaths than the number assumed are measured in terms of the net amount at risk rather than the aggregate face amounts involved. On the level of an individual policy, the savings from a lower death rate than that assumed should be expressed as a percentage of the cost of insurance instead of the tabular rate.

The dividends per $1,000 of insurance provided by an illustrative scale of mortality factors under ordinary life, twenty-payment life, and twenty-year endowment policies, issued at ages twenty-five and fifty-five, and in force for various durations, are shown in Table 27. The mortality savings are assumed to range from 35 per cent at age twenty-five down to 10 per cent at attained ages seventy-five and over, diminishing at the rate of ½ per cent per year of attained age.

TABLE 27

ILLUSTRATIVE MORTALITY SAVINGS PER $1,000
AT VARIOUS DURATIONS AND AGES AT ISSUE*

Number of Years in Force	Ordinary Life, Age at Issue:		20-Payment Life, Age at Issue:		20-Year Endowment, Age at Issue:	
	25	55	25	55	25	55
5.........	$0.65	$2.86	$0.61	$2.73	$0.55	$2.66
10........	0.64	3.23	0.56	2.83	0.41	2.58
15........	0.73	3.49	0.58	2.52	0.27	1.93
20........	0.92	3.40	0.60	1.28	0.00	0.00

* Based on the 1958 C.S.O. Table and 2½ per cent interest, with assumed mortality savings of 35 per cent at age twenty-five, diminishing ½ per cent per year of attained age to 10 per cent at age seventy-five and over.

Three characteristics of mortality savings can be noted in Table 27. In the first place, at any given age and duration, the mortality savings will vary inversely with the size of the premium. That is, the larger the premium, the smaller the mortality savings. Thus, in Table 27, the savings are greatest for the ordinary life policy, next greatest for the twenty-payment life policy, and smallest under the twenty-year endowment. If the savings for a term insurance policy had been shown, they would have been the highest of the four policies, provided the same formula was applicable to term insurance. The explanation for this phenomenon is that—other things being equal—the larger the premium, the higher is the reserve, and the smaller the net amount at risk. The smaller the net amount at risk at any given attained age, the smaller the tabular cost of insurance. Thus, since the percentage of mortality savings at any given age is assumed to be the same, irrespective of the plan of insurance, it follows that the mortality savings will be smallest under the highest premium policy, and vice versa.

The second characteristic that may be noted is that for any particular policy and at any given age of issue, the mortality savings will tend to decrease with duration, with some exceptions. This tendency is attributable to the fact that (1) the net amount at risk—and hence, the cost of insurance—diminishes each year; and (2) a decreasing percentage of the cost of insurance is credited to mortality savings at successive attained ages, because of the shrinking margins in the mortality table. Moreover, the higher the premium, the more pronounced will this tendency be. The decrease is particularly marked in the case of short- and medium-term endowment policies, under which the reserve mounts very rapidly and the amount at risk declines equally rapidly. It should be observed, however, that the cost of insurance does not invariably decrease as the amount of risk declines. Under some policies such as ordinary life, the amount at risk declines at a slower rate than that at which mortality increases, with the result that the cost of insurance (and the mortality factor of the dividend) will increase from one year to the next. This is illustrated in Table 27 by the trend of mortality savings for the ordinary life policy. The exact course of mortality savings under such policies will depend largely upon the scale of percentages adopted in the dividend formula.

The final characteristic that deserves mention is that for any particular policy and duration, the higher the age of issue, the greater the mortality savings. This follows from the higher cost of insurance. In other words, the *decrease* in the scale of percentages from age to age is more than offset by the *increase* in the death rate.

Interest Factor. The interest factor of the dividend formula seeks to credit each policy with its equitable share of that portion of a company's total investment earnings in excess of the sum needed to meet its obligations. It takes the form of a percentage, derived from the difference between the rate of interest assumed in premium and reserve computations and the rate actually earned, which is applied to that sum of money—usually the initial reserve for the policy year in question—assumed to represent the policy's share of the total invested funds. Simple in concept, the interest factor raises several issues in application.

The first complication arises out of the fact that a *rate* of investment earnings must be calculated. Aggregate investment earnings are a known quantity, available from the company's financial and accounting records; but there are several bases which could logically be used to compute the rate of investment earnings. Possible bases include ledger assets, admitted assets, and invested funds. For dividend purposes, however, the question in its simplest form is whether the investment earnings of the company should be expressed as a percentage of total invested assets or as a percentage of only those assets which stand back of or offset those liabilities the valuation of which is based on the assumption that they will be credited annually with interest at a specified rate. Such liabilities are referred to as *interest-bearing liabilities* and include—*inter alia*—policy reserves, funds held under settlement options, dividend deposits, and premium deposits.[4] Naturally, a rate calculated on the basis of this restricted group of assets would be higher than one based on total assets and hence would provide a larger excess interest element in the dividend formula.

Interestingly, the basic issue involved here is how the contingency reserve is to be built up. The contingency reserve enters into the picture in that it is the primary balancing item between total liabilities and interest-bearing liabilities. The effect of computing the rate of investment earnings on total invested assets is to credit the earnings on those assets offsetting the contingency reserve to the latter account, while the effect of computing the rate on the basis of interest-bearing liabilities is to make the earnings on contingency reserve assets available for distribution to policyholders as excess interest.[5]

There is general agreement that the growth in interest-bearing liabilities should be accompanied by an increase in the size of the contingency reserve, and those companies which favor the computation of the earnings rate on the basis of total assets feel that a part of the desired increase should come from the earnings on the contingency fund itself. In fact, such companies may regard the contingency reserve as an interest-bearing liability, on the ground that sound growth requires a constantly expanding fund for contingencies. Under this concept, policies with large reserve accumulations make a heavier contribution to the contingency reserve than those with smaller accumulations, unless an offsetting adjustment is made in connection with

---

[4] Other important noninterest-bearing liabilities are funds set aside for dividend distribution, mandatory security valuation reserves, and unpaid expenses and taxes.

[5] If earnings on the contingency reserve are paid out in the form of excess interest, then one of the other two factors must be reduced accordingly, and vice versa. The dominant requirement of any dividend scale is that it pay out in the aggregate the amount which has been set aside as divisible surplus. Clearly, the disposition of the investment earnings on the contingency reserve has no bearing on the amount of surplus to be distributed to policyholders.

the mortality factor. Contributions to the contingency reserve out of aggregate mortality savings, on the other hand, fall most heavily upon the low-premium, high-protection type of policies.

Those companies which compute the earnings rate on the basis of interest-bearing liabilities only are, in effect, acting on the assumption that each policyholder owns a prorata share of the contingency reserve and is entitled to the earnings from it. Such companies feel that contributions to the contingency reserve can be apportioned among the various policies in a more equitable manner by segregating as accurately as feasible the earnings from the three major sources of surplus and making each class of policies contribute to the contingency reserve on some realistic basis. Needless to say, the excess interest factor in the dividend formula of these companies reflects a higher net rate of interest than the yield on mean assets after federal income taxes.

Some companies pursue an intermediate course and credit a portion of the earnings on the contingency fund to the excess interest factor, and transfer the remainder to an investment fluctuation fund or leave it in the general contingency fund.

A second matter with respect to which differences of opinion and practice exist is the treatment of capital gains and losses on assets other than bonds and stocks. Some companies take these into account in fixing the excess interest factor when they reflect actual market transactions, as opposed to adjustments in book value. It would appear, however, that the more common practice is to transfer such gains and losses to an investment fluctuation fund or to a general contingency reserve. Under the latter practice, net interest earnings are more stable and do not fluctuate with the unpredictable behavior of the capital market. Of course, capital losses during a severe economic crisis may exhaust the special fund set aside to meet such contingencies, making it necessary to reduce the entire dividend scale to absorb part of the losses.

There are also differences among companies as to the treatment of investment expenses. All companies purport to deduct investment expenses from gross investment earnings, but there is no universal agreement as to what constitutes an investment expense. Differences are found particularly in the treatment of general overhead and federal income taxes. A number of companies treat federal income taxes as an insurance expense—as a cost of doing business—rather than an investment expense. This makes a tremendous difference in the net yield.[6]

Even after the net rate of return has been calculated and the excess interest factor selected, there is still the question as to whether the interest factor should be applied to the initial reserve, the mean reserve, or some other actuarial value. The initial reserve has been the traditional base, on the theory that it measures the amount of funds invested on behalf of a particular policy throughout the policy year. This base was adopted when the assumption that death claims are paid at the end of the year had more validity than it does today. Under present claims practices, the use of the initial reserve overstates the excess interest earned. The theoretically correct base is the initial reserve less one half year's cost of insurance. However, the difference between this theoretically correct base and the mean reserve is so small (being a half year's interest at the valuation rate on the initial reserve) that the mean reserve is considered to be a satisfactory approximation.[7]

The rate of interest selected for dividend purposes will not necessarily or usually be the actual rate earned, whether the base be total invested assets or interest-bearing liabilities. Under normal conditions, dividend formulas are modified only at infrequent intervals, which means that the excess interest factor should reflect the general trend of the company's investment earnings and be set at a level which, according to the best judgment of the company, should be appropriate for several years. The factor will usually be based on an interest return somewhat less than that which the company expects to earn in the immediate future; but for short periods of time, it could be based on a higher rate than is actually being earned, the difference being made up out of the contingency reserve.

It is possible that a company might earn a rate of interest less than the rate assumed in the calculation of premiums and reserves. Under such circumstances, the contribution method would call for a *negative*

---

[6] Under a group annuity contract, a company must decide whether to credit the contract with a rate of interest based on the investment earnings of the composite portfolio of the company or one which reflects the various rates of interest at which the funds generated under the contract were invested and reinvested. See Dan M. McGill, *Fundamentals of Private Pensions* (2nd ed.; Homewood, Ill.: Richard D. Irwin, Inc., 1964), pp. 165–71 for a description of the latter approach and the restrictions on its use imposed by the New York Insurance Department.

[7] There are more complicated considerations if a company uses continuous rather than curtate functions.

interest factor—i.e., a *deduction* from the dividend that would otherwise be provided by the mortality and loading factors. Such negative interest factors have been used at times, with the result that the dividends under some policies *decreased* as the reserves *increased*. Other companies, fearful of adverse policyholder and public reaction, have taken the view that a deficiency in interest earnings can be considered a proper charge against the general contingency reserve. In other words, the additional interest earnings needed to meet reserve requirements are drawn from surplus, and the negative dividend factors are eliminated.

The dividend credits per $1,000 provided by an excess interest factor of 1.45 per cent under ordinary life, twenty-payment life, and twenty-year endowment policies issued at ages twenty-five and fifty-five, and in force for various durations, are given in Table 28. The

TABLE 28

ANNUAL DIVIDENDS PER $1,000 FROM EXCESS
INTEREST EARNINGS OF 1.45 PER CENT*

Number of Years in Force	Ordinary Life, Age at Issue:		20-Payment Life, Age at Issue:		20-Year Endowment, Age at Issue:	
	25	55	25	55	25	55
5.........	$0.84	$2.26	$1.54	$ 2.80	$ 2.90	$ 3.12
10.........	1.75	4.30	3.25	5.52	6.17	6.26
15.........	2.77	6.20	5.19	8.42	9.89	9.76
20........	3.86	7.88	7.35	11.79	14.15	14.15

* Based on full net level premium reserves computed in accordance with the 1958 C.S.O. Table and 2½ per cent interest.

factor is applied to the appropriate initial reserves, which are calculated on the basis of the 1958 C.S.O. Table and 2½ per cent interest. For example, the initial reserve for the fifth policy year of an ordinary life policy issued at age twenty-five is $57.97, which is the sum of the fourth-year terminal reserve of $45.42 and the net premium for the fifth year of $12.55. Multiplied by the excess interest factor of 1.45 per cent, this sum produces a dividend credit of $0.84 per $1,000. The initial reserve for the tenth policy year is $120.96, which yields a dividend credit of $1.75.

Contrary to the trend of mortality savings, the excess interest credit increases with duration, if reserves increase, and at all ages of issue and durations is larger for the higher premium forms than for the lower premium policies. This stems from the fact that the excess interest credit is a direct function of the level of reserves. It can be observed that excess interest makes a far greater contribution to the total dividend of a twenty-year endowment policy than does the mortality factor. The same can be said of a twenty-payment life after the first few years. Even under an ordinary life policy, the excess interest eventually surpasses mortality savings. Under a term policy, however, excess interest would be inconsequential, mortality savings being the dominant element.

Excess interest credits are very sensitive to fluctuations in the net rate of interest earnings. This is attributable to the fact that the excess interest factor is in the nature of a residuum. It is the difference between the rate of interest which the company *must* earn to meet its contractual obligations and the rate which it actually does earn. Since the interest requirement at any given time is fixed, any change in the total rate of earnings must be reflected entirely in the excess interest factor. To illustrate, assume that a company whose premiums and reserves are based on $2\frac{1}{2}$ per cent interest is earning a net rate, after federal income taxes, of 4 per cent. Such a company could (but probably would not) use an excess interest factor of $1\frac{1}{2}$ per cent in its dividend formula. If, however, the company's rate of earnings should decline to $3\frac{3}{4}$ per cent, the excess interest factor would have to be reduced to $1\frac{1}{4}$ per cent. Thus, a decline of 6 per cent in the net rate of earnings would cause a 17 per cent reduction in the excess interest factor. An increase in interest earnings would have a similar effect.

The decline in interest earnings during the late 1930's and early 1940's had a marked effect on the dividends of most companies. Endowment and other high-premium types of policies were especially hard hit. Under many of the older policies which had been issued on an interest assumption of $3\frac{1}{2}$ or 4 per cent (rates which were for many years well below those which were being earned), excess interest earnings were completely wiped out; and in all cases, such earnings were drastically reduced. In some cases, as was pointed out above, negative interest factors were introduced into the dividend formula.

Loading Factor. The loading factor of the dividend formula consists of the loading in the gross premium less the amount of expenses assessed against the policy, increased in some companies by one year's interest at the dividend rate. This factor is quite different in nature from the other two factors of the formula. The mortality and interest factors are considered, in a broad sense, to be capable of exact determination. The rate of interest and the reserve to which it applies are definitely ascertainable quantities, as are the ultimate mortality rates and the net amount at risk; and, subject to considerable variation in the details of calculation, these factors can reasonably be assumed to represent the amounts of surplus contributed by individual policies. The contribution from loading, however, cannot be arrived at by any universally applicable rule or formula, but depends upon the method or philosophy of individual companies in the assessment of expenses.

Theoretically, at least, the loading charge in the dividend formula should be based on the same type of cost analysis that should have preceded the computation of the gross premium. If expenses are analyzed carefully and accurately in the preparation of gross premium scales and are apportioned equitably over the various plans, ages of issues, and durations through the loading formula, there is no reason why the same expense charges, suitably modified to reflect subsequent experience, could not—and should not—be used in the dividend formula. Some companies, however, arrive at the loading in a rather arbitrary fashion and justify their actions on the ground that any inequities in the premium loading can be corrected through the dividend formula. This merely postpones the day of reckoning, since the expense charge of the dividend formula, if it is to correct the inequities in the loading formula, must be calculated with all the attention to cost accounting principles and the exercise of judgment that would have had to go into the calculation of a theoretically correct gross premium. There may be an advantage in the latter procedure, however, in that the cost calculations are made on the basis of actual rather than projected experience.

If a cost analysis were made in conjunction with the computation of the gross premium, it may be assumed that the company would use the same expense factors and method of expressing the expenses in the dividend formula. If not, the expense factors developed in connection with the dividend distribution will be similar to those that come out of premium computations and would be expressed in the same general manner. In other words, the expense charge in the dividend formula may be a straight percentage of the premium, a modified percentage of the premium, or a percentage and constant, depending upon the formula used in the leading formula.[8] In the analysis of expenses

---

[8] A formula sometimes used for dividend purposes, but considered defective by many persons, allocates expenses on the basis of a constant or graded percentage of *loading*.

presented in the chapter on gross premiums, a total loading of 16 per cent of the net premium and $3.00 per $1,000 of insurance was developed, of which 9.7 per cent and $1.08 represented actual identifiable expense charges. If the expenses of a particular company should conform precisely to those in the illustration and *were incurred at a uniform rate* throughout the premium-paying period, the dividend formula of that company might be expected to show, for an ordinary life policy, an expense charge of approximately 9.7 per cent of the net premium and $1.08 per $1,000, plus whatever portion of the loading for contingencies the company might decide to withhold for that purpose. Expenses are not incurred at a uniform rate, however; and in practice, the pattern of expense charges, especially during the first few years, is influenced strongly by the manner in which excess first-year expenses are handled.

It is obvious that if all of the expenses of the first year should be taken into full account in determining whether or not a policy is entitled to a dividend at the end of the first year, the expense charge would create a negative factor of such proportions that any mortality and interest savings would be more than offset and no dividend would be payable. In fact, the deficiency might be so great that no dividend would be earned during the second policy year or even during the next few years. There are two sources of surplus, however, which are not usually included in the regular dividend formula, the profits from which can be applied to the reduction of first-year expenses in the aggregate. Previously alluded to, these sources of surplus are savings from select—as distinguished from ultimate—mortality, and gains from lapse and surrender. The savings from select mortality are a direct result of the amount spent in the first year for medical examinations and inspections and can, therefore, reasonably be considered as a legitimate offset to initial expenses. The gains from lapses and surrenders are applied against first-year expenses on the premise that it is desirable, if not necessary, to replace a terminating policyholder with a new one.

If these profits are treated as an offset to excess initial expenses and *in the aggregate* equal or exceed the total *excess* first-year expenses, the same expense charge can be applied in the first year as in subsequent years, and a dividend can be paid at the end of the first year. If —as is more frequently the case—the combined profit from these sources is smaller than the aggregate first-year expenses, a first-year dividend can be paid only if the remaining portion of excess initial expenses is charged against all policies or else is spread, for dividend purposes, over a period of several years.

Those companies that adhere to the philosophy that new business is essential to the continued existence of a company may charge those excess first-year expenses not offset by profits from select mortality and terminations against all policies and pay a regular first-year dividend. Other companies will charge such expenses to the new policies involved but, for dividend purposes, will amortize them over a period of years through a graded expense charge. The amortization period will be long enough to permit the payment of a first-year dividend, a period of from five to ten years usually being sufficient for that purpose. Some companies chart a middle course and charge a portion of the excess expenses to all policies and the remainder to the new policies through a graded expense charge. Under any arrangement whereby the individual policyholder is charged with all or a part of his own excess first-year expenses, the contribution of the loading factor to dividends will be relatively modest during the early policy years but will increase rather sharply after first-year expenses have been fully amortized.

Regardless of the manner in which first-year dividends are derived, or rationalized, most companies make them contingent upon the payment of the premium due at the beginning of the second policy year. This recognizes the fact that, with few exceptions, any dividend payable at the end of the first policy year will exceed the funds then on hand from the policyholder's first premium and, unless offset by the second premium, will represent an out-of-pocket expense to the company. Relatively few companies feel that equity demands such favorable treatment of the terminating policyholder.

In view of the wide differences among participating companies as to the level of gross premiums, amount of loading, and treatment of expenses in the dividend formula, it is not practical to illustrate the loading factor numerically, as was done for the mortality and interest factors. Any figures which might be shown could not be representative and would have only limited significance. Two generalities might be ventured, however. First, the loading factor in the dividend formula of high-premium companies will tend to be larger than that in low-premium companies; and secondly, the loading contribution to dividends, after the first few years, will either remain relatively level with duration or increase slightly. The trend of the contribution during the first few years will depend upon whether the excess first-year expenses are amortized at a uniform rate or at a decreasing rate. In the former case, the contribution will be fairly level during the period of amortization, after which it will increase sharply and then level off; while in the latter case, the contribution will increase each year during the amortization period, after which it will level off. Of course, in a company which treats acquisition expenses as a charge against the whole body of policies, the loading contribution should be relatively constant at all durations.

CHAPTER XVII

Surplus

and

Dividends

(Continued)

ILLUSTRATIVE DIVIDEND COMPUTATION

The principles explained in Chapter XVI can be illustrated by a hypothetical dividend calculation. For this purpose, the tenth-year dividend of an ordinary life policy issued at age thirty-five will be computed. The steps involved will be set forth in proper sequence, after which they will be explained. The steps are as follows:

ORDINARY LIFE POLICY ISSUED AT AGE 35;
RESERVE BASIS: FULL NET LEVEL PREMIUM
RESERVES, 1958 C.S.O. TABLE, AND $2\frac{1}{2}$ PER CENT

1. Gross premium per \$1,000........................... \$23.50
2. Net level annual premium per \$1,000................. 17.67
3. Loading: (1) − (2)................................. 5.83
4. Mortality contribution to tenth-year dividend:
   a) Ninth-year terminal reserve.....................\$150.12
   b) Tenth-year terminal reserve..................... 167.90
   c) Tabular cost of insurance:
      $[4(a) + (2)] (1.025) − 4(b)$..................... 4.08
   d) Mortality charge: $.745 \times 4(c)$..................... 3.04
   e) Return of tabular mortality: $4(c) − 4(d)$........... 1.04
5. Interest contribution: $(.0395 − .0250) \times [(2) + 4(a)]$... 2.43
6. Loading contribution:
   a) Expense charge: $[.132 \times (2)] + \$2.10$.............. 4.44
   b) Return of loading: $(3) − 6(a)$..................... 1.39
7. Total dividend for tenth year: $4(e) + (5) + 6(b)$....... 4.86

The gross premium for the policy in question is assumed to be \$23.50 per \$1,000. This premium was arrived at by loading the net

353

level premium, computed on the basis of the 1958 C.S.O. Table and 2½ per cent interest, by 16 per cent of the net premium and $3.00 per $1,000. This produced a loading of $5.83.

The mortality contribution to the tenth-year dividend is obtained by subtracting the mortality charge from the tabular cost of insurance for the tenth year. The latter is derived by multiplying the net amount at risk, $832.10, by the tabular death rate at age forty-four, 4.92 per 1,000, which yields $4.08 per $1,000. The mortality charge is obtained by multiplying the percentage of actual to "expected" mortality for the attained age in question by the tabular cost of insurance. The rate of mortality in the calculation of an actual dividend is taken from a scale of percentages varying by attained age which reflects the company's own mortality experience during recent years; but in this illustration, the percentage was taken from the scale used in the construction of Table 27. If the actual rate of mortality at age twenty-five is assumed to be 65 per cent of the tabular rate and the percentage is assumed to increase by one-half point for each year of attained age, the assumed actual rate of mortality at age forty-four would be 74.5 per cent of the rate reflected in the 1958 C.S.O. Table. This is, obviously, the same thing as saying that the mortality saving at attained age forty-four is 25.5 per cent of the tabular rate. On the basis of this assumption, the mortality charge would be $3.04, which, deducted from $4.08, gives a mortality saving for the year of $1.04 per $1,000 of insurance.

The interest contribution at all durations is obtained by multiplying the initial reserve for the year in question by the difference between the assumed rate of interest and the so-called "dividend" rate of interest. The latter will usually bear a close relationship to the actual rate of interest earned by the company in recent years; but in any particular year, it might deviate in either direction. In the illustration, the dividend rate was taken to be 3.95 per cent, which, compared to the assumed rate of 2½ per cent, produced an excess interest factor of 1.45 per cent. Applied to the initial reserve of $167.79, this factor produced an excess interest contribution of $2.43 for the year.

The expense charge was assumed to be 13.2 per cent of the net premium and $2.10 per $1,000 of insurance. This charge was based on the assumption that excess first-year expenses had been fully amortized before the tenth year and that such a charge would be sufficient to provide some contribution to the contingency reserve of the company. Nevertheless, the loading was such that a savings of $1.39 was available for dividend distribution, a portion of which may be assumed to have been included in the loading formula for that specific purpose.

On the basis of the various assumptions used in the dividend illustration, a total dividend of $4.86 per $1,000 was derived for the year.

The derivation of dividends for the first twenty years of an ordinary life policy issued at age thirty-five is shown in Table 29. The mortality

TABLE 29

DIVIDENDS PER $1,000 FOR FIRST TWENTY YEARS
UNDER ORDINARY LIFE POLICY ISSUED AT AGE 35*

YEAR (1)	INITIAL RESERVE (2)	AMOUNT AT RISK (3)	MORTALITY RETURN PER $1,000 AMOUNT AT RISK (4)	LOADING RETURN FACTORS Per Cent (5)	LOADING RETURN FACTORS Constant (6)	INTEREST RETURN [1.45% × (2)] (7)	MORTALITY RETURN [(3) × (4) ÷ $1,000] (8)	LOADING RETURN [(5) × NET PREMIUM + (6)] (9)	TOTAL DIVIDEND [(7) + (8) + (9)] (10)
1	17.67	984.36	$0.75	1.0	$0.10	$0.26	$0.74	$ .28	$1.28
2	33.31	968.41	0.78	1.2	.15	0.48	0.76	.36	1.60
3	49.26	952.17	0.81	1.4	.20	0.71	0.77	.45	1.93
4	65.50	935.68	0.86	1.6	.30	0.95	0.80	.58	2.33
5	81.99	918.95	0.91	1.8	.40	1.19	0.84	.72	2.75
6	98.72	901.99	0.97	2.0	.50	1.43	0.87	.85	3.15
7	115.68	884.83	1.04	2.2	.60	1.68	0.92	.99	3.59
8	132.84	867.45	1.11	2.4	.70	1.93	0.96	1.12	4.01
9	150.22	849.88	1.18	2.6	.80	2.18	1.00	1.26	4.44
10	167.79	832.10	1.25	2.8	.90	2.43	1.04	1.39	4.86
11	185.57	814.15	1.34	3.0	1.00	2.69	1.09	1.53	5.31
12	203.52	796.03	1.43	3.2	1.10	2.95	1.14	1.67	5.76
13	221.64	777.76	1.53	3.4	1.20	3.21	1.19	1.80	6.20
14	239.91	759.37	1.63	3.6	1.30	3.48	1.24	1.94	6.66
15	258.30	740.88	1.75	3.8	1.40	3.75	1.30	2.07	7.12
		722.29							
16	276.79		1.87	4.0	1.50	4.01	1.35	2.21	7.57
17	295.38	703.65	2.00	4.2	1.60	4.28	1.41	2.34	8.03
18	314.02	684.95	2.14	4.4	1.70	4.55	1.47	2.48	8.50
19	332.72	666.21	2.29	4.6	1.80	4.82	1.53	2.61	8.96
20	351.46	647.46	2.44	4.8	1.90	5.10	1.58	2.75	9.43

* Net premium based on 1958 C.S.O. Table and 2½ per cent interest.

return in this illustration is based on the percentages of actual mortality assumed in the earlier dividend illustration—namely, 65 per cent of the tabular rate at age twenty-five, increasing one-half point per year of attained age up to age seventy-five. For this particular example, the mortality *savings* range from 30 per cent at age thirty-five to 20.5 per cent at age fifty-four, the twentieth year. The interest return reflects an excess interest factor of 1.45 per cent times the initial reserve for each of the durations involved. The loading return is assumed to be 1 per cent of the net premium plus $0.10 per $1,000 of face amount the first year, increasing 0.2 per cent and $10.10 per $1,000 each succeeding year except the second and third years. This pattern of loading savings indicates that a constantly decreasing proportion of the loading is allocated to the amortization of acquisition expenses. The return from each of the factors shows a steady increase with duration, and the total dividend increases from $1.28 per $1,-000 the first year to $9.43 for the twentieth year.

GENERAL EQUITY OF THE DIVIDEND SCALE

Just as gross premiums and surrender values are tested prior to adoption by asset share calculations, so are proposed and existing dividend scales. The purpose of such a test in the case of a proposed dividend scale is to determine whether—with a given set of gross premiums and surrender values, and with realistic assumptions as to mortality, interest earnings, expenses, and voluntary terminations—the proposed scale of dividends will lead to the accumulation of asset shares which for the various plans, ages at issue, and durations meet the requirements of both adequacy and equity. An existing dividend scale should meet the same objectives and hence should be tested from year to year to ascertain whether or not it does.

If a proposed dividend scale is being tested in conjunction with a *proposed* set of gross premiums and surrender values, any inadequacies or inequities that are disclosed may be corrected through an adjustment in any one or all of the values involved. If the proposed combination of gross premiums and dividends should produce a set of net costs which for most plans, ages at issue, and durations appear to be competitive, the adjustments—if not too substantial—would probably be made in the proposed set of surrender values, especially in the early policy years. If, however, a new dividend scale is being superimposed on an existing set of gross premiums and surrender values, as is frequently the case, the necessary adjustments must be made in the dividend scale. This may result in some distortion of the theoretically correct relationship between the sources of surplus and the contributions of the corresponding dividend factors to the total dividends of some or all policies. However, with asset shares used as a control, there is less need for exactitude with respect to each separate dividend factor, provided the test shows that the over-all dividend payable under each of the plans, ages at issue, and durations conforms approximately to the contributions that such policies are currently making to the surplus funds of the company.[1]

THE EXPERIENCE PREMIUM METHOD

It was noted that under the three-factor contribution plan, the mortality contribution to dividends tends, with some exceptions, to decline with duration, while the contribution from excess interest will definitely increase with duration as long as the actual rate of investment earnings remains fairly stable and as long as reserves increase. The contribution from loading will usually be relatively constant after excess first-year expenses have been amortized, but the savings from this source may fluctuate during the early years of the contract. When these separate factors are combined, the dividends under most policies other than term will tend to increase with duration, which is considered to be a desirable objective by most—if not all—companies. However, the upward trend of dividends is brought about primarily through the influence of the excess interest factor, since the mortality factor declines and the loading factor either remains level or increases slightly. If, for any reason, a company's interest earnings should suffer a substantial decline, it is possible—and even probable—that the dividends on existing policies would decline with duration, which is contrary to the trend that policyholders have come to expect. In an effort to make sure that dividends will always increase with duration, some companies have adopted a variation of the contribution plan called the *experience premium method*.[2]

---

[1] For a description of how asset share calculations can be used to *construct* a dividend scale rather than to verify the general fairness of a scale developed by some other method, see pp. 136–41 of the definitive work by Joseph B. Maclean and Edward W. Marshall entitled *Distribution of Surplus* and published by the Actuarial Society of America as Actuarial Study No. 6 (1937). If the dividend scale were to be developed directly through the asset share approach, the dividend for any particular class of policies in a given year would merely be the difference between the asset share and the cash value with due allowance for a contribution to the contingency reserve and general surplus funds and for any smoothing that might be necessary. The crude results would have to be adjusted, for example, to produce dividends during the early policy years (the payment of which is believed to encourage persistency) and to eliminate distortions produced by the expiration of renewal commissions.

[2] The experience premium method is used for other purposes also. For example, if a company issues both participating and nonparticipating policies the experience premium method provides a means of comparing the anticipated net costs of the two

Under this method, the company calculates a complete set of "experience premiums" for all plans and ages at issue, based on realistic mortality and expense assumptions, but reflecting the same conservative interest assumption that entered into the actual premiums payable by the policyholders.[3] The mortality and expense assumptions used in the calculation of the experience premium are frequently the same as those used in the asset share calculation with which the actual gross premium was tested or derived.

The experience premiums are, of course, lower than the actual premiums payable. The difference represents the *level* dividend which could be paid each year, throughout the lifetime of the policy, from mortality and loading gains, provided future experience as to mortality and expense corresponds to the assumptions that entered into the experience premium. In effect, this procedure tends to provide a smaller mortality gain in the early years than is actually earned and a larger gain than is actually experienced in the later years, while the opposite is true with respect to loading gains. The annual dividends payable under this system consist of (1) the excess of the actual gross premium over the experience premium for the same plan and age at issue, *plus* (2) excess interest earnings calculated in the same way as under the regular contribution plan. The excess interest factor is handled independently of the other two factors because of the difficulty of predicting the future course of interest earnings. If the experience premium were calculated on the basis of the interest rate actually expected to be earned, any material departure of actual earnings from the assumed rate would force a recalculation of the experience premium.

It is plain that with a level contribution from the mortality and loading factors, the total dividend will increase with duration if there

---

competing lines. The technique serves the same purpose in connection with policies issued on different actuarial assumptions. It can also be used to prevent a *decrease* in dividends with duration which is likely to occur in connection with participating single premium immediate annuities (because of the declining principal) and which may occur with ordinary insurance policies during a period of sharply declining interest earnings. Finally, the experience premium method may be used when the anticipated dividends are too small to justify the more cumbersome three-factor contribution method. Thus, flat dividends, based on experience premiums, are usually provided in connection with participating accidental death provisions, disability waiver of premium and income provisions, and term insurance riders.

[3] The rate of interest currently being earned or the one likely to be earned in the future will be used instead of the assumption on which premiums are based (1) if the rate assumed for premium purposes is *higher* than the rate currently being earned and (2) when a level or flat dividend is desired, as for accidental death benefits.

are any excess interest earnings. An excess interest factor of $\frac{1}{10}$ per cent, for example, would provide *some* increase, since, with the exception of term insurance, the base (the initial reserve) would expand with duration. Even if the excess interest factor should decline to zero, there would be no *decrease* in the basic scale of dividends (those stemming from mortality and loading gains). If the excess interest factor should become negative and the original experience premium remained unchanged, dividends would decline with duration. In the event of such a decline in interest earnings, however, a new experience premium would undoubtedly be calculated, with a more conservative interest rate.

Contributions to the contingency reserve may be made out of the difference between the gross premium and the experience premium or out of excess interest earnings—or, what is more likely, out of both sources. Some companies include an allowance for contingencies in the expense loading of the experience premium which would provide a level contribution to the contingency reserve from that source. Such contributions might also be supplemented by a portion of the excess interest earnings.

The principal disadvantage of the experience premium method lies in the unlikelihood that the projected mortality and expense rates will approximate actual conditions over any extended period of time, with the result that new experience premiums will have to be computed from time to time and dividend schedules revised. Of course, this may not be any more of a problem than that faced by other companies in keeping their dividend factors up to date under the unmodified contribution plan. Under both systems, deviations of actual from projected experience can be met up to a point by percentage increases or decreases in the dividend scale; but eventually, in the interest of equity, the scale itself must be revised.

The experience premium method has also been criticized as less scientific and accurate than the contribution plan, in that it does not distribute mortality and expense savings as realized but levels out all such gains on the basis of an assumed future experience.[4] These critics admit, however, that accuracy and equity in the distribution of surplus are, from a practical standpoint, ideals which are largely unattainable and that even under the unmodified contribution plan, the dividends

---

[4] In the terminology of valuation procedures, the experience premium dividend, except for interest, is a *prospective* calculation, while the three-factor dividend is basically a *retrospective* calculation.

allotted to any particular class of policies can only be an approximation to the "true" contributions to surplus from that class.

OTHER CONSIDERATIONS

The foregoing description of the dividend process was oversimplified (for pedagogical reasons) in that it dealt with only the major sources of surplus, and, moreover, ignored several refinements that may be introduced in the interest of equity or under the pressures of competition. It is not necessary to expand the discussion to encompass other sources of surplus, but it does seem desirable to make brief reference to some recent developments that have had an impact on dividend policy.

Reference was made in an earlier chapter to the grading of premiums by size of policy in order to effect an equitable allocation of costs which tend to be relatively constant per policy. This practice naturally raises a question as to whether recognition should be given to variations in per policy costs among contracts issued prior to the introduction of graded premiums. As a matter of fact, many companies which grade the premiums on new policies have introduced the concept into the dividend formula for existing business. In so doing, these companies have been motivated not only by a sense of equity but also by the desire to discourage the surrender or consolidation of old policies to take advantage of the quantity discount on new policies. One procedure is to strip out the per policy expenses (both first-year and renewal) from the loading portion of the basic dividend formula and make a flat per policy charge against the dividend, the dividend becoming x per $1,000 − $K,$ where K is the per policy charge. This is the counterpart to grading the gross premium on new policies by the use of a policy fee. Another approach, which has proved to be more popular, is to include the per policy expenses in the basic dividend formula but grant specific additional dividend credits per $1,000 in various amount bands corresponding to the bands used in the grading of premiums. Even when premiums have been graded by size, it may be necessary to introduce dividend modifications by policy size to reflect changes (upward or downward) in per policy renewal expenses.

Lower mortality among female lives has long been recognized in the form of higher rates for annuities and life income settlements under life insurance policies. Until recently, however, females were granted no rate reduction for life insurance on the grounds that the average amount of insurance per female life was so much lower than that on male lives that the administrative costs more than offset the mortality advantage. Where premiums are graded by size, the justification for ignoring the mortality differential disappears. Thus, most companies now give female policyholders a rate reduction in one form or the other. Some companies use an age setback, as in annuities, with the premiums, dividends, and surrender values being those appropriate for the set-back age. Other companies quote special premiums but provide surrender values appropriate for the policyholder's actual age. Under these circumstances, it may be necessary to make some adjustment in the dividend formula to reflect the lower premium and the more favorable mortality.

Policies which provide unusually high cash values during the early years may be treated separately for dividend purposes. A lower dividend scale may be necessary to offset the additional benefits paid as cash values and as a hedge against loss due to a lapse or surrender rate higher than anticipated. As an alternative to lower dividends, some companies charge a higher premium for these policies. As a further hedge against adverse lapse experience, some companies have also adopted a much flatter commission scale for these policies, which may call for special dividend treatment.

As a part of their service to the private pension institution, many companies offer insurance to participants in pension plans without evidence of individual insurability. To avoid excessive selection against the insurer, the case is underwritten as a whole and the amount of insurance per participant is limited. Nevertheless, the companies anticipate higher mortality on this type of business than on normal issues. To offset the expected higher mortality costs, the companies usually pay smaller commissions and lower dividends than those payable with respect to policies subject to individual selection.

Immediate annuities present unique problems in pricing and dividend policy. In the first place, they are issued in exchange for a single premium or annuity consideration, so that any savings from expense loading would arise only in the first year. In the second place, the reserves under such policies decline with duration, so that excess earnings are likely to diminish each year, in contrast to the pattern under life insurance policies. Finally, unless provision is made for future improvement in annuitant mortality, as with the use of projection factors, declining death rates among the annuitants erode any margins in the mortality assumptions and may eventually produce mortality losses, offsetting the declining gain from excess interest.[5] Thus, unless the margins in the actuarial assumptions are very conservative, which might produce noncompetitive rates, dividends under annuity contracts are likely to be small and to become smaller over time. As a result of these complications, most immediate annuities are written on a nonparticipating basis, even when issued by mutual insurance companies.[6] When the annuities are issued on a participating basis, the contract may specify that each annual dividend, rather than being paid in cash, will be applied to the purchase of a small additional annuity. Under those circumstances, the annual income from the annuity inclusive of dividends, would never decrease but would show a gradual increase, albeit small. Another method of avoiding annual decreases in dividends is to anticipate the total gains over the lifetime of the contract and apportion a prorata share of the gains with each annuity payment. Thus, the dividends would be uniform in amount unless the dividend scale were changed. This will be recognized as an adaptation of the experience premium method of determining dividends. The technique can be applied to life income options as well as immediate annuities.

Deferred annuities with periodic premiums, which are used for retirement purposes, are usually participating during the accumulation period. Except for group annuities (under which employer contributions are applied to the purchase of paid-up units of pure annuities), there is no mortality element prior to the maturity date, the contract simply calling for the accumulation at interest of the gross premiums less expenses. Thus, the dividends consist entirely of excess interest and expense savings. During the liquidation period, these contracts are treated for dividend purposes like immediate annuities, except that under otherwise nonparticipating contracts excess interest may be credited during the *guaranteed* period of annuity payments.

---

[5] The mortality element of an annuity dividend formula involves another complication, this one being philosophical in nature. Within a given class of life insurance policies, mortality gains are created by the surviving members of the group, who are credited with the dividends. With a given group of annuitants, the mortality gains, if any, are created by those who die, while the dividends are payable to the surviving annuitants. This suggests that mortality gains should be discounted in advance and passed along to all members of the original group by means of a lower premium.

[6] State laws that require mutual companies to write business only on a participating basis usually exclude annuities (during the payout period), along with extended term insurance, pure endowments (as a nonforfeiture benefit), paid-up additions, and reinsurance.

SPECIAL FORMS OF SURPLUS DISTRIBUTION

The general rule in most states, including New York, is that divisible surplus must be apportioned and distributed annually. This requirement stems from the 1905–06 investigation of the life insurance industry by the New York State Legislature (known as the Armstrong Investigation) and is designed to prevent the type of abuses that developed under the tontine system of dividend distribution. Under this system dividends for a particular class of policies were accumulated for a specified period, such as five, ten, fifteen, or twenty years and distributed to the policyholders who survived and persisted to the end of the period. Those policyholders who died or surrendered their policies in the interim received no share of the accumulated dividends.[7] In the meantime, the sums set aside for future distribution were not shown on the books of the company as a legal liability but were treated as free surplus subject to the exclusive control of the management. The existence of such a large surplus was an inducement to extravagance on the part of management, especially in the acquisition of new business. Furthermore, the deferral of dividends facilitated the use of misleading "dividend illustrations" based on past results.

Despite the defects in an unmodified system of deferred dividends, there are sufficient theoretical and practical justifications for some degree of deferral that most states permit limited departures, under proper safeguards, from the general requirement of annual distributions. These departures take the form of either *extra* dividends or *terminal* dividends.

Extra Dividends

Extra dividends may follow one of two patterns: a single payment made after a policy has been in force a specified number of years, usually five, or a periodical additional dividend distributed at stated

---

[7] This practice was a modification of an earlier arrangement, originated in 1868 by the Equitable Life Assurance Society of the U.S. and called the *tontine* system, under which a terminating policyholder forfeited not only his prorata share of accumulated dividends but also his claim to a surrender value. The original tontine contracts stipulated that no dividends nor surrender values would be payable until the total premium payments accumulated at 10 per cent compound interest equaled the face of the policy. The system took its name from Lorenzo Tonti, a Neopolitan physician of the seventeenth century, who devised a fund-raising scheme for the French government which embodied the concepts of forfeitures and the benefit of survivorship.

intervals. The single extra payment is usually regarded as a substitute for a first-year dividend, being made available only when dividends are deferred to the end of the second policy year. From a practical standpoint, this procedure has some distinct advantages and can be justified to some extent on equitable grounds. It reduces the strain of initial expenses and may act as a deterrent to voluntary terminations during the early years. It is, in effect, a special system for assessing a larger part of excess first-year expenses against policies terminating during the first few years.

Periodical extra dividends at every fifth year, for example, have little justification in theory, unless it be that regular dividends are calculated on a very safe and conservative basis, with any surplus funds in excess of the regular dividend scale being distributed every five years to the surviving and persisting policyholders. A practical advantage of such extra dividends is found in the fact that, while illustrative net cost figures over a period of years are reduced by these extra refunds, only those policies which remain in force receive the additional payments. This is particularly true of a special dividend payable only at the end of the twentieth year, which is used by a number of companies to improve their showing in net cost comparisons.

For a time, the attitude of the Insurance Department of New York was that these extra dividends were contrary to the requirement of the law that surplus should be distributed annually and not otherwise, and irregular dividends were prohibited. The present statute, however, permits special distributions of surplus, provided the basis of allotment is deemed equitable by the Superintendent of Insurance.

In Canada, companies are permitted to issue policies under which dividends are apportioned only every five years, but the amount of surplus set aside for deferred dividends during each five-year period must be carried as a liability until paid. This latter feature eliminates one of the defects associated with the system of deferred dividends widely used in the United States prior to 1906. Under Canadian practices, it is customary for the company to pay an interim dividend if the policyholder dies during the period of deferral but not if he lapses or surrenders the policy.

Terminal Dividends

Terminal dividends refer to special dividends made available upon termination of a policy through maturity, death, or surrender. Such dividends are usually made available only after the policy has been in force for a specified period of years. Surrender dividends are typically expressed as a percentage of the surrender value, while mortuary and maturity dividends may be a percentage of the face of the policy or of the reserve, the percentage varying by plan and duration.

Terminal dividends are a device for returning to terminating policies all or a portion of their contribution to the surplus of the company. They are made available only by those companies that subscribe to the philosophy that a withdrawing policyholder should receive all or a portion of his contribution to surplus. Those companies that do not provide terminal dividends—and they are in the majority—either feel that each policyholder should make a permanent contribution to the surplus of the company or else view any attempt to allocate the contingency fund to individual policies or classes of policies as impracticable. It will be recalled, however, that the Standard Nonforfeiture Law requires the payment of *surrender* dividends whenever the rate of interest used in the calculation of reserves is more than $\frac{1}{4}$ per cent less than the rate used in the calculation of surrender values.

During the late 1950's such a sharp controversy developed within the industry over the payment of terminal dividends[8] that the New York Insurance Department investigated the matter and after a series of hearings promulgated (by letter dated July 11, 1958) a set of criteria to which terminal dividends paid by companies licensed in New York must adhere. Under these criteria the terminal dividends must (1) be "equitably apportioned by reason of the actual experience for the given class of policyholders and particular plans and policy durations involved, over and above the apportionment for regular annual dividends"; (2) "bear a reasonable relationship to the surplus accumulated by the class of policyholders"; (3) reflect consistent practices with respect to the classification of policies by plans of insurance, years of issue, reserve bases, and other pertinent factors; and (4) be "not disproportionate to the annual dividends paid in preceding years for a given class of policyholders."

The New York ruling also stipulated that (*a*) a company must justify the interval after which terminal dividends are to commence; (*b*) if any terminal dividends are to be paid, they must be applied to all terminations by death, maturity, and surrender, including cases where the proceeds are placed under settlement options or the sur-

---

[8] See Robert T. Jackson, "Some Observations on Ordinary Dividends," *Transactions of the Society of Actuaries,* Vol. XI (1960), pp. 779–80, for a list of the arguments for and against terminal dividends.

render values are applied to the purchase of paid-up insurance and extended term insurance; and (c) a domestic company must obtain annual approval from the New York Insurance Department for the payment of terminal dividends. Foreign companies must comply with the foregoing criteria and rules with respect to policies issued in New York.

A terminal dividend payable at death should not be confused with a *post-mortem* dividend. The latter is a dividend payable at death and covering the period between the preceding policy anniversary and the date of death. It may be computed in various ways, some of which are more scientific than others, but the most common practice is to provide a prorata portion of the dividend that would have been payable for the full year. A few companies pay the full dividend for the year, thus giving effect to the arbitrary assumption that death claims are paid at the end of the year. The loss of interest involved in this assumption is charged to surplus.

Virtually all companies pay post-mortem dividends, the sum being added to the death proceeds under the policy.

DIVIDEND OPTIONS

The policyholder's share in the divisible surplus of the company is made available on the policy anniversary and may be taken in one of four basic forms, at the option of the policyholder. The dividend may be (1) paid in cash, (2) applied toward the payment of the next premium under the policy, (3) applied to the purchase of a paid-up addition to the policy, or (4) deposited with the company to accumulate at interest.

An election as to the disposition of the dividend is usually filed with the company at the time the policy is issued, but a new election can be filed at any time. In most states, if an election is not filed with the company, the owner of the policy must be given written notice of the dividend and to the right to elect the various options. If no election is received within a specified period—usually, three months—the dividend must be applied to the purchase of a paid-up addition, unless the policy provides for some other disposition.

Payment in Cash

In most jurisdictions, the dividend must be made available in the form of cash; but from the standpoint of the policyholder, this application of the dividend has little to recommend it. Other options are usually more attractive.

Part Payment of Premiums

Almost one third of dividends distributed under premium-paying policies are applied toward the payment of premiums for the next policy year. The premium notice sent out in advance of the policy anniversary indicates the amount of the dividend that will be available on that date, and the policyholder need remit only the difference between the gross premium and the stated dividend.

It has sometimes been argued by policyholders who elected this option that the company is under obligation to apply any dividend available on the policy anniversary to the payment of a *partial* premium if the regular premium due on that date is not paid before the expiration of the grace period. The weight of judicial opinion does not support this interpretation.[9] In order to clarify this point, many companies insert a statement in their contracts to the effect that a dividend will be applied toward the payment of a premium due under the policy only if the remaining portion of such premium is duly paid. Some contracts provide that any dividend due at time of premium default will be applied to increase the surrender benefit. Other companies, by the specific terms of their contracts, accept a limited obligation to make automatic application of existing dividend credits, including those being accumulated under the interest option, if such credits are sufficient to pay the whole of the overdue premium or, if not sufficient for that purpose, the whole of any corresponding semiannual or quarterly premium.

Purchase of Paid-Up Additions

Under this option, the dividend is applied as a single premium at the insured's attained age to purchase as much paid-up insurance, payable under the same conditions as the basic policy, as the dividend will provide. The policy may or may not stipulate the rate basis to be used, but it is customary to make the paid-up insurance available at *net* rates. Under such circumstances, this option becomes identical, for all practical purposes, with the reduced paid-up insurance option available in conjunction with surrender values. The similarity is height-

---

[9] *Bush* v. *Prudential Insurance Co.,* 150 F. (2d) 631 (3d Cir., 1945); *Reynolds* v. *Equitable Life Assurance Society,* 142 Pa. Super. 65, 15 A. (2d) 464 (1940); *Price* v. *Northwestern Mutual Life Insurance Co.,* 113 W. Va. 683, 169 S.E. 613 (1933).

ened by the fact that the right to purchase paid-up additions is not usually granted under term insurance policies, corresponding to the usual restriction against *reduced* paid-up term insurance under the surrender options. Thus, the paid-up insurance under both the surrender and the dividend options is either whole life or endowment insurance.

The right to purchase a series of paid-up additions at net rates should be attractive to any policyholder and particularly so to one whose health has become impaired, since the paid-up additions can be purchased without evidence of insurability. The amount of whole life and endowment at age sixty-five insurance that can be purchased at various attained ages for each $1 of dividends is given in Table 30.

TABLE 30

AMOUNT OF PAID-UP INSURANCE PURCHASABLE WITH $1 OF
DIVIDENDS AT VARIOUS ATTAINED AGES

Attained Age	Whole Life Insurance	Endowment at Age 65
20	$3.268	$2.715
25	2.944	2.434
30	2.648	2.179
35	2.380	1.948
40	2.141	1.742
45	1.932	1.560
50	1.753	1.399
55	1.601	1.256
60	1.474	1.125
65	1.368	.....
70	1.284	.....
75	1.217	.....

Basis: 1958 C.S.O. Table and 2½ per cent interest. No loading.

It will be noted that at age forty-five, for example, a net single premium of $1 will purchase $1.932 of paid-up whole life insurance. If the dividend of $4.86 which was calculated earlier were applied under this option, $9.39 of paid-up whole life insurance would be provided. A dividend of the *same* amount would purchase only $9.20 of paid-up insurance the following year; but of course, the dividend would normally be somewhat larger. The amount of paid-up insurance which can be purchased with each $1 of dividends decreases with each year of attained age, because of the higher probabilities of death; but over a long period of years, and with increasing dividends, a substantial sum of paid-up insurance can be accumulated under this option. It is not unusual for the cumulative paid-up additions to amount to a third or a half of the face of the policy by the date of death.

These paid-up additions are themselves usually participating, although only mortality and interest savings are available and one or both of these factors may be modified slightly to absorb any expenses incurred in connection with the insurance.[10] They can be surrendered for cash at any time without surrender of the basic policy; and if the basic policy should be surrendered, the cash values under the paid-up additions would be added to the surrender value of the basic policy in the determination of benefits under any of the surrender options. In the event that the extended term option should be elected, the paid-up additions would be added to the face amount of insurance to be extended.

Purchase of Term Insurance

The contracts of some companies permit the policyholder to apply his annual dividends to the purchase of term insurance. Under the older form of this option, the entire dividend is applied as a single premium—gross or net, depending upon the company—to purchase as much one-year term insurance as it can buy. This use of dividends, while having much to commend it, has never achieved general popularity, possibly because the amount of insurance tends to decline rather rapidly with advancing age.

Under a more recent form of this option, colloquially called the "fifth dividend option" but also known as the "one-year term dividend option," dividends are used to purchase one-year term insurance equal to the surrender value of the policy, with any excess being accumulated at interest to help finance the purchase of term insurance when rates have risen above the level of dividends.[11] The contract or rider specifies a schedule of maximum rates which may be charged for the insurance from year to year, but thus far the companies have usually charged a lower rate determined at the time each dividend is declared.[12] On the basis of current dividend scales and the very low

---

[10] The same sort of adjustment may be made in connection with participating paid-up insurance purchased with the surrender value of a policy.

[11] Some companies permit the excess to be applied under any of the four regular options.

[12] Regulation 39 of the New York Insurance Department has been interpreted by the Department as requiring that the basis of maximum premium rates for one-year insurance be specified in the policy or rider and that such rates be consistent with the company's other term insurance rates. The regulation also requires that the one-year term option must be available under all standard life and endowment policies if it is to be available under any.

premiums being charged, term insurance equal to the growing cash value can be provided for a great many years at most ages of issue.

The fifth dividend option was developed for use in connection with those marketing procedures, such as the split-dollar, minimum deposit, or bank loan plans, under which the policyholder in effect or in fact continuously borrows the full amount of the cash value or the loan value. By electing this option the policyholder can "insure the loan" and make it possible for the beneficiary to receive the original face amount undiminished by any other claims against the policy, at least for many years. It is also said that this option provides a partial hedge against inflation.

The term insurance option in either variation must be elected at time of policy issue, otherwise it is subject to evidence of insurability. Moreover, the option terminates if in any year the dividend is not actually used to purchase the prescribed insurance. The option is usually available under policies subject to a moderate substandard rating.

Deposit at Interest

Dividends may be left to accumulate with the company at a stipulated rate of interest. Such deposits, however, participate in the excess interest earnings of the company, normally being credited with the same excess interest factor as that used in the regular dividend formula. Some companies credit a somewhat lower rate of excess interest, in recognition of the fact that the deposits can be withdrawn at any time and thus require a slightly higher degree of portfolio liquidity. On the other hand, some companies credit a higher rate of excess interest to dividend deposits because of more favorable income tax treatment. (Interest credited to dividend deposits is fully deductible in arriving at the insurance company's Federal income tax liability, whereas under paid-up additions only the guaranteed amount of interest is deductible). In the event of death, the accumulated deposits are added to the proceeds otherwise payable; and in the event of surrender, the deposits are added to the surrender value and may also be added to the face amount extended under the paid-up term insurance option. At most ages and durations, the amount payable in the event of death is less than it would be had the dividends been applied to the purchase of additional insurance; but the total amount obtainable in the event of surrender for cash will be greater, since the whole of the original cash dividends, with accrued interest, remains to the credit of the policy;

whereas if additional insurance had been elected, the accumulation would necessarily have been reduced by the cost of insurance for the dividend additions.

Other Dividend Options

Many policies permit paid-up additions or accumulated dividend deposits to be used to convert premium-paying insurance into fully paid insurance or to mature a policy by payment in full at an earlier date than that called for by the terms of the contract, whether the original maturity would have taken place at the death of the insured, as under whole life policies, or at some stated date, as in the case of endowment policies.

Paid-Up Option. The paid-up option becomes available whenever the reserve value of the dividend additions or deposits, plus the reserve under the basic policy, is equal to the *net* single premium for the policy in question at the insured's attained age. This option is not elected at the time the policy is issued but only when the foregoing conditions are satisfied. At such time, the insured surrenders his paid-up additions or accumulated deposits and receives a paid-up policy in the original face amount. Thereafter, the benefits payable in the event of death are smaller than they would have been under the prior arrangement, but the insured is relieved of any further premium payments. If dividend deposits were used in the exchange, the amount obtainable in the event of surrender would also be somewhat smaller (because of the cost of insurance) than before the conversion. Most companies, in their dividend illustrations, indicate how many years will be required on the basis of their current dividend scale to convert each of their policies into paid-up insurance. According to the estimates of most companies, an ordinary life policy issued at the younger ages (under forty, for example) can be converted into a paid-up policy within approximately twenty-five years through the use of dividend deposits or accumulations. The higher the age of issue, the shorter the period required to pay up a policy.

Sometimes, an option is given to apply each dividend *as declared* to reduce the total number of premiums payable. This is comparable to the *accelerative* endowment plan, which is described below.

Endowment Option. The endowment option becomes available whenever the reserve value of the dividend additions or deposits, plus the reserve value of the policy itself, equals the face amount of the policy. If the reserve value is the same as the surrender value, the option has no significance, since the policy and the accumulated dividends can be surrendered at any time for cash. When the option becomes available before the time at which the surrender value equals the full reserve under the policy, the option represents an additional benefit.

There are two forms of this option. Under the first form, the dividends stand to the credit of the policy until applied to the conversion of the policy into an endowment, so that if death occurs before the endowment option is available, the death proceeds include both the face of the policy and the accumulated dividends. In other words, all dividends remain as *additional* insurance or deposits until the combined value of the policy and dividends equals the face of the policy.

Under the second form, sometimes called the "accelerative" endowment plan, each dividend is applied as declared to reduce the period of the endowment—i.e., to convert the policy each year into a different plan under which the term to maturity is reduced. Other things being equal, the second method will mature the policy in a shorter period than the first, since each dividend is immediately added to the reserve and at no time serves to increase the amount payable in the event of death.

Part Four

SELECTION, CLASSIFICATION, AND TREATMENT OF RISKS

CHAPTER XVIII

Selection
and
Classification
of Risks

PURPOSE OF SELECTION

It has been emphasized in earlier chapters that the essence of the insurance principle is the sharing of losses by those exposed to a common hazard. This is made possible by contributions to a common fund by those exposed to loss from the common hazard. If the plan is to be scientific and equitable, however, each participant must pay into the fund a sum of money reasonably commensurate with the risk which he places upon the fund. To accomplish this objective, an insurance company prepares a schedule of premiums which represents its judgment as to the risk inherent in each category of applicants acceptable to the company. The function of the selection process is to determine whether the degree of risk presented by an applicant for insurance is commensurate with the premium established for persons in his category. If, within each broad risk category, various gradations of risk have been established, as would be true of a company which offers substandard insurance, the evaluation of an application for insurance involves not only *selection* but *classification*.

It is neither possible nor desirable to establish risk categories in which each component risk represents a loss potential identical to that of all the other risks in the category. For practical reasons, the categories must be broad enough to include risks with substantial differences in loss potential. In life insurance, the basis for the risk classification is the age of the applicant. Yet, within each age group, the probability of death is greater for some than for others. These differences in risk stem from physical condition, occupation, sex, race, and other factors. Some persons in the group might be near death, while others might confidently look forward to a long lifetime relatively free of bodily ailments. The relative frequencies of mortality expectation represented in any randomly selected group of persons of the same age would approximate the curve shown in Figure 18, with 100 per cent representing average mortality for the group.

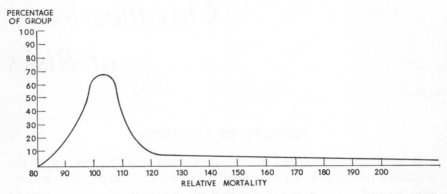

FIG. 18. Relative frequency of mortality expectations of a group of persons at any particular age.

The chart reveals a wide range of mortality expectations for a group of persons falling within a risk category measured by age alone. Clearly, all should not be offered insurance on the same terms. Considerations of equity would suggest that those persons subject to the lowest degree of mortality should pay a lower premium than those who represent an average risk; while those with greatly impaired longevity expectations should be charged more than the standard premium, or even declined altogether.

The insurance company must establish a range of mortality expectations within which applicants will be regarded as normal and hence entitled to insurance at standard rates, or, conversely, the limits beyond which applicants will be considered either superstandard or substandard and subject to a discount or surcharge, as the case might be. In doing so, it should be guided by the principles set forth below.

After the limits for the various risk categories have been established, the company must adopt selection and classification procedures that will enable it to place applicants for insurance into the proper categories. This process is complicated by the fact that applicants for insurance may not fit the curve illustrated in Figure 18. That curve depicts the mortality expectations of a randomly selected group, whereas applicants for insurance do not constitute such a group. The observation has frequently been made that a life insurance company could safely insure the life of everyone who passes any designated location in a typical American city, so long as the practice does not become public knowledge. Unfortunately, the applications received by a life insurance company do not reflect such randomness. There is reason to believe that many who seek insurance have knowledge of an impairment that might be expected to shorten their expectancy or, at least, suspect that they have such an impairment. A company's underwriting procedures must screen out such applicants or classify them into appropriate substandard groups. Thus, it might be argued that the primary purpose of selection is to protect the company against adverse selection. If there were no antiselection, there would be no need for the underwriting process except to separate and classify substandard risks.

GUIDING PRINCIPLES

There are certain fundamental principles which must govern the selection procedures of an insurance company if it is to operate on a sound basis. Some of these principles are mutually inconsistent, which means that a company must fashion its selection program in such a manner as to balance these opposing principles.

Emphasis on the Uncommon Impairment

The selection process is not concerned with hazards or impairments which are common to all persons seeking insurance, since they will operate to increase the mortality among all lives and each participant will bear his proportionate part of the additional mortality costs. If a company were to confine its operations to an area where everyone of insurable age had had malaria, for example, a personal history of malaria could be ignored, provided the mortality assumptions contained adequate margins to take care of the higher mortality that could be expected. The use of tobacco provides an example of more universal applicability. There is little doubt that the use of tobacco has a deleterious effect on the health of the user; yet, the smoking habit is so widespread that the impairment of longevity resulting therefrom is generally ignored in underwriting decisions of insurance companies. The selection procedures of a company seek to identify those factors that set an individual apart from the normal members of a group and tend to produce above-average mortality.

Predominance of the Standard Group

The range of mortality expectations within which applicants will be regarded as normal and hence entitled to insurance at standard rates should be broad enough to encompass the great percentage of applicants.[1] This is particularly important if the company does not offer substandard insurance. An excessive number of rejections undermines the morale of the agency force, increases the cost of doing business, and causes a loss of good will among the insuring public.[2] A disproportionate number of substandard policies may have similar effects. Apart from the practical considerations just mentioned, the broader the base of standard risks, the more stable the mortality experience of the group is likely to be. On the other hand, considerations of equity and competition are involved in this proposition and serve as barriers to an unwarranted extension of the principle.

Balance within Each Risk or Rate Classification

A company must obtain and maintain a proper balance among the risks in each rate classification. This is especially important within the classification of standard risks, which, in view of the principle stated above, is likely to have broad limits. If the over-all mortality of the risks in the standard category is to approximate the theoretical average for the group, which would be the goal of most companies, every risk which is worse than average must be offset by one which is better than average. If the range is broad, the margin by which the inferior risk fails to meet the norm for the group should be counter-

---

[1] That this principle is being observed in practice is evidenced by the fact that 87 per cent of the applicants for ordinary insurance are currently being accepted at standard rates. Only 3 per cent are declined, the remaining 10 per cent being insured at substandard rates.

[2] For the industry as a whole, an excessive number of rejections deprives the insuring public of a valuable economic service and could give rise to demands for governmental intervention.

balanced by the margin by which the offsetting superior risk exceeds the norm. Such precise offsetting or balancing of risks is more of an ideal than an attainable reality; but a rough approximation is feasible for a company using the numerical rating system, under which, as is explained later, the mortality expectation of individual applicants is expressed as a percentage of the average expectation, which is assumed to be 100 per cent.

Irrespective of the underwriting procedures used by a company, if each risk classification is overbalanced with risks whose longevity prospects are less favorable than the assumed average for the classification, the company will end up with excessive mortality costs and—unless it enjoys offsetting advantages in other areas of operations—will have difficulty in maintaining its competitive position. The force of this factor is not diminished by the fact that the over-all mortality experience of the company is improving, unless the rate of improvement is greater than those of its competitors—an unlikely situation.

From the standpoint of maintaining a proper balance within the standard risk classification, the task of the company which does not offer substandard insurance would seem to be greater than that of a company which does offer such insurance. If, in the consideration of a borderline application, the home office underwriter is faced with the alternative of rejecting the risk altogether or approving it at standard rates, he is sorely tempted to follow the latter course of action. If he could place the risk in a substandard classification with a slightly higher premium, he would be under much less pressure to relax his standards. Companies which do not offer substandard insurance are aware of this problem and are constantly on the alert to avoid a relaxation of underwriting requirements.

Equity among Policyholders

The manner in which applicants are grouped for rating purposes should not unduly violate considerations of equity. Some discrimination among policyholders is unavoidable, since all risk classifications must be broad enough to include risks of varying quality. Nevertheless, the spread between the best and worst risks within a classification should not be so great as to produce rank unjustice.

There is a practical side to this matter also, since, if the spread is too great, the better risks may seek insurance with competing companies whose classification system is more equitable, leaving the first company with a disproportionate number of inferior risks.

Compatibility with Underlying Mortality Assumptions

The foregoing considerations tend to be relative matters, being concerned primarily with equity and competition. There is another factor, however, which operates as an absolute regulator of a company's underwriting standards, that factor being the mortality assumptions entering into the company's premiums. All mortality tables used by life insurance companies today reflect the experience of insured lives —of lives which were subjected to some degree of selection. The underwriting standards of a company must reflect at least as effective a degree of selection as that achieved by the companies which supplied the data for the mortality table. Furthermore, the companies which pool their mortality experience for the construction of modern mortality tables employ rather rigorous standards of selection. This is a factor of some importance to companies which, in a desire to capture a larger share of the life insurance market, might be tempted to lower their selection standards. The general improvement in mortality which has been such a prominent feature of the insurance scene during recent decades cannot be expected to nullify the long-run consequences of lax underwriting standards.

FACTORS AFFECTING THE RISK

In order to place an applicant for insurance into the proper risk classification, an insurance company needs reliable information concerning every factor that could be expected to affect to an appreciable extent the longevity of the applicant. As a matter of practice, information is sought concerning the following factors.

Age

The age of the applicant is the most important single factor bearing upon his mortality expectations. Except for the first few years of life, man's resistance to disease and injury weakens with the passage of time, with the result that the probability of death increases with age. Age is such a significant measure of a man's susceptibility to death that it is the point of departure in classifying applicants for insurance. Each applicant is placed within the proper age classification and is then compared to the norm for his age to determine his insurability.

One might assume that such a vital underwriting factor as age would be subject to verification at the time of submission of the application. While, ideally, verification of age would be desirable in all cases, practical considerations militate against the practice. To require proof of age at the time of application would inevitably delay issue of the policy and would be a source of irritation to the applicant. The agency force would object to the requirement, since many applicants would be unable or unwilling to submit documentary proof of the date of birth. Therefore, it is customary to accept the applicant's statement of age, unless there is reason to believe that a misstatement has occurred.

Neither is it customary to require documentation of age at the time of settlement of a claim unless the company has reason to question the accuracy of the stated date of birth. Typical of the circumstances under which a company would require verification of age would be conflicting dates of birth on two or more policies. If a misstatement is discovered after the policy has become a claim, the amount of the claim is adjusted in accordance with the misstatement-of-age clause.

The situation is different with an immediate annuity. Under such a contract, the relationship between the annuitant's age and the amount of the periodic payments is so direct and immediate that proof of age is required at the time of purchase of the annuity.

The age of the applicant enters into the underwriting considerations of a company in another respect. For reasons which will be explained later in this chapter, all companies have upper age limits beyond which they will not write insurance on any basis and somewhat lower limits for the writing of certain types of policies, such as term insurance. The absolute limit may be as low as sixty and as high as seventy-five or more. Under such circumstances, the age of the applicant may determine whether he will be acceptable to the company on any basis. In other words, age alone—irrespective of the other facts of the case—may render a person uninsurable. For that reason, a misstatement of age which induces a company to issue a policy which it would otherwise not issue is grounds for rescission if discovered by the company during the contestable period. Companies also have special underwriting rules for children under which age may be an absolute determinant of insurability.

Build

The build of the applicant—i.e., the relationship between his height, weight, and girth—is one of the basic determinants of his mortality expectation. This was one of the earliest discoveries in the area of medical selection. The earliest attempts to arrive at the ideal relationship between height and weight were rather crude, some drawing their inspiration from the physical proportions of certain ancient Greek athletes, as revealed by statues dating back to the third century B.C. Two statutes in particular which were considered to represent ideal proportions were "The Gladiator" and the "Bronze Tumbler."

The first comprehensive statistical study of the relationship between build and mortality covered the experience on policies issued by the principal companies from 1885 through 1908 and was published in 1913 as the *Medico-Actuarial Mortality Investigation*. The findings of this study, as refined and supplemented by subsequent investigations, served as the basis for the build tables used by life insurance companies in this country for the next several decades. These tables were eventually supplanted by those derived from the findings of the monumental investigation of the Society of Actuaries encompassing the ordinary issues of twenty-six leading companies for the years 1935 through 1953 and published in 1959 in the two-volume work entitled *Build and Blood Pressure Study, 1959*. A build table based upon the latter study and used by a number of prominent companies is reproduced in Table 31.

The upper portion of the table shows various combinations of height and weight, along with the average weight for each height. The lower portion of the table shows in intervals of five percentage points the mortality debits and credits associated with each combination of height and weight, broken down into three broad age classifications. It will be observed that persons in the 20–45 age category can be expected, as a group, to experience mortality 25 per cent higher than normal if they fall within the most extreme underweight classification. Thus, an applicant in that classification would be assigned a debit of twenty-five points for purposes of the numerical rating system. The debit would be only fifteen points if the applicant were in the next underweight classification, and if he fell within the classification represented by the third column from the left, he would receive neither a debit nor a credit. At that point, the underweight condition would be viewed as neutral. Beyond that point as the applicant approaches the average weight for his age and height, he is given credits on the theory that some degree of underweight is conducive to a lower mortality than that associated with persons at or above the average weight. Build again becomes a neutral factor when the weight is average or

TABLE 31
BUILD TABLE—MALE AND FEMALE
AGES 15 AND OVER

Height	Underweight							Average	Overweight															Height
4'10"...	81	87	93	99	105	112	118	124	130	136	143	149	155	161	167	174	180	186	192	198	205	211	217	4'10"
11"...	83	89	95	102	108	114	121	127	133	140	146	152	159	165	171	178	184	190	197	203	210	216	222	11"
5' 0"...	84	91	98	104	110	117	124	130	136	143	150	156	162	169	176	182	188	195	202	208	214	221	228	5' 0"
1"...	86	93	100	106	113	120	126	133	140	146	153	160	166	173	180	186	193	200	206	213	219	226	233	1"
2"...	88	95	102	109	116	122	129	136	143	150	156	163	170	177	184	190	197	204	211	218	224	231	238	2"
5' 3"...	91	98	105	112	119	126	133	140	147	154	161	168	175	182	189	196	203	210	217	224	231	238	245	5' 3"
4"...	94	101	108	115	122	130	137	144	151	158	166	173	180	187	194	202	209	216	223	230	238	245	252	4"
5"...	96	104	111	118	126	133	141	148	155	163	170	178	185	192	200	207	215	222	229	237	244	252	259	5"
6"...	99	106	114	122	129	137	144	152	160	167	175	182	190	198	205	213	220	228	236	243	251	258	266	6"
5' 7"...	101	108	116	124	132	140	147	155	163	170	178	186	194	202	209	217	225	232	240	248	256	264	271	5' 7"
8"...	103	111	119	127	135	143	151	159	167	175	183	191	199	207	215	223	231	238	246	254	262	270	278	8"
9"...	106	114	122	130	139	147	155	163	171	179	187	196	204	212	220	228	236	244	253	261	269	277	285	9"
10"...	109	118	126	134	143	151	160	168	176	185	193	202	210	218	227	235	244	252	260	269	277	286	294	10"
5'11"...	112	120	129	138	146	155	163	172	181	189	198	206	215	224	232	241	249	258	267	275	284	292	301	5'11"
6' 0"...	115	124	133	142	150	159	168	177	186	195	204	212	221	230	239	248	257	266	274	283	292	301	310	6' 0"
1"...	118	127	136	145	154	163	172	181	190	199	208	217	226	235	244	253	262	272	281	290	299	308	317	1"
2"...	121	130	140	149	158	167	177	186	195	205	214	223	232	242	251	260	270	279	288	298	307	316	326	2"
6' 3"...	124	134	143	153	162	172	181	191	201	210	220	229	239	248	258	267	277	286	296	306	315	325	334	6' 3"
4"...	128	138	148	158	167	177	187	197	207	217	227	236	246	256	266	276	286	296	305	315	325	335	345	4"
5"...	132	142	152	162	173	183	193	203	213	223	233	244	254	264	274	284	294	304	315	325	335	345	355	5"
6"...	136	146	157	167	178	188	199	209	219	230	240	251	261	272	282	293	303	314	324	334	345	355	366	6"
7"...	140	150	161	172	183	194	204	215	226	236	247	258	269	280	290	301	312	322	333	344	355	366	376	7"
8"...	144	155	166	177	188	199	210	221	232	243	254	265	276	287	298	309	320	332	343	354	365	376	387	8"

MORTALITY DEBITS AND CREDITS (—)

Ages	Underweight							Average	Overweight															Ages
46 & over...	15	10	5	0	-5	-10	-10	-5	-5	0	5	10	15	20	25	35	50	65	80	95	110	125	150	46 & over
20-45...	25	15	5	-5	0	-5	-10	0	0	5	10	15	20	25	35	45	60	75	90	105	120	135	160	20-45
15-19...	35	20	5	-5	-5	-5	-10	0	5	10	15	20	30	40	55	65	80	100	110	125	145	165	195	15-19

only slightly underweight or overweight. Beyond the first classification of overweight, debits are assessed, the maximum debit for this age category being 160 points. The pattern of debits and credits is similar for the other two age classifications. There is a special juvenile build table for persons under age fifteen.

There are other build tables in common use which differ in both format and substance from the one presented in Table 31.

In connection with overweight male applicants, the company is interested in the distribution of the excess weight. This involves a comparison of the chest (expanded) with the abdominal girth. Among well-built men of average height, the chest measurement (expanded) normally exceeds the abdominal measurement by two inches; but this relationship is likely to be reversed among overweight persons. The companies have prepared charts which assign debits for abdominal measurements in excess of chest measurements, the number of points depending upon the person's age, the percentage of overweight, and the number of inches by which the one measurement exceeds the other; and credits, derived in the same manner, for chest measurements in excess of the abdominal girth. Under the numerical rating system, it is possible for an applicant to be credited with twenty points for a favorable relationship between his chest and girth and to be debited seventy points for an unfavorable relationship.

The chest and abdominal measurements also enable a company to check on the accuracy of reported weights.

Physical Condition

Next in general importance is the physical condition of the applicant. In the short run, this factor may outweigh all others in importance. In evaluating an application for insurance, the company wishes to know whether there are any impairments of body or mind that would tend to shorten the life expectancy of the applicant. Questions designed to elicit information on the physical status of the applicant are included in the application; but if a sizable amount of insurance is involved, the information is confirmed and supplemented by a medical examination.

The primary purpose of the medical examination is to detect any malfunctioning of the vital organs of the body. The heart and other parts of the circulatory system are subjected to special scrutiny. Impairment of the heart may be evidenced by subjective symptoms—such as shortness of breath or pain in the chest—or by objective symptoms—such as changes in the quality of the heart sounds, murmurs, enlargement of the heart, persistently rapid or slow pulse, irregular pulse, poor reaction to exercise, abnormal blood pressure, or abnormalities revealed by X ray and electrocardiogram.

One of the most common manifestations of heart impairment encounters is murmurs. A murmur is any sound other than that associated with the closing of the heart valves. Some murmurs, called *functional,* are considered harmless and consequently are of no significance to the underwriter; others, called *organic,* indicate damage to some part of the heart tissue. The problem is to distinguish between the two. Organic murmurs are very seriously regarded and may cause the applicant to be rated up highly or declined altogether. True functional murmurs are not rated; but if there is any doubt concerning their cause or origin, provision may be made for some extra mortality.

Enlargement of the heart is a condition of underwriting significance, since it is nature's way of compensating for damage to the valves or other section of the heart mechanism. Extra mortality of 50 to 100 per cent can be anticipated from an enlarged heart, without any other evidence of disease.

If the applicant is seeking a relatively large amount of insurance, or if the physical examination points to the possibility of an abnormal heart condition, the company may require an X ray and an electrocardiogram. The X ray can definitely confirm an enlargement of the heart; while the electrocardiogram, a graphic record of the electrical currents produced by the contraction of the heart, may verify a suspected heart condition which was not definitely established by the physical examination. These selection aids are frequently helpful in clearing up doubtful cases in favor of the applicant, enabling him to obtain insurance where he might otherwise be declined.[3]

The functioning of the circulatory system is also tested by measurement of the blood pressure, both while the heart is pumping and while it is at rest. The former is identified as the *systolic* pressure and represents the force with which the blood is driven into the arteries; the latter, called the *diastolic* pressure, represents the resistance which the heart encounters from the blood vessels in forcing blood into the arteries. Pressure is measured by an instrument which enables the medical examiner to determine the amount of air pressure necessary to

[3] Contrary to the general impression, a normal tracing on an electrocardiogram cannot be accepted as conclusive proof of the nonexistence of a heart irregularity, since the valves, and even the muscles, of the heart may be defective without affecting the transmission of the electrical impulses recorded on the electrocardiogram.

obstruct the flow of blood into the arteries and is recorded in terms of the height (in millimeters) of a column of mercury.

Blood pressure tends to increase somewhat with age. The systolic average ranges from 120 at age twenty to 140 at age sixty; the diastolic, from 78 to 90. the *normal* pressure, or that which leads to the best mortality, is lower than the average and seems to be in the vicinity of 115 systolic and 70 diastolic at all ages. For many years, a systolic blood pressure of 100 plus the person's age was considered normal, but insurance mortality studies have clearly demonstrated the fallacy of that rule.

The systolic pressure is more susceptible to emotion than the diastolic. The latter is considered to be a better measure of the constant strain on the heart. Insurance experience indicates that both should be taken into consideration; and if both are higher than normal, the mortality will be heavier than if only one of the two is out of line.

High blood pressure may be a symptom of a condition which itself will impair longevity. It is particularly associated with kidney ailments. A combination of overweight and hypertension is always regarded seriously. Low blood pressure can usually be disregarded unless it is abnormally low or associated with some definite impairment, such as tuberculosis.

The condition of the circulatory system can also be revealed by the pulse rate. The pulse rate is normally the same as that of the heart beat, that is, from 60 to 80 per minute. A rapid pulse is unfavorable, since it indicates that the heart is having to work harder than usual to meet the needs of the body. This may be a sign of an inefficient or impaired heart, or of an infection or other abnormal condition within the body that demands an extra supply of blood. An occasional rapid pulse can be overlooked for underwriting purposes, but a pulse rate that is *persistently* 85 to 90 is regarded as borderline. A rate persistently between 90 and 100 indicates mortality about 50 per cent above normal, while a rate between 100 and 110 results in almost 200 per cent mortality. In general, a slow pulse indicates an efficient heart and is viewed as a favorable sign. An irregular pulse, or one which is slow to return to normal after exercise, is regarded unfavorably.

A standard feature of all medical examinations is the urinalysis. This important diagnostic procedure has a three-fold purpose: (1) to measure the functional capacity of the kidneys, (2) to detect infections or other abnormal conditions of the kidneys, and (3) to discover impairments of other vital organs of the body.[4] The ability of the kidneys to concentrate liquids is revealed by the amount of water in the urine, which is measured by the specific gravity test. Other tests, not a part of the standard urinalysis, measure the ability of the kidneys to excrete. The urine is examined chemically and microscopically for the presence of albumin, pus, casts, or red blood cells, which would indicate a diseased conditions of the kidneys. The presence of an undue amount of sugar in the urine suggests the possibility of diabetes, a condition characterized by an inability to metabolize carbohydrates and caused by a deficiency of insulin. The urinalysis may also reveal abnormalities of the bladder, prostate, and other sections of the urinary tract. Finally, a kidney condition revealed by an urinalysis may point to a circulatory ailment, such as heart disease or arteriosclerosis, since there is ample evidence that a close relationship exists between kidney and circulatory impairments.

In addition to the foregoing tests, the medical examiner will carefully check the other organs of the body for evidence of disease or functional disturbance, giving special attention to any factor or condition that might be related to any previous impairment disclosed by the applicant's medical history.

Personal History

The personal history of the applicant throws important light upon his acceptability to the company. Consequently, in the application, the person seeking insurance is asked to provide details as to his health record, past habits, previous environment, and insurance status.

The applicant's health record is usually the most important of the personal history factors. Complete information as to previous illnesses, injuries, and operations may indicate the necessity for special additional tests or examinations. The findings of the medical examination need to be supplemented by the subjective feelings and symptoms of the applicant. Particular emphasis is placed upon recent illnesses and operations, and it is customary for the company to contact the attending physician or physicians for the medical details that normally would not be known to the applicant and might have a bearing upon

---

[4] The urinalysis is considered to be such a significant diagnostic procedure that the medical examiner is required to certify as to the authenticity of the specimen; for certain combinations of age and amount of insurance, the specimen may have to be forwarded to the home office for chemical analysis and microscopic examination.

his insurability. It is not the practice to consider an application from any person who is currently under medical treatment for any condition or is in process of recovery from any illness.

The company also wants to know whether the applicant has ever been addicted to the use of drugs or alcohol, since there is always a possibility that the "cure" will prove to be only temporary. The personal history may reveal that the applicant has only recently been employed in a hazardous or unhealthful occupation, posing the possibility that he may still retain ill effects therefrom or may revert to such occupation. The personal history may also disclose a change of residence for the purpose of improving the health or an intimate association with a person suffering from a contagious disease, such as tuberculosis.

Finally, the company wants to know whether the applicant has ever been refused insurance by any company or offered insurance on special terms. An affirmative answer would indicate that he once had an impairment, which might still be present. Information as to existing insurance enables the company to judge whether the amount of insurance, existing and proposed, bears a reasonable relationship to the applicant's needs and financial resources.

Family History

Family history is considered significant because of the transmission of certain characteristics by heredity. Build follows family lines; and to some extent, so do structural qualities of the heart and other organs. A greater than average susceptibility to infectious diseases may also be inherited. Hence, the applicant is asked to provide information as to the ages and state of health of his parents and brothers and sisters, if living; or if deceased, their ages at death and the causes of death.

Long-lived parents and siblings at one time were looked upon as assuring a long life for an applicant, even though he were somewhat overweight or possessed some other impairment which would normally place him in the category of borderline risks. On the other hand, an applicant from a short-lived family, unless the deaths resulted from accidents, had to be better than average in other respects in order to be insured at standard rates. Except for cardiovascular-renal diseases and, to a lesser (and declining) degree, tuberculosis, considerably less emphasis is now placed on family history. This is due both to the unreliability of the details of family history recited by the applicant and to the difficulty of tracing the influence of heredity.

There is a statistically demonstrable tendency for the applicant to exaggerate ages at death. Unless parents and siblings are dead or dying, they are generally reported to be in good health; instances of hypertension, diabetes, and other impairments which would be regarded as significant by the home office underwriters are usually not reported. Furthermore, it is not feasible to follow up on the family record. Even if the facts were accurately reported, there would be insufficient evidence to measure the true impact of heredity on longevity. Only data concerning parents and siblings are usually required, whereas hereditary influences may extend back to grandparents and great-grandparents. Moreover, the influence of heredity may not be demonstrable until age sixty or beyond, which is too late to be useful in evaluating the application of a young person whose family record is relatively immature.

Despite the foregoing inadequacies, it has been determined that if a group of applicants—all free of any known personal qualities that would adversely affect their longevity—are divided into classes on the basis of their family record, as revealed in the application, the lowest mortality will be found in the class with the most favorable record, and the highest mortality will be found in the class with the poorest record. The best group shows a mortality of about 85 per cent of the average for all classes, while the poorest group reflects a mortality of about 115 per cent. Therefore, companies usually give a credit of fifteen points for a very good family history and a debit of fifteen points for a very poor history.

In view of its unusual characteristics and importance, tuberculosis is treated as a separate phase of family history and is subject to a special set of ratings. At one time, it was widely believed that the disease was transmitted directly from parent to offspring, but that theory has now been rejected. Today, there are two schools of thought as to the manner in which the disease can be contracted: the "inherited susceptibility" and the "pure infection" schools. The former group holds that tuberculosis can develop *only* in those who inherit a susceptibility to the disease; the latter school believes that it is purely a matter of infection and, if there has been no exposure, a family record of the disease is of no significance. Companies which subscribe to the "inherited susceptibility" concept prescribe a set of ratings that vary with the age of the applicant, the percentage of underweight or overweight, and the number of cases of tuberculosis in the family history, including instances of close association with a tubercular person not a member of the family. The ratings are greatest for underweight persons at the younger ages. Even one case of tuberculosis in the family history results in a rating of 75 per cent. The "pure infection" companies have developed an approach that gives more weight to exposure, and less to age and build.

Occupation

There are many occupations which are known to have an adverse effect on mortality; and insurance companies must make an extra charge for applicants engaged in such occupations. The higher mortality rate associated with these occupations may be attributable to a greater than normal accident hazard, unhealthful working conditions, or the type of individual found in the occupations. The latter hazard is referred to as the "social class" hazard.

The accident hazard, if not the most common, is probably the most obvious. All persons working with machinery are exposed to some accident hazard. Construction workers are exposed to the hazard of falling. Underground miners—in addition to the hazard of machinery—run the risk of explosions, rock falls, and fire. Some electrical workers are exposed to high voltages and some to the danger of falling from high places. Laborers handling heavy materials run the risk of having the materials fall on them. Railroad workers, particularly those around heavy rolling equipment, are subject to a high accident rate. Other groups subject to a higher than normal accident rate include fishermen, lumbermen, and farmers.

Many health hazards arise from the processes associated with a complex industrial civilization, but some of the more important were known to early civilizations. Dust is probably the most serious health hazard. It arises out of such industrial processes as grinding, drilling, and crushing, and is particularly associated with the mining industry. Organic dusts, which are largely derived from substances of animal and plant origin, and are identified especially with the textile industry, produce irritation of the upper air passages and may lead to tuberculosis and other respiratory infections. Inorganic dusts, which are primarily metallic and mineral, will give rise to silicosis if they contain free silica and, in any event, increase the possibility of diseases of the respiratory organs. The lasting effects of exposure to dust make previous employment in the dusty trades an important underwriting factor.

The hazard from poisons exists in a very large number of industries, the number of which has been considerably increased by the expanding use of chemicals in industry. Lead poisoning—largely identified with the mining and smelting of lead but also found in printing, painting, file-cutting, and other processes—is one of the major hazards. Other health hazards include abnormalities of temperature, dampness, defective illumination, infections, radiant energy, and repeated motion, pressure, or shock.

The social class hazard is associated with occupations which employ low-grade labor and pay commensurately low wages. The extra mortality that occurs among such groups is attributable primarily to their unsatisfactory living conditions and inadequate medical care. Their low economic status, however, may reflect substandard physical and mental equipment. There are some occupations which are thought to have a social class hazard not because of low wages but because of the environment in which the persons work. Bartenders, liquor salesmen, and entertainers, for example, are believed to represent a social class hazard purely because of environment.

All companies have prepared occupational manuals in which are listed those occupations which are deemed to have adverse effects on mortality. Because of greater emphasis on industrial safety and more effective public health measures, the number of such occupations is declining steadily. If an applicant is found to be employed in one of the listed occupations, he will be required to pay an additional premium, even though all other factors in his case are favorable. Previous employment in such an occupation may be made the basis of an additional premium if there is reason to suspect that the applicant may return to the occupation. If an applicant is placed in a substandard classification because of an unfavorable current occupation, the rating is usually removed upon a subsequent change to an unrated occupation. The company cannot, of course, increase the premium if a policyholder changes from an unrated to a rated occupation after the policy has been issued.

Credit is given for certain occupations which are subject to more favorable mortality than the average.

Residence

The residence—present or prospective—of the applicant is of importance, since mortality rates vary throughout the world. If the applicant is contemplating foreign travel or residence, the company wants to know about it. It also wants to know whether the applicant has recently traveled or resided in a foreign country, particularly in the tropics. Differences among countries as to climate, living standards, sanitary conditions, medical care, and political stability can be expected to exert a decided effect on mortality.

Generally speaking, policies are not issued by United States companies to applicants whose permanent residence is in a foreign country, even though that country may have a climate and living conditions similar to those of the United States. Unless a company has an organization and representatives in another country, it may not be able to get full information as to applicants for insurance, and practical difficulties may arise in connection with the settlement of claims. Policies are freely issued to persons who plan to be abroad temporarily, provided they do not contemplate an extended stay in countries located in the tropics. A few American and Canadian companies do business in foreign countries, using special premium rates for tropical or subtropical countries to take care of the higher mortality rates.

There are differences in the mortality rate among various geographical regions of the United States, but it is not customary for such differences to be recognized for underwriting purposes. There are some areas of the South, however, in which a few companies will not do business because of the malaria hazard.

Habits

The term "habits," for underwriting purposes, refers to the use of alcohol and drugs. The company is concerned about the former because of the impairment of judgment and reaction during the state of intoxication; it is concerned about the latter because of the effect on the applicant's health. Of course, prolonged, immoderate use of alcohol may also be harmful to the person's health.

An insurance company is not concerned about a prospective insured who uses alcoholic beverages in moderate amounts on social occasions. It is concerned about the applicant who drinks to the point of intoxication. All investigations of the effect of drinking on longevity indicate that substantial extra mortality can be expected from a group of heavy drinkers. As might be expected, the heaviest mortality is found among those who have had to take a "cure." Such persons are carefully underwritten not only because of their impaired physical condition but because of the possibility that they may revert to their earlier drinking habits. Other groups who are considered poor risks are those who drink alone and those who avoid their own social class while drinking. Total abstainers have a lower death rate than those who drink only moderately, and there are some companies in Great Britain who grant a lower premium to those who make an annual declaration that they are nondrinkers.

A person who is known to be a drug addict cannot obtain insurance on any basis. Even after taking a cure, he may be considered uninsurable for as long a period as five years and at best will be rated up heavily for a long period of years because of the possibility of resumption of the habit. For example, a former drug addict may be rated up 200 per cent[5] for the first five or ten years after taking the cure and a rating of 150 per cent thereafter would not be unusual.

Morals

It is surprising to many people that an insurance company would concern itself with the morals of the applicant. It appears to them as an unnecessary intrusion into the personal life of the applicant. Actually, the company is interested in the moral fiber of the applicant, not because it wants to sit in judgment on him, but because it has been clearly established that departures from the commonly accepted standards of ethical and moral conduct involve extra mortality.

Infidelity and other departures from the code of sex behavior are seriously regarded, none the less so because they are frequently found in combination with other types of unsocial behavior, such as overindulgence in alcoholic beverages, gambling, and the use of drugs. The hazards to longevity are the impairment of health and the possibility of violence. The discarded mistress constitutes a menace, as do jealous competitors and gambling associates.

Unethical business conduct is considered to be another form of moral hazard. Companies do not care to insure persons who have a record of numerous bankruptcies, operate businesses that are just within the law, engage in sharp practices, or have a general reputation for dishonesty. The companies fear misrepresentation and concealment of material underwriting facts on the part of such persons. A person who is dishonest in his general business dealings is not likely to make an exception of insurance companies, which have always been prime targets for unscrupulous schemes.

Race and Nationality

With some notable exceptions,[6] the mortality rate is higher throughout the world than in the United States and Canada. A portion of the excess mortality can be attributed to climatic and general living condi-

---

[5] A rating of 200 per cent means that a rate of mortality *double* the normal rate is anticipated.

[6] The lowest mortality rates are found in the following countries: New Zealand, the Netherlands, Norway, Sweden, and Denmark.

tions, but some part of it is due to differences in racial stock. Persons coming to North America from a country subject to a higher mortality rate bring with them that portion of the extra mortality attributable to racial stock and, possibly, a portion of that traceable to the conditions under which they lived. Unless the stock is diluted by intermarriage, a portion of the extra mortality will be passed along to descendants. This extra mortality is taken into account by insurance companies. Some companies will accept only such foreign-born applicants as can qualify for insurance at standard rates, while others will provide insurance to foreign-born persons on whatever rate basis may be appropriate.

Sex

Despite the fact that female mortality in general is lower than that of males, applications from women are carefully scrutinized. There is frequently a question of insurable interest, particularly when the woman is not self-supporting. The medical examination of a female is usually not as effective as that of a male. The history of illnesses may not be revealed in full or may innocently conceal unfavorable facts withheld from the patient by the attending physician. This is especially true of operations involving the female organs. Criticisms of alcoholic habits and morals are more difficult to evaluate. Finally, there is still an element of extra hazard involved in the possibility of childbirth.

At one time, the experience on insured female lives was such that an extra premium was charged—and was justified. Greater participation of women in business, wider acceptance of the idea of insurance for women, and improved mortality incident to childbirth have combined to produce an environment in which women are freely offered insurance at standard rates. The most important factor has been the reduction in the amount of speculation associated with insurance on women. Within the last few years, some companies, in recognition of the lower mortality among carefully selected female lives, have made insurance available to women at lower rates than those for men.

As has been pointed out earlier, the superior longevity of women has long been the basis for higher annuity premiums and lower benefits under life income options.

Plan of Insurance

The plan of insurance is taken into account because policies differ not only as to the amount at risk but also as to mortality rates. Other things being equal, the smaller the amount at risk, the more liberal can be the underwriting standards of the company. Thus, companies tend to be somewhat more liberal in underwriting endowment and limited-payment policies, particularly when the extra mortality from a known impairment is not expected to be felt until middle or later life. For example, the debits for overweight are not as great for endowment policies as for other types.

The mortality under endowment and limited-payment policies is lower than under ordinary life and term policies. This is attributable to the antiselection practiced in connection with the latter two types of policies. The amount of antiselection is believed to be particularly great in connection with term insurance. Some companies automatically include a debit of ten points in considering an application for term insurance, which means that an applicant who is otherwise qualified might be declined simply because he applied for term insurance. Other companies do not include a debit for term insurance but take care of the additional mortality through higher premiums.

The plan of insurance can be especially important in the consideration of substandard risks.

Economic Status

In the eyes of the law, every man has an unlimited insurable interest in his own life. Thus, the burden of preventing overinsurance is placed on the insurance company. The company makes a careful investigation of the applicant's financial status, in order to make sure that his family and business circumstances are such as to justify the amount of insurance applied for and carried in all companies. This investigation also reveals whether the income of the applicant bears a reasonable relationship to the amount of insurance which he proposes to carry. The company is interested not only in preventing too much insurance on the life of the applicant, but also in keeping in force the amounts which have already been issued.

Aviation Activities

In the early days of aviation, any form of flying was considered to be so hazardous—and rare—that the risk was either excluded altogether, through an *exclusion clause,* or made subject to a substantial extra premium. As technical developments and improvement in pilot skills reduced the hazards of flying, underwriting restrictions were gradually relaxed. Today, the risk has been reduced to such a low level, and air travel has become so common, that companies do not consider it necessary to impose any underwriting restrictions on travel as a passenger in any type of nonmilitary aircraft, whether it be a commercial airliner, a company plane, or a personal craft. Furthermore, no occupational rating or restriction is applied to crew members on regularly scheduled commercial aircraft. The treatment of private pilots depends upon the person's age, experience, and amount of flying. For example, most companies will treat as a standard risk an applicant between the ages of twenty-seven and sixty, with at least one hundred hours of pilot experience, who does not fly more than two hundred hours per year. Such a person who flies between two hundred and four hundred hours annually would be charged an extra premium of $3 per $1,000, while flying in excess of four hundred hours per year would involve an extra premium of $5 per $1,000. An applicant under age twenty-seven, otherwise qualified as a standard risk, would be charged an extra premium of $5 per $1,000. The underwriting treatment of a crew member of a military aircraft depends upon his age and type of duty, service with combat aircraft being the least favorably regarded—as one would naturally suppose.

Where there is an indication that the applicant will be engaged in any aeronautical activity that might present a special hazard, the applicant is usually required to complete a supplementary form which will give the company full details of his past and probable future aviation activities, as well as his current status.

It is well to emphasize that in the absence of a specific restriction, all policies cover the aviation hazard in full. In other words, there is no presumption that the aviation hazard is not covered or is subject to a limitation of liability. It is only when the company is put on notice—usually through the applicant's own disclosure—that an unusual aviation hazard is involved that it takes any special underwriting action.

Avocation

Certain avocations are regarded to be sufficiently hazardous to justify an extra premium, at least under given circumstances. Among the avocations that may entail an extra premium are automobile, motorcycle, scooter, and speedboat racing; sky diving; skin diving (to depths over forty feet); ski acrobatics; and mountain climbing. Most of these avocations involve a flat extra premium of $5 per $1,000.

Military Service

For more than one hundred years—at least as far back as the Civil War—American life insurance companies have taken special underwriting cognizance of the extra mortality risk associated with applicants engaged in or facing military service during a period of armed conflict. The underwriting action has taken three principal forms: outright declination of the applicant, limitation on the face amount of insurance issued, or the attachment of a so-called "war clause" which limits the insurer's obligation to return of premium if the insured of premiums, less dividends, with interest.

The use of a war clause has been the most common method of dealing with the extra hazard of military or naval service. Some companies have used a clause, known as the "status" clause, which limits the insurer's obligation to return of premium if the insured should die while *in* military service outside the territorial boundaries of the United States, whether or not the *cause* of death could be attributed to military service. Other companies have used a rider, referred to as a "results" war clause, which limits the insurer's obligation only if the insured's death was the result of military service. While regarded as more liberal to the insured than the "status" clause, this provision invoked the limitation of liability even though the insured was no longer in a war zone at the time of his death. Most companies have been willing to waive these clauses for an appropriate extra premium.

War clauses were widely if not universally used during both World Wars, especially World War II, in policies issued to persons of military age. After the cessation of hostilities, the clauses were generally revoked by the companies without request from the insureds. During the Korean Conflict, war clauses were again inserted in policies issued to young men facing military service and with the termination of hostilities, use of the clauses was again discontinued and such clauses in outstanding policies were voluntarily cancelled by the companies.

With the American involvement in Viet Nam, life insurance companies are again confronted with the problem of assessing the risk in military service. There is no consensus among the companies as to the approach to be followed and a variety of practices can be found. One approach used by a number of companies is to refuse to write any coverage on military personnel at the lower ranks, but to issue insurance in normal amounts to all other military persons, attaching a "results" type of war clause to policies written on persons in combat units or in combat zones.

CHAPTER XIX

Selection and
Classification
of Risks
(Continued)

SOURCES OF INFORMATION

The preceding section reviewed the type of information needed by the underwriting department of an insurance company in considering an application for insurance. This section describes briefly the sources from which this information is obtained. It should be noted that much of the information is obtained from more than one source. This provides the company with the means of verifying information which it considers critical to the underwriting decision and serves as a deterrent to collusion or fraud by any of the parties to the transaction.

The Agent

In a real sense, a company's field force is the foundation of the selection process. The other parts of the selection mechanism can go into operation only after the field force has acted. The home office can exercise its underwriting judgment only on the risks submitted by the agents and brokers. The over-all selection process of a company can be no stronger than its agency force. If the agents submit consistently good business, the underwriting results will be favorable; it they consistently submit below-average risks, the underwriting results will be no better.

Most companies provide their agents with explicit instructions as to the types of risks which will be acceptable and those that will be unacceptable, and instruct them to solicit only those risks which they believe to be eligible under the company's underwriting rules. Where eligibility for insurance is in any way doubtful, some companies, in order to save unnecessary expense and trouble, require the agent to submit a preliminary statement setting forth the facts of the case and the grounds upon which doubt as to insurability is based. Some companies require such a statement in all cases where an application for insurance in any company has been declined, set aside for subsequent action, or accepted at other than standard rates. Under all circumstances, the agent is required to submit, along with the application, a certificate affirming his belief that the applicant meets the underwriting standards of the company, except as noted.

The agent is asked to supply a variety of information in the certificate, the details varying with the company. He is always required to state how long and how intimately he has known the applicant, and to estimate his net worth and annual income. He must provide information about existing and pending insurance, including any plans for the lapse or surrender of existing insurance. He must indicate whether the applicant sought the insurance himself or whether the application was the result of solicitation by the agent. Finally, he is usually required to state whether the application came through another agent or broker.

The degree of selection exercised at the field level depends upon the integrity and reliability of the individuals. There is clearly some selection, since the self-interest of the agent would cause him not to solicit insurance from persons who—because of obvious physical impairments, moral deficiencies, or unacceptable occupations—manifestly could not meet the underwriting standards of the company. Beyond that, the amount of selection is rather limited. Since the agent's remuneration depends upon the amount of insurance he sells, he is likely to submit any application, even though it be borderline, which he thinks stands a chance of being accepted. Hence, the burden of enforcing the company's underwriting standards is thrust upon the home office underwriters, who do not labor under a conflict of interests.

The Applicant

Much of the information needed by a company to underwrite a case is supplied by the applicant himself. This information is contained in the application, which constitutes the offer in the legal sense. Application blanks vary in their content and arrangement; but they usually consist of two parts, the first containing questions of a nonmedical nature and the second including questions to be asked by the medical examiner.

The statements made by the applicant in the first part of the application cover the particulars necessary to identify him, such as his name, address, former and contemplated future places of residence, and place and date of birth. If the applicant has only recently moved to his present residence, the inclusion of former places of residence enables the company, through inspection services, to check with the applicant's former acquaintances. The importance of obtaining the correct date of birth was indicated earlier.

Additional questions in the first part of the application relate to the applicant's occupation, including any changes within the last five years, or any contemplated; his aviation activities, other than passenger flying on regularly scheduled air lines; and the possibility of foreign residence. If there is any unusual aviation hazard, details must be provided in a supplementary form. The application also contains information as to the insurance history of the applicant. This includes details of all insurance already in force on his life, as well as declinations and other actions of underwriting significance.

The foregoing information, together with a statement of the amount of insurance applied for, the plan upon which it is to be issued, the name of the beneficiary, and the respective rights of the insured and beneficiary as to control of the policy complete the first part of the application. This section of the application is usually filled out by the agent on behalf of the applicant, who must sign it and certify as to the correctness of the information contained therein. The signature of the applicant is generally witnessed by the agent, who vouches for him from his personal knowledge.

The answers to the second part of the application must be recorded in the handwriting of the medical examiner, but the applicant is required to sign the form. Several groups of related questions are asked. The first group seeks the details of the applicant's health record, including illnesses, injuries, and surgical operations since childhood. The applicant is also required to give the name of every physician or practitioner whom he has consulted within a specified period of time (usually, the last five years) in connection with any ailment whatsoever. A second group of questions elicits information about the applicant's present physical condition. Another group inquires as to the applicant's use of alcohol and drugs. A fourth group repeats in different form the questions concerning residence and asks whether or not the applicant has ever changed residences or traveled because of poor health. Finally, the details of family history are sought.

The Medical Examiner

In addition to recording the answers to Part II of the application, the medical examiner is required to file a separate report or certificate, which accompanies the application but is not seen by the applicant. The first portion of the report contains a description of the physical characteristics of the applicant which not only provides useful underwriting information but serves to guard against the substitution at the medical examination of a healthy person for an unhealthy applicant. For the latter purpose, some companies ask the examiner to indicate some peculiarity, such as a birthmark, which will establish conclusive identification. The examiner is usually asked also to indicate whether or not the applicant looks older than his stated age.

The basic purpose of the medical examiner's report is to transmit his findings from the physical examination of the applicant. He is required to comment specifically upon any abnormalities of the arteries or veins, heart, respiratory system, nervous system, abdomen, genitourinary system, middle ear, eyes, and skin. He reports the result of the urinalysis and certifies that the urine examined was authentic. He also records the build and blood pressure of the applicant.

In the final section of the report, the examiner is requested to indicate whether he knows or suspects that the applicant is addicted to the use of alcohol or narcotics, or has any moral deficiencies that would affect his insurability.

The medical examiner's report is considered to be the property of the company and is carefully safeguarded at all times.

Attending Physicians

Attending physicians are a source of information on applicants who have undergone medical treatment within a few years prior to applying for insurance. When it appears that the information in the files of the attending physician might influence the underwriting decision of the insurance company, such information is sought as a matter of routine. The insurance companies have enjoyed a remarkable degree of co-operation from the medical profession with respect to inquiries of this nature, all of the relevant information in the physician's files normally being provided. It is customary for the insurance company to reimburse the physician for the expense incurred in supplying the information, a check for a nominal sum usually accompanying the letter of inquiry.

Inspection Report

The company attempts to verify all the information obtained from the foregoing sources by means of an investigation of the applicant by an independent agency. At one time, such investigations were conducted without the knowledge of the applicant, the agent, or the medical examiner; but today, it is common knowledge that such investigations are made. The peculiar advantage of these investigations is that they provide the company with an evaluation of the applicant by a source having no interest in the outcome of the case.

Some of the larger companies maintain their own staff of inspectors, but most companies utilize the facilities of national credit agencies. Member companies of the American Life Convention can use the facilities of the American Service Bureau. In operation since 1920, the bureau is equipped to investigate applicants, agents, medical examiners, and claims.[1]

The request for an inspection report may be made by the home office or by the local agency. In either event, the report is filed directly with the home office of the insurance company; and none of the findings is revealed, either to the applicant or to the agent. In most cases, the actual inspector is known only to the home office.

The thoroughness of the inspection depends upon the amount of insurance involved. When the amount of insurance is not large, the report is rather brief, commenting in a general way on the applicant's health, habits, finances, environment, and reputation. In the case of the smallest policies, the inspection may be waived altogether. When a large amount has been applied for, the report tends to be very comprehensive. It reflects the results of interviews with the applicant's neighbors, employer, banker, business associates, and others who may have had special information. It concerns itself in particular with the business and personal ethics of the applicant. It calls attention to any bankruptcies and fire losses, and comments on the intemperate use of alcohol and other departures from normal social behavior. While not designed to verify the findings of the medical examiner, the inspec-

---

[1] It also surveys agency, underwriting, and medical problems.

tion occasionally uncovers physical impairments that were not revealed in the medical examiner's report. Unfortunately, cases of collusion among the applicant, agent, and medical examiner have been discovered from time to time.

A typical inspection report form is shown in Appendix C.

The Medical Information Bureau

A final source of information is the Medical Information Bureau. This organization, known in insurance parlance as the "M.I.B.," is a clearing house for confidential data of a medical nature on applicants for life insurance. The information is reported and maintained in code symbols, and every effort is made to preserve its confidentiality.

Companies which are members of the bureau are expected to report any impairments designated in the official list. The designated impairments are concerned primarily with the physical condition of the applicant but also include hereditary characteristics and addiction to alcohol and narcotics. Any suspicious tendencies brought out by an examination, if they have a bearing on insurability, are reported, so as to bring the matter to the notice of all companies using the records of the bureau. All impairments must be reported whether the company accepts, suspends, or declines the risk, or offers a modified plan of insurance. However, the company does not report its underwriting decision to the Bureau.

A servicing organization, the Recording and Statistical Company, prints a card for each individual reported to the bureau[2] and provides a duplicate of the card to each member company that wishes to maintain its own set of cards.[3] The card identifies the individual by name, date of birth, and occupation. All the impairments which have been reported are recorded on the card, in code; but the company or companies which reported the impairments are not identified. Strict rules are promulgated for the use and safeguarding of the information, and any violations of the rules are regarded as grounds for withdrawing the service from the offending company.

---

[2] For an interesting description of the work of this organization, see J. C. Wilmerding, "The Medical Information Bureau," *The Journal of the American Society of C.L.U.,* Vol. XX (Spring, 1966), pp. 176–81.

[3] Most member companies, including some of the largest, do not maintain their own set of cards. They find it less expensive and equally expeditious to screen their applications against the checking files of the Recording and Statistical Company, using teletype or postal facilities. Plans are currently underway to automate the entire M.I.B. system.

A company normally screens all of its applications against its file of reported impairments, or, if it does not maintain its own file, against the checking files of the Recording and Statistical Company. If the company finds an impairment and wants further details, it must submit its request through the Recording and Statistical Company. The company which reported the impairment is under no obligation to supply further information; but if it is so minded, it provides the requested information through the M.I.B.

It should be emphasized that there is no basis for the widespread belief that a person who is recorded in the M.I.B. files can no longer obtain insurance at standard rates. The information contained therein is treated like underwriting data obtained from any other source and, in the final analysis, may be outweighed by favorable factors. In many cases, it will merely substantiate impairments revealed in the current application. In other cases, it will enable a company to take favorable action, since favorable results of medical tests are reported as well as the unfavorable ones. In any event, the rules of the M.I.B. stipulate that a company shall not take unfavorable underwriting action *solely* on the basis of the information in the M.I.B. files. In other words, the company must be in possession of other unfavorable underwriting facts or else determine through its own channels of investigation that the condition or impairment recorded in the M.I.B. files is substantial enough to warrant an unfavorable decision.

The M.I.B. files contain information on less than 10 per cent of the insured population.

CLASSIFICATION OF RISKS

Once all available underwriting information about an applicant for insurance has been assembled, the data must be evaluated and a decision reached as to whether the applicant is to be accepted at standard rates, placed in one of the various substandard classifications, or rejected entirely. This is clearly the apex of the selection process and must be accomplished in a manner commensurate with its importance. Ideally, the evaluation and classification system used by a company should (1) accurately measure the effect of each of the factors, favorable and unfavorable, that can be expected to influence the longevity of an applicant; (2) assess the combined impact of multiple factors, including the situations in which the factors are conflicting; (3) produce consistently equitable results; and (4) be simple and relatively inexpensive to operate.

The Judgment Method of Rating

The earliest system used in this country was one which can be termed the "judgment method" of rating. Under this method, the routine cases were processed with a minimum of consideration by clerks trained in the review of applications, and the doubtful or borderline cases were resolved by supervisors relying on their experience and general impressions. The method is still used by many companies, particularly the smaller ones; and in all companies, the element of judgment plays an important role.

The judgment method of rating functions very effectively when there is only one unfavorable factor to consider or where the decision is simply one of accepting the applicant at standard rates or rejecting him altogether. It leaves something to be desired when there are multiple unfavorable factors (offset, perhaps, by some favorable factors) or where the risk, if it does not qualify for standard insurance, must be fitted into the proper substandard classification. To overcome the weaknesses of the judgment method of rating, a method known as the *numerical rating system* was devised almost a half century ago, and is used today by most of the large companies and many of the smaller ones.[4]

The Numerical Rating System

The numerical rating system is based upon the principle that a large number of factors enter into the composition of a risk and that the impact of each of these factors on the longevity of the risk can be determined by a statistical study of lives possessing that factor. It assumes that the average risk accepted by a company has a value of 100 per cent and that each of the factors which enter into the risk can be expressed as a percentage of the whole. Favorable factors are assigned *negative* values, called *credits,* while unfavorable factors are assigned *positive* values, called *debits.* The algebraic summation of the debits and credits, added to or deducted from the "par" value of 100, represents the numerical value of the risk.

---

[4] The system was developed in 1919 by Arthur H. Hunter and Dr. Oscar H. Rogers, Actuary and Medical Director, respectively, of the New York Life Insurance Company. It is described in a paper by Hunter and Rogers entitled "The Numerical Method of Determining the Value of Risks for Insurance" and published in the *Transactions of the Actuarial Society of America,* Vol. XX, Part II (1919).

Naturally, it would be impossible to assign weights to all the factors that might influence a risk. In practice, values are generally assigned to the following factors: (1) build, (2) physical condition, (3) personal history, (4) family history, (5) occupation, (6) residence, (7) habits, (8) morals, and (9) plan of insurance. The values assigned to the various factors are derived from mortality studies among groups possessing such characteristics or, in some cases, estimates of what such mortality studies might be expected to show. For example, if the mortality experience of a group of insured lives with a particular medical history or reflecting a certain degree of overweight has been found to be 135 percent of that among all standard risks, a debit (addition) of 35 percentage points will be assigned to such medical history or degree of overweight. The degrees of extra mortality cited in connection with many of the impairments discussed in the preceding chapter would be the basis for the debits under the numerical rating system.

The operation of the system can be illustrated with the following hypothetical case. The applicant is a married man, aged thirty-two, with two children, living in Philadelphia, Pennsylvania. He is six feet one inch tall and weighs 267 pounds. He is in good physical condition except that, in addition to being overweight, his build is unfavorable, i.e., his expanded chest measurement is one inch less than the girth of his abdomen. His personal health record shows no operations, broken bones, ulcers, or other ailments that would have an adverse effect on longevity. His family is long lived; and the family history shows no tuberculosis, insanity, cardiac conditions, malignancies, or diabetes. He has been employed for several years as a warehouseman in an industrial plant. His habits and morals are good. The plan of insurance is twenty-year endowment.

The company might evaluate the facts as follows: According to Table 31, the applicant is overweight, which would call for a debit of sixty points. The unfavorable build (girth greater than chest expanded) would be the basis for an additional debit of ten points. The favorable family history would be the basis for a credit of fifteen points and the plan of insurance, twenty-year endowment, would call for an additional credit of ten points. The residence is a neutral factor; only debits are assigned to residence, and they are usually assessed only for a foreign or tropical residence. With respect to habits and morals, there is no credit for good behavior, only debits for bad behavior. The occupation is also a neutral factor with no debits or credits. Thus the debits add up to seventy points and the credits add up to only twenty-five. Hence, the numerical value of the risk is 145.

The analysis is summarized below:

Base = 100

Factor	Debit	Credit
Build: overweight...............................	60	—
Physical condition: favorable....................	—	—
Build: unfavorable..............................	10	—
Family history: superior........................	—	15
Occupation: favorable...........................	—	—
Residence: normal...............................	—	—
Habits and morals: favorable....................	—	—
Plan of insurance: 20-year endowment............	—	10
Total......................................	70	25

Rating = 145

It should be noted that credits are generally not allowed where there are other ratable physical impairments or debits for blood pressure or other cardiovascular-renal impairments.

In the foregoing hypothetical situation if the applicant were a longshoreman instead of a warehouseman, the same debits and credits would apply but in addition to the rating of 145, the company would charge an additional flat extra premium of $2.50 per $1,000 or more to cover the occupational accident hazard.

The ratings obtained by this method may go as low as 75 and as high as 500 or more. The ratings that fall between 75 and 125 are usually classified as standard, although some companies, especially those that do not write substandard insurance, may include in the standard category risks that produce a rating of 130, or below age thirty, even 140. Risks which produce ratings beyond the standard limit are either assigned to appropriate substandard classifications or declined. The latter action is taken if the company does not write substandard insurance or the rating is higher than that eligible for the highest substandard classification. Many companies are willing to accept risks that indicate a mortality rate up to 500 per cent of normal.[5] In such a company, the ratings produced by the numerical rating system might be classified as follows:

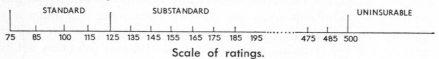

Scale of ratings.

<hr>

[5] Some companies are willing to accept risks which appear to be subject to mortality up to 1,000 per cent of normal.

As will be explained in the following chapter, the broad category of substandard risks is subdivided into several classifications, each with its own scale of premiums. There may be as few as three or as many as twelve substandard classifications. The full significance of the earlier statements concerning the balancing of risks within each classification should now be apparent. With a spread of fifty percentage points in the standard classification, which comprises the great bulk of accepted risks, it is vitally important that each risk which falls within the 100 to 125 range be balanced (in percentage points) by one which falls in the 75 to 100 category. Otherwise, the average mortality for the entire group will exceed the norm of 100.

With a rating of 155, the hypothetical case illustrated above would have fallen into a substandard classification.

The numerical rating system follows much the same procedure as that followed by those who judge a risk without the benefit of numerical values. The same factors are considered, and the final decision is based upon the relationship of the various favorable and unfavorable features of the risk. The numerical method, however, sets up objective standards which assist in the final valuation of the risk and makes for greater consistency of treatment. Lay underwriters can process all applications other than those requiring detailed medical analysis and the inevitable borderline cases. This not only expedites the handling of cases but helps to hold down the expense of the selection process.

Various criticisms have been leveled against the system. It has been alleged, for example, that (1) the system is too arbitrary, (2) there are many impairments concerning which knowledge is too limited to permit the assignment of numerical values, (3) the interrelated factors are nonadditive in so many cases as to nullify the value of the numerical process, and (4) too many minor debits and credits are taken into account in evaluating risk.

Supporters of the system recognize its flaws but feel that it is still superior to any other method that has been devised. They point out that the plan must be—and, in practice, is—applied with common sense. They admit that there are many impairments whose effect on longevity cannot be expressed numerically, but they point out that this constitutes a handicap under any method. They argue that under any system, the cases with interrelated impairments require the expert judgment of the medical and actuarial staff. Whether too many debits and credits are taken into account is a matter of opinion, of course;

but some companies have modified the system to take into account only major impairments.

NONMEDICAL INSURANCE

In citing the medical examiner as a source of underwriting information, the preceding section implied that a medical examination is always a feature of a life insurance transaction. That is not at all the case. A substantial proportion of all new insurance is written without the benefit of a medical examination. For example, neither group nor industrial life insurance ordinarily requires a medical examination. Furthermore, an increasing amount of ordinary life insurance is being sold without a medical examination. While any type of insurance sold without a medical examination might logically be called *nonmedical insurance,* the expression is usually taken to refer to ordinary insurance sold in that manner.

History

Nonmedical life insurance is not a recent innovation. The first life insurance was sold without medical examination. In the early days of life insurance in England, each applicant appeared in person before the directors of the company, who made their decision largely on the basis of personal appearance. The personal inspection of the company directors came later to be supplemented by recommendations of the applicant's friends and associates; and eventually, a medical examination was introduced. The medical examination quickly established its usefulness and was soon regarded as essential.

About 1886, companies in Great Britain began to experiment with nonmedical underwriting. To protect the companies against adverse selection, the policies, which were limited in amount, contained liens during the early years of the contract or else were issued at advanced premium rates. Some companies offered only double endowments on a nonmedical basis. Nonmedical underwriting as it is practiced today, however, was begun in 1921 in Canada. The immediate motivation for the development was the shortage of medical examiners, particularly in the rural areas; but the desire to reduce the expense rate on the predominantly small policies issued in Canada at that time was also a strong influence. The practice spread to the United States around 1925, after the success of the Canadian experiment seemed assured. It gained increasing acceptance during the 1930's, as American experience proved favorable, and then enjoyed its greatest growth when a shortage of medical examiners developed during World War II. The practice is firmly entrenched today in both Canada and the United States.

Underwriting Safeguards

Nonmedical insurance is known to be subject to higher than normal mortality, at least for the first several years, so the companies surround its issue with certain underwriting safeguards. Perhaps the most important safeguard is a limit on the amount which will be made available to any one applicant. As will be explained more fully below, this limit is determined with reference to the extra mortality that can be expected to result from elimination of the medical examination and the savings in selection expenses that will be available to absorb the extra mortality costs. In the early days of nonmedical insurance, the limit was placed at $1,000. When the extra mortality turned out to be lower than expected, the limits were gradually raised. Today, most companies will provide up to $5,000 on a nonmedical basis, subject to appropriate age restrictions, while many will issue up to $10,000 or $15,000 on that basis. The limit generally varies by age groups, the largest amounts being available to the younger age groups. A few companies are willing to write up to $25,000 at the younger ages.

The foregoing limits are applicable to any one application for nonmedical insurance. Some companies will issue additional amounts, subject to an aggregate limit, after a specified period of time has elapsed. Most companies are willing to reinstate the original limits with respect to any insured who, subsequent to obtaining one or more policies on a nonmedical basis, undergoes a medical examination satisfactory to the company. In other words, all nonmedical insurance issued to the person prior to the medical examination would be disregarded, and additional amounts would be made available up to the applicable limits.

A second safeguard imposed by the companies is a limit on the ages at which the insurance will be issued. Studies have shown that the extra mortality resulting from the waiving of the medical examination increases with age and, after a point, will exceed any expense savings that might be available. The point at which the extra mortality costs will exceed the expense savings is obviously a function of the underwriting limit, but most companies regard it to be around age forty or forty-five. Hence, nonmedical insurance is usually not available beyond age forty or forty-five, except in salary savings groups, where the limit may be fifty. There is usually no lower age limit, most companies offering it down to age zero.

A third safeguard is the general limitation of nonmedical insurance to standard risks. As a broad class, substandard risks must submit to medical examinations. An exception is commonly made in the case of risks which are substandard because of an occupational *accident* hazard.

A final safeguard, which is of a more general and pervasive nature, is the intensive cultivation of the sources of underwriting information other than the medical examiner. The companies place a heavier burden on the applicant, agent, and inspector to offset in some measure the loss of the medical examiner's findings. The application form used in connection with nonmedical insurance is elaborate, comprising all the questions usually contained in an application blank as well as those which would normally be asked by the medical examiner. A urine specimen may be required for home office analysis. If the applicant has recently been under the care of a physician, a statement may be required from the attending physician—at the expense of the company. If any adverse information of a medical nature is revealed by the applicant's statement, the inspection report, or other source, the company may prescribe a complete medical examination.

A particularly heavy responsibility is placed on the agent, and great reliance is placed on his judgment and integrity. He must solicit nonmedical applications only from persons who would appear to meet the underwriting requirements of the company from a physical, medical, occupational, and moral standpoint. He must elicit from the applicant and accurately record most of the information that would be sought by the medical examiner. He must file a detailed certificate in which he records his underwriting impressions of the applicant. It is understandable that the privilege of submitting nonmedical business is not bestowed indiscriminately upon the field forces.

Inspection reports are utilized in connection with smaller amounts of insurance than would be true of policies issued on the basis of a medical examination.

At one time, nonmedical business was restricted to rural areas and small towns, where the agent tends to be better acquainted with the applicants and inspection reports tend to be more accurate; but it has now been extended to urban areas. Earlier restrictions on nonmedical insurance for women have largely disappeared. Some companies still have a lower limit for married women than for men.

Economics of Nonmedical Insurance

Several advantages are associated with nonmedical insurance. It lessens the demands on the time and talents of the medical profession, it eliminates the delays and inconvenience connected with medical examinations, and it removes one of the greatest psychological barriers to the sale of insurance. Important as these advantages are, they could not be enjoyed if nonmedical insurance did not rest on a solid economic foundation. It must justify itself on a dollars-and-cents basis.

Insurance issued on a nonmedical basis is known to be subject to a higher rate of mortality than that of medically examined business. This extra mortality is believed to stem from (1) impairments known to the applicant but deliberately concealed and (2) impairments not known to the applicant and of such nature that they could have been discovered by a medical examination. This extra mortality can be measured and expressed as a dollar amount per $1,000 of insurance.

The procedure customarily used to measure the extra mortality is to compare the mortality experience on nonmedical business with the mortality at the same ages, years of issue, and durations on business that was subject to a medical examination. This does not give a direct answer to the question of what the mortality on the nonmedical applicants would have been had they been selected by medical examination, since the two groups being compared might not be comparable in all respects. For example, the two groups might differ as to sex composition, income level, and size of policies. Nevertheless, this method is the best available and is deemed satisfactory.

Studies of this nature reveal that most of the extra mortality occurs during the first ten years after issue, although some extra mortality is observable up to fifteen years. The disparity between nonmedical and medical mortality increases with age of issue, both in absolute amount and as a percentage of the base mortality rate. This would seem to indicate that up to a point, at least, the importance and effectiveness of the medical examination grow greater with age. On the basis of the most recent experience available, which covers the period 1958–63, it would appear that the approximate discounted value of the future extra mortality is as follows:[6]

---

[6] Society of Actuaries, *1964 Reports of Mortality and Morbidity Experience,* Chicago, Illinois.

```
Under age 30.................. $0.75 per $1,000 of insurance
Ages 30–34.................. $1.50 per $1,000 of insurance
Ages 35–39.................. $3.50 per $1,000 of insurance
Ages 40–44.................. $9.00 per $1,000 of insurance
Ages 45–49..................$18.00 per $1,000 of insurance
```

These amounts represent the present value of the extra mortality that was reflected at all durations and not in just one year. In other words, they represent the *aggregate* extra mortality per $1,000 over the lifetime of the policies.

To be offset against these extra death claims are the savings in medical examiners' fees and incidental home office expenses, less the increase in expenditures for inspection reports and attending physician's statements. This net saving, it should be noted, is garnered on every application that does not involve a medical examination, while the extra mortality is experienced only on those policies that remain in force until they become claims—a much smaller number because of lapses and surrenders. The extra mortality costs cited above, however, reflect the smaller number of persisting policies. The savings in selection expenses are expressed as an amount per policy and range from $7 to $15.

Once the extra mortality per $1,000 and the expense saving per policy are known, it is a matter of simple arithmetic to determine the proper limits for nonmedical insurance. If, at ages below thirty, the extra mortality cost per $1,000 is $0.75 and the expense saving per policy is assumed to be $10, the company could safely offer about $13,000 of nonmedical insurance to applicants under thirty. With the same expense saving and an extra mortality cost of $1.50 per $1,000 at ages thirty to thirty-four, the proper limit for persons in that age group would be $6,700. By the same token, the limit for applicants in the thirty-five to thirty-nine category should be about $3,000. Thus, the need for age limits and the equity of variable limits are apparent.

In practice, companies are inclined to offer larger amounts of nonmedical insurance than the above figures would suggest. While the amount made available to any one applicant might seem excessive, all applicants do not request the maximum. Since the company's objective is to break even on its nonmedical business in the aggregate, it may safely set its limits higher than the precise relationship between the expected extra mortality and expense savings would support. Furthermore, at ages under thirty the absolute rate of mortality is so low and the probability of finding impairments on examination so small that the nonmedical rules can be greatly relaxed. Finally, a particular company may set its nonmedical limits on the basis of its own mortality experience and expense assumptions.[7]

Special Branches of Nonmedical Insurance

There are certain special situations in which policies may be issued on a nonmedical basis even when the company does not follow a general practice of issuing nonmedical policies. Two of the most common instances are discussed in this subsection.

Policyholder Nonmedical. Most companies are willing to issue insurance up to a stated limit on the basis of the applicant's declaration of good health if, within a short period prior thereto—such as three to six months—he has obtained standard insurance from the company on the basis of a satisfactory medical examination. The reasoning behind this practice, of course, is that the policyholder's health is not likely to have deteriorated within such a short period of time, and any serious affliction would be apparent to the agent.

Some companies have extended this privilege to policyholders who apply for additional insurance within a much longer period, such as one to five years. Under such circumstances, however, the applicant is required to bring his physical and medical histories up to date, and the case is underwritten on the basis of both the old and the new information. The general experience under this type of nonmedical insurance has not been very favorable and indicates some adverse selection by those applying for it.

This category of insurance without medical examination goes under the name of *policyholder nonmedical,* since it is limited to those applicants who are already policyholders of the company.

Pension Trusts. One of the important contractual arrangements under which retirement benefits are provided to superannuated employees is the individual contract pension trust. Under this arrangement, the benefits are provided through retirement annuity or retirement income contracts purchased by the employer, through a trustee, for each of the employees eligible to participate in the pension plan. Traditionally, if retirement income contracts were used, each employee had to furnish evidence of insurability in the form of a satisfactory medical examination. Within the last few years, however, several

---

[7] See Joseph C. Sibigtroth, "A Survey of Recent Developments in Non-Medical Insurance," *Proceedings* of the Home Office Life Underwriters Association, Vol. XLI, (1960), pp. 140–65 for a more detailed and authoritative discussion of this general topic.

companies have begun to underwrite such plans on a nonmedical basis. In fact, the arrangement goes beyond the conventional concepts of nonmedical insurance. If the *group* is acceptable, the insurance company dispenses with individual underwriting and agrees in advance to accept all applications for insurance. This practice is known as *guaranteed issue*. There is no underwriting beyond a screening of the group.

No published mortality experience is available on these arrangements as yet, but a higher than normal mortality is anticipated. The rate is likely to be higher than that associated with ordinary nonmedical insurance, not only because of the absence of individual underwriting but also because the age distribution of the employees is likely to be higher than that of normal nonmedical groups. In order to offset the anticipated extra mortality under guaranteed issue plans, most companies pay lower than normal commissions and separately classify the policies for dividend purposes.

INSURABILITY OPTION

A number of companies are now offering with all new policies, except those on a substandard basis and short-duration term policies, an option which permits the policyholder, at stated intervals and below a specified age, to purchase specified amounts of additional insurance *without evidence* of insurability. The additional insurance need not be on the same plan as the basic policy to which the option is attached, the option being exercisable in favor of any standard whole life or endowment insurance policies offered by the company. Premiums for the new insurance are payable at standard rates on the basis of the insured's attained age on the option date. If the original policy contains a waiver of premium provision and accidental death benefits, the new policies will, at the insured's option, contain the same features. If premiums are being waived on the original policy at the time an option for additional insurance is exercised, premiums on the new policy are waived from the beginning and will continue to be waived as long as the insured remains totally disabled.

The options vary as to details; but the first provision of this type,[8] which has served as a pattern for most of those introduced later, permits the insured to purchase up to $10,000 of additional insurance

---

[8] This option was first introduced by the Bankers Life Insurance Company of Des Moines, Iowa, under the name of *guaranteed purchase option*. The option of that company is described in an article by Dennis N. Warters, then President of Bankers Life, in the Fall, 1958, issue of the *C.L.U. Journal*, pp. 299–304.

at three-year intervals beginning with the policy anniversary nearest the insured's age twenty-five and terminating with the anniversary nearest the insured's age forty. The amount of insurance which can be obtained on each specified policy anniversary is limited to the face of the original policy or $10,000, whichever is smaller. Additional insurance in an aggregate amount of $60,000 can be obtained under this option without evidence of insurability. At least one company will permit $200,000 of additional insurance to be acquired under such an option. The option is restricted to policies of a specified minimum size —typically, $5,000—and can be attached to only one policy issued by the company. Similar options may, of course, be attached to policies issued by other companies. In most companies, the original policy may be issued on a nonmedical basis. At least one company is willing to make this option available for an appropriate group premium to participants in a group life plan, whether or not the underlying group life plan is underwritten by the company involved.

Some contracts permit the purchase of additional insurance upon marriage of the insured or following the birth of the first child, or subsequent children, of the insured. Some contracts provide coverage automatically for sixty to ninety days after each option date.

The option is available only for an extra premium which varies, not in proportion to the number of option dates remaining, as might be supposed, but with the age of issue. The schedule of annual premiums charged for the option by one company begins at $0.50 per $1,000 at age zero and increases to approximately $2.00 per $1,000 at age thirty-seven. These premiums reflect the company's estimate of the average amount of extra mortality which will be experienced on policies issued without evidence of insurability and, from the standpoint of the insured, may be regarded as the cost of "insuring" his insurability. Premiums for the option are payable to the last anniversary at which it can be exercised—usually, age forty—or to the end of the premium-paying period of the basic policy, whichever is earlier.

The time limitations on the exercise of the options are designed to provide a periodic stimulus to the policyholder to purchase additional insurance as needs dictate and financial circumstances permit.

INSURANCE AT EXTREMES OF AGE

Applications for insurance at both extremes of age must be carefully underwritten. In both cases, the basic obstacle is limited insurable interest—which, if not recognized, may lead to speculation and excessive mortality.

As was indicated earlier, there is great demand for juvenile insurance; and most companies will write insurance on the lives of very young children, even down to one day old. They attempt to cope with the lack of insurable interest in three ways: (1) limiting the coverage to amounts much smaller than those available to adults, particularly at the early ages; (2) seeing that the insurance on the child bears a reasonable relationship to the amounts in force on the other members of the family, especially the breadwinner; and (3) seeking a large volume of juvenile insurance, in order to minimize adverse selection.

From the standpoint of the basic mortality risk, juvenile risks are very attractive. With the exception of the first few weeks after birth, the death rate is very low and does not begin to climb until around age ten. The death rate is high immediately after birth because of the hazards of childbirth to the child, congenital defects, and the naturally delicate physique of a newborn infant. This period of heavy mortality can be avoided by limiting coverage to children who have attained the age of one, three, or perhaps six months. Family economic circumstances seem to have greater influence on mortality at the younger ages than later in life, which makes it necessary to inquire into that factor. In general, the insurance is sold without medical examination.

At the other extreme—i.e., at the older ages—the lack of insurable interest is only one of the complicating factors. In the first place, the volume of insurance issued at ages above sixty or sixty-five is not large enough to yield predictable mortality results. The restricted demand for insurance at those ages reflects the high cost of the insurance, the general inability to satisfy the medical requirements, and the limited need for new insurance. In the second place, a high degree of adverse selection is associated with applications received at those ages. Low volume in itself is suggestive of adverse selection; but when it is accompanied by burdensome premium payments, the environment is even more conducive to adverse selection. This antiselection may be exercised by the insured himself, aware of a serious impairment, or by a third party, perhaps a relative, who seeks insurance on the life of an elderly person for speculative reasons. A third factor, related to the others, is the relative ineffectiveness of the medical examination at the older ages. A routine medical examination does not reveal many conditions of a degenerative nature that can materially shorten the life of the elderly applicant. The story of the elderly person who passes a rigorous medical examination one day only to die the following day is a familiar one.

In the light of these circumstances, all companies establish an age limit—typically, sixty-five or seventy—beyond which they will not accept applications and, in addition, drastically grade down the amount of insurance which they will write on applicants approaching the age limit.

CHAPTER XX

Insurance of Substandard Risks

THROUGH the operation of the numerical rating system or some other method of rating, certain risks considered by an insurance company are classified as substandard. This means that a *group* or *classification* of risks so constituted is expected to produce a higher mortality than that found among a group of normal lives. The group concept must be emphasized, since—as in the insuring of standard risks—there is no certainty concerning the longevity expectations of one individual. All calculations are based on the anticipated *average* experience of a large number of individuals, and the experience of any one individual is merged into that of the group.

This is an elementary concept; but it needs to be reiterated in any consideration of substandard insurance, involving, as it does, extra cost to the policyholder. It is commonly supposed that if an individual is placed in a substandard classification and subsequently lives to a ripe old age, the company erred in its treatment of the case. However, if 1,000 persons, each of whom is suffering from a particular physical impairment, are granted insurance, it is *certain* that the death rate among them will be greater than that among a group of persons of the same age who are free of any discernible impairments. In order to provide for the higher death rates which will certainly occur within the substandard group, the company must collect an extra premium from—or impose special terms on—all who are subject to the extra

419

risk, since it is not known which of the members of the group will be responsible for the extra mortality. It is not expected that every member of the group will survive a shorter period than the life expectancy of a normal person his age. In fact, it is a certainty that this will not be the case; it is known merely that a larger proportion of them will do so than in a normal group. The fact that certain members of the impaired group reach old age is, therefore, no indication that an error was made in their cases. If they had paid no extra premium, a still higher premium would have been required from the others. Generally speaking, nothing could—or should—be refunded to those members of a substandard group who live beyond the normal "expectation," provided that the extra premium charged or other special terms imposed were a true measure of the degree of extra hazard represented by the group.

INCIDENCE OF EXTRA RISK

If a group of substandard lives is to be fairly treated, not only must the degree of extra mortality represented by the group be known within reasonable limits, but also the approximate period in life when the extra mortality is likely to occur. It makes a great deal of difference financially whether the extra claims are expected to occur primarily in early life, middle age, or old age, or at a level rate throughout the lifetime of the individuals. If the extra mortality occurs during the early years of the policies when the amount at risk is relatively large, the burden on the company will be greater than if it should occur at the later durations when the amount at risk is relatively small. Hence, as between two substandard groups representing the same aggregate amount of extra mortality, that group whose extra mortality is concentrated at the later durations should pay a smaller extra premium than that whose extra mortality occurs earlier.

Innumerable variations are to be found in the distribution of the extra risk among the different classes of substandard lives. It is impractical, however, for the companies to recognize all the many patterns of risk distribution. The majority of companies, therefore, proceed on the assumption that each substandard risk falls into one of three broad groups. In the first group, the additional hazard increases with age; in the second group, it remains approximately constant at all ages; in the third, it decreases with age.

Examples of each of these types of hazard are easily found. High blood pressure is an example of an impairment which presents an increasing hazard. Occupational hazards are considered to represent a constant hazard, as are certain types of physical defects. Actually, most of these hazards tend to increase somewhat with age, but they are treated as if they were constant. Impairments attributable to past illnesses and surgical operations are prime examples of a hazard that decreases with time, although all illnesses cannot be so regarded.

TREATMENT OF SUBSTANDARD RISKS

Several methods have been devised to provide insurance protection to impaired lives. With the exception of the lien, most companies utilize all the available methods. In general, an effort is made to adapt the method to the type of hazard represented by the impaired risk, but departures from theoretically correct treatment of the risk are frequently made for practical reasons.

Increase in Age

One method of treatment, widely used in the past and still favored by many companies, is to *rate up* the age of the applicant. Under this method, the applicant is assumed to be a number of years older than his real age, and the policy is written accordingly. The number of years to be added is usually determined by adding to the net premium for the applicant's actual age an amount estimated to be necessary to provide for the extra mortality involved and then ascertaining the insurance age the net premium for which most closely approximates the sum of the first two amounts. For example, the net level premium for an ordinary life contract issued at age twenty-five is, according to the 1958 C.S.O. Table and 2½ per cent interest, $12.55 per $1,000. If an applicant for such a contract, aged twenty-five, should be placed in a substandard classification which is expected to produce an extra mortality equivalent to $3.67, the correct net premium for the applicant would be $16.22 per $1,000. The net level premium in the standard table closest to this amount is $16.43, which is the premium for age thirty-three. Therefore, the applicant is rated up eight years and is thereafter treated in all respects as if he were thirty-three years of age. His policy would contain the same surrender and loan values, and would be entitled to the same dividends, if any, as any other ordinary life contract issued at age thirty-three.

This method of dealing with substandard risks is suitable only when the extra risk is of a decidedly increasing type and continues to increase indefinitely at a greater rate. This can be demonstrated by reference to a group of substandard risks, aged twenty-five, who are rated up to age thirty. Since the death rate at age twenty-five, according to the 1958 C.S.O. Table, is 1.93 per 1,000 and the rate at age thirty is 2.13, provision is made for only 0.20 of one extra death per 1,000 during the first year of insurance. By the tenth year, however, the margin has more than quadrupled, being the difference between 2.40 at actual age thirty-four and 3.25 at assumed age thirty-nine, or 0.85 per 1,000. Thirty years later, the margin has increased to 6.69 per 1,000. Moreover, the higher the age at issue, the more rapidly the margin for additional mortality increases. If the true age of the applicants in the foregoing example had been thirty-five, the extra deaths per 1,000 provided for during the first, tenth, and thirtieth years would have been 0.74, 2.68, and 16.57, respectively.

Although few impairments give rise to such a consistent and rapid increase in the rate of mortality as is provided for by the rated-up age method, the method is considered to be appropriate for all types of substandard risks where the extra mortality, *in general,* increases with age.

The chief appeal of the method, from the standpoint of the insurance company, is its simplicity. The policies can be dealt with for all purposes as standard policies issued at the assumed age, no separate set of records being required. No special calculations of premium rates, cash and other surrender values, reserves, and dividends are involved. From the standpoint of the applicant, the method is attractive, in that his higher premium is accompanied by correspondingly higher surrender values and dividends (if participating). Thus, a portion of each extra premium is refunded as a dividend, and another portion is applied to the accumulation of larger surrender values that would be available under a policy issued at the true age. If the policy is surrendered for cash, the additional cash value is equivalent to a refund of a portion of the extra premium paid. In order to protect themselves against the use of the surrender privilege for this purpose, some companies add a slight loading to the original extra premium.

Endowment policies do not lend themselves to this method quite as readily as do the other types of policies. If the contract is written for a relatively short term, and particularly if it matures at a comparatively young age, the amount of extra mortality provided for, even by a substantial increase in age, may be very small. Unless the policy is a long-term endowment or is issued at a relatively high age, the number of years that must be added to the true age of the applicant may be so great as to appear unreasonable to the applicant. On the other hand, the amount of extra mortality that must be taken care of under endowment contracts in general is likely to be lower than that under other types of contracts because of the smaller amount at risk per $1,000 of face amount and the frequent maturity of the contracts before the period of greatest extra mortality.

Extra Percentage Tables

A more common method of dealing with risks which present an increasing hazard is to classify them into groups on the basis of the *percentage* of standard mortality to be expected, and to charge premiums that reflect the appropriate increase in mortality. The number of substandard classifications may vary from three to twelve, depending to some extent upon the degree of extra mortality the company is willing to underwrite. Some companies are unwilling to underwrite substandard groups whose average mortality is expected to exceed 200 per cent of standard; and they usually establish three substandard classifications with expected average mortality of 150, 175, and 200 per cent, respectively. A scale of substandard classifications, widely used by companies offering coverage up to 500 per cent of standard mortality, is shown below:

Class	Mortality (Per Cent)	Class	Mortality (Per Cent)
A......	125	F......	250
AA......	137½	G......	275
B......	150	H......	300
C......	175	J......	350
D......	200	L......	400
E......	225	P......	500

In effect, a special mortality table, reflecting the appropriate degree of extra mortality, is prepared for each substandard classification, and a complete set of gross premium rates is computed for the classification. The gross premium rates at quinquennial ages quoted by one company for an ordinary life contract under Substandard Tables A, B, C, and D, are set forth in Table 32. For purposes of comparison, the rate for a standard risk at each quinquennial age is also given.

Perhaps the most notable feature of these premiums is that they do

TABLE 32

ILLUSTRATIVE GROSS ANNUAL PREMIUM RATES AT QUINQUENNIAL
AGES FOR ORDINARY LIFE CONTRACT UNDER SUBSTANDARD TABLES
A, B, C, AND D

AGE	RATE FOR STANDARD RISKS	SUBSTANDARD TABLES			
		A (125 Per Cent)	B (150 Per Cent)	C (175 Per Cent)	D (200 Per Cent)
15.........	$14.46	$15.74	$16.67	$ 17.53	$ 18.37
20.........	16.15	17.62	18.67	19.68	20.63
25.........	18.21	19.90	21.15	22.33	23.45
30.........	20.81	22.82	24.33	25.75	27.12
35.........	24.14	26.56	28.41	30.19	31.88
40.........	28.45	31.38	33.70	35.93	38.07
45.........	34.01	37.59	40.50	43.32	46.04
50.........	41.31	45.69	49.40	52.99	56.48
55.........	50.99	56.41	61.11	65.71	70.22
60.........	64.03	70.74	76.73	82.67	88.54
65.........	81.82	90.08	97.69	105.34	112.97

not increase in proportion to the degree of extra mortality involved. That is, the rates under Table D, for example, are not double the rates at which insurance is made available to standard risks. Neither are the rates under Table B one and a half times the standard rates. There is a twofold explanation of this apparent inconsistency. In the first place, the rates illustrated in Table 32 are *gross* premium rates, and the amount of the loading does not increase from one rate classification to the other, except for commissions and premium taxes. The loading remains constant, with minor exceptions. In the second place, the percentage of extra mortality is computed on the basis of *actual—* rather than *tabular—*mortality. The premiums for standard risks are calculated on the basis of the 1958 C.S.O. Table, which contains a considerable overstatement of mortality at the young and middle ages; but the additions to the standard premium to arrive at the substandard rates reflect only the excess of the mortality for the substandard classifications over the *actual* mortality of the standard risks. Hence, the rates for the substandard classifications are not proportionally greater than even the *net* premiums for the standard risks.

The extra mortality provided for under this method is relatively small at the early ages, unless the percentage of extra mortality is high, since the normal or base rate of mortality at such ages is small. As the base death rate increases, however, the margin for extra mortality increases very greatly. This explains why the method is appropriate for substandard risks whose impairments are expected to produce an increasing rate of extra mortality. Like the increase-in-age method, substandard tables should, in theory, be used only when the hazard is expected to increase at an *increasing* rate; but in practice, they are used for all types of impairments which are expected to grow worse as the years go by.

The reserves under policies issued in accordance with extra percentage tables must be calculated on the basis of the mortality assumptions underlying the premiums, requiring separate classification records and tabulations. Surrender values may be based on the special mortality table or may be the same as those allowed under policies issued to standard risks, depending upon company practice and state law. Many companies do not make extended term insurance available under extra percentage table policies, especially at the higher percentages; and those that do, compute the period on the basis of the higher mortality rate, even when only the normal surrender value is allowed.

Extra percentage tables are sometimes used as a basis for determining the extra premiums needed under other methods of underwriting substandard risks. Thus, the risk may first be assigned to an extra percentage table, after which the rating is translated into the equivalent age markup. This is a convenient method of determining the necessary step-up in age when statistics are available as to the additional mortality to be expected from a particular impairment.

Flat Extra Premium

A third method of underwriting substandard risks is through the assessment of a flat extra premium. Under this method, the standard premium for the policy in question is increased by a specified number of dollars per $1,000 of insurance. Assessed as a measure of the extra mortality involved, the flat extra premium does not vary with the age of the applicant. It may be paid throughout the premium-paying period of the policy or may be terminated after a period of years, after the extra hazard has presumably disappeared.

The flat extra premium method is normally used when the hazard is thought to be constant—as with deafness, partial blindness, and so forth; or decreasing—as with a family history of tuberculosis or the aftermath of a serious illness or surgical operation. It is widely used to cover the extra risk associated with certain occupations. When used for this purpose, the extra premium usually ranges from $2.50 to $10 per $1,000 of insurance. Unless a permanent impairment is involved, the extra premium is generally removed if the insured leaves the hazardous occupation.

At first blush, a flat extra premium for an extra hazard that adds an approximately constant amount to the rate of mortality at each age would appear to be a fair arrangement. In practice, however, it works out equitably only if an allowance is made for the fact that under most policies, the amount at risk is not a level sum. Except for term policies, the net amount at risk decreases with each year that elapses. Thus, a flat extra premium becomes an increasing percentage of the amount at risk and, in effect, provides for an increasing extra risk.

When the extra risk is constant, the extra premium for a whole life or endowment contract should diminish each year in the proportion that the amount at risk decreases. In order to avoid the labor and expense that would be involved in such an annual adjustment, and in recognition of the fact that the flat extra premium is of necessity an approximation, most companies compute the flat extra addition on the basis of the *average* amount at risk. Some companies vary the extra premium with the plan of insurance, charging less for endowment policies than for policies with lower reserve elements.

The flat extra premium is not reflected in policy values and dividends. It is assumed that the entire amount of the extra premium is needed each year to pay additional claims and expenses, the dividends and guaranteed values being identical with those of a comparable policy without extra premium. Thus, the policyholder must regard the flat extra premium as an irrecoverable outlay, except through premature death.

Liens

When the extra mortality to be expected from an impairment is of a distinctly decreasing and temporary nature, such as that associated with convalescence from a serious illness, neither an increase in age, a percentage addition to the rate of mortality, nor a flat extra premium is an appropriate method of dealing with the risk. A more suitable method—from a theoretical standpoint, at least—is that of creating a lien against the policy for a number of years, the amount and term of the lien depending upon the extent of the impairment. If adequate statistics are available, it is possible to calculate the term and amount of the lien which would be the equivalent of the extra risk undertaken. If such a method is utilized, the policy is issued at standard rates and is standard in all respects except that, should death occur before the end of the period specified, the amount of the lien is deducted from the proceeds otherwise payable. The method is frequently refined to provide for a yearly reduction in the amount of the lien, on the theory that the hazard is of a decreasing nature.

The lien method is presumed to have a psychological appeal, in that few persons who are refused insurance at standard rates believe themselves to be substandard risks and the others tend to be resentful of the company's action. If the only penalty involved is a temporary reduction in the amount of protection, most applicants are willing to go along with the company's decision, confident that they will survive the period of the lien and thus "prove" the company to have been wrong. The plan appeals to the applicant's sporting instinct.

A practical and serious disadvantage of the method is that a comparatively large lien is necessary to offset a relatively small degree of extra mortality. Furthermore, the reduction occurs in the early years of the policy, when the need for protection is presumably the greatest. Frequently, the beneficiary has no knowledge of the lien; and the failure of the company to pay the face of the policy may be the source of great disappointment and resentment, to the detriment of the company's reputation in the community. There is also a possibility that such liens are in conflict with laws in certain states which prohibit any provision which would permit the company to settle a death claim with a payment smaller than the face amount. These are known as "no-lesser-amounts" statutes.

The lien system has not been widely used in the United States,[1] but is used extensively in Canada and Great Britain.

Other Methods

A method of dealing with substandard risks when the degree of extra mortality is small or when its nature is not well known is to make no extra charge but to place all of the members of the group in a special class for dividend purposes, adjusting the dividends in accordance with the actual experience. It is apparent that this method can accommodate only those impairments which produce an extra mortality not in excess of the normal dividend payments. Moreover,

---

[1] The *concept* of the lien is used by many companies in connection with pension trusts. Whenever an eligible employee cannot qualify for insurance on a standard basis, the premium can remain unchanged, with the amount of protection being appropriately reduced. If the extra risk is assumed to be temporary, the policy, *in form,* provides an increasing death benefit, rather than a declining lien.

a sufficiently large number of such risks must be underwritten to yield an average experience.

Some impairments can be dealt with by merely limiting the plan of insurance. The extra mortality associated with some impairments is largely postponed to advanced middle age or old age. Such impairments could be underwritten at no extra charge by endowment contracts maturing before the impact of the extra mortality. Moderate overweight is typical of impairments adaptable to the endowment plan at standard rates.

A negative illustration of this approach is found in the almost universal refusal of the companies to offer term insurance on a substandard basis.

REMOVAL OF SUBSTANDARD RATING

It frequently happens that a person who is classified as a substandard risk and insured on that basis by one company subsequently applies for insurance with another company, or even the same company, and is found to be a standard risk in all respects. Under such circumstances, the natural reaction of a person is to request the removal of the substandard rating. The question is whether the company should remove the rating.

Theoretically, the rating should not be removed, unless the impairment on which it was based was known to be temporary or was due to occupation or residence. At the time the policy was originally issued, the petitioner was placed in a special classification of risks, the members of which were presumably impaired to approximately the same degree. It was known by the company that some of the members of the group would die within a short period, while others would survive far beyond their normal expectancy. It was likewise known that the health of some of the members would deteriorate with the passage of time, while some would grow more robust. By the time the insured under consideration had been found in normal health, the health of many others in his original group had undoubtedly worsened. Many of them could not now get insurance on any terms, while others would be insurable only at a greater extra premium than that charged. If the company is to reduce the premiums of those whose health has improved, it should be permitted to increase the premiums of those whose health has deteriorated. Since the premiums of those in the latter category cannot be adjusted upward, the premiums of those in the former category should not be reduced.

As a practical matter, the company is virtually forced to remove the substandard rating of one who can demonstrate that he is currently insurable at standard rates. If it does not do so, the policyholder will almost surely surrender his extra rate insurance and replace it with insurance at standard rates in another company. Knowing this, most companies calculate their substandard premiums in the first instance on the assumption that the extra premium will have to be removed on those persons who subsequently qualify for standard insurance. Thus, the common practice is to remove the extra premium upon proof by the insured that he is no longer substandard.

Where an extra premium has been imposed on account of occupation, residence, or a risk which is temporary in nature, it is proper to discontinue the extra premium upon termination of the condition which created the extra hazard without prior adjustment in the substandard premium. It is necessary to exercise care in such cases, however, particularly when the source of the rating was occupation or residence. There is always a possibility that the insured may subsequently return to the hazardous occupation or residence, or that his health was affected adversely. Hence, it is customary in such cases to require that a specified period of time, such as one or two years, shall have elapsed after cessation of the extra hazard before the rating will be removed; and occasionally, a medical examination is required. At the end of such period, the adjustment is usually made retroactively to the change of occupation or residence.

VALUE OF SUBSTANDARD INSURANCE

The majority of life insurance companies on the North American continent provide insurance to substandard risks. Several important companies which formerly confined their operations to standard risks are now willing to accept substandard risks. Some of the companies, however, refer to insurance on substandard lives as *classified* insurance rather than *extra rate* or *substandard* insurance. There is a natural reluctance on the part of some to call such business "substandard insurance," since the term suggests that the insurance is lacking in some of the essential qualities of standard insurance. This, of course, is not the case.

Substandard insurance is of great social importance, since it makes insurance protection available to millions of American families which would otherwise be without it. Approximately 10 per cent of all new policies are on a substandard basis. Extensive investigations into the rates of mortality prevailing among various types of substandard groups are continually being undertaken, resulting in further extensions of this class of business and in revisions of the terms upon which the insurance is offered. It is perhaps fair to conclude that life insurance is now available to all except those subject to such excessive rates of mortality as to entail premiums beyond their ability or willingness to pay.

CHAPTER XXI

Reinsurance

REINSURANCE is a device by which one insurance company or insurer transfers all or a portion of its risk under an insurance policy or a group of policies to another company or insurer. The company which issued the policy in the first instance is called the *direct-writing* or *ceding* company, while the company or organization to which the risk is transferred is called the *assuming* company, or *reinsurer*. The act of transferring the insurance from the direct-writing company to the reinsurer is called the cession.[1] If the reinsurer should, in turn, transfer to one or more companies all or a portion of the risk assumed from the ceding company, the transaction is referred to as the *retrocession*. Thus, the original insurer *cedes* insurance to a reinsurer, which may then *retrocede* the coverage to still other companies.

PURPOSE OF REINSURANCE

In life insurance, reinsurance may be undertaken for one of two broad reasons: (1) to transfer all or a specific portion of a company's liabilities or (2) to accomplish certain broad managerial objectives, including favorable underwriting results and the reduction of surplus drain from the writing of new business. Reinsurance undertaken for the purpose of transferring all or a substantial portion of a company's liabilities is called *portfolio* or *assumption* reinsurance. Reinsurance arranged for general business purposes is referred to as *indemnity* reinsurance.

Assumption Reinsurance

Assumption reinsurance may be undertaken for a number of reasons. A traditional use—but one, fortunately, which is becoming of

---

[1] The term "cession" also refers to a document executed by the ceding company in accordance with the reinsurance agreement which describes the risk being transferred and provides a schedule of reinsurance premiums and allowances, if any.

less importance—has been to bail out insurance companies that find themselves in financial difficulties. Rather than liquidate the company, with almost certain losses to policyholders, a procedure is frequently worked out whereby a solvent insurer will assume the policy liabilities of the company in distress in exchange for the assets underlying the liabilities and the right to receive future premiums under the policies. If the assets are not sufficient to offset the liabilities—a likely circumstance—the reinsurer may place a lien against the cash values of the ceded policies until the deficiency can be liquidated through earnings on the policies. Another situation in which all the business of one company may be ceded to another is that arising out of a merger.

In many instances, assumption reinsurance involves only a segment of the business of the ceding company. For example, a combination company[2] may decide to restrict its future operations to ordinary insurance and arrange to cede all of its outstanding industrial business to another company. Likewise, a company may decide to withdraw from one or more states and, in so doing, prefer to reinsure all policies outstanding in that geographical area. Assumption reinsurance is always tailored to the particular facts and requirements of the case under consideration and does not lend itself to generalization. Hence, it will not be further discussed in this volume.

Indemnity Reinsurance

Indemnity reinsurance is characterized by a whole series of independent transactions whereby the ceding insurer transfers its liability with respect to individual policies, in whole or in part, to the reinsurer. It is extremely widespread and may be resorted to for any one of several reasons.

The most fundamental and prevalent use of indemnity reinsurance is to avoid too large a concentration of risk on one life. All companies, including the giants of the industry, have deemed it prudent to limit the amount of insurance which they will retain on any one life. These maxima, called *retention limits,* reflect the judgment of company management as to many factors, but are strongly influenced by the volume of insurance in force, amount of surplus funds,[2a] and proficiency of the underwriting personnel. The limits range from $1,000

---

[2] One which writes both ordinary and industrial insurance.

[2a] A rule-of-thumb, subject to many exceptions, is that the retention limit should be equal to 1 per cent of capital and surplus.

in small, recently established companies to well over $1,000,000 in the largest companies.[3] There may be various limits within one company, depending upon plan, age at issue, sex, and substandard classification. The retention tends to be smaller at the lower and upper age groups and for plans under which the risk element is relatively large. It is clearly to the interest of a company to retain as much of the risk as is consistent with safety, so the retention limit or limits are usually raised as the insurance in force and amount of surplus funds grow. In order to remain competitive and to retain the services of a qualified agency force, a company must be in a position to accept applications for any reasonable amount of insurance, irrespective of its retention limit. Thus, a company must have facilities for transferring amounts of insurance in excess of that which it is willing to retain at its own risk.

A closely related use of reinsurance, as yet limited in scope but receiving increasing attention, is to stabilize the over-all mortality experience of the ceding company. This function is associated with so-called nonproportional reinsurance, one form of which transfers to the reinsurer all or a specified percentage of that portion of aggregate mortality claims for a given period in excess of a stipulated norm. Another form of nonproportional reinsurance provides protection against an undesirable concentration of risk on several lives, such as might be found among the passengers of a jet airliner or the employees of an industrial plant.

A third use of indemnity reinsurance is to reduce the drain on surplus caused by the writing of new business. It was pointed out earlier that the expenses of putting a new policy on the books greatly exceeds the first year gross premium. This alone creates a drain on surplus, but when the insurer must also set aside funds to cover all or a portion of the first year reserve, the strain is intensified. Under certain plans of reinsurance (to be discussed later), the burden of meeting first-year expenses and reserve requirements can be shifted to the reinsurer, thus permitting the ceding company to write all the acceptable business produced by its agency forces.

A fourth use of indemnity reinsurance is to take advantage of the underwriting judgment of the reinsurer. This is most likely to occur in connection with applications from impaired lives. Some types of im-

---

[3] Some newly established companies reinsure all their business for a number of years, although the companies may be motivated by reasons other than, or in addition to, the avoidance of mortality risk.

pairments are encountered so infrequently that even the largest companies do not have much opportunity to develop any experience with them. Those responsible for the selection of risks, upon encountering such an impairment, cannot evaluate the risk with the same degree of confidence that they feel in dealing with the more common varieties of impaired risks. For the sake of their own peace of mind, they are likely to seek the benefit of reinsurance, knowing that the selection of impaired risks is a special service of reinsurance companies. Even though the impairment is a common one and the underwriter has no hesitation about classifying the risk, he may submit the case to a reinsurer to demonstrate to the soliciting agent that the most favorable terms were granted.

A fifth application of indemnity insurance, closely related to the fourth, is to transfer all policies of substandard insurance. This use is brought into play when the ceding company does not write substandard insurance on any basis. Yet, in order to offer a full range of services to its agency force, the company may work out an arrangement whereby it can channel all applications from substandard risks to a reinsurer equipped to classify and underwrite such risks. A variation of this arrangement is to reinsure all policies of substandard insurance that fall within a class above some stipulated percentage of anticipated mortality, such as 200 per cent.

A company may also enter into a reinsurance agreement with another company in order to receive advice and counsel on underwriting matters, rates, and policy forms. This purpose is usually associated with small, newly organized companies which cannot afford a large enough staff to deal with all aspects of its operations. The relationship between the ceding company and the reinsurer is such that the latter becomes thoroughly conversant with the operations of the ceding company and is in a position to provide expert advice. While extremely valuable, this service of indemnity reinsurance is usually subsidiary to the fundamental function of spreading the risk.

Finally, in connection with group insurance and pension plans, the company with which the master contract is placed may transfer portions of the coverage to several other insurers under instructions from the policyholder. Such an arrangement is specially fashioned and arises because the policyholder, for business reasons, wishes to divide the coverage among several insurers while looking to one for over-all administration of the case.

PROPORTIONAL REINSURANCE

A number of plans have been developed for the transacting of indemnity reinsurance. The basic or traditional plans, designed for individual risks, may be characterized as *proportional reinsurance,* since under these plans a claim under a reinsured policy is shared by the ceding company and the reinsurer in a proportion determined in advance. The precise manner in which a claim payment is shared by the ceding company and the reinsurer depends upon the type of plan employed.

Types of Plans

Proportional reinsurance is provided under two distinct plans: yearly renewable term insurance and coinsurance. A variation of the latter plan, called modified coinsurance, has also been developed.

Yearly Renewable Term Insurance. The yearly renewable term plan derives its name from the fact that the ceding company—in effect —purchases term insurance, on a yearly renewable basis, from the reinsurer. The amount of term insurance purchased in connection with any particular reinsurance transaction is the net amount at risk year by year under the face amount of insurance ceded to the reinsurer. This can be illustrated by a $50,000 ordinary life policy issued at age thirty-five by a company with a retention limit of $10,000. Under such circumstances, $40,000 of insurance would ostensibly be ceded to the reinsurer. However, in the event of the insured's death, the reinsurer would pay, not $40,000 but only the net amount of risk under a $40,000 policy. If the insured should die during the first policy year, the reinsurer would be liable for $40,000 less $659.60, the first-year terminal reserve[4] under the policy in question. If he should die during the eighth policy year, the reinsurer would remit $34,480.40, the face amount less the eighth-year terminal reserve of $5,519.60. The reserves under the $40,000 of life insurance ceded to the reinsurer would be held by the direct-writing company and, in the

---

[4] The full net level premium reserve under the 1958 C.S.O. Table and $2\frac{1}{2}$ per cent interest. Small and medium-sized companies, which are an important segment of the reinsurance market, almost invariably use the Commissioners Reserve Valuation Method. On that reserve basis, there would be no reserve under an ordinary life policy at the end of the first year, so that the amount at risk would be the face of the policy.

event of the insured's death, would be added to the remittance of the reinsurer to make up the full payment of $40,000 due under the reinsured portion of the original policy. The ceding company would, of course, be solely responsible for payment of the $10,000 of coverage retained by it—which, in turn, would be composed of the net amount at risk and the accumulated reserves under $10,000 of coverage.

Whenever a policy is to be reinsured on a yearly renewable term basis, either the ceding company or the reinsurer prepares a schedule of the amount at risk for each policy year under the face amount being ceded. The reinsurer quotes a schedule of yearly renewable term premium rates which will be applied to the net amount at risk year by year. These rates are extremely competitive and usually reflect the lower mortality associated with the selection process. The premiums are generally graded upward with duration, a wide variety of schedules being found. Some schedules grade the premium upward over as long a period as fifteen years. There may be no charge, other than a policy fee of nominal amount, e.g., $5 or $10, for the first year of reinsurance coverage. The premium schedule may also reflect, through a policy fee or in some other manner, the amount of insurance involved. The expense loading is lower than in direct premiums, since the ceding company pays all commissions, medical fees, and other acquisition expenses connected with the policy. (Under most reinsurance agreements, the premium tax is borne by the reinsurer in the form of a "refund" to the ceding company.) As a further cost concession, some agreements of this type provide that the ceding company shall share in any mortality savings on the business ceded.[5]

Since it holds all the reserves, the ceding company is responsible for surrender values, policy loans, and other prematurity benefits.

A number of advantages are associated with the yearly renewable term basis of reinsurance. It permits the ceding company to retain most of the premiums, giving rise to a more rapid growth in assets—a matter of special concern to small and medium-sized companies. For the same reason, it may be favored when the reinsurer is not licensed to transact business in the domiciliary state of the ceding company, which would mean that the latter would not be permitted to deduct the reserves on the reinsured policies from its over-all reserve liability. (This same situation may lead to the use of a modified coinsurance arrangement.) This plan of reinsurance is also easier to administer

---

[5] See p. 445.

than the more complicated coinsurance arrangements. Finally, it is thought to be more suitable for nonparticipating insurance where costs are fixed in advance.

Coinsurance. Under the coinsurance plan, the ceding company transfers the proportion of the face amount of insurance called for in the cession form; but the reinsurer is responsible, not for just the net amount at risk, but for its prorata share of the death claim. In the example cited under renewable term insurance, the reinsurer would be liable for the payment of $40,000, irrespective of the policy year in which the insured died. The reinsurer is also responsible for its prorata share of the cash surrender value and other surrender benefits. In effect, the reinsurer is simply substituted for the ceding company with respect to the amount of insurance reinsured.

The ceding company pays the reinsurer a prorata share of the gross premiums collected from the policyholder,[6] and the reinsurer accumulates and holds the policy reserves for the amount of insurance ceded. Inasmuch as the ceding company incurs heavy expenses in putting the original policy on the books, it is customary for the reinsurer to reimburse the direct-writing company for the expenses attributable to the amount of insurance reinsured. This reimbursement takes the form of a "ceding commission," which includes an allowance for commissions paid to the soliciting agent of the ceding company, premium taxes paid to the state of domicile of the insured[7] and a portion of the overhead expenses of the ceding company. This latter adjustment recognizes the fact that not only does a reinsurer incur relatively lower expenses on that portion of the face amount assumed by it, but the average amount of insurance per reinsurance certificate is larger than the average size of the ceding insurer's policy. Hence, the administrative expense per $1,000 of insurance is lower on that portion of the insurance reinsured than on the normal business of the ceding company, and the reinsurer is willing to share the saving with the company which originated the business. There is normally no sharing of medical and other selection expenses, on the theory that such expenses are incurred on a per policy basis and vary only slightly with the amount

---

[6] There are exceptions to this practice. Sometimes, when the ceding insurer offers both participating and nonparticipating policies, all reinsurance will be arranged on the basis of the ceding company's nonparticipating gross premium rates, in order to avoid the complexity of dividend accounting.

[7] In most—if not all—states, the ceding company is not permitted to deduct premium taxes on amounts of insurance transferred to reinsurers. By the same token, reinsurers are not required to pay premium taxes on insurance assumed under reinsurance agreements.

of insurance. The amount of the ceding commission is negotiated between the ceding insurer and the reinsurer.

If the original policy is participating, the reinsurer must pay dividends on the portion of insurance assumed by it according to the dividend scale of the ceding company. This can prove burdensome if the net investment earnings of the reinsurer do not approximate those of the ceding company, or if the mortality under the ceded policies is not as favorable as that underlying the dividend scale. As a matter of fact, the mortality rates on reinsured policies as a whole tend to be higher than those on direct business, possibly due to the larger amounts of insurance involved and the less rigid underwriting standards of the many small and medium-sized companies which rely heavily on reinsurance. The anticipated higher mortality is taken into account in arriving at the ceding commission.

In the event that the original policy is terminated voluntarily, the reinsurer is liable for its prorata share of the cash surrender value. If the policy is surrendered for reduced paid-up insurance, the reinsurer may remain liable for its proportionate share, or its share may be reduced through the payment to the ceding insurer of the appropriate cash surrender value. Should the policy be exchanged for extended term insurance, the reinsurer usually retains its proportionate share of liability, although its share may be reduced by any policy indebtedness. The reinsurer does not ordinarily participate in policy loans, settlement options, or installment settlements under family income or maintenance policies. The reinsurer's obligation in the event of the insured's death is discharged by a single-sum payment to the ceding company.

Modified Coinsurance.   Many companies regard the accumulation of substantial sums of money by the reinsurer as an unessential feature of a reinsurance arrangement and one which can be disadvantageous to the ceding company. Apart from the natural desire of a company to retain control of the funds arising out of its own policies, it may feel some apprehension about entrusting to another company the accumulation of funds necessary to discharge the ceding company's obligation under a policy. This apprehension is heightened by the knowledge that the basic liability of the ceding insurer to the policyholder or beneficiary is not affected by the inability of the reinsurer to make good on its obligation to the ceding company. This problem is of more immediate concern when the reinsurer is not licensed to operate in the home state of the ceding company, since in many states, the latter would not be permitted to include as assets in its balance sheet sums due from the reinsurer. These considerations have led to a modification of the coinsurance method, under which the ceding company retains the entire reserve under the reinsured policy.

Under this arrangement, the ceding company pays the reinsurer a proportionate part of the gross premium, as under the conventional coinsurance plan, less whatever allowances have been arranged for commissions, premium taxes, and overhead. At the end of each policy year, however, the reinsurer pays over to the ceding company a sum equal to the net increase in the reserve during the year, less one year's interest on the reserve at the beginning of the year. In more precise terms, the reinsurer pays over an amount equal to the excess of the terminal reserve for the policy year in question over the terminal reserve for the preceding policy year, less interest on the initial reserve for the current policy year. It is necessary to credit the reinsurer with interest on the initial reserve, since a part of the increase in the reserve during the year is attributable to earnings on the funds underlying the reserve, which are held by the ceding company. The reserves are usually credited with interest at the rate used in the dividend formula of the ceding company or, in the case of nonparticipating insurance, a rate arrived at by negotiation.

It can be seen that under this arrangement, the reinsurer never holds more than the gross premium, as adjusted for allowances, for one year. Under one variation of this method, the anticipated increase in reserves is even deducted in advance from the gross premium.

In practice, when many reinsurance transactions are being consummated on the modified coinsurance plan, the foregoing adjustments are based on the *aggregate mean reserves,* rather than on the individual terminal reserves.

Apart from the reserve adjustment, the modified coinsurance basis is identical with the straight coinsurance basis, and the description of the coinsurance arrangement in the preceding section is equally applicable to the modified form.[8]

The modified coinsurance plan bears such a strong resemblance in net effect to the yearly renewable term basis of coinsurance that one might question why the former plan would ever be used. One answer lies in the fact that the premium paid by the ceding company is geared

---

[8] In the settlement of claims under the modified coinsurance plan, the reinsurer is charged with the face amount of insurance transferred to it, but credited with the reserve on that sum.

to the premium received from the policyholder, rather than being arrived at through negotiation. The second answer is more complex but rests upon the fact that under a modified coinsurance plan reinsurance costs reflect the incidence of expense and surplus drain incurred by the ceding company. Under the yearly renewable term plan, the ceding company is responsible for maintaining the reserves at the proper level, whereas under the modified coinsurance arrangement, the reinsurer, out of the premium received from the ceding company, must each year turn back a sum equal to the increase in reserves (less one year's interest on the reserve at the beginning of the year), as well as the ceding commission. Over the lifetime of the reinsured policy, the total cost of modified coinsurance and yearly renewable term should be approximately the same, but the net cost of reinsurance in the early years would normally be less under modified coinsurance.

Reinsurance Agreement

Arrangements between ceding insurers and reinsurers are generally formalized by a reinsurance agreement. Such agreements describe the classes of risk that will be subject to reinsurance, the extent of the reinsurer's liability, and the procedures by which the transactions are to be carried out. These agreements are broadly classified as *facultative* or *automatic*.

Types of Agreement. The facultative agreement establishes a procedure whereby the ceding insurer may offer risks to the reinsurer on an individual case basis. The essence of the arrangement is that the direct-writing company is under no obligation to cede—and the reinsurer is under no duty to accept—a particular risk. Each company reserves full freedom of action, and each risk is considered on its merits. The arrangement takes its name from the fact that each party retains the "faculty" to do as it pleases with respect to each specific risk. The automatic agreement, on the other hand, binds the ceding company to offer—and the reinsurer to accept—all risks which fall within the purview of the agreement. The agreement sets forth a schedule of the ceding insurer's limits of retention and provides that whenever the ceding company issues a policy for an amount in excess of the limit for such policy, the excess amount is to be insured automatically. The ceding company does not submit the underwriting papers to the reinsurer, and the latter does not have the option of accepting or rejecting the risk.[9]

---

[9] In recent years, there has been developed a modified type of automatic agreement under which the obligation of the reinsurer becomes fixed only after it has had

Under a facultative arrangement, the ceding company submits to the prospective reinsurer a copy of the application from the insured, together with all supporting documents. The ceding insurer also submits a form which specifies the basis on which reinsurance is desired and the proportion of the face amount which the originating company proposes to retain. This form, which constitutes the offer for reinsurance, supplies all information about the risk in the possession of the ceding company, including the amount of insurance already in force on the risk. The agreement normally provides that the reinsurer will notify the ceding company by telegram of its acceptance or rejection of the offer.

Under an automatic arrangement the reinsurer is obligated to accept a specified amount of reinsurance, including amounts for supplemental coverages, on the basis of the ceding company's underwriting appraisal. The maximum amount that can be ceded automatically to the reinsurer depends upon the quality of the ceding company's underwriting staff, as well as its limits of retention. It is fairly common for the reinsurer to obligate itself to accept automatically up to four times the retention of the ceding company. However, when the retention limits of the ceding company are fairly high, the reinsurer may limit its obligation to an amount equal to the ceding company's limit. The agreement specifies that the originating company will retain an amount of insurance equal to its retention limit and will not reinsure it elsewhere on a facultative basis.[10] In other words, if the ceding company should decide to retain less than the full retention indicated for the particular classification in which the risk falls, the reinsurer is relieved of its obligation under the automatic agreement and the entire transaction will have to be handled on a facultative basis. The agreement usually includes also a so-called "jumbo" clause, which stipulates that if the total amount of insurance in force on the life of an applicant in all companies—including policies applied for—exceeds a specified amount, reinsurance is not automatically effected. The agree-

---

an opportunity to screen its files for any unfavorable information relating to the risk. The ceding company sends the reinsurer a notice of intention to bind; and unless the latter notifies the ceding company of unfavorable information on the risk within a specified time, the reinsurance automatically goes into effect. This method, without slowing down the underwriting and issuing procedures of the ceding company, makes available to the issuing company the confidential files of the reinsurer, built up over many years of operation.

Moreover, there are some automatic agreements, under which the ceding company submits the underwriting papers to the reinsurer which has the option of declining to reinsure the risk.

[10] Such a provision is obviously not included in an agreement under which the ceding company is to transfer all amounts of substandard insurance written by it.

ment normally makes provision for facultative reinsurance of those risks not eligible, for one reason or another, for automatic reinsurance.

Cession Form. The reinsurance agreement stipulates that the ceding insurer, after delivering its policy to the insured and collecting the first premium, is to prepare a formal cession of reinsurance, in duplicate, which provides the details of the risk and schedule of reinsurance premiums, including the ceding commission, if any. One copy of the cession form goes to the reinsurer, while the other is retained by the ceding company. The form is identical for both facultative and automatic insurance. In effect, it is the individual contract of insurance; the entire reinsurance agreement is incorporated into it by reference.

The cession form describes the basis on which the reinsurance is being effected—i.e., whether it is yearly renewable term insurance, coinsurance, or modified coinsurance. If one of the coinsurance arrangements is being used, provision is made for the payment of a ceding commission to the direct-writing company.

Provision is also made for the manner in which premiums are to be paid. All premiums are generally payable on an annual basis subject to prorated refunds in the event of terminations other than on policy anniversaries. The reinsurer bills the ceding insurer monthly for reinsurance premiums falling due during that month. The bill also includes first-year premiums arising from cessions of reinsurance received since the date of the previous billing and refunds of premiums due to policy cancellations, as well as other small adjustments which arise from time to time.

Claims Settlement. The policyholder is not a party to the reinsurance agreement and looks to the issuing company to fulfill the obligation of the contract.[11] Consequently, the reinsurance agreement stipulates that any settlement made by the ceding insurer with a claimant shall be binding upon the reinsurer,[12] whether the reinsurance was originally automatic or was accepted facultatively by the reinsurer. Despite this contractual right to settle claims at its discretion, the ceding insurer will invariably consult with the reinsurer in doubtful cases.

---

[11] Under portfolio reinsurance, policyholders are usually given the right to proceed directly against the reinsurer in pressing a claim for settlement.

[12] An exception is made when the entire risk is carried by the reinsurer. Under such circumstances, the agreement provides for consultation with the reinsurer before an admission or acknowledgement of a claim by the ceding company.

If the policy is to be settled on an installment basis, the reinsurer will nevertheless discharge its liability by the payment of a lump sum to the ceding company. This is true not only of settlement option arrangements but of contracts, such as the family income and retirement income policies, which provide for an installment basis of settlement. If a policy is settled for less than the face amount, such as might happen from a misstatement of age or the compromise of a claim of doubtful validity, the reinsurer shares in the saving. If the ceding company contests a claim, the reinsurer bears its proportionate share of the expenses incurred.

Reduction in the Sums Reinsured. Once a sum of insurance has been ceded, the reinsurer remains on the risk for that amount as long as the amount retained by the direct-writing company remains in force, subject to two important exceptions. One exception is concerned with those instances where the total amount of insurance on a particular risk is reduced after a portion of the insurance has been reinsured. This can result from the maturity or expiration of policies in accordance with their terms or through the voluntary termination of policies by nonpayment of premiums. Some agreements provide that the full amount of the reduction shall come out of the sum reinsured (up to the amount reinsured, of course), while other agreements call for proportionate reductions in the amounts held by the two insurers.

The other exception refers to increases in the ceding insurer's limits of retention and is of especial significance to young and growing companies. This provision states that if the ceding company should increase its limits of retention, it may make corresponding reductions in all reinsurance previously ceded. In the case of a $50,000 policy written by a company with a $10,000 retention limit, $40,000 would originally have been reinsured. If the ceding company should later increase its retention limit for that particular class of policy to $20,-000, it would be permitted to recover $10,000 of the $40,000 which it ceded. This procedure is referred to as the *recapture* of insurance.

Recapture is usually permitted only after the policies involved have been in force a specified period of time. This restriction is clearly designed to enable the reinsurer to recover its acquisition expenses. It is customary to restrict recapture of insurance ceded under a renewable term plan to policies in force for five or more years, while amounts ceded on a coinsurance basis must typically remain in force for ten or more years before being subject to recapture. The recapture provision provides an effective method of recovering amounts of insurance previously ceded when the ceding company holds the reserves, as under the yearly renewable term and modified coinsurance arrangements; but it may be ineffective under the coinsurance plan, since the reinsurer is obligated to release only the cash values—not the reserves—for the amounts recaptured. If there is a differential between the surrender value and the reserve under a policy, as there is likely to be, the ceding company may conclude that it is not worth while to recapture the insurance, at least until the differential is insignificant.

Duration of the Agreement. Subject to the provisions described in the preceding section, a reinsurance agreement remains effective with respect to policies reinsured as long as the original insurance continues in force. With respect to new insurance, however, most agreements make provision for cancellation by either party with ninety days' notice. During that period, the agreement remains in full force and effect, and the reinsurer with an automatic treaty must accept new cessions of insurance. It is anticipated that the ceding company can make other reinsurance arrangements within a period of ninety days.

Insolvency of the Ceding Insurer

In general, reinsurance agreements are regarded as contracts of indemnity, and the reinsurer's liability is measured by the actual loss sustained by the ceding insurer. An important exception is recognized in the case of insolvency of the ceding insurer. Virtually all agreements provide that the reinsurer must remit in full to an insolvent carrier which issued the original policy, even though the claim against the latter will have to be scaled down. Many states, including New York, will not permit a ceding company to treat amounts due from reinsurers as admitted assets, or to deduct reserves held by reinsurers from its policy liabilities, unless the reinusrance agreement requires the reinsurer to discharge its obligation in full in the event the ceding company should become insolvent.

It is important to note that a claimant under a reinsured policy issued by a company insolvent at the time of the claim is not permitted to bring action directly against the reinsurer but must look to the general assets of the insolvent carrier for the settlement of his claim. On the other hand, when the issuing company is insolvent, the reininsurer is given the specific right to contest claims against the ceding insurer in which it has an interest, with all defenses available to the ceding insurer being available to the reinsurer.

Experience Rating

It is becoming increasingly common for reinsurance agreements to contain a provision permitting a ceding company to share in any mortality gains or losses arising under policies ceded to the reinsurer. This is a form of experience rating found in many lines of insurance, including the various group coverages written by life companies. In this case, the ceding company is treated as the policyholder, and the mortality refund (or surcharge, as the case might be) is calculated on the combined experience under all policies ceded to a particular reinsurer. This practice was originated in the 1920's but was generally discontinued in the 1930's because of the disastrous claims experience on "jumbo" risks. In recent years, there has been renewed interest in the arrangement, and many variations in practice may be found. A common arrangement is to have the ceding insurer participate in any gains or losses on amounts of reinsurance below a specified limit and not participate in the experience on amounts in excess of such limit. The purpose of this variation is to permit the ceding company to share in the favorable mortality experience of the bulk of reinsured risks, but to avoid the undesirable fluctuations in its over-all experience that might result from unpredictably heavy mortality among very large risks. It should be observed that arrangements which permit the ceding company to share the gains from favorable mortality experience on reinsured risks lessen the importance of recapture provisions.

These mortality refunds are a matter of accounting between insurance companies and should not be confused with dividends to policyholders, although under participating policies, all or a portion of the savings may be passed on indirectly to policyholders. Agreements which provide for sharing of the mortality savings on reinsured risks with the ceding company are usually referred to as *experience rated* agreements.

Supplementary Coverages

The reinsurance agreement covering life risks may or may not apply to supplementary coverages, such as accidental death benefits and total disability benefits. If the basic agreement is facultative, it is likely to cover supplementary benefits as well as the life risk; if it is automatic, a separate agreement may be used for the supplementary coverages, particularly the accidental death benefits.

Many companies have lower limits of retention for accidental death benefits than for basic life risks. For example, a company may be willing to retain $40,000 of coverage under a basic life policy but only $10,000 of accidental death coverage. Therefore, a policy for $20,-000 with accidental death provisions would require reinsurance for the supplementary coverage, but none for the basic coverage. For this reason, the reinsurance of accidental death benefits may be set up under a special agreement.

The reinsurance may be provided on either a coinsurance or yearly renewable term basis, depending upon the plan used for basic life risks. If the coinsurance plan is used, the premium for the accidental death benefits is based on the premium charged the insured, less a first-year and renewal expense allowance. If the renewable term plan is used, the premium is usually a flat rate per $1,000, irrespective of age of issue or the type of contract issued to the policyholder. The benefits are reinsured on a level amount basis, since only nominal reserves are accumulated in connection with such coverage.

Disability benefits may likewise be reinsured on either a coinsurance or a yearly renewable term basis. The premium is the same as that charged the insured, less a first-year and renewal expense allowance. It is customary to limit the reinsurance of disability benefits to an amount not exceeding that attaching to the face amount of life coverage reinsured.

Substandard Reinsurance

The general principles governing reinsurance of standard risks are applicable to substandard insurance. For substandard reinsurance on either the coinsurance or the modified coinsurance basis, the ceding company pays the reinsurer appropriate portions of the additional premiums collected from the policyholder, subject to a ceding commission for reimbursement of the acquisition expenses of the direct-writing company. If the reinsurance is accomplished on the yearly renewable term basis and the substandard risk is classified according to a multiple of standard mortality, the reinsurance premiums are usually calculated on the same multiple of the standard reinsurance rate. If the policyholder were charged a flat extra premium, the ceding insurer would pay the reinsurer the same premium as for a standard risk, plus an appropriate share of the flat extra premium. The flat extra premiums, however, would not be reduced as the net amount at risk declines.

NONPROPORTIONAL REINSURANCE

The great bulk of life reinsurance is transacted on the basis of proportional reinsurance, as described above, but in recent years increasing interest has developed in an approach which relates the reinsurer's liability to the mortality experience on all or a specified portion of the ceding company's business, rather than to individual or specific policies of insurance. Widely used in property-casualty insurance, this approach is referred to as *nonproportional reinsurance,* since the proportion in which the ceding company and the reinsurer will share losses is not determinable in advance. This type of reinsurance coverage is available from both American and European reinsurers in three forms: *stop-loss reinsurance, catastrophe reinsurance,* and *spread loss reinsurance.*[13]

Stop-Loss Reinsurance

Stop-loss reinsurance is highly developed in casualty insurance but it is in a rudimentary stage of development as respects life insurance. Thus, the plan follows no fixed pattern, many variations being found. In essence, however, the arrangement undertakes to indemnify the ceding company if its mortality losses in the aggregate, or on specified segments of its business, exceed by a stipulated percentage what might be regarded as the normal or expected mortality. The agreements commonly invoke liability on the part of the reinsurer if the aggregate mortality of the ceding company exceeds by more than 10 per cent the "normal" mortality, which, of course, must be defined explicitly or implicitly in the agreement. Normal mortality is usually defined as a specified percentage of the tabular mortality for the categories of business covered by the agreement. Thus, if the mortality under the policies subject to a particular stop-loss reinsurance agreement is running around 50 per cent of the 1941 C.S.O. Table, the agreement

---

[13] For a comprehensive treatment of both the theoretical and practical aspects of nonproportional reinsurance, see Herbert Feay, "Introduction to Nonproportional Reinsurance," *Transactions of the Society of Actuaries,* Vol. XII (1960), pp. 22–48, and the discussion of the paper on pages 50–78. On pages 49–50, there is an extensive bibliography reflecting both American and European literature. A highly theoretical and mathematical treatment of the subject can be found in Paul M. Kahn, "An Introduction to Collective Risk Theory and Its Application to Stop-Loss Reinsurance," *Transactions of the Society of Actuaries,* Vol. XIV (1962), pp. 400–423. A nonquantitative description and critique of nonproportional insurance are contained in Walter W. Steffen, "Recent Developments in Life Reinsurance," *Journal of Risk and Insurance,* Vol. XXXI, No. 2 (1964), pp. 265–71.

might stipulate that the reinsurer shall absorb all losses in excess of 110 per cent of the normal level of mortality, defined as 50 per cent of the 1941 C.S.O. Table rates. Another manner of expressing the reinsurer's obligation is to provide that the reinsurer shall indemnify the ceding company for all claims in excess of a stipulated percentage of tabular mortality, such as 60 per cent of the 1941 C.S.O. Table.

Under some agreements the reinsurer indemnifies the ceding company for only a specified percentage, e.g., 90 per cent, of the excess mortality, an arrangement intended to encourage careful underwriting by the ceding company. Under most agreements, the reinsurer's liability during any contract period, generally a calendar year, is limited to a stipulated dollar amount. Under any of these arrangements, if the mortality for the contract period is below the level at which the reinsurer's obligation would attach, the latter makes no payment to the ceding company.

This approach to reinsurance lends itself to great flexibility, since the agreements can be written to cover only selected portions of the ceding company's business, varying levels of mortality, and periods of varying durations.

The premium for stop-loss reinsurance is arrived at by negotiation and involves the use of highly refined actuarial techniques, as well as a large element of judgment.

The basic appeal of this coverage is that it provides protection against adverse mortality experience arising out of an unexpectedly large number of small claims or an unexpected increase in the average size of claims. It is a form of reinsurance on the amounts at risk retained under conventional reinsurance agreements. Since the unit cost of protection under this approach is less than under proportional reinsurance, it is asserted that a company can reduce its total outlay for reinsurance by increasing its retention limits under conventional agreements and reinsuring the retained amounts under stop-loss arrangements. Other advantages associated with this approach are its flexibility (previously commented upon) and its relative ease of administration, attributable to the absence of individual policy records.

Adherents to conventional (proportional) reinsurance arrangements see many practical disadvantages to stop-loss reinsurance. They point out that it is "short term, rate adjustable, cancellable coverage" in contrast to the "long term, guaranteed renewable, fixed premium coverage" available under conventional arrangements. They call attention to the limit on the reinsurer's liability, as well as exclusion of the war risk. They emphasize the restrictions on the ceding company's underwriting practices necessarily imposed by the reinsurer. Finally, they question for a number of reasons whether any cost savings will, in fact, be realized in the long run.

At its present stage of development in the United States, stop-loss reinsurance serves primarily as a supplement to conventional reinsurance arrangements rather than as a substitute for them.

Catastrophe Reinsurance

Like stop-loss reinsurance, catastrophe reinsurance was first developed for property-casualty insurance lines. As its name implies, it usually provides for payment by the reinsurer of some fixed percentage, ranging from 90 to 100 per cent, of the aggregate losses (net of conventional reinsurance) in excess of a stipulated limit arising out of a single accident or catastrophic event, such as an airplane crash, explosion, fire, or hurricane. The level of losses at which the reinsurer's liability attaches may be expressed in terms of dollar amount or number of lives. The contract usually covers a period of one year and sets a limit on the reinsurer's liability for that period. The coverage is attractive to insurance companies that have a concentration of risks in one location, such as might arise under a group insurance policy. The risk involved is essentially accidental death attributable to a catastrophic occurrence.

While the reinsurer's liability under a catastrophe type of agreement is high, the probability of loss is low. Hence the premiums for this type of coverage are generally low. Moreover, being based on reasonably adequate data, they are more readily calculated than premiums for other forms of nonproportional reinsurance. The expense element of the premium is minimized through the use of aggregate reporting procedures.

Catastrophe reinsurance is clearly intended to serve only as a supplement to proportional reinsurance agreements.

Spread Loss Reinsurance

A final type of nonproportional reinsurance is the so-called spread loss reinsurance. Under an agreement of this type, the reinsurer collects an annual premium of a stipulated minimum amount, of which a certain portion, such as 20 per cent, is allocated to expenses and profit, with the balance being credited to an experience refund account until the latter reaches a specified maximum figure, such as the sum of three years' premiums. During any calendar year when the ceding company's aggregate death claims (net of conventional reinsurance payments) exceed a specified limit, the reinsurer pays the claims in excess of the limit, but adjusts the premium to reflect the claims experience. The agreement provides that any amounts paid by the reinsurer for a given year, plus 20 per cent, must be returned to the reinsurer by the ceding company during the next five years. The agreement can be terminated by either party, with proper notice, at the end of any contract year, except that the ceding company cannot terminate the arrangement under circumstances that would cause a loss to the reinsurer. In other words, the reinsurer must be permitted to recover all payments made to the ceding company.

It is apparent that the primary purpose of this type of reinsurance is to spread the financial effects of an unfavorable mortality experience in any one year over a period of five years. About the only risk taken by the reinsurer is the continued solvency of the ceding company. Consequently, the mathematical basis of the premium charge is completely different from the other two forms of nonproportional reinsurance.

Part Five

LEGAL ASPECTS OF LIFE INSURANCE

CHAPTER XXII

Fundamental
Legal
Concepts

IT IS not sufficient that a student or practitioner of life insurance understand only the economic and mathematical bases of the subject; he must also have a firm grasp of the basic legal relationships that have largely shaped its formal structure and influenced its content. The law of life insurance is derived predominantly from the general law of contracts; yet, the general law has been profoundly modified by the needs of the insurance business. On the one hand, the insurance companies have sought to condition and limit the risks which they assume; on the other hand, the insuring public has required and obtained protection against excessively legalistic interpretations of policy provisions by the companies. The resulting law is a compromise between these conflicting demands.

Part V of the text is not concerned with legal abstractions and esoteric concepts. It deals with those concrete legal principles and situations that are certain to be encountered by the field and home office representatives in the ordinary course of business. Most of the principles are encountered on a recurring—if not daily—basis. Recognition of situations and actions which have legal significance will enable representatives of life insurance companies to provide better service to the insuring public and more protection to their company against involuntary assumption of risk and unfavorable litigation.

Comprehension of the basic legal principles underlying life insurance should be enhanced by a brief summary of the forms of law, the American judicial system, the general principles of contract interpretation, and the unique legal characteristics of a life insurance contract.

FORMS OF LAW

American law, despite its varied and complex nature, can be classified into two broad, all-inclusive forms: legislation and case law. Legislation consists of those general rules of conduct promulgated by a legally constituted body vested with the authority and power to issue such rules for all or a given portion of the population. Case law consists of those narrow rules of conduct promulgated by the courts and administrative tribunals in the adjudication of particular controversies. Legislation is found chiefly in statute books and is generally identified as a "law" or an "act," while case law is located in the published and unpublished reports of judicial and administrative decisions. The rule of law represented by legislation is stated in an official, exclusive textual form; whereas a proposition of case law must be inferred from the facts, official determinations, and accompanying official opinions of a judicial or an administrative decision. Thus, case law is flexible in form, while legislation is rigid.

Legislation[1]

The term "legislation" is usually used as if it were synonymous with "statute." In this section, "legislation" is used in a broader sense. It is assumed to include all forms of law which have the characteristic of *textual rigidity*. This is a significant characteristic, since the fixed wording of a statute or some other form of legislative law makes the problems of its interpretation and application substantially different from those of the interpretation and application of case law.

The following forms of legislative law are presented in descending order of political authoritativeness.

The Federal Constitution. The primary functions of a constitution are to establish the framework of the government and to set forth the more fundamental principles that should be operative in any democratic society. Thus, the Constitution of the United States provides for a national government of three co-ordinate branches—the legislative,

---

[1] The materials in this section were drawn largely from Noel T. Dowling, Edwin W. Patterson, and Richard R. Powell, *Materials for Legal Method* (University Casebook Series) (Chicago: Foundation Press, Inc., 1946), pp. 14–29. The classification of laws set forth in this section of the chapter was taken from that source.

executive, and judicial—and sets down in some detail the powers and functions of each. At the same time, it provides safeguards against infringement by the government on the basic human rights, such as freedom of speech, freedom of religious worship, and freedom of peaceful assemblage. In short, the federal Constitution prescribes the powers of the various branches of the federal government and sets forth limitations on those powers as they affect private individuals. With a few exceptions, it does not lay down rules of law which create rights in or impose duties on private individuals.

Treaties. The treaties entered into between the government of the United States and foreign governments often contain provisions as to the rights of aliens which are paramount to state constitutions or statutes. For example, a treaty provision which confers on aliens the right to own or inherit land is given effect despite a statute to the contrary in the state in which the land is located. Thus, a treaty of 1850 between the United States and Switzerland, which provided that the heirs of a Swiss citizen who had died owning land in the United States should be entitled to inherit the land, was upheld by the Supreme Court of the United States in the face of a contrary legal doctrine of the state of Virginia, in which the land was located. In so holding, the court said: "It must always be borne in mind that the Constitution, laws and treaties of the United States are as much a part of the law of every state as its own local laws and Constitution. This is a fundamental principle in our system of complex national polity."[2]

It is pertinent to note that the Versailles Treaty, concluded after World War I, contained a provision dealing with life insurance policies lapsed through the exigencies of war. The treaty provided that: "Where the contract of life insurance has lapsed owing to nonpayment of premiums, the payment of which has been prevented by the enforcement of measures of war, the assured or his representatives or the person entitled shall have the right to restore the contract on payment of premiums with interest at 5 per cent per annum within three months from coming into force of the present Treaty." This provision, while binding on European insurers, never became applicable to American life insurance companies, since the United States failed to ratify the treaty.

Federal Statutes. The federal Constitution was, of necessity, couched in general terms. It was intended that the legislative body,

---

[2] *Havenstein* v. *Lynham,* 100 U.S. 483, 490 (1879).

Congress, would address itself to matters requiring specialized rules and regulations. The statutes enacted by Congress within the scope of the powers given by the Constitution to the federal government are of higher authority than any state constitution or statute. As a matter of fact, the Constitution itself states that the Constitution, the laws of Congress made pursuant thereto, and federal treaties shall be "the supreme Law of the Land."

Not all acts of Congress, however, create "law" in the sense in which the term is generally used. Some acts are directed at one individual by name or a specifically identified group of individuals and are known as "private laws." They do not purport to lay down general rules of human conduct. Statutes of general application are labeled "public laws."

Federal Executive Orders and Administrative Regulations. The President of the United States has a power of rather indefinite scope to issue executive orders which, if they prescribe general rules of conduct, are laws, legislative in form. Within their proper scope, executive orders are paramount to state law. In addition, many federal administrative bodies have power to make general rules, ordinarily identified as regulations. These are legislative in character and, when issued pursuant to a constitutional federal statute, are superior to all forms of state laws.

State Constitutions. A state constitution is, within the proper sphere of its operation, the "supreme law" of the state—subject, of course, to the priority of federal legislative law in its proper sphere. In addition to outlining the framework of government and limiting the authority of state officials, state constitutions often prescribe general rules of conduct of the kind normally associated with acts of the state legislature. The purpose of such a provision is to place the rules contained therein beyond the power of alteration by the legislature.

State Statutes. This is a voluminous body of legislative law, since state legislatures have residuary powers to prescribe general rules of conduct. In other words, they have all powers not specifically denied them by the federal Constitution, federal treaties, federal statutes, and the appropriate state constitution. The operations of life insurance companies and the contents of their policies are greatly affected by state statutes. In fact, most states have enacted so-called "standard" provisions which must be included, in substance, in all life insurance policies issued in the states.

State Administrative Regulations. Administrative bodies or officials, as a group, are endowed with some of the characteristics of all three branches of government—judicial, executive, and legislative. They sometimes have authority, granted by statute, to adjudicate particular controversies and claims and, in so doing, perform judicial or quasijudicial functions. Their decisions, with their accompanying explanations, become precedents of administrative case law. They serve as prosecuting and law enforcement officials, in which capacity they exercise executive powers. Finally, they are frequently empowered by statute to make general rules of conduct in their particular areas of responsibility; and these general rules, as "regulations," have the force and effect of law. In many states, no provision is made for the filing and publication of these regulations, and their legal status is uncertain. In New York, a constitutional amendment specifies that no regulation of an administrative agency of that state, unless it relates to the organization or internal management of the agency, shall become effective until it is filed in the office of the Department of State.

Regulations, orders, opinions, and rulings issued by the various state insurance departments constitute one of the most important sources of law for insurance companies.

Municipal Ordinances. The right to govern certain subordinate units of the state—e.g., cities, towns, and villages—is delegated by the state to municipal corporations which have limited legislative powers with respect to matters of purely local concern. The general rules enacted by these municipalities are usually called "municipal ordinances." In general, they exert little influence on the operations of insurance companies, although New York City, and possibly other municipalities, levy a gross receipts tax on the collection of certain premiums.

Rules of Court. Rules of court are the rules adopted by a court, or by a body of judges, which regulate pleading and other procedural matters, or which regulate the internal organization of the court. They are of interest only to lawyers or persons involved in or anticipating litigation.

Case Law

Case law is a by-product of the settling of disputes. From time immemorial, this has been the special province of the courts, and the great body of case law is composed of judicial decisions. Within the last few decades, however, administrative agencies have become an important source of case law. The decisions of administrative tribunals are referred to as *administrative case law,* to distinguish them from the decisions handed down by the judiciary.

Judicial Decisions. When a court is called upon to decide a case involving a point on which there is no legislation, it will look for precedents among cases previously adjudicated. If it finds an applicable precedent, it will ordinarily settle the current dispute on the basis of the principles enunciated in the earlier case. If the court finds no precedent squarely in point or applicable by analogy, it must originate a rule to resolve the dispute. Presumably, the rule will reflect proper consideration of history, custom, morals, and sound social policy.

In creating new rules, the courts are making case law. The more situations coming before the courts for which there are no existing rules, the more case law there will be. Moreover, each new rule becomes an integral part of the whole body of rules which the courts may use in the future.

American case law of the judicial variety is deeply rooted in the law of England as it existed at the time of the colonization of America. This is natural, since the early settlers brought with them the only law they knew. This law was composed of the rules being followed by the English courts in the settlement of disputes and the statutory enactments of Parliament still in effect. Since the decisions of the English courts were assumed to reflect those principles, maxims, usages, and rules of action which had regulated the affairs of men from time immemorial, they were designated as the "common law" of England. Since that body of principles and rules became the fountainhead of American decisional law, the latter likewise came to be known as "common law." In this sense, the term "common law" distinguishes case law from statutory or constitutional law.[3]

---

[3] It should be noted that in American usage, common law is always the law of some jurisdiction and not a "body of rules universally and automatically applicable like the law of gravitation" (Edmund M. Morgan and Francis X. Dwyer, *The Study of Law* [2d ed.; Chicago: Callaghan & Co., 1948], pp. 41–42). As Mr. Justice Holmes put it: "The common law is not a brooding omnipresence in the sky, but the articulate voice of some sovereign or quasi-sovereign that can be identified. . . . It is always the law of some state" (*Southern Pacific Co.* v. *Jensen, 244 U.S.* 205, 222 [1917] dissent). This view is not universally accepted. Some believe that the common law knows no jurisdictional boundaries. This view is exemplified by the reaction of the court to the assertion of the defendant in *St. Nicholas Bank* v. *State National Bank,* 128 N.Y. 26, 27 N.E. 849, 851 (1891), that the contract in dispute was governed by the common law of Tennessee. The New York court stated: "There is no common law peculiar to Tennessee. But the common law there is the same as that which prevails here and elsewhere, and the judicial expositions of the common law

1. *Common Law Contrasted with Civil Law.* A broader use of the term "common law" distinguishes the entire system of English law from the legal systems developed in other parts of the world. It has acquired special significance in distinguishing between the English legal system—and systems based on it—and the code developed in the Old Roman Empire which today serves as the foundation of the legal systems in continental Europe and in the state of Louisiana.

The Roman civil law originated as the law of the historic city of Rome but was gradually extended to the entire Roman Empire. After the fall of the Roman Empire in the fifth century, this law was compiled into a code called "Corpus Juris Civilis." Since the compilation was carried out during the reign of Justinian, it is often referred to as the "Justinian Code."

The Justinian Code attempted to evolve a rule to cover every possible type of legal conflict. An example is the rule which was developed to settle the question of survivorship when two persons perished under circumstances which rendered it impossible to determine which died first.[4] While there are many substantive differences between the Roman civil law and the Anglo-American common law, the most significant difference lies in the impact on the entire legal system of the adjudication of a particular case. Under the civil law code, a case is brought within one of the general provisions and is settled by application of the rule contained therein to the facts of the case. The decision in a particular case is little influenced by previous litigation on the point involved and, in turn, will exert little—if any—influence on similar disputes arising in the future. Under the Anglo-American system of common law, however, a controversy not covered by legislation is decided only after a guiding rule has been sought in previously litigated cases; and—more important—once a decision is made, it forms the basis for the settlement of future disputes. The more frequently a decision is used as a guide to action, the stronger it becomes as a precedent.

2. *Law versus Equity.* The term "common law" is also used to designate the rules applied by the courts of common law as con-

---

there do not bind the courts here." Again, in *Slaton* v. *Hall,* 168 Ga. 710, 716, 148 S.E. 741, 743 (1929) the court said: "Though courts in the different States may place a different construction upon a principle of common law, that does not change the law. There is still only one right construction. If all the American States were to construe the same principle of common law incorrectly, the common law would be unchanged."

[4] See pp. 594–5 for the rule.

trasted with the rules applied by courts of equity. This is a third meaning of the expression.

The term "equity" is peculiar to Anglo-American law. It arose because of the failure of the common law to give adequate and proper remedy. In the early courts of England, the procedure for pursuing a legal remedy was very rigid. There were a fixed number of "forms of action," and every remedial right had to be enforced through one of these forms. The first step in any action was to apply to the king for a writ, which was a document addressed to the person responsible for the alleged wrong. This writ gave a brief summary of the facts upon which the right of action was based, and contained certain technical formulas indicating the "form of action" being brought and the amount of money damages being sought. The nature of these writs was fixed and could not be substantially altered. A writ had been developed not only for each form of action but also for the facts, circumstances, and events which would constitute the subject matter of the particular action. If no writ could be found in the collection which corresponded substantially to the facts constituting the basis for complaint, the injured party could obtain no relief in the courts. The only course of action available to him was a direct appeal to the conscience of the king.

Over a period of time, the number of direct petitions became so great that the king had to delegate responsibility for dealing with them. Since the appeal was to the king's conscience, he began to refer such matters to his spiritual adviser, the chancellor, who, being an official of the Church, usually favored the ecclesiastical law or the civil law. The practice of delegating cases to the chancellor for his sole decision, once begun, rapidly became the established method of dealing with such controversies. Eventually, a separate court, functioning under the chancellor and called the Chancery Court, was created.

Following the English precedent, the American colonies—and later, the states—established two sets of courts, one applying the rules of common law and called "courts of law," and the other applying rules of equity and good conscience and called "courts of equity." England still maintains separate courts of law and equity; but in this country, the two systems have been merged to the extent that the same court can hear both types of cases. Whether the case is heard in law or equity depends upon the remedy sought. If there is a legal remedy, the action must be brought in law; if there is no legal remedy or the legal remedy is inadequate, the suit can be brought in equity.

The distinction between law and equity is extremely important to life insurance companies. Not only does equity give them access to remedies which would otherwise be unavailable and which are essential to their operations; but suits in equity are, for the most part, tried without a jury, which—in view of the traditionally hostile attitude of juries toward insurance companies—is considered to be a major procedural advantage. Among the equitable remedies frequently invoked by life insurance companies are suits for rescission[5] and restitution, suits for reformation of contracts, and bills of interpleader.

3. *Restatements of the Law.* The development of rules of law through the adjudication of a series of controversies extending over hundreds of years, whatever the virtues of the system, places an increasing burden on the legal profession. Its members must be familiar with an ever-expanding body of law dealing with subjects becoming ever more diverse and complex. Feeling that the accelerating volume of decisional law posed a real threat to the continuance of the common law system, a group of distinguished legal scholars, in the early 1920's, sought the collaboration of leaders in the three branches of the legal profession—judges, practitioners, and teachers—in a project to simplify the system. The purpose of the project was to determine the basic rules of law, as of the date of the inquiry, in certain important areas of jurisprudence and to restate them without reference to the supporting decisions. The determination was to be arrived at after review, analysis, and synthesis of all reported decisions in the areas covered by the inquiry. The restatements were then to serve as new points of departure for the further evolution of the law. It was anticipated that thereafter, persons pursuing a particular point of law would not find it necessary to consult cases decided prior to the restatement of the law.

The co-operation of many legal scholars—particularly, law school professors—was obtained; and with the financial support of the Carnegie Foundation, the project was launched. Over the next twenty-five years, decisions in such important areas as contracts, trusts, torts, agency, and property were studied and restatements produced.

---

[5] When rescission is sought after the death of the insured, it is usually not possible to avoid trial of the issue by a jury.

Thirty thousand cases were analyzed in the property field alone, the restatement embracing four volumes.[6]

These restatements do not cite cases. Their authority is derived from the insight, skill, wisdom, and care of the legal experts who combed the decided cases in their field. They unquestionably represent an accurate formulation of the law at the date of their respective publications. In some courts, the rule given in the restatement on any question of law may be accepted as *the law,* unless a conflicting local decision can be produced.

In order that the lawyers and judges of a particular state can be adequately informed as to the extent to which the decisions of that state conform to—or deviate from—the text of the restatement, local annotations have been prepared in many states for one or more of the restatements.

Administrative Decisions. Reference has earlier been made to the growth of administrative agencies. These agencies, normally created by legislative enactment, are charged with the administration of laws which are general in character and which affect the rights and privileges of private citizens. When they apply a law to a particular set of facts, they are making case law. Their decisions, when officially or unofficially reported and published, have the status of precedents. Precedents in this area, however, are regarded with less sanctity than are judicial decisions and are less likely to be applied to a different set of facts.

An administrative tribunal, unlike the usual court of law, has jurisdiction over a limited class of cases.

RELATIONSHIP OF THE JUDICIARY TO LEGISLATIVE LAW

Attitude of the Judiciary toward Legislation

The courts have always been jealous of their right to create law through the dispute-settling process and, in general, have regarded legislation as an encroachment on their prerogatives. They have long recognized the supremacy of legislative enactments over decision law but have looked upon a statute as something to be contained within the narrowest possible limits. Moreover, they have been unwilling to treat a statute as an exemplification of a general principle or precept worthy of serving as a precedent for the adjudication of a controversy not falling within its precise boundaries. This attitude is criticized in

---

[6] Dowling, Patterson, and Powell, *op. cit.,* p. 257.

the following excerpt from the writings of an able legal philosopher and Supreme Court Justice:

It is the fashion in our profession to lament both the quantity and quality of our statute-making, not, it is true, without some justification. But our role has been almost exclusively that of destructive critics, usually after the event, of the inadequacies of legislatures. There has been little disposition to look to our own shortcomings in failing, through adaptations of old skills and the development of new ones, to realize more nearly than we have the ideal of a unified system of judge-made and statute law woven into a seamless whole by the processes of adjudication.

The reception which the courts have accorded to statutes presents a curiously illogical chapter in the history of the common law. Notwithstanding their genius for the generation of new law from that already established, the common-law courts have given little recognition to statutes as starting points for judicial lawmaking comparable to judicial decisions. They have long recognized the supremacy of statutes over judge-made law, but it has been the supremacy of a command to be obeyed according to its letter, to be treated as otherwise of little consequence. The fact that the command involves recognition of a policy by the supreme lawmaking body has seldom been regarded by courts as significant, either as a social datum or as a point of departure for the process of judicial reasoning by which the common law has expanded. . . .

. . . I can find in the history and principles of common law no adequate reason for our failure to treat a statute much more as we treat a judicial precedent, as both a declaration and a source of law, and as a premise for legal reasoning. We have done practically that with our ancient statutes, such as the statutes of limitations, frauds and wills, readily molding them to fit new conditions within their spirit, though not their letter, possibly because their antiquity tends to make us forget or minimize their legislative origin. . . . Apart from its command, the social policy and judgment, expressed in legislation by the lawmaking agency which is supreme, would seem to merit that judicial recognition which is freely accorded to the like expression in judicial precedent. But only to a limited extent do modern courts feel free, by resort to standards of conduct set up by legislation, to impose liability or attach consequences for the failure to maintain those or similar standards in similar but not identical situations, or to make the statutory recognition of a new type of right the basis for the judicial creation of rights in circumstances not dissimilar. . . .

That such has been the course of the common law in the United States seems to be attributable to the fact that, long before its important legislative expansion, the theories of Coke and Blackstone of the self-sufficiency and ideal perfection of the common law, and the notion of the separation of powers and of judicial independence, had come to dominate our juristic thinking. The statute was looked upon as in the law but not of it, a formal rule to be obeyed, it is true, since it is the command of the sovereign, but to be obeyed grudgingly, by construing it narrowly and treating it as though it did not exist for any purpose other than that embraced within the strict construction of its words. It is difficult to appraise the consequences of the perpetuation of incongruities and injustices in the law by this habit of narrow construction of statutes and by the failure to recognize that, as recognition of social policy, they are as significant and rightly as much a part of the law, as the rules declared by judges. . . .[7]

Justice Stone ended on a more optimistic note, pointing out that the courts, influenced by the emphasis in law schools on the fusion of judge-made and statutory law, are beginning to recognize that "a statute is not an alien intruder in the house of the common law, but a guest to be welcomed and made at home there as a new and powerful aid in the accomplishment of its appointed task of accommodating the law to social needs."[8]

Interpretation of Legislative Law

While the courts have had to recognize the right of legislatures to make new law through statutory enactments, they have retained the right to interpret or construe the law which is made in that manner. They determine the meaning of the words used in the statute and decide whether a particular set of facts comes within the scope of the law. The same function is exercised with respect to the federal and state constitutions. As a part of this function, the courts determine whether or not a particular statute is in conflict with a constitutional provision.

In the process of determining the scope and meaning of statutory and constitutional provisions, the courts have developed a number of rules. These are known as rules of *statutory construction*. The fundamental purpose of all these rules is to ascertain and give effect to the intention of the legislature. One of the most basic rules is that if the language of the statute is plain and unambiguous, and its meaning clear and definite, there is no room for construction. The statute is said to have a "plain meaning," which the courts must enforce irrespective of their opinion of the wisdom or efficacy of the statute. Normally, the meaning of a statute is sought from the words used by the legislature to express its intent; but if the language of the statute is ambiguous and susceptible of more than one meaning, matters extraneous to the statute—such as its title, legislative history, conditions

---

[7] Harlan F. Stone, "The Common Law in the United States," *Harvard Law Review,* Vol. L, No. 1 (1936), pp. 12 ff.

[8] *Op. cit.,* p. 15.

leading to its enactment, and so forth—can be taken into account in an attempt to arrive at its true meaning.

It stands to reason that all parts of a statute must be considered in any attempt to ascertain its meaning. Furthermore, the interpretation adopted by a court must be one which will give effect to the whole statute. Reflecting the traditional conflict between common and statutory law, the courts have decreed that statutes in derogation of the common law shall be strictly construed. Finally, as between two statutes dealing with the same subject matter, the later one in time is to be given effect as the last expression of legislative intent.

Judicial decisions rendered in connection with the construction of statutes are considered to be case law but do not add to the body of common law. On the other hand, by providing a narrow construction of statutes in conflict with common law, the courts minimize the encroachment of statutory law on common law.

AMERICAN JUDICIAL SYSTEM

Classification of Courts

Federal Courts. The federal Constitution provides for one supreme court and such inferior courts as Congress may, from time to time, establish. At the head of the hierarchy stands the Supreme Court of the United States. The Supreme Court has original jurisdiction over all cases involving ambassadors, ministers, and consuls, and those in which a state is a party. In all other cases which can properly be brought before the Supreme Court, the court has appellate jurisdiction. Hence, the principal jurisdiction of the court is appellate. It is the court of last resort for all cases involving *federal* law and for all cases coming to it from the inferior or lower federal courts involving questions of state law.

In 1891, Congress made provision for intermediary courts of appeal, in order to lessen the burden on the Supreme Court. These tribunals are known as the Courts of Appeals, of which there are now eleven.[9] Each of these courts has a minimum of three judges, who preside as a group, there being a total of seventy-eight circuit judges at present. The jurisdiction of the Courts of Appeals is exclusively appellate. In most cases, the decision of a Court of Appeals is final, subject only to being reviewed by the Supreme Court at its discretion.

_____

[9] These tribunals were originally called Circuit Courts of Appeals.

The general courts of original jurisdiction are the District Courts. The country is presently divided into eighty-four judicial districts, with each state having at least one district and no district embracing territory in more than one state. There is one District Court for each judicial district, but most courts have more than one judge. In total, there are roughly three judges for each District Court. The District Courts have jurisdiction over all cases arising under the federal Constitution or laws of Congress and those cases involving litigants with diversity of citizenship where the amount in dispute exceeds $10,000. When the action is in the form of a bill of interpleader or a bill in the nature of a bill of interpleader,[10] the amount in controversy need exceed only $500 and, furthermore, if the amount should exceed $10,000 there need not be diversity of citizenship among the claimants. For purposes of federal jurisdiction, diversity of citizenship is considered to exist whenever the litigating parties are citizens of different states in the United States or one is a citizen of the United States and the other is a citizen of a foreign country. For this purpose, a corporation is considered to be a citizen of the state in which it is chartered. If the jurisdiction of the federal courts is based on diversity of citizenship, the subject matter of the dispute may be state law.

In addition to these courts of general jurisdiction, there are a number of federal courts which have jurisdiction—not always exclusive—over certain types of disputes. Among such courts are the Court of Claims, the Tax Court, and the Customs Court.

State Courts. In each state, there exists—by constitutional provision and legislative enactment—a system of judicial tribunals, which embraces various courts of original jurisdiction and one or more of appellate jurisdiction. Usually, there is one court of unlimited original jurisdiction which has the power to entertain any action, regardless of the amount involved or the nature of the relief requested, although it does not ordinarily have authority over the probate of wills or administration of estates of deceased persons. This type of court usually hears cases at the county seat of the various counties in the state and is known variously as the District, Circuit, Superior, or Common Pleas Court. There are usually several inferior courts, with jurisdiction limited as to subject matter, amount in controversy, or relief sought. These are commonly designated by some such name as Municipal Court, Police Court, Magistrate's Court, or Justice of the Peace Court.

---

[10] See p. 621.

There may be a separate court or a special division of a court to deal with problems of domestic relations or juvenile delinquency. In many states, there is but one appellate tribunal, a court of last resort. In some, however, there is an intermediate tribunal with powers somewhat similar to those of the Courts of Appeals of the United States. The name of the court is not necessarily indicative of its place in the judicial hierarchy. In New York, for example, the general court of original jurisdiction (the trial court) is known as the "Supreme Court," while the court of last resort is known as the "Court of Appeals." In most states, however, the court of last resort is called the "Supreme Court."

Jurisdiction of Courts

The jurisdiction of a court refers not only to its power to hear a case but also to its power to render an enforceable judgment. The constitutional or statutory provision creating a particular court defines its jurisdiction as to subject matter, parties, geographical area, and amounts involved. Jurisdiction over the person of the defendant is of especial importance. This jurisdiction is given effect by a summons from the court in which the case is to be tried, which is usually delivered to the sheriff, to be served upon the individual or organization made defendant to the suit. The summons must be served within the geographical area subject to the jurisdiction of the court issuing the summons. If a person comes into the state or county, as the case may be, and is served with a summons by the sheriff while there, such person is then under the authority and jurisdiction of the court.

If the defendant is a nonresident of the place where the suit is brought, service of process may be accomplished by publication. This, however, does not normally give the court authority to render a personal judgment for damages. Accompanied by proper attachment proceedings, however, service by publication brings under the court's jurisdiction all attached property of a nonresident which lies within the territorial limits of the court, so that such attached property is liable for the judgment debt and may be used to satisfy the judgment. Moreover, under the Unauthorized Insurers Service-of-Process Act, which is discussed in the following chapter, a policyholder residing in one state may obtain and enforce a judgment against an out-of-state insurance company by serving the summons on the insurance commissioner or other designated official of the state of the insured's domicile.

If a particular controversy falls within the jurisdiction of the federal courts, the plaintiff may bring his action in a federal court. If he brings the action in a state court and the defendant acquiesces in the choice of jurisdiction, the case will be tried in the state court. If, however, the defendant does not wish the case to be heard in the state court, he can have it removed to the appropriate federal court.[11] If a case involving a federal question is adjudicated in a state court, the decision of the state court on that question is subject to review by the Supreme Court of the United States, subject to the conditions and limitations imposed by Congress.

Insurance companies may prefer to have their cases tried in the federal courts because of the caliber of the federal judges, as a class, and the less hostile environment. If the sum in question exceeds $10,000, the case usually goes before a federal court, since diversity of citizenship is likely to be involved. In view of the fact that the insurance business is regulated by the states, insurance cases seldom get into the federal courts through the involvement of a federal statute.

Conflict of Laws

The jurisdiction of a court has reference to its power to hear a controversy and to enforce its decision; it is not determinative of the law which will be applied. A court of one state may have to apply the law, either statutory or common, of another state. The manner in which this could come about involves the whole topic of *conflict of laws,* which is one of the most complex and unsettled branches of the law.

The question of which law will govern the validity and interpretation of a life insurance contract is extremely important, since the states have different attitudes toward various company practices and policy provisions. Broadly speaking, the matter is resolved on the basis of the *contacts* which a life insurance contract has with various territorial sovereigns which might be deemed to have an interest in determining the rights and duties of the parties to—and beneficiaries of—the contract. These contacts might arise out of the relationship of the state to the home office, a branch office, the insured, or the beneficiary, to mention only the major possibilities. Theoretically, if a state has *any* relationship to—or contact with—an insurance contract, it has some —though perhaps only slight—claim to a voice in the determination of the rights and duties thereunder. Since, in the typical case, there will be at least two states concerned with the policy—the state in

---

[11] See Morgan, and Dwyer, *op. cit.,* pp. 27–31, for a more detailed statement of the conditions under which a case can be removed to the federal courts.

which the home office is located and the state in which the insured is domiciled—and there can easily be five or more, rules must be developed to determine which state has the paramount interest in interpreting and enforcing the contract.

The rule followed by the majority of jurisdictions is that questions concerning the *validity* and *interpretation* of a life insurance contract will be resolved by the law of the state in which the contract was made,[12] which will be the state in which the last act necessary to bring the contract into existence took place. This is the so-called "place-of-making rule." Since, under the usual circumstances, the contract becomes effective at the moment it is delivered by the agent to the insured and the first premium is collected,[13] the place of making is typically the state in which the insured resides. On the other hand, if the first premium is paid with the application and a conditional receipt is issued contingent on approval at the company's home office, the act which brings the policy contract into existence occurs at the home office of the company, producing a different result. The tradiitional rule is that matters relating to *performance* of the contract are controlled by the law of state where the contract is to be performed.

Disturbed by the fortuitous nature of the place-of-making rule and convinced that all policyholders should be protected by the laws of their states, several courts have adopted the rule that all policies shall be governed by the laws of the state in which the insured is domiciled, irrespective of where the contract came into existence. Other courts— feeling that the control of a state over a company incorporated under its laws assures equality of treatment of all policyholders, wherever they live—follow the rule that the laws of the insurer's state of incorporation shall be applied in determining the validity and interpretation of a life insurance contract. In all these cases, the choice of the governing law is determined by the conflict-of-law rule of the state in which the case is being adjudicated.

The policy may contain a provision that its validity and interpretation shall be governed by the law of a designated state, which may be neither the state of domicile of the insured nor the state in which the home office is located. It appears that the insured or beneficiary can enforce this provision if the laws of the designated state are more favorable to him than the laws which would apply under the conflict-of-law rule, but the insurance company is not permitted to invoke the

---

[12] *Mutual Life Insurance Company* v. *Johnson,* 293 U.S. 335 (1934).

[13] See pp. 485–95 for an explanation of the methods by which life insurance contracts come into existence.

provision.[14] This has led one insurance law authority to conclude that "the general principle that, *in case* of ambiguity in an insurance contract, it will be construed most strictly against the insurer (*contra proferentem*) and most favorably to the insured or beneficiary has been stretched to a principle that *even an unambiguous* provision as to the choice of law will be enforced only if favorable to the insured or beneficiary."[15] In New York a policy may not contain a provision that its validity and interpretation shall be governed by the law of a designated state if the policy is delivered in New York covering a person resident in New York.

In recent years there has been a noticeable tendency for the courts to follow a new doctrine, known as the "center of gravity," or "grouping of contacts" theory, in resolving conflicts of law problems, whether the matter in dispute involves the validity, interpretation, or performance of a contract.[16] Under this theory, the courts, rather than regarding as conclusive the parties' intention or the place of making or performance, lay emphasis upon the law of the state which has the most significant contacts with the matter in dispute. The merit of the approach is that it gives the state with the most interest in the dispute paramount control over the legal issues. The principal disadvantage of the doctrine is the possibility that it will afford less certainty and predicability than the more rigid rules traditionally applied.

It should be noted that when the courts of one state apply the laws of another state, they apply *their* interpretation of what the law is in the other state. This may differ from the interpretation adopted by the courts of the other state.

It was provided in the act creating the federal judiciary[17] that in trying cases based on diversity of citizenship, federal courts would be bound by the applicable laws of the state in which they were sitting (assuming no conflict of laws). In the famous case of *Swift* v. *Tyson,*[18] decided by the United States Supreme Court in 1842, it was held that the word "laws" used in the act referred to statutory law and not case law. Thus, the federal courts were free to apply their own version of

---

[14] See Edwin W. Patterson, *Essentials of Insurance Law* (2d ed.; New York: McGraw-Hill Book Co., Inc., 1957), pp. 54 and 55, nn. 114 and 116, for citations.

[15] *Ibid.,* p. 55.

[16] See J. Edwin Dowling and Richard E. Errvay, *The Life Insurance Law of New York* (New York: The Association of Life Insurance Counsel, 1963), pp. 380–84, including citations.

[17] Judiciary Act of 1789 § 34, 1 Stat. 92 (1879) 28 U.S.C., § 725 (1952).

[18] 41 U.S. (16 Pet.) 1 (1842).

the common law in settling disputes not involving a federal or state statute. This ruling turned out to be highly significant for insurance companies, inasmuch as federal precedents were more favorable to the companies in many respects than the common law of the various states. This happy state of affairs was ended in 1938, when the United States Supreme Court, in the case of *Erie Railroad Company* v. *Tompkins,*[19] overruled its earlier doctrine and held that the federal courts were obliged to apply the common law, as well as the statutory law, of the state in which the case is being heard. Three years later, the Supreme Court held that the federal courts would also have to follow the conflict-of-law rules of the state in which they sit.[20] Thus, "for purposes of diversity jurisdiction, a federal court is in effect, only another court of the state."[21]

GENERAL NATURE OF A LIFE INSURANCE CONTRACT

A valid agreement between a life insurance company and the applicant for insurance, represented by an instrument called the *policy* (from the Italian word *polizza,* meaning "a rolled document"), is a contract and, as such, is subject to the general rules of contract law. However, in adapting these rules, which are familiar to all students of business law, to the life insurance contract, the courts have introduced substantial modifications because of certain peculiar characteristics of the life insurance contract. These characteristics—which, with one exception, are common to all types of insurance contracts—are briefly described herewith.

Aleatory Contract

The agreement contained in a life insurance policy is *aleatory* in nature, rather than *commutative.* In a commutative agreement, each party expects to receive from the other party, in one way or the other, the approximate equivalent of what he himself undertakes to give. Thus, in an agreement to purchase real estate, the buyer agrees to pay a sum of money which represents the approximate value of the property to him, while the seller agrees to sell the property for a price which represents its approximate value to him. In other words, both parties contemplate a fairly even exchange of values.

---

[19] 304 U.S. 64 (1938).

[20] *Griffin* v. *McCooch,* 313 U.S. 549 (1941); *Klaxon* v. *Stentor Electric Manufacturing Co.,* 313 U.S. 487 (1941).

[21] *Angel* v. *Bullington.* 330 U.S. 183 (1947).

In an aleatory agreement, on the other hand, both parties realize that, depending upon chance, one may receive a value out of all proportion to the value which he gives. The essence of an aleatory agreement is the element of chance or uncertainty. The prime example of such a contract is the wagering agreement. The term may also be applied to an industry where the potential gain or loss is governed largely by chance. Thus, the exploration and drilling functions of the oil industry may be described as aleatory in nature. So is prospecting for gold, silver, or uranium.

In a life insurance transaction, the present value of the potential premium payments at the inception of the agreement is precisely equal, on the basis of the company's actuarial assumptions, to the present value of the anticipated benefits payable under the contract. In this sense, the life insurance transaction is not aleatory. Moreover, the sum total of insurance transactions for a company, or the whole life insurance industry, is not aleatory because of the predictability and stability provided by the theories of probability and the law of large numbers. It remains true, however, that a particular policyholder may pay in to the insurance company a sum of money considerably smaller than the sum promised under the contract. Indeed, the face of the policy may become payable after the insured has paid only one install-ment of the first premium. This *chance* of obtaining a disproportionate return from an "investment" in a life insurance policy has motivated —and continues to motivate—many unscrupulous persons to seek life insurance through fraudulent means and for illegal purposes. The rem-edies for breach of warranty, misrepresentation, and concealment are invoked by the companies to protect themselves and society against fraudulent attempts to procure insurance. The requirement of an insurable interest is also designed to deal with the problems created by the fact that the life insurance policy is an aleatory contract.

The aleatory nature of the insurance contract accounts in large measure for the modifications of contract law in the field of insurance.

Unilateral Contract

Most contracts in the business world are *bilateral* in nature. This means that each party to the contract makes an enforceable promise to the other party. The consideration for such a contract is the exchange of mutual promises. Thus, an order from a wholesaler to a manufac-turer for a specified quantity of a particular item at a specified price, if accepted, is a bilateral contract. The manufacturer agrees to deliver the desired merchandise at an agreed-upon price, while the wholesaler agrees to accept and pay for the merchandise when it is delivered.

Under *a unilateral* contract, on the other hand, only one party makes an enforceable promise. This arises out of the fact that the other party to the contract carries out his part of the bargain *before* the contract comes into existence. For instance, if the wholesaler in the foregoing example had remitted cash with his order, the transactions would have become unilateral in nature, inasmuch as only the manufacturer had anything to perform. In general, unilateral contracts are confined to situations in which one party is unwilling to extend credit to the other or to take his word for future performance.

As a general rule, a life insurance policy is a unilateral contract, in that only the insurance company makes an enforceable promise thereunder. The consideration demanded by the company—namely, the application and the first premium, or the first installment thereof—is given by the insured before the contract goes into effect.[22] The insured is under no legal obligation to pay premiums subsequent to the first, although, if he does not do so, the company will be released from its original promise to pay the face of the policy. Nevertheless, he incurs no legal penalties through failure to continue premium payments. On the other hand, the company is obligated to accept the periodic premiums from the insured and to keep the contract in force in accordance with its original terms.

If a life insurance policy is delivered in exchange for the applicant's promissory note or oral promise of the insured to pay by an agent having the authority to waive cash payment of the first premium, a *bilateral* contract is created. The insurer's promise is exchanged for the insured's promise.

Conditional Contract

Closely related to the foregoing is the fact that the life insurance policy is a *conditional* contract. This means that the company's obligation under the contract is contingent on the performance of certain acts by the insured or the beneficiary. This does *not,* however, make the contract bilateral.

A condition is always inserted in a contract for the benefit of the promisor and hence is disadvantageous to the promisee. Conditions are not confined to unilateral contracts; a party to a bilateral contract

---

[22] More precisely, the first premium is usually paid *concurrently* with the inception of the contract.

can condition his promise in any manner acceptable to the other party. Conditions are classified as either precedent or subsequent. A condition *precedent* must be satisfied before legal rights and duties are created or continued, whereas a condition *subsequent* must be fulfilled in order to prevent the extinguishment of rights and duties already created in the contract. Whether a condition is precedent or subsequent depends upon the intention of the parties to the contract. When the intention is not clear, the tendency of the courts is to classify a condition as precedent, in order to avoid a forfeiture.

The legal significance of a condition is quite different from that of a promise. Failure to perform a promise subjects the promisor to liability for damages to the promisee. Failure to perform or fulfill a condition does not subject the person involved (the promisee) to liability for damages, but merely deprives him of a right or privilege which he otherwise would have had. It releases the promisor from his obligation to perform. As Professor Patterson puts it, "A condition is a shield, not a sword."[23]

The promise of a life insurance company is conditioned on the timely payment of premiums subsequent to the first. Payment of these premiums is considered to be a condition *precedent* to the continuance of the contract under its original terms. If this condition is not fulfilled, the company is relieved of its basic promise but remains obligated to honor various subsidiary promises contained in the surrender provisions and the reinstatement clause.

The company's promise to pay the face of the policy is always conditioned on the insured's forbearance from committing suicide during a specified period (usually, one or two years) after issue of the policy and may be conditioned on his death from causes not associated with war or aviation.[24] Finally, the company has no liability until satisfactory proof of death has been submitted by the beneficiary or the insured's personal representative.

Contract of Adhesion

A life insurance policy is also a contract of *adhesion*. This means that the terms of the contract are not arrived at by mutual negotiation between the parties, as would be the case with a *bargaining* contract.

---

[23] Patterson, *op. cit.,* p. 69.

[24] Some would argue that the suicide, war, and aviation provisions are not conditions in the legal sense but rather limitations on the amount of the insurer's liability. The insurer promises to pay a limited amount, if death results from one of the stated causes.

The policy, a complex and technical instrument, is prepared by the company and, with minor exceptions, must be accepted by the applicant in the form offered to him. The prospective insured may or may not contract with the company, but in no sense is he in a position to bargain about the terms of the contract if he does decide to seek insurance. He must reject the contract entirely or "adhere" to it. Any bargaining which precedes the issuance of a life insurance contract has to do only with whether or not the contract is to be issued, the plan and amount of insurance, and—to some degree—the terms of the settlement agreement, although the agreement is actually drafted by the company.

The adhesive nature of the life insurance contract is highly significant from a legal standpoint. This importance derives from the basic rule of contract construction that a contract is to be construed or interpreted most strongly against the party who drafted the agreement. The avowed purpose of this rule is to neutralize any advantage that might have been gained by the party which prepared the contract. This means that if there is an ambiguity in the life insurance policy, the provision in question will be given the interpretation most favorable to the insured or his beneficiary. The view is rather prevalent in insurance circles that in their zeal to protect the insured, the courts find ambiguities in contracts where none exists.

Some who readily admit the soundness of this rule in general and of its application to life insurance policies prior to the turn of the century question its continued application to policies currently being issued, in view of the large number of provisions which are required by state statutes to be incorporated in such policies. Although these statutes do not prescribe the exact language to be used, many states require that the language of all policy provisions, including those voluntarily included, be approved by the state insurance department before sale of the policy form to the public. Such a requirement has the purpose, among others, of preventing the use of any deceptive or misleading language, or any provisions that would be unfair to policyholders. These factors have produced a relaxation of the strict rule of construction in some courts; but in general, all ambiguous provisions of the policy continue to be construed against the insurer.

Contract to Pay Stated Sum

Contracts issued by property and casualty insurance companies are usually contracts of *indemnity*. This means that the insured can collect only the amount of his loss, irrespective of the face of the policy—

except, of course, that the recovery cannot exceed the face of the policy. Moreover, upon payment by an insurer of a loss caused by the negligence of a third party, as in the case of an automobile accident, the insurer acquires the insured's right of action against the negligent third party, up to the amount of its loss payment and any expenses incurred in enforcing its rights. This is known as the doctrine of *subrogation;* and while a provision giving effect to this doctrine is virtually always included in property and casualty insurance policies, it applies even in the absence of a policy provision.

The foregoing is background to saying that a life insurance policy is not a contract of indemnity, but one to pay a *stated sum.* This is presumably based on the assumption that the value of a man's life to himself is without limit; and thus, no sum payable upon his death will be in excess of the loss suffered. Thus, even though the insured has reached an age or a circumstance where he no longer has an economic value, upon his death the company will still have to pay the sum agreed upon. The practical significance of this principle is that the insurance company, after paying the face of the policy, is not subrogated to the right of action of the decedent's estate when his death was caused by the negligence of a third party.

CHAPTER XXIII

Formation of a Life Insurance Contract

TO BE enforceable, the agreement between a life insurance company and the person seeking insurance, represented by a written instrument called the policy, must meet all the requirements prescribed by law for the formation of a valid contract. In this and the following chapter, it will be explained in specific terms how each of these requirements is satisfied in the formation of a life insurance contract.

LEGAL CAPACITY OF THE PARTIES

Parties to the Contract

There are two parties to the life insurance contract—the insurance company and the applicant. The applicant is normally, but not necessarily, the person whose life is the subject matter of the contract. The person on whose life a policy is issued is technically known as the *insured*. A person who takes out insurance on the life of another is generally referred to as the *owner*. The person whose life is insured is not a party to the contract unless he is also the applicant. Occasionally, two or more persons may jointly apply for insurance on the life of another person, as in the case of business continuation agreements. In that event, the joint applicants would constitute parties of the second part.

477

The designation of a third party to receive the proceeds upon maturity of the policy does not make such a person a party to the contract in the technical sense. The third-party beneficiary need not know of the contract at its inception, may disclaim any benefits thereunder, and incurs no duties by virtue of his designation. The beneficiary does acquire certain rights which are enforceable against the company, but he acquires them only through the agreement between the company and the applicant. Furthermore, the beneficiary's rights can be negated by any defenses available against the applicant.

An assignee, while possessing rights quite distinct from those of a beneficiary, occupies a position similar to that of the beneficiary, in that he is an *interested* party but is not a party to the contract in a strict sense.

It is worthy of noting that the voluntary payment of premiums by a person having no other relationship with the policy bestows no contractual rights or privileges on the premium payer.

The relationship between the insurance company and the other contracting party, be he the insured or the assured, is that of conditional debtor and creditor. The insurance company incurs obligations only if certain conditions are fulfilled, and then its duty is only to carry out the terms of the contract. The insurance company is not a trustee in any sense of the word and is under no legal obligation to render an accounting of the premiums received or, in the absence of a showing of bad faith, of the apportionment of dividends.

Competency of the Insurer

In the absence of specific legislation to the contrary, there is no reason why any person who has the legal capacity to enter into a contract cannot become the insurer under a life insurance contract. Freedom of contract is a constitutional and common-law privilege which must not be abridged unless the nature of the subject matter of the contract is such as to make it a proper subject for the exercise of the police power of the state. Insurance—because of its magnitude, nature, and intimate bearing on the welfare of society—has been adjudged a proper subject for the exercise of such power. The United States Supreme Court has ruled that a state may prohibit the making of insurance contracts by persons, either natural or artificial, who have not complied with the requirements of the law of the state. In many states, the statutes specifically prohibit natural persons from acting as life insurers; and even in those states that have not so legislated, the nature of the business—with its need for continuity and permanence of the insurer—has brought about the same result. Hence, while individual insurers were common in the early days of life insurance, today the business is conducted exclusively by corporate insurers.[1]

If a corporation seeking to write life insurance in a particular state is legally organized, the only question that can arise with respect to its capacity to contract is whether it has complied with all the requirements for doing business in that state. The most important requirement is that the corporation obtain a license to do business in the state. In certain lines of insurance, notably health insurance, the transacting of business, frequently by mail, by companies which have not obtained a license in the state where the policyholders reside is a major problem and creates difficulties for policyholders attempting to enforce claims against such unauthorized insurers. In life insurance, however, the problem of the unlicensed or unauthorized insurer is of less serious proportions. A more likely form of noncompliance on the part of a life insurance company would be failure (perhaps through inadvertence) to file policy forms and other blanks as required by law.

A contract issued by an unlicensed insurer is usually enforceable by the policyholder. This rule of law recognizes that a person who is solicited to buy insurance cannot be expected to inquire into the affairs of the insurance company to determine whether or not it has complied with all the statutory and regulatory requirements governing its operations and is fully qualified to enter into the proposed contract. On the contrary, the prospective insured is permitted to assume that the insurer is legally competent to enter into the proposed contract and will not be permitted to erect as a defense against claims its own violation of statutory requirements. In order to assist the insured in enforcing his claims against an unauthorized out-of-state insurer, forty-seven states have enacted the so-called Unauthorized Insurers Service-of-Process Act,[2] which designates the insurance commissioner or some other state official as agent of the unauthorized insurer for the purpose of accepting service of process. Designed to deal with companies which do business by mail, these statutes permit the insured to secure a judgment against the insurer in the courts of his own state, which judgment must be given "full faith and credit" by the courts of all other states in which the insurer has assets. Agents of unauthorized

---

[1] Including fraternal associations and savings banks.

[2] South Carolina has enacted a somewhat similar law.

insurers are subject to both criminal and civil penalties and, in some states, are personally liable for claims under contracts which they sold. It hardly seems necessary to add that an unlicensed insurer cannot maintain an action to enforce any claim arising out of an insurance contract made in violation of the laws of the state in which the suit is brought.[3]

If the insurer is duly authorized to do business in a particular state but has failed to comply with some other requirement of the state law, the validity of its contracts will usually not be affected by the noncompliance. The contracts will be binding upon both parties; but the insurer will be subject to whatever penalties are imposed for the violation of the law; and if the statute requires certain provisions in such a contract, the contract will be deemed to contain such provisions.

Competency of the Applicant

All individuals are presumed to have legal capacity except those comprising the clearly defined groups that are held by law to have no capacity or only limited capacity to contract. For life insurance purposes, the two most important classes of persons with impaired capacity are minors and alien enemies.

Minors—or infants, as they are known to the law—do not lack capacity in the absolute sense and may enter into contracts which are binding on the other party. However, subject to certain restrictions, a minor can disaffirm his contract at any time and demand a return of the monetary consideration that passed to the other party. Limitations on the right of a minor to void his contract are found in the general rules that an infant is bound to pay the reasonable value of necessaries actually furnished to him and that if he can make restitution of that which he received for it, he must do so. Up to this point, no American court has held a life insurance policy to be a necessity for a minor, in the legal sense of the word. Hence, a minor can disaffirm a life insurance contract at any time and recover all premiums paid. A majority of the courts permit full recovery of premiums, with no deduction for the cost of protection,[4] while a few courts authorize the company to retain that portion of the aggregate premiums applied

---

[3] *Farmers etc. Insurance Co.* v. *Harrah*, 47 Ind. 236 (1874); *Isaac Fass, Inc.* v. *Pink*, 178 Va. 357, 17 S.E. 2d 379 (1941).

[4] *Simpson* v. *Prudential Insurance Co.*, 184 Mass. 348, 68 N.E. 673 (1903).

toward the cost of protection.[5] In the latter case, the recovery is limited to the cash value or reserve. It is clear that only by permitting the insurer to deduct the cost of protection does the court compel the minor to make restitution to the other party.

In recognition of the importance of life insurance and of the unfavorable position of a life insurance company in dealing with minors, most states (thirty-two at the present time) have enacted statutes conferring on minors, of a specified age and over, the legal capacity to enter into valid and enforceable life insurance contracts on their own lives. The age limit varies from fourteen to eighteen, with fifteen predominating. A minor who satisfies the age requirement is permitted not only to purchase a life insurance policy but also to exercise all ownership rights in the contract. The statutes usually require that the beneficiary be a close relative, the eligible relationships being set forth in the laws. Since the statutes bestow legal capacity on a minor only for the purpose of negotiating insurance on his own life, he is still under legal disability in dealing as owner or beneficiary with a policy on the life of another person.[6]

A life insurance contract entered into between an American company and a resident of a foreign country is just as valid as one made with an American citizen, unless a state of war exists between the two countries, in which event the contract would be a nullity. In the first instance, the resident of the foreign country would be described as an alien friend; and in the second, as an alien enemy. A contract made with an alien friend is valid in all respects, while one with an alien enemy is void. No difficulties are likely to arise unless an alien friend with whom a contract has been made becomes an alien enemy through the outbreak of hostilities. In that event, it will generally be impossible, as well as contrary to public policy, for the parties to carry out the terms of the contract. In the case of life insurance, premium payments could not be made (unless the company had a branch office in the foreign country), and a question arises as to the status of the policy.[7]

---

[5] *Johnson* v. *Northwestern Mutual Life Insurance Co.,* 56 Minn. 365, 57 N.W. 934, aff'd on rehearing 59 N.W. 992 (1894).

[6] By a recent enactment New York now permits a minor age fourteen and one-half to twenty-one to contract for life insurance on the life of any person in whom the minor has an insurable interest. This change was made in order to permit minor husbands to apply for family policies covering their wives and children.

[7] This problem has frequently originated through the sale of life insurance to an alien residing in the United States who returned to his native country before the outbreak of hostilities.

The rulings of the courts in cases involving this problem have been diverse. In Connecticut, Georgia, and a few other states, it is held that all rights in such contracts are terminated and all equities forfeited. This is a harsh rule and permits the enrichment of the insurance company at the expense of one whose nonperformance was beyond his individual control. A number of states, including New York and New Jersey, hold that the contract is merely suspended during hostilities and can be revived by payment of all past-due premiums. Under this rule, the policy of a deceased policyholder can be revived and the company forced to pay the face amount. This rule obviously exposes the company to a high degree of adverse selection. A third group of courts, including the United States Supreme Court, hold that the contract is terminated with the outbreak of hostilities, but the policy-holder is entitled to the reserve computed as of the date of the first premium in default. The reserve would be paid over to the governmental agency charged with the responsibility of assembling and holding property belonging to alien enemies. Under this rule, no action can be brought to recover the face of the policy, nor is the company under any obligation to revive the policy. None of the solutions to the problem is perfectly satisfactory, but the basis of settlement prescribed by the Supreme Court would seem to be the most equitable.

MUTUAL ASSENT

As in the case of other simple contracts, there must be an expression of mutual assent before a life insurance contract can be created. One party must make an offer to enter into an insurance transaction, and the other must accept the offer. One would naturally assume that the company, through one of its soliciting agents, makes the offer, which the prospective insured is free to accept or decline. That is not necessarily the case. In many situations, the prospect is considered to have made the offer. As a general rule, and subject to the exceptions noted later, the prospect is considered to have made the offer whenever the application is accompanied by the first premium, whereas the company is regarded as the offeror whenever the first premium is not paid (or, at least, definitely promised) with the application. In the first situation, the prospect has indicated his unqualified willingness to enter into a contractual relationship with the company, even to the point of putting up the consideration; while in the second situation, the prospect may refuse, without any legal penalties, to accept and pay for the contract issued by the company. The question of who is the offeror and who the offeree is important in determining the exact time at which the contract comes into existence, which may be of crucial significance. This matter is dealt with in a later section.

The Application

The chain of events which culminates in the formation of a life insurance contract is inaugurated by a conversation between a soliciting agent of the company and a prospect for insurance, during the course of which the prospect is invited or—more accurately—urged to extend an offer to the company. Such invitations to deal have no legal consequences in the formation of the contract, although they may contain representations that will have consequences after the contract is made.[8] If the invitation to deal comes from a broker, the representations will have no legal effect either before or after formation of the contract, since a broker is considered to be the agent of the applicant for the purpose of procuring insurance.[9]

The prospective insured's offer to the company, or his invitation to the company to make him an offer, as the case might be, is communicated in the form of an application. As far as the law is concerned, the application can be oral or written; and in many branches of insurance, such as fire insurance, oral applications are the custom. In life insurance, however, written applications are required as a matter of company practice.

The application for a life insurance contract serves the following purposes:

1. It requests the insurer to issue a specific type of policy, providing a designated amount of insurance, in exchange for a specified premium.
2. It gives the name and address of the applicant, the name and relationship of the person or persons to whom the proceeds are to be paid, and the manner in which the company's obligation is to be discharged.
3. It provides a detailed description of the risk which the insurer is asked to underwrite, including statements or representations as to the applicant's occupation, travel plans, family history, personal medical history, present physical condition, and habits.
4. It puts the applicant on notice, and requires an acknowledgment from him of the fact, that the soliciting agent has no authority to modify

---

[8] See pp. 547–48.

[9] On the other hand, a broker is considered to be an agent of the insurer for the purpose of collecting the first (and subsequent) premium and delivering the policy.

any terms of the application or of the policy to be issued pursuant thereto (the *nonwaiver clause*).

The contents of the application relating to the first two functions constitute the offer in the technical sense, since they fix the terms of the policy to be issued by the company as an acceptance of the offer. While the identification of the person whose life is to be insured is a necessary part of the offer, the detailed description of the risk is not actually a part of the offer. From a legal standpoint, the representations of the applicant as to his medical history, present physical condition, and so on, are merely inducements to the insurer; they are not promises or conditions of the contract. Neither does the nonwaiver clause relate to the offer. It is intended merely to prevent the applicant from successfully contending afterwards that he was misled as to the apparent authority of the agent.[10]

In the typical commercial transaction, the offer becomes a part of the contract ultimately consummated. This is not true of the offer leading to a life insurance contract, unless the application is specifically made a part of the contract. It has long been established—first by court decisions and later by statutes—that once a life insurance policy is issued, the entire contract is contained in the policy. This rule, known historically as the *parol evidence rule* but more recently as the rule of *legal integration,* has been stated as follows: "All preliminary negotiations, conversations and oral agreements are merged in and superseded by the subsequent written contract and unless fraud, accident or mistake be averred, the writing constitutes the agreement between the parties, and its terms cannot be added to or subtracted from by parol evidence."[11]

Since the company places great reliance on the information contained in the application and—in the event of a contested claim—would undoubtedly want to introduce evidence therefrom, it customarily incorporates the application into the contract, by reference as well as by physical attachment of a copy (usually a photostat) of the application to the policy. In many of the states, including New York, there are statutes which require that a copy of the application be physically attached to the policy if the statements in the application are to be treated as representations and are to be introduced into evidence in the event of litigation.

---

[10] The effect of such notice is discussed on pp. 546–47.

[11] H. M. Horne and D. B. Mansfield, *The Life Insurance Contract* (2d ed.; New York: Life Office Management Association, 1948), p. 46.

Effective Date of Coverage

The coverage under a life insurance policy becomes effective the instant the contract comes into existence. The latter event, however, takes place only after certain conditions have been fulfilled, and those conditions can be fulfilled in more than one manner. The procedure by which a contract is brought into existence after submission of the application depends upon whether the latter is regarded as an offer or only an invitation to the company to make an offer. That, in turn, depends upon the time at which and the circumstances under which the first premium is paid. In that regard, it is necessary to distinguish among three different sets of circumstances. The first set of circumstances to be considered is that under which the application is submitted without payment of the first premium.

Application without First Premium. It will be recalled that when the applicant does not tender the first premium with the application, the latter is regarded as only an invitation to deal,[12] and the approval of the application and issue of the policy constitute an offer from the company to the prospective insured which is normally communicated by delivery of the policy. The applicant manifests his acceptance of the company's offer by accepting delivery of the policy and paying the first premium. Most companies specify in the application that the prospective insured must be in good health at the time of delivery of the policy, and some condition the contract on the absence of any medical treatment during the interim between submission of the application and delivery of the policy. All these requirements—delivery of the policy, payment of the first premium, good health of the applicant, and absence of any interim medical treatment—are treated as conditions precedent which must be fulfilled before the contract comes into existence and the coverage becomes effective. Each of these requirements will be discussed.

1. *Delivery of the Policy.* Delivery of the policy is a legal prerequisite to the validity of the life insurance contract only because the companies specifically make it so. Neither by statute nor by common law is the delivery of a formal policy requisite to the completion, validity, or enforceability of a contract of insurance. This is contrary to

---

[12] This is true only when the soliciting agent does not have authority to extend credit. If the agent has authority to take a promissory note or even an oral promise of the insured, in lieu of cash, an application accompanied by such a promise is an offer from the applicant to make a *bilateral* contract—an exchange of the applicant's promise for the insurer's promise.

real estate law, for example, which holds that legal title to real estate is not transferred until the deed is delivered. The company could conceivably communicate its offer to the applicant in some other manner, and the applicant could manifest his acceptance by notification to the company or to the soliciting agent. The controlling reason why the companies make delivery of the policy a condition precedent to the formation of the contract is that it provides a means of establishing definitely the moment at which coverage under the contract becomes effective. Several other actions of the company—such as approval of the application by the underwriting department, issue of the policy, or mailing of the policy to the soliciting agent for delivery—might be construed as the inception of coverage, leading to much confusion and litigation, unless the parties agree in advance that a definitely determinable event, such as delivery of the policy, shall mark the beginning of coverage.

Despite this attempt to achieve certainty, litigation has developed over the meaning of the word "delivery." The issue is whether the condition can be satisfied only by a manual delivery or whether constructive delivery will be sufficient. If it is clearly evident from the terms of the application and the policy that actual, manual delivery is contemplated, the requirement will be strictly enforced.[13] If, however, the requirement is couched in terms of a simple "delivery," the general rule is that the condition can be fulfilled by constructive delivery.[14] Constructive delivery has been held to take place whenever a policy, properly stamped and addressed to the company's agent, is deposited in the mails, provided no limitations are imposed upon the manual delivery of the policy to the insured by the agent.[15] There are a number of decisions, however, which hold that the requirement of "delivery" —and especially "actual delivery"—is itself a condition precedent which cannot be met by a constructive delivery. It should be remarked that the issue of constructive delivery is not material if the other conditions—notably, payment of the first premium and the applicant's good health—are not met.

---

[13] *Pruit* v. *Great Southern Life Insurance Co.*, 202 La. 527, 12 So. 2d 261 (1942).

[14] *Massachusetts Mutual Life Insurance Co.* v. *National Bank of Commerce*, 95 F. 2d 797 (4th Cir., 1938).

[15] *Life and Casualty Insurance Co.* v. *McCrae*, 193 Ark. 890, 103 S.W. 2d 929 (1937); *Republic National Life Insurance Co.* v. *Merkley*, 59 Ariz. 125, 124 P. 2d 313 (1942); *Jefferson Standard Life Insurance Co.* v. *Munthe*, 78 F. 2d 53 (9th Cir., 1935); *Jackson* v. *New York Life Insurance Co.*, 7 F. 2d 31 (9th Cir. 1925).

To a large extent, delivery is a matter of the intention of the parties. It is a question of who has the *right* to possession of the policy, rather than who has actual possession. That being true, possession of the policy by the insured is, at most, only prima-facie evidence of its delivery.[16] The presumption of proper delivery can be rebutted by evidence that the insured obtained possession of the policy by fraud, for the purpose of inspecting it, or in any other manner manifesting a lack of intention on the company's part to effectuate a legal delivery of the policy. On the other hand, it has been held that if the first premium has been paid, the applicant is in good health, and the company has implicitly expressed its intention of being legally bound under the contract by delivering the policy to the agent to be unconditionally passed on to the applicant, the contract is in force; and, although the insured may die without actual possession of the policy, the company is liable for payment of the insured amount.[17]

In view of the foregoing presumption, an agent must observe proper safeguards in relinquishing physical possession of a policy to an applicant before all conditions precedent have been fulfilled. The need for caution is greatly magnified if the policy, on its face, acknowledges receipt of the first premium, which is sometimes the case. The most common circumstance under which the agent may find it necessary to relinquish control over a policy without making a legal delivery is when the applicant expresses a desire to study the policy. In that event, the applicant is asked to sign a receipt in which he acknowledges that the policy is in his hands only for examination and approval, and that he has not paid the first premium. This acknowledgment is called an *inspection receipt*.

2. *Payment of First Premium.* It is customary for the application —and sometimes, the policy itself—to stipulate that the first premium must be paid before the coverage can become effective. Payment of the full amount in cash is usually specified; and unless the company agrees to extend credit, any payment smaller than the full premium will fail to satisfy the requirement. The agent is usually not authorized to extend credit on behalf of the company, but he may pay the premium for the insured and seek reimbursement on a personal basis. If an agent is authorized to accept the promissory note of an applicant in

---

[16] *Eaton* v. *New York Life Insurance Co.*, 315 Pa. 68, 172 Atl. 121 (1934).
[17] *New York Life Insurance Co.* v. *Baker*, 33 F. 2d 434 (7th Cir. 1929).

payment of the first premium, the tendering of such a note by the applicant will satisfy the condition precedent, but failure of the insured to pay the note at maturity may cause the policy to lapse.[18]

Payment by check may be taken as absolute or conditional payment, depending upon the intention of the parties. If the check is accepted in absolute payment of the first premium, failure of the bank to honor the check would not affect the validity of the policy, merely giving the company the right to sue the applicant for the amount of the check. On the other hand, if the check is accepted only as conditional payment, nonpayment of the check would cause the contract to fail. Most companies stipulate that checks are accepted subject to being honored by the bank, which is the common-law rule in the absence of evidence that the check was accepted as absolute payment.

3. *Good Health of Applicant.* The *delivery-in-good-health clause* is a by-product of the process by which risks are underwritten in life insurance. In most lines of property and casualty insurance, the local agent is clothed with the authority to underwrite the risk and bind the coverage. There need be no lag of any consequence between the inspection of the risk and the binding of the coverage. In life insurance, on the contrary, all underwriting information is forwarded to the home office, and the right to bind the risk rests solely with the executive officers of the company. Under such a system, which seems to be the only feasible one, there is an inevitable time lag between the submission of the application and the assumption of the risk by the insurer. In a large case, where the investigation of the applicant must be very comprehensive and the collection of medical data may involve correspondence with attending physicians and requests for supplemental diagnostic procedures, the lag might be as long as a month. The company naturally would like to be protected against a deterioration of the applicant's health during the time it is considering the application. The means which the companies have chosen to accomplish this objective is the delivery-in-good-health clause.

The exact wording of the good-health clause varies from company to company; but the gist of the clause is that the policy shall not take effect unless, upon the date of delivery, the applicant shall be alive and in good health. Some clauses provide that unless the first premium is paid with the application, the applicant must be alive and in good

---

[18] See pp. 500–502.

health upon payment of the first premium. Such a clause has the effect of making the good health of the applicant a condition precedent to the effectiveness of the contract.[19]

The fact that the good-health requirement is a condition precedent, and has been enforced by the courts as such, has great significance in protecting the companies against fraud. In attempting to rescind a contract on the grounds of misrepresentation or concealment,[20] the companies are frequently required to prove that the applicant deliberately misrepresented the facts of the case. In fact, most states have enacted legislation which stipulates that no misrepresentation shall void the policy unless such misrepresentation was made with actual intent to deceive, or unless it would increase the risk. To prove intent to defraud is always difficult and is frequently impossible. The difficulty is avoided with the good-health clause, since intent is not involved. The clause is concerned with the existence of a condition and not with what may or may not have been known to the applicant. If the company can prove to the satisfaction of a court that the applicant was not, in fact, in good health at the date of delivery of the policy, it can avoid liability under the contract. In practice, however, companies generally raise the issue only when they suspect that the applicant did not act in good faith, or when there has been a material deterioration in the applicant's health in the interval between the date of the medical examination and the date of delivery of the policy.

As might be expected, the courts have frequently been called upon to define the meaning of the terms "good health" and "sound health." A Georgia court[21] has ruled that "good health," as used in the context of the clause under discussion, is a relative term, meaning not absolute freedom from physical infirmity but only such a condition of body and mind that one may discharge the ordinary duties of life without serious strain upon the vital powers. A Texas court[22] has stated that "good health" does not mean perfect health, but a state of health free from any disease or ailment that seriously affects the general soundness of

---

[19] Under the laws of some states, including Pennsylvania, if the applicant underwent a medical examination, the good-health requirement can be invoked only with respect to changes in the applicant's health occurring after the medical examination.

[20] Such action must be taken during the period of contestability. See pp. 571–72.

[21] *National Life and Accident Insurance Co.* v. *Bonner,* 58 Ga. App. 876, 200 S.E. 319 (1938).

[22] *Texas Independence Life Insurance Co.* v. *Pickens,* 153 S.W. 2d 884 (Tex. Civ. App., 1941).

the system. A Nebraska court[23] distinguished between a mere temporary indisposition, which does not tend to weaken or undermine the constitution, and an ailment which must be regarded as serious. One of the most comprehensive definitions was supplied by a Kansas court:

> [Good health] is not apparent good health, nor yet a belief of the applicant that he is in good health, but it is that he is in actual good health. Of course, slight troubles or temporary indisposition which will not usually result in serious consequences, and which do not seriously impair or weaken his constitution, do not establish the absence of good health, but, if the illness is of a serious nature, such as to weaken and impair the constitution and shorten life, the applicant cannot be held to be in good health.[24]

There has been a tendency on the part of some courts to narrow the application of the clause to those cases where a change in the applicant's health occurs between the time of the medical examination and delivery of the policy to the applicant. This line of decisions is exemplified by a fairly recent Pennsylvania case,[25] in which the court stated that the good-health clause has no application to a disease the applicant may have had at the time of the medical examination, unless fraud or misrepresentation can be proved, since presumably his physical condition was satisfactory to the company; otherwise, the policy would not have been issued. "The legal scope of that provision is restricted to mean only that the applicant did not contract any new disease impairing his health, nor suffer any material change in his physical condition between the time of such examination and the date of the policy. . . ."[26]

This interpretation of the clause is certainly at variance with the common understanding of the term "good health" and with the legal definition cited earlier, but it is consistent with the apparent purpose of the clause. As a matter of fact, the companies have usually invoked the clause as a defense against a claim only where there has been a change in the applicant's health, or where there has been fraud or misrepresentation in the application.

The burden of proving that the applicant was not in good health at the time of delivery of the policy is usually on the company. A

---

[23] *Gugelman* v. *Kansas City Life Insurance Co.*, 137 Neb. 411, 289 N.W. 842 (1940).

[24] *Klein* v. *Farmers and Bankers Life Insurance Co.*, 132 Kan. 748, 753, 297 Pac. 730, 732 (1931).

[25] *Davidson et al.* v. *John Hancock Mutual Life Insurance Co.*, 159 Pa. Super. 532, 49 A. 2d 185 (1946).

[26] *Ibid.*, 535 and 49 A. 2d 186.

minority of the courts have held that the insured or his beneficiary must prove compliance with the clause.

4. *Medical Treatment after Submission of Application.* Some policies issued today contain a clause which provides that the policy shall not take effect if the applicant has received medical or hospital treatment between the time that the application was signed and the date of delivery of the policy.[27] Like the good-health clause, this clause is designed to deal with a change in the physical condition of the applicant during the time the application is being processed. It is intended to be a condition precedent, and the courts generally treat it as such. In other words, if during the contestable period, the company can prove that the applicant received medical or hospital treatment between the date of the application and delivery of the policy, and failed to disclose the fact to the company, the latter can avoid liability under the contract. If the fact of medical treatment is disclosed at the time the policy is delivered, the company, after consideration of the ailment, may conclude that the applicant's insurability is not impaired and waive the clause. The courts are very zealous in seeking a waiver of the clause in the conduct of the company or its agents.[28]

5. *Justification of Conditions Precedent.* When the premium is not paid with the application, all conditions precedent must be fulfilled before the contract becomes effective. In general, this means that the policy must be delivered by the agent while the applicant is alive and in good health, and the full amount of the first premium must be paid in cash or by a valid check at the moment of delivery. Delivery of the policy and payment of the first premium are supposed to be simultaneous transactions.

Some may feel that this procedure is unduly legalistic and should be replaced by a system under which the company would approve retroactively all applications from persons who were insurable at the time of application, paying the face of the policy to the beneficiaries of those who die before the policy can be delivered and placing into full effect the policies requested by those whose health deteriorates in the

---

[27] Industrial life insurance policies usually contain a provision which permits the company to void the contract (within the contestable period) if within two years prior to application for the policy, the insured received hospital or medical treatment which he failed to disclose or to prove immaterial to the risk.

[28] Some companies invoke the doctrine of continuing representations to deal with changes in insurability during the interim between submission of the application and delivery of the policy. The landmark case in this area of law is *Stipcich* v. *Metropolitan Life Ins. Co.,* 277 U.S. 311, 45 Sup. Ct. 512, 72 L.Ed. 895.

interim. The impracticality of this scheme is apparent when it is realized that in issuing a policy which has not been paid for, the company is making an offer to the applicant which the latter is free to reject without any liability on his part. In other words, the applicant can refuse to take a policy which he requested, even after the company has incurred considerable expense in having him examined by a physician, securing an inspection report, and processing the application through various channels. The company would be exposed to serious antiselection if it should honor all insurance applications from persons who die or suffer an impairment of health before the policy can be delivered, and yet not be able to force those applicants who are still alive and in good health to accept delivery of their policies. Recognizing the advantages to both the applicant and the company of having the coverage attach at the date of application, the companies have devised a procedure to accomplish the objective. This procedure, involving the use of a so-called *conditional receipt,* is described in the following section.

Prepayment of First Premium. The applicant can avoid the legal consequences of the aforementioned conditions precedent by the simple expedient of remitting the first premium with his application for insurance. In that event, the companies generally acknowledge receipt of the premium with a document called a *conditional receipt,* which binds the coverage without reference to delivery of the policy.

There are several forms of conditional receipt in general use today,[29] but the two basic types may be characterized as the *insurability* type and the *approval* type. The *insurability* type of receipt makes the coverage effective at the time of the application, provided the applicant is found to be insurable in accordance with the general underwriting rules of the company. Some receipts make the coverage effective on the date of the application or the medical examination, whichever is later.

The coverage under such a clause is not automatic. The applicant is considered to have made an offer to the insurer, which, by the issuance of the conditional receipt, accepts the offer, subject to a condition—the condition being that the applicant be found to be insurable. If the home office finds the applicant to have been insurable in accordance with its general underwriting rules on the date of the application or medical examination, the coverage attaches retroactively to the date

---

[29] See Samuel F. Fortunato, "Conditional Receipts: Should the Uninsurable Have Insurance?" *The Forum,* American Bar Association, Vol. I, No. 3, April, 1966, pp. 5–22.

cited. If the company finds that the applicant was not insurable at the time he submitted the application, the coverage never attaches under the policy applied for, and the premium is refunded. For the coverage to be binding as of the date of application, the risk must be acceptable to the company under its underwriting rules on the plan and for the amount applied for, and at the premium rate envisioned in the application. If the risk is acceptable, but only on a plan or at a premium rate different from that contemplated in the application, the company is construed to have made a counteroffer which must be accepted by the applicant before the coverage can become effective. A few companies have adopted a form of receipt which provides retroactive coverage under the counterproposal if the applicant, within a specified period, accepts the counteroffer and pays any additional premium that might be involved. If the applicant should die before he has had a reasonable opportunity to accept the counteroffer, he is deemed to have accepted it, and the company is obligated to pay the amount of insurance that would have been purchased on the altered terms by the premium actually paid.

If the applicant is found to have been insurable at the date of application, the coverage attaches retroactively even though, in the meantime, the applicant has died or his insurability has deteriorated. Companies are frequently called upon to consider the application of a person known to have died since applying for insurance, and they are careful not to permit that circumstance to influence their underwriting decision. The same code of ethics is followed in reviewing the applications of persons who have suffered heart attacks or other physical impairments. If the applicant is to receive the fullest benefit of the conditional receipt, it is absolutely essential that the company apply general underwriting standards rather than standards tailored to fit the individual case.

The *approval* type of receipt states that the coverage shall be effective from the completion of the application, provided the company approves the application. The receipt usually mades no reference to the criteria that will be applied in the company's consideration of the application, but under the present state of the law it is clear that the company must act reasonably and apply its customary underwriting standards. Theoretically, the company is not on the risk if the applicant dies before his application is acted upon. Nevertheless, judicial opinion is divided as to whether the insurer should be held liable for payment of the face amount of the policy if the applicant dies before the application is acted upon. There is a judicial trend, noticeable with respect to both the *insurability* and *approval* types of receipts, to find an ambiguity and to hold that there is coverage from the date of the receipt until approval or declination of the application.

In recognition of this trend, a few companies use a form of conditional receipt that places the company unconditionally on the risk from the date of application, usually for a limited period of time, such as sixty days, the insurance remaining in full effect unless and until the application is declined. Under this form, the applicant enjoys coverage for a brief period even when he is definitely an uninsurable risk.

Properly construed, the conditional receipt arrangement offers real benefits to both the insured and the insurer, and is widely used. It protects the applicant against loss of insurability during the period his application is being processed, and it protects the company against a declination of the policy by the applicant after it has been issued—at considerable expense. The arrangement is feasible, since all applicants using the plan pay their premiums in advance, and the company is not exposed to adverse selection. Moreover, the arrangement does not involve any relaxation of underwriting standards.

Advance Payment of First Premium without Conditional Receipt. The first premium may be remitted with the application without a conditional receipt being issued to the applicant. This situation could arise out of the practice of issuing conditional receipts only when the applicant specifically requests immediate coverage or through inadvertence, as where an inexperienced agent failed to issue the receipt. Under such circumstances, the coverage does not attach until the application has been approved and the policy has been "delivered."[30] The applicant is considered to have made an offer which he can withdraw at any time before acceptance by the company. Acceptance is manifested by "delivery" of the policy.

In this case, as with policies whose premiums are not paid in advance, delivery can take the form of an actual physical transfer of the policy from the agent to the applicant, or transmission through the mails in such manner as to constitute constructive delivery. However, if the application requires that the policy be delivered to the applicant while the latter is in good health, mailing of the policy to the agent for delivery to the applicant is not likely to be regarded as constructive

---

[30] A few courts have held to the contrary. Moreover, California has a statute which binds the insurer as of the moment of premium payment if the risk meets the underwriting requirements of the company.

delivery, since a condition has been imposed on its release. Direct mailing of the policy to the applicant would be regarded as a waiver of the delivery requirement, but would be treated as a waiver of the good-health requirement only if the insurer had knowledge of a breach of the condition. The contract would become effective the instant the policy is placed in the mails, even though the insured never receives it.

Delay in Consideration of the Application

A life insurance company owes a moral duty and—in a minority of the states—a legal duty to the insuring public to consider all applications within a reasonable period and to render prompt decisions on the insurability of those seeking insurance. Two questions may arise in case of an unreasonable delay on the part of a company in determining the insurability of an applicant: (1) Does the unreasonable delay constitute an acceptance of the applicant's offer? (2) Is the insurer liable for the damages caused by its delay in case the applicant dies before the application is either accepted or rejected?

It seems clear that no presumption of acceptance should be allowed when the application is not accompanied by the first premium. In that event, no offer has been made to the company, and the silence of the latter could hardly be construed as acceptance of a nonexistent offer. A different situation obtains, however, when the applicant remits the first premium with his application and thus makes a valid offer to the company.

As a general rule, silence is not construed as acceptance of an offer. To the contrary, after a reasonable time, the offeror can assume that the offer has been rejected and he is free to deal with another party. If this were not the rule, people with goods to sell could flood the country with offers which the recipients would be obliged to reject if they were not to become obligated to buy the goods. The writing of rejections could become an intolerable burden. A majority of courts have applied this general rule to the insurer's silence and have held that no matter how long the company delays, its silence will not bind it to a contract of insurance.[31]

A few courts have made a distinction between *unsolicited* offers, the usual kind, and those which are made in response to the activities of agents who are paid to solicit offers, as is the case in life insurance. These courts have held that the insurer's unreasonable delay in reject-

---

[31] *Steinle* v. *New York Life Insurance Co.*, 81 Fed. 489 (5th Cir. 1897).

ing an application constitutes an acceptance which completes the contract.[32]

While in most states, delay in consideration of an application does not make an insurer liable under *contract,* some courts have recognized a liability of the company in *tort*—i.e., a civil liability arising other than from a contract.[33] These courts hold that since the company is operating under a franchise from the state, it is under duty to act promptly and with due care upon all applications received by it. They argue that the state issues a charter or license in order that the public may have access to an important form of protection which, in the public interest, should be made available to all who can qualify for it. The company solicits the application and, having obtained it along with the applicant's consideration, is bound to furnish the insurance which the state has authorized or to decline to do so within a reasonable time. "Otherwise the applicant is unduly delayed in obtaining insurance he desires and for which the law has afforded the opportunity, and which the insurer impliedly has promised if conditions are satisfactory."[34] Failure to live up to this obligation makes the insurer liable to the applicant for damages. If an applicant who was insurable at the time of application dies before the company—in disregard of its duty to act promptly—has approved the risk, many courts would hold that the applicant's estate could recover the amount of insurance applied for. It would seem that if the insurer is adjudged guilty of a tort, the beneficiary would be the logical person to receive damages; but with a few exceptions, the courts hold that she cannot recover, since she is not a party at interest until the coverage becomes effective.

The question of tort liability is not likely to arise under a conditional receipt situation, since the forms in general use provide for retroactive coverage.

Operative Date of Policy

The foregoing discussion was concerned with the determination of the date on which coverage under a life insurance contract becomes

---

[32] *American Life Insurance Co.* v. *Hutchinson,* 109 F. 2d 424 (6th Cir. 1940); Colum. L. Rev. 1072 (1940).

[33] See Edwin W. Patterson, *Essentials of Insurance Law* (2d ed.; New York: McGraw-Hill Book Co., Inc., 1957), p. 78, n. 28, for case citations and a list of the states in which such doctrine has been approved and rejected. Pennsylvania courts have rejected the doctrine.

[34] *Duffie* v. *Bankers Life Assn.,* 160 Iowa 19, 27, 139 N.W. 1087, 1090 (1913).

effective. Such date is usually referred to as the *effective date* of the policy. It may or may not be the same date as that on the face of the policy, which is significant for other reasons. The latter governs the status of various policy provisions after the contract has gone into effect and is sometimes referred to as the *operative date* of the policy.

The policy may bear the date on which it was issued, the date on which the coverage becomes effective, or the date on which it was applied for. The most common practice is to date the policy as of the date of issue, unless there is a conditional receipt, in which event the policy will bear the date of the application or the medical examination, whichever is later. Occasionally, the policy will bear a date earlier than the date of application. This is known as *antedating* the policy and is done only at the request of or with the consent of the applicant, usually for the purpose of producing a lower insurance age and hence a lower premium.[35] The practice is not generally regarded to be in conflict with anti-rebating laws, but several states prohibit it when an age change is involved. Other states have attempted to control the practice by forbidding the issue of a policy which bears a date more than six months earlier than the date of the application, a limitation which many—if not most—companies have voluntarily adopted.

The practice of antedating policies—which, from a legal standpoint, refers to the use of any date earlier than the effective date of the policy—raises three important questions: (1) When does the next premium fall due? (2) From what date does extended term insurance run? (3) From what date do the incontestable and suicide clauses begin to run? When the antedating was done at the request of the applicant and resulted in a lower contract age for the applicant, the overwhelming majority of both state and federal courts hold that the due date of the next premium is established by the date of the policy. Even when the antedating does not benefit the applicant—i.e., no age change is involved—the majority of the courts support the view that the policy date establishes the due date, on the grounds that certainty is preferable to uncertainty. In some jurisdictions, especially Missouri, it is held that the payment of an "annual" premium entitles the insured to a full year of protection and that the due date of the next premium

---

[35] A person's insurance age for ordinary insurance is his age at the nearest birthday. For insurance purposes, he becomes one year older six months and one day after his last birthday. It is possible to obtain a lower insurance age by dating a policy back only one day, but most cases involve a much longer period.

is determined by reference to the effective date of coverage. For this reason, many companies do not refer to the first premium as an "annual" or "quarterly" premium but indicate, rather, the exact period covered by the first premium and the due date of the second premium.

Closely related to the problem of determining the due date of the second and subsequent premiums is the fixing of the period of extended term insurance in the event that there is a default in premium payments. Clearly, it would be to the advantage of the insured and his beneficiaries to have the date of default from which the period of extended term insurance runs calculated by reference to the effective date of the contract, rather than from an earlier date of issue. The timing of the insured's death could be such that the choice of beginning date for the term insurance could make the difference between payment of the face of the policy and total avoidance of liability by the company. It is generally held, however, that the anniversary date fixed for premium payment purposes also controls the inception date for extended term insurance.

With respect to the incontestable and suicide clauses, the general view is that the date of issue establishes the point of departure. A few courts, arguing that the suicide clause is completely independent of the provisions dealing with premium payment, hold that the effective date of the policy controls. Some policies specify a certain date as being the "date of issue" for the purpose of these clauses, which date is usually recognized by the courts.

In summary, then, it may be said that antedating, if done without fraud or mistake and not in violation of a state statute, is given effect whether it benefits the insured or the insurer.

CHAPTER XXIV

Formation of a Life Insurance Contract

(Continued)

CONSIDERATION

Nature

The life insurance contract, like other contracts, must be supported by a valid consideration. A consideration is always given in exchange for a promise and, in the case of a bilateral contract, is itself a promise. The life insurance contract, however, is a unilateral contract, since only the company makes an enforceable promise. The consideration for the insurer's promise is the first premium or, if premiums are to be paid more frequently than annually, the first installment of the first premium. The policies of some companies state that the promise of the company is given in consideration of the *application* and the first premium. This is apparently intended to give greater legal effect to the application, on which the company places such great reliance.

Premiums subsequent to the first are not part of the legal consideration, since otherwise the contract could not come into existence until they are all paid. Rather, they are conditions precedent to the continuance of the contract. The promise of the insurer is conditioned on the continued payment of periodic premiums. If the insured defaults in the payment of a subsequent premium, the company is released from its original promise to pay the face of the policy but remains obligated to honor various subsidiary promises contained in the surrender provisions and the reinstatement clause.

Form

The insurance company is entitled to receive the first premium, or the first installment thereof, in cash; it may, however, agree to accept any valuable property. The premium may be paid in cash, by check, by promissory note, or—in the absence of a prohibitive statute—by services, such as printing work or advertising. Some states forbid an insurance company to accept payment of any premium in services, presumably because the practice lends itself too readily to rebating. By placing an excessive value on the services rendered, a company or its agent could, in effect, refund a portion of the contractual premium charge.

Checks are readily accepted by insurance companies, but they are generally treated as conditional payments. That is, crediting of the premium is usually conditioned upon the honoring of the instrument by the bank upon which it is drawn. Hence, if the check is not honored when presented, the company holds that the premium has not been paid, and its promise is no longer operative. This is true even though the check was tendered to the insurer in good faith by the insured. However, where the insured had sufficient funds in the bank to cover the check and the bank's failure to honor the check was based on a technical defect in the instrument, such as an improper signature or an incorrect date, or a clerical error on the part of the bank, the companies are inclined to recognize a contractual obligation, provided the premium is subsequently paid in cash or by valid check by the insured or his beneficiary.

A company or its properly authorized agent may agree that the check constitutes an absolute payment of the premium. That is, the company accepts the liability of the parties to the instrument in satisfaction of the premium. This occurs when the agent gives the applicant an unconditional premium receipt in exchange for his check. In this case, if the check is not paid when presented, the company may enforce its rights on the instrument but cannot validly claim that the premium has not been paid.

A company may authorize some or all of its agents to accept a promissory note of the insured in payment of the first premium (and subsequent premiums, for that matter). If the note is honored at maturity, no complications are involved; but a real question arises as to the status of the policy in the event that the note is not paid when due. In anticipation of such an eventuality, a company may include on the note, premium receipt, or policy, or all three, a stipulation to the effect that if the note is not paid at maturity, the policy shall be discontinued. If such a provision is included in all three instruments, it will be enforced according to its terms. Hence, as soon as the maturity date of the note arrives and the note remains unpaid, the company is entitled to repudiate the contract. If the aforementioned stipulation is included in the note or in the premium receipt, *but not in the policy,* there is a conflict of opinion as to the rights of the company. Some courts hold that the provision is nugatory, on the grounds that it violates the statute, found in most states, which provides that the policy and the application shall constitute the entire contract between the parties. Other courts uphold the provision, on the grounds that the statute means simply that the policy shall contain the entire contract as of the time it was issued. The courts which entertain this view feel that the statute does not prevent the execution of subsequent agreements. They point out that if the policy is construed to contain all possible agreements relating to the contract, it would be contrary to the statute for the company to agree to an extension of time for the payment of a premium, whereas such agreements are generally recognized. The latter view would seem to be in accord with the evident intention of the parties.

If the forfeiture provision is contained in the policy but not in the note or the premium receipt, there is also a conflict of opinion. In those states in which the entire-contract statute is strictly followed, the provision contained in the policy will be enforced according to its terms. In other states, the decision turns on the interpretation of the note and the receipt. If the note and the receipt evidence an intention on the part of the insurer to accept the note as an unconditional payment, this subsequent agreement will override the provision contained in the policy. On the other hand, if there is no indication of an intention to accept the note as an unconditional payment, the provision in the policy will prevail.

If there is no forfeiture provision in the policy, or the note, or the premium receipt, the note is considered to be an absolute payment of the premium, and the insurance company is limited to its rights on the note in the event that it is not paid at maturity. This is the usual case.

It should be observed that if the insurer or its authorized agent extends credit to the insured, the contract will be bilateral rather than unilateral. In this case, the consideration for the insurer's promise is the insured's promise to pay the amount of the first premium.

An agent who is not authorized to extend credit on behalf of the company may pay the premium for the applicant. In doing so, he is acting as the applicant's agent, and failure of the applicant to reimburse the agent will not invalidate the policy.

LEGALITY OF PURPOSE

General Considerations

To be enforceable, a contract must be entered into for a legal purpose. All contracts are assumed to have a legal purpose, except those that contemplate a course of action that would contravene a statute or some other rule of law. It is not sufficient, however, that the agreement refrain from an act specifically prohibited by law; it must not tend to encourage illegality, immorality, or other conduct contrary to public policy.

Life insurance clearly does not require either party to perform an illegal act and, in that respect, qualifies as a perfectly valid contract. As a matter of fact, it is universally recognized as having a purpose highly beneficial to society and worthy of favorable legislative treatment. On the other hand, it has been recognized that without adequate safeguards, life insurance could lend itself to behavior that would be socially harmful and contrary to public policy. Specifically, it could provide the motivation for wagering, murder, and suicide.

Inducement to Wagering. With respect to the first of these dangers, life insurance, being aleatory in nature, offers the opportunity of a return out of all proportion to the investment in the contract. This characteristic of the transaction early attracted elements of the populace who were hopeful of enriching themselves through the operation of the laws of chance. In eighteenth-century England, life insurance became the means of satisfying a mania for gambling, which was discouraged but not prohibited. Speculative life insurance was likely to be taken out on anyone who was in the public eye. Persons accused of crimes punishable by death and those in disfavor with the royal court were favorite subjects for life insurance contracts. Prominent persons became the object of speculative insurance as soon as press notices revealed them to be seriously ill, and the premium for new policies on such persons fluctuated from day to day in accordance with the reports or rumors on their condition. Newspapers of the day even carried premium quotations on the lives of persons known to be the object of speculative insurance, with the consequences described by a contemporary writer. "This inhuman sport affected the minds of men depressed by long sickness; for when such persons casting an eye over a newspaper for amusement, saw their lives had been insured in the Alley at 90 p.c., they despaired of all hopes, and thus their desolution [*sic*] was hastened."[1] The situation became so intolerable that in 1774, Parliament enacted a law which provided that a person contracting for insurance had to have an insurable interest in the life of the person to be insured and, moreover, upon the death of the insured, could not recover a sum in excess of the monetary interest.[2]

In this country, an insurable interest has always been required; but with the exceptions noted later, no attempt has been made to apply the indemnity concept. In most states, the requirement of insurable interest is not based upon statute, but results from a judicial application of the public policy against the enforcement of wagering contracts. The states of New York, Pennsylvania, and California, among others, have statutes requiring an insurable interest.

Murder of Insured by Beneficiary. The insurable interest requirement originated as a means of controlling wagering in human lives and still finds its greatest significance in that function, but it was also intended to reduce the threat of murder created by the insuring of one person's life for the benefit of another. The thought was that if the class of persons who can legally insure the life of another is restricted to those who are closely related to him by blood, or possess such a financial relationship with him that they stand to gain more by his continued life than by his death, the temptation to murder the insured would be greatly curtailed. A further safeguard is sometimes provided in the form of a requirement that a person whose life is to be insured by another must give his consent to the transaction. Presumably, he will not permit his life to be insured in favor of a person whose integrity is questionable or whose motives he distrusts. The same reasoning underlies the rule, discussed later, that the beneficiary of a policy taken out by the insured himself need not have an insurable interest in the insured. The law presumes that the insured, whose life is at stake, is capable of choosing beneficiaries who will not be moti-

---

[1] David Scott, *Every Man His Own Broker* (1761), quoted in C. Walford, *Insurance Cyclopaedia* (London: Charles and Edwin Layton, 1876), Vol. IV, p. 187.

[2] Stat. 14 Geo. III, Chap. 48 (1774).

vated to commit murder to enjoy the insurance proceeds sooner.

The foregoing deterrents are supplemented not only by criminal penalties for murder but by statutes and judicial rulings which prohibit the payment of insurance proceeds to a beneficiary who murders the insured. This restriction is based on a general rule of law that a wrongdoer is not permitted to profit by his wrongdoing. The insurance company is not relieved of its obligation to pay, the proceeds going to contingent beneficiaries or the estate of the insured, depending upon the policy language and the law in the particular jurisdiction involved.

Suicide. A final area in which there exists the possibility of a conflict between life insurance and the public interest is the treatment of the suicide hazard. Suicide is contrary to many religious laws, and attempted suicide is ordinarily a penal offense. Thus, suicide is contrary to public policy. Any contract that would encourage or act as an inducement to suicide would, by the same token, be contrary to public policy. Some of the early court decisions in this country indicated that death by suicide should not be covered by a life insurance policy. In a leading case, the United States Supreme Court expressed the view that "death intentionally caused by the act of the insured when in sound mind—the policy being silent as to suicide—is not to be deemed to have been within the contemplation of the parties. . . . [A] different view would attribute to them a purpose to make a contract that could not be enforced without injury to the public. A contract, the tendency of which is to endanger the public interests or injuriously affect the public good, or which is subversive of sound morality, ought never to receive the sanction of a court of justice or be made the foundation of its judgment."[3]

This view, which has since been rejected by the American courts but is still the law in England, was not universally entertained; and in order to protect themselves against persons who might apply for insurance with the deliberate intent of committing suicide, the companies adopted the precaution of inserting in their policies a clause which limited their liability to a return of premiums in the event that the insured should commit suicide within a specified period—usually, one or two years—after the date of issue. It was felt that such a clause would properly protect the interests of the companies and yet, after a preliminary period during which any abnormal impulse toward self-destruction should have passed away or else been carried out, would

---

[3] *Ritter* v. *Mutual Life Insurance Co.,* 169 U.S. 139, 154 (1898).

provide coverage against a hazard of life to which all are subject. Such a clause was adjudged by the United States Supreme Court to conserve the public interest, and a number of states have gone so far as to impose statutory restrictions on the right of the companies to avoid liability because of suicide. The most common type of restriction is to limit the period during which a company can avoid coverage of the hazard. The Missouri statute precludes the defense of suicide at any time, unless it can be proved that the insured was contemplating suicide at the time he applied for the insurance.[4] This statute has been upheld by the United States Supreme Court as not being in conflict with the state constitution or the federal Constitution, but the court intimated that the statute was inconsistent with public policy and sound morality.[5] New York prohibits exclusion of suicide while the insured is insane.

For all practical purposes, the requirement of a legal object or purpose is concerned with the issue of insurable interest, and the remainder of this section will be devoted to that subject.

Insurable Interest

Insurable interest is difficult to define precisely. In its broadest sense, it is a "relation between the insured and the event insured against such that the occurrence of the event will cause substantial loss or harm of some kind to the insured."[6] As applied to life insurance, an insurable interest may be defined as such a relationship between the person applying for insurance and the person whose life is to be insured that there is a reasonable expectation of benefit or advantage to the applicant from continuation of the life of the insured or an expectation of loss or detriment from the cessation of that life. It should be noted that this definition does not require a *pecuniary* interest; it is broad enough to recognize a sentimental interest or one based on love and affection. Legal opinion in this country is divided as

---

[4] The Missouri statute reads as follows: "In all suits upon policies of insurance on life, hereafter issued by any company doing business in this state, it shall be no defense that the insured committed suicide, unless it be shown to the satisfaction of the court or jury trying the case, that the insured contemplated suicide at the time he made his application for the policy, and any stipulation in the policy to the contrary shall be void." The difficulty of proving intent is so great that the companies do not usually attempt it. In at least one case, however, the insurer avoided liability by producing a suicide note written by the insured before he applied for the insurance.

[5] *Whitfield* v. *Aetna Life Insurance Co.*, 205 U.S. 489 (1907).

[6] Edwin W. Patterson, *Essentials, of Insurance Law* (2d ed.; New York: McGraw-Hill Book Co., Inc., 1957), p. 154.

to whether a sentimental interest can satisfy the insurable interest requirement; but since a respectable group of courts do support the view that a sentimental interest is sufficient, the definition was made broad enough to encompass both points of view. It should be further noted that the pecuniary interest need not be capable of exact measurement. Nor need it be based on a legal right. It is sufficient that there be a *reasonable expectation* of some financial gain or advantage.

Various relationships can give rise to an insurable interest. Before they are discussed, however, it seems preferable to indicate when the interest must be present.

Incidence of Insurable Interest. In property and casualty insurance, an insurable interest need not be present at the inception of the contract, but it must exist at the time of loss if there is to be any recovery under the contract. The requirements are just reversed in the case of life insurance. In life insurance, an insurable interest must exist at the inception of the contract but need not be present at the time of the insured's death. This striking difference in the application of the requirement results from the fact that property insurance is based on the principle of indemnity, while life insurance is not. To use property insurance terminology, a life insurance contract is a *valued* policy; it is a contract to pay a stated sum upon the occurrence of the event insured against. Since the beneficiary has a legal claim to a fixed sum of money upon the insured's death, he need not prove that he sustained loss by reason of the death.

One may concede that the insurable interest of one person in another person's life should not be the *measure* of recovery and still argue that if the former's interest has become *wholly* extinguished, his right to the face amount of the policy should likewise be extinguished. To permit a person whose interest in the life of the insured has been completely terminated to collect the proceeds upon the insured's death gives the appearance of speculation and offends the sense of justice of many persons. However, the rule was adopted by the courts (English) at a time when surrender values were not available and termination of a policy before maturity meant the forfeiture of all accumulated values. For the courts to force a policyholder to lapse his policy and forfeit the entire investment element because of the extinguishment of an interest which was perfectly valid at the time the policy was issued would have been harsh.[7] The courts were faced with the alternative of

---

[7] As a matter of strict accuracy, the English courts at first held that a policy did become unenforceable as soon as the insurable interest was extinguished (*Godsall* v.

permitting the owner of the policy to collect the full face of the policy or nothing at all. It is probable that if the matter were being adjudicated today, without regard to precedent, the courts would hold that extinguishment of insurable interest terminates a policy and the policy owner would be permitted to recover the cash value as of the date of extinguishment, together with premiums paid thereafter in mistaken reliance on the contract.

As the matter now stands, an incipient interest is all that is necessary to sustain the validity of a life insurance contract. Thus, if a creditor procures insurance upon the life of his debtor and the debt is subsequently extinguished, the creditor may keep the policy in force and collect the full amount of the policy when the insured dies.[8] A policy procured by a partnership on the life of a partner is unaffected by the dissolution of the partnership and the transfer of the policy to a former member of the firm who no longer has an insurable interest.[9] A corporation that procures a policy upon the life of a valuable manager may collect at his death the full amount of insurance, despite the fact that the manager had meanwhile been discharged.[10] A divorce does not deprive a wife-beneficiary of the right to the proceeds of her husband's life insurance, even though she no longer has an insurable interest in his life.[11]

The foregoing rules are not followed in Texas. The Texas courts have traditionally required a continuing interest. That is, a person who takes out insurance on the life of another person must have an insurable interest in the insured at the maturity of the contract in order to receive the proceeds. The recent statute[12] which eliminated the requirement of an insurable interest for the beneficiary or assignee of a policy procured by the insured left undisturbed the mandate of a

---

Boldero, 9 East 72, 103 Eng. Rep. 500 [K.B. 1807]). The insurers did not take advantage of the ruling, however, and continued to pay the full amount of the policy even when the insurable interest was lacking at the date of death. When the matter came up again, almost a half century later, the court yielded to the custom of the insurers and permitted full recovery under the policy (*Dalby* v. *India & London Life Assurance Co.,* 15 C.B. 365, 139 Eng. Rep. 465 [Ext. 1854]). The latter case has served as a precedent for American courts.

[8] *Ferguson* v. *Massachusetts Mutual Life Insurance Co.,* 32 Hun 306 (N.Y. Sup. Ct., 1884), affirmed, 102 N.Y. 647 (1886). Under such circumstances, however, the debtor usually takes over the policy and continues premium payments upon repayment of the debt.

[9] *Gerstel* v. *Avens,* 143 Fla. 20, 196 So. 616 (1940).

[10] *Wurzburg* v. *New York Life Insurance Co.,* 140 Tenn. 59, 203 S.W. 332 (1918).

[11] *Connecticut Mutual Life Insurance Co.* v. *Schaefer,* 94 U.S. 457 (1876). See p. 599 for exceptions to this rule.

[12] Tex. Civ. Stat. art. 3.49-1 (Vernon, 1963). The law was changed in 1953.

continuing interest for the person who procures insurance on another's life.

The discussion in this section has made no reference to policies procured by the person whose life is to be insured, since in such cases, there is no question of a continuing interest. If the view is accepted that a person has an insurable interest in his own life, then certainly the interest continues throughout life.

Relationships Evidencing Insurable Interest. In considering the relationships which give rise to an insurable interest, it is helpful to distinguish between the cases in which the applicant is applying for insurance on his own life and those where he is seeking insurance on the life of another.

1. *Policy Procured by the Insured.* The question of insurable interest is not involved when a person, on his own initiative, applies for a policy on his own life. It is commonly said that a person has an unlimited insurable interest in his own life; but the expression would appear to be inaccurate, since a person does not suffer a financial loss by his own death or, at least, does not survive to claim indemnity for a loss. Hence, it seems preferable to state that the issue of insurable interest is immaterial when a person applies for insurance on his own life. Regardless of how the status of the insured is characterized, the law considers the insurable interest requirement to have been met— for any amount of insurance.

For underwriting purposes, the companies do not accept the view that the applicant has an unlimited insurable interest or that the question is immaterial. The financial circumstances of an applicant are carefully investigated, and the company limits the amount of insurance to that which can be justified by the applicant's financial status and earning capacity.

The law is well settled that when a person procures a policy on his own life, it is not necessary that the beneficiary have an insurable interest in the insured's life, either at the inception of the contract or at the time of the insured's death. Prior to the enactment of the 1953 statute previously referred to, Texas required that the beneficiary have an insurable interest at all times. The law is now unanimous on that point (except in England), the rationale being that the insured should be permitted to dispose of his human life value with the same freedom that he can exercise in disposing of his other property at death.[13] The

---

[13] As a matter of fact, the insured enjoys much greater latitude in disposing of his human life value, since insurance proceeds are not subject to a wife's dower rights (or statutory equivalent), restrictions on bequests to charitable organizations, or claims of creditors (if properly set up).

temptation to murder is considered minimized by the judgment of the insured in choosing the objects of his bounty.

The courts take a different view of the situation when the policy is applied for at the instigation of the beneficiary. Such a transaction may arise out of a legitimate business relationship and have a useful purpose, or it may serve as a cloak for a wagering contract. When the application does not stem from a business or personal situation which would seem to justify the designation of the particular beneficiary as payee and the beneficiary agrees in advance to pay all premiums under the policy, the courts are inclined to regard the transaction as speculative in nature. For example, where a woman was induced to make application for insurance on her life in favor of the mortgagee of her husband's land,[14] her employer,[15] and her sister-in-law,[16] the beneficiary in each case paying all premiums, the contract was declared to be a wager. Likewise, a policy procured at the instigation of a college upon the life of a wealthy man who was a prospective donor to its endowment fund was declared invalid because the college had no insurable interest in his life.[17] The payment of premiums by the beneficiary is not conclusive proof of wagering, but it gives rise to a strong inference. Since the question of insurable interest is of importance only at the inception of the policy, it is immaterial that later, owing to a change of circumstances, the beneficiary assumes responsibility for premium payments in order to keep the policy in force.

In practice, a company makes no distinction between applications submitted at the initiative of the prospective insured and those submitted at the instigation of the prospective beneficiary. In all cases, it requires that the original beneficiary have an insurable interest of some sort as a precaution against wagering, homicide, or other untoward moral hazard. If the prospective beneficiary does not appear to have a legitimate insurable interest, the company will request an explanation of the relationship; and if the explanation is unsatisfactory, it will almost certainly reject the application. Once the policy is issued, however, the company has no right to withhold approval of a change of beneficiary on the grounds that the proposed beneficiary lacks an insurable interest—or on any other grounds, for that matter, except failure to comply with the prescribed procedure for effecting

---

[14] *Hinton* v. *Mutual Reserve Fund Life Assn.* 135 N.C. 314, 47 S.E. 474 (1904).

[15] *Gerald* v. *Metropolitan Life Insurance Co.,* 167 Miss. 207, 149 So. 789 (1933).

[16] *Carter* v. *Continental Life Insurance Co.,* 115 F. 2d 947 (D.C. Cir. 1940).

[17] *Trinity College* v. *Travelers Insurance Co.,* 113 N.C. 244, 18 S.E. 175 (1893). The college was not even permitted to recover the surrender value under the policy.

such a change. Of course, if the circumstances surrounding the request for change of beneficiary are indicative of an attempt to evade the underwriting requirements of the company or the legal requirement of insurable interest, the company may be permitted to rescind the policy, on the grounds of fraud or on the grounds that the entire transaction was a subterfuge for the procurement of insurance by a person lacking an insurable interest in the insured.

The insured may make the policy payable to a third party by means of an assignment; and as a general rule, it is not necessary for the assignee to have an insurable interest. The position of the courts is that it is immaterial whether the insured designates the payee of the policy within the contract itself, as by a conventional beneficiary designation, or by means of a separate instrument—i.e., an assignment. Five states[18] require the assignee to have an insurable interest, at least under certain circumstances. All states require an insurable interest if the insured was induced by the assignee to take out the policy, since that would be tantamount to the assignee's applying for the insurance directly. If there is any indication at the time of application that an assignment is contemplated, the insurance company, as a matter of underwriting practice, will usually require evidence of the insurable interest of the prospective assignee.

Under the doctrine adopted by the majority of American courts, there is nothing to invalidate successive assignments of a life insurance policy once it is validly issued. None of the assignees need have an insurable interest, and the insured need not give his consent to the assignments. This rule is based on the doctrine that a life insurance policy is a form of personal property and should be freely transferable. If a life insurance contract could be sold only to persons having an insurable interest in the life of the insured, the market would be severely limited, and the owner of the policy would be handicapped in disposing of it. Nevertheless, it would probably be held contrary to public policy today for life insurance policies to be sold on the auction block to the highset bidder.

A special set of rules is applicable when a policy is made payable to a creditor of the insured, whether the designation be as beneficiary or as assignee. The creditor situations will be discussed in the next section.

Most policies are issued upon the application and at the initiative of

---

[18] Alabama, Kansas, Kentucky, Missouri, and Texas.

the insured himself. Hence, the foregoing principles may be regarded as those governing the typical situation. The rules applicable to the exceptional cases where the applicant and the insured are not one and the same are set forth in the following section.

2. *Policy Procured by Person Other than Insured.* Contrary to popular belief, in most jurisdictions, consent of the person to be insured is not essential to the validity of a life insurance contract taken out by a person other than the prospective insured. Those states which do require such consent[19] usually make an exception of applications submitted by a spouse on the life of the other spouse or by a parent on the life of a child too young to apply for insurance in his own right. As a practical matter, the signature of the prospective insured is needed on the application in affirmation of the accuracy of the information in the application. Hence, the companies always require the signature of the person whose life is to be insured, except when such person is a minor.

In all jurisdictions, a third-party applicant must have an insurable interest in the life of the person to be insured. This statement presupposes that the applicant will be the owner of the policy and the person to receive the proceeds upon maturity of the contract. A more accurate statement of the requirement—as it is prescribed in some states, at least—is that the *person who procures the policy and is to receive the proceeds* must have an insurable interest in the insured. The New York Insurance Law, for example, states the requirement in such terms and provides that if the proceeds should be paid to a person not having an insurable interest in the insured *at the time the contract was made*, the insured or his personal representative,[20] as the case may be, may maintain an action to recover such proceeds from the person so receiving them.

The insurable interest required under such circumstances may arise out of either a family relationship or a business relationship. If it arises out of a family relationship, it may be based on *love and affection* or on a legal or factual expectation of *financial* advantage from continuance of the life of the insured. Interests originating in business relationships are regarded as economic in nature.

(*a*) Family Relationships.   The doctrine that an emotional attach-

---

[19] At the present time, eleven states—including New York, Pennsylvania, Delaware, and Maryland—require the consent of the person whose life is to be insured, with certain exceptions.

[20] Executor or administrator.

ment constitutes a sufficient insurable interest, apart from financial considerations, has been expounded in various judicial opinions and incorporated into the statutes of several states, including New York and Pennsylvania. The courts which subscribe to the doctrine usually justify their action on the grounds that the natural affection engendered by close ties of blood and affinity operate more efficaciously to protect the life of the insured than would any other consideration. Such an argument tacitly assumes that the primary purpose of the insurable interest requirement is to protect the insured against the possibility of being murdered by those who would profit by his death. It will be recalled, however, that the requirement of an insurable interest was introduced to stamp out indiscriminate gambling on the lives of public men and vocational or professional wagering on the lives of persons with whom the applicant-owner had no business or family ties. This has led to the argument[21] that justification for the love-and-affection doctrine can be found in the "restricted class" concept enunciated by Oliver Wendell Holmes in the landmark insurance case, *Grigsby* v. *Russell*.[22] In his opinion, Justice Holmes recognized the aleatory nature of the life insurance transaction and asserted that the chief purpose of the insurable interest requirement is to limit the opportunities for wagering on the life of a particular individual to that relatively small group of persons having close ties of blood or affinity with the individual or possessing a substantial economic interest in his life. He pointed out that "the whole world of the unscrupulous" should not be "free to bet on what life they choose." It is apparent that the love-and-affection doctrine is quite consistent with that view. Thus, it would appear that the doctrine serves both of the major objectives of the insurable interest requirement: the minimization of wagering and the prevention of murder.

In applying the doctrine, the closeness of relationship needed to satisfy the requirement is of critical importance. The relationship of husband and wife is universally conceded to be close enough, although it is virtually always accompanied by an economic interest arising out of the wife's legal right to support from her husband and the husband's expectation of domestic services from the wife. Likewise, the relationship of parent and child, based on both economic and familial ties, is generally regarded as sufficient to satisfy the law. A growing minority of courts have also recognized the relationship of brother and sister or

---

[21] Patterson, *op. cit.*, p. 179.
[22] 222 U.S. 149 (1911).

brother and brother or sister and sister, and grandparent and grand-child as sufficient.[23] Blood relationships more remote than the forego-ing, such as uncle and niece, uncle and nephew, and cousin of any degree, have generally been rejected as insufficient.[24] Aside from that of husband and wife, no tie growing out of affinity alone—such as an interest of an individual in his father-in-law, mother-in-law, brother-in-law, stepfather, or stepchild—has been recognized as a sufficient insurable interest.

The courts that do not subscribe to the belief that a sentimental value alone will satisfy the insurable interest requirement still find a valid insurable interest in close family relationships, apparently on the assumption that a legal or factual expectation of pecuniary value exists in such cases. Thus, the legal obligation of a man to support his wife gives her an insurable interest in his life, and the legal duty of a woman to render household services to her husband gives him an insurable interest in her life. The father (and in some instances, the mother) is entitled to the services of a minor child and hence has an insurable interest in the child's life. A woman has an insurable interest in the life of her fiancé, at least in those states where the agreement to marry is a legal obligation.

An expectation of financial advantage from the continued life of a person which is not based on a legal obligation is referred to as a *factual expectation*. A factual expectation is generally not sufficient to support a contract of indemnity, such as those found in the property and casualty insurance branches, but it has long been regarded as sufficient in life insurance. In the earliest reported American decision involving life insurance, the Supreme Judicial Court of Massachusetts upheld a policy in favor of the insured's sister, on the grounds that he had been voluntarily supporting her and probably would have contin-ued to do so had he lived.[25] A foster child, though not legally adopted

---

[23] Patterson, *op. cit.*, p. 181.

[24] In a recent case which has caused considerable apprehension on the part of the life insurance industry, the father of a murdered child was awarded $75,000 in punitive damages against three insurance companies issuing insurance on the life of the child to an aunt-in-law who had no insurable interest in the life of the insured. The aunt subsequently poisoned the child to collect the insurance and was executed for the crime. The court held that the failure of the companies to insist on an insurable interest on the part of the applicant was the proximate cause of the insured's death (*Liberty National Life* v. *Weldon*, 267 Ala. 171, 100 So. 2d 696 [1957]). For a complete account of this case and a summary of the insurable interest requirements in every American jurisdiction, see John W. Gillon, "Tort Liability of Life Insurers Resulting from Violation of the Insurable Interest Rule," *Proceedings* of the Legal Section of the American Life Convention, 1958.

[25] *Lord* v. *Dall*, 12 Mass. 118 (1815).

and hence without legal claim to support, has been held to have an insurable interest in the life of his foster father.[26] A woman living with a man under the honest but mistaken belief that she was lawfully married to him was held to have had an insurable interest in his life because of her expectation (possibly misplaced) that he would have continued to support her.[27] An illegitimate child is considered to have an insurable interest in the life of its putative (supposed) father, who has contributed to its support.[28]

It is sometimes said that a *moral* obligation gives rise to a legally adequate insurable interest. Such an interest might be found in a moral obligation to provide support or to reimburse a benefactor for support gratuitously provided. Some courts have accepted that view; but the majority reject it, on the grounds that the obligation is too vague and uncertain.

When an insurable interest is based on a family relationship, there is no legal limit to the amount of insurance that may be validated by it. This is based on the concept that a life insurance policy is not a contract of indemnity and hence does not purport to reimburse a beneficiary for a specific pecuniary loss. It would be extremely difficult, if not impossible, to place a precise valuation on an interest based on love and affection. Interests arising out of a legal entitlement to support could perhaps be valued, but those based on a factual expectation could be measured only in the roughest terms. Interests based on businesss relationships can usually be valued and, in general, can support only an amount of insurance that bears a reasonable relationship to the value of the interest.

(*b*) Business Relationships. A variety of business relationships give rise to an insurable interest. One of the most common is a contractual arrangement calling for personal services of a unique or distinctive character. Innumerable examples of such arrangements can be found in the entertainment world. Thus, a theatrical producer has an insurable interest in the life of an actor who would be extremely difficult to replace in a role which he has contracted to perform over a definite period. Likewise, the producer of a motion-picture film has an insurable interest in the lives of the principal performers, an interest which comes into sharper focus as the film gets into production and

---

[26] *Carpenter v. United States Life Insurance Co.*, 161 Pa. 9 (1894).

[27] *Scott's Administrator v. Scott*, 77 S.W. 1122 (Ky. 1904). In this case, the putative husband was legally married to another woman.

[28] *Overton v. Colored Knights of Pythias*, 173 S.W. 472 (Tex. Civ. App. 1915).

the death of a "star" would disrupt operations and require the refilming of all the scenes in which the deceased appeared. Professional baseball clubs have an insurable interest in the lives of their outstanding performers.

The foregoing examples are based on contractual or legal obligations, but factual expectations may also support an insurable interest. The increasing importance of the business manager has led to the recognition that a corporation or other form of business enterprise may have an insurable interest in the life of a manager or some other official whose services and skill are vital to the prosperity of the enterprise, even though the person has not assumed a legal obligation to work for the firm for any specified period of time. The interest of a firm in its key officers and employees has been recognized by statute in many states and judicially sanctioned in most, if not all, of the other states. Insurance taken out to protect such an interest in called *key-man insurance* and is widely sold.

Another business relationship that gives rise to an insurable interest is that existing among partners in a partnership and stockholders in a close corporation. As was explained earlier,[29] the consequences of the death of a general partner or an active stockholder in a close corporation are such that the parties involved frequently enter into agreements for the disposition of the business interest of any such individuals who might die while still active in the management of the firm. Specifically, the agreement binds the surviving members of the firm to purchase the interest of the deceased member at a price specified in the agreement, and the deceased member's estate to sell his interest. The agreements are usually financed by insurance on the lives of the individuals involved, the insurance on any particular individual being applied for by either the other members of the firm or the firm itself. In such cases, the courts have recognized an insurable interest, based on the factual expectation of a loss in the event that the business should have to be liquidated, capable of supporting the insurance.

Perhaps the most common business or commercial relationship that produces an insurable interest is that created by the lending of money. Despite the fact that the obligation to repay a loan is not discharged by the death of a debtor, the obligation being enforceable against the deceased's estate, a creditor is everywhere conceded to have an insurable interest in the life of the debtor. This rule is based on recognition

---

[29] See pp. 22–24.

of the fact that the creditor may not be able to collect the sum of money due him from the debtor's estate because of insufficiency of assets. The creditor may protect his interest by taking out insurance on the life of the debtor or by requiring the debtor to designate him as payee under a policy taken out by the debtor.

If the creditor takes out insurance on the debtor's life *and pays the premiums,* he is permitted to retain the full amount of the proceeds, even though they exceed the amount of the debt, plus accumulated interest. As a matter of fact, he can retain the full amount of the proceeds, even though the debt has been completely extinguished. The only limitation imposed in most jurisdictions is that the amount of insurance must not be disproportionate to the amount of the debt as it existed at the time the policy was issued or as it was reasonably expected to be thereafter. The purpose of this requirement is to prevent the use of a debt as a cloak for a wagering transaction. In a leading case, a policy for $3,000 taken out on the basis of a $70 debt was held to be a wager and hence invalid.[30] Yet, policies have been upheld where the amount of insurance was several times the debt. A Maryland court upheld a policy for $6,500 on a debt of $1,000,[31] while a New York court validated a policy for $5,000 taken out to protect a debt of $2,823.[32] These liberal decisions are largely due to the notion that a creditor should be allowed to insure the debtor's life for a sum estimated to be sufficient to reimburse the creditor, at the debtor's death, for premiums paid on the policy, with interest thereon, plus the debt and accumulated interest. This formula was first applied by the Supreme Court of Pennsylvania, which estimated the premiums to be paid on the basis of the insured's life expectancy as projected in the Carlisle Tables.[33] The limitation imposed by this rule is a specious one, since the premiums that would be paid during the insured's life expectancy, plus interest, would exceed the face of the policy. By this test, a creditor could justify any amount of insurance on a debt of $1. This rule, however, is not strictly followed by the courts today; and in general, the amount of insurance must bear a reasonable relationship to the size of the debt.

If a debtor assigns an existing policy to the creditor as *security* for a loan, the creditor is permitted to retain only the amount of his interest

[30] *Cammack* v. *Lewis,* 82 U.S. 643 (1872).
[31] *Rittler* v. *Smith,* 70 Md. 261, 16 Atl. 890 (1889).
[32] *Wright* v. *Mutual Benefit Life Assn.,* 118 N.Y. 237, 23 N.E. 186 (1890).
[33] *Grant's Administrators* v. *Kline,* 115 Pa. 618, 9 Atl. 150 (1887).

and must pay the excess, if any, to the insured's estate or third-party beneficiary, as the case may be. The creditor's interest is construed to comprise the unpaid portion of the loan, accumulated interest on the loan, and expenses connected with the loan, including any premiums paid on the policy. The same rule applies when the creditor is designated beneficiary, if it is clear that the arrangement was intended to serve as security for the debt. In general, the creditor's rights are the same when the debtor procures new insurance and assigns it as collateral, provided the debtor pays the premium. Most courts will permit the creditor to retain the full amount of proceeds under any arrangement which contemplates payment of premiums by the creditor.

Occasionally, a policy is assigned to the creditor *in satisfaction of the debt,* and not as security for it. In those instances, the creditor is allowed to keep all the proceeds, even though they greatly exceed the amount of the debt canceled. The validity of such an arrangement has been upheld even when the creditor has induced the debtor to procure the policy.

Legal Effect of Lack of Insurable Interest. A life insurance contract not supported by an incipient insurable interest is a wagering contract and hence illegal. This does not mean, however, that the contract cannot be carried out according to its terms. The courts will not enforce an illegal contract, but they do not necessarily forbid the parties to observe the promises made under the illegal agreement. If an insurance company feels that the applicant honestly believed that he had an insurable interest in the life of the person to be insured, it may honor its promise, despite later evidence that there was no insurable interest. On the other hand, if the company feels that the applicant knew he had no insurable interest and sought the insurance for speculative purposes, it may deny liability, on the grounds of illegality. If the court sustains the company's contention, there will be no obligation under the contract. Not only will the company be relieved of paying the face of the policy (if the insured has died); but, in some states, it will not be obligated to return the premiums paid under the contract. Several states have relaxed the rule against non-enforcement of illegal contracts to allow the applicant or his personal representative to recover all premiums paid where he applied for insurance in the honest belief that he had an insurable interest. In all jurisdictions, recovery of premiums would be permitted if the insurer's agent induced the applicant to apply for insurance by falsely leading him to believe that he had a legitimate insurable interest.

Moreover, the courts have not strictly applied to wagering policies the doctrine that a partial illegality taints the entire transaction and makes it void for all purposes. The rule is frequently modified when a person applies for insurance on his own life at the instigation of a third party who lacks an insurable interest in the applicant, with the third party paying the premiums and being designated beneficiary. From a strict legal standpoint, such a contract is illegal, but the courts may choose to nullify the interest of the offending beneficiary and direct the insurance company to pay the proceeds to the insured's estate. Under such circumstances, however, the courts are practically unanimous in permitting the beneficiary to recover out of the proceeds the premiums which he paid on the policy. The same attitude is taken toward the case where a policy is assigned to a third party without insurable interest who induced the insured to apply for the policy.

FORM

Some types of contracts have to be in a particular *form* in order to be legal. From a practical standpoint, this aspect of the formation of a contract refers to whether or not the contract has to be in writing or can be in oral form.

The Statute of Frauds, which was originally enacted in England in the seventeenth century and has become a part of the statutory law of nearly all the states of the United States, requires certain types of contracts to be in writing in order to be enforceable. The only section of the statute that might be construed to apply to a contract of life insurance is that which requires written and signed proof of an agreement which, by its terms, is not to be performed within one year from its effective date. This provision has been interpreted to apply only to agreements which *cannot possibly* be performed within one year. Since the insurer's promise may have to be fulfilled within one year or even one day from issue of the policy, a life insurance contract falls outside the statute. Hence, it may be said that in the absence of specific legislation requiring a life insurance contract to be in writing, such a contract can be oral in nature.[34]

Georgia has long required life insurance contracts to be in writing,

---

[34] Section 31(1) of the New York Personal Property Law stipulates that a contract must be in writing if the performance is not to be completed before the end of a lifetime. This provision has been construed to require a life insurance policy to be in writing. See *Goldberg* v. *Colonial Life Ins. Co. of America,* 129 N.Y.S. 2d 637, 134 N.Y.S. 2d 865, 308 N.Y. 958, 127 N.E. 2d 99 (1955).

while several states have construed statutes prescribing standard provisions to require such contracts to be in writing. While all states have prescribed a set of standard provisions that must be included—in substance—in all contracts of life insurance such standard provisions do not necessarily invalidate oral contracts. The standard provisions are simply assumed to be a part of the oral contract.

Statutes invalidating any terms in a policy which appear in a type face smaller than a designated size and those requiring a policy to be signed have been interpreted as not requiring a written contract. Charter provisions requiring all contracts to be in writing are usually disregarded by the courts if proof is furnished that an agent of the company led the "insured" to believe that he was covered under an oral agreement.

As a practical matter, oral contracts are rare, and usually occur only when an agent oversteps his authority and the company is estopped from denying responsibility for the agent's conduct. Oral contracts are a fruitful source of misunderstanding and litigation, and are completely unsuitable for a transaction involving life insurance.

CHAPTER XXV

Avoidance
of the
Contract by
the Insurer

THE DECISION of a life insurance company to enter into a contractual arrangement with an applicant for insurance is based largely on the information furnished to the company by the applicant himself. Consequently, it is vitally important to the company that the information be accurate and complete. Unfortunately, the applicant sometimes defaults in his legal duty to supply factually accurate underwriting information; and if the company feels that it has been misled to its detriment, it may seek to avoid liability under the contract it has entered upon. Its action may take the form of either a suit for rescission of the contract, usually but not necessarily instituted during the insured's lifetime, or, more commonly, a defense to a claim brought by the beneficiary after the death of the insured. These rights may have to be asserted, if at all, during a specified period following issue of the policy, depending upon the type of incontestable clause used.[1]

Under proper circumstances, the company can avoid a contract on any one of three grounds: breach of warranty, misrepresentation, or concealment. Each of these grounds is subject to its own set of rules and restrictions and, consequently, will be discussed separately.[2]

---

[1] See pp. 565–68.

[2] For a comprehensive and authoritative treatment of this subject, see Edwin W. Patterson, *Essentials of Insurance Law* (2d ed.; New York: McGraw-Hill Book Co., Inc., 1957), pp. 272–473. Patterson's discussion deals with all forms of insurance, but there are specific references to life insurance.

BREACH OF WARRANTY

A warranty is a technical concept which has acquired peculiar significance in insurance and, in this context, may be defined as a clause in an insurance contract that prescribes, as a condition of the insurer's liability, the existence of a fact affecting the risk assumed under the contract. The doctrine of warranties originated in marine insurance more than two hundred years ago and still plays an important role in that branch of insurance. It was developed for the purpose of controlling the risk associated with a particular insurance venture. If a certain state of affairs was deemed to be a risk-reducing factor and insurance was arranged on the assumption that such a state of affairs would continue throughout the term of the policy, the policy would condition the coverage on the existence of the favorable state of affairs. The policy would *warrant* that the desired conditions would prevail. For example, the frequent wars during the eighteenth century made it highly desirable that British merchant vessels sail under the convoy of British warships, and it was customary for marine insurers to require an insured vessel to sail under convoy or pay a higher premium. If a shipowner warranted that his vessel would sail only under convoy and then permitted it to sail alone, his coverage would be nullified. It was not necessary for the insurer to prove that the breach—i.e., the failure to sail with convoy—materially increased the risk; materiality was assumed. Neither was it necessary to establish bad faith or fraud on the part of the insured. The insurer had only to prove that the warranty was breached. This is still the law in marine insurance.

The use of warranties gradually spread to other branches of insurance where they were less suitable. They were no longer confined to contracts sold to businessmen familiar with trade and insurance practices but were liberally interspersed in contracts sold to the general public, the members of which had no concept of the significance of warranties. Abuses inevitably developed. The situation was particularly bad in fire insurance where there was no incontestable clause to ameliorate the effect of a breach of warranty. The courts strained the law in an effort to protect the insuring public, but most states found it necessary to provide statutory relief for those persons procuring life and health insurance and, less commonly, those seeking other types of insurance. The general effect of the statutory modifications is that no breach of warranty will void a contract unless it increased the risk, contributed to the loss, or occurred with fraudulent intent.

The special legislation directed at life insurance—and, in many states, at health insurance—was brought about by the fact that, for one reason or another, most companies had begun to incorporate the application into the policy, which, according to common-law doctrine, made all statements in the application warranties. To make doubly sure of this result, some companies, by express provision, made the applicant warrant the truth of all statements in the application. This meant that the company was in a position to void the contract if any one statement in the application was not literally true. This caused more than half of the states to enact legislation which, in effect, provides that "in the absence of fraud, all statements in the application shall be deemed representations and not warranties." A few states, including New York, have dropped the words "in the absence of fraud," making the statements in the application representations under all conditions.[3] The significance of this modification of the common law will be apparent after the discussion in the next section.

In those states that have not enacted legislation of the type described in the preceding pararaph, the statements in the application could presumably be treated as warranties, provided the application were made part of the contract. However, the standard provisions for life insurance policies prescribed in all states contain the language quoted above and thus eliminate the requirement of literal accuracy.

The doctrine of warranties is not entirely without significance in the field of life insurance, since in some jurisdictions, conditions precedent dealing with the insurability of the applicant are regarded as warranties. For example, the New York Insurance Law defines a warranty as follows:

> The term "warranty" as used in this section, means any provision of any insurance contract which has the effect of requiring, as a condition precedent of the taking effect of such contract or as a condition precedent of the insurer's liability thereunder, the existence of a fact which tends to diminish, or the non-existence of a fact which tends to increase, the risk of the occurrence of any loss, damage, or injury within the coverage of the contract. . . .

The definition goes on to state that the expression "occurrence of loss, damage, or injury" is deemed to include death. Thus, the delivery-in-

---

[3] The quoted phrase was dropped in the belief that no modern court would permit an insurer to avoid liability for fraudulent *immaterial* statements.

good-health clause and the medical treatment clause would be construed as warranties in New York and several other states.

In a sense, the statement of the insured's age in the life insurance policy is a warranty, since a misstatement of age which reduces the periodic premium payable is clearly material. However, as a result of a standard provision required in most states, the life insurance policy is not voidable because of such a misstatement, but the amount payable is reduced or increased according to the insurer's premium table. The only other adjustment on this type is that found in some health insurance contracts which provide for a reduction in the amount of weekly benefits in the event that the insured should change to a more hazardous occupation.[4]

MISREPRESENTATIONS

Nature and Legal Effect of Representations

Generally speaking, a representation is an oral or written statement made by a party to a contract prior to or contemporaneously with the formation of the contract. It is not a part of the contract but rather is an inducement to the contract. It may refer to facts or conditions existing at the time the statement is made, in which event it is known as an *affirmative representation;* or it may refer to facts or conditions expected to exist in the future, in which case it is referred to as a *promissory representation.* It may be a fact within the knowledge of the person making the statement, or it may be merely an expression of opinion or belief. A representation does not bind the party making it to anything that may happen after the contract is made; if it did, it would be a promise or condition of the other party's promise and would have to be embodied in the contract. It would be the equivalent of a warranty. Finally, a representation need be only substantially true when made.

In life insurance, representations are made by both the applicant and the soliciting agent; but for all practical purposes, only the applicant's statements have legal significance. Hence, the discussion in this chapter will be concerned only with representations of the applicant.

Since representations do not purport to change the *terms* of a contract, they are not subject to the parol evidence rule, discussed

---

[4] There is a statute in New Hampshire [N.H. Rev. Stat. Ann. ch. 407:4 [1955]] which provides for a reduction *in the amount of insurance*—not necessarily the recovery—when, in connection with a fire insurance policy, there occurs a mistake or misrepresentation which contributed to the loss.

earlier, and, in the absence of a prohibitory statute or policy provision, can be oral in form. However, most states have enacted statutes, directed at life insurance and referred to as *entire-contract statutes,* which state, in substance, that the policy and the application attached thereto constitute the entire contract between the parties. These statutes have been interpreted by the courts to exclude all representations of the insured other than those contained in the application attached to the policy. In other words, the application, or a copy thereof, must be attached to the policy if the company is to treat the statements in the application as representations. In addition, most states require the inclusion in every policy of a provision that has the effect of excluding from considerationn all statements of the applicant other than those contained in the application. A typical provision of that nature reads as follows: "No statement of the insured shall avoid this policy or be used in defense of a claim hereunder, unless it is contained in the application and a copy of such application is attached to the policy when issued."

Technically, when the application is made a part of the contract, either by physical attachment to the policy or by reference to it in the policy, all the statements in the application pertaining to the risk become warranties. In order to avoid this untoward result, more than half of the states have enacted laws, previously referred to, which convert statements in the application from warranties to representations. Other states have removed the sting from warranties by requiring that the matter misrepresented be material or, stricter still, have contributed to the loss, before a company can use the breach of warranty as a basis for voiding the contract. Apart from statute or judicial ruling, the policies of most companies provide that all statements in the application shall be deemed representations and not warranties. As a matter of fact, it is customary for the companies to incorporate into one omnibus clause provisions which state that the policy and the application attached thereto shall constitute the entire contract, that statements in the application shall be deemed representations, and that no statement of the insured shall be used to avoid the policy or to contest a claim unless it is contained in the application attached to the policy.

Legal Consequences of a Misrepresentation

A representation has legal consequences only if a person, acting in reliance thereon, is induced to enter into a contract to which he would not otherwise have become a party. If the representation turns out to be false, the aggrieved party can sue to recover damages from the person who made the misstatement or rescind the contract which he was induced to make. The first remedy is available against anyone who *fraudulently* or *deceitfully* makes a misrepresentation, while the second remedy is available only if the person who makes the misrepresentation is a party to the contract. Thus, if a life insurance company is induced to issue a policy because of the fraudulent misrepresentation of the medical examiner, it can recover damages, if any, from the medical examiner, but it cannot rescind the policy unless it can prove that the applicant conspired with the doctor to have the misrepresentation made or, at least, knew of the fraud before the policy was issued. Cases of this sort are occasionally unearthed, but the typical remedy for a misrepresentation in a life insurance application is rescission of the contract.

A misrepresentation does not of itself make a contract void; it only makes it voidable. The aggrieved party may elect to affirm the contract, in which event he is bound by its terms (but not precluded from suing for damages for any fraud involved); or he may elect to rescind the contract. He is under obligation to exercise his option within a reasonable time after discovering the falsity of the representation. In this respect, a misrepresentation differs from a breach of warranty, in that the latter can be offered in defense of a claim even when the company has delayed beyond a reasonable period in making its election between affirmation and rescission. However, this distinction has lost some of its significance because of a number of court decisions which treat the insurer's retention of premiums after discovery of either a misrepresentation or a breach of warranty as a *waiver* or *estoppel.*[5] In any event, the insurer's delay bars its power to rescind, on the ground of misrepresentation, only if the insured was prejudiced by the delay.

An insurance company's notice of rescission must be accompanied by a tender of all premiums paid under the contract. This is necessary, since the purpose of rescission is to wipe out the contract and restore the parties to the position which they occupied before the contract was made. If the insured is still alive, the tender of premiums is made to him, but if he is deceased it is usually made to the beneficiary and in legal effect is an offer of settlement. When the amount of the refund is

[5] See pp. 548–49.

substantial, a prudent insurer seeks a release from not only the beneficiary but also the insured's estate.

To make its rescission conclusive, the insurance company must obtain an adjudication of its power to rescind. This it may do by defending a judicial proceeding brought by the beneficiary to recover on the policy or by instituting a suit in equity to obtain a decree of rescission. In the former case, the question of misrepresentation is usually left to a jury when there is any conflict in the evidence, since the beneficiary's suit to recover the sum payable by the terms of the policy is an *action at law*.[6] Suits in equity are usually tried by a judge who determines both the law and the facts. Insurance companies prefer the latter type of proceeding because of the tendency of juries to favor the adversary of an insurance company.

To obtain a rescission of a life insurance policy on the grounds of a misrepresentation, the company must prove that one or more statements of *fact* in the application were both *false* and *material* to the company's decision to approve the application. It is not necessary, unless required by statute, to prove that the statement was made with intent to deceive the insurer. While considerable authority can be found for the argument that only a *fraudulent* misrepresentation of a material fact will provide grounds for rescission, a majority of cases hold that an innocent misrepresentation of a material fact suffices to make a policy voidable. The doctrine is well established that the test of a misrepresentation is the *effect* on the insurer, and not the *culpability* of the insured or his agent in making it. By the same token, it is held that a fraudulent misstatement of an immaterial fact will not make a policy voidable. The purpose of rescission is to protect the company—and, indirectly, its policyholders—against an increase in risk arising out of a misrepresentation, and not to punish the insured whose dishonesty caused the company no harm.

An important exception to the rule that a misrepresentation need not be fraudulent exists when the misstatement is concerned with a matter of opinion, belief, or expectation. It is not sufficient that the applicant's belief as to the status of a matter material to the risk turned out to be erroneous. If the applicant's statement accurately reflected his state of mind at the time he made the assertion, no misrepresentation occurred. A statement of opinion is false only if the person

---

[6] Section 4101 of the New York Civil Practice Law and Rules permits an insurer when sued by a beneficiary to have its equitable defense or counterclaim for rescission tried before a judge without a jury.

making it does not have such an opinion at the time the statement is made. Therefore, to void a policy on the ground of a false statement of opinion, the insurer must prove that the insured spoke fraudulently. This leads to the conclusion that a statement of opinion must be *false, material,* and *fraudulent* before it makes a policy voidable.

If the statement in the application is qualified by words denoting mental processes, such as "in my opinion" or "to the best of my knowledge and belief" or "the above is as near correct as I can recall," it is clearly one of opinion or belief. However, even unqualified statements will be construed by the courts to be statements of opinion if the fact to which they relate is deemed to be one not susceptible of accurate and conclusive determination by the insured. In other words, an unqualified assertion as to a situation or an event about which there may obviously be differences of opinion may be construed as a statement of opinion.

A statement by the applicant that he "is in good health" has been held to be a statement of opinion[7] since it calls for an inference rather than a report on observed facts. Statements as to the future are construed as expressions of intent or expectation and are thus opinions, rather than representations of facts. The following questions taken from the application form of a large life insurance company call for a declaration of intentions:

Are you contemplating any hazardous undertaking or any trip or residence outside of this country? (State why, when, and each country.)

Do you contemplate making any aircraft flights in any capacity other than as a passenger?

Do you contemplate any change, temporary or permanent, in occupation? (Details.)

Negative answers to such queries are of no avail in litigation unless the insurer can prove that at the time of application, the applicant had a definite intention of doing the thing which was the subject of the inquiry.

A representation need be true only at the time it is made; it is not necessary that it continue to be true until the contract is consummated. At one time, the federal courts and some state courts accepted the view that a representation had to be true at the moment the

---

[7] *Sommer v. Guardian Life Insurance Co.,* 281 N.Y. 508, 24 N.E. 2d 308 (1939). A *statement* that the applicant is in good health must be distinguished from the requirement that the applicant *be* in good health upon delivery of the policy, which requirement, as a condition precedent, is strictly enforced.

contract became effective, a doctrine referred to as the rule of *continuing representation;* but with some exceptions, the view today is that the intervening falsity of a representation will provide grounds for rescission only if notice of the changed circumstances is fraudulently withheld from the insurer. In other words, the applicant must be aware of the change, must realize that the change is material to the company's underwriting decision, and must deliberately withhold notice of the change to the company. Legally, such subterfuge of the applicant is not construed to be a misrepresentation, but a concealment, which is discussed at a later point in this chapter.

Concept of Materiality

A representation of the insured is of significance only if it is communicated to the insurer and in some way influences its decision with respect to a contract. If a statement of the insured induces the insurer to enter into a contract which it would not have made had it known the true statement of the fact, or would have made only on different terms, the statement is said to be *material*. More accurately, the *facts misrepresented* in the statement are material.

Extent of Falsity. A distinction must be made between the materiality of the subject matter of a question in the application and the materiality of the misrepresentation made in the answer to the question. Not all statements made by the insured in response to questions of the insurer about matters of consequence to the risk are material. To avoid a policy on the ground of a material misrepresentation, the company must prove not only that the insured made a misstatement about a matter of concern to the company, but that the *extent* of the falsity was substantial enough to be of significance. In other words, the *difference* between the actual facts relating to a matter material to the risk and the facts as falsely represented must have been sufficient to induce the company's decision. This is simply another way of saying that knowledge of the true facts would have caused the company to reject the risk or to accept it only on different terms.

The distinction between a material matter and the materiality of a false response relative to the matter can be illustrated in terms of any number of questions in the typical application form. For example, the application form of one large company contains the following question: "Have you now or have you ever had or been treated for any disease or disorder of the nose, throat, lungs, or pleura?" Suppose that an applicant should give a negative answer to that question when, in fact, he had suffered an attack of tonsilitis ten years earlier which was severe enough to require medical treatment. Obviously, the condition of the applicant's throat is material to the company's consideration of the risk; but was the undisclosed attack of tonsilitis ten years ago of sufficient consequence to justify rescission of the policy?

Tests of Materiality. In adjudicating cases involving a misrepresentation, the courts may attempt to test the materiality of the misrepresented facts by reference to the underwriting practices of insurers generally or by reference to the practices of the particular company involved in the litigation. The first test has been characterized as the *prudent-insurer* standard, while the second has been designated the *individual-insurer* standard.

The prudent-insurer standard has been adopted in the majority of jurisdictions, presumably because it is thought to provide an objective standard of judgment on an issue as to which judgments are likely to be subjective or emotional. It is argued that the judgment of the officers of the litigating company is likely to be warped by the general assumption that anyone who dies within one or two years after issuance of the policy must have concealed some physical impairment. Under this standard, the judgment of objective experts on underwriting practices, usually officials of other companies, is substituted for the subjective opinions of the officers of the company which accepted the risk. The test is subject to a fundamental weakness, in that it presupposes a uniformity of opinion and practice which does not exist. The medical directors of the various companies disagree as to the significance of many types of impairments. To rely exclusively on the testimony of outside experts may impose liability on an insurer, particularly a conservative one, for a risk which that company would unquestionably have rejected with knowledge of the facts misrepresented. A weakness of another sort is that the claimant (the beneficiary, as a rule) may have difficulty in persuading qualified experts to testify against the insurance company.

The individual-insurer test is applied in many jurisdictions and has been adopted by statute in several important states. The New York Insurance Law, for example, states: "No misrepresentation shall be deemed material unless knowledge by the insurer of the facts misrepresented would have led to a refusal by the insurer to make such contract."[8] This test conforms to the basic principle of rescission for

---

[8] Sec. 149 (2). For purposes of this statute, a contract issued on the basis of a higher premium is considered a different contract.

misrepresentation and has considerable support in judicial precedents involving transactions other than insurance contracts.

One would naturally assume that in applying this test, the courts would place great reliance on testimony of officials associated with the company involved in the litigation. At one time, however, testimony as to the underwriting practices of the litigating company was, in most jurisdictions, either inadmissible or severely restricted. In some jurisdictions, for example, the only testimony that the medical director was permitted to give was that he had read the application before signing it. Rejection of testimony as to what the company would have done was defended by the courts on the ground that witnesses from one of the parties to the litigation should not be permitted to "substitute" their judgment for that of the jury on the very issue that the jury had to resolve. This meant that the members of the jury had to surmise, from their general knowledge of the human body and the consequences of various diseases, what the insurer would have done had it been in possession of the true facts. This is still the law in some jurisdictions; but most states, by statute or court ruling, have legalized testimony as to the practices of the insurer involved in the litigation. The New York Insurance Law expressly provides that the underwriting practices of the litigating insurer shall be provable: "In determining the question of materiality, evidence of the practice of the insurer which made such contract with respect to the acceptance or rejection of similar risks shall be admissible."[9]

Under this provision, the insurer's medical director or some other qualified official is permitted to testify in court that it is the practice of the company to reject applications that reveal facts similar to those proved in the case under consideration. In fact, if qualified, the witness will be permitted to testify that the insurer, with knowledge of the facts misrepresented, would have rejected the application in dispute. If the testimony is uncontroverted, the evidence is ordinarily (i.e., if not patently absurd) deemed conclusive, and the question of materiality will not go to the jury. In several other states, the insurer is permitted to prove what it would have done had it known the facts later disclosed, but such evidence is not deemed conclusive.

The individual-insurer test enables an insurer to apply its standards of insurability in all cases, including those in which the applicant did not disclose all the facts that the insurer requested. This, of course, assumes that the insurer is permitted to prove its standards of insura-

---

[9] Sec. 149 (3).

bility, rather than leaving the matter to the conjecture of the jury or the judge. The maintenance of underwriting standards benefits not only the insurer, but also the host of honest policyholders who made no misrepresentations. Moreover, the test of what a particular insurance company would have done in a specific factual situation can be more accurately formulated and more reliably proved than what insurance companies in general would have done.

The principal disadvantage of the individual-insurer test is that the proof of materiality comes from the files of the insurance company and the testimony of its officials, and the counsel for the beneficiary has but little chance of controverting it. His only hope is to prove that the company has not consistently followed its alleged practices; but in attempting to do so, he is not permitted to subpoena the records of the insurance company, except in the states of New Jersey and New York. If the company should claim to follow a practice which violates common sense, the beneficiary's lawyer could request the judge to let the question go before the jury. If the request were granted, the outcome would not be very much in doubt.

Some recent decisions have ruled that misrepresented facts are material if knowledge of the facts *might* have caused the insurer to reject the application. This is a much stricter standard from the standpoint of the insured and also one much more difficult to apply in practice. It would treat, as material, facts which would cause the company to seek a further investigation of the applicant, even though in the end, the company would have approved the application. A California statute even holds misrepresented facts to be material if knowledge of them would have led the company to make further inquiries or to delay acceptance of the application.[10]

Statutory Modification of the Common Law

The common-law effect of misstatements by an applicant for life insurance has been modified by statute in many states. The most significant modification is that wrought by the type of statute, enacted in most states and discussed earlier, which converts statements in the application from warranties into representations. The effect of such a statute is to eliminate the conclusive presumption of materiality of statements in the application, forcing the company to prove their materiality.

A second type of statute, far less prevalent, is that which permits a

---

[10] California Insurance Code, Sec. 334.

company to void a contract only if the matter misrepresented increased the risk of loss. Such statutes usually apply only to representations. They were apparently intended to provide a more objective test of materiality than that furnished by the common-law definition. However, any fact that would be considered an inducement to contract under the common-law concept of materiality would, if so unfavorable as to be misrepresented by the applicant, tend to increase the risk. Hence, these statutes by judicial construction have been given the same effect as the prudent-insurer test of materiality.

A few states[11] have statutes that require the misrepresented fact to have contributed to the loss. Illustrative of this type of legislation is the Missouri statute, which reads as follows:

> No misrepresentation made in obtaining or securing a policy of insurance on the life or lives of any person or persons, citizens of this state, shall be deemed material or render the policy void, unless the matter misrepresented shall have actually contributed to the contingency or event on which the policy is to become due and payable, and whether it so contributed in any case shall be a question for this jury.[12]

Under this type of statute, an applicant can conceal or misrepresent a condition which—if known to the insurer—would unquestionably have caused it to decline the risk; and yet, the company will be held liable if the insured's death resulted from a cause not related to the misrepresented condition. For example, if an applicant concealed a serious heart impairment and later met death in an automobile accident not caused by his heart condition, the company would have to pay the face of the policy, despite the fact that it would not have been on the risk if the heart condition had been revealed at the time of application. The position of the insurance companies under such statutes has been made even more difficult by the construction placed on the statutes by the courts. One of the most extreme examples is provided by the construction of the Missouri statute by the Supreme Court of that state. The court ruled that a false statement as to a medical consultation could never be a defense to a claim, since a medical consultation is not capable of contributing to a person's death![13] It would seem that the "matter misrepresented" in such a case

---

[11] Missouri, Kansas, Oklahoma, and Rhode Island. The statutes in the latter three states do not apply if the insurer can show that the answers in the application were made with intent to deceive.

[12] Mo. Rev. Stat. §§ 376.580 & 377.340 (1959).

[13] *Keller* v. *Home Life Insurance Co.,* 198 Mo. 440, 95 S.W. 903 (1906).

would be the ailment disclosed by the consultation, but the federal and state courts in Missouri continue to follow the original ruling of Missouri's highest court.

Source of Litigation

Any statement in the application that is designed to elicit information directly relevant to the risk is a potential source of litigation. Yet, some subject areas of the application seldom serve as the basis for denial of a claim, while others are a fruitful source of dispute. Whether the applicant's answer to a particular question is construed to be a statement of fact or a statement of opinion makes a significant difference.

Answers to questions concerning the amount of insurance carried by the applicant and the disposition of applications submitted to other companies are generally regarded to be statements of fact rather than of opinion. Rarely in recent years, however, has an insurance company successfully invoked an answer to this group of questions as a material misrepresentation. Since the companies that do the bulk of the business are members of the Medical Information Bureau, they will ordinarily have access to information about impairments discovered by other companies. If a company were to be put on notice as to detrimental information in the M.I.B. files, it would be permitted to void the contract only if there were other information of a material nature which the applicant should have disclosed.[14]

Answers to questions about the applicant's past and present occupation, if unequivocal, are regarded as statements of fact. Yet, there are few reported cases where the insurer attempted avoidance of the contract on the basis of a misrepresentation as to occupation. The chief explanation for this is probably found in the fact that the inspection report would be likely to uncover any discrepancy in the applicant's statement as to occupation. Statements as to a change of occupation are considered to be declarations of expectation and could serve as a basis for avoidance only if false and fraudulent.

Answers to questions about family history, in so far as they call for information about events that occurred many years before or happened to relatives long separated from the applicant, are deemed to be opinions. Rarely have answers to such questions been used as a basis for litigation. It would ordinarily be difficult for the insurer to prove

---

[14] *Columbian National Life Insurance Co. of Boston, Mass.* v. *Rodgers,* 116 F. 2d 705 (10th Cir. 1941), certiorari denied, 313 U.S. 561 (1941).

the materiality of the facts misrepresented without also proving that the applicant suffered from a serious medical impairment traceable, in part, to family history. In that event, it would be simpler to avoid the contract on the grounds of the physical impairment. Answers to questions about exposure to contagious diseases, while significant for underwriting purposes, are of little value in litigation because of the difficulty of proving the materiality of the exposure.

Statements of the applicant as to his habits are usually treated as opinions. The questions are directed at the use of intoxicating beverages or narcotics, and call for distinctions of degree, such as infrequent, moderate, or excessive use. Moreover, the applicant is asked to rate himself, which he cannot be expected to do objectively. For these reasons, and because of the fact that the inspection report reveals the most serious cases of addiction to alcohol or drugs, the applicant's statements as to habits seldom constitute the basis for litigation.

Answers to questions about specific ailments or diseases are in most —but not all—jurisdictions deemed to be statements of fact, and not merely of opinion. An applicant is expected to know whether or not he has ever had—or been treated for—disorders of important organs of the body. Some courts infer the applicant's knowledge of the falsity and materiality of his answer from the serious consequences to him of the disease and the treatment.[15] On the other hand, if the evidence indicates that the applicant's physician did not inform him as to the nature of his ailment—for instance, when it was an incurable disease —the applicant's statement as to that particular disease may be treated as an opinion and not sufficient to permit avoidance of the contract by the insurer.

Answers to general questions about medical treatment, consultation, or hospitalization have been the ones most frequently invoked as defenses in recent litigation. The questions usually are directed at such treatment as has taken place only during the last five years, and the applicant is expected to have a sufficiently keen awareness of such events as to provide the insurer with accurate information. With some exceptions, the answers are treated as statements of fact and not of opinion. The fact can, except in those states which have adopted the physician-patient privilege (see below), be proved by the testimony or records of the physician or of the hospital.

Of course, the applicant's failure to disclose, or positive misrepre-

---

[15] See, for example, *Mutual Life Insurance Co. of New York* v. *Moriarity*, 178 F. 2d 470 (9th Cir., 1949).

sentation of, an instance of medical treatment is of itself neither material nor immaterial. The thing that is material is what the company would have learned, with the full co-operation of the physician or the hospital, if it had been put on notice as to the medical treatment and had made inquiry as to its nature. In order to avoid any disputes or disagreements about the materiality of an applicant's misrepresentation of his recent medical history, the New York Insurance Law states that:

A misrepresentation that an applicant for life, accident or health insurance has not had previous medical treatment, consultation or observation, or has not had previous treatment or care in a hospital or other like institution, shall be deemed, for the purpose of determining its materiality, a misrepresentation that the applicant has not had the disease, ailment or other medical impairment for which such treatment or care was given or which was discovered by any licensed medical practitioner as a result of such consultation or observation.[16]

It does not follow that in all cases, the facts misrepresented by the applicant's failure to disclose a medical consultation will be sufficient to avoid the contract. If the consultation was for the purpose of obtaining treatment for a common cold or some other slight ailment of a temporary nature, the facts misrepresented would not, because of their immateriality, constitute grounds for avoidance of the contract.

Many states have enacted statutes which provide that information about a patient's physical condition obtained by a physician through medical treatment or professional consultation shall be regarded as a *privileged communication,* which can be divulged only with the consent of the patient, or—if he is deceased—his personal representative. In those states, a physician is not permitted to give testimony as to his medical treatment of an applicant for insurance unless the latter or his personal representative is willing that the physician's findings be made public. If the physician is not permitted to testify, a suspicion arises that the ailment was one material to the defense of misrepresentation. The suspicion is so strong that, since 1940, the New York Insurance Law has contained a provision that if the insurer proves that an applicant misrepresented the facts relating to a medical consultation and the applicant or any other person claiming a right under the insurance contract prevents full disclosure and proof of the nature of the medical impairment, such misrepresentation shall be presumed to

---

[16] Sec. 149 (4).

have been material.[17] The presumption can be rebutted by evidence from the claimant that the ailment was not material to the risk. This provision, which followed a decision of the highest court of New York to the same effect, has been successfully invoked in New York courts and in federal cases governed by New York law. In other states having the physician-privilege statute, no such presumption of materiality arises.

CONCEALMENT

The doctrine of concealment is the final legal defense of the insurance company in its efforts to avoid liability under a contract which was obtained through the misrepresentation or concealment of material facts. Of the three basic grounds for avoidance, concealment is the narrowest in scope and the most difficult to prove. The three grounds are discussed in this chapter in the order of the success with which they can be invoked by the insurance company.

Nature and Legal Effect of a Concealment

In general law, concealment connotes an affirmative act to hide the existence of a material fact. In insurance law, however, a concealment is essentially a nondisclosure; it is the failure of the applicant for insurance to communicate to the insurer his knowledge of a material fact that the insurer does not possess.

It is general law of long standing that one party to a contract is under no legal obligation during the period of negotiation to disclose to the other party information which the first party knows is not known to the second party and, if known, would be deemed material to the contract. The rationale of this rule is that prices in the market place should be set by the best-informed buyers and sellers; and as a reward for performing this economic function, such persons should be permitted to profit by their special knowledge of affairs. For some years, however, there has been a marked trend in the other direction. Among the numerous exceptions to the general rule are the requirements that one party not actively try to prevent the second party from discovering facts known only to the first party or give deliberately misleading answers to questions designed to elicit information material to the contract.

In insurance, the law of concealment, like the other two doctrines

---

[17] Sec. 149 (4), last sentence.

discussed in this chapter, developed during the eighteenth century out of cases involving marine insurance, and the law still reflects the conditions of that period. The relative inaccessibility of the property to be insured and the poor communication facilities, combined with the aleatory nature of the contract, caused Lord Mansfield, the father of English commercial and insurance law, to hold that the applicant for insurance was required by good faith to disclose to the insurer all facts known to him that would materially affect the insurer's decision as to acceptance of the risk, the amount of the premium, or other essential terms of the contract, whether or not the applicant was aware of the materiality of the facts. Even though conditions affecting marine insurance have changed, the law has not. The person seeking marine insurance today, whether he be the shipowner or shipper, must disclose all material facts in his possession to the insurer; and failure to do so, even though innocent, will permit the insurer to void the contract. Under the British Marine Insurance Act, enacted in 1906, the applicant is even "deemed to know every circumstance which, in the ordinary course of business, ought to be known by him."[18]

In English law, the doctrine of innocent concealment is strictly applied to all branches of insurance. In the United States, it is applied only to marine insurance. The American courts have felt that the circumstances surrounding fire and life insurance are so different from those obtaining in marine insurance—particularly in 1766, when the marine rule originated—that a different rule is justified. Under American law, except for marine insurance, a concealment will permit the insurer to void the contract only if the applicant, in refraining from disclosure, had a fraudulent intent.[19] In other words, *except for marine insurance, a concealment must be both material and fraudulent.* In marine insurance, it need only be material.

Test of Materiality

The doctrine of concealment may be regarded as a special manifestation of the doctrine of misrepresentation. The relationship between a misrepresentation and a concealment has been compared with that existing between the heads and tails of a coin. If a misrepresentation is the heads of a coin, a concealment is the tails. One is affirmative; the other is negative. A concealment is misrepresentation by silence. It has

---

[18] 6 Edw. VII, Chap. 41, Sec. 18 (1).

[19] This is not true in California. The Insurance Code (Section 330) of that state provides that "concealment, whether intentional or unintentional," entitles the insurer to rescind the contract.

legal consequences for the same reason that a misrepresentation does —namely, that the insurer was misled into making a contract that it would not have made had it known the facts. Hence, the general concept of materiality applied to a concealment is the same as that applicable to a misrepresentation: the effect on the underwriting decision of the insurer. "Fraudulent intent" is a subjective concept difficult to prove; many courts take the attitude that if the fact not disclosed by the applicant was *palpably* material, this is sufficient proof of fraud.[20]

The degree of relevance to a risk required of a fact in order to be "palpably" material has never been judicially defined. An illustration was provided in a famous decision by William Howard Taft,[21] then a judge of the Circuit Court of Appeals, who indicated that an applicant for life insurance who failed to reveal to the insurer that he was on his way to fight a duel would be guilty of concealing a palpably material fact. This illustration was almost contradicted by a fairly recent decision that an applicant's failure to disclose that he was carrying a revolver because of his fear of being killed by his former partner, whom he had accused of committing adultery with his wife, was not a palpably material concealment, even though the applicant was murdered a few months later by a person unknown.[22] Experts are occasionally called upon to testify as to the materiality of a concealed fact; but in those cases settled in favor of the insurer, the judge has usually decided from his own knowledge that the fact concealed was palpably material.

The palpable materiality test is applied to the applicant's knowledge of materiality, while both the prudent-insurer and individual-insurer tests of materiality apply only to the *effect* on the insurer. In concealment cases, which are governed by statutes only in California and states that have adopted its laws, the prudent-insurer test seems to be the prevailing one.

Test of Fraud

The test of fraud is whether the applicant believed the fact which he did not disclose to be material to the risk. This test was approved long ago by the highest court of New York in a case involving failure of the

---

[20] If the undisclosed fact is palpably material—that is, if its importance would be obvious to a person of ordinary understanding—it can be inferred that the applicant was aware of its materiality, an essential element in fraud.

[21] *Penn Mutual Life Insurance Co.* v. *Mechanics Savings Bank & Trust Co.,* 72 Fed. 413 (6th Cir. 1896).

[22] *New York Life Insurance Co.* v. *Bacalis,* 94 F. 2d 200 (5th Cir. 1938).

applicant to disclose that he had once been insane.[23] The insurer must prove that an undisclosed fact is, *in the applicant's own mind,* material to the risk. As a general proposition, the insured's awareness of the materiality of the fact concealed can be proved by establishing that the fact was *palpably* material, a characteristic that would be apparent to any person of normal intelligence. However, in concealment cases, as with warranties and representations, the law takes into account the powers of understanding and state of knowledge of the particular applicant involved. Thus, the failure of an applicant who was the state agent for the company to notify the insurer of a cancerous condition of the spleen, discovered after submission of the application but before issue of the policy, was held to be fraudulent in view of the applicant's exceptional knowledge of the materiality of such a condition.[24] On the other hand, the failure of a less sophisticated applicant to disclose a toxic condition of the heart muscle, likewise discovered in the interim between submission of the application and issue of the policy, was held to be not fraudulent when evidence revealed that the applicant had refused to take additional insurance offered to him and had changed the basis of premium payments from monthly to semiannually.[25]

Scope of the Doctrine of Concealment in Life Insurance

The requirement that a concealment be proved by the insurer to have been fraudulent has narrowed the scope of the doctrine in all forms of nonmarine insurance. Its scope has been further narrowed in life insurance through the use of a detailed written application and, in the larger cases, a medical examination. There is a presumption that the application elicits information about every matter that the insurer deems material to the risk; and if the applicant answers fully and truthfully all questions asked in the application, he is under no duty to volunteer additional information. This presumption can be overcome by evidence that the applicant willfully concealed other information which was material to the risk and which the applicant knew to be material. In practice, however, the doctrine is seldom invoked except for the nondisclosure of a material fact discovered by the applicant between the time he signed the application and the time the contract was consummated.

---

[23] *Mallory* v. *Travelers Insurance Co.,* 47 N.Y. 52 (1871). The concealment was held not to be fraudulent.

[24] *McDaniel* v. *United Benefit Life Insurance Co.,* 177 F. 2d 339 (5th Cir. 1941).

[25] *Wilkins* v. *Travelers Insurance Co.,* 117 F. (2d) 646 (5th Cir. 1941).

The general but not unanimous view of the courts is that the applicant under the doctrine of continuing representations, must communicate promptly to the insurer his discovery of such interim facts, if they are so obviously material that the applicant could not fail to recognize their materiality. In one of the early cases on the subject, the insurance company was permitted to deny liability under a policy issued in ignorance of the fact that the applicant had undergone an operation for appendicitis during the period the application was being considered by the home office, even though the applicant was in the hospital at the time the disclosure should have been made.[26] In a later case, involving the interim discovery of a duodenal ulcer, the Supreme Court of the United States had the following to say:

> Concededly, the modern practice of requiring the applicant for life insurance to answer questions prepared by the insurer has relaxed this rule (of disclosure) to some extent since information not asked for is presumably deemed immaterial. . . .
>
> But the reason for the rule still obtains, and with added force, as to changes materially affecting the risk which come to the knowledge of the insured after the application and before delivery of the policy. For even the most unsophisticated person must know that, in answering the questionnaire and submitting it to the insurer, he is furnishing the data on the basis of which the company will decide whether, by issuing a policy, it wishes to insure him. If, while the company deliberates, he discovers facts which make portions of his application no longer true, *the most elementary spirit of fair dealing* would seem to require him to make a full disclosure.[27]

In view of the fact that not all courts impose the duty of disclosure of interim changes and, in any event, violation of the duty must be proved fraudulent, many companies rely on the delivery-in-good-health and medical treatment clauses to protect themselves against interim changes in the applicant's physical condition. These clauses create conditions or warranties which must be fully satisfied before the company can be held liable under the contract.

The applicant is under no obligation to disclose interim developments, however material on their face, when the first premium is paid with the application and a binding receipt, conditioned on insurability at the date of application, is issued. Under such circumstances, the coverage becomes effective as of the date of application—or medical

---

[26] *Equitable Life Assurance Society of United States* v. *McElroy,* 83 Fed. 631 (8th Cir. 1897).

[27] *Stipcich* v. *Metropolitan Life Insurance Co.,* 277 U.S. 311, 316–17 (1928). Italics supplied.

examination, if later—and changes in the insurability of the applicant after that date are supposed to be immaterial to the insurer's deliberations. Of course, interim changes in the insured's physical condition can be used as evidence to support the company's contention that the insured concealed or misrepresented facts known to him when the application was made.

CHAPTER XXVI

Waiver,
Estoppel, and
Election by
the Insurer

IT WAS brought out in the preceding chapter that a life insurance company may be able to avoid liability under a policy on the ground of a breach of condition, a misrepresentation, or a concealment. Not discussed there, but also a possible defense to a suit, is lack of coverage under the terms of the policy. The company, however, may not be permitted to assert any of these defenses, because of additional facts showing that it has waived the defense, has become estopped to assert it, or has conclusively elected not to take advantage of it. Various factual situations constitute the basis for a "waiver," an "estoppel," and an "election," respectively, examples of which will be dealt with in a later section of this chapter. While these are legally distinct concepts, it is customary to refer to them generically as "waiver" and to describe any factual situation which could lead to the loss of an otherwise valid legal defense as a "waiver situation." Simply and broadly stated, a waiver situation is one in which a presumably valid defense of an insurance company to a policy claim has been—or may be found to have been—waived by the company.

If the foregoing definition of a waiver situation seems vague and general, it was intended to be so. The boundaries of waiver law are very indistinct, and the concepts employed tend to be amorphous. This state of affairs is largely attributable to the underlying purpose of waiver law, which, in the case of life insurance, is to protect the policy-

holder and his beneficiaries against a harsh and overly legalistic interpretation of the policy and application. In perhaps no other branch of
the law is there such a universal tendency to make the law fit the facts
and, if that be impracticable, to create new law. It is not without justification that waiver has been described as "a kind of legal mercy, a
way of tempering the wind to the shorn lamb."[1] In the process of providing mercy, the courts "have devised doctrines and asserted principles which are sometimes more creditable to the ingenuity and subtlety
of the judges than easily harmonized with decisions rendered, under
less violent bias, in other departments of the law."[2]

Professor Edwin W. Patterson, Cardozo Professor Emeritus of
Jurisprudence, Columbia University, and an eminent authority on the
law of waiver, ascribes the state of confusion existing in this field
to the use of "flexible concepts to analyze the significance of foggy
facts."[3] There may be hope for improvement, however, since Professor
Patterson has concluded that "the doctrines of waiver, once used as
judicial whitewash to cover a multitude of minor defaults, are now
used more sparingly and with more discrimination."[4]

Inasmuch as the law of agency is at the foundation of most waiver
situations in life insurance, it should be helpful to review the pertinent
elements of that branch of the law before considering the more specific aspects of waiver.

LAW OF AGENCY

Agency may be defined as the relationship which results from the
manifestation of consent by one person that another person shall act
on his behalf and subject to his control, along with the consent of the
other person so to act. The one for whom action is to be taken is the
principal, while the one who is to act is the *agent*. Generally speaking,
any person who has the capacity to make a contract has the capacity
to act as an agent. By the same token, any person who has the capacity to perform a certain act may appoint an agent to perform the act.

In the case of a life insurance company, the agents—in the legal

---

[1] Edwin W. Patterson, *Essentials of Insurance Law* (2d ed.; New York: McGraw-
Hill Book Co., Inc., 1957), p. 476.

[2] John Skirving Ewart, *Waiver Distributed* (Cambridge, Mass.: Harvard University
Press, 1917), p. 192.

[3] Patterson, *op. cit.*, p. 494.

[4] *Ibid.*, p. 483.

sense—include the directors (acting as a body), the officers, home office supervisory personnel, agency supervisors, and soliciting agents. In the business sense, only agency field supervisors and soliciting agents are regarded as "agents." Here, the term "agent" will be used in its broader, legal meaning, with the expression "soliciting agent" being used to designate field sales personnel. Most of the waiver situations involve actions of soliciting agents.

General Rules

There are four general rules of the law of agency which are of particular relevance to life insurance.

Presumption of Agency. There is no presumption that one person acts for another. There must be some tangible evidence of an agency relationship. Thus, if a person claims to represent a certain life insurance company and collects a premium with which he later absconds, the company is not responsible for his actions if it has done nothing to create the presumption that the person is its authorized agent. If, however, the person is in possession of a rate book, application blanks, and receipt forms of the company, a presumption will be raised that the person is in fact representing the company. The presumption could, in all likelihood, be overcome by proof that the company materials were improperly acquired.

Apparent Authority of Agents. Most agency relationships are evidenced by a written instrument which expressly confers certain powers on the agent; it may also expressly withhold certain powers. The agency contract of a life insurance company usually authorizes the field representative to solicit and take applications for new business, arrange medical examinations, and collect first-year premiums. It also sets forth a number of powers specifically denied the agent, including the right to make, alter, or discharge a contract, to extend the time for payment of premiums, to accept payment of premiums in other than current funds, to waive or extend any obligation or condition, and to deliver any policy unless the applicant at that time be in good health and insurable condition.

The power of an agent to bind his principal, however, may well exceed the scope of the principal's express authorization. The latter is construed to convey authority to perform all incidental acts necessary to carry out the purposes of the agency. Such acts fall under the heading of *implied* powers. For example, if an agent is expressly authorized to deliver a life insurance policy which can be properly delivered only upon the payment of the consideration, the agent has the implied power to collect and receipt for the amount due.

The authority of an agent can also be expanded by conduct of the principal or agent which creates a justifiable belief on the part of third parties dealing with the agent that the latter possesses powers which have not been vested in him and may—unknown to the third parties —have been expressly withheld from him. If the third persons can prove that they were justified in relying on the presumption that the agent was acting within his authority, the principal will be "estopped" or precluded from denying that the agent had such powers. In proving justifiable reliance, third parties need demonstrate only that they exercised due diligence in ascertaining the agent's real authority. Authority created in this manner is referred to as *apparent authority*.

The doctrine of apparent authority can be illustrated in terms of an agent who has habitually granted his policyholders extensions of time in the remitting of premiums. If, in the past, the company has not taken action to deal with this infraction of its rules, it would be precluded from denying that the agent had such authority until such time as it notifies the policyholders involved of the limitations on the agent's powers. Such action with regard to one policyholder, however, would not create any presumption as to the agent's power to deal in a similar manner with other policyholders.

Responsibility for Acts of Agents. The principal is responsible for all acts of his agent when the latter is acting within the scope of either his express, his implied, or his apparent authority. This responsibility embraces wrongful or fraudulent acts, omissions, and misrepresentations, provided the agent is acting within his apparent authority. It is likewise responsible for any libel committed by an agent in the pursuit of his official duties. While there is no unanimity in the decisions, the weight of authority is that—in the absence of restrictions —a company is liable not only for the acts of its agents, but also for the acts of the subagents and employees to whom the agent has delegated responsibility; the liability of the company in such situations may depend on whether it has given the agent actual authority, or its actions have created an apparent authority, to delegate responsibility.

Secret limitations on the agent's authority will, under the doctrine of equitable estoppel, be inoperative as to third persons. They will, of course, be effective as between the agent and his principal; and if the agent exceeds his actual authority, he is liable to the principal for any loss or damage. The agent, as might be expected, is also liable to his principal for any loss or damage caused through his fraud, misconduct, or mere negligence.

In the course of their daily business, insurance agents are frequently asked to express an opinion as to the meaning of a particular provision, and it is of some importance to determine the legal effect of such an opinion. The general rule is that no legal effect is to be given to such opinions. This holding is based on the theory that an agent's opinion as to the meaning of any section does not create new or modify old obligations. It is followed particularly where the authority of the agent is limited and the provision involved is clear and unambiguous. In certain jurisdictions, however, a company is bound by the opinions of its agents, especially where the opinion is not inconsistent with the language of an ambiguous clause in the policy and is relied upon by the insured.[5]

Knowledge of the agent as to matters within the scope of his agency is presumed to be knowledge of the principal. This rule is applied even though matters coming to the attention of the agent are not, in fact, communicated to the principal. This rule is of critical importance, since in all their dealings with prospective and actual policyholders, soliciting agents and medical examiners are regarded to be the legal agents of the company. Hence, loyalty to the company, as well as common decency, demands that these field representatives communicate to the company all matters of underwriting or other significance that come to their attention.

Limitation on Powers of Agents. Limitations on the powers of an agent are generally effective when the limitations have been properly communicated and are not in conflict with existing law. All companies communicate to their policyholders by means of a clause in the application blank or in the policy, or in both, the customary limitations on the powers of soliciting agents and other representatives of the company with whom the policyholder may come in contact. Such provision, generally referred to as the *nonwaiver clause,* usually states that only certain specified representatives of the company (executive officers) have the power to extend the time for payment of a premium or to modify the terms of the contract in any other respect. The clause further requires that any modification of the contract must be evidenced by a written endorsement on the contract. The clause used by some companies goes on to state that no knowledge on the part of any agent or medical examiner or any other person as to any facts

---

[5] G. J. Couch, *Cyclopedia of Insurance Law* (Rochester, N.Y.: Lawyers Cooperative Publishing Co., 1929), Sec. 531.

pertaining to the applicant shall be considered to have been made to —or brought to the knowledge of—the company unless contained in the application, including the section completed by the medical examiner.

The nonwaiver clause will not be enforced with respect to acts or statements occurring prior to issue of the policy unless it is contained in the application and the application is attached to the policy. In other words, the applicant cannot be presumed to have knowledge of a limitation in an instrument which will come into his possession only after the transaction has been consummated. On the other hand, it would be assumed that limitations on the agent's authority contained in the application or the policy would be effective with respect to acts done subsequent to delivery of the policy. Unfortunately for the insurance companies, experience has not always borne out this assumption. In one case,[6] the court held that an agent can waive the very clause that says he cannot waive, alter, or modify any terms or conditions of the contract. Having waived the nonwaiver clause, the agent can proceed to waive any provision beneficial to the company. This, it will be recognized, is an extreme point of view.

Brokers as Agents

An insurance broker is a person (individual, partnership, or corporation) who acts as an agent of the insured in negotiating for insurance and in procuring the issuance of an insurance contract. In the eyes of the law, the broker is requested by the prospective insured to act for him, although in practice, the "request" is usually solicited by the broker. The broker usually receives all his compensation (in the form of commissions) from the insurance company, he delivers the policy for the company, and he collects the premium from the insured. As a consequence, the broker has come to be regarded as the agent of the company for the purpose of delivering the policy and collecting the premium. In fact, this status is recognized by statute in some states.

Where the broker is regarded as the agent of the company only for these limited purposes, knowledge of the broker as to facts affecting the risk is not imputed to the company for the purpose of establishing a waiver or estoppel, or for the purpose of obtaining reformation of the contract on the ground of mistake.[7] In many states, however, there is legislation which provides that any person who solicits insurance

---

[6] *West* v. *National Casualty Co.*, 61 Ind. App. 479, 112 N.E. 115 (1916).

[7] *Mishiloff* v. *American Central Insurance Co.*, 102 Conn. 370, 128 Atl. 33 (1925); *Ritson* v. *Atlas Assurance Co.*, 279 Mass. 385, 181 N.E. 393 (1932).

for anyone other than himself and procures a policy from the insurer shall be deemed the agent of the insurer with respect to that policy. Under some of these statutes, the solicitor's knowledge of facts constituting a breach of condition sufficient to make the contract voidable immediately has been imputed to the insurer.[8] This places the company in a position of issuing a policy it knows to be worthless—which, under the doctrine of waiver or estoppel, will preclude it from avoiding the contract on the known breach of condition. A few courts have rejected this imputation of knowledge, on the ground that the statute does not specify the *precise* powers conferred upon the solicitors.[9]

MEANING OF WAIVER, ESTOPPEL, AND ELECTION

It has been intimated that the legal concepts and rules employed in the adjudication of waiver situations have often been lacking in logic and consistency, with the result that the distinctions among waiver, estoppel, and election have become decidedly blurred, perhaps irretrievably so. Basically, however, the legal conceptions of waiver, estoppel, and election are derived from two elemental principles: (1) an individual should be bound by that to which he assents, and (2) an individual whose conduct has led another to act or not to act in reliance upon a belief as to a fact or an expectation as to future performance ought not to be allowed to act in a way contrary to the belief or expectation so created.[10] The first principle is at the foundation of waiver and election, while the second suggests the basis for several varieties of estoppel.

Waiver

The term "waiver" has been used with so many meanings that it almost defies analysis. Some courts try to distinguish it from estoppel, while other courts treat it as synonymous or interchangeable with estoppel. For example, one court might hold that the failure to demand an answer to an unanswered question in an application for life insurance constituted a *waiver* of the right to make the demand, whereas another might hold that the company was *estopped* from demanding the answer. When a court does attempt to distinguish between waiver and estoppel, it ordinarily treats waiver as a manifestation of assent

---

[8] *Welch* v. *Fire Insurance Assn. of Philadelphia,* 120 Wis. 456, 98 N.W. 227 (1940).

[9] *John Hancock Mutual Life Insurance Co.,* v. *Luzio,* 123 Ohio St. 616, 176 N.E. 446 (1931).

[10] Patterson, *op. cit.,* pp. 493 and 494.

and estoppel as nonconsensual, since the purpose of the latter is to redress a wrong and prevent inequitable treatment of one party to a contract by the other. Thus, if waiver is to be given a specific meaning, it would probably be appropriate to define it as "a manifestation of intent to relinquish a known right or advantage."[11] This is quite similar to the definition provided many years ago by the highest court of New York: "A waiver is the voluntary abandonment or relinquishment by a party of some right or advantage."[12]

While the foregoing definitions set waiver apart from estoppel, they do not distinguish it clearly from *election,* which, it will presently be noted, likewise connotes a voluntary act.

Estoppel

The doctrine of estoppel developed centuries ago in the English courts and is a limitation on the right of a person to change his mind. The law recognizes the right of an individual to change his mind, but it imposes certain restraints on that right. The law of contracts attempts to distinguish the serious promise from the casual or jesting promise by means of a *consideration.* In the law of estoppel, a detrimental reliance or change of position by the other party is the test.

There are two broad types of estoppel: *equitable estoppel* (also called *estoppel by representation* and *estoppel in pais*) and *promissory estoppel.* Historically, equitable estoppel, so called because it originated in the equity courts, was the first to develop. It was confined to a representation of past or present fact. There was no element of futurity. This original meaning has been preserved through the years and is reflected in the following comprehensive definition of an equitable estoppel: "An [equitable] estoppel is a representation of fact made by one person to another which is reasonably relied upon by that other in changing his position to such an extent that it would be inequitable to allow the first person to deny the truth of his representation."[13]

The essence of the equitable estoppel is that if a party purports to make a true statement about a past or present fact to another party who relies on the truth of the statement to his substantial detriment, the first party will not be permitted later to deny the truth of the statement. The case is tried on an assumption contrary to fact. Thus, equi-

---

[11] *Ibid.,* p. 495.

[12] *Draper* v. *Oswego County Fire Relief Assn.,* 190 N.Y. 12, 14, 82 N.E. 755, 756 (1907).

[13] Patterson, *op. cit.,* p. 496.

table estoppel is a rule of evidence rather than one of substantive law.

The doctrine of promissory estoppel has developed within the last century and can be distinguished by the fact that it is concerned with a statement of future conduct. It has been defined as "a statement as to his future conduct made by one person to another which is reasonably and foreseeably relied upon by that other in changing his position to such an extent that it would be inequitable to allow the first person to conduct himself differently from that which he stated."[14]

A promissory estoppel has been illustrated as follows.[15] Suppose that A promises to give B $5,000 if B will enter a particular college and receive his bachelor's degree. Suppose, further, that B matriculates at the designated college and has completed all the requirements for the degree except passing the examinations for the final term when A notifies him of an intention to revoke the promise. Since B has made a substantial sacrifice in effort and money to attend college in reliance upon A's promise, the courts would not permit A to revoke his promise. A's promise would be enforced, despite the fact that it was not supported by a consideration.[16] In other words, the law would recognize a valid contract.

The foregoing example illustrates the creation of a new obligation through a promissory estoppel. Some courts will not go that far in applying the doctrine, limiting its application to modifications of existing contracts. The latter application is the typical one in life insurance situations. It is of growing importance.

Election

In its original sense, election means a voluntary act of choosing between two alternative rights or privileges. Thus, if a married man dies testate (with a will), his widow usually has the right to take under the will or under the appropriate intestate law. These are alternative rights, and the widow's act of choosing one is a voluntary relinquishment of the other. The similarity to a waiver is readily apparent.

The concept of election has had only limited application in life insurance. Despite the fact that an election is an overt, manifested intent to be bound, the courts have occasionally found an election in the

---

[14] *Ibid.*

[15] H. M. Horne and D. B. Mansfield, *The Life Insurance Contract* (2d ed.; New York: Life Office Management Association, 1948), p. 81.

[16] Some would argue that B's action is a consideration for A's promise, making A's obligation contractual in nature, rather than one based on estoppel.

inconsistent conduct of the insurer. For example, the acceptance of a premium by the company after the discovery of a material misrepresentation has been viewed as an election by the company not to void the contract.

WAIVER SITUATIONS

In the remainder of this chapter, no attempt will be made to distinguish between waiver, estoppel, and election. The practical effect is the same, irrespective of the particular doctrine which the court uses to justify its decision. The emphasis hereafter is on the types of factual situations in which the courts are likely to invoke one of the doctrines outlined above to deprive a life insurance company of a defense which would have enabled it to avoid the payment of a claim.

Breach of Condition Precedent

The validity of most life insurance policies is contingent upon the fulfillment of three conditions precedent: payment of the first premium, good health of the applicant at the time the policy is delivered, and the absence of new elements affecting insurability (e.g., medical treatment) in the interim between the submission of the application and the delivery of the policy.

Payment of First Premium. The existence of a life insurance policy is usually conditioned upon payment of the first premium, or the first installment thereof, *in cash.* The cash-premium clause is typically coupled with the delivery-in-good-health clause.

The requirement that the first premium be paid in cash has been rather strictly enforced by the courts. Upon proof that the soliciting agent delivered the policy without payment of the premium, or any part thereof in any form, the courts in most jurisdictions hold that the policy is not in force, even though the agent orally assured the applicant that it would take effect at once. The view is that an agent having authority merely to solicit insurance and to collect premiums in cash has no actual or apparent authority to extend credit.

In reaching this conclusion, the courts seem to place great emphasis on the existence of a nonwaiver clause in the *application,* as opposed to the policy. In the leading New York case on the subject,[17] the court, in holding that the requirement had not been satisfied through the payment of the premium by the soliciting agent on behalf of the

[17] *Drilling v. New York Life Insurance Co.,* 234 N.Y. 234, 137 N.E. 314 (1922).

applicant, stressed the fact that the insured *agreed* in the application that the insurance would not take effect unless the premium was paid at the time of delivery of the policy. In another case,[18] the taking of a promissory note, payable to the soliciting agent, was not deemed a waiver of the cash-premium clause, since there was also a nonwaiver clause in the application.

The nonwaiver clause will not prevent a finding of waiver in all cases; it is merely notice to the applicant of the agent's limited authority. If it can be proved that the agent actually has authority to extend credit for all or a part of the premium, his doing so will, in most courts, constitute an effective waiver of the cash-premium requirement. Thus, an agent whose powers extended to the employment of subagents and who had received from his home office detailed instructions as to how to deal with premium notes, was held to have authority to issue a binding receipt in exchange for the applicant's note.[19] In another case, it was proved that the insurer followed a practice of requiring its soliciting agents to remit only the difference between the gross premium and the agent's commission; and—the applicant having paid more than this amount to the agent—it was held that the latter had authority to extend credit for the balance, despite the existence of cash-premium and nonwaiver clauses in the application.[20] In cases of this kind, the formal printed instructions to the agency force will not be conclusive proof of an agent's actual authority, as against proof of what was done by way of relaxation of those rules. To avoid a waiver, a company's action must be consistent with its announced policy.

It is common practice, of course, for premiums to be paid by check. If the check is honored by the bank upon which it is drawn, the premium—for all intents and purposes—has been paid in cash. A check is considered to be a cash payment, likewise, when for a reasonable period of time, the applicant had sufficient funds in his bank account to cover the check.[21] If a check tendered in payment of the first premium is not honored upon presentation within a reasonable time, however, the status of the policy depends upon the terms under which the check was accepted. If the premium receipt states that the check is accepted as payment only on condition that it be honored—a common practice—the policy will not go into force if the check is not honored.

[18] *Bradley* v. *New York Life Insurance Co.,* 275 Fed. 657 (8th Cir. 1921).
[19] *Schwartz* v. *Northern Life Insurance Co.,* 25 F. (2d) 555 (9th Cir. 1928).
[20] *New York Life Insurance Co.* v. *Ollich,* 42 F. (2d) 399 (6th Cir. 1930).
[21] *State Life Insurance Co.* v. *Nolan,* 13 S.W. 2d 406 (Tex. Civ. App. 1929).

If the premium receipt does not so state, however, some courts have construed the issuance of a premium receipt to be an *election* to treat the check as payment of the premium. In that event, of course, the condition of the policy has been fulfilled, and nonpayment of the check merely entitles the insurer to sue the drawer of the check.

A final question relates to policies which contain a clause acknowledging receipt of the first premium. Such a clause might read as follows: "This contract is made in consideration of the application therefor and the payment in advance of the sum of $......, the receipt of which is hereby acknowledged. . . ." Does such a clause prevent the company from showing that the first premium has not been paid? In the majority of cases, it is held that an acknowledgment contained in the policy itself is not *conclusive* (i.e., only prima-facie) evidence of payment, although the burden is on the company to prove nonpayment—a negative sort of undertaking which can be extremely difficult. There are some cases, however, which hold that in the absence of fraud, such a clause is conclusive evidence of payment. A number of states have statutes to that effect. Typical, perhaps, is a provision in the California Civil Code which provides that: "An acknowledgment in a policy of the receipt of premium is conclusive evidence of its payment so far as to make the policy binding, notwithstanding any stipulation therein that it shall not be binding until the premium is actually paid." Presumably, under such statutes, the company—while not being permitted to deny the existence of a binding contract—would still have the right to collect the premium from the insured or his estate, if it were proved that the first premium had not been paid.

Delivery-in-Good-Health and Medical Treatment Clauses. By their very nature, the *delivery-in-good-health* and *medical treatment* clauses are a fertile source of waiver litigation. While the clauses are explicit and unequivocal, if a policy is delivered by an agent with knowledge of a breach of either of the clauses, the presumption can always be raised that the condition was waived by the agent. The issue then turns on the authority of the agent.

The leading case on this subject is *Bible* v. *John Hancock Mutual Life Insurance Company.*[22] It involved an industrial life insurance policy containing a delivery-in-good-health clause and the following medical treatment clause:

This policy shall be void . . . if the insured . . . has attended any hospital, or institution of any kind engaged in the care or cure of human

---

[22] 256 N.Y. 458, 176 N.E. 838 (1931).

health or disease, or has been attended by any physician, within two years before the date hereof, for any serious disease, complaint or operation . . . unless each such . . . medical and hospital attendance and previous disease is specifically waived by an endorsement in the space for endorsements on page 4 hereof signed by the secretary.

The policy likewise contained a clause to the effect that "agents are not authorized to waive any of the terms or conditions of this policy." There was no such clause in the application, which was not attached to the policy.

The applicant, Anna Bible, was a patient in the Hudson River State Hospital, suffering from a manic depressive psychosis. An agent for the John Hancock Company visited her in the hospital and procured her signature to an application.[23] He delivered the policy to her at the hospital in the presence of her husband and collected the first premium. That same agent collected premiums at the hospital at weekly intervals thereafter for a period of three months, the premiums thereafter being collected by another agent. The insured died about twenty months after the policy was delivered, and the beneficiary filed a claim for the benefits. The company disclaimed liability on the ground that the contract had been avoided by the breach of the good-health and medical treatment clauses.

The New York Court of Appeals, however, affirmed a judgment for the plaintiff-beneficiary on the ground that the conditions had been waived. The court pointed out that the agent was more than a soliciting agent; he had the authority to deliver policies and to collect weekly premiums. He thus had the apparent authority to effectuate a waiver or, at least, to acquire knowledge that could be imputed to his principal, the company. The applicant was not put on notice as to any limitations on the agent's authority before the policy was delivered, and the court held that the insured "was not chargeable with notice that the limitation would apply by retroaction so as to nullify a waiver or estoppel having its origin in conduct antecedent to the contract."

The case expresses the rule followed by the majority of courts— namely, that *when an agent with actual or apparent authority to deliver the policy does so with knowledge of facts constituting a breach of either the delivery-in-good-health or medical treatment clause, or both,* the breach is waived.[24]

---

[23] As a matter of fact, several policies were involved.

[24] This rule will obviously not apply when there has been collusion between the agent and the applicant.

The court indicated that there would have been no waiver if the application had contained a clause limiting the agent's authority, and if a copy of the application had been attached to the policy. Inasmuch as the application for ordinary insurance policies (as contrasted with industrial policies) generally contains a limitation on the agent's authority and is customarily attached to the policy, the waiver problem in this area would not be serious if the courts in general share the view expressed in the Bible case. It is a matter of conjecture, however, how far the courts will go in enforcing the limitation-of-authority clause, even when in the application and attached to the policy.

Misrepresentation in Application

The applicant for a life insurance policy must submit a written application in which he supplies various types of information, including that relating to his past and present health. He may also have to undergo a medical examination, including an interrogation by the medical examiner. It is standard practice for the soliciting agent to fill out the application for the applicant, and the medical examiner writes in the answers to the questions which he asks the applicant.

There is always the possibility that the information supplied by the applicant will be incorrectly recorded in the application by the agent or medical examiner. This may occur through inadvertence or through design. Unless there is collusion, the medical examiner has little or no reason to falsify the medical report; but unfortunately, the agent—being on a commission basis—does have an incentive to falsify information that might adversely affect acceptance of the application. If the agent should falsify the answers in the application, he might do so with or without the knowledge of the applicant. If he informs the applicant that he is not recording some item of information correctly, it is likely to be accompanied by an observation that the matter is immaterial and should not be permitted to complicate consideration of the application by the home office underwriting officials. If the truthful answers of the applicant are falsely recorded in the application by the agent or medical examiner, it becomes important to determine the legal effect of such misstatements.

It is a well-settled rule that one who signs and accepts a written instrument with the intention of contracting is bound by its terms. However, if the instrument contains false statements, the aggrieved party has the right to avoid the contract. Hence, in accordance with strict contract law, material misstatements in the application should give the insurance company power to avoid the contract, irrespective of the circumstances surrounding the falsification of the statements. However, the courts, recognizing that a life insurance policy is a contract of adhesion, seldom read by the insured, do not apply strict contract law in these cases. The rule supported by the weight of authority is that if the application is filled out by an agent of the company who—without fraud, collusion, or knowledge of the applicant—falsely records information truthfully provided by the applicant, the company cannot rely upon the falsity of such information in seeking to avoid liability under the contract.[25] The desirability of the rule has been expressed by one court in the following terms: "To hold otherwise would be to place every simple or uneducated person seeking insurance at the mercy of the insurer who could, through its agent, insert in every application, unknown to the applicant, and over his signature, some false statement which would enable it to avoid all liability while retaining the price paid for supposed insurance."[26]

The key to the above rule is that the agent, in filling out the application, is acting for the company, not the insured. In other words, the soliciting agent is, in a legal sense, the agent of the company, the principal. This finding can support either of two legal theories, both of which have been used by the courts to justify their decisions. The first theory holds that there is no deception of the insurance company, since it knew, through its agent, that the written statement or statements were not true.[27] The second theory, more widely used, recognizes that there is deception but holds that since the company, through the knowledge of its agent, knowingly issued a voidable policy, it is estopped from voiding it.

To find an estoppel, the courts must permit testimony, usually from the beneficiary, as to the answers provided by the applicant to the agent. This would seem to be in violation of both the parol evidence rule and an "entire-contract" statute. The courts of New York, Pennsylvania, and a few other states have held that the entire-contract statute does bar testimony to show a waiver or an estoppel.[28] Other

---

[25] In New York, the insured is bound by false answers entered by the agent or medical examiner if the insured certifies as to the answers. *Bollard* v. *New York Life Insurance Co.*, 228 N.Y. 521, 126 N.E. 900 (1920).

[26] *State Insurance Co. of Des Moines* v. *Taylor*, 14 Colo. 499, 508, 24 Pac. 333, 336 (1890).

[27] *Heilig* v. *Home Security Life Insurance Co.*, 222 N.C. 21, 22 S.E. 2d 429 (1942).

[28] See Patterson, *op. cit.*, p. 514, n. 80, for citations.

states with similar statutes have permitted oral communications to the agent to be introduced into evidence, the statute not being mentioned. In Colorado, the highest court faced the issue squarely and held that the statute did not exclude oral testimony to establish waiver or estoppel.[29]

The courts are likewise inclined to find a waiver or an estoppel when the applicant knows the falsity of an answer but the agent asserts that it is immaterial. The view is that the applicant is entitled to rely upon the superior knowledge of the agent or medical examiner, as the case may be. Even a stipulation in the application that oral statements made to the agent shall not be binding upon the company has been held unenforceable. However, where the applicant knows that the agent or medical examiner is not truthfully reporting obviously material facts to his company, the applicant himself is guilty of fraud and cannot invoke the doctrine of estoppel, which requires honest reliance. The applicant's behavior in this situation would be regarded as collusive.

Waiver Subsequent to Issuance of Policy

A breach of condition that occurs after a policy has gone into effect can be waived in either of two ways: (1) by an express statement, usually in writing, of a representative of the insurer having the authority to waive the condition; or (2) by the inconsistent conduct of the company and its representatives.

With respect to the first method, attention must again be directed to the clause embodied in the application for a life insurance policy, stipulating that no provision of the contract can be waived except by a *written* endorsement on the contract signed by a designated officer of the company. This restriction is likely to be enforced with respect to *express* waivers, although the courts occasionally find that the company bestowed the waiver authority on representatives not designated in the nonwaiver clause, even local agents. Moreover, oral statements may be accepted as evidence of waiver. This, it should be noted, is not inconsistent with the parol evidence rule, which applies only to oral statements made prior to or contemporaneously with the formation of the contract. Most of the litigation concerning express waivers involves the authority of the person who allegedly approved the waiver. It is clear that if an important official of the company purports to

---

[29] *New York Life Insurance Co.* v. *Fukushima,* 74 Colo. 236, 220 Pac. 994 (1923).

waive a breach of condition, the waiver will be recognized and enforced by the courts. The validity of other alleged waivers will depend
upon the actual or apparent authority of the company representative
making the utterance.

A waiver after issuance of the policy is more likely to be found in
the inconsistent conduct of the company. It has been said that the
company cannot "run with the rabbits and bark with the hounds."
When the company has knowledge of a breach or nonperformance of
a condition, and wishes to avoid the contract on that ground, it must
pursue a course of conduct consistent with that intention. In their zeal
to protect policyholders, the courts will seize upon inconsistent conduct on the part of the insurer as evidence of an intention not to
exercise its power of avoidance.

An example of inconsistent conduct may be found in the treatment
of overdue premiums. If a company has followed a general practice of
accepting and retaining premiums tendered after the expiration of the
grace period, it will be estopped from denying the punctuality of any
premiums so paid. Perhaps more important, it will be estopped from
insisting on the timely payment of premiums in the future, unless it
makes unmistakably clear to the policyholder or policyholders from
whom overdue premiums have customarily been accepted that future
payments will have to be made before expiration of the grace period.
The same rule applies when a company has established a practice of
sending premium notices, although not required by statute or the
policy. If, without adequate notice to the policyholders, the company
should discontinue its practice, it would probably be held to have
waived its right to insist on payment within the grace period, provided
payment is tendered within a reasonable time. In recent years, many
companies that formerly sent two premium notices—the second sometimes during the grace period—have discontinued the second notice.
The companies were careful to notify their policyholders of the change
in practice, in order to avoid the possibility of a waiver.

Any attempt of the company to collect a premium after the expiration of the grace period may be held to be a waiver, unless accompanied by an invitation to the insured to submit an application for
reinstatement.

CHAPTER XXVII

The Incontestable Clause

THE PRECEDING chapter discussed the impact of the doctrines of waiver, estoppel, and election on the right of a life insurance company to avoid liability under a policy because of fraud, misrepresentation, or breach of condition at the inception of the contract. This chapter will consider an even more restrictive influence—the incontestable clause. This clause, without counterpart in any other type of contract, has been the source of much misunderstanding and considerable litigation. The opinion has been expressed that no other provision of the typical life insurance contract has been the center of so much "controversy, misinterpretation, and legal abuse" as the incontestable clause.[1] While the incontestable clause is no longer the source of much litigation, the provision has a vital bearing on the protection afforded by a life insurance contract and is worthy of careful study.

NATURE AND PURPOSE OF THE CLAUSE

In General

In its simplest form, the incontestable clause states that "this policy shall be incontestable from its date of issue, except for nonpayment of premium." The purpose of such a clause is to enhance the value of a life insurance contract by providing assurances that its validity will not be questioned by the insurance company years after it was issued and has possibly given rise to a claim. It was voluntarily adopted by the companies, partly as a result of competitive pressures, to overcome

---

[1] H. M. Horne and D. B. Mansfield, *The Life Insurance Contract* (2d ed.; New York: Life Office Management Association, 1948), p. 181.

prejudices against the life insurance business created by contests based upon technicalities and to give an assurance to "persons doubtful of the utility of insurance, that neither they nor their families, after the lapse of a given time, shall be harassed with lawsuits when the evidence of the original transaction shall have become dim, or difficult of retention, or when, perhaps, the lips of him who best knew the facts are sealed by death."[2]

The incontestable clause is a manifestation of the belief that the beneficiaries of a life insurance policy should not be made to suffer for mistakes innocently made in the application. After the insured's death, it would be extremely difficult, if not impossible, for the beneficiary to disprove the allegations of the insurance company that irregularities were present in the procurement of the policy. Were there no time limit on the right of the insurance company to question the accuracy of the information provided in the application, there would be no certainty during the life of the policy that the benefits promised by it would be payable at maturity. The honest policyholder needs an assurance that, upon his death his beneficiary will be the "recipient of a check and not of a lawsuit."[3] The incontestable clause provides that assurance. It is based upon the theory that after the company has had a reasonable opportunity to investigate the circumstances surrounding the issue of a life insurance policy, it should thereafter relinquish the right to question the validity of the contract.

Originally introduced by voluntary action in 1864, the incontestable clause had become so firmly entrenched and so obviously beneficial to all parties concerned by the time of the Armstrong Investigation in 1906 that the legislation which grew out of the investigation made mandatory the inclusion of the clause in life insurance policies. Other states followed New York's example so that, today, the clause is generally required by statute. The laws of the various states differ as to the form of the clause prescribed, but none permits a clause which would make the policy in general contestable for more than two years.

Effect of Fraud

It is generally agreed that the original purpose of the incontestable clause was to protect the beneficiary of a life insurance policy against the *innocent* misrepresentations or concealments of the insured. As a matter of fact, there was considerable doubt in the early years of its

---

[2] *Kansas Mutual Life Insurance Co.* v. *Whitehead,* 123 Ky. 21, 26, 93 S.W. 609, 610 (1906).

[3] Horne and Mansfield, *op. cit.,* p. 181.

use that the incontestable clause could operate as a bar to the denial of liability on the grounds of fraud. It is a basic tenet of contract law that fraud in the formation of a contract renders such contract voidable at the option of the innocent party. Moreover, in general, parties to a contract are not permitted to contract for immunity from the consequences of their fraud. These two rules would seem to limit the applicability of the incontestable clause to inadvertent misrepresentations or concealments. Nevertheless, over the years, judicial interpretation has firmly established the principle that the incontestable clause is effective against fraud. Even more to the point, since no reputable life insurance company under ordinary circumstances is likely to contest a policy unless there is evidence of intent to deceive, it may be concluded that the primary function, if not the purpose, of the incontestable clause is to protect the insured and his beneficiaries against the consequences of his fraudulent behavior.

In holding that the expiration of the contestable period precludes a defense even on the grounds of fraud, the courts have been careful to emphasize that they are not condoning fraud. They justify their action on the ground that the company has a reasonable period of time in which to discover any fraud involved in the procurement of the policy and is under obligation to seek redress within the permissible period of time. In line with this reasoning, one court stated:

> This view does not exclude the consideration of fraud, but allows the parties to fix by stipulation the length of time which fraud of the insured can operate to deceive the insurer. It recognizes the right of the insurer, predicated upon a vast experience and profound knowledge in such matters, to agree that in a stipulated time, fixed by himself, he can unearth and drag to light any fraud committed by the insured, and protect himself from the consequences. . . . The incontestable clause is upheld in law, not for the purpose of upholding fraud, but for the purpose of shutting off harassing defenses based upon alleged fraud; and, in so doing, the law merely adopts the certificate of the insurer that within a given time he can expose and render innocuous any fraud in the preliminary statement of the insured. . . .[4]

The incontestable clause has been described as a private contractual "statute of limitation" on fraud, prescribing a period shorter than that incorporated in the statutory enactment. This analogy with conventional statutes of limitations has been questioned by some,[5] but the

---

[4] *Kansas Mutual Life Insurance Co.* v. *Whitehead,* 123 Ky. 21, 26, 93 S.W. 609, 610 (1906).

[5] Critics of this analogy point out that (*a*) the usual statute of limitations begins to run from the time the fraud is discovered, whereas under the incontestable clause, the

basic purpose of the two instrumentalities is the same: to bar the assertion of legal rights after the evidence concerning the cause of action has grown stale and key witnesses are no longer readily available.

The courts recognize that some unscrupulous persons are permitted to profit by their fraudulent action through the operation of the incontestable clause, but they proceed on the premise that the social advantages of the clause outweigh the undesirable consequences. "The view is that even though dishonest people are given advantages under incontestability clauses which any right-minded man is loath to see them get, still the sense of security given to the great mass of honest policyholders by the presence of the clause in their policies makes it worth the cost."[6]

There is a minority view that a policy procured through fraud should be contestable at any time. The fact that the burden of proof is upon the company is deemed sufficient to protect the honest policyholder. An advocate of this view has stated:

> If the laws had exempted cases of fraud from the operation of the provision, or if the courts had interpreted the provision as not applying in cases of fraud, not a single person of the class intended to be protected by the provision could possibly have suffered. Fraud is never assumed to exist; it must be proved affirmatively, and all policies would, therefore, fall into two completely separated groups—those proved to have been secured by fraud and those not so proved. It is, therefore, wholly possible to secure the full protection desired for all policyholders not proved to have secured their policies by fraud without the incidental condonation of fraud.[7]

Despite the general adherence of the courts to the doctrine that the incontestable clause is a bar to a defense of fraud, there are some species of fraud so abhorrent that their nullification through the incontestable clause is regarded to be in contravention of public policy. For example, the incontestable clause has been held not to apply when the contract was negotiated with intent to murder the insured, even

---

period runs from the beginning of the contract; and (*b*) the typical statute of limitations applies to actions and not to defenses such as those invoked by life insurance companies during the period of contestability. See Benjamin L. Holland, "The Incontestable Clause," in Harry Krueger and Leland T. Waggoner (ed.), *The Life Insurance Policy Contract* (Boston: Little, Brown & Co., 1953), p. 58. These critics are content to identify the incontestable clause as a constituent part of the contract and peculiar to a life insurance policy.

[6] *Maslin* v. *Columbian National Life Insurance Co.*, 3 *F. Supp.* 368, 369 (1932); (S.D.N.Y. 1932).

[7] J. F. Little, "Discussion of the Incontestable Clause," *Transactions of the Actuarial Society of America,* Vol. XXXVI (1935), p. 429.

though the murderer was not the beneficiary.[8] In cases where the applicant lacks an insurable interest, the courts generally permit the insurer to deny liability beyond the contestable period.[9] Likewise, in those cases where someone, presumably a healthier person and usually the beneficiary, has impersonated the applicant for purposes of undergoing the medical examination and answering the questions pertaining to the health of the applicant, the courts have uniformly held the purported contract to be null and void, on the grounds that there has been no real meeting of minds.[10] Finally, in a few cases, the courts have recognized execution for crime as legitimate grounds for denial of liability,[11] although in other cases, the company has been held liable.[12]

Meaning of a Contest

A policy can be prevented from becoming incontestable only by appropriate legal action on the part of the company during the contestable period or, under one type of incontestable clause (to be described later), by the death of the insured during the contestable period. The courts hold that there must be a "contest" during the contestable period, and it becomes a matter of interpretation as to what constitutes a "contest" within the meaning of the clause.

In some jurisdictions, a notice of rescission, accompanied by a return of the premium, is deemed to constitute a contest. The majority of the courts, however, have held that the requirement can be satisfied only by a suit for rescission before a court of competent jurisdiction or by a defense to a judicial proceeding in such a court seeking to enforce the contract. In the first instance, the company would be seeking rescission by a suit in equity; in the second case, it would be defending against an action at law instituted by the beneficiary in an attempt to collect the proceeds. A suit for rescission is permitted only when there is no adequate remedy at law; and in most jurisdictions, defense against a beneficiary's action is regarded as an adequate remedy. Equity proceedings, however, are always available to the com-

---

[8] *Columbian Mutual Life Insurance Co.* v. *Martin,* 175 Tenn. 517, 136 S.W. (2d) 52 (1940).

[9] See Holland, *op. cit.,* p. 68, n. 27, for citations.

[10] *Ibid.,* p. 69 and citations in n. 31.

[11] *Scarborough* v. *American National Insurance Co.,* 171 N.C. 353, 88 S.E. 482 (1916); and *Murphy* v. *Metropolitan Life Insurance Co.,* 152 Ga. 393, 110 S.E. 178 (1921).

[12] *Afro-American Life Insurance Co.* v. *Jones,* 113 Fla. 158, 151 So. 405 (1933).

pany while the insured is alive (during the contestable period and, as is pointed out below, are usually available after the death of the insured under certain types of incontestable clause.

Detailed rules of legal procedure have been evolved to establish the precise moment at which a contest has materialized. Once the contest has been joined, the running of the contestable period is stopped; and irrespective of the outcome of the initial contest, the incontestable clause cannot be invoked to forestall any other proceeding. Thus, if a contest is initiated with the insured during the contestable period, the beneficiary may be made a party to the proceedings after the expiration of the period specified in the incontestable clause.

The interpretation of the term "contest" is important in another respect. Broadly interpreted, the incontestable clause could prohibit the denial of any type of claim after the contestable period has expired. It could force the company to pay a type of claim that was never envisioned under the contract. Fortunately, the majority of the courts do not interpret the clause in that manner. They make a distinction between contests that question the validity or existence of a contract and those that seek to clarify the terms of the contract or to enforce the terms of the contract. In one widely cited case, the court said:

> It must be clear that every resistance by an insurer against the demands of the beneficiary is in one sense a contest, but it is not a contest of the policy; that is, not a contest against the terms of the policy but a contest for or in favor of the terms of the policy. In other words, there are two classes of contests; one to enforce the policy, the other to destroy it. Undoubtedly the term "incontestable" as used in a life insurance policy means a contest, the purpose of which is to destroy the validity of the policy, and not a contest, the purpose of which is to demand its enforcement.[13]

The significance of this distinction will be brought out in the discussion dealing with the application of the incontestable clause to other contract provisions.

Inception of the Contestable Period

Where the *operative date* of a life insurance policy coincides with the *effective date,* there is little question as to when the contestable period begins to run. It begins the day following the date on the policy.[14] Where, however, the effective date of protection is earlier

---

[13] *Stean* v. *Occidental Life Insurance Co.,* 24 N.M. 346, 350, 171 Pac. 786, 787 (1918).

[14] There is some case law to the effect that the last day when a contest can be made is, in the case of a two-year contestable provision, the second anniversary

than the date of the policy, some courts have made the beginning of the contestable period coincide with the commencement of insurance coverage, regardless of the date of the policy. On the other hand, where the policy has been antedated so that the date of the policy is earlier than the effective date of coverage, the courts, applying the rule of construction most favorable to the insured, have usually held that the contestable period begins with the date of the policy. This is true whether the clause provides that the policy shall be incontestable after a specified period from the "date of the policy" or the "date of issue." Where the policy makes it clear that the contestable period starts to run only from the time the policy actually becomes effective, there is no reason to apply the rule of construction most favorable to the insured, and the courts will give effect to the contract as written.

TYPES OF INCONTESTABLE CLAUSES

The incontestable clause has gone through a period of evolution, various changes in wording having been made from time to time, usually to nullify the unfavorable interpretations developed out of litigation. The earliest forms were quite simple, and one that was to become involved in a precedent-making court decision read as follows: "After two years, this policy shall be noncontestable except for the nonpayment of premiums as stipulated. . . ." This clause served satisfactorily for many years until the celebrated "Monahan Decision" impaired its usefulness to the companies.[15] In that case, the insured died within the two-year period; and the company denied liability, alleging a breach of warranty. The beneficiary waited until the two-year period had expired and then brought suit against the company. The company defended on the grounds of breach of warranty, but the Supreme Court of Illinois held that the policy was incontestable and found for the beneficiary. This decision, which was accepted as a precedent in virtually all jurisdictions, established the far-reaching principle that the contestable period continued to run after the insured's death.

The practical effect of the Monahan decision was that if the policyholder should die within the contestable period, the company was

of the date of issue, rather than the day thereafter. These rulings were made with respect to policies which state that the policy is contestable for two years after the date of issue.

[15] *Monahan* v. *Metropolitan Life Insurance Co.*, 283 Ill. 136, 119 N.E. 68 (1918).

forced to go into court during the contestable period to seek a rescission if it wanted to deny liability for any reason. If no action was brought before the period expired, the company was estopped from erecting any defense other than lapse from nonpayment of premiums. Much litigation was thus thrust upon the companies to avert claims which they regarded to be unwarranted, to their detriment in the esteem of the public.

In an effort to avoid the undesirable consequences of the Monahan case, many companies adopted a clause which provides that the policy shall be incontestable after it has been *in force* for a specified period. It was believed that with such a clause, the death of the insured would stop the running of the period, since the policy would no longer be in force. When the clause was tested in the courts, however, the decisions, with some exceptions, held that a policy does not terminate with the death of the insured but continues "in force" for the benefit of the beneficiary. In other words, the contract still has to be performed. Thus, this clause has the same weakness as that which was litigated in the Monahan case. Despite this disadvantage, many companies have continued to use the clause, since it permits suits in equity, which are usually tried without a jury.

Those companies that were willing to give up the advantage of suits in equity modified their incontestable clause to make the policy incontestable after it has been in force *during the lifetime of the insured* for a specified period. The courts have uniformly agreed that under this clause, the death of the insured during the contestable period suspends the operation of the clause and fixes the rights of the parties as of the date of death. Under such a clause, if the insured dies during the specified period, the policy never becomes incontestable, and the claimant cannot gain any advantage by postponing notification of claim until the specified period has expired. However, since a legal remedy is available—i.e., a defense against a suit instituted by the beneficiary—the company cannot obtain rescission of the policy by a suit in equity, except during the lifetime of the insured.

A final type of clause that is used by a number of leading companies provides that (with certain exceptions, to be noted) "this policy shall be incontestable after one year from its date of issue unless the insured dies in such year, in which event it shall be incontestable after two years from its date of issue." This clause does not solve the problem created by the Monahan decision, since the death of the insured during the first year does not suspend the running of the period.

However, should the insured die during the first year, the company will have a *minimum* of one year in which to investigate the circumstances of the case and, if desired, to institute a suit for rescission. Under all of the other types of clauses except the one requiring survivorship of the insured, it is possible for the company to have only a few days in which to investigate a suspicious death; in fact, it is quite likely that in many cases, the company would receive no notice of the death of the insured until the contestable period had expired. The clause described in this paragraph is more favorable to the insured than the usual clauses, since, if he survives the first year, the policy becomes incontestable at that time, and if he does not survive the first year, the company's rights are no greater than they would have been under the typical clause. It should be noted, however, that some companies limit the contestability of their policies to one year, whether or not the insured survives the period.

At one time, some companies, in the thought that they were making their policies more attractive, introduced a clause providing that the policy should be incontestable *from the date of issue,* except as to nonpayment of premiums. As it turned out, this clause provided less protection to the insured than any of the other types that have been used. The courts generally regarded this clause as an attempt to provide immunity to the insured against the consequences of his own fraud and refused to enforce it where fraud was involved. The clause protects the policyholder against an innocent misrepresentation or concealment, but does not prevent a defense based on fraud. In other words, the policy *never* becomes incontestable with respect to *fraud.* This unusual and unanticipated result is based on the fact that the clause made provision for no period during which the validity of the policy could be attacked on the ground of fraud.[16]

It is interesting to observe that the policies issued to members of the military and naval service by the federal government under its various insurance programs contained this type of incontestable clause. As a matter of fact, the clause specifically excluded fraud (and certain other conditions) from the benefits of incontestability. Yet, in its

---

[16] There is a minority view that such clauses are enforceable even as against fraud, on the reasoning that if the insurer can properly limit its right to ferret out fraud in the procurement of the policy to a specified period after issuance of the policy, it can delay the issuance until it is satisfied that no fraud is present (*Duvall* v. *National Insurance Co. of Montana,* 28 Idaho 356, 154 Pac. 632 [1916]; *Pacific Mutual Life Insurance Co.* v. *Strange,* 223 Ala. 226, 135 So. 477 [1931]; *Mutual Life of New York* v. *Weinberg,* 319 Ill. App. 177, 49 N. E. 2d 44 [1943]).

promotional material, the Veterans Administration has consistently pointed to the incontestable clause as one of the favorable (to the insured) features of its policies.

MATTERS SPECIFICALLY EXCLUDED FROM OPERATION OF THE INCONTESTABLE CLAUSE

Nonpayment of Premiums

The original incontestable clause excluded the nonpayment of premiums from its operation, and the practice has continued to the present. This exception is not only superfluous today, but has created confusion as to the applicability of the clause to matters not specifically excluded. Payment of the first premium, or the first installment of the first premium, is a consideration of the life insurance contract and is usually made a condition precedent. Unless this requirement is satisfied, there is no contract and hence no incontestable clause. If subsequent premiums are not paid, the contract does not fail as of its inception and may, in fact, continue in force under the surrender provisions.

This has not always been the case, however, and there was probably some justification for the inclusion of the exception in the original clause. Early policies contained no surrender values; and default in premium, even years after issue of the policy, resulted in avoidance of the contract from its inception. It is clear, though, that the termination or modification of a modern policy through nonpayment of premiums is not a contest of the policy. Nevertheless, the historical precedent and the requirements of state statutes have made the exception a fixture.

The express exclusion of nonpayment of premium and other conditions from the operation of the incontestable clause has caused many courts to apply the doctrine of *expressio unius est exclusio alterius*[17] to the attempts of the company to avoid liability under other provisions of the policy. Under such a doctrine, if a particular hazard were not specifically excluded from the operation of the clause, a claim arising from that hazard could not be avoided beyond the contestable period.

Disability and Accidental Death Benefits

It is also customary to exclude from the operation of the incontestable clause the provisions of the policy relating to disability and

---

[17] "The enumeration of some is the exclusion of others," usually paraphrased as "enumeration implies exclusion."

accidental death benefits. A typical clause containing these exclusions might read as follows: "This policy shall be incontestable after it shall have been in force for two years from its date of issue except for nonpayment of premiums and except as to provisions relating to benefits payable in the event of total and permanent disability and provisions which grant additional insurance specifically against death by accident."

If the courts could be relied upon to interpret the incontestable clause in accordance with its basic objective, it would be unnecessary specifically to exclude disability and accidental death benefits from its scope. Unfortunately, they have had some difficulty in distinguishing between a contest involving the validity of the policy and one relating to the coverage of an admittedly valid policy. The distinction is a critical one in connection with disability and accidental death provisions, since it is frequently difficult to determine whether a claim filed under one of these provisions is valid. In order to avoid any possible conflict with the incontestable clause in the adjudication of such claims, the companies chose to keep the provisions entirely outside the operation of the clause. Under the type of clause cited above, the *validity* of the provisions relating to disability and double indemnity can be attacked at any time, even after the expiration of the contestable period. The courts' interpretations frequently turn on th precise wording of the clause; and in some cases, it has been held that the validity of the provisions cannot be questioned beyond the period of contestability. In New York, a provision relating to total disability benefits must be incontestable after it has been in force for three years *without the occurrence of total disability of the insured*. In other words, if total disability begins during the three-year period the provision is contestable at any time.

The exclusion of disability benefits from the protection of the incontestable clause is not in conflict with the intent of the clause. The purpose of the clause is to forestall a contest over the validity of the contract after the insured is dead and cannot defend the representations he made in the application for insurance. Disability claims are filed during the lifetime of the insured, and he can defend his actions, both at the time he applied for the policy and at the time of the claim.

Military or Naval Service

The laws of most states permit, as a specific exception to the incontestable clause, "violation of any provision of the policy relating to naval or military service in time of war." Except during wartime or when war was imminent, it has not been the practice to include in the policy any restrictions as to military or naval service. Even when a so-called "war clause" has been used, it has not been customary to exclude it from the operations of the incontestable clause.

RELATIONSHIP TO OTHER POLICY PROVISIONS

Excepted Hazards

At one time, it was the view of the courts and the state insurance departments that once the contestable period had expired, no denial of liability on the grounds of lack of coverage could be sustained unless the hazard involved in the litigation was specifically excluded in the incontestable clause itself. Moreover, no hazard could be excluded from the scope of the incontestable clause unless such exclusion was recognized in the statute governing the clause.[18] This doctrine was attacked when the Superintendent of Insurance of the state of New York refused to approve a proposed aviation exclusion in a policy of the Metropolitan Life Insurance Company, on the ground that the exclusion was in conflict with the New York statute prescribing the substance of the incontestable clause. The decision of the Superintendent was appealed to the courts, and the issue was resolved in what is known as the "Conway Decision." The New York Court of Appeals, with Judge Cardozo sitting as chief judge, ruled that there was nothing in the law which prohibited the issuance of such a restricted policy. The decision declared that the New York statute requiring an incontestable clause "is not a mandate as to coverage, a definition of hazards to be borne by the insurer. It means only this, that within the limits of the coverage, the policy shall stand, unaffected by any defense that it was invalid by reason of a condition broken. . . . [Where] there has been no assumption of risk, there can be no liability. . . ."[19] Following the Conway decision, the various insurance commissioners reversed their rulings on the inclusion of aviation riders; and today, it is the accepted view that a company may exclude any hazard which it does not wish to cover.

In general, the right to limit coverage has been invoked only with respect to aeronautical activities, military and naval service in time of

[18] This is still the case.

[19] *Metropolitan Life Insurance Co.* v. *Conway*, 252 N.Y. 449, 452, 169 N.E. 642 (1930).

war, and suicide. With advances in aeronautics, the aviation exclusion has lost most of its significance, and with few exceptions war clauses are not currently being added to policies. Limitations on the coverage of suicide, however, are contained in all policies. In New York and a few other states, there are now statutes listing permissible exclusions.

Since the Conway decision, the companies could undoubtedly exclude death from suicide throughout the duration of the contract, unless prohibited by statute. They feel, however, that it is a risk which should properly be assumed by insurance companies, and their only concern is that they not be exposed to the risk of issuing policies to persons contemplating suicide. Consequently, they exclude death from suicide, whether the insured be sane or insane, for the first year or two after issue of the policy, with the risk thereafter being assumed in its entirety by the company. If the insured should commit suicide during the period of restricted coverage, the company's liability is limited to a refund of the premiums paid.

While the suicide exclusion is normally of the same duration as the contestable period, the suicide clause is independent of the incontestable clause. Since most suicide exclusions are of two years' duration and some policies are contestable for only one year, a conflict could develop if the insured commits suicide during the second year of the contract. With few exceptions, the courts have upheld the right of the company to deny coverage of suicide beyond the contestable period.

Conditions Precedent

The incontestable clause is a part of the policy and cannot become effective until the policy has gone into force. There must be a contract before there can be an incontestable clause. Therefore, the incontestable clause does not bar a defense that the policy was never approved.[20]

On principle, it would seem that if a policy provides that it will not become effective until certain conditions have been fulfilled, there would be no contract at all until such conditions had been satisfied. Hence, the incontestable clause itself, being a part of the contract, would not be operative. This would suggest that the incontestable clause should not prevent the insurer from denying liability on the grounds that the applicant was not in good health at the time the policy was delivered or that some other condition precedent was not

---

[20] *McDonald* v. *Mutual Life Insurance Co. of New York,* 108 F. 2d 32 (6th Cir. 1939); *Harris* v. *Travelers Insurance Co.,* 80 F. (2d) 127 (5th Cir. 1935).

fulfilled. However, most of the courts have reached the conclusion that the delivery-in-good-health requirement and other such conditions precedent should be accorded the same treatment as representations. Since the incontestable clause was designed to deal with misrepresentations, it follows that the clause should bar suits based on nonfulfillment of conditions precedent, if, at any time, both parties had treated the policy as having been operative.[21] This is the rule in most jurisdictions.

Misstatement of Age

Most life insurance policies contain a provision which stipulates that in the event of a misstatement of age, the amount payable under the policy will be such as would have been purchased at the correct age by the premium actually paid. In most states, a provision to this effect is required by statute. In jurisdictions where the provision is mandatory, no conflict with the incontestable clause can arise. Even where the clause is not a matter of statute, the right of the company to reduce the amount of insurance after the contestable period has expired has seldom been questioned. This is undoubtedly due to the fact that the misstatement-of-age adjustment was firmly established before any controversy developed over the right of a company to limit the coverage of a policy beyond the contestable period. If it had been held that misstatement-of-age adjustments were subject to the incontestable clause, the companies would probably have found it necessary to require proof of age before issuance of a policy.

It was pointed out in an earlier chapter that a misstatement of age which contravenes a company's underwriting rules may, at the company's option, serve as a basis for rescission. It has been held, however, that such action would have to be taken during the contestable period.[22] If the misstatement were discovered beyond the contestable period, it could still be dealt with in the conventional manner.

Reformation

It sometimes happens that a life insurance policy in the form issued by the company does not represent the actual agreement between the company and the applicant. This may be due to simple clerical errors, such as a misspelled name or an incorrect date, or to more substantial

---

[21] See Holland, *op. cit.*, p. 64, n. 10, for citations.
[22] *Kelly* v. *Prudential Insurance Co.*, 334 Pa. 143, 6 A. 2d 55 (1939).

mistakes, such as an incorrect premium, wrong face amount, inappropriate set of surrender values, or incorrect set of settlement options. The mistake may favor either the insured or the company. The overwhelming majority of such mistakes are rectified without any controversy or litigation. From time to time, however, a policyholder will oppose the correction of a mistake in his favor. In one such case,[23] the policy actually applied for and issued was an ordinary life contract; but through a printer's error, the surrender values shown in the contract were those for a twenty-year endowment insurance policy. The company discovered the error two months after the policy was issued but had to resort to legal action to rewrite the contract.

The appropriate legal action in such circumstances is a suit for reformation of the contract. This is an equitable remedy under which the written instrument is made to conform to the intention of the parties.[24] The party seeking relief must establish the fact that there was either a mutual mistake in the drafting of the written instrument[25] or a mistake on one side and fraud on the other.

The remedy of reformation is clearly available to an insurance company during the contestable period. Moreover, it has long been the rule that reformation to correct a clerical error is not barred by the incontestable clause. A suit to rectify a mistake "is not a contest of the policy but a prayer to make a written instrument speak the real agreement of the parties."[26] In 1948, however, the Ninth Circuit Court of Appeals departed from the rule that had been regarded as well established and held that reformation was in conflict with incontestability.[27] The court reasoned that the words "this contract" appearing in the incontestable clause apply to the printed provisions of the policy of which the clause is a part, and not to the oral conversation and negotiations that preceded the execution of the contract. It was pointed out that "the clause does not say that the insurer shall not contest his liability under the actual agreement; it says *this* contract shall be incontestable." This case was later held to be contrary to the

[23] *Columbian National Life Insurance Co.* v. *Black,* 35 F. 2d 571 (10th Cir. 1929).

[24] The introduction of oral testimony is permitted in such cases, notwithstanding the fact that in so doing, the terms of the written instrument are changed. This is an exception to the parol evidence rule, discussed earlier.

[25] In this connection, it is held that knowledge by one party of the other's mistake is equivalent to a mutual mistake.

[26] *Columbian National Life Insurance Co.* v. *Black,* 35 F. 2d 571, 577 (10th Cir. 1929).

[27] *Richardson* v. *Travelers Insurance Co.,* 171 F. 2d 699 (9th Cir. 1948).

law of California,[28] and the only other reported case since the Richardson decision followed the majority rule that reformation is not barred by the expiration of the contestable period.[29]

Reinstatement

All life insurance policies contain a provision permitting reinstatement in the event of lapse, subject to certain conditions. One of the conditions is usually "evidence of insurability satisfactory to the company." Reinstatement will almost always necessitate a statement by the insured as to the current status of his health and will frequently involve a complete medical examination. It will also involve aspects of insurability other than health, just as at the time of original issue. A question arises as to the legal effect of a misrepresentation or concealment in the reinstatement application not discovered until after the policy has been reinstated. Specifically, can a reinstated policy be rescinded after the original contestable period has expired?

There are conflicting views on this point. One view, greatly in the minority, holds that the concept of incontestability does not apply to the reinstatement process.[30] Under this view, a suit for rescission or a defense against a claim would be subject only to the conventional statute of limitations on fraud—which, it will be recalled, begins to run only *after the fraud has been discovered.*

At the other extreme, and likewise in the minority, is the view that the reinstatement clause is subject to the original incontestable clause.[31] If the original period of contestability has expired before the application for reinstatement is submitted, the reinstated policy is incontestable from the date of reinstatement. If a policy is reinstated during the original period of contestability, the reinstated policy can be contested during the remaining portion of the contestable period.

The majority opinion adopts a middle ground and holds that a reinstated policy is contestable for the same period of time as is prescribed in the original incontestable clause.[32] If the policy was

---

[28] *Mutual Life Insurance Company of New York* v. *Simon,* 151 F. Supp. 408 (S.D.N.Y. 1957).

[29] *Prudential Insurance Co.* v. *Strickland,* 187 F. 2d 67 (6th Cir. 1951). See also G. Frank Purvis, Jr., "Reformation of Life Policies," *Proceedings* of the Legal Section of the American Life Convention, 1957, p. 179.

[30] *Acacia Mutual Life Assn.* v. *Kaul,* 114 N.J. Eq. 491, 169 Atl. 36 (Ch. 1933); *Chuz* v. *Columbian National Life Insurance Co.,* 10 N.J. Misc. 1145, 162 Atl. 395 (Cir. Ct. 1932).

[31] See Holland, *op. cit.,* p. 78, n. 2, for citations.

[32] *Ibid.,* p. 78, n. 3.

originally contestable for a period of two years, the reinstated policy would again be contestable for the same length of time. This is true even when the policy is lapsed and reinstated before the original period of contestability has expired. The reasoning is that the company needs the same period of time in which to detect any fraud in the application for reinstatement as it needed in connection with the original issue. It is hardly necessary to add that the policy becomes contestable again only with respect to the information supplied in connection with the reinstatement process. In other words, the company does not have restored to it the right to question the validity of the contract on the grounds of irregularities in the original application.

CHAPTER XXVIII

The Beneficiary

THE BENEFICIARY is the person named in the life insurance contract to receive all or a portion of the proceeds payable at maturity. The section of the contract dealing with the designation and rights of the beneficiary is, in many respects, the most significant one in the entire contract. It reflects the decisions of the insured concerning the disposition of his human life value. It is the means by which he can provide financial security to his family after he has passed from the scene. In a well-planned estate, the beneficiary designations will be integrated with the election of settlement option in such a manner as most effectively to carry out the insured's objectives.

There are many facets to a study of the beneficiary in life insurance, and the starting point should be a description of the various categories of beneficiaries and beneficiary designations. Emphasis is placed on customary situations and policy provisions, and the student is cautioned that any particular case is decided on the basis of its own facts and the policy wording involved.

TYPES OF BENEFICIARIES

Beneficiaries can be classified from various points of view. For the purposes of this discussion, they will be classified as to (1) nature of the interest, (2) manner of identification, (3) priority of entitlement, and (4) revocability of the designation.

Nature of the Interest

From the standpoint of the interest involved, beneficiaries fall into two broad categories: *the insured* or his estate; and a person or

576

persons other than the insured, normally referred to as a *third-party beneficiary*.

The insured is normally designated as the person to receive the proceeds of an endowment insurance policy or a retirement income policy, since those policies were primarily designed to provide benefits to the policyholder himself. He may designate someone else to receive the proceeds in the event of his death, or he may specify that the proceeds be payable to his estate. Proceeds are usually made payable to the estate only for a purpose associated with the settlement of the estate, such as the payment of last-illness and funeral expenses, debts, mortgages, and taxes. If any proceeds remain after the claims against the estate have been satisfied, they are distributed in accordance with the decedent's will or the appropriate intestate law. It is considered highly undesirable, however, to have the proceeds of a policy payable to the insured's estate when it is intended that they should go to certain specific individuals. The proceeds will be subject to estate administration and may be reduced through probate costs, taxes, and the claims of creditors. Moreover, distribution to the intended beneficiaries will be delayed until settlement of the estate has been completed.

When it is intended that the proceeds be paid to the insured's estate and be subject to the control of the executor or administrator, as the case may be, the proper designation is "the executors or administrators of the insured." If the policy involved is an endowment or a retirement income policy and the proceeds are to be paid to the insured if he survives to the date of maturity and to his estate if he does not so survive, the proper designation is "insured, if living; otherwise to his executors or administrators." The simple designation "insured's estate" would undoubtedly be effective; but such terms as "heirs," "legal heirs," or "family" would not be. When the latter terms are used, the proceeds do not become part of the probate estate. The appropriate intestate law will be followed in determining the legal heirs; but the latter will receive the proceeds directly, being treated as named beneficiaries, rather than heirs. In other words, the proceeds will pass outside the probate estate.

When the insured was the applicant and designates himself or his estate as beneficiary, he is regarded as the owner of the policy and can exercise all rights under the policy without the consent of any other person. The policy is his property and can be dealt with like any other property.

Any person or organization other than the insured who is designated to receive insurance proceeds is known as a *third-party beneficiary*. Three general types of third-party beneficiary can be distinguished. The first is the owner-applicant, sometimes referred to as the "assured." This is the situation in which one person procures insurance on another person's life and becomes the owner of the policy. Ordinarily, the owner will designate himself as beneficiary, although it is not inconceivable that he would direct that the proceeds be paid to someone other than himself, particularly in the event that he should predecease the insured. This type of arrangement is identified with key-man insurance and business continuation agreements, but it is by no means confined to such situations. It may be used by a creditor to protect his interest, or by a family group to provide estate liquidity and minimize death taxes. From the standpoint of ownership rights, the third-party owner occupies the same position as the insured who designates himself as beneficiary. There is the difference—of no legal significance—that the insured owns his policy because he is the only party involved, whereas the third-party owner has his rights established by an express provision in the contract.

The third-party applicant must have an insurable interest in the insured at the inception of the contract. There need be no insurable interest at the date of the insured's death; and the third-party owner, or the beneficiary of his choice, is entitled to retain the full amount of the proceeds.

The second type of third-party beneficiary is the person who has furnished a valuable consideration in exchange for the designation. A creditor may be designated as beneficiary under a policy on his debtor's life, although it is much more common for the policy to be assigned to the creditor. In either event, the creditor is permitted to retain only that portion of the proceeds equal to his interest at the time of the debtor's death. During the insured's lifetime, he could exercise no rights in the policy without the consent or joinder of the insured. Occasionally, a wife is designated beneficiary under a policy as part of a divorce settlement. Her rights would depend upon the terms of the settlement. The designation is usually irrevocable or, if revocable, can be changed only by an appropriate court order.

The third type of beneficiary other than the insured is the person who has furnished no consideration. Technically, this type is known as the *donee* or *gratuitous* beneficiary. This is the typical situation where the insured designates a member of his family as beneficiary for no consideration other than "love and affection." It is not necessary for the donee beneficiary to have an insurable interest, although she usually does. The discussion in the succeeding pages will be directed at the donee beneficiary, unless a specific notation is made to the contrary.

Manner of Identification

Classified as to the manner of identification, beneficiaries may be termed *specific* or *class*. A specific beneficiary is an individual who is designated by name or in any other manner which clearly sets him or her apart from any other individual. A class beneficiary is a person not mentioned by name who belongs to a clearly identifiable *group* of persons designated as beneficiaries.

In making specific designations, it is customary to identify the person both by *name* and *relationship* to the insured, if there is a legal or blood relationship. For example, a wife would be designated as "Mary Smith Doe, wife of the insured." A son would be designated as "Charles William Doe, son of the insured." The full name—i.e., the first, middle, and surname—should preferably be given. The wife's maiden name should be included to prevent confusion and litigation in the event that there should be an antecedent or subsequent wife with the same given name. It invites litigation to designate the insured's spouse simply as "wife," without any name, or to use the insured's name with the word "Mrs." prefixed, such as "Mrs. John Doe." In both of these cases, if the insured should be married more than once, there is likely to be controversy as to whether the designation refers to the woman who was married to the insured at the time he made the designation or the woman who was married to him at the time of his death.

The relationship stated in the designation is regarded as descriptive only and not as a condition of entitlement. That is, if a beneficiary is identifiable by name or otherwise, she will be entitled to the proceeds even though the stated relationship to the insured is no longer applicable—or never was. For example, if a man were to purchase a policy prior to marriage and designate his fiancée by name as beneficiary, describing her as his wife, his death prior to the marriage ceremony would not deprive her of the proceeds. Nor would an invalid marriage have any effect on the beneficiary's entitlement.

A class designation is appropriate whenever the insured desires that the proceeds be divided equally among the members of a particular group, the composition of which may not be definitely fixed as of the time of designation. Examples of such groups are children, grandchildren, brothers, sisters, or heirs. Perhaps the most common class designation is "children of the insured." This type of class designation is especially favored for the designation of secondary or contingent beneficiaries. It may also be used in combination with a specific designation, such as where the insured designates his living children by name and then adds "and any other surviving children born of the marriage of the insured and Mary Smith Doe, wife of the insured."

From the standpoint of the law, class designations are entirely proper. Courts have repeatedly sustained the validity of such designations. From a practical standpoint, however, class designations present the problem of identifying the members of the class. No class designation is entirely free of possible complications. Even the simplest designations can cause difficulties. For example, the designation "children of the insured" would seem to circumscribe the class precisely enough to permit of ready identification; but in discharging its responsibilities under such a designation, the insurance company would have to determine whether the insured was survived by any illegitimate children, children by a previous marriage or marriages, or adopted children. If the surviving children are adults, there is always the possibility that one has severed normal ties with the family, his whereabouts unknown to the other members of the family and perhaps even his existence denied or concealed by them. The designation "children born of the marriage of the insured and Mary Smith Doe, wife of the insured," while quite precise, does not of itself indicate whether adopted children of the marriage should be accorded the same status as natural children. For the sake of clarity, and to avoid possible litigation, some designations include a statement that the word "children" shall be construed as including adopted children. The use of the term "heirs" in a beneficiary designation will make it necessary for the company to refer to previous court rulings as to the meaning of the term in the jurisdiction involved or, lacking these, to seek court interpretation. Then, the company will have to identify and locate the heirs. The perils to the company in this process are such that many companies will not accept the designation of "heirs."

When either the insured or his wife has children by a previous marriage, a class designation must be carefully worded to carry out the insured's intentions. He may wish to provide for all his children and those of his wife by her former marriage, or he may want to confine his bounty to the children of his current marriage. If he specifies that the proceeds are to be paid to "my children" or "children of the insured," his children by any marriage would be included, but the children of his wife by her previous marriage would be excluded. On the other hand, by speaking of "my wife, Mary Smith Doe, and our children," he is not only excluding his wife's children by her former marriage but also any children he may have had by an earlier marriage and any he may have by a subsequent marriage.

Most companies today restrict the use of class designations. They will not accept designations of a class whose relationship to the insured is remote or whose composition will be difficult of determination. Where the class is acceptable, it must be described as precisely as possible. All companies permit the designation of children as a class. This is a useful device in protecting the interests of unborn children. Unless the companies were willing at least to supplement specific designations with a class designation of children not yet born, many children would be deprived of insurance protection through failure of the insured to revise his settlement plan after the birth of an additional child or children. At best, class designations lead to delays in the settlement of death claims. At their worst, they can involve considerable trouble and expense for the company and possibly even the double or multiple payment of some claims.

Priority of Entitlement

With respect to priority of entitlement, beneficiaries may be classified as *primary* and *contingent*. Among the various classes of beneficiary, the primary beneficiary has the first claim to the proceeds if the conditions on which they are payable to her are fulfilled. There may be two or more primary beneficiaries, in which event they will share the proceeds in the proportion specified by the insured. It is not implicit in such an arrangement that the beneficiaries share equally in the proceeds, except as to the members of a class. Class beneficiaries do share equally in the proceeds, since, without mentioning names, it is impracticable to provide disproportionate shares. With respect to her particular share, any one of a group of primary beneficiaries, whether specifically named or designated as a class, enjoys rights in the policy equal to those of any other beneficiary.

The contingent beneficiary, frequently called the *secondary* beneficiary, has a claim to the proceeds which ripens only upon the death or removal of the primary beneficiary. The basic concept of a contingent beneficiary is that of a person or an organization that takes the place of the primary beneficiary in the event that the latter should predecease the insured or lose her entitlement in some other manner before receiving any proceeds. With the increased use of installment settlement plans, however, the contingent beneficiary has assumed importance in another role—namely, to receive the benefits under an installment option payable beyond the death of the primary beneficiary. In this role, the contingent beneficiary can become entitled to benefits even though the primary beneficiary survives the insured. This function is of importance in connection with the interest option, installment time option, installment amount option, and guaranteed installments under life income options.

The two functions of the contingent beneficiary are quite distinctive, and her rights thereunder are quite different. Under the original concept, the contingent beneficiary becomes the primary beneficiary upon the death of the erstwhile primary beneficiary during the lifetime of the insured—subject, of course, to being divested of her position by the insured. In her new status, the former contingent beneficiary succeeds to all the rights of the original primary beneficiary, including those arising under the provisions for optional settlement. Upon the death of the insured, she would be regarded as a "first taker" beneficiary, with all that this status implies under company settlement option practices. She might be given the right to take the proceeds in a lump sum, to elect her own settlement option, and to designate her own contingent beneficiaries to receive any benefits unpaid at the time of her death.

Upon the death of the insured, proceeds payable in a lump sum vest immediately in the primary beneficiary (in the absence of a delay clause), and the interest of the contingent beneficiary or beneficiaries is terminated. Even though the primary beneficiary should die before receiving a check from the insurance company, the proceeds would go to her estate, rather than to the contingent beneficiary. If the proceeds are payable under an installment option, the contingent beneficiary would become entitled to the benefits upon the death of the primary beneficiary. She would be a "second taker" beneficiary, however, and under the practices of most companies, would have to take the proceeds under the distribution pattern prescribed for the primary beneficiary. In other words, a "second taker" contingent beneficiary is not usually permitted to commute the unpaid installments or to elect to have them paid out under a settlement arrangement different from that in effect for the primary beneficiary.

There may be, and usually are, two or more contingent beneficiaries of the first order of priority. The typical insured designates his wife as primary beneficiary and his children, by name or as a class, as contingent beneficiaries. For a lump-sum distribution, the designation might read as follows: "Mary Smith Doe, wife of the insured, if she survives the insured; otherwise in equal shares to the surviving children of the insured." If the proceeds are to be distributed under an installment option, a more complex designation is necessary.

There may be various degrees of contingent beneficiaries, each successive level having a lower order of entitlement to the proceeds. Thus, there may be "first contingent," "second contingent," and "third contingent" beneficiaries.[1] Two levels of contingent beneficiaries are provided for in the following designation: "Mary Smith Doe, wife of the insured, if she survives the insured; otherwise in equal shares to the surviving children, if any, of the insured; otherwise to Harry Doe, father of the insured, if he survives the insured." If the proceeds are to be paid out under an installment option, the agreement usually specifies that any installments remaining unpaid at the death of the last surviving contingent beneficiary shall be paid in a lump sum to the estate of such beneficiary. This obviates the necessity of reopening the estate of the insured to receive the unpaid installments, which—if one or two levels of contingent beneficiaries have passed out of the picture —might precipitate a series of estate reopenings, with considerable expense and little benefit. Many persons designate an educational institution, hospital, or religious organization as the last contingent or ultimate contingent beneficiary.

Right of Revocation

Under modern practice, the applicant for insurance is asked to indicate in the application whether or not he reserves the right to change the beneficiary. If he reserves such right, the designation is referred to as *revocable* and the designee as the *revocable beneficiary*. If the insured does not reserve the right to change the beneficiary, the designation is properly described as *irrevocable* and the designee as the *irrevocable beneficiary*. This distinction is so significant that a

---

[1] In setting up successive classes of contingent beneficiaries, the insured must be careful not to violate the rule against perpetuities or statutory prohibitions against the unlawful accumulation of income.

word on the historical development of the concept of revocability seems warranted.

Historical Development. The early contracts of life insurance in the United States made no provision for a change of beneficiary. The insured simply entered into a contract with the insurance company that upon his death, the company would pay a specified sum of money to the person designated as beneficiary—usually, the wife. Since there were no surrender values or other prematurity rights of significance to the insured, the person entitled to receive the death proceeds was regarded to be the owner of the policy. One of the early students of American insurance law had the following to say about the interest of the beneficiary:

> We apprehend the general rule to be that a policy, and the money to become due under it, belong the moment it is issued to the person or persons named in it as the beneficiary or beneficiaries, and that there is no power in the person procuring the insurance by any act of his or hers, by deed or by will, to transfer to any other person the interest of the person named.[2]

In 1888, the United States Supreme Court defined the interest of the beneficiary in substantially the same terms.[3]

In consonance with this concept of ownership of the policy by the beneficiary, the majority of the early court decisions held that the death of the beneficiary before the insured did not terminate her interest.[4] That is, the insured was not permitted to designate a substitute beneficiary; and upon his death, the proceeds were payable to the estate of the beneficiary originally named in the policy.

Around the turn of the century, some of the larger companies adopted the practice of including in their policies a provision which permitted the insured to substitute a new beneficiary even during the original beneficiary's lifetime, provided he had specifically reserved the right. Moreover, the change could be effected without the consent of the beneficiary. There was some doubt as to the validity of this practice until the standard forms which grew out of the Armstrong Investigation of 1905 and 1906, and became statutory (or compulsory) in New York on January 1, 1907, included a change of beneficiary clause. This clause was supplemented shortly thereafter by

---

[2] George Bliss, *The Law of Life Insurance* (1871), quoted in James S. Burke, "Designation of the Beneficiary," in *The Beneficiary in Life Insurance* (Dan M. McGill, ed. (rev. ed.; Homewood, Ill.: Richard D. Irwin, Inc., 1956), p. 8.

[3] *Central National Bank* v. *Hume*, 128 U.S. 195 (1888).

[4] *Couch on Insurance*, 1006 (1930), and cases cited.

another which stipulated that the beneficiary's interest, whether revocable or irrevocable, would terminate upon her death during the insured's lifetime, with such interest reverting to the insured. The designation of a contingent beneficiary to succeed to the interest of a deceased primary beneficiary was the next logical development.

Status of the Revocable Beneficiary. For some time after the validity of a reserved right to change the beneficiary had become well recognized, the revocable beneficiary was generally regarded to have a vested interest in the policy which could be defeated only by the exercise of the insured's right to revoke the designation. This view became known as the "defeasible vested interest" concept. Under that concept, it was believed that the consent of the beneficiary was necessary to the exercise of any policy rights by the insured other than the right to change the beneficiary. For example, the insured could not surrender or assign the policy, make a policy loan, or elect a settlement option without the consent of the beneficiary. Yet there was nothing to prevent the insured from revoking the beneficiary designation and then exercising the various policy rights and privileges.

During the last quarter century, however, court after court has rejected the defeasible vested interest theory in favor of a more practicable rule which simplifies considerably the administration of policy rights. This modern rule, now prevailing in all but three states, holds that the interest of a revocable beneficiary is, at most, a mere expectancy, which is subject to every other interest created by the insured and to every policy right or privilege exercisable by the insured alone. Under this concept, consent of the beneficiary is not needed for the exercise by the insured of any policy right or privilege. Three states—Colorado, Massachusetts, and New Jersey—still maintain the view that a revocable beneficiary has a vested interest which is subject to divestment through a change of beneficiary accomplished in the manner prescribed by the policy. Even in those states, however, the insured is now permitted to make a policy loan without the consent of the revocable beneficiary.[5]

The interest of a revocable beneficiary, such as it is, terminates

---

[5] *Anderson* v. *Broad Street Bank*, 90 N.J. Eq. 78, 105 Atl. 599 (Ch. 1918); *John Hancock Mutual Life Insurance Co.* v. *Heidrich*, 135 N.J. Eq. 325, 38 A. 2d 442 (Ch. 1944); *David* v. *Metropolitan Life Insurance Co.*, 135 N.J.L. 106, 50 A. 2d 651 (Sup. Ct. 1947); *Strachan* v. *Prudential Insurance Co. of America*, 321 Mass. 507, 73 N.E. 2d 840 (1947); *Muller* v. *Penn Mutual Life Insurance Co.*, 62 Colo. 245, 161 Pac. 148 (1916).

upon her death during the insured's lifetime because of the reversionary clause referred to above. This is true even though there is no contingent beneficiary and the insured fails to appoint a successor beneficiary. Thus, the nature of the revocable beneficiary's interest comes into sharper focus. She has no enforceable rights in the policy prior to maturity and cannot interfere in any way with the exercise by the insured of his rights in the policy. She has an "expectancy" in the proceeds which will materialize only if *all* of the following conditions are fulfilled: (1) the policy remains in force until the death of the insured, (2) the beneficiary designation remains unchanged, (3) the policy is not assigned, and (4) the beneficiary outlives the insured. Despite the fulfillment of these conditions, the beneficiary's interest can be greatly impaired through policy loans negotiated by the insured.

On the positive side, the right of the insured to revoke a beneficiary designation is extinguished by his death, and the interest of the revocable beneficiary vests absolutely at that point. Her interest in the proceeds is, of course, subject to any deferred settlement agreement that might be operative, as well as to the rights of any contingent beneficiaries.

There are circumstances under which an insured who has reserved the right to change the beneficiary will not be permitted to exercise that right. If the policy was procured to secure a debt, or if—by agreement—the named beneficiary is to pay the premiums on the policy, the right to change the beneficiary is forfeited.[6] It has also been held that delivery of the policy to the insured's wife in consideration of marriage gives her a vested interest which cannot be defeated by the designation of another beneficiary by the insured.[7] Similarly, when a wife is designated beneficiary of a policy under an agreement made in contemplation of divorce, or when—by court order—an insured is directed to designate his divorced wife as beneficiary of a policy intended to serve as security for alimony payments or in lieu of such payments, the right to change the beneficiary is relinquished.[8] It should be understood that in all these circumstances, the insurance company would permit a change of beneficiary if it had received no notice of the limitation on the insured's right.

---

[6] *Wellhouse* v. *United Paper Co.*, 29 F. 2d 886 (5th Cir. 1929).

[7] *McDonald* v. *McDonald*, 215 Ala. 179, 110 So. 291 (1926).

[8] *Mutual Life Insurance Co. of New York* v. *Franck*, 9 Cal. App. 2d 528, 50 P. 2d 480 (1935).

Status of the Irrevocable Beneficiary. It is well settled that whenever the insured designates a particular person as beneficiary of a policy and does not reserve the right to revoke the designation, the beneficiary acquires a vested interest in the contract. The exact nature of the interest depends upon the terms of the contract. If there are no conditions under which the beneficiary could be deprived of the right to receive the full amount of proceeds payable under the terms of the policy, her interest would be vested absolutely or unconditionally, and she would be regarded as the sole owner of the policy. She could exercise all policy rights without the joinder of the insured and would even have the right to pay premiums to keep the policy in force. The insured would have no rights in the policy and, consequently, could do nothing with the contract, without the beneficiary's consent, which would in any way diminish or adversely affect the beneficiary's right to receive, at the insured's death, the full amount of insurance provided by the policy. If the beneficiary should predecease the insured, her interest in the policy would become a part of her estate, and her heirs would be entitled to the proceeds upon maturity of the policy.

Such absolute vesting is not common in modern policies. Most policies today provide that the interest of a beneficiary, even one irrevocably designated, shall terminate upon her death during the lifetime of the insured, with all rights reverting to the insured. This is sometimes called a *reversionary* irrevocable designation. Under this type of designation, the interest of the irrevocable beneficiary is only conditionally vested. There is a condition—namely, her death before maturity of the policy—which can destroy her interest. Since the insured can acquire ownership rights in the contract through the death of the beneficiary during his lifetime, he possesses a contingent interest in the policy from the beginning. His interest is considered substantial enough to necessitate his concurrence in all negotiations concerning the policy. Thus, in the usual circumstances, neither the insured nor the beneficiary can exercise any policy rights or dispose of the policy without the consent of the other. For all intents and purposes, the insured and the beneficiary are regarded as joint owners of the policy when the beneficiary designation is irrevocable.

It is possible for an insured to procure a policy under which he would not reserve the right to change the beneficiary but would retain the normal policy privileges.[9] Even though the insured can diminish the beneficiary's interest in such a policy or destroy it com-

---

[9] *Morse* v. *Commissioner,* 100 F. 2d 593 (7th Civ. 1938).

pletely by surrender, he cannot revoke her interest, such as it may be, and give it to another, without the beneficiary's consent. As courts have pointed out, the terms and conditions of the policy are determinative of the rights of the insured and the interest of the beneficiary. In the majority of policies issued today, however, there are no specific conditions that would permit the insured to impair or destroy the interest of an irrevocably designated beneficiary.

Irrevocable beneficiary designations are not widely used. In most situations where their use might be justified, an absolute assignment, ownership policy, or ownership clause is likely to be more appropriate. An irrevocable beneficiary designation does offer the advantage of protecting the beneficiary's interest in the proceeds during her lifetime, and automatically vesting complete ownership rights in the insured in the event that he should survive the beneficiary; but the same result may be achieved by an appropriately worded ownership clause.

SUCCESSION IN INTEREST

Whenever there is only one beneficiary in a beneficiary classification—i.e., primary, first contingent, and so forth—the interest of any beneficiary who predeceases the insured passes in the manner and according to the rules described in the preceding pages, unless the contract provides otherwise. Whenever there is more than one beneficiary in a beneficiary classification, however, a question arises as to the disposition of the interest of any beneficiary who should die before his interest materializes. The problem has frequently arisen in connection with class designations, such as "my children," but it is equally relevant to multiple specific designations.

To pin-point the problem, assume that A, the insured, names his three children, B, C, and D, as primary beneficiaries of his insurance, share and share alike, without designating any contingent beneficiaries, and without specifying what should be the disposition of the share of any child who should fail to survive him. Assume further that D predeceases A, leaving three children E, F, and G. Who is entitled to D's share?

A policy provision on this point is controlling; but in the absence of a pertinent policy provision, D's interest might conceivably be disposed of in one of three ways. It might pass to A's estate, on the theory that where there are multiple designations, the interest of each beneficiary is severable and is contingent on the beneficiary's survival of the insured. The share might pass to B and C, on the theory that the designation of multiple beneficiaries creates a form of undivided interest, analogous to a joint tenancy, with right of survivorship. Finally, the share might pass to D's children, E, F, and G, on the theory that a primary beneficiary has a vested interest in the proceeds which cannot be defeated by his failure to survive the insured.

In the litigation that has developed around this question, there has been no support for the view that the interest of a deceased beneficiary should revert to the insured's estate, despite the fact that this would have been the outcome had the deceased beneficiary been the sole primary beneficiary. The majority of the decisions have followed the rule that the surviving beneficiaries of the classification to which the deceased beneficiary belonged are entitled to take the share of the deceased beneficiary. In the example cited, B and C would be entitled to the full amount of proceeds. This doctrine is known as the "New York Rule," since it was first espoused by the New York courts. From a practical standpoint, much can be said in favor of the rule. Most of the cases involve children, which means that if the share of the deceased child were to revert to the insured's estate, it would ultimately be distributed to the surviving children, the other beneficiaries, reduced by its share of administration expenses and bequests to other persons, including the widow. A substantial minority of the courts have followed the "Connecticut Rule," which holds that the heirs of the deceased beneficiary are entitled to his share. In the above example, E, F, and G would receive the proceeds to which D would have been entitled had he survived A. Each would receive one ninth of the total proceeds, with B and C receiving one third each. This rule is in conflict with the prevailing view of a beneficiary's interest in a life insurance policy, but it reflects the desire of the jurists involved to carry out what they conceive to be the wishes of the insured.

In anticipation of this problem, many companies have incorporated a provision in their policies which—in the absence of contrary instructions from the insured—will control the disposition of the interest of any beneficiary who dies before becoming entitled to payment of his share of proceeds. This provision, commonly known as the "succession-in-interest clause," is applicable to both primary and contingent beneficiaries, and to beneficiaries designated irrevocably as well as revocably. A typical clause might appear as follows:

SUCCESSION IN INTEREST OF BENEFICIARIES

The proceeds of this policy whether payable in one sum or under a settlement option shall be payable in equal shares to such direct beneficiaries as survive to receive payment. The share of any direct beneficiary who dies before receiving payments due or to become due shall be payable in equal shares to such direct beneficiaries as survive to receive payment.

At the death of the last surviving direct beneficiary payments due or to become due shall be payable in equal shares to such contingent beneficiaries as survive to receive payment. The share of any contingent beneficiary who dies before receiving payments due or to become due shall be payable in equal shares to such contingent beneficiaries as survive to receive payment.

At the death of the last to survive of the direct and contingent beneficiaries:

(a) if no settlement option is in effect, any remaining proceeds shall be paid to the owner or to the executors, administrators, successors, or transferees of the owner; or

(b) if a settlement option is in effect, the withdrawal value of payments due or to become due shall be paid in one sum to the executors or administrators of the last to survive of the direct and contingent beneficiaries.

A direct or contingent beneficiary succeeding to an interest in a settlement option shall continue under such option, subject to its terms as stated in this policy, with the rights of transfer between options and of withdrawal under options as provided in this policy.

It will be noted that this clause applies not only to the situations where either a primary or a contingent beneficiary fails to survive the *insured,* but also to cases where a contingent beneficiary fails to survive a *primary beneficiary.* The latter is important when proceeds are being paid out on an installment basis. If the proceeds are to be paid in a lump sum, the problem can be met by specifying in the beneficiary designation that the proceeds will be paid only to those beneficiaries who survive the insured, provided this solution is in accord with the insured's wishes.

The disposition of the interest of deceased beneficiaries envisioned by the succession-in-interest clause does not represent the desires of all policyholders. In designating their children as beneficiaries, many insureds want the share of a deceased beneficiary to go to the latter's children, the insured's grandchildren. This can be accomplished by directing that the proceeds be distributed *per stirpes,* a Latin expression meaning "by the trunk." For example, in designating his wife as primary beneficiary and his children as contingent beneficiaries, an insured could use the following wording: "Mary Smith Doe, wife of the insured, if she survives the insured; otherwise in equal shares to the surviving children of the insured, and to the surviving children of any deceased children of the insured, per stirpes." The expression "per stirpes" means that the issue or lineal descendants of a deceased person take the share of an estate or of the insurance proceeds that the deceased would have taken had he survived. It is used in wills and trusts, as well as in insurance policies. The children represent the parents, and grandchildren represent the children, and so on down the "trunk." As a matter of fact, the words "by representation" are sometimes used in lieu of "per stirpes." The "Connecticut Rule," referred to earlier, embodies the per stirpes concept.

An insured sometimes wants the children of a deceased beneficiary to share equally with the surviving members of the original beneficiary group. In the example used earlier, A might have wanted D's children to share equally with B and C, each taking one fifth of the proceeds. He could have achieved this objective by specifying that the proceeds should go "in equal shares to such of B, C, and D, children of the insured, as may survive the insured, and to the surviving children of such of said children as may be deceased, per capita."

In all these matters, the insurance company accedes to the wishes of the insured, requiring only that his desires be clearly expressed in the designation.

OWNERSHIP RIGHTS

Life insurance policies issued today offer many valuable rights and privileges in addition to the basic obligation of the company to pay the face of the policy upon maturity. Most of these rights—such as surrender options, dividend options, policy loans, assignments, and change of beneficiaries—can be exercised during the insured's lifetime and are referred to as *prematurity rights*. It is essential, therefore, that the ownership of the various rights be clearly established and known to all parties concerned.

When a person applies for insurance on his own life and designates himself or his estate as beneficiary, all ownership rights in the policy are vested in him. The same is true if he designates another person as beneficiary, but reserves the right to revoke the designation. In all but three states, the interest of such a third-party beneficiary is regarded as a "mere expectancy," so tenuous as not to interfere with the exercise of the prematurity rights by the insured. In three states, the interest of a revocable beneficiary is judicially recognized as a qualified or defeasible vested interest which can be divested only by a change of beneficiary. In those states, consent of the beneficiary is necessary to the exercise of all prematurity rights except policy loans and change of beneficiary. When a person applies for insurance on his own life and designates another person as beneficiary without reserving the right to revoke the designation, the insured and the beneficiary are considered to be joint owners of the policy, and neither can exercise any prematurity rights without the consent of the other. It will be noted that in none of these situations is the beneficiary considered to be the sole owner of the policy.

In today's complex world of business and finance, there are more and more situations in which it is desirable—or even essential—that the beneficiary (in the broadest sense) be the absolute owner of the policy. For example, if the insured wants to keep the proceeds out of his gross estate for federal estate tax purposes, he must divest himself of all incidents of ownership. A creditor wants all ownership rights in a policy taken out on the debtor to secure a loan. Partners need to be absolute owners of policies on the lives of fellow partners used to finance business continuation agreements. Employers must be the owners of policies on the lives of key employees.

Sole and complete ownership of a policy can be vested in a person other than the insured in one of three ways. The first is through procurement of the policy by the prospective beneficiary in the first instance. The beneficiary applies for the insurance, with the consent of the insured, and has himself designated as owner of the policy, as well as beneficiary. Some companies have developed special forms, called *owner policies,* for this purpose, while others use regular policies with an ownership clause. This clause declares the beneficiary to be the owner of the policy, any provisions in the policy to the contrary notwithstanding, and specifically states that the beneficiary shall have the right to exercise all the rights which would otherwise be vested in the insured.

The second method consists of the *transfer* of ownership rights in a policy originally issued to the insured by means of an endorsement on the policy. The insured directs the company to vest all his rights, privileges, and options in the beneficiary, and the policy is endorsed accordingly. The endorsement is known as an *ownership clause;* and in some companies, it may be identical to the clause endorsed on a policy at the time it is issued.

The third method is identical with the second, except that it involves the use of an absolute assignment form. This is the oldest procedure and one that is still preferred by many. It will be discussed in detail in Chapter XXX.

The owner of a policy, whether he procured it on his own application or by transfer from the insured, can designate a person other than himself to receive the proceeds of the policy and can reserve the right to revoke the designation. He may also transfer his ownership to another person, provided the transfer takes effect at the time it is made. It is generally agreed, likewise, that an insured—in transferring ownership of his policy to another person—may nominate a successor to take ownership in the event that the original transferee should die before the insured. There seems to be some disagreement, however, as to whether an owner—either as the procurer of the original policy or by transfer from the insured—may himself designate another person to succeed to his ownership in case of his death before that of the insured, other than by a provision in his will. The question is whether such a disposition, to take effect only upon the death of the owner, would be testamentary in nature and hence in conflict with the statutes of wills as they exist in the various states. Because of the uncertainty concerning the matter, some companies will not recognize any disposition of the owner's interest, in the event that he should predecease the insured, other than to the owner's estate. The disposition of the interest by the legal representatives of the owner would depend entirely on the provisions of his will or of the laws of intestacy.

CHAPTER XXIX

The Beneficiary

(Continued)

SIMULTANEOUS DEATH AND SHORT-TERM SURVIVORSHIP

Simultaneous Death of Insured and Beneficiary

It should now be clear that the rights of various parties can be vitally affected by the question of whether the primary beneficiary survives the insured, or vice versa. Under normal circumstances, this is a question of fact which can be easily and conclusively established. If, however, the insured and the beneficiary are killed in an automobile accident, airplane crash, explosion, or other such untoward circumstances, it may well be impossible to determine which survived the other. Inasmuch as valuable property rights are involved in this situation, including the disposition of the estates of the insured and beneficiary, the courts have had to adopt rules which will permit them to solve the dilemma.

The old Napoleonic Code, which was based on the Roman Civil Code, created a set of *conclusive presumptions* as to survival, reflecting the age and sex of the parties involved. These presumptions, at one time embodied in the statutory law of six states, but now in effect only in Ohio, are as follows: A male is presumed to have survived a female if both were between the ages of fifteen and sixty; if both persons were under fifteen, the older—regardless of sex—is presumed to have survived; if both were over sixty, the younger is presumed to have survived, regardless of sex; if one was under fifteen and the other over sixty, the younger is presumed to have survived, regardless of sex; finally, if one was under fifteen or over sixty and the other was between those ages, the latter is presumed to have survived, regardless of sex.

Until recent years, all states not applying the foregoing presumptions followed the English common-law rule, which makes no presumption as to survival. Under this rule, the problem is resolved through the device of placing on one party or the other the legal burden of proving survivorship. If the legal representative (executor or administrator) of the party on whom the burden was placed cannot prove survivorship (and it is assumed in such cases that adequate proof cannot be adduced), it is presumed that the other party survived. With respect to each type of property involved, the burden of proof will be placed on the party who must survive in order to establish entitlement to the property. Thus, the incidence of the burden can vary with the species of property rights involved.

In the case of life insurance, if the policy provides, as most modern policies do, that the interest of a beneficiary shall revert to the insured (in the absence of a contingent beneficiary) in the event of her death during the insured's lifetime, the burden of proving survivorship under the common-law rule would generally be on the beneficiary's estate. This would be true whether the beneficiary designation was revocable or irrevocable. Under an irrevocable designation with no reversionary clause, which is deemed to vest all policy rights absolutely in the beneficiary, the beneficiary's interest would be preserved even though she predeceased the insured.

In an attempt to avoid the litigation inherent in this procedure for establishing survivorship and to provide an equitable basis for disposing of the property of the parties involved, forty-eight states have adopted the so-called "Uniform Simultaneous Death Act." The measure applies to all types of property and property rights. The underlying theory of the act is that, in the absence of evidence to the contrary, each person is presumed to be the survivor as to his own property. In the case of jointly held property, each party is presumed to be the survivor as to his share of the property. The act makes specific references to life insurance, stating that where the insured and the beneficiary have died and there is no sufficient evidence that they died otherwise than simultaneously, the proceeds shall be distributed as if the insured had survived the beneficiary. This is a conclusive presumption, and it applies whether the beneficiary is designated revocably or irrevocably. As enacted in some states, however, the act permits any disposition of the proceeds provided for in the policy.

The objectives of the Uniform Simultaneous Death Act can be

achieved through the inclusion of a so-called *common disaster clause* in the policy. With language similar or even identical to that of the Act, the clause states that when the insured and beneficiary perish in a common accident, the insured shall be presumed to have survived.

Short-Term Survivorship

The Uniform Simultaneous Death Act settles the question of survivorship when there is not sufficient evidence as to whether the insured or the beneficiary survived, but it does not eliminate the possibility of harassing legal action by the personal respresentative of the beneficiary bent on proving that the beneficiary survived the insured. Moreover, it is not effective when it can be proved that the beneficiary, in fact, did survive the insured, even by a moment. In the absence of contrary instructions in the policy, the proceeds would, under such circumstances, go to the estate of the beneficiary.

When there are contingent beneficiaries and the proceeds are held under the interest option or are payable in installments (other than a life income), the short-term survivorship of the primary beneficiary creates no particular problems. The estate of the primary beneficiary would be entitled to one monthly payment at most, and the remainder of the proceeds would go to the contingent beneficiaries. Under all other circumstances, however, the survival of the beneficiary for only a short period is generally considered to be an unfavorable event.

If the proceeds are payable to the primary beneficiary under a life income option, there is likely to be a substantial forfeiture of proceeds, even though there are surviving contingent beneficiaries. If there are no refund features in the option, the company's obligation would be discharged completely by the payment of one monthly installment to the beneficiary's estate.[1] If the payments are guaranteed for a specified number of years, some forfeiture would be inevitable—the extent, of course, varying inversely with the length of the period. There would be no forfeiture, other than loss of interest, under the cash refund or installment refund form of life income option.

If the proceeds are payable in a lump sum and the wife was the primary beneficiary, the proceeds, after probate, may go to relatives of the wife—a generally unintended and, perhaps, undesired result. This would be the case where the insured and beneficiary were not survived by children or grandchildren. Even though there were surviving children, the proceeds would get to them only after having gone through estate administration and suffering some shrinkage. This, however, is

---

[1] The first payment is due immediately after the death of the insured.

the fault of the lump-sum settlement and not the short-term survivorship of the beneficiary. The consequences would have been the same had the insured survived the beneficiary and died shortly thereafter, unless contingent beneficiaries were named to take the proceeds in that event.

In an effort to avoid the undesirable consequences of short-term survivorship of the beneficiary (which is a far more common occurrence than simultaneous death), some companies stipulate that the proceeds will be payable to the beneficiary only if she be alive at the time of payment. Other companies use a provision which states that the proceeds will be payable to the beneficiary only if she survives the insured by a specified period of time, such as ten, thirty, or sixty days. The companies are understandably reluctant to delay payment for a protracted period, but some are willing to defer payment up to 180 days. Such clauses solve the problem very effectively, although no reasonable period would be long enough to cover every case that might arise.

The delayed payment clause has one disadvantage for the policyholder who anticipates a federal estate tax liability. Such policyholder would normally want the proceeds of his life insurance policies to qualify for the so-called "marital deduction," which is a deduction allowed for property passing outright to the decedent's spouse, up to one half of the adjusted gross estate. The vesting of insurance proceeds, or any property includable in the decedent's gross estate, can be delayed up to six months without jeopardizing their qualification for the marital deduction, provided the spouse survives the period and obtains complete dominion over the proceeds. If the spouse does not survive the period, the proceeds do not qualify. This disadvantage of the delayed payment clause has caused some companies to advocate the use of the interest option with contingent beneficiaries, to meet the problem of short-term survivorship of the beneficiary. If the beneficiary is given the unlimited right of withdrawal, the proceeds will qualify for the marital deduction even though she never had an opportunity to exercise the right. If she is injured in a common disaster and dies from her injuries, or dies from any cause shortly after the insured, the beneficiary is not likely to withdraw the proceeds, and they will pass to the contingent beneficiaries. In the event that the beneficiary survives the insured by an extended period, she would be permitted, under the practices of most companies, to elect a liquidation option at contract rates within a specified period, such as one or two years, after the insured's death. The proceeds passing to others on her death would be includable in her gross estate for federal estate tax purposes; but if she dies within a specified period after the insured, the law allows a credit for any taxes paid on the same property in the insured's estate.

Another method of assuring the availability of the marital deduction when there is no evidence of survivorship is through the use of a *reverse* common disaster clause in the insurance policy. This clause makes the presumption that the *beneficiary* survives. Obviously, it should be used only when it is compatible with the over-all estate plan of the insured.

It should be emphasized that a perfectly satisfactory method of dealing with the short-term survivorship hazard is through the use of installment options (except life income options) with contingent beneficiaries. Again, this method would be used only if it meets the distribution objectives of the insured. Perhaps a better way to state the proposition is that neither the simultaneous death of the insured and the beneficiary nor the short-term survivorship of the beneficiary presents any problems when the proceeds are to be distributed under the installment time or installment amount options, or are held under the interest option, with contingent beneficiaries to succeed to the interest of the primary beneficiary.

EFFECTING CHANGE OF BENEFICIARY

As was indicated earlier, the applicant for insurance is always given the opportunity to reserve the right to change the beneficiary. If he does so, he can remove not only the original beneficiary, but also any successor beneficiaries that he might appoint, provided he does not, in the meantime, relinquish the right. This is a matter of contract, and the company cannot refuse to assent to a change of beneficiary on the ground that the prospective beneficiary has no insurable interest, or on any other ground. On the other hand, the company can—and does—prescribe the procedure which must be followed in effecting a change of beneficiary. Such procedure is also a condition of the contract.

All companies require written notice of a change of beneficiary, and most specify that the change must be endorsed on the policy. This is not a burdensome requirement from the insured's standpoint[2] and, in

---

[2] Endorsement is burdensome on the company, and some companies which now require endorsement are searching for a way of avoiding it in the future—for both new and old policies.

the usual case, would pose no difficulties. There are occasionally situations, however, in which the insured is not able to produce the policy for endorsement. It may have been lost, or it may be in the possession of a person who refuses to release it. A common example of the latter difficulty is possession of the policy by an estranged or a divorced wife. In such cases, the company may recognize the change of beneficiary despite the lack of formal compliance with the procedural requirements, but would probably do so only if it were satisfied that there is no danger of the prior beneficiary's establishing a claim. The courts have consistently held that the policy provisions concerning change of beneficiary are for the protection of the company and can be waived under proper circumstances.

Divorce between the insured and the beneficiary deserves special mention. The general rule is that divorce in itself does not terminate the interest of the beneficiary. This is based on the doctrine, mentioned earlier, that the interest of a named beneficiary is a personal one, not dependent on the relationship to the insured which may have been stated in the designation. This general rule prevails in cases where the insured has reserved the right to change the beneficiary but has not done so, as well as in those where the right to revoke the wife's interest has not been reserved; but in the latter situation, a settlement agreement between the divorced husband and wife, or the divorce decree, may affect the wife's rights.

In a few states, this rule has not been followed by the courts, or is modified by statute. In Kentucky, the interest of a wife is *automatically* terminated by divorce, whether she was revocably or irrevocably designated; but where insurance on the life of the husband has been procured by the wife during the marriage and paid for by her with her own funds, the rights of the wife therein are not abrogated or impaired by a subsequent divorce.[3] In Michigan, the wife's interest is automatically terminated by the divorce, whether she was revocably or irrevocably designated, unless the court decree specifies otherwise. In Missouri and Minnesota, divorce does not automatically terminate the wife's interest; but the husband is given the power to change the beneficiary, even though he had named his wife as irrevocable beneficiary. In New York, the aggrieved party in a divorce action may apply to the court granting the final decree or bring an action in supplementary proceedings for an order directing the insurance com-

---

[3] *Ficke* v. *Prudential Insurance Co. of America*, 305 Ky. 181, 202 S.W. 2d 429 (1947).

pany to change an irrevocable beneficiary designation, no legal action being necessary if the designation is revocable.

THE MINOR AS BENEFICIARY

The designation of a minor as beneficiary creates problems that are not ordinarily encountered with an adult beneficiary. Perhaps the most obvious complication is that which may arise if an insured designates a minor as beneficiary without reserving the right to revoke the designation. If, thereafter, the insured should wish to change the beneficiary, assign the policy as collateral for a loan, make a policy loan, or surrender the policy for its cash value, he could do so only with the minor's consent, which he does not have legal capacity to give. The insured might seek to have a guardian appointed for the minor, but it is highly unlikely that a court would permit the guardian to waive the rights of the minor.

Problems will almost certainly arise if the policy matures while the beneficiary is still a minor. The insurance company cannot safely make payment directly to the minor, since the latter is not legally competent to receive payment. Upon the attainment of his majority, he might repudiate the release contained in his receipt and demand payment of the proceeds once again. To protect itself, the company would have to insist on the appointment of a guardian, which involves expense to the minor's estate. In a number of states, insurance companies are authorized by special statutes to waive the guardianship requirement and make payment on behalf of the minor to an adult person, usually a parent or someone standing in place of a parent. However, the amounts which can be distributed under these statutes tend to be nominal, the usual limit being less than $500. A few states permit amounts up to $1,500 to be paid in this manner.

In an increasing number of states, it is provided by statute that a minor who has attained the age of eighteen years shall be competent to receive and give full acquittance and discharge for an amount not exceeding a stipulated sum, ranging from $2,000 to $3,000, in any one year in the form of benefits payable upon the death of the insured, as long as the insurance policy or the policy settlement agreement specifically provides for direct payments to such minor. In some states, the statute applies only to *periodical* payments, not exceeding the specified maximum in any one year. Some statutes permit either a lump-sum payment or periodical payments not exceeding the stipulated sum in any one year. For example, New York has a statute which permits the payment of $3,000 to a minor, either in a lump sum or in periodic payments not exceeding that sum per year. The New York statute also pertains to benefits payable upon the maturity of a policy as an endowment; in a few states, the statue also embraces benefits payable under annuity contracts.

Pennsylvania, alone among all the states, has a statute which permits the insured, in designating a beneficiary, to appoint a guardian of the estate or interest of any beneficiary who shall be a minor or otherwise incompetent. The law further provides that payments of the proceeds by the insurance company to such guardian shall discharge the insurance company for the payment to the same extent as if payment had been made to an otherwise duly appointed and qualified guardian.

Difficulties also exist with respect to the election of settlement options by a minor or a guardian acting on his behalf. The statutes referred to above authorize installment payments direct to minors only when the settlement option was elected by the insured or other owner of the policy. They do not authorize the minor to elect a settlement option. It is quite clear that a minor lacks legal capacity to elect a settlement option; and most companies are not willing to run the risk of repudiation of the contract by the minor, unless the amounts involved are small. However, if the beneficiary is within a year or two of attaining his majority, a company may agree to a settlement involving the payment of interest only, with a provision for payment of principal to the minor upon attaining his majority, or to his estate in the event of his death.

The law is unsettled with respect to the right of a guardian to elect a settlement option on behalf of his minor ward. There are no statutes expressly authorizing such an election, and the few court decisions on the point are conflicting. The basic question involved is whether the election of a settlement option by the guardian is an investment of the ward's funds and, if so, whether it is a legal investment. In a case involving the election of the interest option, the majority opinion held that the right of election was an interest "in the nature of a property right" given by the policy to the beneficiaries which could properly be exercised by the guardian on behalf of the minor beneficiaries.[4] Judge Lehman, dissenting from the majority of the court, took the view that

---

[4] *Latterman* v. *Guardian Life Insurance Co.,* 280 N.Y. 102, 19 N.E. 2d 978, (1939).

the exercise of the right of election was an investment of the proceeds, and that since the investment was not one permitted by statute, the guardian had no right to elect.

A more serious question is involved when the guardian wishes to elect a liquidating option. This runs contrary to the basic rule of guardianship law that the principal cannot be used for the ward's support without court approval. Thus, it seems agreed that a liquidating option can be elected only with court approval, which would be granted only upon demonstration that the action was in the best interests of the ward. Moreover, the election could not operate to deprive the ward of the free and unrestricted use of his funds after attaining his majority. Hence, if the settlement were to extend beyond the ward's age twenty-one, he would have to be given the right to withdraw the unpaid balance at that time. Since the guardian has no authority to dispose of the ward's property after the latter's death, any installments unpaid at the time of the ward's death should be payable to his estate.

Many insureds stipulate that any proceeds becoming payable to a minor will be paid to a trustee, to be administered for the benefit of the minor. This procedure is described in the following section and will not be dealt with further at this point.

If the proceeds are not needed for the maintenance and support of the minor, some companies are willing to accept a provision that the funds will remain with the company, at interest, until the beneficiary has legal capacity to accept them. This is possible under the laws of New York and other states which permit the accumulation of interest during the minority of a beneficiary.

It is worthy of note that under the laws of some states married persons aged eighteen or over attain their majorities.

THE TRUSTEE AS BENEFICIARY

There are circumstances under which it is advisable to have life insurance proceeds administered by a trustee. A trust can serve many useful purposes, but it is especially desirable when there is need for great flexibility in the administration of the proceeds, or when some of the beneficiaries are minors. There appears to be a growing tendency to designate a trustee as contingent beneficiary to administer proceeds for the benefit of minor children, the mother being primary beneficiary. Such an arrangement is called a *contingent trust,* since it goes into effect only if the proceeds become payable to the children while they are still minors. It takes the place of guardianship.

Irrespective of the nature of the trust, the trustee may be a natural person or a corporation, and the designation may be revocable or irrevocable, whichever is consistent with the terms of the trust. If the trust is irrevocable, however, the proceeds are usually made payable to the trustee under the instrumentality of an absolute assignment.

It is highly desirable, if not essential, that there be a trust agreement at the time the trustee is designated beneficiary. If the insured should die before instructions have been provided the trustee, the trust would undoubtedly be dissolved as unenforceable. In such cases, the courts have held that, there being nothing to guide the trustee as to the purpose or manner of distribution of the trust estate, the funds must be paid over to the person or persons presumably entitled to them. If the distributees were children, the proceeds would be paid to duly appointed guardians. The trust agreement need not be a separate instrument, although it normally is. The terms of the trust may be incorporated in the settlement agreement, particularly if it is a contingent trust. The following provision illustrates the latter procedure and also brings out certain other aspects of an insurance trust that should be noted:

Regardless of any provision herein to the contrary, any sum payable as herein provided to any of said children during such child's minority shall be paid to *John Doe,* brother of insured, as trustee for such child. In the event said brother shall fail to serve or shall cease to serve as trustee for such child, because of death or otherwise, any sum payable as herein provided to such child during minority shall be paid to *Richard Doe,* nephew of the insured, as successor trustee. Any permissible right or withdrawal or election of options by such child during minority shall be exercisable by said trustee. All sums payable to said trustee shall be held and expended for the maintenance, support, and education of such minor child in the discretion of the trustee, except as may be otherwise provided in a separate trust instrument; and when such child shall attain the age of twenty-one, trustee shall pay over any unexpended funds. As respects any payment made to said trustee, the company shall be under no liability to see to or be responsible for the proper discharge of the trust or any part thereof, and any such payment to said trustee shall fully discharge the company for the amount so paid. The company shall not be charged with notice of a separate trust instrument, a change of trustee, the death of such child, the termination of the trust, or rights under the trust, until written evidence thereof is received at the home office.

When a trustee is designated as beneficiary, it is usually intended that the trustee shall collect the proceeds in one sum and administer them in accordance with the terms of the trust agreement. There are occasions, however, when the trustee deems it advantageous—either to himself or to the trust beneficiary—to make use of the deferred settlement facilities of the insurance company. It becomes important, under such circumstances, to determine whether a trustee can avail himself of such facilities.

Trustees, as a class, first developed a real interest in insurance policy settlement options in the 1930's, when the going interest rate on new investments dropped below the rate of return guaranteed in insurance company settlement options. Many companies, feeling that trustees were attempting to shift their investment responsibilities (for which they were compensated) to the life insurance industry, and having other reservations about the practice, refused to honor settlement option elections by trustees. Litigation[5] established the right of a trustee to elect a settlement option, unless that right is denied in the insurance policy. Thereafter, many companies inserted a prohibition against the use of settlement options by trustees and have continued the practice to the present.

In the absence of express permission in the trust instrument, there is a serious question whether a trustee has the legal right to use settlement options, even though made available by the insurance company. The issue, as in the case of guardianship, hinges on whether or not a life insurance settlement option is a legal investment for a trustee. Where the investment statute is of the "prudent man" type, a strong argument can be made in favor of the legality of the practice. Many legal experts have concluded, however, that a trustee has an unquestioned right to elect a settlement option only when (1) the trust instrument expressly confers the right and (2) the insurance policy does not deny the right.

REMARRIAGE CLAUSE

When the settlement agreement calls for the proceeds to be paid to the surviving widow under an installment option not involving life contingencies, or to be held at her disposal under the interest option, the insured frequently requests that provision be made for termination of the widow's interest if she should remarry, with the undistributed proceeds going to the children as contingent beneficiaries. Such a provision is called a *remarriage clause*.

All companies discourage the use of a remarriage clause, and many

---

[5] *First Trust Co. of St. Paul* v. *Northwestern Mutual Life Insurance Co.,* 204 Minn. 244, 283 N.W. 236 (1939).

refuse outright to include it in the settlement agreement. When the clause is included, the companies attempt by the wording of the clause to avoid the responsibility of determining whether the widow has entered into a valid marriage. The hazards associated with such a determination are serious enough in ordinary circumstances; but in jurisdictions which recognize common-law marriages, the difficulties are compounded.

The remarriage clause places on the contingent beneficiaries or their guardian the responsibility of providing proof of remarriage of the widow and relieves the company of any liability for payments made to the widow after her remarriage but before proof has been furnished by the contingent beneficiaries. Since the widow will normally be the guardian of the children, there is some doubt that proof of her remarriage will be provided. If the guardian is an outsider, the existence of the clause may not be known to him. If the widow becomes the guardian, it is doubtful that the interests of the secondary beneficiaries would be served any more effectively than if the proceeds had been paid to her as primary beneficiary.

CHAPTER XXX

*Assignment
of Life
Insurance
Contracts*

THE LIFE insurance contract, with its valuable prematurity rights and promise to pay a specified sum of money upon maturity, is an ideal form of collateral for credit transactions. Hence, it is not surprising that the assignment of life insurance policies as collateral security has reached large proportions. They are, in addition, frequently assigned as a means of transferring ownership rights to another person or organization. It is important to note the circumstances under which a life insurance contract can be assigned and the manner in which the rights of the various parties involved are affected by the assignment.

RIGHT OF ASSIGNMENT

Assignment by the Insured or Owner of the Policy

It is a settled rule of law that anyone having an interest in a life insurance contract can transfer that interest, with or without a consideration, to another person. Hence, the contract need not (but frequently does) contain a provision expressly authorizing the insured or owner to transfer his interest; it is an inherent right which can be restricted only by contract. Industrial life insurance policies contain limitations on the right of assignment, but ordinary insurance policies are free of restrictions.

In the usual situation, all ownership rights in a policy are vested in the insured. Among the incidents of ownership is the right to assign the policy. This right carries with it the power to transfer all rights and interests in the policy to another person. When someone other than the insured is owner of the policy, it is customary for the policy to restrict the right of assignment to the owner. This is not a restriction on the assignability of the policy as such; it merely identifies the person who shall have the right to assign it.

The person assigning the policy cannot transfer any greater interest than he possesses or enlarge the obligation of the insurer. This means that he cannot, by his action, impair or defeat the vested interest of another person in the contract. In the typical case, only one other party could be adversely affected by the assignment, and that is the beneficiary. But is the interest of the beneficiary such that it is entitled to protection against infringement? The answer obviously depends upon whether the beneficiary designation is revocable or irrevocable.

If the designation is revocable, the majority rule is that the insured, or other owner of the policy, can assign the policy without the consent of the beneficiary and without complying with the formalities for changing the beneficiary designation. More important, the assignment is held to extinguish the interest of the beneficiary to the extent of the assignee's interest. As might be expected, the majority rule reflects the decision of those courts that view the interest of the revocable beneficiary as a mere expectancy. Those courts that adhere to the defeasible vested interest theory hold that the insured cannot assign the policy without either obtaining the consent of the beneficiary or revoking the designation. The latter step is perhaps the safer course of action, since in some jurisdictions, it may be held that a joinder by a wife-beneficiary is an invalid act if the purpose is to provide collateral for her husband's debts.[1]

It is the rule in all states that when the beneficiary designation is irrevocable, the policy cannot be assigned without the joinder of the beneficiary. The foregoing caveat concerning the wife's approval of an assignment designed to serve as collateral for her husband's debts is appropriate here.

Assignment by the Beneficiary

In the absence of a provision to the contrary, the beneficiary can assign her interest, both before and after maturity of the policy. Prior

---

[1] *Douglass* v. *Equitable Life Assurance Society,* 150 La. 405, 90 So. 834 (1922).

to maturity, her interest is virtually worthless if the insured reserved the right to change the beneficiary. If such right was not reserved, there is something of substance to be transferred; but the interest is contingent upon the original beneficiary's survival of the insured, unless the beneficiary's estate is designated to receive the proceeds if she predeceases the insured.

Upon maturity of the policy, proceeds payable in a lump sum vest in the beneficiary and can be assigned by her, probably without regard to any restrictive provisions in the policy. When the proceeds are held by the company under a deferred settlement agreement, the beneficiary's right of assignment is subject to the rights of the contingent beneficiaries, if any, and restrictive provisions in the policy or settlement agreement. Apropos the latter, it is common practice for the policy or settlement agreement to contain a so-called *spendthrift clause*, which denies to the beneficiary the right to commute, alienate, or assign her interest in the proceeds.[2] Furthermore, the laws of a few states which protect insurance proceeds from the claims of the beneficiary's creditors prohibit an assignment of the beneficiary's interest.

EFFECT OF ASSIGNMENT ON RIGHTS OF BENEFICIARY

The effect of an assignment on the rights of the beneficiary depends not only on the type of beneficiary designation but also on the type of assignment involved. The latter may take one of two general forms: an *absolute* assignment or a *collateral* assignment.

In form, the absolute assignment purports to divest the insured or owner of all incidents of ownership, and to transfer absolutely and permanently all rights and interests in the policy to the assignee. It is designed for those situations, involving a gift or a sale, where the clear intent is to make the assignee the new owner of the policy. The collateral assignment, on the other hand, is the form designed to transfer to the assignee those rights—and only those rights—needed to protect a loan from the assignee to the assignor. It resembles a mortgage of land or a pledge of marketable securities. The arrangement is intended to be temporary; and upon repayment of the loan, the assignment is terminated, with all rights reverting to the insured or previous owner. The assignee's interest in the policy is limited to the amount of the indebtedness and unpaid interest, plus any pre-

---

[2] See pp. 633–35.

miums paid by the assignee to keep the policy in force. For reasons to be explained later, absolute assignment forms have frequently been used when only a security arrangement was intended. In such cases, the assignment is treated as collateral in character and is released upon satisfaction of the assignor's obligation to the assignee. In fact, the courts will enforce such a result if the assignor can prove that, as between the assignor and assignee, a collateral assignment was intended.

If a policy is assigned in absolute *form,* and the parties intended the assignment to be absolute in *substance* as well, the interest of the beneficiary is completely extinguished, provided the designation was revocable or, if irrevocable, the beneficiary joined in the assignment. If an assignment is collateral in *substance,* irrespective of its *form,* the interest of the beneficiary will be extinguished to the extent of the assignee's interest, which is limited in the manner described above. If the insured attempts to assign the policy without the consent of the beneficiary when such consent is necessary, a valid transfer of his interest takes place, but the interest of the beneficiary is not affected. If she is a revocable beneficiary in a jurisdiction which sees a defeasible vested interest, she remains the beneficiary until a change has been accomplished in the prescribed manner. If she is an irrevocable beneficiary, she remains such, and no rights and privileges in the contract can be exercised by the assignee without her consent.

By what legal process is the interest of a third-party beneficiary subordinated to that of the assignee, without a change of beneficiary? The policy instructs the insurance company to pay the proceeds to a designated individual, subject to the right of the insured to substitute a different person. Assignment of the policy does not change those instructions; the beneficiary remains the payee of record. Theoretically, the assignment merely puts the assignee in the shoes of the assignor, who, prior to the assignment, was not slated to receive the proceeds. By what rationale does the new owner *automatically* become the payee of the policy, extinguishing the interest of the original payee?

This poses something of a legal riddle; and for many years, the courts held that an assignment did not, per se, subordinate the interest of the beneficiary. In one of the early cases, the court stated: "After a careful examination of the authorities, I am of the opinion that whether the interest be regarded as vested and defeasible, contingent, a mere expectancy, or whatever the characterization may be, if the policy stipulates the course by which the beneficiary's interest is to be nullified, he cannot be deprived of his right unless the prescribed mode for its destruction is followed. . . ."[3] Today, however, this view is entertained in only three states—Colorado, Massachusetts, and New Jersey—and the dominant philosophy is that the interest of an assignee will prevail over that of a revocable beneficiary.

In general, the courts have based their rulings purely on the intent of the parties. Most of the litigation has involved collateral assignments; and in such cases, there is usually a clear intent to subordinate the beneficiary's interest to that of the creditor-assignee. Since it is generally recognized that the assignee can perfect his claim by observing the formalities of a change of beneficiary, the courts are willing to spare him the trouble of doing so. Consent of the beneficiary to the assignment is regarded in all jurisdictions as conclusive evidence of intent to give a preferred status to the rights and claims of the assignee. In cases involving absolute assignments, not incidental to a credit transaction, some courts have concluded that a formal assignment, with notice to the insurance company, substantially conforms to the requirements for a change of beneficiary and operates as such. This rationale is patently inappropriate for collateral assignments, since the beneficiary of record receives the proceeds in excess of the claims of the assignment.

In all states, it is held that whenever the beneficiary of a policy is the insured or his estate, the claims of the assignee will prevail over those of the executor or administrator of the insured's estate.[4] This is true whether the assignment is absolute or collateral in form. Accordingly, it has been the practice of most companies, whenever the beneficiary does not join in the assignment, to advise the insured to change the beneficiary to his estate before executing an assignment. This is a precautionary measure, designed to avoid litigation by a disgruntled beneficiary. In the execution of assignments incidental to policy loans, the companies *require* this procedure, unless the wording of the policy makes it unnecessary.

This procedure is not without its disadvantages when used in connection with an assignment intended only as security for a loan. Unless the original beneficiary designation is restored after execution of the assignment, any proceeds remaining after satisfaction of the assignee's claims will be payable in a lump sum to the insured's estate.

---

[3] *Anderson* v. *Broad Street National Bank,* 90 N.J. Eq. 78, 105 Atl. 599 (Ch. 1918).

[4] See citations in Harry Krueger and Leland T. Waggoner (eds.), *The Life Insurance Policy Contract* (Boston: Little, Brown & Co., 1953), p. 89, n. 17.

It would be even more unfortunate were the insured to neglect to restore the original beneficiary designation and settlement plan after release of the assignment. Among other disadvantages, it would mean the loss of protection of the cash value and proceeds against the claims of creditors of the insured.

To avoid such undesirable contingencies, many companies have developed administrative procedures that call for reinstatement of the original beneficiary designation immediately following assignment of the policy. In some companies, this involves three separate documents, executed in proper sequence. The first document changes the beneficiary to the insured's estate; the second assigns the policy on a collateral basis; the third restores the beneficiary designation existing before the first document was executed. In other companies, all three actions are accomplished in one document. This document contains a provision similar to the following:

> If this assignment is executed by the insured alone or by the insured and not all the beneficiaries of record, and if the right to change the beneficiary is reserved to the insured, then I, the insured, for the purpose of subjecting to this assignment the designation of beneficiary in force immediately preceding this assignment, (*a*) hereby revoke that designation and designate as beneficiary of the policy at the time of this assignment my executors or administrators; and (*b*) reinstate, effective immediately after this assignment, the designation of beneficiary in force immediately preceding the change of beneficiary made in (*a*) above.

This may appear to be legal legerdemain, but it does take the third-party beneficiary out of the assignment picture. At the moment the assignment is being executed, the estate is the beneficiary; one moment later, the original beneficiary is back in the picture. Any settlement options previously elected by the insured would remain in full force and effect, except that the amount payable thereunder might be reduced.[5]

The foregoing practices are used in connection with the bulk of outstanding policies. However, the recently issued policies of the major companies contain a provision intended to make it unnecessary to follow such a confusing procedure. One such provision reads as follows: "The interest of any revocable beneficiary in this policy and any

---

[5] A shorter provision, designed to accomplish the same objectives as the above-cited clause, reads as follows: "To the extent that he has the right to do so, the undersigned changes the designation of beneficiary in force immediately preceding this assignment and reinstates it to the same effect as if such designation had been executed subsequent to the assignment."

settlement option elected shall be subordinate to any assignment made either before or after the beneficiary designation or settlement option election."

The effectiveness of this type of provision has been upheld[6] even under the laws of New Jersey which, historically, has been one of the states requiring the consent of a revocable beneficiary to an assignment of the policy. Nevertheless, it would seem that an assignee who wants to avoid any possible legal complications upon the death of the insured would be well advised to designate himself as beneficiary. Then, there could be no doubt as to his right to receive the proceeds. This step is neither necessary nor permitted if the A.B.A. assignment form, to be discussed later, is used.

EFFECT OF ASSIGNMENT ON OWNERSHIP RIGHTS

Concept of Ownership

There are two sets of rights in a life insurance policy: those that exist during the lifetime of the insured and those that arise after his death. The first set is known, quite logically, as prematurity rights, and the second set as maturity rights. The most important of the prematurity rights are the right to surrender the policy for cash or paid-up insurance, the right to borrow against the policy, the right to designate and change the beneficiary, and the right to assign the policy. Among the lesser—but still significant—prematurity rights are the right to elect settlement options, elect dividend options, reinstate the policy, convert or exchange the policy for another, and take advantage of the automatic premium loan feature. The maturity rights include the right to receive the proceeds, to elect settlement options (unless usurped by the insured or owner), and to designate direct and contingent beneficiaries (only under certain circumstances).

The concept of ownership of these rights has undergone dramatic development during the last fifty to sixty years. The original concept was that all prematurity and maturity rights were vested in the beneficiary and her estate. In other words, the beneficiary was regarded as the absolute owner of the policy. Once the right of the insured to change the beneficiary was recognized, the insured and the beneficiary were considered to be joint owners of the prematurity rights and the beneficiary the sole owner of the maturity rights—subject, however,

---

[6] *Phoenix Mutual Life Insurance Co.* v. *Connelly,* 188 F. 2d 462 (3d Cir. 1951), reversing, 92 F. Supp. 994 (D. N.J., 1950).

to the right of the insured, if reserved, to divest the beneficiary of all her interest in the policy and the proceeds. Over the years, this concept has been modified until today, in the absence of a contrary ownership arrangement, the insured is regarded to be the absolute owner of the prematurity rights and the possessor of the power to dispose of the maturity rights. If the insured has designated a third person as beneficiary, without reserving the right to revoke the designation, such beneficiary is considered to be the sole owner of the proceeds (when due at maturity), subject to the reversionary interest of the insured; and the insured and the beneficiary are looked upon as the joint owners of all prematurity rights.

Ever since the concept of a beneficiary change was recognized, around the turn of the century, the insured has been identified with ownership rights, either as sole or as joint owner. The most recent development is the complete dissociation or disattachment of the insured from ownership rights in the policy. This development received its impetus from the growth of business insurance, juvenile insurance, and insurance for estate transfer purposes, where there is a distinct need to have ownership of the policy in a person other than the insured; but it was also motivated by the desire of the companies to clarify the ownership status of the various rights in the contract. The dissociation is accomplished by specifying on the face of the policy that a particular person or firm shall be the owner of the policy and restricting the exercise of the various policy rights and privileges to the owner. In most cases, the insured is designated as owner; but the insured, as such, has no rights in the policy. All prematurity rights are vested in the owner, including the right to control the disposition of the maturity rights. The owner is given express authority to designate and change primary and contingent beneficiaries. Furthermore, during the lifetime of the insured, the owner can exercise all the rights and privileges in the policy without the consent of the beneficiary. Thus, it is apparent that the concept of the irrevocable beneficiary is negated with the ownership form of policy. The application makes no reference to the question of whether the applicant does or does not reserve the right to change the beneficiary. If the applicant wishes to create a joint ownership of the policy by the insured and the beneficiary, reminiscent of the irrevocable beneficiary designation, he can designate them as joint owners, with whatever survivorship provisions might be appropriate or desired.

The owner is given the sole right to assign the policy, and the interest of any beneficiary is made subject to the assignment. The assignee does not necessarily become owner of the policy. The policy may stipulate the manner in which a transfer of ownership is to be accomplished, and some policies state that ownership of the policy can be transferred only by a written instrument, satisfactory to the company, endorsed on the policy.

It can be seen that a minimum of *five* parties, other than the insurance company, may be associated with a modern life insurance policy. These are the applicant, the insured, the owner, the beneficiary, and the assignee. In the great majority of cases, the applicant, insured, and owner are one and the same person. Nevertheless, the ownership of all rights and privileges is made crystal clear, irrespective of the number of parties or interests involved. The next problem is to determine what happens to these rights and privileges when the policy is assigned.

Throughout the following discussion, it should be borne in mind that few of the policies involved in assignments to date have contained such a clear delineation of ownership rights as that found in the owner form of policy currently being issued.

Collateral Assignments

A collateral assignment is nothing more than a pledge and is subject to the general rules of law governing such a transaction. The pledgor is entitled to get his property back upon paying the debt when due and, after tendering the correct amount at the proper time, may recover the property in a legal proceeding. On the other hand, if the debt is not paid when due, the pledgee may, under authority of a court obtained in a suit for that purpose—or, more commonly, under the authority of the pledge agreement itself—have the property sold to satisfy his claim, including expenses of sale. The sale can be private, if the agreement gives the pledgee such alternative. The surplus remaining after the pledgee has been satisfied belongs to the pledgor. Since the pledgee is not the absolute owner of the policy, it is doubtful whether he can surrender the policy in the absence of a specific agreement to that effect. If the pledgor of an insurance policy dies before paying the debt for which it is security, the pledgee has a claim against the proceeds of the policy and may enforce it to the extent of his debt and other charges. However, since the collection of the proceeds is not a sale, the pledgee would not have the power, in the absence of an express stipulation, to collect the full amount of the proceeds, holding the excess for the pledgor's representatives.

It was not customary, before the development of the A.B.A. assignment form, for collateral assignment forms to confer on the assignee specific rights and powers in the policy. Hence, when the assignee attempted to surrender a pledged policy or take other action concerning it, most companies insisted that the owner of the policy join in the action. Furthermore, upon maturity of the policy, the assignee was permitted to collect only the amount of the oustanding indebtedness, unpaid interest, premiums paid on the policy, and other expenses incurred in connection with the loan. The remaining portion of the proceeds, if any, was paid to the beneficiary of record.

Many creditors resented having to prove the extent of their interest to the insurance company, preferring to receive the entire amount of proceeds and accounting to the beneficiary for the excess over their claims, as computed by them. To make matters worse, the collateral notes (not the collateral assignment form) used by some banks proved to be defective, in that they failed to give the bank the unquestioned right to pay premiums on the policy in the event of default by the insured and to add the sums thus paid to the principal of the indebtedness. The only recourse of the bank in some circumstances was to obtain title to the policy through foreclosure proceedings, thus establishing its right to pay premiums and to bring these outlays under protection of the collateral assignment. To obviate such difficulties, the A.B.A. assignment form contains a provision which specifically authorizes the assignee to pay premiums and add them to the amount of the indebtedness.

Whatever the impact of a collateral assignment on ownership rights, it is intended to be temporary in nature. Once the loan is repaid by the assignor, the assignment is released, and all ownership rights revert to their status before the assignment. An irrevocable beneficiary, for example, in joining in a collateral assignment, does not relinquish her vested rights in a policy; she merely agrees to subordinate her interest to that of the assignee during the time the assignment is in force. Once the assignment is terminated, the former status of all rights is restored. Repayment of the loan cancels the assignment, even though there may not be a formal release of the encumbrance.

Absolute Assignments

As was pointed out earlier, an absolute assignment in form conveys to the assignee all the title, rights, and interests possessed by the assignor. If the assignor owned all the rights in the policy, or if all persons having an interest in the policy joined in the assignment, the assignee becomes the new owner of the policy and can exercise all the rights therein, without the consent of any other person. The transfer is intended to be permanent. Until recent years, this was the conventional way of transferring ownership of a policy to another person. It was used, for example, when the insured wanted to make a gift of the policy or, on rare occasions, to sell the policy. It was the approved method of divesting the insured of all incidents of ownership in a policy, to the end that the proceeds would not be includable in his gross estate for federal estate tax purposes. In recent years, however, the practice of transferring ownership rights by means of an ownership endorsement has gained favor; and in some of the newest policy forms, it is specifically stated that ownership in the full legal sense can be transferred only by means of a written instrument, acceptable to the company, endorsed on the policy. The forms declare expressly that ownership *of the policy* cannot be effected through an assignment.

Be that as it may, in the days when an absolute assignment was universally regarded as a full and complete transfer of ownership rights, many creditors—particularly banks—turned to it as a more effective method of safeguarding their interests. They began to insist upon an absolute assignment when a policy was being pledged as security for a loan. In this way, they hoped to avoid the restrictions that were frequently imposed upon them in connection with collateral assignments. They wanted the right, without the consent of the insured, to surrender the policy for cash, to borrow the loan value, to elect paid-up insurance, and to exercise any of the other rights and privileges that might protect their interests. They also wanted the right to receive the full proceeds upon maturity of the policy, from which they would deduct amounts due them and pay over the excess to the insured or the beneficiary, as the case might be. In so doing, of course, they would deprive the beneficiary of the privilege of utilizing the policy's settlement options. In most cases, because of the smallness of the sums involved, this was not a serious disadvantage to the beneficiaries; but when the sums involved were substantial and the options were on a favorable basis, this practice of the banks was a potential source of great loss to the beneficiaries.

In many cases, perhaps, the absolute assignment form worked out exactly as the banks and other creditors had hoped it would. In other cases, however, the insurance company, realizing that the policy had been assigned only as collateral, refused to recognize the assignee as sole owner of the policy and insisted upon the joinder of the insured in the exercise of the various policy rights. The companies based their refusal on the failure of the assignment form to mention the specific rights conferred upon the assignee.

Dissatisfaction with the absolute assignment form on the part of both creditor and debtor interests eventually led to the development of a form especially designed for the assignment of life insurance policies. It was developed by the Bank Management Commission of the American Bankers Association, with the collaboration of the Association of Life Insurance Counsel. The official name of the form is "Assignment of Life Insurance Policy as Collateral," but it is popularly known as the A.B.A. assignment form.

A.B.A. Assignment Form

The essence of the A.B.A. assignment form is that it sets forth clearly and specifically the rights which are transferred to the assignee, and those that are not transferred and are presumably retained by the assignor.[7] The assignment is absolute and unqualified, in the sense that the rights vested in the assignee can be exercised without the consent of any other party. It is collateral, in that the assignee's rights are limited to his interest, with all rights reverting to the assignor upon termination of the assignee's interest.

The form states that the following rights shall pass to the assignee, to be exercised by him alone:

1. The right to collect from the insurance company the net proceeds of the policy when it matures by death or as an endowment.
2. The right to surrender the policy for its cash value.
3. The right to assign or pledge the policy as security for loans or advances from the insurance company or other persons.
4. The right to collect and receive all distributions of surplus to which the policy may become entitled during the time the assignment is in force, as well as all dividend deposits and paid-up additions credited to the policy as of the date of the assignment, provided appropriate notice is given to the insurance company by the assignee.
5. The right to exercise all surrender options and to receive the benefits and advantages therefrom.

It seems likely that the form will eventually be amended to add prepaid premiums and premium deposits to the list of benefits to which the assignee is entitled.

---

[7] The full text of the form is printed as Appendix E.

The form stipulates that the following rights shall not pass to the assignee, unless the policy has been surrendered:

1. The right to collect from the insurance company any disability benefit payable in cash which does not reduce the amount of insurance (the so-called *maturity type* of permanent and total disability income provision found in some of the older policies provides for the deduction of each monthly payment from the face of the policy).
2. The right to designate and change the beneficiary, subject to the assignment.
3. The right to elect settlement options, likewise subject to the assignment.

In consideration of the rights vested in him, the assignee agrees:

1. To pay over "to the person entitled thereto under the terms of the Policy had this assignment not been executed" any sums remaining after the liabilities, matured or unmatured, to the assignee are satisfied.
2. Not to surrender the policy or borrow upon it except for the purpose of premium payment, unless there has been a default in the obligations to the assignee or a failure to pay premiums when due, and in any event, not until twenty days after the assignee shall have mailed to the assignor notice of his intention to exercise such right.
3. Upon request, and without unreasonable delay, to forward the policy to the insurance company for endorsement of any designation or change of beneficiary, or any election of a settlement option.

The insurance company is authorized to make payment to the assignee without investigating the reason for any action taken by the assignee, the validity or amount of the assignee's claims, or the existence of any default on the part of the assignor. Upon surrender or maturity of the policy, the assignee is entitled to all the monies due but may, at his option, request a smaller sum. From the standpoint of the assignee, the right to receive the full proceeds eliminates one of the objections to the collateral assignment; but if he wants to permit the proceeds in excess of his claims to be paid under the settlement plan selected by the insured, he may do so. If he requests the payment of a greater sum than the amount of his interest, he becomes what in law is known as a *resulting trustee* for the excess and must account under the principles of trusteeship to the insured or beneficiary, as the case may be, for such sum. In this connection, it is pertinent to observe that bank assignees tend to be reluctant to invoke their right under the A.B.A. assignment form to collect more than their claim upon maturity of the policy. They prefer to avoid the responsibility of determining who under the policy language is entitled to the remainder of the proceeds.

The assignee is relieved of the obligations to pay premiums and policy loan principal or interest; but if he pays any such items out of his own funds, the amounts so paid become part of the liabilities secured by the assignment, are due immediately, and draw interest at a rate not exceeding 6 per cent annually until paid.

Other provisions of the form establish the superiority of the assignment instrument in case of conflict with any provisions of the note for which it is security, grant administrative discretion to the assignee in the handling of its claim, and certify that the assignor has no bankruptcy proceedings pending against him and has not made an assignment for creditors.

This form can appropriately be used with any type of policy form, including the recently issued owner type. It is estimated that at least three fourths of all collateral assignments currently being filed with the companies are on the A.B.A. assignment form, either in its exact form or with slight modifications.

NOTICE TO THE COMPANY OF ASSIGNMENT

If the interest of an assignee is to be protected, the insurance company must be notified of the assignment, preferably as soon as the assignment has been executed. A life insurance policy is not a negotiable instrument; and a transfer of rights in the policy, to be effective, must be recorded with the party who is under obligation to perform. If, without notice of an assignment, a life insurance company, upon maturity of a policy, pays the proceeds to the beneficiary of record, it will be absolved under the general rules of law from any further liability or obligation under the policy, even though a valid assignment of the policy was in effect at the date of the insured's death. To implement the law, and to put all parties on notice, the companies incorporate in their policies a statement that no assignment will be binding on the company unless it is in writing and filed in the home office. This provision has no effect on the *validity* of an assignment, but it has a material bearing on the enforcement of the rights transferred to the assignee.

The issue is broader than the relative rights of the beneficiary and the assignee. At the maturity of the policy, there may be more than one valid assignment of the policy in effect, and the relative rights of the assignees must be resolved. This can happen where one of the assignees failed to demand delivery of the policy with the assignment, or where the insured obtained a duplicate copy or copies of the policy by alleging that he had lost the original. It is conceivable that an insured could innocently or inadvertently assign a policy while a valid assignment of the policy was still outstanding; but in most such cases, the insured is guilty of fraudulent behavior.

Definite rules of law have been evolved to settle the disputes arising over multiple assignments of the same interest. The English rule, adopted in a minority of American jurisdictions, holds that the assignee who first gives notice to the insurance company has prior claim to the proceeds, provided that such assignee, at the time the policy was assigned to him, had no notice of a prior assignment.[8] If he had known of an earlier unrecorded assignment still in effect, he would, of course, have been guilty of fraud in accepting a second assignment of the same interest. The American—or prevailing—rule is that the assignee who is first in point of time will be preferred, regardless of notice to the company.[9] This rule is subject to the important exception that if the prior assignee fails to require delivery of the policy and thus permits a subsequent assignee to obtain delivery of the policy with no notation of the prior assignment, the claim of the subsequent assignee will be superior to that of the original assignee. A third or general rule. applicable under either the English or American rule, is that an assignee not guilty of fraud shall be permitted to retain any proceeds that may have been paid to him. Thus, an assignee with a preferred claim will lose his priority in any jurisdiction if he fails to notify the company of his claim before it has paid another assignee of record. In jurisdictions applying the American rule, the assignee first in point of time will have his interest protected, even under the general rule, as long as he records the assignment with the insurance company at any time prior to payment by the company.

Policy loans or advances made by the company are subject to the foregoing rules. Since assignments involving policy loans or advances are automatically recorded with the company, no difficulties are likely to develop around them. The only time that a company would find its lien against the cash value and proceeds subordinate to that of another

---

[8] See Krueger and Waggoner, *op. cit.*, p. 69, n. 2, for a list of jurisdictions following the English rule. Such important insurance states as California, Connecticut, Ohio, and Pennsylvania follow that rule.

[9] See *ibid.*, p. 70, n. 3, for a list of states following the American rule. New York is on the list.

assignee would be if—with notice of another valid assignment, and without the consent of the assignee—it went ahead and made a policy loan. Presumably, this would happen only through inadvertence. If a valid assignment of the policy had been executed prior to the policy loan but with no notice to the company, the latter would be protected under the exception to the American rule.[10]

Whenever there are conflicting claims for insurance proceeds or other benefits, whether the claimants be assignees or beneficiaries, the insurance company generally seeks the assistance of the courts. To do otherwise would be to invite the possibility of having to pay the benefits more than once. In such circumstances, it files a *bill of interpleader,* an equitable device, and pays the proceeds into court. In taking such action, it admits its obligation to pay, and petitions the court to adjudicate the conflicting claims and determine who is entitled to receive the money. The company discharges its responsibility by paying the disputed sum over to the court. This is an extremely important legal remedy for insurance companies.[11]

OTHER MATTERS RELATING TO ASSIGNMENT

Company Not Responsible for Validity of Assignment

The policy provision pertaining to assignment almost invariably contains a statement that the company shall not be responsible for the validity of any assignment of the policy. Some of the more recent policies broaden the statement to include the word "effect" as well as "validity." This provision is intended to protect the company against suits by a beneficiary or some other person alleging that the assignment was invalid because of the insured's incompetence or because the assignment was tainted with fraud or executed under duress. In the

---

[10] *Patten* v. *Mutual Benefit Life Insurance Co.,* 192 S.C. 189, 6 S.E. (2d) 26 (1939).

[11] Strictly speaking, a "bill of interpleader" requires that the insurance company be entirely disinterested in the outcome of the litigation. Under various state statutes and the Federal Interpleader Statute, the company can file a "bill in the nature of a bill of interpleader" when it does have an interest in the outcome. An example of the latter situation is when the representatives of an insured and the beneficiary killed in a common accident are claiming the proceeds, and the settlement agreement calls for the payment of the proceeds to the beneficiary under a life income option. If the beneficiary is held to have survived, the company may be able to discharge its obligations with one monthly payment. See pp. 596–97. A more common example of the use of a "bill in the nature of a bill of interpleader" is when a company admits a death claim but denies liability for accidental death benefits.

only litigated case on record,[12] an insured and his wife, who was the beneficiary of the policy, executed an assignment at a time when both were of advanced age and lacking in mental capacity. Upon the death of the insured, the company, having no knowledge of the incompetence of the insured and beneficiary, paid the proceeds to the assignee. Subsequently, the wife's guardian sued the company to recover the proceeds, on the ground that the assignment was void. The court refused to hold the company liable for a second payment of the proceeds, giving as one of its reasons the exculpatory statement in the assignment provision.

This clause protects the company only when it has no knowledge of a defect in the assignment instrument or of any irregularity in the circumstances surrounding the assignment. There would seem to be some risk to the company if a defect in the assignment form provided by the company caused loss to an interested party. To date, however, there are no reported cases on this point.

Insurable Interest

The right of an insured or other owner to assign his policy to anyone of his choice, whether or not such person has an insurable interest in the life of the insured, is recognized in all jurisdictions, when no financial consideration is involved. Such donee-assignees have been regarded to be in the same class as donee-beneficiaries as far as insurable interest is concerned. The position of the courts is that it is immaterial whether the insured designates the payee of the policy within the contract itself, as by a conventional beneficiary designation, or by means of a separate instrument, i.e., an assignment. If the applicant for insurance has an insurable interest in the life of the insured at the inception of the contract, an insurable interest on the part of the assignee is not required, either at the inception of the contract or at the time of the insured's death. Of course, if the insured were induced by the assignee to take out the policy, the later would have to have an insurable interest since, in effect, he would be the applicant.

The situation is different when an assignment is made for a consideration. If the policy is assigned to a creditor as security for a debt, the assignee is permitted to retain only the amount of his interest, even

---

[12] *New York Life Insurance Co.* v. *Federal National Bank,* 151 F. 2d 537 (10th Cir. 1945), reversing 53 F. Supp. 924 (W.D. Okla. 1944), certiorari denied, 327 U.S. 778 (1946), rehearing denied, 327 U.S.816(1946).

though the assignment was absolute in form. Thus, it may be said that a creditor-assignee must have an insurable interest in the life of the insured at the maturity of the contract. If his interest is extinguished prior to maturity of the policy, the assignment terminates. On the other hand, an assignment to a purchaser for value is valid in all but five states, irrespective of the question of insurable interest. In other words, in most jurisdictions, a policy can be sold to a person who has no insurable interest in the life of the insured. The rationale of this doctrine was expressed in the leading case of *Grigsby* v. *Russell*, in which Mr. Justice Holmes stated:[13] "Life insurance has become in our days one of the best recognized forms of investment and self-compelled saving. So far as reasonable safety permits, it is desirable to give to life policies the ordinary characteristics of property. . . . To deny the right to sell . . . is to diminish appreciably the value of the contract in the owner's hands."

Briefly, the argument is that there should be a free market for life insurance policies where a person in poor health can obtain the true value of his policy. The minimum price at which a policy should sell is the cash value, but the real value of a policy on the life of a person in poor health is somewhere between the cash value and the face of the policy, depending upon his chances of survival. If a person is ill and needs money for medical treatment, it is argued, he should be permitted to sell his policy to the highest bidder, without regard to insurable interest. The chances of murder are thought to be remote; and in any case, the danger should not be greater than when the insured designates a beneficiary who has no insurable interest.

Five states—Alabama, Kansas, Kentucky, Missouri, and Texas do not follow the majority rule and require the assignee to have an insurable interest when the policy is assigned for value.

---

[13] 222 U.S. 149, 156 (1911).

CHAPTER XXXI

Protection Against Creditors

THE PROTECTION enjoyed by life insurance against claims of creditors is a vast and complex subject, and can be dealt with here in only the most cursory fashion. Emphasis will be on guiding principles, with a minimum of substantiating detail. There are so many facets to the subject that a rather detailed outline is necessary. The most basic dichotomy distinguishes between protection available in the absence of special legislation and that available under statutes specifically designed to give life insurance a preferred status.

NON-STATUTORY PROTECTION

The topic of non-statutory protection can itself be broken down into various subtopics, but the most important distinction to be noted is that between creditors of the insured and creditors of the beneficiary.

Creditors of the Insured

Creditors of the insured may seek to satisfy their claims out of the cash value of a policy still in force or out of the proceeds of a matured policy. The legal principles involved in these two types of action are so different that they must be dealt with separately.

Before Maturity of the Contract. If the policy is payable to the insured or to a *revocable* third-party beneficiary, the insured is the owner of the policy and is entitled to the cash value upon surrender of the policy. The cash value is an asset of the insured and is reflected as such in his financial statements. It would seem, therefore, that in the absence of special statutory rules, the cash value of such an insurance policy would be available to the creditors of the insured on the same basis as any other personal property. Such is not the case, however.

In theory, the insured's creditor is entitled to the cash value of a policy owned by the insured; but in practice, he is generally unable to enforce his rights because of procedural difficulties. The normal collection processes are not effective against the cash value, since the insurance company is under no obligation to pay the money to anyone until the insured exercises his privilege of surrendering the policy. Moreover, the courts are loath to force the insured to exercise his right to surrender. Direct action against the company, in the form of a garnishment or distraint proceeding, has uniformly been unsuccessful, while attempts by judgment creditors to force the insured to surrender his policy have been successful in only a few jurisdictions.

The situation is different when the insured is bankrupt and a trustee in bankruptcy has been appointed. The Federal Bankruptcy Act provides that the trustee of the estate of the bankrupt shall be vested with the title of the bankrupt, as of the date of the filing of the petition in bankruptcy, to all property which prior to the filing of the petition he could by any means have transferred or which might have been levied upon and sold under any judicial process. Since a life insurance policy payable to the insured or a revocable third-party beneficiary could have been transferred, title to it passes to the trustee in bankruptcy. The latter, as owner of the policy, can then surrender it for its cash value. The problem of compelling the insured to perform an act which he does not wish to perform is not involved here. It should be noted, however, that the interest of the trustee in bankruptcy is limited to the cash value of the insurance on the date the petition in bankruptcy was filed. Thus, if the insured should die prior to adjudication of the bankruptcy and before the policy is surrendered, the excess of the proceeds over the cash value must be paid to the designated beneficiary—if any—otherwise to the insured's estate. Moreover, if the insured, within thirty days after the amount of the cash value has been certified to the trustee by the insurance company, pays over to the trustee the sum of money so certified, he is entitled to recover his policy free from the claims of the creditors participating in the bankruptcy proceeding. This provision was incorporated in the act to prevent the hardship which might befall the bankrupt's family if all his life insurance policies were to pass absolutely to the trustee in bankruptcy. Funds borrowed for this purpose can be repaid almost in full from the proceeds of a policy loan. Policies without a cash value do not pass to the trustee in bankruptcy.

Entirely apart from bankruptcy, the federal government has recently been able, in actions brought against the insured, to seize the cash values of life insurance policies in satisfaction of tax liens. Even the tax authorities have not been successful in suits brought directly against insurance companies. Divorced wives also have occasionally been able to satisfy alimony and support claims by actions to seize the cash value of life insurance policies owned by their former husbands.

When a policy is payable to a third-party beneficiary and the right to revoke the designation is not reserved, creditors of the insured have no enforceable claims against the cash value of the policy. This is based on the theory that policy rights are owned by the beneficiary, and the creditors of the insured should not be permitted to destroy or impair the rights of a third-party owner. In any event, the cash value could not be obtained without the consent of the beneficiary; and unless the beneficiary were a co-debtor, she could not be made a party to a suit to compel surrender of the policy. Furthermore, since the insured cannot transfer the policy without consent of the beneficiary, title does not pass to the trustee in bankruptcy. The latter can acquire no greater rights than the bankrupt possesses. Of course, if the insured relinquished the right to change the beneficiary or took out the policy in the first instance in fraud of his creditors, his action may be successfully attacked by the creditors.

After Maturity of the Contract. When proceeds are payable to the insured or his estate, they become available to the estate creditors on the same basis as any other unrestricted assets in the estate. When they are payable to a third-party beneficiary, however, they vest in the beneficiary immediately upon the insured's death, whether the designation was revocable or irrevocable. In theory, therefore, creditors of the insured should have no claim against the proceeds. Nevertheless, in a series of recent cases, the federal government has been permitted to collect unpaid income tax liens out of proceeds payable to third-party beneficiaries, on the theory that the latter are *transferees*. Recovery is allowed only where a valid tax lien had been placed against the cash value during the insured's lifetime and is limited to the amount of the cash value at the date of the insured's death.

Creditors of the Beneficiary

The cash value of a life insurance policy cannot be levied upon by a creditor of a third-party beneficiary, whether the designation is revocable or irrevocable. When the designation is revocable, the insured is the sole and absolute owner of the policy; and when the designation is irrevocable, the insured has rights which cannot be defeated by a creditor of another person. If the insured did not reserve a reversionary interest and the beneficiary was construed to be the sole owner of the policy, it seems likely that the creditors of the beneficiary would have a valid claim to the cash value. Unless the beneficiary was bankrupt, the creditors would experience the same difficulties in enforcing their rights as those encountered by creditors of the insured.

Once the policy has matured, the proceeds are the property of the beneficiary and can be freely levied upon by her creditors, in the absence of the protective provisions to be discussed in the next section.

STATUTORY PROTECTION[1]

All states have seen fit to enact legislation providing special protection to life insurance against the claims of creditors. Such legislation has a long history, the oldest law going back to 1840. The laws are a manifestation of a public policy that sets a higher priority on a man's obligation to his widow and children than on his obligations to his creditors. They reflect a philosophy which has led to laws exempting from attachment by creditors workmen's compensation awards, veterans' benefits, and other similar payments. To a great extent, they duplicate the protection available under case law. In some cases, the protection afforded by statute falls short of that which can be invoked under decision law.

Known generically as *state exemption statutes,* these laws are very diverse in nature. The broadest among them exempt all types of life

---

[1] For a comprehensive and scholarly treatment of the statutory basis for protection of insurance proceeds against creditors, see Howard C. Spencer, "Rights of Creditors," in *The Beneficiary in Life Insurance* (Dan M. McGill, ed.) (rev. ed.; Homewood, Ill.: Richard D. Irwin, Inc., 1956), pp. 41–108. The classification of statutes presented in the succeeding pages is based upon—but not identical with—the classification developed by Spencer.

insurance benefits from attachment by all types of creditors. At the other extreme are laws exempting from claims of creditors of the insured modest amounts of *proceeds* payable to the widow and children of the insured. Some of the laws apply to all types of life insurance, while others protect only some particular form, such as group insurance, pensions, disability income, annuity income, or fraternal insurance. Some protect only insurance taken out by a married woman on the life of her husband. There are statutes which protect the insurance against the creditors of the insured only, creditors of the beneficiary only, or any unsecured creditors, other than the federal government. Finally, some laws protect only proceeds, while others protect all types of benefits, including especially cash values. To make matters more confusing, some states have more than one type of statute.

Types of Statutes

At first blush, it seems impossible to classify such a hodgepodge of legislation. Closer inspection, however, reveals patterns that can serve as the basis for classification. The most apparent breakdown is that between statutes of general applicability and those that apply to specialized forms of life insurance, such as group insurance, annuities, and so forth. The general statutes may, in turn, be classified into six groups.

The first group embraces those statutes that pertain only to policies taken out by or for the benefit of married women on the lives of their husbands. Appropriately known as *married women's* statutes, these were the earliest laws of this type enacted.[2] The early laws protected only a small amount of insurance per married woman, but the amount of insurance exempted under the modern statute is unlimited. As a rule, the protection is effective only against creditors of the insured.

In sequence of time, the married women's type of statute was followed by the so-called *distribution* type of statute. These laws provide, in essence, that proceeds payable to the estate of the insured will pass to his widow and children free of the claims against the estate. It would be assumed that the very language of these statutes would rule out any protection during the lifetime of the insured; but in Tennessee, by a court decision,[3] and in Florida, by statute, cash values are pro-

---

[2] At the time these early laws were enacted, married women did not have legal capacity to own separate property.

[3] *Dawson* v. *National Life Insurance Co.,* 300 S.W. 567 (Tenn. Sup. Ct. 1927).

tected. These laws seldom protect against claims of the creditors of the beneficiary.

A somewhat later type of statute may be called the *procedural* type. The common characteristic of these laws is that they are enacted not as a part of the insurance law, but as one of the general exemptions from execution which are frequently found in civil practice or procedure codes. Since they are general exemption statutes, they usually provide immunity from all types of creditors, including those of the beneficiary. The amount of insurance exempted is usually quite limited, and the cash values are typically not protected. This is perhaps the most heterogeneous group of statutes dealing with the protection of insurance from claims of creditors.

The type of statute which has wielded the greatest influence is that which was first enacted in the state of New York in 1927. It has served as a model for the statutes of fifteen other states and has affected the course of legislation in many other jurisdictions. Thirty states now have statutes either identical with or broadly equivalent to the New York statute. Hence, it may be described as the typical state exemption statute. The use hereafter of the expression *New York* statute will refer to that statute as a generic type, rather than to the specific law of the state of New York, unless the context suggests otherwise.

The New York type of statute applies to all policies of life insurance payable to a person or organization other than the insured or, if different, the person applying for insurance. It protects both the cash value and the proceeds against the creditors of the insured and the person procuring the insurance. The protection is available whether the designation is revocable or irrevocable, and a reversionary interest in the insured is expressly declared to be immaterial. It does not protect anyone against the claims of creditors of the beneficiary.

The broadest protection is available under the so-called *comprehensive* statutes. Found in the states of Arkansas, Kansas, Louisiana, Nebraska, New Mexico, and possibly Georgia (the law in this state is not clear), this type of statute exempts, without limitation, all types of benefits associated with life insurance from the claims of the creditors of the insured, beneficiary, third-party owner, or any other person or organization.

Finally, there are the laws, called *spendthrift statutes* and found in about half of the states, which are concerned solely with the protection of proceeds held under a settlement agreement against the claims of creditors of the *beneficiary*. The statutes are designed to protect the proceeds only while they are in the hands of the company and not after they have been received by the beneficiary. Unlike the other exemption statutes, these laws do not provide automatic protection; they are, instead, permissive in nature. They permit the insurance company and the insured to agree that the proceeds will not be subject to encumbrance, assignment, or alienation by the beneficiary, or to attachment by the creditors of the beneficiary. Such an agreement must be embodied in either the policy or the settlement agreement, and the beneficiary must not be a party to it.

Functional Analysis of the Statutes

Types of Benefits Protected. The minimum objective of state exemption statutes is to provide protection against the claims of creditors of the insured for all or a portion of the proceeds payable to the widow and children of the insured upon the maturity of the policy. The maximum objective, typified by the comprehensive statutes, is to provide unlimited protection to all types of insurance benefits payable to anyone against creditors of every description. An intermediate goal, representing the public policy of most jurisdictions, is to protect—both during the lifetime of the insured and upon his death— the benefits of an insurance policy payable to anyone other than the insured's estate, against the creditors of the insured. The latter objective involves protection of the cash value of the policy; otherwise, the policy may be destroyed by seizure of creditors before it has had an opportunity of serving its basic function—namely, the support of the widow and children after the death of the insured.

Many of the early statutes spoke only of "proceeds." Some courts adopted a narrow construction of the term, but most gave it a broad enough interpretation to include cash values. To indicate that prematurity values are to be protected, many statutes use the language, "proceeds and avails." A few actually use the words "cash value." The result is that practically all statutes, other than the distributive and procedural types, exempt—by specific language or court interpretation—both the cash value and the maturity value.

The word "proceeds" has had to undergo interpretation in another direction. Does it include paid-up additions, accumulated dividends, and prepaid or discounted premiums; or is it limited to the original face amount? The usual interpretation is that it includes all amounts payable upon maturity of the policy.

The exemption of the cash value is of singular importance in connection with the Federal Bankruptcy Act. That act recognizes all exemptions from claims of creditors granted under the law of the state in which the bankrupt resides. Thus, to the extent that a state law exempts cash values, the trustee in bankruptcy cannot take title to the life insurance policies of a bankrupt policyholder. Since the revocability of the beneficiary designation does not affect the exemption, it is apparent that the bankrupt enjoys more protection under the typical state exemption statute than under case law.

As a matter of fact, the treatment of bankrupts under these laws has been the subject of severe criticism by creditor interests. These critics argue that, all too often, a business man in financial difficulty places a substantial amount of assets in life insurance payable to his wife and children, and then—after going through bankruptcy—uses the insurance to re-establish himself in business. Since most states permit a man who has become insolvent to maintain existing insurance, or even acquire new insurance, *for the protection of his family,* without being in fraud of his creditors, there is little that the latter can do to prevent abuse of an otherwise desirable relief provision. Admittedly, the law usually restricts the insurance which an insolvent debtor can acquire or maintain to a "reasonable" amount, but the courts tend to construe the limitation liberally.

Curiously enough, the federal tax authorities have not let state exemption statutes stand in the way of their collection of tax liens. This is true even under the broadest statutes. The government can obtain the cash value of a policy through either forced surrender during the insured's lifetime or collection from the proceeds after his death, provided a lien had been placed against the cash value before his death.

Among the general state exemption statutes, only those of the married women's and comprehensive types protect benefits payable to the insured or the third-party procurer of the insurance. Thus, disability income and annuity payments are usually not exempt from attachment by creditors. In some states, however, these benefits are protected by special statutes. The most liberal of these special statutes is found in New York, where both disability and annuity payments are exempt up to $400 per month, except that 10 per cent of the annuity payments are subject to garnishment, the same percentage applicable to wages. Lump-sum dismemberment benefits are completely exempt. Pennsylvania exempts disability benefits without limit, but protects only the first $100 of monthly annuity income.

Dividends payable in cash are normally subject to seizure. In a few cases, the insured was permitted to accumulate dividends or use them to pay premiums.

Parties Entitled to Protection. Broadly speaking, state exemption statutes protect all third-party beneficiaries against the claims of the insured's creditors. The New York statute and those patterned after it also protect assignees and third-party owners. The comprehensive statutes protect all the foregoing plus the insured. On the restrictive side, the married women's and distributive statutes protect only the insured's widow and children.

As a class, state exemption statutes do not protect the person procuring the insurance from his own creditors. Thus, with the exception of the comprehensive statutes, the insured enjoys no protection against his own creditors. While he cannot be compelled by his creditors to surrender a policy for cash—and thus impair the rights of third parties —if he should voluntarily do so, the funds could be attached by his creditors. It is interesting to note that the cash value and death proceeds of an endowment policy are exempt in many jurisdictions, despite the fact that the insured is beneficiary of the endowment proceeds. Of course, in New York, Pennsylvania, and a few other states, proceeds of an endowment payable to the insured in the form of income are exempt up to the limits of monthly income stated in the law.

Nature of Limitations, if Any. As a rule, the statutes of broad application contain no limitations on the amount of insurance which will be protected thereunder. Several of the statutes, however, predominantly of the procedural type, contain definite limitations, expressed in terms of either the face amount or the amount of annual premiums. For example, the law in South Dakota limits the exemption to $5,000 and to proceeds payable only to a widow, husband, or minor child. The protection is available, however, against all creditors —the beneficiary's as well as the insured's. Arizona and Minnesota restrict the application of their procedural-type law to proceeds payable to the widow or children of the insured, up to a maximum of $10,000.[4] These laws, likewise, are effective against creditors of the beneficiary. Several western states exempt only such amounts of insurance as can be purchased with a maximum annual premium of $500, without specifying the plan of insurance. Idaho restricts its

---

[4] Both of these states, however, have a statute of the New York type protecting third-party beneficiaries without limit.

exemption to insurance purchasable with a maximum annual premium of $250.

As was stated above, when protection is afforded disability and annuity payments, a limit may be placed on the amount of monthly income so exempt.

Type of Creditors against Whom Protection Is Afforded. As has been pointed out earlier, state exemption statutes, as a class, are concerned only with creditors of the insured. A sizable number of statutes, however, provide protection against the claims of *creditors of the beneficiary*. This is true of the comprehensive statutes, which tend to exempt all types of insurance benefits from all types of creditors. The procedural statutes, likewise, usually make no distinction between creditors of the insured and those of the beneficiary, but the exemption is typically available only for such amount of insurance as can be obtained with an annual premium of $500. The law in New York exempts the proceeds and avails of a policy purchased by a wife on the life of her husband against the claims of *her* creditors. Several other states provide a limited amount of protection against the claims of the wife's creditors in connection with policies purchased by the wife with her own funds.

The most prevalent and significant form of statutory protection of insurance proceeds against the creditors of the beneficiary, however, is represented by those statutes that authorize the inclusion of spendthrift clauses in life insurance policies. This type of provision originated with personal trusts and had the dual purpose of protecting the trust income from the creditors of the trust beneficiary and preventing the beneficiary from alienating or disposing of his interest in the trust.[5] The validity of such a restrictive provision was widely debated in this country during the latter half of the nineteenth century; but it was ultimately held to be valid in most jurisdictions, either by statute or by judicial decision. A few states still do not recognize the provision.

Once the validity of a spendthrift clause in a trust agreement was well established, it was a logical development to introduce it into life insurance settlement agreements. Its validity in this setting was very much in doubt, however, since life insurance companies do not segregate assets, accept discretionary powers, or otherwise conform to the trust pattern in the administration of proceeds under a deferred

---

[5] Some courts now allow restraints on alienation of principal, but most continue to restrict the practice to life or income estates.

settlement agreement. To remove any doubts, about half of the states have enacted statutes stating that a spendthrift clause will be enforced if, at the direction of the insured, it is contained in either the policy or the settlement agreement.

The use of spendthrift clauses has become widespread. A typical clause might read as follows: "Unless otherwise provided in this settlement agreement, no beneficiary may commute, anticipate, encumber, alienate, withdraw, or assign any portion of his share of the proceeds. To the extent permitted by law, no payments to a beneficiary will be subject to his debts, contracts, or engagements, nor may they be levied upon or attached." If enforceable, this clause will protect the proceeds while they are being held by the insurance company, but not after they have been received by the beneficiary. The clause applies to debts created after the insured's death as well as those existing at the time of his death.

If the clause is to be enforced, it must be included in the policy or settlement agreement at the request of the insured.[6] This requirement is deemed satisfied, however, by the inclusion of the clause in the printed portion of the policy or settlement agreement, a practice followed by a growing number of companies. The highest state court in New York has held that if the clause is in the policy or settlement agreement, the beneficiary can be given the unlimited right of withdrawal without affecting the validity of the clause.[7] This is an anomaly and inconsistent with the original philosophy of the clause. It means that the beneficiary can have complete control over the proceeds and yet prevent her creditors from getting at the proceeds with any type of legal process. If the clause is in the policy, whether by specific request of the insured or by company practice, the beneficiary can elect to have the proceeds held by the company under a deferred settlement agreement and still enjoy the protection of the clause. It is not believed, however, that under those circumstances, she could reserve a right of withdrawal and retain protection against her creditors.

Properly inserted in the policy or settlement agreement, the spendthrift clause may be enforced despite the absence of a statute spe-

---

[6] *Matulka* v. *Van Roosbroech,* 25 N.Y.S. 2d 240 (N.Y. City Ct. 1940), affirmed, 25 N.Y.S. 2d 247 (Sup. Ct. 1940); *Rath* v. *Kaptowsky,* 393 Ill. 484, 66 N.E. 2d 664 (1946). For a contrary holding, see *Provident Trust* v. *Rothman,* 321 Pa. 177, 183 Atl. 793 (1936). Three states have statutes which permit inclusion of the clause at the request of the beneficiary.

[7] *Genessee Valley Trust Co.* v. *Glazer,* 295 N.Y. 219, 66 N.E. 2d 169 (1946).

cifically authorizing it—provided, of course, that there are no decisions specifically rejecting the spendthrift trust as a matter of policy.

SCOPE OF EXEMPTION STATUTES

There is considerable uncertainty as to the length of time proceeds payable under a life insurance policy are exempt from the claims of creditors and the amount of physical change which they can undergo without losing their exempt status. With respect to claims of creditors of the insured, the proceeds are generally regarded to be exempt as long as they can be identified as such. For example, the courts have almost universally extended the exemption to cover the bank account into which the exempt proceeds have been deposited.[8] Furthermore, it has been held that real estate purchased with insurance proceeds is not subject to creditors' actions.[9]

The law is not as well settled with respect to claims of creditors of the beneficiary. Some statutes which extend their cloak of protection to such claims state specifically that the proceeds shall be exempt from claims of creditors, whether of the insured or the beneficiary, both before and after receipt by the beneficiary. These statutes are presumably enforced in accordance with their intent. Other statutes of this type do not state that the proceeds are to be exempt while in the hands of the beneficiary; and serious question may be raised as to whether, under such statutes, proceeds are protected against the beneficiary's creditors after reaching the hands of the beneficiary, particularly as to debts created after receipt of the proceeds.[10] It seems clear that the protection afforded under a spendthrift clause, even though sanctioned by statute, does not extend beyond the instant of receipt of the proceeds.

---

[8] Isadore H. Cohen, "Exemption of Property Purchased with Exempt Funds," *Virginia Law Review,* Vol. XXVII (1941), pp. 573 and 584.

[9] *Booth* v. *Martin,* 158 Iowa 434, 139 N.W. 888 (1913).

[10] However, in *Reiff* v. *Armour & Co.,* 79 Wash. 48, 139 Pac. 633 (1914), real estate purchased by the beneficiary with exempt life insurance proceeds was held to be not subject to debts created after receipt of the proceeds.

Part Six

SETTLEMENT OPTIONS AND
PROGRAMMING

CHAPTER XXXII

General

Concepts

and Rules

MOST LIFE insurance policies provide that upon maturity, the proceeds shall be payable to the designated beneficiary in one sum, generally referred to as a *lump sum*. However, in recognition of the fact that the needs of the great majority of beneficiaries are better served through the receipt of periodic income than through a capital sum payment, policies of the ordinary category have long contained provisions which permit the proceeds to be taken in the form of income. Collectively, these provisions are known as *settlement options*. They constitute one of the most important features of a life insurance contract and play a vital role in the protection of the insured's dependents. A knowledge of their characteristics and the manner in which they can be used is essential to successful life underwriting.

SETTLEMENT AGREEMENTS

When the proceeds of a life insurance policy are payable in a lump sum, the company's liability under the policy is fully discharged with the payment of such sum. If, however, the proceeds are to be retained by the company under one of the optional methods of settlement, the company's liability continues beyond the maturity of the policy and must be evidenced by some sort of legal document. That document is the *settlement agreement*.[1]

---

[1] Such a document may also be referred to as a *supplementary contract, supplementary agreement,* or *settlement statement*. Some companies do not use a special agreement; the beneficiary simply retains the policy, possibly with an endorsement, as evidence of the company's continuing obligation.

639

The settlement agreement contains the designation of the various classes of beneficiaries and a detailed description of the manner in which the proceeds are to be distributed. During the early development of deferred settlement arrangements, settlement agreements were tailored to fit the exact specifications of the insured and were typewritten in their entirety. As the requests for deferred settlements multiplied, it became necessary—for reasons of economy and administration—to standardize the various arrangements and privileges that would be made available by the company. As a result, the modern settlement agreement is composed primarily of printed provisions, some of which are general in scope and apply to any option that might be elected, and some of which pertain to only one specific option. All of the rights, privileges, and restrictions which the company is willing to make available are included and can be made effective by appropriate action of the insured, which normally takes the form of a check mark in a box opposite the provision in question. The only portion of the agreement that need be typewritten is that concerned with beneficiary designations and any modifications of the printed provisions that are acceptable to both parties. A specimen settlement agreement of the type generally used today is shown in Appendix D and should be consulted.

The typical settlement agreement is one entered into between the insurance company and the insured, or policy owner, to control the distribution of the policy proceeds to third-party beneficiaries after the death of the insured. Depending upon company practice, the agreement may be a basic part of the insurance policy, or it may be separate and distinct from the policy. It can be drawn up at the time the policy goes into effect or at any time prior to the insured's death. The insured can revoke the agreement at any time and substitute a new agreement, although he can revoke the beneficiary designation only if he has specifically reserved such right. He may or may not give the primary beneficiary the right to set aside the agreement upon his death. Upon the insured's death, the company's obligation under the original contract terminates; and it assumes a new obligation, which is defined by the terms of the settlement agreement.

On the other hand, the insured may enter into a settlement agreement with the company to provide payments to himself from the proceeds of a matured endowment or the cash value of a surrendered policy. If the agreement relates to the proceeds of an endowment policy, it can be entered into at the inception of the policy, at any time prior to maturity of the policy, or—subject to company rules—for a period after maturity of the policy. If the insured is to avoid a federal income tax on the "gain" (the difference between the proceeds and the premiums paid), he must enter into the agreement before maturity of the policy or within sixty days thereafter. An agreement to cover the cash value of a surrendered policy would obviously be negotiated at the time of surrender. Separate settlement agreements are not needed for contracts such as the retirement income policy, which by their terms provide for an income settlement.

If the insured did not elect a deferred settlement or did elect one but gave the primary beneficiary the right to set it aside, the beneficiary may—under the rules of most companies—elect a settlement option and enter into an agreement with the company to govern the distribution of the proceeds. The beneficiary is usually given six months after the insured's death in which to elect a settlement option, provided she does not, in the meantime, cash the check proffered by the company in settlement of the death claim. When a period of time elapses between the death of the insured and the election of a settlement option by the beneficiary, a question arises as to whether interest will be allowed on the proceeds in the interim. Company practices differ on this point. Some companies credit interest from the date of the insured's death, some from the date of submission of satisfactory proof of death; others credit no interest until the settlement option has been elected. The latter appears to be a minority practice.

When a beneficiary elects the settlement option, or when the owner of the policy elects a deferred settlement for himself, a spendthrift clause cannot be included in the settlement agreement or—if it is included—will not be enforceable. A spendthrift clause provides that the proceeds shall be free from attachment or seizure by creditors of the beneficiary. While it may properly be embodied in a life insurance policy or settlement agreement procured by one person for the benefit of another, it cannot be incorporated into an agreement at the behest of the party for whose benefit the agreement is being drawn up.[2] This provides an argument for having the insured elect the settlement option on behalf of the beneficiary.

Under the rules of many companies, a settlement agreement entered into between the company and the beneficiary must provide that any proceeds unpaid at the time of the beneficiary's death shall be paid to her estate in a lump sum or else be payable in a single sum or

---

[2] However, as was pointed out on p. 634, election of a deferred settlement by the beneficiary does not necessarily deprive her of the protection of this clause.

installments to contingent beneficiaries irrevocably designated. In other words, the beneficiary cannot designate *revocable* contingent beneficiaries. The companies which impose this limitation fear that the designation of revocable contingent beneficiaries to receive proceeds already in existence at the time the designation is made might be construed as a disposition of property to take effect at the death of the primary beneficiary. If the beneficiary's action should be so construed, the settlement agreement would be ineffectual as to the residual proceeds unless it were executed with all the formalities of a will—which, of course, is not the practice. Some companies feel that such a construction of the settlement agreement is a remote contingency and permit the beneficiary to designate contingent beneficiaries with the right of revocation.

CONTRACT RATES VERSUS CURRENT RATES

As was pointed out earlier, the liability of the company upon the maturity of a life insurance policy is generally stated in terms of a single-sum payment. In making available other modes of settlement, the company promises a set of installment benefits, based on various patterns of distribution, which have a present value precisely equal to the lump-sum payment. The policy contains a set of tables which state for the different options the amount of periodic income which will be payable for each $1,000 of proceeds left with the company. Under each option, a specified *rate* of income per $1,000 of proceeds is guaranteed in the policy; these are referred to as *contract rates*.

From time to time, a company will modify the actuarial assumptions underlying the benefits provided under the optional modes of settlement, which means that the amount of periodic income per $1,000 of proceeds will change. Historically, because of declining interest yields and growing longevity, these modifications have been of such nature as to produce lower benefits per $1,000 of principal. Such benefit modifications are, of course, reflected only in policies and settlement agreements issued after the change. The benefits under existing agreements cannot be curtailed. In order to distinguish the rates of income available under existing policies and settlement agreements from those that are applicable to contracts currently being issued, the latter are referred to as *current rates*. For policies and agreements issued since the last rate change, there is, obviously, no difference between the contract and current rates. For all others, however, the distinction is significant.

Contract rates are always available to the policy owner, except as to options that may be "negotiated"—i.e., options not contained in the original policy. If a policy owner wants the proceeds to be distributed in a manner not provided for in the original policy, and his request is granted, the benefits will almost invariably be based on the rates in effect at the time the option is requested. Thus, if a policy does not contain all the options which the applicant thinks he might want to utilize, he should attempt to have them added to the policy by way of endorsement at the time the policy is issued, or as soon thereafter as possible.

Contract rates are usually available to the beneficiary if she elects a liquidating option (any option other than the interest option) within a specified period after the insured's death—usually, six months to two years. Under the rules of most companies, a beneficiary who is entitled to a lump-sum payment can choose to leave the proceeds with the company under the interest option or one of the liquidating options, provided she evidences her intentions within six months after the insured's death. If she elects an option during that period, benefits will be provided on the basis of contract rates. If within the six-month period, the beneficiary elects the interest option, she can switch to a liquidating option at contract rates up to two years after the insured's death. Moreover, if—during the prescribed period of six months to two years—the beneficiary should elect to have a liquidating option go into effect at some specified date beyond the two-year period, contract rates would apply. On the other hand, if the beneficiary should request a change of option after the permissible period, the benefits would be made available only at current rates, if at all.

The rationale of the restrictions on contract rates should be grasped. They are *not* primarily designed to prevent an indefinite projection of contract rates into an uncertain future. Rather, they are intended to protect the insurance company from adverse mortality and financial selection. For example, if a beneficiary could elect a life income option at any time, her attitude toward that right would be influenced by the condition of her health. If, after the insured's death, her health should deteriorate, she would not consider a life income option, unless it were of the cash refund type. On the other hand, if her health over the years should be excellent, she might elect a life income option as she approached middle or old age. Since beneficiaries as a group could be expected to react in this manner, the company would find itself with an undue proportion of healthy annuitants.

Likewise, if a beneficiary has the choice of withdrawing the proceeds and placing them in some other type of investment or leaving them with the company to be liquidated under one of the installment options, she could be expected to place the investment burden on the company if it provided a higher return than she could obtain in the open market. The reverse would be true if the market yield were higher than that provided by the company. While the behavior of one or a few beneficiaries is of no concern to the company, the adverse action of tens of thousands of beneficiaries could be quite disadvantageous to the company.

If the insured or the beneficiary agrees *in advance* that a life income or other liquidating option will go into operation automatically at a specified time or upon the occurrence of a specified event, contract rates will be made available, regardless of how far into the future the rates are projected. This privilege may not be made available, however, if in the meantime, the beneficiary has an unlimited right of withdrawal (see below), since she would still have an opportunity to select against the company. On the other hand, it is considered unwise from an insurance planning standpoint to commit a beneficiary to a life income option at some distant date, since her health might be poor at that time.

Within recent years, the rate structure of some companies has been modified in a manner to produce larger benefits under settlement options than those available under some contracts previously issued. Such companies, however, have made the more liberal benefits available under all settlement agreements becoming operative after the rate change. Moreover, in order to co-ordinate the "purchase price" of life income benefits under a settlement option with that charged for equivalent benefits under a single premium immediate annuity, many companies will grant a life income of 103 to 105 per cent of the income that could be purchased at current single premium immediate rates if such income would be more favorable than the contractual option income.

RIGHT OF WITHDRAWAL

The beneficiary may be given the right to withdraw all or a portion of the proceeds held by the company under a deferred settlement arrangement. If the beneficiary can withdraw all of the proceeds at any one time, subject only to a delay clause, she is said to have an *unlimited* right of withdrawal. However, if the privilege is subject to restrictions, it is generally identified as a *limited* right of withdrawal.

The right of withdrawal may be limited as to (1) the frequency with which it can be invoked, (2) the minimum amount which can be withdrawn at any one time, (3) the maximum amount that can be withdrawn at any one time, (4) the maximum amount that can be withdrawn in any one year, or (5) the maximum amount that can be withdrawn in the aggregate. The first two types of limitations are imposed by the companies to control the cost of administration, while the last three are imposed by the insured to prevent dissipation or too rapid exhaustion of the proceeds by the beneficiary. The right of withdrawal can usually be invoked only on dates when regular interest or liquidation payments are due. Most companies permit withdrawals on any such dates; but some restrict the privilege to a stated number of withdrawals per year, such as three, four, or six. The minimum amount which can be withdrawn at any one time ranges from $10 to $500, but the most common limitation is $100. Some companies have no minimum requirement.

Most policies reserve the right to delay cash withdrawals under settlement options for a period of up to six months. This is a counterpart to the delay clause required by law in connection with loan and surrender values.

The insured may provide that the right of withdrawal shall be *cumulative*. This means that any withdrawable amounts which are not withdrawn during a particular year can be withdrawn in any subsequent year, in addition to any other sums that can be withdrawn pursuant to the terms of agreement. Thus, if the settlement agreement permits the beneficiary to withdraw up to $1,000 per year in addition to the periodic contractual payments and provides that the right shall be cumulative, failure of the beneficiary to withdraw any funds during the first year would automatically give him the right to withdraw $2,000 during the second year. No withdrawals during the first or second years would bestow the right to withdraw $3,000 during the third year, and so on. A *noncumulative* right of withdrawal, whether exercised or not, expires at the end of the period to which it pertains. Most limited rights of withdrawal are noncumulative.

A right of withdrawal is included in a settlement agreement in order to provide flexibility. It can be invoked to obtain funds for unexpected emergencies or to meet the problem of a rising price level. It is especially desirable during the period when the widow has dependent children under her care. In most cases, however, the right should be hedged with reasonable restrictions, in order to prevent premature exhaustion of the proceeds.

RIGHT OF COMMUTATION

Related to the right of withdrawal is the right of *commutation*. To commute, in this sense, is to withdraw in a lump sum the present value of remaining installment payments. The term is properly applied only to a right attaching to proceeds being distributed under a liquidating option. Hence, it does not apply to proceeds held under the interest option. For all practical purposes, however, the right of commutation is identical with the unlimited right of withdrawal.

The right of commutation is not implicit in an installment arrangement; in order to be available, it must be specifically authorized in the settlement agreement. The right is specifically denied the beneficiary in the spendthrift clause which is sometimes made part of the settlement agreement.

MINIMUM-AMOUNT REQUIREMENTS

In order to hold down the cost of administering proceeds under deferred settlement arrangements, for which there is no specific charge, the companies will not accept a sum less than $1,000 under a settlement option and will not provide periodic installments in amounts less than $10. Some companies impose requirements of $2,000 and $25, respectively. If the proceeds of a policy are split into two or more funds for use with different options, the foregoing requirements apply to each fund. The minimum-payment requirement also applies to each beneficiary. Thus, a policy large enough to satisfy the requirements if payable to the widow alone might have to be paid in a lump sum if several children become payees as contingent beneficiaries.

There is usually a special requirement for proceeds held under the installment amount option. Most companies will not make monthly payments of less than $5 or $6 per $1,000 under this option. The requirement is sometimes stated in terms of percentage liquidation per year, the minimum being 4, 5, or 6 per cent per year. This special rule is designed to assure liquidation of all proceeds and interest within a reasonable period of time.

CHAPTER XXXIII

Structure and Functional Characteristics of Settlement Options

LIFE INSURANCE settlement options, as a group, embody three basic concepts: (1) retention of proceeds without liquidation of principal, (2) systematic liquidation of the proceeds without reference to life contingencies, and (3) systematic liquidation of the proceeds with reference to one or more life contingencies. A number of options have been evolved from this conceptual foundation, but they may be reduced to four fundamental options: (1) the interest option, (2) the installment time option, (3) the installment amount option, and (4) the life income option. These four options will be discussed under the conceptual classification mentioned above.

RETENTION OF PROCEEDS AT INTEREST

Structure of the Option

The simplest and most flexible of all settlement options is the interest option. The fundamental concept underlying this option is that the proceeds will be maintained intact until the expiration of a specified period or until the occurrence of some specific event. It is an interim option, in the sense that it postpones the ultimate disposition of the proceeds and must be followed by a liquidating option or a lump-sum distribution.

The company guarantees a minimum rate of interest on the proceeds, which is payable at periodic intervals, usually monthly. If the policy was of the participating type, the proceeds will be credited with the actual rate of interest earned by the company or, more likely, a rate approximately equal to the interest factor in the dividend formula. This excess interest is usually paid once a year on one of the normal interest payment dates.

The interest on proceeds left with the company may constitute a significant portion of the income of the primary beneficiary. Indeed, it is sometimes adequate for all her income needs. It is not at all infrequent for a life income to be provided the primary beneficiary (usually, the widow) through the interest option, with the proceeds at her death being applied to the needs of the contingent beneficiaries. In order to determine how much principal must be left with the company to provide an interest income of a desired amount, reference can be made to tables such as Table 33.

TABLE 33

AMOUNT OF PRINCIPAL NEEDED TO PROVIDE
STIPULATED PERIODIC INTEREST INCOME
(3 PER CENT INTEREST WITH FIRST PAYMENT BEING MADE
AT END OF FIRST TIME PERIOD)

PERIODIC INCOME DESIRED	FREQUENCY OF PAYMENT			
	Annually	Semiannually	Quarterly	Monthly
$ 10.......	$ 333	$ 672	$ 1,348	$ 4,049
25.......	833	1,679	3,369	10,121
50.......	1,667	3,358	6,739	20,243
75.......	2,500	5,037	10,108	30,364
100.......	3,333	6,716	13,477	40,486

Table 33 is based on the assumption that the proceeds will yield 3 per cent interest. Thus, the annual income per $1,000 is assumed to be $30. However, if payments are to be made monthly, quarterly, or semiannually rather than annually, the amount of each payment will be somewhat *less* than a proportionate share of the annual interest, owing to an adjustment made for loss of interest. If, instead of paying interest at the end of the year, the company pays at the end of the first and each subsequent month, it loses eleven months' interest on the first payment, ten months' interest on the second, nine on the third, and so on. Altogether, it loses $11/24$ of one year's interest. At 3 per cent, the interest on $30 is $0.90, $11/24$ of which is $0.41. Thus, the effective amount of interest earned is $29.59, which divided by twelve, yields

$2.50 as the proper monthly payment, rather than $2.47 (30 ÷ 12). Similar adjustments are made for quarterly and semiannual payments, producing sums of $7.42 and $14.89, respectively.

Functional Characteristics

The primary beneficiary can be given varying degrees of control over proceeds held by the company under the interest option. If the insured wants the proceeds to go intact to the contingent beneficiaries eventually, he will give the primary beneficiary no rights in the proceeds other than the right to receive the interest during her lifetime or for some other specified period. If he wants to provide flexibility to meet unforeseen needs, he may grant the primary beneficiary a limited right of withdrawal. This creates no complications for the insurance company and is always permitted. Further flexibility and control may be provided by giving the primary beneficiary the right to elect a liquidating option within a specified period or at any time. Most companies permit this flexibility; but unless the liquidating option is elected within a stipulated period after the insured's death, the benefits will be provided on the basis of current rather than contract rates. The settlement agreement itself may stipulate that after a specified period of time, or upon the occurrence of a stipulated contingency, the proceeds shall be applied under a liquidating option for the benefit of either the primary beneficiary or the contingent beneficiaries, or both. In that event, contract rates would apply.

The beneficiary may be given complete control over the proceeds by granting her an unlimited right of withdrawal during her lifetime, as well as the right to dispose of the proceeds at the time of her death. One or the other of these rights must be present if the proceeds are to qualify for the marital deduction, which can be very important if the insured has a federal estate tax liability. As was pointed out earlier, the only forms of disposition by the beneficiary that will be permitted by many companies is payment to the beneficiary's estate or payment to irrevocably designated contingent beneficiaries. Some companies are so concerned about the testamentary disposition question that they will grant the primary beneficiary the right to dispose of the proceeds at death only if that be necessary to qualify the proceeds for the marital deduction. If the beneficiary is given an unlimited right of withdrawal, the guaranteed rate of interest may be lower than would otherwise be the case.

Needless to say, if the beneficiary is entitled to a lump-sum settlement but chooses to leave the proceeds with the company under the interest option, she can retain any privileges the company is willing to grant.

Most companies are willing to retain proceeds under the interest option throughout the remaining lifetime of the primary beneficiary or for thirty years, whichever is longer. Thus, the interest option may be available for the use of contingent beneficiaries. A few companies will hold the proceeds throughout the lifetime of the primary beneficiary and the first contingent beneficiary. From the company's standpoint, some limit is necessary in order to control the cost of administration and to avoid an indefinite projection of contract rates into the future. (If the insured or the beneficiary elected a liquidating option for the contingent beneficiaries to commence upon termination of the interest option, contract rates would be applicable).

As a general rule, a company will not accumulate the interest credited to proceeds retained under the interest option. In other words, it insists upon paying out the interest at least annually. This is to avoid any conflict with the law in several states which forbids the accumulation of income of a trust except that payable to a minor beneficiary. By analogy, these laws might be applied to proceeds held by a life insurance company. Most—but not all—companies will permit the accumulation of interest income payable to a minor beneficiary; otherwise, a guardian might have to be appointed.

The unwillingness of the companies to accumulate interest has a profound impact on the technique of programming, as will be apparent later.

SYSTEMATIC LIQUIDATION WITHOUT REFERENCE TO LIFE CONTINGENCIES

Proceeds left with a life insurance company to be liquidated at a uniform rate without reference to a life contingency must be paid out either over a specified period of time, with the amount of each payment being the variable, or at a specified rate, with the period of time over which the liquidation is to take place being the variable. If the period over which the liquidation is to occur is fixed, the amount of each payment depends upon the size of the fund, the rate of interest assumed to be earned, the time when the first payment is to be made, and the interval between payments. If the amount of each payment is fixed in advance, the period over which the liquidation is to take place will be determined by the same factors set forth in the preceding sentence. An option is available for each type of situation. The installment *time* option provides payments over a stipulated period of time, while the installment *amount* option provides payments of a stipulated amount.[1] The two options are based on the same mathematical principles and differ only as to the relative significance attached to the *duration* of the payments, as contrasted to the *level* of payments. If the insured or the beneficiary wants the assurance of *some* income, however small, over a specified period, he should choose the installment *time* option; if, however, the need is for *adequacy* of income, irrespective of its duration, the installment amount option should be chosen. In some situations, the decision will turn on the flexibility obtainable under the two options.

Installment Time Option

Structure of the Option. If a given principal sum is to be liquidated at a uniform rate over a specified period of years, the amount of each *annual* payment can be derived from compound discount tables similar to Table 11 of this volume.[2] For example, if $1,000 is to be liquidated in annual installments over a twenty-year period and the undistributed proceeds are assumed to earn interest at the rate of 3 per cent, the amount of each payment *due at the end of the year* will be $1,000 ÷ $14.877 = $67.22. In other words, the present value at 3 per cent interest of a series of annual payments of $1, due at the end of the year, for a period of twenty years, is $14.877. If $14.88 will provide $1 per year for twenty years, then $1,000 will provide an annual payment as much larger than $1 as $1,000 is greater than $14.88. Such figure is obtained by dividing $1,000 by $14.877, as above.

Amounts payable under life insurance settlement options, however, are due *at the beginning* of the year. As was explained in Chapter IX, this simply means that the present value of the payments under a twenty-year installment time option would be derived by treating the first payment as due immediately and ascertaining the present value of the remaining payments to be made over a period of nineteen years. Reference to Table 11 reveals that the present value at 3 per cent of a

---

[1] These options are also referred to as the *fixed period* and *fixed amount* options, respectively.

[2] See p. 179.

series of nineteen annual payments of $1, due at the end of the year, is $14.324. The addition of $1 to this sum produces the present value of a series of twenty annual payments of $1, the first payment being due immediately. The size of each annual payment that will be produced by $1,000 is determined by dividing $1,000 by $15.324, which yields $65.26.

If the payments under the option are to be made monthly, as they usually are, only one twelfth of the annual payment is due immediately, and the company earns interest on the remaining portion of the annual payment for varying periods of time. It earns one month's interest on the second monthly installment, two months' interest on the third monthly installment, and so forth. Altogether, it *gains* $11\frac{1}{24}$ of one year's interest on the sum of $65.26. At 3 per cent, this amounts to $0.91. Thus, the amount of each *monthly* payment for each $1,000 of proceeds would be $\dfrac{\$65.26 + 0.90}{12} = \$5.51$. The same result could have been obtained by dividing twelve into $67.22, adjusted for the *loss* of $11\frac{1}{24}$ of one year's interest.

The amount of annual, semiannual, quarterly, or monthly payment for each $1,000 of proceeds for any period of years can be computed in the manner just described. Such values for periods up to thirty years are given in Table 34. Under the rules of most companies, thirty years is the maximum period over which proceeds will be liquidated under the installment time option. All policies offering optional modes of settlement contain a set of such values in connection with the installment time option, which values are guaranteed for all settlement agreements entitled to contract rates. These guarantees are important to the policyholder and the beneficiary, and are utilized by the life underwriter in determining how much income will be provided by various policies and options. In other words, the function of this table is to convert a principal sum into periodic income.

Another type of table, not included in the policy provisions, is useful to the life underwriter in connection with the installment time option. This is a table which shows the amount of principal required at various rates of interest to provide a monthly income of different amounts for stipulated periods of varying length. Such a table is fundamentally a table of present values, showing, on a monthly basis, the present worth of a series of payments of varying durations. It is the inverse of the type of table illustrated by Table 34, and is derived from it. For example, if the life underwriter wishes to know how much

TABLE 34

GUARANTEED INSTALLMENTS PER $1,000
OF PROCEEDS (3 PER CENT)

Number of Years Payable	Annually	Semiannually	Quarterly	Monthly
1	$1,000.00	$503.69	$252.78	$84.47
2	507.39	255.57	128.26	42.86
3	343.23	172.88	86.76	28.99
4	261.19	131.56	66.02	22.06
5	211.99	106.78	53.59	17.91
6	179.22	90.27	45.30	15.14
7	155.83	78.49	39.39	13.16
8	138.31	69.66	34.96	11.68
9	124.69	62.81	31.52	10.53
10	113.82	57.33	28.77	9.61
11	104.93	52.85	26.52	8.86
12	97.54	49.13	24.65	8.24
13	91.29	45.98	23.08	7.71
14	85.95	43.29	21.73	7.26
15	81.33	40.96	20.56	6.87
16	77.29	38.93	19.54	6.53
17	73.74	37.14	18.64	6.23
18	70.59	35.56	17.84	5.96
19	67.78	34.14	17.13	5.73
20	65.26	32.87	16.50	5.51
21	62.98	31.72	15.92	5.32
22	60.92	30.68	15.40	5.15
23	59.04	29.74	14.92	4.99
24	57.33	28.88	14.49	4.84
25	55.76	28.08	14.09	4.71
26	54.31	27.36	13.73	4.59
27	52.97	26.68	13.39	4.47
28	51.74	26.06	13.08	4.37
29	50.60	25.49	12.79	4.27
30	49.53	24.95	12.52	4.18

insurance is needed to provide $100 per month for a period of ten years, he divides the amount of monthly income that would be provided by $1,000, found in Table 34 to be $9.61, into $100 and multiplies by 1,000. The amount is found to be $10,406. That is, if it takes $1,000 to produce $9.61 per month for ten years, it takes as much more than $1,000 to produce $100 as $100 is greater than $9.61. Table 35 shows the principal sum needed to produce a monthly income of $10, $25, $50, and $100, for periods up to thirty years. In each case, it is assumed that the first payment is due immediately. The role which this sort of table plays in the planning of a life

TABLE 35

AMOUNT OF PRINCIPAL NEEDED TO PROVIDE GUARANTEED
INCOME FOR VARYING DURATIONS (3 PER CENT)

MONTHS OF INCOME	MONTHLY INCOME			
	$10	$25	$50	$100
12............	$ 118	$ 296	$ 592	$ 1,184
24............	233	583	1,167	2,333
36............	345	862	1,725	3,449
48............	453	1,133	2,267	4,533
60............	558	1,396	2,792	5,583
72............	661	1,651	3,303	6,605
84............	760	1,900	3,800	7,599
96............	856	2,141	4,281	8,562
108............	950	2,374	4,749	9,497
120............	1,041	2,602	5,203	10,406
132............	1,129	2,822	5,644	11,287
144............	1,214	3,034	6,068	12,136
156...........	1,297	3,243	6,485	12,970
168...........	1,377	3,444	6,887	13,774
180............	1,456	3,639	7,278	14,556
192...........	1,531	3,829	7,657	15,314
204...........	1,605	4,013	8,026	16,051
216...........	1,678	4,195	8,390	16,779
228...........	1,745	4,363	8,726	17,452
240...........	1,815	4,537	9,075	18,149
252...........	1,880	4,699	9,399	18,797
264............	1,942	4,854	9,709	19,417
276............	2,004	5,010	10,020	20,040
288............	2,066	5,165	10,331	20,661
300...........	2,123	5,308	10,616	21,231
312...........	2,179	5,447	10,893	21,786
324...........	2,237	5,593	11,186	22,371
336...........	2,288	5,721	11,442	22,883
348...........	2,342	5,855	11,710	23,419
360...........	2,392	5,981	11,962	23,923

insurance program will be illustrated in the programming case presented in a later chapter. It is appropriate at this point, however, to indicate that, while Table 35 is based on the concept of liquidating proceeds over a fixed period, it does not necessarily follow that insurance proceeds whose amount was determined through the application of tables of this type will be placed under the installment time option. It may be more advantageous to use the installment amount option because of the greater flexibility obtainable under that option.

Functional Characteristics. The essence of the installment time option is the certainty of the period over which the proceeds will be distributed. Hence, any developments that increase or decrease the amount of proceeds available are reflected in the size of the monthly payments, and not in the duration of the payments. The additional proceeds payable by reason of the insured's accidental death operate to increase the amount of the monthly payments. Dividend accumulations and paid-up additions have the same effect. If prepaid or discounted premiums are considered to be part of the proceeds, they can be applied under a settlement option and, in the case of the installment time option, raise the level of payments. Under the provisions of some policies, however, such premium deposits are treated as belonging to the insured's estate and do not become part of the proceeds payable to third-party beneficiaries. Policy loans, if still outstanding upon maturity of the policy, reduce the proceeds available and hence the size of the monthly benefits. Some companies permit the beneficiary to repay a policy loan after the insured's death, in order to have the full amount of proceeds payable under a settlement option.

Excess interest, if any, may be paid in one sum at the end of each year or added in prorata proportions to each of the regular benefit payments during the following year.

The installment time option is a very inflexible arrangement. The only flexibility that can be injected into the option is to permit the beneficiary to choose the date on which the option becomes operative, rather than having it go into effect automatically upon maturity of the policy, and to grant the beneficiary the right of commutation. If the option is not to go into operation automatically upon maturity of the policy, the proceeds are held under the interest option until such time as the beneficiary indicates that liquidation should commence. Limited withdrawals are not permitted, presumably because of the administrative expense involved in recomputing the benefits and recasting the agreement after each withdrawal. The companies are willing, however, to permit the settlement agreement to be terminated through withdrawal by the beneficiary of all proceeds remaining with the company.

Installment Amount Option

Structure of the Option. The installment amount option is based on the simple proposition of distributing a specified sum each month, or at some other periodic time interval, until the proceeds are exhausted. Mathematically, it is based on the same compound discount function that underlies the installment time option. The application is different, however.

The principle can be explained in terms of $1,000 to be distributed in equal annual payments of $100, the first payment being due immediately. It is obvious that the liquidation will extend over a minimum period of nine years, since the principal alone will provide payments for that period of time; the problem is to determine how much longer the payments can be continued because of the crediting of compound interest to the unliquidated portion of the principal. The first step is to find in a compound discount table the largest value for an annual payment of $1 which, increased by $1 to take care of the first payment due immediately and multiplied by 100 (since each payment is to be in the amount of $100), can be contained within $1,000. Reference to Table 11 reveals that at 3 per cent interest, the largest such value is $8.5302, which is the present value of $1 per annum for ten years, the first payment being due at the end of the year. Increased by 1 and multiplied by $100, this figure produces a value of $953.02. Thus, a principal sum of $1,000 will provide *eleven* annual payments of $100 each, the first payment due immediately, with $46.98 left over. Improved at 3 per cent compound interest over a ten-year period, this sum will amount to $63.14 at the end of the period and will be added to the last payment. Thus, the original $1,000, improved with interest at 3 per cent, will provide a total of $1,163.14 over the ten-year period.

Tables have been prepared showing the length of time for which payments of various amounts can be provided by varying principal sums, although it is not customary for policies to contain such a table. A table of this type, computed in terms of monthly income only, is presented as Table 36.

Table 36 is not as convenient a tool as Tables 34 and 35, but it can be useful in demonstrating to a policyholder the length of time during which income of a specified amount can be provided by present and prospective insurance, as well as in estimating roughly how much insurance is required to meet certain income needs. For example, to estimate the amount of insurance necessary to produce $200 a month for eight years, at an assumed rate of interest of 3 per cent, a rough interpolation can be made between the time period just under eight years and that just over eight years, as shown on the horizontal line for

TABLE 36

LENGTH OF PERIOD FOR WHICH MONTHLY INCOME IS PROVIDED BY VARYING PRINCIPAL SUMS (3 PER CENT)

DESIRED MONTHLY INCOME	$1,000		$2,000		$3,000		$4,000		$5,000		$7,500		$10,000		$12,500		$15,000		$20,000	
	Yrs.	Mos.	Yrs.	Mos.	Yrs.	Mos.	Yrs.	Mos.	Yrs.	Mos.	Yrs.	Mos.	Yrs.	Mos.	Yrs.	Mos.	Yrs.	Mos.	Yrs.	Mos.
$ 10	9	6	22	10																
15	6	0	13	5	22	10														
20	4	5	9	6	15	8	22	10												
25	3	6	7	4	11	10	16	11	22	10										
30	2	10	6	0	9	7	13	6	17	10										
40	2	1	4	5	6	11	9	7	12	5	20	11								
50	1	8	3	6	5	5	7	5	9	6	15	6	22	10						
60	1	4	2	10	4	5	6	1	7	9	12	5	17	10	24	3				
70	1	2	2	5	3	9	5	1	6	6	10	4	14	7	19	6				
75	1	1	2	3	3	6	4	9	6	1	9	6	13	5	17	10	22	6		
80	1	0	2	1	3	3	4	5	5	8	8	10	12	5	16	4	20	10		
90	0	11	1	10	2	10	3	11	4	11	7	9	10	9	14	1	17	0		
100	0	10	1	8	2	7	3	6	4	5	6	10	9	6	12	5	15	6	22	10
125	0	8	1	4	2	0	2	9	3	6	5	4	7	4	9	6	11	10	16	11
150	0	6	1	1	1	8	2	3	2	10	4	5	6	0	7	9	9	6	13	5
175	0	5	0	11	1	5	1	11	2	5	3	9	5	1	6	6	8	0	11	2
200	0	5	0	10	1	3	1	8	2	1	3	3	4	5	5	7	6	10	9	6

$200 of monthly income. That just under eight years is six years and ten months in the vertical column headed $15,000, and that above is nine years and six months in the vertical column headed $20,000. Since eight years is about halfway between these two time periods, an amount ($17,500) at the mid-point between the $15,000 and $20,000 figures suggests itself as appropriate. The actual amount necessary on a 3 per cent interest basis to provide $200 a month for eight years is only $17,124, but the difference is inconsequential for all practical purposes.

Functional Characteristics. Since the amount of each payment is fixed under this option, any augmentation in the volume of proceeds or interest operates to lengthen the period over which payments will be made, while any diminution in the amount of proceeds shortens the period. Thus, dividend accumulations, paid-up additions, accidental death benefits, and excess interest extend the period of liquidation, whereas loans outstanding at the insured's death and withdrawals of principal by the beneficiary shorten the period. This is true even though the payments are to terminate upon a specified date or upon the occurrence of some specified event, with the balance of the proceeds being distributed in some manner.

A great deal of flexibility is attainable under the installment amount option. In the first place, the beneficiary can be given the right to indicate when the liquidation payments are to begin, as under the installment time option. In the meantime, the proceeds are held at interest, with the interest payments going to the primary beneficiary. The beneficiary can be given either a limited or an unlimited right of withdrawal. Under this option, withdrawals merely shorten the period of installment payments and do not necessitate the recomputation of benefit payments. The beneficiary can be given the right to accelerate or retard the rate of liquidation. That is, she can be given the privilege of varying the amount of the monthly payments, subject to any limitations the insured might wish to impose. For example, the insured might direct the company to liquidate the proceeds at the rate of $300 per month, while giving the beneficiary the option of stepping up the payments to $500 per month or reducing them to any level acceptable to the company. Under such circumstances, the insured is not likely to prescribe any minimum rate of liquidation. The beneficiary can be given the privilege of discontinuing payments during particular months of the year or from time to time. For example, when the proceeds of an educational endowment policy are being paid out to a beneficiary who is enrolled in a college or university, payments can be discontinued during the summer vacation months. Moreover, larger than usual payments can be provided for those months in which tuition and other fees are payable. If a beneficiary under any type of policy finds that the payments under the option will not be needed for a period of time, she can usually arrange to have them discontinued for a few months. Such flexibility stems from the fact that this option is basically little more than a savings account from which withdrawals can be made to suit the convenience of the beneficiary.

Finally, provision can be made for transferring the remaining proceeds to another liquidating option. If the transfer is to take place at a specified date or age, contract rates will be available. If the beneficiary has the right to transfer the proceeds at any time, the conversion will be subject to current rates.

SYSTEMATIC LIQUIDATION WITH REFERENCE TO LIFE CONTINGENCIES

The proceeds of a life insurance policy may be liquidated at a uniform rate over the lifetime of one or more beneficiaries. This is a type of arrangement peculiar to life insurance companies and one which is of very great value. It protects a beneficiary against the economic hazard of excessive longevity; that is, it protects her against the possibility of outliving her income.

Structure of the Life Income Options

Any settlement option based on a life contingency is called a *life income option*. The principle underlying a life income option is identical with that underlying an annuity. As a matter of fact, a life income option is nothing more than the annuity principle applied to the liquidation of insurance proceeds. Hence, there are as many variations of the life income option as there are types of immediate annuities. Reference to the chapter on annuities (Chapter VI) will reveal that among the single-life annuities, there are the pure or straight life annuity, life annuity with guaranteed installments, the installment refund annuity, and the cash refund annuity. There are similar annuities based on two or more lives.

While there is a counterpart among the life income options for every type of immediate annuity, it is not customary for a company to include the whole range of annuity forms in its policies. The typical policy provides for a life income with payments guaranteed for ten, fifteen, and twenty years and the installment refund option. Some companies include the joint-and-last-survivor annuity, and a few show the straight life annuity. Virtually all will make additional options available upon request.

Mathematically, the straight life income option is the equivalent of a pure immediate annuity. To be precisely accurate, it is the same thing as a life annuity due, since the first payment is due immediately upon maturity of the policy or upon election of the option, whichever is later. The monthly income provided per $1,000 of proceeds depends upon the age and sex of the beneficiary and the assumptions as to mortality and interest. While the schedules of income guaranteed under the policies of the various companies are similar, there is currently little uniformity among the companies as to the combination of mortality and interest assumptions used to calculate the income payments. Benefits are provided at *net* rates, there being no charge for the use of the life income settlement.

The life income option with guaranteed payments is mathematically a combination of an installment time option of appropriate duration and a pure *deferred* life annuity.[3] For example, a life income option which undertakes to provide payments of a specified amount to a beneficiary aged forty-five throughout her remaining lifetime and in any event for twenty years, is a combination of an installment time option running for twenty years and a pure life annuity deferred to the beneficiary's age sixty-five. If the beneficiary does not survive to age sixty-five, the portion of the proceeds allocated to the deferred life annuity is retained by the company without further obligation.

Table 37 shows the allocation of proceeds on a $1,000 basis as between the installment time option and the deferred life annuity with varying periods of guaranteed installments. The figures in the table may be treated as dollar amounts or percentages of $1,000. Thus, if proceeds are left to a female beneficiary aged forty-five under a life income option providing 120 guaranteed installments, 39 per cent of the proceeds go into the time option and 61 per cent into the deferred life annuity. Only the amounts shown under the time option will be paid in any event. The amounts shown under the deferred life annuity will be forfeited in each case if the beneficiary does not survive the

---

[3] Such an option may also be viewed as a combination of a pure deferred life annuity and decreasing term insurance, the latter being represented by the guaranteed payments.

TABLE 37

DISTRIBUTION OF PRINCIPAL SUM AS BETWEEN INSTALLMENT TIME OPTION
AND DEFERRED LIFE ANNUITY UNDER LIFE INCOME OPTION WITH
VARYING PERIODS OF GUARANTEED INSTALLMENTS ($1,000 BASIS)

| AGE OF BENEFICIARY | | NUMBER OF GUARANTEED PAYMENTS | | | | | |
| | | INSTALLMENT TIME OPTION: | | | DEFERRED LIFE ANNUITY | | |
Male	Female	120	180	240	120	180	240
30	35	$349	$486	$604	$651	$514	$396
40	45	391	545	673	609	455	327
50	55	461	633	770	539	367	230
60	65	573	762	886	427	238	114
70	75	732	898	971	268	102	29

Rate basis: 1955 American Annuity Table and 3 per cent interest; male ages set back one year and female ages six years.

period of guaranteed installments. The older the beneficiary, the smaller the portion of the proceeds going into the deferred life annuity. This means that at the older ages, a refund feature greatly reduces the amount of monthly payments per $1,000, since the life contingency is being neutralized to a substantial degree.

The installment refund option—which, it will be recalled, promises to continue the monthly payments beyond the annuitant's death until the purchase price of the annuity or, in this case, the proceeds of the life insurance policy have been returned—is a combination of a pure immediate life annuity and decreasing term insurance in an amount sufficient to continue the payments until the proceeds, without interest, have been paid out in full. At the inception, the term insurance is in an amount equal to the proceeds, less the first payment due immediately; but it decreases with each periodic payment and expires altogether when the cumulative payments equal or exceed the proceeds committed to the installment refund option. The cash refund option is likewise a combination of a pure immediate life annuity and decreasing term insurance; but since the refund is payable in cash rather than installments, a slightly larger amount of term insurance is required.

To use a life income option in the programming of a client's estate, the life underwriter needs two types of tables. In the order of use, the first type is one which enables the life underwriter to compute the amount of insurance required to meet the life income needs of the beneficiary or beneficiaries. It shows the amount of principal needed to provide $10 a month under the various life income options for a wide range of male and female ages. The values for such a table, based on one set of actuarial assumptions, are presented in Table 38.

TABLE 38

Amount of Principle Needed to Provide Life Income
of $10 per Month—at Various Ages

Age		Life Income Only	5 Years Certain and Life	10 Years Certain and Life	15 Years Certain and Life	20 Years Certain and Life
Male	Female					
25	30	$3,125	$3,125	$3,125	$3,125	$3,135
30	35	2,985	2,985	2,985	2,994	3,003
31	36	2,950	2,950	2,959	2,967	2,976
32	37	2,924	2,924	2,924	2,933	2,950
33	38	2,890	2,890	2,899	2,907	2,915
34	39	2,857	2,857	2,865	2,874	2,890
35	40	2,825	2,825	2,833	2,841	2,857
36	41	2,793	2,793	2,801	2,809	2,825
37	42	2,755	2,755	2,762	2,778	2,793
38	43	2,717	2,725	2,732	2,740	2,762
39	44	2,681	2,688	2,695	2,710	2,732
40	45	2,646	2,653	2,660	2,674	2,695
41	46	2,611	2,611	2,618	2,639	2,667
42	47	2,571	2,571	2,584	2,604	2,632
43	48	2,532	2,532	2,545	2,564	2,597
44	49	2,494	2,494	2,506	2,525	2,564
45	50	2,451	2,451	2,469	2,488	2,525
46	51	2,410	2,410	2,427	2,451	2,494
47	52	2,364	2,370	2,387	2,415	2,457
48	53	2,320	2,326	2,342	2,375	2,427
49	54	2,278	2,283	2,304	2,336	2,392
50	55	2,232	2,237	2,257	2,299	2,358
51	56	2,188	2,193	2,217	2,257	2,326
52	57	2,141	2,151	2,174	2,217	2,288
53	58	2,096	2,101	2,128	2,179	2,257
54	59	2,045	2,053	2,083	2,141	2,227
55	60	2,000	2,008	2,041	2,101	2,193
56	61	1,949	1,961	1,996	2,062	2,165
57	62	1,901	1,912	1,949	2,024	2,132
58	63	1,848	1,862	1,905	1,984	2,105
59	64	1,800	1,815	1,862	1,949	2,079
60	65	1,748	1,764	1,818	1,912	2,049
61	66	1,698	1,715	1,773	1,880	2,024
62	67	1,647	1,667	1,733	1,845	2,004
63	68	1,597	1,618	1,689	1,812	1,980
64	69	1,546	1,572	1,647	1,779	1,961
65	70	1,497	1,524	1,608	1,751	1,942
70	75	1,253	1,295	1,422	1,621	1,869

Rate Basis: 1955 American Annuity Table and 3 per cent interest; male ages set back one year and female ages six years; no loading.

TABLE 39

MONTHLY LIFE INCOME PER $1,000 OF PROCEEDS
AT VARIOUS AGES

Male	Female	LIFE INCOME ONLY	5 YEARS CERTAIN AND LIFE	10 YEARS CERTAIN AND LIFE	15 YEARS CERTAIN AND LIFE	20 YEARS CERTAIN AND LIFE
25	30	$3.20	$3.20	$3.20	$3.20	$3.19
30	35	3.35	3.35	3.35	3.34	3.33
31	36	3.39	3.39	3.38	3.37	3.36
32	37	3.42	3.42	3.42	3.41	3.39
33	38	3.46	3.46	3.45	3.44	3.43
34	39	3.50	3.50	3.49	3.48	3.46
35	40	3.54	3.54	3.53	3.52	3.50
36	41	3.58	3.58	3.57	3.56	3.54
37	42	3.63	3.63	3.62	3.60	3.58
38	43	3.68	3.67	3.66	3.65	3.62
39	44	3.73	3.72	3.71	3.69	3.66
40	45	3.78	3.77	3.76	3.74	3.71
41	46	3.83	3.83	3.82	3.79	3.75
42	47	3.89	3.89	3.87	3.84	3.80
43	48	3.95	3.95	3.93	3.90	3.85
44	49	4.01	4.01	3.99	3.96	3.90
45	50	4.08	4.08	4.05	4.02	3.96
46	51	4.15	4.15	4.12	4.08	4.01
47	52	4.23	4.22	4.19	4.14	4.07
48	53	4.31	4.30	4.27	4.21	4.12
49	54	4.39	4.38	4.34	4.28	4.18
50	55	4.48	4.47	4.43	4.35	4.24
51	56	4.57	4.56	4.51	4.43	4.30
52	57	4.67	4.65	4.60	4.51	4.37
53	58	4.77	4.76	4.70	4.59	4.43
54	59	4.89	4.87	4.80	4.67	4.49
55	60	5.00	4.98	4.90	4.76	4.56
56	61	5.13	5.10	5.01	4.85	4.62
57	62	5.26	5.23	5.13	4.94	4.69
58	63	5.41	5.37	5.25	5.04	4.75
59	64	5.56	5.51	5.37	5.13	4.81
60	65	5.72	5.67	5.50	5.23	4.88
61	66	5.89	5.83	5.64	5.32	4.94
62	67	6.07	6.00	5.77	5.42	4.99
63	68	6.26	6.18	5.92	5.52	5.05
64	69	6.47	6.36	6.07	5.62	5.10
65	70	6.68	6.56	6.22	5.71	5.15
70	75	7.98	7.72	7.03	6.17	5.35

Rate basis: 1955 American Annuity Table and 3 per cent interest; male ages set back one year and female ages six years; no loading.

The second table needed by the life underwriter is one which shows for the various life income options and range of ages the amount of monthly income that will be provided for each $1,000 of proceeds. After he has determined, through the use of Table 38, how much insurance in multiples of $1,000 is needed, he can demonstrate, through the use of the second type of table, exactly how much income can be provided with the actual and contemplated insurance. The values for such a table, calculated on the same basis as those for Table 38, are shown in Table 39.

Functional Characteristics

Since the life income option contemplates the complete liquidation of the proceeds during the lifetime of the beneficiary, it follows that any circumstances which have the effect of enlarging the volume of proceeds will increase the amount of each periodic payment, while shrinkages in the proceeds will decrease the size of the payments. In this connection, it is interesting to note that excess interest is usually payable only under the annuity form calling for a guaranteed number of payments and, even then, only during the period of guaranteed installments. This is another way of saying that excess interest is payable on the portion of the proceeds applied under the installment time option but is not payable on that portion of the proceeds allocated to the deferred life annuity. Some companies guarantee a lower rate of interest on the installment time option portion of the arrangement than under the deferred life annuity.

As a type, the life income option is extremely inflexible. The benefits are calculated on the basis of the age and sex of the primary beneficiary; and once the payments have begun, no other person can be substituted for the designated beneficiary, even with an adjustment in the benefits. No right of withdrawal is available; but when the benefits are guaranteed for a specified period of time, a few companies will permit the proceeds payable under the installment time option to be commuted. The benefits payable under the deferred life annuity cannot be commuted; otherwise, persons in poor health would be inclined to withdraw the proceeds. If the commutation privilege is exercised with respect to the guaranteed installments, the beneficiary is usually given a deferred life annuity certificate. This certificate provides for life income payments to the beneficiary if she survives the period during which the guaranteed payments were to have been made.

CHAPTER XXXIV

Use of Settlement Options

ADAPTATION OF SETTLEMENT OPTIONS TO BASIC FAMILY NEEDS[1]

In the opening chapter of this text, there were described the basic family needs which can be met through life insurance. For the typical family, these needs can be met only through the proper use of settlement options. The manner in which settlement options can be adapted to these various needs is outlined in this chapter.

Nonrecurrent Needs

Cleanup or Estate Clearance Fund. The first need, in point of time, is a fund to meet the expenses that grow out of the death of the insured and to liquidate the current outstanding obligations. These are claims against the insured's probate estate and must be satisfied before any distributions can be made to the heirs. The size of the fund required for this purpose varies; but for estates of less than $100,000, it will average around 15 per cent of the probate estate. For larger estates, the percentage will be higher because of the progressive nature of death tax rates.

The conventional method of handling proceeds intended for estate clearance is to have them paid to the insured's estate in a lump sum. This is based on recognition of the fact that payment of the claims

---

[1] For a more comprehensive discussion of this topic, see Harry S. Redeker and Charles K. Reid II, *Life Insurance Settlement Options* (Boston: Little, Brown & Co., 1957), pp. 60–96.

against the estate is an obligation of the executor or administrator, the fulfillment of which requires cash within a relatively short time after the insured's death. Within recent years, however, there has been a growing sentiment in favor of leaving the proceeds with the company under the interest option, with the executor or administrator having the unlimited right of withdrawal and the insured's widow or other dependents being designated contingent beneficiaries to receive any proceeds not withdrawn by the insured's personal representative. This arrangement permits the proceeds to earn interest until they are needed by the executor; and if the insurance is more than adequate for the needs of the estate, the excess can go to the insured's dependents without having to pass through the probate estate, with the attendant delay and expense. These advantages are especially important when the potential estate liabilities are large but unpredictable and a substantial amount of insurance is involved. While most companies do not permit executors or trustees to elect settlement options, an increasing number are manifesting a willingness to make the interest option available to an executor during the period of estate administration.

If the probate estate is modest and the insured's widow is the sole or major beneficiary of the estate, it may be advantageous to have the insurance intended for estate clearance payable to the widow under the interest option with the unlimited right of withdrawal. She can use whatever portion of the proceeds is needed to pay the debts of the insured's estate and apply the remainder to her own needs, perhaps in the form of a deferred settlement. This procedure will reduce the cost of estate administration, particularly the executor's fee, and will take advantage of the special inheritance tax exemption available in most states when insurance proceeds are payable to third-party beneficiaries, especially the insured's widow and children. This latter advantage is offset to the extent that payment of the insured's debts out of the insurance proceeds enlarges the taxable distribution from the estate. By using the interest option and a spendthrift clause, the insured can protect the proceeds from the beneficiary's creditors.

The obvious disadvantage of this arrangement is that the beneficiary, through poor judgment, may pay claims which were not valid or, through cupidity and greed, refuse to use the insurance proceeds for the purposes for which they were intended. The latter behavior is, of course, more likely when the beneficiary is not the sole legatee of the estate. This may result in forced liquidation at great sacrifice of valuable assets in the estate. Another hazard of this arrangement, unless properly safeguarded, is that the widow might die before clearing the insured's estate, with the proceeds going to her estate or to minor contingent beneficiaries, either of which situations would make it impossible for the proceeds to be used to pay the insured's debts. To guard against such an untoward development, it is advisable to make the insured's estate the contingent beneficiary if the widow should predecease the insured or die within six months after his death. If the primary beneficiary survives the insured by six months, the children would be the contingent beneficiaries of any unused proceeds.

If the estate liabilities are large and a life insurance trust is going to be used for other purposes, the estate clearance fund can be made payable in a lump sum or under the interest option (if permissible) to the trustee. Under such an arrangement, funds are made available to the executor through a provision in the trust agreement authorizing the trustee to lend money to the estate or to purchase estate assets. Thus, the trust may come to hold assets formerly held by the estate. There will be expense savings in this procedure only to the extent that trust administration is less costly than estate administration.

Mortgage Cancellation Fund. If there is a mortgage on the insured's home and he wants his family to continue occupying the home after his death, he usually attempts to provide enough insurance to liquidate the mortgage upon his death. In many cases, the insurance is provided through a special mortgage redemption policy, embodying the decreasing term insurance principle.

If the mortgage can be prepaid, provision is usually made for a lump-sum payment to either the insured's estate or his widow. This is predicated on the assumption that it takes less insurance to liquidate the mortgage with a single-sum payment than to provide a monthly income equal to the regular monthly payments. If the mortgage has no prepayment privilege or can be prepaid only with a heavy penalty, an income settlement should be arranged to provide funds in the amount and with the frequency required for the mortgage payments. Either the installment time or the installment amount option would be satisfactory, although the time option would be difficult to use if elected before the death of the insured.

Emergency Fund. Perhaps the most satisfactory arrangement for funds being held for emergency needs is the interest option, with a limited or an unlimited right of withdrawal. The widow would normally be the beneficiary. Another method of making emergency funds available is through the installment amount option with appropriate withdrawal privileges. Under this arrangement, a somewhat larger fund would be set aside than would be needed for the regular installments.

Educational Fund. As was indicated earlier, the installment amount option is ideally suited to the liquidation of proceeds intended to finance a college education or professional training. However, the interest option, with appropriate withdrawal privileges, could be used. The payments may be made directly to the student, to the educational institution on his behalf, or to an adult relative or friend.

Income Needs of the Family

Readjustment Income. The readjustment period is the interval of time—usually one to three years in duration—immediately following the insured's death, during which income is usually provided at or near the level enjoyed by the family during the insured's lifetime. Thereafter, the income drops down to a more realistic level.

Theoretically, the income for the readjustment period can be provided by means of the installment time option, the installment amount option, or the interest option with the right of withdrawal. If a step-down within the period is contemplated, which may be advisable if the dependency period income represents a drastic reduction, the amount option should be used. Some estate planners provide the same contractual income during the readjustment period as that of the dependency period, with the thought that the widow can use the withdrawal privilege to cushion the financial shock during the readjustment period.

Dependency Period Income. Broadly speaking, the dependency period extends from the date of the insured's death until the youngest child is self-sufficient or perhaps in college. In programming terminology, however, the dependency period is the interval between the end of the readjustment period and the self-sufficiency of the youngest child. The latter is usually assumed to occur at age eighteen, unless the child is mentally or physically handicapped.

In practice, it will frequently be found that all or a substantial portion of the income needs of this period are met by Social Security survivorship benefits, interest on proceeds being held for other purposes, and monthly payments under family income or family maintenance policies. The latter payments represent a combination of the interest option and the installment time option. Each payment is composed of interest on the proceeds of the underlying whole life policy and a prorata share of the term insurance proceeds which are being liquidated in accordance with the installment time option.

If the needs of this period are not fully met from the foregoing sources, additional income can be provided on the basis of either the time or the amount option. If, at the time the program is being set up, the youngest child is six years old and additional income of $100 per month is desired until the child is eighteen, it would appear to be a matter of indifference whether proceeds in the amount of $12,200 are to be set aside under an installment time option providing $100 per month for twelve years or whether the same sum is to be set aside under an installment amount option providing $100 per month as long as the proceeds hold out, which would be exactly twelve years if there were no withdrawals from the fund and no excess interest were credited to it. Under most circumstances, however, the installment amount option will prove to be more satisfactory.

Of greatest significance, perhaps, is the fact that the right of withdrawal can be granted in connection with the amount option, but not with the time option. In some cases, it may be unwise to give the beneficiary this privilege; but in general, it injects an element of flexibility into the settlement plan which is urgently needed, particularly with the prospect of continued inflationary pressures. Moreover, it should be recognized that moderate withdrawals will not necessarily shorten the period of income payments, since they may be offset in whole or in part by dividend accumulations and excess interest credits.

A second advantage of the amount option is that the potential amount of income does not increase automatically with the passage of time, as it does with the time option. If the time option specifies that a certain portion of the proceeds is to be liquidated at a uniform monthly rate over the period from the insured's death to the youngest child's attainment of age eighteen, the potential monthly income increases each month or year (if the company limits the payment period to multiples of twelve months) that the insured lives after establishing his settlement plan, provided additional children are not born. If the projected income is inadequate or at a minimum level, this is not an unfavorable development. In many cases, however, the proceeds that would have been preserved through adherence to a predetermined monthly income are needed to provide an adequate income to the widow after the children have become self-supporting. The point here is not that the amount option is necessarily to be preferred over the time option, but only that the characteristics of the two options should be recognized and made to serve the objectives of the insured.

A final argument in favor of the amount option in this situation is that provision can be made for increasing the size of the monthly payments to offset the loss of income from Social Security as each child reaches age eighteen. This could be done with the time option also, but it would be extremely cumbersome.

Life Income for Widow. In programming life insurance, it is necessary to break this basic need down into two periods: that running from the eighteenth birthday of the youngest child to the widow's age sixty-two and that extending beyond the widow's age sixty-two. The necessity for this breakdown stems from the fact that the widow's income from Social Security terminates when the youngest child reaches age eighteen (unless the child is totally disabled or is a full-time student) and does not resume until the widow reaches age sixty-two. (A permanently reduced benefit is available at age sixty.) This period is usually designated as the "Social Security gap" or the "blackout period."

The income for the blackout period can be provided in a number of ways, depending somewhat upon the nature of the provisions made for the succeeding period. If no proceeds are to be placed under the life income option until the widow reaches age sixty-two, the interest on the proceeds to be used for that purpose will be available for the blackout period. It will have to be supplemented by income from the liquidation of proceeds under either the time or the amount option. If, on the other hand, the life income option is made operative upon the death of the insured or upon termination of the Social Security survivorship benefits, there will be no interest income during the blackout period from proceeds held under the interest option, but a substantial portion of the income need will be met through the life income option. It is likely, however, that the life income option would have to be supplemented by the time or amount option during the blackout period; otherwise, the income during that period would be smaller than it would be after age sixty-two.

The considerations that argued for the amount option in connection with the dependency period are not applicable to the blackout period, at least not to the same extent. Once the children are grown and on their own, the need for the withdrawal privilege is greatly diminished, although it may still be desirable. The length of the blackout period is fixed unless the youngest child dies before age eighteen, so there is no problem of adjusting the proceeds to a shrinking period. Finally, there is no need to adjust the income during the period to offset the loss of other income sources, as there is during the dependency period. Hence, the installment time option is entirely appropriate for the blackout period, if the withdrawal privilege is not thought to be essential. Regardless of which option is chosen, the widow should be given the privilege of accelerating the effective date of the option if the youngest child dies before age eighteen and the widow's income from Social Security terminates earlier than anticipated.

In most cases, income to the widow after the blackout period will be provided by Social Security benefits and payments under a life income option. At this stage in life, the widow needs the assurance of a definite income for the remainder of her life, and the only practical way of providing that assurance is through the use of a life income option. The interest option can be used if a large sum of insurance is available and the insured desires to preserve the principal for the benefit of contingent beneficiaries. An option other than a life income would also be used if the primary beneficiary is in very poor health or is very old. Otherwise, some form of life income option should always be used to provide a life income to the beneficiary in the later stages of life.

The widow's need for a life income, viewed as a whole and not arbitrarily broken down into the periods when Social Security benefits are and are not available, can be met through two general approaches, each of which has its advocates. The first approach is to start the life income option at the beginning of the blackout period, or even at the insured's death, while the second approach is to defer the life income option until the Social Security payments are resumed at the widow's age sixty-two.

Under the first approach, the amount of monthly income provided under the life income option is that needed to supplement the Social Security benefits payable upon the widow's attainment of age sixty-two. The income will have to be supplemented during the blackout period by sums payable under either the time or the amount option. To minimize the possibility of forfeiture, an annuity form embodying a substantial refund feature is used. Under this procedure, the amount of insurance needed at 3 per cent interest to provide a life income of $250 per month to a female beneficiary aged forty-two, with payments guaranteed for twenty years, is $69,832, or $70,000.

Under the second approach, proceeds needed to supplement the widow's Social Security benefits at age sixty-two are held under the interest option until the widow reaches that age, at which time they are placed under a life income option, with or without a refund feature, depending upon the need for income and the desire to provide benefits to contingent beneficiaries. The interest on the proceeds before the life income option becomes operative is applied toward the income needs of the preceding periods—namely, the readjustment, dependency, and blackout periods. These interest payments will have to be supplemented by benefits payable under the time or amount option, particularly during the blackout period. To provide a life income of $250 a month to a female beneficiary aged forty-two under this procedure would require $71,700. The manner in which it would be accomplished is demonstrated below:

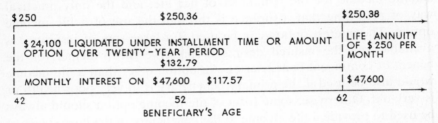

A straight life annuity was used in order to make the arrangements comparable (under the first approach, the refund feature would have expired at age sixty-two); but in an actual case, an annuity form with a refund feature—perhaps 120 guaranteed installments—would undoubtedly have been used. The second approach requires $1,700 more insurance, but the $47,600 set aside for the life income option is protected against forfeiture in the event that the beneficiary should die before reaching age sixty-two. Under the first approach, the portion of the proceeds allocated to the deferred life annuity, approximately 35 per cent of the total, would be forfeited if the beneficiary should fail to survive the twenty-year period. From the standpoint of the first approach, the $1,700 difference in principal needed represents the benefit of survivorship; while for the second approach, it represents the premium paid to avoid the possibility of any forfeiture prior to the beneficiary's attainment of age sixty-two.

ILLUSTRATION OF PROGRAMMING PRINCIPLES

The manner in which the various settlement options can be combined to meet basic family income needs is illustrated in Figure 19.

The techniques demonstrated here are those used in programming an actual life insurance estate, although additional factors must be taken into account in an actual case.

Figure 19 illustrates the programming of the family income needs of an insured who has a wife aged thirty, a son aged six, and a daughter aged one. The insured has been able to devote approximately $700 per month to the maintenance and support of his family. This relatively comfortable standard of living is reflected in the income objectives set by the insured for the family after his death. These

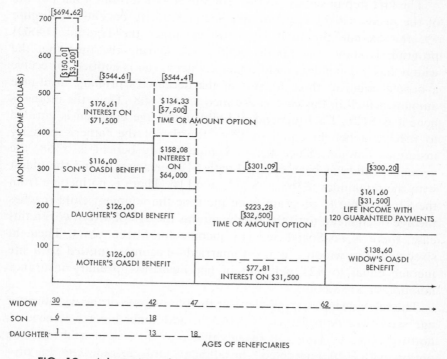

FIG. 19. Adaptation of settlement options to family income needs.

objectives are: $700 per month for the first two years following the insured's death, $550 per month for the next fifteen years (i.e., until the youngest child reaches age eighteen), and $300 a month thereafter as long as the widow lives. It is assumed that the insured is fully covered under the Federal OASDI program for the maximum benefits provided by the 1965 amendment to the Social Security Act.[2] No recognition is given to lump-sum and special needs, the retirement

[2] It will be many years, however, before any case will qualify for maximum benefits.

needs of the insured, the plans of insurance to be used, or other resources of the insured, all of which must be taken into account in an actual case.

In programming the income needs of a family, an assumption must be made as to when the needs commence. The only safe assumption is that the needs begin immediately, since the insured might die at any time. Thus, it is always assumed that the insured dies immediately after the program has been established. That is the assumption in this case.

The first step in setting up the program is to determine what portion of the needs will be met through Social Security benefits. In Figure 19, the income that will be provided under the Federal OASDI program is shown within the solid lines. During the time that the widow has a dependent child under eighteen, she is entitled to receive a benefit equal to three fourths of the deceased's primary insurance amount, which in this case is assumed to be $168. Thus, the mother's benefit is $126. Each dependent child under age eighteen is entitled to receive a benefit equal to three fourths of the father's primary insurance amount. Since the maximum family benefit is $368, the youngest child has been credited with $126 per month and the oldest with the remainder, $368 — $252, or $116. There is no income from the Social Security program from the time the youngest child reaches the age of eighteen until the widow attains the age of sixty-two. In this case, there is no Social Security income for fifteen years. Then, at sixty-two, the widow—if not remarried—becomes entitled to a life income equal to 82½ per cent of her husband's primary insurance amount, or $138.60.

The second step is to supplement the life income of the widow after age sixty-two. Approximately $162 of additional income is needed; and reference to Table 38 reveals that on the basis of a life income option with 120 guaranteed installments, this income can be produced by $31,500 of insurance. The exact income from $31,500 is $161.60 (31×$5.13), as can be determined by reference to Table 39. Since the insured is assumed to die immediately and the life income option is not to become operative until the widow is sixty-two, the $31,500 is placed under the interest option and produces a monthly income of $77.81 ($2.47 per $1,000) for the next thirty-two years. It supplies a portion of the income for the readjustment period, the dependency period, and the blackout period.

The third step is to fill in the income for the blackout period.

Interest on the $31,500 being held for the life income option produces $77.81 per month, but roughly $222 per month more is needed. Reference to Table 35 reveals that $32,314 (22.2 units of $10 a month income) is needed to provide exactly $222 per month for fifteen years. Table 34 then indicates that $32,500 (the closest multiple of $500) will produce a monthly income of $223.28 for fifteen years if applied under the installment time option. However, the $32,500 may actually be liquidated under the installment amount option, even though the amount of principal required was determined by reference to the installment time option.

The $32,500 of proceeds needed for the blackout period is placed under the interest option for the first seventeen years and produces income for the readjustment and dependency periods. Under the assumptions used in this case, the dependency period requirements would be met in full from Social Security benefits and interest on proceeds being held for later liquidation except for the deficit created by the termination of the son's Social Security benefits. This loss is offset by the liquidation of $7,500 of proceeds over the five-year period, with either the time or the amount option being utilized. These proceeds will be held under the interest option for the first twelve years, the total income from interest alone during that period being $176.61 per month. The additional income of $150 per month desired for the readjustment period can be provided by $3,500 placed under either the time or the amount option.

The actual income available during each of the periods is shown in brackets. It is neither possible nor essential to provide the exact amount of income projected for each period. Excess interest and withdrawals will affect the income in any event. The total amount of insurance needed to meet this portion of the insured's program is $75,000. Additional sums would be needed for estate clearance, mortgage redemption, education of the children, and an emergency fund. The retirement needs of the insured could in all likelihood be met from the cash value of a portion of the insurance and hence would not impose an additional burden. In other words, if the insured lives, insurance which was designed to provide income to his family can be used for the old-age maintenance of himself and his wife.

If the probabilities of death and remarriage are ignored, the present value of the Social Security benefits payable during the dependency period alone, the so-called "survivorship benefits," is approximately $55,000. Then, if the widow lives to age sixty-two and remains unmarried, she will become entitled to additional benefits having a present value at that time of $27,000.

The technique of working backwards from the period farthest in the future to the one closest at hand is dictated by the necessity of accounting on a current basis for interest payable on proceeds being held for later liquidation. The periods could be considered in normal sequence if interest could be accumulated. It should not be inferred from this technique that greater importance is attached to the needs of the more remote periods. Actually, a higher priority is normally assigned to the needs which will arise first in point of time. If an inadequate amount of insurance is available, it might all be applied to the readjustment and dependency periods, nothing being allocated to the life income of the widow. If the financial circumstances of the insured later improve, he can purchase additional insurance for the support of his widow in her middle and old age.

The procedure illustrated in Figure 19 is only a graphic portrayal of the income needs of a family and how they can be met through life insurance and Social Security. In order that the objectives may be realized, an adequate amount of insurance must be made available, appropriate settlement options must be elected, and settlement agreements embodying the desired pattern of distribution must be drawn up. The insurance must be made available during the insured's lifetime, of course; but whether the settlement agreement is made effective then, depends upon the wishes of the insured and the estate planning philosophy of the life underwriter. Some life underwriters prefer to follow through with the settlement agreement; but others—mindful of the many changes in circumstances that may occur before the insured dies, and fearful that suitable modifications in the agreement might not be made—recommend that the program, with suitable modifications, be given substance after the insured's death in agreements between the companies involved and the beneficiary.

Part Seven

SPECIAL FORMS OF
LIFE INSURANCE

CHAPTER XXXV

Group
Life
Insurance

GROUP life insurance is a plan of insurance which provides coverage to a number of persons under one contract. It is one of three broad branches of life insurance, the other two being *ordinary* and *industrial*. It is the youngest of the three branches, the first group life plan having been established in 1912.[1] It is also the fastest growing. As of the end of 1965, there were approximately 230,000 plans of group life insurance in operation, and providing over $300 billion of protection.

GENERAL CHARACTERISTICS

Group life insurance possesses a number of distinctive characteristics. Perhaps the most distinctive is the one which has already been mentioned—namely, coverage of more than one person under one contract, with the insurance on each life being independent of that on the other lives. This latter condition distinguishes group life insurance from joint-life insurance, which also covers more than one life under the same contract, but the amount of protection is the same irrespective of the number of lives covered. The number of lives covered under a group life plan ranges from two or more to the millions, the Federal Employees Group Life Insurance Plan being an example of the latter.

---

[1] This was the plan of Montgomery Ward and Company. There were two earlier plans, one written in 1905, which had some of the characteristics of group life insurance, but the Montgomery Ward plan is generally considered to have marked the beginning of true group life insurance.

A second characteristic of group life insurance is that, in general, it is made available to the participating employees without a medical examination or other evidence of insurability. Under certain well-defined circumstances, where there is possibility of individual selection against the insurer, a particular employee may have to present evidence of insurability; but the rationale of group life insurance calls for the underwriting of the group as a whole, rather than the individual members of the group. This has significant implications, which are reflected in a number of statutory and company underwriting rules.

A third characteristic of group life insurance is that it provides low-cost protection. There are two basic reasons for this fact. In the first place, the protection is provided on a temporary basis, no attempt being made to accumulate reserves to meet a contingency converging into a certainty. In other words, the coverage is provided through term insurance. (Exceptions to this practice will be discussed later.) The mortality cost of the term insurance is kept within manageable bounds through the flow of persons, predominantly at the younger ages, into the group. In the second place, mass distribution and mass administration methods are used, affording economies not available under ordinary and industrial insurance.

A fourth characteristic of group life insurance is that, except for the smallest cases, the ultimate cost of a plan is greatly influenced by the mortality among the persons covered by the plan, as well as the expenses incurred in connection with the plan. That is to say, the premiums paid under a group life plan are subject to experience rating. If the plan is large, its cost may be determined entirely by its own experience. The experience of smaller plans is pooled to some degree; but with the exception of the smallest cases the experience of the plan itself has a direct bearing on its premium cost.

A fifth—and final—feature of group life insurance is its favorable persistency rate. Group life insurance is usually installed for a sound business reason and is not likely to be discontinued except in the face of the most pressing financial problems.

GENERAL PRINCIPLES

Since group life insurance is written without evidence of insurability on the part of the individual participants, certain safeguards must be observed if a satisfactory experience is to be obtained. The most important of these safeguards are discussed below.

Insurance Incidental to the Group

The group to be covered by insurance should be formed and maintained for a purpose other than that of obtaining low-cost insurance. Otherwise, there is little doubt that the group will attract an undue proportion of undesirable risks, and difficulty will be experienced in retaining those desirable risks that do join the plan. Furthermore, administration of the plan is likely to be loose and inefficient. The insurance feature should be no more than an incidental benefit of membership in the group.

Flow of Persons through Group

There should be a flow of young, healthy lives into the group. Otherwise, the average age of the group will increase, and the average cost of the insurance per $1,000 will likewise climb. This is especially important when the insurance is on the term basis.

Automatic Determination of Benefits

The amount of protection to be enjoyed by each participant should be determined by a method which precludes individual selection. That is, the participants should not be permitted to choose how much insurance shall be placed on their lives. If the amount of insurance were a matter of individual choice, there would be a tendency for the impaired risks to elect a disproportionately large amount of insurance. This would, of course, increase the average cost of the insurance and could lead to termination of the plan.

Minimum Participation by the Group

Since the group underwriting process does not screen out individual impaired risks, safeguards must be established to produce a normal distribution of risks and to avoid the inclusion of an undue proportion of insurance upon unhealthy lives. It has been found that an average spread of risks can be obtained only if a large proportion of those eligible to participate in the plan actually do participate. Ideally, there should be 100 per cent participation. However, when the participants are required to pay a portion of the cost of the plan, participation must be on an optional basis, and 100 per cent enrollment under such circumstances is largely unattainable. Hence, the companies have generally been willing to write a contributory plan with a minimum participation of 75 per cent. In most states they are not permitted by law to go lower than that for employer-employee contracts. When the plan is noncontributory, 100 per cent participation of eligible persons is required.

Third-Party Sharing of Cost

A portion of the cost of a group life plan should be borne by some party other than the participants in the plan. This tends to improve participation by making the plan more attractive to the individual; it permits a stable rate of contribution from the participants, fluctuations in cost being absorbed in the contribution of the third party; and it gives the third party, who is generally the administering agency, an incentive to make the plan operate along sound lines.

Third-party sharing of the cost is especially important when the coverage is being provided on a yearly renewable term insurance basis, which is the dominant form. If the insured lives contribute on the basis of their attained age, the tendency of the cost to spiral as the years go by will cause a disproportionate number of healthy persons to withdraw from the plan unless a third party—such as the employer—absorbs a portion of the cost. The same tendency will be present if the insured lives bear the entire cost by means of a flat contribution per $1,000 of coverage, irrespective of differences in age. Under such a scheme, the younger members pay more than their share of the cost, and the older members pay less than their share. Under such circumstances, the younger members will eventually realize that they can purchase individual insurance on a more favorable basis and will gradually withdraw from the plan. This will, of course, exert an upward pressure on the average age of the remaining members, producing constantly accelerating costs. The inevitable outcome is termination of the plan. As a minimum, the third party should bear such portion of the total cost of the plan as will permit a contributing member to obtain coverage under the plan on at least as favorable a basis as he can purchase it individually.

Simplicity and Efficiency of Administration

There must be a single administrative organization able and willing to act on behalf of the insured group. The plan itself should be designed to minimize administrative procedures and still retain proper underwriting controls.

If the plan is contributory, there must be a reasonably simple method, such as payroll deduction, by which the master policyholder can collect contributions. An automatic method is essential from both an administrative and an underwriting standpoint. To have to collect contributions on an individual, non-automatic basis on each premium due date would impose an intolerable burden on the administrative agency—normally, an employer. The underwriting significance of an automatic method of collecting contributions is grounded in human nature. It is quite certain that the healthy members will be more inclined to remain in the plan if their contributions are automatically made on their behalf than if they had to take the initiative in remitting their contribution on each due date. Furthermore, once a member has authorized a payroll deduction, it requires some effort to withdraw the authorization. It is assumed, of course, that the impaired lives will remain in the plan regardless of how their contribution is remitted.

There are other aspects of administration which have an impact on participation and, hence, adverse selection. Various forms—such as those dealing with change of beneficiary, change of name, and increases in amount of insurance—must be submitted from time to time. These administrative details are handled by the employer, or other administering agency, with a minimum of effort on the part of the employee. Moreover, the assumption of these administrative responsibilities by the employer reduces the cost of the plan.

STATE REGULATION OF GROUP LIFE INSURANCE

As one of the three branches of the life insurance business, group life insurance is subject to the general rules and standards imposed by state regulatory authorities. In addition, it is subject to special regulation in three important areas: "definition" of group life insurance, standard policy provisions, and rates.

Standard Definitions

Since group life insurance represents a departure from many of the fundamental precepts of ordinary life insurance, the state supervisory authorities, from the beginning, have felt it necessary to define the functions and limit the scope of group insurance. To some extent, they have acted in response to pressure from life underwriter associations, which have felt that group insurance is an encroachment on the natural markets of the individual life underwriter. These associations have been primarily interested in limiting the groups to whom the insurance can be offered and the amount of insurance made available to any one participant.

The earliest attempt to delineate the boundaries of group life insurance was the so-called "standard definition" promulgated by the National Convention (now Association) of Insurance Commissioners in 1917. This definition was short and simple, and is reproduced in its entirety herewith:

Group life insurance is that form of life insurance covering not less than fifty employees with or without medical examination, written under a policy issued to the employer, the premium on which is to be paid by the employer or by the employer and employees jointly, and insuring only all of his employees, or all of any class or classes thereof determined by conditions pertaining to the employment, for amounts of insurance based upon some plan which will preclude individual selection, for the benefit of persons other than the employer; provided, however, that when the premium is to be paid by the employer and employee jointly and the benefits of the policy are offered to all eligible employees, not less than seventy-five per cent of such employees may be so insured.[2]

It will be noted that this definition limited the coverage to groups of *fifty* or more *employees of a common employer* and imposed no limit as to the amount of insurance that could be placed on any one life, provided the amount was determined by a method which precluded individual selection.

This definition was enacted into law by New York State in 1918 and was subsequently adopted by a number of other states, in either its pure or its modified form. Group life insurance, in general, was written within the framework of this definition for the next quarter century. Finally, in 1946, the National Association of Insurance Commissioners, after eighteen months of study, adopted a new definition, which extended the coverage to several types of groups not composed of employees of a common employer, reduced the minimum size of the group, imposed a limit on the amount of insurance which could be placed on any one life, and made other changes. This definition was incorporated in a model group life bill which also contained a recommended set of policy provisions. This so-called "NAIC Model Group Life Bill" has been revised from time to time since 1946; the latest version is presented in its entirety in Appendix F. This model legislation, in one version or the other, has been adopted

---

[2] *Proceedings of the National Convention of Insurance Commissioners* (1918), p. 28.

in verbatim form by several states and has served as the basis for group life legislation in many other states. The essential provisions of the model law will be discussed in context in the remaining sections of this chapter.

Standard Provisions

The original definition of group life insurance was accompanied by a set of six standard provisions recommended to the states for their adoption. The 1946 definition was also supplemented by standard policy provisions deemed appropriate for the expanded scope of the definition. Some of the standard provisions are comparable to those prescribed for ordinary policy forms, while others are directed specifically at group insurance. The standard provisions currently being used are illustrated in the Model Group Life Bill which is shown in Appendix F.

The policy forms used in group insurance must be approved by the state regulatory bodies in accordance with the same procedures prescribed for ordinary insurance. The supervisory authorities will refuse to approve policy language or policy forms which they consider to be discriminatory, ambiguous, or otherwise objectionable. As a general rule, when a group life insurance contract is issued to an organization having participants in more than one state, the law of the state in which the contract is issued will apply.

Rates

In ordinary insurance, the states attempt to assure rate adequacy through minimum reserve requirements. Such a technique is clearly ineffectual in connection with yearly renewable term insurance, the basis on which most group insurance is written, since no policy reserves are required. Hence, in an effort to protect the public from inadequate and unfairly discriminatory rates, several states prescribe a minimum schedule of rates which must be observed in the first year of a group term insurance contract. The company cannot charge less than the minimum scale in the first year, but it may charge more provided no discrimination results. There is no rate regulation in the second and subsequent years, and even the first-year premium can be adjusted retroactively on the basis of the first-year experience.

There is no state prescribed minimum premium requirement for the permanent forms of group life insurance, although the company's rate schedule must be filed with the supervisory authorities.

BASIC FEATURES[3]

Coverage

Eligible Groups. As was pointed out earlier, the original definition of group insurance restricted the coverage to the employees of a single employer. The 1946 definition extended the permissible scope of the coverage by authorizing the issue of group insurance contracts to (1) the trustees of a fund established by two or more employers, two or more labor unions, or one or more employers and one or more labor unions; (2) a labor union for the benefit of the union members; and (3) a creditor to insure the lives of his debtors whose indebtedness is repayable in installments.[4] These are important extensions and have accounted for a substantial volume of group insurance. As a matter of fact, group creditor life insurance is the fastest growing segment of the group field; and as of the end of 1965, there were 59,000 such contracts, covering 56 million debtors with $49 billion of insurance. The multiple-employer plans also cover a large number of persons with a significant volume of insurance.

The laws of many states permit the issue of group insurance to groups not falling within the foregoing categories. Gregg lists *eighteen* additional groups which are recognized in one or more states. Among the groups recognized in many states are the dependents of employees covered under a group plan.

Minimum Number of Lives. The minimum number of lives thought to be essential to the prudent underwriting of group life insurance has declined over the years. The minimum number of lives required for the early group contracts—a self-imposed restriction— was one hundred. By the time the original standard definition was evolved, only five years later, the generally acceptable minimum had dropped to fifty lives, and that was the minimum specified in the definition. The 1946 definition reduced the minimum to twenty-five lives, which has since been reduced to ten lives for groups made up of employees of a single employer. No state now requires more than ten lives, and ten states (Alabama, Alaska, Delaware, Mississippi, Mis-

---

[3] For a comprehensive treatment of the topics discussed in this section, see Davis W. Gregg, *Group Life Insurance* (Rev. ed.; Homewood, Ill.: Richard D. Irwin, Inc., 1957), pp. 21–64. This volume provides excellent coverage of virtually every phase of group life insurance.

[4] As a matter of fact, many states, prior to 1946, permitted the writing of group insurance on groups not composed of the employees of a single employer.

souri, North Dakota, Rhode Island, South Dakota, Tennessee, Wyoming) prescribe no minimum. All group insurers are willing to underwrite groups as small as ten lives, but many will accept groups smaller than that only on the basis of a special contract and special underwriting rules.

The Model Group Life Bill establishes higher requirements for groups not composed of employees of a common employer. Groups composed of employees of more than one employer or more than one labor union must have a minimum of one hundred lives, with no fewer than five in each employer unit. A labor union plan must cover a minimum of twenty-five lives, while a creditor plan must have a minimum of one hundred new entrants per year. Employer trade association plans must contain a minimum of six hundred lives.

The purpose of a minimum-lives requirement is to minimize adverse selection and to reduce the expense rate. The greater the number of persons in the group, the smaller the possibility that the plan was established to provide protection to persons with impaired health, and the greater the chances that the group will contain a normal distribution of healthy and impaired lives.

The spreading of expenses is an important consideration. One of the appeals of group life insurance is the relatively low expense rate, but the rate can be unattractively high if the cost of establishing and maintaining a group plan is not spread over a reasonably large premium volume.

Minimum Proportion of Group. From an underwriting standpoint, all persons eligible to participate in a group plan should be enrolled. Persons who realize they have a health impairment will almost certainly elect to participate, so the persons in good health must be brought into the plan to achieve a proper balance among the risks. Moreover, the more persons enrolled in the plan, the lower the expense rate is likely to be.

Hence, it is not surprising that the standard definitions of 1917 and 1946, and all state statutes directed at group insurance, require that all eligible persons be covered if the plan is noncontributory. If the plan is contributory, at least 75 per cent of the eligibles must be covered. These requirements are enforced by the companies even in states that do not have group insurance statutes.

Eligibility Requirements. In general, group life insurance is intended to provide protection to all regular, full-time employees of a particular organization, or to all such employees falling within a designated classification or classifications. Generally speaking, the employer can set up any classifications that will not operate adversely against the insurance company, except that in some states, classifications cannot be based on age, sex, or race. Part-time and seasonal workers are almost universally excluded.

If a plan is noncontributory, coverage for all eligible employees becomes effective on the date the plan goes into operation, subject to the actively-at-work requirement discussed below. If the plan is contributory, coverage does not become effective with respect to a particular employee until he submits a written request to participate in the plan and authorizes the employer to make the necessary payroll deductions to cover the employee's share of the cost.

Persons hired after the plan goes into effect must be employed a specified period of time before they become eligible to participate in the plan. This is known as the *probationary period,* and it ranges in length from one to six months in the case of group term insurance and up to five years in the case of the permanent forms. A probationary period is usually required by the insurance company as an underwriting precaution and is designed to weed out transient workers, who are generally regarded as marginal, and those in poor health at the time they are hired. If the hiring practice of the employer calls for the passing of a physical examination, the insurer is usually willing to accept a probationary period of minimum length. Administratively, a probationary period serves the purpose of eliminating insurance records on employees who do not remain with the employer long enough to achieve a permanent status.

Normally, insurance on an individual employee will become effective only if he is actively at work on the date he is eligible to participate. This rule applies to employees with the firm at the inception of the plan, as well as to those hired thereafter. It also applies to increases in the amount of insurance as the employee advances from one classification to another. If the employee is not actively at work on the date his coverage is scheduled to become effective, it will become effective only upon his return to active employment.

Like the probationary period, this requirement is imposed for underwriting reasons. An employee must enjoy a minimum state of healthfulness to be actively working at his usual place of employment. The active-work rule automatically eliminates those persons who are ill on the date the coverage is to become effective and never regain their health. For large groups, particularly those collectively bargained, the requirement is sometimes waived, especially at the inception of the plan.

The active-work rule is obviously inappropriate for the coverage of dependents. The same objective is achieved by a requirement that the dependent not be confined to a hospital on the date the coverage would otherwise become effective.

Duration of Coverage. Once the insurance becomes effective for a particular employee, the protection continues as long as he remains in the service of the employer. Temporary breaks in service—such as those arising from sickness, layoffs, and leaves of absence—will not terminate the coverage, so long as premium payments are continued. The master contract usually gives the employer the right to continue premium payments for employees temporarily off the job, provided he does so on a basis which precludes individual selection. Upon permanent termination of service, the coverage continues for thirty-one days beyond the date of termination. During this temporary extension of coverage, the employee has an opportunity to replace the expiring protection with individual insurance, to obtain employment with another firm having group insurance, or to convert the expiring term insurance to a permanent form of insurance.

1. *Conversion Privilege.* The conversion privilege is an important feature of the group term insurance contract. It permits a covered employee to obtain permanent protection without regard to his insurability upon termination of his service or upon termination of the master contract.

If the privilege arises because of termination of service, it must be exercised within thirty-one days after the termination of employment. The conversion becomes effective as of the end of such period, since the group policy automatically provides protection during the period. The employee is permitted to convert all or any portion of his term insurance to any form of insurance, other than term, currently being issued by the insurer. Many companies permit the permanent form to be preceded by a single-premium, one-year term insurance policy, this privilege being required by law in two states. Conversion is permitted only on an attained age basis.

If the coverage terminates through discontinuance of the plan itself rather than severance of employment, any employee who has been insured under the plan for a minimum of five years can convert the smaller of $2,000, or the amount of terminating insurance not replaced by another group policy with any insurer, within thirty-one days after the original group insurance is terminated. The right must be exercised within thirty-one days following discontinuance of the plan, with all other conditions being the same as those described above. The special limitations on the privilege—namely, the minimum period of service and the arbitrary ceiling on the amount of insurance which can be converted—are designed to protect the insurer against the adoption of a group plan by an uninsurable employer simply to take advantage of the conversion privilege.

The mortality on converted insurance has been extremely unfavorable. This is a natural result of the fact that the permanent insurance is made available without evidence of insurability. The picture is distorted somewhat, however, by the tendency of the field forces to replace terminating group insurance with new insurance, if the employee is insurable, since no commission is normally paid on permanent insurance issued in connection with the conversion privilege. The practical effect is that only uninsurable employees are likely to convert their term insurance. To protect themselves against the excessive mortality on the converted insurance, the companies levy a charge, through the dividend or experience account, of $60 to $75 for each $1,000 of insurance converted. This sum is transferred from the group department of the insurer to the ordinary department to cover the anticipated extra mortality on the policies issued by the latter department. This charge is borne by the employer through a reduction in his dividends.

2. *Continuance of Coverage in Event of Total Disability.* Group life insurance policies have traditionally offered some protection against the total disability hazard. The early contracts provided that the face of the policy would be payable, usually in installments, should the employee, while still in the service of the employer, become totally and permanently disabled, as defined in the policy, before attaining age sixty. This was the familiar *maturity* type of provision found in ordinary policies of that period. The experience with this provision during the depression of the early 1930's was so disastrous that it was removed from all new policies and, by agreement with the employers, from many old policies. Nevertheless, a substantial amount of group insurance with this type of clause is still outstanding.

From 1933 through 1937, group life insurance contracts either contained no protection against permanent and total disability or provided for payment of the face amount of insurance on the life of any employee who became permanently and totally disabled before age sixty-five and died within a specified period—usually, one year—after termination of employment, the disability having existed continuously after termination of employment. This provision is commonly referred to as the *extended death benefit* and, in effect, grants a waiver of premium for one year following termination of employment for reasons of disability.

Beginning in 1938, the extended death benefit clause was generally replaced with a provision calling for payment of the face amount of insurance on any employee who becomes permanently and totally disabled before age sixty and remains in that condition uninterruptedly until the time of his death, irrespective of the length of time that elapses between termination of employment and date of death. In effect, this is a *lifetime waiver-of-premium* benefit and is so identified in insurance literature. Most contracts require the employee to present proof annually that he is still totally disabled. The contracts of some companies stipulate that total and permanent disability will be presumed if the employee has suffered the entire and irrevocable loss of sight of both eyes or the loss of use of both feet, both hands, or one foot and one hand.

3. *Continuance of Coverage for Retired Employees.* There is increasing sentiment in favor of continuing a portion of an employee's group insurance coverage after he has retired. It is felt that, as a minimum, enough insurance should be continued to take care of the employee's last-illness and funeral expenses. Theoretically, the employee, upon retirement, could convert a sufficient amount of his group insurance to provide an estate clearance fund; but, as a practical matter, this is not feasible because of the size of the premiums that would be payable at the employee's attained age. For a number of reasons, including the retired employee's limited financial resources and the lack of a convenient method of collecting his contributions, it is generally agreed that the cost of continuing insurance protection for retired employees should be borne entirely by the employer.

There are three general approaches within the framework of group insurance which can be used to provide life insurance protection to retired employees. The simplest and most obvious approach is to continue a portion of the group term insurance for the retired employee, with the employer paying the entire premium on behalf of the employee. The plan may provide for continuation of a flat amount, a flat percentage of the insurance in force on the employee immediately prior to retirement, or a graded percentage of the insurance in force at retirement, decreasing each year until a minimum percentage is reached. The minimum percentage to be continued is generally considered to be 25 per cent and the maximum 50 per cent, unless the original amount of insurance was very modest.

The advantages of this approach are the low initial cost, the ease of administration, and the absence of income tax complications. (The premiums are deductible by the employer and nontaxable to the employee.) The chief disadvantage is the substantial accrued liability which reflects itself in constantly increasing costs until a stable balance has been achieved between active and retired lives. On the assumption that there will eventually be one retired employee for each eight active employees, it has been estimated that the cost of continuing 50 per cent of the insurance in force at the date of retirement for retired employees as a whole will ultimately constitute 74 per cent of the cost of providing protection to active lives.[5] If only 25 per cent of the protection is continued, the cost will be reduced proportionately. Furthermore, all of the additional cost falls on the employer.

In order to level out the cost of continuing term insurance for retired employees, some plans utilize a scheme of advance funding. Funds are accumulated with the insurance company in a special earmarked account, similar to the deposit administration arrangement used in the funding of pension plans, and premiums for retired employees are paid out of the account as they fall due. The account is normally built up through direct employer contributions, dividend and rate-adjustment refunds (which are indirect employer contributions), and compound interest. Employees generally do not contribute to the account. The employer has more flexibility in meeting the cost of insurance on retired lives under this method, and the employees have more assurance that protection will be available in retirement.

The second approach that can be used to provide protection to retired employees is for the employer to purchase a paid-up policy in the appropriate amount for each retired employee. Such policies are made available by the insurer without evidence of insurability or a conversion charge, since, by the terms of the agreement, they are purchased for all employees at retirement or within the period immediately preceding retirement. The purchase may be financed by a single premium at the time of retirement or through a series of annual installments prior to the employee's retirement. The latter method has

---

[5] Society of Actuaries, *Group Insurance* (Examinations Edition, mimeographed; Chicago, 1956), p. 50.

the effect of leveling out the cost and smoothing the fluctuations produced by irregular rates of retirement. The advantages of this approach lie in the absolute assurance to the employees that protection will be continued (no cash values are allowed), the ease of explanation, and the simplicity of administration, there being no need for the employer to maintain contact with the retired employees. The disadvantages of the approach are the taxability of the employer contributions (premium payments) to the employee in the year in which they are made, possible fluctuations in annual cost because of varying rates of retirement, and the increasing cost to the employer.

The third approach is through some form of permanent insurance financed throughout the active working period of the covered employee. Two basic arrangements have been evolved, one involving single premium funding and the other level premium funding. These plans are analyzed in detail at a later point in this chapter and will not be discussed here. Suffice it to say that these two arrangements were developed for the primary purpose of providing protection throughout the remaining lifetime of the covered employee and are generally considered to represent the ideal approach to the problem.

Benefits

The original—and still primary—purpose of group life insurance was to provide funds for the last-illness and funeral expenses of a deceased employee. It was designed to eliminate the need for "passing the hat" among the decedent's fellow employees, an act which usually brought forth a substantial contribution from the employer. In conformity with this elemental purpose, group life insurance contracts typically contain no exclusions, the benefits being payable in the event of death from any cause, occupational or nonoccupational. They do not even include the conventional suicide clause found in ordinary insurance contracts, which omission is justifiable in view of the fact that the insurance is not procured at the initiative of the employee who might be contemplating suicide. If the employee becomes permanently and totally disabled while a participant under the plan, his protection is continued for a limited or unlimited period of time, depending upon the type of disability provision incorporated in the contract. Furthermore, as was pointed out in the preceding section, all or a portion of the protection in effect at the date of retirement may be continued for the retired employee.

Most plans today undertake to provide more insurance than the bare minimum needed for last-illness and funeral expenses. They are designed to replace a portion of the earnings of the deceased employee which would have been devoted to the support of his dependents. Hence, an effort is generally made to establish schedules of insurance which will recognize, to some degree, the needs of the various employees. If the plan is contributory, the schedule must also take into account the employee's ability to pay. Whatever schedule is used, it must—under mandate of law, in most states—operate in such fashion as to prevent any particular employee from deciding how much insurance shall be placed on his life.

Determination of Amount of Insurance on Each Employee. In order to preclude individual selection, the employees to be covered under a group life plan are broken down into various classifications, and each employee in a particular classification receives the same amount of insurance as any other employee in that classification. Schedules are prepared, showing the amount of insurance per employee available to each classification. If an employee moves from one classification to another, the amount of his insurance is appropriately adjusted, although some plans provide that the amount shall not be adjusted *downward*.

Employee classifications for group insurance purposes may be based on one or a combination of three factors: earnings, position, and length of service. Some plans create no classifications, all employees receiving the same amount of insurance.

The most widely used basis for classification is earnings. A common practice is to provide insurance equal to one or two years' salary, to the nearest $500 or $1,000. As a rule, only the regular or base pay of the employee is considered, overtime pay and bonuses being excluded. The high esteem in which this basis of classification is held is largely attributable to the fact that it relates the amount of insurance to (1) the standard of living of the employee and hence to the needs of his family, (2) the ability of the employee to contribute toward the cost of the insurance, and (3) the value of the employee to the firm, to the extent that compensation is a measure of worth. The latter consideration is of particular significance when the plan is noncontributory.

Roughly analogous to the earnings basis of classification is that of position. This basis produces a relatively small number of classifications and has been rather popular when the employees of two or more employers are covered under one plan. A typical position schedule might appear as follows:

Position	Amount of Insurance
Officers and department heads	$15,000
Foremen and salesmen	10,000
All other employees	5,000

Inasmuch as there is a positive correlation between position and compensation, this method of allocating insurance achieves roughly the same results as the earnings basis. On the other hand, it introduces some administrative difficulties in establishing categories and assigning borderline cases.

Allocating insurance on the basis of service is identified with noncontributory plans. It rewards long service and is thought to reduce turnover. At least, it encourages permanence of service. This method recognizes neither need nor ability to pay. In fact, it provides the smallest amounts of insurance to the younger employees, who are likely to have the greatest family needs. This criticism can be leveled against all the bases of classification, for that matter. Under either a contributory or a noncontributory plan, a service schedule has a tendency to increase the average premium cost to the employer, since a constantly increasing percentage of the insurance is on the lives of older workers.

Plans providing the same amount of insurance to all participants are prominent in the field of collective bargaining, especially among multiple-employer groups. Wage rates in the bargaining unit are fairly uniform, so that this basis of allocation closely resembles a salary classification. In more heterogeneous groups, this method is generally unsatisfactory, since it gives no direct recognition to needs and ability to pay.

Minimum Amount of Insurance per Life. The law does not prescribe a minimum amount of insurance on each life covered under a plan of group insurance. Most companies, however, impose a minimum of $500. If the group is small and no other type of insurance is included, some companies require a minimum of $1,000 per life. The purpose of a minimum per life is to produce an aggregate volume of insurance under the plan large enough to permit a reasonable spreading of expenses.

Maximum Amount of Insurance per Life. The original definition of group life insurance contained no limitation on the amount of insurance that could be placed on any one life. For various reasons, including pressure from life underwriter associations, the drafters of the 1946 definition incorporated a limitation of $20,000 per life; this limitation, however, was not enacted into law by all states adhering substantially to the model law. In 1948, the model law was revised to make the limitation apply only to term insurance. After much discussion and debate by interested parties, the model law was again revised in 1953 to provide for a maximum of $40,000 of term insurance per life, subject to the proviso that any amount in excess of $20,000 must not exceed 150 per cent of the employee's annual salary. Under this provision, amounts of term insurance up to $20,000 can be made available irrespective of the salary of the employee. If more than that amount is to be made available, however, the insurance must not exceed the employee's salary by more than 50 per cent.[6] Thus, an employee can receive more than $20,000 of insurance only if his salary exceeds $13,333.33 per year. Employees earning between $13,333.33 and $26,666.66 can receive insurance in amounts up to $1\frac{1}{2}$ times their annual salary. Employees earning more than $26,666.66 must be granted less than $1\frac{1}{2}$ times their annual salary because of the absolute maximum of $40,000.

The foregoing is the limitation contained in the current model law, promulgated in 1956. As of the end of 1965, twenty-five states and the District of Columbia had adopted the limitation of $20,000/$40,000, seven states had limitations other than the foregoing, and eighteen states had no limitation.

Companies have their own underwriting limitations, entirely apart from any statutory limitations. They feel that some maximum limit is necessary in order to minimize anti-selection by the officers responsible for purchasing the group insurance, one or more of whom might be uninsurable or at least substandard, and to avoid undue fluctuations in the claims experience. It is especially important to guard against adverse selection in small groups. The maximum amount of insurance made available for any class of employee normally depends upon the total volume of insurance on the group. An example of one schedule currently in use is as follows:

---

[6] Another way of expressing the limitation is to say that the law permits insurance equal to $1\frac{1}{2}$ times the employee's annual compensation, subject to an overriding maximum of $40,000 and, if the contract so specifies, an overriding minimum of $20,000 per employee.

Total Insurance under Group Policy	Maximum Amount on One Life
Under $1,000,000	$10,000
$1,000,000 but less than $1,500,000	12,500
$1,500,000 but less than $2,000,000	15,000
$2,000,000 but less than $2,500,000	17,500
$2,500,000 but less than $5,000,000	20,000
$5,000,000 and over	Special consideration

Schedules of maximum insurance differ greatly from company to company, depending upon several factors. Many companies take into account not only the total amount of insurance in force, but also such factors as the number of employees insured, the amount of insurance on employees in lower classes, the relationship between the amount of insurance and annual earnings, the existence of other group coverages, and the presence or absence of any indications of anti-selection on behalf of key officers or employees. Virtually all companies will provide as much as $40,000 on one life under proper underwriting circumstances, and individual amounts as high as $100,000 are not unusual. Amounts in excess of the normal limits are sometimes made available for particular individuals upon evidence of insurability.

Financing

A group life insurance plan may be financed entirely by contributions from the employer, in which event it is known as a *noncontributory* plan; by contributions from both the employer and the covered employees, in which event it is known as a *contributory* plan; or, in exceptional circumstances, by contributions from the employees alone. The laws of most states require some contribution from the employer, for reasons previously explained; and even when not required by law, the companies, for underwriting reasons, will generally insist on employer participation in the financing of the plan. Only in the most exceptional cases will a company approve a plan in which the employees are to bear the entire cost.

A number of important advantages are claimed for noncontributory plans. Perhaps of greatest importance is the fact that all eligible employees are covered. This avoids the problems created by the death of an employee who, sometimes without the knowledge of his dependents, elected not to participate in the plan or not to continue his participation. Automatic coverage of all eligible employees also has underwriting implications. A second advantage is the greater simplicity and economy of administration. There is no necessity of soliciting participation in the plan, maintaining a payroll deduction system, and processing evidence-of-insurability forms for late applicants. A third advantage is that the entire cost of the plan is deductible for federal income tax purposes as an ordinary and necessary business expense; whereas under a contributory plan, employee contributions are not deductible. Moreover, the employer contributions are not taxable to the employees as additional compensation except on amounts of term insurance in excess of $50,000 per person[7] and except for group level premium permanent insurance under certain circumstances. Finally, the employer has greater control over the plan, except where a collective bargaining unit is involved.

On the other hand, certain advantages are claimed for contributory plans. The most apparent advantage is that a larger amount of insurance can be made available, assuming the contribution of the employer remains fixed. Thus, the employees are enabled to take advantage of the cost economies associated with group insurance, as well as the opportunity to acquire additional insurance without regard to their insurability. Of course, if the amount of insurance is fixed, employee contributions merely reduce the cost to the employer. A second advantage claimed for the contributory plan is that it permits the employer to channel his contributions to the employees with the greatest need for protection. This is based on the assumption that the employees with the greatest needs will elect to participate. In other words, it is a question of helping those who help themselves. A third alleged advantage is that the employees will have more interest in and greater appreciation of the plan if they make a direct contribution to it. Finally, contributions to the plan give the participating employees a right to express their desires concerning the features of the plan. This is an advantage only from the standpoint of the employees.

The rate at which a particular employee contributes to a group life plan depends upon the type of contract used. If a level premium type of permanent policy is used, the employee will usually contribute on the basis of his age at the time he entered the plan. If the paid-up whole life and decreasing term insurance arrangement is used, he may contribute on the basis of his entry age, or at a flat rate independent of

---

[7] The amount to be included in the gross income of an employee for employer purchased term insurance in excess of $50,000 is determined by multiplying the term insurance premium from a table published by the Internal Revenue Service times the amount of insurance in excess of $50,000 and subtracting any sums contributed by the employee toward the cost of his group insurance (not just the amount in excess of $50,000). The premiums in the Treasury table are set forth by five-year age brackets and are applied on an attained age basis.

his age. If yearly renewable term insurance is used, as it usually is, the employees typically contribute at a flat rate independent of age, although some plans grade the contribution by attained age classifications.

The traditional rate at which employees have contributed toward group term insurance is 60 cents per month per $1,000 of insurance. As a matter of fact, the law in New York and several other states limits the contribution of employees in a standard risk category to 60 cents per month per $1,000, or to such higher rates as will produce aggregate employee contributions not in excess of 75 per cent of the cost of the plan. The mortality experience among standard group plans has been such that employee contributions at the monthly rate specified in the law have exceeded 75 per cent of the cost of the plan. Thus, in effect, the absolute maximum employee contribution for many groups in those states is 60 cents per month per $1,000.

In view of the downward trend in mortality, some of the more recent plans have specified a lower rate of employee contributions than 60 cents per month, a rate of 50 cents being rather common. The rate is frequently reduced below 60 cents per month when the insured group contains a disproportionate percentage of female employees or employees in the lower age ranges.

CHAPTER XXXVI

Group

Life

Insurance

(Continued)

TYPES OF PLANS

Yearly Renewable Term Insurance

The basic plan under which group insurance is provided is yearly renewable term insurance. It is the only arrangement used for the coverage of employee dependents, borrowers from a lending institution, employees of the federal government, and miscellaneous groups, and is the dominant arrangement for the coverage of employees in general.

The yearly renewable term insurance employed in connection with group insurance has the same characteristics as that purchased by individuals. With respect to any particular employee covered by the plan, the protection expires at the end of each year but is automatically renewed for another year without evidence of insurability. The premium rate, however, increases each year, eventually reaching a very high level. Nevertheless, the employee, if he contributes at all, continues to contribute at the same rate, irrespective of his attained age. This is practicable only because the employer absorbs the portion of the cost in excess of the employee's annual contribution. The employer's contribution on behalf of any individual employee increases each year. His contribution on behalf of the entire group of covered employees, however, may remain stable or even decline, depending upon the benefit formula and the age composition of the group. Technically stated, the proportion in which the cost of a group term plan is borne by the employer and the employees as a group depends upon the average annual premium applicable to the plan.

The calculation of the average annual premium per $1,000 for the first year of group term insurance on a hypothetical group of employees is shown in Table 40 and the appended summaries. Only

TABLE 40

CALCULATION OF AVERAGE ANNUAL PREMIUM
PER $1,000 OF GROUP TERM INSURANCE

Attained Age	Number of Employees	Insurance per Employee	Total Amount of Insurance	Annual Premium per $1,000	Total Premiums
20...............	10	$ 5,000	$ 50,000	$ 2.75	$ 137.50
25...............	16	6,000	96,000	2.97	285.12
30...............	18	7,000	126,000	3.15	396.90
35...............	11	8,000	88,000	3.74	329.12
40...............	10	9,000	90,000	5.28	475.20
45...............	9	10,000	90,000	8.08	727.20
50...............	8	10,000	80,000	12.51	1,000.80
55...............	7	10,000	70,000	19.55	1,368.50
60...............	6	10,000	60,000	29.72	1,783.20
65...............	5	10,000	50,000	44.67	2,233.50
Total.........	100		$800,000		$8,737.04

Rate basis: 1960 C.S.G. Table and 3 per cent interest, with loading of 33⅓ per cent of net premium plus $2.40 per thousand on first $40,000 and subject to advance expense adjustment for larger cases.

Annual premium.....................................$8,737.04
Loading (40 × $2.40)............................... +96.00
                                                    $8,833.04
Reduction for advance expense allowance
  ($8,833.04 × .09)..................................... −794.97
Adjusted aggregate annual premium....................$8,038.07
Average annual premium per $1,000 ($8,038.07 ÷ 800)..... 10.05
Employee contribution per $1,000...................... 7.20
Employer contribution per $1,000...................... 2.85
Aggregate employer contribution per year...............$2,280.00

quinquennial ages are given, but the distribution of insurance over the range of ages is fairly realistic. Each employee is assumed to have insurance equal to two years' salary, subject to a maximum of $10,000. The annual premium rates are the minimum required by the state of New York for the first year of insurance.

The first step in deriving the average annual premium is to determine the total premium payable at each age represented by the group of covered employees. This series of values is obtained by multiplying the total amount of insurance at each age by the premium rate for that age. The sum of these values gives the aggregate annual premium which in the illustrative case, is $8,737.04. The aggregate annual premium must be adjusted, however, to reflect a flat $240 per $1,000 included in the loading of the annual premium is applicable to only the first $40,000 of insurance. This adjustment increases the aggregate premium by $96 to $8,833.04. An adjustment in the opposite direction is brought about by application of an advance expense allowance which in this size of case would amount to 9 per cent. This reduction of $794.97 produces an adjusted aggregate annual premium of $8,038.07. The average annual premium per $1,000 is then obtained by dividing $8,038.07 by the number of $1,000 units of insurance— namely, 800—which gives a result of $10.05. Since the annual contribution of each employee, irrespective of his attained age, is $7.20 per $1,000, the employer must bear the difference of $2.85. On the basis of the foregoing assumptions, the employer's aggregate contribution for the first year would be $2,280. However, if the experience under the plan is more favorable than that assumed, there will be a dividend or retroactive rate adjustment which will serve to reduce the employer's cost. Under some plans, the dividend will almost be equal to the employer's contribution and occasionally will exceed it. In the latter case, the excess of the dividend over the employer's contribution must, by law, be applied in some manner for the benefit of the employees.

The premium for a group insurance contract may be paid by the employer annually, semiannually, quarterly, or monthly; but all adjustments in the amount of insurance during the year, arising out of new entrants, terminations, and reclassifications, are made on the basis of the average annual premium, regardless of the actual ages of the employees involved. At the end of each policy year, a new average annual premium is computed, based upon the age distribution of the employees at that time. If premiums are paid more frequently than annually (they are usually paid monthly), the annual premium rates are increased to provide for the loss of interest and the additional expenses of collection.

It can be observed in the rate schedule in Table 40 that the younger employees contribute more under a contributing group term plan than the insurance company charges for their insurance. The minimum gross premium per $1,000 does not exceed $7.20 until the employee is aged forty-four and does not go beyond $6 per year, the other common basis of employee contributions, until the employee is forty-two. This is not considered objectionable, since, if the employee remains with the employer, his projection will eventually cost much more than he pays—$44.67 to $7.20 at age sixty-five, for example. Moreover, at no age does an employee pay much—if any—more than he would have to pay for the same protection purchased on an individual basis.

The contributions made by an employer toward a group term insurance plan are deductible as an ordinary and necessary expense for federal income tax purposes, and (except as provided by the Revenue Act of 1964, for amounts of insurance in excess of $50,000) are not taxable to the covered employees as additional compensation.

Under group term insurance, the employee generally enjoys protection only during such time as he is in the active service of the employer, plus the thirty-one day period immediately following termination of his service. In order to provide for continuation on a permanent basis of all or a portion of an employee's insurance protection, two other plans of group insurance have been developed.

Group Paid-Up Insurance

The basic principle underlying the group paid-up insurance plan is that employee contributions are applied to the purchase of paid-up units of whole life insurance, while employer contributions are applied to the purchase of term insurance. The amount of term insurance that will be purchased for an individual employee in any particular year is the difference between the cumulative sum of paid-up insurance and the total amount of insurance provided the employee under the plan's benefit formula. Since the cumulative amount of paid-up insurance increases each year, the amount of term insurance that will have to be purchased decreases each year, except for increases in the total amount of insurance to which the employee is entitled. For this reason, this arrangement is frequently referred to as "group paid-up and decreasing term insurance."

The structure of group paid-up insurance is illustrated in Figure 20. It is assumed that the employee enters the plan at age thirty and contributes at the rate of $1.30 per $1,000 per month, which is the standard rate of employee contribution under this type of plan, irrespective of the employee's age. In the first year of coverage, all of the insurance is on a term basis, since the employee's monthly contributions are not applied to the purchase of single-premium whole life

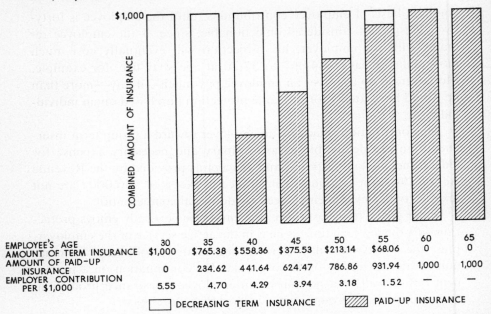

EMPLOYEE'S AGE	30	35	40	45	50	55	60	65
AMOUNT OF TERM INSURANCE	$1,000	$765.38	$558.36	$375.53	$213.14	$68.06	0	0
AMOUNT OF PAID-UP INSURANCE	0	234.62	441.64	624.47	786.86	931.94	1,000	1,000
EMPLOYER CONTRIBUTION PER $1,000	5.55	4.70	4.29	3.94	3.18	1.52	—	—

☐ DECREASING TERM INSURANCE   ▨ PAID-UP INSURANCE

FIG. 20.   Structure of group paid-up and reducing term insurance, basis of $1,000.

insurance until the end of the year. The first year's contributions will purchase $49.30 of paid-up insurance, so that during the second year, there is only $950.70 of term insurance. The second year's contributions will purchase additional paid-up insurance in the amount of $48.05, so that the amount of term insurance is only $902.65 during the third year. By the fifth year, the paid-up insurance has accumulated to $234.62, and the term insurance has declined to $765.38. This process continues until the full amount of insurance is paid up.

The employer's contributions on behalf of this particular employee remain stable over the years. In the first year, his contribution per $1,000 of total insurance is $3.15, since all the insurance is on a term basis. His contribution per $1,000 of combined insurance during the fifth, tenth, and fifteenth years is $2.86, $2.95, and $2.55, respectively.

The amount of paid-up insurance available at age sixty-five depends upon the employee's age of entry into the plan. If he enters at age twenty-five, the standard rate of contribution will cause all the insurance to be paid up at age forty-eight. If he is thirty-five when he enters the plan, $948 per $1,000 of original coverage will be paid up at sixty-five. Entry at forty-five will produce paid-up values of only $558. In order to produce roughly equivalent amounts of paid-up insurance at the age of retirement, regardless of the age at which the employee enters the plan, the employee contribution rate is sometimes graded by age of entry. A typical graded schedule of employee contributions is as follows:

Age of Issue	Monthly Contribution Rate
Under 30	$1.30
30 but under 40	1.60
40 but under 45	2.10
45 and over	2.75

There is no statutory limitation on the rate of employee contribution under group paid-up insurance.

The paid-up whole life insurance is made available to the employees at net rates, the premiums being based on the 1958 C.S.O. Table and 3 per cent interest. It contains liberal cash values which, however, are available only upon termination of employment. Upon termination of membership, the employee can continue the paid-up insurance in full force and effect or surrender it for cash. He is assured of recovering his contributions in full, even if he surrenders the insurance within the first year after it was issued. Upon termination, he can also convert all or any portion of the term insurance on his life, subject to the normal rules applicable to group term insurance.

Inasmuch as employer contributions are applied to the purchase of term insurance, they are accorded the same federal income tax status as contributions made toward conventional group term insurance.

The purpose of group paid-up insurance is to provide protection that will continue beyond the employee's period of service with the employer, particularly throughout the years of retirement. It is not essential that all of the insurance provided under a particular plan be of this nature. As a minimum, a sufficient amount of paid-up insurance should be available at retirement to take care of the normal estate clearance needs.

Level Premium Group Permanent Insurance

Another method of providing permanent protection within the framework of group insurance is to purchase level premium whole life insurance or endowment policies. Such a method is very similar to the paid-up insurance arrangement, the principal difference being that the premiums are not broken down as between whole life and term insurance. The premiums may be paid entirely by the employer or shared in any proportions by the employer and employees. The policies are identical to those available to individual purchasers, except as to such modifications as are dictated by the special circumstances surrounding group insurance. For example, cash values are not available while the employee remains a participant in the plan.

This arrangement lends itself to any kind of permanent policy, the choice depending upon the objective of the plan. If a minimum amount of paid-up insurance is desired at the normal retirement age, some form of limited-payment policy, such as life paid-up at age sixty-five, should be used, or a proportionately larger amount of ordinary life insurance the surrender value of which can be applied to the purchase of paid-up whole life insurance at retirement. If the objective is to accumulate values for the financing of retirement income benefits, a retirement income policy would be appropriate. In the latter case, the insurance serves the dual purpose of providing life insurance coverage during the employee's active working life and monthly income benefits after he retires. As a result, group permanent plans utilizing a retirement income policy or a whole life policy with an auxiliary accumulation fund of some sort are widely used for the funding of pension plans.

Group permanent plans have not been extensively used, except for pension purposes, since an adverse tax ruling was handed down by the federal tax authorities in 1950. This ruling states that employer contributions toward the cost of permanent insurance, not part of a qualified pension plan, shall be taxable currently to the employees as additional compensation, unless the insurance is forfeitable upon separation from service—which, of course, is not usually the case with a plan used solely for life insurance purposes. The ruling goes on to state that if the premium can be separated into portions representing term insurance and permanent insurance, employer contributions will be taxable only to the extent that they are applied to the purchase of permanent insurance. This is the basis for the favorable tax treatment of the group paid-up and decreasing term insurance plan, since the premium is separated into two distinct portions, with the employer contributing the *term* portion. It goes without saying that employer contributions to a group permanent plan are deductible as a business expense.

OTHER ASPECTS OF GROUP LIFE INSURANCE

Master Contract and Certificates

The contracting parties to the typical group policy are the insurance company and the employer. The contact provides insurance on the lives of the employees for the benefit of their dependents. Thus, while there are only two *contracting* parties, there are four interested parties.

The application for the insurance is submitted by the employer, without the signature or other evidence of consent of the employees to be covered. The form calls for identifying information about the employer, the benefit formula, the type of insurance desired, the premium payment period, the probationary and eligibility periods, and the extent of employee contributions, if any. Information about the characteristics and composition of the employee group is supplied in collateral documents.

The agreement between the insurance company and the employer is called the *master contract,* which contains all of the provisions of the plan. Each participating employee receives a certificate which states the amount of insurance for which he is covered, designates the person to receive the proceeds, and sets forth the principal provisions of the master contract pertaining to the rights and priviliges of the employee and his beneficiary. The certificate has no legal status, being neither a contract between the insurer and the employee nor one between the employer and the employee. A specimen group life certificate is reproduced in Appendix G.

The employee is permitted to designate the person to receive the proceeds of insurance on his life and can change the beneficiary at any time, without the knowledge or consent of the existing beneficiary, by filing written notice of the change with the employer. Some policies contain a so-called "facility-of-payment" clause, which is identified with industrial insurance and is described in the next chapter.[1] Virtually all group contracts prohibit assignment of his insurance by the employee.

Proceeds are normally payable in a lump sum; but in recognition of the substantial amounts of insurance now being provided under group contracts, many companies permit an installment settlement. The op-

---

[1] See p. 719.

tions most frequently made available are the installment time and installment amount options, but certain forms of life income option are also permitted by some companies.

Contrary to the practice under ordinary insurance, a misstatement of the age of an employee is usually corrected through an adjustment in the premium rather than an increase or a reduction in the amount of insurance. If the amount of insurance under the plan is determined by the employee's age, a misstatement which affects the amount of coverage must be corrected by an adjustment in the insurance.

Premiums and Dividends

As was stated earlier, New York and several other states prescribe minimum premiums for the first year of group term insurance. In New York, these minimum premiums are based on the Commissioners 1960 Standard Group Table and 3 per cent interest, with loading of 33⅓ per cent of the net premium plus $2.40 per $1,000 on the first $40,000 of insurance in the group. The flat charge of $2.40 per $1,000 is designed to take care of the fixed expenses incurred in the establishment of any plan of group insurance and hence was made to apply to only a limited portion of the total coverage. In recognition of the expense savings associated with the larger cases, advance rate discounts (called advance expense adjustment factors) are provided for plans developing a minimum annual premium volume of $2,400, the discount starting at 1 per cent and grading upward by size to a maximum of 20 per cent on an annual premium volume of $720,000 or more. This rate basis was promulgated in 1961; and the rates derived therefrom are known as the 1961 Standard Group Life Insurance Premium Rates to distinguish them from earlier rate bases, such as, the "T" and "U" rates promulgated in 1926 and 1950, respectively. New York's minimum premium law applies to all group term insurance written in any state by a company admitted to do business in New York.

There is no minimum-premium law applicable to the permanent forms of group insurance, since the reserve requirements to which they are subject are designed to assure adequacy. The group paid-up whole life insurance is usually written on the basis of the 1958 C.S.O. Table and 3 per cent interest, with no loading, while the accompanying term insurance is written on the basis of the 1961 standard group rates. Premiums for level premium group permanent insurance are normally computed on the same basis as those for comparable individual policies, except that the loading is reduced to reflect the economies of group administration.

Extra premiums may be charged if greater than normal mortality is expected because of the nature of the industrial hazard or the class of employees involved. In such event, the extra charge would be applicable to all covered employees or all members of a particular classification, rather than to selected individuals. Since 1941, the companies have been permitted to set their own scale of extra premiums; but if they do business in New York, they must file their schedule of extra premium rates with the Insurance Department of that state. When the plan is written at extra rates, employees may be required to contribute more than 60 cents per month per $1,000, subject to the limitations prescribed in applicable state laws.

Group term insurance rates are usually guaranteed for only one year at a time, although rate increases have been rare. Rate schedules for paid-up whole life insurance are usually guaranteed for five years from the inception of the plan, but the complementary term rates are guaranteed for only one year. Rate schedules for level premium group permanent insurance are generally guaranteed for an initial period of five years, with year-to-year guarantees applying thereafter. However, any rate increases would apply only to policies issued after the change.

The premiums paid under a group contract are subject to reduction for favorable experience. Mutual companies pay dividends, while stock companies grant retroactive rate adjustments. These rate reductions reflect both the experience of the group business of the insurer as a whole and that of the particular plan involved. Great emphasis is placed on the experience of the individual plan; and among the larger plans, the cost is determined almost entirely by the experience of the plan itself.

Dividends and retroactive rate reductions are virtually always credited to the employer. The right of the employer to receive the dividends payable under a group policy is well settled, although in most states, his right is limited to the amount of his contributions. If the dividends exceed the employer's contributions, he must apply the excess for the benefit of the employees in one of the ways prescribed by law.

Administration

The administration of a group insurance plan involves, as a minimum, (1) the maintenance of a record of the employees covered under the plan, showing for each employee his age, the date he entered the plan, the amount of insurance, the coverage on dependents, and the beneficiary; (2) the issuance of group certificates; (3) the compilation of a monthly summary of insurance in force for billing purposes; (4) the submission, adjudication, and payment of claims; and (5) the tabulation of total premiums and claims under the case for the annual review, redetermination of rates, and computation of dividends or rate adjustments.

The coverage and accounting functions may be performed at the home office of the insurance company, a procedure known as "insurer administration." On the other hand, an employer with qualified administrative personnel may perform the functions, a procedure referred to as "self-administration." While the size of the group is not necessarily controlling, self-administration is generally permitted for groups with two hundred or more employees. Appropriate recognition is given in the dividend or experience rating formulas for the administrative functions performed by the employer.

Self-administration of claims, while sometimes permitted, is not as prevalent as self-administration of the accounting functions. The insurance company invariably maintains the record of each policyholder's experience and computes the dividend or rate credit.

CHAPTER XXXVII

Industrial

Life

Insurance

INDUSTRIAL life insurance is the third broad branch of the life insurance business, the other two being ordinary and group. It was originally designed for low-income families who could not afford the amounts of protection and premium payments associated with ordinary insurance. While the amount of insurance per policy is small, averaging around $450, the aggregate amount of coverage is impressive. As of the end of 1965, there were 89 million policies of industrial life insurance in force, providing coverage in the amount of $40 billion.

GENERAL CHARACTERISTICS

Like group insurance, industrial life insurance possesses certain distinctive—though not necessarily unique—characteristics. One of the most distinctive characteristics is the frequency of premium payment. The premium may be paid weekly or monthly, but the great bulk of the insurance is on a weekly premium basis. The payment of premiums on a weekly basis is unique to industrial insurance, but payment on a monthly basis is found in both ordinary and group insurance. A second characteristic of industrial insurance is the limitation on the amount of insurance per policy or per life. The model law on industrial life insurance, promulgated by the National Association of Insurance Commissioners and adopted in substance by a number of states, defines industrial life insurance as "that form of life insurance, the policies for which include the words *Industrial Policy* as part of the descriptive matter; and (a) under which the premiums are pay-

711

able weekly, or (*b*) under which the premiums are payable monthly or oftener, but less often than weekly, if the face amount of the insurance provided in such policy is $1,000 or less." The New York Insurance Law limits the amount of industrial insurance payable on a monthly basis to less than $1,000 *per policy* and the amount of weekly premium insurance to not more than $1,000 *per life,* irrespective of the number of policies or companies involved.

A third distinctive feature of industrial insurance is the collection of the premium by the company's representative at the policyholder's home or place of business. This practice has a long history and significant cost implications. A fourth distinctive feature is that the insurance is normally sold in premium units, rather than units of insurance. The rate books show the amount of insurance on various plans that can be purchased with weekly premiums of specified amounts, rather than the weekly premium for specified amounts of insurance. The premiums are quoted in units of 5 cents, ranging from a minimum of 5 cents to a maximum of $1. Sale of the insurance in premium units greatly facilitates and simplifies the collection and accounting functions. The offering of policies for as little as 5 cents a week brings insurance protection within the means of those with the most limited resources. There has been a tendency in recent years to adopt the sum insured as the unit, with the premiums being the variable, at least for the larger amounts of insurance.

A fifth characteristic of industrial insurance is that it is generally written on all members of the family from birth to age sixty-five or seventy. For many years in this country, insurance on small children was obtainable only under industrial policies. Formerly, insurance could not be effected in some states on the lives of children below the age of one year; but all such limitations have now been removed, and in all states, insurance can be made effective from the date of birth. The common practice of insuring all members of the family led to the development of the family plan, which was discussed earlier.

A final characteristic of industrial insurance that should be mentioned is the general omission of medical examinations. The amounts of insurance involved are too small to justify the expense of medical examinations. For the most part, the company relies on the information contained in the application, which includes a statement by the agent. An examination may be required, usually upon the recommendation of the soliciting agent; but, for financial reasons, such an examination must be less detailed and comprehensive than those prescribed for ordinary insurance. The company has some additional protection in the provision that, subject to the terms of the incontestable clause, the policy is voidable if, within two years prior to issue and without the knowledge of the company, the insured received medical or surgical treatment for a serious condition.

ORIGIN AND RECENT DEVELOPMENTS[1]

Industrial life insurance originated in Great Britain in the nineteenth century. It was the culmination of a long series of attempts to provide life insurance for industrial workers and their families. Throughout the seventeenth and eighteenth centuries, there had been a spectacular growth of local associations known as Friendly Societies and Burial Clubs, which undertook through a system of mutual aid to relieve the worker from financial hardships imposed by sickness and death. With the increasing industrialization of Great Britain in the nineteenth century, and with the migration of workers to cities, the local country groups were to a great extent superseded by larger Friendly Societies formed in industrial centers which, through branches, extended their membership into rural areas.

In the small local clubs, members customarily brought their contributions to social meetings. The larger Friendly Societies, however, found it more expedient to have representatives make systematic visits at regular intervals to the homes of all members.

The financial structure of the Friendly Societies was unsound, in that they operated purely on the assessment basis. Moreover, the management of many of the societies was characterized by inefficiency and dishonesty. The increasing inability of the societies to meet their obligations caused their methods and operations to be investigated by a committee of the House of Commons.

The report of the committee, rendered in 1853, called attention to the defects of the Friendly Societies and Burial Clubs, and to the need for making dependable life insurance available to the lower income groups. Largely as a result of this report, the Prudential Assurance Company of London, which had been writing ordinary life insurance

---

[1] The historical facts in this section were drawn largely from Malvin E. Davis, "Industrial Life Insurance," in *Examination of Insurance Companies,* Vol. 6 (New York: New York State Insurance Department, 1955), pp. 151–53. A comprehensive—though somewhat dated—treatment of the entire subject of industrial life insurance can be found in Malvin E. Davis, *Industrial Life Insurance in the United States* (New York: McGraw-Hill Book Co., Inc., 1944).

for a number of years, opened an industrial branch in 1854. The company applied the principles of ordinary insurance, in that the premiums were varied by age of issue and were computed on a level premium basis. It followed the precedent of the Friendly Society, however, in the administration of premium payments. Premiums were payable weekly and were collected by company representatives calling at the homes of policyholders. This was the beginning of industrial life insurance as it is known today.

At the close of the Civil War, the situation in the United States was similar to that which had prevailed earlier in Great Britain. Life insurance was being conducted on a sound basis by a number of reputable companies, but their clientele was almost entirely in the middle and upper income groups. In general, ordinary policies were issued in minimum amounts of $1,000, with premiums payable no more frequently than four times a year. Although a few companies offered insurance in smaller amounts, with premiums payable more frequently than quarterly, none of them made provision for collection of premiums at the homes of the policyholders. American wage earners were largely limited to insurance sold by organizations operating on the assessment basis.

This situation was corrected with the formation, in 1875, of the "Prudential Friendly Society," later to become known as the Prudential Insurance Company of America. This company was organized to write industrial life insurance along the lines which were proving successful in England and issued the first policy of industrial insurance in America in 1875. Four years later, the John Hancock Mutual Life Insurance Company and the Metropolitan Life Insurance Company, both of which were already transacting ordinary life insurance, undertook the writing of industrial life insurance. Today, with more than two hundred companies transacting industrial insurance, the first three companies to enter the field still account for approximately two fifths of the total coverage although one of those companies discontinued writing industrial life insurance at the end of 1964.

Prior to the middle 1920's, industrial insurance in the United States was written only on a weekly premium basis, and ordinary insurance only on a quarterly or less frequent basis. At that time, some companies began the practice of accepting ordinary premiums on a monthly basis. Since the normal procedures were followed with respect to premium notices and receipts, the companies found it necessary, in order to control costs, to impose a minimum limit—such as $10—on the size of monthly premiums. The combination companies then inaugurated the practice of issuing ordinary policies with monthly premiums of less than $10 and collecting them at the policyholders' homes, in the same manner as weekly premium insurance. These companies also extended the issue of monthly premium insurance to amounts less than $1,000. Such policies were known as "intermediate insurance." They were originally issued in the form of industrial policies but are generally issued now in the form of ordinary policies. In some companies, such policies are known as "debit ordinary." Today, intermediate or debit ordinary insurance, payable on a monthly premium basis and collected by the insurer's industrial agents, is issued in amounts generally ranging from $500 to $5,000. At least one large company is issuing ordinary insurance in such amounts on a weekly premium basis. Whether intermediate policies are issued as industrial or ordinary insurance is primarily a matter of administrative procedure on the part of the insurance company and is of no particular significance to the policyholder, since the principal provisions of the two forms of policies are very similar.

Industrial life insurance has enjoyed tremendous popularity and growth in this country. Nevertheless, the rate of growth in recent years has been much slower than that occurring in the other two branches of the business. To some extent, this slower rate of growth is due to the use of weekly and monthly premium ordinary policy forms for needs that were formerly met with the larger industrial policies. Other factors of a more substantive nature have been at work, however. Since World War II, the rise in income has made it possible for a larger percentage of wage earners to afford ordinary insurance, and the rise in prices has made it seem desirable to purchase the larger amounts of coverage available under ordinary insurance. The growth in the number and coverage of group plans has also had an adverse effect on the sale of industrial insurance. The basic objective of these two plans is identical, at least as respects the wage earner; and the mass distribution and administration of group insurance make it considerably cheaper per dollar of protection. The recent trend toward coverage of dependents under group plans represents a further encroachment on the industrial market. The survivorship benefits under Social Security have undoubtedly affected the sale of industrial insurance. The lump-sum death benefit payable upon the death of the insured worker is in direct competition with industrial insurance; but, of course, it is not available upon the death of the other members of the family. Finally, the amazing growth of the family plan has shrunk the market for industrial insurance. It duplicates the coverage of industrial insurance on the entire family and is administered on a much more economical basis. It has not only impeded the sale of new industrial insurance but has caused a substantial amount of existing coverage to be lapsed or surrendered in favor of the family plan.

PLANS OF INSURANCE

Industrial policies are issued on several different plans of insurance although, because of the smaller sums involved, not on as many plans as ordinary policies. The three most basic plans over the years have been (1) whole life insurance with premiums payable to ages sixty-five, seventy, or seventy-five; (2) twenty-payment life insurance; and (3) twenty-year endowment insurance.

In the early years of industrial insurance, ordinary life policies were the standard form, but it was found that the payment of premiums at the advanced ages was too burdensome for the policyholders of that time. As a result, whole life policies are now available only on a limited payment life basis. Term insurance policies are likewise not offered on a general basis. Because of their relatively low cost, they would seem to be appropriate for the low-income groups, but experience has shown that policies without cash values have no appeal for the type of person who buys industrial insurance.

Twenty-year endowment insurance policies have been especially popular, especially for insurance on the lives of children. The decline in the rate of interest that took place during the 1930's and 1940's, however, had caused the three largest companies to discontinue the writing of short-term endowments on a weekly premium basis. Such policies are issued on a monthly premium basis in amounts as small as $250, as either industrial or ordinary insurance. Since 1938, the New York Insurance Law has prohibited the delivery in that state of any policy of industrial life insurance on the endowment plan, irrespective of the length of the endowment period. This prohibition was partially nullified in 1942, however, when the law was amended to permit the sale of monthly premium endowment insurance policies in amounts less than $1,000, provided the insurance is written on ordinary forms containing no dividend options and no provision for policy loans. There is no significant difference between these ordinary policies and monthly premium industrial policies.

POLICY PROVISIONS

At one time, there were substantial differences between industrial and ordinary policy forms, the industrial policies being more restrictive in nature and scope. Evolutionary changes in industrial policies, designed to adapt them to changing circumstances, have, however, produced a policy form that is very similar to ordinary policy forms, except that in many respects, it is more liberal to the policyholder. The special provisions found in industrial policies are attributable to the manner in which the industrial life insurance business is operated, the limited size of policies, or the nature of the clientele.

Only the distinctive policy provisions are discussed herein. If a familiar policy provision is not discussed, it means that, in substance, the provision is the same as that found in an ordinary insurance policy. The provisions described below are essentially those appearing in the weekly premium industrial policies issued by the three largest writers of industrial business. There is great variety in the provisions of the industrial policies issued by the smaller companies, and they are not always as favorable to the insured as those treated herein.

Option to Surrender within Two Weeks

The policyholder may surrender his policy within a specified period after issue—usually, two weeks—and receive a full refund of his premiums. This provision is intended to give the policyholder an opportunity to study his policy and obtain impartial advice, if desired, before committing his premiums irrevocably. It protects him to some extent from high-pressure salesmanship. If he surrenders the policy within the specified period, he receives free protection from the date of issue to the date of cancellation.

Payment of Premiums

Although collection of premiums at the home of the insured by a representative of the insurance company is a distinctive feature of industrial insurance, this method of premium payment is not specifically provided for in the policy. Hence, if for any reason a premium is not called for when due, it is the responsibility of the policyholder to send or bring the required sum to one of the company offices within four weeks of the due date of the premium.

The policy provides that if weekly premiums are paid continuously without default beyond the grace period for a period of one year to an office of the company that is authorized to receive direct payments, the company will refund at the end of the year 10 per cent of the premiums paid during the year. This is a worth-while saving and helps to bring the cost of industrial insurance in line with ordinary insurance. About one quarter of the weekly premiums of the three largest companies are paid in this manner.

Avoidance of Liability by the Insurer

All industrial policies contain an incontestable clause. The typical clause provides that the policy shall be incontestable after it has been in force during the lifetime of the insured for a period of one year from its date of issue, except for nonpayment of premiums. However, inasmuch as—with rare exceptions—the application is not attached to the policy and does not become part of the contract, misstatements therein cannot serve as the basis for rescission of the contract by the insurer. The company enjoys a measure of protection against the fraudulent procurement of a policy, though, by a provision, generally a part of the incontestable clause, making the policy voidable within the contestable period if, within two years prior to issue of the policy, the insured underwent medical treatment for a serious physical or mental condition without disclosing the fact in his application.

It is not necessary that the applicant, at the time of application, make a statement as to the seriousness of any ailment or condition for which he received medical treatment. He simply reports the fact, in response to a specific question in the application, that he received medical or surgical treatment within a specified period prior to the date of application—usually, five years—giving the date, nature of the ailment or treatment, its duration, and the name of the attending physician or the hospital. By reporting these facts, the insured has fulfilled his obligation; and it is then up to the insurance company, by further investigation, to determine whether the ailment was serious enough to affect the insurability of the applicant. If the company approves the application, it is estopped from later voiding the policy on the grounds that the applicant concealed the seriousness of the condition. If, during the two years prior to the date of application, the applicant underwent medical treatment and failed to report it, the burden, in the event of litigation, is on the insured or any claimant under the policy to prove that the condition was not of a serious nature and not material to the risk.

Industrial policies do not contain a suicide clause, although such a clause would be permissible under the laws of many states. The sums involved are too small for suicide to be a real hazard.

Beneficiary Provisions

The industrial life insurance policy contains two distinctive provisions pertaining to the beneficiary. The first provision is the so-called *facility-of-payment* clause, which is unique to industrial and group policies. In its original form, this clause gave the insurance company the unrestricted right to pay the proceeds to anyone appearing equitably entitled thereto. Under the authority of this clause, the proceeds were normally paid to an adult relative of the insured, by blood or marriage, legally capable of receiving the proceeds, although some companies paid the proceeds directly to the funeral director or other creditor of the insured's estate. In view of the authority vested in the insurance company under this clause, no provision was made for the designation of a beneficiary by the insured.

Mounting criticism of the discretion placed in the hands of the insurance company under the original form of the facility-of-payment clause caused the companies many years ago to introduce the privilege of beneficiary designation by the insured and to modify the scope of the facility-of-payment clause. The clause in general use today provides that if the designated beneficiary predeceases the insured, fails to make claim under the policy within sixty days after the insured's death, is a minor or incompetent, or is the estate of the insured, the company shall have the right to pay the proceeds to the insured's executor or administrator, or to any relative by blood or connection by marriage of the insured appearing to the company to be equitably entitled to such payment. The purpose of this discretionary authority is to permit payment of the proceeds to the proper parties without forcing the payee to incur the expense, trouble, and delay of having an administrator or guardian appointed for a relatively small amount of insurance. Some companies modified their practice only to the extent of permitting the insured to designate a beneficiary. They retain the right to pay the proceeds to anyone, whether a relative of the insured or not, even though a legally competent beneficiary survives the insured and files claim for the proceeds. Such companies frequently pay the proceeds to the funeral director and the named beneficiary jointly.

The second distinctive provision associated with the beneficiary is that which gives the insurance company the right to withhold approval of any original designation or change of beneficiary when the proposed beneficiary does not appear to have an insurable interest in the life of the insured. This provision, not found in ordinary insurance policies, is consistent with the basic objective of industrial life insurance and is designed to assure that the proceeds will go to the insured's dependents, estate, or creditors. It is invoked only when there is clear evidence of intended abuse or misuse of the insurance.

Assignment

As a rule, industrial policies prohibit assignment of the contract. This prohibition is intended to protect uneducated and unwary policyholders from unscrupulous persons who might otherwise induce the insured to assign his policy for a smaller sum than its cash value, or for no monetary consideration whatsoever. It also minimizes legal complications and reduces the possibility of speculative insurance.

The New York Insurance Law requires that industrial policies be assignable to a national bank, state bank, or trust company. Hence, policies issued in the state of New York, and in certain other states, make provision for assignment to such institutions but prohibit transfer to any other type of assignee.

Surrender Values

Industrial policies provide for the same type of surrender options as those available under ordinary policies. Surrender values are computed in accordance with the Standard Nonforfeiture method, with mortality tables reflecting industrial experience being substituted for the C.S.O. Table.

Both paid-up term insurance and paid-up whole life insurance have been used as the automatic surrender option in industrial policies. Paid-up term insurance is the automatic option in the weekly premium policies currently being issued by the two largest combination companies. This benefit is available after premiums have been paid for twenty-six weeks. In some of the smaller companies, paid-up term insurance is available after six weeks.

After premiums have been paid for a period of three full years, the policyholder who defaults in premium payment has the option of taking the cash value or paid-up whole life insurance (or endowment insurance, if the policy is on that plan). In some companies, optional benefits are available only after five years.

Weekly premium policies seldom provide loan values because of the small amounts involved and the disproportionate expense of processing the loans. Monthly premium policies permit policy loans as soon as cash values are available, subject to a specified minimum, such as $10.

Reinstatement

According to their terms, industrial policies can be reinstated within two years from the due date of the first premium in default, unless the cash value has been paid, upon evidence of insurability and good health satisfactory to the company and payment of all overdue premiums, *without interest*. In order to conserve as much business as possible, the companies are more liberal than their policies require them to be. Reinstatement is usually permitted when premiums have been in arrears longer than two years, although in such case, interest at the policy loan rate may be charged on the overdue premiums. Some companies waive evidence of insurability if the policy was in force for a minimum of five years before default in premium. Some companies permit reinstatement without evidence of insurability if the application for reinstatement is submitted within a specified period after lapse, such as sixteen weeks, regardless of the length of time the policy had been in force. In the larger companies, revivals are sometimes allowed without payment of the overdue premiums in cash, the amount due becoming a lien against the policy and bearing interest until paid.

Dividends

Industrial policies of a participating company share in the divisible surplus of the company, but the policyholder has no choice as to the form in which the dividends are payable. Some policies provide that dividends will be credited against future premiums, while others stipulate that dividends will be applied to the purchase of paid-up additions to the sum insured. Under either method, dividends are declared annually. Under the first method, dividends are credited in the premium receipt book in the form of a specified number of weekly premiums. Under the second method, the declaration of dividends takes the form of an announcement, sent to each policyholder, which shows for the various classifications of policies the cumulative amount of additional insurance purchased to date through the application of annual dividends.

Additional Benefits

Industrial policies provide automatically, and without specific additional premium, certain benefits in the event of loss of eyesight or limb or in the event of death by accidental means. The disability benefits available under ordinary policies, usually on an optional basis and for a specific extra charge, are not appropriate for industrial policies because of the small amounts involved and other circumstances surrounding industrial insurance. Instead, the typical industrial policy provides that if, as a result of accident or disease, the insured suffers the loss by severance of both hands or both feet, or one hand and one foot, or the total loss of sight of both eyes, the company will pay a sum equal to the face amount of insurance and will continue the original policy in force for its full amount without further payment of premiums. If the insured loses one hand or one foot, then half the face amount will be paid in cash, and the original amount of insurance will be continued without further premium payments. This coverage continues throughout the duration of the policy, rather than terminating at a specified age, as under ordinary policies. The claim rate is heaviest at the higher ages, the great majority of the claims at those ages arising out of blindness.

The accidental death benefit provided under industrial policies is the same as that available under ordinary policies, except that the former is included automatically and without specific additional premium. When death occurs solely through accidental means under the conditions set forth in the contract, an additional benefit equal to the face amount of the policy is payable. The policies of some companies provide an additional benefit of only one half the face amount if death is the result of a specified type of accident, such as a mining accident. It is generally stipulated that the additional accidental death benefit will be reduced by any amount paid for the same injuries under the specified disabilities provision of the policy.

These additional benefits are not available under paid-up insurance originating in connection with the surrender of the original policy.

Change of Plan

The typical weekly premium industrial policy contains a provision permitting its conversion on an attained age basis to any plan of monthly premium industrial insurance. Some companies will also permit a policyholder to exchange all or any number of his industrial policies, whether of the weekly or monthly premium type, for any plan of ordinary insurance, provided the aggregate face amount of the industrial policies to be exchanged, exclusive of accidental death benefits and paid-up additions, equals or exceeds the minimum amount of ordinary insurance issued by the company at the age of the insured on the plan of ordinary insurance desired.

Settlement Options

In view of the small sums involved, weekly premium policies do not provide for installment settlement of the proceeds. However, the interest and installment time options are available under some monthly premium policies. Under the time option, liquidation can be spread over a period as long as ten years.

ADMINISTRATION

Industrial life insurance is serviced by the so-called *debit* method. In this sense, the term "debit" refers to the entire system for collecting and accounting for premiums payable under industrial policies, the most distinctive feature of which is the house-to-house collection of premiums by a company representative. This method is to be contrasted with the procedure, exemplified by ordinary insurance, under which the policyholder receives a premium notice from the company and is responsible for remitting his premium before the expiration of the grace period to the home office or appropriate branch office. A third method of premium collection is that employed in connection with group and salary allotment insurance. Under that method, the employer, through a system of payroll deduction, collects the premiums of the participating employees and remits them to the proper company office.

The term "debit" is used in three different senses in industrial insurance. The first meaning is that given above—namely, a distinctive method of collecting and accounting for premiums. A second meaning of the term denotes the geographical area serviced by a particular company representative. A third usage of the term refers to the aggregate amount of premiums to be collected by a company field representative within a specified accounting period—typically, a week. Under the accounting procedures of the debit system, the agent is "debited" or charged with the premiums he is supposed to collect and is credited with those he actually does collect. This is the usage which gave rise to the term.

To the extent that ordinary insurance is serviced by the debit method, the following comments apply to it.

Field Force Organization

Companies that transact only ordinary and group insurance may use either the "general agency" or "branch office" system, but companies that transact industrial insurance invariably use the branch office system. The branch office system permits a more direct contact between the home office staff and the field forces, and a better control of the varied field services that are associated with industrial insurance.

A company transacting industrial life insurance divides the territory in which it operates into a number of geographical areas that are called *districts*. A district may be part of a large city, a medium-sized city, or a number of adjacent small towns. Each district is under the direction of a manager or superintendent, who is assisted by one or more assistant managers or assistant superintendents. Their duties include the selection, training, and general supervision of the agents and clerical staff assigned to the office.

Each district is subdivided into smaller areas called *debits*. A debit may comprise an entire community of small size or a few blocks in a large city. Only one agent is assigned to each debit, and he is responsible for servicing all the industrial business of the company in that area, as well as soliciting new industrial insurance.

Premium Accounting

Under nondebit ordinary policies, a premium notice is prepared for each individual policy, and a record of premium and dividend payments is maintained in the home office for each policy. Moreover, an agent's compensation is usually determined on the basis of each individual policy he has sold. In other words, policy-by-policy accounting and record keeping are the rule.

The debit system of premium accounting is based on decentralization of functions and is one of the features that has kept the cost of industrial insurance within reasonable limits. The agent reports on transactions in bulk, referring to individual policies only when they have undergone a change of status. Specifically, he reports on an individual policy only when some change is to be made in it, when premium payments are discontinued, when the policyholder moves to a debit serviced by another agent, or when the policyholder expresses an intention of paying his premium directly to an office of the company.

Premium accounting under the debit system involves three basic records: (1) the policyholder's record of premium payments, (2) the agent's record of premium collections, and (3) the agent's report to the company of premium collections.

The first basic record is called the *premium receipt book*. Each insured *family* is provided with one of these books, which serves as evidence of premium payments under all policies held by the family. Each premium payment is entered in the book by the agent at the time it is made, and the entry is initialed by the agent. The premium receipt book remains in the possession of the family.

The counterpart to the premium receipt book is the *agent's debit book*, which serves as the agent's record of premiums received. There is a page in this book for the policies of each insured family, or premium-paying unit; and the entries on any page of the agent's debit book should conform exactly to the entries in the corresponding policyholder's premium receipt book. The pages in the agent's book are arranged in the same sequence as that followed by the agent in making his collections.

The third basic record in the debit accounting system is the agent's report to the home office of payments received. This report is usually submitted once a month, according to a schedule prepared by the home office, but it contains separate figures for each week in the reporting period. The report shows, for each week in the reporting period, the amount of premiums to be collected (the debit), the amount of premiums actually collected, and a reconciliation of the two sums. The reconciliation is accomplished by adding to the amount of premiums to be collected the premiums received but not due during the period (premiums paid in advance and premiums received on policies in arrears at the time of the previous report), and deducting those that were due but not collected (premiums in arrears and advance payments from a previous period). Certain other adjustments are sometimes necessary to take care of such transactions as payment of premiums by application of dividends.

The agent's account is examined from time to time by an assistant manager to verify that it has been properly completed from the data in the debit book. The accuracy of entries in this book is also verified at appropriate intervals by an assistant manager or home office representative. In the course of this latter type of audit, the premium receipt books of the various families are compared with the debit book entries, and a check is made of the dividends credited by the agent and his other transactions.

The agent's records are kept up to date by means of the so-called *life and lapse register lists,* which are prepared for each debit by the home office once a week and sent to the agent servicing the debit. They constitute an official record of all transactions affecting the insurance in the debit. The life register list reflects all transactions which add policies to the debit, while the lapse register list shows all transactions which remove policies from the debit. Both lists show the number of policies and amount of premiums in force after adjustments have been made for the transactions reported on the list, the life register containing the final summary.

Both the life and lapse register lists serve as the basis for changes in the agent's debit book, and the life register list provides the amount of premiums in force for which the agent must account in his monthly report to the home office. In the larger companies, the basic data needed to produce life and lapse register lists are recorded on punched cards or magnetic tape.

The punched cards or magnetic tape used to produce the life and lapse register lists are an integral part of the home office debit record-keeping system. Out of that system, the company produces its reserves and policy exhibit for the annual statement, makes mortality and other statistical studies, and evolves the basic data for compensating agents for debit business.

Under the debit system, the home office does not maintain a continuous record of the addresses of policyholders, but the agent has such a record in his debit book for premium-paying policies. The home office does have a record of the district and debit in which the policy is in force. On fully paid-up or lapsed policies, the last address at which the policyholder was contacted appears in the home office records. The home office does not maintain a record of premium payments, that information appearing only in the agent's debit book. The home office records simply indicate that the policy is in force in a premium-paying or fully paid-up status, or has been reported as lapsed. For home office purposes, a policy is considered to be in a premium-paying status if premiums are not in arrears beyond the grace period and, hence, is still part of a particular debit. When a policy is reported as lapsed, the date for which the last premium has been paid and the address of the policyholder are included in the report. Such information becomes part of the home office record.

COMPENSATION OF AGENTS AND MANAGERS

Agents

Under the traditional method of compensation, the remuneration of a debit agent consisted of a percentage of the weekly or monthly premiums collected, together with a commission on the net increase in premiums—i.e., the amount of new premiums less the premiums on lapsed policies. The commission on the net increase was usually a stipulated multiple of the increase, referred to in the jargon of the business as so many "times." The multiple frequently varied with the plan of insurance which produced the increase. That is, the number of "times" payable for an increase in premiums for endowment policies was smaller than the "times" payable for an increase in premiums from whole life policies, in recognition of the higher premiums payable under endowment policies. This basis of compensation encouraged the conservation of business, a matter of serious concern from the standpoint of both the company and the policyholders.

The reduction in agents' earnings during the depression of the 1930's, largely attributable to the abnormally high lapse rate of that period, caused the larger companies to adopt a new basis of compensation. The agent's compensation under this revised system is made up of three elements: new business commission, conservation commission, and collection or servicing commission. The largest companies have recently made some modifications in this system. Nevertheless, the basic features of the system still apply in the largest companies and the unmodified system is widely used by the medium and smaller sized companies.

The new business commission is expressed as a percentage of the first-year premiums and is usually the same for all types of debit business—weekly premium, monthly premium industrial, and monthly premium debit ordinary. Under the expense limitation law of New York, the first-year commission rate on industrial insurance must not exceed that payable on monthly debit ordinary, and first-year commissions on monthly debit ordinary must not exceed—in the aggregate—the amount of commissions which would have been payable had the insurance not been on the debit plan. In practical effect, this meant that—in the aggregate—first-year commissions on new debit business must not exceed those that would have been payable had the insurance been written on the nondebit or ordinary basis. The new business commission that has been fairly widely used is 28 per cent of the first-year premiums on endowment insurance policies with premiums payable for thirty years or less and 37 per cent on all other plans of insurance. In some companies, no first-year commission is paid on a policy written within three months before or after the lapse of another policy in the company on the same life or in the same family, a practice which is specifically sanctioned in New York law, provided the commission is not reduced or eliminated for policies sold *more* than three months prior or subsequent to the lapse of the other policy.

The conservation commission is expressed in terms of dollar amounts which vary, within minimum and maximum limits, with the relationship between the renewal lapse rate on the agent's total debit business and the renewal lapse rate for the debit business of the company as a whole. The formula is so constructed that the commission is not affected by the lapse of a policy that has been in force less than one full year. A fairly typical conservation commission is one that varies from $3 to $7 per week.

The collection or servicing commission is expressed as a fixed percentage of the debit premiums collected by the agent. A collection commission of 12 per cent of weekly premiums and 6 per cent of monthly debit premiums, subject to a minimum commission of $35 per week is a fairly typical scale. The higher rate of collection commission on weekly premium business takes into account the fact that the total weekly collection is much smaller than the total monthly collection. In at least one company, the average amount of premium per collection on weekly premium business is just about one half of the corresponding average amount on monthly premium debit business, so that the amount of commission per collection is practically the same. This commission is intended to compensate the agent not only for collecting the premiums but for servicing the policy in all other respects.

If a debit agent is with a combination company, he may usually write any type of coverage offered by the company and is compensated on the basis established for that coverage. Most debit agents with combination companies write a substantial amount of ordinary insurance. In functioning as an ordinary agent, the debit agent need not confine his soliciting efforts to the territory making up his debit.

Managers

Managers and assistant managers are generally compensated by salary, with a bonus which depends upon such evidence of performance as the amount of net new business placed on the books and the relative persistency of the business under their supervision. Not infrequently a portion of the compensation of managers and assistant managers comes from a percentage of the new business and conservation commissions paid to agents in their district.

COST

The cost of industrial insurance per unit of coverage is higher than that of either ordinary or group insurance.[2] This excess cost results from both a higher rate of mortality and a higher rate of expense.

Mortality

There are two basic reasons why the mortality rate among industrial policyholders is higher than that among ordinary policyholders. The first is that industrial insurance is written largely on persons in the low-income groups, which are subject, almost without exception, to a higher death rate at all ages, for both sexes, and with respect to every important cause of death. This higher than normal mortality is attributable to the fact that these persons, *as a group,* work in the more hazardous and less healthful occupations, follow less satisfactory dietary practices, live under less sanitary conditions, and receive less adequate medical care. Moreover, some of the excess mortality seems to be racial in origin. A large percentage of industrial policyholders are Negro, particularly in the South; and this racial group is subject to a higher than normal mortality, some part of which seems to be economic in origin.

---

[2] For a rigorous, mathematical comparison of the cost of insurance protection under industrial and ordinary policies from the viewpoint of the policyholder who is eligible for either industrial or standard ordinary life insurance, see Joseph M. Belth and E. J. Leverett, Jr., "Industrial Life Insurance Prices," *Journal of Risk and Insurance,* Vol. XXXII (Sept., 1965), pp. 367–83.

The second basic reason for the higher mortality among industrial policyholders is the difference in selection standards. Not only is there no medical examination in the typical case, but the range of anticipated mortality within which industrial insurance will be written at standard rates is much wider than that of ordinary insurance and is intended to embrace the great majority of those applying for insurance.

The foregoing factors have caused the companies to construct and use special mortality tables for the writing of industrial insurance. These special tables are recognized in the insurance laws of the various states. The disparity between industrial and ordinary mortality has been narrowing during the last few decades. During the 1930's, the mortality among industrial policyholders was about 40 per cent higher than that among ordinary policyholders. The general improvement in mortality that took place during the 1940's and early 1950's applied with even greater force to industrial policyholders. Thus, the foregoing percentage differential has been substantially reduced.

Expense

The higher expense rate of industrial insurance is due to two factors: (1) the smaller units of insurance involved and (2) the collection of premiums at frequent intervals at the policyholder's home. There are certain types of expenses which do not vary in proportion to the amount of insurance; and when they are spread over the small amounts represented by industrial policies, they produce a disproportionately high rate of expense. These expenses are kept down to the minimum in industrial insurance through the simplified premium accounting system described earlier, the elimination of certain procedures common to ordinary insurance, and simplification of the contract, as by the omission of dividend options and provisions for installment settlement of the proceeds.

The greater part of the higher expense rate associated with industrial insurance is attributable to the collection of premiums at frequent intervals at the home of the policyholder. An analysis of the expenses of one large company made about twenty years ago revealed that about 90 per cent of the excess of industrial over ordinary expenses was due to this additional service to policyholders. While a similar analysis is not currently available it seems safe to say that a somewhat similar result applies today.

Critics of industrial life insurance allege that it is subject to an excessive lapse rate, with consequent loss or added cost to policy-holders. This criticism does not seem to be warranted, particularly in respect to policies issued by the larger companies. The experience of the larger companies indicates that the weekly premium lapse rate is reasonable in relation to that on monthly premium ordinary or indus-trial policies taking into account the greater lapse opportunity for weekly premium business.

It is only logical that weekly premium industrial insurance should be subject to a somewhat higher lapse ratio than ordinary insurance. There are fifty-two opportunities every year for the industrial policy-holder to lapse, as compared to once, twice, or four times for the typical ordinary policy. It would be contrary to human nature for a group of persons paying premiums with a frequency thirteen to fifty-two times that of another group not to succumb to the temptation of lapsing more often than the other group. Moreover, persons who carry weekly premium industrial insurance are more vulnerable to adverse financial developments than are ordinary policyholders and hence should be more prone to surrender their policies for their cash value.

CHAPTER XXXVIII

Total Disability and Accidental Death Benefits

TWO IMPORTANT forms of benefits frequently provided in conjunction with a life insurance policy, whether of the ordinary, group, or industrial variety, are total disability and accidental death benefits. These two benefits are not related and are discussed in the same chapter only for convenience.

TOTAL DISABILITY BENEFITS[1]

The basic purpose of a life insurance policy is to provide protection against loss of income from two major hazards to personal earning capacity: premature death and old age. Disability coverage was introduced into life insurance policies to afford protection against a third major threat to earning potential: physical or mental incapacity.

Total disability coverage, as a part of an ordinary life insurance policy, made its first appearance in the United States in 1896. In that year, the Fidelity Mutual Life Insurance Company of Philadelphia issued a policy containing a provision for waiver of premium or, alternatively, settlement by life annuity, in event of permanent total disability. Eight years later, the Travelers Insurance Company introduced a policy with a waiver-of-premium benefit. Around 1910, companies in general began to write waiver-of-premium coverage. Provision for some form of income benefit upon the occurrence of permanent total disability followed within a few years.

---

[1] For a comprehensive treatment of this subject, see Kenneth W. Herrick, *Total Disability Provisions in Life Insurance Contracts* (Homewood, Ill.: Richard D. Irwin, Inc., 1956).

The decade of the 1920's witnessed a rapid expansion of disability income coverages, characterized by ultraliberal provisions, careless underwriting, lax claims administration, and inadequate rates. With the advent of a major depression in 1929, an avalanche of claims— many of them fraudulent in nature—swept over the companies, producing major underwriting losses and, for many companies, a threat to solvency. In an attempt to cope with the losses, the companies, in 1930, modified their contract provisions, tightened up on underwriting and claims, and raised rates. This was not enough to stem the tide of claims, induced primarily by economic conditions; and in 1932, rates were again increased, and further modifications of a deliberalizing nature were introduced. Many prominent companies ceased to write disability income coverages on any basis. With the end of the depression, underwriting losses disappeared generally; and during the last two decades, the companies have enjoyed reasonable success in writing both waiver-of-premium and income coverages. Many new companies have entered the field, and most of the old companies that withdrew in 1932 have re-entered the field.

Today, all companies write waiver-of-premium coverage, and a substantial number offer disability income. Waiver of premium can always be obtained separately, but disability income is available only in combination with waiver of premium.

Policy Provisions

The general provisions of a total disability agreement apply equally to waiver of premium and income benefits, and can be discussed without reference to the particular type of benefit involved. A high degree of uniformity exists among the disability provisions of the various companies, largely as a result of the promulgation by the National Association (then Convention) of Insurance Commissioners of a set of standard provisions, with the recommendation that they become effective on July 1, 1930.[2] These provisions—some of which were to be mandatory and others of which were to be optional—were given legal status in New York and a number of other states, and have exerted a strong influence on the nature and scope of disability benefits.

Definition of Total Disability. The most basic provision in a disability agreement is that which defines the concept of total disability. Unlike death, total disability is not always a clearly identifiable oc-

---

[2] These provisions were approved by the NAIC in 1929 after more than a year of study.

currence.[3] There is a large element of subjectivity in determining the existence of total disability. Hence, it is necessary to define with some care the event insured against under a disability contract.

The definition of total disability prescribed in the set of standard provisions was "incapacity (resulting from bodily injury or disease) to engage in any occupation for remuneration or profit." While few companies use this exact wording, the substance of the definition is found in virtually all disability agreements attached to life insurance policies today. Moreover, the courts are inclined to interpret variations from the "standard" wording in such a manner as to give effect to the standard definition.

The distinctive features of the definition are that (1) no distinction is made between disability arising out of an accident and that arising out of a disease, as is the case in accident and sickness insurance; and (2) the incapacity must be of such degree as to prevent the insured from performing the duties of *any* occupation for remuneration or profit. The first feature is favorable to the insured, while the second, if strictly construed, would be a decidedly unfavorable feature. Literally interpreted, the requirement that the insured be unable to engage in any form of remunerative activity would exclude all but a few extreme forms of disablement, such as a state of complete helplessness or a total lack of mental capacity. With such an interpretation by the insurance companies and the courts, the total disability clause would be of little value to the insured. Fortunately, neither the companies nor the courts have given the definition such a narrow construction.

The generally accepted interpretation of the definition holds that the insured is totally disabled whenever he is unable, through bodily injury or disease, to perform substantially all the duties of any occupation for which he is qualified by reason of his education, training, and experience. This, it will be noted, is a more rigorous standard than that which would require only that the insured be disabled to such an extent that he is unable to carry out the principal duties of his own occupation—the so-called "occupational disability" standard which is widely applied in health insurance and is sometimes applied, particularly in the South, to life insurance disability clauses. The prevailing interpretation is a compromise, or middle ground, between the occupational disability standard, which is considered to be too liberal, and a standard which would require a state of utter helplessness, which is unrealistically strict.

---

[3] Neither is death in disappearance cases.

Some companies use a "split" definition of disability. During the first two to five years, depending upon the period specified in the contract, the insured must be disabled only to such an extent that he cannot perform the principal duties of his own occupation. After this initial period, the condition would have to be so disabling as to prevent the insured from performing the duties of *any* occupation for which he is suited by education, training, and experience.

A completely different basis for determining the existence of total disability is employed in the total disability contract of Mutual Benefit of Newark, New Jersey—the only company using an approach different from that prescribed in the standard definition. For policyholders with a monthly earned income in excess of a specified amount (currently $200 per month), Mutual Benefit defines total disability in terms of *loss of earned income* rather than in terms of physical or mental incapacity to perform the duties of some occupation. The clause defining total disability states that "the insured will be deemed to become totally disabled on the date when, because of accidental bodily injury or sickness, his average monthly Earned Income for a period of four consecutive months has been reduced to one-fourth or less of such Former Monthly Earned Income. . . ." Under this definition, an insured is treated as totally disabled when, through accidental bodily injury or sickness, he has lost, for a period of four months or longer, 75 per cent of his earned income. For a person having monthly earned income less than the specified amount, total disability is defined in terms of inability to engage in his former occupation or in any other occupation for which he is suited by education, training, or experience. The latter definition is designed for coverage of students, housewives, and others who could not qualify under the earned income test.

Upon the occurrence of certain forms of disablement, the conventional test of total disability is discarded, and the insured is deemed to be totally disabled. These forms of disablement, set forth in the agreement and generally called "specified disabilities," include the entire and irrecoverable loss of the sight of both eyes, or the complete loss of use of both hands or of both feet, or of one hand and one foot. Some clauses require severance rather than loss of use of the limbs. This difference in wording is significant in case of paralysis. After the qualification period (discussed below), the insured would become entitled to total disability benefits even though he were able to perform the normal duties of an occupation compatible with his previous education, training, and experience. In the majority of cases, however, claims arising as specified disabilities would be admissible under any standard of disability. The conclusive presumption of "totality in the case of specified disabilities is essentially an administrative expedient, designed to avoid the difficulties of adjudicating claims on the basis of the conventional definition.

Qualification Period. The early disability clauses purported to provide benefits only for *permanent* total disability, rather than for total disability, per se, or *temporary* total disability. Some contracts contained express language to the effect that the disability had to be founded on conditions which rendered it reasonably certain that the insured would continue to be totally disabled throughout his remaining lifetime. Other contracts merely specified that the disability must be "permanent," without attempting to define the meaning of the term. Irrespective of the terminology employed, the clauses were difficult to administer because of the virtual impossibility, in many cases, of determining whether the condition causing disability would continue throughout the remaining lifetime of the disabled person.

In order to cope with this problem, many companies, around 1920, modified their disability agreements to provide that after a condition of total disability had existed for a specified period of time, the condition would be *presumed* to be permanent *during its further continuance.* A period of six months was originally prescribed, but competition eventually resulted in the adoption by many companies of a ninety-day period.

To establish a claim under the ninety-day clause, it was only necessary to prove that the disability was total and that it had continued for a period of ninety days. This resulted in the approval of many claims based on conditions that did not appear to be permanent, or were clearly of a temporary nature. This clause proved to be so costly that the companies ultimately had to adopt a longer period. The standard provisions, to which reference has earlier been made, prescribed a *minimum* period of four months and a *maximum* period of twelve months.

Today, most disability contracts require that the insured be totally disabled for a period of six months before any benefit rights are established. This is true even though the insured's disability is founded on a condition that is clearly permanent, such as the irrecoverable loss of eyesight or the amputation of physical extremities. The hazard insured against under such contracts is total disability that continues for a minimum period of six months—not *permanent* total disability, per se. Nevertheless, many companies maintain the fiction that their disability agreements cover permanent total disability by continuing to stipulate in such agreements that *permanency* is presumed after the condition of total disability has existed for six months. A few companies still employ clauses that expressly require the disability to be permanent and do not presume permanency after any period of time.

Limiting Age. The insured must become disabled prior to a specified age for total disability benefits to be available. The purpose of the coverage is to protect the earning power of the insured, and there is no economic justification for continuing the projection beyond the period of productive activity. The total disability endorsement has not been deemed an appropriate vehicle for the providing of retirement benefits. Moreover, to continue the protection throughout the declining years of the insured's life would be extremely costly. After a point, it becomes difficult, if not impossible, to distinguish between disability and the normal infirmities of old age.

The first few companies to provide disability protection did not specify an age before which disability must occur; but once the need for such a limitation was recognized, the companies tended to designate age sixty as the terminal age. A few companies adopted age sixty-five as the limit. The standard provisions prohibit the use of an age limitation higher than sixty, except in connection with endowment policies and deferred annuities maturing not later than sixty-five (nor earlier than age sixty). If protection is continued beyond sixty and disability occurs beyond that age, any income benefits must cease at the maturity age.

As a part of the restrictions introduced in 1932, the limiting age was generally reduced to fifty-five, and that is a common limitation found in disability *income* clauses today. The most common limiting age for waiver of premium coverage today is sixty, and there is a trend toward the use of age sixty for disability income coverage as well. Many companies continue the protection to the maturity date of endowment policies and deferred annuities, subject to the limitations set forth in the standard provision.

In administering this provision, the companies stipulate that the insured must be disabled prior to the policy anniversary nearest the limiting age. Thus, the coverage may terminate a few months earlier or later than the nominal limiting age. It is necessary only that the condition of disability have its inception before the policy anniversary nearest the limiting age; the qualification or waiting period can be satisfied after that date.

Benefits. 1. *Waiver of Premium.* The most prevalent type of disability benefit found in conjunction with life insurance policies is the waiver-of-premium provision. This type of benefit is offered by all insurance companies and is included in more than half of the policies currently being issued.

The waiver-of-premium provision becomes operative whenever the insured becomes totally disabled in conformity with the concept discussed earlier and remains in that condition for a period of six months. Once the "permanency" of the condition has been established, the insured is entitled to have waived any premium falling due after commencement of the disability, including any falling due during the first six months of disability. If the insured should pay any premium falling due after the inception of his disability, he is entitled to a refund, provided the premium was not due more than a year prior to receipt by the company of written notice of the disability claim. The standard provisions require the companies to refund any premiums falling due after the commencement of disability and not more than six months prior to written notice of the disability claim, but most companies voluntarily waive any premium falling due within twelve months prior to filing of the claim.

If any premium is in default when proof of claim is submitted and the insured can prove that he became totally disabled prior to the due date of the first premium in default, or within thirty-one days after such due date, he is entitled to have the policy reinstated—provided, of course, that notice of claim is filed within one year from the due date of the first premium in default. If the disability began before the due date of the first premium in default, the policy is reinstated without payment by the insured of the premium in default. On the other hand, if the disability began after the due date of the first premium in default but within the grace period, the premium in default must be paid by the insured, with interest, as a condition precedent to the reinstatement of the policy and the waiving of subsequent premiums.

Waiver of premium does not affect any other provisions of the policy. Cash values increase in the normal manner, and dividends are payable at the same rate as for policies that have not become claims. Normal policy loan privileges are available; and the insured, if he is so minded, can withdraw the annual increment to cash values by means of periodic policy loans. If the amount of insurance is large, the disabled insured can derive a substantial annual income in this manner—but at the expense, of course, of the person who is to receive the proceeds at maturity.

A number of the larger companies automatically include a waiver-of-premium provision in all contracts issued at standard rates. No specific extra charge is made for the coverage, the gross premium for the life insurance contract being increased by an appropriate amount. The advantage to the insured of such a procedure is apparent, but opinion is divided as to the desirability of the practice from the standpoint of the insurance company.

Proponents of the plan argue that it (1) reduces adverse selection by covering the good risks along with the poor, (2) simplifies the underwriting of the life insurance application, (3) avoids loss of life insurance sales through unfavorable underwriting decision on disability application, (4) minimizes administrative expenses, and (5) increases premium volume. Critics of the practice assert that it (1) encourages adverse selection (particularly where large amounts of insurance are involved), (2) hampers the sale of life insurance to those not desiring waiver-of-premium protection (because of the higher premium), and (3) creates an underwriting conflict when the applicant is a standard risk for life insurance purposes but is substandard or even uninsurable for purposes of waiver of premium.[4]

2. *Income Payments.* Disability income coverage is far less common than waiver-of-premium protection, being found in fewer than 5 per cent of policies presently being issued. This type of coverage has been troublesome to most companies and over the years has undergone numerous modifications.

The earliest type of disability income agreement written by old line life insurance companies in the United States was based on the concept that permanent total disability matured the policy, and the agreement provided for payment of the face of the policy in annual or monthly installments (depending upon the agreement) over a specified period of years in the event that the insured should become permanently and totally disabled. If the disabled insured died before the face of the policy had been completely liquidated, the installment payments continued beyond his death until a sum equal to the face had been paid out. If the insured recovered from the disablement before the face of the policy had been paid out, the unliquidated portion of the insurance continued in force under the original terms, except that the premium was proportionately reduced. In some companies, the disabled insured had the option of receiving the face of the

---

[4] See Herrick, *op. cit.,* pp. 124–31, for a discussion of the arguments for and against automatic waiver-of-premium coverage.

policy in installments or having the premiums waived on the policy during the period of disability, the full face remaining payable at death.

This type of provision did not meet with policyholder approval and was soon superseded by an agreement which promised an income benefit that would not reduce the face of the policy. The income was payable in annual installments equal to 10 per cent of the face of the policy, the first payment being due at the end of the policy year in which disablement occurred. This clause was followed (around 1920) by one which promised monthly benefits equal to 1 per cent of the face, likewise not deductible from the proceeds payable upon maturity. This meant, of course, that the disability income was $10 per month for each $1,000 of insurance. This pattern of benefits prevailed until 1932, when the companies, burdened with excessive disability income losses, reduced the monthly income benefits under new contracts to $5 per month per $1,000 of insurance. Many companies discontinued the writing of disability income contracts altogether. Favorable experience with disability income contracts during the last twenty-five years—attributable in some measure to the prosperous economic conditions prevailing during this period—has induced many companies to resume the writing of disability income benefits and has prompted some companies which never wrote the coverage to venture into the field. In the meantime, the monthly income per $1,000 of insurance has again been increased to $10— the limit under the standard provisions—by a majority of the companies. Some companies still offer only $5 per month per $1,000, while a few offer amounts in excess of $10—even up to $20 per month.

During the period of experimentation with disability income benefits, many companies promised that upon expiration of the qualification period, benefits would be payable retroactively for the entire period of disability. This proved to be a very costly arrangement and an inducement to malingering. Consequently, the standard provisions, enacted at a time when the four-month qualification period was in vogue, prohibited the payment of benefits for the first three months of disability. In consonance with this philosophy, benefits under present-day contracts commence with the expiration of the qualification period. For example, under contracts employing a six-month qualification period, the first payment is due at the end of the sixth month. This means that benefits are payable for the sixth month of disability.

Another practice associated with the experimental stage of disability income coverage was the retroactive payment of benefits without any time limit when there was a delay in the filing of the disability claim. This practice was defensible from a theoretical standpoint, but it subjected the companies to a contingent liability of unknown proportions. Claims could be filed under policies that had terminated years before through lapse, expiry, death, or maturity. Policies which had lapsed could be reinstated and used as a source of permanent income. To keep such contingent liability within manageable proportions, the standard provisions imposed a limit of one year on retroactive benefits—both waiver of premium and income payments. The general practice today is to pay benefits retroactively for one year, but not beyond the sixth month of disability.

There is great diversity among the contracts on the market today with respect to the length of the period over which the income benefits will be paid once the qualification period is fulfilled. The original contracts promised to continue the benefits throughout the remaining lifetime of the insured—provided the disability persisted that long. A sizable percentage of current contracts continue to offer a lifetime benefit, particularly those that promise only $5 per month per $1,000 of insurance. Among the contracts providing monthly income of $10 per $1,000, however, the income is generally payable only to a specified age—usually sixty-five but occasionally sixty—with the face of the policy being payable at that age. Such contracts are said to "endow" at the specified age. It should be noted that this is a less liberal provision than one which continues the income throughout the remaining lifetime of the insured, since the present value of $10 per month payable for life from age sixty-five plus $1,000 payable at death is greater, even for a disabled person, than $1,000. Some contracts terminate the income payments at a specified age without paying the face. One other variation is for the contract to pay $10 per month per $1,000 to a specified age or for a specified period, with $5 per month being payable thereafter as long as the insured remains disabled.

The foregoing limitations on the *duration* of income benefits should not be confused with the limitation as to the age before which disability must occur. The limitation on duration becomes operative only if the insured becomes disabled before a specified age. The typical provision stipulates that if the insured becomes totally disabled prior to the policy anniversary nearest age sixty, monthly income benefits at the rate of $10 per $1,000 shall be payable from the sixth month of such disability up to the policy anniversary nearest age sixty-five, at which time the face of the policy shall be payable in a lump sum, or under such settlement option as the insured may elect. If disability occurs after the policy anniversary nearest the insured's sixtieth birthday, the insurance company no longer has any liability under the disability agreement.

The income benefits promised under the conventional disability income contracts are payable irrespective of the level of the insured's earned income at the inception of his disability or of the amount of income provided under disability contracts with other companies. In other words, these contracts, like the life insurance policies to which they are attached, are regarded as contracts to pay a stated sum rather than as contracts of indemnity. Failure to treat these agreements as contracts of indemnity, however, has constituted a basic weakness in the life insurance company approach to the disability hazard and has been a fruitful source of underwriting losses. The more thoughtful persons in the life insurance industry have long recognized the desirability of a clause in the disability agreement which would permit the benefits to be adjusted to the economic loss of the insured. Fear of administrative complications, however, has prevented the general adoption of such a clause. Nevertheless, a few American and Canadian companies, including Mutual Benefit of Newark, have adopted a clause which permits a scaling-down of benefits whenever the aggregate amount of disability income under all contracts exceeds a specified percentage of the insured's earned income. Such a provision is called a *prorate clause*.

The prorate clause of Mutual Benefit, which has been used ever since the company entered the disability income field in 1929, stipulates that in the event that the insured shall become totally disabled and the disability income to be provided by Mutual Benefit and all other companies shall in the aggregate exceed 75 per cent of the insured's former earned income (as defined in the policy), the payments made by Mutual Benefit shall be reduced to such an extent that the insured's aggregate disability income does not exceed 75 per cent of his former earned income. If all companies used such a clause, the liability of the companies could be scaled down proportionately; but if only one or a few use it, the company must be prepared, as is Mutual Benefit, to effect the entire adjustment in its own loss payments.

Contestability. It was pointed out in the chapter on incontestability that the incontestable clauses in general use expressly stipulate that they shall not be applicable to any provisions of the policy relating to permanent total disability benefits—or, for that matter, to accidental death benefits. The reason for this exception has been set forth earlier and need not be repeated here. Suffice it to say that, in the absence of a statutory provision to the contrary, total disability provisions never become incontestable. The insurance laws of New York and South Carolina, however, impose limits on the contestability of such provisions. The New York insurance law specifies that a total disability provision must become incontestable after three years. The South Carolina insurance law stipulates that a disability provision shall be subject to the incontestable clause of the life insurance policy to which it is attached.

Excluded Hazards. Permission is given in the standard provisions to exclude from the disability coverage "certain risks or hazards," provided such exclusions appear in the disability provision itself. This is a right which, with respect to life insurance coverage, was acquired only through litigation. The risks generally excluded are (1) disability arising from self-inflicted injury, (2) disability caused by military or naval service in time of war, and less frequently, (3) disability arising out of a violation of law.

A self-inflicted injury refers to one intentionally caused and would generally be regarded as fraudulent in any event. The hazards represented by military or naval service during time of war are too great to be assumed by any private insurer. Some companies have gone so far as to exclude all claims arising out of war, declared or undeclared, whether the insured is a civilian or in the armed forces. Other companies merely suspend coverage for disability while the insured is in the armed forces in time of war. Disabilities arising out of a violation of law are those sustained as a result of criminal or felonious activity, rather than those resulting from misdemeanors such as violations of traffic regulations. Claims stemming from such risks would probably be excluded on grounds of public policy, irrespective of the policy exclusion.

Rates

The basic principles underlying the calculation of premium rates for total disability benefits are identical with those governing the computation of life insurance premiums. The net single premium is derived by multiplying the probability insured against by the amount at risk multiplied by the present value of $1 for the period the money is to be held. The net single premium is converted into net annual level premiums through the application of the appropriate life annuity due of $1, which periodic premiums are then loaded for expenses and contingencies (and sometimes profits) to arrive at the gross premiums to be charged the policyholders. The application of these concepts to disability coverage, however, is complicated by the fact that (1) the event insured against is not an absolutely identifiable occurrence as it is in life insurance, and (2) the amount at risk is not a constant, as in life insurance, but varies with the insured's attained age and must be derived through the adoption of appropriate actuarial functions.

The basic probability involved in disability insurance is, of course, the chance that the insured will become totally disabled and remain in that condition for a period of six months, or, alternatively, will suffer disability through dismemberment or loss of sight. This is referred to simply as the *rate of becoming disabled*. Such rates have been computed for each attained age within the range of insurability and have been combined with appropriate death rates (most recently those of the 1958 C.S.O. Table) to construct so-called "double decrement" mortality tables, which can be used to calculate premiums for disability coverage.

The amount at risk is either the present value of future premiums to be waived or the present value of a specified monthly income payable as long as the insured remains totally disabled or, depending upon the contract, to the end of a specified period, with the face of the policy to be payable at that time. To measure the monetary obligation involved in such promises, the company must take into account the mutually exclusive probabilities that the disabled insured will recover from his disablement or will die before recovery. In other words, under the typical contract, the company's obligation will terminate only through the insured's recovery or his death. These separate probabilities, discounted for the time period involved, are reflected in an actuarial function known as the *value of a disabled life annuity*. It is computed on the basis of a benefit value of $1 per year or 8.33 cents per month. It is analogous to a life annuity due of $1, except that the probabilities involved are the rates of death and recovery, rather than the rate of survival. Like the life annuity due, there is a different value for each attained age.

To determine the net single premium for a disability benefit of $1 per year, the separate probabilities of the insured's becoming disabled at each age up to the limiting age must be multiplied by the value of a disabled life annuity of $1 for each age involved, with the product being further discounted to reflect the time interval between the payment of the net single premium and the occurrence of total disability —when the disbursement of the funds would commence. According to one widely used table of frequency rates, the probability that a person aged thirty-five will become totally disabled within the year is 2.99 per 1,000. A benefit of $1 per year payable to such person as long as he remains disabled would have a present value at age thirty-five of $4.95, according to the same set of disability statistics. Thus, the sum needed to provide one year's protection against total disability at age thirty-five, with a benefit of $1 per year, discounted at 3 per cent interest, is $0.014. The cost of the second year's protection would be obtained by multiplying the probability that a person now aged thirty-five will become disabled during age thirty-six by the value of a disabled life annuity of $1 per year at age thirty-six, discounted for two years. This process would continue to the last age at which protection is to be available. Using the same data mentioned above, the net single premium at age thirty-five for a disability benefit of $1 per year to continue throughout the lifetime of the disabled person, with the protection to end at age sixty, is $0.775. The net annual level premium payable over the entire period of protection would be $0.775 ÷ 17.06, or $0.045.

Premiums for the early disability contracts issued by American insurance companies were based on disability tables constructed by Arthur Hunter, actuary for New York Life Insurance Company, from the disability experience of American fraternal orders. This experience was not too well suited for use by insurance companies—since the fraternals were conceded to have closer underwriting and claims control than the insurance companies—and, moreover, did not presume permanency after a designated period of time. In order to derive more suitable data for the calculation of insurance company premiums, the Committee on Disability of the Actuarial Society of America made a study of the disability experience of twenty-nine American and Canadian companies for the period 1921–24, the results of which were published in 1926. The study was confined to contracts providing a monthly income (as contrasted with those offering only waiver of premium), which were classified into three groups:

Class   I: Contracts without a ninety-day clause
Class II: Contracts with a ninety-day clause issued by companies having a strict claims practice

Class III: Contracts with a ninety-day clause issued by companies having a liberal claims practice

The report revealed that the companies were experiencing a higher rate of disability than that shown under Hunter's table; but the cases had a lower *claim value,* because of higher rates of termination through death or recovery—as might be expected with a ninety-day clause. On balance, however, the data demonstrated the need for much higher premiums. The study also highlighted the need for a greater degree of uniformity in contract conditions and claims practices, so that loss statistics could be derived on a more comparable basis. This led to consideration of the problem by the National Association of Insurance Commissioners and the eventual promulgation of standard provisions.

The Class III experience was considered to be the most meaningful for rate calculation purposes, and basic actuarial functions (rate of disablement and the value of a disabled life annuity) derived from the data served as the basis of rate-making during the next quarter century. The actuarial functions had to be modified from time to time to reflect changing circumstances, but no new basic data of general applicability were developed until the Committee on Disability and Double Indemnity of the Society of Actuaries made a comprehensive study of the disability experience of the leading companies during the period 1930–50, the results of which were published in 1952.

The experience of the companies was separately analyzed for four different periods and with respect to five different kinds of benefits. The periods were as follows:

Period 1: 1930–35
Period 2: 1935–39
Period 3: 1939–46
Period 4: 1946–50

The following types of benefits served as a basis of classification:

Benefit 1: The "total and permanent" disability clause, under which the probable permanence of disability had to be established on the merits of each case.
Benefit 2: The ninety-day "presumptive" clause, with only waiver of premium being retroactive.
Benefit 3: The ninety-day "presumptive" clause, with both the $10 monthly income and the waiver of premium being retroactive.

Benefit 4: The four-month "presumptive" clause, with only the waiver of premium being retroactive.

Benefit 5: The six-month "presumptive" clause, with only a waiver-of-premium benefit. Benefit retroactive to beginning of disability.

It will be noted that the study did not encompass the type of disability income clause that has been used since 1932—namely, that which provides for a six-month qualification period and $5 or $10 monthly income per $1,000 of insurance, with only the waiver of premium being retroactive to the beginning of disability. Benefit 4 is the closest counterpart to the clause currently being used. Benefit 5 is the waiver-of-premium benefit that has been made available since 1932, the experience thus being significant. The experience for Period 2 is usually regarded as the most representative.

In recent years, premiums for both waiver-of-premium and disability income benefits have generally been based on the actuarial functions derived from the experience of Period 2. Benefit 5 data are used for waiver-of-premium rates; and Benefit 4 data, modified to reflect a six-month waiting period, are used for disability income rates. The

TABLE 41

ACTUARIAL FUNCTIONS AND NET ANNUAL LEVEL PREMIUMS FOR
WAIVER-OF-PREMIUM AND DISABILITY INCOME BENEFITS
AT SELECTED AGES OF ISSUE

AGE	RATE OF DISABLEMENT PER 1,000		VALUE OF DISABLED LIFE ANNUITY OF $1 PER YEAR		NET ANNUAL LEVEL PREMIUM (Premiums and Coverage to Age 60)	
	Waiver of Premium	Monthly Income	Waiver of Premium	Monthly Income	Waiver of $100 of Annual Premiums for Life (Retroactive)	Monthly Income of $10 for Life (6-Month Waiting Period)
20	0.76	2.09	$3.10	$3.90	$0.99	$ 3.17
25	1.00	2.09	2.98	4.24	1.18	3.74
30	1.12	2.29	3.03	4.60	1.41	4.49
35	1.29	2.99	3.25	4.95	1.73	5.49
40	1.64	4.06	3.64	5.29	2.19	6.81
45	2.21	6.15	4.16	5.57	2.86	8.61
50	3.47	9.28	4.82	5.86	3.94	11.11
55	7.12	16.01	5.58	6.20	5.70	14.87
59	11.44	25.18	6.20	6.51	—	—

BASIS: Graduated Rates of Disablement and Graduated Termination Rates of the 1952 Disability Report of the Society of Actuaries, combined with the 1958 C.S.O. Table and 3 per cent interest. Waiver of premium: Benefit 5, Period 2. Monthly income: Benefit 4, Period 2, modified for a six-month waiting period.

graduated rates of disablement and termination are combined with the 1958 C.S.O. Table[5] and 3 per cent interest to determine the necessary actuarial values.

The rates of disablement and the values of a disabled life annuity for Benefits 4 and 5, Period 2, are given for selected ages in Table 41. The net level premiums that would be derived from these functions, when combined with the 1958 C.S.O. Table and 3 per cent interest, are also given in the table. The premiums for the waiver-of-premium benefit are expressed in units of $100 of annual premiums, while the premiums for the disability income coverage are based on a monthly income of $10 during the continuance of total disability, throughout the lifetime of the disabled person.

Gross premiums are derived by adding to the net premium a specified percentage (typically, 15 to 20 per cent) of the net premium, plus a flat amount per $1,000 of insurance, ranging from 10 or 15 cents for waiver of premium to 40 or 50 cents for disability income. Gross premiums for female policyholders are often one and a half to two times higher than the comparable male rates, frequently being double the male rate. The differential is usually smaller for waiver-of-premium coverage and, under the contracts of some companies, may be eliminated altogether.

Reserves

Life insurance companies are required to maintain reserves on both waiver-of-premium and disability income coverages. The reserves on contracts which have not become a claim are computed in the same manner as life insurance policy reserves. The reserve for any policy year is the difference between the present value of future benefits and the present value of future net level premiums. The reserve on a contract which has matured as a claim is simply the value of a disabled life annuity of the proper amount, computed as of the date of valuation. It is comparable to reserves held for life insurance proceeds left under a supplementary agreement.

In New York, for example, the law prescribes that minimum reserves for disability contracts currently being used must be computed on the basis of the Period 2 disability rates of the 1952 Study and Termination rates of the 1952 study combined with the 1958 C.S.O. Table.

Several states—including New York—expressly permit life insur-

---

[5] An assumption as to the death rate among active (nondisabled) lives must be made in order to determine the number of persons at each age who will be exposed to the disability hazard.

ance companies to exclude disability reserves in determining the surrender value of a life insurance policy with a disability rider. Moreover, surrender values are generally not made available under the disability contracts themselves. This provides the insurance companies with an additional safety factor in their rate structure. Reserves for the waiver-of-premium benefit are frequently negative, inasmuch as the decline in the value of the benefit may be more rapid than the increase in the rate of becoming disabled.

Dividends

Disability contracts attached to nonparticipating life insurance policies are invariably nonparticipating themselves. When attached to a participating policy, however, they may be either participating or nonparticipating, depending upon company practice. Participation usually implies sharing of operating gains; but in connection with disability contracts, it has frequently meant sharing of underwriting losses. Such losses are shifted to the policyholders by means of a negative factor in the general dividend formula. The negative factor operates to reduce the dividends payable from operating gains.

The negative factor may be introduced into the dividend formula applicable to all policies issued by the company or only in the formula applicable to policies with disability riders. Many companies feel that any underwriting losses arising out of their disability operations should be borne only by those policies enjoying disability protection, which can be accomplished only by placing such policies in a special classification for dividend purposes. The right to do this had to be adjudicated; but in two famous court decisions,[6] the practice was upheld, on the grounds that the disability endorsement is an integral part of the life insurance policy to which it is attached and is not a severable contract.

Negative dividend factors have never been used in connection with disability contracts otherwise regarded as nonparticipating.

Many companies which once used negative disability factors in their dividend formula are now using a positive factor, their losses having been recovered.

Underwriting

In underwriting applications for disability benefits, an insurance company has two broad objectives: (1) the screening-out of appli-

---

[6] *Rhine* v. *New York Life Insurance Company*, 273 N.Y. 1; 6 N.E. (2d) 74 (1936); and *Rubin* v. *Metropolitan Life Insurance Company*, 296 N.Y. Supp. 908 (1937).

cants who by reason of their age, physical condition, medical history, occupation, residence, or other factors represent poor physical risks; and (2) the minimization of the moral hazard, which plays a major role in disability insurance. The underwriting of the physical hazard is similar to that applied to life insurance applications, the same types and sources of information being utilized. Control over the moral hazard, on the other hand, is sought primarily through limitations on the amount of benefits. The benefits must not be so liberal that the economic condition of the insured would be improved through the occurrence of total disability.

Applications for waiver of premium are subjected to minimum scrutiny because of the relatively small amount of money involved and the consequent absence of a major moral hazard. As was pointed out earlier, some companies automatically issue waiver-of-premium protection in connection with all policies issued on a standard basis. Other companies require compliance with only a few general standards. A few companies underwrite applications for waiver-of-premium coverage as strictly as those for disability income.

Disability income applications are strictly underwritten. Typically, only male risks between the ages of fifteen and fifty are acceptable. The maximum monthly disability income that a single company will issue is about $800. The aggregate amount of monthly income which can be underwritten by all companies combined—without serious moral hazard—is considered to be about $1,200. Most companies wish to limit the aggregate amount of disability income to 50 to 60 per cent of the applicant's earned income. There may also be a limit on the aggregate amount of benefits, including both disability income and waiver of premium, which an applicant will be permitted to acquire.

Generally, only applicants in the white-collar or skilled labor class are eligible for coverage. There are many occupational limitations. The majority of companies do not offer disability income in connection with term insurance. Many are reluctant to offer it with business insurance. Only a few companies will write disability income on women; and those that do, accept only self-supporting women under forty-five whose occupation requires them to leave their residence daily.[7] The limit on the amount of income is usually lower than that applicable to men.

---

[7] Waiver-of-premium coverage is generally available to unmarried, self-supporting women under forty-five or fifty; and a sizable number of companies will write such coverage on dependent married women.

Persons substandard for life insurance for physical reasons can generally not obtain disability income coverage, but a few companies will accept risks—at an extra premium—which are substandard for occupational reasons. Many companies, however, will write waiver-of-premium coverage for persons substandard only because of their occupation.

Claims Administration

The first step in the administration of a claim is notification to the insurance company of the existence of the claim. Notification of claim is generally submitted shortly after satisfaction of the qualification period and in any event during the condition of disability. In the early years of disability coverage, however, it was common practice for the companies to accept notice of claim after the disablement had terminated, with consequent handicaps in ascertaining the validity of the claim. If approved, the claim was generally paid retroactively to the beginning of the disability. In an effort to curb unwise practices in this area, the National Association of Insurance Commissioners recommended—in the form of a standard provision—that the disability contract require submission of written notice of claim during the period of disablement. This was combined with another provision, previously discussed, which imposed limits on the retroactive granting of benefits. Most contracts have incorporated the substance of these standard provisions; but another contract provision—likewise prompted by a standard provision—stipulates that failure of the claimant to give notice during disability shall not invalidate the claim if it can be shown that it was not reasonably possible to comply with the requirement and notice is, in fact, given as soon as reasonably possible. The requirement of notice during disability has frequently been waived in cases of insanity.

Proof of continuance of disability is just as essential as proof of original disablement. The early disability contracts, even though based on true permanent total disability, required that evidence of continuance be furnished every time a premium was waived or an income payment was made. This rather rigorous procedure was modified later to require proof no more frequently than once a year after the first year. With the introduction of the ninety-day clause and the resulting coverage of purely temporary disabilities, a more frequent review of claims became necessary. Such reviews usually involve both an investigation and a medical consultation or examination, and tend to be expensive. Hence, the review procedures of a company reflect a compromise between the desirability and feasibility of frequent reviews. The disability clauses of several companies state that if the insured becomes disabled before age sixty and remains continuously disabled to age sixty-five, the policy will be treated as fully paid (with corresponding cash values and dividends) and no further proof of disability will be required.

If recovery takes place, benefits cease, and the insured must resume premium payments—unless the policy has become paid up. Under the original concept of permanent total disability coverage, recovery would indicate that the disability had not, in fact, been permanent; but under such circumstances, the insured was not expected to refund the payments received or the premiums waived. Under clauses presently being used, recovery is a normal incident and occurs in a high percentage of cases, frequently within a year.

ACCIDENTAL DEATH BENEFITS

A life insurance policy may have added to it, by means of a rider or supplementary agreement, a provision which stipulates that an additional sum—equal to the face of the policy—shall be payable in the event that the insured's death should be caused by accidental means. Such a provision is popularly known as *double indemnity,* since a sum equal to double the face amount is payable upon death from accidental causes. Some policies provide that the additional payment shall be equal to two times the face amount, in which event the provision is known as *triple indemnity.*

There is little, if any, economic justification for this sort of provision. The economic loss involved in the insured's death—the termination of family income from the insured's personal efforts—is the same, regardless of the manner in which death arose. As a matter of fact, the economic loss to the family in an accidental death case is likely to be less than it would otherwise be through the avoidance of a long and costly last illness. There is a further objection to the coverage, on the score that it creates a false sense of security—that it creates an illusion of more coverage than really exists. To the extent that such an illusion dissuades the insured from purchasing a truly adequate amount of insurance, the consequences are harmful. Despite the theoretical and practical shortcomings of the coverage, the double indemnity concept is extremely popular, and accidental death benefits are found in a large percentage of policies. The coverage is relatively inexpensive, and it seems to appeal to people's gambling instincts.

Accidental Death Provision

The traditional form of double indemnity provision provides for payment of the additional benefit in event of death by accidental means from any cause other than those specifically excluded. While death from accidental means may seem to be a clearly identifiable occurrence, experience has shown that the contingency must be precisely defined if the company is to avoid liability for claims not intended to be covered. Accidental death for double indemnity purposes is typically defined as "death resulting from bodily injury effected solely through external, violent, and accidental means independently and exclusively of all other causes and within ninety days after such injury."

The use of the expression "accidental means" is intended to eliminate liability in those cases where the *result* of what happened could be considered as accidental but where the *cause* of that result was not accidental. If a person undergoing surgery were to die from an unusual and unanticipated reaction to the anesthesia, the result would undoubtedly be considered accidental, but the means would not be— unless possibly the apparatus used to administer the anesthesia was operating improperly as the result of an accident. The distinction between accidental means and accidental results can be very tenuous, and there is no assurance in a litigated case that the distinction will be observed.

The requirement that death must be caused *solely* by "external, violent, and accidental means" is intended to avoid liability for claims when disease was the proximate cause of death. This is an important and legitimate distinction, but many borderline cases arise. A person may suffer a heart attack while driving an automobile, the vehicle being wrecked and the driver killed. The insured may fall down a flight of steps as a result of a dizzy spell, suffering a fatal injury. In cases of this sort, it may be difficult, if not impossible, to determine the real or proximate cause of death.

Because of the difficulties associated with the interpretation of the term "accidental means," some companies now insure against "death resulting from accidental bodily injury." More specifically, these companies insure against "death resulting, directly and independently of all other causes, from accidental bodily injury evidenced by a visible contusion or wound on the exterior of the body (except in case of accidental drowning or internal injuries revealed by an autopsy)."

Experience has demonstrated the need for excluding certain causes of death, even though both the means and the result may be accidental. These exclusions are of three kinds: (1) deaths resulting from violations of the law, which are excluded on the grounds of public policy; (2) deaths where an accident was involved but the proximate cause was bodily or mental infirmity; and (3) deaths from certain specified causes, such as the taking of poison and inhalation of gas, where there may be considerable doubt as to the accidental nature of the death. In the latter type of cases, it is difficult to distinguish between suicide and accidental death; and in view of the legal presumption against suicide, a ruling of accidental death would be almost inevitable. Deaths resulting from war, military or naval service in time of war, and operating or riding in any kind of aircraft—except as a fare-paying passenger in a regularly licensed passenger aircraft—are also excluded.

Death must occur within ninety days after the accident and before the insured reaches a specified age, usually sixty-five or seventy. The first limitation is imposed to minimize the effect of other causes, while the second limitation is to hold down costs, since the probability of accidental death increases sharply in later life. Some companies, however, provide double indemnity protection throughout the whole of life.

Premiums and Reserves

When accidental death coverage was first introduced, most companies charged a flat premium, irrespective of age, of either $1 or $1.25 per $1,000, even where coverage extended for the whole of life—as was the practice at that time. With recognition of the fact that the accidental death rate is a function of age, premiums graded by age of issue were introduced.

Rates and reserves for accidental death benefits are now based on the 1959 Accidental Death Benefit Table, which reflects the experience of seventeen large companies. The accidental death rate under this table at selected ages is shown in Table 42.

It can be seen that the accidental death rate (1) decreases up to about age forty-five, (2) is less than one per 1,000 up to about age seventy, and (3) increases rapidly after age seventy, reaching three per 1,000 between seventy-five and eighty. The accidental death rate at the younger ages should be compared with the death rate from all causes at comparable ages under the Commissioners 1958 Basic Table.

TABLE 42

ACCIDENTAL DEATH RATE PER 1,000 AT
QUINQUENNIAL AGES UNDER THE 1959
ACCIDENTAL DEATH BENEFITS TABLE

Age	Deaths per 1,000	Age	Deaths per 1,000
15..........	0.476	50..........	0.465
20..........	0.748	55..........	0.514
25..........	0.490	60..........	0.624
30..........	0.394	65..........	0.809
35..........	0.386	70..........	1.065
40..........	0.395	75..........	1.710
45..........	0.431	80..........	3.277

The net premium rates for accidental death benefits at selected ages and for various periods of protection are given in Table 43.

TABLE 43

NET ANNUAL PREMIUMS PER $1,000 OF ACCIDENTAL
DEATH BENEFITS AT SELECTED AGES AND FOR
VARIOUS PERIODS OF PROTECTION*

Age at Issue	PERIOD OF PROTECTION			
	Age 60	Age 65	Age 70	Whole of Life
25..........	$0.42	$0.44	$0.46	$0.56
35..........	0.43	0.46	0.49	0.64
45.........	0.48	0.51	0.56	0.80
55.........	0.54	0.60	0.67	1.10

*1959 Accidental Death Table Combined with 1958 C.S.O. Table and 3 Per Cent Interest

For many years, reserves for accidental death benefits were held on a one-year term basis, the reserve for any particular policy being the premium for the unexpired portion of the policy year at the rate of $1 per $1,000 of insurance, with appropriate modifications for limited payment policies. The practice today, because of the increase in the accidental death rate at the middle and older ages, is to maintain reserves on the level premium basis.

Part Eight

INSTITUTIONAL ASPECTS OF
LIFE INSURANCE

CHAPTER XXXIX

Regulation

IN THE United States, the business of insurance is more thoroughly regulated and controlled than any other type of private business activity, with the possible exception of the banking business.[1] The insurer is under official surveillance "from the cradle to the grave." From the early part of the nineteenth century until 1944, this control was exercised exclusively by the state governments. Since 1944, it has been recognized that the federal government has the power to control an interstate insurance business, and some federal control has been exercised. However, as will be explained below, governmental control of the insurance business is still exercised almost exclusively by the states.

Insurance is subjected to strict governmental regulation for three basic reasons. The first reason is the number of persons affected by insurance operations. There are few persons in the United States whose lives are not affected by some kind of private insurance. As of the end of 1958, there were 124 million life insurance policyholders alone. The beneficiaries of these policies would constitute another substantial proportion of the population. When account is taken of all the persons carrying other types of insurance policies, it is apparent that insurance is truly "affected with the public interest."

Another reason for the close surveillance of the insurance business is the nature of the insurance transaction. The policyholder pays over a sum of money to the insurance company in exchange for the latter's *promise* to pay an ascertainable amount of money to the insured or his beneficiary upon the occurrence of an event which, in most lines of insurance, may or may not happen. There is no practical way for the policyholder to determine whether the insurer's promise is worth the sum he is asked to exchange for it. As Professor Patterson points out, the insured "may never have occasion to find out, by his own experi-

---

[1] Edwin W. Patterson, *Essentials of Insurance Law* (2d ed.; New York: McGraw-Hill Book Co., Inc., 1957), p. 1.

ence, whether that promise [will] be performed."[2] In life insurance, the insured is asked to pay a present sum of money for a promise which may not have to be fulfilled for many years in the future. The insured builds up an "equity" in the insurer's promise which needs to be protected.

Finally, the contract which describes the obligation of the insurer is unavoidably technical and is drawn up by the insurer. This results in inequality of bargaining power as between the insured and the insurer. In order to protect the interests of the insured, the states regulate the language of the insurance contracts and generally require filing of all policy forms with a designated state official. Moreover, the courts attempt to redress the balance between the two parties by interpreting ambiguous provisions against the insurance company.

REGULATORY STRUCTURE

Early Supremacy of State Control

As early as 1810, state control over the insurance business was instituted, the jurisdiction even being extended to transactions crossing state boundaries. The concept that supervision of insurance should be the exclusive function of the states was based upon the Tenth Amendment to the federal Constitution, which provides: "The powers not delegated to the United States by the Constitution, nor prohibited by it to the States, are reserved to the States respectively, or to the people." Although Article I, Section 8, of the Constitution gives the federal government the power "to regulate commerce . . . among the several states," insurance was not regarded as "commerce" and hence was not thought to be subject to federal control even when operating across state lines. Proceeding on this premise, Massachusetts established an insurance regulatory commission in 1852; and within the next two decades, virtually every state established a special department to supervise the insurance business.

With the establishment of state insurance departments came conflicting and discriminatory legislation and administrative rulings. Conditions in the business became chaotic, and strong sentiment developed in favor of federal regulation.

One of the strongest advocates of federal regulation was Elizur Wright, first Insurance Commissioner of Massachusetts and militant champion of reforms in the insurance business. He urged federal in-

---

[2] *Ibid.*, p. 2.

corporation of insurance companies, and a bill reflecting his recommendations was introduced into Congress in 1866. The bill failed of enactment, and a similar bill introduced in 1868 met the same fate. Failing to achieve their aims through legislative action, the proponents of federal regulation turned to the judicial arena. As a test case, they financed and participated in the defense of an insurance agent who had been indicted for the violation of a state insurance law. The litigation developed when one Samuel B. Paul, an agent representing several New York fire insurance companies in the state of Virginia, refused to comply with the licensing requirements of the state, contending that insurance was commerce and, when conducted across state lines, was beyond the power of the state to regulate. The issue went to the United States Supreme Court, which, in 1869, handed down its landmark decision[3] that "issuing a policy of insurance is not a transaction of commerce" and that insurance policies "do not constitute a part of the commerce between the states."

While only fire insurance companies were involved in the litigation, it was clear that the decision in *Paul* v. *Virginia* was applicable to all lines of insurance, including life. Coming in the early years of insurance supervision, this decision served as the foundation of the entire body of state law that was developed to provide for supervision of all branches of the insurance business.

For seventy-five years thereafter, the Supreme Court, in a series of cases that have come to be known as the "insurance cases," upheld the right of a state to regulate the business of insurance.[4] Each case represented an attempt by the insurance companies to avoid features of state laws that were objectionable to them and, in the broadest sense, constituted an attack against the entire structure of state regulation. The case of *New York Life Insurance Company* v. *Deer Lodge County*[5] was particularly significant, inasmuch as it was the result of a concerted and carefully planned effort to undermine the entire foundation of state regulation by proving beyond doubt that insurance is commerce and, when conducted across state lines, is interstate commerce. The court reaffirmed its familiar but increasingly illogical doctrine that "contracts of insurance are not commerce at all, neither state nor interstate. . . ." In the meantime, all efforts to achieve federal regulation through legislation were unsuccessful. Thus, the insurance

---

[3] *Paul* v. *Virginia*, 8 Wall. 168 (1869).

[4] See J. H. Magee, *Life Insurance* (3d ed., Homewood, Ill.: Richard D. Irwin, Inc., 1958), p. 779, for citations.

[5] 231 U.S. 495 (1913).

industry finally reconciled itself to the legal fiction that insurance, with all its complex ramifications, is not commerce and to the practical fact that state regulation was to be its lot.

SEUA Case and Its Aftermath

In the years following the Deer Lodge County case, the insurance industry lent its support to the movement to strengthen state regulatory activities and to achieve a higher degree of uniformity among state insurance laws and administrative rulings. As a matter of fact, its efforts of this nature extended back to the Armstrong Investigation of the insurance business in 1905. Coupled with this constructive action, however, was certain co-operative activity, identified primarily with associations of capital stock fire insurance companies, which was contrary to the letter, if not the spirit, of the federal antitrust statutes. This activity, which had as its basic purpose the co-operative making and enforcement of rates in fire insurance and related lines, was defended by the companies as necessary to the stability of the business and in the best interests of the insuring public. Moreover, it was not in violation of any state law.

After a thorough investigation of the rate-making and related activities of capital stock fire insurance companies, as revealed initially in the infamous "Missouri rate cases,"[6] the Justice Department of the federal government brought legal action in 1941 against the South-Eastern Underwriters Association—an unincorporated association of 200 stock fire insurance companies doing business in Alabama, Florida, Virginia, North Carolina, South Carolina, and Georgia—alleging a conspiracy to fix and maintain arbitrary and noncompetitive premium rates and to monopolize trade and commerce in violation of the Sherman Antitrust Act. The SEUA did not deny the charges but, relying upon the Paul doctrine, argued that insurance, not being commerce, was not subject to federal antitrust laws. The federal district court which heard the case was influenced by the persuasive precedents found in the earlier Supreme Court decisions and upheld the contentions of the SEUA. The Justice Department appealed directly to the Supreme Court, which—on June 5, 1944—handed down a divided

---

[6] *United States* v. *Pendergast,* 28 Fed. Supp. 601 (1929); *United States* v. *Pendergast,* 34 Fed. Supp. 269 (1940); *United States* v. *Pendergast,* 39 Fed. Supp. 190 (1941); *Pendergast* v. *United States,* 317 U.S. 412 (1943).

decision that insurance is commerce and, when conducted across state lines, is interstate commerce.[7] The court's opinion, by Mr. Justice Black, distinguished the case under consideration from the long line of cases starting with *Paul* v. *Virginia,* pointing out that the earlier cases involved the validity of state statutes, while the SEUA case, for the first time, squarely presented the question of whether the Commerce Clause of the Constitution grants to Congress the power to regulate insurance when conducted across state lines. On the same day, the court held, in a unanimous decision, that a fraternal benefit society was subject to the National Labor Relations Act, since the defendant was an insurance company and its operations affected commerce within the meaning of that act.[8]

The sweeping implications of the SEUA decision presented Congress, the states, and the insurance business with immediate problems of serious import. In the first place, the decision cast doubt on many state regulatory and tax laws which had been enacted without consideration of the Commerce Clause as a possible limitation on state authority. In the second place, it raised questions concerning the application to insurance of various federal statutes which had been enacted without thought to insurance. There was the possibility of duplicative federal and state regulation, as well as outright conflicts between federal and state laws.

Congress stepped into the breach and on March 9, 1945, enacted the McCarran Act, better known as Public Law 15 (of the Seventy-ninth Congress). The act contained a declaration by Congress that continued regulation and taxation of insurance by the states are in the public interest and that the business of insurance shall be subject to such state laws. Congress further declared that silence on its part shall not be construed as a barrier to state regulation or taxation of insurance and that no act of Congress shall supersede any state law on this subject unless the federal statute expressly mentions insurance. The act stated that the Sherman Act, the Clayton Act, and the Federal Trade Commission Act would not be applicable to the business of in-

---

[7] *United States* v. *South-Eastern Underwriters Association et al.,* 64 Sup. Ct. 1162 (1944). This precedent-shattering case was decided by a minority of the full court, the first time since 1879 that a previous decision of the Supreme Court had been reversed by fewer than a majority of the full court. The decision was rendered by only four justices—three dissenting and two not sitting.

[8] *Polish National Alliance* v. *National Labor Relations Board,* 322, U.S. 643 (1944).

surance until January 1, 1948 (later extended to June 30), except that the provisions of the Sherman Act pertaining to boycott, coercion, and intimidation were to be applicable immediately. Upon expiration of the moratorium, the enumerated antitrust laws were to apply to the insurance business to the extent that such business is not regulated by state law.

The states were quick to accept this congressional invitation to assume continued responsibility for regulation of the insurance business. One of the immediate consequences of the McCarran Act was the formation of an All-Industry Committee, composed of representatives of virtually every branch of the insurance business and established to work with the National Association of Insurance Commissioners in developing additional state laws. Their joint endeavor produced significant results. By the end of 1957, for example, virtually all jurisdictions had enacted fair-trade practices laws, patterned roughly after the Federal Trade Commission Act, prohibiting unfair methods of competition and unfair practices in the insurance business. The great majority of states have adopted the Uniform Unauthorized Insurers Service-of-Process Act, in accordance with which a claimant under an insurance policy can institute legal action in his own state against insurers not licensed to do business there. Other uniform state laws were developed through the co-operation of the insurance industry and the insurance commissioners, and adopted by a number of states.

Laws have been enacted in all states regulating the bureaus which collect loss statistics and make rates in the fire, casualty, and surety segments of the business. Rates in these branches of the business have long been made by bureaus acting on behalf of a number of companies, but only since enactment of the McCarran Act have the activities of these bureaus been supervised. In the life insurance field, rates are established by the individual companies and are regulated only through minimum-reserve requirements.

Supreme Court decisions have also served to delineate the extent of state responsibility for insurance regulation. In one case, the court, without reliance on the McCarran Act, upheld a state regulatory law designed to protect its citizens against the activities of unlicensed agents, even though interstate commerce was involved.[9] In another state, the court relied on the McCarran Act to sustain a state premium tax applying exclusively to out-of-state companies, the court assuming that in the absence of that act, the tax would be unconstitutionally discriminatory as against interstate commerce.[10] More recently, the court

---

[9] *Robertson* v. *California,* 328 U.S. 440 (1946).

has held that under the McCarran Act, the Federal Trade Commission does not have jurisdiction over insurance advertising in those states which have enacted their own laws regulating such advertising.[11] The court rejected the Federal Trade Commission's contention that the Act should be construed to permit concurrent state and federal regulation.

Extent of Federal Control

There is a measure of federal control—of a peripheral nature—over the insurance business today, with the possibility that the future will see even more control. The National Labor Relations and Fair Labor Standards Acts, as well as the boycott prohibitions of the Sherman Act, are fully applicable to the business of insurance. Moreover, the provision in the McCarran Act that the Sherman, Clayton, and Federal Trade Commission Acts shall be applicable to insurance to the extent that the business is not regulated by state law offers a basis for the assertion of some federal regulatory power in areas which federal agencies feel to be inadequately regulated under state law. In this connection it is significant that the United States Supreme Court, in a case involving the advertising of mail-order insurance by a company domiciled in Nebraska, held that the regulation of the company by Nebraska does not oust the Federal Trade Commission of jurisdiction in states other than Nebraska.[12] Furthermore, the Supreme Court has held that the Securities and Exchange Commission has jurisdiction over the sale of variable annuities by life insurance companies—on the ground that such contracts are securities rather than contracts of insurance.[13]

The SEUA decision made it clear that the federal government has the ultimate authority to regulate the interstate aspects of the business. The power of the states to regulate this phase of the business is at all times subject to the will of Congress. Whether Congress will be content to leave insurance supervision in the hands of the states will depend upon the effectiveness of state supervision in general and, more specifically, upon the capacity of the states to cope with developments in the insurance business that raise issues of national concern.

---

[10] *Prudential Insurance Company* v. *Benjamin,* 328 U.S. 408 (1946).

[11] *Federal Trade Commission* v. *National Casualty Company,* 357 U.S. 560 (1958).

[12] *Travelers Health Ass'n.* v. *Federal Trade Commission,* 262 Fed. 2d 241, 362 U.S. 293, 298 Fed. 2d 820.

[13] *Securities and Exchange Commission, Petitioner,* v. *Variable Annuity Life Insurance Company of America, and The Equity Annuity Life Insurance Company,* 19 U.S. Supreme Court Bulletin 821 (C.C.H., March 23, 1959); 27 Law Week 4211 (U.S., March 23, 1959).

AGENCIES OF STATE REGULATION

Courts

The courts of a state serve as an agency of control through the adjudication of controversies between litigants. A judicial decision construing a certain clause in an insurance policy regulates, perhaps within a narrow range, the duties of insurers using that clause. If use of the clause is made mandatory for a class of insurers, judicial interpretation of the clause imposes a control that the insurer cannot evade by rewording its contract. Again, the penalties imposed upon those who violate the insurance laws are, with rare exceptions, enforceable only through judicial proceedings. Moreover, insurers and their agents occasionally resort to the courts to overturn rulings of the insurance commissioner. Finally, juries, which have the power to decide disputed questions of fact in insurance contract litigation, are permitted in many states to bring in a general verdict which decides the entire merits of the controversy, both legal and factual. Such verdicts, in a large percentage of cases, are against the insurer.

Legislatures

The legislature of each state has broad powers to enact all legislation, necessary or expedient, for the regulation of the insurance business within its jurisdiction. These powers are limited only by the provisions of the state constitution and of the federal Constitution, as interpreted by the courts. Since no provision of the latter and very few of the former (as a rule) specifically relate to insurance, the limitations are to be found in such general provisions as the federal Due Process Clause: ". . . nor shall any state deprive any person of life, liberty, or property, without due process of law." For reasons given earlier, the insurance business has long been recognized as a proper subject of regulation; and at the present time, the principal limitations on state regulation are that the means adopted by the statute be reasonably related to the protection of the public and that the state shall not exceed its jurisdiction under the division of powers set forth in the federal Constitution.

During the last quarter century, a substantial number of states have enacted comprehensive revisions of their insurance laws, sometimes called "codes," which have swept away the accumulated layers of legislation of many decades and have reduced insurance laws to a uniform style and a fairly systematic order. For the greater part, these laws relate to incorporation, licensing, supervision, and liquidation of insurers, and to the licensing of agents and brokers. A relatively minor portion of the typical law pertains to the enforcement of claims under insurance contracts. Only California and a few other states (which have adopted the California provisions) have "codes" of insurance contract law. The great bulk of that law is to be found in reported judicial decisions.

State legislation regulates not only the thousands of insurers doing business in only one state, predominantly small mutual organizations operating in the fire insurance field exclusively, but also hundreds of insurers doing an interstate business. The great diversity of legislation is no problem, of course, to the insurers operating in only one state, but it is extremely burdensome to insurers operating in many states. The burden of multiple supervision would be much greater but for the uniform legislation developed and sponsored by the National Association of Insurance Commissioners and the high degree of co-operation among the several insurance commissioners exercising administrative control over interstate insurers.

Administrative Officials

In a majority of the jurisdictions, the responsibility for enforcing insurance laws and regulations is lodged in a completely separate and independent department under the direction of a chief official with the title of commissioner, superintendent, or director. In Texas, the responsibility is placed in a three-man board. Many states place this responsibility with a state official who has other duties as well, such as the state auditor, comptroller, or treasurer; or with a bureau of insurance associated with some other department, such as the department of banking.

Massachusetts was the first state to establish an insurance department. In 1852, its secretary, treasurer, and auditor were named to a Board of Insurance Commissioners. Three years later, an independent board was appointed, and a separate insurance department was created—a milestone in the evolution of insurance regulation in the United States. New York was the second state to establish an insurance department and the first to vest the administration of the department in a single official—such action taking place in 1859. Within the next ten years, thirty-five states delegated the task of insurance supervision to either a special department or a specified state official. Such action has now been taken in every state, and the District of Columbia.

Great impetus was given to state insurance supervision by the formation, in 1871, of the National Association of Insurance Commissioners, originally called the National Convention of Insurance Commissioners. The Union then consisted of thirty-six states; and in many of them, problems of insurance supervision had become acute. As each state had jurisdiction over every company doing business within its borders, there was great need for standardization of regulatory requirements and procedures. The National Association of Insurance Commissioners was organized to meet that need. The objectives of the association are to promote uniformity in insurance legislation and administrative rulings, to increase the efficiency of officials charged with the administration of insurance laws, and to protect the interests of policy owners and their beneficiaries. The present constitution provides for an executive committee, an examinations committee, a federal liaison committee, and eleven standing committees, including committees on blanks (reporting forms), laws and legislation, life insurance, taxation, and valuation of securities. There is also provision for special and industry committees.

Early accomplishments of the association include (1) the adoption by all states of a uniform blank for companies' annual financial reports, known as the *convention blank,* since it was developed during the time that the association was going under the name of the National *Convention* of Insurance Commissioners; (2) the acceptance of most states of a certificate of solvency issued by the state in which a company is domiciled, thus eliminating the extra expense and effort that would be involved if each state were to verify the company's reserve calculations; and (3) acceptance of the principle that a deposit of certificates should be required only in a company's home state.

Among the more important recent achievements of the association are (1) the adoption of uniform rules for the valuation of all securities in the annual statement convention blank; (2) the development of a procedure, called the *zone system,* under which the triennial examination of a life insurance company is conducted by a team of examiners from various state insurance departments under the general direction of the insurance department of the home state; (3) the construction of standard mortality tables for the calculation of reserves and other values for ordinary insurance, group insurance, and industrial insurance; and (4) the promulgation of standard laws for the valuation of reserve liabilities and the calculation of minimum surrender values.

SUBJECT MATTER OF REGULATION

An insurance company is subject to state control and supervision from the moment it is organized until the time it finally goes out of existence. Control over the organization of an insurance company is exercised through the incorporation and licensing requirements; control over the conduct of the business is exercised through the power to revoke (or to refuse renewal of) licenses, to carry out periodic examinations of the company, and to impose civil and criminal penalties for various infractions of governing statutes; control over the termination of the enterprise is exercised through the power of the insurance commissioner to apply to a court for the appointment of an official liquidator for an insolvent company or by the commissioner's power, under court order, to wind up a company's business and distribute its assets. It seems logical, therefore, to discuss under the broad headings of "Formation," "Operations," and "Liquidation," the various facets of an insurance company's life cycle which are subject to regulation.

Formation

Two basic steps are involved in the formation of an insurance company: incorporation and the obtaining of a license.

In the early days of insurance in this country, a corporation could be formed only through a special act of the state legislature, which prescribed the powers of the corporation and the conditions to be met by the incorporators. This proved to be a burdensome and unwieldy procedure; and in due course, the states enacted general incorporation statutes, under which charters could be obtained directly from a designated state official, usually the secretary of state. Once the supervision of insurance became the responsibility of a specific state official, the approval of such official was necessary to the incorporation of an insurance company. That is the general situation today.

The conditions laid down for the incorporation of insurance companies are different from those imposed upon the incorporators of other business enterprises. The purpose of these requirements is to obtain a higher degree of competence, honesty, and financial stability in the formation and management of insurance companies than is expected of business corporations generally. Among the special requirements governing the incorporation of a capital stock company is a minimum amount of capital stock, which varies with the lines of insurance to be written; a minimum amount of paid-in or capital surplus, usually 50 per cent of the stock to be issued; minimum number of incorporators, so that the company will not be a close or family corporation; and limitations on the form in which the assets can be held. The requirements for a mutual company are stated in terms of a minimum deposit or guaranty fund, restrictions on investment of the guaranty fund, minimum number and dollar value of applications for insurance, and (in some states) a maximum limit on organizational expenses.

Technically, an insurance company comes into existence upon approval of the application for a charter, or, under the procedures of some states, upon issue of the certificate of incorporation. However, this merely endows the company with juristic personality (status of a person in the eyes of the law) and does not of itself give the company the authority to engage in the insurance business. Such authority is conferred by means of a license. A license, called a *certificate of authority* in some states, is a formal document certifying that the company on whose behalf it is issued has complied with all the applicable laws and is authorized by the state to engage in the kind or kinds of insurance specified. When issued in connection with incorporation, or by the state under whose laws the company is chartered, the license is normally valid for the duration of the charter, which may be perpetual. It does not have to be renewed; but in some states, it can be revoked for cause. In only one state is it necessary for the incorporators of an insurance company to establish the public need or necessity of another insurance company. In Vermont, the incorporators must demonstrate that organization of the company "will promote the general good of the state."[14]

An insurance company must obtain a license from every state in which it wants to do business. The license will contain a recitation of the kinds of insurance business which the company contemplates conducting within the boundaries of the state. The company may not engage in any type of insurance business not authorized by its charter; but it need not, in every or any state in which it is licensed to do business, engage in all the kinds of insurance business authorized by the charter. A license obtained from a state other than the state of incorporation is usually good for only one year and must be renewed annually at a substantial fee. To obtain a license in a state other than its home

---

[14] Vermont Statutes, 1947, Section 9178.

state, a company must comply with all the pertinent laws of the state, which usually involves the depositing of a specified amount of securities with the insurance commissioner or other designated official, to assure payment of claims to policyholders residing in the licensing state.

An alien insurer (one chartered by a foreign country) licensed to operate in New York is required to maintain with an approved trustee in the United States, for the protection of policyholders and creditors in this country, a deposit of securities equal in value to its liabilities in the United States, plus a trusteed surplus at least equal to the amount of capital required of a domestic insurer licensed to do the same kinds of business.

In all states, the insurance commissioner, for sufficient reasons, can refuse to issue a license in the first instance, fail to renew a license which has expired, or revoke a license before the normal date of expiration. The grounds for each of the foregoing types of actions often differ in statutory language but in substance are similar or even identical. The statutory grounds are sometimes general and sometimes specific. The insurance commissioner may be authorized to deprive a company of the privilege of doing business in the state on such broad grounds that his action "is in the public interest"[15] or "will best promote the interests of the people of the state."[16] The specific grounds for refusal or revocation are numerous and varied. Two broad limitations on the licensing authority of a state are that (1) the state, by statute or otherwise, cannot impose as a condition of licensing the waiving or relinquishment of safeguards provided under the federal Constitution; and (2) the insurance commissioner, in the exercise of his broad, discretionary powers, may not impose requirements that go beyond any policy of the state legislature, as manifested by its legislation.

Operations

Once an insurance company is organized, virtually every phase of its operations comes under official scrutiny. Its field representatives must be licensed, its business-getting methods must exclude certain practices, its policy forms must be approved, it must measure up to specified standards of solvency, and its funds must be invested in accordance with the provisions of state law.

---

[15] Massachusetts, Annotated Laws (recompiled, 1948), Supp. to 1954, Chapter 175, Sections 32 and 151.

[16] New York Insurance Law, Sections 40 (4) and 42.

Licensing of Agents, Brokers, and Analysts.   In all states, there are provisions for the licensing of agents and brokers; and in one state, there is provision for the licensing of life insurance analysts.

No person may act as agent within a state without a license to do so, and no insurer may employ or recompense any agent acting without such license. The common requirements for all agents' licenses are an application by the proposed licensee, a notice of appointment by the insurer, and, frequently, some kind of statement or certification by the insurer that the applicant is of good character and qualified. In many states, the applicant is required to pass a written examination given under the auspices of the state insurance department or to complete a prescribed course or courses of learning. The license is usually of indefinite duration, being subject to termination through the licensee's death, termination of his appointment by the insurer, or the revocation or suspension of the license by the insurance commissioner. The grounds on which the insurance commissioner is empowered to revoke or to suspend the license of an insurance agent, often set forth at length, include violation of law in his capacity as agent, fraudulent or dishonest practices, proof of untrustworthiness or incompetence, or a material misrepresentation in the application for his license. Notice of intention to revoke or suspend, and a hearing before the commissioner or a deputy, are usually required.

The requirements for a broker's license are in general somewhat higher than those imposed for an agent's license. Completion of a series of courses in insurance is frequently a condition of licensing. The broker's license must be renewed annually, subject to a renewal fee. The grounds for revocation or suspension of license are substantially the same as those applicable to an agent's license.

Since 1941, California has required that every person who acts as a life insurance analyst be licensed. The term is not formally defined but seems to refer to any person who, independently of his employment by an insurer or insurance agent, purports to give expert advice about life insurance to the public generally. Various categories of persons are exempted from the requirement, including actuaries, bank employees, and active members of the California bar. A written examination is required of the applicant; and the successful applicant must file a surety bond for $2,000, to indemnify any person who may suffer by his fraudulent conduct or his failure to account for monies coming into his possession as an analyst.

Business-Getting Methods.   The states now exercise a substantial measure of control over the methods by which business is acquired by insurance companies and their field representatives. This control has a dual purpose: (1) to enforce a higher standard of competition than that which prevails in most forms of merchandising and (2) to protect the insuring public against practices that could prove to be detrimental to its interests. These objectives are sought through laws which prohibit misrepresentation and twisting, rebating and unfair discrimination, and unfair competition in general.

1. *Misrepresentation and Twisting.* Misrepresentation for the purpose of inducing the payment of an insurance premium was adjudged to be a crime in Massachusetts more than one hundred years ago. During the present century, legislation penalizing such conduct has been widely enacted and has been coupled with prohibitions against *twisting*. Twisting refers to the practice of inducing a policyholder to discontinue an insurance contract with one company and to take out substantially the same kind of contract with another company, by means of misrepresentations or incomplete comparisons of the respective advantages and disadvantages of the two contracts. Inducing a policyholder through misrepresentations or incomplete comparisons to switch contracts within the same company is also regarded as twisting if the policyholder was misled to his detriment.

The misrepresentation statutes usually proscribe any estimates of future dividends by insurers or their agents. Moreover, an insurer is prohibited from guaranteeing future dividends. Dividend "illustrations," usually based on current dividend scales, are not prohibited. Interestingly, one section of the New York Insurance Law prohibits an agent from making a *misleading* dividend estimate, while another section prohibits insurers from making *any* estimates.

2. *Rebating and Discrimination.* Rebating and discrimination are similar methods of unfair competition which overlap to some extent but are not identical. Rebating is the giving of a reduction in premium or some other material advantage not specified in the policy. The most obvious form of rebating would be the waiving by the agent of all or a portion of his commission, with the saving being passed on to the insured in one form or another. Laws prohibiting the practice have three objectives: (1) to assure equitable treatment of all policyholders; (2) to protect the vocational agent from the competition of the avocational or part-time agent, who may be willing to serve his relatives and friends at reduced prices; and (3) to prevent an insurer from impairing its financial solvency through competitive rate cutting.

Rebating can take many forms, and there are numerous administrative rulings with respect to specific practices that may be suggestive of rebating.

While rebating is concerned with the providing of insurance to a particular policyholder or group of persons on more favorable terms than those generally available, discrimination involves a refusal to provide insurance to a particular person or group on terms as favorable as those generally available, or on any terms whatsoever. The statutes do not prohibit discrimination as such—only *unfair* discrimination. Some discrimination among policyholders is necessary to preserve equity, since all policyholders do not present the same degree of risk. Unfair discrimination refers to any inequality of treatment among policyholders which is not justified by underwriting considerations or sound business practices. In life insurance, it is customary to define unfair discrimination in terms of inequitable treatment of individuals of the same class and equal expectation of life, with respect to premiums, dividends, benefits, or policy conditions. While the antidiscrimination statutes do not explicitly prohibit discrimination between different classes of policyholders, there is reason to believe that the insurance supervisory official in most states has discretionary authority to prohibit this type of discrimination.[17]

3. *Unfair Competition.* The statutes discussed in the preceding sections are aimed at specific forms of unfair competition. A number of states have enacted statutes designed to prevent unfair competition in general among insurance companies, the objective being to make state regulation of this aspect of the insurance business sufficiently effective to forestall action by the Federal Trade Commission under the terms of the McCarran Act. These acts usually identify certain practices, such as misrepresentation, twisting, rebating, and unfair discrimination, as unfair trade practices and, in addition, give the commissioner of insurance the authority to seek an injunction, through the attorney general, against other methods that he regards to be unfair or deceptive.

Policy Forms. In most lines of insurance, the policy forms used by the insurers are subjected to some degree of regulation. The primary purpose of this regulation is to protect the policyholders and other persons having rights in the policies against unfair and deceptive

---

[17] See Glenn L. Wood and C. Arthur Williams, Jr., "High Cash Value Life Insurance Policies and Unfair Discrimination," *The Journal of Risk and Insurance,* Vol. XXXI, No. 4 (1964), p. 563.

provisions. The degree of control ranges from the prescription, by statute, of the exact wording of the policy, as in fire insurance, to the mere requirement that the policy form, developed unilaterally by the insurer and without regard to any standard provisions, be filed with the insurance commissioner. The regulation of life insurance policy forms falls in between these two extremes.

Since the Armstrong Investigation of 1905 and the remedial legislation that followed the disclosures of the investigation, life insurance policies, in general, have reflected certain standard provisions. The *substance*—but not the exact wording—of these provisions is set forth in state statutes. The policy forms must be filed with the insurance commissioner, who generally has the authority to withhold approval of any provisions which he regards to be unfair, deceptive, or in some other respect objectionable. He may be empowered to approve provisions which, in his opinion, are more favorable to the policyholders than the provisions prescribed by statute.

Standard provisions have been enacted with respect to the grace period for payment of premiums, incontestable clause, entire-contract clause, misstatement of age, annual apportionment of dividends, surrender values and options, policy loans, settlement options, and reinstatement. Standard provisions for industrial and group life insurance policies are prescribed separately.

Some states restrict, by statute, the causes of death with respect to which the insurer may limit its liability to the reserve at date of death or the premiums paid. The purpose of such statutes is to prevent the insurance company from unreasonably narrowing the scope of the coverage, which might escape the attention of the insured. The New York statute limits excepted causes to suicide (for two years and only while sane), war and military service, aviation, hazardous occupations, and residence (for two years only).

Premium Rates. The right of the states to regulate premium rates was upheld by the United States Supreme Court almost fifty years ago.[18] Today, the regulation of rates extends to fire insurance and allied lines; to all lines of casualty, fidelity, and surety insurance; to some types of inland marine insurance; and to title insurance. The insurance commissioner in every state except Texas is empowered to set aside, reduce, or increase rates filed by or on behalf of fire and casualty insurers if, after a hearing, he finds that the rates are exces-

---

[18] *German Alliance Insurance Company* v. *Lewis,* 233 U.S. 389 (1914).

sive, inadequate, unreasonable, or unfairly discriminatory. In Texas, the Board of Insurance Commissioners has the power to *prescribe* rates and does so extensively.

Life insurance rates are not subject to direct regulation, with the exception of certain minimum rate requirements in connection with group term life insurance and credit life insurance. It is felt that adequacy of rates can be assured through minimum reserve requirements and expense limitations, while competition is expected to prevent excessively high rates.

Financial Condition. The primary purpose of state insurance regulation is to maintain the solvency and financial soundness of the companies providing insurance protection. In states having large domestic insurers, the amount of effort expended in the supervision of the insurers' financial affairs exceeds that involved in all other kinds of supervisory work combined.

The primary concern of the insurance supervisory authorities is that an insurance company maintain, at all times, assets at least equal to its presently due and prospectively estimated liabilities. The liabilities of a life insurance company consist predominantly of its policy reserves. To make sure that these liabilities are properly reflected in the balance sheet, the states prescribe, by statute, the method by which minimum policy reserves shall be computed. The various methods which can be used to calculate legal reserves were discussed in earlier chapters and need not be dealt with further at this point.

The states not only require that there be a sufficient volume of assets to offset a company's liabilities, but they specify the form in which the assets must be held. The funds of life insurance companies are generally invested in fixed-income corporate securities (bonds); real estate mortgages; obligations of the federal, state, and local governments (including certain Canadian obligations); and policy loans. Until recent years, most states have restricted the outright ownership of real estate to that (1) occupied by the company at its home office; (2) necessary for the convenient transaction of its business; or (3) acquired by legal process, such as by foreclosure of mortgage loans. In the latter case, it is generally required that the real estate so acquired must be disposed of within a specified period of time, such as five years. Within the last decade or so, some states have liberalized their laws to permit the investment of life insurance funds in housing projects. The New York law permits a company to invest up to 10 per cent of its admitted assets in such projects. A more recent development has been the liberalizing of state laws to permit the acquisition of certain types of commercial real estate for the production of income, subject to stated limitations and conditions. In New York, the aggregate investments of this type cannot exceed 5 per cent of a company's admitted assets.

Common stock investments are severely limited in all states. Generally speaking, a life insurance company cannot hold common stock, in the aggregate, in an amount greater than 5 per cent of its admitted assets or one half of its surplus to policyholders, whichever shall be the lesser, and there may be a limit on the percentage of the outstanding common stock of any particular corporation that the company may own.[19] There is usually no over-all limitation on the amount of preferred stock which can be held by a life insurance company, but the eligibility requirements with respect to the stock of a particular corporation are rather rigorous. In the aggregate, only about 2 per cent of life insurance companies' assets are invested in preferred stock.

The bases on which the various assets of a life insurance company are to be valued for annual statement purposes are prescribed by the National Association of Insurance Commissioners. The rules are too detailed to be discussed here.

Dividend Policy. A mutual life insurance company has no owners and presumably is operated solely for the benefit of the policyholders. In order to preserve equity among different classes and different generations of policyholders, any funds held by the company in excess of its present and anticipated needs, as determined by the management of the company, should be distributed on some equitable and current basis to the policyholders. To assure this result, the majority of states require that dividends be apportioned and paid annually, and some states place a limit on the amount of surplus that can be accumulated (usually, 10 per cent of the legal reserves). The general purpose of such statutory restrictions is to prevent the accumulation of such a large surplus that the company management might be tempted to operate the company in an extravagant manner, particularly with respect to the acquisition of new business. The requirement of annual apportionment of dividends has the further purpose of prohibiting the deferred dividend (tontine) type of contract, under which dividends were accumulated for a specified period, such as twenty years, and

---

[19] In the majority of states, there is no limitation on the amount of common stock of any particular corporation that a life insurer can hold, but seventeen states impose a maximum limitation of 10 per cent. In New York, the limitation is 2 per cent.

distributed to the policyholders surviving to the end of the period. This is considered to be a mixture of insurance and gambling and, as such, is illegal in most states.

Two other restrictions on dividend policy are sometimes encountered. In a few states mutual companies are usually forbidden to issue nonparticipating policies with certain exceptions,[20] while stock companies which issue participating policies may be subjected to a limitation on the amount that may be transferred from the participating surplus to the stockholders' surplus. The latter limitation is clearly designed to encourage a fair sharing of profits with participating policyholders.

Limitations on New Business. New York, alone among all the states, has established a limitation on the amount of new business which a company can write in a given year. No company operating in New York, and having more than $750 million of insurance in force, is permitted to write, in any one year, a face amount of insurance greater than $200,000,000 or 115 per cent of the volume of business written during the best of the three preceding years. The Superintendent of Insurance, however, is authorized to suspend the limit (subject to such rules and conditions as he may prescribe) for any company if its agency operations are conducted properly and economically, or he may suspend it for all companies if production generally exceeds the statutory limit. Stemming from the Armstrong Investigation, this statute aims to discourage excessive competition and also manifests a policy of antimonopoly, which is to be effected through spreading the business among all available carriers. The statute also contains a limitation on the amount of annuity business that can be written in any particular year.

Limitations on Expenses. New York and Wisconsin have laws which limit the amount of expenses that can be incurred in the writing of new business and maintaining the old business in force. These laws likewise grew out of the Armstrong Investigation and represent an attempt to prevent wasteful competition. The laws are extremely complex and cannot be dealt with here. Wisconsin even places a limit on the amount of loading in the gross premium of any policy—the only state having such a restriction.

Liquidation

If an insurance company gets in a position where it is unable to meet its obligations, the insurance commissioner of the state of incor-

---

[20] For example, New York permits a mutual company to issue nonparticipating policies in connection with extended term insurance, reduced paid-up insurance, immediate annuities and reinsurance.

poration has the responsibility and authority to assume control over the company. If it appears that with proper management, the company can be made solvent again, the insurance commissioner in most states can undertake to rehabilitate the company. If the company is hopelessly insolvent, liquidation proceedings are undertaken.

The original procedure for the liquidation of insolvent insurance companies was for the insurance commissioner to petition the proper court for the appointment of a receiver, who would then liquidate the company under the direction of the court. This is still the procedure in some states; but in a majority of jurisdictions, the insurance commissioner is charged with the responsibility of directly liquidating defunct companies. This is the procedure prescribed in the Uniform Insurers Liquidation Act, which has been adopted by a number of states. Some states have created a liquidation division within the insurance department for purposes of carrying out this function.

If an insurance commissioner has doubts concerning the solvency of an out-of-state company, he may suspend its license to do business in his state. Under such circumstances, he may advise the commissioner of the company's home state of his suspicions or findings and ask that the latter undertake liquidation proceedings, which, of course, would be instituted only after the company in question is given an opportunity to answer any charges made against it.

CHAPTER XL

*Types of Life Insurance Carriers**

IN A vigorous and free society, such as the one that exists in the United States, it is only natural that many different types of insurance organizations are to be found. In this chapter, an attempt is made to describe the essential characteristics of these various organizations through (1) a fairly detailed discussion of commercial life insurance companies—stock companies, mutual companies, and mixed companies—that operate primarily through agents compensated on a commission basis and (2) a brief discussion of certain other organizations, such as fraternal benefit societies, assessment associations, savings banks, and governmental agencies, which either offer life insurance without the service of an agency force, or have other characteristics that distinguish them from commercial life insurance companies.

It is important to recognize that a description of these major categories of insurance organizations cannot be developed in such a way as to encompass all of the possible variations that now exist or may come

* Prepared by Joseph M. Belth, Associate Professor of Insurance in Indiana University's Graduate School of Business.

The author acknowledges the assistance of several insurance professors, company representatives, and government officials who read a draft of this chapter. Particularly helpful were the comments made by Henry F. Scheig of the Aid Association for Lutherans, Robert J. Myers of the Social Security Administration, William T. Beadles of Illinois Wesleyan University, Spencer L. Kimball of the University of Michigan, and John D. Long of Indiana University. However, the author alone assumes full responsibility for the views expressed and for any errors that may remain.

into existence in the near future. Therefore, if one attempts to analyze a company that does not fit neatly into any of the major categories or has characteristics usually associated with more than one category of insurance organization, he may achieve an understanding of the nature of such a company by analyzing the organization from the standpoint of various bases of classification other than those mentioned above. Among the bases of classification not discussed in detail in this chapter are the organizational motivation for forming the company, sources of financial backing, types of insurance offered, distribution methods, types of clientele, territory of operation, place of domicile, reserve methods, and the size and age of the company.

COMMERCIAL LIFE INSURANCE COMPANIES

Most of the life insurance in force today in the private sector of the United States economy has been issued by commercial life insurance companies that operate primarily through agents compensated on a commission basis. These insurers are commonly classified as stock companies, mutual companies, or mixed companies.

Stock Companies

Nature of Stock Companies. A stock life insurance company is a form of legal reserve life insurance corporation in which there are stockholders to receive the earnings of the enterprise. Alternatively, it may be defined as a legal reserve life insurance corporation that currently shows a "capital" item in its balance sheet.

As a general rule, stock life insurance companies operate primarily for the purpose of earning profits for their stockholders. This does not mean, however, that other groups do not benefit from the operations of such companies. For example, stock life insurance companies may provide (1) a worthwhile service to the public in the form of life insurance protection and savings at a reasonable price, (2) an important source of investment funds for business and government, and (3) reasonably remunerative employment opportunities and favorable working conditions for the officers and employees of the insurance companies. In addition to these legitimate purposes for which stock life insurance companies are formed, some companies in recent years have apparently been formed primarily as stock promotion devices,[1] an activity of questionable social desirability.

---

[1] See Spencer L. Kimball and Jon S. Hanson, "The Regulation of Specialty Policies in Life Insurance," *Michigan Law Review,* Vol. 62, No. 2 (December, 1963),

Distribution of Surplus. In the usual case, a stock life insurance company is owned and controlled by its stockholders, because the stockholders elect the board of directors, which in turn is responsible for the appointment and terms of employment of the company's operating officers. Policyholders do not have voting rights, even if their insurance is participating. An exception to this latter rule is the "mixed" company discussed subsequently in this chapter.

It should be noted that it is not correct to say that the stockholders own the surplus of the company. As in the case of corporations generally, the only ways the stockholders of a life insurance company can receive any part of the surplus are through liquidation of the company, which would be followed by a distribution to the stockholders of any assets remaining after satisfaction of the company's obligations, or through the payment of stockholder cash dividends, which are authorized by the board of directors and not by the stockholders. It might be argued that an individual stockholder can obtain his share of the surplus by selling his stock, but whether this approach is available to an individual stockholder depends upon the state of the market for the company's stock. In any case, this latter approach is not feasible for the stockholders as a group.

Since liquidation involves destruction of the company and possibly serious financial loss to all parties concerned, cash dividends constitute the usual method by which stockholders receive a part of the surplus. If the stockholders feel that their cash dividends are not adequate, however, their only recourse is to oust the board of directors and replace it with a new board. This is a difficult task, particularly when stock ownership is widely held, and for this reason the stockholders' "ownership" of the assets represented by the surplus is usually best described as indirect or remote in nature.

Stock life insurance companies generally pay stockholder cash dividends that are quite small relative to the market value of the shares and relative to the stockholder cash dividends paid by other types of business firms. One possible explanation for this practice is the fact that a very important aspect of the operations of life insurance companies is the investment and reinvestment of its assets. Large cash dividends would reduce the amounts available for investment and would therefore prevent the company from utilizing its investment facilities

pp. 173–75; Irving Pfeffer, "Measuring the Profit Potential of a New Life Insurance Company," *Journal of Risk and Insurance,* Vol. XXXII, No. 3 (September, 1965), pp. 413–22; and Jon S. Hanson and Duncan R. Farney, "New Life Insurance Companies: Their Promotion and Regulation," *Marquette Law Review,* Vol. 49, No. 2 (Fall, 1965), pp. 178–88.

to the maximum extent possible. In short, the buyer of life insurance stock presumably invests primarily for capital growth rather than for substantial cash dividend income.

On the other hand, stock life insurance companies often declare stock dividends, sometimes of substantial size, and they also quite frequently utilize the stock split. Neither of these practices, in and of itself, increases the inherent value of a stockholder's interest in the company. However, they are often accompanied by an increase in the market value of the stockholder's interest in the company. For example, the cash dividend rate may remain the same after a stock dividend, and this would tend to offset the proportional decline in market value per share that theoretically accompanies a stock dividend. Similarly, stock dividends and stock splits seem to have some purely psychological but favorable reaction on stockholders and the market in general.[2] Finally, life insurance companies may favor stock dividends over cash dividends because the former are not includable currently as taxable income to the stockholders.

Valuation of Stockholders' Equity. Valuation of the interest of the stockholders is a complex and difficult matter in any type of corporation, but some interesting and unique additional problems are to be found in stock life insurance companies. Four of these special problems of stock valuation in life insurance companies are (1) the conservative manner in which reserve liabilities are computed, (2) the practice of charging off acquisition expenses in the year in which they are actually incurred, (3) the difficulties involved in estimating the present value of the future profits to be generated by business already on the books, and (4) the special problems associated with the sale of participating life insurance policies.

Conservatism is considered to be essential in the computation of the reserve liabilities of a life insurance company because most life insurance policy contracts are long term in nature and because it is important for a company to hold enough assets to be in a position to meet its future obligations with almost complete certainty. Conservative valuation of reserve liabilities is accomplished through the use of (1) "net premium" (as opposed to "gross premium") valuation, (2) relatively low interest assumptions, and (3) mortality tables that produce reserve liabilities larger than would be produced by the use of experi-

---

[2] A description of stock dividends and the arguments for and against their use can be found in most finance or accounting textbooks. See, e.g., Walter B. Meigs and Charles E. Johnson, *Accounting* (New York: McGraw-Hill Book Co., Inc., 1962), pp. 535–37.

ence tables. Thus, the stockholders' equity in a life insurance company, as shown on its balance sheet, is understated to the extent that the company's reserve liabilities are overstated. Adjustment for this conservatism in the valuation of reserve liabilities involves extremely complex calculations and, indeed, requires detailed information on the distribution of a company's business by such characteristics as age, plan, and duration—information that is not generally available to the public. Rules-of-thumb are sometimes used, but they must be handled with caution and with a realization that they may produce results that are quite far from the mark. One such rule-of-thumb, which has been used in the Life Insurance Company Income Tax Act of 1959, calls for decreasing the reserve liabilities of the company by 1 per cent for each one tenth of a percentage point by which the interest rate earned by the company on its assets exceeds the interest rate assumed by the company in computing its reserve liabilities.[3]

Life insurance accounting is sometimes considered as a hybrid form located somewhere between accrual basis and cash basis accounting. One area in which life insurance accounting is essentially on a cash basis is in the treatment of acquisition expenses. These are charged off immediately as expenses in the year in which they are incurred even though the business thus acquired usually will "run off the company's books" over a substantial number of years. The net result of this practice, in the usual case of a growing company, is an understatement of the company's surplus and profit in any given year.[4] Furthermore, the extent of the understatement and the rate of growth in the company's sales are likely to be related—the greater the rate of growth in sales, the greater the understatement of current surplus and profit. This problem has been a source of considerable dispute among some accountants and actuaries. The accountants argue that life insurance companies should follow "generally accepted accounting principles"; the actuaries argue that they are simply following the rules laid down by the state regulatory authorities, who are primarily concerned with solvency rather than the measurement of profitability. At the present time, the problem is being studied jointly by a group of accountants and actuaries.[5]

---

[3] See Chapter XLV for a detailed explanation of the computation of "adjusted reserves" under the Life Insurance Company Income Tax Act of 1959.

[4] For a discussion of this problem, see Reynolds Griffith, "A Note on Life Insurance Accounting," *Journal of Risk and Insurance,* Vol. XXXI, No. 2 (June, 1964), pp. 207–15.

[5] Security analysts as well as accountants have been critical of life insurance

The computation of the present value of the future profits to be generated by the business already on a company's books is an extremely complex task. Not only do reserve valuation practices and the manner in which acquisition expenses are accounted for enter into the picture, but also estimates must be made concerning future interest earnings, mortality rates, lapse rates, and company expenses. Furthermore, the complex calculations that would be needed cannot be undertaken without detailed information concerning premium levels, cash values, and the distribution of a company's outstanding business by such characteristics as age, plan, and duration. As mentioned earlier, this type of information is not usually available to the public. Although rules-of-thumb are used by analysts, these are open to question because of the substantial differences among companies in the variables that enter into the calculations.[6]

Some stock companies have in force only nonparticipating insurance. In such a company, the entire net worth, while available for the protection of policyholders against adverse developments, represents assets held for the ultimate benefit of the stockholders. Many stock companies, however, currently issue or at one time issued participating insurance, either alone or in conjunction with nonparticipating insurance. In the absence of any special charter provisions, statutory restrictions, or other legally binding agreements, the company's entire net worth, after the payment of dividends to participating policyholders, may be viewed in the same manner as the net worth of a stock company that has only nonparticipating insurance in force; that is, the company's net worth, while available for the protection of policyholders against adverse developments, represents assets held for the ultimate benefit of the stockholders.[7] On the other hand, some stock companies with participating business in force have charter provisions that impose special restrictions on the extent to which the stockholders may benefit from the participating business of the company. The effect of such a restriction is to require the company to hold all or almost all of the profits from the participating business, after the payment of

---

company annual statements. See, e.g., Corporate Information Committee of National Federation of Financial Analysts Societies, "Twelfth Annual Report" (1960).

[6] For a comprehensive discussion of this subject, see Melvin L. Gold, "Valuing a Life Insurance Company," *Transactions of the Society of Actuaries,* Vol. XIV (1962), pp. 139–70.

[7] *State of Ohio,* ex rel. *Wade H. Ellis, Attorney General* v. *Union Central Life Ins. Co.,* 13 C.C. (N.S.) 49, 22 C.D. 262 (1910); affirmed 84 O.S. 459, 95 N.E. 1156 (1911).

dividends to participating policyholders, for the benefit of the participating policyholders rather than for the benefit of the stockholders.[8] Furthermore, a few states impose special restrictions in this area and require authorized companies to enter into a binding agreement limiting the extent to which stockholders may benefit from the participating business of the company.[9] When limitations of this kind are in effect, they must be carefully considered in the evaluation of the interests of the stockholders.[10]

Conversion to Mutual Form. Some stock companies have been converted from their stock form into mutual form through a procedure that is called "mutualization." Simply stated, mutualization involves the retirement of the outstanding stock of the company and thereby the elimination of the "capital" item in the balance sheet, together with the transfer of control of the company from the stockholders to the policyholders. Several states have specific statutory provisions that outline the procedure that must be followed in mutualizing a stock company.[11] As a general rule, the mutualization plan is developed and approved by the company's board of directors, and then the plan must be approved by the stockholders, the policyholders, and the insurance commissioner in the company's state of domicile.

The plan must include, among other provisions, the purchase price of the shares and the terms under which they will be purchased. A plan often provides for the establishment of a trust that is designated to receive the shares from the stockholders. Since stockholders representing a majority of the stock must approve the plan initially, the bulk of the stock is usually turned over to the mutualization trustees promptly after the adoption and approval of the plan. This places the control of the company in the hands of the mutualization trustees until

---

[8] *Ohio State Life Ins. Co.* v. *Clark,* 274 F. (2d) 771 (1960); certiorari denied, 363 U.S. 828 (1960).

[9] Limitations of this kind are found in New York, Wisconsin, and New Jersey. A few other states have limitations that are imposed only on domestic companies or that have other special characteristics. Canada also imposes such restrictions. For a detailed description of regulation in this area, see Joseph M. Belth, *Participating Life Insurance Sold by Stock Companies* (Homewood, Ill.: Richard D. Irwin, Inc., 1965), pp. 66–100.

[10] The National Association of Insurance Commissioners is currently studying the question of whether model legislation should be developed in this area. At the time of this writing, the matter has been referred by a special subcommittee of the N.A.I.C. Laws and Legislation Committee to the Subcommittee on Examination Manual Revision of the N.A.I.C. Examinations Committee. The purpose of this referral is to secure, through examinations, the data necessary to determine whether legislation is needed.

[11] See, e.g., *New York Insurance Law,* Sec. 199 (2).

the last shares are received by the trustees, at which time all of the shares can be cancelled.

In theory the process of mutualization is quite simple. In practice, however, there usually will be some stockholders who feel that the price per share is too low, and for that reason they may refuse to surrender their shares and they may take court action in an attempt to block the mutualization. If they fail in court, they have no alternative but to turn in their shares eventually to the mutualization trustees, because no other market for the shares usually exists after adoption of the mutualization plan. Thus, if the plan meets with court approval, all the shares eventually are received by the trustees and the conversion can be completed, but the process of mutualization is usually characterized by a long, drawn out legal struggle that in some cases has stretched over many years.[12]

Mutual Companies

Nature of Mutual Companies. A mutual life insurance company is a form of legal reserve life insurance corporation in which there are no stockholders. Alternatively, it may be defined as a legal reserve life insurance corporation that currently has no "capital" item in its balance sheet.

It is difficult to state a general rule concerning the primary purpose for which mutual companies operate. On the one hand, it can be suggested that the primary purpose of a mutual company is to furnish life insurance protection and savings at as low a price as possible to the policyholders of the company. On the other hand, it can be suggested that the primary purpose of a mutual company is to earn profits, but because there are no stockholders, such profits may take the form of additions to surplus, increased salaries for officers, and/or improved home office and branch office facilities. As in the case of stock companies, mutual companies also provide an important source of investment funds for business and government.

Distribution of Surplus. In theory, the policyholders of a mutual life insurance company own and control the corporation. In practice, however, the widespread geographical dispersion of policyholders, their large numbers, and their relatively small individual financial

---

[12] According to one recent study, twenty-seven stock companies in the United States and Canada have been or are in the process of being mutualized. For a description of many of these mutualizations, as well as a discussion of the various reasons for mutualizations, see Linda Pickthorne Fletcher, "Mutualization of Stock Life Insurance Companies" (Ph.D. dissertation, University of Pennsylvania, 1964).

interest in the company generally cause an over-all pattern of policy-holder apathy, with the result that effective control of the company usually rests with the board of directors and/or the company management. Indeed, this subject has been given considerable thought over a long period of time. For example, in the Armstrong-Hughes investigation in New York in 1905, and again in the TNEC investigation in 1940, serious questions were raised concerning the lack of effective control by the policyholders of large mutual companies.[13]

It was mentioned earlier that it is not correct to say that the stockholders of a stock company own the surplus of the company. Similarly, it is not correct to say that the policyholders of a mutual company own the surplus of the corporation. Rather, the assets represented by the surplus of a mutual company are held by the corporation for the benefit of the policyholders *as a group,* and in the usual course of events the only way an individual policyholder can receive a portion of the surplus is through a distribution of surplus authorized by the company's board of directors.[14] This rule applies not only to existing policyholders but also to former policyholders of the company.[15]

These characteristics of mutual life insurance companies—surplus accumulations derived from the sale of complex long-term financial instruments together with a lack of effective control by the policyholders—have been the subjects of considerable discussion and speculation. For example, how would the existing surplus of a large mutual company be distributed if the company should go out of business? And, in such a situation, how would the surplus generated in the

---

[13] See *Report of the Joint Committee of the Senate and Assembly of the State of New York Appointed to Investigate the Affairs of Life Insurance Companies,* Assembly Document No. 41, Vol. X (Albany, 1906), pp. 366–80. See also *Investigation of Concentration of Economic Power* (Temporary National Economic Committee, Study of Legal Reserve Life Insurance Companies, Monograph No. 28, 76th Cong., 3d sess.) (Washington, D.C.: U.S. Government Printing Office, 1940), pp. 14–27. For some recent observations on this subject, see Allen L. Mayerson, "An Inside Look at Insurance Regulation," *Journal of Risk and Insurance,* Vol. XXXII, No. 1 (March, 1965), pp. 72–73; and Spencer L. Kimball, *Insurance and Public Policy* (Madison: University of Wisconsin Press, 1960), pp. 72–74.

[14] *Greeff* v. *Equitable Life Assur. Soc. of the U.S.,* 160 N.Y. 19, 54 N.E. 712 (1899).

[15] This was the issue in the "Chicago dividend cases." See *Andrews* v. *Equitable Life Assur. Soc. of the U.S.,* 124 F. (2d) 788 (1941); certiorari denied, 316 U.S. 682 (1941). See also *Lubin* v. *Equitable Life Assur. Soc. of the U.S.,* 326 Ill. App. 358, 61 N.E. (2d) 753 (1945).

future by the life insurance already in force be distributed? Fortunately, questions of this kind have not yet required answers because no major mutual companies have gone out of business and it does not appear that any of them will do so, at least in the foreseeable future.[16]

Mutual companies, as a general rule, issue only participating policies. There are exceptions, however. Many mutual companies, for example, issue nonparticipating annuities, and it is also common for mutual companies to issue some of their nonforfeiture options and dividend options on a nonparticipating basis. Similarly, nonparticipating term insurance riders are often attached to basic participating policies.

A few mutual companies offer a regular line of nonparticipating life insurance. At the present time, most states either permit this practice through specific provision in their laws or permit the practice in the absence of any statutory prohibitions. In a few states, however, certain restrictions are present. For example, in New York, domestic and out-of-state mutual companies are prohibited from issuing nonparticipating life insurance (both within and outside New York).[17] In New Jersey, although the law is silent on the subject, the insurance commissioner has imposed certain restrictions on the sale of nonparticipating life insurance by mutual companies. This subject is of considerable current interest because several large Canadian companies that recently mutualized wish to continue issuing nonparticipating insurance.[18]

Conversion to Stock Form. A few mutual companies have been converted into the stock form through a procedure that might be called "stockization." Such a conversion involves the issuance of stock and a transfer of control from the policyholders to the stockholders. Although the procedure sounds simple, it is complicated by the fact that many state laws do not provide for conversions of this kind. In one recent such conversion, a new stock company was formed and the mutual company was then merged into the stock company. Under the

---

[16] For an extremely interesting interchange on this subject between the president of a well-established mutual company and the late Senator Robert S. Kerr of Oklahoma, see *Taxation on Life Insurance Income* (Hearings before the Committee on Finance, United States Senate, 85th Cong., 2d sess., on H.R. 10021) (Washington, D.C.: U.S. Government Printing Office, 1958), pp. 96–103.

[17] *New York Insurance Law*, Sec. 216 (5).

[18] See "Digest of Discussion of Subjects of Special Interest," *Transactions of the Society of Actuaries*, Vol. XVII (1965), pp. D25–36.

plan, the policyholders of the mutual company received preferred shares in the stock company in accordance with their individual interest in the surplus of the mutual company as determined by an actuarial analysis.[19] In the past, serious questions have been raised concerning various conversions of mutual companies into the stock form.[20]

Mixed Companies

Some companies display ownership attributes that represent a blending of the characteristics of both stock companies and mutual companies. Perhaps the clearest example of such a company is one in which part of the board of directors is elected by the stockholders and another part is elected by the participating policyholders. This type of company, which might be properly called a "mixed" company, is provided for in the Canadian statutes, which require that, if a stock company has participating policyholders, at least one third of the directors must be policyholders' directors.[21] However, most American stock companies that sell both lines provide no voting rights for participating policyholders. Some authors refer to a stock company that sells both participating and nonparticipating insurance as a mixed company, but it would seem to be better terminology to reserve this expression for companies in which both stockholders and participating policyholders have voting rights.

A similar concept is embodied in the Minnesota law, which makes it possible to form a domestic "stock and mutual company," in which participating policyholders as well as stockholders have voting rights.[22] The Minnesota law, however, does not provide for a fixed minimum number or proportion of policyholders' directors; rather, stockholders and participating policyholders both vote for all the directors. This arrangement means that the policyholder-stockholder orientation of the board cannot be determined in advance, and also that the relative voting strengths of the policyholders and stockholders may shift with the passage of time.

---

[19] See "Memo Explains How Mutual Life Company Switched to Stock," *The National Underwriter* (Life ed.), March 27, 1965, p. 21. Although the plan has been approved by the insurance commissioner in the company's state of domicile, the case is not yet settled because legal action by one of the policyholders is pending.

[20] See, e.g., *Investigation of Concentration of Economic Power, op. cit.*, pp. 65–70; and Kimball, *op. cit.*, pp. 84–91.

[21] *Revised Statutes of Canada 1952*, Chap. 31, Sec. 6 (5).

[22] *Minnesota Statutes*, Sec. 61.04.

Comparison of Stock Companies and Mutual Companies

A perennial question that arises in discussions of life insurance carriers is whether an insurance buyer should purchase his coverage from a stock company or from a mutual company. This question cannot be answered in generalized form.

It is often difficult for the typical buyer to determine whether a given company is stock or mutual in form. Some stock companies have become mutuals and a few mutuals have become stock companies. A few stock companies have the word "mutual" in their titles, and many mutual companies, including some of the largest life insurance companies in the world, do not have the word "mutual" in their titles. However, even if it is possible to determine readily whether a company is stock or mutual, there are numerous other bases of classification that might be much more meaningful in terms of the objectives of the buyer. Some of these bases of classification are mentioned at the beginning of this chapter. For example, since no one distribution method is necessarily associated with any one type of company, there would appear to be no inherent difference between the two types of companies in the area of advice or service. Therefore, the question of the relative desirability of the two types of companies from the viewpoint of the buyer apparently refers to the subjects of (1) financial strength and (2) the price of protection.

Financial Strength. In the very early years of a stock life insurance company, the amount contributed by the stockholders is likely to represent a substantial proportion of the total assets of the company. Indeed, so substantial is the need for funds in a company's early years that formation of a company on the mutual plan is generally considered impractical. To form a company on a purely mutual basis requires a substantial number of policyholders who are willing to apply for policies and pay initial premiums before the company can actually be launched.[23] Perhaps even more important, however, is the fact that young companies often find it necessary to obtain additional funds again and again before they achieve a level of investment income and

---

[23] It is possible to form a mutual company with a fund of guaranty capital that is to be returned to the contributors as soon as possible. Some of today's major mutual companies were formed in this manner. Until such time as the fund is liquidated, however, the company is essentially a stock company. Indeed, one large company that was originally formed as a mutual company with guaranty capital never liquidated the fund. Today the company is sometimes called a mutual even though its shares of guaranty capital are actively traded in the over-the-counter market in the same manner as the shares of stock companies.

renewal premium income sufficient to support their operations.[24] For these reasons, new companies are invariably formed as stock companies.[25]

With this background, one can see that the contributions of the stockholders have a tendency to strengthen a company during its early years. However, because of the difficulties associated with forming a mutual company, it is unlikely that a prospective buyer would find young mutual companies to compare to young stock companies.

As a stock company grows in size, the contribution of the stockholders tends to decline steadily in importance relative to the stabilizing influence of investment income, renewal premiums, and the margins built into participating premiums if the company offers a participating line. When a stock company is large and well established, the stockholders' equity generally represents a minor portion of the company's total resources that would be available for the protection of policyholders. At the same time, cash dividends to stockholders are usually relatively small and do not constitute a significant drain on the resources of the company.

Furthermore, when a large stock company is compared with a large mutual company in terms of financial strength, consideration must also be given to the participating or nonparticipating nature of the business written by the two companies. As a general rule, if the stock company writes participating business, the latter is likely to represent less than half of the company's total life insurance business. In a mutual company, however, all or almost all of the business is likely to be participating. Since participating premiums generally contain margins substantially larger than the margins in nonparticipating premiums, there is a strong likelihood that the additional value of the premium margins in the mutual company would be at least as great as the value of the stockholders' equity in the stock company. Therefore, from the buyer's viewpoint, it seems clear that neither stock companies nor mutual companies have any inherent advantages over the other in terms of financial strength; indeed, the relative financial strengths of individual companies are very difficult to measure.

Price of Protection.[26]   In a general and theoretical sense, it is

---

[24] See Mayerson, *op. cit.,* pp. 62–64.

[25] See Chapter XLI for a discussion of the process of forming a life insurance company.

[26] The word "price" is used in this chapter to denote the price of only the life insurance protection contained in a policy, in contrast to the word "premium," which

sometimes argued that, other things being equal, a mutual company should deliver protection at a lower price than a stock company because the latter must pay some of its profits to its stockholders. In practice, however, other things are never equal. For example, it is sometimes argued in the opposite direction that a stock company should be able to deliver protection at a lower price than a mutual company because the stockholders "looking over the shoulders of the management" tend to force a stock company into a higher level of efficiency than an otherwise comparable mutual company. Furthermore, in terms of dollars and cents, the only relevant difference between a stock company and an otherwise identical mutual company is the amount of cash dividends paid to stockholders. The presence of this item must be balanced against the fact that the stockholders have made a contribution to the stock company's total resources, and, as mentioned earlier, stockholder cash dividends are usually not very large in relation to the total dollar amounts associated with major life insurance companies.

If a person attempts to make a direct comparison between a stock company and a mutual company in terms of the price of protection, it becomes necessary to determine whether the insurance in question is participating or nonparticipating. Since any attempt to compare participating insurance directly with nonparticipating insurance creates special analytical problems, as discussed later, the only relevant comparisons at this point must involve similar types of insurance. If the buyer has decided to purchase nonparticipating insurance, he is almost forced to buy it from a stock company, since very few mutual companies offer nonparticipating insurance.

If the buyer has decided to purchase participating insurance, he has a choice of company type because participating insurance is sold by all mutual companies and by many stock companies. The problem, then, is to compare the prices charged by stock companies for participating insurance to the corresponding prices charged by mutual companies. In one such study, the author found that the mean of the prices charged by a considerable number of stock companies for participating straight life policies issued to standard males aged thirty-five tended to be somewhat above the mean of the corresponding prices charged by a considerable number of mutual companies.[27]

---

provides for both the protection element and any savings element that might be built into the policy. See Belth, *op. cit.*, pp. 35–49.

[27] *Ibid.*

For several reasons, however, the above results must be carefully qualified. First, and perhaps most important, a substantial amount of price variation was present among both stock companies and mutual companies. The prices of several of the stock companies in the study were well below the prices of many of the mutual companies. In one of the pairs of arrays, for example, the mean of the prices of thirty-seven stock companies was approximately 15 per cent above the mean of the prices of the fifty-one mutual companies. However, the prices of ten of the stock companies were below the prices of twenty-five of the mutual companies.

Secondly, the mutual companies in the study were, on the average, older and larger than the stock companies in the study. This fact suggests the possibility that the age and/or size of the companies might be associated with the prices they charge, and that from the buyer's viewpoint such characteristics might be at least as important as the stock or mutual form of the company.

Thirdly, the results of the above study must be qualified because of the difficulties encountered in securing the necessary data. The companies included in the study were chosen on the basis of availability of data rather than through random sampling techniques. The results are therefore applicable only to the companies studied and cannot be used to make inferences about the life insurance business as a whole.

Participating versus Nonparticipating Insurance

In discussions of the relative advantages of mutual companies and stock companies from the buyer's viewpoint, the discussants are often really referring to the relative advantages of participating and nonparticipating insurance. As suggested above, however, it is important to distinguish between the form of company and the nature of the insurance contract. In the paragraphs that follow is a discussion of the relative advantages of participating and nonparticipating insurance from the buyer's viewpoint, a subject that deals essentially with the relative prices of these two types of contracts.

At the outset it should be noted that it is sometimes difficult to decide what constitutes a "participating" policy. Some companies have begun paying dividends on their "nonparticipating" policies. Other companies have reduced participating gross premiums virtually to the level of nonparticipating gross premiums and project very small dividends that could be eliminated entirely by relatively minor adverse mortality or economic developments. The discussion that follows is based on the type of policy that is usually associated with the word "participating"; that is, a policy whose premium is substantially above the premium for an otherwise comparable nonparticipating policy and with respect to which the company contemplates the payment of fairly substantial periodic dividends.

Direct comparisons between participating prices and nonparticipating prices must be interpreted with care for at least two reasons. First, if dividend projections are used for the participating portion of the comparison, any possible conclusions must be qualified to reflect the fact that the dividends entering into the computation of participating prices are not guaranteed, while the computation of nonparticipating prices is based entirely on contractual guarantees. Secondly, if dividend histories are used for the participating portion of the comparison, any possible conclusions to be drawn for the purpose of providing guidance to new buyers must be qualified because the pattern of dividends probably was affected at least to some degree by economic conditions that are unlikely to be duplicated in the future.

In theory, it seems logical that the price of a participating policy based on dividend *projections* should be lower than the price of an otherwise comparable nonparticipating policy. In other words, because of the inherent flexibility of the dividend aspect of participating insurance, less conservatism is needed in the over-all price structure (which reflects dividends as well as premiums and cash values) of a participating block of business. Whether the price of a participating policy based on dividend *histories* actually proves to be lower than the price of an otherwise comparable nonparticipating policy depends in large measure on (1) the experience of the company issuing the participating policy with respect to the various factors that enter into price and (2) the philosophy of the company with respect to the payment of dividends to policyholders.

In a recent study,[28] the author found that the mean of the prices charged by a considerable number of companies (both stock and mutual) for participating straight life policies issued to standard males aged thirty-five, based on dividend *projections,* did indeed tend to be lower than the mean of the prices charged by a considerable number of stock companies for corresponding nonparticipating policies. When participating prices based on dividend *histories* were compared with

---

[28] See Chapters 5 and 11 in Joseph M. Belth, *The Retail Price Structure in American Life Insurance* (Bloomington, Ind.: Indiana University Bureau of Business Research, 1966).

corresponding nonparticipating prices, however, mixed results were obtained. On policies issued in 1930, the mean of the participating prices tended to be above the mean of the nonparticipating prices; but on policies issued in 1940, the mean of the nonparticipating prices tended to be above the mean of the participating prices.

In view of the results of the above-mentioned study, the pattern of interest rates in recent decades, and the importance of the interest element in cash-value policies, it might be hypothesized that (1) participating insurance tends to be preferable from a price standpoint when the future trend of interest rates is stable or upward and (2) nonparticipating insurance tends to be preferable when the future trend of interest rates is downward. But even if such an hypothesis could be strongly supported, it would not automatically resolve the question of the relative desirability of participating and nonparticipating insurance for present buyers. The prospective buyer would still be faced with an equally difficult task of forming conclusions about the future trend of interest rates. Moreover, the above discussion deals only with the means of arrays, and the price variation present in some of the arrays is of such magnitude that considerable care is needed in the interpretation of the results.

OTHER TYPES OF LIFE INSURANCE CARRIERS

Although most American life insurance is issued by commercial companies of the types described in the preceding section of this chapter, a substantial amount is issued by organizations of other types, including fraternal benefit societies, assessment associations, savings banks, and governmental agencies. In this section of the chapter, these types of carriers are described briefly.

Fraternal Life Insurance Societies[29]

Nature of Fraternal Societies. Fraternal life insurance may be distinguished from commercial life insurance by the fact that the former is issued by fraternal benefit societies while the latter is issued by commercial life insurance companies. Fraternal benefit societies are nonprofit social organizations that operate through the lodge system. Examples of fraternal benefit societies are the Knights of Columbus, the Aid Association for Lutherans, and the Independent Order of

---

[29] For a comprehensive discussion of this subject, see Richard deRaismes Kip, *Fraternal Life Insurance in America* (Philadelphia: College Offset Press, 1953).

Foresters. The life insurance activities of fraternal benefit societies are governed by different sections of the state statutes than those under which commercial life insurance companies operate.

Fraternal benefit societies exist primarily as social organizations that promote good fellowship and cooperation among their members. They may engage in various forms of charitable and benevolent activity, particularly in respect to the needs of their own members. Fraternal benefit societies are characterized by a representative form of government, in that members of local lodges elect their representatives or delegates to the state lodge, which makes decisions on matters pertinent to the state operations of the society, and members of the state lodge elect their representatives to the supreme lodge. societies are also characterized by membership restrictions, in that they often admit only members of a particular nationality, religious group, or occupational group.

Development of Fraternal Life Insurance. The issuance of life insurance by fraternal benefit societies in this country began in the years immediately following the Civil War. There were numerous reasons for the rapid early growth of fraternal life insurance. First, it was generally felt that the commercial life insurance companies were concentrating their efforts primarily in the middle and upper income groups, and that the fraternal approach would be one way in which to make life insurance more readily available to those with lower incomes.[30]

Secondly, level-premium life insurance and the associated concept of a reserve were under attack in several respects. Premium rates were thought to be very high, and there was general public misunderstanding and suspicion concerning the function of the reserve. Furthermore, in most of the states, laws requiring nonforfeiture values had not yet been enacted, and some companies did not provide such values.

Thirdly, many policyholders of commercial companies were disappointed at the size of the dividends they were receiving in relation to the dividends that had been projected at the time of purchase. This problem was particularly noticeable in connection with the use of premium notes, because it had been suggested that dividends would be

---

[30] Industrial life insurance developed in this country at about the same time as fraternal life insurance and was attributed largely to this same feeling concerning the nonavailability of life insurance to persons in the lower income groups. See Chapter XXXVII for a description of industrial life insurance.

large enough to permit the policyholder to pay off the notes with the dividends. Similarly, the problem was quite serious in connection with tontine dividend policies, under which persistency was much higher than anticipated and dividend accumulations for surviving and persisting policyholders were consequently much lower than projected.

Fourthly, it was widely felt that the expenses incurred by the commercial companies in acquiring new business were excessive. Increases in the level of agents' commissions also encouraged the practice of rebating.

Finally, a substantial number of commercial companies failed during this period. Some failures resulted from financial disturbances, such as the Panic of 1873, and others apparently occurred as a natural consequence of the large number of company formations in the years immediately following the Civil War.

Under these circumstances, fraternal life insurance came into existence in this country and flourished to such an extent that, in the latter part of the nineteenth century, its insurance in force approached the amount of ordinary business in force in the commercial companies. As will be seen, however, troubles lay ahead for fraternal life insurance.

The Assessment Principle. In the early development of fraternal life insurance, one of its most important characteristics was its operation on the basis of a postmortem assessment or one of the subsequent modifications of the assessment principle.[31] This general approach was adopted by the fraternals in their belief that the level-premium method and its associated system of reserves were not essential to the sound operation of a life insurance organization. Indeed, much of the appeal of the fraternals was based upon the above-mentioned public misunderstanding and suspicion concerning level-premium life insurance and the accompanying reserves. The fraternals in their early years of operation did not hesitate to disassociate themselves from the reserving techniques of the commercial life insurance companies.

As some of the fraternal societies encountered financial difficulties as a result of the problems associated with the assessment principle, the fraternals began to shift gradually in their attitude toward reserves. Many fraternals, even from their inception, did maintain some reserves, in that their rates of assessment were established at a level somewhat higher than necessary to meet their current benefit pay-

---

[31] See Chapter II for a description of the various forms of assessment insurance and the problems associated with it.

ments. However, these early reserves were by no means comparable to the system of reserves employed by the commercial companies; rather, they were designed to level out fluctuations in current experience. As time passed, however, it became apparent that reserves of the type employed by the commercial companies were essential to the proper functioning of a life insurance organization, and the fraternals gradually moved in that direction.

The transition to a system of reserves was an extremely difficult one for the fraternals because of their history of opposition to that concept as it was practiced by commercial companies. One of the important developments that led eventually to widespread use of reserves by fraternals was the construction in 1899 of the National Fraternal Congress Table of Mortality. Because of opposition within the fraternal ranks to the concept of reserves, however, it was many years before model valuation legislation applicable to fraternals was finally made effective in most of the states.

Other Characteristics of Fraternal Life Insurance. Fraternal life insurance in many ways resembles commercial life insurance. For example, many of the provisions of fraternal life insurance contracts are similar to those found in commercial policies. Also, the use of field representatives by fraternals is often quite similar to the marketing approach of commercial companies, although their functions include the solicitation of new members for their societies. Some societies accept "social members" who do not own insurance; and some societies solicit new members through local lodge secretaries who are not full-time representatives.

One important and distinctive characteristic of fraternal life insurance is its utilization of an "open" contract. The certificate issued to the holder of fraternal life insurance contains not only the benefit provisions but also the constitution and bylaws of the society. The supreme governing body of the society, which consists of representatives elected by the members, can alter the bylaws of the society and thus in effect alter the provisions of the life insurance certificate. However, state laws that have adopted the NAIC uniform code applicable to fraternals require that "no change, addition or amendment shall destroy or diminish benefits which the society contracted to give the member as of the date of issuance."

The "open" contract thus permits a fraternal benefit society that gets into financial difficulties to assess its certificate holders and thus keep itself afloat. This is in contrast to the situation of a commercial life insurance company that issues the typical "closed" contract and gets into financial difficulties. In the latter case, the policyholders cannot be assessed, so the company would be forced to merge with another company, reinsure its business in another company, or go into receivership.

Another distinctive characteristic of fraternal life insurance lies in the area of taxation. Fraternal benefit societies are exempt from most taxes, including the federal income tax and state premium taxes. This favorable treatment is based upon the fact that fraternal benefit societies are considered to be essentially nonprofit organizations that engage in various types of charitable and benevolent activity. In addition, it appears that the societies have been successful in opposing changes in their tax treatment, not only through high-level legislative contacts but also through effective "grass roots" activities by members of local lodges.

Fraternals are subject to regulation that differs in some respects from the regulation that is applicable to commercial companies. Reserve requirements similar to those imposed on commercial companies are now imposed on fraternal benefit societies, but these requirements are not necessarily the same as those applicable to commercial companies. Some states do not require the licensing of field representatives of fraternal benefit societies.

Current Status of Fraternal Life Insurance. Following the introduction and early rapid growth of fraternal life insurance, the amount of fraternal business in force in this country declined absolutely during the period from 1920 to 1940. Since that time, however, fraternal life insurance in force has grown steadily, but at a slower rate than the ordinary business of commercial companies. At the end of 1965, the amount of life insurance in force in United States and Canadian fraternal societies was about $16 billion, in contrast to $521 billion of ordinary and $329 billion of group life insurance in force in United States commercial life insurance companies.[32] The relatively slow growth of fraternal life insurance is perhaps attributable not only to the vigorous promotion of ordinary business by the commercial companies, but also to the rapid rise in the importance of group insurance. At the same time, such far-reaching changes as the growing

---

[32] *Life Insurance Fact Book 1966* (New York: Institute of Life Insurance, annual), pp. 23, 27, 103.

importance of television and the automobile may be reducing the relative importance of the local lodge as an American institution.

Assessment Associations[33]

As mentioned above, the introduction of the assessment principle in this country was attributable in large measure to certain difficulties encountered by the commercial companies with level premiums and the accompanying reserves. The problems of the commercial companies gave rise not only to fraternals, which were generally considered nonprofit in nature, but also to assessment associations, which were regular profit-making organizations.

Although some assessment associations now maintain regular reserves, others do not. Level premiums are often charged, but the association usually has the right to assess policyholders if losses make assessments necessary. Some states prohibit the formation of new assessment associations and require the maintenance of reserves with respect to new members of existing associations. The amount of assessment life insurance in force has been declining steadily, and at the end of 1965 there was about $1 billion in force in United States associations.[34]

Savings Banks[35]

Origin of Savings Bank Life Insurance. The idea of issuing life insurance over-the-counter in mutual savings banks is attributed to Louis D. Brandeis, who was to become an associate justice of the United States Supreme Court. Just prior to the Armstrong-Hughes investigation in New York in 1905, a group of policyholders of the Equitable Life Assurance Society formed a Policyholders' Protective Committee to investigate the situation in that company, and Brandeis was retained as counsel for the committee. While working with that committee, he conceived the idea of savings bank life insurance.

Brandeis was concerned primarily with what he considered to be excessive prices for industrial life insurance. He felt that the mutual savings banks had established a good record of conservative and eco-

---

[33] For a discussion of the relationship between fraternal benefit societies and assessment associations, see J. Owen Stalson, *Marketing Life Insurance* (Cambridge, Mass.: Harvard University Press, 1942), pp. 445–61.

[34] *Life Insurance Fact Book 1966, op. cit.,* p. 103.

[35] For a detailed treatment of this subject, see Donald R. Johnson, *Savings Bank Life Insurance* (Homewood, Ill.: Richard D. Irwin, Inc., 1963).

nomical operations and that they could offer life insurance over-the-counter at prices substantially below those charged by the commercial companies for industrial life insurance. The main reasons for the lower prices, he felt, would be (1) lower acquisition costs (because no soliciting agents would be used) and (2) lower lapse rates (because policyholders would make their purchases voluntarily instead of under the influence of high-pressure salesmanship).

There was strong opposition to the Brandeis plan, not only from life insurance companies, but also from many public officials and even from many of the savings banks themselves. Despite the opposition, however, a bill authorizing the establishment of a system of savings bank life insurance in Massachusetts was signed into law in 1907 and the system went into operation the following year.

In New York, abortive attempts to enact savings bank life insurance legislation were made in 1909 and 1910. No further action was taken in New York until the 1930's. Finally, after an intensive political struggle, a bill was signed into law in 1938 by Governor Herbert H. Lehman, and the system went into operation in 1939.

In Connecticut, after considerable debate, a bill authorizing savings bank life insurance was enacted in 1941 and the system went into operation in 1942. Thus, to date, there are just three states in which savings bank life insurance has been authorized, although there are some fourteen other states that have mutual savings banks. In several of these, including Delaware, Maine, Maryland, Missouri, New Hampshire, New Jersey, and Pennsylvania, consideration has been given to the establishment of savings bank life insurance systems. In these states, however, the proponents have not pressed hard enough and/or the opponents have been too powerful, because no enabling legislation has been enacted.

Characteristics of Savings Bank Life Insurance. In each of the three states in which savings bank life insurance is in operation, the insurance is issued by mutual savings banks that desire to sell such insurance, but the over-all administration of the plan is in the hands of a centralized agency. In Massachusetts, supervision and regulatory control of the system is carried out by the Division of Savings Bank Life Insurance, which is a part of the Massachusetts Department of Banking and Insurance. Actuarial, underwriting, and other services usually performed by home offices of life insurance companies are provided by this Division. In 1938, a voluntary association of issuing banks called the Savings Bank Life Insurance Council was formed, and the

Council has taken over some of the functions of the Division of Savings Bank Life Insurance. There is also a General Insurance Guaranty Fund, to which the individual issuing banks make periodic contributions. It serves as a contingency fund over and above the contingency funds held by the individual banks.

In New York, the central administrative body is the Savings Bank Life Insurance Fund. It handles the functions of all three of the organizations listed above in the description of the Massachusetts system. In Connecticut, the central administrative body is known as The Savings Bank Life Insurance Company.

Savings bank life insurance is further characterized by the unification of mortality. This means that the mortality experience of the issuing banks in a given state is combined so that fluctuations in the mortality experience of individual banks are in effect distributed among all of the banks within a state system.

The insurance department of an issuing bank operates separately from the banking department. The assets of the insurance department are not available for the satisfaction of the liabilities of the banking department, and, conversely, the assets of the banking department are not applicable to the liabilities of the insurance department. Policyholders, therefore, can look only to the assets of the bank's insurance department and the assets in the contingency fund maintained by the central administrative agency in the state.

In the early years of its operation, the Massachusetts system was directly subsidized by the state, which paid some of the system's operating expenses and furnished rent free office space to the Division of Savings Bank Life Insurance. Similarly, the Connecticut system in its early years received a subsidy in the form of rent free office space. In Connecticut and New York, indirect subsidies were paid by the states through the respective state insurance departments, which were involved so closely in the regulation of savings bank life insurance that they were in effect performing some of the functions that would normally be performed by the management in a life insurance company. In recent years, however, these direct and indirect subsidies are no longer in effect, and the three systems of savings bank life insurance are self-supporting and separate from their respective states. The issuing banks in each case reimburse the central agency for its expenses of operation.

Savings bank life insurance operates under three types of restrictions. First, the banks are prohibited from using soliciting agents. This restriction is consistent with the original savings bank life insurance objectives of providing over-the-counter insurance protection and avoiding the substantial acquisition expenses that were being incurred by the commercial companies. In practice, however, some of the functions of the agent are in effect performed by employees of the bank and by the bank through its promotional efforts.

Secondly, the issuing banks in each state may accept applications only from persons who reside in the state or are regularly employed in the state. Although persons who buy the insurance may continue it if they subsequently leave the state, this restriction makes each savings bank life insurance system essentially a one-state operation.

Thirdly, maximum limitations are placed upon the amount of savings bank life insurance that can be issued on any one life. In Massachusetts, the limit is $1,000 times the number of issuing banks in the state. At the present time there are thirty-six issuing banks, so the aggregate upper limit is $36,000. However, any one bank in Massachusetts is limited to $5,000 on any one life, so an individual must purchase separate policies from eight different issuing banks in order to obtain maximum coverage.

In New York, the upper limit on any one life is $10,000 of any policy type plus $20,000 (initial amount) of decreasing term insurance. Thus, an individual can purchase up to $30,000 of decreasing term or a combination of other insurance and decreasing term such that the total is not over $30,000 and the amount of insurance other than decreasing term is not over $10,000. There is no distinction between the aggregate limit and the maximum that may be issued by any one bank, so an individual in New York may purchase the maximum in one policy at one bank.

In Connecticut, the limit is $5,000 on any one life, and the full amount can be purchased in one policy at one bank. Attempts have been made recently to increase the limit to $15,000, but the proposal has been strongly opposed by life insurance agents in Connecticut.

Another characteristic of savings bank life insurance is its low price. It is generally felt, on the basis of limited studies, that the savings banks offer life insurance at prices somewhat below most if not all of the commercial companies. However, although the policy forms are quite similar, there is some question about the comparability of the life insurance sold without agents by savings banks and the life insurance sold through agents by commercial companies. To the extent that agents may offer competent advice and conscientious service to their policyholders, and to the extent that the employees of savings banks may not do so, direct price comparisons between these two sources of life insurance may not be meaningful. On the other hand, it must be recognized that the savings banks may be in a position to offer advice and service equal to or better than that offered by many life insurance agents, and in that sense there may be real price advantages for buyers of savings bank life insurance.

Current Status of Savings Bank Life Insurance. At the end of 1965, there was about $2.1 billion of savings bank life insurance in force in the three states combined.[36] Although this figure is very small relative to the $521 billion of ordinary business in force in the commercial companies, the geographical and amount restrictions under which the savings banks operate must be recognized. For example, the $2.1 billion figure is much more impressive relative to the $79 billion of ordinary business in force in the three states combined. Indeed, in Massachusetts, where the savings bank life insurance system is the oldest of the three, and where promotion is apparently the most vigorous of the three, the ordinary business of the savings banks represents about 6 per cent of the ordinary business in force in the state. It might also be noted that, at the end of 1964, there were only three commercial companies operating in Massachusetts that had more ordinary business in force in the state than the savings banks.[37]

On the one hand, the fairly small amount of business in force in the savings banks is sometimes used as an example of the difficulties involved in marketing life insurance without agents. On the other hand, the life insurance business in general and life insurance agents in particular have strongly opposed the relaxation of the maximum amount limitations and the establishment of savings bank life insurance systems in additional states. The unanswered question, therefore, is whether the savings banks as a medium for marketing life insurance have been unable to secure a substantial share of the market because they do not employ agents, or whether they have been prevented from demonstrating their full potential by the opposition of agents and/or commercial life insurance companies to legislative changes that would permit expansion of savings bank life insurance.

Governmental Agencies

Numerous governmental agencies offer various forms of life insurance protection in the public sector of the United States economy.

---

[36] *Life Insurance Fact Book 1966, op. cit.,* p. 103.

[37] *The Spectator Desk Directory of Insurance 1965* (Philadelphia: The Chilton Company, annual), pp. L236–37.

Among these agencies are the Social Security Administration, the Veterans Administration, and the State of Wisconsin.

Social Security Administration. A very important source of life insurance protection in the United States is the survivors' benefits portion of the Old-Age, Survivors, and Disability Insurance program, which is administered by the Social Security Administration of the federal Department of Health, Education, and Welfare. The original Social Security Act, which was passed by Congress in 1935, provided only for certain retirement benefits and lump-sum death payments that were in the nature of a refund of contributions. In 1939, however, the program was expanded to include life insurance benefits on a monthly basis for certain survivors of covered workers. In 1956, the program was further expanded to provide certain monthly disability benefits. In 1965, hospital insurance benefits for persons aged sixty-five or over and a program of voluntary medical expense insurance for this group were included in the system.[38]

Over the years, the program has expanded not only in terms of additional types of benefits, but also in terms of benefit levels and the percentage of the population that is covered. At the present time, about 90 per cent of the employed population is covered by the system, and the total benefit payments from the system in 1965 amounted to approximately $18.3 billion.[39] The magnitude of the OASDI program may be placed in perspective by noting that the total benefit payments in 1965 by the private life insurance business amounted to $11.4 billion, including policy dividends.[40]

The OASDI system is financed by payroll taxes levied upon both employers and employees. As the program and benefit levels have expanded, payroll tax rates have steadily increased. Payroll taxes are currently levied on the first $6,600 of covered wages earned in a calendar year by an employee from a particular employer. The employee tax rates (an identical tax rate is levied on employers, and a special schedule of tax rates is applicable to self-employed individuals) now scheduled in support of present benefit levels, including the new hospital insurance benefits for the aged, are as follows:

---

[38] It seems likely that the system will soon be referred to as OASDHI—the Old-Age, Survivors, Disability, and Health Insurance Program—but at present it is still referred to as OASDI, supplemented by a new program of hospital insurance benefits and voluntary medical expense insurance for the aged.

[39] *Life Insurance Fact Book 1966, op. cit.,* p. 104.

[40] *Ibid.,* p. 37.

Year	Rate
1966	4.2 %
1967–68	4.4
1969–72	4.9
1973–75	5.4
1976–79	5.45
1980–86	5.55
1987 and thereafter	5.65

The accumulated trust fund is substantially smaller than the estimated present value of the accrued benefits under the program. However, the system is considered to be in "actuarial balance," in that the present value of future tax receipts for the next seventy-five years, together with the existing trust fund, is approximately equal to the present value of future benefit payments and administrative expenses for the same period, based on the assumptions made by the Social Security Administration. At the present time, the system is operating very much like a pay-as-you-go system, because the annual tax receipts plus interest receipts in recent years have been approximately equal to the annual outgo.

The life insurance portion of the program consists of a lump-sum death benefit and an income benefit for survivors. The latter is generally payable to the widow of a covered worker provided that the widow is either aged sixty or has children under age eighteen in her care. The present value of the income benefit may amount to a substantial figure, particularly for the young family of a deceased worker. The actual schedule of benefits is frequently changed by Congress, and the various provisions relative to eligibility requirements are quite complex. For these reasons, detailed information on an individual's OASDI status should be obtained from a local office of the Social Security Administration, which will provide upon request up-to-date literature about the program as well as information concerning the individual's own situation.

Veterans' Administration. Since World War I, the United States government has made life insurance available to current and former members of its armed services. This entry by the federal government into the life insurance business was caused essentially by two factors. First, it was felt by many that the government's program of benefits for the survivors of military men was not adequate at that time, and that provision for life insurance to supplement those benefits would be a desirable part of the over-all program of protection for the families of those serving their country in time of war. Secondly, men entering service at that time virtually lost their insurability, because the commercial life insurance companies either declined to cover the war risk or charged prohibitive extra premium rates to cover it.[41]

The War Risk Insurance Act of 1914 created the Bureau of War Risk Insurance as a part of the Treasury Department. Since marine insurance against war risks was not available from commercial companies, the Bureau was established to provide such protection for shipowners and merchants. In 1917, the War Risk Insurance Act was amended to provide for, among other things, the issuance of life insurance to members of the armed services by the Bureau of War Risk Insurance. The insurance was voluntary and was offered in amounts from $1,000 to $10,000. The plan of insurance was yearly renewable term, and the premiums were net premiums based on the American Experience Table of Mortality and $3\frac{1}{2}$ per cent interest. The federal government bore all the administrative expenses of the insurance as well as the cost of the extra mortality arising from the war. The policy provided for conversion to the usual cash-value plans of insurance within five years after the end of the war. Through the vigorous promotional efforts of the various armed services, some $40 billion of war risk insurance had been placed in force by the end of the war—an amount that exceeded the total insurance in force in all United States commercial companies at that time. After the war, however, the great majority of this insurance lapsed, and only a small percentage was converted into one of the regular plans of United States Government Life Insurance (USGLI).

In 1940, with the enactment of a new draft law, certain modifications in USGLI were felt to be needed. The most important of these changes involved the interest assumption, which in USGLI was $3\frac{1}{2}$ per cent, and the disability income provision, which in USGLI was of the obsolete "maturity" type.[42] The necessary changes were made through enactment of the National Service Life Insurance Act of 1940. The provisions of this act were similar to those governing USGLI, but the interest assumption was changed to 3 per cent, and the only disability benefit automatically included was a waiver of premium provision. Disability income was made available as a supplementary benefit for an additional premium, and evidence of insurability was required for

---

[41] The extra premiums charged to cover the war risk ranged from $37.50 to $100 per year per $1,000 of insurance. See Dan M. McGill, *An Analysis of Government Life Insurance* (Philadelphia: University of Pennsylvania Press, 1949), p. 5.

[42] See page 739.

issuance of the disability income benefit. National Service Life Insurance (NSLI) was made participating, in contrast to the earlier war risk insurance, on which no dividends were paid. Also, the plan of insurance was five-year convertible term, in contrast to the yearly renewable term basis of the earlier war risk insurance. Once again, through the vigorous efforts of the armed services, some $140 billion of NSLI was issued during World War II—an amount that exceeded the total insurance in force in all United States commercial companies at the time. As had happened earlier, however, most of this insurance lapsed with the cessation of hostilities.

In 1951, during the Korean War, the concept of voluntary, subsidized insurance was replaced by that of a gratuitous indemnity for all members of the armed services. The Servicemen's Indemnity and Insurance Acts provided for discontinuation of the World War II type of NSLI and for the automatic free coverage of each member of the armed forces for $10,000 less the amount of any USGLI or NSLI in effect on his life. Within 120 days after discharge, the veteran was permitted to purchase a modified form of NSLI policy—a five-year nonparticipating term policy that was renewable indefinitely, *not* convertible, and based on the 1941 C.S.O. Table of Mortality and $2\frac{1}{4}$ per cent interest. Veterans with service-incurred disabilities, however, were permitted within 120 days of discharge to purchase either a nonparticipating cash-value policy on one of the standard plans of insurance, or a nonparticipating convertible term policy, which could be converted later to any one of the standard nonparticipating cash-value plans.

In 1957, members of the armed services were brought into the Social Security system on the same basis as other covered employees, except that an individual dying without having achieved fully and currently insured status was considered to have achieved such status for the purpose of computing survivors' benefits. At the same time, the gratuitous coverage of servicemen and the issuance of new NSLI to veterans other than those with service-connected disabilities was discontinued. In 1959, holders of the nonconvertible term policies were permitted to exchange them for a nonparticipating cash-value plan or a new type of five-year nonparticipating term policy that was renewable only to age fifty but convertible to a nonparticipating cash-value plan.

In 1965, following the increase in United States participation in the war in South Vietnam, an entirely different approach to the problem of insurance for servicemen was adopted. There was established a system of Servicemen's Group Life Insurance (SGLI or SEGLI) to be underwritten by the commercial life insurance companies. The Veterans' Administration chose the Prudential Insurance Company of America as the primary insurer, which then established an administrative office to carry out the program. Each member of the armed services was blanketed under the plan for $10,000 of insurance, regardless of the amount of USGLI or NSLI in effect on his life, but he was permitted to decline the coverage or elect $5,000 of coverage instead of $10,000. The premium rate was initially $2 per month for the $10,000 coverage, or $1 per month for the $5,000 coverage, with the premiums to be deducted automatically from the serviceman's paycheck. The low premium was made possible through the government's contribution to cover the extra mortality attributable to the special hazards of military service. Within 120 days after discharge, the veteran has the right to convert the coverage to a cash-value plan in any eligible commercial company that has agreed to participate in the program as a "converter" company.[43] The total amount of coverage, estimated initially to be about $28 billion, is distributed among more than five hundred commercial companies that have elected to participate in the program as "reinsurers." Eligibility requirements are the same as for "converter" companies, and the allocation of insurance is made once each year on the basis of a complex formula that reflects both the volume of business in each company that is paid for by government allotments and the volume of the company's other business. In general, the formula results in a larger than proportionate amount of coverage being allocated to small companies and to companies that specialize in government allotment business.

Over the years, life insurance has been offered to servicemen and veterans by the government at prices that are quite low relative to the prices of commercial companies. This is attributable primarily to the substantial subsidies that government life insurance has received from general revenues. Administrative expenses and the extra cost attributable to the hazards of military service usually have been paid from general funds. Policy provisions have been similar to those of commer-

---

[43] To be eligible, a company must meet several criteria. For example, it must be classified as a legal reserve company (or qualified fraternal) by its domiciliary state, it must be at least five years old, and it must be licensed in at least one state or the District of Columbia.

cial companies, but there have also been important differences. For example, particularly in USGLI and participating NSLI, certain of the life income settlement options have been extremely liberal in relation to comparable options in the contracts of commercial companies. At the end of 1965, about $39.4 billion of government life insurance was in force, including about $31.6 billion of participating NSLI, about $6.7 billion of nonparticipating NSLI, and about $1.1 billion of USGLI.[44]

State of Wisconsin. The State Life Fund was established in 1911 by an act of the Wisconsin legislature. This experiment in state insurance grew out of the various investigations that were conducted in the first decade of the twentieth century and the revelations concerning the practices of some commercial companies.

The Fund issues life insurance policies of from $2,000 to $10,000 on the lives of persons who are within the state at the time the insurance is issued. It is under the direct management of the Commissioner of Insurance, who is assisted by other state officials. No additional compensation is paid to these persons for their services to the Fund, and no office rent is paid by the Fund. The policies are issued without liability on the part of the state beyond the assets of the Fund.

The policies issued by the Fund are the standard forms issued by commercial companies. The policy provisions are generally similar to those found in the policies of commercial companies, although fewer settlement options are offered. The price of the insurance issued by the Fund is quite low relative to the prices charged by commercial companies. This difference is attributable to the subsidy received by the Fund in the area of administrative expenses and to the fact that the Fund engages in very little promotional effort. At the end of 1965, about $31 million of life insurance was in force in the State Life Fund, in contrast to about $6 million at the end of 1955.[45]

---

[44] *Life Insurance Fact Book 1966, op. cit.,* p. 102.

[45] *Best's Life Insurance Reports 1966* (New York: Alfred M. Best Co., Inc., annual), pp. 1591–93.

CHAPTER XLI

*Organization and Structure of Life Insurance Companies**

BASIC CONCEPTS OF ORGANIZATION

THE MANAGEMENT of any effective organization recognizes that organizational planning is vital to its profitable growth and development. The basic principles applied by management in various business areas also apply to life insurance companies. The exact form of any organizational pattern is dependent upon the circumstances surrounding the formation and growth of the company as well as on the personalities involved. A company which begins as the idea of one man and grows with the effort and vision of this man and his family will probably have an organizational pattern different from that of a company which results from the merger of several companies of widespread ownership. However, all effective organizations must contain three main elements: (1) levels of authority, (2) departmentalization, and (3) functionalization. The following discussion will consider the essential characteristics of each of these elements and their role in life insurance company organization.

Levels of Authority

As soon as two or more persons work together toward a common objective, an awareness develops that one of the individuals should

---

* Prepared by Dr. Stuart Schwarzschild, Professor of Insurance, and Eli A. Zubay, Professor of Actuarial Science and Mathematics, both of Georgia State College.

have the authority to make decisions that are binding upon the entire group. Most organizations, be they business, religious, charitable, or military, have various levels of authority. At each level, those possessing final authority delegate to subordinates specific authority to make decisions and take certain actions. One of the criteria for a good job of organizational planning is keeping the number of levels of authority to a minimum. This produces short lines of communications and facilitates the making and execution of decisions.

It is also important that the responsibility for a given function be placed with an individual located as closely as possible to the actual point of execution. Of equal importance is the recognition that authority must be delegated along with responsibility. If responsibility is not backed with sufficient authority, indecision and inefficiency will result. There should be a clear statement of the function of each level of authority as well as an explicit statement of the responsibility and authority of every person in the executive, managerial, and supervisory levels.

Stockholders in a stock company, or policyowners in a mutual company, are the primary source of authority. They delegate their authority to the board of directors. The board of directors, in turn, usually will retain some of the authority and delegate the remainder to the executive officers of the company. The latter exercise the direct working control of the business.

The typical life insurance company has four major levels of authority. The highest level of authority is the directorial level, represented by the board of directors and its various committees. The second level is the executive level. Authority at this level is concerned with the company as a whole and is embodied in the president or in the president and a group of his chief general executives, such as the vice-president, the actuary, and the general counsel. Management of the major departments of the life company is the function of the third level of management, the managerial level. Executives at this level are concerned with a particular phase of the company's activities rather than with the operations as a whole. They are usually men with specialized training and knowledge who must translate policy into day-to-day operations. The major responsibility for the day-to-day achievements rests with the fourth or supervisory level of management. This level is characterized by responsibility for a subdivision of a department.

Departmentalization

If the work of an organization is to be performed efficiently, some thought must be given to the assignment of duties and the basis on which these assignments are to be made. The basic principle of departmentalization is that closely co-ordinated activities should be placed with a single group. Three basic plans for departmentalizing a business organization are (1) the functional plan, (2) the product plan, and (3) the geographical plan.

Examples of functional departments would be the actuarial, claims, underwriting, law, investment, and agency departments. Product departmentalization is represented by the ordinary, industrial and group departments. The allocation of responsibility for insurance sales and service for a specified territory or group of states is an illustration of geographical departmentalization. Notice that this illustration suggests that the agency department, which is a functional department, is usually subdivided on a geographical basis; it is not unusual to find all three plans of departmentalization within a given life insurance company.

Functionalization

The simplest form of business organization is the line organization in which all authority comes from a single individual, usually the president. A more common form is the line and staff organization, in which the executive officers are assisted by advisory officers or departments. The law department, for example, can advise the agency department about the contracts the latter is preparing for the general agents, or the actuarial department can advise the agency department concerning the scale of agents' commissions.

In addition to executive or staff officers, an organization may have functional officers who have responsibility for a certain function regardless of its relationship to a department or level of authority; they have the power not only to advise but to act. The medical director, legal counsel, actuary, and controller are examples of officers who exercise control over their functional procedures, regardless of the department or level at which they occur.

Life insurance companies generally operate as "line-staff-functional" organizations. Under this plan the line officials are charged with getting the day-to-day work done; the staff officers are responsible for investigating, planning, and recommending; and the functional officers are charged with getting the job done in certain areas that may cut across departmental lines. The agency vice-president, for example, is a line officer who delegates line authority on a territorial basis to his directors of agencies. He has the assistance of staff officers concerned with research, training, and sales promotion. The decision concerning a particular substandard application submitted by one of the agents may be made by the medical director, a functional officer.

HOME OFFICE ORGANIZATION

The Board of Directors

Stockholders in a stock company or policyowners in a mutual company exemplify the ownership and the primary source of authority in a life insurance company. As indicated earlier, they delegate their authority to the board of directors. The number of directors is usually specified by the company's charter, which also describes the general purposes and powers of the company and the methods by which these powers are to be exercised. The board of directors promulgates the rules and regulations of the company, other than those specifically entrusted by the bylaws to particular committees.

Since so much of the actual management and administration must be carried out by those with the necessary technical knowledge and training, the directors maintain their control by approving or disapproving actions performed or proposed by the officers. In this way, the board fulfills its responsibility for evaluating the progress of the company and fostering long-range planning. The board of directors usually holds monthly or quarterly meetings. In the intervals between these meetings the board's affairs are handled by committees of the board, but the president of the company actually exercises the authority delegated by the stockholders or policyowners to the board.

Committees of the Board

A great deal of the general control of a company's operations is handled by committees appointed by the directors. These groups are set up so that proper action can be taken between board meetings if necessary. Directors with special knowledge and training can be of distinct service by acting on these committees. Liaison is also maintained by requiring that actions of such committees be recorded in the committee minutes and ratified by the full board.

Each of the committees appointed by the directors performs the duties assigned to it by the company bylaws. Each of the committees is usually under the administrative supervision of the president or such other officer as he may designate. Each of these committees usually has the right to make or modify its rules and regulations, subject to the approval of the board of directors. In order to permit these committees to perform efficiently the duties assigned to them, the president may appoint one or more executive officers to each committee. These executive officers are responsible for bringing to each committee's attention the matters requiring committee action, together with appropriate background information and recommendations. In some cases an executive officer is empowered to act for the committee between meetings on any matters within its authority and responsibiltiy and to report his action to the committee at its next meeting.

The number of board of directors' committees and the scope of their duties will naturally vary from company to company. Merely for purposes of illustration let us consider four possible committees: an executive committee, a finance committee, an auditing committee, and a tax committee.

The executive committee (which in some companies is designated as the insurance committee) is concerned with questions of general business methods, lines of business, products, territories, and other matters not under the jurisdiction of one of the other board committees.

The finance committee is responsible for the broad investment policy of the company and decides on the distribution of the funds among the different classes of investments such as bonds, stocks, mortgages, and real estate. This committee also approves the amount of funds maintained on deposit and the selection of the banks in which these uninvested funds are deposited. With regard to mortage loans, this committee establishes general rules concerning interest rates, methods of repayment, and foreclosure procedures.

The responsibility for supervising the accounting system of the company and reviewing the periodic financial statements falls on the auditing committee. A professional auditing firm is normally used by the committee to perform periodic audits. Since this committee operates as a general check on financial transactions, officers of the company do not normally serve as members.

The tax committee is responsible for analyzing and evaluating the income tax implications of any policy, program, or rule, existing or proposed, and for making recommendations about such policy, program, or rule as it affects the company's income tax position. The committee also has the responsibility to recommend on its own initiative changes in any phase of the company's business which in its opinion would bring income tax benefits. The committee is usually authorized to obtain from any department of the company information which it believes may be helpful in discharging its responsibilities.

Interdepartmental Committees

In addition to the committees of the board, a number of interdepartmental committees may be appointed by the chief executive officer to co-ordinate the efforts of the various departments. These committees normally report their findings to the officer responsible for their appointment. Some of the interdepartmental committees which might be appointed are: an insurance committee; a budget committee; a public relations or advertising committee; a manpower and employee benefit committee; a research committee; and a personnel and management training committee.

The *insurance committee* advises on the design of the insurance contract and the specific coverages; the development of the premium rates and the guarantees in the contract; the drafting of the policy; the development of the rules under which policies are issued, serviced, and settled; the servicing of the policies with respect to policy loans, payment of dividends, and changes of beneficiary; the payment of the policy benefits on settlement of the policy as a death claim, matured endowment, or surrender for cash value; the determination of the distribution of the dividends; and the development of changes in underwriting practices.

The *budget committee* is responsible for preparing an annual budget covering the estimated expenses of operating the various functions and departments of the company. This budget proposal is subject to the approval and authorization of the board of directors. The budget committee will usually make periodic reports to the board comparing the actual and budgeted expenditures of the various functions and departments of the company.

The *public relations committee* reviews, recommends, and co-ordinates the policies, programs, and procedures related to advertising, publicity, sales promotions, and public relations generally. This committee will usually supervise the preparation of the annual report to the policyowners or stockholders.

A *manpower and employee benefit committee* will develop rules and regulations pertaining to the employment, dismissal, compensation, and welfare of employees in the home office. (Ordinarily, field office personnel policies would be handled by a separate committee.) This committee might also be charged with evaluating each position within the home office and placing it in a proper grade, making a periodic review of the plans of compensation, reviewing recommendations for changes in compensation for individual employees, and overseeing the company's retirement and pension program.

It will not be feasible for many companies to have a separate *research committee;* instead, they will make each department responsible for research in its area. When, however, a research committee does exist, it may be concerned with product analysis, underwriting practices, operational procedures, and actuarial problems. Product research and new product development would be of interest to this committee. It would study the company's competitive position and report on actions of other companies. It would collect and conduct studies pertaining to underwriting. These would include general studies involving analysis and interpretation of mortality and morbidity data; analysis of statistical information from governmental, insurance, and medical sources; analysis of the rating practices of other companies; comparison of the value and cost of various sources of underwriting information; and the review of intercompany studies pertaining to mortality, morbidity and lapses. There is virtually no limit to the subjects that might be considered by this committee. Other subjects that might be considered are analysis of reinsurance costs, use of operations research techniques in home office operations, testing a new dividend scale, studies of marketing compensation plans, analysis of annual statements of other companies, and labor market studies.

The *personnel and management training committee* is interested in helping each employee to become more proficient in his present job and in providing an adequate number of management trainees to meet the needs of the various departments. A company may offer courses of its own in the various specialities and/or make use of the educational programs of several professional associations and organizations such as the Life Office Management Association, the Home Office Life Underwriters Association and the Institute of Home Office Underwriters (joint program), the Society of Actuaries, the American College of Life Underwriters, the Life Underwriters Association of Canada, and the Life Insurance Agency Management Association. The personnel and management training committee is charged with making these educational programs known to all employees, aiding the various departments in developing their individual orientation programs, and providing to all employees a general understanding of the entire organization and the relationships between departments.

Functional Departments

Earlier it was stated that one of the essential elements of a good organization is departmentalization. To obtain a better appreciation of this principle and a more complete understanding of the broad scope of functions involved in a life insurance organization, let us consider one way in which a home office may be divided into departments. For the sake of simplicity let us assume that this company writes ordinary business only. Even then there is no uniform system of dividing the whole organization into departments. The particular system adopted is largely a matter of convenience and suitability and results largely from the way in which the company developed. In most companies the following major departments would be found: actuarial, underwriting, administrative, agency, law, accounting and auditing, and investment.

Actuarial Department. The main responsibility of this department is to see that the insurance operations of the company are conducted on a sound financial basis. The actuary who heads up this department is responsible for determining adequate premium rates and policy liabilities and for establishing proper surrender values, settlement options, and dividends.

In conjunction with the agency and law departments this department will participate in designing new policies, drafting new policy forms, and getting them approved by the various state insurance departments. The actuarial department also works with the agency department on the preparation of rate books and the development of compensation plans for the agents.

A considerable portion of this department's time might be spent in statistical research, preparing, for example, lapse studies, mortality studies for various standard and substandard groups, and analyses of expenses. The actuarial department is usually responsible for the preparation of statistical reports for various organizations and publications of the life insurance industry.

Routine responsibilities include such things as the maintenance of records of insurance in force, lapses, surrenders, maturities, and changes in the apportionment of dividends to various policies by type.

Other duties of this department include the necessary actuarial calculations for changes in plans, reductions in amounts, changes in benefits, and paying up policies by application of dividends as well as the preparation of written responses to inquiries from policyowners, field offices, and field underwriters about premium rates, policy guarantees, changes in policy contracts, dividends, and policy provisions.

The actuary is responsible, jointly with other officers, for the accuracy of the annual financial statements required by the various insurance departments. He has the main responsibility for furnishing the amount of policy liabilities and other items which are arrived at by actuarial calculation.

Underwriting Department. The principal objective of the underwriting department is to ensure that the actual mortality experienced by the company will not be greater than that assumed in calculating the premium rates; thus, this department collaborates with medical and actuarial personnel in establishing general underwriting standards (including the establishment of substandard classes of risks). It is responsible for communicating with the field force in matters concerning the selection of risks. In addition, this department is responsible for negotiating and managing all reinsurance agreements entered into by the company. The lay underwriter reviews the application, the medical report, the agent's statement, and the inspection report to determine an applicant's insurability from the standpoints of age, build, physical condition, personal and family history, occupation, environment, financial resources and other selection factors. He is aided by the medical director, who establishes medical standards of insurability. The medical director may be the final authority to pass on applications of doubtful insurability from the health point of view. General underwriting control, however, may be exercised by a vice-president who is not a physician.

In some cases it may be the responsibility of this department to keep records on all substandard cases and on a sample of the standard cases, so that the company's mortality experience can be analyzed and underwriting practices evaluated.

Administrative Department. The administrative department, often headed by the secretary of the company, is responsible for providing home office services for the company's field force and policyowners. With regard to policyowners, this service would include the issuance of new policies and the handling of correspondence pertaining to premium payments, claims, loans, changes in beneficiaries, surrenders, and other policy changes.

In many companies this department is responsible for maintaining the basic records in connection with these functions. The administrative department would also perform the premium and commission accounting on which the agents' remuneration is based. It is also responsible for personnel administration and home office planning.

In those companies which do not have an interdepartmental committee concerned with education and training, this department is usually responsible for planning, developing, and administering centralized programs for the orientation, education, and training of all clerical, technical, professional, supervisory, and management personnel. The department also attempts to promote consistent interdepartmental personnel policies and procedures.

In his capacity as secretary of the company, the head of this department would be responsible for compiling the minutes of meetings of the board of directors and of the various committees of the board.

Agency Department. If a company is to experience satisfactory growth and development, it must promote a satisfactory flow of new business and conserve the maximum amount possible of its old business. Thus, one of the responsibilities of the agency vice-president is the recruitment, training, and supervision of the field force. His department is responsible for providing the most effective field service for the policyowners of the company. The vice-president is also interested in market analysis, in the development of sales promotion programs and literature, in studies helping to determine the proper number of and most strategic locations for field offices, and in the maintenance of production and expense records. Members of the agency department work closely with members of the actuarial and law departments in developing new products and policy forms.

Law Department. One of the main responsibilities of the law department is to make certain that the company's operations comply with federal and state laws and insurance department regulations. The law department studies current and proposed legislation affecting the insurance industry so that it can advise the board about this legislation. This department advises the administrative department on questionable claims and represents the company in any litigation. It also performs the necessary title work involved in mortgage loans and real estate investments and is responsible for the legal work on investments other than mortgages and real estate. The law department co-operates with the accounting and auditing department in determining the company's tax obligations. As mentioned before, it participates in the development of policy forms, agents' contracts, or any other contractual forms used by the company.

Accounting and Auditing Department. The accounting and auditing department, under the direction of the vice-president and controller, is responsible for all of the company's general accounting operations and records, the control of all receipts and disbursements, the preparation of financial statements, and the maintenance of budgetary control over department expenses. In an insurance company, with the large number of transactions performed and the huge number of individual items which must be recorded, this bookkeeping activity is a significant part of the company's total operations. The preparation of the various departmental budgets is co-ordinated in this department, and both the home office and field force operations are audited here. The department is also concerned with federal, state, and local tax laws and regulations. The controller is one of the officers who must certify the accuracy of the annual financial statement required by state insurance departments and is the officer primarily responsible for all financial statements. This department furnishes the board with the expense reports and analyses required in their deliberations. It may also have the responsibility for the payroll and may be involved in studying the operations of other departments with a view to work simplification and economy of operation.

Investment Department. The primary function of the investment department is to handle the investment program under policies and recommendations made by the finance committee and the board of directors. These policies are based on reports and studies prepared by this department and cover investment programs for stocks, bonds, mortgage loans, and real estate. In addition to the annual premium income to be invested, there is considerable reinvestment to be performed due to turnover of existing investments including bond maturities, repayment of mortgage loans and sales of assets.

This department is responsible for initiating recommendations to the finance committee for purchases and sales of industrial, public utility, federal, state and municipal obligations, and is responsible for the continuing supervision and evaluation of all such securities owned by the company. The work of this department calls for both security and mortgage analysts. In the larger companies specialization may be carried to the point where, for example, different persons become responsible for particular fields such as industrial, public utility, or state, county, and municipal bonds. Their job is to evaluate portfolio investments and to recommend whether to hold or sell. They also analyze new issues and may negotiate with brokers and investment bankers or directly with borrowers.

The reader should keep in mind that the above description may not fit any particular company; it is presented merely to illustrate one possible type of home office organization.

FIELD ORGANIZATION

Need for a Field Organization

To Produce Volume of Sales. All experience shows that without agents less life insurance would be sold. Notwithstanding the almost universal need for life insurance, relatively few persons voluntarily apply for it; most people have to be solicited by an agent. The unsolicited applications which are received by a company often come from persons who are either uninsurable or insurable only on a substandard basis. Most people tend to defer making provision for obligations which, although of obvious ultimate value, do not seem immediately necessary. The certainty of death, and the possibility of early death, are thoughts upon which most younger people are not likely to dwell. Retirement, too, is a long way off for these persons. Disability is often thought to be something that happens to the other fellow. Today's needs, on the other hand, are immediate and pressing. It requires a major effort to project one's thoughts to a time ten, twenty, or forty years hence. It takes an even greater effort to sacrifice today so that one's dependents, or even one's self, may benefit in the future.

The first companies to sell life insurance policies in the United States had no agents. They sold only a small number of life insurance policies each year, being chiefly concerned with other types of insurance, annuities, or with the banking or trust business. It was only when agents were employed to solicit applications that the volume of life insurance issued increased significantly.

The importance of an agency force in developing and maintaining a life insurance business is clearly seen from the experience of the few companies, and of other special groups or organizations, which operate without agents. An example is the government of Great Britain, which attempted to sell life insurance through post offices for more than sixty years. In 1928 this scheme was abandoned as a failure. In the United States, the state of Wisconsin sells life insurance without the aid of agents and after fifty years of operation had in force some $14 million of ordinary life insurance, out of an aggregate of $9 billion of ordinary life insurance in force in that state—a striking commentary on the agency system.

Another example of the sale of life insurance without agents is found in the savings bank life insurance system which is operated in the states of Massachusetts, New York and Connecticut. Sales are actively promoted by advertising and by other methods; however, in Massachusetts, where the system has been in operation since 1907, the total amount of savings bank life insurance in force is far less than the amount of insurance in force with any one of many regular companies in that state. Currently the new insurance issued by the savings banks in all three states is equal to only a very small part of the new insurance issued in these states by the regular companies.

While the amount of individual life insurance sold without agents increases with the development of mass marketing schemes, such as marketing through credit cards, associations, mutual funds, and lending firms, the amount of new insurance individually marketed through agents continues to dominate the market by a wide margin.

To Render Services. Thus far, the need for agents has been emphasized from the point of view of the volume of insurance issued or in force. Volume and growth, in general, are desirable and beneficial. From the company's point of view, large volume means greater stability and economies of scale. The need for agents, however, is not merely a matter of securing the largest possible amount of new insurance. The need arises also from the social duty of the companies to provide adequate life insurance protection for all who need it and thus to perform in the greatest possible degree the function for which they are organized.

The agency system is sometimes criticized because of its cost, since the commissions and other remuneration paid to agents necessarily increase the cost of insurance to policyowners. Such criticisms generally assume that the costs of the agency system are an expense to the policyowners for which they receive no compensating benefit. This is an unwarranted assumption. Even if the agent did no more than call the prospect's attention to the need for insurance, explain its benefits, and persuade him to apply for a policy, he would be rendering a service of material value. Today most agents do much more than that. They render many types of services—some of them extremely important—which are, in effect, not available at all to the policyowners of organizations which do not employ agents. Any comparison of relative costs of insurance which does not take into account differences in the services rendered is misleading.

Since, as has been already pointed out, comparatively few people—irrespective of their need for it—apply for life insurance until they are solicited by an agent, the agent performs an important social service merely by calling attention to the need for insurance protection and by persuading the prospect to apply for it. The good agent also analyzes the applicant's insurance needs and advises him about the most suitable types of policies, the amounts of insurance required, the cost and methods of premium payment, the more important provisions of the policy contract, the uses of the optional modes of settlement, the most appropriate choice of beneficiaries, and the rights to be given to beneficiaries. If the applicant already has other insurance on his life, the agent will make suggestions for co-ordinating the old and new policies, taking into account any benefits to which the applicant or his dependents may be entitled under governmental or employer programs. It would seem obvious not only that service of this type is valuable, but that it can be furnished only by a properly trained field force.

According to the modern conception of the agent's function, his services do not end with the issue of the policy. Life insurance needs are not static but require frequent review and adjustment to meet changing conditions. This is particularly true of (1) the beneficiary provisions and (2) the prior elections of the optional settlements which are to take effect at the maturity of the policy. For example, children grow up and become self-supporting, or additional children are born. These changes in the family status may require reconsideration of the beneficiary designation. A form of settlement suitable while the beneficiary is young, or while children are young, may become unsuitable later. Policyowners seldom think of such things, and without the continuing advice and service of the agents they would often be overlooked. There are, of course, many other types of services for which the policyowner depends largely on the agent—for example, service in regard to policy loans, assignments, changes in plans of insurance, reinstatements, and so on. Such information and service could be obtained directly from the home office. To most policyowners, however, it is simpler to have the agent take care of such matters, which may be technical or difficult for them.

Still another service furnished by the agent is to assist claimants and beneficiaries when policies become payable at death or by the maturity of an endowment. Here again it is easier for the claimant if the agent obtains, and assists in the completion of, the necessary claim blanks, explains the settlement, and gives advice as to the method of payment to be selected.

Service provided by agents has been discussed here largely because the public, very generally, still lacks knowledge of its extent and an appreciation of its value. The agency system undoubtedly adds to the cost of insurance, but it is a great mistake to assume that the elimination of that cost and the concomitant service would be a gain to policyowners. Under modern conditions, this certainly would not be true.

To Control Field Operations. For companies that have policyowners from coast to coast, there is a rather obvious need to have a field organization of offices distributed throughout the country. This is necessary in order to complete in a timely manner such important business functions as the collection of funds and the scrutiny of claims, as well as serving the customer more efficiently.

The Structure of the Field Organization

Although the structure of the field organization varies among companies, some of the more typical relationships can be generalized. The reader should not, however, expect that a particular company will or should reflect precisely the same structure as is discussed here.

The agent is the foundation of the field organization. He generally operates under the training and supervision of an assistant manager or agency supervisor. The next higher echelon of management is the branch manager or general agent. This, then, is the management structure in the field. The man who supervises and controls field branch managers or general agents may bear a title such as regional vice-president, regional director of agencies, or superintendent of agencies. He may be located either in the home office or in the appropriate regional office. At the top of the agency hierarchy is the agency vice-president, who is directly responsible to the president. In some of the large companies, in order to relieve the agency vice-president of some of his many duties, the position of senior vice-president for marketing has been created as the top position of the marketing structure. In many companies the president devotes a large part of his time and interest to marketing. The responsibilities and interrelationships of the above positions are examined below.

Agent Classifications. Agents are generally classified according to the form of insurance they sell. For example, the "ordinary" agent sells policies which are classified as ordinary; the "industrial" (or "debit") agent sells policies on which the premiums are payable monthly or more frequently and which are classified as industrial (or debit): the "combination" agent sells ordinary policies and industrial policies; and the "group representative" sells group insurance policies.

Whereas the ordinary agent may operate over a rather large area of the state, the debit agent, since he has premiums to collect each week or month, operates over an area that can be efficiently serviced each week. The word "debit" is used to describe the area, the agent, or the company, as well as the amount which the agent is charged to collect each week. This last sense, of course, conforms more precisely with the way the term is used in accounting.

In time, a company will have a certain amount of premium collected each week in a given area. The debit agent collecting this money may be promoted, retired, or die, or his debit may otherwise become open. The new debit agent will, therefore, have an established "book" of business to service, which justifies his starting salary. Besides, he has an established clientele to approach for more life insurance sales. Often a debit develops so much business that the existing agent does not have the time both to service it and also to sell more insurance. At such times a part of the debit is broken off to create a new debit. This allows the original agent more time for selling, which adds to his income; and the new debit provides an existing source of income and customers for a new debit agent.

Agents of companies that sell ordinary and industrial policies may have a debit and also may sell ordinary policies, the premiums for which are collected on the debit or by mail. Such agents are called combination agents. The combination agent not only has his debit territory for industrial and ordinary policies, but he can sell ordinary policies outside of this area. Such agents have increased sales opportunities of more types of contracts and a larger population to which to sell.

Companies generally require that their agents place all of their business with them; however, many companies permit their agents to place with another company, business which the agent's company is unwilling to accept. Such insurance is generally called "surplus" or "excess" because it is for a larger amount than the company has reinsurance capacity or because the risk is more substandard than the agent's company likes to accept.

In communities with over 50,000 population, most companies will use only agents who give their full time to the insurance business. There are many full-time agents in smaller communities also, but if a community has insufficient population for an agent to devote his full time to the life insurance business, companies may permit him to have another occupation. Of course, proper training, development, and supervision can best be achieved if the agents are on a full-time basis and give all of their attention and effort to the life and health insurance business.

Brokers. Another type of life insurance salesman is the broker. A broker may be a general insurance agent who handles all kinds of insurance for his clients, or he may be only in the life insurance business; but instead of representing one company primarily, he sells policies for a number of companies. If he is in the general insurance business, his principal business is likely to be the placing of fire, liability, and other nonlife lines of insurance. Life insurance is likely to be more or less incidental to this other business. Brokers specializing in life insurance have contracts with a number of different companies and submit their business to these companies in accordance with their clients' preferences, the services available from the companies, the cost of the insurance, or on the basis of the commission rates obtainable.

Although the trend in recent years has been toward a more general acceptance of "brokerage" business, some life insurance companies doubt the desirability of this business. It is felt by some companies that brokerage business is likely to be less satisfactory than business written by regular agents who are life insurance specialists, properly trained and equipped to give the necessary information and service. Brokerage business often involves very large cases which may be of marginal or borderline insurability. In such cases, there is a certain amount of "shopping around" in order to obtain the most favorable terms. This, presumably, involves some selection against the company, which may adversely affect mortality experience. Some companies take the view, however, that by exercising proper care in the acceptance of such business, they can protect themselves against the danger of unfavorable mortality experience.

A recent development has been for agents of established companies to organize life insurance companies. These agents then channel a substantial amount of their "excess" business to this company in which they are shareholders and which generally offers them stock options in addition to commissions. Opponents of the development of agent owned companies and of stock options assert that the agent may be led thereby to place insurance where it best serves him rather than where it best serves the buyer.[1]

The scale of commissions paid to part-time agents or to brokers may be lower than that applicable to full-time agents; however, broker commissions are always vested.[2] Brokers generally do not participate in company pension plans or other employee benefits. In the remainder of this chapter, the discussion relates, unless otherwise indicated, to full-time agents.

Supervision. The *agency vice-president* is generally the senior officer, below the president, concerned with marketing. He is often responsible for (1) market development; (2) development, training, and supervision of the home office agency staff; (3) selection and supervision of the various regional vice-presidents; (4) development of a staff for the training of managers, general agents, and agents; (5) sales promotion—advertising, sales material, company magazines, contests, and sales-promoting clubs; (6) budgeting marketing expenses; (7) maintaining production records; (8) research in agent selection, territories, and markets; (9) policyowner service; (10) setting marketing objectives; (11) maintaining favorable relations with other departments of the company; and (12) relations with other companies, trade associations, and the community. Naturally, to handle the many functions of his office, the agency vice-president needs some assistance, and in a number of companies, functions (5), (9), and (12) above will be performed, either entirely or in part, by other departments of the company.

The agency vice-president may have subordinate officers called *superintendents of agencies* or *regional vice-presidents*. These individuals are responsible for the operations of the branch managers and general agents in their territories. They are particularly concerned with the selection of branch managers and general agents to fill vacan-

---

[1] For a discussion of the pros and cons of this development read Robert W. Strain, "Stock Option Incentives in Newly Formed Life Insurance Companies," *Journal of the American Society of Chartered Life Underwriters*, Vol XIX, No. 1 (Winter, 1965), pp. 5 ff.

[2] Vesting of commissions is discussed on page 834–35.

cies that develop, or to expand operations. The regional vice-president makes sure that company procedures, objectives, and required practices are known to the field and are complied with. He also keeps the home office informed concerning field opinions and needs. He advises the home office staff on the probable effectiveness of any changes in the portfolio of policies, systems of remuneration, advertising, or other programs, which may affect the field. He operates directly under the agency vice-president and fills a management position of great importance in communicating effectively with the field.

The effectiveness of the field organization is determined largely by the recruiting of new agents and by the management and direction which the new and experienced agents receive. The *general agent or manager* has the extremely important job of instilling in his organization the desire and will to learn, to serve, to sell, and to succeed. In addition to this important duty of leadership, he must recruit new agents if the agency is to grow; he, or his supervisors, must train them in prospecting and selling, and give counsel and advice where needed. He is responsible not only for the work performed by the clerical staff but also for the correctness of applications and forms turned in by the agency force for transmission to the home office. Some companies expect him to do some selling himself. A few companies discourage this because it may interfere with the recruitment and development of agents. Most companies desire him to be a leading businessman in the community and to participate in civic affairs. In doing so, he not only helps to fulfill the company's social responsibilities but builds prestige for his agency.

The *assistant manager* or *supervisor* is generally a specialist in training new agents and in helping agents on sales interviews. Where there are industrial or combination agents, we generally find a number of assistant managers, each having several debit agents under his continual supervision. The ordinary agent generally has looser supervision and training and therefore fewer supervisors.

Relationship between the Agent and the Company. At one time it was common for the agent to contract with the general agent. Today, even in companies which operate on the general agency system, the soliciting agent more often contracts with the insurance company and not with the general agent. This not only means that the company has greater control over the selection of soliciting agents, but means that in the event of agent turnover the nonvested commissions which would have been earned by the agent revert to the company rather than to the general agent. Although agency contracts vary from company to company some of the provisions which appear in a substantial number of contracts are reviewed here.

1. *Authority.* An agent can only represent another as an agent to the extent of the conferred authority.[3] Authority may be conferred by custom or usage,[4] by the company knowingly permitting the agent to exercise certain authority,[5] as well as by the explicit terms of the agency contract. Additionally, the agent has powers which are incidental to those given explicitly or by custom and use.[6] The authority given the agent is sometimes expressed in the contract as follows: "to solicit applications for insurance, collect first premium thereon, and service such insurance."

The territory in which the agent can represent the company may be specified in geographical terms, be coterminous with that of the agency office, or be limited to those states in which the agent is licensed to represent the company.

The agency contract generally states that the agent has no power to waive any forfeiture or to alter or waive any terms of any policy issued by the company.

Agency contracts generally provide that the contract may be terminated by either party at any time. Generally thirty days' notice is required except when the termination may be effective immediately for some causes, e.g., violation of law or of a contractual provision.

2. *Relationship Established.* In order to avoid the legal burdens of an employer, e.g., liability for social security taxes, unemployment compensation, and workmen's compensation, the contract generally provides that the agent shall be free to exercise his own judgment as to persons from whom he will solicit insurance and the time and places of solicitation. Additionally the contracts generally state that nothing in the contract shall be construed to create the relationship of employer and employee.

3. *Limitation on Representing Other Insurers.* The most significant difference between brokerage and agency contracts is generally in the right to represent or do business with other insurers. The agency

---

[3] *Corpus Juris Secundum,* Vol. 44, "Insurance," section 149, page 821.

[4] *Couch on Insurance* 2d., Section 26:58.

[5] 29 *American Jurisprudence, Insurance,* section 146, page 546: *Pagni* v. *New York Life Insurance Company,* 173 Wash. 322, 23 Pac. 2d 6.

[6] *Thomas* v. *Prudential Insurance Company of America,* 104 Fed. 2d 480 (4th Cir. 1939).

contracts generally provide that the agent shall not represent any other company doing the same kinds of business. Some companies have a tighter restriction and say the agent shall do no business for any other life insurance company. This restriction is often modified by excepting those cases where the applicants for insurance already have the limit of insurance which the company will issue to them, or where the applicants are otherwise not acceptable for insurance by the company. These exceptions to the exclusive representation provision have provided the opportunity for agents to place what is generally called "brokerage," "surplus" or "excess" business with other insurers.

4. *Compensation Arrangement.* The compensation provision of contracts is frequently handled by the attachment of a commission schedule or agreement. This permits the commission provisions to be readily modified for new types of policies, changes in rates and cash value structures, and other changes in marketing strategy, e.g., raising commissions to encourage the sale of a given type of policy.

Commission scales of companies which do business in the state of New York are limited by section 213 of the New York State Insurance Law. Although the commission scales of such companies vary, there is a greater degree of uniformity among companies doing business in New York than among the commission scales of companies which are not limited by expense limitation laws.[7]

The system of agents' remuneration has undergone considerable change and development in recent years. Originally the agent received as a commission only a small percentage of the first premium. Later, as a result of competition, renewal commissions—payable for a limited period of years—were added, and the rate of commission on the first premium was gradually increased. There was, prior to the Armstrong Investigation of 1905, a growing tendency (due in large part to the practice of rebating) to pay higher and higher commission rates, particularly for first-year commissions, and to supplement these in some cases by additional payments, depending on the volume of insurance written. This tendency was checked by the statutory limitations on agents' commissions, which were enacted first in New York in 1909. The New York law placed a top limit on first-year commissions and also limited the number and amount of renewal commissions, but New York has permitted the payment of a small service fee for a further period after the renewal commission has ceased.

Commissions also vary according to the type of policy and age of

---

[7] Illinois and Wisconsin are the only two states in addition to New York which have adopted limitations on expenses.

the insured at the time of issue. Appendix K shows typical commission rates for agents of the ordinary department of a New York company as well as typical commission rates paid by a company not licensed in New York. Commissions have been used instead of a salary primarily because the companies feel that such a system gives the life insurance agent a greater incentive to produce more sales. Another reason for the use of commissions is the fact that the commission arrangement makes the acquisition cost a definite percentage of the premium income. This is a convenient factor in making rates. Also, a company would have to pay a successful salesman a salary equivalent to the commissions he could earn or the salesman would go to a commission-paying company. Since, in effect, successful salesmen will have to be paid a percentage of premium income, companies do not desire to overcompensate the unsuccessful salesman by a salary not related to sales. A final reason for using commissions is that to compensate on a salary basis would make the company liable for social security, unemployment insurance, and workmen's compensation expenses relative to the sales force.

5. *New Agent Financing.* Newly licensed agents, of course, have no immediate commission income. For many years, new agents were expected to finance themselves during their apprenticeship period. Today the company or the general agent often provides funds for the new agent's livelihood until his commission income becomes sufficient. This may be accomplished by advancing the agent funds to be repaid under a formal loan arrangement, or by paying the new agent a salary.

The salary appears to be the more costly, since there is no repayment implied; however, it may not actually be the more costly. The salary plan is a superior bargaining tool and therefore may attract a better prospective agent. Secondly, the salary plan impresses on the manager the fact that, unless he helps the man succeed, the salary payments will for the most part have been of no avail and recruiting the agent may be a net loss. (In practice, of course, even loans to unsuccessful agents are losses since repayment is most unlikely.) Thirdly, under a salary plan, the manager is more able to control the agent's time and work methods than under other plans. The objection to the salary plan is that it reduces the incentive to produce more business than the minimum amount necessary to stay on salary. However, if the salary is not too high, and if the commission scale is high enough to permit the agent to earn commissions above the salary, his incentive should not be affected.

The main features of a typical salary plan in use today are: (1) the amount of monthly salary is based on the agent's minimum living requirements; (2) payment of the salary depends on the fulfillment of specified conditions such as the number of hours worked, or the number of interviews or calls made; (3) if commissions on the basis of a schedule in the agent's contract would exceed the salary, the excess is payable to him, whereas, if the reverse is the case, the salary is not reduced; (4) the salary arrangement continues only for the first two or three years, after which the agent goes on a regular commission basis; and (5) to remain on salary, the agent must have sold each month a stipulated amount of insurance. This last requirement is called "validation." The success of a salary plan depends very largely on the standards of selection of new agents and the care with which they are supervised. Some plans of this type have been very successful.

6. *Nonlevel Commissions.* The growth of a system of paying a relatively large commission on the first year's premium and a smaller commission on renewal premiums is attributable to two factors: (1) company emphasis on the volume of new insurance written, and (2) inability of most new agents coming into the business to make a sufficient income, at least for some years, on a system of level commission rates. The advent of financing programs for new agents destroys in part the logic, if not the prevalence, of the nonlevel commission plan.

From the company's point of view, the nonlevel commission system results in a much higher expense rate in the first year of a policy than in other years. As was pointed out earlier, commissions and other expenses incident to putting a policy on the books, plus the policy's share of first-year death claims, may well exceed the first-year gross premium, forcing the company to modify its reserve structure or to borrow from surplus.

7. *Vesting of Commissions.* Another feature of the commission system, as it existed for many years, was that renewal commissions were nearly always fully vested. Vesting meant that the agent was entitled to the renewal commissions whether or not he remained under contract to the company. The system of vested renewal commissions reflected the view that all renewal commissions were paid as remuneration for securing the business, i.e., for selling, no part being viewed as compensation for "collection" or "service." In the event of a large turnover of agents and a short average period under contract there would be a substantial proportion of all renewal commissions being

paid to persons no longer connected with the company. Such persons would be performing no services for the company or its policyowners.

In general, when changes have been made in the commission system, they have provided for (1) a somewhat smaller rate of first-year commissions offset by increased rates of renewal commissions for the next two or three years, (2) the payment of service fees after all renewal commissions have been paid, and (3) the nonvesting of some or all of the renewal commissions.

8. *Service Fees.* Service fees are usually either a small percentage (such as 2 per cent) of premiums payable after renewal commissions have ceased or, in some cases, a flat amount (e.g., $0.18 per $1,000 of the face amount of insurance). The rationale for service fees is found in the need to compensate the agent for rendering continuing service to policyowners. Consequently, service fees are not vested.

The general effect of all these changes in agent's compensation through the years is that the agent who produces a reasonably good average volume of new business from year to year and who remains with the company enjoys a larger income throughout his whole period of service than under the earlier system.

9. *Noncommission Compensation.* The higher degree of permanence of the agent's service and the development of retirement plans in the American culture have led to the very general adoption of agents' retirement plans. Various retirement plans have been adopted. Under a typical form of agents' retirement plan the agent contributes each year a specified percentage of his commission earnings. The company usually contributes an equal amount, the combined contributions being accumulated at interest during the period of active service and the total accumulation being applied, at the retirement date, to purchase a life annuity on a previously specified basis. Any contributions made by the company under such a plan must be taken into account in determining the total present value of the agent's compensation for comparison with the statutory limitations on agent's compensation in those states where limitations on commissions or expenses apply.

Even while drawing a pension, many emeritus agents prefer to keep relatively active and sell new policies. Because of their wide circle of acquaintances and clients and because of their broad knowledge, they can continue to write a considerable amount of business and still enjoy the advantages of a sedentary life.

A more recent development in agents' contracts is the right to participate in group life insurance and often other forms of group insurance, such as health insurance. The trend has been to increase group insurance benefits for agents, with the company assuming part or all of the cost.

TYPES OF AGENCY ORGANIZATION

The field organization may be structured in one of three different ways. A company may operate with all agents reporting directly to the home office agency department. This type of organization under which the agent is supervised directly from the home office is called the direct agency system. This system works best for a small company operating in a limited territory. As they grow in size, companies have found it necessary to have recruitment and supervision of the agency force at local levels. Such a requirement has led to the organization of the field under either the general agency system, the branch office system, or some combination of the two.

General Agency System

Pure General Agencies. The pure form of general agency is the oldest of the field management systems. Under it the general agent has an exclusive franchise for the sale of the company's contracts in a given territory, frequently the geographic limits of a state. He receives commissions on the business produced, from which he pays commissions to any subagents whom he appoints to develop business and the other expenses of his agency. The difference between the general agent's commission scale and the commissions which he pays his agents is available for the general agent's other expenses and profit. The general agent also receives a collection fee to cover premium billing, collection and record-keeping expenses. As can be readily seen this system permits a young company to add new territories with little or no investment, since the development of the territory is the responsibility of the territorial franchise holder—the general agent. At the same time the general agent is free of home office control except for any limitations set forth in the general agency contract.

Modified Form of General Agency. Although the modifications of the pure general agency relationship have taken many forms, it is possible to delineate some of the frequently found arrangements.

1. *Financial Requirements.* Today in order to start a new agency the outlays for such items as rent, secretarial services, and office

equipment are considerably higher than some years ago. The person who has the initiative and ability to be a successful general agent frequently will not have the capital required to meet the considerable initial outlays and needs for working capital. If companies restrict their expansion activities only to those persons who have adequate financial resources to provide this capital, the companies would have very limited prospects for expansion. Accordingly companies today generally loan to the general agent part or all of these capital needs, the security for the loan being the future commission income of the general agent.

2. *Marketing Control.* Today the appointment of soliciting agents and their rates of compensation are generally subject to home office approval rather than being left to agreements between the general agent and agent. This arises in part out of the desire of the companies to develop an agency force that meets certain characteristics. Furthermore, since today the company often finances part of a new agent's beginning "salary," it naturally desires to have some control over his selection.

In order to obtain maximum results from new marketing developments and to enable the agents to compete effectively with companies that operate through branch offices, companies operating through general agencies frequently provide sales materials to the general agent for the use of his agents. Also in order to develop marketing plans, companies may prescribe that agents complete the prescribed training material and attend specialized training courses.

3. *Premium Collection.* Billing machinery which can process the premium notices automatically from cards or tapes is expensive but can accommodate much more than the billing needs of a general agency. Accordingly, most companies are now billing from the home office and the collection commission is affected thereby. In many cases the premium is still returned through the agency office so that the agency can act quickly relative to contacting policyowners who are delinquent in paying premiums. Although a collection commission is still generally paid, it is greatly reduced below the level that existed when the general agents did all of the billing and collecting.

4. *Miscellaneous.* A final change of considerable significance is that under the pure general agency, when a soliciting agent terminated, the soliciting agent's nonvested renewal commissions went to the general agent. Today the modified general agency only receives the "override" commission and the company does not have to pay the

nonvested renewal commissions that would have been earned by the terminated soliciting agent. This helps to compensate the company for the financing, sales training, and fringe benefit plans it now provides soliciting agents.

Even with these modifications it should be observed that the general agent's income is still a function of the agency's commission income and expenses of operation.

Branch Office or Manager System

The duties and goals of the manager are similar to those of the general agent. However, rather than being an independent contractor he is an employee of the company. It therefore follows that his compensation is not directly related to commissions and office expenses. Nevertheless, he may enjoy changes in his salary and bonuses based on the favorable deviation of his office from the goals set by the home office. However, the goals of the branch office in the branch office system are the goals of the company, whereas the goals of even the modified form of general agency are likely to be those of the general agent.

Financial Arrangements. In the branch office system all office expenses, including the manager's salary and agent training financing, are met from the branch office's budget. To stimulate the manager's development of the branch, his final compensation will be affected by his achievement of company goals. Generally his base salary is revised annually and reflects his standing among the manager heirarchy, his length of service, loyalty, and other attributes. He then will receive additional amounts based upon such factors as increases in commission volume and a low rate of lapse during the early years of a policy's life. Additionally, if the office expenses are lower than the amount budgeted he may share part of this savings.

Marketing Control. To encourage the development of manpower the manager generally receives an override commission on the premiums developed by each new agent during his first year provided the agent remains under contract for a year. The financing costs of new agents are paid by the company, although the manager will generally be charged a portion of the financing costs of those new agents who do not produce a given amount of business in a specified period. If a company desires to develop brokerage business then the manager may receive a special override on such business.

Some companies discourage or prohibit their managers from personal production. The rationale of such companies is that the manager should be available at all times to help the agents in their development and should devote his entire effort to developing a good production organization. However, many companies permit their manager to engage in personal production and receive the same compensation for it as any other agent would. This practice may be justified on the grounds that (1) a manager is a better developer of successful manpower if he remains a successful producer, or (2) the company does not wish to experience the decline in premium income that might result if the manager did not personally produce business, or (3) the company wishes to pay a lower salary with the expectation that with the commission on personal production, the manager will be adequately compensated and motivated.

Miscellaneous. The company generally contributes more significantly to the group life and health insurance, pension and other employee benefit plans for managers than it does for general agents. In regard to vacations, office location and design and other matters of a like nature, the branch manager, unlike the general agent, is subject to home office control.

CHAPTER XLII

*Life Insurance Company Investments**

THE INVESTMENT function is directly related to the accumulation of funds inherent in the business of providing life insurance protection. In addition to initial capital and surplus, sound life insurance operations will generate investible assets through the prepayments associated with level premium insurance and annuities and through deposits left under settlement and dividend options. Like marketing, underwriting and rate-making, the investment of these assets is an important functional area of company management. It can be said that one side of the life insurance business concentrates on the creation of liabilities, while the other side sees to the investment of the assets that must be accumulated to offset these liabilities. In the aggregate, the magnitude and direction of company investments clearly distinguish the life insurance industry as a significant participant in the capital markets. In the discussion which follows, the micro- and macroeconomic distinction will be preserved to enhance an understanding of the company decision-making process and the factors which largely explain the observed economic behavior of the industry.

THE COMPANY INVESTMENT PROCESS

Sources of Investible Funds

The funds which periodically become available for investment in a life insurance company originate in both the insurance and investment

---

* Prepared by J. Robert Ferrari, Assistant Professor of Insurance, Wharton School of Finance and Commerce, University of Pennsylvania.

operations. The funds from insurance operations arise out of the difference between cash receipts (premiums, annuity considerations and other deposits) and cash disbursements (benefits and expenses). The existing investments contribute to investible funds by: (1) earnings from net interest, dividends and realized capital gains; and (2) maturities, prepayments, redemptions, calls and sales. The relative magnitude of these cash flows presents a significant investment problem since a typical, well-established company is likely to be making annual new investments in excess of 10 per cent of total assets. Currently, in the largest companies, this represents yearly investment of well over $2 billion per company. The primary purpose of investment policy is to allocate funds to various categories of investment.

Basic Investment Objectives

The liabilities of a life insurance company are largely composed of the reserves established on behalf of the outstanding insurance and annuity contracts. Therefore, the bulk (80–90 per cent) of liabilities, capital and surplus essentially represent long-term (on the average), fixed-dollar obligations that must be credited periodically with a guaranteed rate of interest. Principles of sound financial management dictate that assets be accumulated in the form and with the maturities consistent with the characteristics of the liabilities that the company has assumed. For a life insurance company, this suggests that a large proportion of assets be long-term, fixed-dollar investments with a yield at least equal to the interest rate guaranteed in the outstanding contracts. The remainder of the assets would be short-term instruments and cash to provide the liquidity necessary to meet current demands. These objectives generally explain the actions of the life companies as evidenced by the preponderance of investments in long-term, fixed-dollar, interest-bearing bonds and mortgages, though individual portfolios can vary significantly depending on the relative emphasis on solvency, liquidity, and yield.

In this context the ideal portfolio would be one which matched the maturities of assets and liabilities, but in practice this is not feasible. The average maturities on available and desirable investments are normally shorter than the duration of insurance liabilities which may extend up to seventy-five years or more. Various writers have expressed great concern over this situation, since unfavorable interest rate movements may expose a company to an "income risk" which can threaten long-term solvency. Since assets are likely to mature one or more times during the expected durations of outstanding contracts, a secular decline in interest rates could result in reinvestment at yields lower than rates guaranteed many years in the past. While historically low-interest rates prevailed in the 1940's, it appears that liquidity, margins in the interest rate assumptions, and various methods of adjustment in dividends and new guarantees are such that the failure to match maturities is of no great concern to most investment managers. The current objective appears to be the acquisition of the longest maturities compatible with the risk, yield and liquidity considerations associated with current strategy.

Although from a legal standpoint the insurance transaction creates a debtor-creditor relationship, the traditions of trusteeship and prudent-man responsibility exert a strong influence on investment policy. In relatively recent times, this conservation viewpoint, with its heavy emphasis on safety, has been relaxed somewhat as relatively greater importance has been attached to higher yields as an investment objective. While a great reluctance to increase risk still prevails, some companies have demonstrated willingness to sacrifice some safety of principal through the acquisition of investments with slightly higher risk but higher expected returns. Perhaps this exemplifies not so much a change in basic investment philosophy as it does increasing competition, more reliance on economic forecasting, and emphasis on portfolio rather than individual risk. The competitive yield objective promises to become increasingly important in the modern life insurance business, which offers investment-oriented contracts like variable annuities and pension-funding instruments in direct competition with other financial institutions for the saving or investment dollar. The apparent conflict between income and safety is, and will continue to be, a fundamental consideration affecting company investment philosophy.

Investment Risk

Like most investors, life insurance companies base their decisions in large part on the relevant risk conditions, attitudes toward risk, and ability to assume risk. These factors are closely related to insolvency, liquidity, rate of return and untenable situations which management wishes to avoid.

Insolvency Risk. The evidence to date indicates that the primary concern of life companies is the risk of legal insolvency, that is, a condition in which admitted assets are less than the liabilities required by law. Many writers refer to this notion rather loosely in a discussion of "safety of principal." This approach usually leads to an inadequate differentiation between risk on individual investment proposals and aggregative or portfolio risk. It is the latter view which spells out most clearly the insolvency risk relevant to company investment policy by considering financial margins of safety and possibilities for diversification.

The threat of insolvency in insurance relates not to real values but rather to an inability to satisfy certain legal standards or regulatory rules of the game. Since legal solvency essentially refers to certain accounting relationships, the risk involved is closely associated with asset and liability valuation requirements and surplus limitations that are unique to life insurance. New York State Insurance Law limits participating policyholders' surplus (including voluntary reserves) to an amount not exceeding 10 per cent of the legal policy reserves and liabilities arising out of such business.[1] For a mutual company this means that surplus is limited to about 9 per cent of assets. Insurers not subject to this restriction tend to have higher proportionate amounts of surplus; however, competition and the relative size of the large mutuals explain why the industry as a whole showed capital and surplus as 8.7 per cent of total assets in 1965. With company surplus limited to such relatively small proportions, it follows that there is little margin for wide independent fluctuations in the values of either assets or liabilities. But, since liabilities are relatively stable and predictable, the primary insolvency risk centers on the potential loss of value of assets.

Valuation requirements promulgated annually by the National Association of Insurance Commissioners prescribe procedures to determine the investments that can be valued in annual statements at stabilized values, such as, amortized values for bonds and adjusted values for preferred stocks.[2] The present rules give partial recognition

---

[1] *New York Insurance Law,* Sec. 207 (1). This restriction reflects the public policy view that, for the most part, excess income from insurance and investment operations should be paid out from year to year as it accrues in order to achieve a more equitable distribution to all policyholders.

[2] "Amortization" refers to the gradual increase or decrease from cost to reflect the approach of payment at par on the maturity date. "Adjusted values" refer to a valuation technique which changes values by only one fifth of the actual change in market prices. See pp. 865–66. The details of the valuation requirements are published annually in the *Proceedings of the National Association of Insurance Commissioners.*

to the going-concern (vis-à-vis liquidation) aspects of company operations by alleviating the ebbs and flows of surplus values that would be caused by valuing all securities at market. It is a well-known fact that the market value of investment assets can fluctuate widely with changes in interest rates and business cycles. Thus, valuation at market would be incompatible with restrictive surplus limitations and would greatly increase the risk of legal insolvency. Also, life insurance companies rarely have to sell securities when the market is depressed, so it would serve no purpose to mark down undefaulted securities that are likely to be held to maturity and to be paid off at par. Bonds in default, preferred stock not in good standing, and all common stock are valued at an "association value," which in most cases is market value or imputed market value when an actual market does not exist. Both mortgage loans on real estate and investment real estate are also valued at amortized values but are not included in the procedures for valuation of securities.

Regulations also provide for valuation reserves called the Mandatory Securities Valuation Reserve (MSVR) which require a company to set aside funds which are not considered part of allowable surplus and which can be used to absorb realized investment losses and fluctuations in the annual statement values of investment securities. The MSVR provides a first line of defense in protecting surplus against declines in market value, but it is limited to a maximum which is approximately 1.5 to 2.5 per cent of assets in the large companies.

In essence, the aggregate risk of insolvency is the probability that assets will decline in value in an amount greater than surplus, contingency reserves and the MSVR,[3] or a decline in assets in excess of 9 or 10 per cent for a typical, long-established company. While a long period of investment earnings lower than the average guaranteed rate could impair surplus, the current difference between expected and guaranteed interest appears to provide a significant margin of safety. In view of the valuation requirements, the primary concern appears to be economic conditions that would necessitate sizable write-downs of bonds and common stock, and cessation of interest income on defaulted bonds and mortgages. Basing assumptions on actual depression experience, one could construct an investment officer's nightmare by assuming a severe economic downturn that caused 10 per cent of a company's corporate bonds and 15 per cent of its mortgages to go into default.

---

[3] This ignores an additional margin of safety that exists in companies where stated reserves are higher than the minimum legal reserve.

Under such conditions it is not unlikely that the defaulted bonds would be written down as much as 70 per cent at the same time that common stock market values declined as much as 50 per cent. For a company with 40 per cent of its assets in corporate bonds and 5 per cent in common stock, the total unrealized loss in asset values in this hypothetical case would be 5.3 per cent of assets. This would obviously be considered an untenable situation, but the loss is still well below the MSVR, surplus and other margins typically available for absorbing losses. Defaulted mortgages do not immediately cause valuation losses since they can be carried temporarily in the real estate account. The impact of cessation of interest income from defaulted issues would depend on the duration of the depression, the initial excess of interest earnings over required interest, and the extent of adjustments in policyholder dividends and new guarantees.

During the 1930's the losses in bond and common stock values due to defaults were ameliorated by moratorium legislation which modified valuation procedures to ease the impact of unrealized losses. This regulatory adjustment, the stabilizing effect of mortgage valuation, mortality and interest rate margins and the ability of the companies to maintain net cash flows even in the worst years all contributed to the survival power that the life insurance industry demonstrated during the depression.

Liquidity Risk. The primary liquidity risk in any business operation is the likelihood that funds will not be sufficient to meet obligations as they mature. This situation is often referred to as technical insolvency. Cash flow analysis of life insurers indicates that liquidity is no particular problem except to the extent that there is too much of it. In *The Investment Process,* Walter states that "For the larger and more mature companies at least, the danger of technical insolvency is, generally speaking, negligible in that inflows are expected to exceed outflows for the foreseeable future, maturities are well distributed, a portion of assets is readily marketable, and a tremendous reservoir of unused borrowing power exists."[4] The only liquidity problems arising in established companies appear to result from insufficient funds to meet an over-zealous amount of forward commitments.[5] However, in

---

[4] James E. Walter, *The Investment Process* (Boston, Mass.: Division of Research, Harvard University, 1962), p. 40.

[5] A forward commitment is an agreement to supply funds to a borrower at some future date and on certain previously specified terms, such as interest rates and maturities.

such cases the normal penalty is not technical insolvency but the embarrassment of negotiating new delivery dates or resorting to borrowing to meet loan commitments.

Income Risk. Previous mention was made of the traditional "income risk" which refers to the possibility that portfolio yield will be less than the rates guaranteed in outstanding contracts; it was suggested that this risk is currently not of particular concern to insurers. There is, however, another income risk associated with investment return, this being the risk of not earning a competitive rate of return on investments. In recent years many companies have conducted aggressive sales campaigns based on their relatively favorable rate of return. In the pension area, where investment results play a fundamental role in the acquisition of new business and the retention of old business, the competition over new money rates attests to the importance of current investment performance to the long-run growth of the insurer. The risks associated with a poor investment return are made more serious by the fact that current investment performance is the cumulative result of past investment decisions. Tactics necessary for improvement may be largely beyond the control of an investment department, at least in the short run. More will be said of this problem in a subsequent discussion of investment performance.

Untenable Situations. Naturally, investment policy must be based on more than a mere classification of risks as insolvency, illiquidity and noncompetitive return. More likely, the collective impact of these factors is exemplified in what might be called "untenable situations" which management wishes to avoid. Interpreting investment risks as to their likely impact on over-all company operations underlines the importance of an aggregate concept of risk (portfolio risk) for investment policy.

In practice, the major danger is not legal insolvency, but rather a solvent level of surplus low enough to place the company in possible jeopardy or to damage its public image. For example, surplus equal to 3 per cent of assets might be determined as untenable. Moreover, an impairment of surplus that would be of such magnitude as to necessitate a reduction in policy dividends would be viewed as an extremely unfavorable development. This condition suggests that investment risks may be viewed differently by the various operating sections of a company. For example, the actuaries tend to consider preservation of surplus as primary, while the marketing forces might see deterioration of the dividend scale as the untenable situation to be avoided. In essence, it is not investment risk but attitudes toward it that shape investment objectives into investment strategy. If management is able and willing to spell out the untenable positions of the company that should be avoided, the proper degree of conservatism or aggressiveness becomes much clearer.

Regulation of Investments

The investment activities of life insurance companies must be conducted within the limitations prescribed by state insurance regulations. Although these laws are the responsibility of the several states, there is significant uniformity, largely attributable to the role of the National Association of Insurance Commissioners in the formulation of investment statutes. Also, because of the high degree of geographic concentration of the domiciled companies, the bulk of the assets of the life insurance industry are regulated by a relatively small number of states. Thus, while the following discussion will emphasize only the provisions of a few important insurance states, these laws are generally representative of the regulatory environment within which the great majority of investment decisions are made.[6]

State laws generally specify investment limitations that can be viewed as being either qualitative or quantitative. The qualitative limitations are aimed at preserving the safety of the assets underlying the policyholder reserves. The quantitative constraints have the dual objectives of imposing portfolio diversification among and within eligible types of investments and preventing undue control by the insurer through proportionately large investment in any one firm.

Qualitative Limitations. The qualitative aspects of investment regulation stem from the specification of eligible types of investment and the minimum quality criteria for individual investments within the eligible categories. Allowable investments tend to be limited to: (1) obligations of the United States government, the states and political subdivisions thereof; (2) corporate debt and equity securities;[7] (3)

---

[6] The New York State Insurance Law is particularly pervasive because of the extraterritorial provisions which require companies licensed to do business in the state to "comply substantially" with New York regulations. *New York Insurance Law*, Sec. 42 (5), 90 (1). For a convenient reference to the laws of representative states see Life Insurance Association of America, *Life Insurance Companies as Financial Institutions* (Englewood Cliffs, N.J.: Prentice-Hall, Inc., 1962), pp. 97–159.

[7] Life insurance companies normally are not permitted to make unsecured investments in unincorporated businesses. Unincorporated entities can obtain life

real estate mortgages; (4) real estate; (5) foreign investments of substantially the same kinds, classes and grade as those eligible for domestic investment; (6) miscellaneous categories, such as equipment trust obligations; and (7) otherwise ineligible investments allowed under leeway or basket provisions.

With regard to each of the eligible types of investment, the laws specify conditions which must be met by each individual proposal which is acquired. Collateral requirements may be prescribed for corporate debt obligations. Safety margins for earnings in excess of fixed charges are required by earnings tests that are applied to corporate debt according to the secured or unsecured status of the issue. Similarly, earnings and dividend tests are often used to determine the eligibility of preferred stock and common stock. Some states require the existence of a market for eligibility of common stock, which may mean that the security has to be listed on a recognized exchange. Eligible mortgage loans are normally defined by a specified loan-to-value ratio, the typical statute restricting the amount of the loan from 66⅔ to 75 per cent of the market value of the property at the time of the loan. This constraint is commonly modified for mortgages insured or guaranteed by the Federal Housing Administration or the Veterans Administration. Foreign investment may be restricted to those insurance companies actually conducting business in the possession or country in question.

Quantitative Limitations. Important limitations are imposed on the amounts that can be placed in eligible investments. The New York Insurance Law will be used to suggest the content and the approximate order of magnitude of the various dollar amount and percentage limitations that may be found in investment statutes.

There are no quantitative limitations on the amount of government bonds that can be held except that at least 60 per cent of the total amount of required minimum capital is to be held in federal, state, and local government securities.

No limit is placed on the aggregate amount of eligible corporate debt obligations held by an insurer. In addition, an insurer can invest in corporate obligations that are not ordinarily eligible for investment provided that the aggregate of such investments does not exceed

---

insurance company funds directly through mortgage loans and policy loans. The companies also make indirect loans by lending to finance companies which in turn lend to unincorporated businesses.

one half of 1 per cent of admitted assets.[8] However, no life insurance company is allowed to invest in the eligible obligations of any one institution in excess of 5 per cent of the total of admitted assets of such insurer.

Investment in the preferred stocks of any one issuing corporation is not allowed to exceed 20 per cent of the total issued and outstanding preferred stock, nor can this amount exceed 2 per cent of the admitted assets of the insurer.[9]

Investment in the common stock of any one institution is not allowed to exceed 2 per cent of the total issued and outstanding common shares, nor can the amount exceed one fifth of 1 per cent of the admitted assets of the insurer.[10] An insurer's aggregate holding of all common stock (valued at cost) is limited to the lesser of 5 per cent of the total admitted assets or one half of the surplus to policyholders.[11]

New York law requires that no mortgage loan made, or acquired, by an insurer on any one property shall, at the time of the investment exceed 75 per cent of the value of the real property or leasehold securing the loan if: (1) the security is primarily improved by a single family residence, (2) the loan is less than $30,000, and (3) the amortization period does not exceed thirty years. In all other cases mortgage loans are limited to 66⅔ per cent of the value of the security except that in either case these ratios may be exceeded to the extent of the guaranteed or insured portions of such loans. A further limitation specifies that no insurer shall invest in or loan upon the security of any one property more than $30,000 or more than 2 per cent of its admitted assets, whichever is greater. In no event is aggregate investment in mortgage loans allowed to exceed 40 per cent of total admitted assets recognizing that guaranteed and insured portions of such mortgages are not included within this 40 per cent limitation.

Life insurance companies complying with New York law cannot have more than 10 per cent of their admitted assets invested in or

---

[8] *New York Insurance Law,* Sec. 81(2).

[9] *Ibid.,* Sec. 81(3).

[10] *Ibid.,* Sec. 81(13).

[11] *Ibid.* Life insurance companies usually show a surplus of less than 10 per cent of admitted assets so the surplus restriction is usually the pertinent measure of the aggregate limit on common stock. Actually, many investment officers would agree that the real limitation on common stock is the cautious attitude created by the procedure of valuing at capricious market values.

loaned upon the securities of any one institution.[12] By a general "lee-way" or "basket" provision, investments which are not otherwise eligible are authorized up to a limit of 2 per cent of an insurer's admitted assets.[13]

Investment Performance

The traditional measure of the investment performance of a life insurance company is the rate of return on invested assets. A portfolio rate of return is essentially a weighted average of the yields produced by the various categories of investments, the weights being the proportion of total investments in each category. The yield on each investment category is itself a weighted average of investments made over time at different rates of return. The result of this procedure is a summary measure of past and current investment decisions. Table 44 illustrates the average net rate of interest that has been earned by the companies in the past. Naturally, the actual performance of any one

TABLE 44

NET RATE OF INTEREST EARNED ON INVESTED FUNDS
U.S. Life Insurance Companies

Year	Rate	Year	Rate	Year	Rate	Year	Rate
1915	4.77%	1928	5.05%	1941	3.42%	1954	3.46%
1916	4.80	1929	5.05	1942	3.44	1955	3.51
1917	4.81	1930	5.05	1943	3.33	1956	3.63
1918	4.72	1931	4.93	1944	3.23	1957	3.75
1919	4.66	1932	4.65	1945	3.11	1958	3.85
1920	4.83	1933	4.25	1946	2.93	1959	3.96
1921	5.02	1934	3.92	1947	2.88	1960	4.11
1922	5.12	1935	3.70	1948	2.96	1961	4.22
1923	5.18	1936	3.71	1949	3.06	1962	4.34
1924	5.17	1937	3.69	1950	3.13	1963	4.45
1925	5.11	1938	3.59	1951	3.18	1964	4.53
1926	5.09	1939	3.54	1952	3.28	1965	4.61
1927	5.05	1940	3.45	1953	3.36		

Source: Institute of Life Insurance. The net interest rate is the ratio of (1) net investment income to (2) mean invested assets (including cash) less half the net investment income. Before 1940, some federal income taxes were deducted from net investment income; beginning with 1940, the rates are calculated before deducting any federal income taxes.

company will vary from the industry average. For example, in 1964, although the average net yield before taxes was 4.53 per cent, a sample of a large number of established companies reveals a range of returns of from 4.14 per cent to 5.79 per cent.

[12] *New York Insurance Law*, Sec. 87.

[13] *Ibid.*, Sec. 81(15). Sentiment among many life insurance company officers seems to favor liberalization of the "basket" provision to something like 5 per cent.

Since the rate of return is greatly influenced by past actions, current investment performance is often more apparent in the periodic changes in the investment return than in the actual return itself. Annual changes in portfolio rates of return are primarily determined by the proportion of existing assets and the amount of new assets that become available for current investments, and the rates at which these investments are made. The current yield is determined by the allocation strategy based on risk, return, and other considerations, and the availability of desirable investments. The relative amount of funds available for investment depends on such factors as (1) average length of investment maturities, (2) company growth, and (3) ability or willingness to supplement or withhold investible funds. Since the rate of return is also a weighted average of returns on investments made in different time periods, it is evident that the rate is influenced by the timing of investible funds with changes in market interest rates. For example, during periods of what prove to be relatively high interest rates, a high asset turnover and a high rate of company growth will have an immediate and persisting favorable influence on the portfolio rate of return. During these same periods, even highly clairvoyant investment departments may not be able to improve appreciably their rate of return if the maturity schedule and poor company growth produce relatively small amounts of investible cash. In general, to assess investment performance properly, allowances must be made for the extent to which the portfolio rate of return is determined by factors which in the short run are largely out of the control of the investment officers. Walter succinctly summarizes the problem and suggests some additional considerations when he states:

As an exclusive measure of comparative performance, the composite rate of return on invested assets is deficient. It weights the results of past investment decisions more than those attributable to current behavior and is affected by asset growth over which the investment staff has but limited control. It further omits capital gains and losses and reflects arbitrary expense allocations.[14]

In recent years a great deal of attention has been given to the rate of return on new investments as a measure of investment performance. This benchmark certainly describes actions of the current investment staff. Also the so-called "new money rates" have become important in the private pension area, since new deposits and reinvestible portions of existing assets can be credited with the most recent investment

---

[14] James E. Walter, *op. cit.*, p. 12.

returns. The relative importance of the new money rate versus the traditional portfolio rate of return in influencing investment policy depends on a company's aggressiveness in the pension field and the direction and magnitude of interest rate changes. The post-war secular increase in interest rates has caused the new money rate in most companies to exceed the portfolio rate by a significant differential. Critics of the new money rate approach have expressed concern over the potential reaction of both insurers and insureds if future interest rate changes are such as to lower the new investment rate below the average portfolio yield.

LIFE INSURANCE COMPANIES IN THE CAPITAL MARKETS

The leading financial instutions in the United States are commercial banks, life insurance companies, savings and loan associations, mutual savings banks, corporate pension funds, nonlife insurance companies, finance companies and open-end investment companies. The most important of these are the commercial banks, which, in 1965, held $377.3 billion in assets, and, together with the Federal Reserve Banks, perform a unique function in monetary policy due to their ability to expand and contract the nation's money supply. In terms of ownership of assets, in 1965 the life insurance industry stood second in importance with $158.9 billion, which exceeded the $129.4 billion of the next closest competitor for the savings dollar—savings and loan associations. From these figures alone it is evident that the life insurance companies in the aggregate exert a powerful influence, both in an absolute and a relative sense, in the capital markets. Their role is made even more significant by the fact that, despite close regulation of investments, the life insurance companies are able to hold a wider range of loan instruments than many of the other financial institutions. Through their size and investment latitude, and their willingness to redirect their lending from one sector to another according to the changing demands of borrowers, the life companies have had a substantial impact upon the markets for government securities, corporate bonds and real estate mortgages.

Since the end of World War II the life insurance industry has experienced an extremely favorable rate of growth as the public displayed an increased demand for life insurance. Since the mid-1950's, however, the relative rate of savings through life insurance has decreased, as evidenced by a shift to term insurance—individual and group—which has little or no savings element. The life insurance industry (as well as banking) has failed to keep pace in competition for the savings dollar with other faster-growing institutions, namely savings and loan associations and corporate pension funds. The companies are also facing increased competition from these two institutions in the search for attractive mortgage loans and corporate bonds which are aggressively sought by savings and loan associations and pension funds, respectively. There is every reason, however, to believe that the life insurance companies will continue to remain a dominant force in the capital markets, particularly in the corporate bond and real estate mortgage sectors.

Historical Investment Behavior

By retracing life insurance company investment behavior from the early 1900's until the present, one can gain valuable insight into the twentieth century financial thinking of these institutions.[15] This span of approximately sixty years may very well prove to be atypical, since it encompassed a rapid sequence of economic depressions, major wars and unprecedented periods of prosperity. However, the investment reactions of the life insurance companies to these extreme events are useful indications of the objectives, attitudes, and true economic role of these institutions.

Table 45 contains the proportionate distribution of the major categories of assets of the life insurance companies in various pivotal years. The changes in asset holdings during these periods serve to illuminate the investment policy of the companies during various economic and political environments.

1917–29. The relative holdings of life insurance companies immediately prior to World War I show heavy commitments to corporate bonds and mortgages and little interest in government securities. This portfolio composition reflects the prosperity prior to the war and is an early example of the tendency of life insurers to give priority to demands in the private sectors of the capital markets and to use governments as a residual source of investments. Railroad mortgage bonds dominated the bond category because of the relative importance of that industry at the time and the desire of the insurers for bonds secured by real property.

The American entry into the war precipitated a strong move into federal government issues as a result of a demand for funds to finance

---

[15] For a detailed analysis of the investment behavior of the life insurance industry see Andrew F. Brimmer, *Life Insurance Companies in the Capital Market* (East Lansing, Michigan: Bureau of Business and Economic Research, Michigan State University, 1962). The following discussion draws heavily from this definitive work.

TABLE 45

Percentage Distribution of Assets of U.S. Life Insurance Companies

Year	Bonds						Stocks	Mortgages	Real Estate	Policy Loans	Misc. Assets	Total
	U.S. Govt.	Foreign Govt.	State, Provincial, & Local	Railroad	Public Utility	Industrial & Misc.						
1917	1.2%	2.8%	5.6%	30.5%	1.9%	.8%	1.4%	34.0%	3.0%	13.6%	5.2%	100.0%
1920	11.3	2.3	4.8	24.3	1.7	.7	1.0	33.4	2.3	11.7	6.5	100.0
1925	5.4	1.3	4.6	19.4	6.0	.8	.7	41.7	2.3	12.5	5.3	100.0
1930	1.7	.9	5.4	15.5	8.6	1.9	2.8	40.2	2.9	14.9	5.2	100.0
1935	12.3	.8	7.3	11.3	9.1	2.5	2.5	23.1	8.6	15.2	7.3	100.0
1940	18.7	1.0	7.8	9.2	13.9	5.0	2.0	19.4	6.7	10.0	6.3	100.0
1945	45.9	2.1	2.3	6.6	11.6	4.3	2.2	14.8	1.9	4.4	3.9	100.0
1950	21.0	1.7	2.4	5.0	16.5	14.9	3.3	25.1	2.2	3.8	4.1	100.0
1951	16.1	1.3	2.5	4.9	16.4	16.8	3.3	28.3	2.4	3.8	4.2	100.0
1952	14.0	1.0	2.4	4.8	16.3	18.7	3.3	29.0	2.6	3.7	4.2	100.0
1953	12.5	.7	2.6	4.7	16.3	19.7	3.3	29.7	2.6	3.7	4.2	100.0
1954	10.7	.5	3.1	4.5	16.0	20.0	3.9	30.7	2.7	3.7	4.2	100.0
1955	9.5	.4	3.0	4.3	15.5	20.1	4.0	32.6	2.9	3.6	4.1	100.0
1956	7.9	.4	3.1	4.0	15.1	20.6	3.7	34.4	2.9	3.7	4.2	100.0
1957	6.9	.3	3.1	3.8	15.1	21.5	3.3	34.8	3.1	3.8	4.3	100.0
1958	6.7	.3	3.3	3.6	14.8	21.8	3.8	34.4	3.1	3.9	4.3	100.0
1959	6.0	.3	3.7	3.3	14.5	22.1	4.0	34.5	3.2	4.1	4.3	100.0
1960	5.4	.3	3.8	3.1	14.0	22.4	4.2	34.9	3.1	4.4	4.4	100.0
1961	4.9	.3	4.0	2.8	13.4	22.6	4.9	34.9	3.2	4.5	4.5	100.0
1962	4.6	.5	4.0	2.6	13.0	23.1	4.7	35.2	3.1	4.7	4.5	100.0
1963	4.1	.6	3.9	2.4	12.3	23.5	5.0	35.8	3.1	4.7	4.6	100.0
1964	3.7	.6	3.8	2.2	11.5	23.7	5.3	36.9	3.0	4.8	4.5	100.0
1965	3.2	.6	3.4	2.1	10.7	24.2	5.7	37.8	3.0	4.8	4.5	100.0

Sources: *Spectator Year Book* and Institute of Life Insurance.

the war effort, a decrease in the availability of corporate debt and a decline in the prices of outstanding governments as interest rates rose. The relatively high yields on governments, combined with unequaled safety of principal, continued to make these loans attractive into the early 1920's.

The 1920's were characterized as a period of continuous economic prosperity. The life insurers reacted to the situation by gradually moving out of governments in order to satisfy the private demands that were both the cause and effect of the economic expansion. The increased importance of mortgages was brought about by the great construction boom in both residential and nonresidential properties, and the expansion in farm mortgage credit up to the mid-1920's. The changing proportions within the bond category were a result of the growth of public utilities, particularly the electric companies, during this period, and the declining relative importance of the railroads.

1930–39. The changes in the distribution of the assets of life insurers during the 1930's are largely explained by the great economic depression which the nation experienced during this period. The economic decline was partially the result of a dearth of capital investment, which, in turn, caused a precipitous decline in the demand for debt in both the private bond and mortgage markets. In addition to the shrinkage of the bond market, the life companies saw many of their bonds fall into default with regard to interest and/or principal payments. They suffered particularly poor experience as a result of the railroad bankruptcies of the 1930's. Nevertheless, the industry was successful in directing funds into public utility bonds as these companies continued to borrow. Mortgage defaults were widespread during the depression, and foreclosed rural and urban properties became part of the insurer's real estate ownership, causing a disproportionate increase in that category. The lack of demand for mortgage loans and the large volume of foreclosures caused the mortgage assets of the industry to decline more than 50 per cent in ten years. Policy loans showed a significant increase as might be expected. The most dramatic change during the depression was the growth of United States Government securities from 1.7 per cent in 1930 to over 18 per cent by the end of the decade. Again, the companies resorted to governments as a residual investment outlet as the private markets declined. Also, since unemployment persisted, the government exerted a demand for funds to finance public works and relief programs.

1940–45. By 1945, life insurance companies held 45.9 per cent of their assets in the form of United States Government securities. The movement into these issues that started during the depression continued, as a result of World War II, up to the mid-1940's. Corporate indebtedness, which had declined during the 1930's, declined even further during World War II. Funds to finance war production were acquired through issues of government bonds and the life insurers participated heavily in these offerings. The continuing decline in mortgages during this period is explained by the general shortage of building materials which caused curtailment of nondefense construction. The decrease in the proportion of assets in real estate reflects the gradual disposal of property acquired through mortgage foreclosures in the 1930's. By 1945 policy loans had declined to 4.4 per cent of assets, indicating an improving economic climate and the increasing willingness of the banks to offer individual loans secured by the investment values in a life insurance policy. This move by the banks obviated the need for an insured to initiate a policy loan in order to acquire the cash value while continuing the insurance protection.

1946–Present. The post-World War II investment behavior of the life insurance companies has been one of fairly stable trends in the changing composition of assets. Since 1945, the holdings of United States Government securities have declined steadily from 45.9 per cent to 3.7 per cent in 1964. Immediately after the war, and continuing for some years thereafter, the large government security holdings were gradually liquidated to finance the bond and mortgage demands of the postwar economic expansion. Up to 1951 the life companies enjoyed the luxury of pegged interest rates on government securities and were not exposed to any risk of capital losses at the time of disposing these issues. After the famous "accord" between the Treasury and the Federal Reserve System the companies had to contend with a more orthodox market, but by this time they had liquidated a large portion of their government bonds. By the end of the 1950's or the early 1960's company holdings of government securities seemed to reach a level which was no longer subject to large discretionary liquidations to take advantage of market opportunities. While the gradual reduction in governments was consistent throughout the entire postwar period, the companies did make greater relative allocations to governments during each of the postwar recessions. The industry figures tend to overstate the position of the large companies in governments because small and new companies invest heavily in these issues.

Railroad and public utility bonds have become relatively less important although the latter still represents 11.5 per cent of total assets. A great deal of the more recent interest in public utility issues has been in communications and gas and natural gas lines. Municipal bonds remained relatively insignificant in new acquisitions, but many companies did place sizable amounts in revenue bonds issued by special authorities. The important place of the life insurers in the bond market is accounted for by their participation in the tremendous postwar demands of commercial and industrial corporations for debt financing. During these expansive years corporate borrowers turned more and more to debt to acquire new funds. The tax deductibility of interest, opportunities for favorable leverage, advantages of capital gains and other factors seemed to recommend financing by retained earnings and external debt rather than by new common stock issues. The insurance industry responded to the apparent needs not only by supplying funds to this market but by taking advantage of the direct placement method of arranging corporate debt transactions. More recently the insurers have been looking to the foreign markets for government and corporate investment outlets but to date foreign lending is dwarfed by the activity in the domestic market.

Mortgages have gradually recovered the relative importance they held before World War I. The life insurers have found the yield differentials between bonds and mortgages sufficient to justify larger current allocations to the mortgage area. The companies have shown increasing interest in commercial and industrial mortgage loans, one of the most obvious examples being high-rise apartment buildings.

Another significant change in company portfolios has been an increase in acquisitions of common stock. This movement has been largely influenced by the liberalizations during the 1950's of the statutory limitations and the slowly changing attitude of the industry as to the propriety of common stock investments.

The current investment policy of the companies in the aggregate can be discerned from the percentage allocation of the funds available for investment. The companies allocated their new investments in 1965 in approximately the following manner:

United States government bonds	8.6%
State and local government bonds	0.8
Foreign bonds	2.9
Corporate bonds	50.4
Real estate mortgages	28.2
Real estate	1.1
Preferred stock	1.2
Common stock	2.5
Policy loans	4.3
Total investible funds	100.0%

These industry figures differ from the allocation strategy of the large, established companies which tend to place smaller proportions in government securities and larger proportions in real estate mortgages. Another factor that lies beneath these figures is the geographical allocation of funds. Sectors of the United States undergoing rapid growth and generating a great demand for funds tend to be more attractive areas for investment because of the relatively high interest rates. The companies with the flexibility to do so have increased their bond and mortgage debt in such states, the most recent example being California. Geography also affects allocation strategies if funds are kept in certain areas to accommodate policyholders and agents, or if allocations are inflexible due to strong ties with branch offices, loan correspondents, or investment bankers.

Summary of Industry Attributes

A number of generalizations, based on observed behavior, can be made concerning the investment characteristics of life insurance companies as they can be expected to exemplify themselves in the capital markets. It is often and tritely stated that the companies attempt to achieve the highest yield consonant with the safety required by the nature of their liabilities. This description is more meaningfully expressed by saying that the industry shows the ability and willingness to respond to changes in the level and structure of interest rates. The clearest examples of this are the movements into and out of the public debt market with changes in the relative demand for funds in the private sector. After a discretionary level of government securities is acquired for liquidity and diversification needs, these instruments come to be regarded as a residual investment outlet. The legal framework, existing yield differentials, and the nature of life insurance liabilities tend to limit current investment activity to high-credit, debt obligation of corporations and amply secured real estate mortgages. The companies demonstrate a marked willingness and ability to vary their investment allocation between bonds and mortgages according to changing yield differentials and market demands. The tax status of the life insurance business is such that the tax-exempt issues of state and local governments have only limited appeal. Common stock would appear to be more suitable as an appropriate investment than the current relative holdings suggest. However, it is unlikely that the companies can or will play a significant role in the equity markets with existing investment attitudes, legal limitations, and valuation requirements.

The life insurance companies should continue to play a major role in the long-term bond and mortgage markets. There is some concern that these investment outlets might fail to provide available investments sufficient to absorb the tremendous investible cash flows of the industry. If this eventuality occurs the companies will probably resort again to government securities. Some of the more progressive companies are already exploring the possibilities of increasing their allocations to investments which traditionally have not been significant outlets for life insurance company funds.

CHAPTER XLIII

Financial
*Statements**

THE NAIC BLANK

THE BASIC financial report of a life insurance company is the annual statement promulgated by the National Association of Insurance Commissioners and known colloquially as the "Convention Blank" or "NAIC Blank." This document sets forth financial and supplemental data of the life insurance company in scope and detail far in excess of what is required from the vast majority of businesses outside the insurance industry. The basic form runs to forty-six pages, including seventeen exhibits, twelve schedules, and various interrogatories, and it is accompanied by twelve pages of official instructions for completion. Since some of the schedules have to be expanded into extra pages to accommodate, for example, the detailed lists of securities owned, a large company may find that its annual statement runs to more than one hundred pages.

The form of this statement is reviewed and revised annually by a standing committee of the NAIC and currently represents the result of an evolutionary process which has been going on for about a hundred years. Through the action of the NAIC the form is standardized for use by each of the states on a uniform basis, although minor variations are required in some individual states.

CONCEPTS OF INSURANCE COMPANY ACCOUNTING

Emphasis on Solvency

The outstanding characteristic of the accounting philosophy which underlies the NAIC statement blank is the overwhelming emphasis upon the demonstration of solvency with its subsidiary effects on the

---

* Prepared by Robert G. Espie, F.S.A., Vice-President and Comptroller, Aetna Life and Casualty.

860

valuation of assets and liabilities and on the usefulness of the official statement as a measure of year-to-year earnings. Solvency has from the beginning been the primary preoccupation of the regulatory authorities because of the great need for protection of the public from the consequences of insolvency and because a failure of management to maintain real solvency may not be obviously discernible until irreparable loss has been inflicted upon innocent parties.

The emphasis on solvency and the difficulty of accurately determining its existence have led to the adoption of valuation conventions which avoid the problem of attaining complete accuracy by assuring that any deviation from complete accuracy in the area of liability valuation is on the side of overvaluation and that any deviation from complete accuracy in the area of asset valuation is on the side of undervaluation. The fact that these conventions may be unrealistic in individual company situations is subordinated to their usefulness and simplicity in demonstrating solvency to regulatory authorities. Further subordinated is the fact that when such conventions overvalue liabilities and undervalue assets by unknown amounts—as compared with theoretical but unknown exact valuation accuracy—surplus is distorted, and earnings, which reflect the change of surplus from one year-end to another, may be doubly distorted.

Measurement of Earnings

The measurement of earnings of a life insurance company from one year to another is rendered difficult not only by the impact of valuation conventions but also by the facts that (1) a comparatively long time must elapse before it can be determined whether the sale of a block of insurance policies has been profitable, (2) the mortality tables allowable for valuation of liabilities normally involve a pattern of mortality rates quite different from those expected by the company when it establishes premium rates, and (3) the net level premium and modified net level premium valuation formulas commonly in use release expense margins in premiums in a pattern quite different from the actual incidence of expenses.

Since the profitability of a block of life insurance policies cannot be determined until the last policy in the block has terminated, it becomes apparent that interim valuations must play a very important role in the determination of earnings and as a corollary any shortcoming in interim valuation must reduce the accuracy of earnings measurement. One of those shortcomings in such valuation is the use, as prescribed by law and regulation, of mortality tables whose mortality levels and patterns of incidence are markedly different from the levels and incidence actually expected by the company when the policy is issued. Thus the reserves during interim years may be higher or lower than the reserves which would have arisen from the use of truly expected mortality. The difference manifests itself as a distortion in surplus and in earnings. Further, the net level premium system of valuation implies that a constant amount of expense loading (excess of gross premium over valuation net premium) will become available each year for the payment of expenses, whereas the actual expenses are typically very unlevel, being heaped at the issue date, followed by lower levels for the renewal commission period, and even lower levels thereafter. Where a modified net level premium method of reserve valuation is used, the lack of correspondence between loading and actual expenses may be less but is still likely to be significant. Differences between the incidence of loading and actual expense emergence necessarily distort *current* earnings although ultimate profitability may work out according to original assumptions.

STRUCTURE OF FINANCIAL STATEMENTS

The financial statements of insurance companies have generally the same structure as the financial statements of other corporations. There is a balance sheet, which on the one side lists assets, and on the other side lists liabilities, surplus and capital, if any. There is a summary of operations designed to show the earnings of the company for the year of account and there is a surplus account designed to reflect the disposition of those earnings, plus the impact of other transactions which do not belong to the particular year of account or which are otherwise not properly chargeable to operating earnings.

The earnings for the year are carried to the surplus account. The surplus account reflects the reconciliation of surplus from one year to another. Total assets are equal to the total of liabilities and surplus and capital.

A balance sheet, summary of operations, and surplus account for a typical stock life insurance company are reproduced at the end of this chapter in all the detail required by the NAIC blank.

Balance Sheet

Assets. The first part of the asset page is devoted to the display of the various kinds of "invested" assets. "Invested" assets consist of bonds, stocks, mortgage loans, real estate, policy loans, premium notes, collateral loans, cash and bank deposits, and any other invested assets of a nature considered allowable for life insurance companies. This area of the asset page normally comprises the vast bulk of the assets of a life insurance company.

The remaining assets comprise items which are not normally thought of as being "investments" but which are of value to the company even though they may not earn interest. They include amounts recoverable from reinsurers, premiums not yet paid, interest and other investment income due and accrued, plus whatever other assets of a similarly miscellaneous nature the company may have.

1. *Classification of Assets.* Peculiar to the insurance business is the classification of assets into ledger assets, nonledger assets, admitted assets, and nonadmitted assets.

Ledger assets, as the name implies, are those which are entered on the general ledgers of the company. They are distinguished in this respect from nonledger assets which are usually determined by inventory methods and determined only at the ends of the periods of account. Nonledger assets are not entered on the books of the company as such. They are entered directly into the financial statement without being carried through the usual paths of voucher to journal, journal to ledger, which distinguishes the ordinary double-entry bookkeeping system. The distinction between ledger and nonledger assets is a purely artificial one and carries no implication as to their quality since any nonledger asset can be converted into a ledger asset by the simple process of spreading it on the books of account prior to the formation of the financial statement itself. For example, some premiums will normally be due and unpaid at statement date; they are normally totaled by inventory methods and entered in the balance sheet as nonledger assets. If a company chose, it could credit premium income and debit a ledger asset account of due and unpaid premiums. By such action the asset would become a ledger asset and enter the balance sheet as such.

A class of assets may have both ledger and nonledger values, which are added together when preparing the balance sheet. For example, common stocks are commonly carried in the ledger at cost, any excess of market value over cost is determined by inventory methods and entered as nonledger, and the total of ledger plus nonledger is carried to the balance sheet.

Quite restrictive rules govern the kinds of assets which may be displayed, and the values which may be assigned to those assets, in the preparation of the balance sheet. Assets considered acceptable for this purpose, valued at amounts considered acceptable for this purpose, constitute admitted assets. Some types of assets are required to be omitted in their entirety for this purpose. Other types may be disallowed in part. An example of an asset which would be considered to be nonadmitted in its entirety might be a deposit in a defaulted bank where the expectation is that there will be no recovery whatever by the depositor. Likewise a premium overdue so long as to be reasonably classified as uncollectible, and for which the insurance company holds no other security, would be treated as a completely nonadmitted asset.

An asset which is not completely nonadmissible may be nonadmissible in part. For example, if a stock has a market value below the value at which it is carried on the books of the company, the deficiency of market value under that cost value is normally classified as a nonadmitted asset. A policy loan which, through clerical error or otherwise, had been made in an amount greater than the security of the policy reserve would be considered to be nonadmissible to the extent by which the amount of the loan exceeds the policy reserve which is its security.

Thus, assets are drawn from the ledgers, they are supplemented by the nonledger assets obtained from inventory techniques, and they are then reduced by whatever amount of the resulting value is considered to be nonadmissible. The transition from ledger values to admitted values is developed in an exhibit showing in columnar form for each category of asset the basic ledger asset if it is a ledger asset, the nonledger amount that is added, the nonadmitted amount that is deducted, and the net admitted asset which is carried to the statement page.

2. *Valuation of Assets.* The rules prescribed for valuation of assets in a life insurance company statement are quite restrictive, are often peculiar to the insurance business, and are, as might be expected, permeated by the emphasis on solvency. In what follows some of the salient characteristics of those valuation rules are described.

(*a*) *Bonds.* Bonds normally comprise a very important element in the investment portfolio of a life insurance company. They are carried under normal circumstances at amortized values. Amortization is an arrangement whereby any difference between the original investment in a security and its final redemption value will be spread over the intervening years in a systematic manner. When a bond is bought at a "premium" over its final redemption value, that premium is written down over the lifetime of the bond by a process of annual decreases in the asset value of the bond matched by annual reductions in the income from the bond. In the case of a bond bought below its redemption value, the "discount" is accrued from year to year increasing the asset value of the bond and similarly increasing the income considered to be derived from the bond. The result of the amortization process is to produce a stable investment return to match the stable interest rate used in the calculation of the corresponding premiums and reserves. Interim vagaries in the market price of the bond in question are considered to be of no practical value since it is assumed that the bond will be held from purchase date until maturity. For quite a few bonds, particularly those acquired through the "private placement" process, there may in fact be no public market quotation of value available and, therefore, the amortized value is the only practical one to use.

Bonds may be valued on the amortized basis only as long as they are in good standing, that is, as long as they are not in default with respect to either interest or principal. If they are not eligible for amortization, they are carried at their market values.

(*b*) *Common and Preferred Stocks.* Common stocks are normally carried in the ledger at their cost. The excess of market value over cost is added by means of the nonledger asset process and any deficiency of market value under cost is deducted by means of the not admitted asset process. The result is to carry common stocks in the balance sheet at current market value. Market values to be used for this purpose are determined from a booklet published periodically by the National Association of Insurance Commissioners. For practical purposes, these market values are those which could be found in a reputable newspaper quoting public stock exchange prices.

Preferred stocks were in former times carried on the ledger at their cost, as is the case for common stocks, and similarly converted to market value through the addition of nonledger or the deduction of nonadmitted values. Recognizing that preferred stocks have an inherent stability of value, and desiring to insulate the surplus of insurance companies from meaningless temporary vagaries of the market, the NAIC promulgated an adjusted basis of valuation for preferred stocks in good standing beginning in the year 1957. On the adjusted basis, the statement value for a preferred stock at the end of any year was taken to be the statement value at the end of the previous year changed by one fifth of the increase (or decrease) from the previous year's statement value to the published market value at the end of the current year. This "one fifth rule" was in use for statements through December 31, 1964 and did, in fact, insulate surplus from the bulk of market fluctuations. It met, however, with some criticism, since it resulted in carrying the preferred stocks in question at values which were neither cost nor market. It was also argued that a preferred stock in good standing was a fixed-income type of security more nearly akin to a bond in its value than to a common stock.

The valuation rule was, therefore, changed by the NAIC to provide that all preferred stocks purchased in 1965 or later would be carried permanently in balance sheets at their original cost. With respect to the portfolio of preferred stocks held at December 31, 1964, companies were given the option of continuing to carry them at their December 31, 1964 balance sheet values or of moving them back to their original cost. As with bonds, the valuation rule is contingent upon preferred stocks being "in good standing." Preferred stocks which are labeled as not being in good standing are required to be carried at their market values.

(*c*) *Other Assets.* *Mortgage loans* on real estate are carried on the books of the company, and in the balance sheet, at the amount of principal originally loaned minus any subsequent repayments of principal.

Real estate is subdivided into three categories. The first category consists of properties occupied by the company, which are valued at their original cost, plus any subsequent capital improvements, and minus any subsequent depreciation. The second category of real estate consists of properties acquired in satisfaction of debt, usually through foreclosure of mortgages, which are normally carried at the amount of the debt. The third category of real estate consists of real estate purchased for investment purposes, normally valued at the investment originally made plus any subsequent capital improvements and minus any subsequent depreciation. Real estate must be carried to the balance sheet at market values if the market values are less than the book values.

Policy loans are under normal circumstances fully secured by the reserve values of the policies in question and are, therefore, carried to the balance sheet at face values. An exception would occur if in any case it should be found that the policy loan exceeded the reserve, in which event the policy loan value would be reduced by a nonadmitted asset entry to the amount of the reserve.

Amounts recoverable from reinsurers are considered to be good assets at their face value provided the reinsurer is not in default. Some states will allow amounts recoverable from reinsurers to be entered as admissible assets only if the reinsurers in question are authorized to do business in those particular states. In such states the reinsurance asset has to be diminished by deduction of any nonadmitted items to bring it to a net admissible statement value. Thus, the total assets and the amount of surplus may not be reported identically in each of the states in which the company is doing business. Where the amounts determined to be inadmissible by one state or another are, in fact, not significant in relation to the total of an insurance company's assets or surplus, a company may reduce the asset (or achieve the same effect on surplus by setting up a special liability) to an amount which is considered admissible in the state which has the most stringent admissibility criteria. The company thereby achieves very desirable uniformity of assets and surplus in its various state filings, the security of the policyholders is not harmed since no actual loss is permanently sustained by the company, and the function of the statement of proving solvency is fulfilled (surplus may, of course, be understated in the process).

Life insurance premiums and annuity considerations deferred and uncollected are shown as an asset even though there may be no enforceable obligation on the part of the policyholder to pay such premiums and considerations and no collateral or other security for their collection. In addition to "uncollected" premiums which have fallen due before the end of the year of account, the asset includes "deferred" premiums which are scheduled to become due between the close of the year of account and the close of the subsequent policy year. Justification for this asset lies in the fact that the corresponding reserves for life insurance policies have been calculated on the assumption that all premiums have been paid for the policy year current at the end of the year of account. Where such premiums have not, in fact, been paid, the reserve liability is, in fact, overstated.

Since the reserve liability assumes that the net premium for the entire current policy year has been paid, rather than the gross, the deferred premiums set up to counter the liability overstatement are first reduced from their gross value to their net. If the "loading" (taken as the excess of the gross premium over the net premium entering into the valuation process) is less than the cost of collection of the premiums in question, conservatism is maintained by the establishment of a specific liability item equal to the excess of the cost of collection over the loading. In this instance, an excess in a liability item is corrected by the establishment of an offsetting asset, then an excess in the offsetting asset is countered by the establishment of a further offsetting liability.

Due and unpaid premiums in accident and health lines are treated differently from due and unpaid in the life insurance lines. Since typical accident and health reserves do not assume that premiums have been paid for the complete policy year, it is not necessary to establish an offsetting asset to counter an overstatement of liability. Therefore, due and unpaid premiums, but not deferred premiums, are entered into the balance sheet. All accident and health premiums due before October 1 and (except for group business) monthly premiums where two or more months are unpaid, are treated as nonadmissible.

Liabilities. The words "reserve" and "liability" are virtually synonymous in life insurance parlance, and are not subject to the same distinctions as in other accounting fields.

1. *Policy Reserves.* The principal liability of a typical life insurance company is its reserve for the fulfillment of unmatured life insurance, annuity, and kindred contracts. The mortality tables, interest rates and calculation methods for determining minimum reserve liabilities are prescribed by state laws, but leave management considerable discretion as to the choice of more appropriate reserve bases as long as they produce larger reserves.

The prescribed mortality standards generally reflect past mortality rates, adjusted arbitrarily in some cases to give the supervisory authorities confidence that they will be adequate for all types of companies without having to inquire into the underwriting or selection practices of each company. The most important table from a historical standpoint is the American Experience Table, which was effectively the minimum mortality requirement for most life insurance up to the promulgation of the Commissioners 1941 Standard Ordinary Table in the years following World War II, and the subsequent promulgation of the Commissioners 1958 Standard Ordinary Table in the early 1960's. Although the most recently adopted tables become compulsory for insurance issued after a certain date, they are not required to be used for previously issued policies and, for technical reasons having to do with dividend distribution and the relationship of cash surrender values to reserves, it is customary to continue until contract termination the mortality basis used for valuation at issue date.

Maximum interest rates generally in the area of $3\frac{1}{2}$ per cent are stipulated by the laws of individual states although 4 per cent was commonly the maximum until the 1940's. Lower interest assumptions may be used and frequently are, the choice being related to the investment outlook at time of policy issue and interest assumptions in the gross premium calculation (but note that the valuation interest may be, and often is, different from the interest rate used in gross premium calculation). Reserves for annuities are likewise subject to minimum standards imposed by states, and companies similarly exercise management discretion in selecting more conservative bases of valuation if they consider that mortality of annuitants or interest obtainable will be lower than the rates stipulated in the minimum reserve standard.

The reserve liability for life insurance may be analyzed algebraically as the present value of the benefits payable minus the present value of the premiums receivable, both being calculated on the reserve assumptions as to mortality and interest. Because of limited calculation facilities in the earlier years of insurance the valuation process for future benefits used the easily handled assumption that death benefits were payable at the end of the policy year of death, and that assumption came to be basic. To refine and conform the assumption to more realistic practices with respect to payment, a company may establish a "Reserve for Immediate Payment of Claims," generally equal to the value of half a year's interest on the death claim. Alternatively, the company may use mathematical formulas derived from calculus techniques which allow for the fact that the death benefit is payable at the instant of death, this type of reserve being referred to as "continuous."

The classic reserve calculation also assumes that the full annual premium is paid at the beginning of each policy year. Where any part of the premium is unpaid for the policy year current at statement date, the assumption of full annual premium payment overstates the true liability and an adjustment must be made. The adjustment consists of the establishment of an offsetting asset of that portion of the current year's premium that is deferred, i.e., that portion which will fall due after statement date and before the end of the policy year, and the portion that is uncollected, i.e., that has fallen due prior to statement date and has not been paid.

Since the reserve calculation assumes that the net valuation premium will be received for the balance of the current policy year and after that point for the remainder of the premium-paying period, it is necessary to adjust for situations where less than full net valuation premiums will actually become available. If the cost of collection of deferred and uncollected premiums—premium taxes, commissions, handling costs—is actually greater than the margin (called "loading") by which gross premium exceeds the valuation net premium the adjustment consists of a special liability called "cost of collection on premiums and annuity considerations deferred and uncollected in excess of total loading thereon."

If the gross premium is less than the valuation net premium (the "loading" is then negative), as sometimes happens in nonparticipating insurance, the adjustment consists of a "Premium Deficiency Reserve" liability computed as the present value of the deficiency during the remainder of the premium-paying period. The older mortality tables tend to generate more of a need for premium deficiency reserves than the modern tables; this is one of the reasons for updating the tables from time to time.

2. *Unpaid Claims.* In addition to the liability for unmatured policies the company will normally have a liability for claims due but not yet paid, in course of settlement, and incurred but unreported. If the claim proceeds are stipulated by the insured or beneficiary to be left with the company and paid out according to a program, the arrangement is usually evidenced by a supplementary contract and liabilities arise for supplementary contracts with (or without) life contingencies. These liabilities are calculated on the same principles as the benefit elements of life insurance reserves, namely, the present value of future amounts payable discounted appropriately for mortality and/or interest.

3. *Expenses.* Typically, no specific reserve is carried for future expenses. Expenses on policies and annuities for which no further premiums are payable are expected to be met out of margins in the reserve assumptions, i.e., actual mortality and interest being more favorable than the assumed rates. Premium-paying policies look for their expenses to the excess of gross premiums over the valuation net premiums, plus margins in the reserve assumptions.

4. *Policyholder Dividends.* Policyholder dividends account for several distinct liabilities. The most obvious is with respect to policyholder dividends due and not yet paid, usually involving questions of lost policyholder addresses or disputes as to the correct payee.

If the policyholder so stipulates, his dividends may be left to accumulate to his credit, improving at interest, creating a liability similar to the deposit liability of a savings bank.

Life insurance companies are required by the states to be very conservative about their liability for policyholder dividends after the statement date. Not only must the company provide for the dividend "earned" up to statement date on the policy year then current, but also it must provide for the dividend expected to be earned during the remainder of the policy year.

Analogously to the declaration of dividends on participating policies, a nonparticipating group policy may have a pricing structure under which the premium is retroactively adjusted to reflect experience. Proper accounting requires that the company provide for the experience refund accrued up to statement date.

5. *Premiums Paid in Advance.* Policyholders may find it useful to pay premiums in advance and companies encourage them to do so by allowing interest on such advance payments. If the advance payment takes the form of a specific discounted amount for each of one or more future premiums payable the company will establish a liability for the then present value, at interest, of the premiums so paid. Apart from the fact that accrual accounting requires this treatment, the company must provide for the contingency that the premium-payer will elect to change his mind and "withdraw" his paid-in-advance premiums, or that he will die and they will automatically be returned to the designated payee. If the advance payments are not specifically linked to particular premiums for particular policies at specific dates, the payments are simply credited to a deposit fund which improves at interest and which gives rise to a similar, but separate, liability.

6. *Foreign Exchange Adjustment.* When a United States company issues a foreign-currency contract it will normally acquire assets and incur liabilities payable in that currency. To the extent that assets and liabilities payable in the foreign currency exist at statement date it becomes necessary to determine the hypothetical foreign exchange effect of converting them from the basis at which they are entered on the books (usually at par of exchange) to the current foreign exchange value. If the result would be a loss, a liability is carried in the amount of hypothetical loss—if a gain, an asset would arise. For example, $100 on deposit in a Canadian bank in Canadian funds when Canadian dollars are at 7 per cent discount would show up in the balance sheet as an asset of $100 under "Deposits in banks" and

an offsetting liability of $7.00 under "Net adjustment in assets and liabilities due to foreign exchange rates." If in addition to the bank deposit the company had a policy reserve liability of $60 on a policy payable in Canadian currency the $100 would still show in the asset, $60 would show as part of policy reserve liabilities and the adjustment liability would reduce to $2.80 (7 per cent of $40). This liability is in the nature of an unrealized capital loss since it represents a decline in the U.S. dollar market value of the net Canadian dollar asset. If the deposit were drawn down and converted into U.S. funds, the statement would show $93 as cash in banks, the same $60 as policy reserve liability, a foreign exchange adjustment asset of $4.20 reflecting the ability to liquidate a nominal liability of $60 for a cash outlay of $55.80, and the operating statement would record a realized capital loss—foreign exchange of $7.00.

7. *Mandatory Securities Valuation Reserve.* Among the liabilities of a life insurance company will be found the "Mandatory Securities Valuation Reserve." This reserve (or liability, if you will) is required by state regulatory authorities as a sort of stabilization fund fulfilling several objectives. First, it contains provision for future losses on the portfolio of bonds carried at amortized values. Experience indicates that a small percentage of bonds currently in good enough standing to warrant valuation on the amortized rather than market value basis will in all likelihood be defaulted in the future. It is also the case that private placements—loans negotiated directly between the borrower and a single large lender, without resort to the normal channels of the public capital market—may by their nature not be susceptible of a simple practical uniform test for determining whether their quality warrants the use of amortization rather than market valuation. For publicly traded bonds and private placements, therefore, it is prudent to set aside a small reserve against the contingency that their balance sheet values may not be ultimately realizable in full.

Although common stocks are carried at market values in balance sheets it is prudent to recognize that realizable values may be significantly less than the market valuation at any particular statement date. An element of the mandatory securities valuation reserve is, therefore, assigned to discounting market values of common stocks in the interest of protecting solvency.

The mandatory securities valuation reserve is also designed to act as a stabilizer. When market values appreciate, or when securities are sold at a profit, a larger-than-normal increase is made in this reserve;

when market values decline or when securities are sold at a loss a smaller-than-normal increase or even a decrease is made. Since changes in this reserve affect surplus, surplus is cushioned to some extent against vagaries of the securities market.

Is the mandatory securities valuation reserve a real liability or is it simply an earmarking of part of surplus? There is no clear-cut answer. On the going-concern principle, it is a real reduction of surplus to reflect future securities losses. On the liquidation concept, it is unnecessary (except to the extent that forced liquidation of large blocks of securities will of itself drive down the market and thereby reduce the realizable proceeds), and would add to the remainder amount distributable to the owners of the business. Since life insurance companies are designed for permanent operation, the going-concern principle seems to have more weight and the concept of the mandatory securities valuation reserve as being a real liability usually prevails.

8. *Catastrophe Reserves.* Another major reserve liability of a significant amount arises out of group insurance operations. The group insurance contract is classically a one-year term type of policy, characterized by a very large amount exposed to risk as compared to premium income. The catastrophe hazard is therefore ever-present. A typical portfolio of $100,000,000 of group term life insurance may be subject to yearly premiums of $700,000 and death claims of $550,-000 consisting of 110 deaths averaging $5,000 per claim. Included in such a portfolio would be numerous individual groups in which 200 or 500 or 1,000 or more employees may be clustered with respect to the effects of epidemic or disaster (cf. the Texas City disaster of 1947). The company must therefore face the possibility that claims amounting to five or ten or more times yearly premium income could be presented at a single stroke. As a measure of protection against such a happening companies have since the 1930's generally followed the practice of annually setting aside an amount in the area of 2 per cent of premiums toward building a "Group Special" or "Group Insurance Contingency" reserve, having a goal of 50 per cent of yearly premiums. A number of companies have recognized similar threats in the group health area and are building special contingency reserves against the possibility of epidemics and analogous morbidity catastrophes.

In theory, reinsurance could be carried for protection of this nature and in theory this protection is needed for all categories of business where the amount of exposure is high compared to the premium. In practice, reinsurance is carried for large exposures in individual term life insurance and individual health insurance operations but catastrophe reinsurance is comparatively uncommon in the group insurance areas.

As in the case of the mandatory securities valuation reserve, the group insurance contingency reserve is properly classifiable as a liability on the going-concern basis and properly classifiable as surplus on the liquidation concept, with the going-concern basis usually tipping the scale.

9. *Other Liability Items.* Apart from liabilities which may be thought of as peculiar to the insurance business, the company must recognize unpaid and accrued commissions, general expenses and taxes, normally shown in ledger accounts for items so recorded and obtained by inventory techniques for others.

Some elements of income to a life insurance company are not reflected in the results of insurance operations because the data for doing so are not available or because the time for doing so has not yet arrived. A company will frequently receive money which is inadequately identified and will have to match the cash asset with a "suspense" liability such as "Remittances and items not allocated" until it can be determined whether it is a premium payment or a mortgage loan payment or a policy loan payment, and so forth. When investment income is received in advance of its due date accrual accounting requires that the receipt be held in a type of suspense liability "Unearned Investment Income" until its due date.

Life insurance companies will also have trustee or quasi-trustee funds such as funds withheld for taxes and not yet remitted to the tax collector, withholding for purchase of savings bonds, escrow funds in connection with mortgage loans, funds held for guarantee of contract performances and the like. They may also borrow money from time to time, particularly where advance commitments of investible funds have been made, and an unusually attractive, but unanticipated, opportunity arises to make a loan which requires prompt disbursement of cash.

Surplus and Capital Funds. Over and above its provision for liabilities a company will hold further funds for the protection of its solvency, as provision against unforseeable contingencies of an unpredictable nature, and as a stabilizer into which extra profits may go in unusually good years and out of which unusual losses may be financed in bad years so that dividends payable will not fluctuate violently from year to year.

Within this general category of capital and surplus funds there may be a wide variety of subcategories dictated by legal requirements, charter provisions, the judgment of management and so on. The most obvious is capital, representing amounts devoted by investors to be permanently exposed to risk of loss as compensation for which the investors expect returns in the form of dividends. The capital may represent funds explicitly given to the company as such and may also contain previous years' earnings which are to be retained permanently. Amounts paid for shares in excess of the par or nominal values of those shares, and not subsequently recommitted to the status of capital per se, may be categorized as "Capital Surplus" or "Paid-in Surplus." Other retained net gains from the operation of the company may be classified as "Unassigned Surplus," "General Contingency Reserve," particular contingency reserves, and so forth. Except for legal technicalities, set up primarily for the protection of creditors, and charter provisions set up for the protection of the comparative interest of various classes of creditors and owners, the subcategories of "Capital" and "Surplus" are of little intrinsic meaning. This tends particularly to be true in the case of a mature life insurance company with a long history of profitable operations.

In the case of a mutual life insurance company it is customary for the founders to invest in a guarantee fund which is similar to capital in that it involves an exposure to loss if the enterprise fails and in that there is normally a return to the capital riskers in compensation for foregoing the use of their principal and exposing it to loss.

Distinctively from capital stock, a guarantee fund will normally be subject to charter limitations on the rate of current return and to charter provisions for the redemption of the fund when the company has accumulated a satisfactory amount of surplus from operations. A mutual company may also be formed by a reorganization of a stock company in which in effect the company buys back its shares from their owners and retires them, leaving only some part of retained gains as surplus.

Summary of Operations

In general format, the Summary of Operations begins with a grouping of income items, followed by a grouping of benefits paid and amounts set aside for future benefits to policyholders and beneficiaries. The next major grouping covers commissions and other expenses, leaving a net gain before dividends to policyholders, before capital gains and losses, and before federal income taxes. Thereafter dividends to policyholders and federal income taxes applicable to operations are deducted, leaving the "Net Gain from Operations after Dividends to Policyholders and Federal Income Taxes (excluding tax on capital gains) and Excluding Capital Gains and Losses."

Blank lines are provided for the write-in of any items not properly falling within the captioned categories.

Each of the captioned lines in the Summary of Operations on page 4 of the annual statement blank is matched on page 5 "Analysis of Operations by Lines of Business" by an identical caption and a columnar display which separates the Summary of Operations into Industrial Life Insurance, Individual Life Insurance, Disability Benefits in Individual Life Policies, Additional Accidental Death Benefits in Individual Life Policies, Individual Annuities, Supplementary Contracts, Group Life Insurance, Group Annuities, Group Accident and Health Insurance, and Individual Accident and Health Insurance. This enables the analyst to study a rather detailed breakdown of Gain from Operations by line of business. This exhibit is also known as the Gain and Loss Exhibit, Part I.

The captions for the lines in the Summary of Operations frequently refer specifically to life insurance and occasionally refer specifically to accident and health insurance, although accident and health insurance is only one of several classes of insurance reportable in the life blank. The reason is that prior to 1947 the accident and health business of life insurance companies had to be reported separately, using the blank designed for casualty insurance. When the life blank was expanded to accommodate accident and health business, the newly introduced lines were kept separate to preserve continuity.

The Summary of Operations is stipulated by caption heading to be on the "Accrual Basis" and the official instructions for completing the annual statement specify that the accrual basis means the earned and incurred basis. This specification, which would appear to be superfluous in the modern accounting world, stems from the background of life insurance accounting based on "cash" and "ledger" transactions.

Despite the stipulation of the use of accrual basis figures the peculiarities of the life insurance business complicate the concept of what constitutes "accrual basis" and therefore it is necessary to examine each class of entry in the Summary of Operations.

Premium Income. Premiums and annuity considerations are converted to the accrual basis by adding the unpaid and deferred premiums to the paid and subtracting the paid in advance, with appropriate adjustment for the unpaid and deferred and paid in advance at the end of the previous year.

The accrual basis premium is applied to "pay for" reserves and additions to reserves out of which benefits will later be paid. It is not "earned" over a period of time in the sense of a prorata payment for coverage; it is "earned" immediately as the consideration for reserve establishment. For example, a single premium for whole life insurance is immediately "earned" as payment for a reserve obligation immediately set up covering the insured for the remainder of his life. A single premium for one-year term insurance is immediately "earned" as payment for a reserve obligation immediately set up covering the insured for his subsequent lifetime but not for more than a twelve-month period. An annuity single premium is immediately earned as payment for the reserve obligation immediately set up to provide for annual payments to the annuitant during his remaining lifetime. The accrual-basis premium is "earned" at its due date, not over a period of time.

Considerations for Supplementary Contracts. When the proceeds of a policy, whether they be in the form of a death benefit, a matured endowment, or a cash surrender value, are directed by the insured to be paid out under a deferred settlement arrangement rather than in a lump sum, it is customary for the company to issue a supplementary contract. The accounting treatment in the N.A.I.C. blank is to record the death benefit, matured endowment, or cash surrender value as an item of outgo and then re-record the same amount as an item of income captioned "consideration for supplementary contracts." Income of this type is subdivided as to whether or not life contingencies are involved. For example, a matured endowment to be paid as an annuity over the remaining lifetime of the insured involves life contingencies, while a death benefit to be paid in the form of an installment amount option does not. Similarly, policy dividends left with the company to accumulate at interest in anticipation of a deferred payout are shown both as disbursements and income.

It may be argued that this accounting treatment inflates income since the funds concerned remain in the possession of the company. However, failure to make matching disbursement and income entries would result in understatement of death benefits and matured endowments and cash surrender values, which might be even more misleading. The prescribed treatment has the merit of disclosure.

Investment Income. Net investment income consists of interest, dividends, and rents earned during the year. To the paid investment income we add the due and unpaid and subtract the paid-in advance at the end of the year, with appropriate adjustment for similar items at the end of the previous year. The word "net" refers to the fact that from the gross income are subtracted expenses and taxes attributable to the investment function and relevant depreciation and depletion. In the case of bonds the amortization process further adds the year's accrual of discount for bonds bought below maturity value and subtracts the year's amortization of premium for bonds bought above maturity value.

Benefit Payments. The disbursement, or more properly, the "charges against income" section provides for separate reporting of death benefits, matured endowments, annuity benefits, disability benefits, surrender benefits and benefits under accident and health policies. These benefits are on an incurred basis which means, for example, that a death benefit is included even if the payee cannot be found and the proceeds have perforce to remain with the company until he is found, and that an amount is included for death benefits with respect to deaths assumed to have taken place but not reported to the company. This latter class of benefit charge is referred to as "incurred but not reported" and is usually estimated from past experience of delays in reporting claims.

The benefits charged against income are the full nominal amounts, without consideration of the impact on related reserves. For example, at the death of the holder of a $1,000 life insurance policy with a reserve of $600, death benefits are reported as $1,000 and on a separate line on page 4 is recorded the negative charge against income by reason of the reserve liability decreasing from $600 to zero. The "mortality cost" to the company is of course only the $400 excess of face amount over reserve and it is this net mortality cost which has to be used in trying to determine whether a company's mortality experience is favorable or unfavorable. The death benefit entry in the summary of operations is not usable for reliably measuring mortality experience.

Benefits paid include payments under supplementary contracts, following out the accounting treatment whereby policy proceeds to be paid in installments are first recorded as benefits, then re-recorded as considerations for supplementary contracts, then finally shown as payments under supplementary contracts when the funds are disbursed to the beneficiary.

Group Conversions. Group conversions arise from the fact that an employee who loses his right to coverage under a group policy, usually by reason of termination of employment, typically has the privilege of acquiring similar coverage under an individual policy through a process called conversion, without having to submit evidence of insurability. Terminating employees who are in insurable condition may or may not avail themselves of the privilege; terminating employees who are quite obviously uninsurable are very likely to do so; therefore the mortality experience of a block of policies obtained by conversion tends to be, and typically proves to be, higher than that of an otherwise similar block of medically examined policies and higher than is contemplated by the premium even after allowance for the saving of examination and other selling costs. The net cost of this extra mortality is known as the "cost of conversion" and it is considered to be a part of the cost of conducting a group insurance operation, not properly chargeable to the individual life insurance operation. In the line-by-line analysis of the Summary of Operations on page 5 of the Statement the group life column will therefore show the cost of conversion (estimated) for the year as a charge against its operations and the individual life column will show a corresponding negative charge. Normally this is an internal transfer within the company, netting out to zero for the company as a whole. Under certain circumstances, however, an employee terminating group coverage in company A may have the privilege of converting to an individual policy of company B, in which case company A will pay the cost of conversion to company B. A will show a positive entry for this caption in the Summary of Operations and B a negative one.

Interest on Policy or Contract Funds. Interest on policy or contract funds will normally arise from crediting interest to the liability for premium deposits. The life insurance policy may also provide for interest additions in the event of an unusual delay in payment of the proceeds.

Reserve Increases. In addition to benefit payments income must be charged with the cost of reserve increases in order to get the full total of benefits paid or set aside for future payment under insurance and annuity operations. Reserve increases are usually determined as the difference between the inventoried totals at successive year-ends. In theory they could be set up by ledger entries on a periodic basis but in practice the clerical cost of doing so would be excessive, and to do so would involve some problems in the basic structure of the NAIC Blank.

The Summary of Operations is charged only with what may be considered as the normal year-to-year increases arising from interest accumulation and advancing age. Where a reserve is specially increased by changing one or more of the reserve assumptions the increase is referred to as "strengthening" and the amount of such increase is charged directly against surplus. The theory is that reserve strengthening is not a cost of doing business for the particular year of account but rather a charge against a number of past years, and that distortion of the current year's gain would result from charging the item to operations. In practice it may be difficult to distinguish whether some types of reserve increases are normal or should be classified as strengthening. If the amounts involved are comparatively small and occur regularly from year to year there may be no point in not charging them against operations.

If a "strengthening" type of reserve increase has an immediate effect on policyholder dividend distribution, the Summary of Operations may include a "gain" from the reduction of incurred dividends for which there would be a corresponding "loss" in the Surplus Account. In this case the effort to eliminate distortion of earnings by charging the strengthening against surplus may of itself create distortion through auxiliary effects on related debits and credits to income. The complete purification of the Summary of Operations into a picture of the earnings for a particular year, with freedom from the impact of events of other years, is *practically* impossible and may in fact be *logically* impossible.

The above remarks with respect to reserve increases and reserve strengthening apply equally, with algebraic reversal, to reserve decreases and reserve "weakening." It should be noted, however, that whereas strengthening is for all practical purposes completely within the discretion of management, weakening of reserves commonly requires the advance approval of the regulatory authorities.

Expense Charges. Commissions are considered to be earned by the agent at the time the premiums are paid. No commission expense is accrued during the period in which the sale proceeds toward completion and the period of time contemplated by the reserve arising from a paid premium is considered to be irrelevant to the question of when the corresponding commission is earned. Commissions paid in advance, usually pursuant to a plan for financing an agent until he is self-supporting out of earned commissions, are treated similarly to salaries paid in advance in that they are not charged against operations until earned. Commissions earned and not disbursed are charged against operations when earned and carried in an unpaid commission liability account until disbursed.

General Insurance Expenses. General insurance expenses include all the usual costs of operating a business and are accounted for as such with one notable exception; those expenses which are attributable to the investment function are segregated and are deducted from gross investment income to get the net investment income entry in the Summary of Operations.

The largest element of expense is the item of salaries, wages and related fringe benefits and the next largest is usually rental costs. Included in rental costs will be the amount charged by the company to itself for the use of company-owned properties, just as the fringe benefits may include premiums paid by the company to itself for group insurance on its own employees.

As is the case with certain other types of fiduciary institutions expenses are accounted for in a conservative manner. No value is placed on inventories of stationery and printed matter, the entire cost being treated as expense. Office furniture and fixtures and equipment may either be charged off fully in the year of purchase or written off via depreciation over the appropriate lifetime as management may elect. The practice of making a complete charge-off in the year of purchase is simple and conservative and involves little or no distortion of earnings if such purchases are reasonably steady as to amount. Where, however, the expenditures are irregular and are material as to amount, as may happen when an office is completely re-outfitted or when an electronic computer is purchased, management may elect the depreciation approach. Note that the depreciation approach and the complete write-off approach produce the same effect on surplus since, with few exceptions, the depreciated value of furniture, fixtures and equipment is considered to be a nonadmissible asset.

Insurance Taxes, Licenses, and Fees. Insurance taxes, licenses, and fees are separately reported, the largest single item being state taxes on premiums, which tend to average 2 to 3 per cent. As in the case of general expenses, any item of taxes which can be attributed to investment income will be so earmarked and deducted in the process of converting investment income from gross to net. Federal income taxes are not reported in this section of the Summary of Operations.

Increase in Loading. Included with expenses is the cost to the company of the "increase in loading on and cost of collection in excess of loading on deferred and uncollected premiums." As was indicated, it is a consequence of the policy reserve assumptions that failure to adjust due and unpaid premiums to their corresponding valuation net premium amounts would result in loading showing up as a profit and would result in cost of collection in excess of loading failing to show up as loss. The change in the amount of these asset and liability adjustments from year to year is properly chargeable to the operations of the year. It is more nearly analogous to an expense than it is to any of the other major groupings of charges against income and so it is reported adjacent to expenses in the Summary of Operations.

Dividends to Policyholders. Dividends to policyholders are charged against operations on an incurred basis, which in this case means the sum of amounts paid or credited to policyholders increased by the provision for dividends payable in the following calendar year and decreased by the corresponding provision at the end of the preceding year. Since the provision for dividends payable in the following calendar year is greater than the amount of dividends "earned" in the current year on a proper accrual basis (see discussion of policyholder dividend liability on page 870–71), the incurred dividends charged to the Summary of Operations represent a definition of accrual basis which is peculiar to the life insurance business.

As is the case with benefits, the dividends charged against operations may not be actual disbursements. They may be left with the company to accumulate or they may be applied as premiums for supplemental benefits, in both cases resulting in an income to the Summary of Operations. If they are applied to reduce premiums the company will receive less than the gross premium but will necessarily have to report as income the full gross premium to allow for the fact that dividends so applied are shown as charges against income. These "inflations" of income are further examples of how the accounting techniques and practices developed for other businesses have had to be modified to suit the needs of life insurance operations.

Federal Income Taxes on Operations. The final charge against operations is for federal income taxes, including those payable to the U.S. Treasury and certain other taxes payable on income or in lieu of income tax to foreign governments. The general criterion is that foreign taxes are properly includible in this item if they are of a type which will qualify for foreign tax credit under the U.S. tax law, regardless of whether the full amount so qualifies.

The federal income tax to be reported as a charge against operations is supposed to reflect only amounts attributable to the operations reported for the year in the Summary of Operations. In particular, taxes on capital gains are reported elsewhere as a deduction from the capital gains themselves. In former years federal income taxes were divided into portions purporting to be charged against insurance and portions purporting to be charged against investment income with the latter part deducted from investment income in the Summary of Operations. Currently no such allocation is made. Also, it is provided that any significant amounts of federal income tax attributable to operations of other years should be charged directly to Surplus Account and not to operations. In practice, the distinction between taxes reportable against current operations and those reportable against surplus is a very difficult one to define in advance for all circumstances and so a large element of management judgment enters into the allocation.

The federal income tax laws applicable to life insurance companies are peculiar to that business and as a result many conclusions drawn from experience with income taxes in other lines of business will be found to be inapplicable to life insurance company federal income taxes.[1] One of the most important points of difference is that the tax is *not* levied on the amount shown in the Annual Statement as earnings before tax. The Federal Income Tax base, generally speaking, consists of (*a*) "Phase I" taxable income which is a measure of the excess of investment income over interest required for the operation of the company, according to a special set of calculation rules, (*b*) "Phase II" taxable income which is a measure of gain from operations according to a special set of calculation rules, and of which only half the excess over Phase I taxable income, if such an excess exists, is taxable currently, (*c*) "Phase III" taxable income which is a measure of how much of the tax-deferred Phase II income has later proved to have been unnecessarily retained in the company on a tax-free basis, again

---

[1] See Chapter XLIV.

determined from a special set of calculation rules, and (*d*) "Phase IV" taxable income which consists of capital gains exclusive of that part of capital gains which accrued before 1959 when the capital gains phase of the law became effective. Since the predominant element of taxable income is the Phase I taxable income, it can readily be seen that the tax payable will not except by sheer coincidence be logically linked to the net gain before tax as reported in the Summary of Operations in the Annual Statement.

Surplus Account

The purpose of the Surplus Account is to reconcile from one year to another the Surplus as Regards Policyholders. To this account will be credited net earnings from the Summary of Operations, plus any other gains not attributable to the normal operations of the year plus any surplus paid in during the year by shareholders. To it are charged any losses from current operations, any other losses not attributable to the normal operations of the year and any surplus distributed to shareholders in the form of dividends. The form of account is a match between the opening balances plus gain items and the loss items plus closing balances. Most of the entries have been discussed above in other connections.

Capital Gains and Losses. Net capital gains are credited, and net capital losses are charged, to the Surplus Account and not to current operations. Capital gains are generally classified as unrealized if the asset in question has not been disposed of and if the profit has not been realized in cash or its equivalent. The most obvious example is an increase in the market value of common stocks owned. While the distinction between realized and unrealized capital gains is maintained in supporting exhibits, the two categories are combined in reporting the effect on surplus.[2] The present practice of reporting all capital gains as credits to surplus and not to current income has the disadvantage of failing to recognize that making long-term investments is an integral part of the life insurance operation and not irrelevant to the main purpose of the company as in most industrial enterprises. A corollary

---

[2] Prior to 1954 realized capital gains were reported as income of the current year in the Summary of Operations. This produced the awkward result that a capital gain would appear for the current year on the sale of any asset whose value had appreciated since purchase even though its value might have declined during the current year. Also, management could create and report increased gain from current operations by the simple expedient of selling an appreciated asset even though the proceeds were immediately re-invested in the same asset at its sales value.

is that deliberate choice by management of a growth security with a low current return may "penalize" current operations as compared with a less profitable investment characterized by high current return and absence of growth potential. A further corollary is that if capital gains are reflected in the net cost of insurance to policyholders the accounting effect will be a reduction in the apparent gain from current operations.

INTERPRETATION OF OPERATING RESULTS

Although the NAIC statement form gives more information about a company's operations than can be found for the operations of most other kinds of businesses, the interpretation of those results is comparatively quite difficult. The intelligent layman analyst must proceed very cautiously or run the risk of serious misinterpretation. There are no magic keys to simplify the analysis of a life insurance company statement.

Mortality

Mortality information would appear to start with the amount of death benefits shown in the Analysis of Operations by Lines of Business on page 5. By itself, however, this is not a good comparison yardstick since it will obviously be affected by the age distribution of business in force, the proportions of medically-examined, nonmedical and converted group insurance, the proportion of substandard risks written subject to extra premium charges, and the company's general philosophy with respect to underwriting standards, rate levels and desired volume of sales. If volume of business is small the death benefit statistics may be subject to fluctuation from the death of a small number of policyholders having comparatively large amounts of coverage. Notably, it tells nothing about the statistics of survivals.

Theoretically, it might be possible to compare the mortality actually experienced against the mortality anticipated by the company in the establishment of its premium scales. In practice, companies consider the mortality assumptions in their tests of nonparticipating premium rates and their tests of participating premium rates and dividend scales to be competitive secrets and publish no such data.

Such comparisons as are internally made for management purposes normally require an intimate knowledge of method by which the statistics are put together, a grasp of the varying degrees of significance of the statistical cells, and an actuarial judgment of the degree of credibility emerging from the averaging process which must be used. There is no simple measurement rule which can be used without sophisticated interpretation, even for the statistics developed for internal management purposes.

The Gain and Loss Exhibit Part II in the statement, subcaptioned "Analysis of Increase in Reserves During the Year" gives figures which purport to show "Tabular cost." "Tabular cost" is a technical term for the excess of the total death benefit expected to become payable during the year computed on the mortality table used for reserve valuation, over the corresponding reserves held. When added to the "Reserves Released by Death" it would give the death benefits payable during the year if, as is not normally the case in fact, the mortality experienced during the year exactly matched the mortality assumption in the reserve calculation.

Companies may internally prepare a ratio of "actual to expected" mortality which, roughly speaking, has a numerator equal to death benefits paid as shown in the Gain and Loss Exhibit Part I minus the reserves released by death as shown in the Gain and Loss Exhibit Part II, and a denominator equal to the tabular cost of mortality from the Gain and Loss Exhibit Part II. A major difficulty with the use of this ratio is that the relationship of the mortality actually expected by management to the mortality used for reserve calculation varies sharply by attained age and is, of course, different for different reserve mortality tables. The usefulness of this ratio therefore depends on the mix of business by attained age, by plan and duration (since the excess of face amount over reserve is considered to be at risk), and by reserve valuation basis.

Prior to 1939 the Gain and Loss Exhibit analyzed the change in surplus for the year to show what purported to be the "gain from loading" (excess of gross premiums over net premiums, minus expenses incurred), "gain from interest" (excess of investment income over interest required to maintain reserves), "gain from mortality" (excess of tabular mortality over actual on net amount at risk), "gain from surrenders" (excess of reserves held over surrender values granted), and so forth. These analyses were technically so defective as to be harmfully misleading and were removed from the blank in the revision effective 1939. It is significant that the best industry talent of that time felt that component analyses were impracticable from a technical standpoint and that there has been no real sign of reversal of this attitude.

Investment Earnings

Investment earnings are displayed in the NAIC Blank on a gross basis, a net basis, and as a ratio of net investment income to mean invested assets, this latter being regarded as the earned interest rate on the company's portfolio. The principal defect in this measure of investment success is that common stocks appear in the denominator at their market values while no recognition is given in the numerator to either realized or unrealized capital gains. Thus, investment in common stock with a high dividend yield and a low growth rate has more of an upward influence on the published earned interest rate than investment in a different common stock with a low dividend yield and a high growth rate, regardless of the relative intrinsic merits of the two investments. No acceptable solution for this problem has yet been found, despite the fact that the published interest rate is of competitive significance.

The rate of yield obtained on new investments is a matter of some significance to the analyst and to management. It is not explicitly shown in the official blank and no regulatory or industry body has yet formulated a generally acceptable formula for its definition.

Although the rate of interest currently obtainable on new investments has long been a factor in the determination of single-premium insurance and annuity rates, the concept has been extended in recent years. Many companies now provide that the interest to be used in dividend and experience-rating calculations with respect to premiums received in a particular calendar year will be based on the experience of the investments made in that year, including subsequent re-investments of the fund where appropriate. The allocation of interest on this basis is called a "year of investment" method. Application of the method is very complicated and the complications will differ from company to company. The NAIC statement form contains an interrogatory as to whether the method is used but does not display the work papers or the results.

Expense Ratios

Expense ratios are very hard to obtain on a useful comparative basis with respect to life insurance operations. First-year expenses are normally much higher than renewal-year expenses and consequently an expense ratio which relates both kinds of expense to total premiums can be quite misleading; the ratio will be distorted upward, if new sales are unusually high, and downward if they are low. Various ratios have been developed relating expenses to premiums, to amounts in force, to number of policies and so forth but none has been free enough from the first-and-renewal distortion problems to have merited general acceptance. Similarly, rules-of-thumb for weighting first-year premiums five or ten times renewal premiums have been advanced and have proved useful, but only as rules-of-thumb subject to all the shortcomings of such rules.

Growth Rates

Growth of business is a vital element in the measurement of the success of any enterprise. The NAIC Blanks give large volumes of data whereby such growth can be measured in terms of sales and in-force by both dollars and numbers of policies, premium income, investment income, assets, operating gains, surplus funds and many subdivisions of most of these categories. Comparison of the various rates of growth from year to year within a company and for a particular company compared to a representative group of competitors will usually tell a very interesting story as to how a particular company has been doing. Even where the statistics of growth are flawed by lack of uniformity in reporting and by differences in the character of individual companies, comparison with reasonably comparable competitors can be quite enlightening.

Generally it will be found for life insurance companies that the NAIC statement form contains ample data for the determination of its progress if the analyst has a real knowledge of the make-up of the data, its value, and its shortcomings. Again, however, as in other forms of business there is no real substitute for analysis of the data in depth and, after all of the data have been digested, there is no satisfactory basis for evaluating the *very* critical element of quality of management, except on the basis of its past history.

USE OF THE ANNUAL STATEMENT

The Annual Statement (and the accounting theory implied in its use) does very effectively the job it was designed to do, namely, to determine whether at any given date the company is solvent enough to warrant its being allowed to sell insurance to the citizenry. From the foregoing, however, it will also be seen that deviations from the accounting practices appropriate for other types of enterprises do exist, some deriving from the conservatism essential to a fiduciary type of business and some from the inherent impracticability of accurately measuring life insurance company earnings for a period as short as one year. It will also be evident that a high degree of familiarity with the principles of actuarial science, the manner in which the life insurance business is conducted, and the technicalities of the Annual Statement form of accounting presentation are needed for its intelligent use.

FINANCIAL STATEMENT OF TYPICAL STOCK LIFE INSURANCE COMPANY IN FORM AND DETAIL SPECIFIED BY N.A.I.C. BLANK

BALANCE SHEET

Asset

1.	Bonds		$274,668,000
2.	Stocks		15,553,000
3.	Mortgage loans on real estate		218,494,000
4.	Real estate		
	4.1 Properties occupied by the Company	$ 2,351,000	
	4.2 Properties acquired in satisfaction of debt	15,000	
	4.3 Investment real estate	4,246,000	6,612,000
5.	Policy loans		8,969,000
6.	Premium notes		0
7.	Collateral loans		0
8.	Cash and bank deposits		4,879,000
9.	——		0
10.	Other invested assets		391,000
10A	Cash and invested assets $529,566,000 (Items 1 to 10)		
11.	Amounts recoverable from reinsurers		388,000
12.	Sundry		1,701,000
13.	——		0
14.	——		0
15.	——		0
16.	——		0
17.	Life insurance premiums and annuity considerations deferred and uncollected		7,336,000
18.	Accident and health premiums due and unpaid		2,273,000
19.	Investment income due and accrued		4,381,000
20.	Net adjustment in assets and liabilities due to foreign exchange rates		0
21.	——		0
22.	——		0
23.	——		0
24.	——		0
25.	——		0
26.	Total		$545,645,000

Liabilities, Surplus and Other Funds

1. Aggregate reserve for life policies and contracts................... $413,421,000
2. Aggregate reserve for accident and health policies................. 8,747,000
3. Supplementary contracts without life contingencies............... 17,127,000
4. Policy and contract claims
    4.1 Life.. 8,140,000
    4.2 Accident and health....................................... 9,903,000
5. Policyholders' dividend accumulations........................... 3,691,000
6. Policyholders' dividends due and unpaid........................ 24,000
7. Provision for policyholders' dividends payable in following
    calendar year
    7.1 Apportioned for payment to _____ 1967.......... $ 2,988,000
    7.2 Not yet apportioned............................. 0   2,988,000
8. Amount provisionally held for deferred dividend policies not
    included in Item 7... 2,000
9. Premiums and annuity considerations received in advance
    less $247,000 discount: including $2,539,000 accident
    and health premiums...................................... 6,458,000
10. Liability for premium deposit funds........................... 2,810,000
11. Policy and contract liabilities not included elsewhere:
    11.1 Surrender values on cancelled policies..................... 0
    11.2 Provision for experience refunds......................... 6,017,000
    11.3 ---- 0
12. ---- 0
13. Commissions to agents due or accrued........................ 440,000
14. General expenses due or accrued............................. 597,000
15. Taxes, licenses and fees due or accrued, excluding
    federal income taxes...................................... 1,686,000
15A. Federal income taxes due or accrued
    (including $__ on capital gains)............................ 2,302,000
16. "Cost of collection" on premiums and annuity considerations deferred
    and uncollected in excess of total loading thereon............... 94,000
17. Unearned investment income................................. 73,000
18. Amounts withheld or retained by company as agent or trustee...... 281,000
19. Amounts held for agents' account............................ 416,000
20. Remittances and items not allocated......................... 1,926,000
21. Net adjustment in assets and liabilities due to foreign exchange rates.. 525,000
22. Liability for benefits for employees and agents if not included above... 1,763,000
23. Borrowed money $---- and interest thereon $----.................... 0
24. Dividends to stockholders declared and unpaid.................. 314,000
25. Miscellaneous liabilities (give items and amounts)
    25.1 Mandatory securities valuation reserve..................... 3,420,000
    25.2 Special reserves—group insurance......................... 13,461,000
    25.3 Reserve for unauthorized reinsurance...................... 1,503,000
    25.4 ---- 0
26. Total Liabilities (Except Capital)............................. $508,129,000
27. Special surplus funds
    27.1 Contingency reserve.............. $9,246,000
    27.2 ---- 0
    27.3 ---- .... 0 $ 9,246,000
28. Capital paid-up........................   6,277,000
29A Paid-in and contributed surplus..........   600,000
29B Unassigned surplus.....................   21,393,000
30. Total of Items 27 to 29B................................. $ 37,516,000
31. Total... $545,645,000

SUMMARY OF OPERATIONS
(Accrual Basis)

1. Premiums and annuity considerations
   1.1 Life.. $ 59,223,000
   1.2 Accident and health.............................. 57,123,000
2. Considerations for supplementary contracts with life contingencies..... 610,000
3. Considerations for supplementary contracts without life contingencies and dividend accumulations............................... 2,646,000
4. Net investment income............................... 22,682,000
5. ----.. 0
6. ----.. 0
7. Total... $142,284,000

DEDUCT:
8. Death benefits..................................... $ 20,550,000
9. Matured endowments................................. 1,780,000
10. Annuity benefits................................... 6,986,000
11. Disability benefits................................ 1,331,000
12. Surrender benefits................................. 3,492,000
12A Group conversions.................................. 0
13. Benefits under accident and health policies........ 49,958,000
14. Interest on policy or contract funds............... 288,000
15. Payments on supplementary contracts with life contingencies....... 1,068,000
16. Payments on supplementary contracts without life contingencies and dividend accumulations............................... 3,348,000
17. Increase in aggregate reserve for policies and contracts with life contingencies....................................... 30,960,000
18. Increase in reserve for supplementary contracts without life contingencies and for dividend accumulations..................... 78,000
19. Increase in group special reserve.................. 905,000
20. Subtotal (Items 8 to 19).......................... $120,744,000
21. Commissions on premiums and annuity considerations.............. 3,140,000
22. ----.. 0
23. General insurance expenses......................... 7,221,000
24. Insurance taxes, licenses and fees, excluding federal income taxes..... 2,406,000
25. Increase in loading on and cost of collection in excess of loading on deferred and uncollected premiums............................... 29,000
26. ----.. 0
27. Total (Items 20 to 26)............................ $133,540,000
28. Net gain from operations before dividends to policyholders and federal income taxes and excluding capital gains and losses (7–27)...... $ 8,744,000
29. Dividends to life policyholders.................... $ 2,981,000
30. Dividends on accident and health policies.......... 0
31. Increase in amount provisionally held for deferred dividend policies... 1,000
32. Total (Items 29 to 31)............................ $ 2,982,000
32A Net gain from operations after dividends to policyholders and before federal income taxes excluding capital gains and losses (28–32)...... 5,762,000
32B Federal income taxes incurred (excluding tax on capital gains)........ 2,444,000
33. NET GAIN FROM OPERATIONS AFTER DIVIDENDS TO POLICYHOLDERS AND FEDERAL INCOME TAXES (excluding tax on capital gains) AND EXCLUDING CAPITAL GAINS AND LOSSES (Item 32A minus Item 32B)............. $ 3,318,000

SURPLUS ACCOUNT
(*left-hand side*)

34.	Special surplus funds December 31, previous year	\$ 9,916,000
35A	Paid-in and contributed surplus December 31, previous year	600,000
35B	Unassigned surplus, December 31, previous year	19,024,000
36.	----	0
36A	----	0
36B	----	0
37.	Net gain (from Item 33)	3,318,000
38.	Net capital gains	850,000
39.	Surplus paid in	0
40.	Net gain from nonadmitted and related items	0
41.	Decrease in mandatory securities valuation reserve	0
42.	Total	\$ 33,708,000

SURPLUS ACCOUNT
(*right-hand side*)

43.	Dividends to stockholders	\$ 1,255,000
44.	Increase in reserve for unauthorized reinsurance	36,000
44A	----	0
44B	----	0
45.	Net capital losses	0
46.	Increase in reserve on account of change in valuation basis	0
47.	Net loss from nonadmitted and related items	160,000
48.	Increase in mandatory securities valuation reserve	1,018,000
49.	Special surplus funds December 31, current year	9,246,000
50A	Paid in and contributed surplus December 31, current year	600,000
50B	Unassigned surplus, December 31, current year	21,393,000
		\$ 33,708,000

CHAPTER XLIV

*Taxation of
Life
Insurance
Companies*

LIFE insurance companies are subject to taxation at all three levels of government found in the United States, namely, federal, state, and local. The federal impost is in the form of an income tax, similar in principle to that levied on corporations generally. State and local levies take several forms, the dominant one being a state tax on gross premiums. At the present time federal income taxes account for about two thirds of the aggregate taxes paid by life insurance companies.

FEDERAL INCOME TAXATION

The development of an appropriate basis for taxing the "income" of a life insurance company has been a vexatious and recurring problem ever since the income tax was introduced into the federal tax structure. The basic notion that gross income minus expenses equals taxable income, which underlies the taxation of corporations generally, does not produce suitable results when applied without modification to life insurance companies. The reasons are found in certain fundamental characteristics of the life insurance transaction and the organizations that provide life insurance services. While there are many facets to the general problem, the most troublesome relate to (1) the long-term nature of the life insurance transaction; (2) the presumed need to maintain the existing competitive balance between stock and mutual companies; (3) the nature and calculation of policy reserves; and (4) the treatment of policy dividends.

Because of the long-term nature of the life insurance transaction, the operating results of a life insurance company for any particular tax year are not conclusive as to the profitability of the business. An operating gain in one year may be offset by an operating loss in a later year, especially if an epidemic occurs or if a catastrophe hazard is present. The profitability of a given block of policies can be conclusively determined only after the last policy has terminated. With an ordinary corporation the receipt of a cash payment normally closes a transaction, while in the case of life insurance the receipt of a payment opens the transaction (as with the first premium) or keeps it open (as with later premiums). All business enterprises face the problem of fluctuating operating results, possibly with alternating gains and losses, but the position of a life insurance company in this respect is somewhat more difficult since it cannot increase premiums on existing business to meet incurred or anticipated losses. On the other hand, the long-run operating results of a life insurance company are more predictable, because of reliance on mortality tables and other actuarial techniques, than the affairs of an ordinary business enterprise.

The need to preserve a competitive balance between two types of corporate organizations having different operating philosophies and methods poses a most difficult problem. The stock company which is operated for the primary purpose of making a profit for its owners could be taxed like an ordinary corporation, with some recognition of the special characteristics of the life insurance transaction, were it not in competition with a type of company whose structure seems to require different tax treatment from the general corporate enterprise. A mutual company has no stockholders and operates on the principle that the policyholders mutually insure each other's lives with claims and expenses being equitably apportioned over the entire group of policyholders and the divisible surplus being distributed in an equitable manner to those who contributed to its accumulation. This mode of operation partakes of the nature of a co-operative and raises a question as to whether the corporation should be regarded as a taxable entity, separate from the individuals who make up its membership. Yet to exempt such a corporation entirely from tax would confer a distinct and perhaps unwarranted competitive advantage over companies which operate on precisely the same basis as mutual companies except as to the disposition of operating gains.[1] In the face of this dilemma, Congress has traditionally fashioned a tax structure that recognizes the special characteristics of mutual companies and then applied the same principles to stock companies with something less than satisfactory results. As will be noted below, the present tax law, enacted in 1959, does make a distinction between stock and mutual companies but with special provisions designed to maintain the competitive balance presumed to exist between the two types of companies.

The special character of policy reserves raises equally troublesome problems. It is generally conceded that a life insurance company should be permitted to deduct from its gross income those sums that must be set aside to meet predictable future obligations. Yet through its choice of mortality and interest assumptions and the method of calculating its reserve liabilities, a company can greatly influence the rate of increase in and the level of policy reserves and, in the absence of restrictions, could control to a substantial degree its income tax liability. The various attempts that have been made over the years to deal with this problem are described below.

The treatment of policy dividends is part and parcel of the broader problem of determining a proper basis for taxing mutual companies. It can be argued with considerable logic that a policy dividend is nothing more than a refund of a portion of a premium originally computed with a deliberate and predictable element of redundacy and, therefore, should be deductible from net earnings by analogy to a price adjustment. On the other hand, to the extent that the dividend arises out of excess interest earnings—an external source of income—one might argue that such portion is profit in the ordinary sense and should be subject to income tax. To tax the entire operating gains, including investment earnings in excess of those needed to support the company's reserve liabilities, arising out of the nonparticipating business of a company, while permitting the deduction of policy dividends in full on participating business would constitute discrimination against non-participating insurance and would upset or distort the competitive balance between stock and mutual companies. Moreover, to place no

---

[1] It should be noted, however, that in Canada mutual companies are free of income taxation while stock companies are taxed at regular corporate rates on amounts credited to the shareholders' account from both participating and nonparticipating insurance.

limits on the deductibility of policy dividends might encourage mutual companies to distribute excessively generous dividends—to the detriment of their surplus position—in order to reduce their income tax liabilities. The Congressional solution to this problem will be noted in due course.

Conceptual Approaches to Taxation of Life Insurance Companies[2]

Conceptually, there are various approaches that might be used to generate an equitable and reasonable amount of tax revenue from the operations of life insurance companies. In fact, several approaches have been used over the years and the present tax law utilizes a combination of approaches. This section analyzes the principal theoretical bases that might be used, while the following section traces the evolution of the tax structure that was established by the Life Insurance Company Income Tax Act of 1959.

Total Income. If life insurance companies were to be taxed on a basis comparable to that applicable to corporations in general, total gross income would be the starting point for the determination of the tax liability. Basically, gross income is composed of life insurance premiums, annuity considerations, and gross investment earnings. Taxable income would be derived by subtracting from gross income (1) expenses (including those associated with the investment function) and other deductions allowed in the Internal Revenue Code for ordinary corporations; (2) total amounts paid to policyholders by reason of death, maturity, surrender, or otherwise, *including policy dividends;* and (3) net increases in policy reserves, as distinct from contingency or other voluntary reserves.

The primary argument in favor of this approach, apart from its general applicability to all forms of business enterprises, is that it treats all forms of income and all lines of insurance in a uniform manner. The tax base is not distorted by the investment-protection mix of the company's ordinary business and both underwriting gains and losses are taken into account. Inequities can result from failure to tax underwriting gains on the elements of a company's business, such as individual term insurance, group term insurance (including credit

---

[2] Background material for this section was drawn from "A Preliminary Statement of the Facts and Issues with Respect to the Federal Taxation of Life Insurance Companies," in *Taxation of Life Insurance Companies*, Hearings before Subcommittee of the House Ways and Means Committee, 83rd Cong., 2d sess., 1954. The same statement was reproduced in Senate Report No. 291, 86th Cong; 1st sess., 1959.

insurance) and health insurance, which generate a relatively small volume of investment income. By the same token, net investment earnings should be offset by any underwriting losses that develop on lines which emphasize the protection element of insurance.

Numerous difficulties arise when an attempt is made to apply the total income approach without modification. One is immediately confronted with the perennial argument that the results of one year's operations do not provide a meaningful tax base when long-term fixed-premium contracts are involved. This argument can be met by permitting the companies to carry their net operating losses backward and forward for a long enough period to ensure stability of results. Conceivably, the companies could be permitted to carry their losses backward and forward without time limit. An ingenious approach to this problem was incorporated into the present tax law, which will be described in detail later.

Another difficulty encountered with the total income approach is the impact on operating results of the methods and assumptions used to compute policy reserves, especially the rate of interest. Since net additions to reserves are treated as deductions from gross income, a company can minimize its tax liabilities by maximizing its reserve liabilities. Two companies with identical operating results could have different tax liabilities purely because of the methods and assumptions used to compute policy reserves. Other things being equal, a company computing its reserves on the basis of the full net level premium method would have a smaller tax liability than one using the Commissioners Reserve Valuation Method or other modified reserve system. This would work a hardship on smaller and newer companies which typically compute their reserves on the basis of the Commissioners Reserve Valuation Method. Similarly, a company could increase its reserve liabilities and, consequently, lower its tax liabilities through the use of conservative mortality and interest assumptions, whether the reserves be computed on the full net level premium basis or a modified standard. If the more conservative assumptions are applied retroactively to increase the reserves on policies issued in earlier years, as was done on a broad scale during the 1940's (when interest rates were falling), the earnings picture is distorted, not only for the prior years but also for the years ahead—and especially in the year or years when monies are transferred from surplus to reserves. During the period when reserve strengthening is being undertaken, a company could manage to avoid any tax liability. In the long run, of course, the additions to surplus will not be affected by the accounting system used to measure year-to-year operating results, but in the short-run serious distortions can occur.

Finally, the issue of policy dividends must be faced when the total income approach is used. The basic elements of this issue have already been identified and need not be repeated here. The pragmatic solutions to this problem have consistently permitted the deduction of policy dividends, at least in part. It should be noted, however, that even if dividends to policyholders are deductible in full by a mutual company (or a stock company issuing participating policies), the portion of net operating gains added to surplus in a particular year would still be taxable. This raises the philosophical issue, previously alluded to, of whether a mutual company is—or should be—a taxable entity, at least partly distinct from its members. The basic question is whether a mutual company (or the participating branch of a stock company) has any income of its own not committed to its policyholders. Those who say not argue that all income attributable to any given block or class of policies will ultimately be returned to the members of the class in one or the other form of benefit. If this actually does occur and all dividends are deductible, then in the final accounting, no tax will have been paid with respect to these policies. On the other hand, if each class of policies does, in fact, make a permanent contribution to surplus, these retained earnings might very logically serve as the basis for a tax. Some would even argue that a temporary accumulation of earnings should be subject to tax, since the accumulation serves a corporate purpose—such as promoting the growth of the company through the financing of acquisition expenses —not identifiable with the individual members of the corporation.

Net Investment Income. A second approach which might be and has been used would be to ignore underwriting results and limit the tax base to the net investment income (gross investment income less investment expenses) of a company. In its most elemental form, this approach would not make explicit allowance for that portion of investment income that must be credited to reserves to meet contractual obligations. In practice, however, implicit allowance has been made by the imposition of a lower tax rate than that applicable to corporations generally. When the method was used, the tax rate was set at a level designed to produce tax revenues approximately equal to those that would result from the taxation of the "free" investment income (net investment income less amounts credited to reserves) at ordinary tax rates. Under this concept, no deductions would be permitted for policyholder dividends.

This basis of income taxation has no theoretical foundation. Its chief, and perhaps only, justification rests on the fact that it avoids many of the practical difficulties associated with most other approaches that might be used. It was proposed by the insurance industry as a method which would provide a stable, substantial, and steadily increasing source of revenue, with the additional merit of great simplicity.

This approach does not avoid the problems created by differences in the reserve requirements of the various companies. Unless the tax rate is to be computed individually for each company—an obviously impractical procedure—the required interest earnings must be calculated for the industry as a whole, with one tax rate applying across the board. Thus, some inequities result among the companies whose experience does not conform to the industry pattern. A second difficulty, associated with any attempt to apply an industry ratio of actual to required investment income, is that the ratio changes over time. To produce consistent results, the tax rate must be changed periodically.

Free Investment Income. A third basic approach, which was utilized in some form for thirty-seven years, would be to tax only the excess of a company's net investment income over the amounts required to be set aside to meet contractual obligations. No recognition would be given to underwriting gains or losses nor to dividends to policyholders. While capital gains and losses might in theory be taken into account, in practice they were not when this approach was being followed.

This approach is clearly more suited to participating insurance than to nonparticipating. It assumes that the only taxable income is that arising out of transactions with outsiders, namely, earnings on investments. Underwriting gains when distributed as dividends to policyholders are considered to be price adjustments. The retention of any part of such gains is assumed to be a temporary phenomenon designed to assure the company's ability to fulfill its obligations to policyholders, such retained earnings eventually being returned to the policyholders. The application of this concept to nonparticipating insurance, which can be expected to generate both excess interest earnings and operating gains, is justified on the grounds that mutual and stock companies must be taxed on the same basis in order to maintain the competitive balance that is presumed to exist.

The free investment income approach can be, and has been, applied on a number of bases. The most obvious basis, but not necessarily the most practicable, is the company-by-company basis. Under this procedure each individual company's tax liability would be determined by the excess of its net investment income over the amounts that must be credited to policy reserves and other interest-bearing obligations. The chief argument in favor of this approach is that the tax reflects the individual circumstances of the companies and hence would appear, at first blush, to be the most equitable arrangement feasible. A subsidiary argument is that the method conforms to the principles applied in the taxation of banks and other financial institutions. The most obvious disadvantage of the method is that it discriminates against the company which establishes its reserves on a conservative basis. If one company computes its reserves on a $2\frac{1}{2}$ per cent interest assumption, for example, while another uses a 3 per cent assumption, actual earnings of $4\frac{1}{2}$ per cent would produce an excess interest factor of 2 per cent in one case and $1\frac{1}{2}$ per cent in the other, although the base to which these factors would be applied would differ. Moreover, the comparability of the tax base with other financial institutions loses some of its validity when differences in the functions and liabilities of the various institutions are considered.

A second basis, designed to deal with inequities associated with the company-by-company approach, is to assume that each company computes its reserves on the basis of the *average* rate of interest used within the industry. Then, each company computes its taxable income as the difference between its net investment income and the amount derived by multiplying the *average rate* of interest for all companies times its policy reserves and other interest-bearing liabilities. The average interest rate used in reserve calculations tends to be rather stable and would not have to be recalculated each year to achieve the broad purposes of the approach. This procedure does not entirely eliminate inequities arising out of different interest assumptions, since the *amount* of reserves to which the *average* rate of interest is applied is affected by the *actual* rate used in the computation of the reserves, as well as by the mortality assumption and the valuation method. This basis is known as the *average-rate* approach to distinguish it from the *industry-ratio* basis which employs a similar rationale but a different technique.

Under the industry-ratio method, the percentage of required to actual net investment income is calculated for the industry as a whole, and any particular company obtains its deduction from net investment income by multiplying this percentage times its own investment earnings. This technique differs from the average-rate approach in that it is a weighted average rather than an arithmetic mean and, moreover, must be recomputed each year to be even reasonably accurate. Since it utilizes a greater element of averaging than the average-rate technique, it ignores to an even greater degree differences among companies as to reserve requirements and actual investment results.

Combinations of these three bases may be used, and the next section will describe various combinations that have been used in the long search for a satisfactory method of taxing life insurance companies.

Distributed Income. Another approach that could be used would be to treat *distributed income* as the tax base and to subject this income to tax at ordinary corporate tax rates. In the case of a stock company, distributed income would be dividends to stockholders. This means that there would be no tax on retained earnings, a departure from general corporate income tax policy which under certain circumstances imposes a penalty tax on undistributed profits. Consequently, this approach is generally regarded as appropriate only for the determination of the *minimum* tax liability of a stock company. In favor of this approach as a minimum tax base, it is contended that while all available income may not be distributed, that portion which is distributed is at least a true measure of the minimum amount of real income.

Difficulties are encountered in attempting to apply this concept to a mutual company, or to the participating branch of a stock company. The only distributions that would be construed as income would be dividends to policyholders. Yet to tax the full amount of policyholder dividends would run counter to the generally accepted notion that refunds based on mortality and expense savings are merely price adjustments and not income in the ordinary sense of the term. Moreover, it would produce an artifical and unjustified distinction between high-premium and low-premium participating companies. Most of the difficulties could be eliminated by taxing only that portion of the dividend distributions attributable to excess interest earnings (computed on either an individual company, average-rate, or industry-ratio basis).

The Conduit Concept. A completely different approach from any of those previously considered was urged upon Congress during the search for a permanent basis of taxing life insurance companies. Under this approach a company's income tax liability would have been measured by the status of its income in the hands of its policyholders. This proposal rested upon the premise that the only income of a life insurance company that should properly be taxed is investment income. Since this income will ultimately be paid to policyholders (and their beneficiaries) as a group, it was argued that the tax on the income should approximate that which would be paid by the stockholders were it to be distributed to them currently or credited to them in the manner of savings bank interest. The proposal called for a tax on the aggregate amount of net investment income rather than just the free investment income. However, under the proposal, deductions from gross investment income would have included not only the expenses directly related to the investment function but all other expenses of the company, including acquisition expenses.

It was recognized that this approach was not appropriate for a stock company, since in the normal course of events the latter would have underwriting gains which would inure to the benefit of the stockholders and presumably should be taxable. Its application to stock companies was urged, however, on the familiar grounds of preserving existing competitive relationships.

In the form in which this proposal was originally made, the tax would have been levied on the company, with the tax *base* being determined as indicated. The tax *rate* was to be that applicable to the lowest bracket of taxable income of individuals on the assumption that it would be utterly impracticable to develop a tax rate that would accurately reflect the composite tax status of the various policyholders. It should be noted, however, that the basic objective of the proposal could be achieved by shifting the tax from the company to its policyholders. The company would compute and report to the policyholders and the tax authorities, the amount of interest credited to policyholders accounts or paid to them directly. While it would be technically possible for this approach to be used, it would place a heavy administrative burden on the companies. Moreover, and more important, it is questionable that a taxpayer on a cash basis could be considered to have constructively received the interest credited to the reserve under his life insurance policy. It has been the consistent view of Congress that interest credited to policyholder reserves should not be includible in the gross income of the individual policyholders.

Evolution of the Present Tax Structure

The present system of taxing life insurance companies has evolved through several stages. During each of these stages, one or a combination of the approaches described above was used.

Period 1909–20. Under the Corporation Excise Tax Act of 1909 and during the early years of the federal income tax, which was instituted in 1913, life insurance companies were taxed under the general principles applicable to ordinary corporations. There was no special section of the law devoted to life insurance companies. In general, a life insurance company included in its gross income the premiums it received, its gross investment income, and its capital gains. Tax-exempt interest was excludible, along with certain other items, and all underwriting and investment expenses were deductible. In addition to the usual deductions, life insurance companies were permitted to deduct (1) sums (other than dividends) paid within the taxable year on insurance and annuity contracts, and (2) the net addition to policy reserves and other contractual obligations. The latter, of course, includes a portion of the gross premiums, as well as interest on the initial reserve at the contractual rate of interest.

This was the *total income* approach, except for a restriction on the deductibility of policy dividends. Dividends were deductible only if paid in cash or applied against current premiums. Dividends used to purchase paid-up additions or left on deposit to accumulate at interest were not deductible. This arbitrary distinction was upheld by the United States Supreme Court.[3]

Period 1921–41. By 1921 the difficulties inherent in the total income approach had become amply apparent and the source of much litigation despite the relatively low rates at which income was taxed.[4] Consequently, the Internal Revenue Code was amended to limit the tax base of a life insurance company to its free investment income. Under the new approach, investment income (by specific definition) included only interest, dividends, and rents. Capital gains and any other type of receipts generally regarded as income were excluded. There were allowed as deductions (1) investment expenses, including taxes, expenses, and depreciation on rental property; and (2) that

---

[3] *Penn Mutual Life Insurance Company* v. *Lederer,* 252 U.S. 523 (1920).

[4] Through 1915 the tax rate was only 1 per cent. It was increased to 2 per cent in 1916, to 6 per cent in 1917 and to 12 per cent in the war year of 1918. The rate was lowered to 10 per cent in 1919.

portion of the net investment income that had to be set aside to meet policy reserves and other contractual obligations.

In order to meet the problem created by differing reserve interest assumptions, Congress stipulated that interest requirements were to be computed on the basis of a uniform rate of 4 per cent, irrespective of the rate or rates actually being used by the companies. In other words, a company would determine its interest requirements by multiplying its policy reserves and other interest-bearing obligations by 4 per cent, without recomputing its reserves on the basis of a 4 per cent interest assumption. This was the *industry-average* approach to the determination of contractual interest requirements, but the 4 per cent rate was chosen arbitrarily and was considerably higher than the average of the rates actually in use at that time. In 1932, the allowable rate of deduction was reduced from 4 to 3¾ per cent, except for those companies whose actual interest assumptions were 4 per cent or higher. Even the new rate was higher than the average of the rates then in use.

From 1921 to 1928, tax-exempt interest was excludible in full from a company's gross investment income, but the law specified that the amount of such interest should be deducted from the amount obtained by multiplying the mean policy reserve by 4 per cent. In other words, the tax-exempt interest reduced the amount of the deduction for contractual interest requirements otherwise allowable to a company. In the landmark case of *National Life Insurance Company of Vermont* v. *U.S.*,[5] the Supreme Court ruled that this treatment of tax-exempt interest was unconstitutional and the decision was made retroactive in effect.[6] Thus, for the entire period 1921–41 tax-exempt interest was excludible without being deducted from the amount computed as necessary to meet reserve requirements.

Through the year 1932, this basis of taxing life insurance companies produced a level of revenue satisfactory to the Treasury. About that time, however, interest rates began to decline drastically and the amount of taxes collected from life insurance companies soon shrank to insignificant levels. In 1937, total income taxes paid by the companies amounted to only $392,000 and in several other years during the decade, the aggregate tax liability of the industry was less than $500,-000. For each of the years 1935 through 1941, the aggregate tax

---

[5] 227 U.S. 508 (1928).

[6] As a result of the decision, refunds in the amount of $36 million were made to life insurance companies for the years 1921–28, out of total tax collections for the period of $112 million.

payments of the companies amounted to only 0.1 per cent of their net investment income, as compared to 1.4 per cent in 1932 and a high of 2.4 per cent in 1926.

To make matters worse, the tax burden was inequitably distributed. In one year a company having only 0.3 per cent of the industry assets paid almost a fourth of the aggregate tax. Another company with only 0.3 per cent of the assets paid 15 per cent of the tax during each of three years. In one year, two companies, which together accounted for about 0.6 per cent of industry assets, paid 58 per cent of the taxes. The over-all situation was aggravated by the fact that most companies had lowered their reserve interest assumption to 3 per cent on all new business, while they were permitted to take deductions on the basis of $3\frac{3}{4}$ per cent interest. The need for new tax revenues to help finance World War II brought matters to a head, and in 1942 Congress adopted a new basis for taxing life insurance companies.

Period 1942–48. The tax legislation enacted in 1942 retained the free investment income concept but promulgated a new basis for computing the deductions for reserve interest requirements of the companies. The new basis combined the *industry-ratio* and *industry-average* approaches.

During this period the Secretary of the Treasury determined and promulgated for each taxable year, on the basis of the preceding year's experience for all companies combined, the composite ratio of needs to receipts. In determining the "needs" of the industry, however, the Secretary accorded a weight of only 35 per cent to the actual interest requirements of the companies, while assigning a weight of 65 per cent to the amount of investment income that would have been required to meet contractual commitments had the reserve liabilities been calculated on the basis of a fixed, assumed industry-average rate of $3\frac{1}{4}$ per cent. It should be observed that the 65 per cent component of the formula was intended to effect a readjustment of the level of reserves for tax purposes,[7] a concept embodied in the present tax law. For the purpose of this computation, preliminary term reserves were increased by 7 per cent to make them comparable to net level premium reserves. The percentage so derived, which became known as the "Secretary's Ratio," was applied by each company to its net invest-

---

[7] The formula was intended to remove *all* effect of the actual rate of interest assumed. It had the approximate effect of defining interest requirements in terms of what they would have been had all reserve liabilities been computed on the basis of a $3\frac{1}{4}$ per cent interest assumption.

ment income (gross investment earnings less expenses) to determine its "reserve and other policy liability deduction," irrespective of the actual relationship between its interest requirements and its net investment income. In determining the percentage of required to actual net investment income, the Secretary included tax-exempt income with other earnings in the denominator, but in applying the Secretary's Ratio the individual insurance company excluded tax-exempt interest from its actual income. This procedure was designed to prevent the double benefit from tax-exempt interest that would have resulted from increasing the "Secretary's Ratio" (if tax-exempt interest had been excluded from the denominator), while at the same time reducing the total investment income of the individual company. The net effect for the industry as a whole, however, was that the aggregate tax liability was increased by virtue of receipt of tax-exempt interest, although the increase did not reflect the full amount of such receipts.

In 1942, the first year to which it was applicable, the Secretary's Ratio was 93.00 per cent, and the aggregate net investment income of the companies was slightly over $1 billion. The exclusion of 93 per cent of the net investment income produced total taxes of $27,427,-000, which amounted to 2.7 per cent of aggregate net investment income. The Ratio declined to 91.98 in 1943, producing an increase in tax revenue (3.1 per cent of net investment income), but it turned upward the following year and continued its climb until it went above 100 per cent. In 1947 and 1948, respectively, the Ratio was 100.66 and 102.43 per cent. During those years, no taxes were paid on life insurance operations, but a small amount of taxes—between $1 million and $2 million each year—was paid on the excess of underwriting gains from health insurance operations over the negative investment income of the companies.[8] The sharp increase in the Secretary's Ratio during the period reflected the joint influence of declining investment yields[9] and the inflexibility of the reserve interest assumptions, especially the fixed $3\frac{1}{4}$ per cent component of the formula.

Period 1949–50. It had become evident during the summer of 1947 that the existing tax law would leave life insurance companies free of income tax on their 1947 life insurance operations. This

---

[8] Since the corporation as a whole was treated as the taxable entity, negative elements in some lines of business were offset against positive elements in other lines.

[9] The downward trend in the rate of return on the composite investment portfolios of life insurance companies reached its nadir in 1947 when the industry return was 2.88 per cent.

was a state of affairs which Congress could neither overlook nor accept as proper. Consequently, negotiations between staff representatives of the life insurance business, the Treasury Department, and Congress were instituted. Many meetings of industry people and conferences with governmental agencies took place. No permanent solution to the tax problem having been evolved, legislation was introduced in October, 1949 to impose a new temporary tax formula for the years 1947 through 1949. The bill failed of enactment largely as a result of objections to its retroactive features. A similar bill limited to the years 1949 and 1950 was enacted in 1950.

The tax formula contained in this bill was similar to that of the 1942 Act with the exception of the method used to determine the "Secretary's Ratio." The Ratio continued to be calculated on an industry-wide basis and to represent the ratio of reserve interest requirements of all companies to the net taxable investment income of all companies. However, in the computation of the composite interest requirements of the industry, the arbitrary weighted rate of $3\frac{1}{4}$ per cent was abandoned and only the actual interest requirements of the various companies were considered. This permitted the ratio to reflect fully the lower interest assumptions adopted for new policies during the 1940's. Thus, Congress retained the *industry-ratio* approach but eliminated the arbitrary *industry-average* component of the formula. The new formula developed "Secretary's Ratios" of 93.55 and 90.63 per cent for the years 1949 and 1950, respectively.[10]

This method was generally referred to as the "1950 stop-gap," since it was meant to be used only until such time as a permanently satisfactory basis of taxing life insurance companies could be developed.

Period 1951–58. In the "stop-gap" legislation of 1951, which continued in effect until 1955, Congress adopted the approach which was earlier described as the "net investment income" approach. During this period the companies paid a tax on their net investment income with no deduction for income required to meet reserve and other contractual obligations. The tax rate was $3\frac{3}{4}$ per cent on the first $200,000 of taxable income and $6\frac{1}{2}$ per cent on the excess. The tax results were the same as if the net investment income of the companies had been taxed at ordinary corporate tax rates (30 per cent on the first

---

[10] It is of some interest that the 1942 formula would have produced a "Secretary's Ratio" of 96.87 per cent in 1950 and hence some tax revenue from life insurance companies.

$25,000 and 52 per cent on the excess) after a deduction of approximately 87½ per cent for required interest. In other words, this approach could be described as the *industry-ratio* method with a fixed or arbitrary "Secretary's Ratio" of 87½ per cent.

The same concept was continued during the years 1955 through 1957 under the "1955 stop-gap" legislation, with the assumed ratio of "needs" to earnings being reduced to 85 per cent except as to the first $1 million of a company's net investment income to which the original percentage of 87½ per cent was still applied. This corresponded to a tax rate of 7.8 per cent of net investment income as against 6.5 per cent for the years 1951–1954. During this period also, life insurance companies were not permitted any deductions for dividends received from other corporations (a privilege available to ordinary corporations) nor were stockholders of life insurance companies allowed the 4 per cent credit generally allowed on dividends received from other corporations.

Summary. From the enactment of the Corporation Excise Tax Act of 1909 until 1921, life insurance companies were taxed on the basis of their total income, including capital gains (and losses). Deductions were allowed for all underwriting and investment expenses; benefits paid to policyholders and their beneficiaries; and net additions to reserves, including the increment attributable to the interest assumption. Dividends to policyholders were deductible if paid in cash or applied against current premiums. Tax-exempt interest, which has been a matter of continuing interest and controversy, was excludible in its entirety.

From 1921 through 1957, some version of the free investment income approach was applied. Under this approach, underwriting gains were ignored in the interest of maintaining existing competitive relationships between mutual and stock companies. Capital gains were also disregarded on the theory that over time capital gains and losses offset each other and nothing would be gained by inclusion of these items in the determination of taxable income. Until 1932, interest requirements were assumed to be equal to 4 per cent of policy reserves and other contractual obligations; from 1932 through 1941 the rate was 3¾ per cent except for policies based on interest assumptions of 4 per cent or more. From 1942 through 1948, the amount of excludible investment income was determined for each company by multiplying its net investment income by a percentage that purported to represent the ratio of interest requirements to net investment income for all companies combined. The percentage was computed by the Secretary of the Treasury, who assigned a weight of 35 per cent to the actual interest requirements of the companies and a weight of 65 per cent to an assumed industry-average rate of 3¼ per cent, with an upward adjustment for preliminary term reserves. For years 1949 and 1950, the "Secretary's Ratio" reflected the actual interest requirements of the companies, the heavily weighted arbitrary assumption of 3¼ per cent having been abandoned. During the period 1951–1957, the net investment income of the companies was taxed, without deduction for reserve interest requirements, at rates designed to produce an aggregate tax liability comparable to that which would have resulted from the use of a "Secretary's Ratio" of 87½ per cent (1951–54) and 85 per cent (1955–57).

Policyholder dividends were not deductible during the period 1921–57, since such a deduction was not compatible with the free investment income basis of taxation. Tax-exempt interest was wholly excludible during the period 1921–42 (as a result of the *National Life Insurance Company* case in 1928) but was treated in such manner thereafter as to result in some tax liability.

CHAPTER XLV

Taxation of
Life
Insurance
Companies
(Continued)

The Life Insurance Company Income Tax Act of 1959[1]

Until the enactment of the Life Insurance Company Income Tax Act of 1959, which was applied retroactively to 1958 operations, the 1942 Act had never been repealed. Its operation was suspended between 1949 and 1957 by the series of "stop-gap" or temporary enactments previously described. Full-scale hearings had been conducted by Congress in 1949, 1950, and 1954. It was in the spring of 1958 during a Senate Finance Committee hearing that it became fully apparent that temporary measures of the type in effect during the years 1949 to 1957 would no longer be enacted and that unless a

---

[1] For a comprehensive and authoritative analysis of the Act, see William B. Harman, Jr., "The Pattern of Life Insurance Company Taxation under the 1959 Act," presented at the Fifteenth Annual Tulane Tax Institute and reprinted by *The Journal of Taxation, Inc.,* 1965. Mr. Harman was a member of the legislative team that drafted the Act and is now Associate General Counsel of the American Life Convention. Much of the factual material for this section of the chapter was drawn, usually without specific documentation, from Mr. Harman's excellent treatise and has

new formula suitable for permanent use were made a part of the tax law, the 1942 Act would again become operative.

The 1959 Act was the result of extensive study by the Treasury Department, the Joint Committee on Internal Revenue Taxation, the House Ways and Means Committee, and the Senate Finance Committee. Its general approach was modified during its consideration by Congress to eliminate inequities among different types of life insurance companies and between life companies and other business enterprises. The legislation that finally emerged from this process is highly complex but the broad principles and basic concepts can be grasped without undue difficulty.

General Features of the Act. The Life Insurance Company Income Tax Act of 1959 embodies the total income approach, which was used with unsatisfactory results during the period 1909–21, but with modifications designed to overcome, or at least ameliorate, the earlier difficulties. All sources of income, including capital gains, are taken into account, but that portion of investment income required to meet contractual obligations is excludible under a procedure for prorating investment income and expenses between the company and the policyholders. Allowable as deductions from gross taxable income are benefit payments and accruals, the portion of gross premiums added to policy reserves, ordinary and necessary business expenses, and certain other items to be discussed later. Tax-exempt interest and intercorporate dividends are prorated between the company and the policyholders in the proportion in which they share the net investment income. Policyholder dividends are deductible up to an amount equal to underwriting gains plus $250,000. Operating losses can be carried backward three years and forward five years. (New companies can carry their losses forward for eight years.)

The essential comparability of this approach to the process by which corporate income tax liability is generally determined may be discerned from the following chart[2] which sets forth in summary form the basic elements that enter into the determination of a life insurance company's tax base:

---

been reviewed for accuracy by Mr. Harman, as well as by other experts on the 1959 Act. Needless to say, final responsibility for the presentation herein rests with the author.

Additional background on the Act may be obtained from Senate Report No. 291, 86th Cong., 1st sess., 1959, and H.R. Report No. 34, 86th Cong., 1st sess., 1959, both bearing the title *The Life Insurance Company Income Tax Act of 1959*.

[2] Taken from William B. Harman, Jr., *ibid.,* p. 687.

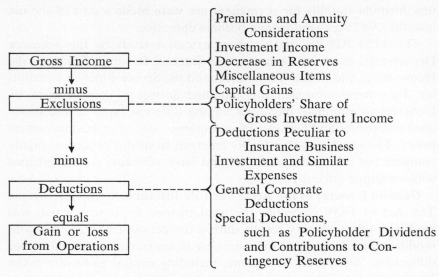

In order to deal with the special problems associated with the life insurance business, the law provides that the tax liability of a particular company shall be computed in four distinct steps or phases. Phase I levies a tax upon the net investment income, after allowance for the interest needed to meet reserve and other contractual liabilities.[3] The allowance for contractual interest obligations is based not upon the actual requirements of the company but rather upon a formula designed to minimize the effects of varying interest assumptions and methods of calculating policy reserves.

Phase II is directed at the underwriting gains of a company and for all practical purposes is applicable only to stock companies. Under this section of the law a tax is imposed on one-half of the excess, if any, of net gains from operations—after certain deductions—over the taxable income developed under Phase I. This is tantamount to taxing on a current basis one-half of a company's underwriting gains, since the taxable investment income is included in the gains from operations and then deducted. The portion of net operating gains not taxable currently (i.e., one-half of the underwriting gains) is placed in a

---

[3] Technically, the sections of the law that describe the procedures or computations by which the taxable income is determined—commonly referred to as "phases" —do not impose the tax liability. The phases, (not a statutory term) are dealt with in Sections 804, 809, and 815 of the Internal Revenue Code, while paragraphs 1, 2, and 3 of Section 802(b) of the Code impose the tax.

special account called the Policyholders Surplus Account (PSA) and is taxed only when distributed to the *stockholders* or transferred to the Shareholders Surplus Account (to be discussed later). Provision for deferral of tax on one-half of the underwriting gains was made in recognition of the long-term nature of the life insurance transaction and the consequent need for contingency reserves. Within limitations to be noted later, this income is not taxed as long as it is retained by the company for the protection of its policyholders. For purposes of the Phase II tax computation, the actual interest requirements of the company are taken into account rather than the "requirements" produced by the Phase I calculation. To the extent that these two sums vary, underwriting gains of a company are not identical to the excess of net gains from operations over the Phase I taxable investment income.

Phase III imposes a tax on distributions to stockholders out of funds not previously taxed under Phase II of the law. In effect, this is a tax on dividends to stockholders paid from funds drawn from the Policyholders Surplus Account. By its nature, this tax is applicable only to stock companies.

Phase IV levies a tax on the excess of net long-term capital gains over net short-term capital losses.[4] Under the "separate basket" concept of the original Act, capital gains were segregated from the ordinary income of a company, with the result that the capital gains tax was not affected by a loss from operations. By an amendment adopted in 1962, the "separate basket" treatment was eliminated and capital gains are now treated as an offset to operating losses, as in the case of other corporations.

The four-phase approach to the determination of a company's tax liability and the deferral of tax on a portion of the underwriting gains should not be permitted to obscure the fact that in the long run the tax base is the gain from operations, with due allowance for policyholder dividends in the case of mutual companies and the participating business of stock companies. This can be observed in the following summary of possible outcomes from a year's operation.[5]

---

[4] What is described in this chapter as Phase IV is nothing more than the alternative tax computation available to any taxpayer. This procedure is not generally referred to as Phase IV.

[5] William B. Harman, Jr., *op. cit.*, p. 689.

Case I serves to illustrate the fact that an underwriting loss offsets taxable investment income and produces a tax base equal to the net

CASE	CURRENT TAX BASE	DEFERRED TAX BASE	TOTAL TAX BASE
I. Gain from Operations *less than* Taxable Investment Income Base	Gain from Operations	None	Gain from Operations
II. Gain from Operations *equal to* Taxable Investment Income Base	Gain from Operations	None	Gain from Operations
III. Gain from Operations *greater than* Taxable Investment Income Base	Taxable Investment Income plus one half of Difference between Gain from Operations and Taxable Investment Income	One half of Difference between Gain from Operations and Taxable Investment Income	Gain from Operations

gain from operations. Case III assumes that amounts placed in the Policyholders Surplus Account will ultimately inure to the benefit of the stockholders and, hence, become taxable.

The taxable income developed under the first three phases of the Act is taxed at the same rates applicable to corporate income generally, namely, 22 per cent on the first $25,000 of taxable income and 48 per cent on the balance of such income. Capital gains are taxed at the usual rate of 25 per cent, unless the alternative tax computation available to corporations generally would reduce the tax to 22 per cent.

Determination of Taxable Investment Income (Phase I). The taxable investment income of a life insurance company is equal to its gross investment income minus (1) expenses incurred in the production of the investment income; (2) the policyholders' share of net investment income (or the interest required to meet contractual obligations); (3) the company's share of tax-exempt interest and deductible dividend income; and (4) the so-called "small business" deduction which is limited to 10 per cent of the net investment income or $25,000, whichever is smaller.

The gross investment income consists primarily of interest, dividends, rents, and royalties. Items of lesser importance include commitment fees and bonuses, prepayment charges or penalties, net short-term capital gains, and income derived from a trade or business other than the life insurance business.

Deductible from gross investment income are all expenses fairly chargeable against such income. These include not only the expenses of the company's investment department but all expenses associated with investment property including state and municipal taxes, depreciation, and depletion. The difference between a company's gross investment income and its investment expenses is called the *investment yield* (rather than net investment income) in the law.

Under a proration concept not used in any previous life insurance company tax law, the investment yield is divided into two shares, one allocated to the policyholders and the other to the company. The policyholders' share, expressed as a percentage of the investment yield, is equal to the interest needed to meet "policy and other contract liability requirements," as computed by the method specified in the law. These requirements relate to policy reserves, pension reserves, and such other interest-bearing items as prepaid or discounted premiums and settlement agreements. The major item among these requirements is interest to maintain policy reserves.

Policy reserve interest requirements are computed on an individual company basis, which represents a major shift in Congressional policy. However, in order to deal with the problem created by differences in reserve interest assumptions, Congress prescribed a procedure for computing interest requirements that reflects the company's own investment experience. The first step in this procedure is to determine the *adjusted reserves rate*. This rate is the lower of (1) the company's net rate of return on investments (i.e., the company's investment yield divided by its assets) for the current taxable year or (2) the average rate of return for the last five years, including the current year. Thus, if a company's net rate of return for the current year were 4.5 per cent and its average rate of return for the last five years were 4.3 per cent, the *adjusted reserves rate* would be 4.3 per cent.

The next step is to determine the *adjusted life insurance reserves*. The purpose of this step is to restate the existing reserves in terms of an approximation of what they would have been had they been calculated originally on the basis of the *adjusted reserves rate*. The adjustment of the reserves is accomplished by the use of an empirical formula which reflects the assumption that an increase of one percentage point in the reserve interest rate decreases the aggregate reserves by 10 per cent, and vice versa.[6] The adjusted life insurance reserves are then multiplied by the adjusted reserves rate to produce an amount that for tax purposes is regarded as the interest required to maintain reserves.

This procedure, which is a crucial element of the 1959 Act, is illustrated in the following oversimplified example.[7]

Step 1. Determination of *Investment Yield*

Gross Investment Income:

Taxable interest	$1,150,000	
Tax-exempt interest	60,000	
Intercorporate dividend income	40,000	
Rents and royalties	200,000	
Short-term capital gain	50,000	$1,500,000

Deductions:

Investment expenses	100,000	
Real estate expenses and taxes	20,000	
Depreciation	24,000	
Depletion	6,000	150,000
Investment Yield		$1,350,000

Step 2. Determination of *Current Earnings Rate*

$$\text{Current earnings rate} = \frac{\text{Investment Yield}}{\text{Mean Assets}} = \frac{\$1,350,000}{\$30,000,000} = .045$$

Step 3. Determination of *Average Earnings Rate*

Current taxable year	4.5%
Immediately preceding year	4.4
Second preceding year	4.3
Third preceding year	4.2
Fourth preceding year	4.1
Total	21.5%

Average earnings rate

$$\text{for five-year period} = \frac{21.5}{5} = 4.3\%$$

---

[6] The validity of this empirical rule has been established by several independent studies. See, for example, Horace Holmes, "Standards of Policy Reserves," *Transactions of the Actuarial Society of America,* Vol. XXXIX, 1938, p. 281 and Alfred N. Guertin, "The Strengthening of Reserves," *Transactions of the Actuarial Society of America,* Vol. XLV, 1944, p. 295. The same relationship was demonstrated by a series of 120 model offices constructed in 1955 by George Davis, Alfred N. Guertin, Richard C. Guest, Norman Hughes, and Henry F. Rood, acting as an actuarial advisory committee to the Treasury Department. The use of this formula was suggested by Walter O. Menge, then President but now Chairman of the Lincoln National Life Insurance Company, during consideration of the 1959 Act and, as a result, this process of adjusting reserves is generally referred to as the "Menge Formula."

[7] This example was adapted, with modifications and extensions, from Stuart Schwarzschild and Eli A. Zubay, *Principles of Life Insurance,* Vol. II, published for the Life Office Management Association by Richard D. Irwin, Inc. (Homewood, Illinois), 1964, pp. 203–7.

Step 4. Selection of *Adjusted Reserves Rate*

The adjusted reserves rate is the lower of the earnings rate for the current tax year and the average earnings rate for the five-year period ending with the current year. Hence, the adjusted reserves rate is the five-year average earnings rate of 4.3 per cent.

Step 5. Computation of the *Average Interest Rate Assumed*

This step is an essential part of the formula for conversion of the actual interest requirements to the adjusted basis. Since a company will normally have business on the books with different reserve interest rate assumptions, reflecting the level of interest rates in the capital market at the time the business was written, it is necessary to compute a weighted average of the assumptions used. The following example assumes that policy reserves have been computed on the basis of three different interest assumptions.

(a)	(b)	(c)	(d)	(e)
				Product of
Assumed	Reserves	Reserves	Mean Reserves	Rate × Mean
Interest	Beginning	End of	$\left(\dfrac{b+c}{2}\right)$	Reserves
Rate	of Year	Year		(a × d)
3.5%	$ 8,000,000	$12,000,000	$10,000,000	$350,000
3.0	4,000,000	6,000,000	5,000,000	150,000
2.5	9,000,000	11,000,000	10,000,000	250,000
	$21,000,000	$29,000,000	$25,000,000	$750,000

$$\text{Average interest rate assumed} = \frac{\$750,000}{\$25,000,000} = .03$$

Step 6. Computation of the *Adjusted Life Insurance Reserves*

As pointed out above, actual reserves are recomputed for purposes of the Phase I tax by assuming that a difference of one percentage point between the *average reserve interest rate* and the *adjusted reserves rate* effects a change of 10 per cent in the opposite direction in the amount of reserves. The procedure for making the adjustment set forth in the tax law appears more complicated than the foregoing statement would suggest but the result is the same. The mean life insurance reserves for the taxable year are multiplied by that percentage which equals 100 per cent *plus* ten times the average reserve interest rate *minus* ten times the adjusted reserves rate. The actual computation is as follows:

$$\text{Mean life insurance reserves} = \frac{\$21,000,000 + \$29,000,000}{2} = \$25,000,000$$

Percentage to be applied:	100%
+10 times 3% (average reserve interest rate)	30
−10 times 4.3% (adjusted reserves rate)	−43
	87%

Adjusted life insurance reserves = $25,000,000 × .87 = $21,750,000

A company valuing its reserve liabilities on the preliminary term basis may adjust them to the net level basis by an approximation set forth in the law or by actual recomputation. Such an adjustment, which, if made, must apply for all purposes of the tax law, would be carried out before the calculation of the adjusted life insurance reserves.

Step 7. Computation of *Policy Interest Requirements*

Adjusted life insurance reserves	$21,750,000
Adjusted reserves rate	× .043
Policy interest requirements	$ 935,250

It should be observed that this procedure results in an overstatement of policy interest requirements when the adjusted reserves rate is higher than the average assumed rate of interest, as is the usual case, and in an understatement of the requirements when the opposite relationship exists. In this example, the actual interest requirements for policy reserves are $750,000, while the restated requirements are $935,250.

In addition to the interest presumed to have been credited to policy reserves, a company is permitted to exclude from its taxable investment income the investment earnings allocated to qualified pension and profit-sharing plans, as well as interest paid on indebtedness, the discount on prepaid premiums, and interest paid or credited with respect to dividend deposits, settlement agreements not involving life contingencies, and other contractual arrangements for which no provision is made in life insurance reserves. In all of these cases, the amount excludible is the sum actually paid or credited.

With the addition of these amounts to the policy reserve interest requirements developed in Step 7, it is possible to determine the proportion in which the policy holders and the company are deemed to share the investment yield. If the interest paid or credited to other than policy reserves is assumed to amount to $77,250, the "policy and other contract liability requirements" will aggregate $1,012,500, and Step 8 can be undertaken.

Step 8. Calculation of *Company's Share of Investment Yield*

$$\frac{\text{Policy and other contract liability requirements}}{\text{Investment yield}} = \frac{\$1,012,500}{\$1,350,000} = .75$$

Percentage attributable to company = 100 − .75 = .25
Company's share of investment yield = $1,350,000 × .25 = $337,500

In arriving at its taxable investment income, a company is permitted three more deductions, called "reduction items" in the law. The first of these, designed to assist small and new companies but available to all companies regardless of size or age, authorizes a deduction of 10 per cent of the investment yield, or $25,000, whichever is smaller.

The second item relates to tax-exempt interest, the treatment of which has been a recurring problem. It will be recalled that under the doctrine enunciated in *National Life Insurance Company* v. *United States* (1928), life insurance companies were to enjoy the full benefit of tax-exempt interest, or, to put it more precisely, no tax was to be levied on tax-exempt interest. In developing a new approach to the taxation of life insurance companies that culminated in the 1959 Act, Congress concluded—and stipulated—that tax-exempt interest should be prorated between the policyholders' share of investment yield and the company's share.[8] This meant that most of such interest would be allocated to that segment of investment yield that would not be taxed in any event, and the company's deduction would be limited to its share. Thus, it appeared to many companies that they were to be deprived of most of the tax advantage associated with tax-exempt interest. The Treasury representatives argued that to treat all tax-exempt interest as belonging to the company would be the equivalent of a double deduction. Not only would the company be permitted to deduct the full amount of the interest from its share of the investment yield, but its share of the investment yield would have been reduced in the first instance by that percentage of the tax-exempt interest allocable to policyholders under the basic proration formula.[9] As might be expected, this issue reached the courts and in 1965 the United States Supreme Court upheld the proration concept, holding that the procedure does not impose a tax on tax-exempt interest.[10] Be that as it may, it can be demonstrated that under the proration approach, a company's over-all tax liability is increased by the receipt of tax-exempt interest.[11]

---

[8] As a matter of fact, the whole concept of prorating investment income and expenses between the company and its policyholders was developed for the sole purpose of dealing with tax-exempt interest and deductible dividend income.

[9] See U.S. Congress, Senate Committee on Finance, *Hearings, Tax Formula for Life Insurance Companies,* 86th Cong., 1st sess., 1959, pp. 50–51.

[10] *United States* v. *Atlas Life Insurance Company,* 85 S. Ct. 1379 (1965). Joined in support of Atlas in this case were some 130 life insurance companies, the National Association of Attorneys General, the Governors Conference, the Port of New York Authority, and a number of other interstate authorities. The state governmental groups regarded the Treasury's position as an encroachment on the tax-exempt status of securities issued by states and municipalities.

[11] See Barnie E. Abelle, Jr., "An Evaluation of the Life Insurance Company Income Tax Act of 1959," *Journal of Insurance,* Vol. XXX, No. 3, Sept., 1963, pp. 412–13.

Dividend income, which presents much the same problem as tax-exempt interest, is treated in the same manner as tax-exempt interest. In most cases, a corporation can deduct 85 per cent of dividends received from another corporation in order to eliminate most of the double taxation that would otherwise result. In the case of a life insurance company such income is prorated between the company and the policyholders, and the company is permitted to deduct only 85 per cent of its *share* of the income rather than the entire amount.[12]

It is now possible to complete the illustration of the process by which a company's Phase I tax liability is computed.

Step 9. Computation of *Reduction Items*

Small business deduction:
$1,350,000 × .10 = $135,000 subject to limitation of .... $ 25,000
Company's share of tax-exempt interest and deductible dividend income:
$60,000 + (.85 × 40,000) = 94,000 × .25 .... $ 23,500
   Total   . $ 48,500

Step 10. Determination of *Taxable Investment Income*[13]

Company's share of investment yield (Step 8) $337,500
Less reduction items (Step 9) 48,500
Taxable investment income $289,000

Determination of Phase II Tax Liability. The first step in the determination of a company's Phase II tax liability is to calculate the gain or loss from operations. This involves consideration of gross receipt items, investment expenses, deductions peculiar to the insurance business, special deductions, and general corporate deductions.

Included among gross receipts are (1) premiums, including discounted premiums, considerations for annuity and supplementary contracts, and the increase in funds held at interest for policyholders and beneficiaries; (2) investment income; (3) decreases in policy reserves; (4) capital gains; and (5) miscellaneous sources of income.

Investment income and expenses are prorated between the company and the policyholders on the basis of their respective shares of the investment yield, as is done in connection with Phase I. However, the

---

[12] The Treasury would argue, of course, that 85 per cent of the other share is also deducted as part of the reserve interest deduction.

[13] This illustration ignores long-term capital gains in an assumed amount of $15,500 which are taxed at a 25 per cent rate under the alternative tax procedure. The law provides for inclusion of long-term capital gains in both the phase I and phase II calculations, with the alternative tax procedure determining whether they will be taxed separately or as an element of the company's over-all tax base.

respective shares are computed on the basis of the company's actual interest requirements rather than the amount derived from the adjustment of reserves carried out in Phase I. Tax-exempt interest and dividend income are prorated between the company and the policyholders as in Phase I, but again the division is based on actual interest requirements.

Since a company is permitted a deduction for an *addition* to policy reserves, it must report as income a *reduction* or *release* of such reserves. Capital gains are included in the total accounting of income in order that they may be offset against an operating loss, but they will be subject to separate taxation under the alternative tax computation (Phase IV) if the latter procedure produces a lower tax liability.

As would be expected, a company can deduct all benefit payments and accruals. It can also deduct additions to policy reserves not attributable to the crediting of contractual interest. (Allowance for the latter item is made by excluding from the company's gross income the policyholders' share of the investment yield, computed on the basis of actual requirements.) If a company strengthens its reserves through a change in mortality or interest assumptions—or a modification in the method of computation—which would, of course, operate to reduce its tax liability, the tax benefits of such strengthening must be spread over the ten-year period beginning in the year following the taxable year in which such strengthening occurs. The small business deduction previously alluded to is also available under the Phase II calculation as a deduction peculiar to the insurance business.

As a consequence of debate over how to treat policyholder dividends, three special deductions were made available. There was fairly general agreement that the portion of policyholder dividends representing return of capital (i.e., mortality and expense savings) should be deductible and the portion representing excess interest should *not* be deductible. This suggested that the deduction for policyholder dividends should not reduce a company's over-all tax base below the investment income tax base developed under the Phase I calculation. The imposition of such a floor on a company's tax base would mean that it would not pay a smaller tax under the total income approach than it had been paying under the investment income approach. However, since newly-formed companies customarily sustain net operating losses for the first several years of their existence, Congress finally concluded that the deduction for policyholder dividends should be permitted to reduce the total income base up to $250,000 below the Phase I taxable investment income as a partial or complete offset to operating losses. The deduction was made available to all companies, irrespective of their size or operating results.

The stock companies protested that the deductibility of policyholder dividends would give mutual companies a competitive advantage (because of the safety cushion provided by redundant premiums) and requested that they be permitted to deduct a comparable amount for purposes of accumulating contingency reserves. They pointed especially to the risks associated with group life and health insurance. Congress responded to this argument by making two more deductions available. The first is restricted to nonparticipating insurance and is equal to 10 per cent of the increase in reserves during the taxable year or, if larger, 3 per cent of the premiums for the taxable year on certain nonparticipating contracts.[14] The second provision permits any company, stock or mutual, to deduct 2 per cent of group insurance premiums (and since 1962, premiums on individual health insurance contracts) until the aggregate deductions equal 50 per cent of the group insurance premiums for the taxable year then current. The amount of the deductions was made to conform to the legal requirements of New York (which mandates the accumulation of contingency reserves for group insurance) in order to eliminate any tax disparities that might otherwise arise.

The sum of these three deductions can not exceed $250,000 plus the amount by which the gain from operations exceeds the taxable investment income. In other words, these deductions, taken together, can not reduce a company's total income tax base to a smaller amount than the taxable investment income less $250,000. As a further restriction, applicable only to stock companies, the deductions permitted with respect to nonparticipating insurance and group and health insurance are added to the Policyholders Surplus Account and hence serve only to defer taxation of the amounts involved. In the event that the sum of these three deductions exceeds the specified limitation, the nonparticipating insurance deduction would be disallowed first, the group and health insurance deduction second, and the dividend deduction last.

In addition to the foregoing deductions, a life insurance company is entitled to all the deductions available to corporations generally, subject to the usual limitations and qualifications.

---

[14] The 3 per cent component of the deduction was primarily intended to provide a safety cushion for term insurance contracts issued or renewed for periods of five years or more, which contracts present a relatively greater mortality risk and accumulate only inconsequential reserves. It was also intended to treat noncancellable health insurance in a manner comparable to life insurance.

The determination of the gain (or loss) from operations and the calculation of the Phase II tax liability are illustrated in the following example, which is a continuation of that used to illustrate the Phase I tax liability.

Step 11. Calculation of *Company's Share of Investment Yield*

$$\frac{\text{Policy and other contract liability requirements}}{\text{Investment yield}} = \frac{\$827,250}{\$1,350,000} = .61$$

Percentage attributable to company $= 100 - .61 = .39$
Company's share of investment yield $= \$1,350,000 \times .39 = \$526,500$

As in Phase I this calculation is made for the sole purpose of allocating tax-exempt interest and deductible dividend income between the company and the policyholders. In this particular computation, however, actual interest requirements were used, which increased from 25 to 39 per cent the percentage of investment yield deemed to be the company's share. This resulted in the allocation of $526,500 of investment income to the company, as compared with $337,500 in Phase I.

Step 12. Computation of *Gain from Operations*[15]

Gross receipts:			
Gross premiums............................		$8,000,000	
Company's share of investment yield:			
Fully taxable income.......................$489,840			
Tax-exempt interest and deductible dividend income............................	36,660	526,500	
Other income..............................		73,500	$8,600,000
Less:			
Company's share of tax-exempt and deductible			
ṭ dividend income........................		36,660	
Deductions peculiar to insurance business......		6,363,340	
General corporate deductions.................		1,000,000	7,400,000
Tentative Gain from Operations...............			$1,200,000
Less special deductions:			
Maximum = $250,000 + ($1,200,000 − 289,000)			
= $1,161,000			
Actual.....................................			700,000
Gain from Operations.......................			$ 500,000

It will be observed that the example shows no deduction for investment expenses inasmuch as investment income was reported on a net basis under gross receipts. This is in accordance with the proration concept of the tax law. The results would be the same if the company's share of gross investment income were reported under receipts, with its share of investment expenses being reported as a deduction.

---

[15] Long-term capital gains have been omitted since under the assumptions of this illustration they will be taxed at 25 per cent under the alternative tax procedure, herein referred to as Phase IV.

Step 13. Determination of Phase II *Taxable Income*

Gain from operations	$500,000
Less taxable investment income (Phase I)	289,000
Difference	211,000
One half of difference	105,500
Taxable income (Phase II)	$105,500

The tax base developed under Phase II is one half of the excess of the gain from operations over taxable investment income. This amount plus the taxable investment income from Phase I produces the total tax base of the company, exclusive of any that may arise under Phases III and IV. If the gain from operations is less than the taxable investment income, the gain from operations becomes the total tax base. If there is a net loss from operations there is no tax liability other than that which might arise under Phase III.

The tax base of a mutual company is usually its taxable investment income less $250,000, since its dividend distributions will normally more than offset any underwriting gains developed under the Phase II calculation.

Determination of Phase III Tax Liability. It will be noted from Step 13 above that only one half of the excess of the gain from operations over taxable investment income is currently taxable. Tax on the other half is postponed until such time as the company, through its own actions, demonstrates that the untaxed earnings are no longer needed for the protection of the policyholders or until the cumulative untaxed sums exceed a specified ceiling. To create a mechanism for the eventual taxation of earnings which escape taxation under Phases I and II, the law provides for the establishment of two tax memorandum accounts, namely, the Shareholders Surplus Account (hereafter referred to as the SSA) and the Policyholders Surplus Account (hereafter referred to as the PSA).

The function of the SSA is to segregate for federal income tax purposes that portion of a stock life insurance company's surplus, accumulated after January 1, 1958, upon which it has already paid taxes or upon which no taxes are levied. In accordance with this function, the following sums are credited to the SSA: (1) all earnings taxed under Phase I or Phase II; (2) capital gains taxed under Phase IV; and (3) amounts transferred from the PSA. Also credited are the small business deduction and the full amount of tax-exempt interest and deductible dividend income, despite the prorating of such income between the company and the policyholders in the Phase I and Phase II calculations. This latter feature is a distinct advantage to the companies since it enlarges the base from which distributions to stock-holders can be made without further tax liability.

The SSA is reduced by distributions to stockholders and taxes paid on sums credited to the account other than by transfer from the PSA. If stockholder dividends in the aggregate never exceed the sums credited directly to the SSA, less taxes thereon, the company will not incur any further tax liability with respect to past operations unless the accumulation exceeds the statutory limitations. (See below). On the other hand, if distributions to stockholders exceed the balance in the SSA, the excess is charged to the PSA at which time a tax at the ordinary corporate rate must be paid on that gross amount which (after taxes) will be equal to the excess distributions. This would create a Phase III tax liability.

The purpose of the PSA is to segregate for federal income tax purposes that portion of a stock company's surplus, accumulated after January 1, 1958, upon which it has paid no tax and upon which a federal income tax will be levied when, and if, any such amounts exceed certain limits or are deemed used for the benefit of share-holders. An obvious source of additions to the account is the portion of underwriting gains not currently taxable, specifically one half of the amount by which the gain from operations exceeds the taxable invest-ment income. The other two items that go into the PSA are the deduction for certain nonparticipating contracts and the deduction for group insurance.

No tax is levied on the sums in the PSA until such time as they are transferred to the SSA or distributions to stockholders exceed the bal-ance in the SSA. Transfers to the SSA may occur (1) at the election of the company, presumably under such circumstances as to gain a tax advantage;[16] (2) when the accumulation in the PSA exceeds certain limits; or (3) when the company ceases to operate as a life insurance company. The tax on sums transferred to the SSA is charged to the PSA, thus enlarging the gross withdrawal by the amount of the tax (as will be demonstrated later).

Congress anticipated the possibility that stock life insurance compa-nies would attempt to escape the Phase III tax liability by limiting their cash dividends to an amount less than the balance in the SSA. In order to close this potential tax loophole and to prevent an unreason-

---

[16] A voluntary transfer might be advantageous when the current tax base does not use up the surtax exemption of $25,000 or when it is anticipated that a tax on the deferred tax account may be "triggered" at some future date when tax rates would be higher.

able accumulation, Congress stipulated that the funds held in the PSA could not exceed the *highest* of three alternative ceilings. Under the first limitation, the amount in the PSA cannot exceed 15 per cent of the company's life insurance reserves at the end of any taxable year. This limitation was designed for well-established companies with a relatively large proportion of cash-value insurance. The second limitation, incorporated into the law for the benefit of newly established companies, states that the balance in the account cannot be greater than one fourth of the difference between a company's life insurance reserves at the end of the current taxable year and such reserves, if any, on December 31, 1958. It is apparent that this limitation would not become effective so long as a company, on the average, can increase its life insurance reserves by more than four times the amounts added to the PSA. The final limitation written into the law with an eye toward the interests of companies that write a great deal of term insurance, health insurance, and group insurance—types of coverages that do not develop large reserves—restricts the accumulation to a sum not larger than 50 per cent of current premium income. While these do not appear to be burdensome limitations, many companies have already incurred a Phase III tax liability.

Under the original Act, there was no provision pursuant to which a company could withdraw funds from the PSA to meet heavy or even catastrophic operating losses, without incurring a tax liability. A 1964 amendment provided limited relief in this regard by permitting —in fact, requiring—tax-free withdrawals of funds credited to the PSA under the nonparticipating insurance and group insurance deductions (which were intended to provide a cushion against catastrophic losses), when it could be demonstrated that such deductions have never produced a tax benefit.[17]

The manner in which a Phase III tax liability (applicable only to stock companies) may be generated is illustrated in the following example which builds on the earlier examples of tax liability determination.

The Phase III tax liability developed in this example is $47,594,

---

[17] Such a situation would exist when these deductions only served to increase operating losses which, despite the loss carryback and carryforward provisions, were never offset against operating gains. This normally occurs during the first several years of a new company's existence when it is writing off acquisition expenses. There is still no provision that allows a company to withdraw funds from the PSA to meet catastrophic losses. These can be dealt with only through the loss carryback and carryforward provisions.

which is derived by multiplying the ordinary corporate tax rate of 48 per cent times the amount, $99,154, that had to be withdrawn from the PSA in order to produce $51,560 for distribution to stockholders. The total distribution to stockholders was made disproportionately large in order to create a Phase III tax liability; in the typical case such a liability will arise only when the PSA exceeds the amount permitted by law.

Step 14. Determination of *Phase III Tax Liability*

Shareholders Surplus Account			
Balance beginning of year			$ 500,000
Add:			
Currently taxable income			
Phase I	$289,000		
Phase II	105,500		
Phase IV	15,500	$410,000	
Permanently untaxed amounts			
Tax-exempt interest	60,000		
Deductible dividend income	34,000		
Small business deductions	25,000	119,000	529,000
Total			$1,029,000
Subtract:			
Taxes for current year		$186,735	
Distributions to stockholders		893,825	1,080,560
Excess distributions to stockholders			$ 51,560
Charged to Policyholders Surplus Account			51,560
Balance end of year			$ 0
Policyholders Surplus Account			
Balance beginning of year			$1,400,000
Add:			
One-half of excess of gain from operations over			
Phase I income		$105,500	
Deduction for nonparticipating insurance		675,000	
Deduction for group insurance		25,000	805,500
Total			$2,205,500
Subtract:			
Distributions to stockholders in excess of balance			
in the SSA		$ 51,560	
Tax on excess distributions[18]		47,594	99,154
Balance end of year			$2,106.346

---

[18] The tax is levied on the gross amount of previously untaxed income that would have to be withdrawn from the PSA in order to produce an after-tax amount equal to the excess distribution to stockholders. The tax is computed in the following manner:

$$\text{Total subtraction} = \$51,560 \times \frac{100}{(100 - 48)} = \$51,560 \times \frac{100}{52} = \$99,154$$

Tax on distribution = Total subtraction − Distribution = $99,154 − 51,560 = $47,594 This procedure is known as "grossing up" the withdrawal. The company must withdraw enough money from its tax-deferred account to pay both its stockholders and the Federal government.

In this illustrative case, the total tax liability for the current year is $234,329, composed of the following elements:

Phase I	$132,220	Phase III	$47,594
Phase II	$ 50,640	Phase IV	$ 3,875

The Phase IV calculation consists simply of multiplying the capital gains rate of 25 per cent times the assumed net long-term gains of $15,500.

TAXATION BY STATE AND LOCAL GOVERNMENTS

State Taxes

The most important form of state tax is the tax levied on life insurance premiums and annuity considerations. This form of taxation goes back to the early 1820's when the State of New York introduced a premium tax to protect its fledgling companies against competition from British companies and companies chartered in other states. In keeping with its purpose the tax was levied only on companies not chartered in New York. Other states followed New York's example and extended the tax to domestic companies in order to provide funds to cover the cost of insurance supervision. Today, all states impose a premium tax of some sort, which has become an important source of general revenue for the states. Only about 5 per cent of the revenue produced by premium taxes is now devoted to supervision of insurance companies, one of the original purposes of the tax.

Taxes on life and health insurance premiums range from 1¾ per cent to 4 per cent, averaging about 2 per cent. About half of the states levy a tax on annuity considerations, but the rate is frequently lower than that applicable to life and health insurance premiums. Some states exempt life insurance premiums and annuity considerations arising out of "qualified" pension plans.

The tax is levied on gross premiums but some states permit dividends to policyholders to be deducted. There may be similar deductions under annuity contracts for refunds to annuitants in case of death during the accumulation period or for amounts paid to pension plan participants in the event of termination of employment. A few states allow a company to credit against its premium taxes any taxes which it may pay on assets located within the state, such as, real estate. In some states where the tax rate is unusually high, a credit is granted for investments within the state, the effective tax rate varying inversely with the volume of investments in the state. Few states, if any, permit a company to deduct premiums on insurance ceded to another company under a reinsurance agreement, since it is customary for the reinsurer to reimburse the ceding company for premium taxes on insurance ceded to the reinsurer. By the same token, a company does not have to pay a premium tax on insurance assumed from another company under a reinsurance agreement.

The domicile of the insured determines the state to which the tax on his premiums is paid. For group insurance and group annuity contracts the premium tax is allocated among the various states on the basis of the amount of premiums generated within the states, although proration may not be required for the smaller cases.

A number of states tax only out-of-state companies, and some tax domestic companies at a lower rate than companies from other states. A few states that have large, well-established domestic companies levy franchise or other taxes in lieu of premium taxes, a practice that gives a competitive advantage to companies of other states.

The premium tax laws of most states have a *retaliatory* feature in accordance with which the tax imposed on a company of another state is fixed at a level not lower than the amount that the other state would impose on a company of the taxing state doing business in the other state. For example, if the premium tax in state A is only 2 per cent, while the rate in state B is 3 per cent, a retaliatory provision in the law of state A would cause companies domiciled in state B to pay taxes of 3 per cent on premiums developed in state A. These retaliatory provisions have had the effect of promoting uniformity in the rate of premium taxation among the states, since if a state imposes a higher tax on companies domiciled in other states, its own domestic companies will have to pay the same rate of tax in the other states.

A few states have premium tax laws that have been characterized as *discriminatory*. The objective of such laws is to tax out-of-state companies at the rate at which they would be taxed in their home states, provided always that the rate is higher than that applicable to domestic companies. For example, a state might tax domestic companies at $1\frac{1}{2}$ per cent and out-of-state companies at $2\frac{1}{2}$ per cent, or at the rate in their home states, *whichever is higher*. Such tax treatment is discouraged by the presence of retaliatory tax provisions in other states. Both retaliatory and discriminatory tax provisions have been upheld as a proper exercise of state police powers.[19]

Taxes other than premium taxes are levied at the state level. Insurance companies pay property taxes, unemployment taxes, license fees,

---

[19] *Prudential Insurance Co. v. Benjamin*, 328 U.S. 408 (1946).

and other levies generally imposed on business enterprises. A few states extend their income tax to life insurance companies. The amounts of revenue produced under the latter have generally been relatively small, but the amount of paper work involved has been a serious burden on the companies. The laws of most states specify that the premium tax shall be in lieu of all other taxes (except for taxes on real and tangible personal property and license fees).

State impositions are not all in the form of taxes. Costs of examination of company finances, records, and practices conducted at regular intervals by state supervisory officials are usually a direct charge against the company examined. Fees are also charged for the issue of agents' licenses and for other services.

Local Taxes

In most jurisdictions, the states have preempted the taxation of life insurance companies as a source of revenue and have not permitted their subdivisions to impose taxes on the companies. In those jurisdictions which do permit local taxation, the local subdivisions have frequently availed themselves of the privilege. In a few cities the tax burden is very heavy. Wherever local taxes are imposed, the maintenance of special records and the filing of documents constitute a serious administrative burden, usually disproportionate to the amount of revenue involved.

CHAPTER XLVI

Tax Treatment of Life Insurance*

BECAUSE of our federal system, there are both federal and state laws affecting this subject, and there are variations among the state laws. Most of them, however, generally follow the federal pattern. There is even an apparently increasing tendency for states to incorporate the federal income tax law by reference, using federal taxable income as the base for the state tax, frequently, however, with some modifications or adjustments. References in this paper to the state laws will be confined to outlining their general nature and indicating those areas where they tend to deviate from the federal rules.

There are three kinds of taxes that are of chief interest to policyholders, in the sense that transactions under insurance and annuity contracts may produce liability for such taxes on the part of the insured, beneficiary, or annuitant. These are the income tax, the estate tax, and the gift tax.

The federal income tax is a net income tax; that is to say, it is based on statutory gross income less the deductions and personal exemptions authorized by statute. Gross income is very broadly defined and includes all items of income from whatever source derived, except such

---

* This chapter is based upon a paper by Stuart A. McCarthy, Vice-President and Associate General Solicitor, The Equitable Life Assurance Society of the United States, which appeared in *Verzekerings-Archief,* Vol. 38, Pt. 4, (Martinus Nijhoff-'S-Gravenhage, Oct., 1961). Appreciation is expressed to the Council of Editors of the *Verzekerings-Archief* for their kind permission to reproduce the material here.

as are specifically excluded. Consequently, includability in gross income signifies that the item in question constitutes income rather than a return of principal under legal and accounting principles and that there is no specific statutory exclusion applicable to it. In some instances, e.g., income from annuities, where opinions may differ as to what is income, Congress has written into the law specific definitions of the extent to which receipts shall be deemed to constitute income.

There is no distinction in the rate of tax according to the source or character of income. All net income after deductions and exemptions is taxed at the same schedule of rates graduated according to amount of net income. The present scale of rates begins at 14 per cent on the first dollar of taxable income and is graduated up to 70 per cent on income which falls into the highest bracket, in the case of individuals. The rate on taxable income of corporations is 22 per cent on the first $25,000 and 48 per cent on the excess.

Capital gains are taxed, but on a basis which is generally more favorable to the taxpayer than in the case of ordinary income.

The federal estate tax is based on the interests in property transmitted at death, rather than on the interests to which the recipient succeeds. It is thus a true estate tax and not an inheritance tax. There is no distinction in the rates by reason of the nature of the property transmitted or the relationship of the recipient to the decedent. Includable in the gross estate is all property in which the decedent possessed an interest at the time of his death, as well as certain other specifically enumerated items such as certain types of lifetime transfers, subject only to the statutory exclusions. The tax is based on the net estate after authorized deductions and an over-all exemption ($60,000 for estates of resident decedents), and is graduated according to the amount of the net estate. The current scale of rates ranges from 3 per cent to 77 per cent.

The gift tax is intended to supplement the estate tax and to prevent evasion of the latter. It is based on net gifts, year by year. The rates are three-fourths of the estate tax rates in the corresponding brackets. It is imposed on the donor and, on a principle similar to that underlying the estate tax, relates to the interest given rather than the interest received. As in the case of the estate tax, the rate is not affected by the character of the property given or the relationship of the donee.

The federal government is practically forbidden by the Constitution to impose any direct taxes on real or personal property. Such taxes are, of course, imposed by the states and municipalities. However, they are not of great significance so far as life insurance and annuities are concerned, since in most instances, even where they reach intangibles, life insurance policies and annuity contracts are exempted, either expressly or by construction.

INCOME TAX LAWS

Treatment of Premiums and Annuity Considerations

Premiums or considerations paid on life insurance or annuity contracts on the life of the taxpayer are regarded as personal, living or family expenses and accordingly are not deductible from gross income in determining taxable income under the federal law.

Moreover, by specific provision of federal law, premiums on a life insurance policy covering the life of an officer, employee or person financially interested in a business carried on by the taxpayer are nondeductible if the taxpayer is directly or indirectly a beneficiary under the policy. This has been construed as forbidding deduction of premiums on partnership life insurance.

It has also been held that premiums on life insurance are nondeductible even though the taking out of the insurance was required by a lender as a condition of making the loan.

The state of New York allows a deduction for premiums on insurance on the life of the taxpayer, not to exceed $150 per annum. This is unusual, however. Other states follow the federal pattern which denies deduction of such premiums.

The federal law permits a limited deduction for medical expenses of the taxpayer, his spouse, or dependent, and authorizes inclusion of premiums on accident and health insurance as a part of medical expenses.

The general rule of nondeductibility of premiums does not apply to an employer's contributions under group insurance or annuity plans. These are discussed below in connection with the employer-employee relationship.

Taxation of Proceeds of Life Insurance

General Rules. Proceeds of life insurance paid by reason of the death of the insured are generally tax-exempt if paid in a single sum. If paid in installments, a portion of each installment representing the interest element may be taxable. This portion is computed by comparing the total of the installments to be paid with the amount that could have been paid in a single sum (usually the face amount of the policy). Where life contingencies are involved, the total installments to be paid are computed on the basis of the mortality table used by the insurer for the particular contract. The surviving spouse of the insured is entitled to exclude from taxable income up to $1,000 per annum of installments which would otherwise be taxable. The amount of life insurance proceeds which may be received in installments tax-free by the surviving spouse, by virtue of this $1,000 annual exclusion, varies according to the terms of the settlement agreement, the mortality and interest assumptions used in the particular contract, and other factors. In a common type of settlement not involving life contingencies it ranges from about $50,000 to about $80,000, depending upon the interest assumptions. This exclusion does not apply to the interest on amounts held by the insurer on deposit at interest. Such interest is fully includible in gross income.

Transfer for Valuable Consideration. Special rules apply where the policy has been the subject of a transfer for a valuable consideration. In the case of such a transfer, the rule is that usually only so much of the proceeds as equals the consideration paid for the transfer plus the premiums thereafter paid by the transferee can be received tax-free. There are a number of exceptions, however, e.g., where the insured is the transferee, where the transfer is to a partner of the insured or to a partnership in which the insured is a member, or to a corporation of which the insured is an officer or stockholder.

Endowment Maturities, Cash Surrender Values, Etc.

Amounts received under life insurance policies other than by reason of the death of the insured include endowment maturity proceeds and cash surrender values. Such amounts are includible in gross income to the extent that, when added to amounts previously received tax-free under the contract, they exceed the aggregate premiums or other consideration paid. The former provision for relief from throwing the taxpayer into an abnormally high income tax bracket through receipt of such an amount in a single year (I.R.C., section 72[e][3]) was repealed by the Revenue Act of 1964. The very complicated and not too helpful general rules on income averaging in sections 1301–1305 may apply in such a situation. If an election is made to receive an amount representing endowment maturity proceeds or cash surrender values in installments, it is taxable as an annuity (see discussion of annuities below).

The taxation of amounts received under life insurance policies under the state income tax laws generally follows the federal rules. The principal exception is that in most states proceeds paid by reason of the death of the insured are fully exempt, whether paid in installments or in a single sum.

Taxation of Annuities

The basis of taxation of amounts received as an annuity under the federal income tax law has been changed several times over the years. The present basis, adopted in 1954, is a modification of the method previously adopted by Canada. It is designed to tax, on a level basis over the whole period of the annuity, the element of the payments which represents interest as distinguished from return of capital. This is done by dividing the "investment in the contract" by the "expected return." The investment in the contract is basically the consideration paid for the contract, reduced by any dividends received under a participating contract before annuity payments commence. The expected return is the aggregate amount of payments expected to be received under the contract. Where life contingencies are involved, the expected return is computed on the basis of actuarial tables promulgated by the Treasury Department.

The result of dividing the investment in the contract by the expected return is the "exclusion ratio." This is the percentage of each annuity payment to be excluded from gross income, the remainder being includible. The exclusion ratio is determined as of the annuity starting date, and normally remains fixed throughout the period of annuity payments. It may, however, change in the event of modification or exchange of the annuity contract.

It will be observed that the principle is similar to the taxation of life insurance proceeds payable in installments by reason of the death of the insured. However, there are two chief differences. First, the investment in the contract is, as above indicated, the consideration paid for the contract, not its value at the time annuity payments commence. The effect is to subject to taxation in the case of a deferred annuity the interest accumulation on the consideration during the period of deferment. In the case of life insurance proceeds, the amount prorated over the period of installment payments, and designed to be received tax-free, is normally the face amount of the policy which could have been received in a lump sum. Hence, the accumulated interest on the premiums is not taxed.

A second difference is that, whereas the determination of life contingencies in life insurance installment settlements is made on the basis of the tables used by the insurer for the particular contract, in the case of annuities the "expected return" is determined on the basis of uniform tables promulgated by the Treasury Department.

The foregoing treatment applies to all forms of annuities, e.g., life annuities, refund annuities, joint and survivor annuities. Included as annuities for this purpose are provisions for payments for a fixed period not involving life contingencies, such as the payment of the proceeds of a matured endowment policy or a cash surrender value in installments for a ten-year period.

An adjustment is necessary for contracts containing a refund feature. Such a feature is present in refund annuities, where there is a guarantee that the total payments will at least equal the consideration. It is also present in contracts which guarantee that payments will be made for at least a stipulated minimum number of years, for example ten years, and for the continuing lifetime of the annuitant thereafter. Where the contract contains a refund feature, the value of that feature must be subtracted from the investment in the contract by use of a table promulgated by the Treasury Department. The effect of the adjustment is to increase the taxable element of the payments to the annuitant over what it would have been without the adjustment, but by way of compensation, any payments of a refund nature to his beneficiary after his death are excluded from her gross income.

The general rules apply to employee annuities, i.e., those which were purchased in part by the employer of the annuitant, subject to some important modifications. First, the investment in the contract is taken as only the employee's contributions. Employer contributions which have been treated as current compensation to the employee, or which would have been tax-exempt if they had been paid to him in cash (except employer contributions made after 1962 which would be exempt as compensation for services performed abroad) are included as employee contributions for this purpose. Second, if the employee's contributions will be returned in annuity payments within three years after the date the first annuity payment is received, the general rule does not apply and instead all annuity payments will be excluded from his gross income until they equal in the aggregate the employee's contributions, and thereafter the whole of each payment as received is includible.

Only a few of the states have adopted the current federal basis of taxing annuities in the sense of writing it into their own income tax laws. However, in those states which have incorporated the federal law by reference, by using the federal taxable income as the base for the state tax, there is an implicit adoption of the federal rule. Among the states which have not adopted the current federal rule either expressly or by implication from the use of the federal tax base, two methods of taxing annuity income are most commonly used. One is the "3 per cent rule," which was in use by the federal government for some years prior to 1954. Under this rule, that part of each year's annuity payments equal to 3 per cent of the consideration for the contract is included in gross income and the remainder is excluded until the amounts so excluded equal the consideration. Thereafter the full amount of the payments is includible. The other is the "excess over cost" rule, which was also used by the federal government at an earlier period. Under that rule, no part of the annuity payments is includible in gross income until the aggregate payments equal the consideration for the contract, and thereafter the full amount of the payments is includible.

Dividends on Participating Contracts

Dividends on participating life insurance policies and deferred annuity contracts are not includible in gross income until, together with any other amounts received under the contract tax-free, they exceed the premium or consideration paid. In practical effect, therefore, they usually go to reduce the premium cost of the contract for purposes of determining gain upon a subsequent transaction such as the maturity of an endowment policy or the surrender of a policy for its cash value. Similarly, in the case of a deferred annuity they reduce the investment in the contract for purposes of the computation of the exclusion ratio at the annuity starting date.

Dividends received on a participating annuity contract on or after the annuity starting date are includible in gross income, as are excess interest dividends under a supplementary contract providing for the payment in installments of the proceeds of a life insurance or endowment policy.

ESTATE TAX LAWS

Life Insurance Proceeds

The payment of the proceeds of life insurance upon the death of the insured may be the subject of a federal estate tax. The proceeds are includible in the decedent's estate if they are payable to his executor or administrator. They are likewise includible if they are payable to any other beneficiary provided the insured had any "incidents of ownership" in the policy at the time of his death. The phrase "incidents of ownership" is not exhaustively defined in either the Internal Revenue Code or the regulations thereunder, but it includes the right to designate or change the beneficiary, the right to surrender the policy for its cash value, and the right to assign or borrow on the policy. Under the current rule, it also includes a "reversionary interest" of a value of more than 5 per cent of the value of the policy immediately before the death of the insured. A "reversionary interest" is a possibility that the policy or its proceeds may revert or return to the insured or his estate or become subject to a power of disposition by him. However, if another person could have terminated the insurance, for example by surrendering it for its cash value, during the insured's lifetime and without his consent, the insured is deemed not to have had a reversionary interest of sufficient value to constitute an incident of ownership. Thus, if a policy of insurance on the life of a decedent was taken out and owned by his wife, who could have surrendered it, borrowed on it or assigned it during his lifetime without his consent, the proceeds would not be includible in his estate even though he might, through surviving her, have succeeded to the ownership of the policy as her heir or legatee.

Payment of premiums by the insured is not significant for this purpose under the present rule. The current rule was adopted in 1954, applicable to the estates of persons dying after August 16, 1954. The law was formerly that proceeds payable to a named beneficiary were includible in the estate in the proportion that the premiums were paid directly or indirectly by the insured, even if he had no incidents of ownership in the policy. Under that rule, it was ineffectual for estate tax purposes to transfer ownership to another than the insured if the insured remained the source of premium payments on the policy.

Under the "incidents of ownership" test, the proceeds of a policy of insurance on the life of a decedent are either includible in his gross estate in full or not at all. There is no evaluation of the respective incidents of ownership. For example, if the decedent could have surrendered the policy for its cash value, it matters not that he may not have had the right to change the beneficiary or the right to assign the policy. Moreover, an incident of ownership held jointly with another person is enough to make the policy includible in the estate.

The federal estate tax is payable by the executor or other personal representative out of the decedent's estate. This is consonant with the nature of the tax as a true estate tax rather than an inheritance tax. Thus, the tax with respect to life insurance proceeds payable to beneficiaries other than the executor is payable in the first instance by the executor out of the general estate rather than by the beneficiaries who receive the proceeds. However, the federal law contains a special provision applicable to life insurance which permits the executor to recover from these beneficiaries the proportionate part of the tax paid which is attributable to the proceeds received by each of them. With respect to most kinds of property, there is no comparable provision of federal law, the ultimate impact or apportionment of the federal tax among the beneficiaries of the estate being left to determination by state law. This is true, for example, of any estate tax paid with respect to annuities.

Transfer of Ownership of Policy

There is no specific provision in the federal statute imposing estate tax on the succession by legacy or inheritance to the ownership of a policy on the life of a living insured. However, the value of a policy so transferred is includible in the estate of the decedent owner, as property in which the decedent had an interest. An example is a policy on the life of a husband owned by his wife who predeceases him. The value of such a policy would be includible in her estate. The valuation of such a policy depends upon whether or not it is still in a premium-paying status. If it is, the value is the interpolated reserve at the date of death of the decedent with allowance for premiums paid beyond that date. The value of a paid-up or single premium policy is determined by the cost of a comparable contract issued by the same insurer at the time of such death.

Marital Deduction

A feature of great practical significance in the present federal estate tax laws is the marital deduction. Under this provision up to 50 per cent of the value of the decedent's estate after claims and expenses, but before taxes, can be deducted to determine the taxable estate if such portion passes from the decedent to his spouse. The concept of "passing" includes not only the bequest, devise, or inheritance of property but also its transfer *inter vivos* or by exercise of a power of appointment and certain other transfers, provided, in any case, that the property is includible in the decedent's gross estate for federal estate tax purposes.

Intended to equalize the advantage formerly held by residents of the community property states over residents of the common law states, the marital deduction has become a major consideration in estate planning. Life insurance proceeds includible in the estate, if left outright to the surviving spouse, qualify for this deduction. Moreover, it is possible to qualify proceeds left to the spouse under an income settlement with contingent beneficiaries provided the spouse is given power of appointment over any amounts which may become payable after her death. Similar rules apply to amounts payable under annuity contracts.

Annuity Contracts

The federal estate tax statutes now contain provisions relating specifically to annuities. Prior to the adoption of the 1954 Code, although it was recognized that the provisions governing life insurance proceeds did not apply to annuities, their precise status under the federal estate tax laws was in doubt. Section 2039 of the Code is broadly worded, and requires inclusion in the decedent's estate of the value of an annuity or other payment receivable by any beneficiary by reason of surviving the decedent, under any form of contract entered into after March 3, 1931 (other than insurance on the life of the decedent) if the decedent was receiving or had the right to receive an annuity under such contract. This language encompasses all of the common forms of annuities, other than straight life annuities, such as refund annuities, joint and survivor annuities, annuities certain, and death benefits, whether payable as an annuity or otherwise, under employee retirement plans.

The valuation of the annuity to the survivor under a contract issued by a life insurance company engaged in the business of annuities is determined by the cost of a comparable contract as of the date of the decedent's death. Thus, in the common case of a joint and survivor annuity on the life of a husband and wife, the valuation of the annuity for life to the surviving wife upon the death of the husband would be determined by reference to the consideration charged by the issuer for a single life annuity to a woman of her age at that time.

If the decedent was not the sole purchaser of the annuity, only such part of the value of the annuity to the survivor as is proportionate to the decedent's contribution to the purchase price is includible in his estate. Thus, in the foregoing example of a joint and survivor annuity, if husband and wife each paid half of the original cost of the annuity contract, only half of the value of her continuing single life annuity would be includible in his estate.

Section 2039(c) provides an exemption from the estate tax for certain employee annuities. This is treated below in connection with the general discussion of employee annuities.

GIFT TAX LAWS

Various transactions involving life insurance policies or annuity contracts may result in a taxable gift. The transfer of ownership of the contract without consideration is an obvious example. The irrevocable designation of a donee beneficiary also constitutes a completed gift. Moreover, each payment of premiums on a policy which has been gratuitously transferred may constitute a further gift.

There is an annual exclusion from taxable gifts of the first $3,000 of gifts to any one person, provided the interest given is a "present interest" as distinguished from a "future interest." The term "present interest" in this context means that there must be a present right to possess and enjoy the property. The unqualified ownership of a life insurance policy is a present interest, even though the policy may not yet have developed a currently obtainable cash surrender value. The 1954 Code appears to have removed any doubt that an unqualified gift of a life insurance policy to a minor is a gift of a present interest notwithstanding that, because of his minority, he may not be able presently to reduce the policy to cash.

There is also an over-all $30,000 exclusion from taxable gifts. This is in addition to the $3,000 annual exclusion, but unlike that exclusion it does not relate to gifts to any one person. It is allowed against the aggregate gifts to all persons made at any time in the lifetime of the donor, whether they be gifts of present interests or of future interests.

In the case of gifts between spouses, the foregoing exclusions ($3,-000 annually and $30,000 lifetime) may in effect be doubled by virtue of the gift tax marital deduction. Another provision permits the spouses to agree that gifts to third parties by either spouse shall be treated as if made to the extent of one half by each spouse. This has the effect that, where only one spouse makes gifts, he may take advantage of the exclusions otherwise available to both spouses with respect to gifts to third parties, if both spouses so agree.

STATE LAWS

Almost all of the states have estate or inheritance tax laws, and a few have gift tax laws. On the whole, however, they are more favorable than the federal law in their treatment of life insurance proceeds. Life insurance payable to a beneficiary other than the insured's estate is generally not taxed under state inheritance tax laws. Where such proceeds are reached by the state laws, there is usually a specific exemption allowable for life insurance proceeds payable to a designated beneficiary, frequently in a substantial amount. However, these exemptions are not available for annuity contracts.

The burden of state inheritance or estate taxes is not entirely superimposed upon that of the federal estate tax, since there is a credit allowed against the federal tax on account of state death taxes paid. Originally permitted in an amount up to 80 per cent of the federal tax, the credit has been limited by subsequent legislation so that it is now a relatively small percentage of the federal tax. For example, on a taxable estate of $100,000 the federal tax is $20,700, against which the maximum credit for state death taxes is $560.

EMPLOYER-EMPLOYEE PLANS

The number and variety of insurance and annuity plans based on the employer-employee relationship is an outstanding feature of the current American economic scene. The development of such plans in the United States, especially within the past forty years and at an accelerated rate within the past twenty years, is probably unparalleled in any other country. Social insurance in the sense of programs or coverage required by law, such as workmen's compensation insurance and the federal Social Security system, is outside of the scope of this chapter. We shall discuss the more common types of benefits provided by employers voluntarily or as a result of collective bargaining with labor unions, especially those types of benefits in which the facilities of life insurance companies are utilized. As will be seen, the tax laws and regulations contain numerous provisions with specific reference to such plans, many of them designed to encourage their establishment and maintenance.

Group Life and Accident and Health Insurance

There are many forms of group insurance, but the oldest and still the most common is that provided under a policy issued to an employer or to the trustee of a trust established by an employer, or an employer and a union, insuring all or a class or classes of his employees for the benefit of a beneficiary other than the employer. The permissible forms of group insurance are governed by state law. The federal tax laws and regulations, however, recognize the institution of group insurance and legislate specifically for it in some respects.

Income Taxation. Premiums paid by an employer for group insurance covering his employees are deductible from his gross income under the federal income tax law. There is no maximum limit on the amount of the deduction, other than the general requirement of reasonableness. However, if the employees contribute to the cost of the insurance, their contributions are governed by the same rules as apply to premiums paid on individual insurance; this means that there is no deduction for such employee contributions to group life insurance.

Section 79, I.R.C., added by the Revenue Act of 1964, modifies the longstanding rule that employees are not required to include the employer's premiums for group term life insurance in their gross incomes for federal income tax purposes. Under this section the employee must include in income the excess of the cost of the insurance on his life over the sum of the cost of $50,000 of such insurance and the amount (if any) paid by the employee toward the purchase of such insurance. The cost of group term life insurance is to be determined for this purpose on the basis of uniform premiums (by five-year age brackets but with ages over 63 taken as age 63) prescribed by the Treasury Department. Exceptions are provided in cases where an employee, who would otherwise be required to include an item of income under this section, is disabled or retired or has designated a charity or the employer as his beneficiary. In the unusual case of purchase of group term insurance under a "qualified" plan (see below, Employee Pension and Annuity Plans), section 79 does not apply, but includibility of the employer's contributions in the employees' incomes is governed by the special rule relating to purchase of life insurance under such plans.

Premiums paid by an employer for group accident and health insurance covering his employees are still excluded from the employees' gross incomes.

The proceeds of group life insurance paid by reason of the death of the employee are governed by the same rules as apply to the proceeds of individual life insurance so paid. Since group life insurance usually does not provide for any nonforfeiture values or for maturity as an endowment, being typically yearly-renewable term insurance, there is no occasion for application of the rules with respect to cash surrender values or endowment maturities.

The proceeds of group accident and health insurance, if paid by reason of the employee's death, are treated as proceeds of life insurance. If paid by reason of dismemberment, they are income tax-exempt. Medical expense reimbursements are similarly exempt. Benefits, attributable to the employer's contributions, for loss of wages during a period of absence from work because of injuries or sickness are accorded only a limited exemption. The excess of the amount received as such benefits over a weekly rate of $100 is includible in gross income. Moreover, even with respect to amounts up to the $100 weekly rate, the exemption does not extend to any benefits payable for the first thirty calendar days of a period of absence, if they are at a rate which exceeds 75 per cent of the regular weekly rate of wages of the employee. If benefits are paid for the first thirty calendar days at a rate which does not exceed 75 per cent of the employee's regular weekly rate of wages, such benefits may be exempt up to a weekly rate of $75, but benefits paid for the first seven calendar days of the period of absence are not exempt unless the employee is hospitalized on account of injuries or sickness for at least one day during the period of absence. But these limitations do not affect the portion of the proceeds, if any, that is attributable to the employee's own contributions to the cost of the insurance. Such portion is considered as tantamount to the proceeds of personal accident and health insurance and accordingly is fully tax-exempt.

Estate and Gift Taxation. Group life insurance stands on the same footing as individual life insurance in respect of the federal estate tax law. Thus, if the employee has the right to designate and change the beneficiary, as he usually does, this would constitute an incident of ownership and so make the proceeds includible in his gross estate. Like individual life insurance, group insurance proceeds may be qualified for the marital deduction.

Because of its nature as term insurance, and certain other provisions usually found in group policies, group insurance does not lend itself to transactions which could be subject to gift tax. However, if in some unusual situation such a transaction should occur, no doubt the same rules would govern as apply to gifts of individual policies.

State Laws. Where states have adopted the federal tax base by reference in their own income tax laws the effect is automatically to conform the state law to the federal, including subsequent amendments. Thus, for example, in those states the subjection to federal income tax of some employer contributions to the cost of group term life insurance for employees has resulted in the includibility in the employees' gross income of the same contributions for purposes of the state income tax. Among the larger number of states which have not adopted the federal base but retain their own definitions of taxable income, only a few have followed the federal lead in that respect. Also, many of the states do not limit the exemption of accident and health benefits for loss of wages as the federal law does. In other respects, what has been said above as to the treatment of group insurance under the federal tax laws holds good for the state laws with very few exceptions.

Employee Pension and Annuity Plans

Although pension plans, sometimes on an informal or unfunded basis, are of long standing, both for governmental employees and in at least some sectors of private industry, the great popularity of funded contractual pension or annuity plans dates from 1942, when the Internal Revenue Code was amended to provide favorable income tax treatment for "qualified" plans. A qualified plan is one that meets certain requirements now contained in section 401 of the Internal Revenue Code. The essence of these requirements is that the plan must not discriminate either in its coverage or in its benefits or contributions in favor of employees who are shareholders, officers, supervisors, or highly compensated, and that contributions under the plan must be irrevocably set aside for the benefit of the participants and their beneficiaries.

There are two chief means of funding a qualified pension or annuity plan. One is through a group annuity contract issued by a life insurance company to the employer. The other is through the establishment of a pension trust, usually with a corporate trustee. A kind of hybrid is the insured pension trust, used mostly by smaller organizations, wherein the pension trustee provides the benefits of the plan through the purchase of life insurance company contracts.

The federal tax laws are designed, generally, to equate the treatment of the employee and his beneficiary under all of these methods of funding.

Income Taxation. The employer's contributions under a qualified pension or annuity plan are deductible from gross income for federal income tax purposes. As in the case of group insurance, there is no specific limitation on the amount deductible. However, the employer must support his claim for deduction by information showing that the method of computing the costs of the plan is in accordance with accepted actuarial principles. Where life insurance company contracts are used to provide the benefits, the premiums charged by the company constitute the cost of the plan.

Not all of the amount contributed to the plan by the employer may be deductible in the taxable year when contributed. The current cost, that is, the cost of the benefits attributable to the current year, is currently deductible, but the deduction of the cost of benefits for past service or other supplementary benefits must be spread over a period of years. Under the method generally used in connection with group annuity contracts, this period must be not less than ten years. Under an alternative method, more commonly used by pension trusts, it is the remaining period of the employee's service to normal retirement date.

If the plan is contributory, the employee's contributions are not deductible. This parallels the rule for group life insurance.

The general rule is that the employer's contributions under a qualified plan are not taxable to the employee. There is one exception, which applies where a pension trust uses life insurance policies to provide the benefits of the plan. In that situation, the excess of the face amount of the policy over its cash surrender value is not regarded as a part of the benefits of a qualified plan, and the employer's contribution for the cost of term insurance in the amount of the excess is currently includible in the employee's gross income.

The benefits of a qualified annuity plan may include, besides the basic retirement benefit, incidental benefits such as life insurance. The taxation of the retirement benefit is, as indicated above, in accordance with the general rules for the income taxation of annuities, with two important exceptions. First, only the employee's contributions are considered in determining the investment in the contract; and, second, if his contributions will be returned in annuity payments within three years after commencement thereof, the special rule applies under which the annuity payments are nontaxable until his contributions have been recovered and thereafter are taxable in full.

The taxation of life insurance proceeds paid by a qualified pension trust is affected by the special rule mentioned above with respect to contributions for the cost of life insurance protection. The excess of the face amount over the cash surrender value of the policy is treated like the proceeds of individually purchased life insurance policies. The remainder, i.e., the portion of the proceeds equal to the cash surrender value, is not regarded as life insurance proceeds but rather as an uninsured death benefit. Hence, it is not entitled to the exemption provided in section 101(a) of the Internal Revenue Code, if it is paid in a single sum, nor is it governed by the proration method in section 101(d) if it is paid in installments. However, it may enjoy the exemption, to the extent of $5,000, which is accorded by section 101(b) to uninsured employee death benefits of any character.

Another incidental benefit of a qualified annuity plan may be a "vesting" right upon termination of the employment of a participant. Thus, it is frequently provided that upon termination of employment after a specified period of employment or of membership in the plan, the employee retains his right to part or all of the annuity, commencing at his retirement date, provided by the employer's contributions under the plan. Such a vesting does not entail any income tax effects at the time of vesting, even if the employee receives title to a deferred annuity contract at that time. However, if he receives a life insurance policy containing a cash surrender value, he may be subject to income tax by reason of such receipt.

Estate and Gift Taxation. As above indicated, the value of the annuity to the survivor of an annuitant under an annuity contract is generally includible in the gross estate of the decedent annuitant. However, section 2039(c) of the Internal Revenue Code contains an exemption in the case of an annuity under a qualified employees' annuity plan. This provision excludes from the gross estate the value of such an annuity or other payment to other than the executor of the decedent, except the part, if any, of such value proportionate to the decedent's contributions under the plan. Thus, under a noncontributory qualified plan the entire value of the annuity would be exempt. The phrase "or other payment" is construed as including a death benefit under a qualified plan, even if payable in a single sum and even though it may constitute the proceeds of life insurance.

A like exemption exists in the gift tax provisions.

Nonqualified Plans. It is, of course, possible to have a nonqualified annuity or pension plan, but the tax consequences and certain other legal consequences make a nonqualified plan unattractive for ordinary business organizations. The employer's contributions to such a plan are not income-tax deductible unless the employee's rights are nonforfeitable (i.e., vested) at the time the contribution is made, and if they are then nonforfeitable, the contribution is includable in the employee's gross income. Nonqualified plans do not enjoy the estate and gift tax exemptions discussed above which are available to qualified plans. A pension trust created in connection with a nonqualified plan is not itself tax-exempt, and therefore its income would be subject to income tax. As a result of these and other legal disadvantages, few employers can afford to maintain nonqualified plans. A possible exception may be found in the case of certain tax-exempt institutions (educational, religious, charitable, scientific, etc., organizations) for whom special treatment is provided.

State Laws. Most of the states have adopted the federal classification of qualified plans and attach the same kinds of tax effects as the federal laws.

CONCLUSION

The foregoing necessarily gives only the highlights of the taxation of life insurance in the United States. It will be evident to the reader that the subject is a very complicated one, involving consideration of the effects of various kinds of taxes imposed by a number of different taxing authorities. It may be stated, as an overall conclusion, that life insurance bears its full share of the burden of taxation, perhaps a larger share than is warranted in view of the beneficent purposes and effects of the institution.

Since taxation in the United States is entirely a matter of statute law, changes in the rules of taxation affecting life insurance may be made at any session of the federal or state legislatures. The foregoing description reflects the situation as of 1966. It is not anticipated that any radical changes will be made in the immediate future.

APPENDIXES

APPENDIXES

Appendix A. Application for Life Insurance Policy

PART I (Doc. 1, Revised Apr. 1963)	APPLICATION TO	For Home Office Use
A 620394	THE [ ] **LIFE INSURANCE COMPANY**	No. ....
	USE FOR INSURABLE AGE 15 OR OVER, EXCEPT FOR ANNUITY OR EMPLOYEE TRUST	To .... Inc.

1A. NAME of proposed insured (the Insured). *Print*
First **John**   Middle **James**   Last **Doe**   Sex: ☒ Male ☐ Female

1B. APPLICANT, if other than Insured. Full name: *Print* **Jane**   **Mary**   **Doe**   Relationship to Insured **Wife**
If Business Organization, "X" type: ☐ Corporation ☐ Partnership ☐ Other Type of Business (Enter)

2. RESIDENCE OF INSURED: Street & No. or R.F.D. *Print* **99 River Street**
City **Harrisburg**   County **Dauphin**
State **Pennsylvania**   Zip Code **17102**

QUESTIONS 4 THROUGH 16 APPLY TO AND MUST BE ANSWERED BY INSURED.

4. How long have you resided in the United States of America? **Life**

5. Do you contemplate leaving the mainland of United States of America for travel or residence? If "Yes," explain in No. 15.   **No**

6A. PRESENT OCCUPATION: Job title & duties If more than one, state all. **Salesman**
Industry **Foods**

How long so employed? If less than 2 years, state previous occupations past 5 years in No. 15.

B. Do you contemplate changing your occupation? If "Yes," explain in No. 15.   **No**

7A. Have you made any aerial flights in the past 3 years **other than** as a fare-paying passenger of a scheduled airline?   **No**

B. Do you contemplate any such flights, or flight training?   **No**

C. Have you ever piloted an aircraft, received flight training, or held a pilot's license, certificate or student's permit? If A, B or C "Yes," submit Aviation Blank.   **No**

8A. Are you a member of, **or do you contemplate joining,** any branch of the Armed Forces, the R.O.T.C., the National Guard or any other component of the Armed Forces Reserve either on an active or inactive status? If "Yes," submit Military Blank.   **No**

B. Are you a member of, **or do you contemplate joining,** the air component of any of the above (or auxiliary, such as the Civil Air Patrol)? If "Yes," submit Aviation Blank.   **No**

9. Have you ever been declined or postponed for life or accidental death insurance or offered a policy with rated-up premium or on plan other than applied for? If "Yes," explain in No. 15.   **No**

10. Is any other insurance on your life pending or contemplated? If "Yes," enter:

COMPANY	LIFE INSURANCE	ACCIDENTAL DEATH (Double Indemnity)	
	$	$	**No**

11. Will the insurance applied for replace insurance on your life in this Company or elsewhere? If "Yes," submit required papers.   **No**

12. When was your last previous examination or application for life or accidental death insurance? Mo. **Dec.** Year **1956** Company **Atlas Life**

13. What is total amount of life and accidental death insurance in force on your life in **other** life and casualty companies? If none, state "None."

LIFE INSURANCE	ACCIDENTAL DEATH (Including Double Indemnity)
$ **10,000**	$ **10,000**

14. Has application ever been made to this Company for insurance or an annuity on your life?

15. Use only for explanations requested above — state question number.

---

3. PREMIUM NOTICES. (Notices will be sent to Owner unless otherwise directed.)
Full Name, Print
Street & No. or R.F.D.
City, State & Zip Code

16A. DATE OF BIRTH: Mo. **January** Day **1** Yr. **1932**

B. Place of birth: **Harrisburg, Pennsylvania**
City   State or Country

C. If foreign born, are you a citizen of the United States of America?

17. AMOUNT AND PLAN APPLIED FOR:
$ **10,000**   **Whole Life**
Amount. Enter in one sum.   Plan

18. Are the following ADDITIONAL BENEFITS desired, subject to Company rules?
A. ACCIDENTAL DEATH.
If "Yes" enter amount below only if other than amount entered in No. 17. $ **Yes**
B. WAIVER OF PREMIUM ON DISABILITY OF THE INSURED.   **Yes**
C. RIGHT TO PURCHASE ADDITIONAL POLICIES.   **No**

19. PREMIUMS PAYABLE: ☒ Annually. ☐ Semi-Annually. ☐ Quarterly.

20. Shall AUTOMATIC PREMIUM LOAN provision become operative according to its terms, if a part of the policy applied for?   **Yes**

21. ANNUAL DIVIDENDS, until otherwise directed, shall be:
☒ A. Applied toward reduction of current premium.
☐ B. Applied to purchase paid-up additions. (If Term plan, B will apply only after conversion and C before.)
☐ C. Left to accumulate at interest. If this election is made enter Owner's Taxpayer Account No.

22A. DIRECT BENEFICIARY: (Print full name).
Jane Mary Doe
Relationship to Insured **Wife**

B. CONTINGENT BENEFICIARY: (Print full name).

Relationship to Insured
(One of the following may be selected by marking with "X")
☐ (1) and any (other) children of the Insured.
☐ (2) and any (other) children of the Insured, except that any amount (or the withdrawal value thereof if a settlement option is in effect) a deceased child of the Insured would have received, if living, shall be payable when due in one sum in equal shares to his or her then living children.
Under (1) and (2) "children" includes child and any legally adopted child, and decisions made by the Company upon evidence satisfactory to it shall be conclusive and fully protect it.

23. Has the premium for the policy applied for been paid to the agent in exchange for the Conditional Receipt with the same number as this application and if so, do you accept and agree to the terms and conditions thereof?   **Yes**

24. **OWNER.** The Owner of any policy issued on this application shall be the APPLICANT unless "A" or "B" is elected.

☐ A. INSURED   ☐ B. INSURED or APPLICANT: Other than { Full Name, Print.   Street & No. or R.F.D. }   Relationship to Insured   Birthdate if under 21   City, State & Zip Code

The Insured consents to this application and declares that all of his answers and statements are complete and true to the best of his knowledge and belief.

It is agreed that: (1) These answers and statements are offered as a consideration for any policy issued on this application. (2) If the premium is not paid when the application is signed, no policy shall be in effect. If, however, a policy is delivered and the premium paid during the Insured's lifetime, the coverage shall be in effect if at the time of such delivery and payment the answers and statements in the application are then true. (3) No agent of the Company is authorized to make or alter contracts, to extend the time for payment of premiums, or to waive any of the Company's rights or requirements.

Executed by Applicant at **Harrisburg, Dauphin, Pennsylvania** on **January** **1** 19 **67**
City   County   State   Month   Day   Year

(SIGNED)   **John James Doe**   (SIGNED)   **Jane Mary Doe**
Signature in full of INSURED if other than the Applicant   Signature of APPLICANT in full

Doc. 1, Part I — (0463)   **PART I**

Appendix A. Application for Life Insurance Policy (Continued)

| APPLICATION PART IIA (Revised Apr. 1963) | | THE [_____] | DECLARATIONS TO MEDICAL EXAMINER | | LIFE INSURANCE COMPANY | | GENERAL AGENCY: CHECK HERE IF DOCUMENT COVERS APPLICANT UNDER PAYOR BENEFIT. ☐ |

1A. INSURED Full name, print. John James Doe   **1B. SEX:** Male ☒ Female ☐

2A. PRESENT OCCUPATION Salesman

2B. MARITAL STATUS: Single ☐ Married ☒ Widowed ☐ Divorced ☐

2C. AMOUNT APPLIED FOR: $ 10,000

3A. FAMILY HISTORY	AGE IF LIVING	STATE OF HEALTH If not "Good" state reason	AGE AT DEATH	CAUSE OF DEATH If Tuberculosis, state date		AGE IF LIVING	STATE OF HEALTH If not "Good" state reason	AGE AT DEATH	CAUSE OF DEATH If Tuberculosis, state date
Father	60	Good			Mother	60	Good		
Brothers: No. Living 1	30	Good			Sisters: No. Living 1	28	Good		
No. Dead 0					No. Dead 0				

	Yes or No	
3. B. Has any member of your immediate family ever had a stroke or cancer, insanity, diabetes, heart or kidney disease?	No	If any of questions 3B through 9B is answered "Yes," enter question number below and state particulars.
C. Have you ever been closely associated with anyone suffering from tuberculosis?	No	
4. A. Have you ever used alcoholic beverages to excess?	No	
B. Have you ever sought help or taken treatment for alcoholic habit?	No	
5. Have you ever used marihuana, morphine, cocaine, opium or any derivatives thereof?	No	
6. HAVE YOU EVER HAD OR BEEN TREATED FOR: A. Rheumatism, rheumatic fever, gout, diabetes, goiter or cancer?	No	
B. Dizzy or fainting spells, epilepsy, paralysis, nervous breakdown, nervous or mental trouble?	No	
C. Raising of blood, tuberculosis, asthma, bronchitis, pleurisy, pneumonia, or lung abscess?	No	
D. High blood pressure, pain or discomfort in chest, a murmur or other disorder of the heart, blood, or blood vessels?	No	
E. Disorder of stomach, liver, gallbladder, intestines, or rectum; ulcer, appendicitis, indigestion, colic or dysentery?	No	
F. Syphilis, renal colic or stone, or any disorder of kidneys, bladder, or reproductive organs?	No	
G. Sugar, albumin, or any other abnormality of urine?	No	
H. Disorder of eyes, ears, nose, throat, or mouth?	No	
I. Disease of skin, glands, bones, joints, spine; or tumors?	No	
J. Any other illnesses, diseases, accidents or any operations?	No	
7. Have you ever applied for disability compensation or pension?	No	
8. A. Have you served with the Armed Forces?	No	
B. Were you rejected or discharged for a physical or medical reason? If B "Yes," state date and reason.	No	
9. A. Have you ever had an Electrocardiogram?	No	
B. Have you ever had an X-ray? If A or B "Yes," state type, by whom made, reason, date and results covering each occasion.	No	
10. Are you now in good health? If "No," state particulars.	Yes	
11. Have you been to or in a clinic, hospital, or sanatorium for observation, operation, or treatment in the last ten years?	No	If "Yes," state below ALL names and particulars covering EACH occasion.
12. Has any physician, practitioner, or healer examined, advised, or treated you within the last five years (this includes your usual medical attendant)?	No	If "Yes," state below ALL names and particulars covering EACH occasion.

NAME AND ADDRESS	REASON	DATE AND DURATION	RESULT
....	....	....	....
....	....	....	....
....	....	....	....

13. Who is your usual medical attendant? Dr. **Have None**   Address

A FEMALE MUST ANSWER THE FOLLOWING:	Yes or No	
14. Have you ever had any menstrual disturbance or complicated or abnormal pregnancy?		If question 14 "Yes," enter dates and particulars.
15. Are you now pregnant? If "Yes," state anticipated delivery date: 19		

I declare that my answers and statements are correctly recorded, complete, and true to the best of my knowledge and belief. In consideration of the issuance of any policy under this application, on behalf of myself or any person claiming any interest in any such policy, unless prohibited by law, I expressly consent to and authorize any physician, practitioner, healer, clinic, hospital or sanatorium at any time to disclose, reveal, or testify as to any facts relating to my present insurability heretofore or hereafter acquired in a professional relationship with me. READ THE ABOVE PARAGRAPH CAREFULLY BEFORE SIGNING.

Signed in my presence: **(SIGNED) John P. Roe** _____ M. D.
Medical Examiner

(SIGNED) John James Doe
Signature of INSURED in full

Date **January 1** 19 **67**
Doc. 1, Parts IIA & III — (0463)

My date of birth is: Mo. **January** Day **1** Yr. **32**
(To be entered by INSURED)   PART IIA

Appendix B. Specimen Whole Life Insurance Contract
The _____ Life Insurance Company

───────POLICY SPECIFICATIONS───────

Date of Issue **JANUARY 1, 1967**

Insured	**JOHN J DOE**	**35 MALE**	Age and Sex
Policy Date	**JANUARY 1, 1967**	**0 000 001**	Policy Number
Plan	**WHOLE LIFE**	**$10,000**	Face Amount

Direct Beneficiary **JANE M   DOE, WIFE OF THE INSURED**

Owner **JOHN J   DOE, THE INSURED**

PREMIUM SCHEDULE

A premium is payable on the policy date and every 12 policy months thereafter during the lifetime of the Insured as provided below:

PLAN AND ADDITIONAL BENEFITS	AMOUNT	PAYABLE FOR
WHOLE LIFE	$ 241.20	LIFE—TO AGE 90
DISABILITY PREMIUM WAIVER	4.90	25 YEARS
ACCIDENTAL DEATH $10,000	8.00	35 YEARS

The first premium is $254.10

TABLE OF GUARANTEED VALUES

End of Policy Year	Cash or Loan Value	Paid-up Insurance	Extended Term Insurance Years	Extended Term Insurance Days	End of Policy Year	Cash or Loan Value	Paid-up Insurance	Extended Term Insurance Years	Extended Term Insurance Days
1	$ 7	$ 10	0	78	13	$ 2,349	$ 4,000	19	84
2	197	410	4	347	14	2,541	4,250	19	98
3	390	800	9	26	15	2,734	4,490	19	91
4	585	1,170	11	333	16	2,928	4,730	19	65
5	783	1,540	13	350	17	3,122	4,960	19	23
6	983	1,900	15	179	18	3,316	5,180	18	334
7	1,184	2,240	16	242	19	3,510	5,400	18	268
8	1,388	2,580	17	207	20	3,704	5,610	18	195
9	1,593	2,910	18	96	@60	4,666	6,550	17	90
10	1,780	3,190	18	239	@62	5,041	6,880	16	227
11	1,968	3,470	18	342	@65	5,589	7,340	15	214
12	2,158	3,740	19	45	@70	6,438	7,980	13	255

Paid-up additions and dividend accumulations increase the cash values; indebtedness decreases them.

HH 1-2a

Appendix B. Specimen Whole Life Insurance Contract (Continued)

OWNERSHIP PROVISIONS

1. THE OWNER

This policy shall belong to the Owner or to the successor or transferee of the Owner. All policy rights and privileges may be exercised by the Owner without the consent of any beneficiary. Such rights and privileges may be exercised only during the lifetime of the Insured except as provided in the Beneficiary and Settlement Provisions.

2. CHANGE OF OWNERSHIP

The Owner may change the ownership of this policy. If ownership is changed, the policy rights and privileges of the Owner may be exercised only if written evidence of change satisfactory to the Company has been filed at its Home Office and this policy endorsed to show the change. The endorsement requirement may be waived by the Company. A change of ownership, of itself, shall not affect the interest of any beneficiary.

PREMIUM and REINSTATEMENT PROVISIONS

1. PREMIUMS

(a) **Payment.** All premiums are payable at the Home Office or to an authorized agent. An official receipt signed by an executive officer of the Company and duly countersigned is available on request.

(b) **Frequency.** Premiums may be paid annually, semi-annually, or quarterly at the published rates for this policy. A change to any such frequency shall be effective upon acceptance by the Company of the premium for the changed frequency. Premiums may be paid on any other frequency approved by the Company.

(c) **Default.** If a premium is not paid on or before its due date, that premium is in default. This policy shall then terminate except as provided in the Grace Period, Extended Term Insurance, and Paid-up Insurance provisions. The date of premium default is the due date of the unpaid premium.

(d) **Grace Period.** A grace period of thirty-one days shall be allowed for payment of a premium in default. This policy shall continue in full force during the grace period. If the

Insured dies during such period, the premium in default shall be paid from the proceeds of this policy.

(e) **Premium Refund at Death.** That portion of any premium paid which applies to a period beyond the policy month in which the Insured died shall be refunded as part of the proceeds of this policy.

2. REINSTATEMENT

This policy may be reinstated within five years after the date of premium default if it has not been surrendered for its cash value. Reinstatement is subject to:

(a) receipt of evidence of insurability of the Insured satisfactory to the Company;

(b) payment of all overdue premiums with interest from the due date of each at the rate of 5% per annum; and

(c) payment or reinstatement of any indebtedness existing on the date of premium default with interest from that date.

HH 1-2

Appendix B. Specimen Whole Life Insurance Contract (Continued)

GENERAL PROVISIONS

1. THE CONTRACT

This policy and the application, a copy of which is attached when issued, constitute the entire contract. All statements in the application shall, in the absence of fraud, be deemed representations and not warranties. No statement shall avoid this policy or be used in defense of a claim under it unless contained in the application.

Only an officer or a registrar of the Company is authorized to alter this policy or to waive any of the Company's rights or requirements.

Policy months, years, and anniversaries shall be computed from the policy date.

All payments by the Company under this policy are payable at its Home Office.

2. INCONTESTABILITY

This policy shall be incontestable after it has been in force during the lifetime of the Insured for two years from the date of issue.

3. SUICIDE

If within two years from the date of issue the Insured shall die by suicide, whether sane or insane, the amount payable by the Company shall be the premiums paid.

4. AGE

If the age of the Insured has been misstated, the amount payable shall be such as the premium paid would have purchased at the correct age.

5. COLLATERAL ASSIGNMENT

The Owner may assign this policy as collateral security. The interest of any beneficiary and any settlement option elected shall be subordinate to any collateral assignment made either before or after the beneficiary designation or settlement option election.

The Company assumes no responsibility for the validity or effect of any collateral assignment of this policy or any interest in it. The Company shall not be charged with notice of any such assignment unless the assignment is in writing and filed at its Home Office.

A collateral assignee is not an Owner and a collateral assignment is not a change of ownership as these terms are used in this policy.

6. CHANGE OF PLAN

The Owner may change this policy to any plan of insurance acceptable to the Company upon payment of such cost, if any, and subject to such conditions as the Company shall determine.

The cost shall not exceed the difference in cash values plus 3½% of such difference for a change made after the first policy year to a plan having a higher cash value and requiring at least five annual premiums after the change.

7. RESERVES AND NET SINGLE PREMIUMS

The Commissioners 1958 Standard Ordinary Mortality Table is used to establish all reserves and net single premiums in this policy except those for the first five years of extended term insurance for which the Commissioners 1958 Extended Term Insurance Table is used. Calculations are based on the net level premium method, continuous functions, and interest at 2¼% per annum. The reserve on this policy shall be exclusive of any additional benefits.

HH 1

Appendix B. Specimen Whole Life Insurance Contract
(Continued)

DIVIDEND PROVISIONS

1. ANNUAL DIVIDENDS

This policy shall share in the divisible surplus of the Company. Its share shall be determined annually by the Company and credited as a dividend. The first dividend shall be payable in equal parts on each premium due date during the second policy year if the premium then due is paid. Each dividend thereafter shall be payable on the policy anniversary.

2. USE OF DIVIDENDS

Dividends credited may be applied under one of the following:

(a) **Paid-up Addition.** Applied to purchase a paid-up addition to this policy. The addition shall share in dividends.

(b) **Dividend Accumulation.** Left to accumulate at interest. Interest shall be credited annually at a rate of at least 2¼% per annum.

(c) **Premium Payment.** Applied toward payment of any premium due within one year if the remainder of such premium is paid in cash or by loan. If such remainder is not so paid, or if this policy is in force as paid-up insurance, the dividend will be applied instead to purchase a paid-up addition.

If none of the foregoing has been elected, dividends shall be paid in cash.

Any paid-up additions and dividend accumulations not required under the Loan, Extended Term Insurance, or Paid-up Insurance Provisions may be surrendered at any time for their then present value which shall not be less than the original cash dividends. Otherwise they are payable as part of the proceeds of this policy.

3. DIVIDEND AT DEATH

A dividend shall be paid as part of the proceeds of this policy for the period from the beginning of the policy year in which the Insured died to the end of the policy month of death.

4. PAID-UP OR ENDOWMENT PRIVILEGE

The Company will endorse this policy as full paid whenever the cash value shall equal the net single premium at the attained age of the Insured. A written request will be required. Any indebtedness shall remain as a lien against this policy.

The Company will pay as an endowment the cash value less any indebtedness whenever the cash value shall equal the face amount. A written request and surrender of this policy will be required.

LOAN PROVISIONS

1. POLICY LOAN

The Owner may obtain a policy loan from the Company upon satisfactory assignment of this policy. The amount of the loan, together with any other indebtedness, shall not exceed the loan value. A loan cannot be granted if the policy is in force as extended term insurance. The Company may defer making the loan for a period not exceeding six months unless the loan is to be used to pay premiums on policies in the Company.

2. AUTOMATIC PREMIUM LOAN

A premium loan shall be automatically granted to pay a premium in default. A premium for any other frequency permitted by this policy shall be loaned whenever the loan value, less any indebtedness, is sufficient for such premium but is insufficient for a loan of the premium in default. A revocation or reinstatement of this provision shall be made by written notice filed at the Home Office.

3. LOAN VALUE

The loan value is the largest amount which, with accrued interest, does not exceed the cash value either on the next

premium due date or at the end of one year from the date of the loan.

4. LOAN INTEREST

Policy and premium loans shall bear interest at the rate of 5% per annum. Interest on policy loans shall accrue from the date of the loan and on premium loans from the premium due date. Interest shall be payable annually. Unpaid interest shall be added to and become part of the loan and shall bear interest on the same terms.

5. INDEBTEDNESS

Indebtedness means all outstanding policy and premium loans on this policy including interest accrued and accruing from day to day. Indebtedness may be repaid at any time and if not repaid shall be deducted as a single sum from any settlement.

Whenever indebtedness equals or exceeds the cash value, this policy shall be deemed surrendered and shall terminate thirty-one days after a notice of termination has been mailed to the last known address of the Owner and of any assignee of record at the Home Office.

HH 1-2

Appendix B. Specimen Whole Life Insurance Contract (Continued)

CASH VALUE, EXTENDED TERM and PAID-UP INSURANCE

1. CASH VALUE

The cash value at any time when all premiums due have been paid shall be the reserve on this policy less the deduction described in section 5, plus the reserve on any paid-up additions and the amount of any dividend accumulations.

The cash value within three months after the date of premium default shall be the cash value on that date except as reduced by surrender of paid-up additions or withdrawal of dividend accumulations. The cash value at any time after such three months shall be the reserve on the form of insurance then in force and on any paid-up additions, plus the amount of any dividend accumulations.

If this policy is surrendered within thirty-one days after a policy anniversary, the reserve shall be taken as not less than on that anniversary.

2. CASH SURRENDER

The Owner may surrender this policy for its cash value less any indebtedness. The insurance shall terminate upon receipt at the Home Office of this policy and a written surrender of all claims. Receipt of the policy may be waived by the Company.

The Company may defer paying the cash value for a period not exceeding six months from the date of surrender. If payment is deferred thirty days or more, interest at the rate of 2¼% per annum from the date of surrender to the date of payment shall be allowed on the cash value less any indebtedness.

3. EXTENDED TERM INSURANCE

If any premium remains unpaid at the end of the grace period, this policy shall be automatically continued in force as nonparticipating extended term insurance. The amount of such insurance shall be the face amount of this policy, plus any paid-up additions and dividend accumulations, less any indebtedness. The term of such insurance shall begin as of the date of premium default and shall be determined by applying the cash value less any indebtedness as a net single premium at the attained age of the Insured. If such term ends on or after attained age 100, paid-up insurance as described in section 4 below will be provided instead.

4. PAID-UP INSURANCE

In lieu of extended term insurance this policy may be continued in force as participating paid-up life insurance. The insurance will be for such amount as the cash value will purchase as a net single premium at the attained age of the Insured. Any indebtedness shall remain as a lien against this policy.

Such paid-up insurance may be requested before or within three months after the date of premium default. A request or revocation shall be made by written notice filed at the Home Office.

5. TABLE OF VALUES

The values shown on page 3 are for the end of the policy year indicated; allowance shall be made for any portion of a year's premium paid and for the time elapsed in that year. Values for policy years not shown shall be calculated on the same basis as this table and shall be furnished on request. All values are greater than or equal to those required by statute.

These values are based on the assumption that premiums have been paid for the number of years stated and are exclusive of any paid-up additions, dividend accumulations, or indebtedness.

In determining the cash values a deduction has been made from the reserve. During the first policy year, the deduction is $16 for each $1,000 of face amount. The deduction decreases by one-eighth in each succeeding year until there is no deduction in the ninth and subsequent policy years.

HH 1-2

Appendix B. Specimen Whole Life Insurance Contract (Continued)

BENEFICIARY and SETTLEMENT PROVISIONS

1. DESIGNATION AND CHANGE OF BENEFICIARIES

(a) **By Owner.** The Owner may designate and change direct and contingent beneficiaries of death proceeds:

(1) during the lifetime of the Insured.

(2) during the sixty days following the date of death of the Insured if the Insured immediately before his death was not the Owner. Any such designation of direct beneficiary may not be changed. If the Owner elects a settlement option, any such designation of contingent beneficiary may not be changed unless the Owner is the direct beneficiary.

(b) **By Direct Beneficiary.** The direct beneficiary may designate contingent beneficiaries under any of the following conditions subject in each case to any remaining rights of the Owner:

(1) If the Owner is designated as the direct beneficiary of death, endowment, or surrender proceeds.

(2) If the direct beneficiary of death proceeds elects a settlement option after the death of the Insured. In this event, the interest in the share of such direct beneficiary of any other payee designated by the Owner shall terminate.

(3) If, at any time after the death of the Insured, no contingent beneficiary of death proceeds is living.

Any such designation made by the direct beneficiary shall be with the right of change.

2. SUCCESSION IN INTEREST OF BENEFICIARIES

The proceeds of this policy whether payable in one sum or under a settlement option shall be payable in equal shares to such direct beneficiaries as survive to receive payment. The share of any direct beneficiary who dies before receiving payments due or to become due shall be payable in equal shares to such direct beneficiaries as survive to receive payment.

At the death of the last surviving direct beneficiary payments due or to become due shall be payable in equal shares to such contingent beneficiaries as survive to receive payment. The share of any contingent beneficiary who dies before receiving payments due or to become due shall be payable in equal shares to such contingent beneficiaries as survive to receive payment.

At the death of the last to survive of the direct and contingent beneficiaries:

(1) if no settlement option is in effect, any remaining proceeds shall be paid to the Owner or to the executors, administrators, successors, or transferees of the Owner; or

(2) if a settlement option is in effect, the withdrawal value of payments due or to become due shall be paid in one sum to the executors or administrators of the last to survive of the direct and contingent beneficiaries.

A direct or contingent beneficiary succeeding to an interest in a settlement option shall continue under such option, subject to its terms as stated in this policy, with the rights of transfer between options and of withdrawal under options as provided in this policy.

3. SETTLEMENT OF POLICY PROCEEDS

(a) **Payment.** All of the policy proceeds or each part, if the proceeds are divided into parts, may be paid in one sum or under a settlement option.

So far as permitted by law no amount payable under this policy shall be assigned or pledged or be subject to the claims of creditors of the payee.

(b) **Availability of Options.** The settlement options shall be available for any direct or contingent beneficiary who is a natural person taking benefit in his own right. In addition, Options B and D shall be available to a corporation as direct beneficiary for its own use and benefit and Options C and F shall be similarly available when the installments depend upon the life of the Insured. Otherwise the settlement options shall not be available.

(c) **Minimum Amount.** The Company shall not be required to apply under or transfer to a settlement option or retain under Option A an amount less than $2,000 for any payee. The Company may pay the withdrawal value of any settlement option where payments to any payee are or become less than $20.

(d) **Date of Settlement.** The date of settlement for any part of the proceeds shall be the date of payment in one sum or if settled under one of the options the date settlement becomes effective.

4. ELECTION OF OPTIONS

(a) **By Owner.** The Owner may:

(1) elect a settlement option for death proceeds during the lifetime of the Insured. Any such election may be changed during the Insured's lifetime.

(2) revoke any existing election and elect a settlement option for death proceeds during the sixty days following the date of death of the Insured if the Insured immediately before his death was not the Owner. Any such election shall be final.

(3) elect a settlement option for surrender or maturity proceeds. Any such election shall be for the Owner as direct beneficiary.

(b) **By Direct Beneficiary.** A direct beneficiary may make an election of a settlement option if no election is in force when this policy becomes payable. Such election shall be subject to any remaining rights of the Owner.

(c) **By Contingent Beneficiary.** A contingent beneficiary may make an election of a settlement option if the policy proceeds become payable to such contingent beneficiary and if no election is in force. Such election shall be subject to any remaining rights of the Owner.

5. INTEREST BEFORE SETTLEMENT

Interest shall accrue on death proceeds from the date of the Insured's death to the date of settlement, but not for more than one year. The rate of such interest shall be at least 2½ % per annum. Interest shall be paid in cash on the date of settlement to the payee then entitled to settlement.

HH 1-5

$\left(\begin{smallmatrix} \text{W. P. 60} \\ \text{A.D.B.} \end{smallmatrix}\right)$

Appendix B. Specimen Whole Life Insurance Contract
(Continued)

6. INTEREST OPTION

Option A: Proceeds Left at Interest

The Company shall pay interest monthly at the rate of $2.06 per month per $1,000. The first payment shall be due one month after the date of settlement. The payments will be increased by dividends as determined by the Company.

The withdrawal value at any time shall be the proceeds held by the Company.

A contingent beneficiary shall not elect or continue under this option beyond his 30th birthday but shall take the withdrawal value or transfer to another option.

7. INSTALLMENT OPTIONS

Option B: Installments for a Specified Period

The Company shall pay monthly installments for a specified number of years as stated in the Option B Table. The first installment shall be due on the date of settlement. Subsequent installments will be increased by dividends as determined by the Company.

The withdrawal value at any time shall be the commuted value of any unpaid installments. Commutation shall be on the basis of compound interest at 2½% per annum.

OPTION B TABLE
Monthly Installments for Each $1,000 of Net Proceeds

Number of Years Specified	Each Monthly Payment	Number of Years Specified	Each Monthly Payment	Number of Years Specified	Each Monthly Payment
1	$84.28	11	$8.64	21	$5.08
2	42.66	12	8.02	22	4.90
3	28.79	13	7.49	23	4.74
4	21.86	14	7.03	24	4.60
5	17.70	15	6.64	25	4.46
6	14.93	16	6.30	26	4.34
7	12.95	17	6.00	27	4.22
8	11.47	18	5.73	28	4.12
9	10.32	19	5.49	29	4.02
10	9.39	20	5.27	30	3.93

Option D: Installments of a Specified Amount

The Company shall pay from a fund established by the proceeds equal monthly installments of a specified amount not less than $5 per $1,000 of the fund. The fund shall be credited annually with interest at the rate of 2½% per annum on the balance and will be increased by dividends as determined by the Company. The first installment shall be due on the date of settlement. Installments shall continue until the fund is exhausted, the final payment not to exceed the unpaid balance.

The withdrawal value at any time shall be the balance in the fund at such time.

8. LIFE INCOME OPTIONS

(a) Description of Options.

Option C: Life Income with Installments Certain

The Company shall pay monthly installments during the period certain elected and thereafter during the remaining lifetime of the beneficiary upon whose life the installments depend. The period certain elected may be 10 or 20 years or a refund period certain such that the sum of the installments certain shall be equal to the proceeds settled under this option, the final payment not to exceed the unpaid balance.

Option E: Joint and Survivor Life Income with Installments Certain

The Company shall pay monthly installments certain for 10 years and thereafter during the joint lifetime of the two direct beneficiaries upon whose lives the installments depend and the remaining lifetime of the survivor. Installments shall be paid jointly and to the survivor. In the event of the death of either of such beneficiaries before the date of settlement, the proceeds shall be payable to the survivor under Option C with installments certain for 10 years.

(b) Amount of Installments. The amount payable under the Option C or E Table shall be determined by the sex and adjusted age of any beneficiary upon whose life the installments depend.

Proof of date of birth satisfactory to the Company must be furnished. The first installment shall be due on the date of settlement. Subsequent installments certain will be increased by dividends as determined by the Company.

The withdrawal value under Option C or E, where available, shall be the commuted value of any unpaid installments certain. Commutation shall be on the basis of compound interest at 3% per annum.

(c) Adjusted Age. The adjusted age shall be the age at nearest birthday adjusted according to the calendar year in which settlement under Option C or E becomes effective.

This age adjustment shall be as follows:

Year of Settlement	1968 or Prior	1969 thru 1973	1974 thru 1978	1979 thru 1988	1989 thru 1993	1994 thru 1998	1999 or After
Age Adjustment	+3	+2	+1	0	−1	−2	−3

(d) Annuity Income Privilege. Instead of the amount of installments for Option C or E determined as provided in (b) and (c) of this section, nonparticipating installments determined in accordance with the terms of Option F, adjusted to provide for the period certain of the option selected, may be elected. The basis for determining the commuted value of unpaid installments certain shall be the same as provided in the Single Premium Refund Immediate Life Annuity issued by the Company on the date of settlement.

Appendix B. Specimen Whole Life Insurance Contract (Continued)

MONTHLY INSTALLMENTS FOR EACH $1,000 OF NET PROCEEDS
OPTION C TABLE
Monthly Life Income with Payments Certain
To Determine Adjusted Age See Section 8(c)

Adjusted Age of Beneficiary		Installment Refund**	Adjusted Age of Beneficiary		10 Years	20 Years	Installment Refund	Adjusted Age of Beneficiary		10 Years	20 Years	Installment Refund
Male	Female		Male	Female				Male	Female			
	10*	$2.51	30	35	$3.07	$3.05	$3.02	55	60	$4.68	$4.33	$4.37
	11	2.52	31	36	3.10	3.08	3.05	56	61	4.79	4.40	4.46
	12	2.54	32	37	3.14	3.12	3.09	57	62	4.91	4.46	4.56
	13	2.55	33	38	3.18	3.15	3.12	58	63	5.03	4.53	4.66
	14	2.57	34	39	3.22	3.19	3.16	59	64	5.16	4.59	4.76
10*	15	2.58	35	40	3.26	3.23	3.20	60	65	5.30	4.65	4.87
11	16	2.60	36	41	3.30	3.27	3.23	61	66	5.43	4.71	4.98
12	17	2.61	37	42	3.35	3.31	3.27	62	67	5.58	4.77	5.10
13	18	2.63	38	43	3.40	3.36	3.32	63	68	5.72	4.82	5.22
14	19	2.65	39	44	3.45	3.40	3.36	64	69	5.87	4.88	5.34
15	20	2.66	40	45	3.50	3.45	3.40	65	70	6.03	4.93	5.49
16	21	2.68	41	46	3.56	3.50	3.45	66	71	6.19	4.97	5.63
17	22	2.70	42	47	3.61	3.55	3.50	67	72	6.35	5.02	5.78
18	23	2.72	43	48	3.67	3.60	3.55	68	73	6.52	5.05	5.90
19	24	2.74	44	49	3.74	3.65	3.61	69	74	6.69	5.09	6.03
20	25	2.76	45	50	3.80	3.71	3.66	70	75	6.86	5.12	6.17
21	26	2.78	46	51	3.87	3.76	3.72	71	76	7.03	5.14	6.34
22	27	2.81	47	52	3.95	3.82	3.78	72	77	7.20	5.17	6.50
23	28	2.83	48	53	4.02	3.88	3.84	73	78	7.37	5.19	6.68
24	29	2.86	49	54	4.10	3.94	3.91	74	79	7.54	5.20	6.87
25	30	2.88	50	55	4.19	4.00	3.98	75	80	7.69	5.22	7.05
26	31	2.91	51	56	4.28	4.07	4.05	76	81	7.84	5.23	7.26
27	32	2.93	52	57	4.37	4.14	4.13	77	82	7.98	5.24	7.49
28	33	2.96	53	58	4.47	4.20	4.21	78	83	8.13	5.25	7.69
29	34	2.99	54	59	4.57	4.26	4.29	79	84	8.26	5.26	7.94
								80	85†	8.39	5.26	8.20
								81		8.51	5.27	8.43
								82		8.63	5.27	8.72
								83		8.73	5.27	9.02
								84		8.83	5.27	9.35
								85†		8.92	5.27	9.62

* and under   *** rates also apply to 10 and 20 year certain periods*   *† and over*

OPTION E TABLE
Monthly Joint and Survivor Life Income with Payments Certain for 10 Years for Beneficiaries of Equal Age
To Determine Adjusted Ages See Section 8(c)

Adjusted Age of Beneficiary	One Male and One Female	Two Male Lives	Two Female Lives	Adjusted Age of Beneficiary	One Male and One Female	Two Male Lives	Two Female Lives	Adjusted Age of Beneficiary	One Male and One Female	Two Male Lives	Two Female Lives
25	$2.65	$2.70	$2.61	55	$3.79	$4.00	$3.63	65	$4.73	$5.11	$4.46
30	2.75	2.81	2.70	56	3.86	4.08	3.69	66	4.85	5.23	4.57
35	2.87	2.95	2.81	57	3.93	4.16	3.76	67	4.97	5.35	4.69
40	3.02	3.12	2.95	58	4.01	4.25	3.83	68	5.11	5.49	4.82
45	3.22	3.35	3.12	59	4.09	4.34	3.92	69	5.25	5.64	4.96
50	3.46	3.63	3.35	60	4.18	4.46	4.00	70	5.40	5.80	5.11
51	3.52	3.69	3.39	61	4.27	4.57	4.08	71	5.53	5.95	5.23
52	3.57	3.76	3.44	62	4.38	4.69	4.16	72	5.69	6.13	5.35
53	3.64	3.83	3.50	63	4.48	4.82	4.25	73	5.85	6.31	5.49
54	3.71	3.92	3.56	64	4.60	4.96	4.34	74	6.01	6.49	5.64
								75	6.19	6.69	5.80

The amount of the payments for any other combination of ages will be furnished by the Company on request.
The maximum monthly income per $1,000 shall be $6.69.

9. LIFE ANNUITY OPTION
Option F: Immediate Life Annuity

The Company shall pay monthly installments during the lifetime of the beneficiary upon whose life the installments depend. The first installment shall be due on the date of settlement. The amount of each installment shall be 104% of the monthly income based upon the Company's Immediate Life Annuity rate at date of settlement and upon the sex and age nearest birthday of the beneficiary upon whose life the installments depend, adjusted to provide for immediate payment of the first installment. This option shall not participate in the surplus of the Company.

10. TRANSFER BETWEEN OPTIONS
A direct or contingent beneficiary who is receiving payment under Option A, B, or D may transfer the withdrawal value to Option B, C, D, or F.

11. WITHDRAWAL UNDER OPTIONS
A direct or contingent beneficiary may elect to receive the withdrawal value instead of continuing to receive payments under a settlement option; except that under Option C or E any beneficiary upon whose life the installments depend may not elect to receive the withdrawal value.

12. POSSESSION OF POLICY
This policy shall remain in the possession of the direct or contingent beneficiaries receiving payments under a settlement option.

13. EXERCISE OF RIGHTS
The policy rights stated in these Beneficiary and Settlement Provisions shall be exercised only by a proper request in writing. All requests must be filed at the Home Office and must be endorsed on this policy unless the Company waives endorsement.

The effective date of a request for designation, revocation, or change of beneficiary shall be as of the date the request was signed. The effective date of an election of a settlement option for death proceeds made by the Owner during the Insured's lifetime shall be the date of the Insured's death. All other requests shall be effective when filed at the Home Office and endorsed on this policy.

The Company shall not be prejudiced on account of any payment made or other action taken by it before a request is filed at its Home Office.

Appendix B. Specimen Whole Life Insurance Contract (Concluded)

WAIVER OF PREMIUM BENEFIT ON DISABILITY

1. THE BENEFIT

The Company will waive the payment of all premiums becoming due during the total disability of the Insured.

The dividends, policy values, and other benefits of this policy shall be the same as if premiums waived had been paid in cash.

2. DEFINITION OF TOTAL DISABILITY

Total disability means disability which:

(a) resulted from bodily injury or disease;

(b) began after the issue date of this policy and before the policy anniversary nearest the Insured's 60th birthday;

(c) has existed continuously for at least six months; and

(d) prevents the Insured from engaging for remuneration or profit in an occupation. During the first twenty-four months of disability, occupation means the occupation of the Insured at the time such disability began; thereafter it means any occupation for which he is or becomes reasonably fitted by education, training, or experience.

The total and irrecoverable loss of the sight of both eyes, or of the use of both hands, or of both feet, or of one hand and one foot shall be considered total disability even if the Insured shall engage in an occupation.

3. PROOF OF DISABILITY

Before any premium is waived due proof of total disability must be received by the Company at its Home Office:

(a) during the lifetime of the Insured;

(b) during the continuance of total disability; and

(c) not later than one year after the policy anniversary nearest the Insured's 60th birthday.

Premiums will be waived although proof of total disability was not given within the time specified if it is shown that it was given as soon as reasonably possible but not later than one year after recovery.

4. PROOF OF CONTINUANCE OF DISABILITY

Due proof of the continuance of total disability may be required once a year. If such proof is not furnished, no further premiums shall be waived.

Any future premiums shall be waived without further proof of continuance of disability if, on the policy anniversary nearest the Insured's 65th birthday, the Insured is then and has been totally and continuously disabled for five or more years since proof of disability was submitted.

5. PREMIUMS

Any premium becoming due during disability and before receipt of due proof of total disability is payable and should be paid. Any such premiums paid shall be refunded by the Company upon acceptance of proof of total disability. If such premiums are not paid, this benefit shall be allowed if total disability is shown to have begun before the end of the grace period of the first such premium in default.

While premiums are being waived, the frequency of premium payment shall remain unchanged. This benefit shall not participate in the surplus of the Company.

6. TERMINATION

This benefit shall be in effect while this policy is in force but shall terminate on the policy anniversary nearest the Insured's 60th birthday unless the Insured is then totally disabled. It may be terminated upon receipt at the Home Office, within thirty-one days of a premium due date, of the Owner's written request.

ACCIDENTAL DEATH BENEFIT

1. THE BENEFIT

The Company agrees to pay an Accidental Death Benefit upon receipt at its Home Office of due proof that the death of the Insured resulted, directly and independently of all other causes, from accidental bodily injury, provided that death occurred within ninety days after such injury and while this benefit is in effect.

2. AMOUNT OF BENEFIT

The amount of this benefit is shown in the Premium Schedule on page 3 of this policy. This Additional Benefit shall be payable as part of the policy proceeds. It shall not participate in the surplus of the Company.

3. RISKS NOT ASSUMED

This benefit shall not be payable for death of the Insured resulting from suicide, whether sane or insane, for death resulting from or contributed to by bodily or mental infirmity or disease, or for any other death which, such as the foregoing, did not result, directly and independently of all other causes, from accidental bodily injury.

Even though death resulted directly and independently of all other causes from accidental bodily injury, this benefit shall not be payable if the death of the Insured resulted from:

(a) Any act or incident of war. The word "war" includes any war, declared or undeclared, and armed aggression resisted by the armed forces of any country or combination of countries.

(b) Riding in or descent from any kind of aircraft, if the Insured participated in training or had any duties whatsoever aboard such aircraft or if such aircraft was operated by or for the armed forces.

4. TERMINATION

This benefit shall be in effect while this policy is in force other than under the Extended Term Insurance, Paid-up Insurance, or Optional Maturity Date provisions but shall terminate on the policy anniversary nearest the Insured's 70th birthday. It may be terminated upon receipt at the Home Office, within thirty-one days of a premium due date, of the Owner's written request accompanied by this policy for endorsement.

HH 1-5. W.P. 60. ADB.

Appendix C. Specimen Inspection Report Form

RETAIL CREDIT COMPANY
LIFE REPORT

CONFIDENTIAL ★★★★

OFFICE

Acct. No.	Dist., Agcy., or Br.		
Date:	Pol. No.		**INSURANCE HISTORY**
NAME:		Date	Acct. No. Amt. or Type Coverage Fam. or Indiv.

Address:
Occupation on
Inq. & Employer:

Date of Birth: A   Health App'd for $ Per   ☐ Hospitalization   ☐ Major Medical Exp.

		NO	YES	
1.	ANY REASON FOR NOT RECOMMENDING APPLICANT?	☐	☐	Feature(s)

	2. On what date was this inspection made?		
IDENTITY	3—A. How many years has each of your informants known him?	A.	
	B. How many days since you or your informants have seen him? *(If not within two weeks, explain fully.)*	B.	
AGE	4. Is there any reason to doubt accuracy of birth date given?		
FINANCES	5—A. What would you estimate his net worth?	A. $	
	B. What is his annual earned income from his work or business?	B. $	
	C. Has he any income from investments, rentals, pension, etc.? *(If so, state source, amount.)*	C.	

		NO	YES	
OCCUPA-TION	6—A. Does the occupation or job differ in name from that given in heading of this report?	A.		
	B. Does he change jobs frequently?	B.		
	C. Has he any part-time or off-season occupation? Does he plan work or travel in foreign countries?	C.		
	D. Does he or his employer sell or manufacture beer, wine or liquor?	D.		
DRIVING RECORD	7. Is he a fast, reckless, or careless driver?			IF YES, See Questions on Back.
AVIATION-SPORTS	8—A. Has he taken flying lessons, either as member of armed forces or as civilian, owned or piloted a plane, or flown in planes not operated by scheduled airlines?	A.		IF YES, See Questions on Back.
	B. Does he engage in hazardous sports? (Racing, skin-diving, sky-diving, etc.)	B.		
HEALTH	9—A. Is there anything unhealthy about his appearance, such as being very thin or having excess weight?	A.		IF YES, See Questions on Back.
	B. Has he any deformity, amputation, blindness, deafness, or other defects?	B.		
	10. Do you learn of any illness, operation or injury past or present?			IF YES, See Questions on Back.
	11. Do you learn of any impairment which caused rejection for military service; or, if he served in armed forces, do you learn he was discharged for medical reasons?			
	12. Do you learn of any member of his family (blood relation) having had heart trouble, cancer, diabetes, tuberculosis or mental trouble? *(If so, who and which disease.)*			
HABITS	13—A. Is he a steady, frequent drinker (daily, almost daily, several times a week)?	A.		
	IF SO, { B. How often?	B.		
	C. How many drinks does he take on these occasions?	C.		
	D. What does he usually drink (beer, wine or whiskey)?	D.		
	14. Does he now or has he in the past used beer, wine or whiskey to noticeable excess or intoxication?			IF YES, See Questions on Back.
ENVIRONMENT	15. Anything adverse about living conditions or neighborhood?			IF YES, See Questions on Back.
REPUTA-TION	16. Do any of following apply to this applicant: Heavy debts? Domestic trouble? Drug habit? Connection with illegal liquor? Irregular beneficiary?			
	17. Is there any criticism of character or morals?			
IF FAMILY POLICY	18. Anything adverse on health or physical condition of other family members? (If so, cover in Remarks.)			

REMARKS: 19. COMMENT BELOW ON TOPICS LISTED AT LEFT; GIVE DETAILS OF "YES" OR INCOMPLETE ANSWERS.

A. BUSINESS:
Employer's name, line and size of business? Name of applicant's job? How long so employed? Cover any indication of frequent job changes or instability of employment.

B. ANSWER HANDY GUIDE QUESTIONS, IF APPLICABLE.

C. PERSONAL: Married, single, or divorced? Any children? Type of associates.

RETAIL CREDIT COMPANY

Signature of person making report_____

Form 1—3-66 U.S.A. ★★★★   OVER—SEE ADDITIONAL QUESTIONS ON BACK   LIFE REPORT

Appendix C. Specimen Inspection Report Form (Continued)

#19 Continued

DETAILS OF APPEARANCE:

20—A. How does he appear unhealthy (complexion, weight, or what)?_____ B. Describe. (If overweight or underweight, give details.)

DETAILS OF HEALTH HISTORY ON APPLICANT:

21. Nature of illness, operation or injury?_____

22. Approximate date it occurred?_____
23—A. How long confined or "laid up"?_____
B. Completely recovered?_____
24—A. Attended by Dr. (Name)_____
Address _____
B. Confined to hospital?_____ If so, name and address:
Name _____
Address _____
25. Any effect on present health?_____ Details:

DETAILS OF DRIVING RECORD:

26. When, where, and under what circumstances does applicant drive in a fast or reckless manner? (Open highway, congested areas, etc.—if known to drive considerably in excess of speed limit, cover.)

27. Any evidence of unsupervised racing?_____ Give details:

ANSWER THESE IF LEARNED IN INVESTIGATION
28. Any arrests?_____ (Approximate dates)_____
29. Charges?_____
If convicted, approximate dates?_____
30. Any accidents?_____ If so, approximate dates and details:
31. License ever suspended or revoked?_____ If so, cause, date and whether he drove without a license?

DETAILS OF ENVIRONMENT:

32. LIVING CONDITIONS:
A. Over-crowded, dirty, unsanitary, etc.?_____ (If so, give details.)
B. If apartment, dark or dirty halls, broken or littered stairs, etc.? (If so, give details.)

33. NEIGHBORHOOD: Deteriorating physically, poor sanitation, vice and crime, vandalism, etc.? (If so, give details.)

DETAILS OF DRINKING HABITS: Give these additional details to show drinking habits as definitely as possible:

34. Classify excessive drinking: ☐ Present ☐ Past

	How often? (Once a week, once a month, etc.)
A. Getting "drunk," stupefied, entirely out of control of usual faculties?	A._____
B. Loud, boisterous, or obviously under influence, although still in possession of most of faculties?	B._____
C. Mild excess, just getting "feeling good"; exhilaration or stimulation?	C._____

35. Do (did) these occasions last for an evening, a day, two days, a week, or for how long?
36. How long has (had) he been drinking to this extent?
37. WHEN WAS THE LAST OCCASION OF THIS SORT?
38. If applicant is an excessive drinker at present, does he drive a car during periods of excess?
39. Has applicant ever taken any "cure" for liquor habit? (If so, when?) Any subsequent lapse?
40. Tell how applicant drinks, if social or solitary, or if because of domestic or other trouble, how it affects him, whether ever arrested, and details to give clear picture of drinking habits; if habits have changed, tell how and how long since change; if reformed, what led to reformation (ill health, domestic trouble or what)?

INSPECTOR: Do not write in this space.
(Use Continuation of Report, Form 5166, for additional remarks.)

1 R—6-66

Appendix D. Specimen Form Relating to Settlement Election and Designation by Direct Beneficiary

DOCUMENT 1569 (Revised May 1966)	THE [_____] LIFE INSURANCE COMPANY [_____]	For Home Office Use ___

BEFORE COMPLETING THIS FORM READ INSTRUCTIONS AND INFORMATION ON BACK OF FORM.

Policy No... 　Date this
form is signed...

Insured (Annuitant)... 　Place...

SETTLEMENT FOR DIRECT BENEFICIARY

$....................... shall be paid in ONE SUM and the remainder of the proceeds settled under:

Select one option only and indicate choice by marking with "X."

☐ OPTION A payable monthly, the first payment being due at the end of such period, with the right of receiving the withdrawal value.

☐ OPTION B in monthly installments for .... years with the right of receiving the withdrawal (commuted) value.

☐ OPTION C in monthly installments certain

(No withdrawal (commuted) value under option C is available to the direct beneficiary.)

　☐ a. for .... (10, 15, or 20) years, and for life. *(Option C for 15 years is not available under periods numbered 5,500,000 and above.)*

　☐ b. under the Installment Refund, and for life.

　☐ c. for .... (10 or 20) years, and for life under the Annuity Income Privilege.

　☐ d. under Installment Refund, and for life under the Annuity Income Privilege.

☐ OPTION D in monthly installments of $................ with the right of receiving the withdrawal value.

☐ OPTION F in monthly installments for life. There is no withdrawal value under Option F and no contingent beneficiary may be designated. Income is payable to the direct beneficiary for life, terminating with the last payment preceding the death of the direct beneficiary. There are no further payments.

The rate for the option elected in this form shall be the greater of (1) the rate in the policy or (2) the rate for the same option in policies regularly being issued by the Company when this settlement becomes effective; and the policy terms relating to such greater option rate shall apply.

CONTINGENT BENEFICIARIES See Special Provision I on back of form.

CAUTION: Use this section only if there is no effective designation of contingent beneficiary. Unless the Owner has directed otherwise, there is no such effective designation under a policy issued after #2,854,028 when the direct beneficiary elects a settlement option for any part of the proceeds.

Subject to my right of change, the following are designated as contingent beneficiaries of the entire proceeds:

FIRST NAME	INITIAL	LAST NAME	RELATIONSHIP TO ME	DATE OF BIRTH

The following may be selected to modify the contingent beneficiary designation by marking with "X."

☐ in equal shares, the survivors or survivor, except that any amount a deceased contingent beneficiary would have received, if living, shall be payable when due in one sum in equal shares to his or her then living children.

The word "children" includes child and any legally adopted child, and decisions made by the Company upon evidence satisfactory to it shall be conclusive and shall fully protect the Company.

I hereby waive and release any ownership rights that I may have and request the Company to proceed as directed above.

The Special Provisions on the back of this form are a part of this designation, election and direction.

The [_____] Life Insurance Company is requested and directed to make this form and the Amendment of Policy Provisions on the back of this form a part of the policy. Any provisions of the policy relating to endorsement of this form shall be deemed complied with when (1) the Company has attached a copy of this form to the policy; or (2) the Company has recorded the form and indicated below that endorsement has been waived.

Witness_____ 　Signature of
Direct Beneficiary_____

| | First Name | Initial | Last Name |

Address to which checks are to be sent: { Street & No._____

City, State & Zip Code_____

Doc. 1569 (Rev. 0566)

Appendix D. Specimen Form Relating to Settlement Election and Designation by Direct Beneficiary (Continued)

SPECIAL PROVISIONS OF DOCUMENT 1569

I. SUCCESSION IN INTEREST OF BENEFICIARIES DESIGNATED BY THE DIRECT BENEFICIARY

Unless otherwise provided in this form the proceeds whether payable in one sum or under a settlement option shall be payable as follows:

At the death of the direct beneficiary payments due or to become due shall be payable in equal shares to such contingent beneficiaries as survive to receive payment. The share of any contingent beneficiary who dies before receiving payments due or to become due shall be payable in equal shares to such contingent beneficiaries as survive to receive payment.

At the death of the last to survive of the direct and contingent beneficiaries due or to become due shall be paid in one sum to the executors or administrators of the last to survive of the direct and contingent beneficiaries.

II. DEFINITION OF SETTLEMENT PROVISIONS

The following terms, if not defined in the policy, shall for purposes of this settlement be defined as follows:

ANNUITY INCOME PRIVILEGE—Instead of the amount of installments for Option C determined as provided in the policy, nonparticipating installments determined in accordance with the terms of Option F, adjusted to provide for the period certain of the option selected, may be elected. The basis for determining the commuted value of unpaid installments certain shall be the same as provided in the Single Premium Refund Immediate Life Annuity being issued by the Company on the date of settlement.

OPTION D — The Company shall pay from a fund established by the proceeds equal monthly installments of a specified amount not less than $5 per $1,000 of the fund. The fund shall be credited annually with interest on the balance and will be increased by dividends as determined by the Company. The first installment shall be due on the date of settlement. Installments shall continue until the fund is exhausted, the final payment not to exceed the unpaid balance. The withdrawal value at any time shall be the balance in the fund at such time.

OPTION F—The Company shall pay monthly installments during the lifetime of the beneficiary upon whose life the installments depend. The first installment shall be due on the date settlement becomes effective. The amount of each installment shall be 104% of the monthly income based upon the Company's Immediate Life Annuity rate on the date of settlement and upon the sex and age nearest birthday of the beneficiary upon whose life the installments depend, adjusted to provide for immediate payment of the first installment. This option shall not participate in the surplus of the Company.

III. MINIMUM AMOUNT PROVISION

The Company shall not be required to apply under or transfer to a settlement option or retain under Option A an amount less than $2,000 for any payee. The Company may pay the withdrawal (commuted) value of any settlement option where payments to any payee are or become less than $20.

IV. ONE SUM PAYMENT

Whenever a settlement option is in effect and this form directs that payment shall be made in one sum, the amount to be paid shall be the withdrawal (commuted) value of the option.

AMENDMENT OF POLICY PROVISIONS
Applying to Policies Numbered Below 4,800,000

Any policy provisions regarding endorsement of any request for designation, revocation, or change of beneficiary or election or change of settlement option shall be amended so that after endorsement of this amendment on the policy the Company may waive endorsement of any future request for designation, revocation, or change of beneficiary or election or change of settlement option.

A request for designation, revocation, or change of beneficiary must be filed at the Home Office and shall then be effective as of the date the request was signed. An election of a settlement option shall be effective when filed at the Home Office. The Company shall not be prejudiced on account of any payment made or other action taken by it before a request is filed at its Home Office.

INSTRUCTIONS AND INFORMATION

This form is for use only with initial elections made by a direct beneficiary at the time of the Insured's death.

Where there is more than one direct beneficiary this form may be used if no designation of contingent beneficiaries or further payees made by the Owner remains effective. A separate form must be completed by each direct beneficiary. Where there is an effective designation of contingent beneficiaries or further payees by the Owner, a special form will be prepared at the Home Office.

Proof of the direct beneficiary's age, satisfactory to the Company, is required if Option C or F is elected.

(Rev. May 1966)

Appendix E. A.B.A. Assignment Form

FORM DESIGNED, PRINTED, AND DISTRIBUTED BY
AMERICAN BANKERS ASSOCIATION
BANK MANAGEMENT COMMISSION

Form No. 10—LIFE INSURANCE ASSIGNMENT   (REVIEWED AND APPROVED 1950)

ASSIGNMENT OF LIFE INSURANCE POLICY AS COLLATERAL

A.   **For Value Received** the undersigned hereby assign, transfer and set over to _____

_____ of _____

its successors and assigns, (herein called the "Assignee") Policy No. _____ issued by the

(herein called the ."Insurer") and any supplementary contracts issued in connection therewith (said policy and contracts being

herein called the "Policy"), upon the life of _____

of _____ and all claims, options, privileges, rights, title and interest therein
and thereunder (except as provided in Paragraph C hereof), subject to all the terms and conditions of the Policy and to all
superior liens, if any, which the Insurer may have against the Policy. The undersigned by this instrument jointly and severally
agree and the Assignee by the acceptance of this assignment agrees to the conditions and provisions herein set forth.

B.   It is expressly agreed that, without detracting from the generality of the foregoing, the following specific rights are included
in this assignment and pass by virtue hereof:
1. The sole right to collect from the Insurer the net proceeds of the Policy when it becomes a claim by death or maturity;
2. The sole right to surrender the Policy and receive the surrender value thereof at any time provided by the terms of the
Policy and at such other times as the Insurer may allow;
3. The sole right to obtain one or more loans or advances on the Policy, either from the Insurer or, at any time, from other
persons, and to pledge or assign the Policy as security for such loans or advances;
4. The sole right to collect and receive all distributions or shares of surplus, dividend deposits or additions to the Policy now
or hereafter made or apportioned thereto, and to exercise any and all options contained in the Policy with respect thereto;
provided, that unless and until the Assignee shall notify the Insurer in writing to the contrary, the distributions or shares
of surplus, dividend deposits and additions shall continue on the plan in force at the time of this assignment; and
5. The sole right to exercise all nonforfeiture rights permitted by the terms of the Policy or allowed by the Insurer and to
receive all benefits and advantages derived therefrom.

C.   It is expressly agreed that the following specific rights, so long as the Policy has not been surrendered, are reserved and
excluded from this assignment and do not pass by virtue hereof:
1. The right to collect from the Insurer any disability benefit payable in cash that does not reduce the amount of insurance;
2. The right to designate and change the beneficiary;
3. The right to elect any optional mode of settlement permitted by the Policy or allowed by the Insurer;
but the reservation of these rights shall in no way impair the right of the Assignee to surrender the Policy completely with all
its incidents or impair any other right of the Assignee hereunder, and any designation or change of beneficiary or election of a
mode of settlement shall be made subject to this assignment and to the rights of the Assignee hereunder.

D.   This assignment is made and the Policy is to be held as collateral security for any and all liabilities of the undersigned,
or any of them, to the Assignee, either now existing or that may hereafter arise in the ordinary course of business between
any of the undersigned and the Assignee (all of which liabilities secured or to become secured are herein called "Liabilities").

E.   The Assignee covenants and agrees with the undersigned as follows:
1. That any balance of sums received hereunder from the Insurer remaining after payment of the then existing Liabilities,
matured or unmatured, shall be paid by the Assignee to the persons entitled thereto under the terms of the Policy had this
assignment not been executed;
2. That the Assignee will not exercise either the right to surrender the Policy or (except for the purpose of paying premiums)
the right to obtain policy loans from the Insurer, until there has been default in any of the Liabilities or a failure to pay any
premium when due, nor until twenty days after the Assignee shall have mailed, by first-class mail, to the undersigned at the
addresses last supplied in writing to the Assignee specifically referring to this assignment, notice of intention to exercise
such right; and
3. That the Assignee will upon request forward without unreasonable delay to the Insurer the Policy for endorsement of any
designation or change of beneficiary or any election of an optional mode of settlement.

F.   The Insurer is hereby authorized to recognize the Assignee's claims to rights hereunder without investigating the reason for
any action taken by the Assignee, or the validity or the amount of the Liabilities or the existence of any default therein, or
the giving of any notice under Paragraph E (2) above or otherwise, or the application to be made by the Assignee of any
amounts to be paid to the Assignee. The sole signature of the Assignee shall be sufficient for the exercise of any rights under
the Policy assigned hereby and the sole receipt of the Assignee for any sums received shall be a full discharge and release
therefor to the Insurer. Checks for all or any part of the sums payable under the Policy and assigned herein, shall be drawn
to the exclusive order of the Assignee if, when, and in such amounts as may be, requested by the Assignee.

G.   The Assignee shall be under no obligation to pay any premium, or the principal of or interest on any loans or advances on
the Policy whether or not obtained by the Assignee, or any other charges on the Policy, but any such amounts so paid by the
Assignee from its own funds, shall become a part of the Liabilities hereby secured, shall be due immediately, and shall draw
interest at a rate fixed by the Assignee from time to time not exceeding 6% per annum.

H.   The exercise of any right, option, privilege or power given herein to the Assignee shall be at the option of the Assignee,
but (except as restricted by Paragraph E (2) above) the Assignee may exercise any such right, option, privilege or power
without notice to, or assent by, or affecting the liability of, or releasing any interest hereby assigned by the undersigned, or
any of them.

I.   The Assignee may take or release other security, may release any party primarily or secondarily liable for any of the Liabilities, may grant extensions, renewals or indulgences with respect to the Liabilities, or may apply to the Liabilities in such order as
the Assignee shall determine, the proceeds of the Policy hereby assigned or any amount received on account of the Policy by the
exercise of any right permitted under this assignment, without resorting or regard to other security.

J.   In the event of any conflict between the provisions of this assignment and provisions of the note or other evidence of any
Liability, with respect to the Policy or rights of collateral security therein, the provisions of this assignment shall prevail.

K.   Each of the undersigned declares that no proceedings in bankruptcy are pending against him and that his property is not
subject to any assignment for the benefit of creditors.

Signed and sealed this _____ day of _____, 19_____

_____		_____(L.S.)
Witness		*Insured or Owner*
		_____
		Address
_____		_____(L.S.)
Witness		*Beneficiary*
		_____
		Address

GROUP LIFE INSURANCE DEFINITION

I. No policy of group life insurance shall be delivered in this state unless it conforms to one of the following descriptions:

(1) A policy issued to an employer, or to the trustees of a fund established by an employer, which employer or trustees shall be deemed the policyholder, to insure employees of the employer for the benefit of persons other than the employer, subject to the following requirements:

(a) The employees eligible for insurance under the policy shall be all of the employees of the employer, or all of any class or classes thereof determined by conditions pertaining to their employment. The policy may provide that the term "employees" shall include the employees of one or more subsidiary corporations, and the employees, individual proprietors, and partners of one or more affiliated corporations, proprietors or partnerships if the business of the employer and of such affiliated corporations, proprietors or partnerships is under common control through stock ownership or contract. The policy may provide that the term "employees" shall include the individual proprietor or partners if the employer is an individual proprietor or a partnership. The policy may provide that the term "employees" shall include retired employees. No director of a corporate employer shall be eligible for insurance under the policy unless such person is otherwise eligible as a bona fide employee of the corporation by performing services other than the usual duties of a director. No individual proprietor or partner shall be eligible for insurance under the policy unless he is actively engaged in and devotes a substantial part of his time to the conduct of the business of the proprietor or partnership.

(b) The premium for the policy shall be paid by the policyholder, either wholly from the employer's funds or funds contributed by him, or partly from such funds and partly from funds contributed by the insured employees. No policy may be issued on which the entire premium is to be derived from funds contributed by the insured employees. A policy on which part of the premium is to be derived from funds contributed by the insured employees may be placed in force only if at least 75% of the then eligible employees, excluding any as to whom evidence of individual insurability is not satisfactory to the insurer, elect to make the required contributions. A policy on which no part of the premium is to be derived from funds contributed by the insured employees must insure all eligible employees, or all except any as to whom evidence of individual insurability is not satisfactory to the insurer.

(c) The policy must cover at least 10 employees at date of issue.

(d) The amounts of insurance under the policy must be based upon some plan precluding individual selection either by the employees or by the employer or trustees.

. . . .

(2) A policy issued to a creditor, who shall be deemed the policy-holder, to insure debtors of the creditor, subject to the following requirements:

(a) The debtors eligible for insurance under the policy shall be all of the debtors of the creditor whose indebtedness is re-payable either (i) in installments or (ii) in one sum at the end of a period not in excess of eighteen months from the initial date of debt, or all of any class or classes thereof de-termined by conditions pertaining to the indebtedness or to the purchase giving rise to the indebtedness. The policy may provide that the term "debtors" shall include the debtors of one or more subsidiary corporations, and the debtors of one or more affiliated corporations, proprietors or partnerships if the business of the policyholder and of such affiliated cor-porations, proprietors or partnerships is under common con-trol through stock ownership, contract, or otherwise. No debtor shall be eligible unless the indebtedness constitutes an obligation to repay which is binding upon him during his lifetime, at and from the date the insurance becomes effec-tive upon his life.*

(b) The premium for the policy shall be paid by the policyholder, either from the creditor's funds, or from charges collected from the insured debtors, or from both. A policy on which part or all of the premium is to be derived from the collection from the insured debtors of identifiable charges not required of uninsured debtors shall not in-clude, in the class or classes of debtors eligible for in-surance, debtors under obligations outstanding at its date of

---

* At a meeting on December 3, 1956 the NAIC Group Life Subcommittee ac-cepted a proposal by the NALU that this sentence be amended by inserting the word "irrevocable" before the word "obligation." The evident purpose was to prevent the use of group creditor insurance to provide coverage in connection with holders of mutual fund shares. However, the subcommittee promised to consider undoing this, by adopting the following minute:

"The Subcommittee agreed to consider any suggestions submitted in connection with the further Amendment of the Group Life Definition to include a category to permit the writing of Group Life Insurance in connection with various kinds of Savings Projects and Revocable Purchase Commitments which extend over a specified period of years."

issue without evidence of individual insurability unless at least 75% of the then eligible debtors elect to pay the required charges. A policy on which no part of the premium is to be derived from the collection of such identifiable charges must insure all eligible debtors, or all except any as to whom evidence of individual insurability is not satisfactory to the insurer.

(c) The policy may be issued only if the group of eligible debtors is then receiving new entrants at the rate of at least 100 persons yearly, or may reasonably be expected to receive at least 100 new entrants during the first policy year, and only if the policy reserves to the insurer the right to require evidence of individual insurability if less than 75% of the new entrants become insured. The policy may exclude from the classes eligible for insurance classes of debtors determined by age.

(d) The amount of insurance on the life of any debtor shall at no time exceed the amount owed by him which is repayable in installments to the creditor, or $10,000., whichever is less. Where the indebtedness is repayable in one sum to the creditor, the insurance on the life of any debtor shall in no instance be in effect for a period in excess of eighteen months except that such insurance may be continued for an additional period not exceeding six months in the case of default, extension or recasting of the loan. The amount of the insurance on the life of any debtor shall at no time exceed the amount of the unpaid indebtedness, or $10,000., whichever is less.

(e) The insurance shall be payable to the policyholder. Such payment shall reduce or extinguish the unpaid indebtedness of the debtor to the extent of such payment."

(3) A policy issued to a labor union, which shall be deemed the policyholder, to insure members of such union for the benefit of persons other than the union or any of its officials, representatives or agents, subject to the following requirements:

(a) The members eligible for insurance under the policy shall be all of the members of the union, or all of any class or classes thereof determined by conditions pertaining to their employment, or to membership in the union, or both.

(b) The premium for the policy shall be paid by the policyholder, either wholly from the union's funds, or partly from such funds and partly from funds contributed by the insured members specifically for their insurance. No policy may be issued on which the entire premium is to be derived from funds contributed by the insured members specifically for their insurance. A policy on which part of the premium is to be derived from funds contributed by the insured members specifically for their insurance may be placed in force only if at least

75% of the then eligible members, excluding any as to whom evidence of individual insurability is not satisfactory to the insurer, elect to make the required contributions. A policy on which no part of the premium is to be derived from funds contributed by the insured members specifically for their insurance must insure all eligible members, or all except any as to whom evidence of individual insurability is not satisfactory to the insurer.

(c) The policy must cover at least 25 members at date of issue:

(d) The amounts of insurance under the policy must be based upon some plan precluding individual selection either by the members or by the union.

(4) A policy issued to the trustees of a fund established by two or more employers in the same industry or by one or more labor unions, or by one or more employers and one or more labor unions, which trustees shall be deemed the policyholder, to insure employees of the employers or members of the unions for the benefit of persons other than the employers or the unions, subject to the following requirements:

(a) The persons eligible for insurance shall be all of the employees of the employers or all of the members of the unions, or all of any class or classes thereof determined by conditions pertaining to their employment, or to membership in the unions, or to both. The policy may provide that the term "employees" shall include retired employees, and the individual proprietor or partners if an employer is an individual proprietor or a partnership. No director of a corporate employer shall be eligible for insurance under the policy unless such person is otherwise eligible as a bona fide employee of the corporation by performing services other than the usual duties of a director. No individual proprietor or partner shall be eligible for insurance under the policy unless he is actively engaged in and devotes a substantial part of his time to the conduct of the business of the proprietor or partnership. The policy may provide that the term "employees" shall include the trustees or their employees, or both, if their duties are principally connected with such trusteeship.

(b) The premium for the policy shall be paid by the trustees wholly from funds contributed by the employer or employers of the insured persons, or by the union or unions, or by both. No policy may be issued on which any part of the premium is to be derived from funds contributed by the insured persons specifically for their insurance. The policy must insure all eligible persons, or all except any as to whom evidence of individual insurability is not satisfactory to the insurer.

(c) The policy must cover at date of issue at least 100 persons and not less than an average of five persons per employer unit; and if the fund is established by the members of an association of employers the policy may be issued only if (i) either (a) the participating employers constitute at date of issue at least 60% of those employer members whose employees are not already covered for group life insurance or (b) the total number of persons covered at date of issue exceeds 600; and (ii) the policy shall not require that, if a participating employer discontinues membership in the association, the insurance of his employees shall cease solely by reason of such discontinuance.

 (d) The amounts of insurance under the policy must be based upon some plan precluding individual selection either by the insured persons or by the policyholder, employers, or unions.

II. No such policy of group life insurance may be issued to an employer, or labor union or to the trustees of a fund established in whole or in part by an employer or a labor union, which provides term insurance on any person which, together with any other term insurance under any group life insurance policy or policies issued to the employer or employers of such person or to a labor union or labor unions of which such person is a member or to the trustees of a fund or funds established in whole or in part by such employer or employers or such labor union or labor unions, exceeds $20,000, unless 150% of the annual compensation of such person from his employer or employers exceeds $20,000, in which event all such term insurance shall not exceed $40,000 or 150% of such annual compensation, whichever is the lesser.

GROUP LIFE INSURANCE STANDARD PROVISIONS

No policy of group life insurance shall be delivered in this state unless it contains in substance the following provisions, or provisions which in the opinion of the Commissioner are more favorable to the persons insured, or at least as favorable to the persons insured and more favorable to the policyholder, provided, however, (a) that provisions (6) to (10) inclusive shall not apply to policies issued to a creditor to insure debtors of such creditor; (b) that the standard provisions required for individual life insurance policies shall not apply to group life insurance policies; and (c) that if the group life insurance policy is on a plan of insurance other than the term plan, it shall contain a non-forfeiture provision or provisions which in the opinion of the Commissioner is or are equitable to the insured persons and to the policyholder, but nothing herein shall be construed to require that group life insurance policies contain the same non-forfeiture provisions as are required for individual life insurance policies:

(1) A provision that the policyholder is entitled to a grace period of thirty-one days for the payment of any premium due except the first, during which grace period the death benefit coverage shall continue in force, unless the policyholder shall have given the insurer written notice of discontinuance in advance of the date of discontinuance and in accordance with the terms of the policy. The policy may provide that the policyholder shall be liable to the insurer for the payment of a pro rata premium for the time the policy was in force during such grace period.

(2) A provision that the validity of the policy shall not be contested, except for nonpayment of premiums, after it has been in force for two years from its date of issue; and that no statement made by any person insured under the policy relating to his insurability shall be used in contesting the validity of the insurance with respect to which such statement was made after such insurance has been in force prior to the contest for a period of two years during such person's lifetime nor unless it is contained in a written instrument signed by him.

(3) A provision that a copy of the application, if any, of the policyholder shall be attached to the policy when issued, that all statements made by the policyholder or by the persons insured shall be deemed representations and not warranties, and that no statement made by any person insured shall be used in any contest unless a copy of the instrument containing the statement is or has been furnished to such person or to his beneficiary.

(4) A provision setting forth the conditions, if any, under which the insurer reserves the right to require a person eligible for insurance to furnish evidence of individual insurability satisfactory to the insurer as a condition to part or all of his coverage.

(5) A provision specifying an equitable adjustment of premiums or of benefits or of both to be made in the event the age of a person in-

sured has been misstated, such provision to contain a clear statement of the method of adjustment to be used.

(6) A provision that any sum becoming due by reason of the death of the person insured shall be payable to the beneficiary designated by the person insured, subject to the provisions of the policy in the event there is no designated beneficiary, as to all or any part of such sum, living at the death of the person insured, and subject to any right reserved by the insurer in the policy and set forth in the certificate to pay at its option a part of such sum not exceeding $500 to any person appearing to the insurer to be equitably entitled thereto by reason of having incurred funeral or other expenses incident to the last illness or death of the person insured.

(7) A provision that the insurer will issue to the policyholder for delivery to each person insured an individual certificate setting forth a statement as to the insurance protection to which he is entitled, to whom the insurance benefits are payable, and the rights and conditions set forth in (8), (9) and (10) following.

(8) A provision that if the insurance, or any portion of it, on a person covered under the policy ceases because of termination of employment or of membership in the class or classes eligible for coverage under the policy, such person shall be entitled to have issued to him by the insurer, without evidence of insurability, an individual policy of life insurance without disability or other supplementary benefits, provided application for the individual policy shall be made, and the first premium paid to the insurer, within thirty-one days after such termination, and provided further that,

    (a) The individual policy shall, at the option of such person be on any one of the forms, except term insurance, then customarily issued by the insurer at the age and for the amount applied for;

    (b) the individual policy shall be in an amount not in excess of the amount of life insurance which ceases because of such termination, provided that any amount of insurance which shall have matured on or before the date of such termination as an endowment payable to the person insured, whether in one sum or in instalments or in the form of an annuity, shall not, for the purposes of this provision, be included in the amount which is considered to cease because of such termination; and

    (c) the premium on the individual policy shall be at the insurer's then customary rate applicable to the form and amount of the individual policy, to the class of risk to which such person then belongs, and to his age attained on the effective date of the individual policy.

(9) A provision that if the group policy terminates or is amended so as to terminate the insurance of any class of insured persons, every person insured thereunder at the date of such termination whose insurance terminates and who has been so insured for at least five

years prior to such termination date shall be entitled to have issued to him by the insurer an individual policy of life insurance, subject to the same conditions and limitations as are provided by (8) above, except that the group policy may provide that the amount of such individual policy shall not exceed the smaller of (a) the amount of the person's life insurance protection ceasing because of the termination or amendment of the group policy, less the amount of any life insurance for which he is or becomes eligible under any group policy issued or reinstated by the same or another insurer within thirty-one days after such termination, and (b) $2,000.

(10) A provision that if a person insured under the group policy dies during the period within which he would have been entitled to have an individual policy issued to him in accordance with (8) or (9) above and before such an individual policy shall have become effective, the amount of life insurance which he would have been entitled to have issued to him under such individual policy shall be payable as a claim under the group policy, whether or not application for the individual policy or the payment of the first premium therefor has been made.

(11) In the case of a policy issued to a creditor to insure debtors of such creditor, a provision that the insurer will furnish to the policyholder for delivery to each debtor insured under the policy a form which will contain a statement that the life of the debtor is insured under the policy and that any death benefit paid thereunder by reason of his death shall be applied to reduce or extinguish the indebtedness.

SUPPLEMENTARY BILL RELATING TO CONVERSION PRIVILEGES

If any individual insured under a group life insurance policy hereafter delivered in this state becomes entitled under the terms of such policy to have an individual policy of life insurance issued to him without evidence of insurability, subject to making of application and payment of the first premium within the period specified in such policy, and if such individual is not given notice of the existence of such right at least 15 days prior to the expiration date of such period, then in such event the individual shall have an additional period within which to exercise such right, but nothing herein contained shall be construed to continue any insurance beyond the period provided in such policy. This additional period shall expire 15 days next after the individual is given such notice but in no event shall such additional period extend beyond 60 days next after the expiration date of the period provided in such policy. Written notice presented to the individual or mailed by the policy holder to the last known address of the individual or mailed by the insurer to the last known address of the individual as furnished by the policyholder shall constitute notice for the purpose of this paragraph.

Appendix G. Specimen Group Life Certificate

THE ———————— LIFE
INSURANCE COMPANY

HEREBY CERTIFIES THAT,

> Subject to the terms and conditions of Group Life Insurance Policy No............
> the life of the Employee named on the back page of this certificate, an Employee of

(Hereinafter called the Employer)

is insured for the amount set forth on such back page. The insurance is to be payable to the beneficiary designated on such back page upon receipt of due proof of the death of the Employee occurring while insured thereunder.

BENEFICIARY: The Employee may change the beneficiary from time to time by written request filed with the Employer, but any such change shall take effect only upon its entry by the Employer on the insurance records maintained by the Employer in connection with the insurance under the contract. Any part of the insurance for which there is no beneficiary designated by the Employee or surviving at the death of the Employee will be payable in a single sum to the first surviving class of the following classes of successive preference beneficiaries: The Employee's (a) widow or widower; (b) surviving children; (c) surviving parents; (d) surviving brothers and sisters; (e) executors or administrators.

In the absence of the appointment of a legal guardian, any minor's share may be paid at a rate not exceeding $50 a month to such adult or adults as have in the Company's opinion assumed the custody and principal support of such minor.

This individual certificate is furnished in accordance with and subject to the terms of the said Group Life Insurance policy, which policy, and the application therefor, constitute the entire contract between the parties. This certificate is merely evidence of insurance provided under said Group Life Insurance policy, which insurance is effective only if the Employee is eligible for insurance and becomes and remains insured in accordance with the provisions, terms and conditions of the said policy.

(FOR additional provisions see subsequent pages hereof)

GROUP LIFE CERTIFICATE

WAIVER OF PREMIUM

CONVERSION PRIVILEGE: A. Upon Termination of Employment. If the Employee's employment is terminated in the class or classes of Employees insured under the Group policy, the Employee shall be entitled to have issued to him by the Company, without evidence of insurability, upon application made to the Company within thirty-one days after such termination and upon the payment of the premium applicable to the class of risk to which he belongs and to the form and amount of the policy at his then attained age, an individual policy of life insurance in any one of the forms then customarily issued by the Company (except a policy of Term insurance, or a policy providing benefits in the event of total and permanent disability or additional benefits in event of accidental death) in an amount equal to, or at the option of the Employee, less than the amount of his insurance under the Group policy at the time of such termination. Such individual insurance policy, if issued, shall become effective on the expiration of the thirty-first day following the day on which occurred the termination of his employment, provided the premium therefor is paid to the Company not later than such effective date.

B. Upon Termination of Policy. If the Group policy is terminated or amended so as to terminate the insurance of any class of Employees in which he is included, the Employee, if he has been continuously insured under said policy for five years or more immediately prior to such a termination, shall be entitled upon such a termination to the same benefits and upon the same conditions and limitations as set forth in the foregoing paragraph upon termination of employment, except that the amount of such converted life insurance shall in no event exceed the lesser of:

(1) $2,000, and

(2) the amount of the insurance on the Employee's life under the Group policy at the date of such a termination less any amount of life insurance for which he may become eligible under any group policy issued or reinstated by the Company or another insurer within thirty-one days after the date of such a termination.

ASSIGNMENTS: No assignment by the Employee of any of the insurance under the policy shall be valid.

INDIVIDUAL TERMINATIONS: The insurance upon the life of the Employee under said Group Life Insurance policy shall cease automatically upon the occurrence of any of the following events: (a) the termination of the policy, (b) the termination of his employment in the classes of Employees insured thereunder.

Note: In case the Employee ceases active work due to sickness, injury, retirement on pension, leave of absence or temporary lay-off, the terms of the Group policy may provide for continuance of insurance for a limited period. The Employee should consult the Employer who is in a position to inform the Employee as to the terms of the policy in this respect.

OPTIONAL MODES OF SETTLEMENT: By giving proper written notice, the Employee may elect (with the right to revoke or to change such election) to have the whole or any part of the amount which would otherwise be payable to the beneficiary in a single sum paid in instalments or in any other manner that may be agreed to by the Company. The amount and terms of payment shall be in accordance with those customarily offered by the Company for group life insurance policies at the time of election. If the Employee does not make an election, the beneficiary may do so after the Employee's death.

MISSTATEMENT OF AGE: If the amount of insurance depends upon the age of the Employee and if there has been a misstatement of the Employee's age, there shall be an adjustment of the amount of his insurance to that determined by his correct age.

EXTENDED DEATH BENEFIT.

A. During Conversion Period Following Termination of Employment. Upon receipt of due proof that an Employee whose insurance under the Group policy terminated due to termination of employment in the class or classes of Employees insured thereunder, died within thirty-one days after such termination of employment, the Company will pay to the Employee's beneficiary the amount of insurance for which the Employee was last insured under said policy.

B. During Conversion Period Following Termination or Amendment of Policy. If an Employee's insurance is terminated due to termination or amendment of the Group policy, and if he has been continuously insured under said policy for five years or more immediately prior to such termination of his insurance, then upon receipt of due proof that the Employee died within thirty-one days following such termination, the Company will pay to the Employee's beneficiary the lesser of:

(1) $2,000, and

(2) the amount of insurance for which the Employee was last insured under the Group policy reduced by any amount for which the Employee became insured under any group policy issued or reinstated by the Company or another insurer within thirty-one days after the date of such termination.

C. During Total Disability Commencing Prior to Age Sixty. If an Employee before attaining 60 years of age and after the effective date hereof but before cessation of his insurance in accordance with the provision hereof entitled "Individual Terminations" becomes totally disabled by bodily injury or disease so as to be prevented from engaging in any occupation for compensation or profit, and

(1) the Employee remains continuously so disabled until his death, and

(2) death occurs either:

(a) within one year after the date of discontinuance of premium payments for the Employee's insurance, or

(b) more than one year after said date of discontinuance but prior to termination of this benefit because of failure of the Employee to submit due proof of continued total disability as required in the following paragraph,

then, upon receipt within one year after the Employee's death of due proof of such continued total disability and death, the Company, provided the Employee has complied with the conditions of this provision hereinafter set forth, will pay to the Employee's beneficiary the amount of insurance for which the Employee's life was last insured under the Group policy, but the amount so payable shall be reduced by any amount payable under Paragraph A or Paragraph B of this provision.

Extension of the death benefit hereunder beyond any anniversary of the date of discontinuance of premium payments for the Employee's insurance shall be subject to the Employee's submitting due proof in writing at the Home Office of the Company within three months prior to each such anniversary that he has been totally and continuously disabled since said date of discontinuance. If the Employee fails to submit such proof within three months prior to any anniversary the benefit shall terminate on that anniversary unless previously terminated because the Employee has ceased to be totally disabled as defined herein.

Extension of the death benefit hereunder shall also be subject to the following conditions:

(1) If an individual policy shall have been issued in conversion of the Employee's insurance under the Group policy, such individual policy must be surrendered to the Company at the time due proof of total disability is first submitted during the Employee's lifetime. Upon such surrender, the Company will refund any premiums theretofore received by the Company under the individual policy.

(2) The Company shall have the right and opportunity to have a medical representative of the Company examine the person of the Employee when and so often as it may reasonably require, but after the benefit has been continued for two full years under this provision, not more than once a year. Upon failure of the Employee to submit to any such examination this benefit shall terminate unless previously terminated because the Employee has ceased to be totally disabled as defined herein.

Upon termination of this benefit, the Employee, unless he becomes insured again under the Group policy within thirty-one days after such termination, shall be entitled to the rights and benefits set forth in Paragraph A of this provision and in Paragraph A of the provision hereof entitled "Conversion Privilege," as if employment had terminated on the date of such termination of benefit.

D. If a benefit becomes payable hereunder after an individual policy shall have been issued in conversion of the Employee's insurance under the Group policy, the amount, if any, paid as a death benefit under such individual policy shall be deemed to be a payment toward the amount of benefit becoming due hereunder and any premiums paid under the individual policy will be paid to the beneficiary thereunder upon surrender of the policy. The designation of a beneficiary under such an individual policy or in the application therefor (if such policy has not been issued) different from the beneficiary under the Group policy shall, notwithstanding any other provision of said Group policy, effect a change of beneficiary hereunder to the beneficiary so designated. While a benefit is continued under Paragraph C of this provision, an Employee may from time to time change the beneficiary by filing a written request with the Company at its Home Office, but such change shall take effect only upon receipt of the request for change at the Home Office of the Company.

Appendix H. Death Rates and Expectation of Life under Various Mortality and Annuity Tables

Age	American Experience 1843–1858		American Men 1900–1915		1941 Standard Industrial 1930–1939	
	Deaths per 1,000	Expecta-tion of Life Years	Deaths per 1,000	Expecta-tion of Life Years	Deaths per 1,000	Expecta-tion of Life Years
0	154.70	41.45	27.85	60.80	. . . . .	. . . . .
1	63.49	47.94	7.39	61.52	31.54	56.43
2	35.50	50.16	4.81	60.98	8.25	57.25
3	23.91	50.98	3.85	60.27	5.20	56.72
4	17.70	51.22	3.55	59.50	4.10	56.01
5	13.60	51.13	3.32	58.71	3.63	55.24
6	11.37	50.83	3.13	57.91	3.29	54.44
7	9.75	50.41	2.94	57.09	3.07	53.62
8	8.63	49.90	2.76	56.25	2.89	52.78
9	7.90	49.33	2.53	55.41	2.73	51.94
10	7.49	48.72	2.37	54.55	2.60	51.08
11	7.52	48.08	2.30	53.67	2.51	50.21
12	7.54	47.45	2.30	52.80	2.50	49.33
13	7.57	46.80	2.37	51.92	2.55	48.46
14	7.60	46.16	2.49	51.04	2.68	47.58
15	7.63	45.50	2.64	50.17	2.86	46.71
16	7.66	44.85	2.86	49.30	3.07	45.84
17	7.69	44.19	3.16	48.44	3.28	44.98
18	7.73	43.53	3.48	47.59	3.49	44.12
19	7.77	42.87	3.75	46.76	3.71	43.28
20	7.80	42.20	3.92	45.93	3.93	42.44
21	7.86	41.53	4.02	45.11	4.13	41.60
22	7.91	40.85	4.12	44.29	4.29	40.77
23	7.96	40.17	4.18	43.47	4.45	39.95
24	8.01	39.49	4.25	42.65	4.60	39.12
25	8.06	38.81	4.31	41.83	4.73	38.30
26	8.13	38.12	4.35	41.01	4.85	37.45
27	8.20	37.43	4.39	40.18	4.97	36.66
28	8.26	36.73	4.41	39.36	5.09	35.84
29	8.34	36.03	4.43	38.53	5.23	35.02
30	8.43	35.33	4.46	37.70	5.39	34.20
31	8.51	34.63	4.48	36.87	5.57	33.39
32	8.61	33.92	4.51	36.03	5.78	32.57
33	8.72	33.21	4.59	35.19	6.02	31.76
34	8.83	32.50	4.68	34.35	6.28	30.95
35	8.95	31.78	4.78	33.51	6.58	30.14

Appendix H. Death Rates and Expectation of Life under Various Mortality and Annuity Tables (Continued)

1937 Standard Annuity—Male 1932–1936		Annuity Table for 1949—Male 1939–1949		Group Annuity Table for 1951—Male 1939–1951	
Deaths per 1,000	Expectation of Life Years	Deaths per 1,000	Expectation of Life Years	Deaths per 1,000	Expectation of Life Years
11.31	68.49	4.04	73.18	....	....
5.11	68.27	1.58	72.48	....	....
3.32	67.62	.89	71.59	....	....
2.16	66.84	.72	70.65	....	....
1.50	65.99	.63	69.70	....	....
1.23	65.08	.57	68.75	.56	....
1.24	64.16	.53	67.78	.52	....
1.25	63.24	.50	66.82	.49	....
1.25	62.32	.49	65.85	.48	....
1.26	61.40	.48	64.89	.48	....
1.26	60.48	.48	63.92	.48	....
1.26	59.55	.49	62.95	.49	....
1.26	58.63	.50	61.98	.50	....
1.26	57.70	.51	61.01	.51	....
1.26	56.77	.52	60.04	.52	....
1.26	55.84	.54	59.07	.53	....
1.27	54.91	.55	58.10	.54	....
1.28	53.98	.57	57.13	.56	....
1.29	53.05	.58	56.17	.58	....
1.31	52.12	.60	55.20	.60	....
1.33	51.18	.62	54.23	.62	....
1.36	50.25	.65	53.27	.64	....
1.40	49.32	.67	52.30	.67	....
1.44	48.39	.70	51.33	.69	....
1.50	47.46	.73	50.37	.72	....
1.56	46.53	.77	49.41	.76	....
1.63	45.60	.81	48.44	.80	....
1.72	44.67	.85	47.48	.84	....
1.82	43.75	.90	46.52	.89	....
1.94	42.83	.95	45.56	.94	....
2.07	41.91	1.00	44.61	.99	....
2.21	41.00	1.07	43.65	1.05	....
2.38	40.09	1.14	42.70	1.12	....
2.56	39.18	1.21	41.75	1.20	....
2.76	38.28	1.30	40.80	1.28	....
2.98	37.38	1.39	39.85	1.37	....

Appendix H. Death Rates and Expectation of Life under Various Mortality and Annuity Tables (Continued)

AGE	AMERICAN EXPERIENCE 1843–1858		AMERICAN MEN 1900–1915		1941 STANDARD INDUSTRIAL 1930–1939	
	Deaths per 1,000	Expectation of Life Years	Deaths per 1,000	Expectation of Life Years	Deaths per 1,000	Expectation of Life Years
36	9.09	31.07	4.94	32.67	6.91	29.33
37	9.23	30.35	5.12	31.83	7.29	28.53
38	9.41	29.62	5.32	30.99	7.72	27.74
39	9.59	28.90	5.56	30.15	8.19	26.95
40	9.79	28.18	5.84	29.32	8.71	26.17
41	10.01	27.45	6.16	28.49	9.29	25.40
42	10.25	26.72	6.54	27.66	9.93	24.63
43	10.52	26.00	6.94	26.84	10.64	23.87
44	10.83	25.27	7.42	26.03	11.44	23.12
45	11.16	24.54	7.94	25.22	12.32	22.39
46	11.56	23.81	8.52	24.43	13.27	21.66
47	12.00	23.08	9.18	23.62	14.27	20.94
48	12.51	22.36	9.89	22.83	15.31	20.24
49	13.11	21.63	10.70	22.06	16.40	19.55
50	13.78	20.91	11.58	21.29	17.55	18.86
51	14.54	20.20	12.54	20.53	18.77	18.19
52	15.39	19.49	13.62	19.79	20.08	17.53
53	16.33	18.79	14.78	19.05	21.51	16.88
54	17.40	18.09	16.08	18.33	23.06	16.24
55	18.57	17.40	17.47	17.62	24.75	15.61
56	19.89	16.72	19.02	16.93	26.59	14.99
57	21.34	16.05	20.69	16.25	28.61	14.39
58	22.94	15.39	22.51	15.58	30.85	13.80
59	24.72	14.74	24.49	14.93	33.33	13.22
60	26.69	14.10	26.68	14.29	36.08	12.66
61	28.88	13.47	29.03	13.67	39.10	12.12
62	31.29	12.86	31.58	13.06	42.38	11.59
63	33.94	12.26	34.37	12.47	45.88	11.08
64	36.87	11.67	37.38	11.90	49.54	10.59
65	40.13	11.10	40.66	11.34	53.33	10.11
66	43.71	10.54	44.18	10.80	57.21	9.66
67	47.65	10.00	48.03	10.28	61.20	9.21
68	52.00	9.47	52.16	9.77	65.36	8.78
69	56.76	8.97	56.64	9.28	69.79	8.36
70	61.99	8.48	61.47	8.81	74.56	7.95

Appendix H. Death Rates and Expectation of Life under Various Mortality and Annuity Tables (Continued)

1937 STANDARD ANNUITY—MALE 1932–1936		ANNUITY TABLE FOR 1949—MALE 1939–1949		GROUP ANNUITY TABLE FOR 1951—MALE 1939–1951	
Deaths per 1,000	Expectation of Life Years	Deaths per 1,000	Expectation of Life Years	Deaths per 1,000	Expectation of Life Years
3.22	36.49	1.49	38.90	1.48	....
3.47	35.61	1.61	37.96	1.59	....
3.74	34.73	1.73	37.02	1.71	....
4.04	33.86	1.87	36.08	1.85	....
4.36	33.00	2.03	35.15	2.00	....
4.70	32.14	2.22	34.22	2.19	....
5.07	31.29	2.48	33.30	2.45	....
5.47	30.44	2.80	32.38	2.77	....
5.90	29.61	3.19	31.47	3.15	....
6.36	28.78	3.63	30.57	3.58	....
6.86	27.96	4.12	29.68	4.07	....
7.40	27.15	4.66	28.80	4.60	....
7.98	26.35	5.25	27.93	5.18	....
8.61	25.56	5.88	27.07	5.81	....
9.29	24.78	6.56	26.23	6.48	25.58
10.02	24.01	7.28	25.40	7.19	24.74
10.80	23.24	8.04	24.58	7.94	23.92
11.65	22.49	8.84	23.78	8.73	23.10
12.57	21.75	9.68	22.99	9.56	22.30
13.55	21.02	10.56	22.20	10.44	21.51
14.61	20.30	11.49	21.44	11.35	20.74
15.76	19.60	12.46	20.68	12.30	19.97
16.99	18.90	13.48	19.93	13.30	19.21
18.32	18.22	14.54	19.20	14.38	18.46
19.75	17.55	15.66	18.48	15.56	17.72
21.30	16.90	16.87	17.76	16.87	17.00
22.96	16.25	18.20	17.06	18.35	16.28
24.75	15.62	19.67	16.37	20.07	15.57
26.68	15.01	21.28	15.68	22.07	14.88
28.75	14.40	23.07	15.01	24.42	14.21
30.99	13.81	25.03	14.36	27.19	13.55
33.39	13.24	27.19	13.71	30.11	12.92
35.98	12.68	29.58	13.08	32.99	12.30
38.76	12.14	32.20	12.46	35.94	11.70
41.76	11.60	35.09	11.86	39.30	11.12

Appendix H. Death Rates and Expectation of Life under Various Mortality and Annuity Tables (Continued)

Age	American Experience 1843–1858		American Men 1900–1915		1941 Standard Industrial 1930–1939	
	Deaths per 1,000	Expectation of Life Years	Deaths per 1,000	Expectation of Life Years	Deaths per 1,000	Expectation of Life Years
71	67.67	8.00	66.70	8.35	79.78	7.55
72	73.73	7.55	72.33	7.91	85.52	7.16
73	80.18	7.11	78.39	7.49	91.83	6.78
74	87.03	6.68	84.92	7.08	98.74	6.42
75	94.37	6.27	91.94	6.69	106.26	6.06
76	102.31	5.88	99.51	6.32	114.40	5.73
77	111.06	5.49	107.65	5.96	123.16	5.40
78	120.83	5.11	116.31	5.62	132.59	5.09
79	131.73	4.74	125.69	5.30	142.74	4.79
80	144.47	4.39	135.74	4.99	153.65	4.50
81	158.60	4.05	146.42	4.69	165.40	4.23
82	174.30	3.71	157.87	4.41	178.03	3.97
83	191.56	3.39	170.05	4.14	191.60	3.72
84	211.36	3.08	183.15	3.89	206.17	3.49
85	235.55	2.77	198.07	3.65	221.79	3.26
86	265.68	2.47	211.80	3.42	238.48	3.05
87	303.02	2.18	227.29	3.21	256.30	2.85
88	346.69	1.91	244.08	3.00	275.28	2.66
89	395.86	1.66	261.70	2.81	295.45	2.48
90	454.55	1.42	280.35	2.63	316.83	2.31
91	532.47	1.19	299.46	2.46	339.45	2.15
92	634.26	.98	321.08	2.30	363.28	2.00
93	734.18	.80	341.88	2.15	388.34	1.85
94	857.14	.64	363.64	2.01	414.58	1.71
95	1,000.00	.50	387.76	1.87	441.95	1.57
96			411.11	1.74	470.40	1.42
97			443.40	1.61	499.83	1.24
98			457.63	1.50	530.13	.97
99			500.00	1.34	1,000.00	.50
100			562.50	1.19		
101			571.43	1.07		
102			666.67	.83		
103			1,000.00	.50		
104						
105						
106						
107						
108						
109						
110						

Appendix H. Death Rates and Expectation of Life under Various Mortality and Annuity Tables (Concluded)

1937 STANDARD ANNUITY—MALE 1932–1936		ANNUITY TABLE FOR 1949—MALE 1939–1949		GROUP ANNUITY TABLE FOR 1951—MALE 1939–1951	
Deaths per 1,000	Expectation of Life Years	Deaths per 1,000	Expectation of Life Years	Deaths per 1,000	Expectation of Life Years
44.98	11.09	38.27	11.28	43.18	10.56
48.44	10.59	41.77	10.71	47.48	10.01
52.17	10.10	45.62	10.15	52.08	9.48
56.17	9.63	49.85	9.61	57.08	8.98
60.46	9.17	54.50	9.09	62.43	8.49
65.08	8.73	59.61	8.58	68.35	...
70.03	8.30	65.22	8.10	75.13	...
75.35	7.89	71.37	7.63	82.69	...
81.05	7.49	78.11	7.17	90.95	...
87.16	7.11	85.50	6.74	99.68	...
93.71	6.74	93.59	6.32	108.71	...
100.72	6.39	102.44	5.92	117.98	...
108.23	6.05	112.11	5.54	127.44	...
116.26	5.72	122.67	5.18	137.07	...
124.84	5.41	134.18	4.84	146.85	...
134.00	5.11	146.71	4.51	156.84	...
143.79	4.82	160.33	4.20	167.12	...
154.21	4.54	175.12	3.90	177.79	...
165.32	4.28	191.15	3.62	188.92	...
177.14	4.03	208.49	3.36	200.59	...
189.71	3.79	227.19	3.12	212.56	...
203.06	3.56	247.33	2.88	225.16	...
217.22	3.34	268.96	2.67	238.52	...
232.20	3.13	292.12	2.47	252.77	...
248.06	2.92	316.83	2.28	268.03	...
264.80	2.72	343.12	2.10	284.46	...
283.51	2.52	370.97	1.94	302.22	...
305.78	2.32	400.35	1.79	321.52	...
331.84	2.12	431.20	1.65	342.53	...
362.12	1.93	463.41	1.52	365.46	...
397.58	1.74	496.87	1.40	390.54	...
438.92	1.55	531.39	1.29	417.98	...
487.28	1.37	566.76	1.20	450.10	...
542.28	1.20	602.71	1.10	489.20	...
610.44	1.04	638.96	1.02	537.61	...
690.72	.88	657.14	.94	597.62	...
800.00	.73	710.90	.86	671.55	...
833.33	.67	745.82	.75	761.72	...
1,000.00	.50	1,000.00	.50	870.43	...
				1,000.00	...

Appendix I. Net Single Premiums Per $1,000, 1958 C.S.O. Mortality Table, 2½% Interest Curtate Functions

ATTAINED AGE MALE*	ENDOWMENT INSURANCE AT AGES				TERM INSURANCE TO AGES	
	55	60	65	70	55	60
0	288.11	263.91	244.45	229.63	73.87	88.93
1	290.29	265.31	245.22	229.92	69.13	84.68
2	296.31	270.66	250.03	234.32	69.22	85.18
3	302.66	276.32	255.15	239.02	69.54	85.92
4	309.22	282.18	260.45	243.89	69.92	86.74
5	315.99	288.24	265.93	240.93	70.36	87.63
6	322.98	294.50	271.60	254.15	70.87	88.59
7	330.18	300.95	277.45	259.54	71.43	89.62
8	337.60	307.60	283.48	265.11	72.05	90.72
9	345.23	314.45	289.70	270.84	72.71	91.87
10	353.08	321.49	296.09	276.73	73.41	93.07
11	361.14	328.71	302.65	282.78	74.12	94.30
12	369.39	336.12	309.36	288.98	74.84	95.54
13	377.84	343.69	316.23	295.31	75.54	96.79
14	386.48	351.43	323.25	301.78	76.21	98.02
15	395.30	359.32	330.40	308.36	76.83	99.22
16	404.31	367.38	337.69	315.07	77.41	100.39
17	413.52	375.61	345.12	321.90	77.92	101.51
18	422.92	384.00	352.70	328.86	78.38	102.60
19	432.53	392.57	360.44	335.96	78.78	103.65
20	442.38	401.34	368.35	343.22	79.15	104.68
21	452.46	410.32	376.45	350.63	79.48	105.70
22	462.78	419.52	384.73	358.23	79.78	106.71
23	473.37	428.94	393.22	366.00	80.07	107.72
24	484.23	438.61	401.92	373.97	80.33	108.72
25	495.38	448.52	410.84	382.14	80.58	109.74
26	506.81	458.69	420.00	390.52	80.82	110.77
27	518.53	469.11	429.38	399.10	81.04	111.80
28	530.56	479.81	439.00	407.90	81.24	112.83
29	542.90	490.77	448.85	416.92	81.41	113.85
30	555.55	502.00	458.95	426.14	81.53	114.85
31	568.52	513.52	469.29	435.60	81.62	115.84
32	581.82	525.31	479.89	445.27	81.65	116.80
33	595.45	537.41	490.74	455.18	81.62	117.74
34	609.43	549.80	501.85	465.32	81.53	118.64

* Except for ages below 15, female values are the equivalent of those for males three years younger. Values for females under 15 (not shown here) are derived on a special extension of the 1958 C.S.O. Table in order to avoid the anomalies that would be introduced by a three-year age setback for females at the younger ages.

Appendix I. Net Single Premiums Per $1,000, 1958 C.S.O. Mortality Table, 2½% Interest Curtate Functions (Continued)

TERM INSURANCE TO AGES		PURE ENDOWMENT AT AGES				WHOLE LIFE INSURANCE
65	70	55	60	65	70	
107.84	130.34	214.24	174.97	136.61	99.28	207.68
104.19	127.42	221.16	180.63	141.02	102.49	207.26
105.22	129.07	227.09	185.47	144.80	105.24	211.05
106.50	130.98	233.12	190.40	148.65	108.03	215.13
107.86	132.99	239.29	195.44	152.59	110.90	219.37
109.31	135.10	245.62	200.61	156.62	113.83	223.77
110.84	137.31	252.10	205.90	160.75	116.83	228.32
112.46	139.63	258.74	211.32	164.99	119.91	233.03
114.15	142.04	265.54	216.88	169.33	123.06	237.90
115.92	144.54	272.52	222.58	173.77	126.29	242.92
117.75	147.12	279.67	228.42	178.33	129.61	248.08
119.63	149.77	287.01	234.41	183.01	133.01	253.38
121.54	152.47	294.55	240.57	187.82	136.50	258.80
123.47	155.22	302.29	246.89	192.76	140.09	264.34
125.40	157.99	310.26	253.40	197.84	143.78	269.99
127.33	160.77	318.46	260.10	203.07	147.58	275.73
129.24	163.57	326.90	266.99	208.45	151.50	281.58
131.13	166.37	335.59	274.09	213.99	155.52	287.52
133.00	169.19	344.53	281.39	219.69	159.67	293.56
134.87	172.02	353.75	288.92	225.57	163.94	299.72
136.74	174.88	363.22	296.66	231.61	168.33	306.00
138.61	177.78	372.97	304.62	237.83	172.85	312.42
140.51	180.73	382.99	312.81	244.22	177.49	318.99
142.43	183.73	393.30	321.22	250.79	182.27	325.71
144.37	186.78	403.90	329.88	257.55	187.18	332.59
146.35	189.91	414.79	338.77	264.49	192.23	339.64
148.36	193.10	425.98	347.91	271.63	197.41	346.87
150.41	196.35	437.49	357.31	278.97	202.75	354.28
152.48	199.67	449.32	366.97	286.51	208.23	361.87
154.58	203.04	461.49	376.91	294.27	213.87	369.64
156.69	206.47	474.01	387.14	302.26	219.67	377.58
158.81	209.94	486.90	397.67	310.47	225.65	385.71
160.95	213.47	500.17	408.50	318.93	231.80	394.03
163.09	217.05	513.83	419.66	327.65	238.13	402.54
165.23	220.66	527.90	431.15	336.62	244.65	411.23

Appendix I. Net Single Premiums Per $1,000, 1958 C.S.O. Mortality Table, 2½% Interest Curtate Functions (Continued)

ATTAINED AGE MALE*	ENDOWMENT INSURANCE AT AGES				TERM INSURANCE TO AGES	
	55	60	65	70	55	60
35	623.76	562.49	513.23	475.69	81.36	119.49
36	638.45	575.49	524.87	486.29	81.09	120.27
37	653.50	588.79	536.76	497.12	80.69	120.96
38	668.91	602.40	548.92	508.18	80.13	121.52
39	684.68	616.30	561.32	519.43	79.37	121.92
40	700.83	630.51	573.97	530.89	78.35	122.11
41	717.35	645.02	586.86	542.55	77.06	122.07
42	734.26	659.84	600.00	554.41	75.43	121.75
43	751.58	674.98	613.39	566.46	73.45	121.12
44	769.33	690.45	627.03	578.71	71.08	120.17
45	787.52	706.27	640.94	591.17	68.28	118.84
46	806.17	722.44	655.12	603.83	64.98	117.08
47	825.30	738.98	669.57	616.69	61.13	114.85
48	844.95	755.90	684.30	629.75	56.66	112.07
49	865.14	773.22	699.32	643.01	51.49	108.68
50	885.90	790.97	714.64	656.48	45.52	104.59
51	907.27	809.15	730.26	670.15	38.66	99.72
52	929.31	827.81	746.20	684.02	30.80	93.96
53	952.07	846.98	762.49	698.12	21.82	87.22
54	975.60	866.71	779.15	712.44	11.60	79.37
55	...	887.03	796.20	727.00	...	70.29
56	...	908.01	813.69	741.82	...	59.83
57	...	929.71	831.64	756.91	...	47.79
58	...	952.21	850.10	772.29	...	33.97
59	...	975.60	869.13	788.00	...	18.13
60	...	...	888.79	804.06	...	...
61	...	...	909.16	820.51	...	...
62	...	...	930.34	837.40	...	...
63	...	...	952.44	854.81	...	...
64	...	...	975.60	872.80	...	...

* Except for ages below 15, female values are the equivalent of those for males three years younger. Values for females under 15 (not shown here) are derived on a special extension of the 1958 C.S.O. Table in order to avoid the anomalies that would be introduced by a three-year age setback for females at the younger ages.

Appendix I. Net Single Premiums Per $1,000, 1958 C.S.O. Mortality Table, $2\frac{1}{2}\%$ Interest Curtate Functions (Continued)

TERM INSURANCE TO AGES		PURE ENDOWMENT AT AGES				WHOLE LIFE INSURANCE
65	70	55	60	65	70	
167.36	224.32	542.40	443.00	345.86	251.37	420.12
169.46	227.99	557.35	455.21	355.40	258.30	429.19
171.51	231.66	572.80	467.83	365.25	265.46	438.44
173.48	235.31	588.77	480.87	375.43	272.86	447.86
175.34	238.90	605.31	494.38	385.98	280.52	457.42
177.05	242.41	622.47	508.39	396.92	288.48	467.12
178.57	245.81	640.29	522.95	408.29	296.73	476.95
179.89	249.07	658.83	538.09	420.11	305.33	486.91
180.97	252.18	678.12	553.85	432.41	314.27	496.98
181.79	255.11	698.24	570.28	445.24	323.59	507.18
182.31	257.84	719.24	587.43	458.63	333.32	517.48
182.49	260.33	741.18	605.35	472.62	343.49	527.89
182.29	262.54	764.17	624.13	487.28	354.15	538.40
181.64	264.42	788.29	643.82	502.66	365.32	548.99
180.49	265.93	813.65	664.54	518.83	377.08	559.66
178.76	267.01	840.38	686.37	535.87	389.46	570.38
176.37	267.59	868.61	709.43	553.88	402.55	581.16
173.25	267.61	898.51	733.85	572.95	416.41	591.97
169.31	267.00	930.24	759.76	593.18	431.11	602.81
164.44	265.68	963.99	787.33	614.70	446.75	613.68
158.54	263.56	...	816.74	637.66	463.44	624.55
151.47	260.53	...	848.18	662.21	481.28	635.42
143.08	256.48	...	881.92	688.55	500.42	646.28
133.19	251.26	...	918.24	716.90	521.03	657.11
121.59	244.70	...	957.47	747.53	543.29	667.89
108.05	236.63	...	...	780.73	567.42	678.62
92.29	226.31	...	...	816.87	593.69	689.26
74.00	215.03	...	...	856.34	622.37	699.82
52.82	200.98	...	...	899.61	653.82	710.27
28.33	184.33	...	...	947.27	688.46	720.60

Appendix I. Net Single Premiums Per $1,000, 1958 C.S.O. Mortality Table, $2\frac{1}{2}\%$ Interest Curtate Functions (Continued)

ATTAINED AGE MALE*	ENDOWMFNT INSURANCE AT AGES				TERM INSURANCE TO AGES	
	55	60	65	70	55	60
65	. . .	. . .	. . .	891.47	. . .	. . .
66	. . .	. . .	. . .	910.93	. . .	. . .
67	. . .	. . .	. . .	931.31	. . .	. . .
68	. . .	. . .	. . .	952.80	. . .	. . .
69	. . .	. . .	. . .	975.60	. . .	. . .
70	. . .	. . .	. . .	. . .	. . .	. . .
71	. . .	. . .	. . .	. . .	. . .	. . .
72	. . .	. . .	. . .	. . .	. . .	. . .
73	. . .	. . .	. . .	. . .	. . .	. . .
74	. . .	. . .	. . .	. . .	. . .	. . .
75	. . .	. . .	. . .	. . .	. . .	. . .
76	. . .	. . .	. . .	. . .	. . .	. . .
77	. . .	. . .	. . .	. . .	. . .	. . .
78	. . .	. . .	. . .	. . .	. . .	. . .
79	. . .	. . .	. . .	. . .	. . .	. . .
80	. . .	. . .	. . .	. . .	. . .	. . .
81	. . .	. . .	. . .	. . .	. . .	. . .
82	. . .	. . .	. . .	. . .	. . .	. . .
83	. . .	. . .	. . .	. . .	. . .	. . .
84	. . .	. . .	. . .	. . .	. . .	. . .
85	. . .	. . .	. . .	. . .	. . .	. . .
86	. . .	. . .	. . .	. . .	. . .	. . .
87	. . .	. . .	. . .	. . .	. . .	. . .
88	. . .	. . .	. . .	. . .	. . .	. . .
89	. . .	. . .	. . .	. . .	. . .	. . .
90	. . .	. . .	. . .	. . .	. . .	. . .
91	. . .	. . .	. . .	. . .	. . .	. . .
92	. . .	. . .	. . .	. . .	. . .	. . .
93	. . .	. . .	. . .	. . .	. . .	. . .
94	. . .	. . .	. . .	. . .	. . .	. . .
95	. . .	. . .	. . .	. . .	. . .	. . .
96	. . .	. . .	. . .	. . .	. . .	. . .
97	. . .	. . .	. . .	. . .	. . .	. . .
98	. . .	. . .	. . .	. . .	. . .	. . .
99	. . .	. . .	. . .	. . .	. . .	. . .

* Except for ages below 15, female values are the equivalent of those for males three years younger. Values for females under 15 (not shown here) are derived on a special extension of the 1958 C.S.O. Table in order to avoid the anomalies that would be introduced by a three-year age setback for females at the younger ages.

Appendix I. Net Single Premiums Per $1,000, 1958 C.S.O. Mortality Table, 2½% Interest Curtate Functions (Continued)

TERM INSURANCE TO AGES		PURE ENDOWMENT AT AGES				WHOLE LIFE INSURANCE
65	70	55	60	65	70	
. . .	164.68	. . .	. . .	. . .	726.78	730.80
. . .	141.54	. . .	. . .	. . .	769.38	740.84
. . .	114.31	. . .	. . .	. . .	816.99	750.71
. . .	82.26	. . .	. . .	. . .	870.53	760.36
. . .	44.49	. . .	. . .	. . .	931.11	769.77
. . .	. . .	. . .	. . .	. . .	. . .	778.93
. . .	. . .	. . .	. . .	. . .	. . .	787.84
. . .	. . .	. . .	. . .	. . .	. . .	796.52
. . .	. . .	. . .	. . .	. . .	. . .	805.00
. . .	. . .	. . .	. . .	. . .	. . .	813.31
. . .	. . .	. . .	. . .	. . .	. . .	821.49
. . .	. . .	. . .	. . .	. . .	. . .	829.51
. . .	. . .	. . .	. . .	. . .	. . .	837.38
. . .	. . .	. . .	. . .	. . .	. . .	845.03
. . .	. . .	. . .	. . .	. . .	. . .	852.42
. . .	. . .	. . .	. . .	. . .	. . .	859.52
. . .	. . .	. . .	. . .	. . .	. . .	866.30
. . .	. . .	. . .	. . .	. . .	. . .	872.78
. . .	. . .	. . .	. . .	. . .	. . .	878.96
. . .	. . .	. . .	. . .	. . .	. . .	884.90
. . .	. . .	. . .	. . .	. . .	. . .	890.61
. . .	. . .	. . .	. . .	. . .	. . .	896.14
. . .	. . .	. . .	. . .	. . .	. . .	901.53
. . .	. . .	. . .	. . .	. . .	. . .	906.81
. . .	. . .	. . .	. . .	. . .	. . .	912.05
. . .	. . .	. . .	. . .	. . .	. . .	917.28
. . .	. . .	. . .	. . .	. . .	. . .	922.54
. . .	. . .	. . .	. . .	. . .	. . .	927.88
. . .	. . .	. . .	. . .	. . .	. . .	933.35
. . .	. . .	. . .	. . .	. . .	. . .	939.06
. . .	. . .	. . .	. . .	. . .	. . .	945.17
. . .	. . .	. . .	. . .	. . .	. . .	951.91
. . .	. . .	. . .	. . .	. . .	. . .	959.49
. . .	. . .	. . .	. . .	. . .	. . .	967.68
. . .	. . .	. . .	. . .	. . .	. . .	975.58

Appendix J. Net Single Premiums, Annuity Due, 1958 C.S.O. Mortality, $2\frac{1}{2}\%$ Interest, Curtate Functions

ATTAINED MALE AGE*	NUMBER OF PAYMENTS						WHOLE OF LIFE
	10	20	30	60x	65x	70x	
25	8.89	15.67	20.69	22.61	24.15	25.33	27.07
26	8.89	15.65	20.65	22.19	23.78	24.99	26.78
27	8.89	15.64	20.60	21.77	23.40	24.64	26.47
28	8.89	15.62	20.54	21.33	23.00	24.28	26.16
29	8.88	15.60	20.48	20.88	22.60	23.91	25.84
30	8.88	15.58	20.42	20.41	22.18	23.53	25.52
31	8.88	15.56	20.34	19.95	21.76	23.14	25.18
32	8.87	16.69	20.26	19.46	21.32	22.74	24.84
33	8.87	15.50	20.16	18.97	20.88	22.33	24.50
34	8.86	15.47	20.07	18.46	20.42	21.92	24.13
35	8.86	15.43	19.96	17.94	19.96	21.50	23.77
36	8.85	15.38	19.83	17.40	19.48	21.06	23.40
37	8.84	15.33	19.70	16.86	19.00	20.61	23.02
38	8.83	15.27	19.56	16.30	18.49	20.16	22.64
39	8.81	15.22	19.40	15.73	17.99	19.70	22.25
40	8.80	15.14	19.23	15.14	17.47	19.23	21.85
41	8.77	15.08	19.05	14.55	16.94	18.76	21.44
42	8.77	15.00	18.86	13.94	16.40	18.27	21.03
43	8.75	14.91	18.65	13.33	15.85	17.78	20.62
44	8.74	14.82	18.43	12.69	15.29	17.27	20.20
45	8.71	14.72	18.19	12.04	14.72	16.76	19.78
46	8.69	14.61	17.93	11.38	14.14	16.24	19.36
47	8.66	14.50	17.67	10.70	13.55	15.72	18.93
48	8.63	14.37	17.39	10.01	12.94	15.18	18.49
49	8.60	14.23	17.10	9.30	12.32	14.64	18.05
50	8.57	14.08	16.79	8.57	11.70	14.08	17.61
51	8.53	13.93	16.47	7.82	11.06	13.52	17.17
52	8.49	13.76	16.13	7.06	10.41	12.95	16.72
53	8.45	13.58	15.79	6.27	9.74	12.38	16.28
54	8.41	13.38	15.42	5.46	9.05	11.79	15.83
55	8.36	13.17	15.06	4.63	8.35	11.19	15.39
56	8.30	12.96	14.67	3.77	7.64	10.59	14.94
57	8.24	12.73	14.29	2.88	6.90	9.97	14.50
58	8.18	12.50	13.89	1.96	6.15	9.34	14.06
59	8.10	12.24	13.49	1.00	5.36	8.69	13.61
60	8.03	11.97	13.08		4.56	8.03	13.18
61	7.95	11.70	12.67		3.72	7.35	12.74
62	7.87	11.42	12.25		2.86	6.66	12.31
63	7.77	11.12	11.84		1.95	5.95	11.88
64	7.67	10.82	11.43		1.00	5.21	11.46

Appendix J. Net Single Premiums, Annuity Due, 1958 C.S.O. Mortality, $2\frac{1}{2}\%$ Interest, Curtate Functions (Continued)

ATTAINED MALE AGE*	NUMBER OF PAYMENTS						WHOLE OF LIFE
	10	20	30	60x	65x	70x	
65	7.56	10.50	11.02			4.45	11.04
66	7.45	10.19	10.62			3.65	10.63
67	7.33	9.87	10.22			2.82	10.22
68	7.21	9.54	9.82			1.93	9.83
69	7.08	9.22	9.43			1.00	9.44

* Female Values are the equivalent of those for males three years younger.

Appendix K. Typical Schedule of Commissions for Career Agency Agreement

New York Licensed Company

LIFE INSURANCE—Ages 0 to 70 inclusive

	(2) 1st Policy Year	(3) 2nd, 3rd, 4th Policy Years	(4) 5th through 10th Policy Years
Life Plans	*Vested*	*Conditional*	*Conditional*
(Participating and Non-Participating)			
Executive Special (NP)	50%*	10%	3%
Family Policy (NP)	50*	10	3
Juvenile 21 Special	50*	10	3
Life Paid-Up at Age 95			
(Non-Participating)	20	10	10
Limited Pay Life and Progressive Protection			
Premiums for 30 years or longer	50*	10	3
Premiums for 20 to 29 years	50	10	3
Premiums for 18 or 19 years	47½	10	3
Premiums for 13 to 17 years	42½	10	3
Premiums for 10 to 12 years	35	10	3
Premiums for 9 years	30	5	5
Premiums for 8 years	25	5	5
Premiums for 7 years	20	5	5
Premiums for 6 years	15	5	5
Premiums for 5 years	10	5.	5
Ordinary Life (see page 3 for			
Convertible forms)	50*	10	3
Progressive Protection (except Limited			
Pay)	50*	10	3
Term Insurance (Non-Participating)			
Decreasing Term	40	5	5
Family Income Agreement	(Same as basic policy)		
Five Year Renewable	40	(2nd, 3rd, 4th, 5th—5% 6th yr. 20%; 7–10—5%)	
Five Year Term—Life	40	(2nd, 3rd, 4th, 5th—5% 6th yr. 25%; 7–10—5%)	
Insurability Rider—			
attached to Life Paid-Up at Age 95	10	(same as basic policy)	
attached to all other policies	40	(same as basic policy)	
One Year Renewable	20	3	3
Ten Year Term	40	5	5 (5th yr. only)
Ten Year Term Agreement—			
attached to Life Paid-Up at Age 95	10	(same as basic policy)	
attached to all other policies	40	(same as basic policy)	
Endowment Plans			
(Participating and Non-Participating)			
Endowment, Premiums for Whole Term—			
Premiums for 38 years or longer	50*	10	3
Premiums for 30 to 37 years	45*	10	3
Premiums for 28 and 29 years	45	10	3
Premiums for 23 to 27 years	40	10	3
Premiums for 20 to 22 years	35	10	3
Premiums for 18 and 19 years	35	6	2
Premiums for 13 to17 years	30	6	2
Premiums for 10 to 12 years	20	6	2
Premiums for 8 and 9 years	15	3	3
Premiums for 5 to 7 years	10	3	3
20 Payment Endowments—			
For 25 years	30	10	3
For 30 years	35	10	3
For 35 years	40	10	3
For 40 years	45	10	3

* 5% additional will be paid for each policy of $5,000 or more written up to and including age 60. In applying this rule, the amount of insurance shall be:

  (a) The single sum insured on an Executive Special policy;
  (b) The primary sum insured on a Juvenile 21 Special policy;
  (c) The basic sum insured on a Family policy, or a Progressive Protection Policy.

(over)

Appendix K. Typical Schedule of Commissions for Career Agency Agreement (Continued)

(1)	(2) 1st Policy Year	(3) 2nd, 3rd, 4th Policy Years	(4) 5th through 10th Policy Years
	Vested	Conditional	Conditional
Life Income Plans			
Life Income at 55, Non-Participating—			
Premiums for 33 years or longer	45%*	10%	3%
Premiums for 30 to 32 years	40*	10	3
Premiums for 23 to 29 years	40	10	3
Premiums for 20 to 22 years	35	10	3
Premiums for 18 and 19 years	35	6	2
Premiums for 13 to 17 years	30	6	2
Premiums for 10 to 12 years	20	6	2
Life Income at 60, 65, 70, Non-Participating—			
Premiums for 38 years or longer	50*	10	3
Premiums for 30 to 37 years	45*	10	3
Premiums for 28 and 29 years	45	10	3
Premiums for 23 to 27 years	40	10	3
Premiums for 20 to 22 years	35	10	3
Premiums for 18 and 19 years	35	6	2
Premiums for 13 to 17 years	30	6	2
Premiums for 10 to 12 years	20	6	2
Premiums for 8 and 9 years	15	3	3
Premiums for 5 to 7 years	10	3	3
Life Income at 50, Participating—			
Premiums for 33 years or longer	40*	10	3
Premiums for 30 to 32 years	35*	10	3
Premiums for 23 to 29 years	35	10	3
Premiums for 20 to 22 years	30	10	3
Premiums for 18 and 19 years	30	6	2
Premiums for 13 to 17 years	25	6	2
Premiums for 10 to 12 years	15	6	2
Life Income at 55, Participating—			
Premiums for 38 years or longer	45*	10	3
Premiums for 33 to 37 years	40*	10	3
Premiums for 30 to 32 years	35*	10	3
Premiums for 23 to 29 years	35	10	3
Premiums for 20 to 22 years	30	10	3
Premiums for 18 and 19 years	30	6	2
Premiums for 13 to 17 years	25	6	2
Premiums for 10 to 12 years	15	6	2
Life Income at 60, 62, 65, 70, Participating—			
Premiums for 38 years or longer	50*	10	3
Premiums for 33 to 37 years	45*	10	3
Premiums for 30 to 32 years	40*	10	3
Premiums for 28 and 29 years	40	10	3
Premiums for 23 to 27 years	35	10	3
Premiums for 20 to 22 years	30	10	3
Premiums for 18 and 19 years	30	6	2
Premiums for 13 to 17 years	25	6	2

* See footnote on page one

2

Appendix K. Typical Schedule of Commissions for Career Agency Agreement (Continued)

(1)	(2) 1st Policy Year	(3) 2nd, 3rd, 4th Policy Years	(4) 5th through 10th Policy Years
	Vested	Conditional	Conditional
Life Income at 60, 62, 65, 70, Participating—Contd.			
Premiums for 10 to 12 years	15%	6%	2%
Premiums for 8 and 9 years	10	3	3
Premiums for 5 to 7 years	5	3	3
Single Premium Insurance (NP)	3	—	—
For Pension and Profit Sharing Trusts Only, Participating and Non-Participating			
Life Income, Class G	10	2	2
Life Income, Guaranteed Standard Issue	80% of Coms. for Plan Selected	Coms. for Plan Selected	Coms. for Plan Selected

Convertible Life Plans, Participating and Non-Participating

Ordinary Life Policy with Conversion Option—(See A below)

Convertible Life Policy—Guaranteed Standard issue only—(see B below)

Years to date of conversion	A. Policy with Option	B. Convertible Policy		
10 or over	50*	40.0	10	3
9	48	38.4	5	5
8	46	36.8	5	5
7	44	35.2	5	5
6	42	33.6	5	5
5	40	32.0	5	5

When the conversion option is exercised, commission will not be allowed on the single premium paid at that time.

NOTES

AGES ABOVE 70. The maximum first-year commissions will be 45% rather than the 50% which applies at ages 70 and below.

RATINGS—Full commissions payable on ratings except in following cases:

Certain temporary Flat Dollar extras for medical reasons. Commissions on extra premium not payable during first year of policy, but are payable thereafter.

Rating for aviation, motor car racing, submarine operation—Commissions never payable on extra premium.

REINSURANCE. Under a policy re-insured, the rate of first year commissions shall not in any case exceed the rate allowed by the re-insuring company.

COMMISSIONS ON SPECIAL CASES shall be at the rates allowed under the Company's rules and practices in effect at the time the premium is due. See Career Agency Agreement for types of cases.

*See footnote on page one.

(over)

Appendix K. Typical Schedule of Commissions for Career Agency Agreement (Continued)

ANNUITIES

(1)	(2) 1st Policy Year Vested	(3) 2nd, 3rd, 4th Policy Years Conditional	(4) 5th through 10th Policy Years Conditional
Annual Premium Deferred Life and Deferred Cash Refund Annuities			
Premiums for 20 years or longer	15	2	2
Premiums for 10 to 19 years	10	2	2
Premiums for 5 to 9 years	5	2	2
Premiums for 2 to 4 years	2½	2	—
Annual Premium Survivorship Annuities			
Premiums for 28 years or longer	40	10	3
Premiums for 23 to 27 years	35	10	3
Premiums for 20 to 22 years	30	10	3
Premiums for 18 and 19 years	30	6	2
Premiums for 13 to 17 years	25	6	2
Premiums for 10 to 12 years	20	6	2
Participating and Non-Participating Retirement Annuity (Pension Trusts Only)	10	2	2
Single Premium Annuities			
Survivorship	3	—	—
Other Plans	2½	—	—

CHANGES IN COMMISSION RATES

The commission rates in all schedules may be changed at any time by announcement of the Company but such change shall not affect commissions on Life Insurance and Annuity policies issued prior to such change.

PROGRAMMED EMPLOYEE PROTECTION INSURANCE

First and subsequent nine years of insurance (10 years) 10%
All commissions are non-vested and payable in accordance with the Company's rules and practices in effect at the time the premium is due.

GROUP INSURANCE

Commissions on premiums for all Group Policies, including Term Policies issued on "Employee Plans," shall be specified in the Company's Standard Commission Schedule applicable to the particular type of Group Policy or Policies, and in accordance with the Company's Group commission rules in force when the new business premium is written.

ACCIDENT • SICKNESS • HOSPITALIZATION INSURANCE

(See Separate Schedule)

4

Appendix K. Typical Schedule of Commissions for Career Agency Agreement (Continued)

Company Not Licensed in New York

SCHEDULE I

Effective Sept. 24; 1964

COMMISSIONS

FIRST YEAR COMMISSIONS: Subject to the provisions of this Agreement, first year commission rates payable on the policies issued on applications written and submitted to the Company shall be as follows: except that (1) for policies sold on female lives for plans available to both males and females, and for which a three year setback applies to the female rates, the setback age will apply in determining the commission rate, and (2) commission on insurance written on the lives of military personnel in the lower four pay grades or their dependents shall be one half (50%) of those commissions shown:

THESE PERCENTAGES APPLY TO THE ANNUAL COMMISSION PREMIUM

A. LIFE INSURANCE POLICIES   Issue Age

	0-9	10-19	20-29	30-39	40-49	50-59	60-69	70-Over
NON PARTICIPATING PERMANENT PLANS								
Executive Special Ordinary Life	80	75	70	65	60	55	50	45
Executive Special Life Paid Up at Age 65	80	74	67	60	53	40	—	—
Ordinary Life	90	85	80	75	70	65	60	55
Life Paid Up at Age 65	90	84	77	70	63	50	—	—
20 Payment Life	80	75	71	67	63	59	55	50
10 Payment Life	60	58	56	54	52	50	47	45
20 Year Endowment	50	50	50	50	50	50	50	50
Endowment at Age 65—Male	80	74	67	60	50	35	—	—
Endowment at Age 62—Female	78	72	65	58	50	35	—	—
Retirement Income at Age 65—Male	75	66	58	50	40	25	—	—
Retirement Income at Age 62—Female	67	58	50	42	30	19	—	—
PARTICIPATING PERMANENT PLANS								
Ordinary Life	85	80	75	70	65	60	55	50
Life Paid Up at Age 65	85	79	72	65	58	45	—	—
20 Payment Life	75	70	66	62	58	54	50	45
10 Payment Life	55	53	51	49	47	45	42	40
20 Year Endowment	45	45	45	45	45	45	45	45
Endowment at Age 65 Male	75	69	62	55	45	30	—	—
Endowment at Age 62 Female	73	67	60	53	45	30	—	—
Retirement Income at Age 65 - Male	70	61	53	45	35	20	—	—
Retirement Income at Age 62 Female	62	53	45	37	25	14	—	—

A. LIFE INSURANCE POLICIES   Issue Age   (continued)

	0-9	10-19	20-25	30-39	40-49	50-59	60-69	70-Over
CONVERTIBLE LEVEL TERM PLANS								
10 Year	—	55	55	55	50	45	40	—
15 Year	—	60	60	60	55	50	45	—
20 Year	—	65	65	65	60	55	—	—
To Age 65	—	70	70	70	60	45	—	—
To Age 75	—	—	—	70	65	55	40	—
DECREASING TERM POLICIES AND BENEFITS								
10 Year	—	50	50	50	45	40	35	—
15 Year	—	55	55	55	50	45	40	—
20 Year	—	60	60	60	55	50	—	—
25 Year	—	65	65	65	60	55	—	—
30 Year	—	65	65	65	—	—	—	—
To Age 65	—	65	65	65	55	40	—	—
SPECIAL PLANS								
5 Year Renewable and Convertible Term	—	—	70	65	60	45	—	—
Executive Special Double Protection to Age 65	80	75	70	65	60	55	50	45
Family Insurance	—	84	77	70	63	50	—	—
Flexible Equity	—	—	75	70	65	60	55	—

SINGLE PREMIUM

Life Insurance .... 3% All Ages
Annuity .... 2½% All Ages

B. HEALTH INSURANCE

	0-9	10-19	20-25	30-39	40-49	50-59	60-69	70-Over
Accident and Sickness	—	32	32	32	32	32	—	—
Major Medical	—	32	32	32	32	32	—	—

Appendix K. Typical Schedule of Commissions for Career Agency Agreement (Continued)

Company Not Licensed in New York

RENEWAL COMMISSIONS: The rate of renewal commissions to be paid to Career Agent for the second through the fifth policy years shall be computed according to the following table:

I. Life Insurance Plans	When 1st year commission is 55% or more	When 1st year commission is less than 55%
All Plans (except those listed below).............. 10%		7½%
(a) Term Plans and Benefits.................. 10%		10%
(b) Executive Special Plans 7½%		7½%
(c) All Participating Plans 7½%		7½%

II. Health Insurance Plans

Guaranteed Renewable   15%

SERVICE FEES: After the fifth policy year service fees shall be payable on the Commission Premium received by the Company during the premium paying period for all policies except Annual Premium Annuities, provided that the Career Agent's Agreement is in effect during such period, and provided that the total first year commissions paid to the Career Agent by the Company on policies covered by the Career Agent's Agreement amount to at least $2,000.00 during each of the two calendar years immediately preceding the calendar year in which the service fees are otherwise payable. Service fees shall be computed as follows:

	Per Cent of Commission Premium
(a) Life Insurance Policies	2%
(b) Health Insurance Policies	10%

VESTING: In the event of termination of this Agreement, first year and renewal commissions on policies, issued on applications written and submitted to the Company by the Agent prior to the date of such termination shall be payable in accordance with the following: (1) if such termination occurs because of death, such commissions shall be payable to Agent's designee, or his estate in the event of his failure to name a designee, as though this Agreement were still in effect; (2) if termination occurs for any reason other than death after this Agreement has been in effect for two full years, first year commissions due for policies written prior to termination shall be paid and renewal commissions shall be paid for as many years as this Agreement shall have been in effect, except that no such commissions shall be payable for policy years after the fifth, or until such renewal commissions expire, whichever is sooner; or (3) if termination occurs for any reason other than death while this Agreement has been in effect less than two years, first year commissions due for policies written prior to termination shall be paid and no other commissions shall be payable after the date of such termination. Other than as specifically provided in this paragraph no commissions shall be payable after the date of termination. All renewal commissions after termination of this Agreement shall be reduced by a collection charge of 2% of the renewal premiums.

GENERAL PROVISIONS: Commission rates payable on plans other than those included in the Schedule I may be fixed by the Company by special agreement. Commissions payable on premiums for additional benefit provisions, except level term or decreasing term or dependents insurance benefits, shall be at the same rates as those provided for the principal policies in which such provisions are included, unless otherwise specified herein. No commissions shall be payable on preliminary term insurance premiums, temporary extra premiums of five (5) years or less, or on premiums waived under any provision. Renewal commissions shall not be allowed on premiums paid in advance until their respective due dates. On amounts of insurance in excess of the Company's limits of retention the Company reserves the right to adjust commissions on the amount reinsured.

INDEX

Index

A

A.B.A. assignment form, 615, 617–19
Accident and health insurance
  estate tax treatment, 944
  gift tax treatment, 944
  income tax treatment, 943, 944
Accidental death benefits
  age limitation, 754
  definition of contingency insured against, 753
  exception to incontestable clause, 568, 569
  exclusion, 753
  family
    income policy, 111
    life insurance policy, 115
  under group contracts, 24
  under industrial life policies, 722
  under term contracts, 50
  Intercompany Accidental Death Table, 754, 755
  lack of economic justification, 752
  military or naval service, 753, 754
  policy dividends, effect on, 335, 340
  premiums and reserves, 754, 755
  reinsurance of, 445
  triple indemnity, 752
Accidental Death Benefits Table, 1959, 754, 755
Acquisition expenses
  under adjusted premium method, 302–4
  dividends, impact on, 349–51, 359, 364
  expressed as percentage of the premium, 253–56
  limitations on, 304, 305, 778
  nature of, 247
  under reinsurance agreements, 436, 437
  reserves, impact on, 271–74
  savings under nonmedical insurance, 309, 412–14
  surplus, impact on, 271–74
  surrender values, impact on, 292, 293, 301–4
Actuarial assumptions
  as to extended term insurance, 158
  interest assumptions in general, 180, 181
  for reserve valuation purposes, 240–42, 895, 897, 898, 904, 905, 918, 921
  reserves of interest assumptions, effect on, 235–39

Actuarial assumptions—*Cont.*
  reserves of mortality assumptions, effect on, 235, 236
  selection procedures, effect on, 380
  for surrender value purposes, 297, 303
  under nonmedical insurance, 413, 414
Administrative law, 457, 458, 460
Admitted assets, 863–65
Adverse financial selection
  under settlement options, 643, 644
  surrender values, effect on, 295
Adverse mortality selection
  under annuities, 94, 101, 102
  under assessment insurance, 29
  automatic waiver of premium, 738, 739
  under group life insurance, 681, 682, 686–88, 690, 694, 696
  extended term insurance, impact on, 322, 323
  surrender value, impact on, 294
  as justification for selection procedure, 377
  at the older ages, 418
  under policyholder nonmedical, 414
  reinstatement of suspended policies, 482
  under settlement options, 102 n, 643, 644
  and term conversion privileges, 49
  under term insurance generally, 44, 396, 406
  under term policy, 45
  traceable to renewal privilege under term policy, 45
  under yearly renewable term insurance, 31, 32
Age of applicant
  maximum age limitation, 381, 417, 418
  misstatement of age clause, 381, 523
  proof of age, 381
  as a selection factor, 380, 381
Age setback, 101, 103, 162
Agency, law of
  agency contract, 831, 832
  agent, definition of, 543, 544
  apparent authority of agents, 544
  brokers as agents, 546, 547, 828, 829
  falsification of application by agent, 555–57

1001

Agency, law of—*Cont.*
  implied powers of agents, 544, 545
  nonwaiver clause, 484, 546, 547, 551, 552
  presumption of, 544
  principal, definition of, 543
  responsibility of principal for acts of agents, 545, 546
Agency organization, 821, 826, 836–39
Agent
  apparent authority, 544, 545, 831
  brokers as agents, 547, 548, 828, 829
  compensation arrangements, 829, 832–36
  definition of, 543, 544
  falsification of application by, 555–57
  financing of new agents, 833–34
  implied powers of, 544, 545
  legal status of, 485
  nonwaiver clause, 484, 546, 547, 550, 551
  presumption of agency, 544
  responsibility for acts of, 544, 546
  secret limitations on authority, 544–46
  service fees, 835
  as source of underwriting information, 398, 399
  types of, 827, 828
  use of inspection receipt, 487
  vesting of commissions, 834, 835
Aleatory contracts, 471, 472, 502, 503, 512
Ambiguous provisions, construction of, 474, 475
American Annuity Table, 1955, 103, 154, 155
American Experience Table of Mortality
  characteristics of, 146, 147
  contribution of Sheppard Homans, 46 n, 147
  criticism of, 148, 149
  reserves, effect on, 236–39
American Men Mortality Table
  general characteristics, 147, 148
  group insurance, use for, 148
American Service Bureau, 402
Amount of insurance to be carried, 18
Annual statements, 860 ff.
Annuities
  actuarial considerations, 102–4
  adverse selection, 101, 102
  age setback, 102
  annuity certain, 80, 87
  the annuity principle, 81–83
  apportionable, 85, 86
  calculation of prospective reserve, 234, 235

Annuities—*Cont.*
  cash refund annuity, 88, 661
  classification of, 83–85
  deferred annuities, 83, 84, 91, 92, 204–6
  definition of, 81
  derivation of net single premium, 198–206
  estate tax treatment, 940, 941
  "exclusion ratio," 935
  50 per cent refund annuity, 89
  function of, 82, 83
  immediate pure annuities, 84–86, 201–4, 660
  immediate refund annuities, 85–90
  income tax treatment, 935–37
  installment refund annuity, 88, 661, 936, 940
  joint
    and last survivor annuity, 96, 97
    life annuity, 96
    and one-half annuity, 98
    and two-thirds annuity, 97
  life
    certain, 81, 204, 234
    due, 208, 231–33, 252–56, 279
    with guaranteed payments, 87, 936–40
  modified cash refund annuity, 89
  participating, 104, 361, 362
  proof of age, 381
  pure deferred life annuity, 87, 204–6, 213, 214, 660
  retirement annuity, 92–95
  straight life annuities, 84, 85
  trend of annuitant mortality, 102
  types of, 81
  uses of, 105, 106
  variable annuities, 98–101
Annuity Table for 1937
  current use, 103
  derivation of, 150, 151
  reproduction of, 199
Annuity Table for 1949, 152, 153
  projection factors, 152
  source of data, 152
  use of, 153
Annuity tables
  American Annuity Table, 1955, 103, 154, 155
  Annuity Table for 1949, 152, 153
  Combined Experience Table, 297
  distinction between male and female mortality, 104, 150, 154
  Group Annuity Table for 1951, 152–54
  Standard Annuity Tables for 1937, 17,

Annuity tables—*Cont.*
103, 150, 151, 199
use of projection factors, 103, 142, 152–55
Antedating of policies, 497, 498, 564, 565
Antidiscrimination statutes, 249
Application for life insurance
attachment to policy, 484, 555
as consideration for contract, 499
entire contract statutes, 485, 524
as offer to insurance company, 483, 484
parol evidence rule, 484
as source of underwriting information, 399–401
when submitted by broker, 483
warranties in, 522, 524
Armstrong Committee, 290, 363, 560, 584, 585, 775, 778, 788
Assessment insurance, 27–29, 798, 799
Asset share calculation
as basis for surrender values, 293–96
in gross premium calculations, 258–60
nature of, 238
relationship between various actuarial values, 311–14
surrenders, effect of, 258, 259
to test equity of dividend scale, 356, 357
to test trial gross premium, 268, 271
validation period, 271
Assignee, 503, 510, 515–16, 614–19, 622, 623
Assignment
A.B.A. form, 615, 617–19
absolute form, 608, 609, 615–17
by the beneficiary, 607, 608
bill of interpleader, 621
change of beneficiary prior to, 610–12
as collateral for loans, 21, 22, 515–17, 610–12, 614, 615, 616–18
collateral form, 609–12, 614, 615
company not responsible for validity of, 621, 622
group life insurance, 708
insurable interest of assignee, 407, 410, 515–17, 614–18, 622, 623
by the insurer or owner of policy, 606, 613
multiple assignees, 620, 621
need for beneficiary's consent, 607, 610
notice to insurer of, 619, 620
payment of premiums by assignee, 615, 618
policy loans, 610, 611, 616–18, 620

Assignment—*Cont.*
of proceeds, 608
resulting trustee status of assignee, 618
rights of assignee, 615–19
rights of beneficiary, effect on, 608–12, 619
under industrial life policies, 720
Automatic premium loan
advantages and disadvantages, 326–28
extended term insurance, compared to, 327
types of, 325, 326
under term insurance, 50
Aviation exclusion, 396, 397, 570, 571

B

Beneficiary
as applicant for insurance, 511–17, 576
Armstrong Investigation, 584, 585
assignment on rights of, effect of, 608–12
beneficiary's death, effect of, 586, 587
class, 579–81
common disaster clause, 596
contingent or secondary, 581–83, 641, 642
contingent trust for minor beneficiary, 603
creditor, 507, 510, 515–17, 578
defeasible vested interest concept, 585, 592, 610, 612, 613
designation
of beneficiary by third party owner, 593
in consideration of marriage, 586
of guardian as beneficiary, 601
divorce of, 121, 407, 578, 586, 599, 600
educational fund, 668
effecting change of, 599, 600
emergency fund, 667, 668
of estate clearance fund, 577, 665–67
facility of payment clause, 708, 719, 720
"first taker," 582
heirs as, 577, 580
under industrial life policies, 719, 720
insurable interest, 503, 505–14, 578, 579, 720
insured or his estate as beneficiary, 576, 577, 610
key-man insurance, 20, 578
of lump sum proceeds, 577
method of designation of, 583, 584, 587
minor as, 481, 600–604

Beneficiary—*Cont.*
mortgage cancellation fund, 15, 667
per capita distribution, 583
per stirpes distribution, 590, 591
primary, 581
readjustment income, 668
remarriage clause, 605
reverse common disaster clause, 598
reversionary revocable designation, 587
right
to change beneficiary, 583, 584
to select settlement options, 640, 641
rights
of irrevocable beneficiary, 587, 588, 607, 608, 612–14
of revocable beneficiary, 585, 607, 608, 612–14
short-term survivorship of beneficiary, 596–98
simultaneous death of insured and beneficiary, 594–96
specific, 579
succession in interest, 588–91
third party beneficiary, 578
trustee as, 603–5
Uniform Simultaneous Death Act, 595, 596
Benefit
of selection, 143, 144, 156, 289, 290, 341, 350
of survivorship, 197, 198
Bernoulli's Theorem, 136
Bilateral contracts, 472, 473, 485, 501, 502
Bill of interpleader, 466, 621
Bottomry and respondentia loans, 182
Branch office system, 838, 839
Broker
as agent, 547, 548
legal status of, 483
Build and Blood Pressure Study 1959, 382
Business continuation insurance
insurable interest, 515
need for, 22, 23
use of joint life policies, 67, 68

C

Capital gains
accounting for, 884
impact on dividend policy, 335, 345
tax treatment of, 903, 911, 913, 920 n, 921, 924, 928
Carnegie Foundation, 461
Case law
common law, 458–61

Case law—*Cont.*
definition of, 454
development of, 458
forms of
administrative decisions, 462
judicial decisions, 458–62
relationship to legislation, 462–64
restatements of the law, 461, 462
Cash surrender values
when available, 315, 316
delay clause, 316, 317, 745
under industrial life insurance policies, 720, 721
Cash values
as a basis for loans, 21
under ordinary life insurance, 60–62
use for retirement purposes, 16, 63
Check, payment of premium by, 488, 500, 552, 553
Civil law
contrasted with common law, 459
development of, 459
presumptions as to survival, 594, 595
College Retirement Equities Fund, 100
Commissioners 1958 Extended Term Insurance Table, 158
Commissioners 1960 Standard Group Table, 159, 160, 708
Commissioners 1961 Standard Industrial Table, 160, 162
Commissions
ceding commission under reinsurance, 437
as a form of acquisition expense, 248
under guaranteed issue policies, 415
as a percentage of gross premium, 253, 254, 256
scale of, 832, 833
vesting of, 834–35
Common disaster clause, 596
Common law
concepts of, 459–61
civil law, contrasted with, 459
"equity," contrasted with, 459, 460
restatements of the law, 461, 462
source of, 458
statutory modification of, 531–33
statutory or constitutional law, contrasted with, 458
Commutation privilege
definition of, 646
under installment time option, 655
under life income option, 664
Commutative contract, 471
Compound discount
application, 7–9
to installment amount option, 656–58

Compound discount—*Cont.*
  application—*Cont.*
    to installment time option, 651–54
    of the values, 179, 181
  bank discount method, contrasted with, 175
  concept of, 170
  derivation of present values, 171
  modification for payments at beginning of year, 180
  present value
    of annual payments, 177–79
    of 1 at various rates of compound interest, 173, 174
Concealments
  distinguished from misrepresentation, 537, 538
  interim changes in health, 539–41
  laws relating to, 531–33
  in marine insurance, 537
  nature and legal effect of, 536, 537
  palpable materiality, 538, 539
  scope of doctrine of concealment, 539–41
  test
    of fraud, 539
    of materiality, 537, 538
Conditional contract, 473, 474
Conditional receipt, 492–94, 541, 553
Conditions
  precedent
    absence of medical treatment, 485, 491
    definition of, 472
    delivery of the policy, 485–87
    delivery-in-good-health clause, 485, 498–501, 527
    exemplified by premium payments, 474
    incontestable clause, relationship to, 571, 572
    justification of, 491, 492
    medical treatment clause, 491
    payment of first premium, 485, 487, 488
    premium subsequent to first, 499, 500
  subsequent
    conditions found in life insurance policy, 474
    definition of, 473
Conflict of laws; *see* Laws, conflict of
Consideration for contract
  extension of credit, 485, 487, 488, 551, 552
  form, 500–502
  nature of, 499
  payment by check, 488, 500, 552, 553

Contingencies
  allowance for, 183, 256, 337, 913, 922, 926
  reserves for, 337, 344, 345, 358, 359
  surrender values, effect on, 295, 296
Contingent trust for minor beneficiary, 603
Contract of adhesion, 474, 475, 760
Conversion; *see* Exchange of policies
Conway decision, 570, 571
Corpus Juris Civilis, 459
Cost of insurance
  dividends, effect on, 340–43
  level premium plan, relationship to, 36–38
  under joint life policies, 67
  retrospective reserves, with respect to, 226–29
Court of Claims, 466
Courts
  American
    classification of
      federal courts, 465, 466
      state courts, 466, 467
    conflict of laws, 468–71
    jurisdiction of, 467, 468
  Federal
    jurisdiction of, 465, 468, 470, 471
    structure of, 465, 466
    types of, 465, 466
  state
    classes of, 465, 466
    jurisdiction of, 468–71
Credit insurance,
  nature of, 20, 21
  uses of, 53
Creditor
  as assignee, 507, 510, 610, 611, 614, 619
  as beneficiary, 507, 510, 515–17, 578
  insurable interest of, 507, 510, 515–17, 615–18, 622, 623
CSO 1941 Table
  death rates under, 163–65
  general characteristics, 148
  margins of safety, 143
  reserves, effect on, 237, 238
  sponsoring body, 149
CSO 1958 Basic Table, 162–65
CSO 1958 Table, 155–59
Customs Court, 465

D

Death of applicant prior to consideration of application, 493
Decision law; *see* Case law

Defeasible vested interest of beneficiary, 585, 592, 610, 612, 613
Deferred survivorship annuity, 121, 123
Deficiency reserves
  accounting for, 870
  competition, effect on, 156 n
  as incentive to development of 1958 CSO Table, 155
  nature of, 242, 243
Definitions of insurance, 25, 26
Delay clause, 316, 317, 645
Delay in considering the application, 485–87
Delivery of the policy
  as condition precedent, 485, 486
  constructive delivery, 486, 495
  legal effect of, 486, 492, 495
Delivery-in-good-health clause
  as condition precedent, 484, 489, 527
  meaning of good health, 489, 490
  as substitute for doctrine of concealment, 540, 541
  waiver of, 553–55
  as warranties, 523, 540, 541
Dependency period income, 13, 14, 668–70, 673, 674
Disability income benefits
  Accidental Death Benefits Table, 1959, 754, 755
  assignment, effect of, 618
  duration of benefits, 741
  under family income policies, 110
  group life insurance, 690
  incontestable clause, exception to, 568, 569
  under industrial policies, 722
  maturity type of clause, 618, 690, 739
  prorate clause, 741, 742
  protection against claims of creditors, 631
  reinsurance of, 448
  retroactive payment of, 740
  under term insurance policies, 50
Discrimination, 773, 774
Diversity of citizenship, 466, 468
Dividends
  accelerative endowment option, 371, 372
  accounting for, 777, 870, 871, 882
  accumulations, 367, 370–72
  acquisition expenses, effect of, 349–51
  allowance for under retroactive conversion of term insurance, 47
  annuity contracts, 103, 361, 362
  application under variable annuities, 99
  computation of, 353–56

Dividends—*Cont.*
  concept of, 331
  contribution plan, 340
  to convert policy to paid-up or endowment policy, 64
  deposit at interest, 370, 371
  differentiation as to sex, 350, 351
  disability benefits, effect of, 749
  endowment option, 371, 372
  equity of, 356, 357
  excess interest factor, 220, 345, 346
  experience premium method, 357–59
  on extended term insurance, 325
  extra dividends, 363, 364
  family life insurance policy, 115
  fifth dividend option, 369
  first year dividends, 350, 351, 359
  grading for policy size, 360
  under group life insurance, 680, 685, 709, 710
  guaranteed issue, effect of, 419
  impact of acquisition expenses, 349–51
  income tax treatment, 937
  under industrial life policies, 721, 722
  interest factor, 220, 343–48, 353–56, 358, 370, 887
  legal restrictions on dividend policy, 777, 778, 870, 871, 882
  loading factor, 257, 340–43, 348–56, 358
  as a margin for adverse mortality, 45
  mortality factor, 341–43, 353–56, 358
  mortuary dividend, 364
  negative dividend factors, 340, 346, 749
  new money or investment year concept, 344, 887
  options, 366–71
  paid-up additions, 367–69
  paid-up option, 371
  part payment of premiums, 367
  payment in cash, 366, 367
  post-mortem dividends, 366
  projections, 795, 796
  under reinsurance agreements, 436–39
  selection, gains from, 350
  settlement dividends, 364, 365
  source of surplus, 332–34
  specific margin in premium for, 257, 275
  stock
    company, 330, 331, 782, 783
    dividends, 783
  under substandard insurance policies, 421, 422, 426–28
  surrender dividends, 309–11, 365, 366
  surrenders, gains from, 334, 335, 350
  tax treatment, 370, 895, 898, 937

Dividends—*Cont.*
  terminal dividends, 309–11, 364–66
  Tontine system, 363
Divorce of wife-beneficiary, 121, 507, 578, 586, 599, 600

E

Educational fund, 15, 668
Election
  nature of, 542, 543, 548–51
  to waive cash payment of premium, 552, 553
Emergency fund, 15, 667, 668
Employer welfare plans, 24
Endowment insurance
  adaptability to joint life policies, 66
  benefit of survivorship, 197, 198
  calculation of prospective reserve, 234
  double endowments, 72, 409
  early uses of, 77, 78
  as element of life income policy, 123
  limited payment plans, 72, 73
  mathematical view of, 73, 74
  maturity date, 72
  misuse of, 76, 77
  nature of, 71
  net level premium, derivation of, 213
  net single premium, derivation of, 195–98
  payor clause, 78
  to provide old-age income, 80
  semi-endowments, 72
  settlement plan for educational funds, 79
  surrender values prior to Guertin legislation, 298
  whole life insurance, relationship to, 59
Entire contract statutes, 485, 624, 556
Equity
  equity courts and rules
    as contrasted with law, 459–61
    development of, 460, 461
    "forms of action," 460
    life insurance companies, significance to, 461
  reinstatement, 574
  rescission and restitution, 461, 489, 509, 510, 525–27, 563, 564, 566
Erie Railroad Company v. *Tompkins,* 470
Estate
  clearance fund
    beneficiary of, 577, 665–67
    interest option, use of, 667
    lump sum settlement, use of, 665, 666
    as a nonrecurrent need, 12, 13
    trust, use of, 667

Estate—*Cont.*
  tax treatment of life insurance
    accident and health insurance, 944
    annuities, 940, 941
    employee pension and annuity plans, 947
    group life insurance, 944
    "incidents of ownership" test, 938
    marital deduction, 939, 940
    ownership, transfer of, 939
    proceeds, 937–40
    reversionary interest, 938
    state laws, 942
Estoppel
  agent's authority, secret limitations on, 535, 536
  apparent authority of agents, 544, 545
  equitable estoppel, 549, 550
  misrepresentation in application, 555–57
  nature of, 542, 543, 548, 549
  promissory estoppel, 549, 550
Evidence of insurability
  upon exchange of retirement annuity for life insurance policy, 95
  exchange of policies, with respect to, 64
  family life insurance policy, 116
  industrial life insurance, 612, 613
  under juvenile insurance, 129
  under survivorship annuity, 120
  waiver
    for group life, 680, 684
    for paid-up additions, 368
    for term conversion, 46
    under renewal provisions of term insurance, 44, 45
Exchange of policies
  family income policy, with respect to, 112
  under group life insurance, 689, 690, 705
  under industrial life policies, 723
  joint life policies, with respect to, 67
  ordinary life, with respect to, 64
  retirement annuity for life insurance contract, 94, 95
  term insurance, with respect to, 47–52
Expenses
  acquisition expenses, 248, 253–55
  analysis of, 887, 888
  classification of insurance company expenses, 247–49, 264
  derivation of expense rates, 252–56
  as an element of loading, 248
  expense margins as source of surplus, 257
  federal income taxes, 345

Expenses—*Cont.*
as function of size of policy, 68, 69, 247–51
under industrial life insurance, 730, 731
investment expenses, 247, 345
maintenance, 255, 256
savings under nonmedical insurance, 409, 412–14
settlement of claims, 255, 256
state regulation of, 727, 728, 788
stock company expenses, 264
surrender expenses, 296
underwriting expenses, 249, 250, 253–56
under variable annuities, 99
Extended term insurance
actuarial bases of, 158, 322
advantages and disadvantages, 324, 325
allowance for extra mortality, 158
under antedated policies, 497, 498
calculation of, 322
compared to automatic premium loan, 327
dividends, 325
under endowment policies, 321
margins for administrative expense, 158
under ordinary life insurance, 62
under reinsurance agreements, 438
under substandard insurance, 425

F

Face amount plus cash value policy, 127
Facility-of-payment clause
under group life insurance, 708
under industrial life policies, 719, 720
Family
income policy, 108
life insurance policy, 114–16
maintenance policy, 112
plan, 114–16
Farr, William, 136 n
Federal Bankruptcy Act, 631
Federal Constitution, 455
Federal Courts of Appeals, 465
Federal District Courts, 466
Federal Trade Commission Act, 764, 765
Females
under insurance contracts, 158, 159, 216, 217, 395
life income options, 661–63
treatment of under annuity contracts, 102, 395
Forfeiture of equities, 481, 482

Fraternal life insurance societies, 796–801
Fraud
good-health clause as protection against, 489
incontestable clause, effect of, 560–62
moral hazard, 393, 394, 402
Friendly Societies and Burial Clubs, 713, 714

G

General agency system, 836–38
Gift tax treatment
employee pension and annuity plan, 947
group life insurance, 944
individual life insurance, 941, 942
Grace period, 367, 558
Graded premium policies, 68, 69, 249, 250
Grigsby v. *Russell,* 512
Gross premiums
acquisition expenses, 248, 252–55
antidiscrimination statutes, 249
asset share calculation, 258–60, 265–73
concepts of, 246, 247
contingencies, allowance for, 183, 256
expense rates, derivation of, 251–57
expense rates graded by size of policy, 68, 69, 249–51
insurance company expenses, nature of, 247–49
loading formula, 249, 260
nonparticipating premiums, 260 ff.
participating premiums, 251 ff., 264, 265
termination rates, 264, 267
underwriting expenses, 248, 249, 253–56
Group Annuity Table for 1951
margins of safety, 143, 154
projection factors, 153–55
source of data, 153
use of, 156
Group life insurance
actively-at-work rule, 688, 689
administration of, 682, 683, 710
adverse mortality selection minimization of, 681, 682, 686–88, 690, 694, 696
amount of insurance per employee
determination of, 681, 694, 695
maximum, 686, 687, 695, 696
minimum, 685, 686, 695
assignment, prohibition against, 708
contingency reserves, 873, 874, 922, 925, 926

Group life insurance—*Cont.*
  conversion privilege, 689, 690, 705, 879
  coverage for retired employees, 690–93
  deposit administration funds, 692
  dividends, 709, 710
  eligibility requirements, 688, 689
  eligible groups, 681, 686
  employee's contribution, rate of, 699, 701–3, 706
  employer participation in financing, 672, 677–79
  estate and gift tax treatment, 944
  expense rate, reduction of, 686, 687
  experience rating, 680, 685, 709
  facility-of-payment clause, 708
  Federal Employees Group Life Insurance Plan, 679
  federal income tax treatment, 692, 698, 703, 706, 707, 943, 944
  financing, 697–99
  general characteristics, 24, 679, 680
  general principles, 680–83
  group creditor life, 686–87
  influence of *NAIC*, 159, 684
  master contract, 707
  medical examination, requirement of, 697, 698
  minimum number of lives, 684, 686, 687
  minimum proportion of group, 682, 687, 688
  misstatement of age, 708
  parties to the contract, 707
  permanent forms of insurance
    level premium policies, 693, 698, 699, 706, 707
    paid-up policies, 693, 698, 699, 703–6
    for retired employees, 692, 693
  premium rates
    level premium policies, 706, 709
    loading, 701, 708, 709
    paid-up insurance, 703–6, 709
    state regulation of, 160, 685, 699, 701, 705, 708
    yearly renewable term insurance, 701–3, 708, 709
  probationary period, 688
  settlement options, 708
  standard definitions, 683, 684
  Standard Group Life Insurance Premium Rates, 1961, 160, 708
  standard provisions, 685
  state regulation of, 683–85, 699, 701, 705, 708

Group life insurance—*Cont.*
  termination
    of employment, 689, 693
    of plan, 689, 690
  total disability coverage, 690, 691
  yearly renewable term
    allocation of cost between employer and employees, 700–703
    average annual premium per $1,000, calculation of, 701, 702
    conversion of, 689, 690, 879
    cost implications, 680
    federal income tax treatment, 689, 690
    rate of employee contribution, 698, 699, 701, 702
    for retired employees, 691, 692
Guaranteed dividend policy, 127
Guaranteed issue, 415
Guardianship of minor beneficiary, 601, 602, 605
Guertin
  Committee, 148, 149
  legislation
    development of new mortality table, 148, 149
    purpose, 149
    Standard Valuation Law, 278, 285–89, 301–4
    surrender dividends, 309–11

H

Homans, Sheppard, 46 n, 147
Human life value
  diminishing nature of, 9, 10
  measurement of, 6–9
  source of, 3–6
Hunter, Arthur H., 405, 745

I

Income and principal policy, 125–27
Income tax treatment of life insurance
  annuities, 935–37
  cash values, 934, 935
  employee pension and annuity plans, 945–47
  excess over cost rule, 937
  exclusion ratio, 935, 936
  group life insurance, 943, 944
  premiums and annuity considerations, 933, 943, 945
  proceeds
    general rules, 934
    transfer for valuable consideration, 934
  three per cent rule, 937

Incontestable clause
accidental death benefits, 568, 569
under antedated policies, 497, 498
aviation clause, 570, 571
conditions precedent, 571, 572
contest, meaning of, 563, 564
Conway decision, 570, 571
disability clause, 568, 569, 742, 743
excepted hazards, 569, 570
fraud, effect of, 560–62
fraudulent acts beyond scope of, 562, 563
in government life insurance policies, 567
incontestability from date of issue, 567
incontestable period, inception of, 564, 565
industrial life insurance policies, 491 n, 718
military or naval service, 569, 570
misstatement of age, 381, 572
Monahan decision, 565, 566
origin of, 560
purpose of, 559, 560
reformation, 573, 574
reinstatement, 574, 575
as special statute of limitation, 561, 562
as standard provision, 560
suicide clause, 570, 571
types of, 565–67
Indemnity, principle of, 475, 476, 506, 507, 516
Industrial life insurance
accidental death benefits, 722
administration, 723–27
agent's debit book, 725
agent's report of premiums collected, 725, 726
amount of insurance per policy or per life, 711, 712
assignment, right of, 720
change of plan, 713
children, insurance of, 712, 715, 716
collection commission, 728
compensation
of agents, 727, 728
of manager, 729
conservation commission, 728
debit, concepts of, 723, 724
disability benefits, 722
discount for direct remittance of premiums, 718
dividends, 721, 722
expense rates, 730
facility of payment clause, 719, 720
family plan, impact of, 715, 716

Industrial life insurance—*Cont.*
field force organization, 724
Friendly Societies and Burial Clubs, 713, 714
general characteristics, 711–13
group life insurance, impact of, 715
incontestable clause, 491 n, 718
intermediate insurance, 715
lapse rates, 731
life and lapse register lists, 726
medical examination, omission of, 712
medical or surgical treatment, 713, 718, 719
monthly debit ordinary insurance, 715, 727
mortality, 729, 730
NAIC, influence of, 160, 161, 711, 712
new business commission, 727, 728
option to surrender within two weeks, 717
origin of, 713, 714
plans of insurance, 716
policy loans, 721
premium
accounting, 724–27
collection, 712, 717, 718
payment, frequency of, 711
receipt book, 725
Prudential Friendly Society, 714
recent developments in, 715, 716
reinstatement, 721
Social Security, impact of, 715
suicide clause, 719
surrender values, 720, 721
Influenza epidemic of 1957–58, 157
Inspection receipt, 486
Installment
amount option
"blackout" period, 670–76
common disaster and short-term survivorship problem, 596–98
dependency period income, 669
educational fund, 15, 668
emergency fund, 668
excess interest, 658
flexibility, elements of, 658, 659
mortgage cancellation fund, 667
readjustment income, 668
structure of, 655–68
use of, 13, 14
withdrawal privilege, 658
time option
"blackout" period, 670–76
common disaster and short-term survivorship problem, 596–98
commutation, right of, 665

Installment—*Cont.*
 time option—*Cont.*
  dependency period income, 669
  excess interest, 655
  under family income policy, 108, 109
  mortgage cancellation fund, 667
  present value of annual payments, 651–54
  purpose of, 651
  readjustment income, 668
  structure of, 651–54
  use of, 13–15
  variation of amount of proceeds, effect of, 655
  withdrawal privilege, 655
Insurability option, 416, 417
Insurable interest
 of assignee, 506, 509, 514–16, 615–18, 622, 623
 of beneficiary, 503, 507, 578, 579, 720
 business relationship evidencing, 514–17
 of creditors, 507, 511, 516–18, 615–18, 622, 623
 as deterrent to murder of insured, 503, 512
 as deterrent to wagering, 502, 503, 512
 factual expectation, 511, 513, 514
 family relationships evidencing, 511–13
 Grigsby v. *Russell,* 512
 incidence of, 506–8
 lack of, 517, 518, 563
 legal obligation, 511–15
 love and affection, 511, 512
 moral obligation, 514
 nature of, 505, 506
 policy procured by insured, 508–11
 policy procured by person other than insured, 511–17
 in Texas, 507, 508
 valuation of, 514–17
Interest
 assumed earnings rate for actuarial computations, 180, 181, 240, 263, 264
 assumption on reserves, effect of, 238–41, 904, 905, 918, 921
 assumptions
  under annuity contracts, 102, 240
  under life insurance contracts, 180
  reserves, effect on, 238–41, 904, 905, 918, 921
 bases for measuring interest returns, 76, 343–45, 887
 capital gains, 335, 345, 903, 911, 913, 920 n, 921, 924, 928

Interest—*Cont.*
 compound discount
  application of the values, 178, 180
  bank discount method, contrasted with, 174
  concept of, 170
  modification for payments at beginning of year, 180
  present value
   of annual payments, 177–80
   of 1 at various rates of compound interest, 172, 173
  present values, derivation of, 171
 compound interest
  annual payments, accumulation of, 174, 175
  concept of, 167
  interest, accumulation of, 168, 169
  modification for payments at end of year, 176, 177
  values, derivation of, 176
  definition of terms, 167, 168
  excess interest factor, 332–34, 342–47, 648, 665, 668, 674
 Interest option
  for benefit of minor, 602, 603
  "blackout" period, 670–76
  common disaster and short-term survivorship problem, 596, 598
  dependency period income, 668, 669
  emergency fund, 667
  estate clearance fund, 667
  excess interest, 648
  under family income policy, 622, 623
  flexibility, elements of, 649, 650
  interest, accumulation of, 603, 650
  permissible duration, 650
  readjustment income, 668
  structure of, 647–50
  testamentary disposition question, 649
  withdrawal privilege, 649
 Investment features of life insurance policies
  endowment insurance, 73, 74
  as a function of the level premium plan, 36–39, 840
  ordinary life, 60, 61
  yield on, 56, 75, 76
 Investment statutes; *see* Regulation of investments
 Investments of life insurance companies
  capital markets, impact on, 852–58
  classification of, 55, 56, 856–58, 862–68
  direct placement, 857
  earnings on, 56, 76, 77, 887
  expenses connected with, 247, 345
  income risk, 846

Investments of life insurance companies
—*Cont.*
insolvency risk, 842–45
investment performance, 850–52
"Leeway" or "basket" authority, 850
liquidity risk, 845–46
mandatory securities valuation reserve, 335 n, 844, 845, 872–74
nature of, 56
new money rate of return, 851–52
objectives, 841–42
organization for, 822
regulation of, 776, 777, 843, 844, 847–
50, 864–68
safety of, 55, 56
valuation of, 776, 777, 843, 844,
864–68

J

Jenkins, Wilmer A., 151, 154
Joint life insurance, 66, 67, 68
Jumping juvenile policy, 129, 130
Justinian Code, 459, 594
Juvenile insurance
economic basis of, 11
educational needs, 15
jumping juvenile, 129, 130
legal limitations, 114, 128
payor clause, 78
underwriting of, 417

K

Key-man insurance, 19, 20, 53, 54, 514,
515, 578, 582

L

Lapse
distinguished from surrender, 296,
297
rates under industrial insurance, 731
Law of average, 136, 137, 472
Law of mortality, 135
Laws, conflict of
bases used to resolve conflicts, 469–71
"center of gravity" rule, 470
Erie v. *Tompkins*, 470
grouping of contacts theory, 470
"place-of-making" rule, 469
Swift v. *Tyson*, 470
Ledger assets, 863–65
Legal integration, rule of, 484, 556
Legal limitations on new business, 778
Legislation
attitude of the judiciary toward, 462–64
definition of, 454
forms of
administrative regulations, 457

Legislation—*Cont.*
forms of—*Cont.*
federal
constitution, 454, 455
executive orders and administrative regulations, 456
statutes, 455, 456
municipal ordinances, 457
rules of court, 457
state
constitutions, 456
statutes, 456
treaties, 455
interpretation of, 464, 465
private laws, 456
public laws, 456
rules of statutory construction, 464,
465
Versailles Treaty, 455
Level premium plan
decreasing term insurance, applied to,
111
legal reserves, effect on, 33
nature of, 32–36, 54, 55
net amount at risk, effect on, 33–36
relationship to cost of insurance, 36–38
term insurance, applied to, 33–35
whole life insurance, applied to, 35, 36
Lew, Edward A., 151, 154
Licensing of agents, brokers, and analysts, 772
Licensing of insurance companies
as a condition of doing business, 770
reinsurance agreement, impact on,
435–38
Unauthorized Insurers Service-of-Process Act, 467, 479, 480
validity of contract, impact on, 479,
480
Life annuity due, use of
in developing expense rates, 252–56
in preliminary term valuation, 280
in premium calculations, 208
in prospective reserve calculations,
231–33
in settlement options, 208
Life expectancy
meaning of, 141
use of, 7
under various mortality tables, 163–65
Life income
option
cash refund annuity, 88, 661
as combination of annuity certain
and pure deferred life annuity,
87, 660

Life income—*Cont.*
option—*Cont.*
common disaster and short-term survivorship problem, 596–98
excess interest, 664
with guaranteed installments, 87
inflexibility, elements of, 664
installment refund annuity, 88, 662
programming, use in, 673–76
as pure annuity, 660
structure of, 658–61
use of, 14
for widow, 14, 670–76
policy, 122, 123
for widow, 14, 670–76
Limited payment life insurance
joint life insurance, adaptability to, 66
nature of, 65, 66
net level premium, derivation of, 212
net single premium, derivation of, 193–95
prospective reserve, calculation of, 234, 235
Loading of net premium
adjustment for premiums paid more often than annually, 215
classification of insurance company expenses, 247–49, 264
concept of, 183
disability benefits, 748
expense rates, derivation of, 252–56
gross premium, relationship to, 246
loading formula, 249, 260
margins in, 242
modified reserves, relationship to, 274–76
statutory limitation on, 778
under substandard insurance, 424
term insurance, 44
Lump-sum settlement
beneficiary of, 577
common disaster and short-term survivorship problem, 596–98
estate clearance fund, 665, 666
under family income policy, 109, 110
mortgage cancellation fund, 667
use of, 12, 13

M

McCarran Act, 763–65
Mandatory security valuation reserve, 335 n, 844, 845, 872–74
Marital deduction, 597, 598
Materiality
of concealments, 537, 539
definition of, 528
falsity, extent of, 528, 529

Materiality—*Cont.*
individual-insurers standard, 529–31
laws relating to, 529, 530, 532, 535, 536
prudent-insurers standard, 529, 530
of representations, 528–33
tests of, 529–31
Medical consultation, 401, 412, 532–36
Medical Information Bureau, 403, 404, 533
Medical treatment clause, 491, 523, 540, 541, 553–55
Medico-Actuarial Mortality Investigation, 382
Military or naval service
accidental death clause, 753, 754
disability clause, 743
incontestable clause, 569, 570
underwriting for, 396, 397
Minors
accumulation of interest for, 603, 650
as applicant for life insurance, 480, 481
as beneficiary of estate clearance fund, 667
contingent trust for minor beneficiary, 603
guardianship, 601, 603
legal capacity of, 129, 480, 481, 600–604
right
to disaffirm, 480
to receive proceeds, 600, 601
to select settlement options, 601–603
Misstatement of age, 381, 523, 572, 708
Mixed companies, 790
Modified life policies, 125
Modified reserves
acquisition expenses, impact of, 276–78
Armstrong Committee, 290
borrowing from reserves, limitations on, 283
Commissioners Reserve Valuation Method, 285–89
full preliminary term valuation, 278–83, 300, 301
Illinois Standard, 283–84
New Jersey Standard, 284
Ohio Standard, 284
select and ultimate method, 290
statutory approval, 278
surrender values, impact on, 300, 301
tax liability, impact on, 897, 898, 905, 918, 921
Monahan decision, 565, 566
Moral hazard, 393, 394, 402, 749, 750
Mortality
analysis of, 885, 886

Mortality—*Cont.*
annuitant mortality, 101, 102, 201
under assessment insurance, 27–29, 798, 799
under converted policies, 49
distinction between male and female mortality, 103, 150, 154, 156–59, 395
dividend formula, factor in, 341–43, 353–56, 358
Negro mortality, 150
under nonmedical insurance, 412–16
rates, derivation of, 138–40
under reinsurance agreements, 437, 438
source of surplus, 332–34
substandard risks, 419, 420, 423–26
unification of mortality under savings bank life insurance, 803
under yearly renewable term insurance, 31, 32
Mortality Tables; *see also individual tables*
additional decremental factors, 145, 146
age setback, 102, 103, 162
aggregate table, 145
American Experience Table, 46 n, 146, 147
American Men Mortality Table, 146, 147
Basic Tables of Society of Actuaries, 145, 262, 263, 265
central death rate, 140 n
Commissioners 1958 Extended Term Insurance Table, 158
Commissioners 1960 Standard Group Table, 159, 160, 708
Commissioners 1961 Standard Industrial Table, 160, 162
CSO 1958 Basic Table, 162–65
CSO 1958 Table, 155–59, 162
CSO 1941 Table, 143, 148, 149, 163–65, 188, 744, 747
elements of, 140–42
extra percentage tables for substandard risks, 423–25
Ga 1951 Table, 143
graduation of data, 142, 143
National Fraternal Congress Table of Mortality, 799
population
data, 135, 136
tables, 134, 156, 162–65
probability of death, 140 n
projection factors, 102, 152–54
radix, 140, 141
reserves, effect on, 156, 236–38

Mortality Tables—*Cont.*
safety, margins of, 102, 156–58, 181
select table, 144, 145
Standard Industrial 1941 Table, 149, 150
Table X$_{17}$, 155–58
Table X$_{18}$, 156–59
ultimate table, 144, 145
Mortgage cancellation fund, 15, 667
Mutual companies
conversion to stock form, 789, 790
distribution of surplus, 787–89
dividend projections, 795, 796
nature of, 787
nonparticipating insurance, 789, 790
stock companies
comparison with, 791–94
competition with, 893–95, 899, 901, 902
Mutualization of stock companies, 786, 787
Multiple protection policy, 118, 119
Murder of insured by beneficiary, 503, 504

N

National Association of Insurance Commissioners
annual statement reporting requirements, 862
asset valuation rules, 865, 866
minimum standards for reserve and surrender values, 147–49, 157–59
Model Group Life Bill, promulgation of, 684
model law on industrial life insurance, 711, 712
mortality tables, development of, 147–49, 155, 157–61
standard disability provisions, 733, 751
uniform state laws, development of, 764, 767, 768
National Fraternal Congress Table of Mortality, 799
National Office of Vital Statistics, 136
National Service Life Insurance, 808, 809
Nature of life insurance contracts, 461–66
Needs approach to life insurance
dependency period income, 13–14
educational needs, 15
emergency needs, 15–18
estate clearance fund, 12, 13, 577, 665–67
life income
for insured, 15–16
for widow, 14

Needs approach to life insurance—*Cont.*
mortgage redemption, 15, 667
readjustment income, 13
Net amount at risk, 36–38, 67, 226–29, 340–43, 435–38
Net premiums
benefit of survivorship, 197, 198
net level premium
concept of, 207–9
deferred annuity, 213, 214
endowment insurance, 212, 213
life annuity due, 208
life annuity, similarity to, 207, 208
limited payment life, 212
ordinary life, 210–14
premiums payable more often than annually, 182, 185, 214–16
term insurance, 209, 210
net single premium, 187
aggregate approach, 183–85
concept of, 204–6
deferred whole life annuity, 195–98
endowment insurance, 200–203
immediate whole life annuity, 201–4
individual approach, 187
paid-up term insurance, 320–22
purchase of paid-up additions, 367, 368
rate computations, assumptions underlying, 186, 187
reduced paid-up insurance, 318–20
term insurance, 189–93
whole life insurance, 193–95
underlying assumptions, 183
New money rate, 344, 887
"No-lesser-amount" statutes, 427
Non-admitted assets, 863–65
Nonledger assets, 863–65
Nonmedical insurance
expense savings, 248, 413
extra mortality, 412, 414
guaranteed issue, 415
history of, 409
insurability option, 416, 417
pension trusts, 415
policyholder nonmedical, 414
underwriting safeguards, 409–12
Nonwaiver clause, 484, 546, 547, 551, 552
Numerical rating system
as basis for substandard classifications, 407, 408
criticisms of, 408
description of, 405, 406
as a means of achieving equity, 379
operation of, 406, 407

O

OASDI, 14, 17, 18, 63, 80, 146, 668, 670–76, 806, 807
Omnibus clause, 524
Operative date of policy, 497, 498
Oral contracts, 518, 519
Ordinary life insurance
endowment insurance, viewed as, 59
joint life insurance, adaptability to, 66
net level premium, derivation of, 210–12
net single premium, derivation of, 193–95
prospective reserve, calculation of, 230–33
retrospective reserve, calculation of, 221, 225
surrender values, derivation of, 304–6
distinctive features, 59–65
nature of, 58, 59
reserve under full preliminary term valuation, 279–81
use of, 20
Owner policies, 592
Owner-applicant, 477, 511–17, 578
Ownership
clauses
as alternative to irrevocable beneficiary designation, 588
family life insurance policy, 116
as means of transferring ownership, 592
of policy
by beneficiary, 584, 587, 607, 608, 612–14
family life insurance policy, 116
by the insured, 585, 591, 592, 607, 608, 612–14
by the insured and beneficiary jointly, 585, 587, 592, 607, 612–14
maturity rights, 602–4
ownership clause, 588, 592
by person other than insured, 592
prematurity rights, 591, 592, 612–14
right by owner to assign policy, 606, 607, 613

P

Parol evidence rule, 484, 566
Parties to life insurance contract
group life insurance, 707
legal capacity
alien enemies, 455, 481, 482
applicant, 480–82

Parties to life insurance contract—*Cont.*
  legal capacity—*Cont.*
    insurer, 478–80
    minors, 480–82
    Unauthorized Insurers Service of
      Process Act, 467, 479, 480
    Versailles Treaty, 455
    war, effect of on, 455, 481, 482
  ordinary insurance, 477, 478
Paul v. *Virginia,* 761, 763
Payment of premium
  under antedated policies, 497, 498
  by check, 488, 500, 552, 553
  as condition precedent, 475, 477, 478
  as consideration for contract, 499, 500
  extension of credit for, 475, 477, 478,
    551, 552
  incontestable clause, relationship to,
    566
  premium receipt, 501
  prepayment of first premium, 492–95
    without conditional receipt, 494
  by promissory note, 500–502
  waiver of late payment, 558
Payor clause, 78
Pension trusts, 414, 415, 427
Per capita distribution of insurance proceeds, 591
Per stirpes distribution of insurance proceeds, 590, 591
Peterson, Ray M., 153, 154
Plans of insurance, 129
Policy loans
  as an asset, 866
  by assignee, 616–18
  change of beneficiary prior to, 610, 611
  delay clause, 645
  extended term insurance, effect on,
    322, 323
  impairment of beneficiary's interest
    through, 586
  under industrial policies, 721
  joinder of beneficiary, 585, 610, 611
  premium loan; *see* Automatic premium
    loan
  recording of, 620
  to redeem policy under bankruptcy pro-
    ceeding, 626
  under reinsurance agreements, 438
  under substandard insurance, 421
Policy-writing fee, 249, 250
Population tables, 135, 156, 162–65
Premium
  notice, 367, 374
  taxes, 248, 254, 256, 437, 438, 928, 929

Prepayment of premiums
  as an alternative to retroactive conver-
    sion, 48
  extended term insurance, effect on,
    322
  premium deposits distinguished from
    discounted premiums, 48
Privileged communications, 535
Programming life insurance
  dependency period income, 13, 14,
    668–70
  educational needs, 15, 668
  emergency needs, 15, 667
  estate clearance fund, 12, 13, 655–57
  life income
    for insured, 15, 16
    for widow, 14, 670–76
  monetary evaluation of needs, 16–18
  mortgage redemption, 15, 667
  readjustment income, 13, 668
  techniques, 671–76
Promissory note, use of
  bilateral contract, creation of, 473,
    485 n
  payment of premium by, 500–502
  validity of contract, effect on, 487,
    488, 492–94
Proportion of personal income devoted
  to insurance and annuities, 18, 19
Protection of insurance benefits against
  creditors
  alimony and support claims, 626
  annuity payments, 631
  bankruptcy of insured, 625, 626, 631
  against creditors of beneficiary, 628,
    634, 635
  against creditors of insured, 624–26,
    633
  disability income benefits, 631
  Federal Bankruptcy Act, 625, 631
  insolvent insured, 631
  limitations on, 632
  non-statutory protection, 624–27
  parties entitled to protection, 632
  proceeds, 626, 630, 631, 634, 635
  "proceeds," meaning of, 600
  spendthrift clause, 630, 633–35
  spendthrift statutes, 629, 630, 634, 635
  state exemption statutes, 627, 630
  statutory protection, 627–30
  surrender values, 624–26, 630
  tax claims of federal government, 626,
    631
  temporal scope of, 635
Provident Savings Life Assurance Society of New York, 46 n

Prudential Friendly Society, 714
Pure endowment, 71, 284–88

R

Readjustment income, 13, 668, 673, 674
Rebating, 773, 774
Reduced paid-up insurance
    administrative expense, 251 n, 319,
        320
    advantages and disadvantages, 317,
        320
    nature of, 318
    under ordinary life policy, 62
    proportionate paid-up insurance, 318 n
Reformation of contracts
    as equitable remedies, 461, 573
    incontestable clause, relationship to,
        573, 574
Regulation
    by administrative official, 767, 768
    All-Industry Committee, 764
    certificate of authority, 770
    convention blank, 768, 860
    by courts, 766
    discrimination, 774, 775
    dividend
        estimates, 774
        policy, 777, 778
    expenses, limitations on, 304, 305, 778
    federal control, extent of, 765
    Federal Trade Commission, 765, 774
        Act, 764, 765
    financial condition, 776, 777
    fraternals, 796–801
    of group life insurance, 685–87
    incorporation
        requirements, 769, 770
        by special legislative act, 769
    of industrial life insurance, 711, 712,
        716, 720, 727, 728
    insurance "codes," 766, 767
    investments
        of guardians, 602
        of insurance companies, 776–77,
            843, 844, 847–50, 864–68
        "Leeway" or "basket" provision, 850
        prudent man statutes, 605
        of trustees, 604, 605
    legal limitations on new business, 778
    by legislatures, 766, 767
    licensing
        of agents, brokers, and analysts, 772
        requirement, 770, 771
    liquidation, 778, 779
    McCarran Act, 763–65
    NAIC, role of, 764, 767, 768
    Paul v. *Virginia,* 761, 763

Regulation—*Cont.*
    policy forms, 774, 775
    premium rates, 775, 776
    reasons for, 759, 760
    rebating, 773, 774
    Securities and Exchange Commission,
        765
    SEUA decision, 762, 763, 765
    Standard provisions, 775
    state control, establishment of, 760–62
    twisting, 773
    unfair competition, 774
    Wright, Elizur, 760, 761
    zone system for triennial examinations,
        768
Reinstatement, 574, 575, 738
Reinsurance
    accidental death benefits, 445, 446
    acquisition expenses, 436–38
    assumption, 431, 432
    automatic agreement, 440, 441
    catastrophe, 449
    ceding commission, 437
    cession form, 442
    claims settlement, 442
    coinsurance, 436–38, 446
    concept of, 431
    definition of terms, 431
    disability benefits, 445, 446
    duration of agreement, 443
    experience rating, 445
    facultative agreement, 440, 441
    indemnity, 432, 434
    insolvency of the ceding insurer, 444
    "jumbo" clause, 441
    as a means of obtaining advice and
        counsel, 433, 435
    modified coinsurance, 438, 439
    non-proportional, 447–50
    policy dividends, 436, 437
    premium payments, method of, 441,
        442
    of Provident Savings Society, 46 n
    recapture clause, 443
    reduction in sums reinsured, 442, 443
    reserves, 435–39
    retention limits, 432, 439, 440, 445
    rights of policyholder against rein-
        surer, 442, 444
    spread loss, 449, 450
    stop-loss, 447–49
    of substandard risk, 433, 446
    yearly renewable term insurance, 435,
        436, 445
Remarriage clause, 605
Representation
    affirmative, 523

Representation—*Cont.*
  concept of materiality, 528–31
  continuing, 528
  laws relating to misrepresentation, 489,
    523, 524, 529–33, 535, 536
  legal consequences of misrepresenta-
    tion, 525–28
  misrepresentation distinguished from
    concealment, 537, 538
  nature and legal effect of, 523, 524
  of opinion, belief or expectation, 526,
    527
  privileged communication, 535
  promissory representation, 523
  source of litigation, 533–36
Rescission and restitution
  as a contest, 563, 564
  as equitable remedies, 461
  grounds for, 525–27
  on grounds of misrepresentation or
    concealment, 489, 525–27
  for lack of insurable interest, 519, 520
Reserve strengthening, 240, 241
Reserves
  acquisition expenses, impact of, 276–
    78
  Armstrong Committee, 290
  as base for excess interest factor, 345-
    46
  borrowing from, limitations on, 283
  Commissioners Reserve Valuation
    Method, 285–89
  company tax liability, impact on, 895,
    897, 898
  contingency, 244, 337, 344, 345, 873,
    874, 921, 922, 925, 926
  deficiency, 242–44, 870
  full net level premium valuation, 219,
    314
  full preliminary term, 278–83
  gross premium valuation, 219, 242
  Illinois Standard, 283, 284
  initial, 220, 345, 346
  interest assumption, effect of, 238–41
  level premium plan, relationship to,
    32–36
  mean, 220, 345, 346, 439
  methods of determining, 221 ff.
  modified plan, 219
  mortality assumptions, effect of, 158,
    236–38
  New Jersey Standard, 284
  Ohio Standard, 284
  prospective, 218, 230, 233
  under reinsurance agreements, 435–39
  retrospective, 219, 221–29
  safety margins, 241, 242

Reserves—*Cont.*
  select and ultimate method, 290
  statutory regulation, 230, 868–69
  statutory standards for minimum, 147–
    49, 157–59, 219, 241, 278, 287,
    868, 869
  strengthening through lower interest as-
    sumption, 240, 241, 879, 880
  surrender values, relationship to, 297,
    299, 300
  under term insurance, 33–36
  terminal, 220, 345, 346
  types of, 435–38
  voluntary, 244, 245
Restatements of the law, 461, 462
Retirement
  annuity
    basis of cash value, 93
    cash option, 94
    distinctive characteristics, 92–94
    as element of retirement income pol-
      icy, 116
    exchange for life insurance contract,
      94, 95
    surrender values, 93, 94
  income contract, 116, 118
Return premium policy, 125
Reverse common disaster clause, 598
Rogers, Oscar H., 305
Rules of statutory construction, 464, 465

S

Savings Bank Life Insurance, 801–5
Securities and Exchange Commission,
  765
Selection of risks
  age of applicant, 380, 381
  alcohol and drugs, use of, 306, 307,
    534
  American Service Bureau, 402
  attending physician, 401, 402, 411
  aviation activities, 395, 396
  blood pressure, 382, 385, 386
  build, 381–84, 406, 407
  Build and Blood Pressure Study, 1959,
    382
  distinguished from classification of
    risk, 375
  economic status, 396, 397
  family history, 388, 389, 404, 405,
    533, 534
  guiding principles, 378–81
  heart impairments, 385, 386
  inspection report, 402, 411, 412
  insurability option, 416, 417
  insurance, amount of, 396, 533
  judgment rating, 404

Selection of risks—*Cont.*
juvenile insurance, 417
maximum age restrictions, 417, 418
medical examination, 400, 401, 409, 485–88, 495
medical examiner, 401
Medical Information Bureau, 403, 404, 533
Medico-Actuarial Mortality Investigation, 382
military service, 396, 397
morals, 393, 394, 402, 406, 407
nonmedical insurance; *see* Nonmedical insurance
numerical rating system, 379, 407, 408
occupation, 390–92, 400, 416, 417, 429, 533
overweight and underweight, effect of, 382–84
personal history, 387, 388, 390, 396, 397, 534, 535
physical condition, 384–87, 406, 407
plan of insurance, 395, 396, 406, 407
privileged communication, 535
purpose of, 375, 376
race and nationality, 394
reinsurance as aid to, 433, 434
rejections, effect of, 378
residence, 391, 392, 400, 406, 407, 429
role of field agent, 398, 399, 411
sex, 395
substandard risks; *see* Substandard risks
tuberculosis, 390
uninsurability, 378, 379
urinalysis, 387, 388
Servicemen's Group Life Insurance, 810
Settlement
agreement; *see* Settlement, options
options
administrative costs, 650, 655
adverse selection under, 102
basic annuity forms, relationship to, 85
commutation privilege, 646
contract v. current rates, 642–44
dependency period income, 668–70
educational fund, 668
election by
beneficiary, 640, 641
guardians, 601, 602
insured, 640, 641
minors, 600
trustees, 603–5
emergency fund, 666, 667
family income policy, 109, 110
flexibility, elements of, 641, 645, 646

Settlement—*Cont.*
options—*Cont.*
under group life insurance, 707, 708
under industrial life insurance, 723
life income for widow, 670–72
minimum amount requirements, 646
mortgage cancellation fund, 667
readjustment income, 668
settlement agreements, 639–42
testamentary disposition question, 593, 652
time limitation on election of, 653, 654
use in programming, 671–76
withdrawal privilege, 654–56
SEUA decision, 762, 763, 765
Short-term survivorship of beneficiary, 596–98
Simultaneous death of insured and beneficiary
common disaster clause, 596
delayed payment clause, 597, 598
English common law, presumptions under, 595
marital deduction, 597, 598
reverse common disaster clause, 598
Roman Civil Code, presumptions of, 594, 595
Uniform Simultaneous Death Act, 595, 596
Society of Actuaries
basic tables of, 145, 262, 263, 265
Committee on Disability and Double Indemnity, 746
development of 1958 CSO Table, 155–59
Source of litigation, 533–36
South Sea Bubble, 78
Special or preferred risk policies
justification of, 68, 69
limitations on, 69, 249
nature of, 68
Spendthrift clause, 608, 630, 633–35, 641, 646
Standard Annuity Table, 1937
characteristics of, 150, 151
use of, 16, 103
Standard Industrial 1941 Table
general characteristics, 149, 150
margins of safety, 143
Standard Nonforfeiture Law, 301–12, 315, 720
Standard provisions of life insurance contract
change of beneficiary clause, 584, 585
as form of legislative law, 456
incontestable clause, 560, 775

Standard provisions, life contract—*Cont.*
  legal effect of ambiguity in, 475
  total disability provisions, 733, 746, 751
Standard Valuation Law, 285–90, 301–4
State exemption statutes, 627, 630; *see
  also* Protection of insurance benefits against creditors
Statute of Frauds, 518
Statute of limitation, 561, 562
Stock companies
  distribution of surplus, 782, 783
  income tax treatment, 895, 898, 913,
    922, 924–27
  mutual companies, comparison with,
    791–94
  mutual companies, competition with,
    893–95, 899, 901, 902
  mutualization, 786, 787
  nature of, 781
  participating insurance, 785
  valuation of stockholders' equity,
    783–85
Subrogation, doctrine of, 475, 476
Substandard risks
  aviation activities, effect of, 395, 396
  dividend adjustments, 427, 428
  extra percentage tables, 423–25
  flat extra premium, 425, 426
  incidence of extra risk, 420, 421
  liens, 426, 427
  numerical rating system, use of, 407,
    408
  occupation, effect of, 391, 392
  rated-up age, 421–23
  reinsurance of, 446
  restrictions on plan of insurance, 428
  standard mortality, impact on, 379
  substandard rating, removal of, 428,
    429
  theory of, 419, 420
  unavailability of nonmedical insurance,
    411
  value of substandard insurance, 429,
    430
Succession-in-interest of beneficiary
  Connecticut rule, 589, 591
  New York rule, 589
  per capita distribution, 591
  per stirpes distribution, 590, 591
  succession-in-interest clause, 589, 590
Suicide clause, 474, 497, 498, 504, 505,
  570, 571, 719
Surplus
  account in financial statement, 884,
    902
  acquisition expenses, impact of, 276–
    78

Surplus—*Cont.*
  adjustment in asset values, 335
  capital gains, 335, 345
  contribution plan, 340
  criteria for apportionment of, 337, 338
  divisible surplus, 335–37, 340
  excess interest, 220, 332–34, 343–48,
    353–56, 358–64
  gains and losses, concept of, 330, 331
  gains from surrender, 344, 345, 350
  legal limitations on, 244, 245, 777,
    843
  loading savings, 332–34, 348–56, 357
  mortality savings, 332–34, 338–41,
    353–58
  permanent contribution to, 259, 365
  sources of, 332–34
Surrender
  charge, 297, 298, 300, 306
  options
    automatic, 315–19, 720
    automatic premium loan; *see* Auto-
      matic premium loan
    cash, 315–18, 720, 721
    delay clause, 316, 317, 645
    exercise by assignee, 614–18
    extended term insurance, 320–25,
      720
    under industrial life policies, 720,
      721
    reduced paid-up insurance, 318–20
      720, 721
    Versailles Treaty, 455
  values
    adjusted premium method, 302–6
    asset share as basis for, 295
    charge, 297, 298, 300, 306
    claims of creditors of insured, 624–
      26, 630
    defects in old nonforfeiture legisla-
      tion, 299–301
    definition of
      lapse, 296, 297
      surrender, 296, 297
    dividends, 309–11
    equitable treatment of withdrawing
      policyholders, 291–93
    under family income policy, 115
    impact of
      acquisition expenses on, 292, 294
      adverse financial selection on, 295,
        304
      adverse mortality selection on,
        294, 304
      contingency reserve on, 295, 296,
        304
      profit allowance on, 296, 304

Surrender charge—*Cont.*
values—*Cont.*
surrender expenses on, 296, 304
income tax treatment, 934–35
under industrial life policies, 720, 721
legislation prior to Guertin Legislation, 297–301
liens against, 426, 427, 432
under ordinary life policy, 60–62
modification of adjusted premium method, 306–9
nonforfeiture factor, 308
Standard Nonforfeiture Law, 301–11
statutory standards for minimum values, 147–50, 157–59, 220, 221, 296–98, 301–4, 720
under life income policy, 123
under substandard insurance policies, 421, 422, 425–27
under term policies, 50, 52, 301, 315
Survivorship annuity, 119–22, 126
Swift v. *Tyson,* 470

T

Table X₁₇, 155–58
Table X₁₈, 156–58
Taxation of life insurance companies
accounting for taxes, 881–83
Federal income tax
adjusted reserves rate of interest, 905 n, 915–18
average reserve rate of interest, 915–18
capital gains and losses, 903, 911, 913, 920 n, 921, 924, 928
company-by-company approach, 900
conduit approach, 901, 902
Corporation Excise Tax Act, 903, 908
deductible dividend income, 914, 920, 921, 924, 927
distributed income approach, 901
fraternals, 800
free investment income approach, 899, 900, 903, 904, 908, 909
group and health insurance deduction, 922, 925, 926
reserve methods and assumptions, impact of, 895, 897, 898, 904, 905, 918, 921
income from pension assets, 918
industry average approach, 900, 904, 905, 907
industry-ratio approach, 900, 905, 907

Taxation of insurance companies—*Cont.*
Federal income tax—*Cont.*
investment yield, 915–18
Life Insurance Company Income Tax Act of 1959, 910–13
loss carryback and carryforward provision, 877, 911, 926
Menge formula, 916 n
National Life of Vermont v. *U.S.,* 904, 909, 919
net investment income approach, 898, 899, 908
nonparticipating insurance deduction, 922, 925, 926
Penn Mutual Life Insurance Company v. *Lederer,* 903
Phase I, 913, 914
Phase II, 913, 920–924
Phase III, 913, 924–27
Phase IV, 913, 928
policyholder dividends, treatment of, 895, 898, 901, 903, 921
policyholders' surplus account, 913, 922, 924–27
proration concept, 915, 919, 923
"reduction items," 918, 919,
Secretary's Ratio, 905–9
shareholders' surplus account, 913, 924–27
small business deduction, 914, 921, 924
special deductions, 921, 922
stock and mutual companies, competition between, 893–95, 899, 901, 902
stockholder dividends, treatment of, 895, 898, 924–27
stop-gap legislation, 907–9
tax-exempt interest, 903, 904, 906, 909, 911, 914, 919, 921, 922, 924, 927
total income approach, 896–98, 903, 908, 911, 912
U.S. v. *Atlas Life Insurance Company,* 919
local taxation, 931
state taxation
discriminatory, 929
franchise, 929
miscellaneous, 929–30
premium, 928–29
retaliatory features, 929
Tax Court, 466
Term insurance
accidental death benefits, 50
adverse selection associated with, 44, 396, 406

Term insurance—*Cont.*
  attained age conversion, 47, 48
  automatic conversion, 49, 50
  convertibility, 46–51, 112, 115, 116
  decreasing term, 29, 52, 108, 109, 117
  disability benefits, 50
  disadvantage of, 32, 46, 111, 112
  dividend treatment, 341, 362
  extended term insurance, 62, 158; *see
    also* Extended term insurance
  fallacious arguments in favor of, 54–
    57
  family income policy, in, 108, 109
  family life insurance policy, in, 114,
    115
  family maintenance policy, in, 112
  increasing term, 52
  life expectancy contracts, 50
  limit on renewability, 32, 45, 46
  loading of net premiums, 44
  long-term contracts, 49–51
  modified life policies, in, 125
  multiple protection policies, in, 118,
    119
  nature of, 43, 44
  net level premium, derivation of, 209,
    210
  net single premium, derivation of, 189–
    93
  prepayment of premiums as an alter-
    native to retroactive conversion,
    48
  relationship to endowment insurance,
    71
  renewability, 44–46
    limitations, 49, 112
  reserves, effect on, 244, 245
  retirement income contract, in, 116,
    117
  retroactive conversion, 47
  return premium policy, in, 125
  surrender values, 50, 51, 301, 315
  term
    expectancy contracts, 50, 51
    to sixty-five, 51
  use of, 20, 50, 53, 54, 111
  yearly renewable term, 29–32, 187,
    188; *see also* Yearly renewable
    term insurance
Terminal dividends, 309–11, 364–66
Termination rates, 264–67
Testamentary disposition question, 593,
  642, 649
Theory of probability
  life insurance, application to, 134–37,
    472
  simple probability, 133
  statement of the theory, 133, 134

Tontine system, 363
Tort liability, 495–97
Total disability benefits; *see also* Disability income benefits
  age before which disability must
    occur, 736, 737
  automatic waiver of premium, 738,
    739
  claims administration, 733, 751, 752
  class III rates, 745, 746
  Committee on Disability and Double
    Indemnity, study of, 746–48
  contestability, 742, 743
  dividends, 749
  early development, 732, 733
  excluded hazards, 743
  female applicants, 750
  Fidelity Mutual Life Insurance Com-
    pany, 732
  under group life, 690, 691
  Hunter's Table, 745, 746, 748
  income payments, 335, 340, 445, 578,
    579, 618, 631, 690, 722, 719–22
  under industrial life insurance, 722
  modification of coverage, 733, 736,
    737
  moral hazard, 749, 750
  Mutual Benefit definition, 735
  NAIC, standard provisions of, 733,
    746, 751
  occupational disability, 734
  "permanent," definition of, 735, 736
  premium rates
    early actuarial functions, 745, 746
    for females, 748
    increases in, 733
    loading of, 748
    underlying principles, 753–55
  prorate clause, 741, 742
  qualification period, 735, 736
  rate of becoming disabled, 744, 747
  reserves, 748, 749
  retroactive benefits, 738, 739
  specified disabilities, 735
  substandard risks, 750
  total disability, definition of, 733–35
  underwriting, 749, 750
  value of disabled life annuity, 744,
    747
  waiver of premium, 50, 115, 681, 722
    732, 737–39
Twisting, 773

U

Underwriting
  expenses, 248, 249, 253–56
  medical examinations, expense of, 248

Underwriting—*Cont.*
  nonmedical insurance, 248
  preferred risk policies, 68, 69
  of term insurance applicants, 43
Uniform Insurers Liquidation Act, 779
Uniform Simultaneous Death Act, 595,
    596
Uniform state laws
  Model Group Life Bill, 684, 685, 687,
    688
  Model law on industrial life insurance,
    711, 712
  standard
    definitions of group life insurance,
      683–85
    disability provisions, 733, 746, 751
    policy provisions, 560, 584, 585, 685,
      765
  Standard Nonforfeiture Law, 301–11,
    315, 720
  Standard Valuation Law, 285–89, 301–4
  Unauthorized Insurers Service-of-Proc-
    ess Act, 467, 479, 480, 764
  Uniform Insurers Liquidation Act, 779
  Uniform Simultaneous Death Act, 595,
    596
Uniform Unauthorized Insurance Service-
    of-Process Act, 467, 479, 480, 764
Unilateral contracts, 472, 473
Unsolicited offers, 495, 496
U.S. Government Life Insurance, 808

V

Valued policy, 475, 476, 506
Variable annuities
  accumulation units, 98, 99
  annuity units, 99
  arguments for and against, 101
  authority to write, 100
  CREF, 100
  regulation by SEC, 765
  theory of, 98
Versailles Treaty, 455

W

Wagering
  in early years of life insurance, 502,
    503
  insurable interest requirement, rela-
    tionship to, 503
Waiver
  acts of brokers, 547, 548
  conditional receipt, 553
  by express statement, 557
  by inconsistent conduct, 558
  of late payment of premium, 558
  nature of, 542, 543, 548, 549

Waiver—*Cont.*
  payment of first premium, 551–53
  premium notices, 558
Waiver of premium (total disability)
  automatic waiver of premium, 738, 739
  as earliest type of benefit, 732
  family life insurance policy, 115
  under group life insurance, 695
  under industrial life policies, 722
  nature of the benefit, 737–39
  reinstatement, 738
  retroactive waiver, 738
  under term policies, 50
Waiver of unpaid installments of annual
    premium at death of insured, 216
War Risk Insurance, 807, 808
Warranties
  development of, 521, 522
  in life insurance, 522–24
  in marine insurance, 521
  statutory modification of, 522, 523
Whole life insurance
  functions of, 70
  income and principal policy, as element
    of, 126
  life income policy, as element of, 123
  nature of the hazard, 36, 58
  net single premium, derivation of, 193–
    95
  principal types of, 58
Wisconsin State Life Fund, 811
Withdrawal privilege
  dependency period income, 669
  emergency fund, 667, 668
  estate clearance fund, 666
  under installment amount option, 658
  under installment time option, 655
  under interest option, 649
  under life income option, 664
  readjustment income, 668
  types of, 644–46
Wright, Elizur, 46 n, 297, 760, 761

Y

Yearly renewable term insurance
  adverse selection, 31, 32
  under group life insurance, 680, 689–
    92, 698–703
  nature of, 30–32
  net premiums, derivation of, 187, 188
  under reinsurance agreements, 435,
    436
  War Risk Insurance, 808
Yield on life insurance company invest-
    ments
  bases for measuring, 76, 343–45, 887
  level of, 56, 76, 77, 887

This book has been set in 11 point Times Roman, leaded 2 points, and 10 point Times Roman, leaded 1 point. Part titles and numbers are in 18 point Spartan Heavy. Chapter numbers are 14 point Times Roman; chapter titles are in 24 point Times Roman. The size of the type page is 27 by 45 picas.